# THE DILOGGÚN

## The Orishas, Proverbs, Sacrifices, and Prohibitions of Cuban Santería

ÓCHA'NI LELE

Destiny Books
Rochester, Vermont

Destiny Books
One Park Street
Rochester, Vermont 05767
www.InnerTraditions.com



**Library of Congress Cataloging-in-Publication Data**

Lele, Ócha'ni, 1966–
The Diloggún : the orishas, proverbs, sacrifices, and prohibitions of Cuban Santería / Ócha'ni Lele.
p. cm.
Includes bibliographical references and index.
ISBN 978-089281912-6
1. Orishas—Cuba. 2. Santería—Cuba. 3. Divination—Cuba. I. Title.

BL2530.C9L93 2003
299'.674—dc21

2003053174

Printed and bound in India by Replika Press Pvt. Ltd.

10

Text design and layout by Virginia Scott Bowman
This book was typeset in Janson with Greymantle as the display typeface

*For Ogúndei, Evaristo Perez, ibaé. We all miss you.*
*For Cynthia Perry. Thank you for believing in me.*
*For my godfather, Banacek Matos. Thank you . . .*
*for everything you gave me.*

# ACKNOWLEDGMENTS

It is said that Olódumare spread his knowledge and wisdom throughout the world so that each person could have a small part. Since 1989 I have immersed myself in the culture of orisha worship, and no matter how much I learn I realize that there is so much more to be learned. A book as vast as this represents countless hours of travel, questioning, study, note taking, and work. I am indebted to the many people who have encouraged, supported, and instructed me; I need to acknowledge them all here.

I am indebted to those who gave me my foundation in the religion, setting me on the path that led to the completion of my research: Auria Gonzalez (omo-Oshún), Rigoberto Rodriguez (omo-Oshún, ibaé), and Juan Gonzalez (omo-Yemayá, ibaé), gentle tutors who taught me the basic oral meanings of the parent odu and their special rituals. To my many sponsors and godparents in the religion, I am always in your debt: my first godmother, Baba Lade; my first yubonna, Odofemi; and my ex- and onetime oriaté, Afolabi. Although I am no longer a godchild in that house, the training and teaching that I received as I was given my elekes, warriors, Olokun, Ibeyi, santo lavado (Obatalá), and nganga (the cauldron of Palo Mayombe) were instrumental in this volume's research. I spent many months in Michigan questioning, observing, and learning; it was through participation in that ilé ocha that I learned the manipulations of obí and diloggún, the oracles of the orishas. I also need to thank Akin Babatunde, Ogúndei (ibaé), Paul Bennet, Reynaldo Ruiz, Omolotiwa, Dr. Mary Curry (ibaé), and Christine Jaffe for all their support and help throughout these writing projects. Special thanks and love also go out to Omolotiwa, Oshunguere, Oshunare, and Adeobe for accepting me with open arms when I literally "showed up" on their front doorstep. Thank you! You have all been the most incredible and gracious hosts!

Although Palo Mayombe is a religion separate from Lucumí practice, my experiences in this Congolese faith were instrumental to my spiritual development and, hence, my work as an author. I need to thank all those in my munanso who gave me foundation and initiation: my Tata, Tiembla Tierra Sambia Empungo (Banacek Matos); my Yayi, Chola Cuatro Vientos (Keisha Lago); and the witnesses to my rayado, Lucero Malembo Malongo, Lucero Tata Entoto, Siete Sayas Sirena de Madrugada (Dr. Miriam Bonet), and Matojo que Crece. They gave me strength when I felt that I had none, courage when I was afraid, and foundation when the very walls around me were crumbling. How can I thank these people enough for giving me back my life? I cannot. I also need to thank Eva Shangó (Obadeoba), an espiritista with the most incredible egun and muertos, for helping me give my own spiritual court strength, light, and elevation. Her work as an espiritista is incredible, and I owe my own spiritual development as an espiritista to much of her work. Elba Oshún (Oniosún), her "partner" in the religion, has been very sweet and very kind, and I thank her for her work as well in elevating my spiritual court. Finally, I need to thank Naomi Alejandro (siete rayos), Madre Nganga from the rama Vititi Congo, for her many hours of visits and discussions on the religion Palo Mayombe. She was a fountain of knowledge, one that I drank from quite frequently.

I also want to thank the following people for their support over the years:

- Susannah Noel, the editor for my first book, *The Secrets of Afro-Cuban Divination.* I learned so much by working with her on my first major project. Susannah, you have no idea how your ripping and shredding of my first manuscript molded my work to date as an author. Just don't do it again—ever!
- Doris Troy, the editor for my second book *Obí, Oracle of Cuban Santería.* She picked up where Susannah left off and helped my writing acquire the final bit of polish it needed. Doris, you did a beautiful job with that volume, and I thank you for it!
- Laura Schlivek, my project editor throughout all my work with Inner Traditions. Laura, you are incredible, providing me with encouragement and motivation when I am about to give up. Thank you for your mentoring.
- Jon Graham, my acquisitions manager at Inner Traditions. When no one else there believed in my proposals, you did, and I am grateful for your belief in my work. I am sure that the orishas thank you as well for ensuring that the beauty and complexity of our faith is out there for the world to read about and understand.
- Nancy Ringer, who attacked and edited this project with an almost religious zeal. You did a wonderful job, Nancy.
- Cynthia Perry, my benefactor and patron, the one person who believed in me and my work so much that she was willing to give up everything to ensure that my dreams came true. Cindy, how can I thank you for being there when times were rough? How can I thank you for continuing to push me toward my dreams and goals? I cannot. But at least you know that you have my undying love and gratitude.
- Mark Benezra, owner of Original Publications, for allowing me to quote freely from Awó Fá'Lokun Fatunmbi's *Awó: Ifá and the Theology of Orisha Divination.* As always, on a personal level I must thank him for his time and encouragement early in my writing career. The man is nothing short of brilliant, and he was, in the day, a cherished mentor.
- Marjorie Stevens and Ann Refoe, two teachers who realized that I had talent as a writer and encouraged me to write "feverishly." Teachers are the most important influence in our lives, and they can never be given enough praise. To both of you, know that whenever my pen hits paper, you are both there in my prayers and thoughts.

The blessings and love that I have to give go out to you all. I thank each of you for believing in me when I did not believe in myself. ¡Aché! To all of you!

# CONTENTS

# AN INTRODUCTION
## TO THE LUCUMÍ RELIGION

Although the Lucumí faith is a modern religion flourishing on American soil, it is heavily rooted in the past, a surviving spiritual evolution of ancient Yoruba beliefs. The Yoruba were a proud nation of warriors who occupied southwestern Nigeria, an area in which their modern-day descendants still thrive. These Africans developed a religious city-state system whose brilliance in some ways exceeded that of the classical Greek and Roman empires, for while those ancient European civilizations are no more, the Yoruba culture lives on. History tells us that the Yoruba nation was founded by a holy man, Odúduwa, who established the first holy city at Ilé Ifé. As the ethnic group spread, entire city-states sprang up around the worship of various *orishas,* or gods. Ilé Ifé belonged to Obatalá, Oyó to Shangó, Ilobu to Inle, Ketu to Ochosi, Inisa to Otín, and Ilesa (Ijesa region, Iwo and Edo) to Logun Ede. Each city-state had its own priesthood devoted to the orisha protecting the city. Thus, initiates in Ilé Ifé were brought into the mysteries of Obatalá, whereas those who entered the priesthood in Oyó received Shangó, and Ketu priests were bound to Ochosi. Uniting all these city-states, no matter the god served, were three concepts: Odúduwa, the common ancestor; Elegguá, the orisha who opens the doors from our world to that of the divine; and Olódumare, the supreme god. While the people of each individual province had their own orisha to worship, with Odúduwa in their blood, Elegguá at their feet, and Olódumare in their heaven, all were one nation.

The religion, whether one speaks of the ancient Yoruba, the modern Yoruba, or the Lucumí, teaches that the ultimate creative force, Olódumare, divided itself into innumerable aspects—the orishas. Only by worshiping and studying each orisha can one slowly acquire greater knowledge of the vast divine whole. Each orisha is a living, spiritual personification of limited *aché* (a word translating loosely as "power, grace, and life"). The aché of an orisha depends on the aspect of Olódumare from which it spawned. Obatalá, a deity who can be either male or female, comes from the most vast and wise aspects of Olódumare; he is also known as the "King of White Cloth," the cloth being the pure white light from which all things coalesced. Yemayá is the sweet, life-giving, mothering principle of unknowable deity; like a mother, she is swift to protect and defend her children. Ochosi, the hunter, hunts not only to feed Olódumare but also to feed his people; he taught humans how to hunt for food and was born of the aspect of Olódumare that represents the principle "To live, life must feed on life." Olokun, the hermaphroditic deity ruling the depths of the ocean, draws her aché from the part of Olódumare that is secret, mysterious, and unknown; hence her home is in the depths of the ocean, where none may descend while living in the flesh. Ainá, mistress of flame and constant companion to Shangó, is the limitless fire of Olódumare's existence.

Modern African Yoruba religion and the Cuban-American Lucumí faith share the same basic beliefs, though both are as far removed from the principles of ancient Yoruba worship as they are in distance from each other. While New World slavery was an unforgivable heresy of Christian people, it was the catalyst for the Lucumí evolution; had it not been for the slave trade, our gods would never have come to American soils. The Middle Passage from Africa to Cuba brought together diverse ethnic groups, many of which had had no prior contact with one another. The few African nations that had been acquainted with their neighbors were not always on good terms; they warred, and this weakened each group, making them prone to European conquest and kidnapping. Of all the New World territories involved in slave importation, Cuba boasted the longest history. While slaves were imported to Brazil in 1538 and to the colonies of North America in 1619, in Cuba they arrived as early as 1521. The Cuban influx was tremendous: In the 241-year period from 1521 through 1762, an average of five hundred Africans per year were brought to the island as slaves, totaling 120,500 blacks. These, and their captive-born descendants, were forced to work for a greedy population, a light-skinned race too lazy to labor and produce for itself. Of all the New World regions, Cubans held on to the slavery system the longest; not until 1870, twenty years after the abolition of slavery in Brazil and ten years after abolition in the United States, did slavery come to an end in Cuba. The Lucumí faith was molded during this 349-year period in Cuba.

Realize, however, that the gestation period for the emerging Lucumí practices was prolonged. Only a minority of the Africans captured in the early years of the slave trade were Yoruba, and religious practices of those Yorubans did not survive much beyond the first generation in Cuba. The Portuguese, British, French, Dutch, and Spanish traders raided vast areas, not focusing on any one tribe. Blacks were brought from both coasts and the central region. The borders of the raiding region ran south to Mozambique, Zimbabwe, and Angola and extended north to Kenya and Senegal. Because of its strength, the Yoruba nation was initially avoided; those few brought as slaves were political prisoners of other tribes. Widespread raiding of the Yoruba began in 1763, however, with the highest numbers being captured through 1774. For eleven years, the Yoruba comprised a dominant proportion of new Cuban slaves, and they and their descendants increased their ethnic presence on the island. After 1774, the number of first-generation Yoruba slaves dwindled, but slavers continued to capture them until 1789. During this twenty-six-year period (1763–89), 15,600 slaves flooded Cuban ports, most of them Yoruba. By 1789 the Yoruba were among the largest, "freshest" African populations on the island. With a number of descendants who remembered fragments of the oldest Yoruba religious traditions and first-generation "imports" who were familiar with current religious practices, the radical changes in slavery made during the year 1789 gave the Yoruba population an overall cultural advantage that other groups would not share.

For it was in 1789 that Charles IV, king of Spain, issued "The Royal Document on the Trades and Occupations of Slaves." The official Spanish opinion on the value, lives, and worth of slaves had never before been determined; Charles defined their duty by royal decree: From the age of seventeen through the age of sixty, all blacks in good health were to toil ceaselessly in Cuban fields, producing for the master class at all costs. Manual labor was for the black hands. White hands were not to be soiled; instead, they were to handle the mental tasks of continuing society. The royal decree also defined the master class's duty to its servants: Being good Catholics, all who used slave labor were to teach their charges the one true, holy religion of the Roman Catholic Church. While Christians believed that blacks were subhuman, Church doctrine taught that they still had souls; the masters could own their slaves' bodies, but only God could claim what lay beneath their flesh. The slaves' souls were to be nurtured in the name of Mother Rome. Because all was done in the name of God, the document forbade slave labor on the high holy days of the Church, especially the feast days of Spanish saints. On these holy days, blacks were to attend mass and receive communion; thus would they find salvation and be free in the afterlife. Every day after laboring long hours in the field, the slaves were to recite the rosary in their homes. The royal decree promised rewards for the slaves: In return for total submission to both the masters and the Church, they would be given free time to entertain and work for themselves.

Although meant to ensure total domination over both the bodies and the souls of black slaves, Charles's decree would, in time, have the reverse effect. It became the foundation that nurtured, rather than destroyed, African traditional religion.

Arising from the foundation of "The Royal Document on the Trades and Occupations of Slaves," the framework for the continuation of native African religions was built by two men, Father Juan Matienzo and Bishop Pedro Augustín Morrell de Santa Cruz. Both had great zeal for black religious education.

Father Matienzo authored guidelines for each slave's religious upbringing. He believed that blacks were mentally comparable to children and could learn something new only by comparing it to something familiar. He knew the trauma of forced separation from their homelands broke their spirit and realized that their longing for the old ways burned in their hearts. Matienzo sought to use this trauma and yearning to build a bridge from the Africans' paganism to the holy Catholic Church. He encouraged both fellow priests and laymen to allow slaves to retain some of their native customs while worshiping the white supreme God. He theorized that slow acclimation and carefully calculated abdication of superstitious practices would lead each African to salvation. Having attained salvation, one by one the Africans would abandon their heathen practices.

Unknown to him, Matienzo's work failed miserably. For with their mouths the African slaves prayed openly on the rosary to the Virgin Mary and the Father, Son, and Holy Ghost, but in their hearts they longed for their native gods, crying to them for peace and release from their prisons. Some slaves, say the Lucumí elders, did look upon the saints with an open mind, but instead of a holy Christian persona, they saw in the faces of the saints their own tears and, behind these, the faces of their own orishas staring back. At this point, the elders say, the holy Catholic saints looked down in pity and despair at what their own people were doing, and the orishas, in their infinite wisdom, worked through the saints to carry their followers through the hardships of slavery. When the first Yoruba prayed on the rosary, Cuban society felt the first stirring of Santería in its midst.*

Along with Father Matienzo, Bishop Pedro Augustín Morrell de Santa Cruz crusaded for black spiritual redemption. For his work, he borrowed a custom originating in fourteenth-century Seville, Spain, and an organization known as the *cofradia*, or the religious brotherhood for laymen. In Spain, each cofradia was dedicated to a specific saint and headed by the priests of the local church dedicated to that holy persona. Every week, members of the cofradia met in their church; the brotherhood provided religious instruction, fellowship, and support for both lifetime Catholics and new converts.

Through centuries of usage in Spain, the concept had proved valuable for the conversion of souls; it was a peaceful, although subversive, way to immerse the newly converted into Catholic culture. Bishop Morrell rationalized that the success of the cofradia in Spain could translate into success with the conversion of slaves, and if the slaves were truly converted to the Holy Mother Church, they would be more easily controlled and more productive to Spanish society. Because most Cuban churches were built in the cities themselves, the organization of the cofradia became an urban phenomenon, licensed and overseen by the existing municipalities and parishes. Soon, each church sponsored one in the name of its patron saint.

Though the municipality licensed it and the church parish directed it, for the cofradia to have full impact, it was essential that it be governed by laymen. Lay leadership had brought success in Spain, and Bishop Morrell believed it would work in Cuba

---

*Throughout this book, I will refer to this religion as both Santería and the Lucumí faith. The term Santería, which translates as "worship of the saints," is actually a misnomer. Slave traders and masters applied this term in distaste for how the Africans seemingly worshiped and revered the holy Catholic saints over God himself. In truth, the Catholic saints are not worshiped in this religion, although they do have the adherents' reverence for helping to save the worship of orishas from extinction. Many believers, however, retain their Catholic ties to some degree, using the term *Santería* for their beliefs affectionately. When I use *Santería*, I use it with this same affectionate spirit, and not as the slur that white and Hispanic slavers intended.

as well. Because blacks did not trust their masters, and with good reason, priests turned over the governing of each brotherhood to the most prominent and well-respected Africans among the slaves. These Africans, of course, had proved themselves to the parish by taking the sacraments and praying daily on the rosary. Leading a cofradia meant more freedom for a slave, so these positions were sought eagerly. Little did the masters know, however, that the most respected men and women among the slaves were the priests and priestesses of each ethnic group's tribes.

The heads of the cofradias were known as godfathers and godmothers of those they represented. It was here, in the cofradia, that the custom of referring to one's Lucumí priestess or priest as one's godmother or godfather began. The first job of the godparent was religious instruction, assisting in catechism. Part of that instruction was to teach the converts about the holy saints. Openly, godparents taught the traditional beliefs about the saints. Secretly, they taught African myths about the sacred spirits and showed how they shared attributes with the saints.

Very quickly, the various ethnic groups brought together in a cofradia saw that all their spirits were related, although at the same time vastly different, and that they could, in secret, hide the worship of their spirits behind the guise of the saints. Thus began the amalgamation and sharing of religious beliefs between the once conflicting tribes; the cofradias also initiated the syncretization of African spirits with the saints of the Catholic Church. The final job of the cofradia's godparents was to represent their charges at baptism, and this spawned the Lucumí custom of being baptized a Catholic before being allowed entrance into an *ilé ocha*, or spiritual house of an orisha.* The slave masters and Catholic clergy rejoiced, for it seemed that the Africans were catching on to the new religion very quickly. They gathered earlier on Sundays than did most whites for church services, and they stayed together until the late hours of the night, praying and praising the saints and God, although oftentimes in their native tongues. The celebrations of Catholic feast days for the saints became more colorful, flavored with African soul and spice; every slave who could attended and worshiped with great zeal. Because the program seemed to work so well, the cofradias were given more prominence and more freedom. The Holy Mother Church believed it was winning more souls for God.

During this time, four major ethnic groups were represented among the Cuban slaves: the Bantu, the Yoruba, the Ibibio/Ibó/Ijaw, and the Fon (Arara). While Bishop Morrell introduced the cofradia, Father Matienzo still insisted on letting the Africans continue their simplest ethnic customs. To do this, *cabildos*, or ethnic clubs, were established under the rule of the cofradia. The reorganization of cofradias along tribal lines, so the clergy theorized, would bring greater depth to the new Catholic devotees. Cabildos were licensed by cities through the church and allowed the various ethnic groups to study Catholicism together as a single ethnic group. Every Sunday and on the holy feast days the cabildos met to dance, sing, and worship God. The most popular of these were Cabildo Arara Sabalu Africano, Cabildo Arara Dahome, and Cabildo Arara Cuevano, all for the Arara tribes; Cabildo Macongo and Cabildo Mumbale, for the Bantu; and, most important for us, the Lucumí peoples, Cabildo Africano Lucumí. It was in Africano Lucumí that the Yoruba came together every Sunday to worship their orishas through the guises of the saints. They used the cabildo to keep their own religion alive secretly, for to be found out would mean an end to their religious freedom.† In Cabildo Africano Lucumí, the orisha Obatalá became known as Our Lady of Mercy, Oshún became Our Lady of Charity, Yemayá

*The Catholic baptism is becoming a dying practice among the new generation of Lucumí priests. In the days before the faith came to the United States, not only would the initiate be baptized in the church before the weeklong consecration as an orisha priest or priestess, but also, after the consecration was completed, the godparent would take the *iyawó* (the "bride," or new initiate) into a church so he or she could pay homage to the saints who helped save the faith from extinction. At this time, the iyawó would light a candle for the saints and pray while the godparent explained which orisha's worship was hidden behind that persona's face.

†This fear for loss of the slaves' newfound religious freedom gave birth to the ironclad tradition of Lucumí secrecy. To survive, we had to hide. This, fortunately, is something we no longer endure.

syncretized with the Virgin of Regla, Babaluaiye was Saint Lazarus, Oyá was known as Saint Teresa, and Shangó became Saint Barbara. The African feast days of the orishas were changed to match the feast days of the Catholic saints. And it was at this time that the slave masters nicknamed their charges' worship Santería. But while the Africans' seeming distortion of Catholicism to focus on the saints worried the slave masters, it also allayed their fears, for they believed that, in time, the blacks would "get it right" and worship the one true God.

As the Lucumí cabildos grew more joyous and bold in their celebrations, the master class came to regard them as a necessary nuisance. On Sunday nights and holy feast days, cabildo members met until late in the night, with seemingly ceaseless chanting and singing, continual drumming, and garrulous praising of saints in both Spanish and broken Yoruba. By 1800, while the actual cofradias still met in their allotted churches, the cabildos were banished outside the city walls. The master class saw this as a blessing, for no longer were they subjected to the noise. The evolving Lucumí adherents also saw this as a blessing, for no longer were they subjected to curious eyes or the danger of discovery. With this even greater freedom, the liturgies we came to know as Lucumí were solidified. While the previous years had brought changes and fragmentation, the continued influx of slaves into this more open cabildo society brought cohesion and solidification. During the country's last period of slavery, 1821–70, 16,700 more slaves per year were brought into the country. The Yoruba were a minority among these, but their numbers were still sufficient to renew and replenish the faith. Nigerian-initiated priests and priestesses of the orishas came together in large numbers, many having exposure to one another for the first time. To strengthen the faith and save it from future degeneration, the modern initiations of giving *elekes* (a series of ornate beaded necklaces presented in a special baptism ceremony), giving *warriors* (the compilation of the orishas Elegguá, Ogún, Ochosi, and Ósun presented to worshipers), and *asiento* (the Cuban-styled initiation that includes the giving of multiple orishas) were crafted. The new rituals of *obí* (coconut divination) and *diloggún* (cowrie-shell divination) were devised. By 1870, we had arrived: We were known even among the master class as the Lucumí, and we continue to flourish today.

Lucumí traditions are communal; one cannot be a priest alone, nor can one work the religion alone. Anyone who claims to be a *santero* (priest) or *santera* (priestess) arrives at that title through the toil and labor of his or her elders, and the names, both common and Lucumí, of those elders are not held in secret but recited proudly. Those who are knowledgeable and well versed in Lucumí traditions can recite from memory the lineage of their teachers reaching back decades.* Beyond the recitation of lineage and the personal acknowledgment of elders, initiates have one final document proving their initiation and lineage: the *libreta* (notebook) given to the iyawó after the ceremonies of the asiento are completed. Although the libreta contains sensitive information concerning a priest or priestess's *itá* (the life reading given to a new initiate at a divination ceremony) that need not be shared with others, the first few pages themselves are open to inspection by any who ask respectfully. On the first pages of this document are recorded the priest or priestess's full name, the date of his or her initiation, the signature of the godparent, the signature of the *yubonna* (the godparent's assistant in all ceremonies), and the signatures of all those who attended and put aché on the iyawó's head.† Those who sign the book, and the initiate's own godparents, are easily verified; being a religion of community,

*By reciting these lineages, Lucumí priests and priestesses can determine their relationships to each other within the religion. It is said that although our ranks increase geometrically, someone will "know someone who knows someone" or we will discover a common spiritual ancestor. Religiously, it is a very small world! Unfortunately, because of the politics behind the slave trade, not many initiates today can trace their lineage more than one or two generations into Africa. This, one day, might be an exciting area of research for someone with more time on his or her hands than myself.

†The godparent gives each priest or priestess who works at a iyawó's initiation an envelope with a small *derecho* (the sacred fee for the energy they bring). Before the godparent hands out this envelope, however, each working priest or priestess is required to sign the initiate's libreta, including the *oriaté* (an expert in Lucumí rituals). Therefore, if there are no signatures, there is no proof of initiation.

it is expected that an initiate will retain ties with some or all of these people for life. Quite simply, priests or priestesses without libretas, with libretas containing unverifiable signatures, or who cannot state the names of their godparents should be treated cautiously.* The Lucumí religion itself may be described as a process of spiritual evolution. One cannot simply pick up a Lucumí manual and become a practitioner, although books themselves can be useful guides to one's religious life. Those outside our faith are known as *aleyos*, or strangers; they have little faith and no involvement, but sometimes, out of desperation, they come to the priesthood for help when life becomes unbearable. In time, some aleyos might come to worship and adore the orishas, taking the elekes initiation.† Here, the aleyo begins by acknowledging the ancestors, the past from which he is born. Then he is stripped and bathed in an herbal elixir known as *omiero*. (In a manner similar to baptism, the omiero bath washes away the aleyo's past sins and transgressions, which stood in the way of his evolution.) Once bathed, he is dressed in white; with two or more priests or priestesses (normally, the godparent, the yubonna, and an oriaté) in attendance, the aleyo is presented with four beaded necklaces: the elekes of Obatalá, Yemayá, Oshún, and Shangó. The godparent chants, the priests or priestesses sing, and one by one the necklaces are draped over the believer's neck. He is now an *aborisha*, a believer and worshiper of the orishas, and the priest or priestess who puts the beads around his neck becomes the aborisha's godparent. The shrines in the godparent's home are the sanctuaries of the orishas; it becomes the aborisha's church, and it is to these orishas that he comes to worship.

After the vestment of the elekes, for most the next step in the religion is the reception of the warriors. The warriors are a conglomeration of four titanic orishas: Elegguá (fate or destiny), Ogún (the warrior and the lord of iron), Ochosi (the hunter), and Ósun (who watches over the initiate's head, or spiritual consciousness). Elegguá can take on many different forms; however, in almost all manifestations he comes as a cement head adorned with cowries. The specific Elegguá received by the aborisha is determined by a reading with the diloggún. Ogún's mysteries come with a cauldron containing several iron tools; among these is a metal crossbow and arrow, the symbol for the orisha Ochosi. Ósun's mysteries are kept inside a small metal cup adorned on top with a metal rooster and having four bells hanging from its edges. With the reception of these four powerful spirits, the aborisha finally begins his or her true walk in the religion. The godparent giving these orishas explains, upon their reception, how the initiate is to care for them and details the many chants, prayers, and *eboses* (offerings) that may be made to appease and work with them. It is said that those in possession of the warriors are in total control of their own destinies.

While there are other initiations an aborisha might take, such as that of Olokun (the primordial hermaphroditic ocean orisha), Orisha Oko (who represents the fertility of the earth), and *santo lavado* (the washing of one's guardian orisha), for most the next step in the religion is the weeklong ceremony known as *ocha* (also known as *kariocha* or *asiento*). The rites of ocha, which have been passed down orally, are a series of ceremonies that initiate an aborisha into the mysteries of his or her guardian or crowning orisha‡ and through which the aborisha is consecrated as a priest. Most initiates receive not only their guardian orisha but also the following orishas: Elegguá,

*I have put this information here for a very specific reason; once, someone very close and dear to me was defrauded of money by a priest who was, quite simply, a fake. Although the amount of money she paid for useless ritual services was minimal, the repercussions this event caused in my own family were irreparable. Forewarned is forearmed. Note that there is another way to verify the legitimacy of a santero's orishas: If the asiento is done correctly and properly, a special piece is included with each orisha's diloggún. The revelation of the identity of this special piece, however, is not to be found in this book.

†To honor our history in Cuba, some ilé ocha still require baptism as a Catholic before the reception of the elekes. This, again, is a dying practice among Lucumí adherents.

‡The concept of a guardian or crowning orisha is central to the Lucumí faith. It is believed that each person is ruled by one orisha, and when the ritual of asiento is given, that one spirit is put to the initiate's head and is worn, briefly, as a crown. Afterward, the initiate becomes a iyawó (bride) of that spirit and is properly initiated into the mysteries.

Obatalá, Ogún, Oshún, Oyá, Shangó, and Yemayá. In the ceremony of ocha, the initiate's head (spiritual consciousness) is reborn through the godparent's work, and the intiate's orishas are born anew from the godparent's *soperas* (the bowls wherein the sacred stones and implements of each orisha are kept). Once all this is done, the initiate becomes a iyawó, a bride of the spirits, and has finally settled into his or her new life. The state of being a iyawó lasts for a year and seven days; when this time has passed, the initiate is considered a priest or priestess.

The cost of the asiento ceremonies increases yearly with inflation. Bolts of cloth, several tureens, dozens of freshly picked herbs, many animals, countless implements (made of gold, silver, bronze, copper, and wood), and various other expenses are necessary for the rites of ocha. It is not unusual for the adherent to save four thousand to ten thousand dollars to cover the extensive costs of catering, clothing, work, and other items that go into "making the saint."

While these are the basic initiations that one follows when becoming involved in the Lucumí faith, at each level the goal is the same: worship of the orishas. As it is practiced today, Santería can be divided into two active aspects that feed on each other: worship and divination. Worship takes many forms. Daily worship in the home consists of the priest or priestess and the aborisha pouring water and giving prayers to Olódumare, Elegguá, the *egun* (ancestral spirits), and the guardian orisha. These offerings are intended to cool the divinities, and they, in turn, cool the worshiper so that the day is blessed. On Mondays, Elegguá (fate, destiny, the opener of all roads) is propitiated and plied with offerings of wine, rum, and cigars. On a weekly basis, one's patron orisha is refreshed with special oils, prayers, and libations.* Orisha priests and priestesses will present a wide array of meats, drinks, and thanksgiving offerings throughout the year on behalf of other aborishas and initiates. Votive offerings are made infrequently, as are propitiatory sacrifices. Finally, there is the yearly or anniversary offering of the *ilé ocha*, when initiates and godchildren come together to drum, dance, chant, and sing on the holy day of any one spirit. Worship easily becomes a daily, weekly, monthly, and yearly affair for the faith's adherents.

The second aspect of Santería, divination, is grossly misunderstood, sometimes even by those who adhere to its practices. People in all ages and cultures have sought shades of the future, desiring knowledge of what is to come. Pagan practices have always incorporated the art of divination in their religions; from the Greek oracle at Delphi to the Ogham of the Celts, divination has been a part of, not separate from, religion. In today's New Age movement, however, divination is often an act performed outside one's spiritual faith. No longer are gods, goddesses, or spirits consulted. Some people patronize fortune-tellers and psychics in the hope of gleaning the inner intentions of a lost lover, while others seek a quick peek at future careers and prosperity. Although some use spirit guides in their consultations, and this is closer to the African spiritual systems that survived, many still credit the entire act of divining to the higher, inner self, and this is anathema to African beliefs.

It is the love of our African souls, our ancestors, our roots, and our orishas that brings us each, in time, to the Lucumí religion. Yet it is the desire to worship the orishas better, to care for them as they wish to be cared for, that brings us to the oracles. Through the *odu*, the "random" patterns produced by sixteen cowrie shells on the mat, we learn of each spirit's will. Our destiny, goals, loves, and losses are displayed with each sacred mandala. Divination is an act that feeds our worship, and the worship then given fulfills the prophecies of divination. This book concerns itself with that aspect of the orisha traditions that was nourished by the Caribbean's lush, tropical climate—the true art of divination.

Because our religion survived centuries of slavery through the safeguard of seclusion and stone-silence, as I present this book I realize that many see this writing as the breaking of an ancient, secret code. Although traditional Yoruba religion is very open

*Aborishas, adherents who are not priests or priestesses, try to visit the godparent weekly to bring offerings to the godparent's crowning orisha. If the guardian orisha of the aborisha is known, weekly worship of that spirit takes place in the godparent's home as well.

about its practices and tenets, even about the secrets of its odu, the Lucumí religion still shrouds itself in darkness and mystery. The silence is unbreakable, sometimes even among adherents. While silence was a valid survival mechanism through the heresy of slavery, the mystery it engenders causes us further loss and fragmentation; those elders who hold the secrets of our religion are slowly dying out, and without careful instruction, many of our mysteries are in danger of loss. This same secrecy allows those without *santo* on their heads (those who have not been initiated) to move in our midst, taking advantage of those seeking the true religion of the orishas by claiming initiation they do not have. This was the true goal of slavery: to destroy our culture and make us subservient to a ruling class; by hiding, we open ourselves to our own loss and destruction. Our own internal growth threatens our ranks as well. The Lucumí faith itself is legal now (since the U.S. Supreme Court ruling in the case of the Church of the Lucumí vs. the city of Hialeah, Florida); it attracts a hugely diverse new following, and older heads cannot keep up with the demands of training a new priesthood. I will agree with my critics that my book cannot and should not take the place of a living teacher for initiates, but I offer it as a detailed reference to help serious students (and some elders) retain the enormous volume of information required of them when accessing the oracle known as the diloggún.

Although this volume might seem massive, it should not be approached as a definitive treatise on the many patterns that can fall when using the diloggún. This work is certainly more comprehensive than my previous work, including 1,200 pages of manuscript and over 400,000 words on the subject. It will fill yet another void of knowledge among orisha adherents in the New World. However, even something of this scope cannot be exhaustive. Although oral, our holy book is vast, larger in scope than that of any other world religion, and it is far more ancient than any other living faith. These writings are but a minute part of those things I have learned from my elders, and while this book seems large, in truth the odu are even larger. I, a single man, cannot capture all the myth, magic, history, or teachings in my writings. This book can serve as a resource, but ultimately one must depend on one's elders and godparents as guides in the religious world. That is how I learned, not from books, and that is how others should learn as well. Between my writings and our elders' teachings, the true secrets and mysteries of our faith will be captured for future generations. Ultimately, that is the true vision of my work: preservation and continuation for our future. May this vision never die.

# ONE

# MANIPULATING THE DILOGGÚN, THE ORACLE OF THE ORISHAS

## An Introduction to the Diloggún

While many consider the diloggún to be merely an oracle, in truth it is a unique spiritual process of rituals, liturgies, and discoveries. The diloggún is based on an oracular system used in Nigeria, the holy land and origin of the Yoruba tribes, the predecessors of the Lucumí. There, before humans knew of orishas or odu, there was only Orúnmila. Born from Olódumare herself, Orúnmila was the great witness to creation and knew all things. He incarnated among mortals, bringing his infinite knowledge of odu and divination to earth. Orúnmila's teachings are known as *Ifá.* The sacred science of Ifá was first passed to Asheda (the first *babalawo,* or Ifá priest) and then to Akoda (the second babalawo). Together, these two men spread Orúnmila's cult of divination among the Yoruba, and from it the original sixteen-cowrie-shell oracle evolved.

Yet the forced transplantation of Africans to Cuba brought the necessity for change. Political factors behind slave trading ensured that many babalawos were left in Nigeria, and without the cult of Ifá, orisha worshipers in the New World lacked an advanced oracle. With only a broken knowledge of the 256 odu, the sixteen-cowrie-shell system in the New World grew slowly and painfully. It remained incomplete until the arrival in the early 1900s of four titanic priests and priestesses: Mama Monserrate, Octavio Sama, Timotea Albear, and Ferminita Gomez.*

Although the dates of her birth, initiation, and death are not remembered in our lineage of the religion, we know that Mama Monserrate rose to power among the priesthood sometime in the late 1800s to the early 1900s, amid a period of religious oppression by the Catholic Church. For thirty years (roughly 1880–1910), it became the Church's mission to stamp out all surviving remnants of African culture on the island of Cuba; to be a santero or santera was considered a criminal act. In spite of this, Monserrate immersed herself in the culture and was crowned with (initiated to) the orisha Aganyú. Her name in Lucumí became Obatero. We know little about her mundane life; however, we do know from oral history that Obatero spoke rarely on religious matters, even within the *igbodu* (the sacred room where the orishas are born and initiates are crowned). However, when Obatero's mouth opened,

*My information on the history of the religion and our oracle, the diloggún, is based on the oral history of my elders. In places, this information might differ from the scant documentation left by historians. Remembering that all history is written by the victors, in spite of what may exist in official documentation, I trust the oral version of these histories more than the written record. It is left up to the reader to do his or her own research among both written scholars and oral versions remaining in his or her own line of the religion. Somewhere between the two, perhaps the truth will be found.

all were silent. Her peers respected her words as if they were dictates from the orishas themselves. Although she was influential in her time, it would be decades after her death before others credited her as the true initiator of our faith in Matanzas, Cuba.* For by her hands were many heads crowned, and by her teaching did the codification of the Lucumí faith begin. Under Mama Monserrate's crown, Cuban priests began to establish Lucumí as a liturgy unto itself, although the system was still experimental and developing with each religious function. Obatero was illiterate, but those who could read and write took copious notes of her style, and these fragmented libretas formed the foundation for many of our religious practices. Of all the heads (initiates) born from this priestess, only two were destined for a greatness beyond her own: Octavio Sama, known in Lucumí as Obadimelli, and Ferminita Gomez, known as Ochabi.

Octavio Sama's name, like Mama Monserrate's, is all but lost except in myth and oral history. He is known to most religious lines of the Lucumí faith, but each branch has its own stories about this powerful man's priesthood. In my own line, it is said that Octavio came to Cuba as a slave with his mother. In his homeland, Octavio was preparing for initiation to Ifá and, as is the custom there, spent years of his youth working to master the verses of Ifá. His initiation, however, would never take place, for the slave traders ripped him from his homeland before it could happen. In Cuba, Monserrate saw Octavio's potential and crowned him with the orisha Oshún by Cuban rites. Once Oshún was installed in his head, however, the orisha Aganyú took possession of him. Although the ceremony was finished and Oshún was in Octavio's head, Monserrate put Aganyú on Octavio's shoulder. Octavio's initiation gave birth to the custom of crowning Aganyú through Oshún (a process known as *Oshún oro Aganyú*).

After his crowning, Octavio's aché seasoned. With Oshún on his head but possessed by Aganyú,† he became known as the "man with two crowns." He was a genius, blessed with superior skills at divination. His itá forbade his initiation to Ifá, so as a iyawó Octavio applied his knowledge of Ifá's 256 odu to the sixteen signs of the African diloggún. During his priesthood, he completed a reformation of the entire system, creating the 256 patterns of diloggún divination used in Lucumí ritual.‡ Unlike his godmother, Mama Monserrate, Sama had a basic education and was able to write fragmented notes about the system he perfected. These libretas have been saved, copied, and photocopied; most are passed down by elder initiates and oriatés today.

In time, Octavio crowned another Cuban, Nicolas Valentin Angarica.§ Among the Lucumí, Angarica was known as Obatola, and under his godfather's guidance he became a powerful, respected oriaté in Matanzas and beyond. Though he was illiterate himself, one of his godchildren penned a book, *Manuel del Oribate*, from Obatola's basic teachings. While not the most detailed or reliable text, this tome is still copied, reproduced, and sold in *botánicas* (religious supply stores often found in Latin American communities) across the United States. Although it has many shortcomings, this book is regarded as an underground classic of our faith.

During Octavio Sama's work as an oriaté, he befriended another slave brought from Nigeria named Timotea Albear. In Lucumí, she was known

*The Spanish word *matanza* translates to "slaughter" or "carnage." Many credit the naming of this part of Cuba, Matanzas, to the number of slaves put to death there.

†When Octavio Sama moved to Havana in the late 1920s, he took the secrets for the direct crowning of Aganyú with him. It is believed that Mama Monserrate did not continue the custom of directly crowning with Aganyú in Matanzas, because no other priest or priestess of Aganyú was made by her hands during her lifetime. Most of the remaining Aganyú initiations done in Matanzas after Mama Monserrate's death were performed via Oshún oro Aganyú.

‡Another ancestor of note is Eduardo Salako, who lived and died in Matanzas. While he had little to do with the structure of the diloggún (the focus of this book), Salako, under Mama Monserrate, became a major architect of many of our religious practices. He was a member of the Lucumí Society in Matanzas, which, we believe, owes it existence to the work of Monserrate as well.

§Nicolas Angarica was born sometime in 1901. His date of death is unknown to us; however, *Manual del Oribate* was published in 1952, and we know Angarica was not alive at that time.

as Ayái La Tuan. Timotea, a priestess of Shangó, had completed the initiation rites while still a child in Africa. Although Octavio spent his childhood in Africa studying the odu of Ifá, Ayái's specialty had been cowrie-shell divination. Some elders say that this priestess had already begun to divine using composite castings of the shells. When Timotea and Octavio met, her skills were already beyond those of most male oriatés in Cuba, and with Octavio's guidance, she became proficient in the new form of Lucumí diloggún. In time, Timotea was regarded as the first female oriaté of the Lucumí faith.* This, however, was not her most important contribution to Lucumí history. During her priesthood in Cuba, the religion was growing, yet it was also in danger of fragmentation. To keep the cults of all our spirits alive, Timotea created our method of asiento, the giving of multiple orishas when an initiate is crowned. She was a true pioneer in the New World and finished most of the Lucumí codification.†

Ferminita Gomez (also called Ochabi) was the second most influential godchild of Mama Monserrate. Of all the women crowned in the early 1900s, none was more influential or powerful than she. Before her crowning, Ferminita was marked a child of Oshún by her godparents, Adele and Kudasi (their real names are lost to us). Though Ferminita had prepared to be a child of Oshún, Yemayá took possession of Ferminita before the ceremony could begin and demanded to be installed in Ferminita's head. The igbodu was in an uproar; this was Yemayá's first possession in Cuba, and neither Adele nor Kudasi could crown her children. Only one woman was available who knew the secrets for crowning Yemayá: Mama Monserrate. She was called in to finish the work, and Ferminita became her godchild. After the asiento, Ferminita's itá told that she was to receive a very special orisha: Olokun. Olokun was given to her by the hands of Yenye t'Olokun, a babalawo crowned directly in Africa with this orisha *before* he was initiated to Ifá. Ferminita firmly established Olokun's worship throughout Matanzas and the rest of Cuba; Olokun still lives with her descendants of both spirit and blood. Beyond Olokun, Ferminita's most important contributions to us were her clearly written libretas, which detail the Lucumí practices prevalent in Matanzas during her lifetime. Copies of her pages are jealously guarded, even today.‡

Many say that the religion was codified in Havana; in truth, though, the earliest traces of Lucumí codification are found in Matanzas. From Matanzas, the bare bones of our religion, the rituals in practice, were spread throughout Cuba, fleshed out further by the elders' aché. However, we owe our oracle, our asiento, and our liturgy to the work of these four amazing priestesses and priests: Obatero (Mama Monserrate), Obadimelli (Octavio Sama), Ayái La Tuan (Timotea Albear), and Ochabi (Ferminta Gomez). Through their work, especially the knowledge and aché of Obadimelli, the final reformations to our divination system were completed and a new oracle was born to the religion: the diloggún.

The word *diloggún* itself may be described in two fashions. First, when speaking of diloggún, one may be referring to the cowrie shells of a particular orisha, which a Lucumí priest or priestess receives upon initiation. As described in the introduction, in the ocha ritual an adherent is crowned with the guardian or crowning orisha and also receives several other orishas. An orisha is composed of three material elements: *otanes* (stones), implements, and diloggún. The otanes form the body of the deity; they are stones upon which sacrificial offerings to the orisha are given. The implements are the metal or wooden tools sacred to the orisha, the symbols

*Timotea Albear married Bernabe Menocal, a famous babalawo, and moved to Havana; there, she was regarded as the first great Havana oriaté. She died sometime in 1935. Her children, and her children's children, still practice the religion; some migrated to the States in the early 1950s.

†Note that while Albear's contributions to Lucumí liturgy were phenomenal, she was by no means the only influential oriaté initiated and tutored by the prolific Octavio Sama. Others who came along from Octavio's work include Tomas Romero, Liberato Valdez, and Nicolas Angarica, among others less noted.

‡Though I am not able to retain a copy of Ferminita's libretas myself, I have been given several opportunities to read and study her writings. They are an unmatched contribution to our religious practices.

by which it does its work on earth. The diloggún, or cowrie shells, are the most important aspect of an orisha, for within these cowrie shells resides the soul of the deity. All the spirits have eighteen shells in their diloggún, except for Elegguá, who has twenty-one shells, because twenty-one is his sacred number and is shared with no other spirit.

The second way of defining *diloggún* is as the set of sixteen shells an italero selects for use in divination, and for the purposes of this book, this is the usage I intend when I speak of casting or reading the diloggún. The shells are believed not only to house the soul of an orisha but also to be its mouthpiece; through the shells and the sacred alphabet of the diloggún, an orisha is able to speak to a priest. In its natural state, a cowrie shell has on one side a smooth, rounded back and on the other side an elongated, serrated opening resembling a mouth. Before initiation, the initiate's godparent painstakingly sorts through bags of cowrie shells, picking the largest, strongest, and most beautiful to house the orisha's soul. With a knife or file, the godparent removes the rounded back of the cowrie; the rounded hump is "popped off" so that the back is flat. The godparent files down the new surface so that it has no ragged edges. During the rites of ocha, the otanes, implements, and shells are consecrated, born from the godparent's own orishas with the aid of the herbal elixir omiero. Once born, the orishas can speak through the shells.

To read or cast the diloggún, the diviner selects sixteen shells at random from an orisha's set of cowries. He sets the remaining shells to the side, with the natural "mouth" facing down. Cowries left to the side are known as *adele* (witnesses), and while they must be present for divination, they remain unused. The mechanically opened side of the shell has a value of zero; the natural mouth has a value of one. When the diloggún (the set of sixteen cowrie shells) is cast on the diviner's mat, a numerical value from zero to sixteen is obtained by adding up the values of the shells depending on which mouths face up. The number corresponds to a particular letter in the sacred alphabet of the diloggún, and the orisha invoked uses this numerically founded alphabet to speak to the priest.

To comprehend the diloggún's system, think of it as a vast, limitless book that chronicles creation, beginning with the first stirring of Olódumare. If the diloggún is the complete book, each odu is a single chapter of that book. The sixteen major chapters or divisions of the diloggún are known as the *parent odu*. Each parent odu has a name (letter) and a number associated with it. To effectively employ this oracle, one must know all sixteen names and their numerical equivalents. They are:

**1** Okana
**2** Eji Oko
**3** Ogundá
**4** Irosun
**5** Oché
**6** Obara
**7** Odí
**8** Eji Ogbe
**9** Osá
**10** Ofún
**11** Owani
**12** Ejila Shebora
**13** Metanla
**14** Merinla
**15** Marunla
**16** Merindilogún

The number of mouths displayed in a single casting of shells corresponds to the number of a parent odu (hence, if five open mouths fall on the diviner's mat, the odu Oché is open).

Just as the chapters in many books are divided into smaller sections, so each odu has smaller divisions, called the *omo odu* (children of odu). Each omo odu is a part of a spiritual family linked by the parent odu that gave it birth, just as each subheading of a chapter is part of the chapter's greater whole.

By casting the diloggún, an *italero* (an expert in the reading of the diloggún) accesses one of these chapter subsections on behalf of a client. The diviner himself does not know, initially, which section of the book to read. He must first gently awaken the orisha whose diloggún is being cast with an invocation known as *mojubando*, a litany paying homage to Olódumare, the earth, the ancestors, and that particular orisha. (Note that for almost all sessions, barring an itá, an italero consults with Eleggua's shells.) Speaking through the two castings of cowrie shells the italero makes, the orisha identifies which part of the diloggún applies to the client. The first casting names the parent odu, and the second the omo odu, narrowing the reading down to 1 of 256 possible combinations. The first casting is modified by the second. For example, if the italero's first casting of diloggún results in a mandala of nine open mouths on the mat, the parent odu is Osá. Casting the cowries a second time, if the italero counts three mouths, the odu Ogundá has fallen. The resulting odu is Osá Ogundá, and the italero knows he must search his memory for the meanings of that particular composite letter.

Each of the odu forms a spiritual organism, a complete entity that forebodes various blessings (known collectively as *iré*) or misfortunes (known collectively as *osogbo*). After casting a composite letter, the italero uses eight *ibó* (divination tools) to extract from it the qualities of iré and osogbo. Depending on the question asked, the ibó are used in a number of pairings; together, italero and client manipulate the cowries and ibó in tandem to determine the orientations of the odu. From these are the predictions of any one letter drawn and the eboses needed to placate volatile essences determined. Harmony is created. Evolution unfolds.

Throughout this text, I will explore not only the manipulations of this oracle but also the metaphysics and meanings behind each letter of diloggún. Remember that although the odu contain all the facets of our faith and lives, they are not stagnant, unchanging, mere collections of sacred stories and scripts conceived centuries ago. Each of the letters is alive in the universe and in our lives. They are organisms of energy, creatures of symbiosis awaiting connection with our own human energies as they are opened on the mat. A divination session, then, becomes the most important focus of Lucumí worship. The sacred shells reveal the forces at play in an adherent's life, and these energies are redefined and placated as the orisha priest manipulates the letters in an attempt to help his client evolve. Diloggún is an oracle, yes; yet it is also a long, arduous road to change and personal transformation. It is the heart of Lucumí worship.

## Opening the Diloggún

There are two styles for preparing the divination room. The most traditional uses a mat on the floor. Diviner, assistant, and attending priests and priestesses sit on the mat; in front of the diviner, seated on a low stool, is the client. Only he sits above the rest. In contrast, some diviners prepare a table with enough chairs to accommodate the client, godparent(s), diviner, and any priests or priestesses who are acting as assistants or students.* For this scenario, the diviner lays a grass mat on the working surface. The room is set up so that the client sits on one side of the table with his or her godparents, and the italero and other elders/students sit on the opposite side of the table. No matter how the diviner chooses to read, whether on a mat or on a table, a *jícara* (gourd) filled with water, a lit cigar, and a lit candle are placed on the divination surface to give aché and strength to the spirits consulted;† beside these are placed the diloggún of the orisha and the complete set of ibó used for the reading. The symbols for the eight ibó are *efun* (a white, powdery chalk), a black stone, two bound cowries, a seashell, a piece of bone, a guacalote seed, a doll's head, and a piece of broken china or pottery. The assistant making a record of the reading is provided with a pen and plenty of paper.

After arranging the room and seating everyone properly, the diviner's assistant records the client's full name, as it was given to him or her at birth, at the top of a piece of paper. If the client is a married woman, the assistant records her full birth name plus her married name. This information is kept

*In Lucumí worship, to properly learn the oracle one must undergo an apprenticeship with a competent italero or a period of study with an oriaté. Books such as this one are valuable guides and study texts for the casting of diloggún, yet they cannot replace the intimate environment provided by a novice-elder relationship.

†Not all diviners agree with this setup. No matter how the working area is prepared, at the very least the jícara of water, the shells, and the ibó are necessary. The rest of the elements laid out depends on the diviner's beliefs and preferences.

nearby so that the diviner can refer to it during the *mojuba* (prayer); naming the client in full is integral to the invocation of that person's ancestors, known as egun, during consultation. When the initial preparations for the room and the written record are complete, the diviner takes the efun and rubs it over both his hands until the palms, fingers, and thumbs are covered in white. He does this to the client as well (for one needs clean, pure hands before handling the shells of an orisha). Now, he instructs the client to take the derecho (the small fee, usually twenty-one dollars, that is sacred to the orishas) and fold it tightly into a small ball. The client crosses himself with the derecho, marking the four quarters of his body, then gives it to the diviner. This is an important moment in the reading, for with the passing of this money, the energy exchange among the client, the italero, and the orisha begins; from this moment the oracle is considered open and there should be no interruptions. As a final preparation, the italero marks a white chalk circle on the grass mat, drawing double lines through the four cardinal points: north, south, east, and west.

Before praying to the orisha, the priest holds a jícara of fresh water in his left hand and, using the fingers of his right, sprinkles three dashes of water before the orisha's shells with the following words.

> *Omi tutu; ona tutu, aché tutu. Tutu ilé. Tutu Laroye. Tutu Arikú Babawa.*
>
> Fresh water, freshen the road to the orisha, refresh my power. Freshen my home. Freshen Elegguá in his path of Eshu Laroye.* Bring us freshness that has no end.

One offers this simple libation before praying to any orisha to bring coolness and freshness to our roads, to our aché, to our homes, and to Eshu Laroye, an avatar of Elegguá. Heat or stagnation in these areas could hinder the consultation. Our world is a place of hot and cold, stagnation and refreshment, growth and decline; when working with the orishas, however, we put ourselves in a place where only evolution can be found. One works to remove those things that overheat and destroy life. Eshu Laroye is both honored and refreshed by this ritual gesture. He is the companion of Oshún, the orisha who makes life worth living, and he is one of Elegguá's most mischievous paths. If we desire our prayers to reach the orishas, we must first honor and cool him so that he will help, and not hinder, our communication. It takes only a moment to do this, yet it is one of the most crucial points in our invocation.

Having refreshed ourselves, our homes, and Eshu Laroye, the ritual of mojubando begins. The italero selects sixteen of the shells and places the rest to the side with the ibó, facedown. While chanting, the italero holds these sixteen shells and adds to them the derecho that the client has provided for the consultation. He rubs these briskly yet gently between his hands to slowly awaken the orisha soul sleeping in the cowries. If the diviner's hands are too small to hold all the shells and the derecha, he may place them on the mat and rub them in a circular, clockwise motion. This gentle manipulation of the shells continues until all the prayers are complete.

> *Mojuba Olófin. Mojuba Olorún. Mojuba Olódumare. Mojuba Olójoni. Oní Odún Mocuedun. Olorún Alabosúdaye. Olorún Alabosúnife. Olorún Alayé. Olorún Elemí. Olódumare Oba aterere kaje. Olódumare, mojuba gbogbo ikú imbelese. Olódumare, ibaé bayé tonú. Mojuba atijó ojo. Mojuba atiwó orún. Mojuba ayái odún, oní odún, odún olá. Mojuba Orún. Mojuba Oshúkua. Mojuba ile ogere a foko jerí.*
>
> Homage is paid to the part of God closest to the earth. I pay homage to the God in the heavens, God who is eternal and everywhere. I pay homage to the one who owns this day. Today, I greet you! Olorún, who is the keeper and protector of the earth. Olorún, the one who protects the first, holy city of Ifé. Olorún,

*Eshu Laroye is one of the many avatars of Elegguá. Many orishas have different avatars, also known as paths. The avatars are related to the orishas' many incarnations on the earth; many orishas have spent mortal lives among humans. One of the mysteries of the asiento is that when an aleyo is crowned and becomes a iyawó, in some ways he or she also becomes an avatar of the guardian orisha. Only those avatars of significant religious, historical, or political importance are remembered specifically and become paths of that orisha. Note that while many specific avatars are agreed upon by most believers, the subject itself is one of considerable debate among the more knowledgeable ilé ocha.

living one and owner of the earth. Olorún, you who owns all spirits. Olódumare, the one who encompasses the entire Cosmos. Olódumare, I pay homage to all the ancestors that sit at your feet now. I praise the creative forces and those that have sacrificed their own lives for the continuity of life. I pay homage to the awakening sun, the sunrise. I pay homage to the dying sun, the sunset. I pay homage to all eternity: yesterday, today, and tomorrow. I pay homage to the sun. I pay homage to the moon. I pay homage to Mother Earth.

Beginning with the first three sentences of the mojuba—"Mojuba Olófin. Mojuba Olorún. Mojuba Olódumare"—the supplicant invokes and addresses the powers of creation, the very forces that began the universe aeons ago. Because all things human and divine are descended from and created by the collective forces known as God, before beginning to address the orisha the supplicant must give honor and respect to God. The intonation begins with Olófin, a force that some consider an ancient, all-powerful aspect of God—the part of creation that is closest to the earth and the most easily approachable. *Olófin* is a Lucumí contraction meaning "owner of the palace," the palace being all of the earth, the majestic home in which dwells the spirit of the divine. Through Olófin we pray to Olorún and Olódumare, for those aspects of the divine are the most primal and farthest from creation. *Olorún* is yet another Lucumí contraction, meaning "the owner of heaven." Olorún is seen in the daytime sky, its symbol being the sun, and although one does not worship the sun itself, praise is given to it as the symbol of Olorún on earth. Olódumare, as was mentioned in the introduction, is the ultimate creative force that gave birth to the orishas. *Olódumare* is a contraction meaning "the owner of odu and the womb." Odu is a woman, and the womb is part of the feminine reproductive system. Thus, although Olódumare is beyond gender, it is not incorrect to think of it as the Great Mother, the starry night sky from which all is born.

*Mojuba Orúnmila Eleri ikin. Mojuba igba Irunmole ojukotún. Mojuba igba ojukosí. Mojuba Irunmole wamale. Mojuba Akoda. Mojuba Asheda. Mojuba ejubona Mefa. Mojuba gbogbowan Obá Ilé Ifé. Mojuba Odúduwa. Mojuba Oranmiyan. Mojuba Arabá lotu Ifé. Mojuba Olokun. Mojuba Olosa. Mojuba awon iyá afinju eje. Mojuba Ajé-ogunguluso Olambo yeye aye. Mojuba itá Merindilogún. Mojuba Orún Okó. Mojuba okún Okó. Mojuba Okiti awo Okó. Mojuba ará. Mojuba ilé. Mojuba yeye. Mojuba baba. Mojuba gbogbowan Imale Iju. Ibaé tototo Olódumare y mojuba. Kinkanmaché Orún, mojuba.*

I pay homage to Orúnmila, the witness to creation and the recorder of all the odu. I pay homage to the two hundred divinities on the left side of God. I pay homage to the two hundred divinities on the right side of God. I pay homage to the divinities that came to the earth. I pay homage to Orúnmila's first student. I pay homage to Akoda's first student. I respect all those who teach others the sacred path of Ifá. I pay homage to all the chiefs of the sacred city and cradle of civilization, Ilé Ifé. I pay homage to the founder of the Yoruba empire. I pay homage to Odúduwa's son. I pay homage to all the diviners who live in the sacred city. I respect the spirit of the ocean that first owned all the land. I pay homage to the spirit of the lagoon that first formed as land arose from the sea. I pay homage to the council of the Mothers, the beautiful birds [the Witches] who are the Mothers of the forest. I pay homage to the spirits of the forest who have come to the aid of the Mothers of the forest again and again. I pay homage to the sixteen odu of creation, the containers of all existence. I pay homage to the stone of heaven, the immovable stone of Olódumare. I honor the strength of the stone and the mystery of the stone of creation. I pay homage to the body. I pay homage to the earth and the land. I pay homage to all the mothers and my Mother. I pay homage to all the fathers and my Father. I pay homage to all the invisible spirits who are present at this time. I give all my praise to the spirit of creation, and give my humble thanks. For all the blessings that come to me from heaven, I give thanks.

These litanies are not used by all ilé ocha. In the Lucumí religion, there is a divide, an irreconcilable chasm, between those houses that work closely with Ifá and the babalawos and those that do not. Much of this chasm stems from the work of Ferminita Gomez (see page 11), who some say "reclaimed" our religion from the hands of Ifá. The priests of Orúnmila, the babalawos, however, are still indispensable to the religion. The babalawos perform many functions that an orisha priest or priestess cannot fulfill. No matter how little or how much time we spend in this religion, we all come, at some point, to the feet of Orúnmila. If a member of the Lucumí faith has received anything from the babalawos, even if it was only a reading, it is in good taste to offer these few lines of praise to the mysteries of Orúnmila. As with any other aspect of this religion, when in doubt as to what should be done, question the godparents. They know what is best for spiritual evolution.

> *Mojuba gbogbowan Olodó ará orún: oluwos, iyaloshas, babaloshas, omo-kolaba egun imbelese Olódumare. Mojuba gbogbowan Olodó ará orún: oluwos, iyaloshas, babaloshas, omo-kolaba egun elelegba* lagba-lagba imbelese, timbelese Olódumare.*
>
> I pay homage to those who have gone to the river and who are now citizens of heaven, the dead priests and priestesses who rest with Olódumare. I pay homage to all the oluwos, iyaloshas, babaloshas, and babalawos who have Olófin, the dead who are at the feet of God. I pay homage to those who have gone to the river and who now live in heaven with Olódumare: oluwos, iyaloshas, babaloshas, and babalawos who have Olófin, and also the dead of Elegguá who are now at the feet of God.

By now, the diviner has not only addressed the primal powers of creation but also begun to pray to the dead elders of our faith. These elders made the rites of ocha while living and have now passed beyond the land of the dead to Olódumare. They sum up the powers of heaven, the invisible realm, those forces that we call *ará onú*, or the inhabitants of heaven. By honoring these greater powers, the italero ensures that only positive energies are called to the mat. He proceeds with all their powers and blessings behind his actions. Then the focus is narrowed a bit; the italero begins praying for and to the ancestral priests and priestesses who lived and died in the service of the orisha whose diloggún is being consulted (in this case, the children of Elegguá). One of the mysteries of this religion is that of egun and ancestral reverence; it is believed that each of us, while on earth, is the child of a specific orisha, and beyond death, our energies melt and merge into the whole of that sacred spirit. Indeed, the orishas themselves were once human, and upon their earthly demise they moved beyond the grave and back into the whole whence they came. The fact that these spirits were born to earth makes our own egun, from the most distant past, the mothers and fathers of God.

Having addressed the greater forces of creation and the body of egun that makes up a specific orisha, the supplicant then begins to narrow his focus once more. He moves into prayer for the egun of his spiritual family that gave birth to his *orí*, or consciousness. He also prays to those egun of his family line that brought his physical head/body to birth. Among our faith we say that we stand on the shoulders of those who have come before. Though it is an orisha to whom one prays, one would not be praying to this force had the ancestors not given birth to both the physical and spiritual heads. The next part of the mojuba pays homage to these ancestral forces, asking for their blessings, their strength, their knowledge, and their aché before invoking the macrocosmic forces known as the orishas. It brings our invocations full circle and narrows us down magically to this one moment when we celebrate our humanness, our weakness, and our strength, and it gives us sacred time and space in which we may call upon our gods.

> *Ibaé bayen tonú gbogbo egun ará orún orí emi nani [your name in ocha or your given name if ocha has not been made].*

*Elelegba* is a Lucumí contraction that means "the dead priests and priestesses of Elegguá." To describe the priests and priestesses of the other orishas, use with the orisha's name the prefix *ol* (for a name beginning with a vowel) or *olo* (for a name beginning with a consonant). Examples: olobatalá, oloshún, oloshangó, oloyá, oloyemayá, ologún, olochosi. In the case of the orishas who are not crowned on the head but are given *oro in santo* (crowned through the ritual of another orisha), the prefix *omo* is used, with a hyphen. Examples: omo-Ibeyi, omo-Ainá, omo-Inle, and so on.

I give homage to all the ancestral forces that join me on my journey, I who am known as _____.

*Ibaé bayen tonú gbogbo egun ará orún orí iyá [use* baba *in place of* iyá *if the godparent is a man] itobi mi, [name of one's godparent]. Ibaé bayen tonú gbogbo egun ará orún orí yubonna mi, [name of one's yubonna]. Ibaé bayen tonú gbogbo egun ará orún orí igboro kale ile. Ibaé bayen tonú gbogbo egun, gbogbowan Olodó, lagba lagba otokú ará orún timbelaye, imbelese Olorún, Olódumare.*

I pay homage and give my respect to all the ancestors that accompany the head of my godmother/godfather, [name of godparent]. I pay homage and give my respect to all the ancestors that accompany the head of my yubonna, [name of yubonna]. I pay homage and give my respect to all the ancestors that accompany the priests and priestesses visiting my house. I give my respect and pay homage to all the dead, all those who have gone to the river and are now my spiritual ancestors; I pay homage to all those in heaven who are now at the feet of Olódumare.

*Ará orún, ibaé bayen tonú. [Name of deceased priest or priestess] ibaé.*

Those who now live in heaven, my respects are paid to those who have gone to the other land in the sky. [Name of deceased priest or priestess], homage is paid.

*[Name of deceased priest or priestess] ibaé.*

Homage to individual deceased priests and priestesses continues until all the ancestors in one's spiritual lineage have been named.

*Ibaé gbogbo egun iyá mi, [name of one's mother]. Ibaé gbogbo egun baba mi, [name of one's father].*

My respects are paid to the ancestors of my mother, [the name of one's mother]. My respects are paid to the ancestors of my father, [the name of one's father].

*[Name of deceased family member, starting with the most recent death], ibaé.*

This continues until all the known deceased ancestors in one's blood lineage have been named.

Having honored creation and egun, the mojuba becomes a prayer for the protection and health of all priests and priestesses and brothers and sisters in the ilé ocha, or family of the orisha, of which the supplicant is part. Whenever a ritual of ocha is done, its energies unfold to incorporate all those who might be present and those who are not. Through these rites, it is hoped that the blessings gleaned from these prayers will better not just the person praying but also the entire ilé ocha. And the supplicant asks permission of his godparents and elders to proceed with his religious practices, even though they may be physically removed from the sacred space, because the heads that gave birth to the supplicant are always spiritually present with him.

As names are called for the blessings, those who are present for the divination will answer, "Aché!" to give strength to the prayer that was said for them and to thank the supplicant for his blessings.

*Kinkanmaché iyá/baba tobi mi [one's godmother or godfather].*

*Kinkanmaché yubonna mi [one's yubonna].*

*Kinkanmache Oluwo [one's godfather in Ifá].*

I ask for protection, blessings, and the good things in life for my godmother/godfather, my yubonna, and my godfather in Ifá.

*Kinkanmaché [one by one, the names of all the living godparents, the grandparents in ocha, and so on, of your own godparents, followed by the names of those priests and priestesses who are present].*

*Kinkanmaché orí, Eledá emi nani [one's own name in ocha if ocha has been made].*

*Kinkanmaché gbogbo kaleno, igboro, abure, ashire, oluwos, iyaloshas, babaloshas kale ilé.*

So that nothing bad can happen to those who are present in my home: my brothers, sisters, sons, daughters, visiting priests and priestesses, priests of Ifá, the mothers, the fathers, and the keepers of the spirits who have come to my house.

Finishing this part of the process, the italero begins an intonation to all the orishas that are considered *fundamento* (those given in the ritual of ocha). The correct order of invocation of the fundamento orishas for a priest of Obatalá is Elegguá, Oshún, Yemayá, Shangó, and Obatalá. If an orisha other than Obatalá has gone to the head, that orisha is prayed to last and Obatalá is prayed to second. For instance, a priest of Oshún would pray in the order of Elegguá, Obatalá, Yemayá, Shangó, and Oshún. A child of Yemayá would pray to Elegguá, Obatalá, Oshún, Shangó, and Yemayá. A child of Shangó would pray to Elegguá, Obatalá, Yemayá, Oshún, and then Shangó. The priest of Elegguá would begin with Elegguá and end with Elegguá.

One petitions Elegguá first because he alone opens the doors to the divine, and then each spirit, ending with the italero's guardian, is given a brief series of praises. During this litany, the italero explains to the orishas that the client has come for a consultation at their feet. It is important to name the client in full: first, middle, last, and married name if any. License must be granted by the spirits to proceed, so the italero asks their permission before proceeding. It is also traditional to ask that the results of this session prove beneficial not only for the querier but also for the diviner, his ilé, and the attending priests and priestesses.

Until more complex prayers, praises, and call names are learned, the following series of simple prayers may be used by the novice. It is written for a child of Obatalá, and it is assumed that he is consulting with Elegguá's diloggún.

> ***Eshu Elegguá olo gbogbo na mirin itá alagbana babá mi unlo na burukú nitosi le shonsho. Kuelu kuiko odí. Kosí ofo; kosí ejo; kosí aro; ni oruko mi gbogbo omo nile fu kuikuo. Adupe, babá mi Elegguá.***
>
> Owner of all four corners, elder of the roads, my father, take all evil away, so that we can walk with good health. Let there be no illness; let there be no loss; let there be no revolution; let there be no death. In the name of all the sons of this house, I thank you very much, my father Elegguá.
>
> ***Oshún yeye mi oga, mi gbogbo ibu laye nibo, obgo mo orisha lo uwe nitosi gba ma abukon ni omi didun nitosi oni aláfia ati ayo. Obínrin kuelu re aché, wiwo ati re maru asho gele nitosi yo ayaba ewa kuela re reri ati aye sugbon be toni sho nitosi ko mo nigbati wa ibinu. Obínrin ikú, iko Olófin, adupe.***
>
> My mother, owner of all the rivers of the world, where all the children of the orishas go to bathe and to receive the blessing of the sweet water and to have happiness and joy. Woman with her skirt and five scarves to dance, beautiful queen with her laughter and joy, but we have to be careful because we don't know when she is angry. Woman who deals with the dead, messenger of Olófin, we thank you.
>
> ***Yemayá orisha obínrin dudu kuele remaye, abaya mi re oyu ayaba, ano rigba oki. Mi iyá mayele, oga ni gbogbo okun, yeye, omo eya lojun. Oyina ni re ta gbogbo okun nibe iwo ni re olowo nitosi re omo teriba adupe iyá mi.***
>
> Black female goddess with her seven face marks, queen divine, receive my salvation. We greet you, other, owner of all the seas, mother, daughter of the fish. There, afar, is your throne below the sea, where you keep your riches for your obedient son. Thank you, my mother.
>
> ***Shangó, babá mi, kawo ilemu fumi aleya. Tilanshani nitosi ki ko gbamu mi re oro niglati wa ibinu ki kigbo ni na orin ati gbogbo omo ninin gbodo wi kuelu kuikuo beru nitosi dilowo kawo kawo ile mi iwo bagbe babá mi ki awa na kue ni okán nitosi junle ni iwaye ne re elese ati wi Shangó alamu obá layo ni na ile ogbe o mi.***
>
> My father Shangó, god of thunder, control my home. Give me the radiant salvation so that your word does not catch me when you are angry, you who scream in the sky. All your sons here below say with respect, and to honor you, control our homes. Remember, my father, that we call on you from our hearts, we kneel before you to ask, god of thunder, merciful king, happiness on earth. Shelter us.
>
> ***Obatalá okunrin ati obínrin ni laye eledá ni gbogbo na dara dara ati burukú obá ati ayaba,***

*afin oga ni na bala ati gbogbo na shish baba alaye alabo mi ati mi gbogbo na ejun, dara dara baba wa afin alano. Jekua baba mi, adupe.*

Obatalá, great male and female deity, world creator of all good, health, and evil, king and queen, albino owner of purity and of all justice, father who shields, grand protector of all the world, my protector and of all good and healthy things, our merciful albino father, hail, my father; thank you!

Now, for the benefit of the client, who, unless he has been immersed in this religion for some time, will not have understood any of these litanies, the diviner prays in English:

I come to you all today on behalf of [client's full name]; he has come to consult with the diloggún, and I ask for the aché to proceed and make contact with Olorún, egun, and the orishas on his behalf. Let the results of this consultation be beneficial for him, for me as his diviner, and for all the members of this house.

At this point, the italero again prays in Lucumí; this time, however, the invocation is directed at the orisha whose shells are being read. Normally, the diloggún of Elegguá is used, and the following prayer illustrates the process of invocation. Godparents will give their protégés more traditional litanies.

*Mojuba Elegguá, babá mi. Agó, Elegguá, Baralayiki, Eshu Odara. Mojuba Eshu lona. Kosí ikú; kosí arún; kosí ofo; kosí arayé. Babá, fun mi iré owó, iré omo, iré omá, iré arikú babawa.*

I pay homage and salute Elegguá, my father. With your permission, Elegguá Baralayiki [a praise name for invocation], Eshu Odara [another praise name for Elegguá]; I salute you, Elegguá of the roads. May death be no more, may sickness be no more, may loss be no more, may troubles be no more. Bring me the blessings of money; bring me the blessings of children; bring me the blessings to tell good from bad, the blessings of good health and immortality of the soul.

Now the diviner begins to pray against all the evil and osogbos that might stand in the way of a beneficial reading.

*Kosí Ikú. Kosí ofo. Kosí ano. Kosí inya. Kosí fitibo. Kosí akopa. Kosí inya. Kosí fitibo. Kosí akopa. Kosí tiya-tiya. Kosí araye. Kosí gbogbowan osogbo unlo. Fun iré owo. Iré omo. Iré arikú babawa. Ko un soro ofo pa oda oda pa ofo. Ko un soro ofun malobe malobe ofun.*

May death be no more. May loss be no more. May sickness be no more. May war be no more. May nothing be overwhelming. May nothing be disrespectful. May there be no arguments. May there be no gossip or evil words. May all misfortunes be no more. So that we may have the blessings of money. So that we may have the blessings of children. So that we may have blessings and not see Death. So that the bad is not spoken or mistaken for the good. So that the good spoken is not mistaken for the bad.

Once the prayer has been intoned, the diviner (still holding the diloggún and derecho in his left hand) touches the client's body in the main centers of aché, naming each part in Lucumí as he does so.

Orí inu—the head
Eshu ni pacuó—the back of the neck
Esika meji—the shoulders
Okokán—the heart
Inú—the stomach
Akwá meji—the arms (here, one touches the inner folds of the elbows)
Onukun meji—the knees
Elese meji—the feet
Owo osi owo otún ono wale—the hands

At this point many italeros place the diloggún gently in the client's hands; this is done with care, with reverence, for the diloggún are the mouthpieces to odu, the sacred alphabet of the orishas, and the very soul of the spirit being consulted. The gentle circular movements of the italero's hands, the force of a prayer in the orisha's native tongue, and the skill with which the diloggún has been handled all serve to gently awaken this force. Now, this titanic orisha waits to hear the client's troubles.

He may think silently about the difficulties in his life, or he may speak aloud to the orisha about the reason he is at its feet. When the client is finished, the italero retrieves the shells, raises them again in his left hand, and says, "*Ocháreo*" ("We join to the orishas"). The shells are cast to the mat while those present says, "*Adaché*" ("Of our own free will"). The first odu is marked as the diviner counts the shells falling mouth up, and it is written down at the top of the sheet of paper. Once the first odu is recorded, the diviner places the derecho to the right of the mat beside the ibó, picks up the shells in his left hand, and casts them, calling, "Ocháreo," while those present answer, "Adaché." This second odu is counted and recorded on the paper beside the first, creating a composite, or omo, odu. For example, if the first odu that fell was six, Obara, and the second the fell was seven, Odí, the composite odu is 6-7, or Obara Odí. The diviner then proceeds to use ibó to mark the odu's orientation.

## Using Ibó in Divination

While it may seem that the initial manipulation of the diloggún is a process completed by the diviner alone, in truth it is a complex interplay of energies. The diviner sets these energies in motion by awakening the spirit sleeping in the shells. He does this by license of the orisha crowning him, the spirit put to live inside his head. In our example, this is Obatalá; he gives the priest the aché to divine. The ritual of diloggún is a spiritual dance between these two titanic forces that results in the opening of odu on the mat. Once the odu is opened and identified, a vortex awakens, for each odu in itself is a vast container of spiritual possibilities. This vortex extends to encompass the diviner, the client, and any others present for the session. The divination process has now only begun. For while there are 256 odu, 256 basic possibilities in the universe, each person is individual and unique, and no two will harmonize with the same odu in the same way. The client's own orí identifies how an odu affects him and how he, in turn, affects the odu. To make the client's orí speak within this vortex, the diviner employs special tools known as ibó.

During the ritual, a client's orí uses the eight ibó to answer questions posed by the diviner. The questions themselves have been devised over the centuries to encompass all that humans face, the many blessings or misfortunes encountered during the course of their lives. They have only yes or no answers. Methodically, the priest asks each question of both the orisha consulted and the client's orí and then gives two ibó, one for a yes answer, one for a no answer, to the client. The client takes one ibó into each hand, without revealing to the diviner which ibó goes in which hand. The priest then casts the shells on the mat again, and the resulting odu offers the orisha's interpretation of the orí's answer. Depending on which odu is revealed, the diviner directs the client to open one of his hands; the ibó in that hand reveals whether the answer is yes or no. Note that it is from the client's own hands that this information is revealed; therefore, there can be no prejudice on the diviner's part. Together, the diviner and client work with the ibó to determine several spiritual qualities inherent in the original composite odu: its orientation, degree of orientation, predictions, prohibitions, taboos, and eboses. Each odu is a container with limitless contents, and not all of its possible messages will apply to everyone at every session. Methodically the opening letter is explored for those messages that apply to the client.

The eight ibó employed in divination follow.*

**otá:** Otá is a smooth black stone. Traditionally, one finds this symbol in the woods; remember that the stone must be small enough that a client can hide it in a closed fist. Of all the earth's creations, stone is the most durable. It withstands time, and instead of being destroyed by the centuries, it becomes smooth and polished as it ages. Therefore, one uses otá to represent the immortality and stability of both the soul and spiritual truths. While otá answers in the nega-

*Note that while all eight ibó are standard among diviners, there are variations as to how one employs these tools. Divination with cowries is a learned skill with specific rules; however, many priests and priestesses employ their own artistic flourishes when utilizing the eight ibó. That is why, before marking anything with the shells, one identifies the positive and negative symbols to the orisha with the initial prayer described on page 21. By doing this, there is never any confusion among the diviner, the orisha, or the client's orí.

tive and pairs with any of the seven remaining ibó, almost always one uses it with efun. Sometimes its oracular meaning changes to the affirmative depending not only on the question asked, but also on the ibó with which one pairs it.

**efun:** Efun is a white, soft, loosely compacted chalk prepared from crushed and powdered eggshells. While normal chalk is hard and difficult to crush, efun coats objects with ease. Applying too much pressure crushes it into nothing. Obatalá and Olófin own this ibó, as the two claim all things that are white. During the course of divination, one pairs this symbol with the otá, especially when determining the qualities of iré as opposed to those of osogbo or when determining the eboses needed to bring a client back into alignment with his destiny. Efun always marks the affirmative (yes) answer. Since Obatalá and Olófin can speak in all odu, whenever the italero is unsure of which ibó to use for a positive response, he picks efun.

**ayé:** For this ibó, one uses an elongated, spiral shell; the species of shell is not important, but it must be a saltwater shell. Remember that it must be small enough to be secreted in a client's closed fist. The ayé's use is limited in questioning. One uses it to ask questions about relationships and marriage, questions relating to illness, and questions relating to water orishas. When found in the client's hand, it answers in the affirmative. Normally, one pairs it with the otá.

**owó:** When used as ibó, this symbol takes one of two forms: two cut cowries tied with the cut sides together or a single uncut cowrie a bit larger than those used for the orisha's diloggún. During the course of a reading, one may pair it with two other ibó: efun, in which case owó marks the negative, or otá, in which case owó marks the affirmative. Financial questions demand the use of this symbol. Note that it is not very popular with most italeros, but the oriaté frequently employs owó in his readings. It is a mark of superior skill to use the proper tool for the proper job.

**apadí:** The symbol for this ibó consists of a small piece of broken pottery or china. Among less skilled diviners, apadí is not very popular. One uses it when marking those things concerning arguments or wars.

**gungun:** This ibó is a bone taken from the left hind leg of a goat. Always, one pairs this symbol with otá, using it to mark the affirmative to questions dealing with the dead, egun, or those spirits said to dwell in heaven with Olódumare. While most diviners avoid the use of this ibó, it is essential to these questions; they cannot be properly marked without its use.

**ewe ayó (more commonly known as osán/sesán):** This ibó is the seed of the guacalote tree. It conceptualizes both offspring and, curiously, illness. One's children and progeny are found here because the seed holds the potential to become a tree and create thousands of new seeds; illness is found here because the fruit hiding the seed must rot before a new tree can grow. Whenever it is used in a reading, this ibó will normally respond in the negative.

**orí ere (also known as orí agboran or eri-aworan):** For this ibó the diviner uses a tiny doll's head, one that a client can hold secretly in his closed fist. Most italeros and oriatés use the head of a tiny jester's doll. One uses this for concerns of the client's orí; always, it answers in the affirmative.

While each line of questioning has its own rules to follow, the basic format for using ibó remains the same: First, the diviner picks two ibó; his choice of ibó will be determined by the question he intends to ask. If chosen by odu as possible answers to his question, one ibó answers in the affirmative and the other answers in the negative. (Unlike other oracles, the diloggún system allows no room for vague responses.) Cupping the two ibó in his left hand, the diviner touches each to the open mouths on the mat, asking his question, in Lucumí if possible.* The ibó are then given to the client while the diviner intones

> *[Name of the affirmative ibó] lo si wayu, [name of the negative ibó] beko, [name of the affirmative ibó again] ke ibó.*
>
> [Affirmative ibó] answers yes, [negative ibó] answers no, [affirmative ibó] is blessed/preferred.

This short prayer asks that the best answer come from the divination; it also identifies, to both the orisha consulted and the client's orí, which symbol answers yes and which answers no. Once the client has these tools in his hands, he is instructed to shake them together briskly and then to separate one into

*Some diviners will, toward the end of a session, allow the client to ask secret questions of the oracle. To do so, a diviner will place the two ibó reverently in the client's hands and allow him to whisper his concerns to the orishas (having first instructed the client that only questions with yes or no answers are appropriate). Once finished, the client returns the symbols to the diviner so he may touch them to the diloggún and complete the process.

each closed fist. There they will remain until odu demands the revelation of one symbol.

Now the diviner gathers the sixteen shells in his left hand, gently tapping them on the mat three times. After the third strike, he brings up his hand, opening it so that the entire diloggún rolls out. He counts and marks the number of mouths displayed, determining whether an elder or a younger odu is open. The letters with elder status are

| | |
|---|---|
| Okana—1 | Ejila Shebora—12 |
| Eji Oko—2 | Metanla—13 |
| Ogundá—3 | Merinla—14 |
| Irosun—4 | Marunla—15 |
| Eji Ogbe—8 | Merindilogún—16 |
| Ofún—10 | |

If one of these eleven signs opens, the diviner chooses the ibó present in the client's left hand. This is the answer to the question posed. If any of the remaining five odu opens with this casting, both fists remain closed while the diviner gathers and casts the shells again.

The five remaining signs are the younger odu. Their order of seniority from youngest to oldest is

| | |
|---|---|
| Oché—5 | Osá—9 |
| Odí—7 | Owani—11 |
| Obara—6 | |

To effectively employ the younger odu in the process of picking hands, one must remember them in exactly this order. When a younger odu opens on the mat with the diviner's initial casting, he instructs the client to keep both hands closed while he gathers the sixteen shells a second time. Again, he strikes his left hand on the mat three times, letting the shells fall after the third strike. Once more, he counts the number of open mouths displayed. If the first throw of cowries is younger than the second, he directs the client to open his right hand. If the first odu is older than the second, the client should open his left hand. Thus does the oracle mark its own answer.*

Those are the basic rules, but as with all rules, there are exceptions. Diviners agree that Obara (6) and Osá (9) are of the same age, even though they have younger/older status in their ranking among the younger odu. Obara ranks as younger than Osá because Olódumare created it after Osá. However, if the odu marked when determining the hand of ibó is either 6-9 or 9-6, one chooses the left hand out of respect for these two letters. In this way there will never be a war between the two signs. There will also be times when a younger odu falls twice and becomes a *meji*, or twin, of itself (5-5, 7-7, 6-6, 9-9, or 11-11). This makes the letter one of the sixteen primaries, and these demand the opening of the left hand. Finally, there are two additional rules concerning the elder odu Elleunle (8) and Irosun (4). When Elleunle or Irosun falls, the answer is always yes, the affirmative. After marking this, the diviner directs the client to open his left hand. If the affirmative ibó is found there, all is well. If the negative ibó is found there, the italero knows that there is a spiritual war going on within this person, and even he does not agree with what the orishas have marked. Make this an issue for discussion, as it will bring spiritual ruin if not addressed.

During the initial casting of the cowries or the marking of ibó, yet another sign may develop and fall in the diloggún: the odu that is but a shadow, Opira. When the shells fall with all mouths face-down and closed, we say that Opira has come to the house, and for a time, the routine process of diloggún becomes suspended so the diviner may attend to this catastrophic symbol. The circumstances with which this letter deals are cataclysmic: natural disasters, insanity, mental instability, famine, death, and general calamity in the client's life. So severe are some of this sign's predictions that most priests close the oracle immediately, telling the client that "the shells have left my hand." Together, diviner and client seek out an Ifá priest to remove the osogbo opened when Opira fell on the mat. For those houses that do not work closely with a babalawo, however, there is a set of rituals

*Two special notes concerning the hands during this process: First, the right hand is considered younger than the left hand. This serves as a good device for remembering the hand to be chosen. Second, an answer found in the left hand not only is stronger but also will be made more immediately manifest than if it were found in the right hand. An iré marked in the left hand is a good blessing; if an osogbo is marked in the left hand, we say that the curse is already upon this person.

to clear the dangerous pattern. If the ibó are in the client's hands, they remain there while the diviner performs this cleansing. First, the priest or priestess who works as the diviner's assistant turns over all the shells, displaying the mouth of each cowrie. He or she puts all sixteen shells in a jícara of fresh water, taking the entire gourd to the front door immediately. The water cools the heat of Opira just a bit, so the assistant must be careful to allow none of it to fall on the floor between the diviner's mat and the front door.

The assistant opens the front door and, standing just inside the front door and covering the opening of the jícara loosely with the fingers of one hand so none of the shells flies out, flings the water far out into the street. He or she then inverts the gourd on the ground just outside the door, allowing the diloggún to fall into a new pattern. Lifting the gourd, the assistant counts the number of shells falling faceup, calling out this number to the italero. He or she places the cowries back in the jícara, closes the front door, and pours fresh water over the diloggún. The assistant then returns the diloggún to the diviner to continue the session.

The marking of Opira continues thus: First, the diviner asks if the sign fell for the client; if the answer is no, the diviner asks if it fell for himself. If the answer is still no, the questioning goes on to the client's godparents and then to the priests or priestesses who are present. If the oracle answers no to all these, the questioning continues on to the members of first the godparent's ilé ocha and then the diviner's. Once an affirmative answer is found, that information is noted and the reading may continue. If Opira cannot be marked on anyone in this line of questioning nor on any ilé ocha represented in the room, both the client and diviner should see the priests of Ifá. The reading is closed. If Opira is marked, the one for whom it has been marked should have a session with the diloggún immediately so that its heat may be placated. In any case, the diviner cannot read for anyone else that day until he reads for himself first.

After extracting and recording the opening odu for this session, the diviner proceeds with the divination in a set pattern. The first question asked with the ibó is intended to reveal the opening orientation of the odu, or whether it opens in good fortune. For this, efun and otá are chosen. Holding them in his left hand, the diviner asks, "Iré ni?" which means, "Is a blessing predicted through this letter?" and then touches the positive ibó (efun) to each of the mouths open on the mat, keeping the negative ibó (otá) securely behind this and hidden in his hand. He hands the two pieces to the client, giving him the efun first and the otá second, saying, "Efun lo si wayu, otá beko, efun ke ibó" ("Efun answers yes, otá answers no, efun is blessed/preferred"). Assuming that this is the client's first reading, the diviner explains which ibó will answer yes and which will answer no. As described above, the client is advised to shake both together briskly, take one into each hand, and hold them tightly in closed fists. The diviner then takes the diloggún firmly in his left hand and, striking the table three times, lets the shells fall after the third strike. Following the rules for determining which hand to pick, the diviner chooses the appropriate hand to get the answer to the question "Iré ni?"

## When the Reading Opens in Iré

If in answer to the question "Iré ni?" the diviner finds the ibó efun, blessings come with this casting of the diloggún.* The diviner takes back both ibó from the client and proceeds in a set traditional pattern to extract the rest of the odu's prognostications. For all these manipulations two ibó are used: efun and otá. The efun answers in the affirmative to the question, always meaning "yes," while the otá answers in the negative, always meaning "no."

Most italeros categorize the myriad blessings possible in the odu as having twenty-five origins. However, many also personalize this categorization with their own line of questioning. The standard

*If the otá is found in the chosen hand, the answer to "Iré ni?" is no; the odu comes with misfortunes. When this happens, one begins the process for extracting the exact misfortune predicted. For this procedure, turn to "When the Reading Opens in Osogbo" on page 27.

list follows, along with an explanation of what an affirmative answer from the ibó means. Begin with the question "Iré ariku?" and proceed to the end of the list. If the ibó marks none of these, one says that the source of iré is unknown and not firm; an ebó (offering) is necessary and the reading continues as if it had opened in a mild osogbo. Blessings come only through the client's good works and good behavior.*

**Iré arikú?** An affirmative answer to this question brings health, vitality, longevity, and immortality of the soul. Many consider it to be one of the best types of iré the orishas may give; it is sought after, and this is why diviners ask this question first. The word arikú has many translations, the most common being "not to face an untimely death."

**Iré elese eledá?** This phrase translates to "Goodness at the feet of one's orí?" Here, the odu tells the diviner that luck and evolution come from the client's own orí, his higher self and spiritual head; it also alludes to blessings brought by one's guardian orisha.

**Iré otonowá?** This phrase translates to "Goodness from heaven?" Many also ask, "Iré elese otonowá?" which means, "Goodness at the feet of heaven?" This is a favored blessing; it shows that all the client gains from life comes to him by laying himself down at the feet of Olódumare and all the spirits in heaven.

**Iré elese ocha?** This phrase translates to "Goodness at the feet of the orishas?" Here, it is said that the client's evolution and blessings will come through one of the orishas who speak in the odu. The diviner now deviates from the normal process of questioning. Using the efun and otá, he begins to question the oracle as to which orisha brings the blessings. Starting with the first orisha to speak in the parent odu open on the mat, and continuing in order until the oracle points out which spirit is bringing iré, the diviner asks, "Iré elese [the name of the orisha]?" Unless the iré in this sign is firm and manifest in this life (see page 26), this is the spirit that demands ebó as larishe (a remedy to overcome osogbo and bring iré).

**Iré elese egun?** This phrase translates to "Goodness at the feet of one's ancestral spirits?" This orientation, when marked, says that the iré of odu manifests through one of the many egun that work on behalf of the client. These egun can be either blood or spiritual ancestors. In some ilé ocha, diviners insist on marking which egun accompanies the client to bring iré; however, this is excessive and unnecessary. Egun work together on behalf of a single person. Although one may work with many spirit guides or Congolese spirits to further evolution, they are not egun—they are just spirits. When iré elese egun is marked, the diviner lets the client know that his blessings are coming about through the work of ancestral spirits, and if eboses are called for (eboses is the plural of ebó), they are directed toward egun and not the spirits of another tradition.

**Iré elese ará onú?** This phrase translates to "Goodness at the feet of the spirits of heaven?" Many confuse iré elese ará onú with iré elese egun; however, there is a distinction between one's egun (physical and spiritual ancestral spirits) and ará onú (the inhabitants of heaven). One's egun are a part of one's spiritual and genetic heritage. If a client cannot claim blood lineage or a direct spiritual link through the initiations of this religion, then he cannot claim a particular spirit as egun. Egun follow an individual his whole life. They are a collective energy that works continually for his evolution if they are given love and spiritual care. Ará onú are different. These spirits are unrelated to the client physically and spiritually; they are foreign souls that for whatever reason have taken an interest in this person. They can come from any cultural or spiritual background, for heaven does not discriminate on the basis of religion, and in the end, we all worship one creative force. Offerings made to ará onú may be undertaken at the same time as those made to egun; however, the client should be told the distinction between these two types of spirits.†

**Iré ayé?** This phrase translates to "Goodness through the increase of fortune?" It is self-explanatory: If the client does all he is told by this odu, his fortunes will increase.

**Iré elese elenú?** This phrase translates to "Goodness from the speaker's tongue?" Blessings brought by this are twofold. First, Elegguá owns the tongue; the propitiation of this ori-

*When the diviner cannot mark a specific iré, the odu promises a blessing, but the blessing is not specified. When this happens, the diviner continues his questioning of the oracle as if it has fallen in an osogbo. Immediately, he begins the process of extracting an ebó to harmonize the client with the odu. For this procedure, turn to "Marking the Eboses, or Remedies of Odu" on page 30.

†An additional note: The spirits of ará onú do not include "familiar spirits" or those types of spirits seated in the *nganga* (pot or cauldron) of the *palero* (there are odu that point out the workings of these types of beings). Any spirit tied or bound to any object or any place cannot be said to exist in heaven. They are earthbound spirits and can bring few blessings on their own.

sha is essential to making manifest the blessings promised. Second, it is by the client's own tongue, his own words, that he will receive blessings.

**Iré lowó?** This phrase translates to "Goodness and evolution through works [the client's own hands]?" Here, one knows that the client is in total control of his own destiny; by his own hard work he will grow and evolve. Advise him to work hard, for through his own hands will salvation from difficulties be found.

**Iré dedewan t'Olokun?** This phrase translates to "Blessings from the depths of Olokun?" Whatever good is promised by this odu will come from Olokun and the depths of the ocean. The client might need to receive Olokun, since having this orisha brings the mysteries of the sea into one's home. Later, if the diviner determines that the iré is not firm, Olokun will require some type of ebó to stabilize the iré. Note that this blessing is extremely powerful if marked by the pattern Irosun.

**Iré ashegunota?** This phrase translates to "Blessings from the stones of the orishas?" Some diviners ask a variation of this question, "Iré elese ashegunota?" which means, "Blessings at the feet of the stones of the orishas?" An affirmative answer to this question means that the good fortune comes from one of the otanes of the orishas. When this blessing is marked, the normal line of questioning deviates just a bit, as it does for "iré elese ocha," because the diviner must ascertain which orisha brings the blessing. Working through the list of orishas that speak in the parent odu, in the order in which they are listed, the diviner asks, "Iré elese [name of orisha]?" After marking the orisha, depending on whether or not the blessing is firm, the diviner prescribes a variety of eboses to that spirit. Often, the client who comes in an unstable iré ashegunota needs to receive that spirit. The client must search for the orisha's otanes (stones) in nature himself.

**Iré elese araoko?** This phrase translates to "Goodness at the feet of the fertile land?" The one for whom this blessing comes needs to travel away from the city and spend time in the country. While a short vacation might do, for many this blessing suggests a permanent move to a more rural setting. Initiates might need to receive the orishas tied with the earth's fertility cycle, such as Orisha Oko, Korikoto, Ochumare, and Osain.

**Iré elese abure?** This phrase translates to "Goodness at the feet of a brother or sister [either a blood relative or a member of one's house of ocha]?" This blessing suggests that one needs to strengthen the ties binding both one's physical family and one's spiritual family.

**Iré elese obini?** This phrase translates to "Goodness at the feet of a woman?" A female (known or unknown) to the client will bring a blessing.

**Iré elese okuni?** This phrase translates to "Goodness at the feet of a man?" A male (known or unknown) to the client will bring a blessing.

**Iré elese omo?** This phrase translates to "Goodness at the feet of a child?" From one of the client's own children a blessing will come. If the client is childless, the iré still comes from a child. Note that for childless married couples (and sometimes childless unmarried couples), this marks unexpected conception and pregnancy. Additionally, no matter the odu in which this blessing comes, when iré elese omo opens, the diviner prohibits the client from having or recommending an abortion. To do so forever destroys the iré of the odu, and no amount of eboses will ever bring it back.

**Iré elese arubo?** This phrase translates to "Goodness at the feet of the elders?" This blessing comes through the hands of an elderly person. Note that no matter the odu through which this iré comes, Obatalá and Olófin are involved in the client's life, and both dictate that he spend more time concerned about the elders in his family. Their needs are to be tended. "Elders" in this case equates to those of both age and ocha. (Remember, some who are young in age have years in the religion—this makes them elders, too.) Also, those with gray hair, even if young, are to be respected, because good advice could come from them.

**Iré ibujoko?** This phrase translates to "Goodness and blessings of change?" Some italeros ask, "Iré elese ibujoko?" which means "Blessings at the feet of change?" When this iré is marked, the odu forebodes many changes for the client, and it is by accepting these changes that blessings come. The odu itself might mandate changes in lifestyle and behavior, and life itself can alter catastrophically. Pliability is called for in one's outlook.

**Iré aláfia?** This phrase translates to "Blessings of peace?" It means what it says: Peace is coming to the client's life. The odu opened might suggest several ways for the client to find his peace; he must conduct himself according to the odu's advice.

**Iré elese babatobi?** This phrase translates to "Blessings and goodness at the feet of one's godfather?" Initially, it marks the need for the client to become closer to his godfather in the religion, for it is through him that evolution comes. This type of iré often falls in Iroso Ogbe (4-8). It comes for those who are in dire need of the religion yet are too poor to afford the ceremonies of the orishas. When it comes, the diviner needs to keep the client's financial state in mind. This blessing comes not only for the client but also for the godfather.

**Iré elese iyatobi?** This phrase translates to "Blessings and goodness at the feet of one's godmother?" The same considerations for iré elese babatobi apply in this orientation.

**Iré banda loguro?** This phrase translates to "Blessings and goodness from the depths of the earth?" Some diviners will ask, "Iré elese banda loguro?" which translates to "Blessings and goodness at the feet of the depths of the earth?" Both questions have the same implications. This orientation implies that one's evolution rises from the depths of the earth; it is one of the more mysterious blessings, and it usually requires the reception of the darker orishas: Orisha Oko, Korikoto, Babaluaiye, Naná Burukú, Nanumé, Yewá, and spirits with similar natures. Some diviners prescribe eboses to be done in dark, mysterious places such as caves, cemeteries, and heavily wooded areas.

**Iré elese ewe?** This phrase translates to "Blessings and goodness from gambling?" When this type of iré comes, it shows that the predicted evolution comes from mild gambling. Unless the iré is firm and manifest in this life, however, more money will be lost than won. It also implies that one who takes risks in life, dreaming impossible dreams and working to attain them, comes out ahead of those who take few chances.

**Iré elese orí yoko?** This phrase translates to "Blessings and goodness at the feet of a tied head?" In other words, the client finds his destiny fulfilled by initiation to his orisha. When this blessing comes, if the iré is not firm, the diviner marks eboses to the client's guardian orisha. If the guardian orisha is not known, the diviner uses the shells to mark the client's guardian orisha at this time, before the session is closed. No matter which odu is open for this blessing, the ultimate ebó is for the client to make ocha.

**Iré iyekú?** This phrase translates to "Blessings and goodness through tragedy?" Some diviners ask the question "Iré elese iyekú?" which means "Blessings and goodness at the feet of tragedy?" Both have the same spiritual implications. This blessing marks many unfortunate events in the client's life before his evolution comes; almost always, it arrives through death and inheritance. It can also mark lawsuits and personal injury claims. In iré iyekú, the diviner explores options for ebó so that the tragedy implied is minimal compared to the blessings obtained.

After determining which type of blessing is predicted, the diviner writes the odu that marked the positive ibó under the opening odu on the piece of paper; beside this, he records the iré predicted. If none of the blessings are marked, the iré is not firm; the diviner cannot and must not ask for firmness or for firmness to manifest in this life (the next two questions). The proper procedure in this case is to searche for an ebó that will make the iré manifest firmly in this sign; see "Marking the Eboses, or Remedies for Odu" on page 30.

If a type of iré is marked, the diviner then determines if the predicted blessing is firm. Two questions are asked: "Iré yale?" ("Is the blessing firm?") and "Iré yale timbelaye?" ("Will the blessing manifest in this life?"). If the answer to "Iré yale?" is no, then the predicted iré is *kotoyale*, or incomplete. The diviner must mark ebó, and he does not ask the second question. If the answer to "Iré yale?" is yes, the oracle is telling the diviner that the client's source of blessing is strong, mounting behind him to push him toward his destiny. The diviner then presents the second question to the oracle. If the answer to "Iré yale timbelaye?" is no, then the iré is complete yet not stable *(tesi-tesi)*, and ebó is required.

If the answer to the second question is also yes, the oracle has answered that not only is the predicted iré firm, but it also will manifest in this life. The oracle is telling the diviner that the odu's energy has been in effect for some time, and the client has navigated himself well through its energies. He is in alignment with his destiny. The particular composite odu that has opened will tell the client what forces are in effect in his life and how they will affect him. Marking the iré as iré yale timbelaye, the oracle closes itself, and the diviner will not need to mark or prescribe ebó.

A negative answer to either question does not close the oracle, and the diviner needs to follow the procedure for marking ebó as described on page 30.

## When the Reading Opens in Osogbo

If in answer to the question "Iré ni?" the odu points to the hand containing otá, the oracle is telling the diviner that the reading opens in osogbo (misfortunes are predicted). When this happens, the italero must mark the osogbo predicted by odu. Just as in marking iré, the diviner asks his questions in a specific order until the proper osogbo is found. The following list is the order in which these osogbos are questioned. In attempting to mark osogbo, efun is never used as an ibó. Instead, otá (as the negative) is paired with one of the remaining six symbols (as the affirmative) to obtain yes or no answers.

**Ikú?** Literally, this word means "death." To ask the oracle if ikú is the osogbo predicted, the diviner chooses the otá (stone) and gungun (bone) as ibó. The shells mark this misfortune when the bone is in the chosen hand. Unlike other oracles such as cards, dominoes, and runes, for the diloggún death means just that: death. The client's life is in danger. Other osogbos in this list are more appropriate for concepts such as "the death of a way of life," "the death of one's mode of current living," and "the death of unneeded, unnecessary things." To die before one's time is a major misfortune in Lucumí belief, and the orishas work with their adherents to ensure that each individual lives his maximum allotted time on the earth.*

**Ano?** Ano translates to "illness." When asking the oracle if ano is the osogbo predicted, one chooses the ayé (seashell) and otá (stone) as ibó. If the ayé is in the chosen hand, this misfortune is marked. Some type of disease will visit the client if the odu cannot be placated.

**Eyo?** The diviner uses the otá (stone) and apadí (pottery shard) to question this osogbo. Eyo brings legal complications, bad tongues, and unforeseen tragedies. If the apadí is in the chosen hand, this misfortune is marked upon the client. There will be many arguments and tragedies in this person's life unless both the odu and the orishas are appeased.

**Arayé?** The diviner attempts to mark this osogbo using the apadí (pottery shard) and the otá (stone). If the apadí is in the chosen hand, arayé misfortune is on the client. Arayé refers to arguments, evil tongues, and witchcraft. It is a hot osogbo, and any eboses marked by the odu must be done immediately if the client hopes to avoid it.

**Inya?** For this question the diviner chooses the apadí (pottery shard) and otá (stone) as ibó. If the apadí is in the chosen hand, this osogbo is marked upon the client. Simply, inya means "war."

**Ona?** When questioning ona, the diviner once again uses the apadí (pottery shard) and otá (stone) as ibó. If the pottery shard is in the client's chosen hand, this osogbo is marked on him. The word ona translates as "afflictions," and the type of misfortunes it brings to the client can be vague and unspecified. His home, body, and family are all affected under this orientation. Although he may not speak specifically in the odu opened on the mat, Eleggua is the orisha demanding propitiation when ona is predicted; he can block all roads to destruction and open paths to evolution.

**Ofo?** For this osogbo, apadí (pottery shard) and otá (stone) are again the ibó to use. Apadí marks the affirmative answer. The word ofo translates as "loss"; when this osogbo comes, every aspect of the client's life suffers: business, personal, economic, and so on.

**Ogo?** When asking the question "Ogo?" the diviner has two choices to pair with the otá (stone): the apadí (pottery shard) or the ayé (seashell). If the apadí or ayé is in the chosen hand, this osogbo is marked. The word ogo translates as "witchcraft," and it can come from any number of sources. If not fought, it will destroy the client's life.

**Akoba?** This is a general osogbo telling the diviner that things are not good in the client's life. To attempt to mark akoba, the diviner picks the apadí (pottery shard) and otá (stone) as ibó. Finding the apadí in the chosen hand signifies that akoba is the osogbo.

**Fitibo?** When asking the question "Fitibo?" the diviner picks the gungun (bone) and the otá (stone). Finding gungun in

*An untimely death, not death itself, is a curse. Realize that not everyone comes into the world with the promise of a long, full life. Some agree before Olódumare (God) to be born and die young, just as some agree to hard, meaningless lives. Destiny is a personal thing, and it is never easy to divine. While it is possible to extend one's destiny and grow beyond what one was promised in heaven, this is not the only goal of divination. The ability to change one's destiny is an exception, not a rule. What is promised is that each of us, if we listen to the orisha's advice and make ebó, will live the full amount of time that we were granted by Olódumare before our descent to earth. And if a hard life is our lot, to some degree that, too, can be lessened. Those who truly live and grow while working through their destiny can have their burden in life lessened and enjoy more than what was originally bargained for in heaven.

the chosen hand marks death. In this case, death is close, as opposed to ikú, which predicts eventual death. In our own house we have seen the differentiation of these two misfortunes thus: When fitibo opens on the mat, the client is in danger of violent acts resulting in accidental death from the moment he walks out the diviner's door. When ikú opens, death may be accidental; the accident, however, is far into the future. Ikú also points out death from slow, wasting diseases; fitibo marks more sudden illnesses such as heart attack.

**Égba?** To question this osogbo, the diviner chooses the ayé (seashell) and otá (stone) as ibó. If the ayé is in the client's chosen hand, égba is marked. The word égba means "paralysis," and it signifies the loss of all that is good in the client's life. Although this orientation will never be specific as to what is to be paralyzed, depending on the odu opened, paralysis of the body or part of the body is a possibility. A Latin American singer (who shall, for legal and ethical reasons, remain nameless) received Babaluaiye (an orisha, the father of sickness and infectious disease) as the ebó against certain "égba elese lowó" (paralysis from his own hands). An accident left him paralyzed, with his spine severed. Although doctors told him that there was no hope of ever walking again, within a year this entertainer was back on the road!

**Oran?** For this question, the diviner uses the apadí (pottery shard) and otá (stone) as ibó. If the apadí is in the chosen hand, the odu marks oran as the osogbo. Oran signifies moral and legal crimes; therefore, the client himself is creating his own osogbo. While ebó can help alleviate this negative orientation, in the end it is up to the client to stop creating his own osogbo.

**Epe?** When asking "Epe?" the diviner picks the otá (stone) and osán (guacalote seed) as ibó. If the osán is in the chosen hand, epe is marked. Epe literally means "curse," and although many priests and priestesses who retain Catholic ties might immediately be tempted to denounce the evil afflictions of witchcraft sent by others, it is important for the diviner to hold his tongue until the exact origin of epe is known (even God can curse!). Note: We differentiate between epe and ogo for many reasons, the most obvious being that a curse is a direct, malefic attack, whereas ogo can be sent with good intentions yet still have destructive effects on the client's personal destiny.

**Ewon?** To attempt the marking of this osogbo, the diviner uses the apadí (pottery shard) and otá (stone) as ibó. The apadí answers in the affirmative. Ewon means "imprisonment." Sometimes it denotes physical incarceration; however, the client might also become a prisoner of his own life, thoughts, emotions, and habits.

After determining which type of osogbo is predicted, the diviner writes the odu that marked the affirmative ibó under the opening odu on the piece of paper; beside this, he records the osogbo predicted. If the oracle marks none of the osogbo in this list, the osogbo is said to be *eshe*, or general afflictions. The odu falling when the diviner tried to mark ewon is written down and "eshe" is written beside it.

Now the diviner must determine the origin of the osogbo—that is, what spiritual principle is bringing this misfortune upon the client through the odu that opened on the mat. To do so, the diviner phrases his question a specific way:

> *[Name of osogbo, as determined from the previous list] elese [origin of osogbo, chosen one at a time from the following list]?*
>
> Does the [name of osogbo, as determined from the previous list] come at the feet of [origin of osogbo, chosen one at a time from the following list]?

In other words, if eshe is the osogbo afflicting the client, the diviner would first ask, "Eshe elese otonowá?" If the answer is yes, the diviner knows that the client's osogbo originates in otonowá. If the answer is no, the diviner moves on to the next question: "Eshe elese eledá?" If the answer to this question is yes, the client's osogbo originates in eledá. If the answer is no, the diviner continues to the next question, and so on, until he unveils the origin of the osogbo.

As is the case in marking the osogbo, the otá serves as the negative answer to the diviner's question; it is paired with one of the remaining seven ibó, which symbolizes the affirmative answer.

**Otonowá.** To attempt to mark otonowá as the origin of the client's misfortune, the diviner uses efun (chalk) and otá (stone) as ibó. If the efun is found in the chosen hand, the osogbo comes "elese otonowá." Otonowá is a Lucumí contraction meaning "from heaven," and the diviner may take its unveiling to mean that Olófin, Olorún, and Olódumare are sending the osogbo. Although one or more orishas might stand up in the reading to offer their advice and help if the client performs ebó, he must make direct petitions to Olorún if the osogbo is to be lightened or lifted. The diviner spends time explaining ethical action and moral responsibility in relation to this person's troubles. God demands nothing but the best from each of us, and only our best should be given back to God.

**Eledá.** When attempting to mark eledá as the origin of the client's osogbo, the diviner picks the orí ere (doll's head) and the otá (black stone) as ibó. Finding the orí ere marks this origin. In questioning eledá, the diviner has asked if the osogbo comes "at the feet of the client's own head." This means that the client's own orí brings about any ill luck or harm. No matter the orishas standing up for ebó, the client needs a rogación (a cleansing of his head) and an eborí (a feeding of his head) to align once more with both his higher self and his guardian orisha. Note: The diviner should pay careful attention to the orisha who owns the original composite odu opened on the mat, for that spirit might assist the client in attaining his balance. In this case, the rogación is done at the feet of that orisha so he or she may bless the client's head.

**Egun.** For ibó, the diviner picks the gungun (bone) and otá (stone). If the gungun is displayed in the client's chosen hand, the oracle affirms that the ancestral spirits are the source of the client's osogbo. Remember: Egun are ancestors of both the physical and spiritual families. When egun is marked, many diviners try to mark the specific spirit that brings these calamities; however, in our own house we find this to be a ludicrous practice. Egun denotes a collective force of spirits that work to help the client evolve, and osogbo from them results from either negligence of these forces or the futile attempt of the spirits to push this person closer to his true path. Knowing that an osogbo comes from egun is enough; the diviner and client will work together to propitiate this collective force as a whole.

**Lowó arayé.** When marking this origin, the diviner picks the apadí (pottery shard) and otá (stone) as ibó. Lowó arayé means "the curses of evil eyes, tongues, and circumstances." If the client's hand reveals the apadí, this origin is marked.

**Ará onú.** To determine if ará onú is the origin of the client's osogbo, the diviner uses the otá (stone) and efun (chalk) as ibó. Ará onú denotes the citizens of heaven, those spirits who rest with Olódumare; therefore, if efun (the affirmative answer) is in the chosen hand, the odu emphasizes that the misfortunes are punishments sent by heaven, the invisible realm.

**Ocha.** When questioning ocha as the origin of the client's osogbo, the diviner picks the efun (chalk) and otá (stone) as ibó. If ocha is marked, it shows that the client's troubles are brought to him at the feet of the orishas. Now the diviner determines which spirit brings the osogbo to the client. Working through the list of orishas who speak in the parent odu, the diviner now questions the oracle as to who sends "punishment." Use the ayé (seashell) and otá (stone) when questioning if this comes from a water orisha, such as Yemayá, Olokun, Oshún, or Inle. Even though this orisha might remain silent throughout the rest of the reading, the diviner marks ebó to this spirit; and if it will take no ebó, he tells the client to appease that force constantly.

**Tiya-tiya.** When questioning tiya-tiya, the apadí (pottery shard) and otá (stone) are the appropriate ibó to use. Tiya-tiya denotes arguments, gossip, and slander as the cause of the client's osogbo. No matter the advice given in the odu itself, with this orientation the client must be on guard against the slander of others; he must also ensure that he takes no part in any argument or gossip that might come his way.

**Obini.** When questioning obini, the diviner uses the apadí (pottery shard) and otá (stone) as ibó. Obini means "woman"; if the odu reveals the apadí in the client's chosen hand, his misfortunes are brought to him "at the feet of a woman."

**Okuni.** Just as with obini, the diviner here uses the apadí (pottery shard) and otá (stone) as ibó. Okuni translates as "man"; therefore, if the apadí is in the chosen hand, all the client's troubles come to him "at the feet of a man."

**Abure.** In questioning abure, the diviner uses the apadí (pottery shard) and otá (stone) as ibó. Abure means a sibling of blood or ocha. If the apadí is revealed in the client's hand, his misfortunes come "at the feet of a sibling."

**Lowó.** Lowó is Lucumí for "the client's own hands" or "the client's own works." To determine if lowó is the origin of the osogbo, the diviner chooses the apadí (pottery shard) and otá (stone) as ibó. If it reveals the apadí in the chosen hand, the odu marks lowó. Simply stated, what the client has sown, he will reap; his own hands will cut off his evolution.

**Ogo.** Ogo is a Lucumí word for "witch," "witchcraft," or "sorcerer." To question ogo, the diviner chooses the ayé (seashell) and otá (stone) as ibó. If the ayé is chosen, the odu reveals ogo as the origin of the client's osogbo. The origin itself, however, is interesting, for while it marks magic as the source of the client's ills, sometimes it can be the client's own mystical involvements that bring his ruin. The specific odu that opened on the mat will give hints as to whether this is the case.

**Alaleyo.** Alaleyo is a Lucumí contraction meaning "those who are outsiders to the faith" or "commoners who live in the world." To mark alaleyo as the origin of the client's osogbo, the diviner picks the osán (guacalote seed) and otá (stone) as ibó. The guacalote seed marks this as the origin. Alaleyo is an interesting but not precise concept, and it puts the client on guard against others whose true intentions are not known. Note that if the opening odu marks any person or type of people as the origin of danger, and alaleyo has opened as the origin of osogbo, the diviner must caution the client to stay away from those people at all costs. They will be his ruin.

After determining the origin of the predicted osogbo, the diviner writes the odu that marked the affirmative ibó under the osogbo's odu on the piece of paper; beside this, he records the origin that was revealed. If the oracle marks none of the possible origins of the osogbo, we say that the osogbo comes *elese elenú*, or from the client's own tongue. The odu thrown for alaleyo is recorded with this phrase listed beside it.

## Marking the Eboses, or Remedies for Odu

By now the diviner knows the opening odu and its orientation (iré or osogbo); he also knows the type of blessing or misfortune promised; and, in the case of osogbo, he knows the origin of the client's troubles. Remember that if the diloggún presents any iré yale timbelaye (guaranteed to manifest in this life) the odu is closed; it requires no further manipulations. In every other situation, there is more work to do.

The diviner now attempts to mark an ebó to resolve, stabilize, and harmonize the odu in the client's life. Of all the eboses a sign might prescribe, this offering or sacrifice is the most important; it will help the client evolve. To begin extracting the odu's major ebó, the diviner selects the efun (chalk) and otá (stone) to use as ibó throughout the entire process. One uses efun because it belongs to Obatalá and Olófin; they are the most forgiving of all the orishas, and with their influence any osogbo can be soothed. For this reason, efun always answers yes and marks the ebó, while otá answers no and signifies the need to manipulate the oracle further until finding a resolution.

To begin the search for the major ebó, begin with these four initial questions.

**Larishe si?** With this question, the diviner asks the open odu if there is a remedy to its unbalanced nature. If the casting he makes points to the client's hand that holds efun, the answer is yes. Of the four questions, "Larishe si?" is the best to receive an affirmative answer for. More than just an ebó, the marked offering will soothe what seethes about the client. Next the priest investigates the various types of ebó one may offer to the spirits. (See pages 31–33 for a complete listing.) The proper question to ask is "Larishe [name of ebó]?" ("Is the remedy [name of ebó]?") This continues until the priest receives an affirmative response to a particular ebó. Now the diviner must determine which orisha claims this ebó. Chapters 2 through 13 of this book, each of which is devoted to a particular odu, each contains a section titled "The Orishas Who Speak in [odu's name]." The orishas listed in that section are those who may claim an ebó when the odu of their chapter is open. Naming the orishas who might claim an ebó for the particular odu that is open, one by one and in the order in which they are listed in this book, the priest asks, "Ebó [marked ebó] elese [orisha's name]?" until he finds the proper spirit. (Efun continues to mark the affirmative and otá the negative.) In addition, using his own aché, the diviner determines the materials for the ebó, the length of time it remains with the orisha, and the method of disposal once the offering is removed from that spirit's shrine.

**Ocha onire?** This question translates to "Will an orisha give a blessing?" If it points to efun in the client's hand, the diloggún emphasizes that one of the orishas comes to bless his adherent. Realize, however, that while blessings are beneficial, they are not remedies. Although some spirit has taken an interest in the client and will help him, there will still be instability. The diviner's next step is to determine which orisha blesses the client. As described above, the diviner works through the list of orishas who might claim an ebó for the particular odu that is open, in the order in which they are listed in the relevant "The Orishas Who Speak in [odu's name]." The question in this case is "[Orisha's name] onire?" ("[Orisha's name] gives the blessing?") He names each spirit in turn until he finds efun in response to the question. Next, the diviner determines what the spirit wants as ebó. Working through the list of eboses given on pages 31–33, he asks, "[Name of ebó] elese [marked orisha's name]?" ("An offering of [name of ebó] at the feet of [marked orisha's name]?") As always, efun marks the affirmative. After determining both the orisha and the ebó, the priest uses his aché to decide exactly what to give, how long it remains, and the method of disposal once the ebó is lifted (removed) from the shrine.

**Egun onire?** Translated into English, this means "Will egun give a blessing?" If the diloggún points to efun, egun onire has been marked. Because the ancestors are petitioned as a collective force, immediately the diviner begins to mark the type of ebó needed, working through the list on pages 31–33. He asks, "Ebó [type of ebó] elese egun?" ("An offering of [type of ebó] at the feet of egun?") Once the type of ebó is determined, the diviner uses his aché to detail the materials for the offering, how long it is to remain, and the method of disposal once the ebó is lifted from the shrine.

**Igboro larishe?*** Translated into English, this means "Does an initiate present have a remedy?" Efun answers yes. When the diloggún marks igboro larishe, the orisha whose shells are on the mat is telling the diviner that someone present at the divination knows the ebó to soothe the odu and help the client evolve. After the diviner delivers the reading, initiates present will have the chance to advise the client from their own experiences with this letter. The diviner records their advice on paper as if the oracle presented it itself.

If the diviner has asked all four questions and the answer to each is no, the odu prescribes no ebó at this time to bring harmony. The diviner will have to search deeper into the odu itself to help the client find his evolution.

If the diloggún has marked larishe si, ocha onire, or egun onire, the diviner must mark an appropriate ebó. The types of eboses found in the diloggún are as follows.

*If there are no priests or priestesses present at the reading other than the diviner, he does not ask this question.

**Adimú.** An adimú is an offering, almost always something edible. Most diviners who mark adimú as the needed ebó prescribe some type of cooked food. This ebó does not call for animal sacrifice; an adimú is anything simple and cool, whereas blood is complex and hot.

**Aladimú.** This marks any type of offering based on what the diviner knows the orisha likes. It can be either food or a nonedible item, such as candles, flowers, or votive statues.

**Eboshure.** This is an offering of anything edible. Normally, eboshure consists of fruits, grains, or vegetables as opposed to the cooked foods often prescribed in adimú. Any food presented in an eboshure remains with the orisha until it begins to spoil.

**Ebó keun edun keun.** This is a daily cleansing done before the orisha's shrine. Each day, a different item is used for the cleansing. This type of ebó is always done with fruits or grains; never is an animal sacrifice used.

**Koshé ocha.** This translates as "the reception of an orisha." If the list of eboses for each composite odu (as described in chapters 2 through 13) details that a certain orisha should be received, then the diviner does not need to mark which spirit the client needs. If no orisha is listed as an ebó for a particular odu, the diviner should work through the list of orishas who speak in an odu until one is marked.

**Ebó misi.** This marks a spiritual bath (herbal waters) to be taken by the client. The diviner marks the items to be used and the number of times the bath is to be taken. Some odu include directions for specific spiritual baths; when this is the case, those directions should be followed.

**Yoko ocha.** This ebó marks that salvation is to be found by being crowned. If the client's guardian orisha is not known, this letter will not close until the diviner uses the shells to determine this information. If the client's guardian orisha is known, we say that the client is a "prisoner" of ocha; he is required, by his guardian orisha, to be initiated. Until he makes ocha, he will not find true happiness.

**Ocha onire.** The diviner attempts to mark this ebó only if the diloggún has answered positively in the initial questioning to larishe si; he does not attempt to mark it if the diloggún has revealed ocha onire or egun onire. This ebó shows that an orisha will remove the volatile heat of the letter. The diviner must mark both the orisha and the ebó required by that orisha. The questions to be asked are "[Name of the orisha] onire?" and then "Ebó elese [name of the orisha]?" If the orisha wants nothing, we say that he or she loves the client freely and no offering is required. A token adimú, however, should still be given.

**Egun onire.** The diviner attempts to mark this ebó only if the diloggún has answered positively in the initial questioning to larishe si; he does not attempt to mark it if the diloggún has revealed ocha onire or egun onire. This marks that egun will remove the volatile heat of this letter. The diviner must determine if they want anything in return for their help, asking, "Ebó elese egun?" If no ebó is required, we say that these spirits love the client freely; however, a token adimú is still necessary.

**Orúnmila onire.** In this orientation, Orúnmila stands up on behalf of the client. The orisha priest or priestess is powerless to mark ebó to Orúnmila; only a babalawo may prescribe his eboses. For this reason, many diviners do not try to mark Orúnmila onire. If, however, the question has been asked and the answer is yes, the reading continues in a normal fashion and the remedy to the osogbo is written, "Orúnmila onire; the client must go to a babalawo for a reading." This is the extent to which a cowrie-shell diviner can mark ebó to Orúnmila.

**Olorún onire.** This marks that the blessing will come at the feet of Olorún and Olódumare. The ebó for this is for the client to salute the sun every morning.

**Orisha onire.** This signifies that the blessing or release from osogbo will be brought by the more obscure, mysterious orishas, those that know the secrets of life and death itself: Orisha Oko, Yewá, Oba, Naná Burukú, Babaluaiye, Nanumé, and so on. First the diviner must determine which of these orishas speaks in the odu that has opened, and then he must mark which of them is giving the blessing to clear the sign. Once this information is known, eboses to the orisha are marked. If the orisha will accept no ebó, and if the letter will not close out, the client is marked for the reception of this orisha. The diviner should mark this and then close the reading. Note that it would be wise for the client to receive this spirit's eleke no matter the ebó marked in the letter. Also, if eboses for a composite odu (as described in chapters 2 through 13) mark the reception of a dark, obscure orisha, that is the orisha to be received; the diviner does not need to mark it because the odu already has.

**Igboro larishe.** The remedy will come from one of the priests or priestesses present at the mat. They should be allowed to give the client eboses (but not advice unless the diviner specifically asks for it later). Any ebó prescribed by any priest or priestess in the room should be written in the record as if odu prescribed it itself.

**Ebó kere.** Ebó kere is a beautiful yet complicated set of offerings. It consists of several spiritual cleansings for the client. First the diviner needs to ascertain the orisha taking ebó kere. Then he must mark a series of offerings to be given and used for the cleansings. The length of time, in weekly increments, must also be marked. For example, the oracle answers yes to ebó kere, and the diviner discovers with ibó that Yemayá is to receive the offerings. Since her number is seven, he decides that each offering should remain with her for seven days, and he marks the following items for a period of seven weeks: a watermelon, molasses, seven coconuts, plantains, a ñame, flowers, and a basket of fruit. After the offerings are marked, he then uses the oracle to mark where each offering should be taken after it is removed and the next given. The oracle answers that the offerings should be taken to the lake for disposal.

**Sarayeye.** This marks that a spiritual cleansing is needed. It is customary for the diviner first to attempt to mark sarayeye to egun. If the oracle will not let this ebó go to egun, the diviner marks it to an orisha, working through the list of orishas that speak in the sign. After the proper spirit is determined, the item with which the client should be cleansed is marked. Sometimes this is an animal. In sarayeye, however, no sacrifice is dictated, so it is customary for the animal to be set free after the cleansing. (If a blood sacrifice is needed for a cleansing, the odu dictates eyebale, or the sacrifice of an animal.) The method of disposal should be marked as well (if the cleansing is done with an animal, the oracle should dictate where the animal is to be set free).

**Koborí eledá.** This ebó prescribes an offering made to one's orí. Usually this is a rogación, but the diviner must mark the items needed for the cleansing. Depending on the problems faced by the client and the odu that fell, the rogación may need to be done at the feet of a specific orisha. The odu will dictate whether this is the case. This type of offering will not dictate the "feeding" of the orí with sacrifice; such an ebó would be marked through eyebale.

**Kaure.** These are prayers; the diviner marks whether they are made to egun or to an orisha. If the prayers are for an orisha, he must mark which one. The prayers should be dictated to the client. In kaure, it is customary for the client to make adimú with a candle before the prayer and with fruits once the prayers are complete.

**Eyebale.** If the oracle marks none of the ebó listed above, the offering required is eyebale, or the sacrifice of an animal. It is important to note that eyebale is always a last resort for ebó. Life on all levels is a precious gift, and it is taken, reverently, only when there are no other options. Blood offerings are very hot and volatile. If the oracle has not yet determined whether the offering goes to egun or to an orisha, the diviner now asks, "Eyebale elese egun?" ("Does the animal sacrifice go to egun?") If the answer is no, he must ask, "Eyebale elese orisha?" ("Does the animal sacrifice go to the orisha?") If both egun and orisha refuse eyebale, the oracle dictates that the sacrifice goes to the client's own head. A rogación is given, and with this cleansing an animal sacrifice is offered directly to the client's crown (the area that links the physical head on earth with the spiritual head in heaven). Only in this way will the client's issues be resolved, for in this case we say that his own spiritual and physical orí is causing confusion in the reading.

Note that in many houses of ocha, eyebale is not the last larishe included in the pattern of questioning. If the oracle answers negatively to the question of eyebale, many diviners say that the larishe is "ko larishe" ("no larishe"). This interpretation, however, is frivolous; odu would not answer yes to the question "Larishe si?" only to tell the diviner that the ebó required is "ko larishe." It is possible that this confusion arises from an exception to this line of questioning. In some of the odu, when a letter will not close, specific orishas must be questioned in turn about the possibilities of larishe and ebó. Out of respect for both the odu opened and the orisha questioned, the possibility of eyebale is given as a direct choice during questioning. When eyebale is refused, certain eboses are then considered marked as the offerings that will bring the client back into alignment with his destiny, turning osogbo into iré. (When this alternative pattern of questioning is needed, the reader will find it flagged in the relevant chapter of this book.)

All of the ebó information should be written in the reading's record by the diviner's assistant.

Once the diviner has completed the processes detailed above, the initial manipulations of the diloggún are complete. The odu has been opened, its orientations determined, and the initial larishes prescribed to bring the client back into alignment with odu, egun, and orisha. It is now time for the diviner to impart what he has learned to his client.

## Giving the Reading

By this time, the initial manipulations of the diloggún are complete; the diviner has performed the mojuba and has marked the orientations, and the diviner's assistant has recorded all the information gleaned from this. Before anything else is done, the diviner should perform any gestures, prayers, or rituals associated with the odu opened. These are described, in full, in the introductory sections of chapters 2 through 13 of this book. (Before attempting divination, all diviners should be thoroughly familiar with this material.)

Now the diviner proceeds with the reading of the odu appearing on the mat. The initial steps to giving the reading must be followed to ensure that odu is properly placated. First, the diviner calls off the name of the sign that has opened, followed by a complete rendition of the orientation and prescribed larishe in both Lucumí and the native language of the client. The initial manipulations have yielded the writing/interpretation of one or more sacred sentences by the diloggún, and this initial pronouncement is essential to the final interpretations of odu.

As an example, turn to the illustrations of properly recorded readings given at the end of this chapter. In the first example, the diviner would begin his reading with the words "Irosun Ogbe: ona elese ocha, elese Olokun. Larishe si: koshé Olokun." He then translates the phrase into English (if the client's native language is English): "Irosun Ogbe: closed roads and afflictions at the feet of the orisha Olokun. There is a remedy: the reception of Olokun." For the second example, the diviner would begin with "Obara Meji: iré elese elenú. Iré yale. Larishe si: adimú elese ocha, Shangó." In English, the diviner would then say, "Obara Meji: Blessings and goodness come through one's own tongue. The iré is firm but not guaranteed to manifest now in one's life. There is a remedy: an adimú at the feet of the orisha Shangó." Our third and final example of a recorded reading marks the following: "Ejiogbe Oché: ikú elese otonowá. Igboro larishe." This translates as "Ejiogbe Oché: Death comes at the feet of heaven, Olódumare. Good advice comes from an initiate that is present."

It is not important for the diviner to explain the steps involved with the larishe at this time. Instead, he must let the client (who by this time will be both worried and confused about the process of divination) know the essentials of what is predicted, along with any pronouncement of his problem's solution. To do this, the diviner, keeping in mind the information he has learned so far, gives one or more of the many proverbs associated with the open odu. In our first example, Irosun Ogbe, the most relevant proverb to match both the odu and the prescribed larishe would be "Nobody knows what lies at the bottom of the sea." We pick this proverb from those associated with the parent odu (Irosun) and not those of the composite, for Olokun is the depths of the sea, and it is her reception that will clear the initial osogbo predicted in the sign. After rendering a proverb, many diviners then tell one of the many *patakís*, the sacred stories associated with the composite odu. Since this reading seems to revolve around the orisha Olokun, the diviner might wish to deliver the story about the shoemaker's apprentice, in which Olokun is one of the major characters.*

In the second example, the proper proverb could be "With your tongue, you may save or destroy the town. Control the tongue." It could allude directly to the firm iré coming through the client's own tongue, and it could also explain why the client might not have this iré manifest in his life: His tongue is out of control. The diviner would then tell the patakí of this odu titled "The Food of Obatalá," for this story revolves around Shangó (to whom ebó must be made) and the tongue.

In our third example, the diviner might begin his reading by reciting the proverb "Lies bring revolution" or, from the parent odu, "The head carries the body: Do not lose the head." Both allude to falsehood and destruction, and our final example foreshadows death if the head is lost. The patakí "The Truth Is Sweet Like Honey" could be told, for it teaches the results of ethical actions in this odu, and any osogbo brought by heaven is an evil visited upon one who is truly deserving of such things. God never makes a mistake!

Now, it often happens that a client comes to the mat with a specific problem, and the opening odu, larishe, proverb, and patakí seem to have little, if any, bearing on the trouble he faces. If the client begins to ask questions because of this, the diviner should silence him and explain that before the session ends, the oracle will answer his questions in full, and if not, the client will have three chances to ask specific questions to clarify his concerns. While odu might have been approached because of a specific trouble, omo odu concentrates on not just one aspect of life, but the entire spectrum of life concerns that a person can face. Just as a physician treats not just a specific symptom of disease but a total organism, the odu reaches into the full vortex of the client and his environment to determine what is out of alignment. Once odu has determined this, it works gently to pull this person back into focus, back into his personal destiny and harmony with both orí and orisha. A single problem faced by anyone can have roots that extend through many different aspects of life. A single symptom cannot be treated alone.

Now that these initial steps have been taken, the diviner faces his most difficult task: turning the massive amount of information contained in both the parent and the omo odu into a cohesive whole, weaving a reading out of the divinatory meanings given in each letter. Throughout, the diviner should keep in mind the orientation of the letter; if an osogbo has opened and the odu contains specific messages that should be delivered only in iré, obviously they will not apply to the client's situation at this time. The diviner begins by assessing how the parent odu relates to the "sentence" the diloggún has written for this client. Once he has his plan of delivery in mind, the diviner relays these meanings slowly and deliberately, remembering that, as he speaks, the assistant

*Note that not all diviners employ the art of storytelling in their craft. Unfortunately, the recitation of these patakís during the divination process is a dying custom among priests. It is, in my opinion, one that should be thoroughly revived, for it is through these stories that one learns about the orishas in this religion.

will have to write down his words. Once the options for discussion are exhausted in the parent odu, the diviner begins to relay the meanings of the composite opened on the mat, and these words are recorded by the assistant as well.

The final two steps to a proper reading are the enforcement of taboos and the explanation of larishe. The diviner must once again think about the phrase delivered from the initial manipulations of odu. If the client has offered any information about his present life circumstances, the diviner considers these as well. Finally, having weighed the seriousness of what the odu has uncovered, the diviner prescribes prohibitions based on the parent odu. (Chapters 2 through 13 each list the prohibitions of the odu they feature in the section titled "The Prohibitions of [Odu's name].") These prohibitions are dutifully recorded by the assistant so that, after the reading, there will be no question about what the client should or should not do based on the orisha's advice.

If the reading opened in a firm iré, these prohibitions are guidelines by which the client should consider living. If the reading opened in an osogbo, the prohibitions are strict taboos that should not be broken if the client aspires to goodness and evolution. For most clients, the prohibitions apply for a period of twenty-one to twenty-eight days, the normal passage of time for the energy of a single odu. However, if a serious osogbo opens, the diviner may prescribe these prohibitions for a longer period. If this reading is a *bajado* (done to determine one's guardian orisha), the prohibitions should be followed until the client makes ocha; if this reading is an itá, they apply for life.

Now comes the explanation of the larishe. Since the larishe that has been prescribed is already recorded, the assistant may cease writing unless the diviner is moved by the orishas to add more information. The following items must be detailed for the client: the nature of the spirit who claims larishe, the type of ebó marked for larishe, and what steps are necessary to fulfill the offering. The diviner must ask his client, "Do you have any questions about this ebó or any of the material that we have gone over?" This is the client's one chance to clarify all the information brought up during the session.*

Now the diviner has his first chance to close the session. The question "Eboda ke un soro?" ("Is the conversation here sufficient?" or "Has all been accomplished?") is put to the oracle. If the answer is yes, the priest instructs the client to kiss his fingers and then to touch the mat, showing respect for the odu that opened and the orishas who spoke. Once this is done, the diviner gathers the diloggún from the mat. He cups it in both hands and blows on the shells, saying, "*Tó, aché!*" to allow the spirit to depart.

If the answer to the question is no, the odu and the orishas have more business with the client that they would like to discuss. Perhaps it is only another ebó that is needed. The diviner must once again embark upon the questioning used to mark the ebó, beginning with "Larishe si?" The pattern described in "Marking the Eboses, or Remedies for Odu" (page 30) is strictly followed. If an ebó is marked to some orisha or egun, the diviner explains the implications of the offerings demanded and the nature of the orisha or egun that wants the sacrifice in relation to the odu that opened on the mat.

If this process has been exhausted but the oracle still refuses closure, it is directing the diviner to mark one or more of the many eboses linked with the composite odu, as described in "The Eboses of [composite odu's name]" in each of the following chapters.† Each odu will have its own process for

---

*If the prescribed larishe was igboro larishe (which means the remedy will come from an initiate at the mat), now the initiates present may begin to advise the client based not only on their own experiences with the odu, but also on the eboses they might have done in the past to help appease the letter that fell. This conversation begins with the eldest head present and continues until everyone who desires to speak has had a chance. The advice given by the initiates is noted in the reading's record.

†Many diviners will repeat the questioning that begins with "Larishe si?" only one additional time during the course of a session. If two larishes have been marked and still the odu refuses closure, they turn to the many eboses contained in the open odu. In our house, however, we let the oracle take us through this phase of questioning as many times as it will allow. In this manner, we feel, the orisha's diloggún is allowed to speak, marking only those things that are truly essential to the client's evolution. This point, however, cannot be argued; each diviner must do what he or she feels is proper.

determining these eboses, and the reader is directed to study the description of eboses given for each composite. Once an ebó is accepted, the diviner should attempt the process for closure again. If the sacrifices marked for the composite odu are not sufficient to close a reading, the diviner then works through the potential additional eboses listed for the parent odu, as described in "Closing the Session: Further Eboses of the Parent Odu, [parent odu's name]" in each of the following chapters.

If the reading comes to the point which there is no more larishe and no more eboses in the composite and parent odu, it is time to allow the oracle to rest. Diviner, client, and all initiates present must now talk, honestly. Something is amiss in the reading, and it can be sorted out only by a thorough conversation with those in the room. The diviner may wish to discuss, in depth, all the implications contained in the parent odu and composite odu. After the diviner has had an honest talk with the client, the oracle is again asked for closure. If it will not close, and the diviner is very experienced, it is time to turn to the eboses of the omo odu as a parent odu. (For example, if the odu is Ejiogbe Okana (8–1), the diviner would now turn to the eboses given for Okana as a parent odu.) After marking one of these, the diviner again asks for closure. If even now the oracle will not close, it is time to call a more experienced elder, no matter the experience of the diviner himself. The session has missed something essential, something important, and it will take one with more wisdom to bring the reading to an end.

Once the oracle has been closed and the orisha dismissed, the assistant gives the top part of the paper, which contains the odu, to the diviner and the bottom part, which contains the taboos, prognostications, and eboses, to the client. If the client is a godchild, the godparent keeps the entire record on his or her behalf.* Under no circumstances is the client to have the numbers of the odu that has fallen, nor is the odu that was opened to be discussed again beyond what was marked during the reading.† The client must give eboses as soon as possible, in the order that they were prescribed. The initial larishes are to be done first, followed by the eboses of the composite odu, and then the eboses of the parent odu. Once these works are complete, the advice given by each initiate at the mat is followed to ensure that the energies of the letter are properly placated. When the client is ready to give his eboses, he should bring the ingredients for each to the diviner's or godparent's home, preparing as much as he can with his own hands. Work is aché, and the one mandated to make the offering must prepare it with his own hands. Only after all this work has been done has the client fulfilled his obligations to the orishas, and only then will the evolution promised by the oracle begin to affect his life.

Before a novice begins to work with the consecrated diloggún of an orisha, it would be wise to follow these steps in learning how to manipulate the diloggún. First, the material in this chapter should be read many times until the general flow of a reading is understood. Then the details of this system should be memorized. The names and meanings of ibó should be memorized, as well as the situations in which a specific ibó is used to mark the orientation/larishe of a specific odu. Second, the concept of elder/younger odu must be understood and committed to memory, for if there is any mistake in picking the appropriate hand of ibó, the oracle's messages will not be correctly deciphered and the reading will be of little use to the client. Third, study the Lucumí vocabulary essential to the delivery of a reading; those words and phrases included in this section are integral to the process of divination. Commit them

*Godparents should always be in attendance at a godchild's diloggún session. If they cannot go, a stand-in should be appointed.

†The odu are living organisms of energy, and if the client has the name and numbers of an odu in his possession, he can unwittingly call that energy to himself again and again, creating devolution instead of evolution. Once the eboses for a letter are done, the client should no longer dwell upon the odu that opened. There are two exceptions to this rule: the reading of itá and the reading of the head. Itá, given when a client makes ocha and becomes a iyawó, will affect this person for life; the letters revealed at itá mark and mold his destiny. The reading of the head is like an itá for an aleyo or aborisha: It is the main energy pattern that rules his life until ocha is made.

to memory. Finally, an unconsecrated set of cowrie shells should be opened, and the would-be diviner should find a friend who is also studying divination to practice both manipulation and picking hands of ibó. Having a third party present to follow the guidelines in this section, pointing out mistakes as they come up, will help the entire learning process. Only once these steps have been followed and the material of this chapter mastered should the initiate throw his first hand of consecrated shells under the guidance of an elder.

## Examples of Recorded Readings with the Diloggún

It is important that the date of the reading goes in the upper left-hand corner, followed by the client's full birth name plus the marriage name (if it applies) and then the date of the client's birth. This information makes it easy for the diviner, the godparent, and the client to look back over the reading at a later date, not only to determine its accuracy but also to ensure that the eboses were fulfilled.

### 12/10/96 Juan Ramírez-Rodríguez 10/10/62

**4-8 Irosun Ogbe** [This is the odu opened when the diloggún was cast.]*

**4 osogbo** [This is the odu cast when the question "Iré ni?" was asked. The answer was no; the odu Irosun demanded that the left hand be opened to find the oracle's answer, and the otá was there. Both the odu that fell and the fact that the reading is in an osogbo are marked in the record.]

**5-5 ona** [The odu marking the osogbo in this sign was Oché Meji. The ibó used for questioning this osogbo are the apadí (affirmative) and the otá (negative). Although Oché is the youngest odu, the fact that it opened in a meji made it an elder, so the diviner chose the left hand, revealing apadí.]

**4 elese ocha** [This odu marked the origin of the osogbo as coming at the feet of ocha. Irosun is an elder odu, and whenever an elder falls the left hand is chosen. Otá and efun were the ibó used, and efun was found in the client's left hand. In elese ocha, the next step is to determine the orisha bringing the osogbo.]

**4 Olokun** [Again, Irosun opened on the mat, and the left hand was chosen. Efun was there, and Olokun was marked as the origin of this osogbo.]

**8 larishe** [Odu offered a way to escape the osogbo that was hanging over the client at this time. The odu that fell was Eji Ogbe, the oldest of all the odu. This odu answers yes to all questions, so there was no need to open a hand. However, on a whim the diviner picked the client's left hand, and he found the otá there. The oracle was pointing out that the client is either at war with himself over finding a way out of difficulty or will perhaps later disagree with the larishe the odu has prescribed.]

**4 koshé ocha** (Olokun) [When Irosun fell at koshé ocha—the reception of an orisha—and unveiled the efun in the client's left hand, this ebó was marked as the larishe required by the odu. Since this reading is filled with Irosun, having opened with Irosun and marking most of its orientations in Irosun, the diviner decided by his own aché that Olokun was the orisha the client must receive. His decision was further reinforced by the fact that Olokun was the orisha bringing afflictions through the odu. Also, one of the many eboses marked in Irosun Ogbe is the reception of Olokun.]

[Now that all the orientations and larishe have been marked, the diviner begins with his reading, and the assistant begins writing.]

> *Irosun Ogbe: ona elese ocha, elese Olokun. Larishe si; koshé Olokun.*
>
> Irosun Ogbe has opened on the mat; there are closed roads and afflictions at the feet of the orishas. These are brought by Olokun. There is a remedy to the troubles that you now have; you must receive Olokun. Remember this: Nobody knows what lies at the bottom of the ocean. In this sign we say, "Maferefún Olokun!

*When this odu opened, the diviner folded up the derecho, crossed himself, and returned it to the client. In Irosun Ogbe, the diviner may not charge the client for the reading, nor may he charge for the work he does in performing prescribed eboses. All his work must be done for free, with the client providing only the material for the ebó. Many diviners have become unscrupulous in their manipulations of Irosun Ogbe, delivering the many eboses that can be marked in this sign as advice instead of actual ebó. In this way, they feel they can get around the prohibition of not charging for their work. This is an unethical practice among santeros, and to my knowledge all who do this lose many times more than they gain financially when the orishas later prescribe outrageously expensive eboses for the simplest of their own problems brought to the diloggún.

Maferefún Ajé Shaluga!" (Maferefún means "praise be to" or "all power be to.") Let me tell you a story.

## The Story of the Shoemaker's Apprentice

Many centuries ago everyone on earth walked unshod. Yet one man, an old, wise man, discovered the method of making shoes. Not wanting to cut his feet anymore on sharp rocks or thorns, he made a pair of shoes for himself, and when others saw how easily and comfortably he walked, they wanted shoes as well. He made shoes for his family first, perfecting his technique, and then he began to make them for everyone who lived in his town. Because no one else knew how to make shoes, the old man quickly became rich, and the more shoes he made, the more shoes others wanted. He was overworked, and in time he hired a young boy to whom he could teach his art.

So happy was this poor young man to have employment that he went before the ocean, Olokun's home, every day before going to work, and there he gave thanks for the blessings in his life. In return, Olokun gave him even greater good fortune by bringing the old man and his business new customers. Eventually the shoemaker's apprentice had enough money to make an ebó, and he gave toasted corn, smoked fish, and jutía (a large African rat) soaked with palm oil to the street corner, feeding Elegguá, and for the Queen of Oceans he threw a large watermelon into the waters. Elegguá accepted his offering—the first the young boy had ever given him. But being at times an evil spirit, he decided that now was the time to test the young man's faith, bringing him a bit of trouble before he increased his fortune. Elegguá went to the shoemaker (who never made ebó to any orisha) and told him all the boy did at the ocean and the street corner, saying that he did not do it in thanks but in the hopes of bringing ruin to the old man's work. The shoemaker was terrified by the news and fired the boy, paying him for the work he had done that day.

The young man did not lose faith. He took what money he had to make yet another ebó to Olokun and Elegguá. Having made his offerings, he was once again broke, and he soon found himself hungry. He began to walk to another nearby town. Elegguá smiled to himself, for in spite of the great evil he had visited upon the apprentice, the boy had not lost faith. Truly, he was worthy of blessings.

The boy walked a great time and arrived at a spot where a man sold food; he got a jícara of this, which cost ten cents. After finishing it, he told the man that he had no money. This angered the man and began a fight that drew all the townspeople. They were quick to judge the boy and ordered that if he could not pay for his food, he should be punished severely. Another old man happened to be walking by, and when he learned of the boy's predicament he offered to pay for his food. Satisfied, the crowd broke up and the old man and the boy were alone.

"Why have you done this?" the old man asked the boy.

"Sir," he said, "I was fired this morning and I had no work. I was starving."

The old man asked if he wanted work, and the boy said that he did. "Good, follow me!" When they had walked a long way and the old man was sure that they were alone, he told the boy, "Look, your work will be simple." He pointed toward a cave. "We will remove this stone there; it is a hindrance to us. This is the door to a cave, a narrow entrance that would not have room enough for me. But for you, it will be easy to slip inside. Once inside, your work will be to chip away the great stone until the opening is large enough for me to pass through."

He gave the boy a hammer and chisel, and the boy entered and saw that the cave held within a fortune in gold and gems. He began to pick at the boulder, and when he was done, the old man asked him what was inside. Immediately the boy thought to himself that he did not want to lose his job, and he responded that he had seen nothing. This went on for three days; each morning, boy would meet his employer at his home for breakfast, and then they would go to the cave to work on increasing the entrance. But on the fourth morning the young man found his employer had died in the night; he was still in bed, sleeping the sleep of ikú.

The boy tended him well and buried him. Then he worked for another week, making the opening of the cave large enough that he could pass through with its riches, and when he was done, a large palace was built above the very cave that made him wealthy. With his newfound wealth, he soon became the owner and master of the entire countryside.

He bought a white horse and went to his town. No one recognized him. He went to the old shoemaker, who barely remembered him, but upon recognizing him was astounded and afraid of his success. Yet the boy understood the old man's plight and did not reproach him for past evils; he treated him well and spoke only about business.

He saw the shoemaker was spanning hard times and made

a deal with him to alleviate his troubles. Investments were made to increase both their fortunes, and the old man lived a life far more prosperous than any he had ever known. The shoemaker's shop became a string of shops, an empire; yet the years passed and this old man died. He left everything to his old apprentice, who soon became the richest man in all the land by making shoes.

[After the story, the diviner's assistant continues to write the things that the priest delivering the text of odu says. Once the reading has been delivered and all the odu marked and closed, the top portion of this paper stays with the godparent/diviner, while the bottom part is given to the client so that he knows exactly what was predicted and which eboses to make.]

### 3/16/96 Stephen Bernard Jones 12/22/72

**6-6 Obara Meji** [This was the composite odu that opened on the mat.]

**8 iré** [The diviner asked the diloggún, "Iré ni?" The odu Eji Ogbe answers yes in all cases; however, the diviner opened Stephen's left hand anyway to see which ibó was there. It was efun, which shows that the client's orí is in agreement with the orisha.]

**6-6 elese elenú** [This odu marked the type and origin of the iré: elese elenú. Since Obara is one of the younger odu, a second casting of shells was done. It became a meji. This made Obara an elder, and the diviner opened the client's left hand. It held the efun.]

**8 iré yale** [The iré marked in this odu was firm; it was not, however, guaranteed to manifest in this life. Issues were still pending with both the odu and the orisha, so the diviner's next step was to determine if a larishe will hold the iré firm for the client.]

**6-8 larishe si** [There was a larishe. Obara, a younger odu, preceded Eji Ogbe, the oldest odu; in other words, the first throw was younger than the second, so the diviner opened the client's right hand. Efun was there. Normally, an answer found in the right hand is not as strong as that found in the left; however, because Eji Ogbe fell as the second odu, the diviner was assured that a good delivery of Obara Meji plus strong ebó would hold the iré firm for his client.]

**4 adimú** [Irosun marked the left hand, and efun was there. The ebó was marked as adimú.]

**6-6 elese Shangó** [Obara Meji opened again for the question "Adimú elese Shangó?" Since this is an elder odu, the diviner chose the left hand, which revealed the efun. The adimú went to Shangó.]

[Now that the opening odu and its orientations are known, the priest delivers the reading while the assistant records his words.]

> *Obara Meji: iré elese elenú, iré yale. Larishe si; adimú elese ocha, elese Shangó! Kawo Kabiosile! Maferefún Shangó!*
>
> Obara Meji has opened on the mat. Blessings and goodness will come through one's own tongue; the iré promised by odu is firm but not guaranteed to manifest in this life. There is a larishe; there is a way to lock in what the sign and the orishas promise. Make adimú to Shangó, who speaks strongly in this letter. Remember this proverb: With your tongue you may save or destroy the town. Control the tongue. Let me tell you a story.

### The Food of Obatalá

Shangó was but a youth when Obatalá gave him his aché. So young was he that none of the elder orishas believed he deserved their respect; indeed, many of them were insulted that the wise Obatalá would endow such a young orisha with so much power. Their envy grew in time to disdain and distaste for Shangó, and every day it came to pass that one or more of the orishas would go to the King of White Cloth with tales of Shangó's youthful exploits. Many of these were lies crafted to make Shangó a lesser spirit in Obatalá's eyes, while others were half-truths embellished with outrageous tales of dishonor. Obatalá was no fool and he could tell when the orishas were lying to him, yet so bad were the stories that he had no choice. He called Shangó to his palace and said, "My son, I gave you your aché because, in my eyes, you are a noble orisha. Yet to be what you are at such a young age, you can no longer be a child; you must be above all reproach. You must never beat around the bush with others; always speak what is on your mind. And never ever put yourself into a situation that seems compromising. Give no one any reason to speak badly about you!"

"Father, what do the others say about me?" Shangó asked;

and he listened sorrowfully as the orisha told him all the stories. "But Father, none of that is true! What am I to do?" Obatalá thought for a moment, and then he said, "My son, I want you to prepare a meal for all my children and for me; I want you to cook the best food there is in the world for all of us to eat!"

Shangó was puzzled at this advice, but he knew Obatalá could see much farther and more clearly than he, so he prepared what he believed to be the best food in the world for all the orishas to eat. His meal was simple, consisting of a roasted cow's tongue. As the orishas gathered for the dinner in their father's opulent palace, Obatalá questioned, "Shangó, tongue is the best food in the world?" Shangó answered, "Yes, Father, for good aché is the best thing in the world, and the tongue is full of aché!" All the orishas were stunned at Shangó's youthful wisdom. "Aché!" they all answered, and then they began to feast.

A few days passed, and Obatalá returned to tell Shangó that he had prepared the best food in the world for his children, but now it was time for him to make the worst food in the world for him and his children. Shangó, once again, prepared cow's tongue (for he now began to understand Obatalá's plan—and wisdom). As all the orishas gathered for dinner, Obatalá asked, "Shangó, if again you make us all the same thing, having told me it was the best, why do you now make it and say that it is the worst?" And to this Shangó answered, "Because, my father," and he looked slyly at all the orishas seated for dinner, "a good tongue will save us all, and a bad tongue will destroy all that Olófin has created!"

Obatalá looked at all the orishas seated in his palace. Once again, they realized that Shangó was very wise, and they all hung their heads in shame. "You are right, Shangó," said Obatalá. "From this day forth, in the odu known as Obara Meji, is born this saying: A good tongue will save us all, and a bad tongue will destroy us. And all that speak of you, Shangó, for all eternity, and no matter what is said, good or bad, you will always be the one who owns the tongue and the good and bad that comes from its aché."

Shangó smiled and said, "Kawo Kabiosile!"

[After telling this story, the diviner begins to relay the meanings of the parent odu that applied to this client's life; he then relays the messages of the omo odu in full. All these things are carefully recorded by the assistant. Once the reading is complete, the diviner is given the top part of the paper that records the odu and orientations, while the client is given the bottom part in which the advice is written out in full. Thus is the session ended.]

### 4/15/97 Kevin Lee Smith 5/17/59

**8-5 Ogbe Oché** [This is the odu that fell on the mat for this client.]

**9-9 osogbo, ikú** [The answer to "Iré ni?" was no; the oracle predicted osogbo. The assistant did not record this odu; there are some houses that do not follow this custom. Ikú, however, was marked with Osá Meji. While Osá is a younger odu, the fact that it is meji made it an elder and the diviner chose the client's left hand. Gungun and otá were the ibó used, and gungun was in the left hand, marking ikú.]

**8 elese otonowá** [Eji Ogbe marked otonowá as the origin of the osogbo.]

**4 igboro larishe** [Because this elder odu opened, the diviner picked the left hand, which held the efun. Again, in this house the odu marking the fact that there was no larishe is not recorded; this is customary in some ocha houses.]

[Now that the opening odu and its orientations are known, the priest delivers the reading while the assistant records his words.]

> *Ogbe Oché: osogbo, ikú—elese otonowá—igboro larishe. Maferefún Obatalá. Maferefún Oshún.*
>
> Ogbe Oché opened on the mat. Death is coming for you from heaven, from Olódumare. The diloggún says that there is a larishe, but it will come in the form of good advice from an initiate present. That advice will come only after you hear what the oracle has to say. Remember these two proverbs: Lies bring revolution; and the head carries the body. Do not lie, and do not lose your head. Now, let me tell you a story.

## The Truth Is Sweet Like Honey

There was once a time when the Irunmole, the first orishas, walked upon the earth among humans. Orúnmila was no exception, and he spent his days traveling to visit those who were sick and in need. Humans who had emotional, spiritual, and physical diseases sought out the great diviner, and with Ifá he was able to cure the ills that plagued humanity. Many saw the work the orisha did and gave him praise, but others were jealous of the diviner's success. Those who were wicked slandered Orúnmila: "While you travel, who cares for your wife?" they asked. "You are unable to keep your woman; you are unable to keep your heart free of adultery. And you who have no stable home try to create stability in the lives of others?" The questions turned to taunts, sneers, and gossip; soon the evils were too great for the mighty Orúnmila to bear. Saddened and weak, he sought out one of his own disciples for advice. He wanted to know if he should stay home, ceasing his good works, or if he should continue to travel and help his fellow humans. The babalawo's pronouncement was simple: Continue to work on earth. The advice was simple: Continue to ignore the slander as you search out new work. The ebó was simple: Offer strong liquor and sweet honey to Ifá before continuing your work. Orúnmila made the ebó of Ogbe Oché and set out to continue his work.

The slander reached new heights, and in every town it seemed that fewer and fewer humans sought out Orúnmila's divine advice. Yet one day a saddened woman came to him and begged to see Ifá. She was close to suicide, yet the words of the oracle so inspired her that within days it seemed her spirit was renewed, and all she touched became sweet like honey. The woman praised the awó to all her friends: "The words that he speaks with his oracle are the truth; they are sweet, like honey, even though one's life be bitter like strong drink." Soon her own friends came to him for advice, and their friends as well. Inspired by their kind words, Orúnmila began to work longer and harder, and this newfound praise spread throughout the nearby cities. Wherever he went, he found humans who wanted his help. Slander gave way to truth, and he became highly respected at home and abroad. More followers came to Ifá, and with these were born more diviners to his cult. Orúnmila had nothing but praise for his babalawo and gratitude to Olódumare, for they had helped him find wealth and power. Refusal to listen to gossip and slander had brought fulfillment from his work; the truth of Orúnmila was spread, and the truth became sweet like honey. Soon this odu gave birth to the saying the diviner tells his client when Ogbe Oché opens on the mat: The truth is sweet like honey.

[At this point one of the initiates present, an elder who had ten years in Obatalá's priesthood, began to look distressed, almost as if she were "biting her tongue." The diviner noticed this, and, remembering that good advice would come from an initiate present, he prompted her to speak. Her words were written in the record of the reading.]

"I know that you are having problems at work with your nursing supervisor [the client was a nurse]; you feel that she is unfair and you speak badly behind her back. Don't do this anymore. Leave your problems at the feet of your Eleggúa and offer him the honey and strong liquor; he will give you strength to do your work properly, and he will sweeten your supervisor's position toward you. Your own feelings toward this person might be unfounded; she might only be doing her job, and she feels your resentment so that it is taken out on you. Break the cycle at your end, and all will come out well. Otherwise, you might be in danger of losing your job."

[Although this advice did not directly affect the osogbo predicted in this sign, the diviner later questioned Eleggúa about the ebó the initiate prescribed. Eleggúa accepted it as the solution to this person's problems at work and then stood up to claim eyebale as the means to overcome the prediction of the odu. This elder, also, with the diviner's consent, gave many more pieces of advice that she believed came through her egun—and in Ogbe Oché, it is possible for egun as well as any orisha to speak. The oracle prescribed a few more eboses for the composite odu and then closed out easily.]

# TWO
# THE FAMILY OF OKANA

## The Proverbs of Okana

- If there is nothing bad, there can never be anything good.
- Without bitterness, one cannot know when there is goodness.
- The world was created by one.
- Your friend of yesterday shall become your enemy of today.
- A snake can beget only a snake.
- A witch can beget only a witch.
- The heat of the fire never conquers the spoon, and the spoon never melts in the soup.

## The Orishas Who Speak in Okana

| | |
|---|---|
| Elegguá | Obatalá |
| Ogún | Aganyú |
| Babaluaiye | Shangó |
| Orisha Oko | Egun* |

## The Message of Okana

Opening with only one mouth on the mat, the diloggún sits before the italero in a volatile pattern. Okana has come to the house, bringing fear and apprehension to those not well versed in the diloggún's mysteries. This sign is perilous and fraught with danger. Being almost opira (the absence of open mouths) itself, the reading is almost lost here; such are the spiritual currents surrounding the client that the orisha consulted has all but refused to speak on his issues. Yet one shell remains open; a single mouth speaks on this person's behalf. It is a tenuous thread, a minute spark of light, a solemn prayer spoken against insurmountable odds. Remember that the entire world was created by one: one spirit, one force, one moment. All of this is referenced by Okana. Creation, however, implies destruction. It brings tragedy, travesty, and turmoil. Creation is never painless. It is always selective in what it saves or destroys as new things are born. If nothing else, the opening of one mouth is a moment of spiritual tension, and those present for the reading will feel this. It can be an unpleasant experience.

Born of Ofún (ten mouths), Okana shares its parent's evolutionary powers; however, its aché tends toward destruction. It bears down fiercely on those things in the client's life that must be changed but are immovable by nature's kinder forces. Its powers are random and wanton. Because this sign alludes to things that are doubled or twinned, problems it flags are easily doubled, and under its influence the client's life could become more severe. The odu tells us that the client sitting before the orishas exists in this pattern; he already knows and feels this power,

*While egun are not orishas, many of the orishas were once egun. That is, some orishas lived mortal lives and died. For this reason, one's egun have the option to speak in many odu. One should keep in mind, however, that the egun are not orishas, and not all orishas have been egun.

and this is why he has come to the diviner's house.

Okana also tells us that the client's attention wavers, and already he is not listening to what the orishas say. His attention falters even before the admonitions of this odu are delivered. To dominate the client's attention and make him listen, the diviner gives the sacred gesture of this sign: He pulls both of his ear lobes simultaneously. Then he snaps his fingers in front of the client's eyes three times. With the client's attention now focused, the diviner chants the prayer of this sign:

*Okana sode*
*Okana oke*
*Osode omo*
*Ariku Babawa.*

The initiates present in the room bow their heads in silence during this prayer. No one speaks or even whispers while the italero intones the chant. Once finished, he gathers the shells and places them gently in the jícara (gourd) of fresh water used to give a libation to the orishas. The spiritual heat radiating from the shells is fierce; by putting them in water, the diviner soothes them. After submersing all the pieces of the diloggún, he gives the gourd to the youngest initiate present. (If the diviner is reading alone, he fulfills this part of the ritual himself.) The initiate (or the diviner) carries the container of water to the front door. He opens the door wide so fresh air enters the house. Covering the opening of the jícara loosely with the fingers of one hand so none of the shells flies out, he flings the fresh water far out into the street. The water takes the heat of Okana with it, sending it back to Earth. She is vast enough to cleanse the letter's negativity. Keeping the gourd covered, the initiate brings it back to the mat and turns it upside down so the shells fall into a new pattern beneath the gourd. The initiate casting this letter puts his left foot on top of the gourd. This ensures that the pattern falls beneath his feet and not on him. In many houses of ocha, the diviner repeats this gesture three times, tapping his left foot on top of the upside-down gourd.

The initiate who took Okana's heat from the house lifts the gourd gently, ensuring that none of the shells is disturbed by its removal. The italero counts the number of mouths displayed. He marks this in the reading's record, and the session continues. Casting the shells again, the diviner marks the final letter forming the composite odu.

It is important to note that the true composite of Okana comes from the first pattern marked (Okana) and the final pattern just cast; it excludes the letter read after Okana's heat was removed from the house. The sign thrown upon the floor for that process is said to have "come in at the door." This sign represents the client's salvation; it removes the osogbo he faces and stands up to save him. Throughout the consultation, the italero should consider the letter that came at the door, for the orisha owning it will demand ebó before allowing closure of the odu. It also gives the italero clues as to what the future beyond one mouth holds for the client. It further defines this session, and one or more eboses from that odu may be required to cleanse the client of negativity.

Many orishas might choose to speak in Okana, and in this odu the admonitions are stern. The spirit whose shells are cast has the first option. Elegguá follows; he owns Okana, and he alone has the aché to overcome many of its obstacles. Ogún is fierce here, and while he may not speak kindly to the one opening in this sign, his words are more gentle, more hopeful, than if he were speaking in his true home, Ogundá. Babaluaiye follows Ogún, and when he speaks the diloggún reeks of sickness and disease, yet it also offers hope that what ails the client can be cured. Know that the path back to good health will not be an easy one. Orisha Oko is found here, but in his guise as the devourer of the dead and the decayer of the earth. Remember, however, that his decay feeds new life and new ideas. Finally, Obatalá (the most forgiving, yet in Okana one of the most stern), Aganyú, and Shangó also speak in this sign, claiming eboses and offering advice for the client's evolution. Most important to this letter, however, are the client's own egun. Okana is dark and mysterious, and through this letter one's forgotten ancestors (both of spirit and of blood) come to claim the recognition that is theirs by right. Although they come last in this list, often the odu will not close out unless ebó is marked to them.

The sign Okana is harsh and heated; to quote from an earlier work, it is "an expression of peace wrought by the destruction of discord (hence its volatile nature)."* Fá'Lokun Fatunmbi, a prominent yet controversial babalawo, writes of this odu:

> Ifá teaches that in Okanran [another name for this sign] Shangó becomes incarnated as an orisha by the principles of justice that are manifest through creation. The historical Shangó was an effective warrior who unified the eastern portion of the Yoruba nation. After his victories on the battlefield, Shangó became abusive in his use of power and was transformed by his own sense of guilt and shame. This does not mean the creator is an unforgiving Deity. By incarnating Shangó as an orisha, the universe allows for transformation through tragedy and crisis. False pride and egotism can create an illusion of accomplishment and honor, but the laws of nature are such that the illusion cannot be sustained by itself indefinitely.†

Keep in mind that Okana is a letter of instant and random transformation brought by the client's own actions. He has spent his whole life working up to the energies encompassed by this odu. Overcoming them will prove to be no simple task.

The easiest way to begin a study of Okana is with an examination of it in iré (blessings). "Iré ni?" is the first question put to the oracle after marking an odu. It means "Are blessings predicted?" Having iré marked in Okana means only one thing: In time, the client will overcome his problems. The type of iré marked (there are twenty-five possible origins) will identify the client's source of strength. Even if Okana brings blessings, realize this: Okana has no iré. When it marks itself thus, the sign is all but taunting the client. Trials and tribulations will still come; danger and disaster lurk around each bend. The odu in iré, however, becomes a process of transformation. Just as coal is pressurized into a diamond or sand melted into pure glass, so will this person become something more than he now is. This process will not be complete until Okana's influence has passed. This client must modify his behavior, not according to his standards, but by those of the orishas. He must listen carefully to the advice given, follow the prohibitions set forth by the diviner, and make ebó. Unfortunately, unless the answers to the next two questions asked by the diviner are "yes," one also knows that the client probably will not do all these things as he should.

Having determined iré and its source, the italero continues to question the oracle. He asks, "Iré yale?" ("Is the iré firm?") Answering yes, Okana tells the diviner that the client's source of help is strong, and even though he might not adhere to all the prescriptions given in this session, spiritual forces are mounting to carry him through hardship. The diviner then asks, "Iré yale timbelaye?" ("Will this iré manifest in this person's life?") Of the three questions the diviner has asked so far, this is the most important. Answering yes to iré yale timbelaye, Okana gives closure to itself; it says the odu's energy has been in effect for some time, and the client is on the verge of breaking out of what has been a horrid cycle. If the answer to all three questions has been yes, the oracle is closed, and the diviner does not need to mark or prescribe ebó. If, on the other hand, the oracle ended its positive answers after iré or iré yale, larishe must be asked and ebó marked. They are essential to the client's evolution.

Even when this odu opens in iré, the diviner should know this: The client at the mat does not like to hear the truth about himself. Okana is a severe sign opening only when severity is called for. It is not flippant and is never frivolous in its appearance. Its series of ritual gestures is an attempt to impress, symbolically, the need to listen. Do not be afraid to tell the client all this odu has to say, for when one forebodes disaster but the listener does not take heed, the diviner will be known as a true prophet when that disaster occurs. The reading of this sign brings the priest respect from this person and others. Being belligerent, this client might not

---

*Óchání Lele, *The Secrets of Afro-Cuban Divination: How to Cast the Diloggún, the Oracle of the Orishas* (Rochester, Vt.: Destiny Books, 2000), 56.

†Awó Fá'Lokun Fatunmbi, *Awó: Ifá and the Theology of Orisha Divination* (New York: Original Publications, 1992), 129–30.

listen at all. Once the first negative comments pass the diviner's lips, his attention will waver. In spite of this, the diviner must continue. Know that even those diviners who are close to a client find that in this sign their own well-meaning advice falls on deaf ears. Indeed, the argumentative tone taken by the client at the mat makes others slow to give good counsel. Tell the client who has come with an iré this: The letter, while harsh, does not come without offering help. It shows that the client can find a way to make present difficulties work out, but this is true only if he follows the letter's advice.

Since Okana brings no true iré, the diviner begins his assessment of this sign as if it had brought an osogbo. When it opens, deliver a stern warning: Life now enters a chaotic period. This is a letter that cares not what one was or what one is. Many who open in one mouth have lived saintly, intelligent lives. When the sign is marked with iré, is not unusual for the client to be a humanitarian, a volunteer worker, or even a social activist. Good things have been wrought by this person's hands. If the italero knows this person well and knows such things to be true, he can also know this: The power given, the authority bestowed because of this person's good works, has been abused. Those who rise, yet rise too quickly, tend to fall more rapidly. Selflessness has become selfishness. Modesty has given rise to immodesty, and humbleness, by recognition of its virtues, has become degradation.

No matter how much good this person has done, he has wrought much evil, and this is what brings Okana upon him. Know that under these circumstances Okana does come with just a bit of hope, for just as good has wrought evil, the darkness that the client enters will once again lead to light. To get there, however, he must still travel through the darkness of this odu.

Certain conditions are shared by all who open in a composite of Okana, no matter whether the sign's orientation is iré or osogbo. Okana's energy affects one's head; it clouds the mind, making rational thought impossible. It also weakens the heart, suppressing and sustaining emotional imbalances until one wallows in tears and misery. Unable to trust either thoughts or feelings, one easily becomes a victim of one's environment. One becomes prone to accidents, theft, violence, treason, and false friends. Okana brings imbalance on inner and outer levels; the only way to overcome this imbalance is to slow down and take some time to oneself. The frantic pace at which one lives must be left behind until the abilities to think and to feel *appropriately* are restored. For the client at the mat, life's momentum has been accelerated for some time, and he is now accustomed to it. The need to slow down and seek solace exists, yet this person will not admit his needs. Tell him this: He needs to slow down, or the orishas will force him to slow down. Once the body, mind, and heart are exhausted, weakness and sickness will come. If this happens, the client will be able to do nothing more beyond recover.

Okana is synonymous with exhaustion. This person is so worn out that he is not capable of clear, rational, or original thought. Complacency is not unusual because this person is just too exhausted to do anything else. During the consultation, thoroughly assess the most common reason for this exhaustion: sleep deprivation. A client who opens in Okana is sleep deprived; he is often a chronic insomniac. When sleep does come, it is fitful, filled with dreams and nightmares. These are dredged from the depths of the client's soul; they are reflections of what is buried deep within, the darkness that this odu symbolizes. Often, sleep is disturbed by egun. They have been ignored and now they clamor for attention. Overwork and overextension of one's physical resources may also contribute to exhaustion. This client might be working beyond his optimal level. He knows this, but the drive to succeed and prosper beyond his peers will not let him rest. He may be worried about his station in life: Finances, goals, careers, and marriages all can be a source of despair.

Tell the client this: He has many problems in his life, yet has no time to solve those problems. Usually, he thinks that he can work out his turmoil by talking to others. Because the one who opens in one mouth is usually the confidant to the world, he figures that those whom he has helped will be willing to help him. Yet he lays down his troubles at the feet of those who do not care and who do not listen. When this person's life begins to fall apart (and on his present path, it will), those whom he has helped most intimately (emotionally, intellectually, and even financially) will turn their backs on him, ignoring his pleas for help. Note that this odu demands that the client avoid others who do not listen, who do not communicate openly and honestly. At this time, he needs avenues for clear communication and expression. In Okana, he also needs to avoid behaving with harshness and impatience, for they will drive away the few true friends he has.

Okana tells us much about this person's character, the parts of himself hidden from public view. Even if this client appears happy and carefree, deep within is a darkness that threatens to overwhelm. The smile he wears is a mask, and the kind words he speaks are lines learned much as an actor assuming a character. This person is a molded container for much darker thoughts and energies. Emptiness sums up his life. Often a client comes to the mat in Okana because he questions everything: his work, his family, his existence, even God. The depth of these inner feelings is heavily dependent on the odu's orientation. The darker and more dangerous the osogbo, the more dangerous the darkness within the client. Suicidal ideation is not uncommon. Insane fantasies brew within. Implore this person never to act on a whim and never to act in anger. Just as this darkness will rise and engulf, so must it recede and unveil. Once it is gone, the client is cleansed.

Know that this person argues with himself; he hears voices, mostly negative, and struggles to keep those voices at bay. In iré or a moderate osogbo, these voices are fragmented parts of himself. They are random, errant pieces of his own personality with which he argues and against whom he struggles. Many think this person is deep, pensive, and frequently lost in thought. In actuality, this client wars with himself. In a serious osogbo, these voices do not originate with the client. Instead, they come from the dead, and they taunt him. The diviner must be careful when dealing with a client who has an osogbo from spiritual realms, for he is under attack by dark forces. In these cases, psychosis and schizophrenia are imminent. It is important to prescribe much work, including a series of masses and rogaciónes, for the client's egun so that he will not fall into a psychotic nightmare.

From Okana, the diviner knows that the client is involved in the shadier aspects of life. In some cases this sign flags only minor moral transgressions, but sometimes the composite odu that opens on the mat warns of major conflicts. The client must stop all such actions now, for Okana brings retribution, and others will discover what is going on. If this person is in a relationship, he must not be involved in adultery. He should take no part in lies, gossip, or treason. If this person is involved in business transactions, he must be honest. Those in positions involving cash transactions are warned to keep their hands "out of the till." Okana cautions the one at the mat to be careful and to work diligently. If this person's livelihood comes in a position involving documentation, those documents must be kept carefully, for some aspect of record keeping may come back to haunt him. Even if this person does nothing wrong, others will falsely accuse him when problems arise. He has no true friends at this time; when osogbo comes, it is "every man for himself." To survive the energies in play now, he should conduct himself by the highest legal and moral standards possible.

Illegal activities may find a way to creep into the client's life even if caution is exercised. Purchases of used goods should be avoided. If the client is determined to buy a used item from another person, he should investigate its origin. It may be stolen. If someone asks to store an item in the client's home, the request should be politely refused for the same reason. Anything bought, held, or found could be illegally obtained property.

Honesty is the best policy for the next month or so. If the truth cannot be told, nothing should be said. If the client cannot act honorably, nothing should be done. Cursing in the form of profane language should not be employed, nor should a client involved in the occult cast curses. These things will only intensify the erratic energy of this odu. Avoid both minor arguments and major debates, as well as any rally, cause, or confrontation in which the client has much emotional involvement. Any type of disagreement now will serve only to block the paths remaining open.

The next twenty-eight days will not be a good time for parties or social gatherings. Now is the time to be alone, to think, to plan. One should find somewhere safe, a quiet place in which to sort out all difficulties before they become all-consuming. The client might believe that all is well or will be fine, and that there is no need for solitude. This is a person who resists rest and solitude, preferring to talk out troubles with others. But now no one cares about the client's problems; no one wants to help. Only the orishas care. The reason for openness, honesty, peace, and solitude is simple: Like attracts like. Bitterness and intrigue will block out the good things that life has to offer. Negativity and impatience ensure continual failure.

Random violence and planned attacks are also a danger now, both by and for the client. Ensure personal safety at all times. Guarding one's physical safety, however, should not extend to the carrying of weapons, especially when Okana Ogundá (1-3) is the odu in effect. Do not buy large knives or guns for the home; if the client already owns these weapons, they should be safely locked away. In Okana Ogundá, not only can the accident be in the home, but also it may be brought by someone from outside the home. Children are especially vulnerable in this pattern; Okana Ogundá kills innocence by fire. If young ones are in the client's home, do not leave them alone, untended, or unguarded, and make sure those weapons or tools that can kill or maim are removed from the house. "Out of reach" is a misnomer in this odu, for to innocence, all things are in reach.

Whenever Okana is oriented to an osogbo, it is extremely hot and volatile. Any violence or altercation will bring trouble with the law, so the client must conduct himself well at all times. There should be no attacks, no simulated violence, nor even any harsh physical activity or practical jokes. In this letter, danger lurks in darkness, so the client should keep a light on in the bedroom when asleep at night and not go out after dark until the energies of this odu have passed. Those who work third-shift jobs dealing with the public are under the scrutiny of vagrants and robbers and for the next nine days should be overly vigilant and cautious.

The diviner must prescribe one strong prohibition in any osogbo: If the client hears signs of violence, he must not check it out with his eyes. He should secure himself so that the violence cannot touch him and then call the authorities, saying only that he has heard a strange disturbance. If he is asked to do a visual check, he should refuse. He should not admit to witnessing any act of violence, for then the danger of this letter might carry over into the courtroom.

In either ano or ikú, the letter foretells illness, disease, and death brought about by accident or violence, and the client must guard his safety at all times lest he become a victim of another's evil. He should not go out at night or alone during the day. Windows and doors to cars, homes, and offices should be kept locked at all times. Roadways are hot in this letter. If the client must drive about during the day (he should *not* drive at night), he should wear his seat belt. He should not drive at an excessive speed or become angry or display anger toward another driver.

When arayé opens as the osogbo, the client is overly stubborn and hardheaded. This will be both his disgrace and his downfall. No matter how sternly the diviner delivers the reading, the client will not heed his advice. The diviner should tell the client this. Then he should deliver the full list of prohibitions and meanings for Okana, telling the client that he ignores these things at his own peril. This way, when the dangers in this sign are finally manifested in the client's life, the diviner can be assured that he did all that was humanly possible to keep this person from harm. His downfall will be his own doing.

There are many other issues flagged by this odu, and the diviner may wish to discuss those appropriate from this list:

- Okana warns of potential accidents. Many of these can occur in one's own home. Okana attracts dirt and clutter, so one should keep the house as tidy as possible to prevent accidents. Keep clutter out of stairwells, off steps, and away from stoops. Make sure the house is well lit at night. Identify and secure sources of fire, for fire is a particular danger here. Finally, monitor the very young and very old carefully; they are most prone to accidents under Okana's influence.

- Okana is synonymous with exhaustion. Examine the client for signs of sleep deprivation, including bloodshot eyes, dark circles, stooped shoulders, low energy level, and frequent yawning. Chronic insomnia is one of this odu's most frequent problems. The cause of insomnia should be determined and dealt with before the session's closure. If nothing else, prescribe a rogación to clear the head of what ails it.
- Okana signals that the client's thoughts and emotions are clouded by wants and desires. To pass safely through this tumultuous period, the client must focus on essentials, not extras.
- This client has come to the diviner seeking help, yet he has no faith. He does not believe in the orishas, nor does he believe in their religion. Even if the client professes faith, it is in his head and not in his heart. His negativity and stubbornness have closed the gates to the divine. The diviner must make an issue of this, exploring the client's doubts. He must discover exactly what brought this client to the mat. Whatever reason the client gives will not be the entire truth; there is more beneath the surface. The client should be told this; when he realizes the diviner and the orishas can see deeply inside, he may be more likely to listen to them.
- Okana flags serious financial difficulties. If the client is solvent now, soon he will not be. The diviner should counsel this person about his spending habits, encouraging him to work harder and save more.
- Children figure prominently in this sign. When the odu brings iré, it flags someone who works well with children. Be cautious, however, if the odu Okana Ofún opens on the mat; it may signal that this person has much aché with children, but a child (or perhaps a child's parent) will make accusations of harm and molestation. If Okana opens in an osogbo and children live in this person's house, one could be ill. The moment sickness is seen in a child of the client's home, he or she should be taken to a physician; a small health problem may become very serious without proper medical intervention. Okana in osogbo marks depression, tears, mental illness, and suicide in children. It also brings them accidental death. Any child with whom this client associates could become sad, sick, depressed, or misguided in life, and this will soon become apparent.
- If the client feels that his life is unbearable, two of this odu's proverbs sum up succinctly what this energy is trying to teach. First, if there is nothing bad, there can never be anything good. And second, without bitterness, one cannot know when there is goodness. These proverbs are self-explanatory and can be used to assure the client that if he heeds the advice of this odu, better times will come.

## The Prohibitions of Okana

Because Okana is such a heated and volatile odu, even if its orientation is iré these prohibitions should be prescribed by the diviner to keep the client on a path to evolution. If the letter's orientation is osogbo, the prohibitions of not only this odu but also those of the letter that came in at the door should be prescribed. Remember, the letter that came in at the door gives clues as to why Okana opened, and it holds the key to the client's evolution.

- Conduct oneself legally and ethically at all times to avoid altercations with the law.
- Purchase goods only from reputable sources where the goods' origins are easily identifiable (such as department stores). Avoid garage sales, pawn shops, items sold through classified ads, and other secondhand sources, for Okana warns that whatever the client wants to buy could be stolen property. Keep receipts, warranties, and serial numbers; if the client must buy something secondhand, make sure that these papers are provided. Beware of those selling electronics, computers, and household appliances for unbelievably low prices, and do not buy jewelry on the street. Do not accept expensive gifts from new acquaintances, lovers, or coworkers. Politely and humbly refuse gifts from anyone other than a close friend or relative.
- The tongue has aché in this sign; however,

it will manifest only the bad, not the good. Measure spoken and written words carefully. Do not quote anyone unless one is sure that the quote is correct and proper credit is given. When quoting another's spoken words, make sure that witnesses can verify what was said, and make sure that the reputation of those witnesses is untainted. Okana can flag lawsuits for writers, authors, journalists, public speakers, and professional commentators. Avoid profane language, heated arguments, and debates, for they can agitate the volatile nature of Okana. Do not gossip. Do not spread gossip. If one's tongue does not wag, it cannot whip.

- Parties and social gatherings easily deteriorate among children of Okana. Do not go to any gathering of three or more people. Avoid social occasions or places where liquor or other alcoholic beverages are served, including restaurants. Do not partake of any intoxicant, hallucinogen, or narcotic. If a social gathering is unavoidable, do not eat or drink there, because the food may be poisoned (accidentally with bacteria from improper cooking or intentionally with poison or witchcraft). Guard one's drink at all times, never leaving a glass unattended. Watch the server carefully. Ask for unopened bottled water when one dines at a restaurant, and if one leaves the table, ask for a fresh bottle of water upon returning. Never drink that which is left behind.
- Now is not the time to date anyone unknown or unfamiliar. Strangers could poison or drug one.
- Violence and weapons are a danger in this odu. One must ensure one's own safety at all times: Lock doors and windows. Go out only in daylight hours and only in the company of a close friend. Do not carry weapons, as they are easily turned against the wielder. Do not keep guns or knives at home. Children are especially vulnerable to weapons kept in the home, and other adults or teenagers living with this person could become a source of violence. Remember that there is no such thing as make-believe violence, and there are few funny practical jokes. Avoid roughhousing, and never compromise the feelings of others.
- Shun adultery and domestic violence. Do not mistreat a spouse or lover; a broken heart or trampled pride could easily create violence.
- Be cautious around animals; never taunt or mistreat them. Even one's own pet could scratch, bite, or attack.

## Marking Ebó in Okana: Initial Considerations

Okana marks volatile spiritual currents as the root of one's issues; the letter requires much spiritual work to avoid and overcome osogbo. Note that when Okana opens on the mat, no one, not even an aleyo present but uninvolved in the session, may leave before performing a specific ebó for Elegguá. On behalf of all present, the diviner smears a piece of raw beef liberally with red palm oil, showing it to Elegguá as he wraps it in brown paper. While reciting prayers to Elegguá for the removal of Okana's heat, he rubs all present from head to toe with this package, beginning with the client and ending with himself. After cleansing everyone, the meat sits with Elegguá overnight. The next morning, the ebó goes to the woods; again the diviner offers a prayer to Elegguá, leaving with the words "Eshu batie sode," meaning, "Eshu takes the osogbo [of the reading]." (Eshu is another name for Elegguá.) After returning home, the diviner casts the oracle for himself to ensure that he does not suffer from Okana. He performs any cleansings or eboses marked by the diloggún immediately. In this way is the work of Okana complete, and the diviner is assured that neither he nor anyone else comes to harm by its destructive energies.*

Beyond the traditional ebo for Elegguá, several other eboses must be prescribed in Okana. An aborisha without elekes who opens in Okana must receive them as ebó. The aché bestowed by this baptism and the beads of Obatalá, Yemayá, Oshún, and

*These cleansings and eboses are necessary so that only the client will face what his odu brings. Remember: All those present for a reading are affected, temporarily, by the odu opened. At the mat, it enfolds them all with its energies.

Shangó negate much of Okana's volatility, soothing the client and washing him of his past. In this way, future evolution comes. If the prescription of the elekes plus the eboses marked during the reading aren't enough to close the odu for the aborisha, the diviner should also give the eleke of the orisha whose diloggún he consulted or the eleke of an orisha who speaks in Okana (see the list on page 42). To see if this is an option, the diviner works through this list of orishas, asking, "Ebó eleke de [orisha's name]?" If the eleke of an orisha is marked but the odu still refuses closure, each spirit who has offered an eleke might need ebó. To see if this is an option, the diviner should ask of each orisha, "Ebó elese [orisha's name]?" If the answer is yes, the diviner should use the shells to mark the appropriate offering from the list of eboses in chapter 1.

If the client has already received elekes, in Okana the initiation of the warriors is the next consideration. The reception of Elegguá, Ogún, Ochosi, and Ósun is a powerful way to leave this odu's osogbo behind. When the odu mandates the reception of the warriors, the diviner must keep some important points in mind. First, houses that give Elegguá to noninitiates must mark the path of Elegguá required before bringing Okana to closure. Second, the elekes of Elegguá and Ogún must be prepared and washed with these warriors. Do not give the beads of Ochosi unless the oracle will not close; there are other odu and other circumstances for which one should save these. Finally, if Okana has already prescribed the initiation of the elekes for the client, do not prescribe the initiation of the warriors in the same session unless there is absolutely no other way to settle the osogbo of Okana. One should wait for another reading before this initiation is considered.*

The final consideration for ebó in Okana is that four potent spirits influence the entire family: Elegguá, Shangó, Aganyú, and egun. Elegguá always speaks in all of Okana's composites, but he never speaks alone; one of the other three dominating spiritual forces will accompany him. The diviner must always mark an ebó to Elegguá and one of the other three spirits to placate this sign, even if they did not speak to the client during the reading. Elegguá must be included in an ebó in Okana, for he works with all the other spirits, even egun; it is he who can help or hinder the process of invocation, evolution, and supplication. In Okana, his goodwill is essential to evolution. The part of each ebó given to Elegguá must go to him before any offering to Shangó, Aganyú, or egun is placed.

*Many consider it foolish to read odu for a client more than once every three months; some diviners make their clients wait six months before they may be seen again. Initiations are potent, powerful milestones in one's life; do not give them haphazardly but at specific points in a client's evolution. In this way, initiations can make the monumental changes for which they are meant. In casting diloggún and prescribing ebó, remember one important rule: Less is always more.

### Traditional Eboses in Okana

When marking the eboses or larishes for any odu in the family of Okana, note that certain substances are traditionally used. If an eyebale is marked, the diviner should choose from the following list, if possible: a rooster, two pigeons, a guinea hen, or, when four legs are needed, a goat or a ram. For adimú, the traditional offerings are honey, cornmeal, bananas, plantains, toasted corn, smoked fish, jutía, two coconuts, or a ñame (a type of yam). Other prepared adimú for specific orishas follow.

## Ebó Elese Elegguá y Aganyú o Elegguá y Shangó

### *(Ebó at the Feet of Elegguá and Aganyú or Elegguá and Shangó)*

Since Aganyú and Shangó are father and son, they share the same tastes in adimú, and these offerings may be adapted for either orisha. Their sacred numbers differ, however, so one must change the numbers involved in the recipes when preparing the ebó. The eboses in this section are described as if one were giving them to Elegguá and Aganyú. At the end of each recipe, the appropriate adaptations are given if one desires to make that dish for Shangó.

### *Vegetable and Fruit Towers*

In ocha, a tower made of an orisha's favorite vegetables and fruits is often used as an ebó. This offering builds a symbolic spiritual bridge between earth and heaven, or supplicant and orisha. It is important to incorporate Elegguá into the ebó. Before preparing a tower, the priest presiding over the ebó must lift Elegguá from his shrine, putting him at Aganyú's feet. Once this is done, the client must supplicate Elegguá with a basic ebó before beginning any work for the other orisha. If one does not supplicate Elegguá first, the entire process will result in failure. The client may light a red seven-day candle for Elegguá and rub him liberally with epó (red palm oil). After this anointment, the client should sprinkle jutía and smoked fish heavily over the orisha's crown. Once all these things are done, the tower for Aganyú can be prepared and presented. Elegguá remains with Aganyú until the client has removed the tower from Aganyú's shrine.

This tower requires the following ingredients: okra, a box of cornmeal, cheesecloth, honey, epó, jutía, smoked fish, a white or red platter, a red cotton cloth, a red and white flag (a construction-paper cutout glued to a toothpick will suffice), a white seven-day candle, and a red seven-day candle. The client needs a large sheet of brown paper for the disposal of the ebó.

Cut the okra into several small, uniform pieces and remove the seeds carefully.* Bring a large pan of water to a boil, and add to it the okra and the cornmeal. Boil rapidly until the okra is soft, then strain the matter from the liquid using the cheesecloth. Once the okra and cornmeal mixture is cool, add a liberal amount of honey, epó, jutía, and smoked fish. Mash everything until a thick paste forms.

On the platter, form the paste into a large tower. Drape a red cotton cloth over the top of the tower and insert a small red and white flag at the very top. Paying *foribale* (salutation) to Aganyú, the client puts the tower platter over his opened sopera (bowl), praying to him for release from all his trials and tribulations and asking for those things in life held dear. Once his prayers are over, the client lights the two seven-day candles, one white and one red. The tower is left over Aganyú's shrine until the candles burn out; once the fire consumes them, wrap the tower in brown paper and take it to the woods. Discard the ebó at the foot of a palm or ceiba tree. Before leaving, the client should again pray to Aganyú, asking the orisha to lift his osogbo and to fulfill his dreams.

If the diviner prescribes the use of this tower for Shangó, make no changes to the recipe. Make sure that Elegguá sits at Shangó's feet before the tower is prepared and that the client propitiates him first.

### *Towers of Boiled Ñames*

Aganyú also accepts towers made of boiled ñames. Again, put Elegguá at the foot of Aganyú's shrine before preparing the ebó. The client should supplicate Elegguá with the following adimú: a red seven-day candle, plenty of epó, and a whole, uncooked ñame. The red candle is lit to Elegguá; the client lifts him from his terra-cotta dish and anoints him with a liberal amount of epó. Once oiled, Elegguá is put back into his dish, and the client presents him with the ñame. The ñame given to Elegguá remains with the orisha until it rots. It is a good omen for a vine to grow from it; however, the vine must not grow to a height taller than the client. Cut it back frequently.

This tower requires the following ingredients: a fresh ñame, goat's or cow's milk, a platter (white or red), nine cowrie shells, a red flag (a construction-paper cutout mounted on a toothpick is fine), and two seven-day candles, one red and one white.

Wash, peel, dice, and boil the ñame until it is soft. Strain the softened pieces out of the water and mash them with milk until a paste forms. On the platter, form a tall tower with this paste. Place the nine cowrie shells around the tower's peak, inserting the flag in its highest point. Light the two seven-day candles at the base of Aganyú's shrine and leave the tower on top of Aganyú's open sopera for nine days. At the end of nine days, the client should wrap the tower in brown paper and discard it at the foot of a ceiba or palm tree deep in the woods.

To prepare this tower for Shangó, make two minor changes to the recipe. First, adorn the tower

*The seeds themselves make a wonderful adimú to egun, who may also need propitiation in this family of odu. Save them in a small bowl, and put the seeds to the bóveda (the altar set up to honor and propitiate egun) after the tower is presented to Aganyú.

with six cowries, not nine. Second, leave the ebó with him for six days, not nine.

### *Saraeko*

Normally saraeko is a simple, uncooked porridge. However, this recipe takes the basic porridge two steps further: Not only is it cooked, but also it is solid. To make this version of saraeko, gather the following ingredients: one box of cornmeal, a can of goat's milk, 5 tablespoons of white sugar, half a stick of cocoa butter, a roll of aluminum foil, two white platters, a large quantity of toasted corn, smoked fish, jutía, epó, honey, and guinea pepper. The client will need two large sheets of brown paper for this ebó's disposal as well.

In a large saucepan, mix together the cornmeal, goat's milk, white sugar, and cocoa butter. Add enough tap water to cover all the ingredients. Cook over medium heat, stirring constantly, until most of the liquid is boiled away. Remove the pan immediately from the stove. As it cools, the porridge will congeal and thicken.

Once the cooked mixture is cool, cut ten large pieces of aluminum foil. Divide the porridge in ten equal portions, placing one in the center of each piece of aluminum foil and molding each into the shape of a rectangle. Fold the foil over each rectangle, as if you were making a tamale.

In a big saucepan, bring a large quantity of water to a boil over high heat. Gently slide all ten tamales into the boiling water. Let them boil for 15 minutes.

While the tamales are boiling, prepare the two platters for the ebó. On each, make a large bed of toasted corn. Garnish the corn liberally with the smoked fish, jutía, epó, and honey, as well as nine grains of guinea pepper. When the tamales are done, remove them from the water and allow them to cool before opening the foil. On one platter, place a single tamale; this goes to Elegguá. On the second platter, place nine tamales; this goes to Aganyú.

Leave the adimú with each orisha for nine days. At the end of this time, wrap Elegguá's in brown paper and discard it at a crossroads. Wrap Aganyú's adimú in brown paper also, but leave his at the foot of a palm or ceiba tree in the woods.

To adapt this adimú for Shangó, make nine tamales, not ten. Give three of these to Elegguá and six to Shangó. Leave the adimú with both orishas for six days instead of nine.

### *Plantain Adimú*

A simpler adimú to appease Aganyú can be made with the following ingredients: twelve fresh green plantains, a can of goat's milk, two plates (white or red), and honey.

Bring a large saucepan of water to a boil over high heat. Peel the plantains, then put them in the boiling water to cook. Once the plantains are soft, remove the saucepan from the stove and strain the plantains from the water. While they are still hot, mash the plantains with just enough goat's milk to form a thick paste. Make twelve balls from this paste. Smear them with honey, then place three on a plate for Elegguá and nine on a plate for Aganyú.

This adimú remains with both Elegguá and Aganyú for nine days. At the end of this time, wrap each adimú in separate pieces of brown paper. Take Elegguá's to the crossroads, and leave Aganyú's at the foot of a ceiba or palm tree.

To adapt this adimú for Shangó, use nine plantains, not twelve, and form nine balls, not twelve. Three of the plantain balls go to Elegguá and six balls go to Shangó. Leave this offering with both orishas for six days, not nine.

### *Boli*

Boli is not only an ebó for Aganyú, Shangó, and Elegguá but also a traditional food staple of the Yoruba. It is simple to prepare.

Preheat the oven to 350 degrees Fahrenheit. While the oven heats up, peel twelve ripe plantains and lay them in a large baking dish; make sure the plantains do not touch or they will stick. Grease the pan with just a dab of epó or other thick vegetable oil before baking, if desired. Put the baking dish on the center rack, and bake until the plantains begin to brown (this can take just a few minutes, so watch carefully).

Remove from the oven. Serve three to Elegguá and nine to Aganyú. The diviner uses his own aché to determine how long this ebó remains with the orishas and the proper means of disposal.

To adapt this recipe for Shangó, simply prepare

nine plantains instead of twelve. Give three to Elegguá and six to Shangó.

### Fried Plantains

Fried plantains are not only an ebó for Aganyú, Shangó, and Elegguá but also a food staple among Cubans. To prepare fried plantains as an adimú, provide at least three ripe plantains and some vegetable oil (epó may be used as well). Use more plantains if desired.

Preheat 1/3 inch of oil in an iron skillet over low heat. It is important to use low heat; cooking at a higher temperature will result in plantains that are burned on the outside and not cooked on the inside. While the pan heats, peel each plantain, cutting them into 1/4-inch-thick rounds. When the oil is hot, put the rounds in the pan. Fry until the bottoms are golden, then flip each piece and fry until the other side is golden. Remove from the pan and place on a paper towel or napkin to absorb the extra grease. Serve a third of the fried plantain slices to Elegguá; give the remaining portion to Aganyú or Shangó.

The diviner uses his own aché to determine how long this ebó remains with the orishas and the proper means of disposal.

### Fried Sweet Bread

If Aganyú speaks harshly to the client, the following adimú will appease and pacify him. Provide the following ingredients: one loaf of sweet bread, a dozen eggs, a can of goat's milk, epó, two plates (red or white), white sugar, and honey.

From the loaf of sweet bread, cut twelve slices. In a large mixing bowl, scramble the eggs thoroughly until they form an even, golden color; mix a small amount of the goat's milk into this. Place a large skillet on the stove over medium-high heat and drop a tablespoon of epó into it. While the pan heats and the epó melts, soak one piece of sweet bread in the egg and milk mixture. Once it is saturated, pan-fry the bread on both sides in epó. Once it is fried, place the bread on a plate and sprinkle liberally with white sugar. Repeat this process for each slice of bread.

Once all twelve slices are fried, put three on one plate for Elegguá and nine on another plate for Aganyú. Drizzle the fried bread liberally with honey and serve to the orishas immediately. Leave the ebó overnight; the following morning, wrap the contents of the two plates in separate pieces of brown paper. Elegguá's adimú goes to the crossroads; Aganyú's goes to the foot of a palm or ceiba tree.

To adapt this recipe for Shangó, fry nine pieces of sweet bread, not twelve. Three go to Elegguá; give six to Shangó.

### Epó Biscuits

One final cooked food may be made in this odu to appease these orishas. At the priest's house, the client should bake twelve biscuits and grease all twelve lightly with epó. Three go to Elegguá, and nine go to Aganyú. This adimú remains with the orishas overnight before it is discarded. The diviner uses his own aché to determine the proper means of disposal.

To adapt this ebó for Shangó, bake nine biscuits. Three go to Elegguá and six to Shangó.

### Nine Plantains

When Aganyú speaks directly to the client in Okana, after all the required eboses are finished the client may return to this orisha to make one final adimú and a single, special request. For this ebó, provide the following ingredients: a sheet of brown paper, nine green plantains, epó, and red ribbon.

On the brown paper, the client writes his request, his prayer for evolution. At Aganyú's shrine, he pays foribale and reads aloud what he wrote. He then smears each plantain with epó. When the last one is covered, the written request is secured in the middle of all the fruit with a piece of red ribbon. The fruit and the message sit with Aganyú for nine days; at the end of this time the plantains are taken to the woods and left at the foot of a tree, preferably a palm or ceiba tree.

To adapt this ebó for Shangó, one must provide six green plantains, not nine. They are left with Shangó for six days before being removed and left at the foot of a tree.

## Ebó Elese Shangó y Elegguá
### (Ebó at the Feet of Shangó and Elegguá)

The four recipes given here are appropriate for Shangó but not always for Aganyú. To my knowledge, traditional Yoruba *amalá-ilá* made with yam flour (not cornmeal) must never be given to Aganyú. Traditional Cuban amalá (made with cornmeal) and amalá-based recipes are, however, appropriate for Aganyú. The changes, when needed, to the recipes to adapt them for Aganyú are noted below. The final ebó in this section is specific to Shangó and may not be adapted for his father.

### *Amalá-Ilá*

This traditional Yoruba recipe not only is favored as adimú for Shangó in Nigeria but also is a favored dinner dish among Yoruba families. Traditional amalá is made with *elubo,* a flour made from yams, a food staple in Nigeria. After harvest, the tubers are dried thoroughly; when tough, they are ground and pounded to form a powdery flour. Elubo is difficult to procure unless one is lucky enough to live near a traditional African grocery store. In Cuba and the United States, amalá is usually made with cornmeal. While Shangó loves the cornmeal version of amalá, there are times when he appreciates the trouble one goes to in preparing the more traditional fare.

To prepare traditional amalá-ilá as an adimú for Shangó, one needs six pieces of okra and 6 cups of elubo flour.

Chop and dice the six pieces of okra. Put the diced okra in a small saucepan, adding enough water to cover them plus one extra inch of water. Bring this to a rolling boil; reduce the heat, cover, and simmer for 15 minutes. While the okra simmers, bring 4 cups of water to a rolling boil in a large saucepan. Slowly, add the elubo 1 cup at a time, stirring well until it dissolves in the water. Depending on how thick one wants the amalá, all six cups may not be necessary. Reduce the heat and continue to stir until the elubo is at its desired consistency. Remove from the heat, but continue to stir another minute or two so that it does not stick to the pan or burn. Strain the okra from the water.

There are three ways to serve traditional amalá-ilá to Shangó. First, the amalá (made with elubo flour) may go in a large bowl and the ilá (boiled okra) in a smaller bowl, and they are served side by side. Second, one may mix the ilá into the amalá and serve in one large bowl. Third, one may use the ilá as a garnish on top of the amalá, not stirring it into the mixture. No matter how it is served to him, Shangó will love this traditional African recipe. Note that this is never appropriate for Aganyú.

The diviner uses his own aché to determine how long this ebó remains with the orishas and the proper means of disposal.

### *Sweet Amalá*

This traditional Cuban recipe substitutes cornmeal for elubo. Because cornmeal lacks the natural sweetness of the yam-based flour, honey is added to the recipe to help it acquire a more palatable taste. To make sweet amalá, one needs two ingredients: 2 pounds of cornmeal and a jar of honey.

In a large saucepan, bring 8 cups of water to a rolling boil. Add the cornmeal, reducing the heat to medium. Stir constantly so the mixture does not burn. Once it begins to thicken, reduce the heat to low, continuing to stir. When enough water has evaporated that only a thick paste remains, remove the pan from the heat. Stir in honey until the dish is sweetened to taste and serve immediately, while it is still warm.

In Okana, a portion of this offering should go to Eleggua first, although it is not necessary to sit him at Shangó's shrine for this. The larger portion goes to Shangó. The ebó remains with the orishas overnight. The next morning, use obí to determine how they want their ebó discarded. Note that if one prepares this recipe for Aganyú, no changes are made to the recipe.

### *Sweet Amalá and Bananas*

If the osogbo of Okana is severe, sweet amalá may be enhanced to placate the odu. These additional ingredients are needed: 3/4 cup of epó, wax paper, and nine peeled bananas.

After making the sweet amalá, let it cool. Then brush nine pieces of wax paper lightly with epó. Divide the sweet amalá into nine equal portions, and roll each flat with a rolling pin that has been greased with epó. Place a banana on each flat piece of amalá. Roll each piece of amalá tightly around the banana and squeeze the ends shut so the banana is totally enclosed. Place three of these banana rolls on a small platter for Elegguá and the remaining six on a serving plate for Shangó. Leave the adimú with them overnight, and the next morning, using obí, determine how they want their ebó discarded.

To adapt this ebó for Aganyú, increase the cornmeal used to make sweet amalá by 1 pound. The extra amalá is necessary because one prepares twelve peeled bananas, not nine. Three are for Elegguá and nine go to Aganyú.

#### *Sweet Amalá and Pumpkin*

In Okana, one final ebó may be made to appease Shangó. To complete this adimú, several items are needed: sweet amalá, a pumpkin, a white plate, okra, and two white seven-day candles.

Prepare the sweet amalá first. Give Elegguá a small portion, then take the rest of the items for ebó before Shangó's shrine. Put the pumpkin on the white plate and cut off its top. Pour the sweet amalá into the pumpkin. Cut the okra into six equal pieces and place them over the amalá. Light the two white candles to Shangó, and pray to him while giving foribale.

The plate with the pumpkin is left over Shangó's *batea* (the wooden tureen in which Shangó's secrets are housed) for six days; at the end of this time, the pumpkin is discarded at the foot of a palm or ceiba tree in the woods. Note that this ebó is never appropriate for Aganyú.

## Ebó Elese Elegguá y Egun
### *(Ebó at the Feet of Elegguá and Egun)*

#### *Oguidí*

Oguidí is a homemade candy adored by egun; it is also favored by Elegguá. To prepare this dish, one needs the following ingredients: one box of cornmeal, a cinnamon stick, 1 cup of brown sugar, vanilla, aluminum foil, honey, and molasses.

Soak the entire box of cornmeal in a bowl of fresh, cool water for three days. This ensures that the cornmeal will begin to ferment. After three days, add the cinnamon stick, brown sugar, and a dash of vanilla to the water and cornmeal. Put the mixture over low heat and cook, stirring continually so that it does not burn, until the water is all but evaporated. Form two tamales of equal size from this cooked mixture, using aluminum foil to enclose them. Bring a large pan of water to a boil, carefully drop in the tamales, and boil for 15 minutes.

When the tamales are cooked, pluck them from the water and remove the aluminum foil. Two platters should be prepared, with one opened tamale on each. Give one platter first to Elegguá and then place the second before egun. While the candy is at its respective shrine, cover it with honey and molasses while praying for sweetness to come back into one's life. These offerings sit with the spirits for three days. At the end of this time, each should be wrapped in brown paper and taken to a cemetery.

#### *Plátanos Borrachos*
#### *("Drunken Plantains")*

Several ingredients are needed to prepare this dish: epó, nine ripe plantains, one cinnamon stick, a few star anise seeds, 1 cup of honey, 1 cup of dry red wine, $^1/_2$ cup of sugarcane syrup, and aluminum foil.

Preheat the oven to 350 degrees Fahrenheit. While the oven is heating, lightly grease a baking dish with epó. Peel the plantains and place them side by side in the baking dish. Crush the cinnamon stick and star anise seeds and mix them into the honey; pour this mixture over the nine plantains. Then mix together the wine and sugarcane juice and pour this mixture over the nine plantains as well. Cover the baking dish with the aluminum foil, place it in the oven, and let bake for 45 minutes. Then remove the aluminum foil from the dish and let bake another 5 to 10 minutes, or until the juices have thickened (watch carefully so that the plantains do not burn). Remove the dish from the oven and let cool.

Place Elegguá with egun and serve the dish to both of them, together. This ebó should be allowed to remain with them for three days. At the end of this time, the food should be wrapped in brown paper and taken to a cemetery.

# The First Composite Odu of Okana, Okana Meji (1-1)

## The Proverbs of Okana Meji

- The speaker will die by his own tongue.
- If there is no evil, there can be no good.
- With one, the world began.
- It is through deep sadness that one masters discouragement.
- He who does not have anything will want to have it all.
- The same knife that cuts the bread can cut the flesh.
- The same knife that slices the bread can kill a man.
- Just as a snake shall always give birth to a snake, so does a witch give birth to a witch.
- Just as goodness gives birth to goodness, so shall evil always conceive evil.
- The heat of the fire never melts the spoon, and the spoon never breaks in the soup.
- The one who has nothing wants to have it all.
- One should not wish for more than can be handled.

## The Message of Okana Meji

When a casting of one mouth repeats itself, the odu Okana Meji is open on the mat. Through this pattern of the diloggún, Shangó was born among mortals, later cheating death and ascending to become an orisha. While the act of ascension is marked beyond this family of signs, those forces setting Shangó's transformation in motion were born here. Shangó's eternal bond with Obatalá originates here as well; the elder spirit is the younger's mentor. The letter also speaks of an ebó made by Oyá and Shangó while they still walked on earth. The two wished to be powerful and went to the diviners to mark ebó. Once ebó was made, Shangó spat fire when he spoke angrily, and Oyá's mouth made sparks as well. Okana's aché provides raw emotion and creates psychic energy in humans.

This odu alludes to twins and doubles, making Okana Meji (a twin of itself) especially powerful. It symbolizes dual forces at work; furtive, covert, and unseen, they overwhelm. Know that this odu speaks backward, and no matter how eloquently this reading is delivered, the client will hear the opposite of what has been said.

In this odu, the diviner must give homage to both Shangó and Elegguá, saying, "Maferefún Shangó! Maferefún Elegguá!" The propitiation of these two orishas is essential to overcoming the osogbo of Okana Meji, and the diviner must keep this in mind. If an ebó is marked to appease either orisha in this sign, the key to evolution is that both orishas must be given the same ebó at the same time. Whatever is claimed by Elegguá must be given to Shangó as well, and vice versa. The diviner must also pay homage to Oyá, saying "Maferefún Oyá!" Because whatever Elegguá and Shangó will not overcome on the client's behalf, she can. Okana Meji is dangerous, yet Oyá thrives on danger. She can destroy in an instant what rises to engulf the client. Know, however, that her solutions can be as terrible as the osogbo opened. Finally, the diviner says, "Maferefún Obatalá!" Amid darkness, Obatalá is light; when death threatens, he is salvation. Being the most forgiving of all the orishas, Obatalá's permeation throughout this odu can be one's redemption, and when all else fails it is to this orisha the diviner must turn for a solution.

Understand that this letter brings no iré. It only promises a difficult passage from troubles if the advice of the orishas is heeded. The eboses prescribed must be made quickly, and if the osogbo is severe, anything marked must be doubled. Otherwise, tears and torment will come before evolution.

The client should be told that Okana speaks of his mother. She has saved this child's life many times. If the two are separated now, this chasm must be healed; otherwise the client's life will be in danger. If the mother is dead, danger is already upon this person. A mother who opens in Okana Meji must be led to make sacrifice on behalf of her children; without ebó, she will watch them die. No matter who sits before the diloggún, a stern warning must be delivered: There will be three sudden deaths before Okana Meji has passed. While the three deaths may not be those of close friends or relatives, the passing of each will touch this person's life in intimate, strange ways. The word *danger* sums up this odu, and the one sitting at the mat must take heed.

This letter also brings up the following concerns:

- If there is no illness or disease in the client's house, soon there will be. He must take care of himself to avoid this. Also, this osogbo can afflict an elder; summon a doctor immediately if an elderly person in the client's house becomes ill.
- When Okana Meji opens in an osogbo that speaks of illness, disease, death, tragedy, or accidents, the outer "twos" of the body are in danger: the legs and the arms. Of these, the legs are more vulnerable. Caution the client to walk instead of run and to avoid participation in contact sports. Avoid cramped sitting positions. Broken bones are not uncommon. Tissue injury is imminent. Advise the client of the seriousness of this; if any tissue injury is sustained, surgery may be the final result. In Okana Meji, such procedures are more risky than the injury.
- Others speak ill of the client, even in his own home. In his absence, one of these people may leave something bad for him or steal something good from him. One of these people wishes the client's death, and his furtive assaults will not stop until after the client is dead and buried. In its worst osogbo, this pattern marks potential murder attempts.
- The client is very desirous of the opposite sex, but sexual appetites must be restrained.
- This letter speaks of evil between the client and another person with three children. There could be issues pending between these two. As with all things of Okana Meji, be cautious.
- This person is being held back by bad luck and unusual circumstances. He has economic and emotional difficulties. The client must work hard to regain and maintain his stability, because once it is lost, it may be lost for good.
- The orishas are not happy with this person, and they give him nothing without a price. His life is hard: Hard labor is his lot in life, and he will have to work hard to overcome this.
- This client abhors hearing the truth about himself; the more the diviner says, the less he will listen. This odu, nevertheless, demands that the diviner tell the client all prohibitions, prescriptions, and interpretations.

## The Prohibitions of Okana Meji

- Okana Meji gives specific directions for one's conduct among family and friends. It says one is angered by those one loves; one shows this anger and can be abusive. This emotion must be suppressed. When angry, take care that the arms stay close to the body. Touch no one. Children must be watched carefully and treated well. Measure one's words before addressing any child.
- In relationships, adultery is to be avoided. One should have only one lover and never date outside an established relationship.
- During sexual relations, proper birth control must be used. Pregnancy is taboo in this sign; it will bring serious health concerns for both the mother and the unborn child. In Okana Meji, the wage of conception is death.
- Okana Meji is a sign of addiction. All drugs, vices, and alcohol must be prohibited.
- Avoid the sacrificial foods of Aganyú, Shangó, and Elegguá.
- Do not go walking alone during the day, and stay indoors at night. Tragedy comes for the one who breaks this taboo.

## The Eboses of Okana Meji

Okana Meji demands that all its offerings be doubled. The larishe that has come to soothe this sign's initial osogbo must be doubled if it is to be of any use. For example, if the larishe is a hen given to Oshún, two hens must be given to Oshún. If the larishe is a ñame given to Elegguá, two ñames must be given to Elegguá, and two must go to Shangó as well. (Keep in mind that as a general rule for marking eboses in Okana Meji, what Shangó receives,

Elegguá also must receive, and vice versa.) These parameters must be carefully worked out in the diviner's head and written in the record of the reading or else the client will not evolve.

Quite a few works must be done when this letter falls. Okana Meji is severe, and this person needs all the spiritual help he can get to overcome its vibrations. First, the dead claim ebó in Okana Meji. Someone in this person's family died without proper burial. This sign marks miscarriages on the client's mother, possibly even abortions, and each of these children was resigned to death without proper burial or memorial services. A series of three masses must be given to appease the client's unknown and unnamed dead. Only in this way will egun stand aside and let this person evolve. The diviner should ask, "Ebó elese egun?" to see if the egun will take ebó from the client.

If the client is a mother, she must make sacrifices to save her children from death; the diviner must ask the diloggún which orisha stands up to offer larishe for this. If no larishe can be found, the ebó is a rogación for each child at the feet of his or her guardian orisha.*

In addition, Okana demands that the client have a rogación.

Know that in this odu, Elegguá is very hungry and he wants to eat. While the following ebó will not lift the osogbo of this sign, it can be used to help bring one's dreams or desires in life to fruition. Realize that this ebó must be done with a good, clean heart and that only one's purest goals or aspirations should be brought to the orisha. Elegguá does not like to be tricked, but at times he likes those with a "tricky nature." He likes to make deals and pacts, and in this sign he will do so if the client truly deserves all that he asks for. For the ebó, the client brings a rooster before Elegguá, and he makes preparations for its sacrifice while the animal sits near the orisha, stirring up his appetite. When all is ready, the sacrificial songs begin, but then the ritual is interrupted, briefly, while the client puts the rooster to the side and begins to have a long, honest talk with his Elegguá. From the heart, he tells the orisha about his life and where he wants it to go. The client must not be motivated by greed; instead, he must pour out his heart and highest aspirations. Using obí (coconut divination), the client then determines if Elegguá agrees to all that has been said. Only a casting of *ejife* or *aláfia meji* (both positive symbols) may be taken as an assurance of Elegguá's agreement. Note that Elegguá may not be fed until some type of deal is struck between the client and the orisha, and the ritual may not end until Elegguá has been fed. A pact between the two must be carefully bargained. This is a dangerous ebó, but if it is done with an honest heart, the client will come away with a clearer understanding of what Elegguá will and will not bring into his life.†

Having considered all of the above, if the diloggún will not close, the diviner should investigate the following:

- The diviner has already prescribed a rogación, but the client's head may need to be fed as well. The diviner should ask, "Eborí?" If the answer is yes, the proper sacrifice to offer is two white doves or pigeons.
- The client could have unresolved issues with the four orishas who might stand up to help this person avoid osogbo: Elegguá, Shangó, Oyá, and Obatalá. The diviner should consider asking, "Ebó elese [orisha's name]?" If the answer is yes, he marks the offering with the shells.
- Shangó and Obatalá could be standing up together to claim ebó. Remember that in this sign the two orishas are close; Shangó worships the ground that Obatalá walks on because the elder orisha gave Shangó much of his aché. To see if they require ebó, the diviner should

*If the guardian orishas of the children are not known, these rogaciónes may be done at the feet of Obatalá.

†Note that many old libretas have said that the true secret of this odu is to present a rooster to Elegguá, ask for the opposite of what one desires, and then take away that rooster, so that Elegguá is not fed at all. Therefore, in anger Elegguá will make sure the client does not receive what he asked for. This is dangerous, and those who have given an ebó to Elegguá in such a manner have seen their lives fall apart, ruined beyond belief. It's true that they received the opposite of what they asked for. However, Elegguá is an orisha and knows what lies in our hearts. To deceive him is to deceive ourselves, and Elegguá will find a way to get the sacrifice that was denied, and more.

ask, "Ebó elese Shangó y Obatalá?" If ebó is needed, the diviner should work through the list of eboses described in "Marking the Eboses, or Remedies for Odu" (page 30) until the dilog-gún marks one. Keep in mind that if Shangó takes an ebó here, Elegguá must be offered the same; however, because it is important that the ebó made to Shangó be done with Obatalá at his side, Elegguá should be given his part of the offering first and separately.

- If Shangó and Obatalá do not need an ebó, or if the odu will not close even after that ebó is marked, Shangó and Oyá could be standing up together to claim ebó. To see if they require ebó, the diviner should ask, "Ebó elese Shangó y Oyá?" If the answer is yes, the diviner should, as before, mark the appropriate ebó with the dilog-gún. Again, remember that anything Shangó claims must be duplicated for Elegguá, and that Elegguá's should be given his part of the offering first and separately. Once given the ebó, Shangó and Oyá will destroy with fire all that stands in the way of this person's evolution.
- If the odu still will not close, the diviner should ask if Ogún is standing up for ebó, questioning, "Ebó elese Ogún?" If Ogún does stand up for ebó, he should be given an earthenware jar filled with rum and a plate of roasted meat smeared liberally with epó, all served on a bed of palm fronds. This is Ogún's first and only option for ebó in this odu; the diviner may not mark any other ebó for Ogún unless it comes later as a consideration through the eboses for the parent odu, Okana (see page 85). Anyone present for this ebó should take a single palm frond home and put it just outside the front door before going inside. This act honors the pact created by the client and Ogún. Ogún will destroy the enemies in this person's life, all those who have tried to alter or hinder his destiny. When they are destroyed, the client will claim their luck. Those who have palm fronds at their front door will be spared Ogún's wrath.
- Finally, Aganyú, Yewá, or Yemayá could also be standing up in this odu for ebó. The diviner should consider each one in turn, asking, "Ebó elese [orisha's name]?" If the answer is yes, the diviner should use the shells to mark an appropriate offering.
- As a last resort for initiates only, the diviner might consider the reception of either Aganyú or Yewá.* To see if the reception is necessary, he should ask, "Koshé [orisha's name]?"

If these options have been exhausted and closure is still not allowed, the diviner must turn to the eboses listed under the parent odu, Okana. (See page 85.) Something there is necessary to bring evolution and closure for this sign.

## The Second Composite Odu of Okana, Okana Ejioko (1-2)

### The Proverbs of Okana Ejioko

- Do not hurt yourself when throwing arrows.
- Do not hurt your best friend when throwing arrows.
- When you release arrows, release them with care.
- Carelessness will injure both you and your best friend.
- He who taunts the cat will be scratched by the cat.
- The young one disrespects the elder.

### The Message of Okana Ejioko

When one mouth (Okana) is followed by two (Eji Oko), Okana Ejioko is the composite opened on the mat. This odu goes by several other names: Okanran Ejioko, Kanran Ejioko, Okana Oyekun, Kanran Oyekun, Kana'yeku, and Okanran Oyekun. It is an interesting pattern, one that has much to do with death and the dead, and speaks of another religion that has become strongly absorbed into our own:

*Consider the reception of Yewá only if the client's life represents the fullest and harshest osogbo of Okana. Yewá is a severe spirit, making the most dramatic changes and demands in one's life.

Palo Mayombe, a sect of Palo, a Congolese spiritual tradition encompassing magic and mysticism. In fact, in one of the patakís for Okana Ejioko, the orishas Shangó and Orúnmila walk on earth among mortals as practicing paleros (Palo priests). If a child of Shangó opens in Okana Ejioko, this person could have issues pending with the Palo Mayombe; he should be taken to a competent palero for a spiritual investigation. Likewise, one who is destined for Ifá could also need to investigate Palo Mayombe. Before the client does anything else in the Lucumí faith, he must settle these issues so that the Congolese spirits who walk with him do not stand in the way of his future evolution with the orishas.

Okana Ejioko is a hot letter full of advice for the client; all of it must be heeded if he hopes to grow in life. In this sign, it is said that those who are younger will always disobey those who are elder. However, if youth aspires to be more than its parents, the wisdom of age must be heeded. The main advice of this pattern revolves around respect for the elders. It must be given, even when undeserved.

This is a time for unconditional generosity. The client should be counseled to give freely of his food and drink, even to his enemies. It is also said that if arrows are thrown, the client or his best friend could be hurt. These "arrows" apply to every aspect of the client's life, and especially gossip. This letter can also bring up health issues concerning the client's heart; monitor it carefully, and become concerned if it "misses a beat."

Be wary that nothing is missed. This letter demands careful attention and alertness to all things. Somewhere in this person's life is a hole, a vast chasm that is growing and into which many things will be lost. The client should not become lost in large issues; he must pay attention to small issues, as well, for through such small holes much can be lost. Emptiness is the greatest hole here, and one must find something to fill it before it becomes overwhelming. Mental illness, instability, and suicide are all dangers in this odu. Warn the client: "Do not take your own life, and do not wish you were dead, for these are the greatest sins."

The diviner should also explore the following issues with the client:

- Visitors will come to the client's door; they will be both announced and unannounced. Unless it is impossible to receive these callers, none should be turned away. Graciously, the client must entertain his visitors. They should be offered food and drink. Those who come to him on the street begging alms must be given something as well, and he should keep aside a very small amount of money in his pockets to be prepared for this. Goodness is lost when others are turned away hungry.
- One's lover is both a joy and a sorrow in this odu, and one never knows the love one has until it is gone. Do not argue with the lover; walk away, cool down, and come back when the head is clear.
- A war is coming to the client's life; it is not here now, but soon will be. When this war comes, the client must have a rogación before Obatalá to keep his head cool and clear. He must then feed Elegguá a single rooster if he hopes to win this war.

## The Prohibitions of Okana Ejioko

- Travel at this time is not recommended because accidents are a danger. Travel over water should be avoided at all costs. If a trip is pending and Okana Ejioko comes in osogbo, the trip will bring disappointment and, if ebó is not done, possibly disaster. If Okana Ejioko comes in iré, the trip will go well, yet it may not live up to one's expectations. Note that this trip could involve a visit to someone who is ill.
- Avoid violence. Avoid lifting one's hands against another in anger, and avoid anything that will bring contact with the law. If one is living outside the law in some way, all such activities should stop now.
- Do not keep items that belong to others in the home, in the car, in the office, or on one's own person. The law may conduct a search, and any such items found could bring one under suspicion.

## The Eboses of Okana Ejioko

When Okana Ejioko has opened on the mat, three issues should be explored. The first issue revolves around Shangó. If the letter comes in a weak iré, Shangó is trying to bring blessings; however, the client's life is not stable enough, nor is his head clear enough, to see that blessings are coming. To solidify this person's aché with Shangó, especially if the client is a child of Shangó, the diviner should consider a rogación for the client at Shangó's feet. After this rogación, prepare an adimú for Shangó, giving Elegguá a share of the offering.

Okana Ejioko also flags issues with Orúnmila. Because Orúnmila cannot speak directly through the shells, the diviner may wish to send the client to a babalawo for a session with Ifá.

Finally, the odu says there could be issues pending with the *nkisi* (forces of nature) of the Palo Mayombe, especially if the client is a child of Shangó or Orúnmila. Unless the italero is also *rayado* (initiated to the priesthood of Palo Mayombe), a competent priest in that religion must be consulted to assess the client. An initiation to Palo may be a part of his spiritual destiny.

Once these issues have been explored, the diviner has his first chance to close the oracle. If it remains open, the following eboses should be considered:

- In this odu the reception and propitiation of the Ibeyi (the divine twin children of Shangó and Oshún) can be important. To see if the Ibeyi require ebó, the diviner should first ask, "Ebó elese los Ibeyi?" If ebó can be marked, it can be given to either the client's Ibeyi (if he has received them) or the godparent's Ibeyi (if he has not received them). The next consideration is the reception of the Ibeyi, which the diviner questions by asking, "Koshé los Ibeyi?" If their reception is marked, they must be taken as soon as possible. A huge party should be thrown in their honor once the client has received them.
- If the client is an aleyo and the oracle still will not close, the diviner should turn to the eboses of the parent odu, Okana (see page 85), to find something that will satisfy the osogbo that has opened.
- If the client is an initiate and the oracle still will not close, the odu might be indicating that a *tambor* (sacred festival of an orisha) is the solution to this person's troubles. The diviner should investigate this possibility, asking, "Tambor de santo?" If the answer is yes, he must determine whether the tambor is necessary for, in turn, Elegguá, Ogún, Ochosi, Ibeyi, Babaluaiye, Orisha Oko, Obatalá, Aganyú, or Shangó, asking, "Tambor elese [orisha's name]?" Note that if a tambor is marked during an itá for a iyawó through either Elegguá or the guardian orisha, the client is automatically marked to give a drum to all the orishas in time.*

If none of these eboses will close the odu for an initiate, the italero must turn to the eboses of the parent odu, Okana, to find closure for the oracle. (See page 85.) Something there is needed for the client's evolution.†

# The Third Composite Odu of Okana, Okana Ogundá (1-3)

## The Proverbs of Okana Ogundá

- Revolution and blood [will come] through the nose or anus.
- The dead are not really dead.
- Your dead enemy still wishes the worst for you.
- A good rooster knows when to crow.
- A good penis knows when to rise.

## The Message of Okana Ogundá

Okana Ogundá, also known as Kanran Ogundá, opens when one mouth, Okana, is followed by three mouths, Ogundá. The diviner must begin this session by paying homage to Elegguá and Ogún, saying,

*The protocol for giving drums to the spirits is that one must give a drum to one's godparent's guardian orisha (from whom one's spiritual consciousness was born) before playing a drum for any of one's own orishas.

†Okana Ejioko can also mark the need for an aborisha to attend a tambor given by another initiate. If this sign refuses closure, this prescription may be made.

"Maferefún Elegguá! Maferefún Ogún!" These two spirits stand as warriors behind the client, offering their support through the trials and tribulations he must face, and they will work hard to remove this sign's osogbo if they are propitiated.

The diviner also pays homage to Obatalá, saying, "Maferefún Obatalá!" For while Elegguá and Ogún come to fight, Obatalá comes to calm, to soothe the volatile essences unfolding in Okana Ogundá. In this odu Obatalá protects the client, offering his strength to the client's head so he can make wise, rational decisions amid what amounts to his own karma (for lack of a better word in this religion). The client should have a rogación at Obatalá's feet, even if Obatalá claims nothing from this session. If Obatalá takes ebó, it cannot be given until after the rogación is complete. And if Obatalá demands eyebale as ebó, the diviner knows the client is entering a war; his own orí should be fed two white pigeons or doves before Obatalá is fed.

Finally, the diviner must say "Maferefún Shangó!" Shangó is capable of becoming the client's salvation; he may have the remedy to what ails the client.

Okana and Ogundá are extremely hot signs, and their union demands extreme caution on the diviner's part. The opening of this odu requires a special ebo for both Okana and Ogundá after the oracle has closed. (See "The Eboses of Okana Ogundá" on page 63 for details.)

Before entering into the delivery of the reading, the diviner must keep some important points in mind. Okana Ogundá is one of the most dangerous signs in the diloggún. The client's own "karma" has opened this odu, yet it comes not as a punishment but as a raw cleansing. It portends a perilous yet cleansing journey. Know that Okana Ogundá is incapable of true iré. If the odu is marked with iré, the blessing is offered only because some spiritual force somewhere has taken pity on this person, and to that source the client must travel. His faith must be pure and his heart strong as he accepts this spiritual help. Unfortunately, Okana tells us that the client is weak; his head is weak and his faith is weak. Speed and time are of the essence in this odu. The client must be told to complete his eboses quickly, no matter the cost or effort. Once all is done, he would be wise to return to the diviner for divination to see what new things the orishas have in store. This is the best advice one can give for now.

This pattern forebodes seven warnings: revolution, sickness, tragedy, enemies, arguments, violence, and legal complications. Which of these might apply directly to the client can be determined by the orientation—iré or osogbo—that has come and by the origin of that orientation. Regardless of the orientation, the following point should be kept in mind: The client must guard against bloodshed in his own home, for once blood begins to flow here, the evil that will come cannot be stopped. The evil will enter the client's home by his own stupidity; it can come through the front door, the back door, or even an open window. For now, when he is home the client should bar himself and his family behind locked doors and closed windows. When he is not home, he should lock the house securely. He should abstain from hoarding weapons, for they could be turned against him. He should not drink, entertain guests, or open the door for unexpected visitors. If the client is a priest or priestess for whom a sacrifice is pending, he or she should not shed blood in the home; all sacrifices should be done in the godparent's home, for now. Finally, blood could flow even from the nose, mouth, or anus; this marks disease, and the client must go to a physician.

Outlaws and bandits often open in Okana Ogundá, and for them it means that the law is on its way. To save himself, such a client must move. He must destroy anything obtained illegally or remove it from his home, leaving behind no trace of evidence. By swearing before the orishas that he will never break the law again, he might be saved. He should tell no one his business or his plans, and he must separate from all those who break the law to make a living.

In Okana Ogundá, even a law-abiding citizen should avoid all possible contact with the law. He should not speed or be a witness to accidents or crimes. He should not drink when away from home or use illegal intoxicants. He should not sign contracts at this time, for they will contain traps. Most important, the client must stay away from officers of the law; if he sees a police officer, he should move and look the other way.

In addition to these considerations, when Okana Ogundá opens on the mat, the following items should be explored with the client:

- Okana Ogundá speaks of a tragedy in the house or brought to the house. If the client follows the precautions given earlier for guarding against bloodshed in the home, much of this osogbo can be avoided. Regardless of these precautions, some evil will still come; pray that it is minor.
- If the client has not already lost something precious, he soon will. As above, much of this osogbo can be avoided if he follows the advice given previously. Gold, jewels, and important papers should be kept locked in a bank vault. Valuables should not be displayed in public. This odu promises that if something turns up missing, one day it will be found. However, it will be necessary to call the law to reclaim it.
- If the client is in a relationship, his significant other could have a secret so terrible that it will destroy the relationship when it is revealed. No matter: His current relationship is all but doomed to failure.
- Threesomes of the heart will bring tragedy. If this person has two lovers in his life, he is already in danger. The odu offers a warning: He should not seduce another person's spouse.
- The client has a terrible enemy he is not even aware of. The enemy is not, nor may have ever been, a friend or even an acquaintance. Know that if a random violence occurs in this person's life, it is not truly random but planned long ago.
- If Okana Ogundá comes in an osogbo marked as ano or ikú, it flags health concerns for the abdomen and throat. Something is wrong in the client's abdomen. Right now it is so small that not even a physician can diagnose it, yet one day it will become something big. If the client is a woman, she may have reproductive troubles; she may have had miscarriages in the past and may have miscarriages in the future. There could also be sickness in the throat. Again, something small can become something big. One day, either a minor medical procedure or a major surgery could be performed on either the abdomen or the throat.
- The client (if a woman) or the client's wife (if a man) may have aborted a child in the past because she doubted its paternity. If conception is difficult now, it is because of this abortion.

## The Prohibitions of Okana Ogundá

- Okana Ogundá prohibits most forms of travel, especially to the ocean or over the water. If one has a trip pending when this letter falls, postpone it for eight days, traveling only on the ninth day or later. Before leaving, however, Elegguá must be asked to mark ebó to ensure safe travel. (He must not be asked to allow the trip during the eight-day prohibition; the letter forbids this.)
- Do not smoke in bed. Before retiring for the night, extinguish all sources of open flame, including candles lit to the orishas. Note that in this odu, fire does not kill those who are sleeping; it is the smoke that chokes the breath.
- In Okana Ogundá, all drugs, vices, and alcohol are taboo. Refuse to be the third party in any illicit dealings, and do not go to dark places or social gatherings, especially if alcohol and drugs will be served. While one will harm oneself when intoxicated, one is also a danger to those who are sober.

## The Eboses of Okana Ogundá

The first two eboses that must be prescribed are the closing eboses for both the parent odu, Okana, and the omo odu, Ogunda: the cleansing of the diviner and the client to Elegguá and Ogún and the cleansing of all others present at the reading to Elegguá. These eboses are mandatory regardless of whether the composite odu opened in iré or in osogbo, and they must be made as soon as the oracle has closed. (See page 49 for a description of these cleansings.)

The next considerations for eboses in Okana Ogundá center on egun. Egun have much to say in this odu. The diviner must prescribe three spiritual masses for the client, and the prescriptions of the *espiritistas* (spiritual mediums) must be followed exactly.*

Elegguá and Ogún demand attention here; if the client does not have his warriors, he must get them. If the client has the warriors, the diviner might consider investigating whether Elegguá and Ogún together will take ebó, asking, "Ebó elese Elegguá y Ogún?" In this odu, note that if either Elegguá or Ogún has claimed to have larishe (the solution to the client's osogbo), what is done for one must be done for the other or else the sacrifice cannot bring evolution.

Finally, in Okana Ogundá the head can become one's salvation, but only if it is not weak and confused. The diviner must offer the client a rogación at the feet of Obatalá to bring strength and coolness to his orí.

Once the diviner has delivered his reading in full and the client understands all that has been said, he should ask, "Larishe Shangó?" If the answer is yes, Shangó has become the client's salvation; he has the solution to the osogbos opened at the mat. The diviner should mark an ebó to him.

If the odu will not close at this point, the diviner should consider asking the egun if they require any further eboses, saying, "Ebó elese egun?" If the answer is yes, the diviner uses the shells to mark an appropriate offering.

If none of these prescriptions will bring closure for an aleyo or aborisha, the diviner should turn to the list of eboses given for the parent odu, Okana (see page 85). If the client is an initiate, the diviner should continue with the line of questioning given here.

If no orishas or egun will take ebó, or if the letter still refuses closure, the next option is the sacrifice of a four-legged animal. The proper sequence for questioning if this ebó is marked is Elegguá, Ogún, Ochosi, Babaluaiye, Orisha Oko, Obatalá, Aganyú, Shangó, and egun.

If a four-legged offering is marked, the diviner must also determine if itá is required after the ebó is completed, asking, "Itá elese [marked orisha's name]?" (If a four-legged animal is to be given to egun, itá is not an option.) If both the sacrifice of a four-legged animal and an itá are marked for an orisha the client lacks, he must also receive that spirit.

If a four-legged animal is not required, the client could need to receive Ochosi, Orisha Oko, Babaluaiye, or Aganyú. To see if the client needs any of these orishas, the diviner should question each in turn, asking, "Koshé [orisha's name]?"

If neither the four-legged offering nor the reception of Ochosi, Orisha Oko, Babaluaiye, or Aganyú is accepted, the next possibility in this odu is the reception of the knife. (This ceremony, known as *pinaldo*, gives a priest or priestess the right to sacrifice four-legged animals.)

If after these eboses are investigated the odu still will not close, the diviner must turn to the eboses of the parent odu, Okana. (See page 85.)

Once the odu gives closure, the closing eboses for Okana and Ogundá must be made. Two pieces of beef must be oiled with epó and wrapped separately in brown paper. All people present at the reading must gather before the diviner's warriors while he prays to both Elegguá and Ogún to lift the osogbos brought by this sign. Once the prayers are finished, the diviner cleanses himself with the meat, using one piece for Elegguá and the other for Ogún. He then cleanses the client in the same manner. Once this is done, the priests and priestesses who are present, in the order of their elder status (beginning with the eldest and continuing down to the youngest), cleanse themselves with the meat that belongs to Elegguá. They are followed by the aborishas and then the aleyos. (Only the diviner and the client cleanse themselves to Ogún; the rest of those present at the reading cleanse only to Elegguá.) Once everyone in the house has finished this ebó, the room is opened and all should leave. The next morning, the diviner must take these eboses to nature: Elegguá's goes to a crossroads, and Ogún's goes to a railroad track. Note that all who were present for the reading must have a session with the diloggún as soon as possible.†

*The Lucumí mass involves the use of espiritistas, who extract from egun their wishes and advice for the supplicant.

†If the odu comes in a severe osogbo and will not close, Ogún may be demanding that all should be cleansed to him as well. This is the exception, and not the rule.

## The Fourth Composite Odu of Okana, Okana Irosun (1-4)

### The Proverbs of Okana Irosun

- There is fire within and fire without.
- One cannot expect thunder when the sky is blue.
- In the dry season, no rain will fall.
- [There will be] a revolution inside the body.
- [There will be] hemorrhages of the mouth, the nose, and the anus.
- In the land that you travel, do what you see.
- When in Rome, do as the Romans do.
- By speaking backward, things will come out right.

### The Message of Okana Irosun

This odu opens when a casting of one mouth, Okana, is followed by a casting of four mouths, Irosun. It is also known as Okana Irosun, Okana Iroso, Kanran Irosun, and Kanran Iroso. When it falls, the diviner faces a person who must make ocha; it is part of his destiny. The diviner should begin the reading by stating this and, if the client is an aleyo, advising him to receive the elekes and warriors as soon as possible so he has a foundation in ocha.

Fate is fickle in this sign, and the client must learn patience and perseverance if he is to overcome adversity. Know that in this odu, Impatience once went for divination because he was not happy with his life. The diviners told him to be careful and avoid haste, for those who try to change their own destiny can make matters worse. In a similar vein, if this client curses his own lot in life, he will find that things get worse and not better.

Spiritual heat is wrought by this letter. Okana Iroso signals that someone has placed a curse on the client, and it must be fought with spiritual cleansings. This sign also portends revolution within the body; it may soon turn against the client through sickness. He must take care of his health and see a physician if any symptoms of sickness arise, especially in the eyes. Abdominal pains warn that a trip to the physician is necessary. Emphasize that the client should watch for bleeding of the mouth, nose, and anus; these should be given prompt medical attention. Also, he should go nowhere that would bring embarrassment if the truth were known. Since the law figures prominently in this odu, he should do nothing illegal, no matter how minor.

In addition, the following considerations should be kept in mind:

- Obstacles come not only in this person's spiritual path but also in his physical path. The client must watch where he walks, being cautious of holes, ditches, rocks, and anything else that could be strewn in his way. He must pay careful attention to the road when driving, because animals or people could throw themselves in front of his car.
- In Okana Irosun, enemies can turn one's own words into powerful weapons. The client must measure his words carefully around others.
- The client must protect his head and his eyes, for they are vulnerable to injury. If he is a risk taker, enjoying dangerous contact sports, he should abstain from them for at least a month.
- The client's lover may become seriously ill while this odu is in effect.

### The Prohibitions of Okana Irosun

- When visiting the home of another, especially the home of religious elders, have good manners and follow their customs. There are too many wars between houses about whose ways are more correct, whose are proper and whose are not. To avoid conflicts, follow the advice of the elders of the house one is visiting; if one is asked about one's own customs, then one may instruct.
- Avoid the following foods: apples, cashews, red plums or prunes, red beans, red foods, red drinks, mangos, the heads or tails of animals, fish (including sardines), grains, seeds, grainy foods, grainy fruits, and tripe. Avoid the consumption of blood by making sure that all meat is well drained of its fluids.
- Wear clothing in good repair. Do not wear torn

or ripped or dirty clothes. Do not wear clothing with lace, holes, or eyelets. Fringes are taboo, as is the color red.

- Avoid holes. Holes in the house must be covered or repaired. Do not look through holes, jump over holes, or keep things in holes. Do not get inside holes or tight spaces.

## The Eboses of Okana Irosun

In Okana Irosun, there are serious spiritual issues that must be explored; however, the manner in which they are considered will depend on the client's status in the religion. If the client is an aborisha whose head has not been marked (he does not know who his crowning orisha is), issues among Shangó, the client's orí, and the godparent's crowning orisha are pending. To settle these issues, a rogación must be given at Obatalá's shrine to strengthen the orí. Then an adimú must be presented to Shangó and the godparent's crowning orisha. If the oracle will not close, Shangó and the godparent's crowning orisha might each want a specific ebó in place of a simple adimú. To determine if this is the case, the diviner should ask, "Ebó elese [orisha's name]?" When these adimús or eboses are lifted from the orishas' shrines, they must be replaced immediately with coconuts: two for Shangó, two for orí, and two for the crown. The coconuts should remain until all the client's issues are settled, with new coconuts being given as replacements when the existing coconuts go bad.

If this client is an initiate or an aborisha whose head has been marked, these eboses are similar, except that the rogación given to Obatalá is done before the sopera of the client's crowning orisha instead.

The final issue that demands exploration is the client's relationship with egun. In Okana Irosun, ebó must be made first to the client's Elegguá and then to his egun. These eboses should sit with egun and Elegguá for three days, and each night a mass should be given for the client's ancestors. The client must do all that the espiritistas tell him to do. When the three days and three masses are completed and the eboses given to Elegguá and egun are lifted, another adimú should be left with egun.

Once all these things have been prescribed, the diviner has his first chance to close the odu. If it will not close, he should consider the following things:

- The dead could be standing up for a specific ebó. The diviner should ask, "Ebó elese egun?" If the answer is yes, the diviner works through the possible eboses (as described in chapter 1) to determine what egun require.
- The Ibeyi (the twin orishas) can be an integral part of this sign. If the oracle refuses closure and the client does not have these orishas, the diviner should investigate whether their reception is necessary, asking "Koshe los Ibeyi?" If the answer is yes, the client must receive them as soon as possible. If the client already has the Ibeyi, the diviner should investigate whether they need ebó, asking "Ebó elese los Ibeyi?" If the answer is yes, the diviner uses the diloggún to mark the proper ebó from the list given in chapter 1. If the Ibeyi ask for ebó yet accept nothing, the proper sacrifice to give them is a party thrown in their honor. This must be done as soon as possible, for the Ibeyi will work miracles in the client's life.
- Olokun is important in this odu as well. If the client does not have Olokun and the letter refuses closure, the diviner should attempt to mark her reception with the shells, asking "Koshé Olokun?" If the client already has Olokun, the diviner should question whether she needs ebó, asking, "Ebó elese Olokun?" If the answer is yes, she stands up for ebó, the diviner uses the diloggún to mark the proper ebó from the list given in chapter 1. In the rare occasion that Olokun stands up for ebó yet will not mark any, the proper offering is a feathered animal and then an *agbán* (a ritual cleansing with various types of foods and grains). With this ebó, Olokun will clear all osogbo from the client.
- If the client has received Elegguá, this orisha might be standing up for more carga and reinforcement in his clay tray; the diviner should try to mark this. If the client is a priest or priestess

and the answer to this question is no, then the diviner should ask if Elegguá wants a crown. Once he has his crown, he will give this person a kingdom.

If the odu still will not close out, the diviner needs to have an honest talk with the client about his commitment to the religion. If the client is an aleyo, the diviner should place a *mazo* (a heavily beaded necklace draped over an orisha's shrine) over him and lead him to salute his guardian orisha. He or she is now in bondage to ocha. If the client is an initiate, he is being led to assess his life as a priest of the faith. After exploring this issue with the client, the diviner should again ask the oracle for closure. If it refuses, he must investigate the options for ebó under the parent odu, Okana. (See page 85.)

## The Fifth Composite Odu of Okana, Okana Oché (1-5)

### The Proverbs of Okana Oché

- Jealousy is the mother of mistrust.
- Jealousy is the cause of destruction.
- Your jealousy will destroy everything.
- If you don't know what to do for yourself, what can anyone else tell you?
- He who tries to teach Ochosi how to shoot is like a man trying to tell a woman how to give birth.

### The Message of Okana Oché

When one mouth is followed by five, Okana Oché, also known as Okanran Oché and Kanran Oché, has opened on the mat. The diviner says, "Maferefún Elegguá! Maferefún Obatalá! Maferefún Oshún!" These three orishas dominate this sign, each with its own aché. As always, Elegguá is fate and destiny; it is by his goodwill that the client can move from osogbo into iré. No matter which orisha takes ebó in this odu, Elegguá must be also receive his share. Obatalá lends his cool, calming nature to the person who has come in this pattern of extremes. This person's head could easily become heated, overwhelmed by the spiritual currents dredged forth from this sign. It will take all this orisha's strength to cool it. Finally, Oshún is firm here as well; Oché is her pattern, and she rules all things that are brought when it appears. Depending on the orientation of this odu, the aché of these three orishas might be needed to help clear the client's paths.

Okana Oché emphasizes that the client's emotions can lead his head astray. Above all else, he must suppress this tendency, because in this sign being swept away by extremes is a danger. Love and hate, happiness and unhappiness, anger and contentment—all must be tempered. No single emotion is as extreme in this odu as jealousy. Okana Oché signals that the client is jealous of acquaintances, friends, family, and lovers, and his jealousy is slowly deteriorating these relationships. Arguments with loved ones are also a danger through this odu; the client should be encouraged to be gentle with those whom he loves. He needs to practice honest communication to keep osogbo at bay. Envy is hot in this letter; know that the client is envious of all whose fortunes are greater than his own. His envy has brought secret enemies, because he aspires to be more than they (and for all the wrong reasons). Caution is advised in Okana Oché; a friend of whom the client is envious is planning the client's demise.

The client's body is sickened through witchcraft or poison. Before this odu has passed, blood might run from the nose, mouth, anus, eyes, vagina or penis, or ears. Illness could develop in the feet, legs, or abdomen. Impotence could afflict men, and frigidity might develop in women. Infections of the reproductive tract could render a client of either sex infertile. If problems in any of these areas arise, the client must go immediately to a physician for a complete checkup. The diviner should then be consulted again for an ebó to heal the disorder.

Okana Oché also marks mental and nervous disorders in one or more members of this person's family. Once a sufferer is identified (the illness will become obvious in time), he or she should be brought back to the diviner for ebó. This letter provides solutions to heal mental afflictions.

Currently, this person's roads are broken; the paths laid toward attainment are cut short or blocked. This letter cautions the client that no matter what happens, he must persevere over aggression and obstacles. Even in osogbo, problems are not as insurmountable as they seem; while the ideal end result might not be achieved, one can emerge from Okana Oché victorious. The client's salvation is simple: ebó.

## The Prohibitions of Okana Oché

- It is forbidden for one to have altercations with Oshún's children. It is also guaranteed that a child of Oshún will come to one's house to start trouble. When this happens, do not try to settle the argument alone. Leave the problems to Oshún, and let her deal with her own child.
- The following foods are taboo: roasted or burned meats and vegetables, canned foods, pumpkin, squash, gourds, reheated foods, cold leftovers, beets, eggs, watercress, goat, fowl, red snapper, and shellfish.
- When one is eating, foods that are not part of the same dish must be kept separate; do not mix anything on the plate.
- The sacrificial foods of the orisha who stood up in this reading to claim larishe, plus the foods sacred to Oshún, might be limited or taken away altogether. The diviner, taking into account the orientation of the odu, will determine if this is necessary.
- Abortions are taboo. Do not recommend one, and do not have one.
- Respect all bodies of water. Do not jump or dive into pools, lakes, or the ocean. Never go swimming in the river, and ask permission before driving or otherwise crossing over one. Enter all bodies of water feetfirst, never headfirst.

## The Eboses of Okana Oché

When Okana Oché opens on the mat, it flags several eboses that the client should perform regardless of the odu's orientation. First, odu tells us that something is not right in this person's environment. He must thoroughly clean his home, including the closets, drawers, and cabinets and beneath furniture. Any areas that are dark, closed, or infrequently opened must be aired out and examined thoroughly; there could be sickness or witchcraft brewing in these places. To move negative energy out of the house, the client should open all windows and doors while cleaning. Begin at the point farthest away from the front door and work toward it. Once the home is physically clean, it must be spiritually cleansed with candles, holy water, floor washes, and incense. If the osogbo of Okana Oché is severe, a cleansing with two white doves should be performed, and these should be set free at the front door, allowed to take the remaining osogbo away to heaven and Olófin.

Second, once this cleansing is complete, the client must host a spiritual mass for egun in his home. In this sign, they do not feel properly seated or welcomed into the client's life; a mass will settle them appropriately. If the odu refuses closure after these two eboses, egun might need additional offerings. The diviner should question, "Ebó elese egun?" If the anwer is yes, one must use the diloggún to mark the appropriate ebó.

Two eboses are required in the event that the client has or develops two specific conditions. First, if either the client or a member of his family develops abdominal pains over the next six months, a rogación must be performed over the stomach in front of Oshún. It is performed exactly as one would cleanse the head, except that the affected person lies on a mat before the orisha's shrine and the cleansing is limited to the abdominal region. If abdominal troubles are affecting conception or unborn children, additional eboses (such as a sacrifice to Oshún and the abdomen) might be required when the rogación is performed. Second, if either the client or a member of his family develops neurological, psychological, or emotional problems, a rogación should be given to the affected person's head in front of Oshún's shrine. She will clear those things heating the orí, giving the sufferer a safe space in which to heal.*

Elegguá could be standing up together with

*In both cases, proper medical and supportive care must be sought out as well, for while Oshún removes the spiritual causes of disease in this sign, the body and mind will need professional care to support the healing processes invoked.

Obatalá or Oshún for ebó in this odu. To determine if this is the case, the diviner asks, "Ebó elese Elegguá y Obatalá?" and "Ebó elese Elegguá y Oshún?" If the answer to either question is yes, the diviner marks the required ebó with the diloggún.

If none of these prescriptions is enough to close the sign, consider the following:

- A series of five spiritual masses, one per week, might be needed by this client's egun. The italero should question this as an option for ebó.
- If the odu remains open, as adimú, the client must offer calabazas to the following orishas: Elegguá, Oshún, and Shangó. When the calabazas begin to rot, remove them, according to the appropriate method of disposal as determined by obí.
- Additional eboses could be required by Elegguá, Oshún, Shangó, Obatalá, Aganyú, or egun. The diviner should consider asking, for each in turn, "Ebó elese [orisha's name]?" If one of these orishas is marked, the appropriate ebó should then be marked as well.

If the odu still will not close, the diviner must turn to the eboses of the parent odu, Okana (see page 85), to find something that will fulfill the odu, bringing evolution.

## The Sixth Composite Odu of Okana, Okana Obara (1-6)

### The Proverbs of Okana Obara

- Do not lose your head, because the dead are waiting for you.
- Do not lose your head, because you will lose yourself.
- Do not lose your head.
- If you don't lose your head, you can save yourself.
- The favor that you have done will cost you your life.
- There are times when one should show a hard hand and times when one should show a gentle hand.
- The dead are walking.
- Only when the hand goes down does the drum sound; when the hand goes up, the drum is silent.
- Do not lose your head, because death is waiting for you.
- Lose your head and you will lose yourself.
- Death is looking for a new victim.

### The Message of Okana Obara

Okana Obara is opened when an initial casting of Okana, one mouth, is followed by Obara, six mouths. The letter is also known as Okanran Obara and Kanran Obara. Among the many stories associated with this odu is one about the goat. He wanted to be popular and spent his time doing favors for others. The good he did was never returned, and the goat lost his own head. In this letter's lore, even Shangó gave away too much of himself, and as was the case for the goat, it cost him his head.

When this odu opens on the mat, the diviner must pay homage to Shangó by saying, "Maferefún Shangó! Kawo kabiosile!" Shangó's aché is essential to the client's evolution; however, his help will come neither easily nor cheaply. The diviner also says, "Maferefún Orisha Oko!" Okana Obara makes the earth hot and ready to swallow up the client; Orisha Oko controls the fecundity of the earth and so can offer assistance to the client. Finally, the diviner should say, "Maferefún Elegguá! Maferefún Ogún! Maferefún Orúnmila!" All three of these spirits stand up in this letter. Although he does not speak directly in the diloggún, Orúnmila could be pointing this person toward Ifá. This issue should be explored with a babalawo.

Know that this sign brings no iré. It signals that death is searching for a victim, and all who are close to the client are in danger. While odu marks the client as the source of this pattern, such is its strength that it enfolds all about him. At this moment, none is closer to this person than those sitting at the mat. Death now knows them all and will stalk them one by one. Those in the diviner's home are also in danger, but they will not suffer the more volatile essences of this odu. Know that everyone concerned will be plagued with bad luck, setbacks, and suspicious circumstances. All must avoid darkness (physical and spiritual), underhanded behavior, moral and legal transgressions, and accidents (brought by one's own hands or the hands of others). All forms of violence, even arguments, should be avoided. Okana Obara is a sign demanding secrecy, but not the kind required by covert operations or unethical actions. Remember that punishments are severe in Okana's family, with this odu bringing death as the ultimate equalizer.

Okana Obara alludes to the fact that the client's physical head has been separated from his spiritual head; there is a vast gulf, a dark chasm, between these two parts of himself. Without his spiritual head watching over its earthly counterpart, the client is left to guide himself through the trials and tribulations around him. If the physical head gets too hot, there will be nothing to keep him safe and out of harm's way. Without focus, he will lose his life.

This is also a letter of cyclic events. It flags multiple rhythms playing through the client's life. Many liken these events to the playing of a drum. "Only when the hand goes down does the drum sound; when the hand goes up, the drum is silent." The first half of this proverb alludes to those drastic circumstances calling this person to attention, those moments in which anger, fear, surprise, and even manic happiness can strike him. The second half of the proverb tells us that after each major event in this person's life, there can be a period of rest, silence, and recovery. But just as the beat of the drum depends on the drummer's own whim and sense of rhythm, so is the client at the mercy of his own fate for these periods of events and nonevents in his life.

The following considerations should also be explored with the client for whom Okana Obara has fallen:

- To save himself, the client in this odu must work to change his own nature. He is too good, too forgiving, and too giving. He must refuse to do favors for others and must work instead to collect the debts that are owed to him.
- This sign tells the diviner that many of the client's relationships are inherently abusive. The ones who ask the most of the client are the ones who like him the least; he has enemies, and some pray for the day when he will fall. He must save himself while he still can and not worry about what happens to others around him.
- Money and financial concerns figure into this odu. If the sign comes in iré, it still marks an initial loss; however, the client will recover. This sign in iré hints at inheritances and winnings, so the client should play an occasional lottery ticket. *Note:* He should never buy more than one. *Okana* means "one"; therefore, only one is needed to bring blessings. Any more than one is simply a waste of resources.
- In osogbo, Okana Obara promises only financial setbacks. Money could even be lost or stolen. The client should try to work hard and save or he will fall behind.
- Neighbors pry in this odu, and many will want to know what happens inside the client's home. It is unwise for the client to be too friendly with his neighbors. The spiritual charm known as *ojo y lengua* ("the eye and the tongue") should be washed in Shangó's omiero and hung over the inside of the client's front door. It keeps away evil eyes and gossip. Daily, some jutía should be sprinkled to Elegguá and just outside the front door as well. If the client is a priest, he should give a ñame to Obatalá to bring peace. These precautions will ensure that his home is kept cool, safe, and protected.
- The client must care for his feet; they will ache and swell. If the odu has opened in an osogbo marked as ano or ikú, injury or disease could come to the body's extremities, with the feet and legs being the most vulnerable.
- If the client is male, women can be both his luck and his disgrace in Okana Obara. If he is with a lover now, much of the good that he has left in life is due to her; he must show appreciation for this. Another woman will soon be coming into this man's life. She will tempt him. He must stay true to his current lover or else all of his luck will be gone. Other women will come to ply him with affection and ask him to do things that

he knows he should not do. He must be wary of them, for they will bring tragedy.

## The Prohibitions of Okana Obara

- The color red is a danger in this odu. All who are present for the reading are prohibited from wearing anything red for the next twenty-one days. The client is prohibited from this color for the next three months or, if the reading is an itá, for life.
- The favor that one does can cost one's life; do not do favors for others. It is in this manner that all of one's luck, and even one's life, can be lost.
- Do not consume peanuts or cashews.

## The Eboses of Okana Obara

The diviner must prescribe a rogación for all those present at the reading, to take place immediately after delivery of the reading and closure of the oracle and before Elegguá's traditional Okana ebó (the red meat smeared with epó) is given to him. The diviner cleanses the head of the client first and then the heads of the initiates, in the order of eldest to youngest. Once this series of rogaciónes is complete, the eldest priest present cleanses the head of the italero. Until the rogaciónes are done, the room is sealed; initiates may neither enter nor leave the home. If any refuse the rogación, leaving before this ebó is finished, they take the entire osogbo of Okana with them, cleansing the diviner's home with their own bodies. They become the ones stalked by Ikú; however, to ensure that the osogbo does not try to return, the diviner should still complete the series of cleansings.

The client who has brought Okana Obara to the mat also has a series of eboses to fulfill. Obatalá brings forgiveness and salvation in this odu; the client must have a rogación at Obatalá's feet within a few days.* Upon its completion, the client should resolve to change his behaviors, wearing white for sixteen days as a symbol of his commitment.

As soon as possible, the client also needs to make ebó to Shangó through one of his priestesses (not a priest). To see if Shangó will mark a specific offering, the italero must ask, "Ebó elese Shangó?" If the answer is yes, the diviner should use the shells to mark the appropriate offering. If the answer is no, the priestess whom the client seeks out must dictate the ebó. If the client is an initiate, he should also give his own Shangó a white ceramic horse as soon as possible.

If the client is an initiate, he is marked to receive Orisha Oko. The reception of this orisha is not optional; it is mandatory in this sign.

Finally, if this person has young children, they are in danger from this odu. Each should be given a rogación before Obatalá immediately.† Know that each child is now marked for ocha, and to evolve, each must make ocha as soon as possible. Frequent offerings should be made to the godparent's Obatalá as well to ensure the spirit's goodwill.

Having explained all these prescriptions, the diviner now has his first chance to close the odu. If this letter refuses closure, Shangó or Obatalá could be standing up for more specific eboses. The diviner should ask of each, "Ebó elese [orisha's name]?" If the answer to either is yes, he should mark the ebó they require.

If the oracle still will not close and the client is an aleyo, the diviner should turn to the eboses of the parent odu, Okana (see page 85). Something there is needed for this person's evolution.

If the client is an initiate who already has received Orisha Oko and, thus, was not marked to receive this orisha now, Orisha Oko might require ebó, and the diviner must ask, "Ebó elese Orisha Oko?" If the answer is yes, the diviner must mark the appropriate ebó.

If the odu continues to remain open, the reception of one or more orishas who speak in Okana (see the list on page 42) might be necessary. Naming the orishas one by one, the diviner should ask, "Koshe

---

*A rogación known as *sodidé* (a Lucumí word meaning "to arise") should be performed for the client if the osogbo is severe. Sodidé not only cleanses one's head but also elevates one's soul. To give a rogación sodidé, the priest begins at the feet, not the head, and works upward to the head. In the odu Okana, a rogación sodidé should always be given at the shrine of either Obatalá or the guardian orisha.

†Again, if the osogbo of 1-6 is severe, perform the rogación *sodidé* to elevate each child's soul.

[orisha's name]?" Once a spirit's reception is marked, the odu should again be asked for closure.

If these eboses are not enough to close the odu, the diviner should turn to the eboses of the parent odu, Okana, to find a way of bringing closure to the oracle.

## The Seventh Composite Odu of Okana, Okana Odí (1-7)

### The Proverbs of Okana Odí

- You are trying for the impossible.
- You have wealth and fortune, but you are not lucky in love.
- One who dreams with the dead or with the sea cannot fear either one.

### The Message of Okana Odí

While most patterns of Okana can be dangerous and volatile, Okana Odí is one of the few carrying hidden iré. To find the blessings, the client must remain cool and calm; he must listen to all that the diviner has to say and he must make ebó in a timely manner. This odu marks the birth of a true diloggún diviner. Divination is a skill this person will and should acquire. Yet this is also the letter in which a hole is dug; when it opens in osogbo, the diviner knows that he sits before a client who faces severe dangers. How did this person come by this osogbo? Okana Odí says that this person reaches for impossible things. While reaching in itself is not bad (the diviner would not want to discourage him from dreaming), the client reaches for so many things beyond his grasp that he misses those things within his grasp. To save him from exhaustion, the orishas have closed many of the roads in his life; once ebó is made, they will slowly open them again. The diviner must advise the client, however, that he must slow down his pace; life is meant to be savored, not devoured. The diviner should tell him that large goals, while overwhelming in the beginning, are more easily obtained when broken into smaller ones. If he heeds these words, his life will become cooler and sweeter.

The following points should also be explored with the client:

- This client has a love that was denied due to friends, family, or society. He has paid many times over for this.
- This person will soon be slandered by a sibling of blood or ocha. He should not return evil with evil. He must let the godparents know what is happening, and then leave everything at the feet of the orishas.
- Yemayá is this person's salvation. He should leave all his troubles at her feet so she can fight. The client must not fight his own wars.
- If the client's mother is deceased, her spirit is close to him.
- Insomnia and bad dreams plague this person.

### The Prohibitions of Okana Odí

- Do not eat the following foods: shellfish, rabbit, rooster, fish, alcohol, coffee, the tail of animals, or the heads of animals. Do not consume any food with blood.
- Do not enter the woods without first offering a sacrifice.
- Do not do collective or volunteer work.

### The Eboses of Okana Odí

Okana Odí is complex, and when trying to close the oracle or mark ebó the diviner will need to keep several options in mind. The first considerations depend on the client's mother. If she is still alive, odu demands that she sit before Yemayá for a rogación. To this rogación the priest should add four live snails. If the mother is not in the religion, or if she will not consent to this rogación, the client must have the rogación in her name. If the client's mother is deceased, the following eboses should be done as soon as possible to bring rest to her soul and evolution for the client:

- The client must have a rogación before Yemayá's shrine in his mother's name. Add four live snails to the traditional elements.
- After the rogación, the client should set up a

white table in the mother's name and offer a full mass in her honor.

- At the end of the mass, a feathered animal must be sacrificed to the client's mother at his egun shrine. If the mass was not done in the client's house, he should bring his *opá ikú* (the ritual staff used in egun worship) to be fed in the priest's home. If the client does not have an opá, he is now marked to receive it as ebó.
- The day after the sacrifice, the client must return to the priest's house to have a rogación for himself before Yemayá's shrine.
- After the rogación, Yemayá Asesu* should be fed feathers in the kitchen-sink drain. Unless the priest's path of Yemayá is Asesu, his own Yemayá may not partake of this sacrifice.

If this series of prescriptions is not enough to close Okana Odí, there could be further issues with Yemayá. To see if she requires anything else, the diviner should ask, "Ebó elese Yemayá?" If possible, whatever Yemayá marks as ebó should be given at the ocean or the largest body of water possible.

Note that once all these eboses are done, the client must never again neglect his mother in life or in death; she risked her own life to give him birth and, if for no other reason, must be loved for this.

If the oracle still will not close, the diviner should turn to the eboses for the parent odu, Okana (see page 85). Something there is necessary to bring evolution to this person.

# The Eighth Composite Odu of Okana, Okana Ogbe (1-8)

## The Proverbs of Okana Ogbe

- The war is silent and you already know it.
- Do not ask that which you already know.
- When you think you are about to be robbed, shut your door tightly and use your head.
- What you are coming to see you will already know ahead of time.

*Like Eleggua, Yemaya has many avatars. Asesu is one of them.

## The Message of Okana Ogbe

When a casting of one mouth, Okana, is followed by a casting of eight mouths, Eji Ogbe, the odu Okana Ogbe is open. This letter is also known by the names Okana Unle and Okana l'Ogbe. Opening thus, the diviner begins the reading with a proverb: It is not wise to ask that which is already known. What does the client already know? He knows there is a silent war going on. He knows he is in danger of robbery. He knows he might have to steal something before too much time has passed. The diviner must insist that this person keep all the doors to his home closed and locked and all other entrances, including windows, secure, even when he is at home. The client must be warned not to steal, for theft will only aggravate his situation. He must think through all actions before undertaking them. He must be cautious against accidents, and to avoid a fatal accident he must travel as little as possible. The diviner must tell the client that the orishas are trying to help him as much as they can, but they need attention (ebó) in order to work as well as they should.

If Okana Ogbe has opened in iré, the letter points out the possibilities of longevity, a good life, and all the wonderful things that Olófin has to offer—if the client follows the advice of the orishas. Even in iré, however, these blessings can be transient, and every bit of good will be followed by something bad.

If Okana Ogbe comes in osogbo, the diviner must tell the client that paralysis in either his body or his environment is a danger. He may find himself without work, basic necessities, or even a home if he is not careful. An ebó will help raise up this person so that this osogbo is not suffered.

The following issues should also be explored with the client:

- If the client owns a dog, he must be told to care for this animal well, even spoil it. This dog has a keen intelligence burning within, and it knows more about what goes on in the client's home than the client himself does. Whenever the client is tempted to talk freely to others about things that should not be spoken, he should talk to the dog instead; the dog will never betray his master. If treated well and with respect, this animal could save the life of its master one day.

- This person will be trusted with secrets; he will overhear many important conversations. These secrets will be empowering. However, the client must not share what he knows with anyone.
- To avoid tragedy, the client must keep his eyes and ears open at all times. In this way may he save his own head.

## The Prohibitions of Okana Ogbe

- If Okana Ogbe is in osogbo, especially ano or ikú, the following foods are prohibited: eggs, sweet potatoes, peanuts, fruits with grainy seeds, sesame seeds, white beans, pork, tripe, fish, animal heads and tails, reheated foods, alcohol, white drinks, and palm wine.
- If the sign opens in iré, alcohol should be ingested only in moderation.
- If this reading is the itá of an initiate, alcohol is forbidden for life.

## The Eboses of Okana Ogbe

As soon as possible, the person opening in Okana Ogbe must have a rogación at the feet of Obatalá and then offer some type of adimú to the orisha. For the next eight days the client must dress in white to seal in the iré that Obatalá can bring. This mandatory ebó may need to be personalized, and the diviner should ask several questions to see if any adaptations are necessary. To see if the head needs to be fed, the priest must ask, "Eborí?" If the answer is yes, in addition to the materials for the rogación the client needs to bring two white pigeons or white doves for his head. If eborí is prescribed by the odu, after the eight days in white have passed the client must return for one final rogación at Obatalá's feet. Also, Obatalá might wish to have a specific ebó, not just an adimú chosen by the client. To see if he would prefer something specific, the diviner should ask, "Ebó elese Obatalá?" If the answer is yes, this ebó should be marked by the diviner and presented with the final rogación after the eight days in white.

Obatalá and Elegguá might stand up together for ebó in this odu. The diviner must ask, "Ebó elese Obatalá y Elegguá?" If the answer is yes, the appropriate ebó is a rooster for Elegguá and two white pigeons or a white rooster for Obatalá. Complete this ebó on the same day as the initial rogación; present the sacrifice before giving the rogación. The orishas should be fed side by side, but no part of the pigeons, if they are used, should touch the image of Elegguá.

Having made these prescriptions, the diviner may now try to close the odu. If the sign refuses closure and the client is an initiate, the diviner turns to the eboses of the parent odu, Okana (see page 85), to find a way to bring closure to the oracle.

If the client is an aleyo and odu refuses closure, there is one final avenue of exploration. The diviner must thoroughly consider which orisha is standing up to protect the client in this odu. If the sign offered larishe, the diviner considers the spirit to whom larishe is mandated. In Okana Ogbee, it is not unusual for that spirit to be Obatalá. If the client has not yet had a bajado, Obatalá could be his guardian orisha. The diviner must prescribe eboses to the guardian orisha so that this person can find evolution. Also, if this client has a daughter, she could be a child of Oshún, and this should be explored by the diviner.

If these considerations are not enough to close the oracle, the diviner may now turn to the eboses of the parent odu, Okana (see page 85).

# The Ninth Composite Odu of Okana, Okana Osá (1-9)

## The Proverbs of Okana Osá

- Failures from the past will impede the future.
- Envy breeds gossip.
- Divorce [is coming].
- Friend will kill friend.
- Treason, revolution, and falsehood [are coming].
- A fight between husband and wife can bring only tragedy.
- Your best friend is your worst enemy.

## The Message of Okana Osá

When a casting of one mouth (Okana) is followed by a casting of nine mouths (Osá), the sign Okana Osá has fallen on the mat. In this odu the diviner must say, "Maferefún Elegguá! Maferefún Oyá! Maferefún Aganyú!" for all three spirits are strong here. The diviner should point out to the client that this sign brings up special issues with Oyá and Aganyú; the two orishas stand close, and they love the client dearly. They are now his guardians, his protectors, and his teachers. If the client is an aleyo whose head has not been marked, one of these two might claim it. Oyá will bring issues with egun to the mat; she also brings issues with the market and the breath. Aganyú comes as the volcano and marks explosions in this client's life. Both orishas must be saluted and propitiated, and eboses must be marked to thank them for their assistance.

Shangó is also firm in this odu, and the diviner must say, "Maferefún Shangó! Kawo kabiosile!" This letter tells of a time when Shangó, Ogún, and Ochosi hunted game for Obatalá during a period of drought and famine. All three killed game; all three ate their kills without sharing. Yet when they came back before Obatalá with empty hands, only Shangó owned up to his failure. For this, his admission of guilt, Shangó received his crown, while Ogún and Ochosi were denied to wear the same.

A variety of issues must be explored with the client who opens in Okana Osá. First, the diviner must tell him that a great treason could come to his life involving two other people. The easiest way to avoid this tragedy is for him to refuse to be a third party in anything; however, he will find that this is all but impossible. If he does become involved in some type of threesome that brings tragedy or despair, he must own up to his actions. If he admits his guilt, he will emerge unscathed and crowned, like Shangó.

This odu signals quick changes in luck and life; it is the explosion going off daily in the home. Its nature is transience, yet the client at the mat must stand firm against it. Enemies will come and go while this letter is in effect, and the client must guard himself so that he does not fall victim to their evil.

Know that Okana Osá marks a client who will become a great diviner. This person will learn to read the shells, to prescribe eboses, and to placate osogbos. This knowledge will not come easily; perhaps the greatest gift this letter can bring is the gift of empathy, for when the time comes for this person to cast his first hand, he will have experienced many of life's tragedies and he will know what it is like to come before the orishas when all else has been abandoned. He will receive wisdom not only from the elders but also at the hands of the orishas themselves. Despair and loss can be life's best teachers.

The following points should also be explored with the client:

- Married couples tend to argue while this odu is in effect. To avoid arguments, the client must be good to his lover for the next twenty-eight days. Know that in this sign, one's best friend can and should be one's lover; the client should consider this daily so that nothing bad happens.
- If the client wants to achieve anything special, he must seek out the orishas for advice. Because it is not wise to consult the diloggún too often, he may bring important questions to the orishas with the obí. He must make no important or life-altering decisions without consulting them first. Remember that in this pattern, Oyá and Aganyú have the client's best interests in mind.
- There are many evil eyes and tongues upon this person. The diviner must mark ebó to solve osogbo. Because Shangó and Elegguá both speak in this odu, if gossip and rumors become too harsh, the client should make an ebó to both with a cow's tongue. They will shut the mouths of all who speak evil about him.
- While the client will have to work hard once this odu has fallen, the sign itself indicates that hard work will pay off in the end. It is important that amid all the change and chaos that comes, the client keeps his eyes set on one important goal. Do this, and his environment will not overwhelm him.
- The person for whom this odu has fallen lives outside the law. He must change his ways or suffer.

## The Prohibitions of Okana Osá

- The following foods should be avoided: rooster, mutton, liquor, white and red beans, and coconut.
- Do not run, carry weapons, open doors after dark, smoke, go to places where death may be found, or let sick people sleep in one's house.
- Follow all the prohibitions of both Oyá and Aganyú; remember that one of these might become one's own crown.

## The Eboses of Okana Osá

Okana Osá focuses on five spiritual forces: egun, Oyá, Aganyú, Shangó, and Obatalá. The most important issues center on the egun. No matter the orientation of this sign, they demand ebó. The client must host a series of spiritual masses in his home to bring the ancestors peace, evolution, and refreshment. If the client does not have a bóveda, he must. If he does not have an opá ikú, he must. An unadorned shrine is as useless as no shrine at all; daily, the client should provide fresh water, candles, cigars, flowers, and prayers for those that brought him to birth. Before ending this session, the diviner must allow egun to personalize the sign with their own sacrifice, asking, "Ebó elese egun?" If the answer is yes, he must mark the ebó they require. Once the dead are fulfilled, the client will begin to evolve.

Okana Osá is volatile, affecting the head. As soon as possible the client must have a rogación at Obatalá's feet. The rogación must involve nine elements to strengthen the head sufficiently. As soon as this rogación is complete, the client should give an adimú of nine cool fruits on a white platter to Oyá and then to Aganyú, setting each platter over each orisha's sopera.

If Okana Osá opens in an osogbo and will not close, Obatalá, Oyá, or Aganyú could be demanding additional offerings. To investigate this option, the diviner must ask of each, "Ebó elese [orisha's name]?"

The continued refusal of the oracle to close demands that the diviner dig deeper into the odu to find something to bring closure. If the client is an initiate, he could have additional issues with Oyá or Aganyú. If he has not received either spirit, the reception of one or both could be essential to his evolution. The diviner must ask "Koshé Oyá?" and then "Koshé Aganyú?" to see if either is necessary.

Having exhausted all these options, if the letter still does not offer closure, the diviner must then turn to the eboses of the parent odu, Okana (see page 85). Something there is needed for the client's evolution.

# The Tenth Composite Odu of Okana, Okana Ofún (1-10)

## The Proverbs of Okana Ofún

- He who aims at too much gets very little.
- He who is overly fond of gold will never get any.
- He who embraces a lot cannot carry much more.
- He who embraces a lot cannot squeeze very hard.
- He who wants a lot accomplishes very little.
- He who strives for gold gets copper instead.

## The Message of Okana Ofún

Okana Ofún, also known as Okana'fún, Kanran Ofún, and Okanran Ofún, opens when a casting of one mouth, Okana, is followed by a casting of ten mouths, Ofún. It is a dangerous pattern, filled with warnings for the client. He must obey the following prescriptions for twenty-eight days:

- A child is in danger. He must be saved, for one day he will do something special.
- The client has bizarre, surreal dreams, some of which may serve as warnings against danger.
- Evil magic or witchcraft is in the street or at the front door, and the client must be wary of strange objects and powders.
- The client must be cautious against all accidents, especially when driving. If a dog or other animal is killed while he is behind the wheel, he should stop and take care of the body properly. If the animal is still alive, he must take it to a veterinarian.

Additionally, the following items should be explored with this person:

- The client's lover or spouse is a concern in this odu. Okana Ofún signals that the client should treat his significant other well. Marital arguments could escalate into something more severe at this time.
- The client spends too much time on the street; he should go home before sunset. When there, he should spend quality time with family and close friends. The street holds too much danger for him now, and while he is there, he cannot be home taking care of personal business.
- The client must respect his elders. Good advice comes from them; he must heed them.
- This person has a scar on his body; if this odu is not heeded, there will be another.
- In the client's extended family, an imperfect child might soon be born.
- Something important to the client will be lost unless he is vigilant over his personal affairs. Once it is lost, it will not be noticed or recovered until it is too late.

The diviner must tell the client that Okana Ofún brings danger and difficulty, and the orishas are loath to help because they have been disregarded in the past. The client must not ignore them now.

## The Prohibitions of Okana Ofún

- Do not consume the following: entrails, tripe, white beans, peanuts, eggs, sweet potatoes, rooster, mushrooms, and alcohol.
- Avoid places in which many people have died or places where both egun and ikú travel, such as funerals, cemeteries, hospitals, nursing homes, wakes, and memorials.
- Limit the amount of time spent in dark or poorly lit places. Make sure that the home is well lit at all times so that the dead do not gather, and keep the home clean and immaculate.
- When eating, feed the dead first so that they do not feast on one's plate.
- Do not open the door during mealtime, for in this way evil comes.
- Do not sleep in total darkness, and do not get up to open the door or answer the phone after retiring for the night.
- When going out during the day, do not wear ripped, torn, or mended clothes.
- When walking, be careful not to step on blood.

## The Eboses of Okana Ofún

Okana Ofún is a sign of poor housekeeping and hygiene. When this odu opens in an osogbo, the diviner must prescribe a thorough housecleaning in honor of the orishas. Beginning with the back of the house and working toward the front door, the client should scrub one room at a time, not forgetting to clean and sanitize closets, linens, clothes, drawers, rugs, corners, trash cans. He should wash and paint walls, shampoo carpets, and throw out anything that is broken, ripped, torn, or in bad repair. Once the physical cleansing is complete, the client should perform a spiritual cleansing of his home using elements such as candles, incense, holy water, two coconuts, and two white doves or white pigeons. After the physical and spiritual cleansings are complete, the client must never let his home fall into disarray again. To do so is to attract the negative forces that this cleansing removed.

Having made this prescription, the diviner may attempt to close the odu. If the oracle refuses closure, the following considerations should be investigated:

- Another option for ebó in Okana Ofún centers on the warriors. To determine if the warriors require ebó, the priest asks, "Ebó elese los guerreros?" If the answer is yes, the proper adimú is saraeko (see page 52).
- This odu can flag issues with Obatalá. The client should be given a rogación of ten elements at this orisha's feet. Once this is done, a white seven-day candle and an adimú of cool fruits should be left at his shrine.
- If the rogación is not enough to close the letter, the diviner should ask, "Ebó elese orí?" If the answer is yes, two white pigeons or white doves should be fed to the client's head to give it strength.

Once this list is exhausted, if the odu will not close, the diviner must turn to the eboses of the parent odu, Okana (see page 85), to find ebó that will bring closure to the oracle.

## The Eleventh Composite Odu of Okana, Okana Owani (1-11)

### The Proverb of Okana Owani

- He who is stubborn and a pest ends up bad; his bones will rot in jail.

### The Message of Okana Owani

When the initial casting of one mouth, Okana, precedes a second casting of eleven mouths, Owani, the odu Okana Owani is open on the mat. In this odu the diviner says, "Maferefún Elegguá! Maferefún Ogún! Maferefún Babaluaiye!" for all three are strong in this odu, and the aché of each might be needed to overcome osogbo.

In this sign, even the most casual client has unresolved issues with the warriors, and if he has not received them, he must. Also, the issues pending with Babaluaiye are so strong that the diviner will need to explore the client's relationship with him. In Okana Owani, it is unusual for a reading to close out unless extensive spiritual work with these orishas is prescribed; the diviner must keep this in mind as well.

Before going into the meat of this session, the diviner must ask the client if he has a large rock in his yard or perhaps one he found and brought home. If the answer is yes, two issues must be considered. First, someone may have died where the rock was found; this stone could be a powerful spirit capable of working good (in iré) or ill (in osogbo) for the client. Second, the stone might be the foundation for an Elegguá. The client must bring the stone to the italero to determine this information.

The diviner must also realize that he faces one who thinks poorly of this religion and of the orishas. These negative thoughts may even have found their way into his words. The diviner must advise this client that he must never think or speak ill of this religion again, nor may he blaspheme against the orishas or God. To do so will incur the wrath of those spirits from whom he seeks help. Even though the orishas are slow to anger, once angered they are difficult to appease. The client is a wanderer: He roams from faith to faith looking for help and commits himself to a religion only as long as help is forthcoming. When life becomes hard, he begins to wander again. His spiritual life is a mess; his head is overwhelmed and his soul is laden with burden. In Okana Owani, if the client can truly put his heart into the religion and his faith in the orishas, he will evolve. His evolution will be slow, but it will come.

When this letter comes in osogbo, it is very specific as to the danger the client is facing. For the next eleven days, the client should avoid arguments with other people; he should live a monastic life, venturing out of the house only for necessities such as work and shopping. He must speak no evil during this time. Not following this prohibition is an invitation to all types of accidents, violence, and even altercations with the law. The client must not raise his hands in anger toward anyone in his family, for in a blind rage someone could be hurt or killed, and the person with whom one fights will never forgive. A shove or a push could result in death—one way that Okana Owani might bring the client to the hands of justice. The client must make an ebó to Elegguá or Ochosi immediately and follow these prohibitions.

The house in which the client lives is cold, damp, and dark. Already this person thinks about moving; now he must move. The home's atmosphere is not fit for dwelling. If the client is a man, his lover cares for him very much, yet is often unacknowledged. If the client is a woman, she loves her partner with all her heart, yet feels slighted most of the time. Communication is needed between the two, and arguments must be avoided if the relationship is to be saved.

The following points should also be explored with the client:

- This odu speaks of inheritances and how they could be lost. If the client is the youngest of three siblings, one day the older siblings will

cheat the client out of money from an inheritance. If a parent or another family elder dies, the client must ensure that his interests are protected or he will be left with nothing. Note that if this client is the eldest of three, the diviner must warn him not to cheat his youngest sibling out of his or her inheritance. The orishas will punish him for this.
- This person has many goals and detailed plans; however, he never acts on them as he should. This causes him to lose much of his luck.

## The Prohibitions of Okana Owani

- Do not consume sesame seeds, grains, fruits with grainy seeds, alcohol, corn, or red foods. When cooking any meal, prepare extra food in case unexpected visitors show up. If visitors do not come, give some of the extra food to egun and save the rest for a later time.
- The roads are too hot and volatile for travel when this letter appears, and danger comes early in the morning. To avoid accidents, do not drive before noon.
- Do not despise anyone; treat everyone well. Be gracious to those who visit unexpectedly.
- At all costs, avoid promiscuity.

## The Eboses of Okana Owani

Depending on the client's situation, there are a few options for ebó to consider. First, if the client is sick or if the sign opened in ano or ikú, offer Babaluaiye a sacrifice. If this person has not received Babaluaiye, the diviner must ask the following questions, in this order:

- First the diviner asks, "Koshé eleke de Babaluaiye?" If the answer is yes, the client must have a rogación before this orisha's shrine. After this, he must receive Babaluaiye's eleke around his neck.
- Regardless of the answer to the first question, the priest now asks, "Ebó elese Babaluaiye?" If the answer to this is yes, the diviner must mark an appropriate offering.
- Regardless of the answer to the second question, the diviner now asks, "Koshé Babaluaiye?" If the answer is yes, the client must receive this orisha.

No matter how the diloggún answers these questions, its prescriptions must be fulfilled in the order in which they were marked. If both the eleke and ebó were prescribed, they must be fulfilled on the same day. The rogación and eleke are given first, and then the client presents his ebó. The reception of Babaluaiye, being an expensive ceremony, may wait for some time until the client has the derecho; however, if a great deal of time must pass between the opening of odu and the reception of the orisha, the client must give frequent adimú to Babaluaiye so that he knows the client is serious about fulfilling ebó.

The next set of concerns center on Elegguá and Ochosi. These two orishas stand up in odu to direct the client toward his destiny; at this time, their main concern is bringing him out of osogbo. To see if they require anything as ebó, the diviner should ask, "Ebó elese Elegguá y Ochosi?" If the answer is yes, he must mark the required ebó with the shells. Since these two spirits take responsibility for guiding the client in this odu, their ebó should be fulfilled immediately.

The final option for ebó in this sign comes with egun. To see if they require anything, the priest should ask, "Ebó elese egun?" If the answer is yes, the diviner should mark the appropriate offering with the diloggún. If egun will not mark a specific ebó, in Okana Owani the proper offering for them is a series of spiritual masses. These must be performed weekly in the client's home and continued until the egun stand up in a mass to say that they have had enough.

If the client is an aleyo and the odu will not not close, the diviner must now turn to the eboses of the parent odu, Okana (see page 85), to search for something that will bring closure. If the client is a priest or priestess, the diviner has one final option for ebó: the reception of Ochosi. To see if this is needed, he asks, "Koshé Ochosi?" If the answer is no, or if the the marking of Ochosi's reception is still not enough to close the odu, the diviner must then turn to the eboses of the parent odu, Okana (see page 85).

## The Twelfth Odu of Okana, Okana Ejila (1-12)

### The Proverbs of Okana Ejila

- Do not try to put out a fire with a mouthful of water.
- More money comes, and more is wanted.
- Do not fight fire with a few drops of water.

### The Message of Okana Ejila

When one mouth on the mat is followed by twelve, the odu Okana Ejila (also known as Okana Oturupon) is open. Both Shangó and Aganyú speak strongly in this sign; they advise the client to listen well because what they say will be said only once. This sign speaks of tragedy, revolution, entanglement, evil, and bad luck. When it falls on the mat, we say that one should not try to put out a fire with a mouthful of water, and until now this is what the client has been doing in his life. He must be encouraged to know his limits and work accordingly, to know what is possible and stay within his resources. Many pressures will come to bear on this person, which will put him at his breaking point. He should not be afraid to ask for help and advice, especially from the orishas and the elders of this religion, for with their guidance most things can be overcome. But the client must be careful, for in this pattern temporary instability and insanity are foretold.

The client should watch where he walks in the street, for Shangó and Aganyú will put something there that will be this person's salvation. When it is found, he must guard it well.

If this letter falls in iré, from this moment on the client will prosper and evolve in life as long as he heeds the advice of the orishas. He will have many enemies in his life, but they can be overcome.

If an osogbo falls in this sign, the client is in danger of fires and accidents. He must do ebó quickly and be cautious in all things. There will be much weeping over financial difficulties, but the orishas say not to weep. He must be sure to thank the spirits for the blessings that he has; in this way, more blessings will come. An osogbo also indicates that this person has issues with Ifá that must be resolved. As soon as possible, the diviner must take him to a babalawo.

The following points should also be explored with the client:

- This odu signals hypochondria. The client always complains about minor health issues, and many of these are not issues at all. He must be careful lest he will bring real sickness upon himself.
- If the client is planning a journey, he must have a rogación before Obatalá. Otherwise, he could suffer mishap.
- The client desires to moves away from his present home. While this is a good idea, the client is not properly prepared for such a move. He must take his time and plan the move carefully.
- In this sign, the client's worst enemies eat and drink in the same place as he. He must be wary.

### The Prohibitions of Okana Ejila

- Avoid the following foods: ram, eels, fowl, okra, pumpkins, squash, calabazas, and papaya. If food or drink is offered by a stranger, client, or coworker, accept but do not consume it. Observe the traditional taboos, and especially the food prohibitions, given to initiates of Oyá. In this odu, Oyá can be one's salvation if she is given proper respect.
- Do not argue, fight, gossip, travel, or stop fights.
- When the child of another cries, do not comfort it. Accusations will be made. Do not baby-sit for anyone.
- Anything that is broken must be thrown in the trash. Do not keep broken or burned items at home.
- When it rains, do not get wet.
- Do not handle explosives or gunpowder.

## The Eboses of Okana Ejila

The opening of Okana Ejila on the mat flags special considerations, and the diviner must make the following ebó prescriptions. First, this odu is so hot that only Obatalá can bring coolness to the client's life. As soon as possible, this person must have a rogación before Obatalá's shrine. At the ceremony's conclusion, he must receive a fresh eleke of Obatalá around his neck. If the client comes to the oracle with illness already upon him, or if ano or ikú is the osogbo that has opened, he must receive an idé (a bracelet beaded in the colors of the orisha to whom it is dedicated) of Obatalá as well, to be worn on his left wrist and never removed. (Barring the reception of Obatalá through santo lavado, Okana Ejila is one of the few letters that allow an aleyo to wear an *idé* of santo.) The client may also need to make ebó to Obatalá once the rogación and reception of these items are complete. To determine if ebó is required, the diviner must ask, "Ebó elese Obatalá?" If the answer is yes, he should use the shells to mark the appropriate ebó.

Two other orishas also demand attention in this odu: Elegguá and Shangó. Before attempting to close the oracle, the diviner must give each the option to claim sacrifice, asking, "Ebó elese [orisha's name]?" If the answer is yes, the appropriate offering must be marked with the shells.

If after these prescriptions have been made the odu refuses closure, the client might need a *niche osain* (an amulet made of herbal, mineral, and animal substances and beaded in the colors of the orisha to whom it is consecrated) to accompany the eleke of one or more orishas. For each of the orishas for whom an eleke has been marked (more than one spirit might mark a niche osain), the diviner should ask, "Koshé niche osain de [orisha's name]?" If the answer is yes, the niche osain should be made with twenty-one herbs sacred to that orisha, washed in omiero, and fed with the otanes of that spirit. Note that this niche osain should be given when the eleke is invested.

If the client is an aborisha and the oracle still refuses closure, the diviner must turn to the eboses of the parent odu, Okana (see page 85), to find closure for the session. If the client is an initiate, the diviner has two final options in the composite itself. Both concern the orisha Osain. First, this spirit might be standing up to claim ebó, and to see if this is necessary, the diviner must ask, "Ebó elese Osain?" If the answer is yes, the diviner uses the diloggún to mark the appropriate offering. If the answer is no, the final option is Osain's reception, and the priest must ask, "Koshé Osain?" Claiming neither of these, the oracle is directing the diviner to look to the parent odu, Okana (see page 85), to bring closure to the session.

# The Thirteenth Composite Odu of Okana, Okana Metanla (1–13)

## The Proverbs of Okana Metanla

- You are a prisoner of ocha.
- That which you complain about is your own fault.
- Death comes through the mouth, by poison.
- The irresponsible leader is killed so another may take his place.
- The careless leader is killed and his position is usurped.
- The incompetent boss loses his employees through anarchy.

## The Message of Okana Metanla

When a casting of one mouth is followed by thirteen mouths, the odu Okana Metanla (also known as Okanat Irete) is open. It marks a client for whom making ocha is both destiny and salvation. Commitment to this path will be but the first step to leaving behind the unpleasantness of the past and opening the doors to a more bountiful future. Even if the client has come only for a reading, the diviner should spend some time explaining these things, the basic precepts of our faith. He must tell the client about the steps to becoming a priest or priestess: marking the orisha of the head, receiving the elekes from the godparent, and taking the initiation of the warriors.

The diviner should advise the client to look at all areas in his life where leadership is held: friendships, relationships, work, and so on. If there is any area in which he feels that he is a leader, the "boss," he needs to have caution, for the leadership in these dealings is about to be overthrown. This could mean that both friendships and love affairs will come to an end, and if the client is in a supervisory position at work, there could be either a demotion or loss of employment altogether.

## The Prohibitions of Okana Metanla

- Avoid the following foods: hen, banana, okra, black-eyed peas, corn, and corn flour.
- Beware of adultery; do not seduce or flirt with another's spouse, for this will bring osogbo into one's life. Do not date women with fair skin or skin that is fairer than one's one. If dating another who has recently broken up with a lover, ensure that the former relationship is over before beginning something new. In this letter, the ex-lover comes back to reclaim the former, and often the ex-lover wins.
- Do not entertain guests. If there are guests in the home, do not throw things at them; hand things to them instead. Do not let guests sleep in one's home overnight, because in this letter someone who does not live in one's house could die there.

## The Eboses of Okana Metanla

In this letter, the client needs to have the elekes, and with them he should receive the eleke of Babaluaiye. He must also receive the warriors as soon as possible, for they will fight all the osogbos predicted in this sign.

If the client has a dog, he has marked himself for the reception of Babaluaiye; until this orisha can be received, the client should make frequent ebó to him. To find out if the spirit wants a particular ebó, the diviner should ask, "Ebó elese Babaluaiye?" If the answer is yes, the diviner uses the diloggún to mark the appropriate offering.

If these prescriptions are not enough to bring the odu's closure, the diviner must consider the options for ebó in the parent odu, Okana (see page 85).

# The Fourteenth Composite Odu of Okana, Okana Merinla (1-14)

## The Proverb of Okana Merinla

- You will sell your own luck.

## The Message of Okana Merinla

When one mouth comes to the mat followed by fourteen, Okana Merinla (also known as Okana Ika) is open. In osogbo, this sign emphasizes all the warnings and prohibitions of the parent odu, Okana. Even if the sign comes in iré, it should be treated as having all the precautions of Okana in osogbo.

The major warning that should concern the diviner is that against robbery and confrontations with the law, because loss, revolution, and vengeance are all foreshadowed here. The client's own "karma" is mounting up against him. If the eboses are done in a timely manner, however, the effects of the osogbo may be delayed and lightened to a degree. The client must still follow all the prohibitions and advice given at this time.

Curiously enough, one for whom this letter falls can be an extremely lucky person, but his luck is given away through stupidity. To prove his luck, the client may wish to play an occasional game of chance, such as the lottery. His winnings will not be big, but he will have enough small wins to prove that there is a chance for recovery from present circumstances.

## The Prohibitions of Okana Merinla

- Avoid pork and monkey meat.
- When dining, do not eat or drink from small bowls. When food is served in a small bowl, ask, if it is appropriate, for a large mug instead. If it is not appropriate, do not consume the food.
- This letter enforces fidelity to one's spouse. If one has been considering divorce, reconsider,

and stay in the relationship for at least another three months. Let the spouse instigate divorce if he or she wants to leave. If this reading is an itá, choose one's mate wisely, for divorce is now prohibited.

## The Eboses of Okana Merinla

The larishe and eboses prescribed by Okana should be done swiftly, for this sign moves to bring osogbo quickly once identified. First, of course, the initial considerations for eboses in Okana must be investigated (see "Marking Ebó in Okana: Initial Considerations" on page 49). In addition:

- The client must never wear black. Instead, he should wear white as much as possible to honor Obatalá.
- The client needs to be taken to a babalawo immediately for a complete assessment by Ifá.

If the odu refuses closure even after these prescriptions, the elekes of one or more orishas speaking in this odu (see the list on page 42) could be necessary for protection. To find out if an eleke of any of these orishas is necessary, the diviner should ask of each, "Ebó eleke de [orisha's name]?" Note that more than one orisha could stand up in this odu to offer protection through his or her eleke. After marking an eleke, the diviner should explain to the client why this spirit is offering his or her protection in this odu (using his own aché to deliver this information). After explaining the relevant material to the client, the diviner may attempt closure again.

If this is not enough to close the oracle, those spirits who offered protection through their elekes might also be standing up for ebó. The diviner must ask each spirit for whom the client will receive an eleke, "Ebó elese [orisha's name]?" If the answer is yes, the diviner must mark appropriate sacrifice.

If none of these considerations brings closure, the divine must turn to the eboses of the parent odu, Okana (see page 85).

# The Fifteenth Composite Odu of Okana, Okana Marunla (1-15)

## The Proverbs of Okana Marunla

- Death is not far.
- There is no recuperation from exhaustion.

## The Message of Okana Marunla

When one mouth on the mat is followed by fifteen, the odu Okana Marunla (also known as Okana Iwori) is open. When it falls for an initiate, he is marked to give a drum for Shangó, who will save him from all osogbo, including death—and Ikú is not far away.

Recently, the client may have begun to save a lot of money without really knowing why; saving is out of character for this person. Unconsciously, he may have been putting away money to pay for initiations of the orishas and egun. While the odu demands that the client continue to work hard and save, it also demands that the client learn to honor the body and understand its need for rest, sleep, recreation, and proper nourishment. The diviner should not allow this person to become overextended through work, for the client will not recuperate from exhaustion. Nor will the client recuperate easily from poverty, despair, homelessness, or depression, so the quest for initiation into the orisha's mysteries must be tempered with patience. The priest or priestess who stands as a godparent to this person must ensure that the aborisha receives only that which is needed for his spiritual evolution at this time, and no more. Once the aborisha becomes involved more deeply in the religion, his enthusiasm must be tempered with restraint. He will become a santero when the time is right, and if ebó is done as needed, the orishas will reward his patience and faith with the means for initiation.

## The Prohibitions of Okana Marunla

- Do not eat yams, rooster, corn, and corn flour. Respect the sacrificial foods of the orishas, using them as offerings for the spirits and not as meals for oneself.

- When dining in the house of strangers, be wary of what is served, and make sure one knows how the food is prepared. Do not eat foods that are raw or not well cooked. Food offered with insistence should raise a flag. It must not be consumed, because intentionally or unintentionally, something could be wrong with it.
- Do not buy, carry, or own weapons. Be very wary of guns around children and teenagers, because there could be a fatal accident. If one has a handgun, sell or dispose of it. If one has a rifle or shotgun, keep it unloaded and under lock and key.
- Do not take or borrow the belongings of others. Do not pick up, use, or carry anything that belongs to another. Personal possessions should not be loaned out, and do not be generous with one's own money or belongings.
- Do not go out in the first rain after this odu opens; instead, stay home. After this, one may go out, but do not get wet in the rain for three months, or, if this reading is itá, ever.
- Do not seduce another's spouse or lover. Before having sex, make sure one knows one's intended lover. This person could have another lover on the side.
- Do not pretend to be rich or have money, and do not carry valuables or wear expensive jewelry in public. It will attract thieves.
- Have nothing to do with holes. Don't wear them, buy them, dig them, or walk over them.

## The Eboses of Okana Marunla

The larishe and eboses prescribed by Okana should be done swiftly, for this sign moves to bring osogbo quickly once identified. First, of course, the initial considerations for eboses in Okana must be investigated (see "Marking Ebó in Okana: Initial Considerations" on page 49). In addition:

- The diviner must find out if Shangó requires a specific ebó, asking, "Ebó elese Shangó?" If the answer is yes, the diviner uses the shells to mark the appropriate ebó. If the answer is no, the client should give an adimú (anything his heart tells him to give) to Shangó anyway to ensure the orisha's goodwill.
- The client needs to be taken to a babalawo immediately for a complete assessment by Ifá.

If the eboses prescribed thus far are not enough to close the oracle, the elekes of one or more orishas speaking in this odu (see the list on page 42) could be necessary for protection. To find out if an eleke of any of these orishas is necessary, the diviner should ask of each, "Ebó eleke de [orisha's name]?" Note that more than one orisha could stand up in this odu to offer protection through his or her eleke. After marking an eleke, the diviner should explain to the client why this spirit is offering his or her protection in this odu (using his own aché to deliver this information). After explaining the relevant material to the client, the diviner may attempt closure again.

If this is not enough to close the oracle, those spirits who offered protection through their elekes might also be standing up for ebó. The diviner must ask each spirit for whom the client will receive an eleke, "Ebó elese [orisha's name]?" If the answer is yes, the diviner must mark appropriate sacrifice.

If Okana Marunla still will not close, the diviner must turn to the eboses of the parent odu, Okana (see page 85). Something there is needed to bring evolution.

# The Sixteenth Composite Odu of Okana, Okana Merindilogún (1-16)

## The Proverbs of Okana Merindilogún

- Food, because it did not make ebó, went in smelling good and came out smelling foul.
- When the mouth ate the food, the food was defecated for being disobedient.

## The Message of Okana Merindilogún

When one mouth is followed by sixteen mouths, the sign Okana Merindilogún (also known as Okana

Otura) has come to the house. Defecation was born in this odu. Whenever this letter falls on the mat, it carries all the warnings of its parent odu, Okana; treat the letter as if it fell in severe osogbo even if its orientation is in iré.

Food, because it did not make ebó, went in smelling good and came out smelling foul. The mouth ate it, and it was defecated for being disobedient. The diviner must warn the client not to become as food, disobedient and foul. Okana Merindilogún is a sign of abdominal and intestinal trouble, and when it opens on the mat it is not unusual for the client to experience minor stomach discomfort before it closes. This odu warns against diphtheria, colitis, stomach ulcers, Crohn's disease, and loose stools. If the client experiences abnormal bowel movements or intestinal pains, especially after eating, he should go to a physician at once.

## The Prohibitions of Okana Merindilogún

- Avoid the following foods: alcohol, corn, yam, pork products, rooster, rabbit, turtle, crab, and the meat of scavenger animals.
- Do not smoke cigarettes or cigars; in this sign, they are poison. If one is a lifetime smoker, have a physical and a chest X ray immediately; there could be something wrong with the lungs.
- Do not work for free or one will lose one's luck. Do not engage in volunteer programs, mentoring programs, relief programs, blood drives, fund-raising, or any type of work in which one does not get paid. Do not give gifts unless it is an appropriate occasion (such as Christmas or birthdays).
- Control the tongue and measure one's words. Do not lie or gossip, for these things will bring osogbo.

## The Ebó of Okana Merindilogún

The larishe and eboses prescribed by Okana should be done swiftly, for this sign moves to bring osogbo quickly once identified. First, of course, the initial considerations for eboses in Okana must be investigated (see "Marking Ebó in Okana: Initial Considerations" on page 49). In addition, the client needs to be taken to a babalawo immediately for a complete assessment by Ifá.

If the eboses prescribed thus far are not enough to close the oracle, the elekes of one or more orishas speaking in this odu (see the list on page 42) could be necessary for protection. To find out if an eleke of any of these orishas is necessary, the diviner should ask of each, "Ebó eleke de [orisha's name]?" Note that more than one orisha could stand up in this odu to offer protection through his or her eleke. After marking an eleke, the diviner should explain to the client why this spirit is offering his or her protection in this odu (using his own aché to deliver this information). After explaining the relevant material to the client, the diviner may attempt closure again.

If this is not enough to close the oracle, those spirits who offered protection through their elekes might also be standing up for ebó. The diviner must ask each spirit for whom the client will receive an eleke, "Ebó elese [orisha's name]?" If the answer is yes, the diviner must mark appropriate sacrifice.

If Okana Marunla still will not close, the diviner must turn to the eboses of the parent odu, Okana (see page 85). Something there is needed to bring evolution.

## Closing the Reading: Further Eboses of the Parent Odu, Okana

Having exhausted the options of larishe and ebó in the composite odu, the diviner must turn to the parent odu to find a method of closure. Okana contains within itself many offerings and rituals to placate both the letter and the orishas that speak in it.

Before progressing with any of the eboses in this list, the diviner must mentally review the larishe prescribed in this odu, as described in "Marking Ebó in Okana: Initial Considerations" (page 49). He must also consider that Okana can demand the doubling of all offerings marked. Having come this far without closure, the odu requires that the prescribed eboses be doubled. For example, if the larishe of a composite odu is a hen to Oshún, two hens must now be given to Oshún. If the larishe is a ñame to Elegguá, two ñames must be given to Elegguá, and two must go to Shangó as well (since their offerings must be duplicated). The diviner must work out these guidelines carefully in his head and write them in the record of the reading or else the client will not evolve.

Now the diviner should ask for closure. If closure is not allowed, the remaining items in this list should be explored.

- The diviner should determine if the client needs a rogación by asking, "Eborí?" If the answer is yes, the client should have a rogación at the feet of the first orisha to stand up in this odu, and his head should be fed two white pigeons or two white doves. If a rogación and/or eborí are marked, the diviner should ask, "Sodidé?" If the answer is yes, the rogación should be done in reverse, beginning with the feet and ending with the head. Okana is a harsh odu that drags one down; one's spiritual head gets caught up in the dross world of matter. A rogación sodidé will lift one's soul back into the spiritual world. It is a good treatment for darkness and depression.
- If the odu still will not close, the next question the diviner should ask is "Ebó elese Elegguá?" If the answer is yes, the diviner should smear three fresh fish liberally with red palm oil and give them to Elegguá. They should remain with Elegguá overnight and be disposed of the next day, in a method determined by the diviner. The fresher the fish, the more aché they will have.*
- If the letter still will not close, the next question the diviner asks is "Ebó elese los guerreros?" If the odu accepts this sacrifice, feed the warriors feathered animals as follows: a rooster shared among Elegguá, Ogún, and Ochosi; a pigeon to Ogún and Ochosi; and a pigeon to Ósun.
- If the oracle continues to refuse closure, the next question the diviner asks is "Ebó elese Ogún?" If the answer is yes, the client should give Ogún a knife smeared with red palm oil; feed both the knife and Ogún a rooster. With this sacrifice, Ogún will fight with the knife and the client will not have to fight alone. This orisha will protect him from all harm and accidents involving iron. Note that if the client has received the warriors, this ebó may be done to his own orisha. The knife may not go inside an orisha's cauldron. Having a knife in an orisha's cauldron signifies that one has received the initiation known as *pinaldo* (the ceremony giving a priest or priestess the right to sacrifice four-legged animals). Know that a priest or priestess who gives this ebó should consider receiving the knife soon.

If the client has received Ogún, after the above ebó is complete the client should bring a ñame before Ogún's shrine, and with this the diviner cleans the client spiritually. The root is then given to the orisha, and the vine is allowed to grow freely until it is as long as the client is tall (it must never be allowed to grow taller than he). This ñame is left there until it dies.

If the osogbo is severe and the client has not received Ogún, after giving Ogún the knife and rooster, the diviner should liberally smear a piece of red meat with red palm oil and clean the client with this. The meat is left with Ogún, and the next day he must be asked for the method of disposal. The client should remove the meat and take it to its proper place as dictated by Ogún.

- If no other ebó will suffice, ask Elegguá if the home of the client needs his protection. If the answer is yes, both dirt and ashes must be taken from the four corners of the client's home, wrapped in red cloth, and given to Elegguá. He will guard the foundation of the client's home.
- Finally, it is possible that the client needs to receive Aganyú. The diviner should use this ebó only as a last resort, asking first "Ebó elese Aganyú?" and then "Eleke de Aganyú?" If neither the ebó nor the eleke of this orisha will satisfy the letter, the diviner then asks, "Koshé Aganyú?" If the answer is yes, the client

*If this ebó is prescribed for a client who likes to fish and eat fish, prohibit the act of fishing and the consumption of fish for three months. If this reading is an itá, this prohibition might become necessary for life.

must receive Aganyú as soon as possible. Note that Aganyú may be received only by initiates. Aborishas who have not ocha done may either make ebó to Aganyú or receive his eleke for protection.

If the diviner has come this far into the letter and nothing will satisfy Okana, he has two options. The first is to call upon an elder for help and guidance; something has been missed, and this must be determined. The second option is to consider the eboses of the secondary letter that has opened, for something in that family might be needed to close odu. For example, if the sign 1-3 (Okana Ogundá) has opened and refuses to close, one might need to make an ebó from the family of Ogundá. Not all houses, however, agree on this point; it is something to be considered.

Remember also the letter that came in the door. At this point, the italero might need to consider the eboses of that odu (as parent odu). Something there might be necessary to placate Okana.

When no other ebó will satisfy the letter, the sacrifice needed is the giving of a four-legged animal to the orisha whose diloggún has been consulted. There is no need to ask the oracle for closure—a sacrifice of four legs will automatically suffice to close the odu. The sacrifice must be done soon. No itá is given for this ebó. To examine the deeper spiritual issues that have opened on the mat, however, this client should be taken to Ifá soon. Something important has been missed, and neither the diviner nor his elders have the aché to determine what this might be.

# THREE
## THE FAMILY OF EJI OKO

### The Proverbs of Eji Oko

- The brothers are enemies.
- An arrow arises between brothers.
- The knot tied in the rope does not stop it from being strong.
- There will be arrows among friends.
- There will be war among brothers.
- Today, your own brother is your enemy.
- A lying woman loses her husband.
- A lying man loses his wife.
- Spouses who lie deserve separation.
- One who lives near the market will always hear its noise.
- There will be wars among families.
- Where there are arguments, there can be no peace.
- When the ram moves, it turns its head from right to left.
- Enjoy the moment, for it is all you have, and it, too, will soon be gone.
- The sound of the mortar echoes from where it is used.

### The Orishas Who Speak in Eji Oko

| | |
|---|---|
| Elegguá | Ibeyi |
| Ogún | Obatalá |
| Ochosi | Orúnmila |
| Oyá | Shangó |
| Orisha | Oko |

### The Message of Eji Oko

Opening with two mouths on the mat, the oracle sits before the italero in a dark, mysterious pattern. The odu Eji Oko seethes with mystery, change, separation, and imagination. This pattern has no parent in the diloggún; born of Olódumare's unfolding, it emerged after Eji Ogbe and stands in opposition to that sign, in the west.* Eji Oko preceded material existence: There were no humans, no animals, no plants, no earth, no moon or sun until after this energy coalesced. It formed even before the existence of the orishas, when there were only the Irunmole, the first orishas born in heaven from Olódumare and odu. Eji Oko is the balance to Eji Ogbe. Eji Ogbe is light; Eji Oko is darkness. Eji Ogbe stands at the east and is the harbinger of creation, life, light, and awakening; Eji Oko bars the west, turning all back into primal darkness. It begins the cycle of death, decay, and destruction, yet it feeds the cycle of life, growth, and creation through its work. Its spiritual implications are nothing short of awesome.

Having Eji Oko open before him, the diviner knows he will be bringing forth the client's own secrets from this primal darkness. Two mouths alludes to cycles; it is the energy that controls the seasons, the patterns of sun and moon, and the fertility and fecun-

*Eji Ogbe (eight mouths) was the first odu born; it is said to stand in the east.

dity of the earth. Of this letter, Fá'Lokun Fatunmbi writes, "Oyekun Meji [another name for Eji Oko] . . . symbolizes all those forces that can never be known. It is an image of those forces that create the night."* Yet this odu does not manifest through the height of any one cycle; rather, it is the end, death, which renews the energies expended. Fá'Lokun continues, "The transition from death to that which lies beyond is similar to the transition from womb to birth. All growth requires discarding that which is no longer effective. The passage from childhood to adulthood represents the death of a child. The passage from adulthood to elder status represents the death of a vigorous life to embrace the physical limitations of old age."†

The opening of this sign on the mat marks a passage whose path is ephemeral and fleeting. Like the arrows of Ochosi, this one moment flashes, often unnoticed; once Eji Oko has made its mark, the portal by which one transcends or descends may never again be crossed. Once childhood is left behind, it cannot be reclaimed; once the wisdom of old age is found, the body can never again be young. This odu tells us to enjoy the moment, for it is all we have, and it, too, will soon be gone. To honor the pattern that has opened on the mat, the diviner hooks the index fingers of both his hands together as if simulating the shooting of an arrow; he does this first to the right, and then to the left. This gesture honors both the odu and Ochosi, who owns Eji Oko. The client, and sometimes those present for the reading, is directed to make this gesture as well. Once this is done, the diviner chants the prayer for this odu:

*Eji Oko, temitan temishe*
*Ajuba oloko. Tela oko.*
*Temoran temishe. Mojiwo loko.*

Those present will bow their heads in silence while the diviner chants. After he is done, to honor both the opening odu and the orisha who owns it, many will mutter, "Maferefún Eji Oko! Maferefún Ochosi!"

In this letter are many spirits who might choose to speak. The one whose shells are being cast has the first option, and most of what this orisha says will come to pass quickly. Elegguá follows; while he does not own Eji Oko, he is comfortable in the rapid transitions it represents. When the letter's osogbo is severe, Elegguá can overcome the insurmountable in the client's life. Ogún is fierce in Eji Oko, yet his ferocity is not directed toward the client. Eji Oko marks the shortest path to attainment, and Ogún works tirelessly against the obstacles that might be in the way of this person's evolution. Ochosi's influence is felt throughout all sixteen composites of this odu, but he owns Eji Oko; while he may not speak first, he will have something to say before the reading has closed out. Oyá, while considered to be the gatekeeper to the cemetery, is also the orisha of fast change and tumultuous cycles. Although many consider her true home to be Osá, she is found in this odu as well. When she chooses to speak, she does so sternly, warning the client that change is coming fast and hard; and the orientation of this odu will strongly affect what she has to say. Orisha Oko lives here too; being the spirit that controls the fecundity and decay of the earth, he calls this letter of the diloggún home. The Ibeyi come next, and in all patterns of Eji Oko these spirits might stand up to speak, mark ebó, or demand their reception into the client's life. Obatalá and Orúnmila might stand up here as well (both can influence all the odu, although Orúnmila speaks only through his babalawos), and Shangó could mark and claim ebó in all the composites of Eji Oko.

To understand the action of Eji Oko, visualize the sacred implement of Ochosi: the crossbow. Loaded with a single arrow, it is a powerful weapon, one that can pierce the heart and kill all that stands in its way. Its effectiveness depends on the skill of the hunter. He must have a keen eye, capable of judging distance. He must have a powerful, steady arm that can load the arrow quickly and remain still while the body takes aim. He must be capable of long, slow, even breaths so that his form remains motionless while the mind adjusts his aim. The motion of his target, the distance between it and the hunter, the horizon, the wind—all these things

---

*Awó Fá'Lokun Fatunmbi, *Awó: Ifá and the Theology of Orisha Divination* (New York: Original Publications, 1992), 6.

†Fatunmbi, *Awó*, 131.

are measured in a single moment before the arrow flies. Ochosi makes the hunt seem simple and effortless; one quick, fluid series of motions, and the prey falls, dead. Yet if there is an error in any of these motions, the moment is wasted and the target missed. Opening in Eji Oko, the client is cautioned that his life is coming to a single, concentrated moment of time in which his thoughts, actions, and aim must be brought together skillfully; he must, like the hunter, focus on his target. Like the sailing arrow, he will either miss his mark or kill his prey. There is no middle ground.

The foreshadowed moment of change in the client's life speaks of both greater and lesser transitions. The lesser transitions will be exposed in the client's daily life as changing energies that move him toward evolution (in iré) or devolution (in osogbo). The diviner opening the diloggún must consider the client's current station in life; if this person is not careful, all his accomplishments, goals, and work might change. One who is in a relationship, or even married, could lose his lover; one with a stable job could find himself unemployed or suddenly dissatisfied with his work. Relationships could change, finances could crumble, and one's own home might be lost. The orientation of this sign will determine if these things are to happen for the better or for the worse. The diviner must advise his client accordingly.

Greater transitions and cycles with the religion itself might begin. To quote from my previous work, "Greater cycles will speak of one's place in our faith. The wanderer who has come for a reading will find himself drawn into the religion. For him, the initiation of the elekes is integral. Those who have their beads will find themselves thrust forward to take the warriors and perhaps ocha, the crowning of the head. Santeros for whom this sign falls will prosper in the religion. Some odu demand the reception of the knife, while others will forebode the initiation of godchildren to the religion."*

To help the client evolve spiritually, the diviner must keep these greater transitions in mind. He must determine the client's religious status and then delineate the next step into the faith. Although many say that the Lucumí faith is a "rich man's religion on a poor man's salary," odu will not demand something impossible of a person. If he is meant to take the next step, the orishas will provide the resources he needs. It is important for the diviner to tell the client this, for if he misses the opportunity, Eji Oko promises that it will be a long time before it is offered again.

The easiest way to begin a study of Eji Oko is with an examination of it in iré. If the answer to the diviner's question "Iré ni?" is yes, the diviner can already make many assumptions about the client and how he will progress. This odu has come as one of evolution; the rapid changes predicted by the oracle will serve to bring increased blessings to the client's life. Change is not easy and growth is never painless, but if this person commits himself to evolution, his blessings will increase. The letter foreshadows unexpected travel and, in fact, can flag the need for physical travel. Iré can manifest through unexpected offers, so if the chance for personal or business travel arises, the client must not turn it down. On this path his abundance may begin. Also, unlike the iré in other signs, Eji Oko in iré can mark a variety of nightly visual or audio hallucinations. This person will experience surreal dreams and tragic nightmares. Visions, sounds, foul smells, and sweet aromas might come. When they do, this person should exercise vigilance and caution. They will warn either of blessings that are present but about to be missed or of impending tragedy.

Having determined iré and its source, the italero continues to question the oracle. If the iré is marked as iré yale (firm iré), Eji Oko is telling the diviner that the client's source of help is strong; the orishas are mounting behind this person to thrust him toward his evolution and destiny. If the iré is then also marked as iré yale timbelaye (iré manifest in the client's life), Eji Oko is giving closure to itself. It tells the diviner that the odu's energy has been in effect for some time, and the client has conducted himself well through its energies. The force of his conduct, his prior good deeds, his adherence to his own destiny, and his worship of

---

*Óchàni Lele, *The Secrets of Afro-Cuban Divination: How to Cast the Diloggún, the Oracle of the Orishas* (Rochester, Vt.: Destiny Books, 2000), 74–75.

the orishas—all have already given him the tools to facilitate his own evolution. The letter has opened now to tell him what forces are in effect and what is coming his way.

Although Eji Oko might have opened in an iré, the diviner must consider one important point in his reading: Eji Oko is always a pattern of cyclic evolution. It marks cataclysmic change before evolution, and it guarantees that the one at the mat will stumble frequently before walking on clear, solid ground. This letter marks both the heights and depths of mortal existence, each low becoming another high before it is thrown into darkness, despair, or destruction. It brings decay, yet just as composted matter fertilizes the earth so that new life can grow, so will this person's life be made fertile for rebirth. Those things unessential to the client's evolution will be destroyed. The elements of his life that should have prominence will move to the forefront, and the new space in his life created by Eji Oko will help them grow and develop. The exact composite opened, along with the orientation of iré, will help the diviner determine what will be destroyed and what will be saved.

The diviner must completely assess the client's life at this time. In iré, it is not unusual for this person to have experienced devolution in one or more areas of his life. His health may be failing. He may be emotionally drained; relationships, friendships, and marriages could all be strained to the point of loss. Financially, materially and economically, this person could be on the brink of disaster. Two mouths on the mat guarantees that, although the client may experience a low point in his life, evolution will begin again. Good things are coming, and the client should be assured of this. The greatness of this pattern demands that the client work hard through these trials, for the more force he puts into his own restoration, the farther he will go in life when Eji Oko begins to rebuild what it has destroyed. The diviner should tell the client, "There has been decay, but there will be growth; there has been illness, but there will be health. You are coming to rebirth and renewal, and you must be ready to claim these blessings as they come. When they come, you must be rested and ready to move forth, for like Ochosi's arrows you will have to fly flawlessly to your target or miss altogether."

The greatest blessing that Eji Oko in iré can bring is economic wealth. If all the requirements of odu are fulfilled, and if the client listens intently to the advice being offered, he will plant seeds of prosperity and achievement that will grow throughout his life. Note, however, that abundance will not come immediately. Instead, it will develop slowly throughout this person's life, growing in size as he continues to work with the orishas. The client must not ruin this opportunity by working his own will in the world; he must make his life malleable in the hands of Olódumare and the orishas. They will guide him to his destiny. The firmer the iré of Eji Oko, the greater this person's achievement will be. Although the sign might not require any ebó, the diviner should still prescribe something for those spirits speaking in this odu; as the client sows, so shall he reap. In iré, the diviner should also tell the client that blessings will come from a relative who lives in the country, and this iré will be made manifest by taking a trip to visit this relative, establishing a closer relationship with his kin. The client should keep this prediction in mind for the rest of his life.

Because Eji Oko in iré puts the client firmly on the path to evolution, now is the time for the diviner to prod this person deeper into the religion's mysteries. For one who has nothing of ocha, the first step is the investment of the elekes. Being one's baptism into the religion, this ceremony is profound and powerful. The washing and consecration of one's body in omiero, the strengthening of the head with a rogación, the liturgy of prayers and songs culminating in the final investment of the necklaces of the orishas—all serve to break the client's final ties with a physically and spiritually impoverished past. He arises renewed, invigorated, and refreshed, ready to evolve amid the chaos that was his life. If the client already has the elekes, he should be pushed to take the initiation of the warriors (Elegguá, Ogún, Ochosi, and Ósun). With these four titanic orishas in his life, the client will have no more personal wars, no more fruitless struggles. He who has these spirits has no enemies and no impediments; the orishas take on all his adversaries, clearing the path to evolution. If the client has had both of these initiations, he should be led gently to asiento, for Eji Oko says that this is where he will find his destiny fulfilled.

If Eji Oko has come in osogbo, the diviner may assume that the client's mind is agitated; his head is heated and filled with many thoughts. He has secret plans that are delusions and sets goals that are impossible to attain. He likes to speak to himself in secret, criticizing his faults rather than encouraging his dreams. Bitterness sums up this client's life. Warnings given in this pattern are meant to help the client overcome his own sourness. He must be reminded that life easily becomes a reflection of the mind. Blocks will remain in this person's path until his temper is controlled and his cursing of others stops. This cursing extends not just to deliberate magical attacks but also to profane language empowered by raw anger. Such outbursts gather energy. Not every curse that the client sends reaches its intended goal; many of them manifest in his own life. And the client's life reflects the very things that he criticizes in others. The diviner must emphasize these points: The client must not threaten and must not curse. The client's disposition must change, or the ebó marked for Eji Oko will only slow down, and not reverse, the negative changes that are coming. The obliteration of negative thoughts and impulses should be extended to all who live or visit this person's home. No one should be allowed to swear, curse, or blaspheme in his house.

Under Eji Oko's influence in osogbo, one can easily become temperamental even if this is not one's true mental state, and temper will bring troubles upon the client. He must be warned never to threaten or raise his fist against anyone. He must make no threats of harm in public or private, and he should never confide thoughts of violence, even to a friend. He must keep his temper under control at all times and avoid even simulated gestures of violence. The diviner should tell the client that, in spite of all the bad in his life, he can have luck and goodness again if he follows this counsel. However, positive energy will be able to manifest only once these negative traits are given up.

If Eji Oko comes in any type of osogbo, the diviner should also relay to the client the following considerations:

- Eji Oko portends the announcement of a great tragedy in the client's family. While the client will be a part of this tragedy, he must ensure that he is not the cause of it, and he must not be caught in the middle of it. Divisions and differences are coming to blood relatives, and their parents will suffer. While eboses made through Eji Oko will calm some of these energies, they will not cure them. Caution is the rule here.
- In all composites of Eji Oko, the law is prominent. Not only the client but also his relatives could be falsely accused. It is not unusual for criminals to open under Eji Oko in osogbo. If the client is willfully breaking the law, time is of the essence if he hopes to avoid prosecution. He must change his ways tonight and make ebó to Ochosi immediately in penance for what he has done.
- Just as journeys figure prominently in this odu when iré is predicted, so do they influence one's destiny when osogbo has come. The client must be cautioned against journeys beyond his normal travel. If he must travel, the client should ask the orishas' permission to go. If they give permission, he may make ebó and travel, but he should stay only as long as necessary. If the orishas forbid him to travel, he must not go. A journey at this time will mark the beginning of the client's ill fortune.
- The client who opens in Eji Oko in osogbo believes himself to be hard and strong, yet he is soft and weak. His false perception of self could cost him everything.

With ano as its osogbo, Eji Oko carries severe health warnings. Even though the client believes he is in perfect health, odu announces that he is fragile. The client is in danger of falls, and the resulting fractures can become a serious threat to the client's health. The bones in his legs and waist could become dislocated, and all the double organs, including the sexual organs, kidneys, and lungs, are in danger. Skin eruptions, headaches, and bleeding are signs that something is amiss. If the client is elderly, he is particularly susceptible to cold drafts; a blast of cool air in a heated room could be crippling. Whatever his age, the client must see a physician at the first sign of illness.

If the orientation of Eji Oko is ikú, not only do all these health warnings apply, but also we say that Death is looking for a victim, and what he cannot take through sickness he will take through accident. To avoid tragedy, the client must heed the prohibitions given below.

No matter the orientation of Eji Oko, the one for whom this odu opens has become suspicious of everything and everyone. His friends, his family, his lover—all have given him reason to doubt their sincerity, and he has come to a point in his life where he trusts no one. Some of his suspicions are warranted, for Eji Oko tells us that key points of this person's life are in danger. His job might be stable, but because of a friendship at work it might soon be in jeopardy. A traitor in the client's workplace betrays all confidences bestowed upon him. The diviner must tell the client, "Remember that while you should be friendly at work, you have no true friends there. Speak of nothing more than daily niceties. In this way will you save your job."

If gossip at work is ruining the client's reputation, he must turn to Shangó for help. He should bring to the orisha a raw cow's tongue smeared with epó. It should be split down the middle, and a brown piece of paper on which the names of all his coworkers have been written should be stuffed inside. The tongue should then be sewn back together with red and white thread. Once done, this ebó should be served to Shangó on a red platter and left with him overnight. The next morning, it must be taken to the base of a ceiba or palm tree, along with a derecho of six cents. Shangó will sew shut the mouths of all who gossip about the client.

The family life of one who has opened in Eji Oko is far from pleasant. Even if the pattern has given iré, the client's own family has all but turned its back. Relatives (except for his parents) are wishing evil things on the querier. Brothers rise against brothers in Eji Oko, and sisters squabble ceaselessly. If the pattern manifests in an osogbo, these altercations and disagreements could become violent. No matter what happens, the client may not divorce himself from his family; he must stay close, especially to his own parents, but he may shield his goals, dreams, and personal desires from them for a time. If wars arise, he may protect himself, but he may not attack in return. He who flings arrows in anger will miss his mark, and his enemies will continue to evolve. If his family life becomes unbearable, the client should turn to Ochosi for his help, praying for peace and justice. Ochosi will protect him from harm at the hands of his own relatives. Many problems in the client's family are caused by outsiders. If the client can identify such sources, they can be dealt with and removed.

Eji Oko raises many other issues for the client. No matter the orientation of the odu, the diviner should explore the following during his reading:

- This odu warns that two blood relatives will fight for the same goal. It marks jealousy and sibling rivalry. Such rivalry, if it comes to pass, can escalate into a physical confrontation. While one must always fight for the things one considers dear in life, if possible, one must avoid wars with those of one's own blood. In this odu, the family can become divided, but one's family should be a source of strength.
- Eji Oko also warns that a relative might be cursing the client with witchcraft. The orientation of the odu will reveal if this is the case. Protective measures must be taken.
- One who has opened in Eji Oko is prone to violence and arguments. For the client to work through this tendency, his orí must be kept cool and refreshed. A rogación, or even a series of rogaciónes, might help. To lose one's temper in this odu is to lose one's blessings.
- Eji Oko points out that one's economic evolution begins with hard work. To achieve what he wants in life, the client must work hard. There is no other way.
- If the client grew up in the country, he should return to the country. One day he will own land and a house.

- In all things, this client should keep his own counsel. Goals, plans, and aspirations must not be spoken to the wind or else his energy will disperse.
- Eji Oko warns us that someone may be trying to trick or lie to the client about financial affairs. When it comes to money, he should not trust friends, family, or lovers until the energy of this odu has passed. And he must be wary of business dealings or partnerships.
- A child known to the client might soon fall ill, and the illness could involve a journey.
- If the client lives with anyone, a roommate (even if a family member) wants him to leave. If the client lives alone, his neighbors want him to move. If the client lives alone and has no neighbors, a tragedy might force him out of his house. He must be careful and cautious or else he may find himself on the street.
- Eji Oko speaks of the influence of twins in the client's life. The diviner must assess just how deeply this influence affects him. The manifestation of twinhood has many possibilities: The client could be a twin (whether his twin is alive, has died, or was stillborn); his own children may be twins; he may have twin siblings; he may have twin relatives in his extended family; or he may have ancestral relatives who were twins. If Eji Oko has come in iré, the Ibeyi must be received. If it has come in an osogbo, the Ibeyi must be properly propitiated with ebó.
- The client has many egun supporting his actions. However, a spirit among them does not belong to the client. In iré, it wants to help; in osogbo, it burdens the client and might be a "sending" from another person who wishes the client ill. Regardless of the odu's orientation, in time this errant spirit will do more harm than good. It should be removed by giving egun a *misa* (a ritual, also known as a séance, intended to honor the dead).
- There are disturbances in the client's house at night. If children are in the client's house, they cry out in their dreams. One of these children is having visions of Obatalá and might be his child. This should be looked into as soon as possible.
- Before this odu has passed, some aspect of the client's job will change. He must be prepared and work hard to ensure that the change is for the good.
- In the client's home is a stone that brings iré. This stone must be found and fed so that greater luck will come. It should be read by a priest; it could be either a foundation for egun or an Eleggúa.
- The client should keep his home well lit and warm. If it is summer, he must not leave the air conditioner running for too long. The odu Eji Oko needs warmth and light to prosper.
- The air in the client's home could be bad. In the winter, the client should fill his home with plants and make sure they have lots of sun. In the summer, he must air out the house frequently.

## The Prohibitions of Eji Oko

Eji Oko is an odu of rapid movement and speed; it alludes to one moment that can change the course of the client's life forever. In this pattern, obeying taboo is urgent. The client might not have the skill or awareness to judge all the current events in his life, and he certainly will not be aware of all that goes on behind his back. Yet he can control his actions, and the taboos that can be prescribed in Eji Oko will help him avoid many of the tragedies and obstacles predicted. Unless this reading is an itá or bajado, the prescribed taboos must be followed for twenty-one to twenty-eight days. If the reading is a bajado, the taboos must be followed until ocha is made. If the reading is an itá, they apply for life. Realize that each of Eji Oko's sixteen composites has its own taboos, which will enhance and build upon those given here.

- One's words affect one's life. Therefore, profane language must not be used. Do not take God's name in vain; do not curse or blaspheme. Bragging is also taboo. Do not speak of one's own good fortune to others, for in Eji Oko one's words dissipate into thin air. Those who should not hear will hear what is said. Envy and jealousy will gather. The very act of speaking will diminish the speaker's effectiveness. Finally, measure one's words before speaking. Speaking impulsively will cause one to sound like a fool and irritate others.

- In Eji Oko, when one lends out something, one also lends out one's luck, and neither the item loaned nor one's luck will come back. When borrowing from others, one also takes on their osogbo; it will come with the item loaned. Therefore, do not lend out any of one's belongings. Do not pawn personal items. Do not purchase items on credit, except in the case of an emergency. Do not borrow anything from others.
- In Eji Oko, it is said that the servant moves in while the master is forced out. No one beyond one's family or lover should live in one's own home, and even this should be avoided if at all possible.
- The law is hot and already on one's trail. Do not break the law in any way lest one be taken into the court system and Ochosi's home, the jail. Do not let lawbreakers into one's home, and do not associate with those who must hide to make a living. Do not argue, fight, or even make simulated actions of violence. If someone attacks, one must not fight; instead, run. Do not associate with those who work in the legal profession, and do not talk to law enforcement officers.
- If a court appearance is scheduled during the period of prohibitions, do everything legal to avoid it. Try to not be called as a witness, and do all that is possible to avoid jury duty. Do not step foot in a police station, a police car, a court, or a jail, if possible. Avoid civil litigation as well.
- Have nothing in religious imagery that is not made of expensive materials such as wood, stone, metal, and glass. Do not keep religious icons made of plaster; they draw bad energies to one's home. If one already has some of these, the diviner must ask the orishas if they need to be thrown away. Do not give them away or else the receiver will suffer as well.
- Eji Oko speaks of accidents at one's workplace; exercise caution, and do nothing that one is unqualified to do.
- Eji Oko speaks of danger from beneath the earth. Do not go into basements, and do not live in a house with a basement. Caves contain danger, so stay out of those as well, or else something bad will be brought back from beneath the earth. Holes and excavations are also dangerous, so stay away from them.
- Watch what one eats and drinks. Illness can come from what one puts into one's mouth.
- The streets are dangerous between noon and 6:00 P.M. Do not go out walking, driving, or riding during this period.
- Do not dress like a friend, for one may be mistaken for that friend, and unhappy events intended for that friend may be brought to one's own feet instead.
- Avoid extremes of temperature. Guard against drafts and cold winds, especially when outdoors in cold temperatures, and make sure that one's hair is not wet when going outside. Do not bathe in or drink hot water; all liquids put on the skin or ingested into the body must be of tepid temperature.
- Do not wear any clothing, including hats, that is binding or restrictive. Women should not wear girdles, and neither women nor men should wear pants or belts that are tight in the waist. This unneeded pressure will cause or complicate the health problems inherent in the odu.

## Marking Ebó in Eji Oko: Initial Considerations

Despite its severe pronouncements, Eji Oko is a very spiritual odu. It is one of the four primaries that opened creation, and it can open one's eyes to the soul of nature, the vast, spiritual world that hides behind matter. One might describe the client's next stage of evolution in Eji Oko as an awakening: No matter his position in the religion (casual client, aleyo, aborisha, initiate, or godparent), this person's current state of being is about to be destroyed, and he will, if the diviner is careful with this reading, emerge into a new state of being. The initial considerations for ebó in Eji Oko are intended not to help the client destroy osogbo but to facilitate his spiritual awakening. They are catalysts for his evolution. The true issue at stake here is the state of the client's soul and his journey to become something more than he is currently. Eji Oko promises that soon this client will question his place in our faith, and his "karma" will thrust him forward to a new level of participation.

If Eji Oko has come in iré, the Ibeyi must be received. If it has come in an osogbo, the Ibeyi must be properly propitiated with ebó.

In Eji Oko, if the client has not yet received elekes, he must now, as ebó. While not the same as the Christian rite of baptism, the investment of the elekes has a symbolism similar to that of baptism. The client begins by acknowledging the ancestors, the past from which he is born, and then he is bathed with omiero, washing away the past sins and transgressions that stood in the way of evolution. His body receives its first consecration to the orishas. After this, a rogación is given to strengthen the head, and perhaps for the first time in his life the client develops a bond with his higher self, his counterpart in heaven. The ceremony culminates with the investment of five necklaces: the elekes of Obatalá, Yemayá, Oshún, Ochosi, and Shangó.* Then, dressed in white and seated on the mat, catered to and cared for as if he were a helpless child, the newly made aborisha receives his first glimpse of what his life would be like as a iyawó. The entire ceremony is a moving experience, one that removes the client from mundane issues and helps him see what is truly important: his own soul and God.

In this odu the warriors—Elegguá, Ogún, Ochosi, and Ósun—dominate. Because Eji Oku deals with evolutionary cycles, and because the warriors work together to help the aborisha evolve, in this sign no ebó is more potent than the initiation of the warriors. Even if the client has not received his elekes, this initiation should be taken as soon as possible, for Eji Oko promises fast, unannounced change, and only the aché of these spirits can help him emerge unscathed. If it is financially impossible for the client to receive the warriors now, the client must give an ebó to Elegguá, Ogún, and Ochosi. Using the diloggún and his own aché, the diviner should mark an acceptable offering for these spirits. If the client is making ebó to the diviner's or godparent's orishas, nothing goes to Ósun. Instead, he must have a rogación at the feet of Obatalá.

Because Ochosi rules this odu, it is possible that he will need individual eboses in order for the reading to close out. Appropriate offerings for him in the odu Eji Oko follow.

### Traditional Eboses in Eji Oko

Certain types of animals and food offerings are traditional to this pattern. For animals, the diviner can pick from the following list: a rooster, two pigeons, two birds that have been caught by the client and not bought, and a goat or ram (when four legs are needed). For simple adimú, the diviner should first try to pick from the following offerings: two coconuts, two eggs, two fresh fish, two dishes of cooked food favored by the orisha speaking in this sign, epó, smoked fish, jutía, efun, and honey.

## Cleansing at the Feet of Ochosi

When Ochosi comes to claim ebó and the diloggún marks a cleansing at his feet, the following rituals will cleanse the client and placate the orisha.

### *Cleansing with Guinea Eggs*

As soon as possible, the client must provide the following elements: a large blue cloth, a white plate, seven guinea eggs, epó, honey, anisette, a cigar, and cascarilla. The diviner must prepare this ebó. The blue cloth is laid on the floor before Ochosi, and in

*The usual elekes ceremony calls only for the necklaces of Obatalá, Yemayá, Oshún, and Shangó. When the elekes are prescribed through the odu Eji Oko, however, Ochosi's eleke is given as well. For now, he acts as the client's guide to evolution.

the middle of this the diviner sets the white plate. He smears each guinea egg with epó and honey and places them on the white plate. Then he sprays them with the anisette and fumigates them with cigar smoke. The diviner also sprays anisette on Ochosi, and he sets the smoking cigar in Ochosi's clay dish. Finally, the diviner sprinkles the cloth, plate, and eggs with cascarilla.

Now the client begins his ritual cleansing. Every day for the next seven days, he stands before Ochosi, praying for evolution. He uses one egg each night to cleanse himself, rubbing his entire body with it. After cleansing with an egg, the client places it on the blue cloth beside the plate, not on the plate; he does not use it again. After the seventh egg is used, the client lifts the white plate from the cloth. He ties the blue cloth securely, with all seven guinea eggs inside it. The client takes it immediately to the woods. When he finds a dead tree, he smashes the blue cloth into it, so that all seven eggs break. He then places the cloth on the ground, sets a derecho of seven cents next to it, and leaves the woods without looking back.

### *Cleansing with Coconuts*

Cleansings before Ochosi may be done with coconuts. The client should bring the following items to the diviner's home: a large yellow cloth, a large blue cloth, a small basket, a smaller square of yellow cloth, a smaller square of blue cloth, sandpaper, seven coconuts, a paintbrush, yellow paint, and blue paint. The diviner prepares the ebó in front of Ochosi.

He lays the large square of yellow cloth on the floor and lays the large square of blue cloth over it but at a forty-five-degree angle, so that the overall appearance is that of an eight- pointed star. He sets the basket in the center of the cloths and lines it with the smaller pieces of yellow and blue cloth. These cloths, too, should be laid down to form an eight-pointed star.

While the diviner is setting up this altar before Ochosi, the client must sand the seven coconuts that he brought for his ebó; once he removes all the hairs, he paints each coconut half yellow and half blue. When the seven coconuts are dry, the diviner places these in the basket.

Now the client begins his ritual cleansing. Every day for the next seven days, the client stands before Ochois and cleanses himself with one coconut. He rubs it over his entire body, praying for release from osogbo. When he is finished, he places the coconut on the large square of cloth, not back in the basket; he does not use it again. After the last coconut is used, the diviner lifts the basket from the cloth and ties all seven coconuts in the large pieces of blue and yellow cloth. The client takes this bundle to the woods and leaves it at the foot of a dead tree, along with a derecho of seven cents.

If Ochosi has also demanded an adimú from the client, the day after the coconut cleansing is complete (the eighth day after the ebó was begun), the client should return to the diviner's home with the following items: a large quantity of toasted corn, a bottle of anisette, and seven cigars wrapped in blue and yellow ribbon. The client fills the basket with corn, and the bottle of anisette and the cigars are placed on top of the corn. This adimú stays with Ochosi indefinitely. It will bring the client luck.

## Adimú for Ochosi

### *Fruits*

The simplest adimú one may present to Ochosi is the fruit known as melón de castilla. The client must give seven of these melons and pray for evolution. One may also present simple adimús of mangos and almonds—both are delicacies to this orisha.

The offerings remain with the orisha until they begin to spoil; they are then discarded in the woods.

### *Three Gourds*

To appease Ochosi with adimú, the client brings the following ingredients for ebó: three jícaras, plenty of toasted corn, grains, and cornmeal.

Set the three gourds before Ochosi and have the client pay foribale to the orisha. The priest then fills each gourd with a different ingredient: toasted corn in one, grains in the second, and cornmeal in the third.

This simple adimú remains with Ochosi for three days. At the end of this time, the client discards all the elements under a bush in the woods.

### *Seven Gourds*

When Ochosi claims an adimú in Eji Oko, the following ebó will placate him. To make this offering, the client must bring to the diviner's or godparent's house the following ingredients: seven gourds, a large amount of toasted corn, seven pennies, smoked fish, jutía, guinea pepper, honey, epó, anisette, a blue seven-day candle, and a yellow seven-day candle.

Once these items are assembled, the client puts everything in front of Ochosi and gives foribale; the diviner prays over him to Ochosi and lifts him up. The seven gourds are placed in a semicircle before Ochosi and are filled with all the ingredients except the candles. The two seven-day candles are lit, and this offering stays with the orisha until the candles burn out.

When the candles burn out, the client removes the ebó and takes it deep into the woods, leaving it at the foot of a dead tree.

### *Goat Steak*

When the osogbo of Eji Oko is harsh and volatile and Ochosi demands ebó, the following adimú may appease him. The client must provide these ingredients: epó, cocoa butter, a goat steak, toasted corn, a white platter, jutía, smoked fish, and honey.

Preheat a large skillet; grease it with both epó and cocoa butter. While the pan heats, rub epó and cocoa butter into the steak. Prepare a bed of toasted corn on the white platter, garnishing it with the jutía and smoked fish. Fry the steak lightly on both sides, keeping the center pink. Place the steak on the bed of toasted corn. Present this adimú to Ochosi and drizzle honey over it while praying to him for iré and sweetness. Leave the steak with Ochosi overnight; the next day, the client must take the ebó to the foot of a dead tree deep in the woods.

### *Pear Amalá*

If Ochosi has stood up in Eji Oko to claim adimú, amalá may be made to satisfy him. For this, the client should bring to the diviner's house the following ingredients: honey, cornmeal, brown sugar, and six pears.

In a large saucepan, combine 2 cups of water, 1/2 cup of honey, 1/2 cup of cornmeal, 1 tablespoon of brown sugar, and the six pears, diced into small squares. Bring this mixture to a boil; reduce the heat and allow to simmer, stirring constantly, until a thick porridge forms. Serve to Ochosi while steaming hot.

Leave this ebó with the orisha overnight; the next day, the client must discard it deep in the woods.

### *Fried Yellow Corn*

For this ebó, the client must provide the following: 2 pounds of hard yellow corn (chicken feed), epó, an onion, and a coconut.

Soak the corn overnight in cold water so that it becomes soft, then strain it. In a large frying pan, melt 2 tablespoons of epó. Grate the onion and add it and the softened corn. Fry until the mixture is thoroughly cooked. Place the sautéed corn and onion on a terra-cotta plate; over this, sprinkle freshly grated coconut. Serve to Ochosi while still hot.

The next day, the client must remove the ebó and take it deep into the woods, leaving it at the foot of a dead tree.

### *Roasted Corn*

Ochosi loves roasted corn on the cob. Slather seven roasted ears of corn with plenty of epó, and serve these to him on a terra-cotta dish. For a more visually appealing presentation, save some of the green husks from each fresh cob, and use them to line the dish. The diviner must use obí to determine the proper method of disposal for this ebó.

## Ochosi as Protector

There are times when Ochosi stands up in Eji Oko to warn a client that an enemy will soon harm him. If the name of this enemy can be determined, or if the name is already known, this simple ebó will render him harmless. On a brown piece of paper and using a lead pencil (not ink), the client writes the enemy's name. He smears the back and front of the paper with epó, then folds it three times. He impales the paper on one of Ochosi's arrows.

Blowing anisette and cigar smoke over the orisha, the client prays to Ochosi that the named enemy is rendered harmless by the forces of justice. To finish this ebó, the client lights two white candles to the orisha in the name of justice. He will protect the client from this enemy.

## The First Composite Odu of Ejioko, Ejioko Okana (2-1)

### The Proverbs of Ejioko Okana

- There is sickness in the veins.
- The shadow is behind you.
- Release arrows with care.
- Your own carelessness will injure you and your best friend.
- Youth will always disrespect age.
- If you throw arrows, you will hurt only yourself.

### The Message of Ejioko Okana

When an initial cast of two mouths, Eji Oko, precedes a cast of one mouth, Okana, the odu Ejioko Okana is open on the mat. This sign is known as Oyekun Okana, Yeku Okana, Oyekun Kanran, Yeku Kanran, Oyekun Okanran, and Yeku Okanran. It marks an important stage in human evolution: the consumption of meat. When first created, humans were vegetarians and foragers; they had no capacity for agriculture and were forced to consume what the land provided. In regions of sparse vegetation, they starved. When there was drought, they starved. When this sign unfolded, it taught humans how to hunt; it taught them how to preserve, store, and cook animal foods so there would be no food-borne illness. Some credit this sign with the development of kosher in the Jewish faith; however, since it also teaches the consumption of blood supplements (vitamins being the modern counterpart), the development of kosher does not belong here. (Kosher demands the absence of blood.) With the knowledge given by Ejioko Okana, early humans were protected against starvation and nutritional deficiencies. Its aché enabled our race to grow and populate colder climates, depending on animals, not plants, for food.

In this odu, the aché of the warriors is vital. The diviner pays homage to Elegguá, Ochosi, and Ogún, saying to each, "Maferefún!" It will take the strength of all three to fight the osogbo inherent in this sign. Ejioko Okana can bring little iré. When it is marked as iré, it marks only that, with proper ebó, the client can find safe passage away from difficulties.

Ejioko Okana brings dire warnings of sickness for not only the client but his family as well. The legs, feet, and blood are affected in this sign, and if anyone related to the client complains of an affliction in these areas, that person should see a physician immediately. If a man has opened in Ejioko Okana, the diviner must tell him that he is in danger of catching a venereal disease. For now, he must limit or avoid sexual activities; also, the diviner should consider what this implies for a client who is either married or in a committed relationship. Since many sexually transmitted diseases are asymptomatic, the diviner should advise a sexually active male to be screened for these diseases immediately. He must also warn the client that adultery and unfaithfulness will bring an unwanted pregnancy.

The client's home and hearth figure into this odu as well. The orisha whose diloggún is consulted does not like the atmosphere in which the client lives. It is too cold, too dark, and too unhealthy. The client must remedy these conditions immediately. He must ensure that his home is clean and pure and give it light and warmth.

Spiritual darkness comes with those who frequent the client's house. He lets enemies in. This pattern warns of seven enemies in the client's life. Not all of these are known to him, but some do enter his house. One of these will steal something valuable. Three work continually to cause his fall, and three are working witchcraft at his door.

This odu also indicates that a negative spirit tries to pose as the client's egun. It waits at the client's front door, looking for a chance to enter. The client's egun must be strengthened so that this spirit can be sent away.

Also, client's neighbors are curious about what goes on in his home. They might soon cause trouble.

Many do not like him or the way he lives, and they want him to move out.

In any casting of Ejioko Okana, the diviner must keep the following points in mind:

- The greater the osogbo, the greater the danger of sickness. If ano or ikú is marked, sickness is already festering in the client's blood. Before this odu passes out of his life, the client may need medication for an infection.
- If the client is a man, he will fight with his lover. The discord is caused by his own wandering nature. If the man does not change his ways, he may find himself alone and lonely.
- If the client is a woman, she must not trust her lover implicitly. Her man could pass on a venereal disease acquired through adultery.
- Something bad is buried in or around the client's home. It could affect his health or physical safety. This person should consider moving as soon as possible. Know that Ejioko Okana is associated with environmental poisoning.

## The Prohibitions of Ejioko Okana

- Because this odu forebodes illnesses of the blood and sexually transmitted diseases, sexual encounters outside of a committed relationship are forbidden. Adultery is forbidden as well. If one has indulged in unsafe sexual practices, have a thorough health screening now.
- Avoid the following foods: beans, grains, peanuts, alcohol, yams, goat's milk, and goat meat.
- Food-borne illnesses are a danger in this odu, as are deliberate poisonings. When eating away from home, be careful. Limit one's consumption of foods in restaurants, and be careful in the homes of others. Do not eat reheated foods. Do not leave drinks lying about. If one leaves a beverage unattended, do not drink it; obtain a new drink instead.

## The Eboses of Ejioko Okana

When Ejioko Okana opens on the mat, several issues must be explored. The first issue revolves around egun. Coming in a weak iré, Ejioko Okana shows that the client's ancestors are trying to bring blessings, but the client's life is not stable enough and his head is not clear enough to see that blessings are coming. To solidify this client's aché with egun, the diviner should prescribe several things. First, he should set up a bóveda for his ancestors, both spiritual and physical. Fresh flowers and white candles should grace it, and he should renew the waters weekly. If the client does not have an opá ikú, provide and feed one. Finally, offer a series of masses for this person's ancestors. His spiritual court is in disarray, and only a skilled espiritista or medium can help him settle these issues. The client should follow exactly the advice given during these rituals. The diviner should note that Ejioko Okana gives egun the right to personalize eboses. To see if egun require further eboses, after making the above prescriptions, the diviner should ask, "Ebó elese egun?" If the answer is yes, the diviner uses the diloggún to mark the appropriate ebó.

The next issue revolves around the Ibeyi. In all composites of Eji Oko, these twin spirits are essential; however, in Ejioko Okana they can provide the means for evolution in even the harshest osogbo. If the client does not have the Ibeyi, he is marked for their reception. If the client already has the Ibeyi, the diviner should find out if they need ebó, asking, "Ebó elese los Ibeyi?" If the answer is yes, the diviner uses the diloggún to mark the appropriate offering. If the answer is no, in this pattern it is wise, nevertheless, to offer them something from the heart to enlist their aid. Note that if a client faces insurmountable odds in his life, accompanied by a volatile osogbo in this odu, he might opt to cater a large party in honor of the Ibeyi. At the end of this party, once all the children have gone home, the diviner should bring two white pigeons before the orishas, cleanse the client with them, and then sacrifice the birds. One week after the party and sacrifice, the client gives the Ibeyi twin dishes of fruit and candy. Then they will overcome sourness with sweetness.

After exploring these issues with the client, the diviner has his first chance to close the diloggún. If the odu remains open, he should investigate the following:

- The client may be unsettled issues with Ifá. A man might need *mano de* Orúnmila (an initiation ceremony); a woman might need *kofá de* Orúnmila (also an initiation ceremony). Seek out a competent babalawo as soon as possible to investigate these issues.
- If difficulties with close friends or relatives bring the client to the mat, these problems come because of a wrong he once did. The diviner must explain this to him; he will understand. There is an ebó to resolve these issues. First, the client must seek forgiveness from the ones he wronged, and he must atone materially for what he did (by giving a gift). Then the client should lavish gifts or adimú on the diviner's Eleggua. These gifts must come from the heart and should not be prescribed; the more the client gives, the greater the iré from this ebó.
- If the client likes to enter many contests, this odu also prescribes ebó to increase his chances of winning. To Eleggua (his own, his godparent's, or the diviner's) he should give a large basket of fresh sweet fruits. The orisha will work to increase his luck at games of chance.
- If the client is having difficulties achieving his goals, as ebó he should feed feathered animals to Eleggua and Ochosi together. He must pray to Eleggua that all obstacles are removed and petition Ochosi to show him the shortest path to what he desires.
- If the odu still will not close, the diviner asks, "Ebó elese Eleggua y Ochosi?" If the answer is yes, he uses the shells to mark the appropriate offering.
- If the oracle continues to refuse closure, the elekes of Eleggua and Ochosi might be necessary for the client. The diviner asks, "Elekes de Eleggua y Ochosi?" If the answer is yes, the diviner should make sure a tiny bow and arrow are included in Ochosi's eleke to mark it as having come from Eji Oko.

If the odu will not close after these options have been investigated, the diviner must turn to the eboses of the parent odu, Eji Oko (see page 132). Something there is needed to facilitate the client's evolution.

## The Second Composite Odu of Ejioko, Ejioko Meji (2-2)

### The Proverbs of Ejioko Meji

- A woman who lies will lose her husband.
- A man who lies will lose his wife.
- Lies will dissolve the marriage.
- The knot tied in a rope does not stop it from being strong.
- What you build with your head is destroyed with your feet.
- Lovers who lie deserve to lose.

### The Message of Ejioko Meji

When the first casting of two cowries repeats itself, the pattern Ejioko Meji, also known as Oyekun Meji and Yeku Meji, is open on the mat. Many say that this letter's aché caused the son of God, Jesus Christ, to incarnate among mortals. It is also the sign in which Ikú rejoiced at human creation; all the animals on the earth were formed, in part, to satisfy Death's taste for meat, but when he took his first human life he discovered that ours is sweeter and more fulfilling. As centuries passed, more varieties of animals were formed to satisfy Death's hunger, yet none sated his cravings like human flesh. The aché of Ejioko Meji also gave Ochosi his formidable hunting skills, and through the hunt he became known as the deliverer of divine justice. To right a wrong committed before Olófin, Ochosi's arrows (a gift from Obatalá) took the life of his own wife. Since that day, Ochosi fights for justice, no matter what it costs him or those around him.

By opening on the mat, this odu makes two major predictions for the world in general: Two good, important people will die. One will die in a country setting, and the other will die in an urban area. These deaths will somehow touch the client's life.

In Ejioko Meji, all of the client's current relationships are under the orishas' scrutiny. In iré, their cautious observance and subsequent reaction will be gentle. However, the diviner must still advise caution. The client must learn to live by a simple rule: Treat others as he would have them treat him. If he offers good intentions and honorable actions, they will be returned to him. If he offers evil, evil will be returned swiftly. Lies, deceit, gossip, and treason will dissolve even the most solid of his relationships.

If Ejioko Meji comes in osogbo, many of the client's closest friends could abandon him. Many of his friendships are all but dissolved now, and they will only get worse unless the client changes his ways. Monogamous relationships, especially marriages, will suffer. When an osogbo is present in Ejioko Meji, the diviner knows that the client and his lover or spouse lie to each other; even their friends participate in these lies. Treachery, despair, deceit, jealousy, and adultery are all hidden. This odu tells the one at the mat that if he values his significant other, all this must end now. He should also be aware that his lover has lied to him many times. Those who lie deserve their losses, and in a volatile osogbo the relationship might already be unsalvageable.

Ejioko Meji in osogbo also tells us that two people known to the client will die before the year is done. If the client wants to travel to these funerals, he should come back to the orishas to mark ebó before going. Ikú might be stalking a new victim close to the recently deceased; under the influence of Ejioko Meji, he might choose the client. Only ebó will cleanse him of this osogbo.

The diviner should know that the warnings and prohibitions of this odu are strong; even if the odu opens in iré, these warnings and prohibitions must be detailed carefully so that the client has no misunderstanding. The changes this client desires in his life will come if he heeds this advice. They will come slowly, but once they come, his life will change quickly, always for the better. Until this time, the client should make ebó frequently and zealously so that his luck is not missed.

Regardless of the odu's orientation, before ending the session the diviner must also explore with the client the following points:

- The orishas are not pleased with the client's current living conditions. Witchcraft could be buried at the front door. To fight it, the client should pour copious amounts of fresh water at his doorstep daily, praying to Olófin, Olorún, and Olódumare. His home is too cold, sterile, dark, and unkempt. He must clean it and give it more light and warmth.
- This odu signals that the client's neighbors are nosy; they want to know what goes on behind closed doors. Someone is envious and wants the client to move.
- This odu announces tempests and storms at sea; it also announces problems with water at home. The client should keep this warning in mind.
- Ejiokok Meji can forebode health concerns centering on the legs and blood. The client must be watchful for signs of this, for these illnesses could be serious.
- If the client lives with children, he should watch over them carefully. Innocence is in danger in this odu, and something bad will happen if he is not cautious.
- The client's work or livelihood could be in danger. He must guard his job and work wisely. To avoid tragedy, he should not commit to purchases now but, rather, save his money for a rainy day.

## The Prohibitions of Ejioko Meji

In this odu, all the prohibitions of the parent odu, Eji Oko, apply.

## The Eboses of Ejioko Meji

Ejioko Meji speaks of death and the dead; therefore, the diviner must focus on the client's issues with egun. In this odu, the most ancient spirits, forces whose names have been forgotten by their descendants, clamor for attention. Alien spirits gather as well, and many of these will try to pose as the client's egun; they must be removed. Souls gather at both his front and back doors. One in particular is malicious. It might be a malicious sending from another person, and it waits for the client's demise. Egun must be propitiated before any other ebó for Ejioko

Meji is done. The client must feed the opá ikú in his house. If he does not have one, he must find one. Immediately, the diviner must hold a mass to help elevate the client's egun. Given the light (the mass) and strength (the sacrifice) of these propitiations, the client's egun will hold evil at bay. The client must follow the advice of the espiritistas exactly, and once the first mass is complete, he must give egun another adimú. Until the client's life is settled, he should host a monthly mass for his ancestors.

Because Ejioko Meji affects the head with rapid change, the client must have a rogación before Obatalá's shrine. After the rogación, the diviner should prepare four coconuts for ebó by sanding them smooth and painting half of each white and the other half red, with a thin black line separating the two halves. Every day for the four days after the rogación, the client should cleanse his head and body with one coconut, leaving the coconut with Elegguá after the cleansing. Each coconut should be used only once. On the fifth day, the client must take the four coconuts to a crossroads. Obatalá will see them, and once the ebó is complete, he and Elegguá will deliver blessings from Olófin.

Ejioko Meji also carries heavy aché with twins, and the client's relationships with twins must be established. If he has ancestral twins, two masses should be said in their names and a small shrine to these egun built. If the client has twin children, they should both receive Elegguá and the Ibeyi so they grow with blessings. If the client is the survivor of a set of twins, a mass should be said and a small shrine kept in the deceased twin's name. If the client is himself a twin, the diviner should find out whether he was the first- or second-born of the two. The first twin is guarded by Shangó, and if the client was firstborn, Shangó might want ebó. Yemayá guards the second-born of twins, and if the client was second-born, she might want ebó. To see if the appropriate orisha requires ebó, the diviner should consider asking, "Ebó elese [orisha's name]?" If the answer is yes, the diviner should mark the appropriate offering with the shells. If the answer is no, the client should still give some form of ebó, anything his heart tells him to give. And Oshún, as the mother of twins, should be given ebó in either case.

Now the diviner has his first opportunity to close the oracle. If the above prescriptions are not enough to close the odu, the diviner should consider the following points:

- The client's egun may require a specific ebó. To find out if this is the case, the diviner can ask, "Ebó elese egun?" If the answer is yes, the diviner uses the shells to mark the appropriate offering.
- Additional work with either the client's orí or Obatalá could be necessary. The diviner should ask, "Eborí?" If the answer is yes, two white pigeons should be fed to the head. The diviner might also ask, "Ebó elese Obatalá?" If the answer is yes, an appropriate ebó should be marked with the diloggún.
- If Ejioko Meji has opened for an aleyo and refuses closure, it marks the need for this person to attend a tambor held in honor of the orishas. When the deities possess their initiates during this ceremony, the client must pay homage to as many of them as possible. Any and all spirits who come will have much advice to give to this person.

If the oracle still will not close and the client is an aleyo or aborisha, the diviner should explore the options for ebó in the parent odu, Eji Oko (see page 132). If the client is an initiate, the diviner should explore the following considerations:

- Having fallen for a priest or a priestess, the odu could be marking a tambor as the solution to the client's troubles. Using the diloggún, the diviner should ask if the drum is to go to the orisha of the diloggún being consulted. If this spirit refuses the drum, the diviner should ask the same question for each of the spirits given in the client's ocha.
- If a tambor has been marked as ebó during an itá of either Elegguá or the crowning orisha, the client is marked to give all his spirits a drum during the course of his life. Making a commitment to this, and the playing of the first sacred drum, will put this person on the path to spiritual evolution. The orisha that gave birth to the client's head (the godparent's crown) must be

given a drum before any of the client's orishas may have one.

- If this client's osogbo is great and his lot in life already tragic, a severe ebó can be used to bring luck back into his life quickly: two jutías sacrificed to Elegguá. Only an oriaté may give this ebó. This sacrifice is expensive (jutía must be imported) and is to be used only as a last resort, when all else fails. Those animals substituted for jutía in the United States, such as opossum, are not acceptable for this ebó.

If nothing in this list will satisfy the odu, the diviner must turn to the eboses of the parent odu, Eji Oko (see page 132). Something there is needed for the client's evolution.

## The Third Composite Odu of Ejioko, Ejioko Ogundá (2-3)

### The Proverbs of Ejioko Ogundá

- Where there are arguments, there is no peace.
- With the tongue is one's game developed; do not argue.
- Do not leave security for uncertainty.
- A bird in your own hand is worth more to you than two in your friend's hands.
- A bird in the hand is worth two in the air.
- Today cannot be like tomorrow.
- One does not know today what will be done tomorrow.
- Death is on your trail.
- The face of the vulture bulges forward and his stomach protrudes backward.
- Be happy with the things you have.

### The Message of Ejioko Ogundá

The odu Ejioko Ogundá, also known as Oyekun Ogundá and Yeku Ogundá, opens when the initial cast of two mouths is followed by three mouths. When this sign falls, the diviner calls out, "Maferefún egun!" This praise is offered not only for the client's egun but also for the ancestors of all the priests and priestesses present for this reading. Each must make ebó to his or her own ancestors once this letter closes; see "The Eboses of Ejioko Ogundá" (page 105) for a description of this particular ebó. Remember: When an odu opens, it enfolds all present; the egun in Ejioko Ogundá are so strong that everyone in attendance at the reading must make this ebó. Those who fail to make this offering will find their own spirits demanding more elaborate eboses when they, in turn, sit for a session with the diloggún.

After explaining this ebó to all, the diviner pays homage to Shangó, Elegguá, Ogún, Ochosi, and Orúnmila, saying to each, "Maferefún!" Their aché and blessings are important to the client, and each might claim some form of ebó before the session ends.

Ogún is fierce in this odu; he has much to tell this person. The diviner must relay the following points to the client as Ogún's own words. First, Ogún has come in this odu to warn the client that although he thinks himself popular, having many friends, in truth he has very few. Those who are closest to him wear masks to hide their true intentions. The client must be wary; he must look for those who are wearing masks and try hard to see what lies beneath these. Second, the client frequently puts his trust in others, yet he is notorious for trusting the wrong people. Until he can be assured of another's true friendship, he should trust no one. He should remember that secrets told are no longer secret. Minding this simple rule will go a long way toward solving many of the client's difficulties. Third, Ogún says this person has begun many projects over his life, yet he has finished very few. Ogún wants the client to focus on one thing at a time, completing one project before beginning another. This will bring evolution. Fourth, Ogún warns against threesomes of the heart, especially with a married person. And finally, if a woman close to the client becomes pregnant, he must not counsel her either for or against an abortion.

In this odu, the diviner must also keep the following points in mind:

- The client must be told the following: The number three is both a blessing and a curse in his life. His mother has been pregnant with at least three children. If she does not have at least three living children, it is because she suffered abortions or miscarriages. This client may have three lovers, and in heterosexual relationships he could have children in all three. His legitimate wife, if she is healthy, will become pregnant with three children. If three live children are not born during this marriage, it is because she will suffer miscarriages or abortions.

- The client's home has a negative energy inside of it, and this negativity attracts more of the same. In a serious osogbo, the letter indicates that evil spirits are attracted to the client's home. He must work to remove the negative energy, thoroughly cleaning his home and avoiding arguments in the home.
- The client must be on guard against police intervention in his life. If he calls them for help or another calls them against him, the result will be the same: disaster. Until the influence of Ejioko Ogundá has passed from his life, he must tread carefully.
- Avarice and greed will bring this person's downfall. He must not covet what another has or work with lust for results.
- The client will need to take a short trip soon. If the letter comes with iré, the trip will go well. If it falls in an osogbo, it will go poorly. If the osogbo is volatile, the client is prohibited from traveling for eight days following this odu's opening. After this period of time, he may travel safely, but not joyously; the trip will still be a disappointment.
- Three enemies are close to this client and they want to cause his downfall. They might even be "friends" who know his innermost secrets. The best advice the diviner can give is that the client should be cautious.
- Any sickness or disease predicted through this odu is likely to manifest in the veins and legs. The client should monitor these areas, and any pain, swelling, or discoloration there demands a visit to a physician. If the client is a diabetic, he must be extremely careful with his feet. Pain in the waist is a warning of serious illness as well.

## The Prohibitions of Ejioko Ogundá

- Ejioko Ogundá forbids the killing of turtles, whether for sacrifice to the orishas or for their meat.
- Do not become the third party to any endeavor, and do not accept anything from others third-hand.
- Avoid threesomes of the heart, especially with someone who is already married or dating.
- Do not counsel any woman for or against an abortion.
- Do not lend or pawn items. If one must be rid of them, either give them away or sell them outright. Do not reclaim any item lent or pawned before Ejioko Ogundá opened on the mat; with it, one would reclaim one's bad luck.
- Do not keep plaster images or icons from other religions. They will bring tragedy to one's home.
- Do not wear tight shoes, tight pants, or any item of clothing that binds around the waist.

## The Eboses of Ejioko Ogundá

Ejioko Ogundá has many considerations for ebó. First, one's head is one's salvation, yet the implied osogbo of this sign will heat the orí unbearably. The client must have a rogación before Obatalá's shrine, and after this the priest must cleanse him with red meat and epó before Ogún's shrine. This cleansing will give him a clean space for evolution.

The propitiation of Elegguá and Ochosi is essential to this odu, and if the client has any issues with these two orishas, the diviner may ask the following questions: "Ebó elese Elegguá?"; "Ebó elese Ochosi?"; and "Ebó elese Elegguá y Ochosi?" If the answer to any of these is yes, the diviner will mark the appropriate sacrifices using the shells.

The client also has issues with egun to be settled. The diviner should prescribe a series of three masses. To find out if the egun require further ebo, the diviner must ask, "Ebó elese egun?" If the answer is yes, he uses the shells to mark the appropriate offering.

The diviner should tell the client to visit a babalawo for a session with Ifá; many issues in his life can be settled only through Orúnmila. For a man, Ejioko Ogundá hints that mano de Orúnmila is needed, and for a woman, kofá de Orúnmila. An accurate assessment by Ifá will determine if this is necessary.

The diviner must also explore the following eboses:

- If the client has been physically attacked or his property vandalized, a particular ebó to Ogún will strengthen his defenses and destroy all his enemies. The diviner should put a piece of iron ore in Ogún's cauldron and pour omiero over it. He should then sacrifice a rooster to Ogún and, after the sacrifice, sprinkle plenty of smoked fish and jutía over him while the client names his enemies and all the wrongs that others have done to him. Ogún will render these people harmless, punishing them for the evil they have wrought.
- If gossip and bad tongues plague the client, have him prepare an adimú of cow's tongue for Shangó. He should bake the tongue with plenty of epó and serve it to Shangó on a bed of toasted corn.
- Ejioko Ogundá signals that the client must make frequent adimú to his Elegguá. This orisha will work to ensure that his secrets are not betrayed by those who know them.
- A serious osogbo marks the client as being argumentative and hardheaded; this is because Ikú is on his trail, and he knows it. He also has a close friend or relative (a wife, child, or lover) who is equally argumentative; he and this person are having many troubles. They must come together to sacrifice a rooster to Elegguá and leave an adimú with him once the sacrifice is complete. Elegguá will save both, healing their relationship.
- If a relative is ill and in danger of death, it is possible to extend, and possibly save, this person's life with a particular odu: the sacrifice of a ram to Shangó. Shangó can, if nothing else, relieve the pain and suffering while extending the afflicted one's final days.

After considering all these as options for ebó, the diviner asks the oracle for closure. If the sign remains open, Eji Oko may be marking the client for the reception of the Ibeyi. If the Ibeyi have already been received, the diviner must find out if they are standing up for ebó, asking, "Ebó elese los Ibeyi?" If the answer is yes, he should mark an appropriate sacrifice for them using the diloggún.

If the oracle remains open and the client is an aleyo, the diviner now turns to the eboses for the parent odu, Eji Oko (see page 132). Something there may be necessary to bring closure.

If the client is a priest or a priestess, a sacrifice of four legs is needed. If the odu still refuses closure and came in an osogbo of ano or ikú, the diviner must mark sacrifices to Ogún and Ósun (the client's orishas). After these sacrifices, he must feed the earth beneath the client's shadow.

If the oracle continues to refuse closure, the diviner turns to the eboses for the parent odu, Eji Oko (see page 132). If nothing there can satisfy the odu, the proper ebó to mark is the reception of the knife. This prescription in itself will close the odu.

After the letter is closed, everyone present for the reading must prepare an ebó for egun; this may be done collectively or individually. (If the ebó is given collectively, however, everyone must present some type of adimú—even something simple, like a candle—to his own egun when he returns home.) The proper offering for egun in Ejioko Ogundá is *natilla* (a type of pudding) served in a gourd; take this to a hollow tree in the woods along with several simple foods (fruits and cooked grains will suffice) and beverages (coffee and rum are preferred).

To prepare natilla for egun, the following ingredients are necessary: 3/4 cup of evaporated milk, 1/4 cup of water, one cinnamon stick, 1 1/2 tablespoons of sugar, 1 1/2 tablespoons of cornstarch, one egg, 1/4 teaspoon of vanilla extract, and instant cocoa.

Mix the evaporated milk with the water. From this mixture, measure out 1/4 cup and put this aside, saving it for later. Crush the cinnamon stick, and stir the resulting cinnamon powder and the sugar into the remaining milk-and-water mixture. Microwave on high power for 1 minute and 35 seconds. Blend the 1/4 cup of reserved milk-and-water mixture by hand with the cornstarch and the egg. Combine with the microwaved mixture and mix well. Put the combined mixture in the microwave and cook on medium-high power for 2 to 3 minutes, or until the mixture is thick. Then stir in the vanilla extract and mix well. Darken the pudding by adding instant cocoa a teaspoon at a time, stirring vigorously, until the desired color is attained. Serve the natilla to egun in a gourd.

## The Fourth Composite Odu of Ejioko, Ejioko Irosun (2-4)

### The Proverbs of Ejioko Irosun

- There is a rocky path before you.
- Remove from your path that which bothers you, and you will walk with ease.
- Things pawned are things lost.

### The Message of Ejioko Irosun

When an initial casting of two mouths, Eji Oko, precedes a second casting of four mouths, Irosun, the pattern Ejioko Irosun has opened on the mat. This odu also goes by the names Oyekun Iroso, Oyekun Irosun, Yeku Iroso, and Yeku Irosun. With this sign open, no matter its orientation, the diviner knows that the client is to blame for his own problems; the obstacles he faces are self-imposed, and if he works to remove them, he will walk far on his own without the orishas' help. The problems the client cannot solve by himself may be brought by witchcraft and negative spirits; once ebó is made, the orishas can take care of them. Any severe, volatile osogbos that come in this casting must be read as punishments from the orishas, and the client needs to own up to his wrongdoings before he can have evolution. The focus of this sign, for the diviner, is to determine how to placate the orishas and how to cleanse the negative energies from the client's life. This will not be an easy task, especially since the client must take responsibility for his own actions.

Ejioko Irosun flags a client for whom personal relationships are in danger. Because he has a selfish and self-serving nature, many of his friends are not happy with him. He must learn to be more honest and open if he is to save his relationship with them. Note that being honest and open does not equal telling all that one knows; the client will have some secrets he'll need to keep. If the client is in a committed relationship, it is in danger as well. Another person is vying for his lover, and when the time comes he will have to surrender that relationship. In this odu, the client must not compete for another's affections. If love is not given freely, it is not given truly but, rather, is sold to suitors. This odu also indicates that when the client courts his next lover, he should sacrifice a rooster to Elegguá to avoid rivalry. If marriage does come of his next relationship, Elegguá requires a goat as ebó—this will keep his lover honest. Once married, the client must never surrender what belongs to his heart: his lover. Divorce becomes taboo in this sign.

The diviner begins the reading by offering praise, saying, "Maferefún Shangó! Maferefún Olokun!" Both orishas are close to the client and want what is best for him. However, the two orishas must be placated with ebó before iré will come. Olokun comes to tell the client no one knows him as well as he; only he knows the client's thoughts, plans, dreams, and desires. He knows what is in his heart, things of which even the client is not aware. One day, Olokun will bring all these longings to light. Shangó comes to warn the client of the bad that might still befall him. He wants this person to watch his path and where he walks. He must always have his eyes open; he must not let himself stumble or fall. Shangó tells us that many evil eyes watch the client, and many bad tongues wag about his affairs. He will destroy these people in his own good time. If someone in this person's home is sick, Shangó says to take him to a physician immediately—he could die in the client's home. Shangó also says that if the client suffers pains in the eyes, head, or neck, he should see a physician and then come back to him for a rogación. Shangó will bring healing.

In a reading of Ejioko Irosun, the diviner must keep the following points in mind:

- This odu, even in iré, brings serious stressors to the client's life; he must give himself adequate time for rest, sleep, prayer, and meditation so that he does not become overwhelmed. In osogbo, this person could lose his head over minor issues. The diviner must advise caution in all personal dealings so the client does not do something he later regrets.

- Unbalanced people will be attracted to the client while this odu is in effect. He must guard his personal safety and beware of those whom one would label "crazy." To associate with such people will be his downfall.
- Ano or ikú marks sickness on not only the client but also his family. Over the next year, the client could be required to travel to visit those who are sick or hospitalized.
- The letter can bring danger, treason, traps, and prison. Legal papers are not always what they seem. The client should consult an attorney for even the smallest legal matters.

## The Prohibitions of Ejioko Irosun

- Do not eat any type of grains or any food containing the heads, feet, or intestines of animals. If meat served at a meal has bones, do not suck or gnaw on them, because Ejioko Irosun indicates that one might choke on bones.
- In this odu, open holes are the means by which one's luck is lost and misfortune enters one's life. Be careful when around any type of hole. Do not look into peepholes, and do not wear torn or ripped clothing. If holes are inherent in an article's design, do not buy it; if it is already among one's possessions, throw it away. Do not wear any clothing made of lace or containing eyelets.
- Do not wear any red clothing.

## The Eboses of Ejioko Irosun

The first considerations for ebó in Ejioko Irosun center on Elegguá. He speaks strongly in this odu and gives the client foundation in all things. To properly placate him, the diviner must work out the following issues:

- A client who has not received Elegguá must take the initiation of the warriors. Once Elegguá, Ogún, Ochosi, and Ósun are seated in the client's house, evolution will come.
- If the client is an aborisha who received the warriors through Ifá, an Elegguá of ocha must be prepared. Without this, the client cannot evolve in the religion.
- If the client received Elegguá through ocha, that Elegguá is demanding special treatment. The client must worship him as if he were the guardian orisha. The diviner should consider packing additional *carga* (secret ingredients that strengthen Elegguá's aché) into his image.
- The diviner should also consider finding out if Elegguá will take a specific offering, asking, "Ebó elese Elegguá?" If the answer is yes, the diviner uses the shells to mark the appropriate ebó.
- If an initiate has opened in Ejioko Irosun, Elegguá is demanding a crown. In this odu, he says that he is king, and if treated like the king of this client's life, he will give him a kingdom.

In addition, in Ejioko Irosun, the Ibeyi are necessary for the client's evolution. If he does not have them, he must receive them; if he has them, he must give them a party.

After considering these options, the diviner has his first chance to close the oracle. If the odu remains open, he must explore the following possibilities with the client:

- Shangó is also important in Ejioko Irosun, and he might need ebó. The diviner should ask, "Ebó elese Shangó?" If the answer is yes, the proper adimú to give is a stalk of green plantains. When presenting these to Shangó, the client pays foribale, praying to the orisha about the problems he faces. Shangó will help the client win his battles and wars. When the plantains begin to rot, the client must remove them and discard them at the foot of a palm or ceiba tree.
- Egun can also stand up for attention and ebó. The diviner should ask, "Ebó elese egun?" If the answer is yes, he must mark the required offering using the diloggún. If egun will take no

ebó, the diviner might wish to prescribe a series of masses for them.

- The Ibeyi could be standing up for further eboses. To find out if this is the case, the diviner should also ask, "Ebó elese los Ibeyi?" If the answer is yes, the diviner uses the diloggún to mark the proper offering.
- Olokun is important in this letter as well. If the client does not have him, he might need this orisha; the diviner should ask, "Koshé Olokun?" If the client already has Olokun, he should give one of the following eboses: a blue plate to sit on, a beaded fishnet to cover Olokun's sopera, a beaded mazo, or a mask. If Olokun already has these items, or if the odu still will not close, the diviner should find out if she needs a different specific offering, asking, "Ebó elese Olokun?" If the answer is yes, the diviner uses the diloggún to mark the appropriate offering.
- If the oracle remains open, the next option for ebó in Ejioko Irosun goes to Yemayá and Oshún. Since they are sisters, they will take ebó together. To attempt to mark this ebo, the diviner asks, "Eyebale y adimú elese ile Yemayá y elese ile Oshún?" If the answer is yes, the client must offer a sacrifice and an adimú to Yemayá and Oshún in their respective houses, the ocean and the river. If possible, he should make the ebó to both in brackish water, where the river meets the sea.

If the oracle refuses closure and the client is an aborisha, the diviner should consider the eboses of the parent odu, Eji Oko (see page 132).

If the client is an an initiate, the guardian orisha could be standing up for a crown. The diviner should ask, "Corona para [orisha's name]?" If the answer is yes, an appropriate crown must be bought or made.* If the answer is no, the diviner should consider the eboses of the parent odu, Eji Oko.

*Only orishas considered royalty, such as Shangó, Yemayá, Oshún, Obatalá, Oyá, and Elegguá, may wear crowns. If the client's guardian orisha is not royalty, do not ask this question.

## The Fifth Composite Odu of Ejioko, Ejioko Oché (2-5)

### The Proverbs of Ejioko Oché

- Where there are riches, there is tragedy.
- Money will bring tragedy.
- You called Death; now he is looking for you.
- Let us not die as a friend of the house of strangers.
- May we not die in the house of mourning.
- When death comes, let us praise those friends of brave character.
- A shrewd man will never die inside.
- Feathers improve the beauty of the bird.

### The Message of Ejioko Oché

When an initial cast of two mouths, Eji Oko, precedes a cast of five mouths, Oché, the odu Ejioko Oché is open on the mat. This sign is also known as Oyekun Oché and Yeku Oché. When born among the odu, Ejioko Oché revealed one of the most tragic principles created by Olódumare: fear. So great is Fear in creation that he is considered an orisha, although he was never born physically on earth. He has no face and no name; he hides in darkness. He speaks in whispers that stir the soul and suffocates one's spirit. He has no shrine and takes no followers, and he is dreaded by both mortals and immortals alike. Yet it is said that fear also prepares our minds for ocha; those who open in this odu are marked to become priests or priestesses of our faith, but they will not commit to doing so until they have felt true fear. The diviner should tell the client this; he should also tell him that he has yet to learn what true fear is. Soon, he will know.

When this odu opens, the diviner exclaims, "Maferefún Elegguá! Maferefún Oshún! Maferefún Shangó! Maferefún Olokun!" The aché of these four spirits is essential to the client's evolution; they will all help him overcome the fear foretold in this sign.

The odu brings many warnings to the client, and he must heed its advice if he hopes to evolve amid chaos. First, Oshún speaks firmly here. She stands up in this orisha's diloggún to say that the client once made a promise to her, and now she comes demanding payment. If the client cannot remember making such a promise to Oshún, the diviner should mark an ebó to Oshún so that she is appeased. Whether Ejioko Oché opens in iré or osogbo, Oshún can bring or block blessings as she sees fit, and now her goodwill is essential to the client's evolution. Oshún also appears here to warn the client of health issues. The blood, stomach, legs, feet, and all the internal organs of the abdominal region might suffer illness or decay. This warning is especially serious if an osogbo of ano or ikú is marked. He must also be wary of diseases that can rot or decompose living flesh, such as sores, bacterial infections, ulcers, and cancers. Ejioko Oché demands that the client care for himself; he must eat well, rest adequately, and give up vices.

Shangó offers advice to the client as well. He says that the client is poor now, living in self-imposed poverty and despair, but soon his luck will change. How quickly the change happens will depend on the iré or osogbo opened. As an omen that his luck will change, the client will find, or he will be given, a thunderstone (a sacred stone belonging to Shangó and believed to be created when lightning touches the earth). When he receives the stone, he must wash and feed it with his godparent's Shangó as soon as possible. From that moment on, he must treasure it, for if he loses it, he also will lose the gifts Shangó wants to bring. He should carry the thunderstone with him every day; if the stone is small, he might mount it as a pendant. Shangó also wants the client to say a special incantation several times each day while going about his normal affairs. When outdoors, the client should look at the sky and reach his hands up to heaven, saying, "Olófin, I am so bored." In time, Olófin will hear his cries and the heavens will open, providing new, more exciting and profitable opportunities.

In all castings of Ejioko Oché, the diviner should keep the following possibilities in mind:

- Through the action of Ejioko Oché, the orishas are bringing change, worry, and revolution to the client's life. Note that these are not punishments but tools for personal growth. To make this person's transitions less severe, the diviner must detail all the prohibitions of this sign, even if it has come in iré.
- The client's family makes unrealistic demands. The diviner should advise the client not to allow this.
- This client has many self-destructive tendencies and in darker osogbos may be suicidal. In a volatile orientation, Death could even come because the client has been calling him. The diviner should warn the client to change his ways immediately and make ebó lest he be in danger. Note that already this person has strange dreams and nightmares and perhaps also insomnia and an irrational fear of the dark.
- The client is overworked and overwhelmed, yet he is also bored with his life. If he has patience and thinks all things through, new and more exciting opportunities will come.
- The client's home is under both scrutiny and attack. First, Oshún is not pleased with how the client lives. This person must clean his home and then give it light and warmth. Also, the client's neighbors and acquaintances are nosy. He should let no one other than close, trusted friends inside. Finally, someone wants this person to move, and if that person is angered, he will stop at nothing to make this happen.
- In this odu, not only the client but also his lover and children are marked for ocha. In time, all of them will come to the feet of the orishas.
- Money will come to the client through the country. The diviner should tell him to keep this in mind.
- If the client is single but semi-involved in a relationship, he may be thinking about taking a wife or permanent lover. Two others will be vying for the affections of the person he has in mind. If the client hopes to win, he must sacrifice a rooster with plenty of fresh honey to Elegguá and then provide the orisha with a basket of fresh, sweet fruits. The client will then attain his heart's desires.
- If the client is in a position of authority, his subordinates are giving him trouble. The diviner should have him bring a bolt of white cloth to

Obatalá as a sacrifice; the orisha will then soothe the tension in the workplace. The client should give a bolt of appropriately colored cloth to any other spirit who stands up in this reading as well.

## The Prohibitions of Ejioko Oché

- Because Ikú can be close by in this odu, avoid wakes, funerals, nursing homes, hospitals, and sickbeds. These are places that Death visits regularly, and since he is already looking for the one who opened in this odu, this one will be recognized in such a place. Likewise, limit one's time outdoors after dark and stay away from dark places like clubs, bars, and movie theaters.
- If illness takes one to Oshún for a rogación, vices become taboo. Give up tobacco, alcohol, gluttony, and addictions. The foods of Oshún (such as gourds, squashes, and pumpkins) also become taboo in this letter when illness or disease is present.
- When Ejioko Oché comes in osogbo, travel becomes taboo. If one must travel, before leaving return to the diviner and make an adimú to his Elegguá and Oshún. The trip might still bring disappointment, but at least one will be safe.

## The Eboses of Ejioko Oché

When this odu opens on the mat in anything but the firmest iré, a few initial eboses must be considered. First, the client has an unpaid promise to Oshún; he must now pay it, for she will withhold evolution until he does. If the client cannot remember making any promises or having incurred any debts to Oshún, the diviner must make find out if she is standing up for ebó, asking, "Ebó elese Oshún?" If the answer is yes, the diviner uses the diloggún to mark the appropriate offering.

If the client does not have the Ibeyi, he is now marked for their reception. If he has them, he should offer them a simple ebó of whatever his heart tells him to give.

This sign reveals that the client's own guardian orisha has brought punishment and revolution. If the client's guardian orisha is not known, the issue is between the client and his godparent's guardian orisha. Whichever the case, that spirit must be propitiated. To find out what is needed to settle this debt, the diviner should ask, "Ebó else [guardian orisha's name]?" If the answer is yes, he should mark the appropriate ebó using the diloggún.

Two other options for ebó come in this sign when the client is ill. When disease is present in the blood, stomach, legs, feet, or internal organs of the body, the client must have two rogaciónes before Oshún. The first goes to his head and the second to his abdomen. Afterward, the diviner must cleanse the client with two pigeons and a hen; these are then fed to Oshún. By completing these rogaciónes and following his physician's advice, the client's life will be saved. The second option for ebó manifests when an impending operation has brought this client to the mat and is directed to Ogún. To determine if this orisha will stand up to defend the client in Ejioko Oché, the diviner asks, "Larishe elese Ogún?" If the answer is yes, the diviner will mark an appropriate ebó. If the answer is no, the client's life lies in the hands of his physician; his own "karma" and lack of self-care have brought him to this point, and he is left to pray to his orí and God for his own salvation.

If the prescription of these eboses is not enough to close the session, the diviner must explore the following:

- Egun can stand up in this sign for both spiritual work and ebó. If the letter refuses closure, they, like Oshún, are announcing their displeasure with the client's living conditions. Immediately, this person's home must be physically cleaned and spiritually cleansed. The client must tend his bóveda well, providing it with fresh water daily and white flowers and candles weekly. Once these things are done, a series of at least five weekly masses (one per week) should be hosted in the client's home. Finally, egun must be given the option to claim ebó; to see what they require, the diviner should ask, "Ebó elese egun?" If the answer is yes, he uses the shells to mark the appropriate offering.

If the client is an aleyo or aborisha and the odu still will not close, the diviner must turn to the eboses of the parent odu, Eji Oko (see page 132). Something there is needed for the client's evolution.

If the client is an initiate, the diviner should investigate the following eboses:

- The client might need to receive Ochosi. The diviner should ask, "Koshé Ochosi?" If the answer is yes, until preparations can be made the client should at least receive the spirit's eleke; he must first have a rogación before his godparent's crowning orisha and leave adimú to that spirit.
- If the odu still will not close, the client must host a tambor in Oshún's honor. She will come down and remove all that stands in the way of the client's evolution.

If this pattern continues to remain open, the diviner must consider the eboses of the parent odu, Eji Oko (see page 132). Something there is necessary for the client's evolution.

## The Sixth Composite Odu of Eji Oko, Ejioko Obara (2-6)

### The Proverbs of Ejioko Obara

- The orishas bring a revolution.
- Men should not tell secrets to women.
- Women should not tell secrets to men.
- Wars are begun when someone wants what another has.
- Brothers will war among themselves.

### The Message of Ejioko Obara

When the initial cast of two mouths, Eji Oko, precedes a cast of six mouths, Obara, the odu Ejioko Obara, also known as Yeku Obara and Oyekun Obara, is open on the mat. This sign alludes to the horse and the ox as beasts of burden; both wanted to find fame and fortune on the earth, so they went to the diviners in heaven to find out what they had to do before descending. Ebó was marked but never made. Humans soon enslaved both animals to do their heavy work for them. This odu warns that the client's life is at a turning point, and if he does not listen and do all that he is told, he will live a life of servitude, one filled with burdens and despair.

When this pattern opens, the diviner says, "Maferefún Shangó! Maferefún Yemayá!" These orishas are the client's salvation and will demand ebó of him in exchange for their help. Obatalá can bring blessings in this sign, so the diviner also exclaims, "Maferefún Obatalá!" As his final praises, the diviner says, "Maferefún Elegguá! Maferefún Ochosi!" These two spirits dominate all patterns of Eji Oko, and rarely will a sign in this family close without their intervention.

With Ejioko Obara on the mat, the first thing the diviner should tell his client is that a war is coming between brothers and sisters of ocha. If the war has not yet begun, it soon will, and the client must do all that he can not to be involved. The orishas of those who fight among themselves will bring more revolution and strife to their lives, and this war will not be fought only on the earth. Each involved will try to move the powers of heaven against the other. Know that while this odu tells the client he must not be involved in this war, it also foreshadows his eventual involvement. The fact that he is in this ilé ocha will drag him into the middle of strife and intrigue. Before the war has passed, some of his own spiritual family might wish him harm. Take note that this pattern also speaks of love spells and sorcery; others could lay obstacles in the client's path through witchcraft. Enemies will speak behind this person's back, but timely ebó will lessen the effects of these things.

Each orisha who stands up in Ejioko Obara brings his or her own advice to the client. Yemayá and Shangó come because they love this person dearly; however, if the odu has opened in an osogbo, they also come to claim past debts that are owed to them. The diviner must explain this to the client sternly: "In the past, you have prayed for favors from both Yemayá and Shangó. Promises were made, but these are unfulfilled. They must now be paid." The client must be forced, at the mat, to talk about the prayers he has offered to these two spirits and the promises in his heart for them at that time. Any promises he made to these orishas are written in the record's reading; they are now eboses needed to placate this odu. The client must offer them immediately. If the client cannot or will not speak on this matter, the diviner must question the oracle to see if Shangó, Yemayá, or the two together will accept ebó; see "The Eboses of Ejioko Obara" on page 114.

While Obatalá is the most forgiving of all the orishas, in this odu he is stern. Three times he has tried to bring blessings to the client's life. Three times the blessings that Obatalá gave were lost. The client, through his own carelessness, has given away much of the good in his life. He has not fulfilled his mundane obligations to family and friends, nor has he lived up to his religious obligations. It is time for the diviner to be stern; he must instill responsibility and respect in this person or else he will not evolve. The diviner must assure him, however, that if he does all things as he should, Obatalá will try one more time to bring a very special blessing into his life. The client must not miss this final opportunity, for it will not be given again.

Finally, Elegguá and Ochosi are here, gently leading the client to iré by cautioning him against many things. First, they tell the client that he goes through life too quickly; he runs from place to place without watching where he is going or what goes on around him. He must slow down. His haste causes him to miss much, including the blessings that the orishas try to bring to him. Women figure prominently in this person's life, and they are both a curse and a blessing. The client must abstain from telling women his secrets; one will soon betray him. (Likewise, if the client is a woman, she should refrain from telling men her secrets, because one will soon betray her.) Elegguá and Ochosi want to tell this person that they are working together to bless his life; before this sign closes, the diviner may need to prescribe ebó to these spirits together.

The diviner should also explore with the client the following points:

- This client suffers from insomnia and does not sleep well, which may be due to the many spirits surrounding him.
- The client's legs are prone to injury; he must protect them. Diseases of the blood are a risk here as well.
- In osogbo, this odu speaks of random violence. If the client is not careful on the streets, he may be hurt. The diviner must advise him to use caution when outdoors, especially when traveling to strange places.
- During the course of the next few months, this person will have many important tasks and errands to complete. In Ejioko Obara, it is vital that the client complete these tasks on his own. He must not send others to do them in his place. If he does, he may be cheated out of something important.
- The client himself causes many of his own problems. If the client is a woman who has come to the oracle because she cannot have children, her infertility is her own fault as well.
- Any osogbo brought by this odu will eventually abate on its own. The diviner should tell the client not to hide from his troubles because they will go away, and if he works to resolve them, they will leave him in better shape than he was before they came.

## The Prohibitions of Ejioko Obara

- Avoid unnecessary travel to strange or foreign lands. If one must travel, never go alone; go with a trusted friend.
- Never send others to do a job that should be done by one's own hands.
- If Shangó or Oshún claims any ebó during the course of this reading, do not consume any type of gourd, out of respect for these two orishas.

## The Eboses of Ejioko Obara

Shangó and Yemayá are the first concerns for ebó in this sign. As described above, any promises the client made to these orishas in the past but did not keep must now be marked as ebó. If the client cannot remember having any unkept promises to them, the diviner must ask the following series of questions: "Ebó elese Shangó?"; "Ebó elese Yemayá?"; and "Ebó elese Shangó e Yemayá?" If the answer to any of these questions is yes, the diviner must mark the appropriate offering using the diloggún. Until he makes this ebó, the client can have no evolution.

Obatalá might also offer a remedy to keep this person from missing the blessings inherent in the odu. The diviner must check this by asking, "Larishe elese Obatalá?" If the answer is yes, the diviner will mark an appropriate offering with the shells.

Now the diviner has his first opportunity to close the odu. If the odu refuses closure, the diviner should investigate the following:

- Eboses may be required for Elegguá and Ochosi. To check this, the diviner may ask, "Ebó elese Elegguá?" and "Ebó elese Ochosi?" If the answer is yes, the diviner uses the shells to mark the appropriate offering.
- If the odu still refuses closure, the client may have issues pending with the Ibeyi. If the client has not received these orishas, he is now marked for their reception. If he already has them, the diviner must find out if they require ebó, asking, "Ebó elese los Ibeyi?" If the answer is yes, the diviner marks the offering with the diloggún.

If this letter still refuses closure after all these options have been explored, the diviner should turn to the eboses of the parent odu, Eji Oko (see page 132). Something there is needed to bring the client's evolution.

## The Seventh Composite Odu of Eji Oko, Ejioko Odí (2-7)

### The Proverbs of Ejioko Odí

- He who eats a lot will die, killed by his own mouth.
- He who eats like a glutton dies like a fish, through the mouth.
- The flames come from beneath.
- The fires shall burn below.

### The Message of Ejioko Odí

When the first casting of two mouths, Eji Oko, precedes a cast of seven mouths, Odí, the odu Ejioko Odí is open on the mat. This sign is also known as Oyekun Odí and Yeku Odí. Although Orúnmila cannot speak through the diloggún, it was by this odu's grace that he brought all the oracles to earth, so when this pattern falls on the mat, many diviners say, "Maferefún Orúnmila!" With these oracles, humans were enabled to speak with the orishas, the spirits of creation, and find their paths to evolution. With this marvelous gift, Orúnmila brought all who live on Earth the means to find wealth, health, love, prosperity, abundance, happiness, and all the things that make life worth living.

The diviner will also say, "Maferefún Yemayá!" Yemayá speaks strongly in this odu. Whether the odu comes in iré or osogbo, it marks the client as having issues with her. If the client has not already had his head (guardian orisha) marked, he may be her child. Yemayá's advice here is stern. She says that if good is always done, evil can never be returned. All the wrongs done to this person thus far should be left at her feet with a simple adimú, and she will deal with them herself. If evil was wrought by a relation of blood or of ocha, her punishments will be severe indeed. Yemayá also warns the client to take health issues more seriously. At this time any illness, even a cold, warrants a trip to a physician and a rogación before her shrine. If sickness comes in either the groin or the abdomen, the client must wear his elekes, being careful to wear Yemayá's for a total of twenty-eight consecutive days. Thus will she remove all that is wrong.

The diviner must tell the client, also, that this pattern marks him to make ocha, and he should begin to plan for this event.

If Ejioko Odí opens in iré, the client at the mat will be gifted with brilliance when it comes to divination. Whether this person's path is with the orishas or with Ifá, he will learn all that these oracles have to teach and one day will be a well-known and sought-after diviner.

In this odu we say that the world once became evil and rotten, and Olódumare sent Orúnmila down to cleanse it and reclaim it from evil. If Ejioko Odí has come in osogbo, this quality could manifest in the client's life: His life, in general, could be going bad.

In addition, the diviner must explore with the client the following points:

- Because Ejioko Odí marks the descent of all the oracles to earth, and because it foreshadows greatness at divination, this client must learn to speak "words of truth." The tongue has aché, and one's words are forces for manifestation. The client must be told to speak the truth at all times or say nothing at all. By doing this, he will honor both Olófin and his own head.
- Just as the odu were the first children of Olódumare, so does this odu presage the birth of a new child to the client's family. If the client is a woman, she will have a child blessed by God.
- In this odu, it is important that the diviner ask the client how many children were born to his mother. If his mother bore three, all were born for greatness, yet because of their quarreling, this greatness may never come. The diviner should advise cooperation in the family unit.
- In this person's home someone might soon become ill; when this happens, the client must bring that person to the diviner or to his godparent. He or she will require the assistance of the orishas for a healing.

## The Prohibitions of Ejioko Odí

- Measure one's words before speaking. The tongue does have aché, but it will beat one with its own words. Do not speak ill of others, and do not gossip.
- Evil will come to those around one; refuse to participate in it. Here, we say that the world was rotten and had to be cleansed of evil. Make sure one does not need to be "cleansed" by God.
- Do not consume shellfish or seafood for twenty-eight days; abstain from raw seafood and raw shellfish for life. Poisons could come to the body through these things.

## The Eboses of Ejioko Odí

This odu indicates that the client has issues to be settled with Yemayá, and the diviner must consider many options for ebó. If the client has not had the initiation of the elekes, he must have at least her eleke, and he should wear it daily. He must also have a rogación before her shrine, leaving adimú to Yemayá when it is done. Yemayá should be given her chance to claim something from the reading; to see what, if anything, she requires, the diviner must ask, "Ebó elese Yemayá?" If the answer is yes, the diviner uses the diloggún to mark the appropriate ebó.

The initiation of the Ibeyi is important in this odu. If the client does not have them, he must receive them. If he has them, the diviner must find out if they require ebó, asking, "Ebó elese los Ibeyi?" If the answer is yes, the diviner uses the diloggún to mark the appropriate ebó.

If these considerations are not enough to close the reading, the diviner must turn to the eboses of the parent odu, Eji Oko (see page 132). Something there is necessary for the client's evolution.

# The Eighth Composite Odu of Eji Oko, Ejioko Ejiogbe (2-8)

## The Proverbs of Ejioko Ejiogbe

- Others want to destroy the king by killing him with arrows.
- Those in this world should not become entangled with those in the next.
- There will be competition between brothers.
- The one who was born to be a head should not end up in the tail.

## The Message of Ejioko Ejiogbe

When a casting of two mouths, Eji Oko, is followed by a casting of eight mouths, Eji Ogbe, the odu

Ejioko Ejiogbe has come to the mat. This pattern is also known as Ejioko Unle, Ejioko l'Ogbe, Oyekun l'Ogbe, and Oyekun Unle. Through this odu the first "reading of the year" was performed: Olófin had finished his work at creation, and a new year was about to begin. He sat down with the diloggún to cast a sign telling him how the new year would progress. Since this time, elder priests and priestesses have continued this custom in their own ilé by opening an odu on December 31 of every year to represent the coming new year.

The diviner thanks Olófin for creating this custom, saying, "Maferefún Olófin!" He also pays homage to Obatalá, Yemayá, Olokun, the Ibeyi, Oshún, and Oyá, saying to each, "Maferefún!" Before this letter closes, many of these orishas will stand up to speak, and most of them will claim ebó.

Ejioko Ejiogbe is filled with blessings, but while it can bring limitless iré, it also carries hidden danger. Remember that Eji Oko speaks of crucial turning points in a person's life, fleeting moments that, once passed, will change the course of one's life forever. The odu Eji Ogbe speaks of life and death; it enforces the difference between the two, reminding us that some things in creation must never become "crossed." Eji Oko alludes to crossroads; Eji Ogbe forbids crossings. The client exists in a stressful time, and the diviner must help him sort out his life now, before the reading ends.

With this odu on the mat, the diviner knows that the client has not fulfilled all his religious obligations as he should. This sign tells us that, a long time ago, a series of cleansings, perhaps even eboses, were prescribed for this person. They were essential to his evolution, but they were not done. Because of this, the client has many troubles, his mind is clouded, and he has difficulty realizing his goals and dreams. The italero who has opened the diloggún must talk honestly with the client about his past in this religion; he must examine the prescriptions that have been given to this person before and those prescriptions that were not fulfilled as they should have been. While the odu that brought these prescriptions has passed, the need for completing those eboses has not. This odu, Ejioko Ejiogbe, now prescribes these eboses once more. The diviner must record them in the record of the reading so the client will do them immediately.

In this pattern we pay homage to Obatalá because, although Eji Oko is the parent odu open, Eji Ogbe dominates the reading. Eji Oko brings rapid changes, thorough transformations, and passages into new eras of development; Eji Ogbe says that most of these transitions will affect the client's head and personal outlook on life. Regardless of the odu's orientation (iré or osogbo), the changes brought by this pattern will be stressful, and when the head becomes hot or overwhelmed the client must turn to Obatalá to refresh his orí. As ebó, the diviner must prescribe a series of eight weekly rogaciónes before Obatalá's shrine. The rogaciónes will strengthen the client for the trials and changes that lie ahead. Note that no matter whose diloggún is used or the reason that this consultation was given, Ejioko Ejiogbe suggests that if the client's head (guardian orisha) has not been marked with a bajado or with Ifá, he could be Obatalá's child.

Yemayá (the giver of life on earth) and Olokun (the aché of the ocean) are also powerful in this sign. Both orishas bring change, and change is always stressful, but these changes will refresh and renew the client; they will give him a new lease on life. The diviner must mark ebó to these two powerful orishas in the ocean, if possible, or to the diviner's own orishas if it is not possible to travel to the ocean soon.

This sign makes a very important prediction for the client: Sometime in his past, roughly eight years ago, he lost something valuable. This lost item could be anything—a possession, a jewel, money, or a friend. Ejioko Ejiogbe promises that this item will be found again, although it might not be reclaimable. The orientation of the odu (iré or osogbo) will determine whether this finding will be met with rejoicing or sadness. The client should be careful, for once he has found what was lost, his life will become strange, exotic, and chaotic. Ejioko Ejiogbe can also become an odu of loss if one is not careful, and the client must take care to guard his most precious possessions.

In addition to these considerations, the diviner must keep the following in mind:

- The connection with twins is overwhelming in this odu. The most obvious is that this client is a twin himself. Because Ejioko Ejiogbe speaks of the crossing between life and death, it is possible that the client's twin is dead; he or she may have been miscarried, stillborn, or killed. Another possibility is that one of the client's ancestors was a twin or that he has twin children. The diviner must investigate these options, for they will have an effect on the eboses for this odu.
- This odu foreshadows competition between brothers, whether of blood or of ocha. The client should be careful and prepared just in case a "war" breaks out.
- This person's fortune could come by the sea, river, or a large body of water; if he is not living near such a body of water now, he should consider moving to such a location. Also, when looking for work, the client should consider employers based on their proximity to such bodies of water. Note that if this person is not living by a large body of water now, one day he will.
- The diviner should ask the client if it is his nature to loan things out, and then ask what things he has loaned out to others. He must then direct the client to reclaim these items, if possible, for the person who borrowed them has borrowed his luck as well. As long as these items are out of the client's control, so is his evolution.
- This person does not sleep well. He hears voices and music at night; much of these auditory hallucinations come from the dead; the music he hears is the drums of our ancestors at their celebrations. Initiation is coming for this person; he cannot escape it, and until he commits to this path he will continue to be disturbed with these dreams.
- The client likes to confide his dreams and desires in others; this must stop. Now, Elegguá is his true confidant, and he should confide all in him and no one else.

## The Prohibitions of Ejioko Ejiogbe

- One's stomach is delicate; pay careful attention to one's diet, especially when away from home. Do not consume alcohol or other intoxicants, for these will rot one's flesh. Avoid hot, spicy foods, as these will trouble one's digestion. Do not eat food that is improperly served, too hot or too cold, or not thoroughly cooked.
- Do not wear dark or overly bright colors. Dress in white as much as possible. If white is not possible, dress in the lightest colors possible.
- Do not allow outlaws, bandits, or con artists in one's home.
- Do not sign legal papers unless a lawyer is present to review them. Do not answer questions from the authorities without legal counsel.
- Do not loan out or give away old clothing; when another wears one's clothing, he wears one's luck as well.
- Ensuring the safety of oneself and one's possessions is crucial under the influence of this odu. Do not wear jewelry out into the street. Do not take large sums of cash when traveling. Make sure one's home is properly attended, guarded, and locked at all times.

## The Eboses of Ejioko Ejiogbe

When Ejioko Ejiogbe opens on the mat, a handful of initial eboses must be prescribed:

- An ebó made to Ochosi for luck and evolution is mandatory. The client takes several handfuls of almond leaves and covers Ochosi completely with them. Every day for the next four days, he lights two white candles to the orisha, blowing plenty of anisette over his shrine. After the four days of ebó, he discards the leaves under a bush in the woods.
- Because this odu forebodes that the client's fortune will come by the sea, a large river, or another large body of water, he should make ebó to Yemayá, Oshún, and Inle in a place where brackish water exists, a location in which the river and the sea meet. To begin, in the

diviner's home the client should lay a large grass mat before Yemayá, Oshún, and Inle. On this mat, he offers dozens of fresh fruits to the three orishas. After seven days, he adds fresh fruit and takes the entire offering to the chosen location as ebó.

- The diviner must mark ebó to Yemayá and Oshún in the ocean, if possible, or to the diviner's own orishas if it is not possible for the client to travel to the ocean soon.
- Because this odu can become volatile, the client's head could become overwhelmed or exhausted. To calm the passions and keep his head cool, the client must have a series of eight weekly rogaciónes before Obatalá's shrine. If a hot osogbo comes, the diviner should also feed both the client's orí and Obatalá two white pigeons.
- If the client is a twin and his sibling has died, he must set up some type of shrine to honor his twin's soul and tend it well. He also must receive the Ibeyi.
- Finally, before leaving the diviner's home the client should be cleansed with two coconuts. After the cleansing, the diviner must place the coconuts in a basket and set them under running water until the client has left.

If the letter will not close off after these initial eboses have been prescribed, the diviner should consider the following:

- Because the Ibeyi once saved Obatalá from death by treason and poison, they can be essential in this odu. If the client does not have them, he must receive them; if he has them, the diviner must find out if they will take ebó, asking, "Ebó elese los Ibeyi?" If the answer is yes, the diviner marks the ebó with the diloggún. If the answer is no, the client should, nevertheless, be advised to tend his Ibeyi, spoiling them with sweet food and toys.
- If the client does not have Olokun, the diviner should see if his reception is necessary, asking, "Koshé Olokun?" If the answer is no, or if the client already has Olokun, the diviner must find out if Olokun will take an ebó, asking, "Ebó elese Olokun?" If the answer is yes, the diviner uses the shells to mark the appropriate offering. If the answer is no, the client should, nevertheless, be advised to attend an agbán for Olokun as soon as possible.
- If the oracle still refuses closure, any of the following orishas could require ebó: Obatalá, Yemayá, Oshún, and Inle. To see what, if anything, these orishas require, the diviner must ask, "Ebó elese [orisha's name]?" If the answer is yes, the diviner uses the shells to mark the appropriate offering. After each ebó is marked, he should attempt to close the oracle.

If the diviner has investigated all the possibilities for eboses but the oracle remains open, he must turn to the eboses of the parent odu, Eji Oko (see page 132). Something there is needed for the client's evolution.

## The Ninth Composite Odu of Eji Oko, Ejioko Osá (2-9)

### The Proverbs of Ejioko Osá

- Your best friend wants your lover.
- There are rumors and confusion in your family.
- Salvation comes by making ocha.
- Your best friend would steal your own wife.
- There is a revolution in your house.
- Tragedy comes with your best friend.
- No one trades on the palm tree without making money.
- [There will be] revolution, troubles, and fires.

### The Message of Ejioko Osá

When a casting of two mouths, Eji Oko, precedes a casting of nine mouths, Osá, the odu Ejioko Osá, also known as Yeku Osá and Oyekun Osá, is open. The diviner exclaims, "Maferefún Oyá!" Many times the client has been hunted by Ikú, and Oyá herself has stood up to protect him from an early demise. The diviner also says, "Maferefún los Ibeyi!" The sacred twins have worked to keep him safe when no other orisha would. Ejioko Osá signals, however, that their protection now wears thin, and Oyá has much to say to this person. Through this pattern, she announces that sickness, treason, and revolution are near; before these energies have passed, the client's life could become tumultuous. The client must persevere, for Oyá will use these energies to bring change to his life. She warns that the client must guard his health, for if sickness comes, it will be severe. In Ejioko Osá, it is not unusual for the diseased to die. If he comes to the mat because of sickness, the client should be told his health will get worse; if he comes in perfect health, someone close to him may fall fatally ill.

In any type of osogbo, Ejioko Osá marks on the client disharmony, obstacles, fires, revolutions, tragedies, and domestic disputes. While the larishe of this sign (if any) and prescribed eboses might help lessen the severity of these events, they are not a total solution. What the client faces amounts to his own karma, and he must work through it. The osogbos of ano and ikú bring their own special difficulties. With these, the one at the mat could have problems in his blood, veins, lungs, or throat; these regions are most vulnerable in the darker, colder months of the year. Any minor symptom could become a major complaint, so the client must monitor his health.

The diviner should also explore with the client the following points:

- Ejioko Osá is a harsh odu for the client and his family; it guarantees that one who is afflicted with terminal illness will not recover. Many times we say that the odu itself is illness with no security or salvation.
- Ejioko Osá is an odu of obstacles. The diviner must determine what the client brings to the mat in terms of goals: material, emotional, spiritual, and physical. Because the conversation during a session with the diloggún is inspired by both the orishas and the odu, before attempting closure the diviner and his client should determine what obstacles stand in the way of achievement of each of these goals. Any ebó demanded by the diloggún or prescribed by the diviner will help destroy these obstacles.
- Fires and revolutions could manifest in both the streets and the client's home. The client must be cautious both within and without his residence.
- Ejioko Osá guarantees that a tragedy can separate this person and his best friend. To save this friendship, the client must work hard to ensure that no arrows fly between them. Know that if the client is married or has a lover, his best friend is desirous of that person.
- The client's true salvation comes by making ocha. Even if this is a casual reading for a new client, the diviner must recognize that this person's life will not improve until he begins to explore this religion. Once ocha is made, his paths will be easy to travel.

## The Prohibitions of Ejioko Osá

- In this odu, open sources of flame are a danger. Have no more than two candles lit in the home at any one time. Do not leave candles burning unattended.
- Do not let others sleep in one's home; someone could die under one's own roof.
- Unless it is absolutely necessary, do not go to hospitals, nursing homes, cemeteries, funerals, or wakes. If a visit to one of these places is necessary, ask Oyá and Elegguá for permission before going, and cleanse oneself thoroughly upon returning home.

## The Eboses of Ejioko Osá

When Ejioko Osá opens on the mat, it signals that the client requires the eleke of Oyá. If the client does not have this eleke, he should receive it after having a rogación (with nine ingredients) at Oyá's feet. And because Oyá has defended his life at least three times, she may want ebó in exchange. To see if she requires anything, the diviner asks, "Ebó elese Oyá?" If the answer is yes, he must mark the appropriate offering using the diloggún.

Elegguá can claim ebó in Ejioko Osá. If the odu comes in iré, the diviner asks, "Ebó elese Elegguá?" If the answer is yes, the diviner uses the diloggún to mark the appropriate offering. If, however, the letter has opened in a mild osogbo, the ebó to be offered is automatic: feathers. If the osogbo is hot and volatile, a goat is the sacrifice mandated.

The Ibeyi are important to this odu; if the client does not have them, he must receive them. If he has them, the diviner must investigate whether they require ebó, asking, "Ebó elese los Ibeyi?" If the answer is yes, the diviner uses the diloggún to mark the appropriate offering. If the client's life is sour and hopeless, this odu indicates that he must host a party in honor of the Ibeyi, inviting as many children as possible. This will turn the osogbo of this odu into iré.

Finally, if the client struggles against insurmountable odds and is male, he should be sent to a babalawo to receive mano de Orúnmila. If the client is a woman, she must receive kofá de Orúnmila. Should the client already have this initiation, consultation with Ifá is still required; ebó must be made to his or her Ifá, and only Orúnmila may dictate what this ebó is to be.

If the eboses prescribed so far will not bring closure to Ejioko Osá, the diviner should turn to the eboses of the parent odu, Eji Oko (see page 132). Something there is needed for the client's evolution.

## The Tenth Composite Odu of Eji Oko, Ejioko Ofún (2-10)

### The Proverbs of Ejioko Ofún

- He who rises early has money in his pocket.
- Olódumare helps those who wake early.
- He who wakes early will always have the blessings of the orishas.
- During holy week, cover the mirrors.

### The Message of Ejioko Ofún

When a casting of two mouths, Eji Oko, precedes a casting of ten mouths, Ofún, the odu Ejioko Ofún is open on the mat. This letter is also known as Oyekun Ofún and Yeku Ofún. From this sign is born the custom of covering all the mirrors in the house during the Catholic holy week. Ejioko Ofún is a volatile odu, bringing equal amounts of good and evil not only to the client's life, but also to the lives of those present for the reading.

Before determining the orientations of this sign, the diviner should say, "Maferefún Babaluaiye! Maferefún Elegguá! Maferefún egun!" All three orishas stand strong in this odu. Having uttered these reverences, the diviner then marks the heads of all present with efun, drawing a small dot to cover the area known as the "third eye," the region of the pineal gland between and slightly above the two eyes. Everyone must allow this dot to remain on his or her face until well after nightfall. It is a spiritual charm against death, disease, illness, and decay, a minor purification and protection that will help all present walk away from the mat with blessings.

This odu affects many separate areas of the client's life, and the diviner should explore all of them before attempting to close the oracle.

- Babaluaiye, Elegguá, and egun are working together to bring blessings to the client's life. If the letter comes in an osogbo, they are there helping him overcome osogbo. While his life might seem bad now, one day it will be good.
- The client will take vacations and long trips before the year is out. He will not only travel outside his country but also might live outside his motherland.
- Travel might become necessary because the client will have to visit a sick relative. He might also travel to meet relatives he has never met before.
- This odu, although shared by Elegguá and Babaluaiye, is ruled by egun. This is the reason that the heads of all present are marked with efun. Everyone's ancestral spirits (of blood and of ocha) are coming to offer support, guidance, and blessings. They also come to claim ebó. Whatever eboses are marked for the client's egun must be done by all who are present for this reading if they hope to evolve.
- Tell the client that he dreams of the dead; much of his aché comes from them. Their rituals should always be worked, with regular offerings put out for them.

- One of the letter's many proverbs is "Olódumare helps those who wake early." The client's eyes must be open; he must always watch out not only for danger and intrigue but also for blessings and abundance. And he should awaken before sunrise.
- Ejioko Ofún marks unplanned pregnancy and childbirth. If ebó is not marked and made, the child will be delivered by caesarean section. Danger exists for both the mother and the infant, with birth defects being a possibility.
- Ejioko Ofún also carries many health warnings. The most dangerous center on the client's children; he must watch them carefully and pay attention to them constantly. Intestinal trouble, inflammation of the inner organs, venereal disease, and blood-borne pathogens are all a danger. Both the elderly and children should receive prompt medical attention if they become ill.
- At work, this person is lazy. The odu signals that he must not be lazy if he hopes to keep his job; he must work hard. There is a lot of gossip at this person's workplace; he must fight it so that it does not ruin his livelihood.

## The Prohibitions of Ejioko Ofún

- An "exchange of the head"—when one's head is touched by another's—is a danger in this sign. When an "exchange of the head" occurs, one's head absorbs the other's osogbo. Do not let anyone touch one's head. Do not share scarves or hats. Do not let one's head covering fall on the floor; if it does, kiss the hat and put on another.
- Gossip will be one's downfall. Do not gossip. If one listens to gossip, do not act on it or repeat it.
- For the seven days following the opening of this odu, do not gaze at oneself in mirrors or reflective surfaces. For this time period and during the Catholic holy week, cover all the mirrors in one's house.

## The Eboses of Ejioko Ofún

Ejioko Ofún flags issues with the client's egun, who must be propitiated. The first prescription is that of several spiritual masses to give light and progress to the client's ancestors and spirit guides. There is no set number of masses to mandate; however, the diviner might suggest one per week until the client's egun say they have had enough. The client must follow the prescriptions of the espiritistas exactly. If the client does not have a bóveda, one must be set up; ensure that a competent espiritista comes to offer the first prayers, blessing the altar. Finally, in this odu egun must be allowed to personalize these eboses; they hold the keys to the client's future evolution and must be the focus of his spiritual life. To see if they will mark an ebó, the diviner must ask, "Ebó elese egun?" If the answer is yes, the diviner uses the diloggún to mark the appropriate offering.

Whatever eboses are marked for the client's egun must be done by all who are present for this reading.

In addition to propitiation of the egun, the following eboses must be explored:

- Before leaving the diviner's house, the client should give a saraeko (see page 52) to Elegguá. The diviner should also give Elegguá the chance to claim an ebó, asking, "Ebó elese Elegguá?" If the answer is yes, the diviner marks the appropriate offering with the diloggún.
- The client must also give Babaluaiye adimú immediately, before leaving the diviner's house if possible. Something simple—a loaf of bread and unsalted wine (such as dry white wine)—will suffice. As soon as possible, the client should have a rogación before Babaluaiye's shrine and must be given the orisha's eleke. The orisha should be given his chance to claim ebó; the diviner must investigate this option by asking, "Ebó elese Babaluaiye?" If the answer is yes, the diviner should mark the appropriate offering.

Now the diviner has his first chance to close the oracle. If the odu will not close, the client might need to receive Babaluaiye. To see if this is necessary, the diviner should ask, "Koshé Babaluaiye?"

If the reading still will not close, the diviner should turn to the eboses of the parent odu, Eji Oko (see page 132). Something there is needed for the client's evolution.

## The Eleventh Composite Odu of Eji Oko, Ejioko Owani (2-11)

### The Proverbs of Ejioko Owani

- All your birds will die in a cage.
- Children should not be in prison.
- Birds are saddened and die in cages.
- Children must not live like convicts, in prison.
- Hate is borne of love, and love of hate; remember this.

### The Message of Ejioko Owani

When a casting of two mouths, Eji Oko, precedes a casting of eleven mouths, Owani, the odu Ejioko Owani, also known as Oyekun Owani and Yeku Owani, is open. It is a volcanic combination, one that reverberates with the aché of many orishas, and before the letter closes most will demand their chance to speak and claim ebó. The diviner begins by paying homage to Shangó, Aganyú, Elegguá, the Ibeyi, and Ochosi, saying to each, "Maferefún!" All speak here, and in this sign their words may not be kind.

The diviner should begin to explore this letter by telling the client, "In this odu, the influence of Shangó and his father, Aganyú, is strong. They speak to you now, but they will speak only once. Pay attention and heed what is said!" These two orishas focus on three concerns: the law, health, and children. The diviner must slowly and methodically explore this odu by determining its orientation, orisha, and eboses and then thoroughly discuss the parent odu, Eji Oko (see page 132), with the client before exploring the composite odu itself. To help this person evolve, the diviner would do best to treat Ejioko Owani as if it had fallen in osogbo, even if iré is marked; by doing so, the blessing will not be missed.

No matter which orisha speaks or stands up to offer help, the diviner should mark eboses to Elegguá and Ochosi. Elegguá will keep open the avenues of escape, while Ochosi can point out the quickest path to release. Together, these two warriors create a formidable team that can overcome all difficulties.

Regarding legal matters, in Ejioko Owani any deals this client makes outside the law, no matter how minor they are, will bring severe retribution. Intrigues in the home have drawn the attention of neighbors, and they could be the source of many problems. The client must close the blinds and draw the curtains. These issues need to be taken care of before the client's life falls into disarray. He must avoid gossip and not investigate any strange events; they will reek of illicit dealings. Important information about the client and those close to him should not be given away. Many of this person's actions are violent; they make people afraid, and they could lead to jail. He must avoid raising his hand against anyone in his family for this same reason.

The health concerns of Eji Oko—the blood, waist, and legs—are joined here with the health concerns of Owani—the liver, kidneys, and genitals. Sexually transmitted diseases are a possibility. The client's family will also experience multiple health concerns; someone in the family is sick right now and does not know it. This person should have made ebó yesterday to counteract an illness that will come tomorrow. The diviner should mark the ebó required, and the client should perform it as soon as possible. Without ebó, the health problems in the client's family will be severe.

It is said that birds die in cages. Parents should think of their children as birds; they are not meant to live lives of restriction or imprisonment; and no matter how terrible a child's actions might be, he is not a criminal. Children are just that: children. They respond to the examples set by peers and parents. This odu also forebodes that father and son will fight.

If the client has orishas, he should guard them well, perhaps even moving them to a new place for a while. Someone might steal one or more of their implements or even try to destroy their diloggún.

## The Prohibitions of Ejioko Owani

- Do not ever live in a house built on the bank of a river. One day, the river will rise in anger and destroy all that one has worked so hard to obtain.
- Avoid the following foods: rabbit, pigeon, and melons.
- One's trustful nature gets one into much trouble. Do not tell one's goals and plans to anyone. They must be kept secret, revealed only after the goals are obtained.
- In business dealings, be cautious. Do not make deals that are shady or on questionable legal grounds. No matter how minor these details are, they can bring severe legal consequences.
- Keep windows and blinds closed and all the doors and windows to one's home locked so that others cannot see into or enter one's home.

## The Eboses of Ejioko Owani

When reading Ejioko Owani, the diviner's first consideration for ebó centers on the orishas Elegguá and Ochosi; the two work together here to bring the client's evolution. Elegguá is fate or destiny, and he is trying to bring the client into alignment with his goals and aspirations. Ochosi stands here to show this person the shortest route to attainment. Opening in any of the odus of Eji Oko marks the client to receive the warriors. If he already has the warriors, the diviner must ensure that he has the elekes of both Elegguá and Ochosi. The client must wear these daily for twenty-one days. If the client has both the warriors and the elekes of Elegguá and Ochosi, then the diviner must give Elegguá and Ochosi the option to claim ebó either separately or together, asking, in turn, "Ebó elese Elegguá?"; "Ebó elese Ochosi?"; and "Ebó elese Elegguá y Ochosi?" If either orisha claims an ebó individually, the diviner must use the diloggún to mark the appropriate offering. If the orishas demand ebó together, the proper offering to give is a sacrifice of feathers. *Note*: When these two orishas claim ebó together, they are also warning the client that soon he will have to flee. This flight could be emotional, physical, or even spiritual; when he runs, the client will have these spirits assisting his escape.

If the client has already received his warriors, once a year he must sacrifice to them behind the front door of his residence. This ebó will keep osogbo at bay beyond his front door, so that it does not enter his house.

The second option for ebó centers on Shangó and Aganyú. Just as he did for the orishas Elegguá and Ochosi, the diviner must ensure that the client has the elekes of both Shangó and Aganyú. Likewise, the two must be given their chance to claim ebó together or separately. If they claim ebó individually, the diviner should mark the appropriate offering using the diloggún. If Shangó and Aganyú claim ebó together, the proper offering is a sacrifice of feathers, shared between father and son.

Finally, the Ibeyi are important to this sign as well. If the client does not have them, he must receive them. If he has them, the diviner must give the Ibeyi a chance to claim ebó, asking, "Ebó elese los Ibeyi?" If the answer is yes, the diviner uses the diloggún to mark an appropriate ebó.

This odu also suggests eboses for specific circumstances. If the client comes to the mat for any of the reasons listed below, the ebó described will help him evolve out of his difficulties.

- When a woman has come to the oracle because her womb is barren, the orisha whose diloggún was consulted might have the remedy to her problems. After delivering the reading, which addresses the pressing spiritual and physical issues of the client, the diviner should give her the ibó efun and otá and allow her to speak her original concern openly to the spirit consulted. The diviner touches the ibó to the shells on the mat as he says, "Efun lo si wayu, otá beko, efun ke ibó." He returns the ibó to her so that she can take them into separate closed fists while he gathers the diloggún and asks, "Larishe si?" If the casting directs the diviner to the client's hand that holds efun, the orisha is answering that a larishe is possible to help the client with her concern. The diviner should mark the appropriate ebó with the diloggún.

- If the client has come to the mat because he or someone related to him is sick, this odu provides ebó to help heal that person. The afflicted one brings two roosters and two coconuts to Elegguá and Ogún. The diviner uses first the coconuts and then the roosters to cleanse the person (one of each for Elegguá and the others for Ogún). The diviner then sacrifices one rooster to Elegguá and the other to Ogún. They will help heal the client of illness.
- If the client is a man who has come to the mat because he has recently lost his wife to another man, he must sacrifice a rooster to Ogún as soon as possible. If he does not, one day he could lose his life due to adultery.

If the eboses prescribed so far are not enough to bring odu's closure, the diviner must turn to the eboses of the parent odu, Eji Oko (see page 132). Something there is needed for the client's evolution.

## The Twelfth Composite Odu of Eji Oko, Ejioko Ejila (2-12)

### The Proverbs of Ejioko Ejila

- Failure comes when one does not make ebó.
- He who does not pray will not find luck.
- When entering a dance, the dancer opens his hands in anticipation.
- After dancing, the dancer brings down his hands before sitting.
- He who does not petition the orishas fails in all his endeavors.

### The Message of Ejioko Ejila

When two mouths, Eji Oko, are followed by twelve, Ejila Shebora, Ejioko Ejila is open. This odu is also known as Oyekun Ejila and Yeku Ejila. When this sign was born on the earth, it taught humans how to recognize animals that were dying of sickness. It also taught us that it was taboo to eat those found dead. By its aché was the new race of carnivores saved from terrible and untimely death.

When Ejioko Ejila falls on the mat, the diviner snaps his thumb and the third finger on both hands once; this gesture helps those present for the reading to avoid all danger. He immediately says, "Maferefún Aganyú! Maferefún Shangó! Maferefún los Ibeyi, Taewó and Kaindé!" These four powerful orishas stand up on behalf of the client; even in the darkest osogbo, they will help him through all his difficulties. Aganyú has come to insist that his son, Shangó, and his grandchildren, the Ibeyi, are the client's salvation. In this sign, he speaks only once, and if the client ever doubts his words, he will never speak them again. The client must fulfill any eboses claimed by these spirits immediately. If he does not, he will not evolve.

The diviner should also keep in mind that Elegguá, Obatalá, Oshún, and Ochosi can speak up here on the client's behalf as well. If the client's head (guardian orisha) has not been marked yet, there may be a war among these spirits (excluding the Ibeyi) as to who will rule the client's orí in ocha. No matter who claims him, however, the client will always be protected by the Ibeyi and will have the blessings of Oshún.

In any type of iré, this letter showers good news and blessings upon the client. It is a sign of good health and well-being; energy, vitality, and youthfulness are some of the many gifts that it can bring. However, even when firm, the iré can be lost when the client does not follow the advice or taboos of this sign, so the diviner must spend time carefully detailing the odu's message and prohibitions. To evolve, the client must put away extraneous things. This sign in iré encourages travel, even brief trips, so if the chance comes for the client to go away for a time, he must do all that he can to go; good fortune will come. In osogbo, this advice is reversed: Travel is not a good idea now; if the option to travel, even for short trips, is offered, it must be turned down. The client must commit himself to living a careful, cautious life. He must also be prepared for bad news to come, and if he lives with others, this news will be the source of many arguments in the home. He should live and move slowly. He should avoid running, jumping, climbing, or making sudden movements, for in Ejioko Ejila the risk of a fall is imminent and can cause serious injuries. The sign can bring tragedy, revolution, ill fortune, and new enemies, so the client must be cautious.

No matter the orientation of odu, the diviner should explore with the client the following points:

- In this odu, it is not uncommon for the client to have two lovers. Even if the client is ethical in his actions, letting each know about the other, this behavior allows the luck of Ejioko Ejila to be lost or the osogbo to be made hotter. One or both lovers must be given up. The client must be prepared for the abandoned lover to feel scorned and try to create trouble.
- This is an odu of family and family ties. So that there are no misunderstandings between parents and their children or between siblings, the client should seek their advice and counsel on important matters that can affect them. However, not all the advice they give will be good. This odu emphasizes the need to discuss and listen, but it does not require that the client follow that advice. He must try to look at both sides of the coin and then make an informed decision.
- Even in iré, this sign is dangerous for writers/authors, celebrities, political figures, and those in positions of authority. If the client is in one of these positions, his image and conduct will come under scrutiny. While he cannot hide, he should try to keep his personal life private and beyond reproach. Without such cautions, his job or position could be lost, and public shame and scandal will come; the greater his status, the greater the shame.
- The law figures prominently in this odu. The client must obey the law and try to avoid any altercations with authorities. Incarceration may come by mistake, and while the client will be cleared of wrongdoing, this incarceration will bring public shame.
- The client should be very observant when walking outdoors. He will soon find something valuable. If the odu opens in osogbo, however, the item in question could bring more evil than good. If possible, the client should try to find the true owner of the object.

## The Prohibitions of Ejioko Ejila

- Be cautious of what one eats. Make sure that all meats are well cooked and prepared hygienically. Meats that are spoiled must not be cooked and consumed, nor may leftovers that have been improperly stored. Be wary of precooked meals and canned foods. In this odu, there is danger of food-borne poisons or illness.
- In this odu, hunting is taboo.
- Legal entanglements could arise, and one must avoid those who live outside the law to make a living. Have a lawyer review all contracts before signing them.
- If the odu opens in osogbo, do not travel for twenty-eight days. After this period of time, consult with the orishas before traveling, making ebó before leaving.

## The Eboses of Ejioko Ejila

When this odu falls on the mat, it warns that a powerful elder in one of the ilé ocha represented at the mat may soon die, regardless of the odu's iré or osogbo. If only one ilé ocha is represented, this warning falls on it. If more than one house is represented, the diviner has the option to determine upon whose house this osogbo falls. He should ask this question: "Osogbo de ikú elese ilé ocha de [priest's or priestess's name]?" The diviner should not attempt to mark this osogbo on any specific elder's head, for the death will not be sudden but will come slowly, and there will be time to fight it. When an elder in the house marked becomes ill, all members come together to make sacrifice in that person's name to Orisha Oko. It will take both feathers and four legs to fight this impending doom. The afflicted elder should also be given a rogación before Obatalá, using, in addition to the traditional ingredients, the flesh of four snails. If all is done as it should be done, the elder will recover.

Ejioko Ejila is a powerful odu, and to help the client soothe its energies and evolve amid the chaos it can bring (even in iré), the following eboses must be prescribed:

- In Eji Oko, an initial consideration for ebó is

the reception of the elekes. If the client does not have the elekes and is not in the financial position to take that initiation now, it is mandatory that he now have a rogación before Obatalá's shrine and receive Obatalá's eleke. The need for this eleke comes from the vast number of orishas trying to accompany the client's head in this odu; without Obatalá's calming influence, his orí will become overheated and overwhelmed. For the next twenty-one days, the client must wear the eleke during the day, and every day upon awakening he must say, "Maferefún Obatalá!" After this time period, if the client heeds all the advice given in this odu, he should be ready to take the initiation of the elekes.

- During this reading, if Elegguá stands up to take or prescribe ebó (or if his diloggún is the one consulted), the client should wear his eleke daily as well; Elegguá will bring him luck through this odu.
- In this odu, as in many of Eji Oko's composites, the aché of the Ibeyi is necessary for the client. If he has not received them, he must; if he has them, they may be standing up for ebó. To see what they require, the diviner should ask, "Ebó elese los Ibeyi?" If the answer is yes, he marks the appropriate ebó with the diloggún.

Now the diviner has his first opportunity to close the oracle. If it refuses closure, Elegguá, Ogún, Obatalá, Shangó, or Aganyú could be standing up to claim ebó. To determine if this is the case, the diviner should ask, "Ebó elese [orisha's name]?" If the answer is yes, he marks the appropriate ebó with the diloggún.

If the prescriptions determined so far will not close the odu, the diviner should turn to the eboses of the parent sign, Eji Oko. Something there is needed for the client's evolution.

# The Thirteenth Composite Odu of Eji Oko, Ejioko Metanla (2-13)

## The Proverbs of Ejioko Metanla

- For each dead king, [there is] a new king.
- For each new king who dies, a new one must be crowned.
- You want to be very wise, and you fool only yourself.
- There is a spark of goodness with all things evil.

## The Message of Ejioko Metanla

When a casting of two mouths, Eji Oko, is followed by one of thirteen mouths, Metanla, the odu Ejioko Metanla is open. This sign has many other names: Oyekun Metanla, Yeku Metanla, Ejioko Irete, Oyekun Irete, and Yeku Irete. Opening with this pattern, the diviner pays homage to Babaluaiye, egun, Shangó, the Ibeyi, Elegguá, and Yemayá, saying to each, "Maferefún!" These orishas and egun are firm in this odu and each may speak; however, none speaks as strongly as Babaluaiye.

When Ejioko Metanla opens on the mat, everyone present at the reading is marked for a cleansing before Babaluaiye (see page 127). If the reading opens in iré, Babaluaiye has marked this ebó as an evolutionary tool. He wants to bring blessings to all those at the mat but cannot do so until the energies of each have been cleansed. If the reading opens in an osogbo, however, Ejioko Metanla becomes a pattern of debt and disappointment. The client has issues to settle with Babaluaiye. The essence of this sign is so volatile, so severe, that in osogbo all who are present are influenced by its erratic vibrations, and all must make ebó or suffer, for Babaluaiye has saved this client many times, and here he has come to claim what is rightfully his: the offering promised him for favors given. After prescribing the initial ebó to all present, the italero must prod the client to remember his debts to Babaluaiye. If he can remember nothing, the diviner must still mark some form of ebo to the orisha so that he will harbor no ill will. Until Babaluaiye is properly propitiated, the client cannot evolve beyond his present difficulties.

No matter this sign's orientation, the diviner must tell the client this: Of all the odu in the family of Eji Oko, Ejioko Metanla is the biggest provider of wealth and prosperity. If the client follows the advice given in this odu, all those things that he desires will come. All that he touches will prosper. This is not the case now, but things will change.

With this sign on the mat, the diviner knows that his client has no fixed residence, no stable place to call home. Either he moves around frequently or there is insecurity in his home. Someone living with him or near him harbors ill will; if the client lives with family, this raises a whole set of negative issues (his own blood wishes him ill). His neighbors want to know what goes on inside his home; they are nosy, and the things they think they know anger them. Many pray to God that he will move. All of this ill will and instability causes a lot of negativity around the client. However, the eboses prescribed in this odu will help him soothe his environment. At all costs, this person must work to achieve a stable home life.

Also, the diviner must keep the following points in mind:

- This person must take good care of his first three children because they will come to his rescue at a critical moment in his life. If he does not already have a child who has curly hair, he can look for one in his family. Tell him to develop a close relationship with this child. He must not rely on support from his wealthy brothers because they will abandon him in his hour of need.
- The client's job is in danger, and to save it he should work diligently and conscientiously.
- This person must respect the advice of both his elders and the orishas; he must listen to what they say if he is to prosper under this odu.
- Obatalá is essential to this pattern. The client must depend on him for all things.
- Any illegal activities in the client's life, even minor ones, must be put aside in this odu. They will eventually catch up with him.
- This odu tells the client that a friend will soon give him advice; it might seem good, but in truth it will be bad. The friend gives this advice because he wants the client to fall. Ejioko Ejila indicates that if the client makes ebó to Elegguá and his own head and then follows that bad advice, he will prosper, to the horror of his ill-intentioned "friend."
- If this is a major reading, such as a bajado or an itá, this odu tells the diviner that the client will one day marry a wife who will bring abundance to his life. This woman will then give birth to a child whose head is destined for greatness.

## The Prohibitions of Ejioko Metanla

This odu mandates a severe prohibition for everyone present at the reading: Do not venture out of the home for the next seven days unless it is for something essential, such as work or food. Danger lurks outdoors. If one cannot avoid going out, do not go out alone, especially after dark.

Other prohibitions for the client are as follows:

- Do not indulge in alcohol or other intoxicants either in the home or while out and about; one must be in full possession of one's faculties at all times.
- Dogs are sacred to Babaluaiye; if one owns a dog, treat it well.
- If this letter comes in osogbo, travel is taboo for twenty-eight days. If an unavoidable trip is pending, put it off for at least seven days; the orishas will not compromise on this.

## The Eboses of Ejioko Metanla

When this pattern falls on the mat, everyone present for the reading is marked to give the following ebó to Babaluaiye.

Those who have received Babaluaiye may do this ebó before his shrine; those without Babaluaiye will have to set up a small spiritual altar in a quiet corner of the house.

Beginning the night after the reading, gather a large piece of sackcloth, a yellow seven-day candle, two large gourds, toasted corn, epó, grated coconut, smoked fish, and jutía. Place the sackcloth on the floor and set the two gourds on it. Offer a prayer to Babaluaiye; while praying, light the yellow candle and fill one gourd with toasted corn, epó, grated coconut, smoked fish, and jutía. Take one handful of the mixture from the gourd and cleanse oneself. After the cleansing, place the handful of mixture in the second gourd. Every night for the next six nights (for a total of seven nights of cleansings), repeat the prayer and the cleansing with a fresh handful of the mixture. After the seven nights of cleansing are complete, wrap both gourds and their contents tightly in the sackcloth. Take this ebó to the woods and leave it under a bush, along with a derecho of seventeen cents. Then return to the diviner's house with a feathered animal for Babaluaiye. Before his shrine, the diviner will cleanse one with it and then make a sacrifice.

While everyone present for the reading will have to do this ebó, the client himself may have additional issues with Babaluaiye. The diviner should also consider the following questions:

- "Ebó elese Babaluaiye?" If the answer is yes, the diviner should mark the appropriate offering with the diloggún, giving the orisha a chance to personalize what he desires from the client. Note that if the ebó required is a rogación, it should be given in front of Babaluaiye's shrine; after the cleansing, the client must receive the orisha's eleke.
- "Koshé Babaluaiye?" If an ebó is not enough to settle the issues with Babaluaiye, or if no ebó can be marked, the diviner must ask this of the diloggún. This spirit's reception could be essential for the client's evolution. Note that if Babaluaiye will take no ebó but his reception by the client is marked, the client must have a rogación in front of Babaluaiye's shrine as soon as possible and also receive the orisha's eleke. This will put his feet on the path to evolution while plans are being made for Babaluaiye's reception.

In addition to these issues with Babaluaiye, the diviner should consider the following:

- Shangó is strong in this sign, and if the client has received mano de Orúnmila or kofá de Orúnmila, there may be issues between Orúnmila and Shangó. The proper ebó in this circumstance is to put a washed thunderstone next to the client's Ifá. If the client has not received his Ifá, the diviner must determine if Shangó requires ebó, asking, "Ebó elese Shangó?" If the answer is yes, he marks the appropriate ebó with the diloggún. If Shangó does claim an ebó, in addition to what he asks for, the client should buy and wash a thunderstone and keep it at Shangó's shrine.
- Olokun might also demand ebó in this odu. To see what he might require, the diviner should ask, "Ebó elese Olokun?"
- Elegguá might block closure in this sign unless he is propitiated. The diviner should ask, "Ebó elese Elegguá?" If he stands up to claim ebó, the proper offering is a rooster sacrificed to Elegguá and a white pigeon sacrificed to the client's orí. With this ebó, the client's destiny will finally come.

If, having explored all these options, the diviner still cannot close the reading, he should turn to the eboses of the parent odu, Eji Oko (see page 132). Something there is necessary for the client's evolution.

## The Fourteenth Composite Odu of Eji Oko, Ejioko Merinla (2-14)

### The Proverbs of Ejioko Merinla

- There is envy between brothers.
- It is of more value to have a lot of small things than a few big things.
- The sleeping shrimp is taken by the current.

### The Message of Ejioko Merinla

When a casting of two mouths, Eji Oko, is followed by one of fourteen mouths, Merinla, the odu Ejioko Merinla is open. This odu goes by many other names: Oyekun Merinla, Yeku Merinla, Oyekun Ika, Yeku Ika, and Ejioko Ika. Even in iré, this is one of the more volatile letters in this family. When it comes, it announces tragedy, distrust, and revolution. Many people around the client wish evil on him. Sickness and disease are close; the legs, veins, and soft body tissues could become injured, infected, or inflamed. Ejioko Merinla speaks of poisons that cause rot and decay. The heart and lungs have already suffered deterioration, and while this might be so minor that even a physician would not notice, the damage is there, and one day it could become a serious problem if the client does not look out for his own health. In this pattern, smokers often suffer emphysema and cardio-obstructive pulmonary disorder (COPD). While the client might think his life is a mess now, even more destructive currents are coming, and if he is not ready and prepared, he will be swept away like the sleeping shrimp. Awareness and vigilance are the keys to averting tragedy here.

## The Prohibition of Ejioko Merinla

- Do not hunt, trap, kill, or abuse animals.

## The Eboses of Ejioko Merinla

As is described in the initial considerations for ebó in Eji Oko (see page 95), if the client has not taken either or both the elekes and warriors, he must commit to these initiations as soon as possible. While the energies of odu will pass in time, the osogbos wrought in this sign cannot be completely removed until he has them. The client's life is at a turning point, but things will not turn or improve until he is firmly seated in this religion with the orishas.

This odu marks the need for the client to salute the sun every morning after awakening, giving honor and praise to Olódumare, Olorún, and Olófin. Afterward, he must pray directly to Shangó, supplicating him through the heavens. This personal ritual continues for a full month. His salutations will help him overcome the difficulties he faces. The diviner should check to see if Shangó needs anything else in return for his help, asking, "Ebó elese Shangó?" If an ebó is needed, the diviner must mark it using the diloggún, and the client must fulfill this obligation immediately. Once Shangó is propitiated, evolution can begin.

Having made these prescriptions, the diviner may try to close the reading. If the diloggún remains open, he must turn to the eboses of the parent odu, Eji Oko (see page 132). Something there is needed for the client's evolution.

# The Fifteenth Composite Odu of Eji Oko, Ejioko Marunla (2-15)

## The Proverbs of Ejioko Marunla

- An inconvenience may cost you your life.
- Be prepared for news of a tragedy.

## The Message of Ejioko Marunla

When a casting of two mouths, Eji Oko, is followed by one of fifteen mouths, Marunla, the odu Ejioko Marunla is open. This odu is also known as Oyekun Marunla, Yeku Marunla, Ejioko Iwori, Oyekun Iwori, and Yeku Iwori. It is a pattern of tears, depression, and darkness; even in iré, it marks terrible tragedy upon the head of its owner. This letter brings suicide and suicidal ideation not only upon the client but also on those closest to him. Here, we say that one should be prepared for word of bad news; evil is all around, and it will come whether the client is prepared or not. Personal safety is compromised, and a minor inconvenience can escalate to life-threatening proportions. Ejioko Marunla also marks the death of an elder; if anyone in the client's ilé becomes ill, that person should be taken to a physician immediately. In this sign illness, even something minor, can destroy a life, so any sickness demands medical attention.

The diviner should also keep in mind the following points:

- No matter how bad things get for this client, food, and the means to buy it, will always come to him. As long as he works hard, he will never have to worry about starvation.
- If the client has children, he should be told that soon his problems will be over. If he does not

have children, he should be told that they will eventually come.

## The Prohibitions of Ejioko Marunla

- Do not hold or organize meetings. Do not belong to clubs of any kind.
- Do not be outside in the rain. If it begins to rain while one is out, go home or take shelter. Avoiding rain will ensure one's peace and prosperity.

## The Eboses of Ejioko Marunla

- To appease this letter, the client must have received the elekes, the warriors, and the Ibeyi. If these initiations have already been taken, then the warriors or the Ibeyi might be standing up for ebó; the diviner should try to mark this.
- If someone in the client's family becomes ill, the odu requires, as an ebó, that this person be taken to the doctor, even if there is no money available for medical treatment. The one who becomes ill should come to the diviner as soon as possible for a reading.
- This odu marks the client to make frequent ebó and adimú to Ogún. If Ogún has not stood up for larishe in this sign, the diviner must mark several eboses to him before attempting to bring the odu to closure.
- Sacrifices should be offered to Eleggua and Olokun. The diviner, using his own common sense and knowledge of the orishas, will determine which sacrifices are appropriate.
- Every day, pray to Olódumare for evolution, as he is the one to bring it.
- This client should make a huge feast in honor of his ancestors.

Now the diviner should attempt to close the odu. If the prescriptions he has made are not enough to close the odu, he should turn to the eboses for the parent odu, Eji Oko (see page 132). Something there will be needed to bring the client's evolution.

# The Sixteenth Composite Odu of Eji Oko, Ejioko Merindilogún (2-16)

## The Proverbs of Ejioko Merindilogún

- Do not tell what should be kept secret.
- Do not offer what you cannot give.
- Do not give those things that are not yours to give.

## The Message of Ejioko Merindilogún

When the initial cast of two mouths, Eji Oko, precedes a cast of sixteen mouths, Merindilogún, the odu Ejioko Merindilogún is open. This sign is known by many other names: Ejioko Otura, Oyekun Otura, Yeku Otura, Yeku Merindilogún, and Oyekun Merindilogún. Many say that this pattern alludes to the transfiguration of Christ. Through this odu Orúnmila taught humans how to offer ebó to both himself and the rest of the orishas, providing salvation to all on the earth. This pattern is so hot and volatile that the client must make ebó if he hopes to persevere. Even in iré, this sign can be dangerous, and any blessings brought will be ephemeral unless the client propitiates the spirits to hold them firm.

The diviner begins his assessment of this letter by paying homage to Elegguá, Ogún, egun, Shangó, and Orúnmila, saying to each, "Maferefún!" All five are strong in this odu, and all might claim ebó or offer advice before the reading closes.

In Ejioko Merindilogún, it is said that the orishas are annoyed with the client, even if the odu comes in iré; if the letter has come in an osogbo, the spirits might be angry with him. To begin a thorough assessment of this odu, the diviner should consider the client's status in the religion. Is he a casual or first-time client, an aborisha, or an initiate? A client who is not in the religion (an aleyo) should be asked, "What do you want from the orishas?" Ejioko Merindilogún tells a first-time client that he does not belong here. He has no respect for the faith and no love for our spirits; he comes only for a quick fix to his problems. While the odu will mark many eboses to solve what ails him, the orishas emphasize that they are more than a problem-solving mechanism: They are parts of God. After this reading, the diviner should advise the client to make ebó but never return unless he comes with love and faith in his heart. Without love and faith, the orishas might not help him again.

An aborisha who comes in Ejioko Merindilogún has annoyed the spirits that he is supposed to be worshiping. He comes again and again for readings, and usually he makes ebó, but although he has been told many times to receive certain orishas, to advance in the faith, he has not. He must consider this, and he must start doing all that he is told.

An initiate who has taken the asiento ceremony, or even an aborisha who has many orishas in his life (including the warriors, the Ibeyi, Olokun, and Babaluaiye), should be told that the orishas are upset with him because they feel abandoned. Again and again, this person professes his love and faith, but he does not act as he should, nor does he give his orishas the worship they deserve. This is why his life is a mess. The orishas are also annoyed because only they have the strength to protect this person from his enemies and from other bad spirits, yet he turns to foreign faiths and foreign philosophies to solve his many problems. And now he comes to the mat as a last resort. While the orishas are now forgiving, this is the last time they will forgive their adherent. The diviner should tell the client all this.

When the odu comes in osogbo, the diviner should make many specific predictions for the client. In ano or ikú, this sign can bring sickness; the veins, legs, and abdominal region will all be affected. There can be death through negligence, and an ancestor whose death was caused by this client will come back to exact revenge. Others are jealous of the client's lover or spouse.

## The Prohibitions of Ejioko Merindilogún

- All the taboos of the parent odu, Eji Oko (see page 132), are in effect. They are essential to keeping one on the path to evolution.
- When buying religious supplies, do not go to one's favorite botánicas or stores; one has acquired enemies in these places, and they will bring danger and treason. Instead, seek out new sources for supplies. Do not buy kola nuts or coconuts from previous markets; pick a new source, and go there.
- An initiate loses the right to sacrifice guinea hens in this odu; this right is lost for life, even if the reading is not itá.
- Do not make fun of the elderly or the deformed. They are Obatalá's children.

## The Eboses of Ejioko Merindilogún

When Ejioko Merindilogún opens, there are specific eboses for certain circumstances. The diviner must keep the following in mind:

- If the client is an engaged male, his fiancée is a blessing from Olokun. She might even be Olokun's child. In iré, the letter promises that blessings and financial success will come with this marriage. Ebó must be given to Olokun in thanks for this. In osogbo, it is imperative that the man receives Olokun in order to hold on to both his fiancée and his blessing. To determine a remedy to solve this osogbo until Olokun's reception, the diviner should also ask, "Larishe si Olokun?"
- When Ejioko Merindilogún has fallen for a pregnant woman or a man whose woman is with child, the birth of the child heralds great iré. The birth of twins is foreshadowed and, if it comes to pass, brings even greater blessings. From heaven, this unborn child has planned its parents' future prosperity, and once on the earth it will seal these things. A sacrifice of feathers must be made to Elegguá immediately, and the client must receive the Ibeyi if he does not already have them. Note that if the pregnancy is proceeding poorly, the diviner may determine if a remedy is needed, asking "Larishe si?"
- If a child's sickness has brought the client to the mat, the diviner must then ask, "Larishe si,

Elegguá?" If Elegguá does not have a remedy, the child might soon die.

- When Ejioko Merindilogún comes for one who is affluent, the diviner is assured of two things. First, this fortune was accumulated through deceit and dishonesty. Second, in time, this fortune will be squandered and lost. To prevent this, the client must resolve to change his ways immediately. A client who is an initiate must also receive Ochosi. For a client who is an aborisha, the diviner must ask, "Ebó elese Ochosi?" If the answer is no, the aborisha will one day fall and lose all he has. If the answer is yes, the diviner marks the appropriate ebó with the diloggún.

If after these prescriptions are made the odu will not close, the five spirits who speak in this sign—Elegguá, Ogún, egun, Shangó, and Orúnmila—might be standing up to claim ebó. To see if any of these will accept an offering, the diviner might ask, "Ebó elese [spirit's name]?"

If the oracle still will not close, the diviner must turn to the eboses listed below for the parent odu, Eji Oko. Something there is needed to close the session.

## Closing the Reading: Further Eboses of the Parent Odu, Eji Oko

Having exhausted the options that are given in each of the omo odu, the diviner must now turn to the sacrifices and offerings that can satisfy the parent odu, Eji Oko, in order to close the reading.

- The diviner should first ask, "Eboshure elese Eshu?" If the answer is yes, the client must save a portion of all his meals for the next three, seven, or twenty-one days (the diviner should mark the length of time with the shells). He must wrap this portion in a brown paper bag and, at the end of the meal, take the bag to a street corner or crossroads, leaving it there for Eshu in the street.*
- Next the diviner might ask, "Ebó elese Elegguá?" If the answer is yes, the ebó is eyebale—in this case, the sacrifice of a rooster to Elegguá.†
- The next ebó to be marked is for Ochosi. The diviner asks, "Ebó elese Ochosi?" If the answer is yes, the diviner must mark the ebó that is required by this orisha. If the answer is no, and if the client is an initiate, the diviner should find out if his reception is needed to satisfy this odu, asking, "Koshé Ochosi?"
- The next ebó that this letter could require is an offering to the earth and Orisha Oko. The diviner should ask, "Ebó elese Orisha Oko?" If the answer is yes, he marks the appropriate ebó with the diloggún. If the answer is no, and if the client is an initiate, this orisha's reception might be needed. The diviner should ask "Koshé Orisha Oko?" If the answer to this is yes, arrangements must be made for his reception immediately.
- Next, the diviner should petition the Ibeyi for their help, asking, "Ebó elese Ibeyi?" If the answer is yes, the proper ebó for them is twin baskets of fruit.
- If none of these is accepted, or if the odu still will not close, the diviner must tell the client that he needs a rogación before the shrine of his guardian orisha; during this ritual, the client's orí should be fed two white doves or pigeons to give it strength. After this, the client should put a chair behind his front door and sit in it to meditate every day. During his meditations, he should pray to Olófin, Olorún, Olódumare, and egun.
- If the letter still will not close, the client may have issues with one of the many orishas who speak in this sign—Elegguá, Ogún, Ochosi, Oyá, Orisha Oko, Ibeyi, Obatalá, Orúnmila, and Shangó. One or more will require either ebó or reception into the client's life. For both initiates and noninitiates, the diviner should consider asking, "Ebó elese [orisha's name]?"

*Even if the client has received Elegguá, he may not make this ebó to him. It must go to Eshu in the street.

†If the client has received Elegguá, this sacrifice is made to his own Elegguá.

- For initiates, the reception of Ogún* (caracoles), Ochosi, Oyá (for children of Yemayá who don't have her), or Orisha Oko might be mandated. To investigate this possibility, the diviner should ask, "Koshé [orisha's name]?"

If this list is exhausted and the odu still refuses closure, the diviner has two options. First, he may call an elder in the religion, for something important in the sign could have been overlooked. Second, he may look at the list of eboses given for the omo odu as a parent odu. (For example, if Ejioko Okana opened on the mat, the diviner would then turn to the eboses given for Okana as parent odu.)

*Initiates do not normally receive the shells of Ogun when making ocha; these are given at a separate time, usually after the year and seven days of white are complete. The reception of Ogun's shells bestows upon the initiate the right to sacrifice feathered animals. He may, however, kill only those animals whose life can be taken quickly with his bare hands.

# FOUR

## THE FAMILY OF OGUNDÁ

### The Proverbs of Ogundá

- Tragedy, deception, and despair are near.
- Tragedy is brought by making the wrong decisions.
- Tears can turn into laughter, but laughter will again become tears.
- That which was lost will eventually come back.
- Good deeds will not go unrewarded.
- Evil deeds never remain unsanctioned.
- On entering a low door, one must bow the head.
- Beware of those who come bearing gifts.
- As you have sown, so shall you reap.
- Those who fight with the sword will die with the sword.

### The Orishas Who Speak in Ogundá

| | |
|---|---|
| Olófin | Obatalá |
| Ogún | Ayao |
| Yemayá | Aganyú |
| Elegguá | Babaluaiye |
| Ochosi | |

### The Message of Ogundá

Opening with only three mouths on the mat, the diloggún sits before the diviner in a dangerous pattern, one fraught with peril. The odu Ogundá demands fear and respect, for it seethes with volatility; it is an energy that demolishes all God creates. This reading will be hot; spiritual currents and tides that are tumultuous and tortuous surround this client. Even though an omo odu has yet to be cast, the diviner already knows much of what lies ahead for this person: Tragedy, despair, and deception are near, perhaps already upon him. Ogundá speaks of loss, tears, manic laughter, evil deeds, treason, and wars. This client has caused much evil, and his deeds will have their own treacherous rewards. This client might walk proudly, but the doors to evolution are low, and he will be forced to bow his head before he can progress. This odu is one of karma; the sign Ogundá is the client's fate and punishment, but it is also his cleansing. If nothing else, the odu portends a time of growth through destruction.

Born of Odí (seven mouths), Ogundá is the antithesis of its parent sign. Yet to understand Ogundá, briefly one must examine its parent. Odí as a collective force is firm, maternal, nourishing; while demanding of her creations, she is fierce to protect them when danger arises. Ogundá's mother represents rest, completion, a seal that can balance and stabilize energies. It is the true home to Yemayá, mother of this world, and it brings great blessings to those whom it rules. Ogundá, on the other hand, is harsh, random, fierce, hot, transient in essence, and destructive in nature. Many compare its nature to that of time—in time, all things come to birth, and in time, all things come to death. Time is both a friend and an enemy of creation. Time consumes his own children; he eats all that he creates. Ogundá, too, is a force capable of destroying its own children. Ogundá births bloodshed and war, yet like all the odu it can still be a catalyst for evolution. All that Odí holds dear is ripped away, torn apart, forced to evolve separately or be destroyed by Ogundá. The client for whom this pattern falls, unfortunately, is caught up in the maelstrom.

To illustrate the power and aché of Ogundá, one must study its actions in nature. Its most obvious association is with those things that are hard, sharp, severe, or metallic. Ogundá is iron; it rules all those things made of this metal. In thinking of weapons and of war, one realizes the power of this odu; unchecked, it is a wanton, wayward force that can kill randomly and on a large scale. Think then of surgeons and the scalpel they wield; the scalpel is but another form of a knife, a tool born in this family of odu. Yet while a knife can kill, when the force of Ogundá is guided by trained, skilled hands, the tool of death becomes a tool of healing. It cuts; it makes one bleed; and it scars the body. Through its destructions, however, it gives new life by the resection of diseased tissue. Agriculture, technology, weapons, war, civilization, and health—all have come by the use of iron and other metals. All have brought blessings. All have wrought much evil. All have come by the grace of Ogundá. The diviner knows that for the client to evolve in this odu, he must learn to temper the sign's vast energy with his own restraint; he must learn to wield Ogundá as skillfully as a surgeon wields the knife. He knows, also, that this may prove an impossible task.

Once Ogundá is cast on the diviner's mat, the reading is suspended before the omo odu is opened. Temporarily, this odu enfolds the diviner and those in the room in its energy; the erratic vibrations brought by this pattern will bring fear to those who know the meanings of this sign. To protect himself, the diviner pats his abdomen three times with open palms. Still holding his hands open, he lifts them to just below his jaw, palms facing heaven and balanced as if they hold a delicate powder on their surface. Inhaling deeply, the priest blows a steady puff of air over both palms, directing his breath at the client. Through this gesture, any osogbo brought to the priest who has opened Ogundá is sent back onto the one who has come to be read, and those present in the room often follow suit to protect themselves. The diviner must not allow the client to perform this series of gestures; this is his reading, and this odu marks his life. He must accept it and work with those energies until they are gone.

Having performed the gestures of Ogundá, the diviner continues with the sacred prayer of this sign:

*Ogundá meji.*
*Tesi tesi. Faraye afesuye.*
*Lesi losun. Ogundá etaji feranje.*
*Afesuye.*
*Be Ósun. Lenu Ósun.*

Those present bow their heads in silence while the diviner chants this brief prayer. After he is done, to honor both the opening odu and the orisha for whom it was named many might mutter, "Maferefún Ogundá! Maferefún Ogún!"

Through this odu, a variety of spirits might choose to speak or make their influence known. No matter whose shells are consulted, in Ogundá Olófin himself comes to offer his help to the client. He wants this person to evolve beyond his present difficulties; he wants him to move out of the energies manifest and into something new and beautiful. However, this mighty orisha can do little here beyond offering blessings and support. He will neither take ebó nor offer advice. The simple fact that Olófin is present should be enough to instill faith in the client. A good heart, a pure soul, higher aspirations, and clean living will help this person elevate himself beyond the portents revealed by this odu. No matter which composite opens, no matter which spirits give advice or claim ebó, the diviner must tell his client that with God's help, eventually all things are possible. The client should pray to Olófin before praying to any other spirit, for all must come to bow at Olófin's feet. Only the goodwill of heaven can overcome that which ails the client. And this is what Olófin brings: the goodwill of heaven.

Beyond Olófin, the orisha whose shells have been consulted will have the first chance to speak; this is the spirit who brought Ogundá to the mat, and it is this force that must advise how the client may placate and cool the odu. Know this: Even if the odu comes in iré, this orisha's words will be harsh. Ogundá rarely brings blessings. Always, it marks turmoil first, alluding to the serious state in which the client's life has fallen. This force has come to chastise, maybe even to punish.

When the letter opens in iré, the diviner should tell the client this: "Of all the odu this spirit could open, Ogundá has come. It brings iré, but the truth is that three mouths offers few blessings. Your goodness comes because this orisha, by his good graces, has chosen to give you this consultation. Listen now to what you are told. Make the ebó you are supposed to make. Change your ways and change your heart, and maybe, just maybe, you will get through what is coming. Maybe you will evolve. Know that things will not be easy; they may even get more difficult. There is no absolution for your past transgressions, but through hard work you are being offered a chance to grow. Do not waste this chance." These words hold true for all the composites of Ogundá in iré, and for his own good, the diviner may not make his words any less harsh. The client's life might depend on them.

When the letter opens in iré, it indicates that the orisha whose shells have been consulted makes certain promises if the spirit's words are heeded. First, a client who owns his own businesses will find that it prospers; however, economic growth will come only after a period of strife and struggle. A client who holds a job or has a full-time career will face worry, doubt, and hard work; his livelihood could even be endangered by coworkers. He will experience a lot of work, much overtime, and bad luck on the job. But in the end, if he perseveres through this and continues to work hard, he will be rewarded financially. A better job could come. Riches can come to this client, but they come only with a lot of work and extensive personal sacrifice. Lawsuits, tragedies, deaths, or accidents might come while Ogundá is in effect, but with Ogundá in iré these setbacks will gather greater wealth as they are settled. Inheritances might even come from long-lost relatives. None of these things will be easy; they will put the client through hardship after hardship. The final results, however, will be well worth the effort put into them.

The diviner must remember, however, that even in iré Ogundá is harsh, heated, and volatile. Of itself, it can bring few blessings, yet if the client is skillful in his dealings, blessings can be created. The diviner must tell this person that he has come to a time and a place in his life where destruction is imminent; his life is not as it should be, and unless he gives himself up to the will of the orishas, it will not get better. Ogundá speaks of change and destruction, and in iré it will destroy those things in the client's life that are outworn or useless. Unfortunately, many things in this person's life are useless, and his life will be ripped apart so that something new is created. He should not fight this destruction but should, rather, go with it, setting his sights on higher, loftier goals for himself. Once old and useless things are destroyed and trampled, new things can be built. Think again of the surgeon; he wields a knife to excise decaying, diseased tissues from the body. It hurts; it maims; it scars. Yet from this process is the body able to heal, to build anew and become stronger. The surgery takes only moments, but the healing takes weeks, sometimes longer. So it is with the client's life: The orishas are the surgeons, and Ogún wields the knife. The client should be afraid, yet he must plow ahead bravely. Evolution will come after the pain.

We say that civilization was built with Ogundá; under the skillful eye of Ogún we evolved from a race of scavengers to a race of hunters and then to a race knowing the secrets of agriculture and husbandry. Each of these transitions brought much good, yet they also thrust us into new situations that brought evil. Think of the great transitions that occurred as society moved from a base of agriculture and husbandry to one of industrial power; the industrial revolution brought many changes to our lives, but not all were good. Even today, as we head deep into a new age of technology and information, we encounter as much destruction as growth. Though it seems that civilization has moved away from the ancient times of ancestor reverence and orisha worship, in truth we are thrust deeper into its mysteries. At the core of all our develoment are Ogundá, the sign of revolution and upheaval, and Ogún, who controls the metals and machines that make our technology possible. While the changes predicted for the client's life might affect no one but him, they will be as far-reaching and potentially disastrous as the revolutions we have seen in our own society.

Iré yale is a better omen than iré alone. When firm blessings are predicted, the diviner may continue to advise the client: "The orisha knows your heart and knows your thoughts. While you began with good intentions, in time you walked a crooked path. For a time that worked, but now you must pay for your wrongdoings. While in some ways giving you iré yale is too good for you, your past goodness should not be totally unrewarded. Even Olófin wishes you the best, and all the orishas must answer to him, as we answer to them."

If iré yale timbelaye has opened, however, these predictions change for the worse. The orisha whose shells are being consulted is still wishing the client the best, yet will offer no ebó to resolve this person's conflicts. This spirit will give only advice, and the client is left to work out his issues alone. If he perseveres, it is only because Olófin gives blessings; even with Olófin's blessings the path that he walks will not be easy. No matter what has brought the client to the mat, the diviner must divulge these warnings. When iré yale timbelaye has come with Ogundá, there will be tears.

After the orisha whose shells are being consulted has had the chance to speak and mark ebó, often Ogún stands up; Ogundá is his home, and rarely will it close out unless he has had his say and his chance to mark ebó. While Ogún's words might be harsh to the one at the mat, the client must turn to Ogún to resolve the difficult issues of Ogundá. No other orisha knows the trials and tribulations that Ogundá brings better than he. Ogún can quell the osogbo of this odu.

Yemayá, too, can speak through Ogundá, but her influence here is both pained and severe. If she takes ebó in this sign, it will be no simple affair. After her, Elegguá and Ochosi can speak or claim offerings; like Ogún, they can become the client's salvation in this odu. Obatalá speaks here as well, and always he teaches that honest effort and a pure soul can bring salvation. Know, however, that Obatalá can be a harsh, severe orisha, and when all else fails he can be the greatest warrior among them all. Aganyú and Babaluaiye also speak through Ogundá, but their influence will always be harsh. Beware if Aganyú speaks; the client could be scarred by fire or iron before this letter has passed. Babaluaiye, as well, has little good to say in Ogundá; his influence can mark massive disease or decay requiring surgical intervention.

In contradiction to the other families of odu in the diloggún, Ogundá is often easiest to work with when it opens in an osogbo. Having a specific osogbo reveals not only the sources of the client's ills but also ways of avoiding them (through taboo) and fixing them (through ebó). When the sign opens in osogbo, the diviner knows that the client's life is filled with arguments and tragedy; this person often finds himself at odds with those he cares about the most, and at times there seems to be no resolution to these problems. His personal desperation devolves into fights, struggles, and arguments. Ogundá brings separation to siblings, friends, and lovers, and many of these separations are brought about by the client's own argumentative nature. If he wishes to keep his loved ones close, he must not fight with them so much. Know that this pattern marks the existence of a person who is jealous of all the client's relationships. This person does much to cause the separation arising in the client's life. If the client can identify this troublemaker, he can neutralize his influence.

Men and women who open in Ogundá will have separate but similar issues. Women in Ogundá often have suffered at the hands of men. It is not uncommon for odu to tell the story of a woman who has loved another with all her heart yet lost her soul. This pattern speaks of yearning, heartache, and desperation. It also speaks of violence, and many women opening in Ogundá have suffered from domestic abuse. Physical beatings, mental anguish, and emotional torment might lie in the woman's past, and even in the present. If the woman who has opened in this odu does not change her ways, these energies can carry over into her future, and she could suffer death, dismemberment, or disfigurement at the hands of an abusive mate. A far darker portent of Ogundá is rape, and the possibility that a child was conceived of this union. Note that the seduction of a minor by an adult is the equivalent of rape; the diviner must question the client about this as well. An even darker warning comes for a woman with a daughter: If these energies are in the mother's past, they may come in the daughter's future as well. The client must be vigilant and try to protect her daughter.

Men who open in Ogundá can have similar issues. The diviner, however, should determine the sexual orientation of his client. Homosexual men will suffer as a woman in this sign, while heterosexual men will become the adversary. A man opening in Ogundá can be violent, quick-tempered, and given to random malicious acts. The degree to which these tendencies manifest depends on how well disciplined he has become over the years. In the most extreme osogbos, the client might have been, or will become, a rapist, arsonist, or spouse abuser. In the more gentle osogbos, he will be given to heated arguments and minor violence. These behaviors are both marked and prohibited by this odu. In other words, the orisha who speaks will no longer tolerate this behavior, and if it continues, his punishments will be extreme. Already this person's life is falling apart, and Ogundá guarantees that continuing in this manner will make it worse.

Relationships suffer in this odu, and there are many warnings the client should keep in mind while this letter is in effect. If he is single, he may often experience unreturned love, and at this time two options might seem feasible to him: obsession or stalking and love magic. Because Ogundá can bring incarceration, the client would be unwise to pursue someone whose affections are not returned. This person could find himself in the hands of the police. Love magic is taboo as well; the client is in no state to attempt such an undertaking, and if he does, he will be the one enchanted. Under Ogundá's influence, a single woman, or a woman who has recently ended a relationship, is in danger of doing something foolish to gain or hold a lover. She must never act out of desperation for love. The world is full of men, each better than the next, and the client should hold on to her own heart until one worthy of it can be found. Sick affections are born in this odu; a client of either gender must keep this in mind so that he or she does not become caught up in them. Just as Ogún once raped his own mother and then punished himself for his crimes, so will he punish those who force their affections on another.

Ogundá's energy brings arguments, and those who open in this sign and are involved in committed relationships or marriages could suffer as well. Men will be tempted to raise their hands in anger against their wives, and wives will goad their husbands into a rage. Both must step away from these situations. Not only love but also freedom, and perhaps even one's life, may be lost. Ogundá foretells pregnancy, yet it also indicates that the child could be lost through an accident or disease. For a woman, the time of pregnancy is also the time in which her husband will be the most tempted to leave. A man in Ogundá is forbidden to engage in infidelity of any kind, whether he is married or just living with a lover. He is also advised not to leave his wife; no one but she can put up with his miserable ways. And a client of either sex must be counseled to change his or her argumentative ways, lest a spouse or lover leave.

The diviner may assume that the client has many enemies in his environment that he might not be aware of. To keep himself safe from harm, the client must leave behind his life of arguments and violence. He must avoid verbal disputes, no matter how minor, and definitely avoid physical altercations. He must not even harbor thoughts of arguments or violence. Now is a time to promote calm and security.

Through Ogundá, many become careless with their words. The client must be reminded that many hold evil intentions toward him. He should not express his secret desires to anyone, not even a close friend, and he should avoid large social gatherings.

There are dangers for this person on the streets as well, especially at night. He must not go out of the house at night. He should not raise his hand in anger against another person or carry or use weapons, for they not only can kill the innocent but also can be turned against their owner. Even if he fights only in self-defense, the client will find himself entangled in the legal system. And the law is hot for the client right now. The diviner must tell the client to measure his words carefully when speaking to civil authorities or law enforcement. He must never take the law into his own hands, even if his personal property is in danger. In this odu, when a thief comes in through the front door, one should run out the back. Anyone who fights, uses weapons, or attacks another while under the influence of Ogundá risks his own life and liberty. Ogundá is the home of false accusations. The law could take the client even if he is innocent.

In Ogundá, the osogbo ano flags severe health complications, including loss of blood, intestinal trouble, and kidney dysfunction. Diseases that waste the abdomen, womb, and colon are all a danger as well. The heart is in distress; the client must avoid vices. He also must take good care of any puncture wounds, bites, or infections. Ogundá gives birth to tetanus, so the client should have a tetanus booster vaccination if he sustains a puncture wound. The client's back is weak, and he must avoid heavy lifting, frequent bending, and swift movements. If back pain develops, it demands immediate medical attention. The client must avoid back surgery at all costs until the orishas say it is safe, and he must avoid surgical intervention in other regions as long as there is an appropriate medical alternative.* Now is not the time for elective surgeries, especially cosmetic procedures; this odu warns of excessive scarring and infection. If surgery is imminent, the client should conduct background checks on all the potential surgeons, choosing one with the most experience and the best record. Before surgery, the client should make ebó to Ogún so that the surgeon's metal instruments will bring health and healing, not death.

In addition, all composites of Ogundá may bring up the following issues, which the diviner should explore with the client:

- Those opening in Ogundá often have had both a head injury and an injury from fire or iron that resulted in a scar. The diviner must ask the client if both are true. If the answer is no, injury becomes a danger in this pattern, and the client must guard himself against this.
- This odu is hot, and no matter its orientation it can bring a variety of ills to this person's life, including curses, fights, dangerous jokes, street violence, gossip, legal entanglements, tragedies, and personal attacks (by friends and acquaintances). The client must guard himself against these things.
- Something the client thought he lost, whether a person or a possession, will return to him. Something the client wants to discard will suddenly appear new and useful. That which was thrown away he will regret. Tears in all cases will turn to joyful laughter.
- Ogundá forebodes the danger that the client might become the unwitting slave or instrument of another's dark, sinful desires, as well as a danger of imprisonment and tragedy. The client must be on guard against overt or covert manipulation, for it is through this that false accusations will come.
- In business dealings, Ogundá gives severe warnings. Unknowingly, the client could be caught in something illegal. If he has business partners, one of them is working against the law, and all will suffer for it. If the client has come to the orishas because he is about to start a business, now is not a good time, especially if partners are involved. The client should wait at least a month before negotiating and signing a contract. Even then, legal papers will not be what they seem, so he should hire a lawyer to review them. And before signing a contract, the client should come back to the diviner to make ebó.
- The client should avoid traveling, even for business. Offers for unplanned trips or long journeys are key points in this sign; while the client is on a journey, the evil intentions of another will become known, and while the client is away, malice will be wrought at home.

*When treating illness, there are two types of interventions—medical and surgical. Medical interventions are based on drugs and lifestyle changes, while surgical interventions rely on the mechanical resectioning of diseased tissues. When Ogundá comes, it emphasizes the need for medical over surgical interventions when possible.

- This person has enemies who watch him and want to harm him; some might even use occult means to bring his destruction. Ebó will fight this. So envious are others that they will stop at nothing to ruin him: Slander, libel, gossip, violence, and intimidation will be their tools. Because Ogundá warns against invoking the legal system now, this person must depend on the orishas to protect himself. There is no other way.

## The Prohibitions of Ogundá

When Ogundá comes, the diviner has several general prohibitions to discuss with the client, regardless of whether the odu opens in iré or osogbo. If the client aspires to move beyond the turmoil of his life, he must consider these prohibitions to be strict taboos that he cannot break. The client should follow all prescribed prohibitions for a period of twenty-one to twenty-eight days, unless this reading is a bajado, in which case they must be followed until ocha is made, or an itá, in which case they apply for life.

Note that each of the sixteen composites of Ogundá has its own specific prohibitions. The diviner should prescribe the prohibitions of the composites only if the reading opens in osogbo; in this case, the taboos of the composite odu will keep the client from further spiritual, mental, emotional, and physical harm.

- Ogundá is home to Ogún, who lives along railroad tracks. For now, do not travel by train, and avoid places where there are large stores of iron, such as railroads. If travel over a track is inevitable, one would be wise first to pay homage to Ogún. Stop and look both ways, even if a train is not coming; before driving or walking over the tracks, Ogún's home, cross one's arms and say, "Bendición, Ogún!" (*Bendición* means "blessings.")
- Do not go outdoors at the following times: noon, 3:00 P.M., 7:00 P.M., and 9:00 p.m. These times and numbers are sacred to Ogún. If the osogbo of the letter is severe, all outdoor activities should be restricted between the hours of noon and 9:00 P.M.
- Do not ride horses, even for recreational purposes. There is danger of an accident, and paralysis could be the end result.
- Avoid any means of mechanical transportation that travels on less than three "feet," such as motorcycles, bicycles, skates (while they have several wheels, they use only two feet), and skateboards (again, many wheels but only one platform).
- When walking, do not cross over ditches or trenches. Do not jump over holes. Instead, walk around them.
- Avoid traveling, even for business. Offers for unplanned trips or long journeys are key points in this sign; while the client is on a journey, the evil intentions of another will become known, and while the client is away malice will be wrought at home.
- Ogundá brings ambush from behind: Protect one's back at all times. When in a strange place, stand close to an exit with the back to the wall. When standing on the street, keep one's back to the wall so one can see in all directions. Do not stand at or near corners. Do not stand in a group, especially one that is facing the same direction. And never, ever ignore this advice at night.
- Guns, knives, chains, and clubs are all forbidden. Do not carry or use them.
- To avoid injury to the back, avoid lifting heavy objects and do not lean back in a chair.
- Do not consume rooster, alcohol, or illegal intoxicants. Do not eat the sacrificial meats of Ogún and Elegguá. If a child of Ogún, do not eat the sacrificial meats of Shangó, and if a child of Shangó, do not eat the sacrificial meats of Ogún. Consuming these animal products will not only anger the orishas and cause spiritual damage but also bring a variety of physical and gastrointestinal problems. Do not fish, because fish can be one's salvation. Do not eat any fish, especially those that are caught with a hook.
- Do not neglect your health. Have a complete physical now. If this reading is an itá, the iyawó should schedule an appointment before the three-month ebó and have a physical every year for the duration of his life.

- To prevent accidents, avoid situations in which falling is a possibility. Do not climb ladders. Avoid heights or scaling high places; do not reach above the head. Never perform acrobatics or do maneuvers that stretch the body beyond its normal range of motion. An accident now could be fatal.
- Under the influence of this odu, one may attract people who are intoxicated, medicated, or mentally unstable. Keep away from them. If one is in a medical profession in which one sees these types of people on a daily basis, be very cautious at work.
- The head is not meant for carrying loads. Use it to think. Carry loads only with the hands.
- Be cautious of those who ask for things to be done that were never done before.
- Do not hold any item for another person; false accusations could result.
- Do not harbor thoughts of revenge, violence, or anger. Do not harm another, even if there is just cause.
- Do not engage in practical jokes. Do nothing to compromise the safety, feelings, or integrity of another.
- Never confide secrets to another; they are secrets only if no one else knows them.
- While this odu forbids uninvited guests (even unexpected visits by friends), one is allowed to entertain by invitation. However, Ogundá foretells danger of robbery from a visitor, so do not allow strangers into the home, and be vigilant over those with whom one is familiar. Keep personal belongings private and secure.
- To avoid the prospect of witchcraft being turned against oneself, avoid using or association with those who use witchcraft and the occult.

## Marking Ebó in Ogundá: Initial Considerations

Because the diloggún is a tool for one's evolution, each odu prescribes many eboses to put a client back into alignment with his destiny. While the client might have come to the oracle with simple, mundane issues, the opening of three mouths on the mat flags serious, volatile osogbos at work in not only the client's life, but also the lives of those seated in the room for instruction and of those there to give spiritual support to the client (such as one's godparents). When Ogundá opens on the mat, no one, not even those aleyos present but uninvolved in the session, may leave until performing a specific ebó for Ogún. On behalf of everyone present, the diviner smears a piece of raw beef liberally with epó. He wraps the beef in brown paper, shows it to Ogún, and petitions him to cleanse all in the house. Beginning with himself and then moving from the client to the godparents, priests and priestesses in elder status, aborishas who have taken initiations, and then aleyos who have taken nothing of ocha, the diviner rubs everyone in the house from head to toe with the ebó. After all are cleansed, the diviner leaves the meat to sit with Ogún overnight. The next morning, he takes the ebó into the street, saying, "Eshu batie sode."* ("Eshu takes the negativity [of the reading].") After returning home, the diviner casts the oracle for himself to ensure that he does not suffer from Ogundá. In this way, the diviner is assured that neither he nor anyone else will be harmed by Ogundá's energies.

Note that if the oracle refuses closure no matter what the diviner tries to mark or discuss, this initial prescription of ebó might need alteration. The orishas may decide that it needs to be taken not to the street but to the trash, a crossroads, railroad tracks, a river, a lake, the ocean, or the woods. A diviner with the knowledge, aché, and experience will know when this needs to be altered to bring closure to odu. Also, those people present at the reading who have received the warriors should perform this same ebó to their own Ogún when they return home to ensure that the harsh energies of Ogundá have been removed. Those aleyos who were in the diviner's home during the reading who have not received the warriors might consider sitting for a session with the diloggún soon. They may need to take the initiation of the warriors for their own spiritual protection.

*If a dog is found wandering in the street, feed this meat to him.

Having made this initial prescription of ebó, the diviner now must consider whether his client is an aleyo, an aborisha, or a priest. His religious status will determine how the italero is to consider the initial marking of ebó in Ogundá. An aleyo (an outsider who is just a casual client with nothing of ocha) opening in Ogundá will need the initiation of the elekes to evolve beyond the harsh osogbo made manifest in odu. The aché of Obatalá, Yemayá, Oshún, and Shangó is needed to overcome the tragedies of three mouths. If the osogbo is severe, and if the diviner has received the shells of Ogún, he should give the client the eleke of Ogún as well. Although it is normally saved for the investment of the warriors, Elegguá's eleke should be given at this time, also. Know that once the aleyo has received these things, he is no longer aleyo; now he is aborisha, an adherent of the orishas. In time, the investment of the elekes will draw him closer into the ilé ocha.

If the client is an aborisha who has received the elekes but not the warriors, the initiation of the warriors is the next step to take. Just as our baptism (the reception of the elekes) is a potent ebó against the osogbo of Ogundá, so is the reception of Elegguá, Ogún, Ochosi, and Ósun a powerful way to leave behind this odu's osogbo. If the reception of the warriors is marked because of this odu, the diviner should keep some important points in mind. First, if his ilé ocha is one that gives Eshu (another name for Elegguá) to those who have not yet made ocha, he must mark the path of Eshu before bringing Ogundá to closure. Also, in this odu the diviner must fortify Ogún's cauldron. Although most ilé ocha give the aborisha only the stone of Ogún plus his farming tools, in this odu it is essential that the orisha has a full set of implements so his aché is strong. Include a piece of railroad track, a chain, a bellows, and three, seven, nine, or twenty-one railroad spikes and horseshoes. Increase Ochosi's implements, especially if he stands up during the reading for ebó. Instead of just his stone and crossbow, include three crossbows and add a small set of deer antlers to the cauldron; this is especially important in the composite odu Ogundá Osá, where the pact between Ogún and Ochosi to always live, work, and eat together was made.*

For those who already have the elekes and the warriors, or for priests and priestesses of this faith, there are further initial considerations in this odu. Since Ogundá is hot and volatile, the head of one who opens in this odu is easily clouded and weakened by these energies. The diviner should prescribe one or more rogaciónes. If the composite odu has come with a larishe, the rogación should be given before the orisha claiming larishe, and if the client has not received that spirit, he must receive that spirit's eleke now.

Finally, in all patterns of Ogundá, Ogún himself must be given ebó. The sacrifices on the following list are all appropriate to offer him in this family of odu.

## Adimú

### *Seven Gourds*

A simple adimú to appease Ogún may be made of the following ingredients: seven large gourds, toasted corn, seven pennies, guinea pepper, rum, honey, coconut oil, molasses, epó, smoked fish, and jutía.

To prepare this offering, place the seven gourds before Ogún and fill them with the toasted corn. Lay a single penny in the center of each gourd, on top of the corn, and place a single guinea pepper over each penny. Sprinkle the remaining ingredients liberally over all.

This adimú should remain with the orisha for three, seven, or twenty-one days; the diviner will determine the exact length of time using the dilogún. To discard the ebó, the client should take all seven gourds to a set of railroad tracks.

### *Watermelon*

Ogún adores watermelon. While many believe this fruit is suitable only for Yemayá and Olokun, it is a suitable adimú for Ogún as well. To serve

*Not all *ramas of ocha* (spiritual lines) give a stone for Ochosi in Ogún's cauldron. Ochosi is a separate orisha that must be received after the ocha ceremony. However, a single stone washed for this orisha does have aché. Some lines give only a crossbow and arrow to symbolize the pact between Ogún and Ochosi to work together. It is only one of the minor differences among the different ramas of ocha.

the fruit to the orisha, the client should purchase a large watermelon and cut it into three equal parts. Put each part in a large jícara or on a large plate and serve to Ogún, allowing it to remain with him overnight. The next morning, the client discards the watermelon at a set of railroad tracks.

In severe osogbos, this adimú should be composed of three large watermelons served to Ogún whole.

### *Stuffed Fish*

When Elegguá stands up for ebó in the reading, prepare this ebó to satisfy both him and Ogún. The client should bring the following ingredients to the diviner's home: guinea pepper, honey, molasses, smoked fish, jutía, coconut oil, ten fresh fish, epó, rum, and toasted corn.

Mix together enough guinea pepper, honey, molasses, smoked fish, jutía, and coconut oil to stuff all ten fish. Having stuffed the fish, preheat a frying pan over medium-high heat and drop a liberal amount of epó into the pan. Fry the fish in the heated oil. As they fry, spray rum infrequently over the fish to season and add the chef's aché to them. Fill two terra-cotta plates with the toasted corn, and when the fish are done, put three on one plate for Elegguá and seven on the second plate for Ogún. Present the plates to the orishas, leaving them overnight.

The following morning, the client wraps both eboses in brown paper. Elegguá's goes to the crossroad; Ogún's should be left at the railroad tracks.

### *Steak*

Ogún loves to eat, and when a hot, volatile osogbo comes in Ogundá, the following dish can placate him. To prepare this ebó, the client will need to provide the following ingredients: a large steak, epó, manteca de cacao, smoked fish, jutía, and toasted corn.

Season the steak with epó, rubbing a large amount of oil into both its sides. Once it is saturated with epó, coat the steak liberally with the manteca de cacao as well. Sprinkle a liberal amount of smoked fish and jutía on both sides of this steak, rubbing them into the meat well. Preheat a skillet over medium-high heat. Drop a generous amount of epó into the pan. Fry the steak in the oil until it is browned but still pink on the inside. Serve the steak to Ogún on a bed of toasted corn.

While presenting this adimú, the client should pay foribale to the orisha, praying for his support and protection. The ebó sits with the orisha overnight, and the next morning the client wraps it in brown paper and discards it at the railroad tracks.

### *Mashed Ñame*

A simpler adimú for Ogún consists of seven balls of mashed ñame. To prepare this ebó, the client brings the following ingredients to the diviner's house: a large ñame, white rice, toasted corn, coconut oil, manteca de cacao, honey, molasses, rum, guinea peppers, smoked fish, and jutía.

Peel the ñame and dice it into small squares. Boil the squares in water until they are soft. While the ñame is boiling, cook the white rice (do not use salt). Once both the rice and the ñame are done, put them into a large mixing bowl with manteca de cacao and mash everything together until a thick paste forms. Mold the paste into seven individual balls. Lay a bed of toasted corn on a white plate. Smear each ñame ball with some coconut oil before placing it on this bed. Drizzle honey and molasses and spray a shot of rum over all the balls. Put one guinea pepper on top of each ball, then sprinkle the smoked fish and jutía over the entire plate.

When serving this adimú to Ogún, the client should pray for the spirit's blessings, protection, and goodwill. The adimú should remain with the orisha for seven days; at the end of this time the client places the balls in a brown paper bag and discards them at the nearest railroad tracks, along with a derecho of seven cents.

## Cleansings

### *Seven Pears*

A simple cleansing to Ogún consists of seven pears, one of the orisha's favorite fruits. The client should bring the pears to the diviner's house. Before Ogún's cauldron, the diviner rubs the client from head to toe with each pear. The fruits should remain with Ogún for seven days. At the end of this time, the client wraps them in brown paper and discards them at the nearest railroad tracks.

### *Seven Guinea Eggs*

Another cleansing before Ogún's shrine requires the following ingredients: a large green cloth, a small white saucer, seven guinea eggs, epó, honey, rum, a cigar, and cascarilla.

To prepare this cleansing, the diviner lays the large green cloth on the floor before Ogún and places the white saucer in the center of it. One by one, he presents each guinea egg to Ogún and then anoints them with the epó, honey, rum, cigar smoke, and cascarilla. After anointing each egg, he places it on the white saucer. Once he is done, the diviner blesses the client before Ogún's shrine and offers a prayer to Ogún. Now the cleansing begins.

Once every day for seven days, the client lifts one egg from the saucer and uses it to cleanse himself by rubbing his body with it. Once he has used an egg for cleansing, he places it on the cloth, not on the saucer. On the seventh day, after the final egg is used, the client removes the saucer from the cloth. He ties the eggs securely in the cloth and takes this bundle to the nearest railroad tracks, along with a derecho of seven cents.

## Spiritual Baths

Because Ogundá is so volatile, many diviners will prescribe a series of spiritual baths for the client. While the priest should prepare them, the client may administer them in his own home. Before he can take a spiritual bath, however, the bathtub must be clean; the client must scrub it thoroughly so that there is no trace of dirt. Next he fills the tub with warm, fresh water.

To begin his bath, the supplicant stands, naked, in the tub. The prepared bath is contained in a large bowl, which he pours over himself from the shoulders down the body.* Once he has scrubbed and soaked thoroughly, the client should drain the water so a normal shower may be taken. He dries off with a white towel and dresses in white. After the bath, he must avoid sexual activity for twenty-four hours.

Several formulas for spiritual baths for Ogundá follow.

### *Albahaca, Toronjil, and Hierba Buena*

The priest soaks equal amounts of the herbs albahaca, toronjil, and hierba buena overnight in a large quantity of fresh water. The following morning, he strains the herb matter from the liquid, wringing the herbs by hand until the water is a dark green. He adds to the liquid the juice of one watermelon, a bit of rum, and equal amounts of river water and well water, and then he bottles the liquid in seven different jars. The client bathes in the contents of a single jar every night for seven nights. Instead of using normal deodorant soap, he bathes with a pure cocoa butter or castile soap. After the seventh bath, the client returns to the diviner's home for a rogación before Obatalá, who owns all heads. Ogún should sit at Obatalá's feet during the rogación so he can witness the event. The client should give a basket of cool fruits to both spirits when the rogación is complete.

### *Verdolaga, Bleo Blanco, and Sauco Blanco*

For this bath, the diviner bathes the client himself and gives a rogación when the bath is complete. The day before this ebó is made, he soaks equal amounts of the herbs verdolaga, bleo blanco, and sauco blanco in a vat of cool, fresh water. The next morning, he strains the herbs from the water, wringing them out until the water is deeply tinted. The diviner then adds to the bath white flower petals, efun, cow's milk, goat's milk, coconut milk, grated coconut, shredded cocoa butter, and rice milk, and he sets the vat with the spiritual bath in front of Obatala's shrine so that the orisha may bless it.

When the client comes to the diviner's home, he must bring a white towel and white clothes, and he must wear old clothes that can be ripped off and thrown away. With the client standing in fresh water, the priest rips off the old clothes and then bathes the client from the shoulders down. After letting him soak, the diviner directs the client to take a shower,

*Because one's head belongs to an orisha (and probably not to the one to whom the bath is consecrated), it must be protected from the initial pouring of water. One must never pour a spiritual bath over the head. However, if the head becomes wet later during the cleansing process, that is fine; it will refresh the orí.

dry off, and dress in white. The diviner gives the client a rogación before Obatalá, first placing Ogún at Obatalá's feet to witness this cleansing. The next morning, the client takes the old clothes and the remnants of the rogación to a hill in the woods.

*Pomegranates*

This simple bath will not only cool and cleanse the client but also satisfy the need to pacify Ogún with an adimú. Depending on the severity of the osogbo brought to the mat, the client should provide three, seven, or twenty-one pomegranates. The priest places them on a white plate and leaves them over Ogún's cauldron for three days. After three days, the priest removes the pomegranates from Ogún. Instead of discarding these, however, he cuts them open and scoops out the juice and seeds. He mixes the juice and seeds with as many different kinds of fresh waters as possible; lake, river, brook, tap, rain, and sea water may all be used. The client pours this spiritual bath over himself from the shoulders down. After this cleansing he should take a quick shower before drying off and dressing in white.

*Laurel, Romerillo, and Maravilla*

Crush equal amounts of the herbs laurel, romerillo, and maravilla in a large quantity of fresh water until it tints green from the juices. Strain the herb matter from the water and pour the liquid into seven bottles. The client should bathe with the contents of one bottle per night for seven nights, dressing in white during this time.

*Obatalá's White Bath*

Because Ogundá is so hot and volatile, Obatalá's white bath is an appropriate ebó in this family of odu; his cooling, calming nature will help the client evolve beyond the harsh energies of this letter. To prepare this bath, the diviner mixes the following eight ingredients: cow's milk, goat's milk, coconut milk, florida water, white flowers, grated coconut, crushed cascarilla, and grated cocoa butter. He leaves the bath mixture, in the vat in which it was mixed, in front of Obatalá for four hours. At the end of this time, he bottles it in eight separate bottles.

The client should bathe in the contents of one bottle every night for eight nights, dressing in white the entire time. After the eighth bath, he should come back to the priest's house for a rogación in front of Obatalá. After the rogación, he should prepare a simple adimú to appease Ogún.

### Traditional Eboses in Ogundá

Certain types of animal and food offerings are traditional to use in Ogundá. For eyebale, the diviner should try to pick from the following list: a rooster, three hens, three pigeons, and a goat or a ram (when four legs are called for). For adimú, the diviner should pick from fresh and smoked fish, jutía, a knife, three coconuts, a white sheet, cornmeal, red meat (beef), and seven or three ears of corn.

# The First Composite Odu of Ogundá, Ogundá Okana (3-1)

## The Proverbs of Ogundá Okana

- Your dead enemy wishes the worst for you.
- The dead are not so dead.
- They run, and they do not know why they run.

## The Message of Ogundá Okana

Ogundá Okana opens when a casting of three mouths, Ogundá, is followed by a casting of one mouth, Okana. The odu is also known as Ogundá Okanran, Ogundá Kanran, and Ogundá Kana. Because Ogundá and Okana, two volatile patterns, have crossed paths here, their union demands caution from the diviner. They bring no iré, and their opening requires that the closing eboses for both Okana and Ogundá be done. (See "The Eboses of Ogundá Okana" on page 147.)

When Ogundá Okana falls, the diviner pays homage to Elegguá, Ogún, Obatalá, and Shangó, saying to each, "Maferefún!" Obatalá and Shangó stand up in this pattern to bring blessings to the client; they also come to fight the osogbos that are inherent in this sign. Before the odu has closed out, all four orishas may require eboses.

The first advice the diviner should give the client who has opened in this pattern is this: Around him are many who run in panic, yet none understands the reason why he runs. Their own panic is a mystery. A frantic pace permeates the client's life from without, and if he succumbs to this hurry, this haste, it will make him prone to accidents. Now, while life accelerates, the client must try to rest and stay calm. He needs strength not only for himself but also for others.

This odu signals that the client is carrying a huge burden, one of much importance to his life; it has weight, and before this sign has passed he may be forced to make an important decision about this burden and his life in general. Left to his own devices, this person will make the wrong decision. He does not think about events or situations until it is too late and he cannot do anything about them. This tendency toward procrastination has wrought much evil in his life. Here, at the mat, the diviner must lead the client to pour out his heart and soul to the orishas. He must impress upon the client that the oracles will help him along the path of evolution; odu can help us all achieve our destinies flawlessly. Evolution, however, requires honesty with oneself and faith in one's orishas. As this person's troubles are poured out, the spiritual entities who have come to the mat will hear them; before they let the odu close, they will advise him and prescribe ebó. If the client begins to change his life or make decisions here at the mat with the diviner's orishas present, later he will not be forced to make quick, unplanned changes in his life.

In addition to these concerns, the diviner should also explore the following items with the client:

- Due to exhaustion and lethargy, this person cannot think clearly or rationally. The diviner should advise against quick, uninformed decisions. When a need to do something drastic arises, the client should take a few deep breaths, relax, and walk away from the situation. As soon as possible, he should return to the diviner and consult with his orishas.
- Ogundá Okana warns of thieves and cautions against thievery. Those who must lie or steal to make a living will fall while those who are honest or sincere will rise. This odu also warns that a thief could be visiting the client's home on a regular basis. If an important item turns up missing, it was stolen by a friend or close acquaintance. If this client has roommates, he should consider living alone; he does not live with honest people. If he lives with family, he should know that his own blood relatives will steal from him should the chance arise.
- This pattern tells the client that his friends are involved in personal wars and disputes. He may get caught in the middle of several disagreements. Here, there is danger: His friends, relatives, and acquaintances might all tell him lies or half truths, hoping to make him take sides. In all patterns of Ogundá, the number three is a danger. There are two sides to every disagreement, but if the client gets involved, he creates a threesome. He must refuse to be involved in any such disputes.
- This odu speaks of jealousy. While the client is jealous of others, they are envious of him as well. Those who are overwhelmed with greed and envy may try to start verbal or physical fights with this person; he must walk away from them. In Ogundá Okana, the best defense against osogbo is a quick retreat to safety.
- Relationships in this sign are tricky. In iré, relationships can have problems, but in osogbo they can be worse. The client should also treat his lover carefully and thoughtfully, but even then they will still have problems.
- Conception and pregnancy under this odu's influence will be not a joy but a curse. For now, the client should use proper birth control or abstain from sexual activities.
- At home the client must be cautious. Falls, fires, domestic violence, break-ins, and robberies are all dangers. He must be vigilant over his personal safety.
- In any osogbo, this odu can bring blood loss through disease or injury. In ano or ikú the loss

of blood is imminent and may occur through internal bleeding, anemia (either physiological or nutritional), or accidents. Blood-borne pathogens introduced by sharp objects (infection), intestinal disease and decay, renal disease, and back pain are also a danger.

- In a severe osogbo, the client is so bored with life that suicide may soon seem a viable option. The diviner must counsel him never to consider this; one day, his life will change for the better.
- While Ogundá Okana carries a lot of osogbo, it also brings some iré in the form of an unexpected item—a letter, a package, a gift, or some news—the client will receive. If the client accepts the item graciously and with proper etiquette, more blessings will follow.

## The Prohibitions of Ogundá Okana

- Metal poses a great danger; with metal, one could be wounded by one's own hands. Be careful of metal objects at home, at work, and on the street. Do not carry or wear metal objects, especially weapons. They could be turned against their owner.
- Alcohol will cloud the mind and anesthetize good judgment. If one consumes alcohol, it will at those times when one is in greatest need of all one's faculties. Therefore, avoid alcohol. Avoid other forms of intoxicants as well.
- Driving will become hazardous during the day, but it can become suicidal at night. Limit one's driving to the hours between sunrise and sunset.
- Long trips are taboo for eight days; shorter trips may be taken during the day.
- For the next eight days, be sure to be indoors, at home, after sunset.
- Women must not become pregnant at this time; conception will not be healthy now for either mother or child.

## The Eboses of Ogundá Okana

Regardless of its orientation, Ogundá Okana requires the prescription of two closing eboses, one for Okana and one for Ogundá. They must be made as soon as the oracle gives closure. The diviner must oil two pieces of beef with epó and wrap them separately in brown paper. All those who were present for the reading must gather before the diviner's warriors while he prays to both Elegguá and Ogún to lift the heat of this sign. Once the prayers are finished, the italero cleans himself with one piece of meat to Elegguá and the other to Ogún. He then cleanses the client in the same manner. The initiates then clean themselves to both orishas, followed by the aborishas. After everyone has finished this ebó, the diviner opens the room, and all should leave. Each must make the same ebó to his or her own Ogún upon arriving home. The next morning, the diviner who performed the reading must take the meat packages to nature: Elegguá's goes to the crossroads and Ogún's goes to the nearest railroad track. Note that all who were present for this reading (even aborishas who were in the house but not at the mat) should have a session with the diloggún as soon as possible.

Once the closing eboses of Ogundá Okana are done, another ebó should be made to Ogún to protect the client from a road accident. The diviner must rub a piece of red meat with epó and seal it in a brown bag. The client rubs this meat on all four tires of his car, plus the front and back fenders. Before driving, he should present this meat to Ogún, leaving it with the diviner's orisha overnight; the next morning he returns and takes this ebó to the nearest crossroads. Having done this, the client is free to drive on short trips as directed by this odu.

After prescribing these eboses, the diviner must tell the client about the rest of the offerings that he has to complete to bring closure to this odu. Ogún, Obatalá, and Shangó receive first consideration in this odu. Here Ogún is hot, and he must be cooled before the client can work through the osogbos brought in this sign. Obatalá balances the heat of Ogún, trying to refresh the client so that he may work through his difficulties calmly. Shangó is here as a warrior, and he will fight all that tries to harm this client. The day after this reading, the client must shower and dress totally in white, then return to the diviner's home with a two baskets of cool, fresh fruits for the orishas Ogún and Shangó, plus the elements needed for a rogación. Note that nothing red may be brought before Ogún or Shangó, for that color is hot and this person needs coolness in his life. Pears, bananas, pomegranates, and coconuts are good choices for them. First, one basket of fruit is presented to Ogún. The priest then sits the client in front of Obatalá and gives him a rogación of the head. Then the second basket of fruit is put on top of Shangó's sopera. There, the client pays foribale and prays to Shangó to remove all the osogbos that stand in the way of his evolution.

After detailing these eboses, the diviner has his first attempt to close the odu. If it will not close, he must consider the following items:

- If Ogundá Okana will not close, the meaning of the sign has altered slightly. The orisha Ogún stands up to say that the client has not truly heard all that was said in this reading; the client has a knife or machete in his house that he keeps as a weapon, and might carry a weapon on his person (he could have it even now). He does not intend to give up this weapon, nor will he refuse to use the weapon should the chance arise. Ogún has already seen this in his heart, and it angers the orisha. Now he demands that the client turn over the weapon to him as ebó. If there is a gun in the client's house or on this client now, it must be given to Ogún as well. He will wield those weapons for the client and keep him safe if he follows all that this odu has to say. This way, the client will not be harmed by his own actions.
- If the client is a pregnant woman, she must make ebó to Ogún immediately since he rules this sign. The proper ebó is two ñames: one for the mother and one for the unborn. If the letter will not close, Ogún may be demanding more. To find out if this is the case, the diviner should ask, "Ebó elese Ogún?" If the answer is yes, the diviner uses the diloggún to mark the appropriate offering.
- If this odu still will not close, Shangó could be demanding additional eboses. To determine if he needs anything, the diviner should ask, "Ebó elese Shangó?" If the answer is yes, the proper adimú is a stalk of green plantains. The plantains should be left with Shangó until they begin to turn brown, and then the client must wrap them up in brown paper and take them to the foot of a palm tree.
- In this odu, Obatalá can stand up for additional eboses as well. If Ogundá Okana will not close, the diviner might consider asking, "Ebó elese Obatalá?" If the answer is yes, the diviner should mark the appropriate sacrifice using the diloggún.

If the prescriptions made thus far will not close the reading, the diviner should consider the eboses for the parent odu, Ogundá (see page 172). Something there is necessary for the client's evolution.

## The Second Composite Odu of Ogundá, Ogundá Ejioko (3-2)

### The Proverbs of Ogundá Ejioko

- With your tongue, you make dangerous games.
- Where there are arguments there can be no peace.
- Arguments bring bad spirits.

### The Message of Ogundá Ejioko

Having opened in a pattern of three mouths followed by two mouths, Ogundá Ejioko, also known as Ogundá Oyekun and Ogundá Yeku, has come to the mat. This sign speaks of women, lovers, and money; its passage will affect all these areas in the client's life for the good (in iré) or the bad (in osogbo). Men who open in this odu must be very careful in their dealings with women; one could love him too much and may try to tie him down with an unplanned pregnancy. Even though this odu is not one under which a woman can easily conceive, she will try, and she might even lie about her pregnancy if she feels the client is going to leave her. This man must make sure that it is he who leaves her and not she who leaves him, because if she is the first to go, the client's luck will go with her. This pattern says that tragedy comes through women; the client must be wary of them.

If the client is a woman, the diviner knows that she is in a bad relationship or has recently gotten out of one. She is desperate and has come to the mat seeking hope and help. The diviner must tell her that there is none. If she is pregnant, it is by her own choice, and life will be difficult for both her and her unborn child unless she makes ebó to absolve her transgressions. If she is not pregnant, her desperation is leading her to it. Tell her that this path is wrong and she will suffer from it. Assure her, however, that if she walks away from her estranged lover now, he will suffer. This is what she wants to hear.

This letter flags specific dangers. The client argues continually about the same subjects; this must stop. Tongues play dangerous games: A friend will soon betray the client by telling things that should be kept secret. The diviner should warn the client not to confide his secrets in others until the effects of this odu are gone. He must keep his thoughts, goals, aspirations, and plans to himself and achieve them alone; only in this way will he have victory. Dangers also come through affairs of the heart. The client must not become entangled in threesomes, nor may he make an advance toward a married or engaged person. Blood and personal relationships also figure in this odu. Those in the client's family who have died are still with him, and they are in need of spiritual assistance. He has many fake friends who secretly create chaos and many true friends who unknowingly bring turmoil. He must exercise caution in all personal relationships; until someone has proved himself, the client should not trust him.

When this odu opens on the mat, the diviner says, "Maferefún Shangó!" Shangó alone can save the client from all the danger brought by Ogundá Ejioko. If the client works with him, prays to him, and makes ebó to him, this orisha will make sure he overcomes all that he faces. If the client has wars, he must leave them at Shangó's feet; if others bring treason and treachery, he must tell Shangó, and Shangó will fight back. The diviner must reassure his client, saying, "You no longer walk alone; Shangó walks with you, and he will fight for you. Give to him all that you face: your fears, your darkness, and your dreams. He will fight for what you need, and he will take away that which hurts you." The diviner must also tell the client that Shangó says he has three sworn enemies. These evil ones want the client's death, but it is they who will die. The client must beware, for when these three are finally dead, his own life will be in danger. If the client walks closely with this religion, coming back every six months for a reading and to make ebó, the orishas will warn him in plenty of time before his own life is in danger, and he will be able to avoid an early death.

The diviner must also keep in mind the following points:

- The client should monitor his health, especially that of his heart. To preserve his health, he should consume neither chemicals nor intoxicants.
- This person's home may not be stable; someone wants him to move away from where he lives. Someone who visits this person's home might rob it, while another could leave malicious witchcraft behind.
- Women are taboo in this sign, even for women. One might bring treason. The client must be cautious in all dealings with women and not reveal any secrets to them. While it is not a prohibition, the client is warned against trusting his wife or female lover with too much personal information. So dangerous are women during this period that the mate could cause the client's death by accidental treason.

## The Prohibitions of Ogundá Ejioko

- One argues about the same subjects again and again; this must stop. Do not argue with anyone, and do not let others argue in one's home.
- Danger comes through affairs of the heart. Do not become entangled in threesomes, and do not make an advance to a married or engaged person.
- Dealings with women can become taboo in this sign, even for women. Do not trust any woman with one's secrets; this will be one's downfall.

- Do not leave the door to one's house open or unlocked. Something or someone that one does not want in one's house will come. Take precautions against robbery, for when one is robbed (or even assaulted), dealing with the police will bring a whole new set of issues to one's life.
- Do not pawn one's valuables. If one has pawned jewelry, gold, or anything valuable, buy it back immediately, even if one must borrow the money from another person to do so. Through the pawning of items, one is losing one's luck bit by bit, and when the item is lost one's luck will go altogether. Pawning one's belongings is tantamount to pawning one's life.

### The Eboses of Ogundá Ejioko

In this pattern, the diviner has many options for ebó to explore. The first consideration is for the client's egun. The dead are close to him, yet they are not there to help him but to demand help from him. If this person does not have a bóveda, he must prepare one. If he has a bóveda, he should provide it with fresh water daily and give weekly offerings of flowers and candles. An osogbo in Ogundá Ejioko demands that the client receive his opá ikú; if he already has one, it must be fed again.

A client who has come to this oracle with no grounding in our religion must have a series of three masses prescribed. The espiritistas present will have much to say regarding the client's relationship with his ancestors. Their spiritual prescriptions will help him evolve as he helps his ancestors evolve.

If a woman comes to the orishas for healing and this odu opens, the following ebó is mandated: The diviner must use a rooster to cleanse her body and then sacrifice the rooster to Ogún. He must then give Ogún seven squash or calabazas, along with seven gourds packed with cornmeal, toasted corn, epó, jutía, smoked fish, and honey. Into each gourd he should plant a small, hooked guava branch.

If a man who is unsure of his lover's fidelity opens in this odu, he must give all the warriors together a large basket of toasted corn, and the diviner should feed them a rooster all together. This ebó will ensure that adultery does not cost the client his life.

Having explored these eboses, the diviner is given his first chance to close the odu. If it will not close, he must explore the following options:

- The client's egun may require further ebó. To determine if they require a specific sacrifice, the diviner should ask, "Ebó elese egun?" If the answer is yes, he uses the diloggún to mark the appropriate offering.
- The client could have unresolved issues with Shangó. To determine if this orisha requires anything, the diviner must ask, "Ebó elese Shangó?" If the answer is yes, then the client owes a spiritual debt to this orisha, and it must be paid. If the client is an aleyo, he may have made a promise in return for favors but not kept his word; the diviner should try to mark his promise as the ebó first so iré will come from it.
- The Ibeyi could be a necessity; the diviner should ask if the client has already taken this initiation. If not, they are marked; if he has them, these two orishas might be standing up for ebó. To find out what they require, the diviner asks, "Ebó elese los Ibeyi?" If they answer that they will take an ebó but will mark nothing, the proper ebó is a party. The bigger the party, the greater the blessings that will come of this ebó.

If the diviner cannot close his session after exploring these possibilites for ebó, he must consider the eboses for the parent odu, Ogundá (see page 172).

## The Third Composite Odu of Ogundá, Ogundá Meji (3-3)

### The Proverbs of Ogundá Meji

- Ogún splits a fish in halves.
- Tears turn into laughter.
- That which was lost will eventually come back.
- Good deeds will not go unrewarded.
- Evil deeds never go unsanctioned.
- On entering a low door, we automatically bow our heads.
- The drunk believes one thing and the bartender thinks another.

- To offer a toast, one must first learn how to drink.

## The Message of Ogundá Meji

When the initial cast of three mouths repeats itself, Ogundá Meji has come to the house. It is a severe pattern that will test the will and strength of the client. It brings no true iré to the one at the mat, even if it is marked as iré. In fact, it is best that this sign come in an osogbo, for then the odu announces the origin of all the tragedies foretold and the diviner is better equipped to deliver his reading. In osogbo, the diviner can mark eboses to help the client overcome his tragedies, and the client is empowered to evolve.

This odu gave birth to the custom of brushing one's teeth and rinsing the mouth with water first thing in the morning. Such is this odu's harshness that it also gave birth to the autopsy. Strangely enough, the orí owes its existence to this pattern, and the client's orí can be his salvation from the harshness of Ogundá Meji. Elegguá's red, white, and black necklace originates here, and it is to Elegguá that the client must turn to find a solution to many of this pattern's ills. Remember, however, that Ogún owns the parent odu, Ogundá; it was named for him, and his propitiation is essential to the client's evolution. Before digging into this reading, the diviner must pay homage to the powers represented here—Ogún, Elegguá, and orí—saying to each, "Maferefún!"

No matter Ogundá Meji's orientation, the letter may be summed up by two words: *treason* and *tragedy*. Some great unforseen force is coming from which the client may not or cannot recover. Through the words, actions, and false accusations of those with whom the client associates, he could be imprisoned. Know that much of this letter's osogbo comes from services the client has rendered or favors he has done for others. Good deeds may have gone unreturned or even been paid back with evil. The diviner must tell the client that Olófin knows what is in his heart, and while the reward for his kind actions may not come soon, it will come eventually. Although the client may not be able to rationalize the forces in his life now, the diviner must tell him that he has done three favors for others, deeds that went unrewarded and are now forgotten. Those who received this unacknowledged goodness will have their own evil repaid with evil one day.

Ogundá Meji, particularly if it has come with an osogbo of ano or ikú, speaks of some very serious concerns for the client. He must make ebó rapidly and must begin seeing a physician for a yearly physical. A disease brews deep within the client's body; now, it might be small and undetectable by even the most advanced medical equipment, but its smallness will not last forever. Bit by bit it will consume the client, and one day it will kill him. The cause of his demise may not be discovered until after his body is opened in death. Ogundá Meji afflicts the intestines; there could be decay there. It also affects the heart and the blood; coronary disease is a danger. If this person is not careful, blood-borne pathogens could enter his body. Note that vices such as drinking, smoking, taking drugs, and being promiscuous are all avenues through which these possible afflictions could be exaggerated or introduced into the body.

In addition, the diviner should explore with the client the following issues:

- Soon, someone will come to the client asking him to do a favor: The size of the favor does not matter; it could be small or big. The client must not grant this favor, for if he agrees to it, the last of his luck will leave him. Unfortunately for the client, he will not realize what he is doing or what he has done until it is too late.
- Three very important women figure in this person's life; however, they have no idea how special they are to the client. He should tell each of them how much she means to him. He should also buy each a small token of his gratitude to show that she is are appreciated.
- For the one who has come in Ogundá Meji, the next seven days are very volatile. While nothing particularly disastrous might happen during this time, it lays the foundation for future tragedies and osogbo to enter his life. Because there are serious issues at home that must be considered, the client should spend the next five days at home with his loved ones. He must

allow no one to visit and prevent arguments in the house. If callers phone, he should say that he is too busy to talk. For the seven days following the reading, the client must not be out in the street, especially after dark. He should avoid both friends and strangers during this time. And he must treat the taboos of Ogundá as if they were the mandates of Olódumare himself. If the client follows these prescriptions, he will avoid complicating his life with more tragedy.

- If the client has a daughter, he must treat that child well. No matter how bad life becomes for this person, he must ensure that all his children, especially his daughter, are treated well. If he avoids his responsibility as a parent, his daughter will die. The diviner should tell the client that he must be the parent he himself never had.
- If the client has a daughter who is of the legal age to marry, she currently has two suitors; neither is right for her. The client should gently discourage these relationships. However, he must not oppose the next suitor to follow these two; if he does, he will destroy his own relationship with his daughter.
- If the client is a married woman, she is fighting another woman for her husband's love. This competitor is, more than likely, a child of Oyá. The client must beware for her safety and her marriage. Although any ebó marked in this sign will give her the upper hand, there is only one true solution: She must go to a babalawo and receive kofá if she hopes to win.

## The Prohibitions of Ogundá Meji

- If this pattern has opened in any osogbo, do not go out for seven days. Danger is in the street, and it is looking for the one who has opened in Ogundá Meji.
- Do not lift anything heavy, or else one risks straining the back. Even if one abides by the rules, lower back pain might come; if so, the pain originates in the kidneys. Avoid coffee, dark sodas, and teas until this odu has passed.
- Weapons are now taboo. Do not carry or use them.
- Avoid sleight of hand as well as sly tricks. Do not play jokes on anyone; do not wear disguises; and do not try to be tricky.
- Restrain the hands. A slight push or shove could kill someone.
- In Ogundá Meji, women seek the love of foreign, exotic men. A lover taken under this sign's influence will bring danger or even death. Now is not the time to begin a new relationship.

## The Eboses of Ogundá Meji

During the time that Ogundá Meji is in effect, the client's head could become overwhelmed; his orí will all but abandon him. The diviner must prescribe a rogación before Obatalá's shrine as soon as possible. Once this rogación is complete, the client should give two equal adimús to Obatalá and Ogún; he must give Obatalá's first and Ogún's second. Cool, sweet, fresh fruits are best in this odu; avoid the color red or anything dark. Do not give candles, for while they give light, they also put out heat.

Also, the client's egun not only demand attention but also offer support if the client appeases them. The diviner must prescribe work with the client's bóveda, directing the client to change the water frequently and provide fresh, cool fruits and white flowers on a weekly basis.

After all these prescriptions have been made and discussed, the diviner has his first chance to close the oracle. If this sign will not close, he should explore the following possibilities:

- The client could have further issues with Obatalá, egun, and Ogún. One or more of these might need additional eboses. To determine if these spirits will take more eboses, the diviner should ask, "Ebó elese [spirit's name?]" If the answer is yes, he should mark the proper eboses using the diloggún.
- In this odu, Oshún is the orisha to petition to bring sweetness back into the client's life. To determine if she is demanding anything specific, the diviner must ask, "Ebó elese Oshún?" Even if she will not take ebó in this odu, the client must be directed to offer her something; her

goodwill is needed to fight the harshness found in Ogundá Meji.

If the odu still will not close and the client is an aleyo or aborisha, the diviner must turn to the eboses of the parent odu, Ogundá (see page 172). Something there is needed for the client's evolution.

If the client is an initiate, the odu may be trying to mark him for the reception of the knife. To find out if this is the case, the diviner should ask, "Ebó de pinaldo?" If the answer is no, he should then continue with the eboses of the parent odu to find a method of closure.

## The Fourth Composite Odu of Ogundá, Ogundá Irosun (3-4)

### The Proverbs of Ogundá Irosun

- A single man can save his people.
- There are traps, treasons, and deceptions.
- A tree is honored for its complicated shape.
- One should not punish the son of an honorable man.
- Albinos are honored because of Obatalá.

### The Message of Ogundá Irosun

Ogundá Irosun is said to have come to the mat when three mouths (Ogundá) are followed by four mouths (Irosun); the odu is also known as Ogundá Roso. We know Ogundá Irosun as the pattern giving birth to all judgments and tribunals; before it has passed, the client may face many of these himself. Ogún and Ochosi walk closely together in this letter, and they may be the client's salvation. The diviner must pay homage to both, saying, "Maferefún Ogún! Maferefún Ochosi!" He also pays homage to Oyá, Shangó, and Elegguá, saying to each, "Maferefún!" The osogbo of this letter can become great. Its essence is so volatile that the aché of all five orishas may be required to help the client evolve.

The italero must first consider the sign's orientation, because it will determine the type of issues the client has with Elegguá. If the odu opens in iré, the diviner knows that Elegguá comes to fight the client's battles, and he pays homage to him, saying "Maferefún Elegguá!" Elegguá is fate or destiny, the one orisha who can open all the roads to heaven or close them at his whim. Coming with blessings, Elegguá promises this client his support. However, he insists that he be treated as if he were the orisha of this person's head. If he is given a crown and treated like a king, he will create for his child a kingdom.

If the odu opens in osogbo, it announces Elegguá's displeasure with the client. If it is Elegguá's diloggún that has been consulted, the focus is no longer on the client's problems but on the problems Elegguá has with him. Elegguá must be placated, and it is up to the diviner to find out what he wants. If Elegguá cannot be appeased out of his osogbo, this person will soon find all the doors, roads, and paths in his life closed. The client must obtain his goodwill again.

In addition to judgments, tribunals, and the possibility of false testimony, this pattern alludes to the client's greatest secret: He has difficulty limiting himself to just one lover. Monogamy is not ingrained into this person; when he is with just one lover and not juggling two, still he lusts after another. If the client is married, he may have had at least one affair. At some point, the client has lived between two lovers, sharing a home with one before moving in with the next. The odu signals that his behavior is wrong; it is unethical and it must stop. The client may have only one lover. Having two at once is forbidden; he must make up his mind between the two. He must be cautioned that the lover he drops will become consumed with rage and jealousy, although it might not be openly shown, and will cause trouble. While such trouble is the client's own fault, he should nevertheless guard himself against it.

This person will soon have a chance encounter with an older woman. The daughter of this woman will be important in the client's life. She will be a child of Oshún, and she will bring either joy or tragedy, depending on the odu's orientation. The client should be prepared for this.

The diviner should also keep in mind the following points:

- Because the tribunal is born here, the client should be prepared for scrutiny by his peers, on both a personal and a professional level. He must consider ethics before acting or speaking.
- If ano or ikú is foretold, the client could have decay in the blood, intestines, heart, or head. Cancers and ulcers are not uncommon. This person could be overdue for a complete physical with blood work; if that is the case, the diviner should prescribe a physical as if it were an ebó. Ano and ikú could even predict a sickness or death in the family. A small inheritance could come of this tragedy.
- The client must be careful with his child or children. Not only could one succumb to sickness or accident, but also others might bring false accusations as to how they are treated. These accusations could create problems with the law. The client must avoid being alone with the children of others; at all times he should have his own children or another adult present.
- Robbery and petty theft are dangers in this odu. This will be wrought by the hands of a friend, maybe even a lover. The client should be wary.
- No matter the orientation of this odu, the client must be careful to treat Elegguá well. If he is not well kept, he will close the client's roads until he gets what he wants.
- The diviner should tell the client that the oldest child in his family has issues to be settled with the orishas. His destiny could be to become a priest of ocha. This child must be brought for a session with the diloggún as soon as possible.

## The Prohibitions of Ogundá Irosun

- Do not drink alcohol or consume illegal intoxicants. These will bring one's downfall.
- Do not sacrifice animals in one's home, especially if this sacrifice is offered on behalf of a godchild or client. To do so is to invite one's own downfall.
- Romantic triangles are prohibited. Avoid the number three in personal relationships.
- Do not sleep away from home, especially when intoxicated.
- Do not associate with anyone who works outside the law, especially escorts or prostitutes. This will put one into a compromising situation.
- Travel is prohibited for eight days following the opening of this odu.

## The Eboses of Ogundá Irosun

When this odu falls on the mat, many diviners reinforce the client's warriors by adding a small set of deer horns to Ogún's cauldron; this strengthens Ochosi and gives greater aché to the bond these two orishas share. If the client is about to receive his warriors, these antlers must be washed when the orishas are born. If the client already has the warriors, the antlers should still be washed, and Ogún and Ochosi together should be fed a rooster and two pigeons immediately. Know that when marking ebó in Ogundá Irosun, any ebó claimed by Ogún must be given to Ochosi, and vice versa.

Obatalá's calming influence is necessary in this odu. The client must prepare an ebó for him and receive a rogación before his shrine. The diviner will use his own common sense and knowledge of the orisha to determine an appropriate ebó.

When the rogación is finished, the client should provide Ogún with an ebó consisting of a rooster and a gourd filled with toasted corn, honey, jutía, and smoked fish. After the sacrifice, Ogún must not be washed for three days. After this period, he may be washed, and then the client should take the gourd to the nearest railroad tracks. If the osogbo of Ogundá Irosun is severe, an old, rusted piece of iron should be put into his cauldron before he is fed; and when Ogún is cleaned, the iron should be washed and sanded until it looks almost new.

The client's egun are also a concern; the diviner should prescribe three masses for them. As they are given light and evolution, so will they help the client evolve.

If the odu opens in ososgbo, Elegguá must be given ebó. If he does not mark a particular ebó, the diviner must still prescribe offerings and sacrifices for this orisha, using his own aché to determine what is appropriate. The client must obtain his goodwill again.

If Ejioko Irosun refuses closure, the diviner should explore the following points:

- If the osogbo is severe and the odu will not close out, Ogún may require not one but seven gourds filled with toasted corn, honey, jutía, and smoked fish.
- Obatalá, Ogún, and egun could be standing up for additional eboses. To determine what, if anything, is needed, the diviner asks, "Ebó elese [spirit's name]?"
- Olokun is also important in this letter, and if the odu will not close, it may wish to mark the client for his reception. The diviner should investigate this option by asking, "Koshé Olokun?" If the answer is yes, he may then ask for closure. If the answer is no, or if the client already has Olokun, Olokun may be standing up for ebó. The diviner should then ask, "Ebó elese Olokun?" If the answer is yes, he uses the diloggún to mark the appropriate offering.
- Oyá, Shangó, or Elegguá could be standing up for ebó. If Oyá stands up for ebó, once it is fulfilled the client should have a rogación at her feet with nine things, and he must be given her eleke. If Elegguá takes ebó, once that ebó is done he must be given a crown. If Shangó takes ebó, he has come to defend the client, and after the ebó is complete, he should be given a baseball bat beaded in the colors red and white.

If this is not enough to close the odu, the diviner should turn to the eboses of the parent odu, Ogundá (see page 172); something there is needed for the client's evolution.

## The Fifth Composite Odu of Ogundá, Ogundá Oché (3-5)

### The Proverbs of Ogundá Oché

- The dead are standing and waiting.
- Don't retrieve what has been discarded.

### The Message of Ogundá Oché

When three mouths are followed by five, Ogundá Oché has come to the mat. This odu is hot and volatile. It is credited with having given birth to rape and bodily violation, and both men and women are in danger of these things. It is the odu in which the curse was born in the land of the orishas, and having opened thus the client himself could be cursed. It is also the pattern in which Olófin speaks his sacred word for the first time. The diviner must consider these issues first, no matter the odu's orientation.

Seven orishas stand strong in this odu: Olófin, Orúnmila, Ogún, Elegguá, Oshún, Shangó, and Babaluaiye. All may speak or claim ebó before this session closes, and all are essential to the client's evolution. The diviner honors these orishas by saying to each, "Maferefún!"

This sign is an enigma among the family of Ogundá. It is very sensitive to its origin of iré or osogbo. While no odu in three mouths can truly bring iré, if the letter is marked for iré it can, in time, bring great evolution to the one for whom it has been cast.

Ogundá Oché says that the child will conquer the parent, but to understand the full implication of this, the diviner must determine one piece of information: Was this client oppressed by his parents or will he himself be the parent who is conquered?

Because Ogundá Oché is the odu where rape was born, a man who opens in this sign may be of the mind-set to rape, or he may have been the victim of rape and sodomy as a child. The woman who opens in this sign may have been raped or may be putting herself in a position where rape is inevitable. Any person who comes in this pattern may have had a traumatic childhood: Physical, mental, emotional, and spiritual abuse figure greatly in this person's past. Broken hearts and crushed souls open in this sign. The diviner must proceed carefully and cautiously; if the client is receptive to the reading, tears will come before the reading is done.

Many other issues demand investigation in this odu. The diviner must consider the following:

- In this odu, Oshún may speak. Women in particular will have many issues with her. If the odu opens in any type of osogbo, the client can have trouble with the blood, intestines, and heart; if the client is a woman, she also can have trouble with her reproductive organs. If she is pregnant, if she is trying to become pregnant, or if conception occurs in the next five months, it is important that she return to the diviner for a rogación of the abdomen. A child conceived while this odu is in effect may be delivered by caesarean. Heavy periods, menstrual retention, or pains in the abdomen demand that the woman seek medical help.
- Ogundá Oché is known for bringing fever and tetanus. Puncture wounds demand medical attention.
- If the client is an aleyo, ask him if he knows his father. If he does not, his father may have been a crazy man. Currently, he could be either institutionalized or dead.
- In Ogundá Oché, one's curiosity is one's downfall. The client should stay out of other people's business.
- The diviner must tell the client that he made three promises that he has not kept. Ogundá Oché signals says he must do what he promised or else tragedy and treason will find him.
- Finally, if the client is not Ogún's child, he is blessed by him. The diviner should make sure that this session is not given closure until an ebó is marked or prescribed to Ogún.

## The Prohibition of Ogundá Oché

- Do not ever cut one's hair short. If it is short at the time of the reading, it must be allowed to grow. If it is long, it must stay long. If the need to cut the hair arises, one must reconsider; if it still seems unavoidable, one must consult with Oshún. Know that if Oshún does allow one to cut one's hair, she will demand something big in return.

## The Eboses of Ogundá Oché

Ogundá Oché makes the reception of the warriors mandatory, and it sends the client to Ifá to receive either kofá or mano de Orúnmila. If the client has not yet received the warriors, in this odu it would be wise for him to receive them from a babalawo before receiving Elegguá from ocha.

Because the client is blessed by Ogún, the diviner must mark or prescribe an ebó to Ogún before attempting to close the oracle.

The dead are here, too, waiting, and the italero must determine that for which they are waiting. The next question for the diviner to ask is "Ebó elese egun?" If the answer is yes, the diviner must use the diloggún to mark what is needed.

The diviner must also consider and explain the following options for ebó:

- If the client has an illness affecting the abdominal region, the ebó necessary is a rogación of the abdomen and head at the feet of Oshún.
- If this sign comes in either ano or ikú and later the client falls ill, the following ebó must be made: A rooster is given to Elegguá, followed by two roosters given to Ogún. Oshún is then fed five small hens. If surgery is inevitable, the client should have a rogación of the abdominal region at Oshún's feet.

Now the diviner has his first opportunity to close the oracle. If the oracle refuses closure, he must consider the following:

- Oshún is very important in this letter; if it refuses closure, she may be standing up for ebó. To find out if she is standing up on the client's behalf, the diviner should ask, "Ire elese Oshún?" If the answer is yes, the diviner should then ask, "Ebó elese Oshún?" If the answer is no, we say that Oshún protects the client for free, yet the client should still offer some small adimú to her in gratitude. If the answer is yes, the diviner should mark what is required with the diloggún.
- If the client is an initiate, he may need to receive Inle. To determine if this is the case, the

diviner should ask, "Koshé Inle?" If the answer is no, or if the client already has Inle, the orisha might want ebó. If the client is an aborisha or an initiate, the next question for the diviner to ask is "Ebó elese Inle?" If the answer is yes, the diviner must then mark the ebó needed.

If the prescriptions made thus far are not enough to close Ogundá Oché, the diviner must then turn to the eboses of the parent odu, Ogundá (see page 172).

## The Sixth Composite Odu of Ogundá, Ogundá Obara (3-6)

### The Proverbs of Ogundá Obara

- The never-ending war cannot end.
- Return what the visitor offers.
- The one who does not want soup gets three bowls, all full.
- The great has the same value as the small.
- There are two sides to every coin.
- There are two versions to every story.
- Listen before you act.
- One must learn to listen before one speaks or acts.

### The Message of Ogundá Obara

When the initial cast of three mouths, Ogundá, precedes a cast of six mouths, Obara, the letter Ogundá Obara has come to the mat. The diviner says, "Maferefún Orúnmila! Maferefún Elegguá!" Although Orúnmila does not speak in the dilog-gún, his influence is felt here. Elegguá has much to say to the client, particularly about his home and family. He says that the atmosphere is hot and volatile due to the arguments and fights in the client's residence. If the client has received Elegguá and keeps him in his home, he is withholding his blessings because of this discord. Keep in mind that in this religion one's home is one's church; the orishas live with us, and we with them. The things that go on inside the four walls of our homes affect these spirits, and they prefer peace and calm. Unfortunately, now that Elegguá is bothered by what goes on in his home, the mere cessation of fights and arguments will not be enough to appease him. The diviner must find some ebó to placate the client's Elegguá so things in the home return to normal. Sometimes, the ebó will include the removal of all who do not belong in his house. In Ogundá Obara, Elegguá's goodwill is essential to one's evolution. Even in iré, this person is surrounded by tragedy, and he will need to make ebó if he is to remain safe.

The diviner must also discuss with the client the following points:

- Three family members are in danger, and one or more of these might live with the client. Before the year is out, one could fall ill and die. Ebó made through this odu will ensure that a life is saved.
- In this pattern, the small blessings in the client's life have the same value as the great blessings in his life. He must give thanks for all that he has, no matter how small the blessing might seem.
- Dreams come frequently to this client; the night before the reading he may have had a very special dream. The diviner must ask if the client can remember this dream. He must give thanks for these dreams, because they bring him warnings, messages, and luck.
- One day this client is rich and the next he is poor. This odu tells him to save his money; he should not spend it foolishly. Gambling is an unwise endeavor now. The diviner should tell the client that money could come to him through a woman. He must focus on holding on to this woman when she arrives, and not the prosperity that she brings. If he loses her, he will lose the luck she brought as well.
- This odu is hot, and in a tragic osogbo death could come by robbery, attack, vandalism, or mugging. Sickness might come in the blood, stomach, intestines, or heart. The client could suffer from anemia, and unless he eats well this will get worse. This person must always be cautious about both his health and his personal safety.

## The Prohibitions of Ogundá Obara

- Many times in the past one has thought and spoken poorly of the orishas. One is prohibited from ever speaking poorly of this religion or its priesthood again. To do so is to risk the orishas' wrath.
- Do not help another lift, move, or carry anything. If someone falls, do not help that person up from the floor. Those whom one lifts will continue to rise, and the helper will fall in those people's place.
- When eating away from home, be cautious of what is consumed. Never eat or drink in the home of a stranger unless the food or drink comes in a sealed container.
- Ruin comes by fire. Do not leave sources of flame untended. Do not smoke in bed.
- Do not use squash or gourds for anything except ebó.

## The Eboses of Ogundá Obara

When Ogundá Obara opens on the mat, the diviner knows that the client has issues to be settled with both Elegguá and Shangó. To soothe the erratic vibrations of this odu, he must give adimús of fresh, sweet fruits to both orishas. Because their placation is essential to the client's evolution, before attempting to close the odu the diviner must ask, "Ebó elese Elegguá?" and "Ebó elese Shangó?" If either will claim ebó, the diviner should mark something suitable with the diloggún. If the client is an initiate, it is possible that his orishas will want to take ebó together. The diviner should consider asking, "Ebó elese Elegguá y Shangó?" If they will take an offering together, the diviner should mark the appropriate offering with the diloggún. When the ebó is fulfilled, Elegguá should be sitting at Shangó's feet.

As ebó, the client should also be told that he has issues with Ifá, and he must be sent to a babalawo for a consultation.

The diviner now has his first chance to close the reading. If it will not close, he should explore and consider the following:

- The client could have unsettled issues with Ogún. To determine if he requires anything, the diviner asks, "Ebó elese Ogún?" If the answer is yes, the diviner uses the diloggún to mark the appropriate offering.
- Each orisha who has spoken or stood up in the reading should now be marked to receive an adimú of fresh squash or calabazas. The offering should be allowed to sit with the orisha until it begins to spoil.
- If the letter still refuses closure, the client has issues pending with Osain. The diviner must determine if the client needs a niche osain, asking, "Ebó niche osain?" If the answer is yes, the diviner next questions which orisha needs the osain, asking for each of the orishas that speak in this odu, "Niche osain elese [orisha's name]?" If the answer is no and the client is an initiate, the diviner may then ask if the client needs to receive Osain, saying, "Koshé Osain?" If after this question the oracle still will not close, the diviner must turn to the eboses of the parent odu, Ogundá (see page 172).

# The Seventh Composite Odu of Ogundá, Ogundá Odí (3-7)

## The Proverbs of Ogundá Odí

- What is known is not questioned.
- Look at what is in front of your eyes.
- Guess the riddle.
- That which you know, do not ask.
- Do not sit in a seat without a bottom.

## The Message of Ogundá Odí

When a casting of three mouths, Ogundá, is followed by one of seven mouths, Odí, the odu Ogundá Odí, also known as Ogunda'di, has opened on that mat. In this pattern Judas's treason against Christ was born, and before the energy of Ogundá Odí has passed the client will suffer betrayal by a friend.

In this odu, four orishas are strong, and the diviner pays homage to each, saying, "Maferefún Elegguá! Maferefún Ogún! Maferefún Oshún!

Maferefún Yemayá!" Before the session has closed, each of these orishas may speak and take ebó from the client.

Ogundá Odí is extremely sensitive to its orientation of iré or osogbo. In iré, the diviner may tell the client that luck is close, and once the harsh energies of Ogundá have passed this person will emerge unscathed, blessed by good fortune. Much of this luck will come through the grace of Oshún's children. The client must spoil her and be kind to her priestesses. Once luck comes, the client must not change the way he looks at the world or the way he conducts himself around others. This luck is so close; the diviner should tell him to open his eyes and look for it. It is already there.

Ogunda Odí in osogbo marks problems with the blood, especially the loss of blood or its vitality. Anemia, diabetes, and sepsis are all possibilities. There are also warnings of abdominal and intestinal trouble and heart failure. The client should stop poisoning the rivers of his body and take good care of his body. The client's back may suffer injury if he does not modify his behavior, and the kidneys are also under a lot of stress. Lower back pain could signal either muscle strain or problems with the internal organs; in this case, the client should consult a physician.

The client has a bad temper, and it causes many arguments with those he loves. Arguments that begin while this letter in osogbo is in effect can escalate into violence. Coolness and calmness are the qualities needed now. The client should not raise his hand against another or abuse—physically, emotionally, or mentally—anyone in his family.

This odu in osogbo also insists that the client not tell what he knows to others. The things he says will be used against him later.

Regardless of the letter's orientation, until its energy passes, life will be full of Ogundá's trials and tribulations. The diviner must carefully delineate all that this letter has to say; the prohibitions of both the parent odu, Ogundá (see page 172), and the composite, Ogundá Odí, are essential to the client's safety. The client must turn to Yemayá to lead him through these troubles; she is a firm mother in this sign and can lead him out of the chaos that has become his life. Speaking through Ogundá, however, Yemayá identifies issues that should concern the client: domestic abuse, infidelity, and child abuse. She will not tolerate these things. If the client is the abuser, she will punish him; if he is the abused, she will avenge him. In the case of the former, the client can make no ebó for forgiveness; he must stop his ways and pray for the best. In the case of the latter, if the client prays to Yemayá and makes ebó, she will release him from his hard life.

In addition, the diviner should keep the following in mind:

- This pattern has much to say about the client's love life; when it opens, no matter its orientation, it says that his wife or lover will cheat on him. He must be on guard against this. The client himself is not loyal to his lover; his eyes wander, and if he has not already, he will have an adulterous affair. Once this happens the orishas will separate this person not only from his legitimate significant other but also from his hidden affair. He will be left alone with no one. This happened to him once in the past, and still he has not learned his lesson.
- The client should be wary of his neighbors. This client stays up late at night, and those who live near him see the lights on. They wonder what could be happening at such a late hour. They see the client coming and going, and their curiosity overcomes them. Many harbor ill will and jealousy; one in particular hates the client and the way he lives. They might call the police, making false statements. The client must beware of neighbors who suddenly try to become friendly with him; they are nosy and will bring treason and intrigue to his life.

## The Prohibitions of Ogundá Odí

- Oshún will not tolerate poor treatment of her children. If one befriends any child of Oshún, be careful. To slight her child is to insult the orisha.
- Yemayá will not tolerate abusive behavior. It

must end now. Nor will she tolerate her children in abusive relationships. Those must end now.

- If ano or ikú comes, do not drink dark liquids, especially sodas. These are poisons to the body.
- Do not lift, carry, push, pull, or move heavy objects. One's back is weak and may be injured.
- Give respect to both the river and the ocean; ask permission before crossing them, and do not swim in either.

## The Eboses of Ogundá Odí

If the prescription of the eboses listed in "Marking Ebó in Ogundá: Initial Considerations" (see page 141) is not enough to close the oracle, the diviner should explain the following eboses to the client. First, Yemayá watches over him, and he should wear her eleke every day so she can protect him wherever he goes. Second, the client needs to be cautious with his head; no one should touch it. His orí needs to be strengthened with a rogación. If he is well, the rogación should take place at the feet of his guardian orisha, but if he is ill, it should be done at the feet of Yemayá. She will fight all his battles and be his therapist; he must leave all his problems, fears, and wars at her feet. Because Yemayá stands up so strongly in this letter, the diviner should check to see if she wants ebó, asking, "Ebó elese Yemayá?" If the answer is no, she protects the client for free, but he should still offer her a token adimú. If the answer is yes, the diviner must mark the appropriate ebó with the diloggún.

Oshún also wants to bring blessings to this client, but he may need ebó as well. To determine if this is the case, the diviner should ask, "Ebó elese Oshún?" He must mark what she requires with the diloggún. Note that if both Yemayá and Oshún take ebó in this odu, once those eboses are done the client should offer a fresh basket of fruits to both spirits in a place where the river meets the sea.

This odu flags an interesting potential situation for the client that should, if it is encountered, be enacted as if it were ebó. The client is destined to meet a woman who is a child of Oshún; he will meet this woman in a public place, and she will be carrying a heavy load in a basket. When he sees this woman, he must offer to carry her load for her. If she accepts, he is to do exactly as she asks with this basket. Once this task is fulfilled, Oshún will bring great blessings to his life.

If the oracle still will not close, the diviner must prescribe that Elegguá should receive a part of every ebó marked for the other orishas in this sign. Elegguá might also want something else, and the diviner should then ask, "Ebó elese Elegguá?" If the answer is yes, the diviner should mark the appropriate offering using the diloggún.

If these eboses cannot close the sign, the diviner must turn to the eboses of the parent odu, Ogundá (see page 172). Something there is needed for the client's evolution.

# The Eighth Composite Odu of Ogundá, Ogundá Ejiogbe (3-8)

## The Proverbs of Ogundá Ejiogbe

- Because of your infidelity, your grave has been dug.
- Dishonesty kills the liar.
- Treachery shall destroy the treacherous.
- Those who call black "white" and white "black" are being watched by Olódumare above.

## The Message of Ogundá Ejiogbe

When the first casting of Ogundá, three mouths, is followed by a casting of Eji Ogbe, eight mouths, the odu Ogundá Ejiogbe has opened on the mat. This sign is also known as Ogundá Ogbe, Ogundá Unle, and Ogundá l'Ogbe. Stern in all its pronouncements, this pattern is the birthplace of both treason and infidelity. The client will soon experience these things in his own life. Once this letter opens on the mat, the diviner should say, "Maferefún Olófin! Maferefún Obatalá! Maferefún Ogún!" No matter whose diloggún is consulted, these three powerful spirits dominate the energies of this odu. Note that Ogundá Ejiogbe puts the client in bondage to ocha; a commitment to this religion and to its principles will save this person from the dark paths that he has trodden opening in his life new roads that previously were no more than mere hopes and dreams for the client. It may take some time before this person will be ready for initiation, but continuous work and perseverence will be rewarded by the orishas. Also, for a man Ogundá Ejiogbe hints that he might need to make Ifá; the diviner should relay this information to the client and and send him for a reading with a babalawo.

In this pattern, we say that because of this person's infidelity, his grave has been dug; the client is marked as having a tendency to get involved with the wrong people, especially those who are married, and this behavior must end. There is anger in the client's home; if the client is a man, he is abusive to his wife. False love permeates the client's life. He says he loves others, but he is lying; others say that they love him, but in truth they do not care about him. The client must be cautious with passion and distrust the passions of others. Tears are being shed now for the anger and arrogance this person brings. The diviner should tell the client that he should consider packing a suitcase when he goes home; if the client is a man, his lover or spouse will want him to move out, and he should leave immediately. If the client is a woman, she will discover the infidelity of her spouse, and perhaps the abuse of which he is capable. She should leave that very night.

The diviner should also keep in mind the following points:

- Ogún demands that projects begun by the client be finished by the client. The client should leave nothing undone and work alone as much as possible. Only in this way can he have victory.
- The client should be cautious around women, especially married ones. If the client is a man, he should be advised not to have affairs with married women or to become involved in threesomes or romantic triangles.
- The client must not recommend abortion or divorce to anyone. He must stay out of others' personal business.
- Health concerns in this odu center on the back, kidneys, and abdominal region. Stomach upsets, ulcers, and cancers could all be a problem. The client should take good care of his body and see a physician for any complaints.
- Tumors and head trauma will bring seizures; at the first sign of seizure activity, the client should see a physician immediately. If a seizure comes, it signals that all of the osogbo of Ogundá Ejiogbe is already upon the client.

## The Prohibitions of Ogundá Ejiogbe

- Obatalá and Olófin advise coolness in one's life, and this extends to the foods one eats. Avoid hot and spicy foods, which can cause poor digestion and bowel irritation.
- The head is even more delicate than the stomach; care for it. If contact sports cannot be avoided, wear protective headgear at all times. Let no one touch the head or hair.
- Frequent headaches will come to those overwhelmed by stress; in this sign, it is taboo to do more than one can handle.
- Dark colors are taboo in this odu; wear white or the lightest colors possible.
- Do not make sacrifices in one's own home.
- Mice are taboo. Neither harm them nor kill them. Do not lay mousetraps.
- Do not steal or use anything that causes a habit or a vice.

## The Eboses of Ogundá Ejiogbe

At the mat, before this letter is closed, the diviner must drape a mazo over the client, like a banner, and direct the client to salute Obatalá, his godparents, and the diviner. After this, the diviner should explain that the client is destined to make ocha and will not find his evolution until he has done so. The diviner should discuss with the client the next step into the religion; it is now marked as ebó. As soon as possible, two things must be accomplished: a rogación at Obatalá's shrine and a bajado to determine this person's crowning orisha.

This odu also brings issues with Ifá, and as soon as possible the client must be sent to a babalawo. Men should be prepared to receive mano de Orúnmila, and women should be prepared to receive kofá.

Once all these issues have been explored and recorded, the diviner has his first chance to close the oracle. If the letter will not close, the odu may be trying to mark ebó for both Eleggua and Obatalá. The diviner should ask, "Ebó elese Eleggua y Obatalá?" If the answer is no, they protect this person for free, yet a token adimú should still be made to them. If the answer is yes, the diviner must use the diloggún to mark the ebó needed.

If the odu still will not allow closure, the diviner must turn to the eboses of the parent odu, Ogundá (see page 172).

## The Ninth Composite Odu of Ogundá, Ogundá Osá (3-9)

### The Proverbs of Ogundá Osá

- Flies cannot enter a closed mouth.
- Olófin splits the difference.
- In union, there is strength.
- While the vulture knew where to menace, it never knew where to sleep or find food.

### The Message of Ogundá Osá

When an initial cast of three mouths, Ogundá, precedes a cast of nine mouths, Osá, the odu Ogundá Osá, also known as Ogunda'sa, is open on the mat. The diviner immediatley pays homage to Olófin, Ogún, Ochosi, and Yemayá, saying to each, "Maferefún!" Before this letter has closed, each of them may have something to say to the client, and all may claim ebó.

This pattern is volatile and heated; it is dangerous for both the client and the diviner. We say that it gives birth to slander, gossip, and lies; these things affect the client now. In this odu Ogún and Ochosi made a pact to live together, and in this sign Ogún, shamed by his wife Yemayá, cut off her head.

This letter has much to say about the client and the way he lives his life. With Ogundá Osá on the mat, the diviner knows that the client is solitary, living in a self-imposed loneliness; he may have a spouse, a lover, or friends, yet still he has an emotional solitude that keeps others at a distance. This person may wish to leave his lover, but he cannot. Many bad eyes and tongues surround him; people who gossip and wish evil behind his back speak sweetly and kindly to his face. These persons must be discovered, for in secret they can bring ruin. The client is hardheaded; the diviner knows that he will not receive these words well, yet he must be forced to hear them if he is to evolve.

So that the client can overcome the volatility of this letter, the diviner must also discuss with him the following points:

- From the mouths of others comes gossip, lies that border on slander, and the client will not be able to recover from the damage they cause. If the client tells the truth or, if he cannot tell the truth, remains silent, Ogún will defend him.
- The woman who opens in this odu is in danger from her husband; she could be maimed or killed.
- In Ogundá Osá, men are physically weaker than women but are more easily pushed to violence. In this sign, the strong woman will suffer.
- Many will try to cause trouble for the client. Someone who visits may rob the client, while others will speak badly about what goes on in his home. He must be careful about whom he trusts and let only those who are trustworthy into his home.
- Hard economic times are coming; the client may need to move. He may lose his home and his possessions due to bad luck.

### The Prohibitions of Ogundá Osá

- Do not carry weapons at this time; leave all weapons to Ogún. He will fight the battles that need to be fought.
- The hands are the first weapon of choice; restrain these at all times. Do not raise them in anger or make threatening gestures.
- Postpone any trips for the next eight days. If the osogbo is severe, do not travel for twenty-eight days.
- If one cannot speak kindly to one's spouse, say nothing at all for now.

- Do not lie; through lies one will lose Ogún's goodwill and strength.

## The Eboses of Ogundá Osá

Before attempting to close the oracle, the diviner must tell the client that he needs a set of washed deer antlers for Ochosi; these are to live in Ogún's cauldron. The diviner should prepare these antlers as soon as possible. This honors the pact that the two spirits have to always work and live together.

Ogundá Osá indicates that the client has developed a special relationship with Ogún; for whatever reason, this orisha favors him. To ensure his continued goodwill, the client must spoil him, giving him special treats infrequently. If Ogún has claimed nothing so far in this reading, the diviner must also ask, "Ebó elese Ogún?" If the answer is yes, the client should consider making this ebó monthly.

This odu also recommends that the client go to a babalawo to receive kofá or mano de Orúnmila.

Now the diviner has his first opportunity to close the oracle. If the letter refuses closure, the client may have issues pending with Aganyú. The diviner should ask, "Ebó elese Aganyú?" If the answer is yes, the diviner marks the appropriate offering with the shells. If the answer is no and the client is an initiate, he might need to receive this orisha, and the diviner should ask, "Koshé Aganyú?"

An initiate in this odu may also need to receive Osain. To determine if this is the case, the diviner should ask, "Koshé Osain?"

If none of the prescriptions made so far is enough to close Ogundá Osá, the diviner should turn to the eboses of the parent odu, Ogundá (see page 172).

# The Tenth Composite Odu of Ogundá, Ogundá Ofún (3-10)

## The Proverbs of Ogundá Ofún

- If you are cursed, forgive those who curse you.
- He who forgives is saved; he who does not is doomed.
- You were cursed from your mother's womb.
- A liar lies and is destroyed by his lies.
- The wicked one will display his wickedness openly, and this shall destroy him.
- The treacherous one will do untold harm to himself.

## The Message of Ogundá Ofún

Ogundá Ofún falls when an initial casting of three cowries is followed by ten. This sign is hot and volatile; it is in effect for the client, and if it is not properly placated, it can overwhelm the italero who has opened it. His first prescription will be a rogación for himself and a cleansing to Ogún for all others present in the house, to take place immediately after the reading has been brought to an end. (See "The Eboses of Ogundá Ofún" on page 164.)

When this pattern opens, the diviner should say, "Maferefún Oshún! Maferefún Elegguá! Maferefún Ogún! Maferefún Ochosi!" Oshún does not speak kindly here. Ogundá Ofún signals that the client's connection with her is strained; she wants to bring blessings, but she cannot. If the odu opens in osogbo, it may signal that Oshún is angry with the client. Ogundá Ofún speaks of wars, treason, and legal entanglement. Three powerful orishas—Elegguá, Ogún, and Ochosi—offer their help in exchange for the client's worship and adoration. To evolve, he must give it to them.

In this odu we also honor a spiritually powerful plant known as prodigiosa. This plant is all but immortal; the more one cuts away from it or tries to destroy it, the more vigorously it grows. So things are in the client's life: Whenever he or anyone else tries to take away the bad, more bad comes. Yet when the good is cut away, it comes back more vigorously, too. As ebó in this odu, the client might wish to grow prodigiosa in his home. It will bring many blessings.

In any orientation of this letter, the greatest danger is that of an operation. Even if the client is unaware of any sickness in his body, his health must be screened carefully, for Ogundá Ofún is known for making internal troubles where none existed before. As is common in the family of Ogundá, the abdominal region is the area most commonly affected; the stomach, intestines, and kidneys could all be diseased. The client could also have problems in the blood or with the heart, so he must treat his body well. The first unusual symptoms warrant a visit to the family physician.

Personal relationships are also a source of trouble in this letter. The client should be advised that friends will cause more worry and strife than will enemies. He must never tell secrets, for they are a source of much gossip, and bad tongues abound when this letter falls. Arguments will ensue, and although many times the client will be in the right, his logic will fall on deaf ears. The disputes will create violence, hatred, and envy, so he must keep the facts to himself for now. When arguments begin, especially with the client's spouse, he should walk away and cool down first. The client should avoid cursing and retribution; when others do him wrong, he should go immediately to the orishas and tell them the entire situation. They will take care of everything.

In addition, the client must keep the following points in mind:

- He must be careful against wounds, especially cuts and punctures. These could bring infection, fever, tetanus, and disfigurement.
- The client must respect the elders in both ocha and the family, for their advice at this time is invaluable.
- If any pains develop in the bones or muscles and last for more than a day, the client should visit the doctor. The pain could signal a serious health problem.
- This odu can be an indicator of legal issues.
- The client is cursed. The greater the osogbo, the greater his curse. The witchcraft against this person is so strong that it will bring death unless it is fought. Before it passes, blood might be spilled.
- This odu speaks of anorexia, bulemia, and malnourishment. The client could be starving himself to death.

## The Prohibitions of Ogundá Ofún

- Keep one's home clean and pure. Do not let trash or dirt accumulate in the house.
- Dress in white for twenty-one days. Do not wear dark colors.
- Avoid heavy lifting; permanent back injuries are a danger in this odu.
- Do not curse or seek retribution for wrongs done to one; instead, bring all wrongs done to one to the orishas.
- Do not carry weapons.

## The Eboses of Ogundá Ofún

When Ogundá Ofún has come to the mat, it is of the utmost importance that the cleansing ebó for Ogún be performed (see page 141). After the session has closed and Ogundá's ebó has been completed, the eldest priest or priestess present must give the diviner a rogación to cool his head. The rogación should be given at the feet of the diviner's crowning orisha; it will take all the aché of his crown to calm his orí. If Ogundá Ofún opened in a volatile osogbo for the client, this ebó should be reinforced by feeding the diviner's orí two white pigeons. Note that the diviner is prohibited from performing any eboses for the client until his own head has received a rogación.

Before leaving the house the next morning to discard Ogundá's ebó, the diviner must wash his head with holy water from seven churches (if he is a spiritual Catholic) or natural water from seven different locations in nature (if he is pure Lucumí). Note that since Yemayá and Oshún own all the world's waters between them, the water from their soperas may be used as well. To further soothe the energies of this odu, the diviner might prepare for himself a spiritual bath from these waters with purple flowers.

The ebó marked for the diviner may also be necessary for the client. After making his initial prescriptions, the diviner should ask, "Ebó elese orí?" If the answer is yes, the client is marked to have a rogación at the feet of Obatalá or, if he is an initiate, at the feet of the diviner's crowning orisha. When the initiate client returns home, he may give adimú to his own crown.

In addition to prescribing the closing ebo for Ogún, if Ogunda Ofún opens in osogbo, the diviner must also prescribe ebó to Oshún. To see if she will mark a specific offering, the diviner asks, "Ebo elese Oshún?" If the answer is yes, the diviner uses the diloggún to mark the required sacrifice or offering. If the answer is no, Oshún still requires ebó, but the diviner uses his own intuition and aché to determine what she might want. Her propitiation is essential; she must be given something.

The following eboses are also considerations in this sign:

- If the client is in trouble with the law, he should make ebó to Ochosi immediately. The appropriate offering is for the client to sprinkle Ochosi liberally with efun and light two seven-day white candles while the client prays for his help. The diviner then feeds two pigeons to the orisha. The head of each pigeon should be speared on a separate arrow after the animal is killed. After the sacrifice, an additional two seven-day white candles should be lit to Ochosi. The orisha should not be cleaned of the sacrifice until the candles have burned out.
- If sickness and disease have brought this client to the mat, surgery may be imminent. He must make ebó to Ogún, and the diviner should mark what is necessary. If no ebó can be marked, a sacrifice of feathers should be made.
- Upon returning home, the client should put a mixture of water, honey, and cornmeal in a gourd; this ebó goes to the warriors Elegguá, Ogún, and Ochosi. The next morning, he should throw the offering to Eshu in the street.
- As ebó, this client should clean his house thoroughly, putting all his empty bottles and containers in the trash and removing the trash immediately. Bad spirits and energies can hide in these containers. The client should wear white every day for seven days. Prodigiosa should be used in a series of spiritual baths; depending on the orisha who has stood up in Ogundá Ofún, other ingredients may be added.

While they are not mandatory, additional considerations for eboses in this odu center on Oshún, Elegguá, Ogún, and Ochosi. If any of these orishas gave advice during the reading, the diviner may consider marking eboses to them, asking, "Ebó elese [orisha's name]?" If the answer is yes, he uses the shells to mark the appropriate offering.

Finally, the diviner considers a prescription of three masses to egun.

Having considered these options, the diviner now has his first chance to close the oracle. If it remains open, he should turn to the eboses of the parent odu, Ogundá (see page 172).

## The Eleventh Composite Odu of Ogundá, Ogundá Owani (3-11)

### The Proverbs of Ogundá Owani

- Hypocrisy is a part of our own education.
- One leader throws a stone, and all his people are blamed.
- Do not take on the troubles of others.
- Get away first, for the law is after you.
- Your openness with others is what causes you to fall.

### The Message of Ogundá Owani

When the initial cast of three mouths, Ogundá, precedes a cast of eleven mouths, Owani, the odu Ogundá Owani has come to the house. When this sign opens, the diviner pays homage to Elegguá, Ogún, and Ochosi, saying to each, "Maferefún!" Before this odu closes, all three may have much to say to the client. In a pattern as hot and volatile as this, the aché of all three will be needed to keep the client out of harm's way.

This sign, no matter its orientation, demands that the client give thanks to the spirits for the good he has, even though evil is all around him. Elegguá says that this person should go to church, dressed in white, and pray to the saints that helped save this religion from extinction in Cuba. Bad times are coming, and this person must pray to Obatalá for protection, strength, and purity of soul.

This letter, even when it falls in iré, embodies all the evil and bitterness of its parent odu, Ogundá. Any osogbos that fall now are not to be blamed on others; the client can blame only himself for them. Karma can be a terrible thing, and this is what brings his difficulties. The diviner must advise the client to move and think quickly, for the law is literally at his front door. Some evil will try to visit itself upon his home; so severe is this warning that the client might wish to stay with a relative or trusted friend for a day or two. We say here that the client must run, although he does not know what it is he is running from; justice, or even Ochosi, might be after him to punish him for past transgressions. The client's adversaries will cause immediate destruction. This person has one strong, powerful enemy. He or she wants the client's destruction at all costs and will stop at nothing until he is destroyed. It may be necessary to call in the law. The cause of all this, of course, is nothing short of the client's own trusting nature. The client must be silent and move in silence if he is to overcome the evils this pattern can bring.

## The Prohibitions of Ogundá Owani

- In an osogbo, do not wear tight collars, necklaces, scarves, or other binding materials around one's neck. Limit jewelry, and do not wear more than two elekes at a time.
- Do not leave others unattended around one's own orishas, and always keep the orishas in a secure, safe place. Remember: Ocha cannot take care of those who do not care for ocha. If the osogbo of this sign is severe, lock the shells in a safe place, and move the otanes temporarily to a new location.
- Do not keep broken pots, and do not plant seeds in pots that are broken, cracked, or chipped.
- Avoid parties, large groups of people, and places in which people "party" and use intoxicants; the orishas say that these things are not meant for one now.
- Street corners are sources of danger; stay home.
- Do not become involved in love triangles or illicit relationships, for these will bring only scandal and harm.

## The Eboses of Ogundá Owani

When Ogundá Owani opens, Elegguá automatically takes an ebó of cooked red, white, black, and garbanzo beans. After this ebó sits with Elegguá for three days, the client should take it to the shore of a small lake or lagoon. If possible, this ebó should be prepared before the client leaves the diviner's home.

Now the diviner has his first opportunity to close the letter. If it will not close, the diviner must explain to the client that Elegguá wants three newly hatched chickens ("peeps"). If the client does not have the warriors, this sacrifice is made to the diviner's Elegguá. Ogún, too, requires ebó. The priest should cut a length of chain equal to the client's height and give this chain to Ogún. Afterward, the diviner should feed Ogún a rooster. As was the case with Elegguá, if the client does not have the warriors, this ebó should be given to the diviner's Ogún.

Now the diviner may ask the oracle again for closure. If the letter still will not close, Elegguá and Ochosi together may be standing up for ebó. The diviner should ask, "Ebó elese Elegguá y Ochosi?" If the answer is yes, the proper ebó is to give feathers to both.

The diviner should also consider the following:

- If the possibility of legal proceedings has brought the client to the mat, he should give to Ochosi an ebó of four white seven-day candles, three bows and arrows, jutía, and smoked fish. If the client faces imprisonment, the sacrifice of a feathered animal to Ochosi is called for.
- If this sign comes in either ano or ikú and later the client falls ill, the following ebó must be made: A rooster is given to Elegguá, followed by two roosters given to Ogún. Oshún is then fed five small hens. If surgery is inevitable, the client should have a rogación of the abdominal region at Oshún's feet.

If these eboses will not close the letter, the diviner should then turn to the eboses for the parent odu, Ogundá (see page 172).

## The Twelfth Composite Odu of Ogundá, Ogundá Ejila (3-12)

### The Proverbs of Ogundá Ejila

- If one puts one's heart into one's work, all things will come out well.
- In the house of a blacksmith, there is a wooden knife.
- The nail dressed himself well, and it cost him his job.

### The Message of Ogundá Ejila

When an initial cast of three mouths, Ogundá, precedes a cast of twelve mouths, Ejila Shebora, the odu Ogundá Ejila has come to the house. The diviner says, "Maferefún Babaluaiye!" This orisha stands strong here, and before the diloggún allows closure he may offer advice to the client and take ebó from him.

The diviner should note that the client for whom this letter falls lives an awful life filled with stress, economic disaster, violence, and abuse. However, if the odu falls in iré yale, it marks a guarantee is that from this moment on the client's life will get better and he will experience evolution. (This guarantee an anomaly in the family of Ogundá.) An orientation of just iré promises that if the advice of this reading is heeded and the proper eboses done, the client will find eventual freedom from difficulties, but it will come slowly. All osogbos demand extreme caution; if a client who opens in an osogbo does not follow the advice of this reading exactly, his situation will only get worse.

When a woman's reading opens in Ogundá Ejila, she wants to leave her husband or lover, yet she is afraid to leave. Perhaps she fears violence, or perhaps she fears being alone, or perhaps she is just afraid that she will be making a huge mistake in abandoning the relationship. Until she decides for herself what it is she wishes to do, she should avoid arguments and violence with her mate. She must also avoid infidelity and must not raise suspicions prior to her leaving. If her mother is still alive, the client might consider paying her a visit; she will have advice and may even be able to offer some help in the situation.

The diviner must also explore with the client the following points:

- A red woman will bring tragedy and deception. The client should beware of women with a ruddy or sunburned complexion, with red hair, or who wear red. This color on a woman announces that his destruction could be imminent.
- This client must go to his mother as soon as possible, seeking her advice on all things. Through his mother's advice will many of his problems be resolved.
- A client who wants to leave his or her lover but cannot is tied with witchcraft. This spell must be broken.

### The Prohibitions of Ogundá Ejila

- Do not carry or allow oneself to come into proximity to weapons. Avoid those who have to carry a weapon for either work or protection; danger comes from such people.
- Do not argue with those in authority or positions of power. This taboo applies to police, rescue personnel, and anyone else who wears a uniform. Definitely, do not argue with one's boss, or one's job will be lost.
- Do not wear or borrow another's clothing. Do not allow personal items to be borrowed or worn by someone else. This includes combs, brushes, towels, bedsheets, personal hygiene products, and anything else that has intimate contact with one's body.
- Do not have fires lit while sleeping, and have no source of flame in the bedroom. Do not smoke in bed or after sleeping. Never leave sources of fire unattended. Before leaving home, unplug electrical appliances that are not in use.

## The Eboses of Ogundá Ejila

Before attempting to mark the eboses listed below, the diviner may ask the odu for closure. If it remains open, the diviner should begin his line of questioning in this odu with Babaluaiye. To find out if this orisha requires ebó, he should ask, "Ebó elese Babaluaiye?" If the answer is yes, the diviner uses the diloggún to mark the required offering. If the answer is no, we say that Babaluaiye is standing up in the reading to defend the client for free, but the client should still present him with a token adimú to ensure his goodwill. The diviner should also consider whether the client needs to receive Babaluaiye, asking, "Koshé Babaluaiye?" If the answer is yes, until this initiation is given, the client should at least have Babaluaiye's eleke.

If the letter still will not close, Elegguá and Ochosi may be standing up together for ebó. To determine if this is the case, the diviner asks, "Ebó elese Elegguá y Ochosi?" If the answer is yes, he should mark something suitable using the diloggún.

If these eboses are not enough to close Ogundá Ejila, the italero should turn to the eboses of the parent odu, Ogundá (see page 172). Something there is necessary to close the sign.

# The Thirteenth Composite Odu of Ogundá Metanla (3-13)

## The Proverbs of Ogundá Metanla

- In a clean gourd, one drinks water that does not stain the tongue.
- Water from a clean well will not stain the mouth.

## The Message of Ogundá Metanla

Opening in a pattern of three mouths followed by thirteen, the odu Ogundá Metanla, also known as Ogundá Irete, has come to the house. When it falls, the diviner says, "Maferefún Obatalá! Maferefún Elegguá! Maferefún Ogún! Maferefún Oshún! Maferefún Oyá!" All five orishas are firm in this pattern; all may speak, and all might claim ebó before this session is closed.

Another orisha must also be considered in this sign, and for this the diviner must determine one piece of information: Does the client know his guardian orisha? If the client is an initiate with ocha or an aborisha whose head has been marked, Ogundá Metanla flags issues between this person and that spirit. If the client is an aleyo who has not had a bajado, these issues lie between him and the godparent's crown. If the odu comes in iré, these issues are mild. There is a separation among the physical head, the orí, and the orisha, and a rogación will put the client back in harmony with these forces. If the odu has come in any osogbo, the separation is severe, and the orisha might even be angry with this person. The diviner must examine this situation carefully, for unless it is resolved, the client can have no evolution.

In addition to the client's issues with the crown orisha, Ogundá Metanla marks debts to Oshún. The diviner must explore this issue thoroughly with the ibó and shells so the client can appease this orisha. She fights many battles on his behalf, attacking gossip, loose tongues, witchcraft, robbery, and health problems dealing with the kidneys and abdomen.

This pattern signals that an army of enemies is pursuing the client; unfortunately, not all these enemies are human, nor are they alive. The armies of the dead could be amassed for attack; it will take all the strength of this person's egun, and frequent eboses to the orishas, to overcome them. The client must not fight his battles alone. He must depend on his elders, his godparents, and his orishas now, because he does not have the foresight to defend or attack on his own. If the client is afraid of problems with his enemies, he should run and not fight, for fighting will only complicate matters for him.

The diviner should also explore the following issues in conjunction with this odu:

- Three people are planning to enter into a war with this person. He must be vigilant or else he will be harmed by them.
- This sign foreshadows decapitation. Three people will lose their heads in confrontations with others, and one of these heads might become lost, literally.

- This person shows a lack of consideration and respect for others. He must end this behavior now.
- This client has a charm or a niche osain and doubts it powers; he might even be thinking about throwing it away. He might also doubt his own orishas. This letter warns that he must not get rid of these things. They are his salvation, and his own doubt is part of his curse.

## The Prohibitions of Ogundá Metanla

- This odu predicts that one day a Cuban finch *(mariposa)* or other songbird will fly into one's house through an open door or window. It brings luck. Do not frighten or kill this bird. It will leave the house in its own time.
- The prohibition against weapons is strong in this odu. Do not carry clubs, guns, knives, or anything else that can be used as a weapon.
- Have only one lover at a time.
- Some say that Ogundá Metanla prohibits the diviner from keeping the client's derecho. Those who follow this custom will give back the derecho and not charge the client for ebó.

## The Eboses of Ogundá Metanla

The issue between the client and his or his godparent's crown must be examined carefully. If Ogundá Metanla has come in iré, the diviner should prescribe a rogación at the feet of that spirit. If the rogación is prescribed for an aleyo to the godparent's crown, the diviner should consider making it a rogación sodidé; it is dangerous for one who has nothing of ocha to be out of alignment with his godparent's crown, and a rogación sodidé will lift him up into the light and protection of that orisha.

If Ogundá Metanla comes in any type of osogbo, the diviner can assume that this orisha is angry with the client, and ebó is required to set things right. To determine if any ebó can be marked, the diviner must ask, "Ebó elese [orisha's name]?" If the answer is yes, he uses the diloggún to mark the required offering. If the answer is no, the client must still give ebó, presenting this orisha with an offering from the heart. In this circumstance, it is very important that the diviner speak honestly with his client and determine the reason for the orisha's anger so that spirit can be placated.

Egun are prominent in this odu. While they do not speak directly in this sign, they are the client's foundation and must be strengthened if he hopes to persevere beyond the inherent osogbo of this letter. The diviner should prescribe a series of three masses for the ancestors; the client must follow the prescriptions of the espiritistas exactly. If the client's mother is deceased, this odu demands that she be given her own mass. She needs light and elevation. In return, she will nurture the client in death as she nurtured him in life.

The diviner now has his first opportunity to close the oracle. If it will not close, he should consider the following options:

- If the client possesses a niche osain or charm for one of the orishas, it should be washed again in omiero and fed so it is recharged.
- The client may have a debt to Oshún. To determine if this is the case, the diviner must ask, "Ebó elese Oshún?" If the answer is yes, the diviner must use the diloggún to mark an appropriate ebó.

If the prescriptions made thus far are not enough to close the letter, the diviner must turn to the list of eboses given for the parent odu, Ogundá (see page 172).

# The Fourteenth Composite Odu of Ogundá, Ogundá Merinla (3-14)

## The Proverb of Ogundá Merinla

- Death is on its way for sure.

## The Message of Ogundá Merinla

When the initial casting of three mouths, Ogundá, precedes a casting of fourteen mouths, Merinla, the odu Ogundá Merinla is open on the mat. This sign is also known by the name Ogundá Ika. In this pattern, and in the remaining two signs of this family (3-15 and 3-16), we say, "Death is on its way for sure." These signs are volatile and explosive in nature. The client exists in a very harsh energy, and his life will reflect this. Know that if this person has girls living in his house (whether or not they are his own flesh and blood), one of them is in danger of rape or bodily harm. A cleansing ebó will protect this child; the cleansing must be given to all the women living under his roof or the osogbo may "switch heads." See "The Eboses of Ogundá Merinla" for a description.

Once the client has left the diviner's home, some of the energies of Ogundá Merinla might remain behind. Before going to bed, the italero must divine for himself. If the odu he opens marks any eboses, he should perform them immediately. He may do no work for anyone else until these eboses are complete. Only in this way will the diviner save himself from harm.

## The Prohibitions of Ogundá Merinla

- Do not let any stranger into the home, even if a friend vouches for that stranger. This person could not only rob or vandalize the home but also hurt those living there.
- Do not fight, argue, use weapons, or entertain violence.
- Do not become entangled in a discussion involving oneself and two others. Always avoid social gatherings that revolve around the number three.
- For seven days after this odu opens, do not let anyone else sleep in one's house except those who already live there. Do not let anyone sleep in one's bed except for oneself and one's lover or spouse.
- Do not go out into the street at night.

## The Eboses of Ogundá Merinla

The first consideration for ebó in Ogundá Merinla is designed to protect the young women in the client's home. All must be brought before the diviner's Ogún and cleansed with red meat saturated with epó, much like the closing cleansing ritual prescribed for Ogundá.

If the larishe prescribed for Ogundá Merinla is not enough to close this letter, as ebó the client should be given a small knife or a small razor that he should keep hidden somewhere on his person for a period of twenty-four hours. No one should be allowed to see or touch this blade. Once twenty-four hours have passed, the client should return to the diviner's home so that the blade may be given to his Ogún. (If the client has had the initiation of the knife, it may go to his own Ogún.) Ogún may require an ebó when this is done; to find out if this will be necessary, the diviner should ask, "Ebó elese Ogún?" If the answer is yes, he must then mark what Ogún requires using the diloggún.

- If the diviner has prescribed ebó for all the women in the client's home and the odu remains open, the youngest child could be in severe danger. Once all the women are cleansed with the beef and epó to Ogún, each should have a rogación and be given Ogún's eleke. This prevents the osogbo of the youngest from jumping to the head of an older child. The youngest girl must then be cleansed with a rooster; afterward, the diviner feeds the rooster to Ogún.

If these eboses are not enough to close the odu, the diviner should turn to the eboses of the parent odu, Ogundá (see page 172). Something there is needed to close the sign.

# The Fifteenth Composite Odu of Ogundá, Ogundá Marunla (3-15)

## The Proverbs of Ogundá Marunla

- The tree that is cut down makes a thundering noise.
- Death is on its way for sure.

## The Message of Ogundá Marunla

When the first casting of Ogundá, three mouths, is followed by Marunla, fifteen mouths, the odu

Ogundá Marunla, also known as Ogundá Iwori, is open. While an odu normally encloses all who sit at the mat for a session, such is this odu's strength that its explosive force extends to the streets. Before this reading has closed, a strange accident may occur in the diviner's own neighborhood. All present must remember: In Ogundá, one is forbidden to go outside and check out a disturbance. Any strange noises outside must be ignored; the reading must continue. The police may be called if necessary, but no one in the diviner's home should admit to witnessing any accident or crime. Nor may anyone give out his or her name; all should try to remain anonymous.

This odu, even if it is marked as iré, must be delivered as if Ogundá had come with the harshest osogbo. It is an evil omen that the client will regret for months to come.

The best advice the diviner can give is that the client should be careful in all things. The diviner must read for himself when the client leaves his home.

## The Prohibitions of Ogundá Marunla

- For a total of twenty-eight days, the following prohibition applies to all who were present for the reading: If one hears a disturbance outside one's home, do not go outside to check it out. The police may be called if necessary, but one must not admit to witnessing any accident or crime, and one must refrain from giving out one's name, making every effort to remain anonymous.
- All the prohibitions of the parent odu, Ogundá (see page 172), apply to the one at the mat. If any are broken, the client will find himself caught in a vicious cycle from which there will be no recovery.
- When this reading is over and the closing ebó done, go straight home and remain there for seven days. To venture out is to risk illness, accidents, and death. Only after seven days have passed may the eboses of this pattern be done.

## The Eboses of Ogundá Marunla

If the letter will not close, the diviner must let the client know that he has issues with both Yemayá and Ogún that need to be resolved. He must receive their elekes and wear them every day for twenty-eight days. If this prescription is not enough to close the odu, the diviner must then try to mark an ebó to the orishas, asking "Ebó elese Ogún?" and then "Ebó elese Yemayá?" If the answer is yes, he uses the diloggún to mark the required offering.

If this letter still refuses closure, it might be marking the client for the initiation of Babaluaiye. To determine if this is the case, the diviner should ask, "Koshé Babaluaiye?" If the answer yes, the client must receive this orisha as soon as possible. In the meantime, he should receive the eleke of Babaluaiye.

If these eboses are not enough to close the odu, the diviner should turn to the eboses of the parent odu, Ogundá (see page 172). Something there is needed for the client's evolution.

# The Sixteenth Composite Odu of Ogundá, Ogundá Merindilogún (3-16)

## The Proverbs of Ogundá Merindilogún

- There will be kidnapping, blackmail, and robbery.
- Death is on its way for sure.

## The Message of Ogundá Merindilogún

When the first casting of three mouths, Ogundá, is followed by one of sixteen mouths, Merindilogún, the odu Ogundá Merindilogún has come to the mat. This odu is also known as Ogundá Otura. It is the last and most destructive odu in the family of Ogundá; however, the destruction foretold in this pattern comes not from the client's environment but from within himself. This letter speaks of suicide, and although the energy of the odu might pass in a few weeks, the tendencies marked within this person will never pass unless he gets counseling. For the rest of his life, he will be marked by the possibility of self-destructive tendencies. Since like attracts like, during the course of his life this person will encounter many people who tend to have suicidal thoughts and feelings; over time, he will know many who take their own lives. Ogundá Merindilogún is a letter of darkness and a mark of depression; unless the client can go within himself to change the way he thinks or feels, no one else can help him.

Oshún stands up in this letter to demand payment for promises rendered; the diviner must mark what is needed. Note that if the client pays his debts and prays to Oshún, she can help bring the sweetness he needs back into his life. The orishas, however, can work miracles only when we let them.

The diviner should explore with the client the following points:

- This letter foretells suicide. If the client himself is not suicidal, someone close to him will try to take his own life.
- The law and war pursue this person; he cannot outrun them, and he will have to face them.
- The client has treasonous friends, but he cannot and must not fight with them.

## The Prohibitions of Ogundá Merindilogún

- All the prohibitions of Ogundá apply in this odu. If one breaks them, one does so at one's own peril.

## The Eboses of Ogundá Merindilogún

Ogundá Merindilogún marks the client as having debts and issues with Oshún. If the client does not know what that debt could be, the diviner must attempt to mark an ebó to her, asking, "Ebó elese Oshún?" If the answer is yes, the diviner should use the diloggún to mark an appropriate offering. If Oshún will not mark an ebó, the client should, nevertheless, offer an adimú to try to ensure her goodwill. If the client is suffering from a disease of the abdominal region, he must not only give an ebó to Oshún but also have a rogación at her feet.

If after these investigations the letter will not close, the diviner must turn to the eboses of the parent odu, Ogundá (see below). Something there is needed to bring closure.

## Closing the Reading: Further Eboses of the Parent Odu, Ogundá

Having exhausted the options for larishe and ebó in the composite odu, the diviner must now turn to the parent odu to find a method of closure. Ogundá contains within itself many offerings and rituals to placate both the composite odu and the orishas that are speaking. The eboses for the parent letter are as follows.

- Ogún may be standing up for additional eboses. The diviner should ask, "Ebó elese Ogún?" If the answer is yes, the proper ebó is the sacrifice of a rooster and two pigeons. The diviner should use each animal to cleanse the client to Ogún. If this offering is not enough to satisfy Ogún in Ogundá, each day for three days following this ebó an adimú of freshly cooked food should be prepared for him. When an offering is removed, the client should seal it in a brown paper bag, cleanse himself with it from head to toe, and take the offering to the nearest railroad tracks. Then he should return to prepare the next dish for Ogún. On the fourth day, when the third adimú is removed, he should light two white seven-day candles to Ogún.
- Eleggua, too, could be standing up for ebó. The diviner asks, "Ebó elese Eleggua?" If the answer is yes, the diviner should feed him a rooster at the nearest railroad tracks, leaving the bird's carcass there. For three, seven, nine, or twenty-one days after this, as ebó to Eleggua the client should put a small portion of all his meals in a brown paper bag and leave it at a crossroads the next morning.
- Ochosi may also require ebó. To determine if this is the case, the diviner asks, "Ebó elese

Ochosi?" If Ochosi takes ebó, he should be fed two pigeons; the heads from these are impaled on his arrows. While the animal's carcass should be disposed of immediately, the heads should be left with him until the third day after the sacrifice. When the birds are removed, Ochosi is cleaned, rubbed with epó, and given a basket of cool fruits.

- Yemayá, Obatalá, Aganyú, and Babaluaiye may also require ebó. To investigate these options, the diviner asks, "Ebó elese [orisha's name]?" If any of these orishas will take ebó, the proper sacrifice is feathers. The diviner should cleanse the client with the animals before the ebó is made.
- For aborishas and initiates, the reception of Babaluaiye is an option; the diviner asks, "Koshé Babaluaiye?" If Babaluaiye's reception is not necessary, his eleke may be. The diviner asks, "Ebó eleke de Babaluaiye?" If the answer is yes, the client must have a rogación before Babaluaiye's shrine before the eleke is given.
- For initiates, the reception of Aganyú is an option; the diviner asks, "Koshé Aganyú?" For both aleyos and initiates, the eleke of Aganyú is also a possibility. The diviner asks, "Ebó eleke de Aganyú?" If the answer is yes, the client should have a rogación in front of Aganyú's shrine before the eleke is invested.
- Eborí is also a possibility for Ogundá. The diviner should ask, "Eborí?" If the diloggún marks this as ebó, two pigeons are fed to the client's head first, and then two more are given to Obatalá. The client must also have a rogación before Obatalá's shrine.
- If none of the eboses investigated so far will close the letter, the client must be chained to the earth (he must wear on his left ankle a chain that has previously been fed to the earth), and the earth itself should be fed a rooster and grains so that it will not claim the client before his time.
- A special ebó must be done by initiates of Shangó if the reading is obtained with Elegguá's diloggún. Both Shangó and Ogún are put on the floor; the client's Elegguá sits between them. Elegguá is given a white chicken in sacrifice; the client should be cleansed with the chicken before it is killed. After Elegguá eats, Shangó and Ogún share two white roosters and one guinea hen between them. The client should be cleansed with these animals as well. After the sacrifice, all the carcasses go into a bag, along with toasted corn, jutía, smoked fish, epó, honey, rum, dried coconut, and nine guinea peppers. The client takes the bag to the woods and cleanses himself with it before leaving. Note that if Ogundá comes during the itá of an initiate of Shangó in either Elegguá or Shangó, this ebó must be done annually on his birthday.

When no other ebó will satisfy the letter, the proper ebó is the sacrifice of a four-legged animal to the orisha whose diloggún has been consulted. After the sacrifice is prescribed, it is not necessary to ask the oracle for closure; eyebale of four legs will close this odu. The sacrifice should be done as soon as possible. No itá is given for this ebó. Note that if the client is an initiate and the sacrifice of four legs is marked in Ogundá, this person is marked to receive the initiation of the knife. If the sacrifice of four legs is marked for an aleyo or aborisha, ocha is now mandated.

# FIVE

# THE FAMILY OF IROSUN

## The Proverbs of Irosun

- You cannot go to the ocean and avoid walking on the sand; you will leave a trail.
- Nobody knows what lies at the bottom of the sea.
- Nobody but Olorún and Olokun knows what lies at the bottom of the sea.
- Beneath all water and land, the fires still burn.
- Unseen things are best left unseen.
- Open the eyes; there is much to see.
- The fire is beneath.
- All fingers are children of the same hand, and none can separate.
- The child is born properly but becomes crooked and evil in time.
- You stand properly and you stand crooked.
- The child born healthy and strong grows weak from lack of care.

## The Orishas Who Speak in Irosun

| | |
|---|---|
| Shangó | Borosía |
| Eleggua | Oba |
| Olokun | Orúnmila |
| Yewá | Obatalá |
| Dada | Aganyú |
| Boromu | Ochosi |

## The Message of Irosun

Opening with four mouths on the mat, the oracle sits before the italero in an elusive pattern. Irosun, a sign seething with mystery, despair, and deceit, has come to the house. While all the letters of the dilog-gún bring enlightenment and evolution, Irosun's nature is to hide more than it reveals, to bring more questions than answers. It is a paradox unto itself, and no one can fully understand its implications. We say that only Olorún and Olokun know what Irosun holds. Nevertheless, a competent diviner can turn Irosun's unknowns into self-discovery and growth if he has studied the letter.

Born from the odu Owani (eleven mouths), Irosun is a foundation built from one's past. In my previous work I wrote of the parent, "Owani is an odu very rooted in the past, yet fulfilled only in the present. It is a sign of introversion and intro-spection, and a letter that encourages the sacrifice of the superfluous for the accomplishment of one goal."* At the core of Owani is the power to birth innovative people: prophets, geniuses, artists, politi-cians, visionaries, and social pioneers. This energy carries over into Irosun; the one who opens with

*Óchání Lele, *The Secrets of Afro-Cuban Divination: How to Cast the Diloggún, the Oracle of the Orishas* (Rochester, Vt.: Destiny Books, 2000), 290.

four mouths may have creative potential, but it is so deeply buried that it is all but lost. It may never manifest unless the client understands Irosun's implications.

Like the creative energy buried deep in Irosun, the client's life is caught up in dark, swirling currents from which there seems no escape. Intuitively, he already knows this, and it is what brings him to the diviner's mat. The client feels forlorn and perhaps hopeless. However, if he opens his eyes now to see what lies before him, there is hope that he will reclaim his destiny. The symbol of Irosun is the eye, and through this reading the diviner must impress upon the client the importance of opening his eyes to the world around him.

Having cast four mouths, the diviner now makes the sacred gesture of this odu. He touches the mat with the middle fingers of both hands, keeping the remaining digits suspended in the air. Without moving any of his fingers, he brings up both hands, and with the middle fingers, he stretches both of his lower eyelids down. This pantomime not only calls everyone's attention to the opening of the odu on the mat but also serves to warn all present to open their eyes wide so they miss nothing. Once these gestures are complete, the diviner chants the prayer for this odu:

*Aparatita ebebe kiki enu akolaba.*
*Enu lashe inafokosi moro oroni.*
*Foko kosí mala yoko esi misan.*
*Ina un yobe ina un yoko.*
*Apendeure achawo onadereko apan.*
*Apal'Eshu apal'Eshu lenu Ogún ni.*
*Dagbonide Ósun apendemi.*

Those present bow their heads in silence while the diviner chants this brief prayer. After he is done, to honor both the opening odu and the orishas who own it, those who know the odu might mutter, "Maferefún Irosun! Maferefún Olorún! Maferefún Olokun!"

In this letter, many orishas might choose to speak. The spirit whose shells have been cast has the first option, and what he has to say will be deep. Realize, however, that this spiritual force has a message not only for the client but also for the diviner and for those present at the mat. First, with this initial cast of four mouths, the orisha of the dilogún warns that the client may have come to test the diviner's skills. Although the person at the mat could have come innocently for a reading, in the most extreme cases the client might be an initiate, a priest or priestess of ocha, scouting new houses of ocha, looking for new, more knowledgeable godparents. The client could also be a babalawo spying. If the diviner senses treason, he should state a proverb applying to all sixteen composites of Irosun: "You cannot go to the sea and avoid walking on the sand; you will leave a trail." Although the diviner cannot prove treason immediately, the casting of Irosun guarantees that one day treason will be uncovered.

Second, by opening this reading in Irosun, the orisha consulted may be throwing up a red flag against the possibility of a godparent/godchild relationship. It warns that romantic desires and fantasies could develop between the client and his godparent (who could be the italero). In this religion, the godparent is the spiritual parent; he may not initiate a lover into the mysteries of the orishas because this would constitute an incestuous relationship. Those not directly involved with this client's spiritual growth must be wary, for although his deception cannot be pinpointed at this time, unethical issues might soon arise. Note that the diviner and those present at the reading should tell none of these things to the client. This information must be kept secret among them. Although the diviner and current godparents are bound to perform the prescribed eboses, they would be wise not to give anything of ocha beyond ebó to this person until they know his intentions. In time, Irosun guarantees that they will know all.

In addition to the orisha whose shells are cast, the following may stand up in all composites of Irosun to offer advice or claim ebó: Shangó, Elegguá, Yemayá, Olokun, the Ibeyi, Yewá, Oba, Obatalá, Aganyú, and Ochosi. Four other spirits—Dada, Boromu, Borosia, and Orúnmila—will not speak directly in the shells, but their influence can affect its closing. Dada is in the court of Shangó; Boromu and Borosia are both in the court of Odua, and they will stand up only for those in the priesthood. When any of these three makes its presence known in this family of odu, there is only one issue to settle: the spirit's reception. When Orúnmila comes, a female client could need kofá de Orúnmila and a male client could need mano de Orúnmila. Either could need an Elegguá from Ifá. Therefore, the odu may not close until the italero prescribes a visit to a babalawo for the client. Until these issues are investigated by Ifa's priests, any iré promised in a letter influenced by Orúnmila will be slow in coming.

When Shangó speaks through Irosun, his words are not always kind and gentle, yet they are the client's salvation. In almost any osogbo he comes not only to reprimand but also to protect the client, keeping him safe with harsh love. A true godsend, his intercession unveils secret enemies, traps, and treasons that have been laid for the client. He warns, "Open your eyes and watch where you walk. Thus, you will not fall." With Shangó's goodwill, osogbos the client may never see will be removed so they cannot touch him. This pattern has many token offerings the client may give Shangó for his supplication. *Pañuelos* (ornate, decorated silk cloths in an orisha's sacred colors), beaded nets, and cooked foods will all bring his favor upon the client. A beaded double-headed ax, a sword, and even a beaded bat might all be washed in omiero and given to Shangó; with these, he will fight the client's battles. A white ceramic horse would be an appropriate adimú, for with it Shangó can carry the client to safety.

Of all the spirits who speak in Irosun, Olokun and Olorún are the only ones who know this sign's full implications. Unfortunately, most of what they know cannot be told in the language of mortals. Yet this much can be expressed: The client's own eyes are closed to what goes on in his environment. Others have laid traps and planned deceit, and the mighty Olokun has kept his eyes on them. Now that the client has come to the oracle, Olokun insists that he open his eyes. Olokun points out the client's naïveté. He must stop looking within and stop wandering around aimlessly in the world. He must spend time learning to see what things are worth his effort and who is worthy of his loyalty and trust. Olokun says that the client, like Irosun, is lost. If he would focus on the present, he would feel unwound and disjointed. Upon hearing these words, the client's emotions could come boiling to the surface, and the diviner must be prepared for this. He should advise the client not to become lost in these feelings, for as his depths are cold and crushing, so is the weight of this sign when Olokun speaks. He must stay focused on Olokun, Olorún, and the advice given at this session, for though the odu itself is lost, the client should not lose himself.

Rarely will a pattern of Irosun close unless Elegguá has his chance to speak and claim ebó. Irosun deals with fate and destiny, and no orisha knows these qualities better than Elegguá. He was present at the client's birth; he was present when his destiny was chosen. Placation of this spirit can put the client on the path to evolution.

Oba is here, too. She speaks of the great sorrow existing within the client, of the tears that overwhelm him. When she comes in four mouths, she comes as one's savior from oneself. Yewá is next. Even when she does not speak she is here. Her influence is shadowed through all sixteen composites. Yet when Yewá stands up in Irosun, the sign's implications become severe. Her mystery is deep, more frightening than that of Olokun. Remember that four mouths always alludes to the depths, and Yewá herself is the depth of the grave, the wet earth.

Obatalá, Babaluaiye, Aganyú, Ochosi, and egun may all also speak through Irosun. However, what they bring to the mat is heavily dependent on the composite odu opened.

Before assessing the client who has opened in Irosun, the diviner must realize that this is perhaps the most mysterious pattern an initiate may read. It hides more than it reveals, and no matter how carefully this session is delivered, all present at the mat will leave with unanswered questions. To understand the mystery of this odu, one must visualize Olokun's realm: the vast ocean. Standing on the shore, one can see miles over its surf until a gentle curve removes the ocean's edge from view. What lies beyond the curve is lost to one's sight; it cannot be known until it chooses to come closer. Yet the surface of the ocean, even that small part that can be seen with the naked eye, hides more than it will ever reveal. Below the surface of the water lies a vast realm, a chasm of darkness, and below this lies even more land remaining forever unknown. There is earth below the sea, but none can travel to its deepest depths where only Olokun lives. Irosun alludes to this mystery. It tells us that mysterious forces are at work, but they can never be known.

Because this odu is so complex, the easiest way to begin its study is to examine it in iré. If the odu opens in iré, the diviner can make many assumptions about the client and how he will progress. In iré, this odu speaks of evolution. The client has been facing many mysteries; he is filled with many questions and concerns, and up until now there have been no answers offered. Through four mouths, two vast spiritual forces—Olokun and Olorún—have become the client's allies. They know all, and they will help the client discover what he seeks to know. However, the journey toward discovery is never an easy process, especially when one seeks to know oneself. It is a dangerous, arduous road. The diviner must tell the client to open his eyes. He is walking through life with his eyes closed, and there is so much to see. He must master the skill of discernment; he must learn to see what is real, friendly, and helpful, and what is not. The diviner must also tell him this: One grows not by imagining forces of light but by illuminating what already lies in darkness.

If the iré is marked as iré yale (firm blessings), Irosun is telling the diviner that the client's source of help is strong; the orishas are mounting behind this person to thrust him toward his evolution and destiny. Imagine, for a moment, the vastness of the ocean and its powerful currents; they are gathering to propel the client toward his goals. Think about the fire beneath the earth; this is the fuel for his desires. Meditate on the mystery of the grave's depths; even this can motivate him to accomplish more. All these are sources of strength in Irosun.

If the iré is marked as iré yale timbelaye (firm iré manifest in the client's life), Irosun gives closure to itself. It tells the diviner that its energy has been in effect for some time, and the client has conducted himself well through its energies. The force of his conduct, his prior good deeds, his adherence to his own destiny, and his worship of the orishas—all these have already given him the tools to facilitate his own evolution. The letter has opened here to tell him what forces are in effect and what is coming his way.

Because Irosun unveils mysteries while forcing one to evolve, in iré the diviner should assess the client's position in our religion. Now is a time of initiation, and timely initiations ensure this person's growth. (The initiations the diviner should encourage the client to undergo are described in "Marking Ebó in Irosun: Initial Considerations"; see page 180.)

When Irosun comes in osogbo, the inner darkness of this odu manifests without; the client is caught in its web, a sticky tangle of deceit and treachery, and he may know true terror before this energy lifts. No matter the osogbo opened, the diviner must tell the client, "You live in great spiritual darkness; so deep is this blackness that you can't see the road before you, and you have lost your way. There is no light; know that all around you is much to be seen, yet Irosun also says that things unseen, for now, are best left unseen. The darkness you are in is forcing you to slow down, to cease movement, and while all your goals seem unreachable, for now this can be a good thing for you. Look within; there is light there. Stop, rest, and plan. Make the eboses of this sign. Once you have rested, once you have regrouped, once you make sacrifice, the light will shine without again. You will see with new eyes, and you will grow."

Irosun in osogbo speaks of separation. Parent and child, husband and wife, godparent and godchild, friends and lovers—a great distance unfolds between them. The client cannot hold close all whom he considers dear, and now he must evaluate which people are the most important influences in his life, which give back as they receive from him. The diviner must ask the client, "You have nurtured many, but who nurtures you? You have shared with many, but who shares with you? You keep the best interests of others in mind, but who watches out for you?" Those people who return the client's care are those whom the client should hold close while Irosun tries to rip away all others. The client must learn to be discerning; many around him lie to hold him close for their own benefit, and he must see through these lies or be destroyed. If the client learns discernment, the prophesied separation between all can become a selective separation from those unnecessary persons. This odu, however, indicates that this lesson may be beyond the client, so he must live by making ebó.

In Irosun's osogbo, one suffers by reaching too far. The diviner knows that the client has overstretched himself. Changes are coming that will force him to cut back. He should be mindful of this impending current. His finances could crumble. A breadwinner in the household could lose his job through negligence, accident, or oversight, and it could take months to recover from this. The diviner must tell the client that now is a time not to go into debt but to work out of debt. Now is a time to save rather than spend.

In an osogbo with Irosun, Elegguá can be one's greatest ally, and the diviner must explore the client's relationship with him. Elegguá can help or hinder as he sees fit.

Irosun in osogbo also touches upon many other subjects. The diviner may explore them all with his client.

- In osogbo, health concerns focus on the eyes; the client must go to an ophthalmologist for an exam. They also focus on the "twos" of the body: the legs, feet, arms, hands, ears, kidneys, lungs, and lymphatic systems. If the client experiences any physical discomfort from any of these organs or limbs, he should consult a physician. He must protect the eyes and abdominal region well, especially if this letter comes in ano, for blows to these will cause serious injuries. He must also protect his head. He should not participate in any sport without the proper safety equipment. When traveling in a car, he should wear a seat belt; when riding a motorcycle or bicycle, he must always wear a protective helmet and goggles.
- The client has begun many projects, yet cannot decide which to finish first. Because of this, money is pulled in with one hand and thrown out with the other. He must set goals and keep them secret, and he must finish one project at a time.
- The client will one day make ocha, even if he has come only for a reading. His love for this religion and the orishas will grow.
- The client has either a birthmark or a scar; one day, he may be scarred again.
- The client should be cautious around fire and electricity. Candles burning in the home should not be left unattended; any frayed electrical wiring should be replaced. When leaving home, he must extinguish all candles and unplug all electrical appliances not in use.
- Religious "headhunters" will come after this person and tell him that his spiritual initiations were not done correctly. They will try to make the client abandon his spiritual family for another house of ocha. He must not listen; they want him only for his money.

No matter the orientation of Irosun, iré or osogbo, the diviner has many issues to discuss with the client. Like the odu in which he has opened, the client sitting before the shells is deep and mysterious. Although he thinks he knows himself well, that he is in touch with the depths of emotions and feelings that course within him, in truth he has yet to tap into more than the surface reflection. Much as a glacier shows only a fraction of its mass above the ocean, the client reveals only a small piece of himself. No one—not even the client himself—truly knows himself. This odu points out that only Olokun and Olorún know all; these mighty orishas know even those things the client does not know about himself.

A generalization that holds true for most clients opening in Irosun, regardless of its orientation, is this: They come with big smiles, pleasant faces, and relaxed demeanor, yet their seemingly happy, hopeful faces are a mask. Under this mask is darkness; bright eyes hold tears and smiles hide depression. For some, the surface is no more than a conditioned response to the turmoil seething inside. Alone, this person cries. All around him are false friends, enemies, gossip, bad tongues, evil thoughts, and treason. Deception hides, waiting for its chance to come out. The diviner, as a counselor, should tell this person not to let the actions of others bring him down. He must refuse to let others bring despair; those around him will take falls, but he should not try to catch them, for he will then fall himself. This mask is a good defense; however, the client himself should not believe that his mask is his true face. For the client, the first step toward healing is to admit that he is sick; the second step is to accept help and treatment. The orishas will be this person's physician.

When making new friends, the client should proceed slowly and cautiously. He is innately naïve, and others sense this. People will take advantage of him. As a rule, the client should look at others with distrust. He should be polite, of course, but only as polite as well-mannered society dictates. He should do no favors for others unless something is given immediately in return. Irosun is a sign of reversal. In this odu, we say that perceived friends are enemies, and perceived enemies are actually friends. The client must be ever vigilant against fraud and deceit. In business, he must remember that there are no true friends, only clients and salesmen. If someone wants to begin a business with or for the client, he must make sure that a fair contract is first issued and signed. He should do nothing on faith and should, instead, have all legal documents scoured by an attorney. He should do nothing by good word alone and should, instead, have all promises put into writing. He must not cosign for a loan, for it will be he who pays off the debt. In the end, however, if he follows the advice of the orishas, the client need not worry, for they will provide for him.

Through the energy of Irosun, the client will feel disoriented. A female client might be tempted to describe herself as "hormonal"; a male client might say that he is weak. The diviner must advise this person to not become lost in these energies. The client must keep his eyes focused ahead at all times. He must visualize his goal and pursue it in a straight line. Even if weakness ensues, even if the client feels exhausted and wants to rest just for a moment, he should continue his journey. Olófin will watch what tries to strike from above, and Olokun will be vigilant over those things that come from within. The power of this sign guarantees that if the client moves continually and ethically, he will have the assistance of all the spirits who stand up in odu. He must be steadfast; the diviner must tell him to let naught stop or turn him away from his plans and aspirations. But while the orishas watch the heavens and his back, the client is on his own to watch his path. He must keep his own counsel and let no one interfere with his progress. If he follows this advice, all will come to closure, and he will attain his goals.

Relationships become tricky in this odu. If the client is a man, even in iré, he could lose his wife to adultery. Initially, the client's behavior led his spouse to these actions. She felt unwanted and unloved, and her own attempts to rekindle passion went unnoticed. Now, however, she is falling in love with the new suitor. This person's influence sways her to argue, but the client must refuse to participate in quarrels with his spouse if he hopes to save the marriage. If a relationship or marriage is worth having, it is worth fighting for, and the client must now fight for his lover.

Irosun signals that a woman is watching the client. She is evil; her thoughts are no good, and she speaks badly of everyone she knows. She is looking for a way to bring ruin, perhaps even imprisonment, to the client. Gossip about loved ones began with her mouth, but when it reaches the client's ears, he should pay it no mind. The eboses prescribed will protect the client from her.

Irosun may forebode the birth of twins into the family. It also points to the reception of the Ibeyi, the sacred twins, and the client must soon welcome these orishas into his home.

In any orientation there are other issues to consider. Keep the following in mind at all times:

- The client is depressed or prone to depression. In this odu tears well to the surface; they are not seen by others but are shed in darkness or behind closed doors.
- The client has been deceived frequently and is being deceived now. The diviner should tell this person, "Do not let what others do to you destroy you. Do not let what they say about you ruin your self-esteem." While he might appear confused, unable to rationalize this advice, in truth the client will understand. In self-defense

or embarrassment, however, he will not admit that these things are true.

- Irosun's influence is hectic. At this time the client has a lot of goals. In iré, he is working toward these, but unless his iré is marked as iré yale timbelaye, he may not reach them. The diviner should ask the client to assess the reasons for this himself. In osogbo, this pattern points out that the client's tendency is to daydream rather than to work. He lacks the motivation to put plans into action.
- This pattern predicts that one day the client will run into an attractive business proposition. The orientation of this odu determines the outcome of this. In iré, all will go well. In osogbo, he must be wary.
- Irosun advises the client to assess his workplace. If nothing else, four mouths points out that this person is working under duress; stress is eating him alive. In osogbo, this sign signals that some aspect of his job is destroying his health. Be wary.
- The client's home is vulnerable. Four mouths guarantees that one day this person will be robbed.

## The Prohibitions of Irosun

Irosun is an odu of deception, darkness, and mystery. No matter how competent the diviner or how honest the client, the full implications of any composite odu, especially in osogbo, will never be understood. To overcome adversity, the prescription of taboo is necessary. Within the family of Irosun are many prohibitions that the diviner should prescribe, and within each composite are prohibitions that become mandatory when osogbo falls.

For all composites of Irosun, the diviner should consider the following:

- Irosun speaks of the open hole and the evil it contains. While under this odu's influence, open holes are means by which much of one's luck will be lost and misfortune will enter one's life. Be cautious around holes of any kind. Do not look through holes, especially peepholes. Never wear clothing that is torn or ripped or that contains lace or eyelets outside of one's home.
- Do not wear red clothing. It draws too much attention to the wearer, and the color itself is spiritually hot. Likewise, red furniture in one's home is dangerous. Cover or upholster it.
- Do not speak to anyone over a fence. Go around it; do not be separated from the other person. Never jump over a fence, even when one thinks what lies on the other side is known. In addition, neither jump over ditches or step over ropes or hoses.
- Cats are taboo. None should be brought home. If one already owns a cat, treat it with love and respect. To harm the animal is to lose one's luck.
- Keep one's home immaculately clean and well lit at all times to avoid dangers and accidents.
- To ensure one's health, do not eat grains or grainy foods. Consume nothing made from animal heads or intestines. If the meat eaten at a meal has bones, do not gnaw or suck on them, because choking is a danger.
- Cap or discard all open bottles at home immediately. Luck escapes with these.
- Elegguá controls one's comings and goings. When one must travel, consult with him first. If Elegguá says not to go and the trip is for pleasure, abide by his advice. If the trip is for business, one has two options: Ply Elegguá with ebó or stay home.
- Do not make fun of beggars and vagrants, for these are favored by Babaluaiye. Give alms to the poor regularly.
- To avoid ruin, keep away from those who must hide to live, and keep nothing that should be hidden.
- Do not hide money at home. Do not let strangers see one's valuables.

## Marking Ebó in Irosun: Initial Considerations

Irosun marks hidden forces as the source of the client's issues; secrets lie in the depths of this person's being, and only one orisha may see what is unseen or know what is unknown: Olokun. In considering eboses for Irosun, the diviner must first consider the client's status in this religion: aleyo, aborisha, or initiate. If the client is an aleyo, the diviner must prescribe a rogación before Olokun's shrine and the investment of Olokun's eleke. If the client is an aborisha or initiate, the diviner must determine if Olokun requires ebó from this person, asking, "Ebó elese Olokun?" If the answer is yes, the diviner marks the appropriate offering with the diloggún. An aborisha or initiate who has not already received Olokun is marked by four mouths for his reception. His birth marks a spiritual maturation in this person's life, and his agbán will remove the hindrances in this person's life. In this odu, once the client brings Olokun home, two more eboses must be done for him. First, the client should purchase a blue crystal plate; his sopera lives on top of this. Second, the client should buy an ornate blue mask for Olokun. Prop this against the front of his tureen so that when others look upon him, all they see is a large mask. With this, he will hide what needs to be hidden and reveal only what needs to be revealed.

Opening in Irosun, an aleyo with nothing of ocha should be led, gently, to take the elekes. The investment of the necklaces of Obatalá, Shangó, Oshún, and Yemayá is a powerful way to stabilize the iré Irosun can bring. This sign is a calling to priesthood, although the client's priesthood may be far in the future. Treated as a iyawó for one night, the recipient of these elekes will feel what his future religious life might be. He already searches for these mysteries.

An aborisha who already has the elekes must be pushed to receive the warriors. In the quest for self-knowledge, Elegguá, Ogún, Ochosi, and Ósun are necessary guides. They bring stability to the client's life. Because Irosun is lost, the client will need the warriors as allies in order to navigate the currents Irosun brings.

An aborisha who has already received the elekes and warriors should be led gently to asiento. Put the basket received from Olokun's agbán before his shrine. There, the client puts all the things that he needs for a santo, even the money for the derecho. It is upon the crowning of asiento that all life's mysteries will unfold, and it is Olokun who will be the guide to this gate.

Those clients who already have Olokun now have issues with the Ibeyi twins, Taewó and Kaindé. The diviner should consider asking, "Ebó elese los Ibeyi?" If the answer is yes, he must use the diloggún to mark an appropriate offering. If the Ibeyi refuse ebó, nothing short of their reception will help this person. Their birth and their birthday party will remove both the tears he cries and the sourness he faces.* He will evolve. (Note that if the reception of Olokun has been prescribed in this sitting, the initiation of the Ibeyi must not also be prescribed unless there is no other way to achieve closure of the odu.)

For priests and priestesses of Oyá, another orisha must be considered for ebó: Yewá. She is rarely spoken of, yet she is among the most severe and powerful in the Lucumí pantheon. For initiates of Oyá, Yewá is just as important as Olokun. Oyá is the gateway to the grave; Yewá is the grave that feeds on one's death. Although their domains are unique, Olokun and Yewá share spiritual similarities: Olokun is the wet, damp earth that lies at the bottom of the sea, and Yewá is the wet, damp earth that lies at the bottom of the grave. In time, all die and are sent to Yewá's domain, the grave; in time, all things that die find their way to Olokun's domain, the bottom of the sea. While many fear Yewá, and with good reason, for a priest or priestess of Oyá she can provide stability in this life and the next. The diviner has two options. The first is to ask, "Ebó elese Yewá?" If the answer is yes, the diviner uses the diloggún to mark the ebó. If ebó alone will not satisfy her, or if she will not take ebó, the diviner then asks, "Koshé Yewá?" If she comes, the priest or priestess will have multiple blessings in his or her life.

The final consideration for ebó in Irosun is directed toward two potent spirits: Shangó and Olokun. Even if all the requirements of odu are

*Most ilé ocha give a special children's party in honor of the Ibeyi after their birth; others save this tradition for use only as ebó. The preferences of one's godparents should be obeyed when these two orishas are received.

fulfilled and neither of these spirits speaks directly to the client, one or both should be given ebó to placate the odu. The sacrifices used most often in Irosun follow.

### Traditional Eboses in Irosun

Certain items are traditional for use as ebó in Irosun. Whenever possible, for eyebale the diviner should pick from the following list: a chicken, two roosters, and four pigeons. If an adimú-type offering is needed, he should pick from the following: a ñame, an arrow, smoked fish, jutía, a white sheet, four small sacks, and four cakes.

## Ebó Elese Olokun
## *(Ebó at the Feet of Olokun)*

Note that all the eboses in this section are written for the orisha Olokun. Many say that Yemayá speaks beside Olokun; this, however, is not the custom of our house. I have been taught that while Yemayá can speak in some composites of Irosun, her true aché is in the family of Odí (seven mouths). However, if Yemayá does stand up in a composite of Irosun, a competent priest can adapt these eboses for her as well.

### *Ekru-aro Adimú*

When osogbo comes through Irosun with Olokun requesting an adimú as the larishe, a dish known as *ekru-aro* will appease her. The client should provide the following ingredients: a pound of black-eyed peas, two eggs, seven squares of aluminum foil, and some cotton twine.

Wash the peas well, removing all dirt, debris, and foreign objects; in a large saucepan, soak them overnight. The next morning, rub all the peas well, removing their shells. Mash the peas until they form a thick paste, adding minimal amounts of water, if needed. Beat the eggs and mix them into the mashed peas. Divide the mixture into seven equal portions, wrapping each portion in aluminum foil and tying it with string so it does not open. Cook in boiling water for 30 minutes. Cool, unwrap, and serve on a blue dish to Olokun. Using obí, the diviner asks Olokun when and where he wants his ebo discarded.

### *Seaside Cleansing*

To soothe himself and remove harmful energies or to solicit assistance in making important decisions, the client might prepare the following ebó for Olokun. First, the client should dress in his oldest clothes, items that he no longer wears or needs, and gather fresh white clothing to change into.

He takes to the sea a jar of molasses and seven pennies. Entering the sea by walking sideways, with his left side facing the ocean (one must never enter the ocean face-first as this is considered "taunting" the orisha Olokun), the client wades out until he is waist deep. He pours a clockwise circle of molasses around himself, drops the seven pennies to the bottom of the ocean, and washes his face with seawater, praying to Olokun to remove the osogbos that hinder him in life. The supplicant backs out of the water and changes into the white clothing; then he throws the old clothes far out into the sea. With these, Olokun will take away whatever hinders the client's evolution.

*Note:* The client must not lose the jar in the sea. If he is not sure he can complete this ebó without losing the glass jar, he should pour the molasses into a jícara and bring the gourd out into the water with him. If the gourd is lost in the ocean's waves, it will eventually decompose without polluting the water.

### *Ebó for Eshu and Olokun*

Three paths of Elegguá have special aché with Olokun: Eshu Aniki Olokun, Eshu Ayé Belleburo, and Eshu Ayé. In the religion it is said that Eshu Aniki Olokun dredges up the wealth from the depths of the ocean (Olokun's realm) and puts it into the hands of Eshu Ayé Belleburo; Belleburo then puts the wealth of the ocean into Eshu Ayé's hands. Eshu Ayé distributes the wealth as he sees fit. If the client has one of these three Eshus from ocha and also has Olokun, he can give the following ebó to the two orishas to bring increased abundance to his life.

Put Eshu at Olokun's feet. Gather the following

ingredients: gofio, molasses, seven pennies, seven nickels, seven dimes, seven quarters, two gourds, honey, jutía, smoked fish, a red seven-day candle, and a blue seven-day candle.

In a large mixing bowl, combine the gofio and molasses until a thick paste forms. From this paste, fashion seven balls of equal size. Insert into each ball one penny, one nickel, one dime, and one quarter, packing the ball again so the money is sealed inside. Place three balls in a gourd for Elegguá and the other four in a gourd for Olokun. Take the gourds, honey, jutía, smoked fish, and candles to Olokun's shrine. There, light the red candle to Elegguá and the blue candle to Olokun, praying for one's desires. Give Elegguá his gourd first and Olokun hers second. Still praying, pour a liberal amount of honey over both adimús and then sprinkle the jutía and smoked fish over them. The ebó stays with the orishas until the candles are consumed. Dispose of the gourds in the ocean.

Note that the client who has one of these three Eshus in ocha has aché with both that orisha and Olokun; all eboses given to Olokun should be shared with this Elegguá. The two together will bring special blessings to his life.

### *Watermelon Prayer*

When all the requirements for Olokun in Irosun are fulfilled, one may make a special prayer and request to her. For this ebó one will need a blue platter, a blue seven-day candle, a white seven-day candle, a watermelon seven pieces of paper, seven pennies, molasses, and a large piece of blue cloth.

Place the large blue platter on the floor in front of Olokun; on either side of this set one candle. Place the watermelon on top of the plate. Write one's wish on each piece of brown paper. Cut seven holes in the top of the watermelon, and put one piece of paper into each hole. Place a penny on top of each piece of paper, then pour molasses freely over the fruit, making sure that some goes into each hole.

Before Olokun, pray for one's desire and light the two candles before taking one's leave. When both candles are burned out, lift the watermelon from the plate and wrap it in the blue cloth. Discard the ebó in the ocean, throwing it as far out into the waters as possible.

## Ebó Elese Shangó
## *(Ebó at the Feet of Shangó)*

All the eboses in this section are written for the orisha Shangó. Note that Aganyú and Shangó are father and son; many of these offerings can be adapted for Aganyú. If Aganyú stands up in a reading of Irosun for ebó, an experienced priest may adapt these offerings for him.

### *Plantain Adimú*

To prepare the following adimú for Shangó, collect six green plantains, smoked fish, jutía, honey, and guinea pepper.

Peel and boil the plantains until they are soft; mash these together in a large bowl with a liberal dash of smoked fish and jutía. Over this, pour a liberal amount of honey. Mix everything into a thick paste. From this, form six large balls of equal size. Insert one guinea pepper into each ball. Serve the six balls on a plate to Shangó, and while praying to him for peace and evolution, drizzle honey freely over them.

This ebó remains with Shangó for six days. After this time, discard the ebó at the foot of a palm tree in the woods.

### *Plátanos en Tentación*
### *(Plantains in Temptation)*

This is a wonderful dish to prepare for Shangó when he demands propitiation. It may also be made for other orishas who like the plantain as ebó, such as Ogún, Elegguá, and Aganyú. To prepare this, collect three tablespoons of butter plus enough to grease a pan, three ripe plantains (they should be a golden yellow hue), 1/3 cup of white sugar, 1/3 cup of brown sugar, 1/8 teaspoon of cinnamon powder, 3 tablespoons of dry cooking wine (unsalted), and two cinnamon sticks.

Preheat the oven to 375 degrees Fahrenheit. Lightly butter a baking dish. Peel each plantain and place them side by side in the dish. In a mixing bowl, stir together the white sugar, brown sugar, and cinnamon powder. Sprinkle half of this mixture over the plantains, then pour the wine over them. Lay the two cinnamon sticks over all three bananas. Cut the 3 tablespoons of butter into small pats and put these pats over the bananas so that they are covered completely. Bake for approximately 1 hour, keeping an eye on the plantains so that they do not burn.

Upon removing the plantains from the oven, sprinkle the remaining sugar and cinnamon mixture over them immediately. When they are cool, put the plantains on a serving dish and leave them with Shangó overnight. The next morning, use obí to determine how he wants his ebó discarded.

## Cuban Amalá-Ilá*

This recipe is among the most popular for making amalá-ilá for Shangó. To prepare it, one needs a 2-pound box of yellow cornmeal, salt, a large onion, six cloves of garlic, one pound of okra, 3/4 cup of epó, 1/2 teaspoon of cumin powder, 1 teaspoon of oregano powder, 1 (16-ounce) can of tomato sauce, 1/2 cup dry red wine, six raw okras, and a large red bowl.

To prepare the amalá, put the cornmeal and a dash of salt into a large pan with eight cups of water. Stir continually over medium-high heat until it boils. The moment it begins to boil, turn the heat to low and continue stirring until the mixture is very thick. Remove from the stove and pour into a large bowl.

While the amalá cools, peel and dice the onion finely. Peel and mince the garlic. Combine the onion and garlic in a small mixing bowl; set aside. Cut the okra into small slices; set aside. Heat the epó in a skillet over medium heat until it is melted. Add the garlic and onion and sauté, stirring continually, until the onion becomes transparent. Immediately, add the sliced okra, cumin powder, oregano powder, tomato sauce, and red wine. Reduce the heat to low and cook, stirring continuously, until the mixture is thickened. Remove from heat.

Stir the okra stew into the amalá, and mix well. Pour into a large red bowl, garnish with the six whole okras, and serve to Shangó. Leave this adimú with him overnight; the next morning, use obí to determine how he wants his adimú discarded.

### *Sweet Amalá Bundle*

To prepare this adimú for Shangó, gather 2 pounds of cornmeal, honey, a large bundle of fresh plantain leaves, and epó. Preheat the oven to 350 degrees Fahrenheit. In a large saucepan, bring 8 cups of water to a rolling boil. Add the cornmeal to the boiling water, reduce the heat to medium, and cook, stirring continually so the cornmeal does not burn. When it thickens, reduce the heat to low, continuing to stir. When all the water evaporates, leaving a thick paste, remove the amalá from the stove; stir in just enough honey to sweeten it to taste. Keep stirring until the saucepan cools so that the amalá does not burn.

Rinse the plantain leaves well so that there is no trace of dirt on them. Shake the excess water from them, and allow them to dry on a paper towel. With a brush, grease a 3-inch-deep baking pan liberally with epó. When the plantain leaves are dry, brush both sides of each leaf with epó as well. Carefully place the leaves in the baking pan so that each leaf overlaps the next by one third of its width and half the length of each lies outside the pan. (Arranged in this manner, the leaves can be folded into a bundle that will contain the amalá.) Press down on each leaf with one's palm so that the epó forms a seal and holds the leaves together. Once this bed of leaves is formed, pour the amalá into the baking pan. Fold the plantain leaves over the amalá, sealing with more epó if necessary. Bake for at least 15 minutes but no more than 30 minutes, watching carefully so that the plantain leaves brown lightly but do not burn.

After removing the pan from the oven and while the amalá bundle is still hot, place a serving platter on top of the baking pan. Turn the bundle upside down so it slides out onto the platter. Leave the pan in place for 5 minutes; it will help the bundle retain its form as it cools. After the bundle cools, serve it to Shangó immediately. The ebó remains with him overnight. The next morning, use obí to determine how he wants his ebó discarded.

*The traditional Yoruba recipe for this adimú is given on page 54.

## The First Composite Odu of Irosun, Irosun Okana (4-1)

### The Proverbs of Irosun Okana

- That which you imagine is true, so tell no one.
- Only Olorún and Olokun know what is at the bottom of the sea.
- Those who rail in defense against insults from others must continue to suffer.
- [There will be] a revolution in the body.
- Blood from the nose, mouth, or anus [will flow].
- Namesakes never kill one another.
- There is gain from the ground.
- One's enemy does not wish one to survive trial by ordeal.

### The Message of Irosun Okana

When four mouths on the mat are followed by one mouth, the odu Irosun Okana has come to the house. This sign is also known as Irosun Kanran, Irosun Kana, and Irosun Okanran. When this odu falls, the diviner says, "Maferefún Orúnmila! Maferefún Elegguá! Maferefún Obatalá! Maferefún Ogún!" All four spirits stand up in this sign to offer their protection, and in the trials that lie ahead the client will need their goodwill. Irosun Okana is a severe odu, opening when severity is called for. Even if it comes with iré, it marks all the tragedies of Irosun, the parent odu, on the client. It can create disappointment, gossip, and envy. So close are these negative energies that the diviner can be assured someone is planning a trap for the client. Iré shows that the orishas offer escape, and the iré marked tells the client where to turn for spiritual help.

Osogbo in this odu marks specific tragedies on this person, and he must work hard to avoid them. Fires in the home, cancers of the head and abdomen, and adultery are serious concerns. The love of an exotic person may seem tempting, but the client should avoid it; courtship outside his current relationship will bring danger.

Regardless of the odu's orientation, the diviner should keep the following in mind:

- A pregnant woman who opens in this odu has reason to worry about her relationship or marriage; her lover does not think the child is his. The diviner should ask the woman if she has been faithful, for in this sign she might be carrying another man's child. Likewise, a man who comes in this odu might be expecting a child; unfortunately, it may not be his.
- Gossip plagues this client; he is the victim of many evil tongues. When he hears what others say, he becomes angry. The diviner should tell the client to neither listen nor respond to others' accusations. He must keep silent on these things. For just as many speak evil words, others are saying good things, and in the end the truth will come out.
- This client brings a lot of worry to the mat. The diviner should tell him that most of his assumptions are true; however, this odu forbids the client to speak of these worries.
- The client is actively seeking to court another. The person he courts can bring only tragedy and tears; the courtship must not be pursued.
- Orúnmila is very close to this client and has much to say, but he cannot speak through the diloggún. The diviner should send the client to a babalawo as soon as possible for a consultation.
- Something frightening will happen to this person at night; it could even happen in his own home, while he is sleeping.

### The Prohibitions of Irosun Okana

- Do not smoke in bed or keep an open flame in the bedroom. Do not have ashtrays, candles, lighters, lamps, or electrical appliances near one's bed.
- Gossip is prohibited in this odu.
- Adultery is taboo.
- When leaving home, unplug all electrical appliances not in use.
- Do not keep broken appliances in the house.

### The Eboses of Irosun Okana

When Irosun Okana falls on that mat, it marks the client as someone who must make ocha; however, the diviner may not wish to give this information at this time. He must consider the client's position in the religion. Is he an aleyo or an aborisha? If the client is an aleyo who has nothing of ocha, the diviner should direct him to take the elekes as ebó. They will set his feet firmly on the path to ocha and will elevate him to the status of an aborisha.

If the client is an aborisha who has the elekes but not the warriors, the diviner should prod him into this next step as ebó. If the diviner's ilé ocha has the custom of marking Eshu before one makes ocha, he must mark the proper path of Elegguá now.

If the client has committed to the religion and has both the elekes and the warriors, the diviner should tell him that he is now marked for ocha. The diviner should put Obatalá's mazo around the client's neck as a banner and direct him to salute Obatalá, the godparents, and then the priests and priestesses present in elder status. This ebó is strong in this odu, so strong that it will save the client's oldest child from death. It must be fulfilled in as timely a manner as possible.

The second consideration for ebó in this pattern centers on Ogún. Remember that in either iré or osogbo, Irosun Okana tells the diviner that there are obstacles in the client's life. Ogún wants to destroy all that stands in the way of the client's evolution. To do this, he must take something from the client. If the odu has already claimed larishe for Ogún, all is well; nothing further is needed. If Ogún has not yet claimed anything, the italero must find out if he will take ebó, asking, "Ebó elese Ogún?" If the answer is yes, the italero uses the shells to mark the offering. If the answer is no, the client should still offer some form of ebó; as he gives, so shall he receive.

The final consideration in this odu is the client's issues with Ifá. Orúnmila wants to advise this person but cannot do so through the diloggún. As ebó, the diviner must tell this person to go to Ifá for a thorough assessment.

After explaining all these prescriptions, the diviner has his first chance to close the diloggún. If the odu will not close, the client has further issues to resolve with the orishas Obatalá and Elegguá. The client should give Elegguá an adimú; the diviner may consider marking something for him with the diloggún or picking something suitable using his own aché. Place Elegguá at Obatalá's feet and give him the ebó there. Afterward, the client should have a rogación at Obatalá's feet.

If this prescription is not enough to close the odu, the diviner should consider asking, "Eborí?" If eborí is marked, the diviner must feed two white pigeons to the client's head after he gives the ebó to Elegguá.

If these considerations are not enough to close the odu, the diviner must turn to the eboses of the parent odu, Irosun (see page 210). Something there is necessary for the client to find evolution.

Note that if the eboses of neither the composite nor the parent are enough to close Irosun Okana, the diviner should offer Ogún a four-legged sacrifice to bring this session to closure. There are two variations for this eyebale. In the first method, the diviner gives Ogún the four-legged animal along with seven gourds filled with a mixture of cornmeal, mashed ñame, honey, epó, and red ocher. This ebó remains with him until the sacrifice of four legs is cleaned from his otá; however, he may not be cleaned for four days. Then the client must have an itá with Ogún. In the second method for eyebale, a large animal trap (such as an iron bear trap) is put beside Ogún's cauldron, and the blood of the animal is allowed to pour over this as well. In the center of this trap the diviner places a single gourd filled with a mixture of cornmeal, mashed ñame, red ocher, and rum. This ebó sits with Ogún for three days. At the end of this time the client takes the gourd to the nearest railroad tracks, and he cleans Ogún after the ebó's disposal. The bear trap is oiled with epó; it stays with him indefinitely and is part of his tools.

## The Second Composite Odu of Irosun, Irosun Ejioko (4-2)

### The Proverbs of Irosun Ejioko

- Your luck escapes through holes.
- Things loaned are things lost.
- No one knows what lies at the bottom of the sea.

- The dead stand in waiting.
- By not knowing what we have to do, we finish up by doing exactly nothing.
- By not knowing what we should not do, we make the same mistake over and over again.
- There is a rocky path before you.
- If you remove your shoes, you cannot walk with ease.
- Not even a donkey stumbles over the same stone twice.

## The Message of Irosun Ejioko

When the initial cast of four mouths, Irosun, precedes a cast of two mouths, Eji Oko, the odu Irosun Ejioko, also known as Irosun Oyekun and Irosun Yeku, is open on the mat. Even before the qualities of iré and osogbo are extracted, the diloggún has delivered an important message: A priest or priestess of one of the ilé ocha represented at the mat is in danger of death. With this warning, however, an ebó is offered to save the life of this elder. (See "The Eboses of Irosun Ejioko," on page 188.)

The diviner pays homage to the orishas to whom the client must turn for guidance and solace, saying, "Maferefún Obatalá! Maferefún Shangó! Maferefún Ogún! Maferefún Ochosi!" Obatalá is the salvation of the client's orí. Dark times are coming for the client, and he will have to work hard if he is to get through the osogbos that lie before him. The orí, however, can be weakened and overwhelmed amid all the changes, and only Obatalá can save it. Shangó comes here as a fierce warrior, as does Ogún; these two will ride into battle for this client, destroying all those who oppose his work in the world. Their help, however, does not come without a price; the client will have to make ebó to both if he hopes to enlist their help.

The diviner must keep in mind that Irosun Ejioko holds within its grasp both death and the grave. Its image is that of a coffin, and if an osogbo of ano or ikú has opened, this coffin has been built for the client. If an accident does not take him, disease or illness could. This person believes that he is in perfect health, but the odu signals that this could change with a moment's notice. At the first sign of illness the client must see a physician. Bones in his legs and waist could become dislocated, and all the double organs of the body are in danger. The diviner must caution this person to monitor himself for skin eruptions, headaches, and bleeding, for all these are signs that his health is suffering. He must be wary of his own personal safety, for death is looking for a victim, and already Ikú might be on his trail.

In addition, the diviner should keep the following in mind:

- When a client opens in either iré or a gentle osogbo, he is facing financial difficulties. These, however, will improve once the proper eboses are made. If a serious osogbo has opened and no larishe was prescribed, things will get worse before they get better. Unless the client is a very hard worker, he may soon be fired or forced to quit.
- The client's greatest danger comes from the opposite sex. He must be wary in dealings with people of the opposite sex.

## The Prohibitions of Irosun Ejioko

- Do not pawn personal possessions. Much of one's remaining luck lies with these things, and to pawn them is to pawn one's luck.
- Do not loan one's personal possessions, for things given out will not be reclaimed. Once this session is over, try to reclaim those things that one loaned out prior to this reading.
- Dishonesty, adultery, and gossip are all forbidden in this odu.
- All open containers and bottles in the house must be closed or thrown away.

When Irosun Ejioko comes in an osogbo of ano or ikú, the following prohibitions also apply.

- Falls are a danger and may cause possibly mortal injuries. Do not climb ladders or stand on stools, chairs, or tables. Heights and unstable terrain must be avoided. Be very cautious near holes; walk around them and not over them.
- Keep the home warm and well lit; do not let it become dark or cold.

- Do not dress like a friend.
- Avoid street corners between noon and 6:00 P.M.
- Be very careful at work; do not perform dangerous jobs or duties for which one has not been trained.

## The Eboses of Irosun Ejioko

When Irosun Ejioko comes, it delivers a very important message to the priests and priestesses present: An initiate could die soon. If initiates of more than one house of ocha are present at this session, the diviner must try to determine upon whose head (in which house) this osogbo falls. He may ask, "Osogbo de Irosun Ejioko elese ilé de [initiate's name]?" If the diloggún will not mark the ilé upon which this tragedy falls, we say it is inevitable and prepare for the worst. If the house can be marked or only one house of ocha is represented, the following ebó can save the life of the elder: Give eight white doves or white pigeons, eight white roosters or hens, four plates, and a new silver bell to Obatalá. This ebó is given on behalf of all the elder heads in the house. During the next year, if any of the elders falls ill, the stricken one must have a reading, and the prescribed eboses must be fulfilled immediately. If possible, all the elders of the house should be gathered when the eboses for the stricken elder are done so they can all be cleansed with the sacrificial offerings. They must be given rogaciónes before leaving, as well.

If Irosun Ejioko opens in an osogbo of ikú, the client must have the same ebo recommended to save the life of the elder. It must be done quickly so that the osogbo of odu does not destroy his life.

Regardless of its orientation, the odu mandates an ebó to Ochosi for luck and evolution. The client must take several handfuls of almond leaves and cover Ochosi completely with them. Every day for the next four days, he lights two white candles to the orisha and blows plenty of anisette over his shrine. After the fourth day of ebó, he takes the leaves to a bush in the woods.

Shangó and Ogún both speak strongly in this sign, and they must be given a chance to claim ebó if a larishe has not been marked to them. To determine if either requires ebó, the diviner asks, "Ebó elese [orisha's name]?" If the answer is yes, he uses the diloggún to mark the required offering. If the answer is no, the client might be wise to offer an ebó anyway, so that no issues exist between himself and these two orishas.

Finally, the client must be directed to give Elegguá adimú. The diviner may choose an appropriate offering with his own aché; he does not need to mark it with the shells.

Having explained these prescriptions, the diviner now has the first opportunity to close the oracle. If the letter refuses closure and the client is an aleyo or an aborisha, the diviner must turn to the eboses of the parent odu, Irosun (see page 210). If closure will not come and the client is a priest or priestess, the orisha whose diloggún has been consulted might be marking a tambor as the solution to the client's problems. The diviner must ask this orisha if a tambor is required, asking, "Tambor elese los santos?" If the answer is yes, he should then ask if the orisha whose diloggún has been consulted will take the tambor, questioning, "Tambor elese [orisha's name]?" If the orisha of the diloggún refuses the tambor, the diviner should try to mark the tambor to one of the orishas given in the initiate's ocha.

There are some traditional eboses in this odu for the orishas:

- For the client's guardian orisha, give eight pigeons (if the orisha will eat pigeon), eight coconuts, and four plates.
- For Elegguá, cornmeal and a rooster can be used as an ebó. This same offering may be given to Shangó.
- For Obatalá, one may give a white rooster or two white pañuelos.

# The Third Composite Odu of Irosun, Irosun Ogundá (4-3)

## The Proverbs of Irosun Ogundá

- The law of the funnel is this: Keep the wide end of all things for yourself and the narrow end for everyone else.

- Only Olorún and Olokun know the mysteries that lie at the bottom of the sea.
- A single man can save his people.

## The Message of Irosun Ogundá

When the initial cast of four mouths, Irosun, precedes a cast of three mouths, Ogundá, the odu Irosun Ogundá is open on the mat. The diviner pays homage to Olokun in this odu, saying, "Maferefún Olokun!"

One day Olokun arose from the ocean and tried to take all the land back into the sea. As Olokun was rising over dry land, Olófin and Obatalá went to Orúnmila for divination; each had a rogación of his head in accordance with odu. "Where," cried Olófin before Olokun, "will your children live if you destroy the earth?" Olokun wanted back his domain, for when the land had lain all under the oceans, he had ruled the entire earth, but he also loved each of his mortal children dearly. He went to Orúnmila to talk to him. "Olófin and Obatalá did their ebó first," Orúnmila said, "and there is nothing that you can do. If you rise against land, you destroy your followers." Olokun could not bear to destroy his own, and he remained at the bottom of the sea. Just as he could not bear to see his children suffer, Olokun cannot bear to see the client suffer now.

The client also pays homage to Ogún and Ochosi, saying to each, "Maferefún!" These two orishas made a pact to always work together. The skills lacked by one the other had, and they found that together their effectiveness at hunting was doubled. When this odu opens, the diviner knows that these two orishas are working together to bring the client's evolution.

Finally, the diviner says, "Maferefún Shangó!" In this odu Shangó comes as a fierce warrior. He will protect the client through the trials and tribulations that lie ahead.

The odu Irosun Ogundá is hot and volatile; so many orishas act and interact in this sign that the client's life can become complicated. Under the influence of Irosun Ogundá, regardless of its orientation, a variety of accidents and disasters can occur in the client's life. Most of these incidents will be caused not by the hands of others but by the client's own temper and lack of judgment. He must be calm; his head must be clear and stable as he fights the osogbos that lie ahead.

The diviner should explore with the client the following considerations:

- The client lives a bad life, and the diviner should tell him so. His priorities are not straight, and often he takes advantage of others. This must stop.
- The client faces a danger of fire in the kitchen. He might be a poor cook; he does not pay attention to what he is doing in the kitchen. The stove, the trash, and kitchen appliances might all catch fire before this odu has passed.
- This person brings a lot of suffering to himself by his own words. He speaks but does not believe in what he says.
- This odu marks the possibility of witchcraft against the client. If it opens in osogbo, the witchcraft could be a malicious magical sending. The diviner must mark an ebó and many spiritual baths to remove the witchcraft.

## The Prohibitions of Irosun Ogundá

- Do not carry or use weapons.
- Do not threaten, curse, or wish ill upon anyone. Even if another aggravates a fight, back away. Running away would be better.
- Do not strike one's lover, especially if one's lover is a pregnant woman. Even a minor hit or slap could cause her to miscarry, and the orishas will hold one responsible for the death of the child.
- This odu forbids adultery and threesomes. If an adulterous relationship is consummated, it will be one's demise.

## The Eboses of Irosun Ogundá

When the odu Irosun Ogundá opens, many eboses must be prescribed to keep osogbo at bay. First, the client must have a rogación at Obatalá's feet, and immediately after the rogación he must offer the following adimú to Elegguá and Olokun: Mix dark molasses and gofio until they form a thick paste. Mold the paste into ten balls. Put three of these balls in a jícara to Elegguá and seven in a jícara to Olokun. Before these two orishas, the client should ask Olokun to save his life, for he is her child, her supplicant.

If the client does not have his warriors, he must receive them. If he has his warriors, he must honor Ogún's and Ochosi's pact to work together by washing a set of deer antlers for Ochosi and placing them in the iron cauldron.

One more ebó is mandated: Fill a large jícara with toasted corn, toasted cornmeal, jutía, and smoked fish. Drizzle honey on it for sweetness. Give this ebó to the warriors (the client's warriors if he has them, and the diviner's warriors if he does not) for three days; at the end of three days, the client discards the gourd and its contents in the woods.

Now the diviner has his first opportunity to close the reading. If this odu will not close, he should explore the following:

- In Irosun Ogundá, Ósun was cursed to stand guard over Obatalá's palace day and night, never sleeping. If the odu has opened in osogbo, Ósun may require ebó. The diviner should ask, "Ebó elese Ósun?" If the answer is yes, Ósun's carga must be reinforced; it must be opened and doubled. The diviner greases the inside of Ósun's cup with epó and the outside with coconut oil. Then he feeds Ósun a pigeon. Even though Ósun should already have a pigeon head inside him, the head from this pigeon sacrifice should go inside as well to give him more aché.
- Olokun, Obatalá, Ogún, Ochosi, or Shangó could need ebó. To determine if this is the case, the diviner should ask, "Ebó elese [orisha's name]?" If the answer is yes, the diviner should use the diloggún to mark an appropriate offering and then ask the oracle for closure.

If the eboses marked thus far are not enough to close the odu and the client is an aleyo or an aborisha, the diviner should turn to the eboses of the parent odu, Irosun (see page 210). Something there is needed for the client's evolution.

If the oracle will not close and the client is a priest or a priestess, the diviner should explore the following options:

- The spirit whose shells are being consulted might need a four-legged sacrifice. The diviner should ask, "Ebó elese [orisha's name]?" If the answer is yes, the ebó of four legs is marked. No itá is given with the sacrifice; this reading is the itá.
- If the orisha of the diloggún will not accept a four-legged sacrifice, a different orisha who speaks in Irosun might require this eyebale; the diviner must consider this. If this is the case, an itá is given.
- If the sacrifice of a four-legged animal cannot be marked, or if it will not close the odu, the client could need the initiation of pinaldo (knife). The diviner must ask, "Koshé pinaldo?"

If none of these eboses will close the odu, the diviner now turns to the list of eboses for the parent odu, Irosun (see page 210). Something there is needed to bring the client's evolution.

## The Fourth Composite Odu of Irosun, Irosun Meji (4-4)

### The Proverbs of Irosun Meji

- No one knows what lies at the bottom of the sea.
- All the fingers are children of the same hand, and none can separate.
- The fire is shut off not only with water but also with intelligence.
- The tree that is born crooked will never straighten up.
- You stand properly, and you stand crooked.
- The child is born properly but becomes crooked and evil in time.
- One man alone saves the town.
- You cannot go to the sea and avoid walking on the sand; you will leave a trail.
- The caged bird misses his home.
- The son who was born strong, healthy, and straight is now crooked from lack of care.

## The Message of Irosun Meji

When a cast of four mouths doubles itself, Irosun Meji is open. The diviner says, "Maferefún Shangó! Maferefún Yewá! Maferefún Odua! Maferefún Olokun!" These four orishas speak strongly in this odu.

Once the orientation of iré or osogbo is marked, the diviner puts the mazo of Obatalá on the client, draping it over his left shoulder and under his right arm, like a banner. Once the session closes, this person must salute Obatalá,* the diviner, and his godparents. He is now bound to make ocha, and the diviner must explain this to him. Although this person has come for no more than a reading, he is destined to be a great head in the religion; how soon his advancement will come or how far he will go depends on the orientation of this odu. The eboses prescribed in this sign will strengthen his life and assist in his personal evolution, but he will have no happiness or true iré until this final step is taken. Before ocha comes, however, the client will consider abandonment of his ilé ocha. Headhunters will come proclaiming that the client's ilé has no knowledge and no foundation. He must pay them no mind. Deception permeates this letter, and the client must be on guard against it continually.

In Irosun Meji, Elegguá demands worship and supplication. Although another orisha may claim the client's head, he must treat Elegguá as if he were his patron. Elegguá loves the client, and by working closely with him the client will surmount all this odu's troubles. However, Irosun Meji also warns against fanaticism. Elegguá says the client is a pest to the orishas at times, and he badgers his godparents relentlessly. This person gets overwrought, bringing sorrow when he thinks he is a joy. He spends too much time with his spiritual family. The diviner must remind the client that quantity never equals quality. By putting distance between himself and his godparents, he will bring them closer together. The diviner should tell the one at the mat, "You come to the religion hoping to find a family. Now, Elegguá tells you to go home; you have one there." The diviner should let this person know that if blood relatives have brought tears, so will those related in spirit. A foundation outside the ilé ocha must be laid so that when they begin to create problems, the client can endure.

When Irosun Meji comes in an osogbo, it flags specific health concerns. The client could have trouble with his eyes and his sight; he must be sent to an ophthalmologist for an exam. Spiritually, the eyes are a source of weakness; he should wear clothing that draws attention away from them. If the client wears glasses, they must be tinted. Choking and drowning are also dangers in this sign. The client must be careful when eating; he should chew food carefully and drink slowly.

The biggest health risk in Irosun Meji, however, comes not from disease or decay but from compromised personal safety. The client should check the locks on his car, garage, house, and windows immediately. If the locks are insufficient or broken, he should replace them; if they are still functioning, he should reinforce them.

The diviner must also keep in mind the following points:

- The client must guard against depression. Even in iré, Irosun Meji marks suicide and suicidal tendencies. This letter indicates that the client cries inwardly, not showing the world his true feelings.
- This pattern speaks of memory loss. If it comes in a severe osogbo, the client's orí will be affected.
- Elegguá demands that the client make peace with his family. The diviner should tell the client, "Forgive your mother. She will never change, but she deserves forgiveness." He will understand these words.
- This letter forebodes money through a family inheritance. However, the inheritance will cause fights in the family.
- This person has siblings he has never met. One day, he will meet them without knowing who they are.

*If a bajado has been done for the client, or a *planté* (life reading) with Ifá, the client salutes his guardian orisha. If this information is not known, the client salutes Obatalá, because he owns all heads, even though not all heads are destined for his priesthood.

- Because Irosun Meji warns of traps and treason, the client must be wary of others. He should keep his dreams secret; by sharing his hopes and aspirations with others, he loses the energy to make them real. The diviner must tell the client that he has many secrets, and he should not give them away unless he receives something equally valuable in return.
- This sign promises that there will be a lot of gossip surrounding the client's ilé ocha. He must be careful regarding whom he lets into his spiritual family until the true intentions of potential members of the family are known.

## The Prohibitions of Irosun Meji

- If one has received orishas, and especially if one is a priest or priestess, their implements must be kept under lock and key. Do not leave others around their shrines unattended. One day, someone will steal something from one's tureens.
- Contact lenses are taboo. If one wears glasses, the lenses must be made of safety glass; they must not be fragile.
- For twenty-eight days, do not gargle. Be careful when eating. One may choke under Irosun Meji's influence. Drowning is also a danger, so be wary of any body of water.
- Limit travel to daylight hours. Travel at night will bring danger.
- Beware of those of mixed ancestry. A light-skinned mulatto could be a source of danger and despair.

## The Eboses of Irosun Meji

In making eboses in Irosun Meji, the client must use the *achotele*—the four colors of Ósun (white, yellow, blue, and red). After an ebó is done but before it is discarded, the client should cleanse his body and head with four strips of cloth in these colors. He should then put the cloths in the bag with the ebó and discard them together. In addition, the Ósun of everyone present for the reading should be reinforced with these colors.

When a reading of Irosun Meji opens on the mat, there are many considerations for ebó.

- The client must obtain a silver coin (American, pre-1964) and wash it during the *lavatorio* (the ceremony in which an orisha is born) of each orisha he receives from this point onward. If others in the ilé ocha receive orishas or if an asiento is done, the client should go there to work, and while he is working the godparent must wash the coin with one or more orishas. This ebó is a powerful amulet for those who open in Irosun Meji. The client should always carry the coin and never spend or pawn it. To lose it would be to lose the luck this odu brings.
- The client's Ósun should be reinforced as is described for Irosun Ogundá (see page 190).
- The priest washes a ceramic pumpkin in Oshún's omiero. The client should put money in this for Oshún every week as a devotion. This way, the client will never be poor.
- As a child, this person played or wanted to play a musical instrument; the desire was quelled and not followed through. Elegguá wants this person to play that instrument again. When it is not being played, it should be left with the orisha. The happiness the client had as a child will slowly come back to his life.
- If the client has not received his warriors, he must now. If he has his warriors, they might need ebó. To determine if this is the case, the diviner should ask, "Ebó elese los guerreros?" If the answer is yes, he uses the diloggún to mark the proper offering.
- Oba or Shangó might also stand up in this odu for ebó. To see if either requires ebó, the diviner should ask, "Ebó elese [orisha's name]?" If the answer is yes, the diviner uses the diloggún to mark an appropriate offering.
- If an initiate has opened in a severe osogbo, the diviner knows that Shangó has all but left him due to disobedience. The only way to bring Shangó back to the otanes is for the client to feed him a ram and sit for itá.

If these eboses are not enough to close the letter and the client is an aleyo or an aborisha, the diviner should now turn to the eboses of the parent odu, Irosun (see page 210). Something there is needed for the client's evolution.

If the letter will not close and the client is an initiate, the diviner should consider the following eboses:

- In a cave, the client should feed Oba two white hens. Before beginning the sacrifice, he should lay Oba on a white plate. After Oba has been fed, the client must take a piece of rock from the cave and use it to make a four-faced Eshu; this path of Eleggua has no name but lives at the feet of Oba. It will take all the carga of Eleggua. However, each of the four faces must be given a separate, special ingredient: efun in one face, ósun in another, charcoal in the third, and dirt from the cave itself in the fourth. No diloggún is washed for this Eshu, and he is used for no one except the client. He is a personal Eshu and will never give birth to another Eleggua.
- The diviner should warn the initiate who has opened in Irosun Meji to take care of his health. To seal good health and prosperity for this person, as an ebó the client plays a drum to Elegguá. Unless the odu will not close, a *fundamento* (consecrated drum) is not necessary in this odu.

If at this point the odu still refuses closure, the diviner must examine the eboses of the parent odu, Irosun (see page 210). Something there may be needed for the client's evolution.

If after all of these eboses have been investigated Irosun Meji still will not close, a cleansing is mandated for all who were present when the odu opened. This ebó is done as a group ritual, with the diviner presiding. Take to a palm tree a dark rooster and toasted corn, epó, efun, jutía, smoked fish, and rum. The supplicants cleanse themselves to the tree with all these objects. The diviner then sacrifices the rooster to the tree's roots and, once the tree is fed, nails the bird to the tree with a square-headed nail. The bird's carcass is left there; all cleanse themselves with the four colors of Ósun before leaving.

## The Fifth Composite Odu of Irosun, Irosun Oché (4-5)

### The Proverbs of Irosun Oché

- Death is taking a stroll, looking for someone to take.
- The dead circle like vultures, looking for someone to take.
- The dead are out and about, looking for someone to capture.
- Don't let the spirits of the dead catch you.

### The Message of Irosun Oché

When the initial casting of four mouths, Irosun, precedes a second casting of five mouths, Oché, the odu Irosun Oché is open on the mat. This sign alludes to the spider's special talent of spinning a sticky web. The client must be cautious, for, like a spider, someone is spinning a sticky web that will, in time, catch him.

The diviner pays homage to Shangó and Oyá, saying to each, "Maferefún!" Both are strong in this odu, and both come to fight on the client's behalf. He will need their strength and protection, because Irosun Oché is a powerful odu that can cause great wars and strife to break out among men with little provocation. The diviner pays homage to egun as well, again saying, "Maferefún!" Egun are here, but in this volatile pattern, death and the dead (not egun) come with them. If the client is not careful, he could lose his life. Finally, the diviner says, "Maferefún Orúnmila! Maferefún Ogún! Maferefún Elegguá!" What Shangó and Oyá cannot settle, these orishas will. Know that Irosun Oché sends the client to Ifá once he has made all the eboses demanded of this sign; he has issues to be settled by the babalawos.

When this odu opens in iré, it signals that the client is blameless for the bad in his life; bad things happen to good people for no reason, and the diviner's job here is to help the client avoid the bad that is looking for him. In osogbo, however, the client must take responsibility for his own actions. All of the bad coming is a direct result of his unethical actions and poor choices, and in the end only he can save himself. In this odu, the diviner knows that Death himself is out looking for a new victim. Only the client's orí can save his life; the diviner must consider this when marking ebó. If ano or ikú is the osogbo predicted, the client could have inflammation or decay in the abdomen, circulatory system, feet, legs, or shoulders. If the client's health was poor before, it will only get worse in the future, so he must take care of himself. And no matter the osogbo opened, any pains in the client's bones or teeth demand ebó to Obatalá, and troubles in the abdominal region dictate ebó to Oshún.

The diviner must also explore the following issues with the client:

- If the sign comes with a firm iré, it marks the arrival of money through gifts, inheritances, or games of chance. The client does not deserve this good fortune, however, so when it comes he must be thankful for the source of goodness.
- Any osogbo in this odu marks disappointment, disillusionment, despair, hypocrisy, envy, gossip, and deception. Remember that this odu says the client deserves the bad it brings; he must work hard to overcome these negative energies.
- In all orientations of Irosun Oché, the respiratory system is delicate; the nose could be hurt or injured, and infection could enter the lungs. One day, surgery on the nose could be required.
- One of the client's issues is his mouth; he speaks ceaselessly, and rarely do his words mean anything. If he hopes to evolve, he must shut his mouth.
- The client has a terrible crush on someone. He must be careful if he acts on this; how he goes about making his intentions known can bring iré or osogbo to his life.

## The Prohibitions of Irosun Oché

- When this odu opens in an osogbo, use calabazas, gourds, and squash only for ebó and nothing else.
- Open holes are the means by which luck can be lost and misfortune can enter one's life. Be cautious around holes of any kind. Do not look into peepholes, and do not wear torn or ripped clothing outside the house. Do not wear any clothing that incorporates lace or eyelets.
- Do not consume grains or any food made from the heads or extremities of animals.

## The Eboses of Irosun Oché

Irosun Oché requires two initial considerations for ebó. First, the sign mandates a rogación for the client's head to strengthen his orí. If his guardian orisha is known, the rogación should be given at the feet of that spirit. Afterward, the client should offer his guardian an adimú of coconuts. If the client's guardian orisha is not known, the rogación is given before Obatalá. If possible, this rogación should be done before the client leaves the diviner's home.

Second, egun need ebó. The diviner must prescribe a series of three masses immediately; after each of these, the client should give adimú to his egun. He must follow the prescriptions of the espiritistas exactly.

Now the diviner makes his first attempt to close the oracle. If it ends in failure, the diviner should ask, "Ebó elese [guardian orisha]?"; if the client's head has not been marked, the diviner might ask, "Ebó elese [godparent's crowning orisha]?" He might also consider asking, "Ebó elese Obatalá?" and "Ebó elese egun?" If the answer to any of these questions is yes, the diviner uses the shells to mark the offering.

If the odu still remains open, the following become issues:

- Shangó and Oyá could be demanding ebó, and at this point they must be given ebó together. What is done for Shangó must be done for Oyá, and what is done for Oyá must be done for Shangó. If neither has taken ebó in this odu, the diviner should ask, "Ebó elese Shangó y Oyá?" If the answer is yes, he will use the diloggún to mark an ebó.
- Elegguá and Ogún can claim ebó in this sign together or separately. The diviner should consider asking, "Ebó elese Elegguá?" and "Ebó

elese Ogún?" If both take ebó, Eleggua must be given his first. If Oyá and Shangó are taking ebó in this pattern, Elegguá must have his ebó first, followed by Oyá and Shangó and then Ogún.

If the odu still will not allow closure and the client is an aleyo or an aborisha, the diviner should turn to the eboses of the parent odu, Irosun (see page 210).

If this letter will not close and the client is an initiate, the diviner has one more consideration for ebó: the reception of Dada. The diviner must ask, "Koshé Dada?" If the answer is yes, the client needs an Ósun equal to his own height.

If the odu still will not close, the diviner must now turn to the eboses of the parent odu, Irosun. Something there is needed for this client's evolution.

## The Sixth Composite Odu of Irosun, Irosun Obara (4-6)

### The Proverbs of Irosun Obara

- The explosion of the volcano is your daily life.
- Cats walk on fences; people should not.
- Make up your mind.

### The Message of Irosun Obara

When an initial casting of four mouths, Irosun, is followed by one of six mouths, Obara, the odu Irosun Obara has come. Immediately, the diviner should say, "Maferefún Shangó! Maferefún Babaluaiye!" Both orishas are firm in this sign. Within the patakís of this odu is a story of Babaluaiye's despair:

His grief in life was so great that he lost his memory. He forgot his immortality and walked on the earth among humans, starving and begging for alms. His clothing was torn; it barely covered his emaciated body. As the townspeople taunted him, throwing water behind his back, Shangó rode through town on his white horse. When he saw Babaluaiye his heart was torn with grief for him, and it was filled with anger toward the crowd. He beat them all away and gave the father of the earth his own rich cloak. Babaluaiye's confusion lifted. This gentle kindness brought back his memory.

Since that time, both orishas have championed the causes of the poor. Know that if this client is on the verge of poverty, despair, or vagrancy, Babaluaiye and Shangó both watch over him; they will raise him up. How soon, how fast, and how high depend on the client's actions and the orientation of this odu.

The diviner also pays homage to the Ibeyi, saying, "Maferefún los Ibeyi! Maferefún Taewó and Kaindé!" When Irosun Obara has come to the mat, it signals that the client has issues with the twins that need to be resolved.

Among the lore of this sign is a story about a king whose twin brother died at birth. The king's mother made ebó to her dead son's spirit, as did the king himself when he grew to adulthood. All the king's affairs went well, but when he stopped caring for his dead brother's soul, he eventually lost his own life.

In this odu, the client is marked as having some connection to twins. He could be a twin or the survivor of twins; he could have twin siblings or twins among his ancestors; or he could be destined to have twin children. If nothing else, the client has issues pending with Taewó and Kaindé; they want to bring blessings into his life but will need ebó before they can do this. The diviner should explore this issue before bringing the session to closure.

When Irosun Obara opens on the mat, the first message the diviner should deliver is this: A powerful spirit surrounds the client constantly. In iré, it is trying to help, but much of its help amounts to no more than meddling in the client's personal life. It is not evil, but it is confused, and without the client's prayer and offerings it does not know how to improve his life. The diviner should advise the client to spend more time at his bóveda, giving this spirit fresh water and white candles; he should pray to all his egun and let all of them know what he needs. In this way he will achieve evolution. In osogbo, this spirit is no ally; it is an enemy, and it has been sent to harm him. If the client has a lover or spouse, the diviner should question this relationship. If it is filled with problems, they are caused by this spirit. This malevolent spirit could even try to kill his significant other. Immediately, the client must reinforce his egun with sacrifice and give a series of three masses in their honor. They will remove this spirit.

In addition to all these concerns, the diviner should keep in mind the following points:

- Danger is coming to the client's home; he has been warned of this many times through bad dreams. He should pay attention to the nightmares if he hopes to avoid tragedy. The diviner should tell him that he awakens frequently, small fragments of the dreams barely eluding his waking mind. He will understand.
- Danger can come to this person by three routes: fire, electricity, and accidents. All of these will occur in his home if he is not careful.
- This client, if male, must be careful around women who are involved or married. Issues could arise.
- The client should watch his wallet; it may be stolen.
- If the client is in an established relationship, someone might want to steal his lover away. He must watch for this.

## The Prohibitions of Irosun Obara

- This odu forbids adultery, promiscuity, and random sexual encounters. All of these can cause a loss of money, property, health, and good fortune.
- The danger of fire through this odu is great. Do not leave open sources of flame unattended. Keep electrical appliances that are not in use unplugged.

## The Eboses of Irosun Obara

When the odu Irosun Obara has opened in an osogbo and will not close after the initial larishe has been prescribed, the client must make the following sacrifices to the earth and Orisha Oko: Gather a pumpkin, seven pieces of coconut, epó, seven guinea pepper grains, a candle, a rooster, and several types of grain. Place these items on the ground and dig a large hole in the earth. Hollow out the pumpkin; place seven pieces of coconut smeared with epó inside it. Put a single grain of guinea pepper in the center of each. Light the candle and insert it into the pumpkin. Then place the pumpkin in the hole. The priest cleanses the client with the rooster and sacrifices the animal to the earth. He throws the carcass in the hole, and all sing to Orisha Oko while cleansing themselves with grains. When everyone is done, the priest presiding over the ritual fills in the hole; no one speaks during this work. Now that Orisha Oko and the earth have been fed, neither he nor the earth will feed upon the client's body.

If the client is an initiate, another ebó must be prescribed. The client decorates a red cloth with many cowrie shells; the design should be aesthetically pleasing. This cloth is draped over Shangó's tureen and left there. As soon as possible, this initiate must receive Babaluaiye. When Babaluaiye is brought home, the red cloth is taken from Shangó's sopera and put over Babaluaiye's. It is never removed from him, for it honors the pact that the two orishas have to live together and the promise Shangó made to watch over Babaluaiye always.

Once these things have been explained, the diviner has another chance to close the odu. If it remains open, he must consider the following options; the client could have further issues pending with Shangó, Babaluaiye, and the Ibeyi. To determine if they require anything, the diviner should consider asking, "Ebó elese [orisha's name]?" If the answer is yes, the diviner uses the shells to mark an appropriate offering.

If the odu will not close and the client is an aleyo or aborisha, the diviner must now turn to the eboses of the parent odu, Irosun (see page 210).

If the odu will not close and the client is an initiate, one final consideration remains: the reception of Orisha Oko. To investigate this option, the diviner asks, "Koshé Orisha Oko?" If the answer is yes, the client must receive Orisha Oko before the ebó of feeding the earth.

The diviner now asks again for closure. If he is refused, he must turn to the eboses of the parent odu, Irosun.

## The Seventh Composite Odu of Irosun, Irosun Odí (4-7)

### The Proverbs of Irosun Odí

- All that glitters is not gold.
- Think with the head and not the feet.
- If the head does not sell you, no one can buy you.
- The head moves the feet, but the feet are taking the body to the auction block.

### The Message of Irosun Odí

When four mouths are followed by seven mouths, Irosun Odí is open. Immediately, the italero says, "Maferefún Obatalá! Maferefún Yemayá! Maferefún Olokun!" All three orishas dominate this sign. They offer their protection and have much advice to give to the client. Obatalá is here to say that the client must lean upon him. Spiritually, this person is not clean, and Obatalá wants to cleanse him of all that stands in his way. Olokun herself cares for this person as if he were her own child, and if the client spoils her with frequent adimú, she will not only save him but also lift him up. Finally, none in Irosun Odí protects the client as fiercely as Yemayá. She has watched over this person; she has seen how others try to beat him down as he follows his spiritual path. She tells the client, "Keep doing good so that sorrow will not be known." Irosun Odí signals that Yemayá is mounting to curse those who curse the client and bless those who offer help. Her protection is so strong that if the client has not had a bajado, he might be her child.

With Irosun Odí open on the mat, the diviner can infer that the client's finances lack stability. Money has been tight, and things will only get worse in the next few months. However, if the client lives frugally and works hard, his financial troubles will become a thing of the past. The client has recently acquired the bad habit of lavish spending (lavish compared to what he earns), and the odu mandates that he stop this. The client is forbidden to spend his money on anything but the basic necessities of life. Instead, he must save. No matter how severe financial barriers become, he must not cry in misery; his despair will only make matters worse. He must account for all the blessings the orishas have given and offer thanks. They will, in their own time, provide more.

If Irosun Odí has opened in any osogbo that suggests malicious witchcraft or cursing, such as araye, ogo, or epe, the initial larishe prescribed by the letter is essential to dispelling the sorcery. This larishe should be the first ebó done by the client. If no larishe was prescribed, it is up to the diviner to help the client fight the sorcery by prescribing *trabajos* (works) that will help cleanse the witchcraft. This odu signals that a woman whose complexion is darker than the client's sent the initial energies of the curse. The curse is bringing small accidents to the client's life, but in time these small incidents will become great. The client should be cautious when away from home. For now, going out after dark is not wise, nor is announcing his itinerary. After the odu is closed, the diviner might wish to instruct the client on ways in which witchcraft can be fought.

The diviner might also wish to explain to the client the following points:

- This person has a very close friend with whom he spends a lot of time. Both are marked for a small series of tragedies when this odu opens. This friend should be brought for a session with the diloggún. For a couple of weeks, these two should spend less time together. If the osogbo of the odu is severe, both should have a rogación at the feet of Obatalá; they could be marked for accidental death, and only Obatalá can save them.
- When the client is sad, he should smile, even though it hurts. This will bring a blessing to his life.
- The diviner should advise the client to think with his head rather than his feet, for only thus can he avoid traps and treason.
- Blessings predicted in Irosun Odí usually center on children. The client must be respectful of youth, never allowing a child to be hurt (emotionally or physically) in his home. This pattern foreshadows that the client will raise a child who is not his own. This child is a special gift from

Yemayá. She raised many children that were not her own, yet loved them as if they were.

- For young women, Irosun Odí forebodes the death of a child.

## The Prohibitions of Irosun Odí

- Do not cry or beg for money; instead, be thankful for what one has and work hard.
- Do not step over hoses.
- Do not jump over fences, look through fences, or speak through fences. In all cases, walk to the other side.
- When going away, do not announce one's travel plans to others.
- Never loiter in the streets; keep moving.

## The Eboses of Irosun Odí

When the oracle has opened in this odu, the diviner should try to close it after he has prescribed the initial eboses and larishe of Irosun. If this proves fruitless, three orishas could be standing up for ebó: Obatalá, Yemayá, and Olokun. To determine if any of these three requires ebó, the diviner should ask, "Ebó elese [orisha's name]?" If the answer is yes for Yemayá or Obatalá, in this odu the proper ebó is a rogación before their shrines. After the rogación is complete, the client should offer the orisha an adimú of sweet, cool fruits. If Olokun stands up in this odu for ebó, the client should give the ebó to both him and Elegguá. The proper ebó in this case is ten balls formed from gofio and dark molasses and drizzled with sweet honey. The client should give three balls to Elegguá and seven to Olokun. They remain with the orishas for three days. At the end of this time, the client should take Elegguá's ebó to a crossroads and Olokun's to a large body of water. (The ocean is the best choice, but those who are landlocked must choose the largest they can find.)

If sickness has been foretold in this odu, the client should have a rogacion of not only his head but also his entire abdominal region before the shrine of Yemayá.

Now the diviner may ask the oracle again for closure. If it remains open, he should turn to the eboses of the parent odu, Irosun (see page 210). Something there is needed for the client's evolution.

# The Eighth Composite Odu of Irosun, Irosun Ogbe (4-8)

## The Proverbs of Irosun Ogbe

- The one born for the head must not be left in the tail.
- A king dies, and a king is born.
- You were born to be the head but chose to stay in the tail.

## The Message of Irosun Ogbe

When the first casting of four mouths, Irosun, is followed by one of eight mouths, Eji Ogbe, the odu Irosun Ogbe has come to the house. This sign is also known as Irosun Unle, Irosun Umbo, and Irosun l'Ogbe. This sign gave birth to the custom of taking a iyawó to the river before initiation; it is said that Oshún, in her form as a vulture, flies to heaven to tell Olódumare what is about to be done.

The diviner opens by saying, "Maferefún Oshún! Maferefún Elegguá! Maferefún Orúnmila! Maferefún Olokun! Maferefún Ósun!" All of these orishas stand up in this sign, and before the letter has closed many will speak or claim ebó. If the client is a priest or priestess, the diviner also says, "Maferefún Ajé Shaluga!"

When this pattern opens on the mat, the diviner may not charge the client for the reading or for the larishe. If the client cannot afford the derechos for the eboses of this odu, the diviner may not charge for those either.

When Irosun Ogbe opens, the diviner has a lot of general advice to deliver to the client. First, the eboses prescribed must be done in a timely manner, for they are marked here to help the client avoid the defamation and ungratefulness that accompany this sign. Irosun Ogbe brings sickness to the client and the client's family; it also marks traps, treason, and despair. If the sign has come in a severe osogbo, it brings disappointments, disillusionment, restlessness, hypocrisy, gossip, and envy; these energies may be just beginning now, but as time goes by they will strengthen. The eboses will calm and balance the energies of this odu so the client may avoid needless suffering.

Elegguá speaks strongly in this sign, especially if it is his diloggún that has been consulted. When an aborisha opens in Irosun Ogbe, Elegguá may pronounce that he needs to make ocha. In this sign, it is not uncommon for an "Irosun Umbo santo"—an asiento done for free—to be marked. In this situation the one who comes to the mat needs santo desperately; the orishas love him, but they know that he cannot afford the full expenses of initiation. They also remember all the blessings and love that they have poured out upon this ilé ocha, and the Irosun Umbo santo is both a test and a payback. If the santo is marked in Irosun Ogbe, the head of the client is in debt to his elders; he must give them all his loyalty and love.

Elegguá says that the client has issues with his siblings of either blood or ocha; a fight will come soon. The orisha forbids the client to fight with his brother. Always, they must come together as friends. The sign warns of robberies, and Elegguá hints that the thief could be the client's own flesh and blood. The client must take steps to protect his possessions. Elegguá also advises the client of the following four things: First, a woman is very jealous of the client. She will cause him much harm. The client should be wary of all vices for now, for she will use them against him. Second, if a large sum of money is due, even an inheritance, the client must make ebó to Elegguá so that the money is not lost or stolen. Third, Elegguá says that the client's abdomen, head, and pelvic regions could suffer from ulcerations; he should be aware of physiological changes in those areas. Finally, Elegguá advises that the client maintain calmness and peace in all things.

In addition, the diviner should consider the following points:

- The client should remove anything black from his home, for black absorbs all light, leaving darkness; it will bring more negativity into the client's life.
- This pattern enforces the need for cooperation. The client needs unity in his life; he must treat others with respect and avoid wars, fights, and struggles.
- The client must learn to avoid discrimination but to be discriminating in all things.
- Irosun Ogbe tells the diviner that many are coming to his own ilé ocha seeking various levels of initiation. The diviner must be selective about whom he initiates; the orishas are testing him. While we often say that this is a rich man's religion on a poor man's salary, no matter how desperate he is, the diviner is being warned to measure his godchildren by their hearts and not their wallets.
- If the sign brings ano or ikú for the client, he must be on guard against the following health problems: diabetes, ocular deterioration, renal dysfunction, parasites, and cardiovascular disease.

## The Prohibitions of Irosun Ogbe

- To soothe this odu, one must promote calm and clarity in his life. Do not argue, fight, or raise one's voice to others.
- One's neighbors are nosy. They may come to make friends, but their intentions are not good. Do not mingle with one's neighbors.
- Irosun Ogbe prohibits bathing or swimming in the ocean. Also, do not jump or cross over holes, ditches, creeks, or rivers.
- Food taboos now include pigeon, dove, and sheep (mutton).

## The Eboses of Irosun Ogbe

The diviner must remember that when Irosun Ogbe opens on the mat, before he attempts to mark iré or osogbo, he must return the derecho the client has given him for the reading. Once this is done, the odu tests the diviner further: He must tell the client that he will perform any larishe prescribed or ebó marked for free. And if the client cannot afford the materials for the ebó, the diviner's ilé ocha will provide what is necessary.

Now the diviner should ask the oracle for closure. If he is refused, he must explore several options:

- The next question the diviner asks the oracle should be "Ebó elese eledá?" If the answer is yes, he must prescribe a rogación for the client at the feet of Obatalá before he leaves the diviner's home.
- If the odu still will not close, the client may also need to feed his orí. The diviner asks, "Eborí?" If the answer is yes, the day after the rogación the client should return to the diviner's house with two white doves or white pigeons. The diviner uses these offerings to feed his orí and gives his head a rogación before Obatalá.
- If the oracle still refuses closure, the diviner should consider asking, "Ebó elese Elegguá y Obatalá?" If the answer is yes, the diviner uses the diloggún to mark an appropriate ebó. Elegguá is brought to Obatalá's shrine, and the ebó is offered there.

If at this point the oracle still will not close, the diviner should turn to the eboses of the parent odu, Irosun (see page 210).

If even the eboses of Irosun are not enough to close the odu, the diviner must ask, "Koshé ocha?" ("Should ocha be received?") If the answer is yes, the diviner must drape Obatalá's mazo over the client and direct him to salute Obatalá, the diviner, and the godparents. An asiento is prescribed, and it must be performed as an Irosun Umbo santo; in other words, the diviner's ilé ocha must perform the ceremony for free. (The client is expected to pay as much as he can for the expenses: the room, the herbs, the animals, the clothes, and the food. The ilé, however, must work for free, and what the client absolutely cannot provide, they must. )

With this prescription, the odu is now closed.

## The Ninth Composite Odu of Irosun, Irosun Osá (4-9)

### The Proverbs of Irosun Osá

- [There will be] treason among friends.
- Watch where you walk.
- Look forward and look backward.
- Take care where you walk.

### The Message of Irosun Osá

When the initial casting of four mouths, Irosun, is followed by a casting of nine mouths, Osá, the odu Irosun Osá is open. In this sign, the first orisha to be honored is Obatalá, in his incarnation as Ochanlá; the diviner should say, "Maferefún Obatalá! Maferefún Ochanlá!" Irosun Osá is a hot letter. Even in iré, it can wreak havoc in the client's life. Obatalá, however, is the essence of all things pure and cool, and if the client follows all that Obatalá says, he will emerge unscathed. When things are at their worst, the client must turn to Obatalá for peace and closure. The orisha says that the client must be patient and think calmly, for while his life can be bad, it cannot stay bad forever. Obatalá warns of tragedies, deceit, gossip, and false friends. Amid all this, he tells the client to stay true to himself and his ideals. When confusion comes, and it will, the client should return to the diviner or his godparents for a rogación of the head at Obatalá's feet; with this cleansing, clarity will return.

Oyá is the next orisha to be honored; the diviner should say, "Maferefún Oyá!" While Obatalá in this sign promotes peace, Oyá is here to tell the client how he may avert tragedy. This person's home is neither neat nor clean, and Oyá says this mess is offensive. If he will not clean his home for himself, he should clean it for her. In the end, this person's safety could depend on it. Fire is a danger in this odu; as soon as he gets home, the client should inspect his home with this in mind. He must not leave open flames unattended, especially at night in his bedroom. If electrical appliances are not in use, he should unplug them, and he should examine the cords of all appliances to make sure they are not frayed. Oyá says that even if this odu comes in an iré, illness is marked on both the client and his family. Irosun Osá forebodes death from disease. Oyá might mark death on the first who falls ill in the client's family after the letter falls, so the client should make ebó quickly, and when sickness occurs, the afflicted one must seek medical attention.

The diviner also celebrates Shangó and Oshún in this odu, saying to each, "Maferefún!" Shangó comes here as a fierce warrior to fight all those who try to harm the client. Although this is a hard odu, Oshún is sweet toward the client. Both orishas tell the client it is time for him to work hard and settle his affairs; he must wander aimlessly no more but must focus on very specific goals that he hopes to achieve. The client should spoil both orishas when this pattern opens. As soon as possible, he should make *chekete* and, placing Shangó and Oshún side by side, serve it to them together, praying for what is in the heart; they will hear, and answer. The client must make an additional ebó to Shangó. His sacred stone is the thunderstone, and over the next year the client must give him six large ones. It is said that lightning never strikes twice, and since thunderstones are made by lightning strikes, once the client gives these six to Shangó he will settle his affairs and wars. He must also be certain to bring sweetness and beauty to Oshún, giving her honey and satin pañuelos made in her colors. With these eboses, she will bring beauty back to the client's life.

In addition, the diviner should explore with the client the following:

- This client is the center of attention; his own friends could cause him setbacks.
- Here, we say that one's enemy is close, so close that it could be one's own neighbor. The client should be wary of prying eyes.
- If the diviner is reading for an initiate, even if the intitiate is his own godchild, he should know that the client knows more about the religion than he does. The reason for this person's greater knowledge should be a concern for the godparent.
- When Irosun Osá opens on the mat, it indicates that now is the perfect time for the client to learn a new skill or trade. If possible, the client should go back to school, earning a vocational certificate or even a degree.
- While this pattern can bring a lot of tragedy at its onset, as it passes it can bring a lot of iré. Love and relationships will be renewed; things that were thought lost will be found.

## The Prohibitions of Irosun Osá

- In Irosun Osá, if one is an orisha priest, do not leave one's soperas unguarded. If others from this religion visit one's home, watch them. Lock the shells in a safe place, perhaps even a bank vault. One should not keep money with one's soperas.
- Open fires are taboo in one's home, as are dirt and clutter.

## The Eboses of Irosun Osá

This is an intense odu, especially for aleyos and aborishas. When it opens in any type of osogbo, it marks many eboses for the client. First, he should receive the Ibeyi and Olokun; it is not essential that he receive them immediately, but until he has them he will not evolve very far in life. This odu foreshadows the need for initiation, and eventually this client will have to make ocha. Also, if the client's crowning orisha is not known, he should have a bajado soon.

Once these issues have been discussed, the diviner may ask the oracle for closure. If it will not close, he must explore the following issues:

- Obatalá, Oyá, Shangó, Oshún, and egun could be standing up for ebó. To determine if any will claim an offering, the diviner must ask, "Ebó elese [spirit's name]?" If the answer is yes, he uses the shells to mark the required offering.
- Shangó and Oyá could be demanding ebó together, as could Shangó and Oshún. To determine if an offering to either pair is necessary, the diviner should consider asking, "Ebó elese Oyá y Shangó?" and "Ebó elese Shangó y Oshún?" If the answer is yes, he uses the shells to mark the offering.

- If none of these options is enough to close the odu, Elegguá might need ebó alongside Obatalá, Shangó, Oyá, or Oshún. The diviner may check this by asking, "Ebó elese Elegguá y [orisha's name]?" If the answer is yes, the diviner will use the diloggún to mark the appropriate ebó.

If the odu still will not close, the diviner must consult the options given for the parent odu, Irosun (see page 210).

## The Tenth Composite Odu of Irosun, Irosun Ofún (4-10)

### The Proverbs of Irosun Ofún

- No one listens to a blabbermouth.
- The arrow of disobedience strikes one's mother.

### The Message of Irosun Ofún

When the initial cast of four mouths, Irosun, is followed by one of ten mouths, Ofún, the odu Irosun Ofún is open. In this sign the diviner says, "Maferefún Ochanlá! Maferefún Obatalá!"

Among this odu's patakís is the story of a time when the forests were scarce of animals. Ochosi, the most skilled hunter of all the spirits, had overtracked and overkilled his game. Obatalá forbade Ochosi to hunt, but Ochosi so loved his sport that he was disobedient. By accident, he shot his own mother with an arrow when he returned to the forest.

The diviner pays homage to Ochosi, saying, "Maferefún Ochosi!" For while his disobedience cost his mother her life, Ochosi comes here to teach the client about the virtues of obedience so he does not suffer a similar fate. The diviner also pays homage to Oyá, saying, "Maferefún Oyá!" Of all the orishas, few know as well as she the meaning of true loneliness, and it is she who keeps the client company on his journey. Note that Irosun Ofún gives birth to loneliness, and in time the client could find himself abandoned by all his friends. Last, the diviner pays homage to Babaluaiye, saying, "Maferefún Babaluaiye!" This sign gives birth to initiation into Babaluaiye's cult, and the opening of this sign marks the client as destined to become a Lazarero (initiate to the cult of Babaluaiye).

Because Irosun Ofún has opened on the mat, the diviner knows that the client suffers silently, and much of his suffering is due to his loneliness. He is separated from those he loves, and if this odu comes in osogbo, the client's separation brings deep spiritual darkness. The diviner must investigate this person's family, especially his relationship with his mother and the women of his family; if nothing else, he must tell him to forgive his mother, because she will never change. This odu tells the diviner that the client's mother has suffered herself because of this person's past errors, and she now deserves all the love this client can give her.

The diviner also knows that the client's own nature drives away people in his life. No one likes a blabbermouth, and this odu says the client is this. The italero must tell the client to refrain from talking too much, because his constant talking keeps true companionship at bay. Remind him that listening is a passive, absorptive skill, and by taking in the words of others he will draw others closer. Yet he must also be selective about those to whom he listens. Irosun Ofún is a mysterious odu that hides more than it reveals; it brings traps, treason, and deception. The client must listen, yes, but he should trust no one implicitly until that person's true intentions are known. In time, the client's circle of friends and acquaintances will grow.

The diviner must be careful when delivering the advice of this sign. Irosun Ofún guarantees that the client will think the italero is lying for personal gain when ebó is prescribed. Perhaps the best advice to give here is this: "You have many personal issues. Resolve these before the orishas will speak on anything. Give the sacrifices and offerings that must be given; only then will you evolve." Although this odu says the client may not complete his eboses, he must be invited to return for another reading once they are completed.

In addition, the diviner should keep the following in mind:

- The client is destined for jail. Although the time he spends incarcerated will be short, he will experience fighting within prison walls. He has only one way to avoid this: making ebó.

- When ano or ikú comes in Irosun Ofún, it marks severe health warnings. Even though this person thinks himself to be in perfect health, his body is delicate, and he must keep this in mind. The client could have an abdominal disease that may result in an operation. His head and skin are delicate, and cancer is a concern in these areas.
- Metal has scarred or will scar this person's body.
- The client has a birthmark or mole that should be removed. If it is not removed, one day it will cause problems.

## The Prohibitions of Irosun Ofún

- For twenty-one days, the aleyo or aborisha must dress in white. If social situations require more formal dress codes, avoid wearing black. Wear the lightest colors possible.
- Be very careful around children, especially the children of others. Unfair accusations might be raised.
- Respect all the foods of Obatalá, especially milk, white bread, and eggs. A priest or priestess must avoid these foods altogether.
- Limit the consumption of dark liquids.

## The Eboses of Irosun Ofún

When Irosun Ofún opens on the mat, the reception of Babaluaiye is mandatory. Because this reception will take some time to prepare for, the client must immediately have a rogación at Babaluaiye's feet. Once he is cleansed, he should be given Babaluaiye's eleke.

Another ebó is mandatory if the client has a dog. The diviner or any other initiate present at the mat who has a dog must do this ebó as well. Attach a short chain to the dog's collar and take him out into the street. There, let the dog loose and walk back to one's home alone. Leave the front door open. When the animal returns on his own, the luck that has left will return as well.

The diviner should now ask the oracle for closure. If the pattern will not close, Obatalá, Oyá, Ochosi, or Babaluaiye might need ebó. To see if this is necessarsy, the diviner must ask, "Ebó elese [orisha's name]?" If the answer is yes, he uses the diloggún to mark the ebó.

If the eboses prescribed thus far are still not enough to close the odu, the diviner should turn to the eboses of the parent odu, Irosun (see page 210). Something there is needed for the client's evolution.

# The Eleventh Composite Odu of Irosun, Irosun Owani (4-11)

## The Proverbs of Irosun Owani

- White is beautiful; wear it more often.
- One foot stands in the house and the other stands in the grave.

## The Message of Irosun Owani

When an initial casting of four mouths is followed by one of eleven mouths, the odu Irosun Owani has come to the mat. In this sign, the diviner says, "Maferefún Obatalá! Maferefún Yewá! Maferefún Oshún! Maferefún Shangó!" All of these spirits stand up here. This pattern is harsh, and even in iré it will bring out all the worst of Irosun. It marks illness upon either the client or someone in his family; we say that one foot stands firmly on solid ground, yet one foot is firmly in the grave. The client should watch his step lest both feet land on the wrong side. With this sign open, the diviner knows that the client's spirit is strong; if he listens to the advice of the reading and makes ebó, things will come out well. The young children and elderly adults around him, however, are not strong. If one of them falls ill, he or she should be taken to a physician immediately.

In addition, the diviner must explore the following points:

- This letter marks death, and the client must guard his safety and health at all times.
- The client should be careful when drinking fluids, especially water. This sign indicates a danger of choking and of pneumonia brought by aspiration.

- The client must be very wary of pains that come in the abdomen; if such pains occur, he must have a physical and return to the diviner to make ebó.
- The client should not cry in misery over money; finances will begin to settle as this odu does the same.

### The Prohibitions of Irosun Owani

- Do not gargle. Do not suck the meat off bones. Do not eat quickly or while standing up; instead, sit down and chew slowly.
- Except for making ebó, one must not go to the cemetery. When making ebó at a cemetery, do not go in alone; be accompanied by a priest or priestess.
- Do not wear black or dark colors.

### The Eboses of Irosun Owani

When Irosun Owani has opened on the mat in an osogbo, the client has many considerations for ebó. To begin, as ebó he must wear white for twenty-one days. If his job demands a specific dress code, he should wear the lightest colors possible. He must also pray to Obatalá for salvation daily; if the osogbo is severe, he should have a rogación before Obatalá immediately. If sickness comes to the client or to someone in the house, the diviner must wash a silver idé in Obatalá's omiero and put it on the client's wrist; he must never remove it.

After these prescriptions have been made, the diviner should ask the oracle for closure. If he is refused, he must consider the following:

- Elegguá and Yewá may require ebó. The diviner should ask, "Ebó elese Elegguá?" and "Ebó elese Yewá?" If either orisha claims ebó, the proper offering is a dish of baked red snapper garnished with tomato and gofio. If both take ebó, the eboses should be prepared together and Elegguá given his portion first. If neither the diviner nor the godparent has received Yewá, this ebó may be made to Yewá on a grave in the cemetery. The diviner must then receive Yewá. Also, if this client is an initiate, after making ebó he should make preparations to receive Yewá as well.
- If the oracle still will not close, the final options for ebó in this sign center on Oshún, Shangó, and Babaluaiye. The diviner must ask, "Ebó elese [orisha's name]?" If the answer is yes, the diviner will use the diloggún to mark the ebó required.

If these eboses are not enough to close the odu, the diviner must consider the eboses of the parent odu, Irosun (see page 210). Something there is needed for this client's evolution.

## The Twelfth Composite Odu of Irosun, Irosun Ejila (4-12)

### The Proverb of Irosun Ejila

- The hen was born to have chicks.

### The Message of Irosun Ejila

When a casting of four mouths, Irosun, is followed by one of twelve mouths, Ejila Shebora, the odu Irosun Ejila, also known as Irosun Oturupon, has opened on the mat. In osogbo, this odu predicts many misfortunes: traps, treason, hypocrisy, envy, and deception. Irosun Ejila warns that none of these is of the client's doing; they are sent by another through a deliberate or unconscious curse, and the ebó of the clay vessel (see "The Eboses of Irosun Ejila," on page 205) will clear these volatile energies.

Irosun Ejila signals that much of the sorrow in the client's life is caused by loneliness and lack of children. If the client is married, birth control should not be used until another child is born, for a spirit that wants to come through as a baby is standing close. The orishas and Olódumare have decreed the birth of this child, and it is in the client's destiny. Until the child is allowed birth, the client's life will remain empty and unfulfilled. If the client is single, the diviner should advise him that children are marked for the future, and he must not try to avoid this eventuality. Abortion of the client's next conceived child will not be tolerated; it will anger the orishas, especially Oshún.

## The Prohibitions of Irosun Ejila

- Do not become involved in any illegal or immoral schemes presented by a sibling of blood or of ocha. Shangó promises that all these will end in failure.
- One has bad intentions for another person; these plans must not be carried out. Harbor no jealousy or evil thoughts. Shangó stands up in this letter to offer his protection, and the evil that others do or have done should be left at his feet.
- Do not arouse any hot emotion in another person; be careful with the heart and to whom it is given. Mak ship, or fe feelings are arouses stro and disaster.
- Do not carr of weapons. for either w from these p
- Do not allov aborted.

## The Eboses of

The diviner shoul he has marked th ations for ebó in Ir the diviner should magic may be at w ebó will clear these

The client shou water and take it j must then allow it t ing on the ground. V allowed to evaporat sweep up the clay s the trash. The broo ... clear these pieces must also be thrown away. After this, the door must be refreshed with a libation of cool water given to Olódumare every day.

If the ebó of the clay pot will not close the sign and the client is an aleyo or an aborisha, the diviner should turn to the eboses of the parent odu, Irosun (see page 210). Something there is needed for this person's evolution.

If the client is a priest or a priestess, the diviner has one more consideration for ebó. This client might need Dada and an Ósun equal to his own height. To determine if this is the case, the diviner asks, "Koshé Dada?" If the answer is yes, then preparations should be made for the ceremony as soon as possible.

If the odu still remains open, the diviner must consider the eboses of the parent odu, Irosun.

# Composite Odu of Metanla (4-13)

## osun Metanla

lowly, but still he will reach

vly; yet it always catches up. the plants will not produce.

## sun Metanla

nouths is followed by one of a, the odu Irosun Metanla, te, has opened on the mat. efun Babaluaiye!" The ori- rn the client that sickness ust mark an ebó to him. If it adopting a new dog as a luaiye first, because dogs ient already has a dog, he for the reception of this ives with the client, the for to honor this animal

This odu signals that the client has some debt to Babaluaiye, and the diviner must explore this issue. Even if the client is not in the religion, perhaps at some time he made a deal with "God" to cure an illness in himself, someone in the family, or someone to whom he was close. Now, from the client sitting before the shells with an unpaid debt to "God," Babaluaiye claims the payment of that debt as his own, for all the orishas are a part of God.

The odu also indicates that past moral and legal indiscretions the client has committed are catching up. He thought that he had left these indiscretions behind, but until his karmic and legal debts have been paid, they will not disappear into the past. Also, in this letter the diviner must advise the client that he moves too quickly in life, exhausting himself. He must slow down or his health will suffer. Slow movement equals careful movement, and in the end diligent work will still help him attain his goals. The client has many unfulfilled emotional and physical needs, and they will be realized only if the eboses of this letter are done.

In addition, the diviner should keep in mind the following points:

- If the letter comes in firm iré, it promises that an unexpected amount of money will soon come the client's way.
- In osogbo, the odu brings disappointment, hypocrisy, envy, and gossip.
- The client should not go to the ocean until the energy of this odu has passed; there is danger there.
- Someone in the client's home or family might need to go see a babalawo for a reading; Orúnmila has much to say to that person.

### The Prohibitions of Irosun Metanla

- The prohibition against weapons is strong in this odu. Do not carry clubs, guns, knives, or anything else that can be used as a weapon.
- Having two or more lovers at the same time is now taboo. Keep only one lover at a time.
- In this odu, one severe prohibition is mandated: Do not go out into the street for four days. There is danger outdoors, and one should stay at home instead. If going out is unavoidable, do not go out alone, especially after dark.
- Do not indulge in alcohol or other intoxicants; one should be in full possession of one's faculties at all times.

### The Eboses of Irosun Metanla

Before the diviner attempts to close the odu, he must inform the client that the following eboses are necessary:

- The client must take the initiations of the elekes and the warriors and should then begin preparing for ocha.
- If the client's guardian orisha is not known, it must soon be determined.
- If this client is a priest or a priestess, he or she must receive Dada and an Ósun equal to his own height.

Once these eboses are recorded, the diviner may try to close the oracle. If it will not close, he should consider that Babaluaiye figures prominently in this odu, and the client may need to receive his eleke as ebó. The diviner should ask, "Ebó eleke de Babaluaiye?" If the answer is yes, the client is marked to receive the eleke of Babaluaiye. If the answer is no, or if the oracle still will not close, the diviner should determine if Babaluaiye requires ebó, asking, "Ebó elese Babaluaiye?" If the answer is yes, the diviner should use the shells to mark the appropriate offering. If the oracle still will not close, the client may need to receive Babaluaiye; the diviner should ask, "Koshé Babaluaiye?" If the answer is yes, the reception ceremony should be done as soon as possible.

If none of these eboses will close the odu, the diviner should consider the eboses of the parent odu, Irosun (see page 210). Something there is needed for the client's evolution.

## The Fourteenth Composite Odu of Irosun, Irosun Merinla (4-14)

### The Proverb of Irosun Merinla

- No one but Olokun and Olorún knows what lies at the bottom of the sea.

## The Message of Irosun Merinla

When the initial cast of four mouths, Irosun, precedes a cast of fourteen mouths, Merinla, the odu Irosun Merinla, also known as Irosun Ika, is open on the mat. Through this letter Oshún brought money, riches, and happiness to the world; if the client's reading falls in firm iré, she is bringing these blessings slowly to the client's life. If he follows all the advice of Irosun, he will soon receive an unexpected amount of money. The diviner might want to mark a token ebó to Oshún to ensure her favor. And the client would be wise to spend time during the day praying to her, saying "Maferefún Oshún" once upon awakening and once before going to bed at night; indeed, he should recite this as if it were a mantra many times throughout the day. The client should also visit the river often, for this is where he will find strength.

Whenever the letter falls in osogbo, the client is pining for riches, children, and all the wonderful things that life has to offer; and although the letter itself might offer a larishe, one of the eboses given for this odu should be done to ensure that the client's many dreams and desires become reality.

## The Prohibition of Irosun Merinla

- This letter enforces fidelity to one's spouse. Divorce is now taboo. If one has been considering divorce, reconsider, and stay in the relationship for at least another three months. Let one's spouse instigate divorce if he or she wants to leave. If this reading is an itá, one must choose one's mate wisely, for divorce is now taboo for life.

## The Eboses of Irosun Merinla

If this letter marks any type of osogbo, several eboses are automatically marked for the client, and they must be done as soon as possible:

- Both the elekes and the warriors are needed in this odu; the client must receive them as soon as possible. The elekes of the orishas who have stood up in this reading should be given as well.
- If the client is childless yet wants a child, in this odu the following ebó will help: Fill a large basket with black-eyed peas and leave this in the home for five days. On the morning of the sixth day, take them to the river with prayers for Oshún.
- If the client wants wealth and love, in this odu the following ebó will help: Give the Ibeyi a party, inviting as many children as possible. The divine twins love to be surrounded by laughing children, so serve sweet foods and provide a piñata and other games. Throw money and coins to the children if one desires riches, and serve as many candies and pastries as possible if one desires love. Let the children do whatever they want, and do not yell at them or discipline them while the party is being celebrated.

Now the diviner has his first chance to attempt to close the odu. If it will not close, the client may have issues with Oshún; she may require ebó in order to bring some of the riches and wealth born to the world in this letter to the client's life. The diviner must ask "Ebó elese Oshún?" If the answer is yes, he uses the shells to mark the offering.

If these prescriptions are not enough to close the odu, the diviner must turn to the eboses of the parent odu, Irosun (see page 210). Something there is necessary for the client's evolution.

Once the reading has been closed, the diviner must direct the client to salute Obatalá, saying, "Maferefún Obatalá!" He should repeat this phrase daily, saying it once upon awakening, once upon retiring, and several times throughout the day. He should keep up this spiritual practice for the rest of his life.

# The Fifteenth Composite Odu of Irosun, Irosun Marunla (4-15)

## The Proverbs of Irosun Marunla

- Do not take what is not yours.
- Only Olokun and Olorún know what lies at the bottom of the ocean.
- They give you food and drink, yet you speak evil of that given freely.

## The Message of Irosun Marunla

When a casting of four mouths, Irosun, is followed by one of fifteen mouths, Marunla, the odu Irosun Marunla has opened on the mat. This odu is also known as Irosun Iwori. With this odu open on the mat, the diviner should tell the client that he is ungrateful for the many blessings and offerings that others have given him, including those brought by the orishas and God. He must cease his ungratefulness now, or all good in life will be withdrawn. He should never take anything that is not his, nor should he accept things without giving something in return, even if that something is no more than a humble "thank you."

## The Prohibitions of Irosun Marunla

- Do not hold or organize meetings. Do not belong to clubs of any kind.
- Do not be outside in the rain. If it begins to rain while one is out, go home or take shelter. Avoiding the rain will ensure one's peace and prosperity.

## The Eboses of Irosun Marunla

Before the diviner asks the oracle for closure, he must explain to the client that he is close to death by disease or accident. In this odu, however, an ebó to Yewá can save him. He must bake a red snapper with tomato and gofio, adding to it nine sweet balls of gofio and nine slices of tomato. He should then take this dish to the cemetery, asking Yewá to have mercy and offer her protection.

The diviner should then ask the letter for closure. If he is refused, he should ask, "Ebó elese Yewá?" If the answer is yes, the diviner must use the diloggún to mark ebó to her.

If the odu still will not close and the client is an aleyo or an aborisha, the diviner should turn to the eboses of the parent odu, Irosun (see page 210). Something there is needed for the client's evolution.

If the letter will not close and the client is an initiate, the reception of Yewá may be necessary. As a last resort, the diviner should ask "Koshé Yewá?" If the answer is yes, the client should be given Yewá's eleke immediately so that he is under her protection until the ritual can be done.

If this odu continues to remain open, the diviner must turn to the eboses of the parent odu, Irosun (see page 210).

# The Sixteenth Composite Odu of Irosun, Irosun Merindilogún (4-16)

## The Proverbs of Irosun Merindilogún

- Do not do that which you know not how to do.
- A single link of chain does not break.
- A chain is only as strong as its weakest link.

## The Message of Irosun Merindilogún

When an initial casting of four mouths, Irosun, is followed by one of sixteen mouths, Merindilogún, the odu Irosun Merindilogún, also known as Irosun Otura, has opened on the mat. This odu is very powerful and greatly influenced by its orientation of iré or osogbo. The diviner must proceed carefully and cautiously when giving this reading so that he does not miss any point important to the client's evolution.

Although Orúnmila cannot speak directly in the diloggún, the italero begins this session by paying homage to him, saying, "Maferefún Orúnmila!" He tells the client that he must go to Ifá for a consultation soon; he has issues with the babalawos that can be resolved only at Orúnmila's feet. The diviner also pays homage to Ogún and Oshún, saying to each, "Maferefún!" These two orishas offer the client their help and support during the trials and tribulations that lie ahead. Before this odu has closed, they may claim ebó.

The diviner must also explore each of the following issues:

- One's words have power in this odu. The client would do better to speak one sincere word of kindness to someone who suffers than to speak a thousand empty, meaningless words of support. Those who suffer do not need to hear about the client's trials and do not want to hear him say, "Cheer up! Things will get better!" When there is no reason to be happy, one cannot be happy. Instead, when those around the client are suffering, he should let them know that he is there and gently help them focus on the good that exists in their lives.

- Those who are closest to this client are those who think the worst about him. They are filled with envy and jealousy, and they want to harm him in any way possible. He should not enter into arguments or even altercations with his friends, for disputes will only make matters worse. He must be aware that this problem exists and take steps to prevent further issues.
- The abdominal region could become a source of discomfort or disease; the client should monitor that area for symptoms. If any irregularities are present, the diviner should attempt to mark ebó by asking, "Larish si?" If the answer is yes, the diviner uses the diloggún to mark the appropriate offering. The client should also see a physician for treatment.

## The Prohibitions of Irosun Merindilogún

- Do not consume grains, grainy foods, or any food containing animal heads or intestines, especially sausages. These bring sickness to the client.
- Choking is a danger. If meat is served on the bone, cut the meat off the bone before eating. Do not gnaw or suck on the bone.
- Have no source of open flame in the home. Unplug all nonessential appliances when they are not in use.

## The Eboses of Irosun Merindilogún

The diviner should attempt to close the oracle after the larishe and the initial eboses for Irosun have been marked. If the oracle refuses closure and the client has both the elekes and the warriors, he should make a special ebó for Ogún: Purchase a length of chain equal to the client's height plus two additional links. Separate one link from this length of chain by cutting the second-to-last link on the chain; discard the cut link and retain the single separated link. Wash both the chain and the single link in Ogún's omiero. After this consecration, feed them, together with Ogún, a single rooster and one pigeon. Then put the length of chain in Ogún's cauldron. The client should carry the single link of chain with him at all times. Remember the proverb "A single link of chain does not break." This ebó will solve most of the osogbos brought by Irosun Merindilogún.

If the osogbo is severe, wash a chunk of iron ore for Ogún as well, and feed it and Ogún's stone a rooster. Then place the rock inside Ogún.

If these eboses will not close the odu, or if the client is an aleyo who has neither warriors nor elekes, the diviner should investigate the following possibilities:

- The elekes of one or more orishas speaking in this odu could be necessary for protection. To determine if this is necessary, the diviner should ask, "Ebó eleke de [orisha's name]?" After marking an eleke, the diviner should explain to the client why this spirit is offering his or her protection in this odu (using his own aché to deliver this information). After explaining the relevant material to the client, the diviner should attempt closure. Note that more than one orisha could stand up in this odu to offer protection through his or her eleke.
- If the oracle still will not close, those spirits who offered protection through their elekes might also be standing up for ebó. Each spirit who has marked his or her eleke as larishe in this odu must be asked, "Ebó elese [orisha's name]?" If any stand up for ebó, the diviner should use the diloggún to mark the appropriate sacrifices.
- Ogún and Oshún might be standing up for ebó together. The diviner should ask, "Ebó elese Ogún y Oshún?" If the answer is yes, the diviner should use the diloggún to mark an appropriate offering. This ebó should be given to both at the same time, with Ogún set at Oshún's feet.
- If the osogbo is severe and the odu remains open, Elegguá may be demanding itá to solve all this client's issues. The diviner should ask, "Itá

elese Elegguá?" If the answer is yes, arrangements for an oriaté to sacrifice four legs (a goat) must be made, and itá is given the day after the sacrifice.

If all these options have been explored and the oracle continues to refuse closure, the diviner should turn to the eboses of the parent odu, Irosun (see page 210). Something there is needed for this client's evolution.

If nothing else can bring this sign to closure, the client has issues with Ifá. A trusted babalawo should be sought out as soon as possible to assess this client's spiritual issues.

## Closing the Reading: Further Eboses of the Parent Odu, Irosun

Having exhausted the options for larishe and ebó in the composite odu, the diviner must turn to the parent odu to find a method of closure. This sign, Irosun, contains within itself many offerings and rituals to placate both the letter and the orishas that are speaking in it. The eboses for the parent odu follow.

- When neither the larishe nor the eboses of the composite will close out Irosun, this letter becomes hot, and the "ebó of hot and cold water" should be done at the conclusion of the reading to soothe the heat of this pattern.

  This ebó requires only two gourds or small bowls. Fill one with hot tap water and the other with cold tap water. Then turn on all the cold-water faucets in the house. While the faucets are running, all the people in the home should stand just inside the front door. The diviner opens the door wide and flings the hot water from inside his house into the street, casting it as far as it will go. All then go outside and face inside the house. The diviner now flings the bowl of cold water into the house. Everyone can now reenter the house and turn off all the cold-water faucets. However, leave the front door open until the water in the house is dry. This simple ebó should be repeated by all present for this reading in their own homes.
- Irosun is dark and mysterious; because it alludes to the client's past, it also alludes to his ancestors, both physical and spiritual. If a casting of four mouths refuses closure, the italero must focus on the client's issues with his egun. Through this odu's energy, the most ancient and forgotten spirits, forces whose names are no longer known to their descendants, clamor for attention. To evolve, the client must propitiate egun. In Irosun, the proper method is through a series of four masses. Four espiritistas, mediums who are capable of passing their own egun and guides, must be present at each mass. Unlike other masses, in which a bóveda is set up and the congregation sits in a semicircle before the white table, the four mediums must sit at the white table and the client and godparents must sit in a semicircle before them. While others may be present at the spiritual mass, the entire focus is on the client. The prescriptions given by the espiritistas must be followed exactly. After marking this ebó, the diviner should give egun a chance to personalize it, asking, "Ebó elese egun?" If the answer is yes, he uses the diloggún to mark the appropriate offering.
- No matter which orishas stand up in a composite odu, in all patterns of Irosun the following spirits may speak or claim ebó: Shangó, Elegguá, Olokun, Yewá, the Ibeyi, Dada, Boromu, Oba, Obatalá, Babaluaiye, Aganyú, and Ochosi. For an initiated client, the diviner may consider asking, "Ebó elese [orisha's name]?" For an uninitiated client he may ask the same question, but he must not ask it of Dada and Boromu. These two have significance only for initiates.

There are traditional offerings for the above-mentioned orishas in the odu Irosun. As ebó, the diviner should consider the following:

- When either Shangó or Aganyú stands up at this point to claim ebó, the diviner should prescribe a thorough housecleaning. The client should begin at the back of his house and work toward the front door. He should clean all his closets, drawers, and dark spaces, especially under and behind furniture. Everything should be scrubbed and sanitized. Unused papers, trash, and broken appliances must be removed. Anything not in good repair, even clothing, must go.

- For Shangó, further prescriptions are appropriate. The client should sew an ornate red pañuelo for the orisha, draping this over the batea. He should also consider giving him a mazo or a set of beaded tools. If Shangó has offered a larishe for the odu, the client should sew a red cotton flag for him and adorn it with cowries and some of Shangó's symbols (such as the double-headed ax or a thunderbolt). The client should hang this flag over the front door to honor Shangó and then perform Irosun's ebó of hot and cold water.
- If Elegguá's shells are being used for this consultation, or if Elegguá stands up during the reading, the diviner should add more carga or aché to the client's Elegguá. If the client's Elegguá came from Ifá, a babalawo must do this, and the client must now receive Elegguá from ocha. The diviner must also determine if Elegguá needs a crown; in Irosun, Elegguá is a king and must be treated as such.
- Many considerations are possible for the orisha Olokun. The first option for ebó to Olokun is made with a fishing net. First, the client offers an adimú of fresh fruits to Olokun in the ocean. He then casts the net far out to sea and draws it in slowly. The client should take the net home and drape it over the back door. This simple ebó will catch evil before it sneaks in and keep the client's blessings from escaping. Other options for ebó for Olokun include ornate blue masks, handmade pañuelos, and life-sized tools used by sailors such as oars, anchors, ship's steering wheels, and floats (the glass type).
- When Yewá claims ebó in Irosun, a red snapper is her adimú of choice. It must be baked and garnished with fresh sliced tomatoes and gofio. If none among the diviner, client, and godparent has Yewá, the ebó must be left for her on the oldest grave in a cemetery.
- If the Ibeyi claim ebó in this sign, give them two pigeons each and twin baskets of fruit.
- If an osogbo comes "elese elenú" ("by the speaker's own tongue"), the following adimú may be given to the Ibeyi and Elegguá: Place Elegguá between the two Ibeyi. Serve all three equal bowls of alphabet soup. Light white candles to all three, praying that one learns to speak appropriate words at appropriate times. These three spirits will bless all that one says, helping one find the proper words for every occasion.
- When Oba claims ebó in Irosun and the client is an initiate, the client takes the orisha to a cave and puts her on a white plate. There, he feeds her two hens.
- For aborishas, the diviner may also consider the reception of Olokun, the Ibeyi, or Babaluaiye, especially if their influence is specific to the composite odu opened.
- For initiates, the diviner may consider the reception of Olokun, Yewá, Dada, Boromu, Oba, Babaluaiye, Aganyú, and Ochosi, especially if their influence is specific to the composite opened at the mat.

If this list is exhausted and the odu still refuses closure, the diviner has two options. First, he may call an elder in the religion, for something important in the sign could have been overlooked. Second, he may look at the list of eboses given for the omo odu as a parent odu. (For example, if Irosun Oché has been cast, the diviner would now turn to the eboses of Oché as a parent odu for closure.)

# SIX
# THE FAMILY OF OCHÉ

## The Proverbs of Oché

- Oché is the blood that runs through the veins.
- Everything in this life has its time.
- In iré, we say that all food tastes sweet; in osogbo, we say that all food tastes sour.
- Just as there are rivers in the earth, so are there rivers in the veins.
- While your tongue is your luck, it is also your disgrace.
- There is a proper time for everything.
- One's luck is a fickle thing.
- It is the needle that pulls the thread.

## The Orishas Who Speak in Oché

| | |
|---|---|
| Oshún | Oyá |
| Elegguá | Yemayá |
| Orúnmila | Ochosi |
| Obatalá | |

## The Message of Oché

Opening with five mouths on the mat, the dilogqún sits before the italero in a sweet, beautiful pattern. Oché, a nurturing sign filled with the energies that sustain the viability of life, has come to the house. Born last among all the odu, Oché is an afterthought of God, the final seal on creation, yet it brings all carnal and soulful pleasures to the world. It is said that when creation stood at its final threshold, Olódumare looked down on the earth from heaven and wondered, "What more can I give the world?" He looked at its vastness and beauty. His love poured forth, a sacred river of blessings that began with his heart. As the blessings gathered throughout the land, they formed the mighty, coursing rivers; sources of fresh water swelled across the globe and Oché was born. God smiled, for only then were all things complete. From Oché was born Oshún: The youngest odu created the youngest orisha. All the Irunmole in heaven smiled at their radiance and delicacy. None knew, however, that behind their elegance lay the most powerful energies in the world.

After all things were made, one by one all the odu opened on earth; they descended from heaven to live among both humans and orishas, and their energies flourished. All prospered. Yet Oché, the last to be born, remained closed and hidden. The full force of its blessings was withheld. All the spirits and humans forgot about Oché and Oshún; life was hard, and all toiled ceaselessly to survive. Alone and isolated, Oshún grew ill and weak, and still Oché withheld the sweet, life-giving waters that were hers to give. Oshún was dying, and creation, without her blessings, began to wither. It was Oyá, the lady standing between this world and the next, who first felt creation's death rattle; and she went to Shangó for help. He was a diviner by birth but had not yet exercised this right, and Oyá, who knew the secrets of life and death, persuaded him to open the diloggún for the first time. Beside Oshún's deathbed he cast the sixteen shells; the entire universe watched as the oracle fell, fearful yet titillated with its first casting. All the odu were there, vying for the honor to be first, to be the sign that would heal Oshún and save Olódumare's work in the world—all except Oché, who remained closed and forgotten. Yet when the diloggún opened for the first time, it marked five mouths. Oché was forced to open, and cascades of fresh water coursed through the land again. The last to be born was the first to arrive when life itself was endangered. Oché renewed creation; Oché healed Oshún. She became the queen of life.

Because of its blessings, Oché is a sign demanding respect. Having cast five mouths, the diviner suspends the reading to perform the sacred gesture of this sign. He places both hands on his thighs, resting them there for a moment before placing them on the sides of his legs. Those who have ocha follow the italero's lead. Those whose heads were born from this sign carry their reverence just a step further; crossing their arms over their chests and bowing their heads, they, along with the diviner, silently intone the sacred prayer that honors this odu:

*Oché muluku muluku oyo bata*
*Lowo'che muluku*
*Lodafun aktampo lori ilumana*
*Oché ibade Yewá koide saba indore ebó.*
*Ibaé owó, ibaé omo, ibaé Iyalode abe.*

After this prayer is intoned, to honor both the opening odu and the orisha who owns it many will mutter, "Maferefún Oché! Maferefún Oshún!" This letter demands strict ritual attention and observance and commands fear and respect. Of all the odu in the world, none influences our lives more than five mouths. Within its grasp are all things bittersweet and all the blessings that make life worth living. Its opening on the mat is one's salvation, for just as Oché renewed creation, it can renew one's life. Many are doubly blessed by being born through Oché. However, having one's head born in five mouths is both an honor and a curse. Controversy surrounds this odu, and depending on the house of ocha and the oriaté who performs the ceremony of itá, a iyawó opening in Oché can lose the right to read an orisha's diloggún, to give an orisha, or even to work this religion for another. The controversy surrounding Oché is born of its power and mystery; and the implications of this sign should never be underestimated.

The orisha whose shells are cast has the first option to speak in this odu. If this is the first time Oché has opened for a client, these are perhaps the most important words he will ever hear: The diviner sits before one who, by right of birth, is called to be a priest of this faith. The orisha consulted says that the client's head, or guardian orisha, must be marked soon by an oriaté. Once the guardian orisha has been brought down, initiation will soon follow. If the client is an aleyo who has been involved in the faith for some time, the diviner knows that he has felt cheated, fooled into parting with his hard-earned money for things of the spiritual world. Perhaps the client has come from another house where his previous godparents were scandalous or of ill repute. All this will change. For until Oché opened to reveal this person's destiny, nothing could be done to help him; no amount of ebó could encourage his evolution. His past involvement in the religion only cleared the osogbos hindering his evolution, and all the scandals of the past were a result of his malicious karma. The client was locked in poverty and despair. These locks are now broken. His life was bitter and sour. Now, Oché brings just a taste of sweetness. The client will have evolution and prosperity, and the bitterness of the past will serve only to make the future taste sweeter. The diviner must tell the client to consider this day, upon which five mouths opened, to be day of rebirth and renewal of his faith.

Oshún must be given much praise and honor for testing this client's will and determination as he sought to find a path to the orishas. He has faced trials by fire; those fires are now quenched. He has experienced much crying, wailing, and gnashing of teeth; those things are over. His wounds have been dressed and they will be healed. Since the client first sought out the Lucumí gods, he has been in search of a family, a religious haven in which these mysteries could be explored. Oché says the searching may end: The client is home. The diviner must give the client Oshún words: "You had luck once, and that luck was lost. You had true love once, and that love was let go, thrown away, killed by lack of trust and nurturing. These were but a few of the tests that you had to go through to find evolution. If one were to eat sweet food every day, there would be no way to know what sweetness is. Without bitterness, Oshún tells you that even the sweetest foods would taste bland. The difficulties you have experienced serve as pointers toward evolution. Keep those things in the past, remember them, and never allow yourself to become caught up in them again."

In Oché, Oshún says the client stands on the shoulders of those who have come before. She insists that this client make use of the strong foundation laid through his own hard work and that of his ancestors and his immediate family. As frequently as possible, this client must come to Oshún's sopera and pray. He must pay any debts he owes her. He should offer her sweet adimú and ask her for guidance. If he pampers her in this way, she will pamper him in return. The diviner must tell the client, however, that because Oshún's interest in him is so strong, many of her children will be drawn to his life. Because Oshún loves him, the Oshún in their heads will love him as well. In spite of this love, he must be wary of Oshún's children. It is taboo to argue with her chosen, even when they are wrong and one is right. He should be careful to bring none of them to shame or cause them to feel humility. Oshún's children will bring joy and heartache to his life. If he makes their acquaintance, he should get to know them slowly, holding them at arm's length until he is sure he can enter into a friendship with them.

Elegguá is the next to speak in Oché, and he gives witness to all that Oshún has to say. Although she owns this odu, if the client hopes to evolve, he must propitiate Elegguá. If Oshún wants to give the client a kingdom, Elegguá has the power to block this blessing if he is not pleased. Likewise, when Oshún is angry, Elegguá is the only one who can save the client from her.

After Elegguá comes Orúnmila. Although he will not speak in the shells, Orúnmila can make his influence known. There will be times when Oché will not close out until the italero says, "There are issues with Orúnmila, and you must be seen by a babalawo to settle these." After Orúnmila, the orishas Obatalá, Oyá, Shangó, Yemayá, and Ochosi may all speak or claim ebó, but their issues will be heavily dependent on the composite odu that opens. In any pattern of Oché, however, it is appropriate to say "Maferefún!" to them all even before the composite is known.

The easiest way to begin a study of Oché is to examine it in iré. In iré, the odu speaks of evolution. The client's life will become sweeter, but this sweetness will not come easily, nor will it come without a cost. The diviner should ask, "Without bitterness, how could you know what sweetness is?" The client who is marked with iré in Oché has come from a sour past. His life on many levels was bitter and hard. Now the client has begun to work off his karmic debts; there may be more bitterness, but interspersed with life's sour tang will be a sweet flavor. The diviner should tell the client, "If you follow the advice of this reading, if you heed the words of Oshún, if you make ebó, and if you heed the taboos of this letter, life will get better. You have Oshún's blessings." The source of iré is integral to this reading; it tells the client whence his spiritual strength and help come. He must turn to this source lest his blessings be lost.

If the iré is marked iré yale (firm iré), the odu tells the diviner that the client's source of blessing is strong; Oshún and Oché mount behind him, pushing him toward his destiny. If the iré is also marked iré yale timbelaye (firm iré manifest in the client's life), Oché gives closure to itself. It tells the diviner that this pattern's energy has been in effect for some time, and this person has navigated himself well through its energies. He is in alignment with his destiny. Five mouths has opened here to tell the client what forces are in effect and what he will walk away with.

When any composite of Oché opens in iré, the diviner should explore with the client all the following points:

- The client must always have respect for nature, especially the river, for it is Oshún's true home. He should give to her small offerings and always ask her permission before crossing or swimming in its waters. If the client is a iyawó sitting for either itá or a reading, he is now prohibited from swimming or bathing in rivers until the end of his year as a iyawó.

- This respect for nature must extend to the natural homes of all the orishas. As ebó, the client must spend time in the home of his patron, doing something to clean up the area (removing trash, planting, et cetera) and leaving it in a better state than he found it.
- As soon as possible, the client should rearrange all his furniture at home, cleaning everything. This renews the energy there so it does not stagnate.
- Oshún and Elegguá want this person's home to be happier and fresher. He should play beautiful, uplifting music daily to remove any harsh vibrations from his home.
- When this sign is marked as iré yale or iré yale timbelaye, the client should play the lottery occasionally and sparingly. Infrequent, mild gambling will bring some financial blessings. The diviner must caution frugality in this, for if the client throws away his money unwisely, he will anger Oshún and destroy this blessing.

In osogbo, Oché raises a variety of health concerns, especially if the osogbo is marked as ano or ikú. Oché rules most of the body, in particular the blood, the pelvic region, and the electrical/chemical stimuli of the nervous system. When this odu's energy is not balanced, afflictions of the areas that it rules can manifest in the client's life; hypoglycemia, diabetes, sepsis, and many types of poisoning are all possible. Sexual and reproductive disease, digestive disturbances, and intestinal trouble are also problematic for women, and sometimes for men as well. If the client experiences any symptoms of sickness in any of these areas during the next year, he should see a physician immediately and have a complete checkup. Oché also warns that the client should take time for adequate rest, sleep, and recreation, for his nerves are unstable and exhaustion could debilitate his health.

Sometimes health afflictions in this odu are only temporary. If so, they are Oché's method of getting the client's attention and bringing him back into alignment. It is not unusual for one who opens in Oché to suffer temporary sexual dysfunction under this sign's influence. However, if the loss of sexual function is long-lasting or if sterility or impotence ensues, the client must see a physician immediately. If the client is a woman, the italero must warn her that Oché forebodes unwanted pregnancies. If having a child is impossible or not realistic now, the woman should either abstain from sexual relations or use proper birth control at all times.* For Oshún, abortion is not a viable option; having one will only incur her wrath, and the mother will suffer permanent sterility or even death. A man who opens in Oché is forbidden to suggest an abortion to anyone, for the mother of the unborn will come to regret it, and she will see the man who advised it as the source of her despair.

In osogbo, Oché also addresses issues of home and hearth. The home should be a source of rest, pleasure, and solitude, but for this client often it is not. Oshún wants the house to be clean, well lit, and comfortable at all times. She finds that the atmosphere is often repressed and oppressing. The client should be advised to lighten up his home with laughter and music. He should also entertain close friends at his home.

Regardless of the odu's orientation, the diviner must keep an important point in mind when reading Oché: It is the youngest odu, yet it is one of the most powerful and most awesome. It holds in its grasp all things bittersweet. Oshún, the goddess of love, money, eroticism, and fertility, owns this odu; while she is the most beautiful of all the orishas, she can also be the most antagonistic and the most horrible when offended. Crying profusely, this sweet orisha expresses her joy, her happiness, and her love; laughing, she forebodes things evil and sinister and displays her displeasure at mortals. Like Oché, Oshún is the youngest of her kind. She is small and fragile to behold, but she is also the strongest and most powerful orisha, having learned to wield those

*If Oché comes in a severe osogbo for a woman, the diviner should question her about possible past abortions. Those who use abortions in lieu of birth control anger Oshún, and serious ebó is needed to overcome her anger.

things that make life bearable like a two-edged sword. Make her proud, spoil her, and give her the due that she deserves, and Oshún gives freely of her blessings. Make her angry or scorn her, and those things that make life sweet are withheld; one has only bitterness. The client must not fooled by this letter's youth or folly. Under the influence of this sign, all things small become great and powerful, and under its effects, even the strongest mountain can be felled.

Even in iré yale timbelaye, many osogbos are inherent in this pattern, and these must be kept in mind by the client. Most have to do with envy and evil thoughts. These negative feelings caused the client's original fall and many of his problems, and they will bring him many problems again if he does not overcome them. When an aleyo comes in Oché for the first time, it marks him as coming from an impoverished background; while he may have basic necessities and even a few luxuries, life has yet to live up to his expectations. He has a tendency to look covetously at the possessions of others, to desire the things that others have for no other reason than to feel equal. The italero must tactfully tell this person that the possessions of others have little bearing on his own self-worth; with the exception of a few people who were born into this world with excellent karma, most have to work hard to attain a life of luxury and wealth. The diviner must warn the client not to judge others by their possessions: clothes, jewelry, cars, houses. He must learn to look only at the person and the energy he or she embodies.

Also, the diviner should warn this person not to criticize those of whom he is envious; he must never belittle those who are wealthy or better off behind their backs. Bitterness and sweetness will attract more of the same. A secret of prosperity for those who open in Oché is emulation: Learn from the elders and those who have wealth. Listen to how they achieved satisfaction and how they balance their lives. The client will also be encouraged if the italero shares this one small secret revealed by Oché: Others see the client as being prosperous and having luck himself. He, too, is the recipient of others' envy and evil intentions. What is poor to one is rich to others. If the client thanks Oshún for the many blessings she has given, more will come.

Another secret to making the most of Oché's power is to learn two important qualities: humility and gratitude. True humility opens one up to infinite possibilities. Those who are unassuming and unpretending have nothing to live up to beyond what they already are. Humility is equitable with submission, and by submitting to divine will one moves effortlessly toward one's destiny. Oshún achieved her own stature by being humble; she earned love and respect through her unassuming ways.

Gratitude is the continual acknowledgment of the good in one's life. No matter how sour life is, there is always something to be thankful for. The diviner should tell the client, "You have a home? It may not be the home you desire, but having a place to live is more than many have. Offer thanks. You have health? Many are dying. Offer thanks. You have friends or family? Many are alone in this world. Offer thanks. Once you learn to appreciate and manage the gifts you already have, the orishas will trust you with more."

An initiate who has made ocha—or even a iyawó sitting for itá—has special concerns with five mouths, even when it comes in iré. This person will, at some point, become disillusioned with the religion of the orishas. His disillusionment will come not because the gods are treating him badly but because those with whom he associates are self-centered and vain. (Again, he must be wary of Oshún's children, for while she is wonderful, oftentimes they are not.) If the client is an initiate surrounded by many godchildren, they will be the source of worry, anger, and disdain. Oché points toward unrealistic demands and impossible requests. The italero, as an elder and guide, must inform the client that leaving this faith would bring his final destruction; he must advise him, instead, to go into seclusion if his faith begins to crumble. He should keep company only with those other initiates and godchildren whom he trusts and loves, and who give trust and love in return.

Everyone who has made ocha eventually comes to this realization: Some godchildren are family, and some godchildren are clients—and this division must always be kept in mind. For a time, the client would be wise to treat the religion as if it were a business, a source of income. Those who try to stay close to him for reasons beyond the religion are truly family. They are the ones to whom he should devote his time, energy, and teachings.

Also, the diviner must counsel the initiate client not to give away the knowledge of ocha for free. Others must earn it through hard work and perseverance. He must not teach others the mysteries of this faith but, instead, let them learn it by working hard at religious functions. The child of Oché does, in time, learn all things under heaven and earth, yet the learning must be accomplished through blood, sweat, and tears. Should not others have to work at least this hard?

Finally, the italero should give the initiate who has come for a reading this warning: If ever he thinks about leaving this religion and can find no reason to stay, he must not give away or throw away the orishas. Instead, he should wrap them carefully in cloth and store them, for many years later the day will come when he regrets his loss—and the orishas will still be there, waiting.

Oché in any orientation signals that the client will move three times over the next few years; after the third move, he will have found his true home. With each move, the client should leave behind the broom he uses in each dwelling so that it does not take the negativity of the old home into the new. And before moving any furniture or personal possessions, the client should move the orishas and their implements into the new home; they should be given their choice of where to live in the house, with the client using obí to determine their wishes. Finally, the client should always begin the move in the morning and finish in the evening; he must leave behind whatever he cannot move in one day. Once everything is unpacked, he should throw a housewarming party in honor of Oshún; she will bring many new blessings to this client's life.

Oché warns the client to be neither a nag nor a pest when dealing with friends and family; one who opens in this odu is marked as having a tendency toward obsessive-compulsive disorder (in varying degrees). The client tends to bother the same people with the same requests. They want him to lighten up. The diviner should tell the client to wait some time before he repeats a request. He must strive to avoid bitterness in his personal relationships, either speaking sweetly or not speaking at all. Remember: Oshún owns honey and all things sweet, and with this she can tame even the strongest of spirits (she once tamed even Ogún with her honey). For the client to have his way with others, he must be kind, not demanding. Bitterness always brings more of the same.

The client's family has been, or will become, a source of worry. He will face many trials and tribulations with his blood relations. He must not allow them to become a source of stress; he must try not to get caught up in family difficulties. He should give help when help is needed, but he should not lose sleep over family problems. The diviner should also tell this person this: In time, even his mother will come to forgive him (he will understand). He must listen but not speak; watch, but not act. In time his family will change their ways, and if they do not, all will suffer save the client.

The client must be on guard against war, envy, strife, and gossip between those he calls family, of blood or of ocha, especially if the letter comes in osogbo. The client should love his relations of both blood and ocha from a distance; in this way, they can never bring harm or disappointment. For now, it is the only sensible way for him to deal with them.

Oché can portend incest (either spiritual or physical) between the client and his relations, which would greatly anger Oshún. If the client begins to desire anyone he is related to by blood or ocha, he should immediately remove himself from that person's presence and not go back alone for some time. If anyone related by either blood or ocha shows interest in him beyond that of friendship, he must avoid that person indefinitely. This odu also reminds the italero that nothing of ocha may be given to anyone with whom he, himself, had a romantic involvement or with whom he would like to have a romantic relationship. Ocha intermixed with a romantic relationship is akin to incest.

The following concerns are also highlighted in Oché and should be explored by the diviner:

- Beyond the health concerns already mentioned, Oché portends problems with the legs, knees, ankles, feet, waist, and spine. Past illnesses, too, will recur, for the client has not modified the behavior that brought them on. Proper health care begins with proper hygiene: Daily showering and deodorizing will do much to improve the health, as will a thorough airing and cleaning of the home. The client should keep his nails clean and his feet covered with socks and shoes. Tetanus infection is a danger; now would be a good time for the client to get a tetanus booster and update all immunizations.

- The client should not rely on home remedies for health care. If he is sick, he should see a physician for proper medical advice.
- The client should keep his kitchen immaculately clean and clear of spoiled foods, for Oché warns of poisons that accompany what one eats. He must be careful when eating away from home. In the home of another, he should not eat food that is given with insistence; it might harbor malicious witchcraft or even poison. (The poison could be intentional or unintentional.)
- At times the client is happy and at other times he feels like crying; these moods swing interchangeably. The diviner must tell the client that like attracts like. If he wants happiness, he must pretend to be happy. Similarly, he should not nag or become a pest to others, for as he treats them, so will he be treated. Sourness will affect his health, his finances, and his relationships; every aspect of his life can be destroyed by a negative attitude.
- This person has dealt with many different priests and priestesses of this and other religions in the past. He speaks ill of them, but he must not any longer. Speaking ill of those who have tried to help him is how he loses much of his luck.

## The Prohibitions of Oché

Oché is both sweetness and sourness; it alludes to all the blessings that make life bearable (if one has them) or unbearable (if one lacks them). In iré, the prohibitions are key to making sure Oché's goodness is not lost. In osogbo, the prohibitions are urgent and mandatory to ward off or minimize dangers and negative energies. The italero must depend on his own aché and the diloggún to determine appropriate prohibitions for his client.

- Severe food restrictions come with five mouths in osogbo. Do not consume eggs, reheated foods, watercress, canistel, malanga, shrimp, squid, octopus, or freshwater fish. Any food product that was cooked and then canned, frozen, or boxed is forbidden. If one has been forbidden any foods before, Oché makes them forbidden again—for life. Know that Oché, in osogbo, tells the diviner that this person did not follow these previous taboos.
- Do not loan out any item that has touched one's body or borrow any item that has touched the body of another. Prohibited items include, but are not limited to, shirts, pants, underwear, bed linens, towels, washcloths, soaps, shampoos, and combs.
- Measure one's words before speaking. Never use profanity; blasphemy will be one's downfall.
- Do not participate in, listen to, or repeat gossip.
- Do not brag about one's good fortune, for in this way will others wish and bring evil.
- Do not pawn personal items, no matter how desperate one becomes for money.
- Do not share knowledge freely. After learning something new, keep it a secret.
- For a woman, beware of an impending pregnancy. If one becomes pregnant, abortion is forbidden.
- For a man, do not advise others to have abortions.
- If this reading is an itá, the one sitting at the mat may never initiate a child of the orisha with whom the itá is had: The aché of this spirit is too important to be given away to another. Never open the diloggún of that orisha unless absolutely necessary.*
- Do not keep any spoiled foods in one's kitchen or refrigerator. Do not let any food spoil on any of the orishas.
- Do not wear yellow.

*In our house, the one at the mat may initiate children of the other orishas and still give the orisha for whom Oché Meji fell.

## Marking Ebó in Oché: Initial Considerations

Each odu prescribes many eboses to put a client back into alignment with his destiny. Oché is a sign of spiritual evolution; it is the youngest, yet the most powerful. To bring the most iré from this session, the diviner must be thorough and skillful in his assessment of the client's life, taking many factors into consideration.

If this is the first time that Oché has opened for a client, the diviner knows that Oché has come to bring renewal and refreshment; it has come to save the client, just as it saved the world when it opened with the first historical casting of the diloggún. The diviner should tell the client this. Now the diviner must consider the client's place in the religion. If the client is an aleyo with nothing of ocha, he must receive the elekes. If his guardian orisha is not known, he should receive the elekes in the name of Oshún; she will bring sweetness to his life. If the client is an aborisha who has already received the elekes, the diviner must prescribe the warriors; the intervention of Elegguá will open the client's path to attainment. Finally, if the client has both the elekes and the warriors but has not yet made ocha, the diviner must tell him that the greatest ebó and leap of faith lies before him: asiento. Only when his orisha is crowned on his head will he finally become all that he is meant to be.

Also, although there is a list of eboses in each composite odu, there are certain types of spiritual advice and offerings that must accompany all sixteen of these patterns when they open on the mat. Consider the following for all castings of Oché:

- The diviner should drape a mazo over the client's neck and direct him to salute his guardian orisha (or Obatalá, if his guardian orisha has not been identified), his godparents, and then the diviner. He is now bound to make ocha, and the diviner should advise that he receive both the elekes and the warriors as soon as possible. If the guardian orisha has not been determined, the client should have a bajado soon as well. If the client cannot make ocha for some time, this letter demands that every month he have a rogación before Oshún and have his head washed with the herbs of ocha and Oshún so that his luck and health will improve.
- The client might need a rogación at the feet of an orisha who has stood up in this sign. To mark this, the diviner should ask for each orisha who has stood up, "Eborí elese [orisha's name]?"
- If the eboses prescribed thus far are not enough to close the composite odu, the diviner should explain the following: If the client has any trips or vacations planned, he should first consult Oshún and ask her permission to go. She takes a special interest in the affairs of the client. If Oshún tells him that he should not go and the planned trip is for pleasure, he should not go. If Oshún tells him that he should not go and the planned trip is for business, he must try to mark an ebó to her as a means of appeasement.

The final consideration for ebó in Oché is that Elegguá and Oshún influence the entire family. While Elegguá speaks in all composites, he never speaks alone; he is always accompanied by Oshún. A part of each ebó must go to Elegguá, and it must go to him before giving any part of the offering to Oshún. The sacrifices most often used for these two spirits follow.

### Traditional Eboses in Oché

Certain types of offerings are native to Oché's energy. Whenever possible, the diviner should include elements in ebó from this list. For sacrifice, pick from the following: five hens, a guinea hen, and five small "peeps" (newly hatched chickens). If an adimú-type offering is required, the diviner should pick from the following: a jar of honey, five freshly smoked fish, five pumpkins, gourds or calabazas, five red parrot feathers, and five peanuts.

## Ebó Elese Eleggua y Oshún
## *(Ebó at the Feet of Eleggua and Oshún)*

These eboses are appropriate in three situations:

- The client is an initiate whose crowning orisha is Oshún. In this case, place Elegguá with Oshún, and give the eboses to them both, at the same time.
- The client is a child of Oché (Oché opened in either Elegguá or the crowning orisha in the iyawó's itá). Set Elegguá with the crowning orisha and adapt the ebó so it is appropriate for the crown. (An experienced priest or priestess will know how to make these adaptations; if the diviner is a novice, an experienced elder must be consulted to make the appropriate changes.)
- Both Elegguá and Oshún stand up for ebó in Oché and the odu will not close. These eboses may also be used in an attempt to settle issues with both orishas.

### *Calabaza Soup*

To prepare this dish the client will need the following ingredients: 3 pounds of calabaza, six cloves of garlic (four whole, two minced), a 2-inch cinnamon stick, 1 tablespoon of butter, one medium onion (diced), 1/4 teaspoon of saffron threads, 3 cups of chicken broth, 1/2 cup of cream, freshly ground pepper, 6 tablespoons of sour cream for garnish, and 2 tablespoons of toasted pumpkin seeds for garnish.

Cut open the calabazas and scoop out all the seeds and fibers. Cut the gourds into 2-inch pieces. Place the pieces of calabaza in a large saucepan and add enough water to cover them. Add four whole cloves of garlic and the cinnamon stick. Bring to a boil, then cover, reduce the heat, and allow to simmer for 20 minutes, or until the calabaza pieces are extremely soft.

Pour into a strainer. Pick out and discard the garlic cloves and cinnamon stick. When the calabaza pulp is cool, peel and discard its skin. Purée the pulp, then set it to the side.

Melt the butter in a large saucepan over medium-high heat. Add the diced onion and sauté until it is soft. Then mix in the two minced garlic cloves and the saffron threads. Add the calabaza purée and mix well, then pour the chicken broth over all, again mixing well. Turn up the heat and bring the soup to a boil; then reduce the heat and let simmer for 15 minutes, stirring frequently so the soup does not burn. Finally, remove from heat and stir in the cream and ground pepper to taste.

Divide the soup among six bowls. Give one bowl to Elegguá; before his shrine, garnish it with a scoop of sour cream and some of the toasted pumpkin seeds. Give five bowls to Oshún, garnishing them before his shrine. This ebó remains with the orishas overnight. The following morning, pour the soup into a river.

Small, hollowed-out pumpkins may be used to serve this ebó in place of bowls. For this option, add coins and cowries to each pumpkin to bring prosperity back into one's life.

### *Celebration for Oshún*

In Oché, Oshún may want the client to give her a huge party with lots of music. The bigger the party, the greater the blessings this orisha will bestow. When the throne to Oshún is built, Elegguá must sit at her feet, and the plaza of fruits should include gourds, calabazas, pumpkins, and squash. If Oshún takes this ebó but the odu still will not close, the party may need to include a *guiro* (ceremonial drumming). The diviner should check this with the shells, asking, "Guiro de Oshún?" If a guiro will not satisfy her, a drum may be needed to placate her. To find out if she requires this, the diviner must ask, "Tambor de Oshún?"

### *Fruit and Caramel Basket*

If the client is trying to obtain a special blessing from Oshún, he can offer the following ebó to both her and Elegguá. As soon as possible after the reading, the client returns to the diviner's house with a large, round wicker basket that has two handles. He lines the interior of the basket with one yellow cloth and one white cloth and then fills the basket with a large variety of fruits, including bananas and plantains for Elegguá and oranges for Oshún. Over the fruits, he casts handfuls of sweet caramels. He places the basket before Elegguá and Oshún.

Every day for the next five days, the client should return to the orishas, lighting a white candle for both spirits and praying for his evolution. After his prayers on the fifth day, client and priest take the entire basket to the river. Each holds it by one handle, and they set it on the riverbank so that it just barely touches the water but is not submersed in it. The priest offers one final prayer for the client's evolution. With this ebó, the orishas will bless this client.

### *Herbal Bath*

If the oracle has determined that the client needs a spiritual bath to remove osogbo, the following will help. The client will need to provide myrtle, vervain, lettuce, lavender, watercress, claret, honey, cinnamon, five egg yolks, two yellow candles, and a complete change of white clothes. The diviner steeps the myrtle, vervain, lettuce, lavender, and watercress in a large pot until the water is dark with their juices; he then strains the herbs from the water, wringing their juices into the water. To the liquid he adds the claret, honey, cinnamon, and egg yolks. The priest uses this bath to wash the client from the shoulders down, and then the client is allowed to soak and bathe himself freely.

After a quick shower to remove the residue, the client dries off, dresses in white, and is taken before Oshún's sopera. There, he salutes her and lights the two yellow candles, praying that this cleansing is made complete by her aché.

If the osogbo of this sign is severe, repeat this bath nightly for a total of five nights.

### *Sacrifice of Chickens*

The client places five small freshwater fish in five small gourds. Over each fish he places one peanut and one parrot feather. He presents these gourds to Eleggúa and Oshún. Then the priest sacrifices five small chickens to them both, allowing the blood from the sacrifice to drip into the gourds. Five days after this ebó is made, the client takes everything to the river with five cents for Oshún.

### *Sacrifice of Goat*

If the initiate's osogbo is severe and the odu will not close out, Oshún may be demanding a crown from this person. She might also wish to give him an itá. An oriaté should be found to sacrifice a goat to her. Eleggúa must share in this sacrifice. The skin from this goat should be saved, cured, and used to line a crown for the orisha. When the crown is ready, the client gives a huge party for Oshún, and five parrot feathers are put in the crown.

For the next ten years, on the anniversary of this ebó, a party is thrown in Oshún's honor and five more feathers are added to the crown, until there are a total of fifty-five in the crown.

## Adimús for Oshún

When Oshún requires adimú in Oché, the diviner may prescribe freely from the following dishes.

### *Sweet Pastries*

This ebó will sweeten both the orisha and the client's head. The client returns to the diviner's home with five sweet pastries. The client serves these to Oshún on a terra-cotta platter draped with yellow cloth, and leaves them with her overnight. The next evening, the client returns for a rogación at Oshún's feet; when all the elements of the rogación have been applied, some of each sweet pastry is added to his head before wrapping it in white cloth. If the client has not taken the elekes yet, the diviner should present Oshún's necklace to him at this time. If the client already has the elekes, the diviner should drape the mazo of Oshún over him, so that it passes over his left shoulder and under his right arm, and then direct him to salute Oshún. He is now in bondage to make ocha. In either case, when the rogación is removed, the client discards it in the river.

### *Sweet Baked Oranges*

Oshún adores this adimú. To prepare it for her, the client must provide the following ingredients: 2 pounds of sweet potatoes, half a stick of butter, 1/4 cup plus 4 tablespoons of sugar, 1/4 cup of orange juice, four egg yolks, five fresh oranges, four egg whites, yellow food coloring, cinnamon, and honey.

Preheat the oven to 375 degrees Fahrenheit. Peel the sweet potatoes, boil them until they are soft, then mash well. To the mashed sweet potatoes add the butter, 1/4 cup of sugar, orange juice, and egg yolks. Mix thoroughly. Cut the tops off the five oranges and remove the pulp from the inside, leaving only the shells. Fill each orange shell with the mashed sweet potato mixture, packing well. Place the five oranges on a baking sheet and bake for 15 minutes.

While the oranges are baking, beat the egg whites on high speed until they form a thick foam. Add 4 tablespoons of sugar, continuing to beat the mixture until it is shiny. To make the meringue pretty, add a few drops of yellow food coloring and continue to mix until the color is even. When the meringue "holds" the imprint of the mixer, it is done. After the oranges are finished baking, top with meringue, using a pastry bag. Sprinkle lightly with cinnamon and glaze the outer shells with honey. Serve this to Oshún on a terra-cotta plate draped with yellow cloth. Allow the ebó to remain with her overnight.

To discard this ebó, the client takes the oranges to the river and leaves them on the riverbank.

### *Ochinchin*

When Oshún demands adimú, this special omelette will sate her and bring special blessings to the client. To prepare this, the client provides the following ingredients: five eggs, a dash of milk, five large shrimps, and watercress or spinach.

Crack the eggs into a large mixing bowl and add a dash of milk. Whip the eggs well until blended. Lightly grease and preheat a skillet over medium heat; once the skillet is hot, pour the egg and milk mixture into the pan. Let the eggs solidify slowly; when bubbles begin to form in the eggs, place the shrimps and watercress (or spinach) in the center of the omelette. Fold the omelette in half, and when it is thoroughly cooked, remove from the pan. Serve this to Oshún on a white or yellow plate, leaving the ebó with her overnight.

The next morning, the client discards the ochinchin in a river with five pennies, talking to Oshún there about one's desires, dreams, and aspirations.

### *Natilla*

To prepare natilla as an adimú for Oshún, the client needs to provide the following ingredients: 1 cup of evaporated milk (one can), 1 1/2 tablespoons of white sugar, a cinnamon stick, salt, 1 1/2 tablespoons of cornstarch, one egg, and 1/4 teaspoon of vanilla extract.

In a large microwavable bowl, stir together the evaporated milk and 1/4 cup of water. Remove 1/4 cup of the mixture and set this aside in a small bowl. To the large bowl of water and milk, add the sugar, the cinnamon stick, and a pinch of salt. Microwave this mixture on high for 1 minute and 25 seconds.

To the smaller bowl of milk and water add the cornstarch and the yolk of one egg. Whip well. Once the mixture in the microwave is done, stir the cornstarch mixture into the heated liquid, stirring continually until the ingredients thicken. Reset the microwave to medium-high heat and cook for at least 2 minutes, until the mixture is thick. Remove. Add the vanilla extract and stir, then serve this to Oshún in an attractive bowl. The client later discards this ebó in the river.

### *Olelé*

Assemble the following ingredients: 1 pound of black-eyed peas, two eggs, a pinch of saffron, a medium onion (diced), a red bell pepper (diced), six cloves of garlic (diced), 3 tablespoons of epó, 1/2 cup of tomato sauce, 1/4 teaspoon of powdered black pepper, and aluminum foil.

Soak the beans in water overnight. The next morning, drain off the water and rub the peas gently to remove their shells. Mash these well to create a paste. Then mix in the eggs and saffron; set this mixture to the side.

In a large skillet, melt the epó over medium heat. Add the diced onion, pepper, and garlic and sauté until the onion becomes translucent. Add the tomato sauce and black pepper. Stir continually for 3 minutes, or until the tomato sauce becomes shiny. Add the bean mixture and stir well. Remove from heat.

When this is cool, divide it into five equal portions and wrap each in a square of aluminum foil. Tie the squares securely. Bring a pot of water to a boil. Drop the foil-wrapped packages into the water and boil for 30 minutes. Drain and cool. Serve the olelé to Oshún on a terra-cotta platter. The next day, the client discards this ebó in the river.

## The First Composite Odu of Oché, Oché Okana (5-1)

### The Proverbs of Oché Okana

- Things are done for ungrateful people.
- Your enemy will do you evil, and yet he will do you good.
- Jealousy is the mother of mistrust.
- Your jealousy will destroy all for which you have worked.

### The Message of Oché Okana

When an initial cast of five mouths, Oché, precedes a cast of one mouth, Okana, the odu Oché Okana is open on the mat. This pattern is also known as Oché Kana, Oché Okanran, and Oché Kanran. As it opens, the diviner says, "Maferefún Oshún!" Oché in all its composites is Oshún's home, and here she always has the first chance to speak. Before delving deeply into this sign, the diviner should tell the client all Oshún has to say: "Oché Okana has opened for you on the mat. Maferefún Oshún! Of all the signs that could have opened, of all the orishas who could speak, it is this beautiful woman who has come to bring you blessings. Indeed, she has already brought you blessings, for here she tells you that all you have, all that you have been given, is a gift from her. And all the osogbo or negative influence that exists in your life comes not from the saints but from your own hands. If you do nothing else once you leave here, this mat, this room, you must pray to her and thank her for the blessings that she has brought you. In time, she will offer you more."

The client may not believe the diviner's words at first, for no matter the orientation of Oché Okana, his life can be filled with despair. The sign indicates that the client has many evil eyes on him and many sharp tongues lashing him. These negative influences, however, come from his own misdeeds and improper actions in the world. The diviner should tell the client that if he lives according to the words of this odu, he will rise above this turmoil, for though his enemies can visit evil upon him now, in the end they will bring him only good. The client at the mat is nervous and filled with conflicting thoughts and emotions that not even he can sort out. Now, before Oshún and all the spirits, the client must be forced to voice his thoughts, both the good and the bad. He must pour out his heart and his soul to the orishas. Only in this way can his healing begin.

In this odu, the diviner also pays homage to Elegguá, Obatalá, and the client's crowning orisha (if it is known), saying to each, "Maferefún!" All these spirits stand up on behalf of the aborisha and initiate alike. While it is Oshún who takes the client to santo, it is Elegguá who opens the roads so evolution may be found; the client should ply him with adimú so that his roads remain open and clear. Obatalá is the orisha who formed all heads on the earth; even if the client is a child of another orisha, he must turn to Obatalá for peace and clarity of mind on the road to ocha. The client should also give ebó to his guardian orisha, if it is known. If the guardian orisha is not known, the client should pay foribale and give thanks to the godparent's guardian orisha and the godparent's head, for through them the client will be reborn.

In general, the diviner should know that Oché Okana is an elusive, mysterious odu. When it comes in iré, the diviner should advise the client to play the lottery sparingly, for he is slowly acquiring good luck. In an osogbo, the pattern becomes one of setbacks, illness, death, traps, and myriad accidents. No matter the odu's orientation, the client will experience sudden pains in his body, and illness is always a breath away. This person neglects his health, and if he does not begin to pay attention to it, his body will begin to decay in minor ways. If the client is male, he is interested in someone and this person does not trust him; he should be told that the relationship is not permanent, and in time the orishas will bring a new mate. If the client is a woman, she is secretly in love with a man, and she must get this person out of her head, for although a long-term relationship is possible, this man is not the right mate for her. He could even bring danger. Both men and women opening in this sign should enter into relationships with those of red or ruddy complexions cautiously;

Oché warns against it. While a period of arguments with and treason among friends is quieting down now, it is not over. These discords will escalate again.

In the osogbo orientations of *ano* (sickness) or *ikú* (death), the letter Oché Okana brings up some serious health issues for the client. He may experience pain or swelling in the legs, knees, calves, or feet. If he holds a job that demands long hours of standing, he must care for his feet, taking frequent breaks so they are not injured. He should beware of cuts, scrapes, abrasions, and bruises, for these are means by which infection or decay can enter the body. If any unusual symptoms develop or persist in association with such injuries, the client must see a physician immediately. Decomposition is possible in the abdominal region; pains there demand medical attention as well. For women, this decomposition extends to the reproductive organs; men could be affected with impotence or venereal disease. Those who open in an osogbo of ano or ikú might consider a rogación of the abdomen as a preventive measure. Finally, blood-borne pathogens are also a danger in this sign, particularly for health care workers; the client should take measures to prevent infection.

## The Prohibitions of Oché Okana

- One has had but not obeyed food prohibitions in the past. The diviner will identify prior food prohibitions, then say, "You did not follow all these as you should. This brought you many tragedies, and you never realized why these bad things happened." All food prohibitions that were not obeyed in the past must be made again. One is also forbidden to consume calabazas, gourds, pumpkins, squash, melons, and eggs. For five days, sweets are also forbidden. If this taboo is broken, the sweetness in one's life will disappear as well.
- Conception and pregnancy are forbidden for five months following the opening of this sign. Women must use proper birth control, and men must do the same. If a woman is pregnant or conceives under this sign, she must have a rogación of the abdominal region before Oshún; the priest then cleanses her and the unborn child with five hens and sacrifices the hens to Oshún. This ebó can save the life of the mother and child. Know, however, that the woman still might have a difficult pregnancy and labor.
- Do not sit at a table with many people; one will be tempted into giving away one's secrets.
- Do not swim or bathe in the river. Before crossing a river, give proper respect to Oshún.
- If Oché Okana has come in Elegguá, Obatalá, or the crowning orisha, one must respect that spirit's diloggún, using it very sparingly. If one gives away, sells, or throws those shells on the mat too often, someday one could lose the aché they represent.
- If this reading is an itá, one may not hereafter crown a child of Shangó.

## The Eboses of Oché Okana

Oché Okana marks the client for ocha. In time, Oshún herself will bring this person to the river. Until ocha can be made, however, several eboses must be done to help carry this client to his initiation. To begin, if the client's guardian orisha is not known, an oriaté should be brought in to determine this information. If the guardian orisha is known, or once the guardian orisha has been identified, the client must have a mass for his egun; these spiritual forces, in addition to Oshún and his guardian orisha, will carry him through to his crowning. The client must follow exactly the advice of the espiritistas present. After closing the mass, the diviner bathes this person thoroughly in omiero and gives him a rogación at the feet of his crowning orisha. He will be exhausted after all this and should be allowed to sleep on a mat in front of his crowning orisha's shrine. The next morning, after removing the rogación, the diviner gives the client another bath in omiero and makes eboses to Elegguá, Oshún, and the client's crowning orisha.

Once these eboses have been done, the client's feet are firm on the path to ocha. Every month, he must have a rogación before his crowning orisha; this will keep him focused on his goal.

The diviner must also explore with his client the following ebosees:

- If the odu comes in an osogbo of ano or ikú, or if the client suffers any abdominal disease, he should have a rogación of the abdomen before Oshún's shrine.
- In this odu, as ebó Ogún must be fed a knife beside his cauldron. Both Ogún and the knife should share two pigeons and a rooster. Afterward, the client should hide the knife behind the front door of his home to protect it from danger.
- If Oché Okana has fallen for an aleyo or an aborisha, he should wear a red parrot feather in his hair for twenty-eight days.
- If Oché Okana has fallen for an initiate, he should wear a red parrot feather in the hair at all orisha functions. If this reading is an itá, he must wear one every day for the rest of his life.
- Elegguá and Obatalá can claim ebó in this odu as well. To find out if they require anything, the diviner should ask, "Ebó elese Elegguá y Obatalá?" If the answer is yes, he uses the diloggún to mark the appropriate ebó.

Now the diviner asks the odu for closure. If it will not close, Oshún could be standing up for ebó. The diviner should ask, "Ebó elese Oshún?" If the answer is yes, he uses the diloggún to mark the appropriate ebó.

If the prescriptions made thus far are not enough to close the odu, the diviner must turn to the eboses of the parent odu, Oché (see page 257). Something there is needed for the client's evolution.

# The Second Composite Odu of Oché, Oché Ejioko (5-2)

## The Proverbs of Oché Ejioko

- Money brings tragedy.
- Do not abandon certainties for the unknown.
- In the soapmaker's home, everybody slips.
- In the house, little by little, everyone must make ocha.
- Where there is money, tragedy comes.

## The Message of Oché Ejioko

When a cast of five mouths, Oché, is followed by one of two mouths, Eji Oko, the odu Oché Ejioko, also known as Oché Oyekun and Oché Yeku, has fallen. Many credit this sign as having given birth to the odu Metanla (thirteen mouths). Oché Ejioko is an odu of sickness and epidemics; pandemics—illnesses that circle the globe—can be spawned here. This is also the odu of flies and mosquitoes, messengers of Babaluaiye. They bring sickness, and the client must learn to avoid them. This pattern is harsh, but its severity can become the client's salvation.

Here, the diviner says, "Maferefún Oshún! Maferefún Yemayá! Maferefún Ochosi! Maferefún Babaluaiye!" Oshún and Yemayá come to bring blessings to the client; however, the circumstances into which he has thrust himself prevent him from accepting these blessings. Ochosi also speaks in this odu, showing the client the shortest route to evolution. And Babaluaiye is here to heal the illnesses that Oché Ejioko marks on the client. Before this odu closes, all four orishas might stand up here to claim ebó or mark larishe.

Regardless of the odu's orientation, the diviner should explore the following concerns:

- No matter what brought him to the mat, spiritually this person is in debt to Yemayá. The diviner must prod the client to speak about his relationship with her. Any promises he has made in the past are now due; they should be recorded as if they were ebó prescribed by odu.
- Likewise, this person is in debt to Oshún. The diviner must have the client speak honestly about his relationship with her. Any promises he has made in the past are now due; they should be recorded as if they were ebó prescribed by odu.
- A trip to the forest could bring luck to the client; he must plan a day to go there.
- Oché Ejioko signals that a powerful spirit has accompanied the client to the mat. It tries to help him but often makes a mess of his affairs. This spirit needs light, warmth, refreshment, and guidance if it is to help the client evolve.
- If the client is male, he finds himself enamored

of a married woman; her husband is a dark-skinned man. Odu advises the client to stay away from her, for her husband could kill him.
- In this person's house, everyone will, in time, come to the feet of the orishas.

## The Prohibitions of Oché Ejioko

- Do not wear the color yellow; this color belongs only to Oshún.
- There is danger from disease by flies, mosquitoes, and other pests. Avoid outdoor activities early in the morning, late in the evening, or at night. If one must go out during these times, especially in wet areas, take protective measures against bugs and insects. Do not eat outdoors, and do not go on picnics. Keep the doors and windows (or at least the screens) to one's home closed.
- Do not live in damp, swampy areas.
- This odu speaks of external parasites and parasitic infections. Guard against lice, ticks, and fleas.

## The Eboses of Oché Ejioko

In Oché Ejioko, one's egun are one's foundation. The diviner should prescribe a series of five masses to take place as soon as possible. Before the mass, everyone present for the mass must be cleansed with an incense of cinnamon and dried orange peels. After all are seated at the bóveda and the espiritistas have offered their opening prayers, everyone present for the mass must cleanse him- or herself to the bóveda with a mixture of river water, holy water (the waters of Yemayá and Oshún may be used for this), rainwater, honey, and cinnamon. The client provides five sweet adimús for egun; they may use these to cleanse the client, bringing sweetness back into his life. The client should be directed to follow all the prescriptions of the espiritistas exactly, for they will provide the foundation for his evolution.

If the oracle will not close, the italero should consider whether the client's egun require further eboses, asking, "Ebó elese egun?" If the answer is yes, he uses the diloggún to mark the appropriate offering.

Oché Ejioko flags issues with Oshún, Yemayá, Babaluaiye, and Ochosi. If none of these claimed larishe during the course of the reading, the diviner can determine whether any will take ebó by asking, "Ebó elese [orisha's name]?" If the answer is yes, he uses the diloggún to mark the appropriate ebó.

If the odu remains open, the client may have deeper issues with Babaluaiye. The diviner should consider asking, "Ebó eleke de Babaluaiye?" If the answer is yes, the client is marked to receive the eleke of Babaluaiye. The diviner should also ask, "Koshé Babaluaiye?" If the answer is yes, the client is marked to receive the orisha Babaluaiye.

Oché Ejioko demands the reception of the Ibeyi; if the client does not have them, he must receive them. If he has them, the diviner should find out if they require ebó, asking, "Ebó elese los Ibeyi?" If the answer is yes, he uses the diloggún to mark the appropriate ebó.

In addition, the diviner should consider the following options for ebó:

- If the client is ill or if the osogbo of ano or ikú comes, he must turn to Oshún, Yemayá, and Babaluaiye for help. The client must have a rogación of the abdomen before both Yemayá and Oshún. At the end of the rogación, each orisha must eat feathers. The animals' blood must drip over this person's stomach. The client should also cleanse himself to Babaluaiye with two yellow candles, seventeen different types of grains, and sackcloth. At the end of the cleansing, the client should provide Babaluaiye with an adimú of dry white wine and a loaf of bread.
- Slowly, everybody in this person's house needs to make ocha. As ebó, the client should bring them one by one for a session with the diloggún.

If these options do not close the odu and the client is an aleyo or aborisha, the diviner should turn to the eboses of the parent odu, Oché (see page 257). Something there is needed for the client's evolution.

If the oracle refuses closure and the client is an initiate, the orisha whose diloggún is being consulted could be marking a tambor as the solution to all the client's troubles. The diviner should ask first if a tambor is required. If the answer is yes, he must mark the orisha who will claim the tambor, questioning, in turn, the orisha of the diloggún, Yemayá, Oshún, Elegguá, Ochosi, Babaluaiye, and egun. If a tambor is required but none of these spirits will take it, the diviner should continue his questioning with the rest of the orishas the client received in his ocha.

If after this process the odu still will not close, the diviner must turn to the eboses of the parent odu, Oché. Something there is needed for the client's evolution.

## The Third Composite Odu of Oché, Oché Ogundá (5-3)

### The Proverbs of Oché Ogundá

- Do not pick up that which you dropped.
- Do not recover that which you left behind.
- Do not go out to look for that which has been abandoned.
- Your enemy will do you evil, and yet he will do you good.
- Do not pick up what was discarded.
- Only the knife knows where the heart of the ñame lies.

### The Message of Oché Ogundá

When a casting of five mouths, Oché, is followed by a casting of three mouths, Ogundá, the odu Oché Ogundá has opened on the mat. This powerful odu has much to say to the client; the diviner must proceed carefully so that he does not miss anything.

Among the lore of this odu is the story of a town in which all the evil people gathered together with one purpose: to overthrow their king. The king was honest and pure, and he had a sincere heart. Olófin himself saw what was happening and intervened; he destroyed the evil townspeople and reinstated the king. Something similar could happen in the client's life, so his heart must remain noble.

In this odu, the diviner must begin the reading by honoring four orishas: "Maferefún Oshún! Maferefún Obatalá! Maferefún egun! Maferefún Inle!" Before this odu has closed, the diloggún will raise issues with all four. If these issues are not examined and settled carefully, the client will not have evolution.

Oshún has much to say to the client who opens in Oché Ogundá. In this odu, we say that only the knife knows where the heart of the ñame lies; in other words, only the client knows what he wants and why he has come to the orishas for help. Regardless of the client's desires, Oshún wants one thing: his head in ocha. Even if this client is not her child, Oshún loves him as if he were, and she should be adored as a good son adores his mother. Oshún has all that this client wants, and she will give him these gifts as he earns them.

This letter signals many serious health concerns, and they are especially dangerous if the osogbo has come in ano or ikú. Oché rules the abdominal and genital areas. Ogundá foreshadows disease that requires surgical intervention and resection. The client must be watchful for damage or disease in these areas. Impotence in men is a strong possibility. This is an "affliction of disobedience" in this sign; when it comes, the man knows that he has offended Oshún and must return to make ebó. Sterility is a danger for women. Under no circumstances should any person opening in this odu have a vasectomy or tubal ligation; these sterilization procedures are permanent, and in the future this person will want to have children.

The diviner should also keep the following points in mind:

- Oshún's children will always be a source of problems and heartache for the client. He must be careful with them, for Oshún forbids the client altercations with them.
- Any strange lumps, pains, or swellings in the genital region warrant an immediate visit to the doctor.
- The client must pay attention to matters in his physical and spiritual family. When conflicts arise, he should put his blood family first and his ocha family second.
- For a woman who opens in Oché Ogundá, the menstrual cycle is strongly affected by

her thoughts and actions. Stress could dry up her womb or make it overactive. Anemia can become a chronic condition if she does not promote calm in her life.

- In Oché Ogundá, men and women must have clearly defined marital relations. The client should tend to concerns at home before dealing with problems elsewhere.

## The Prohibitions of Oché Ogundá

- Be cautious of papers and contracts; do not sign anything unless it is approved by an attorney. Be wary of what one reads, for not all written is true.
- Anything that brings sadness must be taken away; tears will bring more of the same.
- Do not be overpowering or overwhelming to others; sweetness always brings more of the same.
- Do not speak with sadness; one's words must be happy, gentle, and kind.
- This is an odu of possible enslavement, and one must not be a slave to anything, including habits, people, and vices.
- Take care around needles and sharp objects, especially if one's work is in the field of health care. Disease could enter the body through a cut or puncture wound.
- Do nothing illegal. Do not visit another person in jail.
- Do not tell secrets to women, and remain cautious around men.
- A woman who opens in Oché Ogundá may never put a knife to her head; her hair must be allowed to grow. Only her godparents may trim the ends. A man who comes in this sign must consult with Oshún before cutting his hair. It, too, may need to grow long and beautiful. In both cases, allowing the hair to grow long honors Oshún.
- Do not work with metals or weapons. They can lead to injury.

## The Eboses of Oché Ogundá

In Oché Ogundá, red coral brings blessings. As a general rule for life, any eleke that the client receives from this moment on must contain red coral. He also should try to use coral in as many eboses to Yemayá and Oshún as he can, and he should hoard this stone for his own personal use.

In this odu, ebó centers on four spirits: Oshún, Obatalá, egun, and Inle. For each except Inle, the diviner should consider asking, "Ebó elese [spirit's name]?" If the answer is yes, he uses the diloggún to mark the appropriate ebó. Once Oshún, Obatalá, and egun have had a chance to claim ebó, the diviner should tell the client that he needs to give five masses to his egun. The client must then follow exactly the prescriptions of the espiritistas, for both he and his egun will benefit from them. If the client does not have his opá ikú, he should find one and have it fed. If he has no bóveda, he must set one up as soon as possible. He must provide sweetness for his ancestors, giving them honey, candy, cakes, and cookies frequently as adimú. Remember: Distributing sweetness will bring more of the same to one's life.

Inle cannot speak directly, but the orisha whose diloggún is consulted can speak on his behalf. If the client is an initiate, the diviner should ask, "Koshé Inle?"* If Inle's reception is not mandated, or if the client is an aleyo or an aborisha, the diviner should ask, "Ebó elese Inle?" If the answer is yes, he should use the diloggún to mark an appropriate offering. If neither Inle's reception nor an ebó to him is required, the client must have a rogación in front of Yemayá, and he should be given Inle's necklace at that time.

To help the client discover his heart, his purpose in the world, he should have a rogación at Oshún's shrine. Once his head is clear, the priest places a ñame on a white plate and hands the client a new, clean knife. The client inserts the knife slowly into the ñame, feeling for its heart. When he finds it, he cuts the root in two. He smears it with honey and leaves it with Oshún for five days. At the end of this time, the client takes the offering to the river and discards it.

Oché Ogundá marks the client to live his life by

*If this reading is an itá with Yemayá and Inle's reception is marked for the initiate, hereafter Inle must always sit at Yemayá's feet.

making ebó to Oshún. On the third of each month he should spoil both her and Elegguá, giving sweet adimú to each orisha. Whenever he is in doubt or danger, he should petition Oshún for a total of five days with five different adimús, leaving each with him for just a day and discarding them in the river. With such placation, Oshún will never fail him.

The diviner must prescribe an adimú to Oshún now to prevent abdominal disease in the client. If the client is an initiate, the odu might mark the reception of the knife; the right to use the knife removes the need to be under the knife. A client who is already experiencing abdominal disease should have a rogación at Oshún's feet after the adimú is offered.

Now the diviner has his first chance to close the odu. If these prescriptions are not enough to close the odu and the client is an aleyo or an aborisha, the diviner must turn to the list of eboses for the parent odu, Oché (see page 257). Something there is needed for the client's evolution. If the client is an initiate, however, the diviner has a few more eboses to consider:

- The client could need to receive Ochosi. To determine if this is the case, the diviner should ask, "Koshé Ochosi?" If the reception of Ochosi is marked, the client should have a rogación at Ochosi's feet as soon as possible, afterward receiving his eleke, while arrangements are being made for his reception.
- *Caracol de Ogún* (the diloggún of Ogún) is a possibility in this sign. To find out if it is needed, the diviner asks, "Koshé los caracoles de Ogún?" If the answer is yes, the ceremony should be performed as soon as possible, and it should include an itá.
- Oshún may require an ebó given in the river. To determine if this is the case, the diviner asks, "Ebó elese Oshún en el rio?" If the answer is yes, the proper offering is two hens and plenty of honey given in the river.
- If the oracle continues to refuse closure, it may be demanding the sacrifice of a four-legged animal. First the diviner asks the oracle if a sacrifice of four legs is needed. If the answer is yes, he then asks the oracle if the orisha speaking (the orisha whose diloggún has been cast) claims the sacrifice. If the answer is yes, the sacrifice is marked and no itá is needed. If the answer is no, the diviner then tries to mark the sacrifice to one of the orishas given in the client's ocha, in the order in which they are petitioned by the client. If the sacrifice is marked to one of these orishas, an itá is required for the client.
- If the oracle still will not close, the reception of the knife is mandatory.

If the oracle still refuses closure, the diviner must turn to the list of eboses given for the parent odu, Oché (see page 257). Something there is needed to bring the client's evolution.

If the eboses of the parent odu will not close the odu for an initiate, the following sacrifices should be offered: five hens to Oshún, three roosters to Elegguá, and eight white pigeons to Obatalá. The carcasses stay in the house until midnight and then are removed by the priest. The client must return home before sunrise. If this ebó will not close the odu, the diviner should turn to the eboses of the omo odu, Ogundá.

## The Fourth Composite Odu of Oché, Oché Irosun (5-4)

### The Proverbs of Oché Irosun

- If the rain does not fall, the corn does not grow.
- Freshwater fish cannot go to salt water.
- Your enemy will do you evil, and yet he will do you good.
- The dead are looking for someone to capture.
- Do not let the spirits of the dead catch you.

### The Message of Oché Irosun

When a casting of five mouths, Oché, is followed by a casting of four mouths, Irosun, the odu Oché Irosun has fallen. This is a mysterious sign, giving birth to mysterious things. The menstrual cycle of women is born in this odu, and all are mandated to pay homage to women and their mysterious powers.

Elegguá was born in a seashell through this sign; his birth here will have various implications for the client. Some say Oché Irosun separated the salt waters from the fresh waters; all agree that it alludes to the rain that falls from the skies. In iré, rain will be abundant; in osogbo, drought is possible. Finally, the song "Ogundá Arere . . ." was first sung in this pattern.

Many orishas stand behind the client's evolution in this odu, and homage must be paid to each. The diviner should say, "Maferefún Orisha Oko!" for here he is firm; even an aborisha may need to receive him. He also says, "Maferefún Oshún! Maferefún Olokun! Maferefún Yemayá!" All three speak in this odu, and each could offer advice or claim ebó.

As is the case in all patterns of Oché, Oshún speaks first. No matter its orientation, Oché Irosun signals that Oshún is upset with the client. In iré, the odu tells us that a long time ago this person sought a favor from Oshún, and she agreed to do it in return for a price. The blessing was given, but the price was never paid. The client's life is now in turmoil. He suffers in minor ways; afflictions have come from seemingly nowhere. These are Oshún's way of bringing him back to the shells so she can have her ebó. The client must reveal what it was that he promised her.

In osogbo, the issue goes deeper. The client has done something to anger Oshún, and she wants retribution. Carefully, the diviner must try to mark a larishe that will pacify Oshún. Until she is appeased, the client can have no evolution.

Oché Irosun also flags the possibility of sickness and disease; these concerns become more pressing if the odu opens in an osogbo of ano or ikú. For a woman, the reproductive system might suffer; her menstrual cycles could be suspended or overactive. Menstruation could come painfully, excessively, randomly, or not at all. Even though this woman might be unaware of this fact, the odu indicates that in her past she conceived and miscarried a child.

In either sex, the blood and stomach could decompose, inviting a host of diseases and illnesses. The client must monitor his health and treat his body well. He should take care to eat healthfully, for anemia and vitamin deficiencies are at the root of his complaints. The client must be on guard against sexually transmitted diseases. Sexual dysfunction, especially in a man, warrants a physical.

The diviner should also explore the following predictions:

- Because Oché Irosun implies Oshún's anger, her children are especially dangerous for the client. Until she is placated, one of her initiates may unknowingly try to exact punishment.
- While moving to a new home could be a good idea, the client may not move without the permission of his guardian orisha.
- Many enemies surround the client, and not all of them are known. He should be careful in all his personal dealings.
- A very close friend or family member may soon be arrested; the client should do all that he can to free this person from jail.

## The Prohibitions of Oché Irosun

- Do not swim or bathe in rivers or the sea. When at these places, one must pay proper respect to the forces they embody.
- Invitations for various parties, gatherings, or events will be extended. Do not accept.

## The Eboses of Oché Irosun

When Oché Irosun has opened on the mat for an aborisha or an initiate (but not an aleyo), Oshún and Yemayá want this person (whether male or female) to live with a woman as a roommate; heeding this advice will bring iré. Also, as soon as possible, the aborisha or initiate should give the following ebó to Oshún: Put five cobs of corn in a basin of river water. Place this at her shrine until they begin to take root. When this happens, luck will come. Before removing the ebó, use obí to determine how they should be discarded. Finally, the aborisha or initiate must receive Orisha Oko. Until preparations for this ceremony can be made, the client should wear the orisha's eleke, and he should be given a rogación at Orisha Oko's shrine.

If the client is an initiate and the odu has opened in an osogbo of ikú, the client should keep two quail in the house as pets. Their cooing can scare away Death himself.

When Oché Irosun opens for a woman of child-bearing age, she must have a rogación of her abdomen (first) and her head (second) before Oshún and Yemayá. Afterward, she must give these two orishas a sweet adimú in exchange for the cleansing.

Now the diviner has his first chance to close the odu. If it will not close, the diviner should explore the following options:

- The client could have further issues with Oshún, Yemayá, Shangó, egun, and Orisha Oko. To determine if any of these spirits is demanding ebó, the diviner should ask, "Ebó elese [spirit's name]?" If the answer is yes, he uses the diloggún to mark the offering.
- Olokun could also be demanding ebo or, perhaps, that the client receive him. The diviner must ask, "Ebó elese Olokun?" If the answer is yes, he uses the diloggún to mark the offering. If the answer is no, or if the odu continues to refuse closure, the diviner asks, "Koshé Olokun?" If the reception of Olokun is marked, preparations for this ceremony should begin as soon as possible.

If the prescriptions made thus far are still not enough to close Oché Irosun, the diviner should turn to the eboses of the parent odu, Oché (see page 257). Something there is needed for the client's evolution.

# The Fifth Composite Odu of Oché, Oché Meji (5-5)

## The Proverbs of Oché Meji

- The needle pulls the thread.
- The cat wears gloves.
- Talking a lot will tire one's tongue.
- Promises made must be kept.
- Those things that are up are about to be down, and those things that are down are about to be up.
- The hen has a decaying orifice; she cannot lay eggs.
- One's luck is a fickle thing.
- If you talk too much, you will tire out both your tongue and your companions; do not talk so much.

## The Message of Oché Meji

When a casting of five mouths repeats itself, Oché Meji is open. This sign is beautiful and powerful yet also harsh and heated. For every blessing it brings to the client, it will take something away. For all the good that can be said, even this can be matched with evil. The diviner must be careful with his delivery of this session.

Oshún is of utmost importance in this odu; although she was once a minor spirit among the saints, her works in Oché Meji elevated her to grand status. Once, the Iroko (the orisha who spans the sky and the earth, the sacred tree before which all the orishas gather) grew proud and arrogant, and he sought to flood the world. Oshún convinced Olódumare to bring an end to the flood. Ogún once left civilization, and it crumbled; he hid in the woods, and not even the strongest orishas could bring him back out. Oshún, by her sweetness and grace, brought him back to civilization. For saving the world time and time again, Oshún is celebrated; the diviner says, "Maferefún Oshún!"

The diviner also pays homage to the orishas enamored with Oshún, saying, "Maferefún Iroko! Maferefún Ogún! Maferefún Obatalá! Maferefún Shangó! Maferefún Ochosi! Maferefún Elegguá!" Oshún enchanted Obatalá with her purity; he taught her to read the shells. She enraptured Shangó's heart; he lavished her with gifts. She inflamed Ochosi with her vulnerabilities; he taught her to fight and defend herself. She befriended Elegguá with her purity; he helps her for free. Even when all these spirits are angry, if Oshún's favor can be obtained no one in heaven or on earth will destroy this client. These orishas will all defend him fearlessly when Oshún stands up for him. Even Orúnmila loves Oshún's favorites, for she was the first *apetebi*, the first woman on the earth to assist him in his work.

The custom of tasting honey was born in this odu. Ikú himself tried to poison Oshún when she would not be his wife, and all the aché of heaven and earth was needed to heal her. Since that day, honey is never given as adimú unless the supplicant first tastes what is offered.

This odu indicates that spirits of the dead frequently manifest to the client. His home is frequented by egun. The egun must be given several masses and offerings to help with their spiritual progress and evolution. One spirit who visits the client is especially troublesome, frequently awakening those who reside in the home. A cleansing of the house will remove this unwelcome spirit. Also, if the client is not aware of his home's history, he should investigate it; Oché Meji warns that someone died in or near the dwelling, and this spirit needs a mass in order to be put at rest.

Oché Meji also signals that the client is close to a guide, a Gypsy-type woman who once consulted the cards. Working with her will increase the client's ability to consult with cards or glasses of water. The odu mandates that the client begin this kind of work, for he has much talent for witchcraft.

This sign flags certain health concerns, as well, and if it comes in an osogbo of ano or ikú, the client must pay careful attention to these warnings. They are not typical of the rest of Oché's composite odus. The client must be cautious of his bones and jaw, for they could suffer trauma and breakage. He must protect his head, both physically and spiritually, at all times. A bath of Oshún's herbs applied to the head, plus a later rogación, should offer stability and protection. In Oché Meji, the client's bowels can become twisted; he could have physical problems in the intestines or the digestive tract. Acid is abundant in his stomach, which could lead to ulceration. His blood, too, is very acidic. To remove many of the health complaints that are now just brewing in the body, the client must suppress any vices he now indulges in.

In addition, the diviner should keep in mind the following points:

- Jewelry and other valuables or heirlooms should not be pawned; they contain the client's luck.
- Soon, the client could have a complete reversal of fortune and luck. He must hold on tightly to those things that are dear and let the rest go. He can save only so much for himself.
- If the client is a woman, she is not a virgin. If she has a child, the one she says is the father is not the father.
- This is an odu of empty promises, things that remain unfulfilled. To gather iré to himself, not only should the client try to make good on all the promises he has made to others, but also he should collect on all the promises that others have made to him.

## The Prohibitions of Oché Meji

- In this odu one can be very vulnerable to infection and community-acquired illness. The following taboos are meant to guard one's health: Do not sit on public toilets. When eating, do not share drinks or eating utensils. If eating in another's home, use only disposable cups and plates. Avoid public places like restaurants. Never accept a drink that has been opened; always ask for a closed bottle.
- Do not consume leftover, boxed, or reheated foods. Do not consume any red foods.
- Do not make empty promises; better yet, make it a habit never to promise anything to anyone.
- Do not hold grudges against others. If someone treats one badly, let go and move on.
- Do not pawn jewelry.
- When this odu comes in an osogbo, all vices and addictions must be suppressed; do not be a slave to any addiction. Follow all the prohibitions of Oché. Also, if this reading comes during the first itá, the iyawó may not cross over or come near a river during the entire year.

## The Eboses of Oché Meji

When a casting of Oché Meji has fallen on the mat, the diviner sits before someone who is destined to become a great spiritualist; his evolution in this direction will come.

If the client does not have a bóveda for egun, he

should set up one. If he does not have an opá ikú, he should provide one. If the client has an opá, it must be strengthened; the diviner should feed it a rooster and, one week after this sacrifice, oil it with cocoa butter.

Oché Meji marks a series of five masses to egun, one per week for five weeks. The client's egun are in need of light and evolution, and these masses will resolve this problem. He should pay attention to all the espiritistas do, for one day he will be a great medium. (And the diviner may encourage that the client attend masses regularly.)

Finally, a spirit skilled at consulting cards accompanies this client. The diviner should investigate this situation spiritually. It is a powerful guide, and to help establish a relationship with it, the client should construct a bóveda just for this spirit.

Oshún speaks strongly in Oché Meji, and this odu holds many possibilities for ebó to her. To bring warmth and blessings to his home, the client should throw a party in Oshún's honor. The more people he invites and serves, the greater the blessings Oshún will bring. The client must make sure that five perfumes are available to all who come; each guest should spray himself and Oshún with one of these scents. The food at the party should include five sweet dishes. Remember: Oshún is the orisha of all sweetness, and five is her number. The day after this party, when the house is clean, the diviner feeds three baby chicks to Elegguá and two hens to Oshún. This sacrifice will clean all the remaining osogbos from the client, setting his feet firmly on the path to evolution.

Now the diviner has his first chance to close the oracle. If Oché Meji will not close, the diviner should investigate the following possibilities:

- Elegguá or Oshún could be demanding ebó. To find out what else these orishas require, the diviner should consider asking, "Ebó elese Elegguá?" and "Ebó elese Oshún?" If the answer to either question is yes, he uses the diloggún to mark the appropriate offering.
- If the odu still will not close, Oshún may require the following ebó: The diviner prepares Oshún's omiero with five of her herbs. Before making any ebó for the client, the priest washes his own head carefully with these waters. Next he washes the client's head, and then he gives him a rogación before Oshún's shrine. Afterward, he presents five calabazas first to the client's orí and then to Oshún. The client is now prohibited for life to consume any gourd.
- If the odu still will not close, the diviner may consider asking, "Eborí elese Oshún?" If the answer is yes, the diviner must feed the client's head two white pigeons or doves before his head is washed in Oshún's herbs.
- Iroko, Ogún, Obatalá, Shangó, Ochosi, Babaluaiye, or Elegguá could be claiming an ebó. The diviner should ask, "Ebó elese [orisha's name]?" If the answer is yes, he uses the shells to mark the required ebó.
- If the client is an aleyo or an aborisha, he could need Babaluaiye. The diviner should consider asking, "Koshé Babaluaiye?" If his reception is mandated, the client should wear his eleke; he should be given the eleke after having a rogación at Babaluaiye's shrine.

If the odu still refuses closure and the client is an aleyo or an aborisha, the diviner should turn to the eboses of the parent odu, Oché (see page 257). Something there is needed for the client's evolution.

If Oché Meji will not close and the client is an initiate, it could be marking two other possibilities:

- A tambor for the godparent's crown could be the solution to all that ails this client. Since the godparent's crown birthed the initiate's head, it will also align his head with his destiny. The diviner should ask, "Tambor elese [orisha's name]?" If the answer is yes, the ceremony should take place as soon as possible. In the meantime, the client should have a rogación before that orisha's sopera. He must offer the orisha a sweet adimú afterward.
- Iroko's reception could be mandated. To determine if this is needed, the diviner should ask, "Koshé Iroko?"

If odu still will not close, the diviner should now turn to the list of eboses for the parent odu, Oché. Something there is needed for the client's evolution.

## The Sixth Composite Odu of Oché, Oché Obara (5-6)

### The Proverbs of Oché Obara

- The tongue is the body's whip.
- The bell sounds loudest in your own backyard.
- He who speaks much makes many mistakes.
- The drunk thinks one thing, and the bartender thinks another.
- Do not lead the blind, for when they know as much as you, they will stab you in the back.
- Look for happiness and love at home before you seek it somewhere else.
- Your enemy will do you evil, and your enemy will do you good.
- The house will find ruin.
- The bell sounds for the pleasure of the world.
- The bitterness of the world is carried with you.

### The Message of Oché Obara

When an initial cast of five mouths, Oché, precedes a cast of six mouths, Obara, the odu Oché Obara is open on the mat. Immediately, the diviner says, "Maferefún Shangó! Maferefún Oshún! Maferefún Yemayá! Maferefún Taewó and Kaindé! Maferefún Elegguá, Eshu Aye! Maferefún Ideu! Maferefún Obatalá!" For Shangó and Oshún were once lovers, and while Shangó was away at war, Oshún gave birth to twins, the Ibeyi. All the world accused her of evil since only animals could give birth to more than one child at once. Alone, in shame, Oshún abandoned her children to Yemayá, who accepted them as if they were her own. Oshún wandered in grief. Eshu Ayé (Elegguá) found her alone and close to starvation, and he brought her home. Oshún would eat meat only from female goats. However, Eshu Ayé had only male goats, and so while he fed them to her, he did not tell her where the meat came from. After many weeks, Oshún discovered the animals Eshu Ayé had been feeding her, and in anger she castrated them all. Thus did their meat become sweet and delicate like that of the female goat, and since that time, Oshún prefers their meat above all else.

Eventually, Oshún's grief over Taewó and Kaindé returned, and she wandered away from Eshu Ayé's home. Misery, hopelessness, and shame swept through her; as she became lost in despair, love and sweetness left the world. Finally, even Olódumare felt her pain, and he decreed that Oshún's womb would conceive once more; she would have a male infant whose aché would remove her tears. Ideu was born. His birth dried her tears, but fear gripped her heart like a vise. Even as sweetness and beauty returned to all things, Oshún was afraid: Obatalá himself decreed that all male children born to the orishas would be put to death. Before any could see Ideu, Oshún dressed him as a girl in beautiful dresses of yellow silk. When others came to see the newborn, she presented him as her "daughter." Thus was Ideu's life saved. In time, Obatalá took back his decree, but Ideu chose to continue wearing dresses: In a dress was his life saved, and in a dress was his life lived.

Therefore, having cast this odu on the mat, the diviner pays homage to Shangó and Oshún for giving birth to the Ibeyi, to Taewó and Kaindé for being a source of both joy and sorrow, to Yemayá for raising the children Oshún had not the strength to care for, to Eshu Ayé for saving Oshún when she could not care for herself, to Ideu for drying his mother's tears and bringing sweetness and joy back into the world, and finally to Obatalá for taking back his decree so no male born to an orisha was ever again murdered in the land of the orishas. The diviner will need to examine the implications of this sign and its lore carefully, for all these spirits and all these issues could have some bearing on the client's life.

After this long list of spirits, the diviner pays homage to two more, saying, "Maferefún Oyá! Maferefún egun!" Their energy also manifests in this letter, and the client has much to do with the dead. The client's egun must be given masses, for only by helping the spirits evolve can this person find evolution. His house must be spiritually and physically cleansed if troublesome spirits are to be removed. One of these is in turmoil, and it awakens the client frequently at night by sitting on the edge of his bed. A cleansing will remove this presence.

A woman whose reading opens in this sign may have many special concerns. If she has children or is pregnant, gossip surrounds them; others say that she does not know who the father is or that the man she calls their father is not their real father. The odu speaks of both pregnancy and sickness in the womb. The client's menstrual cycle suffers some irregularity. She may have a nervous disorder or suffer decomposition of the blood and intestines. She should offer adimú to Oshún to avoid sickness in the abdominal area; if she already suffers from abdominal complaints, she should have a rogación at Oshún's feet.

In addition, the diviner should keep the following points in mind:

- In this sign, the client could have so much money that he does not appreciate it. If he doesn't change his attitude, a large amount of money could disappear soon.
- The client offers his opinion at times when it is not asked for.
- The client should look for prosperity where he is before he seeks it elsewhere.
- This person needs to communicate with his godparents more often so that there is no misunderstanding.
- Many people around this client do not understand what he does religiously, and if they were to know all his plans, they would do all that they could to stop him. When it comes to ocha, this person must not tell others what he plans to do.

## The Prohibitions of Oché Obara

- Maintain a tight grip on one's finances; do not give anything away. A santero who works the religion must not do it for free; he must always charge, and charge well, for his work.
- Do not pawn personal possessions; one may, however, sell them outright.
- Oshún forbids one to move from one's present home. If the need to move arises in the future, one must return and consult with her before making any definite plans.
- Do not work at third-shift, late-evening, or early-morning jobs; one is meant to work while the sun shines.
- Alcohol is taboo; never let anyone drink at an orisha festival held for one's own spirits.
- Never walk before the orishas nude or in one's underwear.
- Do not go to bed immediately after a large meal; always wait at least five hours after a meal before retiring. Do not eat after sunset.

## The Eboses of Oché Obara

When Oché Obara opens on the mat, the diviner has many initial considerations for ebó. First, the client needs Elegguá in the path of Eshu Ayé. He will walk closely with this person, opening doors that were once closed. If the client's avatar of Elegguá is Eshu Ayé, a smaller one should be made in a tiny conch shell; it must have foundation (it must contain an otá inside the image), and the client must carry it with him at all times. In this case the diviner might wish to determine whether the client's Eshu Ayé requires ebó, asking, "Ebó elese Eshu Ayé?" If the answer is yes, the diviner should use the diloggún to mark what is needed.

By opening in Oché Obara, the orisha whose diloggún is being consulted demands that the client speak to him while sounding a cowbell; the normal instrument for this orisha should be kept at the shrine but rarely used.

Finally, anyone who opens in Oché Obara must wear a red parrot feather in the hair when going to an orisha function or festival.

Having made these prescriptions, the diviner can now attempt to close the odu. If it will not close, he should investigate the following:

- If the client comes because of bitterness in his life, this odu prescribes a unique ebó that may be used to soothe differences among family, lovers, and friends: The client should invite everyone involved to dinner. While waiting for the entrée, he should serve a bit of a sweet dessert, insisting that everyone eat it while waiting for the meal. Once the dessert has been consumed, he serves the entrée, which should be bitter, and finishes the meal by offering yet another dessert. The sweet that was turned to sour will be turned to sweet once more.

- Eleggua wants this person to know that if he ever experiences a "holocaust" in his own life, there is a remedy: with Oshún and the Ibeyi near Elegguá, the sacrifice to him of an uncastrated goat. The client must have itá the next day and do all the eboses that Elegguá prescribes. The bad times will then turn to good.
- If the odu has opened in osogbo, the client may have further issues to address with Oshún. The diviner should prescribe that the client offer five *cappuccinos* (a Cuban pastry) to Oshún and, the following day, have a rogación before her shrine, with a portion of each pastry used on the client's head. If Oshún requires an adimú, the client should present her with five sunflowers on a yellow plate, and pour honey and cinnamon liberally over this. Note that if egun (especially the Native American spirits) stand up for adimú in this odu, a single sunflower on a terra-cotta plate may be offered; it should be covered with honey and cinnamon as well.

If the odu refuses closure at this point and the client is an aleyo or aborisha, the diviner should turn to the eboses of the parent odu, Oché (see page 257). Something there is needed for this person's evolution.

If Oché Obara will not close and the client is an initiate, the diviner should ask, "Eyebale elese Oshún?" If diloggún marks eyebale as ebó, Oshún wants to be fed two hens in her own home, the river; once the sacrifices are done, the client should leave an adimú of sweet foods on the riverbank. By marking this ebó, Oshún says that this client once had a special place for her in his heart, perhaps even a special routine. It ended. She wants that place in his heart and that special routine once more. After making this ebó, the client should present her with a large jar of honey containing a honeycomb and wrapped in yellow cloth and yellow ribbons. Every day before leaving home, the client should cross his tongue with a bit of this honey and say, "Maferefún Oshún!"

If this prescription will not settle the client's issues with Oshún and the oracle still will not close, the orisha may be standing up for a new home, and the client should offer her a new sopera. If this new prescription is still not enough to close the odu, the diviner must consider the eboses of the parent odu, Oché (see page 257). Something there is needed for the client's evolution.

## The Seventh Composite Odu of Oché, Oché Odí (5-7)

### The Proverbs of Oché Odí

- The one who owes and pays is free of debt.
- Your enemy will do you evil, yet he will do you good.
- Prepare for war.
- You are free because of lack of proof.
- Do not push your luck.
- You will get caught with your finger in the pudding.

### The Message of Oché Odí

When a casting of five mouths, Oché, is followed by a casting of seven mouths, Odí, the odu Oché Odí has opened. Having cast this odu, the diviner must pay homage to Orúnmila, Shangó, Elegguá, Yemayá, Oshún, Osain, Ogún, and Inle, saying to each, "Maferefún!" Each of these orishas may influence this person's evolution.

This letter is very tricky; its orientation of iré and osogbo heavily influences the reading, but each orientation carries a piece of the other. This melding comes from the odu's patakís. One tells of the time when war was imminent in the world, and Orúnmila walked the earth announcing, "It is going to rain weapons." Only a few came outside to catch the gifts that were falling from heaven, and they hoarded the weapons in case of war. Most of the earth hid. Orúnmila once again walked about, saying, "It is going to rain gold." Everyone came out for a chance at catching gold, but instead the wars began, and those who had come out at Orúnmila's first warning won.

Oché Odí is also the odu in which the air plant and the orchid were born; these can have many uses as ebó. It also speaks of parasites and parasitic infections; worms, lice, fleas, fungal infections, and other opportunistic organisms can infect the client.

Because iré can bring osogbo and osogbo iré, the diviner should treat Oché Odí as if it had fallen in an osogbo. If one prepares for the worst, when good comes one is joyous. If the sign opens in iré, the client has a clear road to travel. Yet if he strays from his path, he will be hit with all manner of setbacks. Health issues are always a concern in this sign. The diviner must tell the client to practice perfect hygiene. He should keep his feet, toenails, hands, and fingernails clean and dry at all times. He should wash his hands frequently, for most infections are acquired through the hands. Bacterial infections and food-borne parasites are also a danger. The client must demand cleanliness in the preparation of cooked foods; he must ensure that meats are well done and vegetables or fruits washed well. Fungal infections, sexually transmitted diseases, and hepatitis are all also close; the client should not participate in behavior that would put him at risk of contracting these diseases. Note that if the prohibitions of both Oché Odí and the parent odu, Oché (see page 257), are prescribed and followed, many of these dangers will be avoided. Also, this sign warns of illness to the stomach and intestines; profuse internal bleeding is possible in the elderly. This person's cholesterol could be too high.

The diviner should also keep the following concerns in mind:

- This sign says that he who owes should pay his debts; if he does, he will be free, absolved of guilt. The diviner should encourage this client to assess the debts and favors he owes to other people; these must be paid. He should also encourage the client to assess the debts he owes to the orishas; these, too, must be paid. Paying his debts is the easiest way for the client to facilitate his evolution.
- In osogbo, the client can be a bitter ingrate; he thanks no one for the good anyone does. This behavior must change.
- This odu signals that the client is a pest and, at times, a snob. He must remember that bitterness will always attract more of the same.
- A child of Yemayá or an initiate of Obatalá who opens in Oché Odí often has something wrong in his blood. The diviner should advise that the client have bloodwork done with his family physician.
- Men who open in this odu can have serious concerns with women. If the client is a man and has recently ended a relationship, he is crying on the inside over this. The diviner should tell him there is hope: If he changes his ways, she might take him back, and they can be together happily for a long time. A man who lives with a woman will find her pregnant, and this will not be a joy for him. He is afraid of fatherhood and commitment, which is why he has not married her. A married man will find himself tempted to take a lover on the side; he must not do this. (The diviner should note that married men who come in this odu often court the affections of other married women.)

## The Prohibitions of Oché Odí

- Do not eat leftovers, reheated foods, stale foods, or boxed foods. One's health depends on wholesome, fresh food.
- Do not consume the internal organs of animals.
- Do not eat, pick, buy, sell, or give away any type of gourd: Save gourds only for ebó.
- Do not eat white flour, gumbo, or okra.

## The Eboses of Oché Odí

Oché Odí marks the client as a child of two waters, but this can have varying meanings, depending on the type of reading given and the client's initiatory status. One who opens in Oché Odí is being blessed by both Yemayá and Oshún; in this way he is a child of two waters, and he should offer both orishas an ebó. The diviner should examine the larishe of Oché Odí carefully; if either Yemayá or Oshún claimed an ebó, he should consider it claimed by both. The ebó should be given first to the orisha who claimed it and then to her sister. The diviner might also consider asking whether the two will take something special together, querying, "Ebó elese Yemayá y Oshún?" If the answer is yes, he uses the diloggún to mark the offering. Once he has given the two this ebó, for luck he should give an ebó—a plaza of fresh fruits would be the best choice—to Inle in brackish water, a place where the river meets the sea.

Another way in which the client could be a child of two waters is if this odu comes in an itá for Yemayá or Oshún or if it falls for either the head or the feet to head for a iyawó. No matter which of these two orishas claims his head, the client will always be mistaken for a priest of the other. He must never correct this mistake, for in truth both Yemayá and Oshún lay claim to his head. Daily, he should pray to both, and when he offers an ebó to one, he must offer it to the other as well. He should keep the soperas of these orishas at equal height and put them side by side with the Elegguá of his ocha between them. Every year the iyawó should travel to a place where the river meets the sea; there he must sacrifice to both orishas, give them a plaza of sweet fruits, then bathe in the water and take some home for spiritual baths. The diviner should now tell the iyawó that Yemayá and Oshún will always work together to save him; when there is great need in his life, he must adore them both.

After making these prescriptions, the diviner now has his first chance to close the oracle. If it remains open, the diviner should consider the following possibilities:

- The client has issues with his egun; he must keep a spiritual bóveda and tend it well. The diviner might consider asking if the egun require ebó, questioning, "Ebó elese egun?" If the answer is yes, he marks the offering with the shells.
- The client could have issues with Shangó, Elegguá, or Ogún. They might need ebó. To determine if this is the case, the diviner should ask, "Ebó elese [orisha's name]?" If the answer is yes, he marks the offering with the shells.

If these eboses will not close the odu and the client is an aleyo or aborisha, the diviner should now examine the eboses for the parent odu, Oché (see page 257). Something there could be essential for the client's evolution.

If the odu will not close and the client is an initiate, he might need spiritual work with Aganyú. First the diviner should ask, "Ebó elese Aganyú?" If the answer is yes, he marks the offering. If no ebó is needed, or if the odu will not close even after ebó is marked to Aganyú, the diviner should consider the reception of Aganyú, asking, "Koshé Aganyú?"

If these considerations will not close the odu, the diviner should now turn to the eboses of the parent odu, Oché. Something there is needed to bring the client's evolution.

## The Eighth Composite Odu of Oché, Oché Ogbe (5-8)

### The Proverbs of Oché Ogbe

- Do not cry in misery; it will only make things worse.
- Everything in life has its own time.
- Lies bring arguments.
- There are disturbances in your house due to liars.

### The Message of Oché Ogbe

When an initial cast of five mouths, Oché, precedes a cast of eight mouths, Eji Ogbe, the odu Oché Ogbe is open. It is also known as Oché Unle, Oché Ejiogbe, and Oché l'Ogbe. Of all the odu in this family, Oché Ogbe is among the most beautiful. Through it were all the world's rivers born. Rain fell from heaven; it sought its mother, the ocean, and cut the riverbeds in dry land during its journey. Gold, silver, and amber were born here, too; all the riches of the world first appeared as Oché Ogbe unfolded.

Ideu's influence is strong in this odu. While many elders claim that Ideu was born in Oché Obara (5-6), others argue that only the prophecy of his birth was told in Oché Obara. These elders say that he was born here, in Oché Ogbe, for as his birth healed Oshún's misery, so can it heal the client's. Regardless of the orisha's birthplace, the diviner pays homage to him for bringing sweetness back to the world, saying, "Maferefún Ideu!" With Ideu's influence, this sign becomes one of renewal; it destroys sadness. But the diviner should know this: No matter who speaks or claims ebó here, the client is sad. His heart may be broken; his spirit is weak. Depression and darkness threaten to overwhelm him, and at its worst this letter speaks of suicidal ideation and tendencies. It marks life's final sojourn: death. This trip, however, is not an osogbo brought from God, the orishas, or other spirits; it is brought by the client's own head and heart. The solution to his troubles lies with the advice of three spirits: Oba, Oshún, and egun.

With this odu open on the mat, the diviner begins by saying, "Maferefún Oba!" This orisha's presence radiates in this odu. To honor her, for she so rarely speaks in the diloggún, many diviners will tell the story of her oppression. Once, when her husband, Shangó, forsook her, Oba abandoned the world of the living for the land of the dead. Such was her insecurity and desire for love that she mutilated her own body. When Shangó saw what she had done, he was filled with disgust. He sent her away. Forlorn and lost, she banished herself to the cemetery. The client may be in a similar circumstance. For him, life has become a prison; he faces traps and entanglements, and he cries tears of oppression. He harbors memories bitterly, and these memories are so tragic that they can kill. His depression is almost manic. Oba knows this pain; she wants no one to suffer as she—not for love, not for money, and not for friendship. Oba demands worship. The client must honor her by going out to have fun. He must forget about the past, dress up, and act grand! He also must learn to speak his thoughts, emotions, and desires, to communicate his feelings to others. And he must never sacrifice his physical or emotional health for love.

The diviner also says, "Maferefún Oshún!" She knows much about this person's tears and heartbreaks, for she is the orisha of sweetness and love, the one who gives the gifts that make life worth living. She has tried many times to make this person happy, but his refusal to accept her blessings and his blindness to the good that he has in life make her angry; he makes her weep. Oshún wants to cry over this person no more. In spite of the bad in his life, he also has good, and it is a gift from Oshún. The client must look for the good that exists, the blessings Oshún has brought, and he must thank her for them. Wallowing in self-misery only angers her.

The diviner pays homage to egun as well, saying to them, "Maferefún!" In this odu, egun come first to chastise and then to bless. Their warning is this: Death haunts the client. However, it is not looking for him. Instead, he is calling it. He yearns for it; he dreams about it. He desires rest amid chaos. But his ancestors do not want him with them yet; they want him to live out a full life and to prosper on earth. They know how he feels. They know his tears and depression. The diviner should deliver this message: "No one loves you like your family, yet those who have gone before do not want you with them yet. They want to live through you, to help you achieve all that they could not." This is their blessing—to help him do what they could not. All the client's ancestors suffered trials and tribulations while they were alive. If this person will listen to them, work with them, and honor them, he will have the experience of countless lifetimes behind him. With egun's help, he can only prosper.

In addition, the diviner should consider the following issues:

- The client is suffering pains in the hips, feet, and knees. If ebó is made, these will pass.
- While Oshún loves the client dearly, he must be warned never to make promises to her that he cannot keep. If he does not keep a promise to Oshún, he will lose her favor.
- No one knows the good one has until it is lost. The client must remember this counsel and give thanks for his blessings every day.
- If the client lives with a lover, the diviner should tell him, "Treason will happen between your friend and your lover, and it will happen under your own roof."
- If the client guards something in a trunk or chest, it might be stolen. He should take care to protect it.

- A war might arise between this client and a *mayombero* (a priest of Palo Mayombe). He must be careful; he could lose everything in this war.
- A pregnant woman who opens in Oché Ogbe has special concerns with Oshún. The child was conceived under duress; it came through sadness but will bring blessings. The expectant mother must do all she can to bring this child to the world. Caesarean section is dangerous in this odu, but with ebó the health of mother and child can be saved. Obatalá himself will assist Oshún with this. The ebó mandated for expectant mothers is detailed in "The Eboses of Oché Ogbe" (see below).

## The Prohibitions of Oché Ogbe

- When Oché Ogbe falls on the mat, the orishas warn that vices will cause an early death. Smoking, alcohol, drugs, and recreational sex are all taboo.
- Do not sell anything that belongs to one's orishas. One might be tempted to sell the orishas themselves, but this would be tantamount to selling one's own soul.
- If one has a nganga or charm of palo, guard it. Small items will be lost; large ones will be stolen.

## The Eboses of Oché Ogbe

When Oché Ogbe opens on the mat, it provides many spiritual prescriptions for the client's evolution. First, the diviner must tell him to attend to his egun well. The client's sadness can be so deep that, subconsciously, he wishes to be with them; this information should not be relayed to the client, as he might be suicidal or harboring suicidal tendencies. However, he must be told that a bóveda, an opá ikú, and a mass are all required. As he gives egun firmness in this world, his chance to escape prematurely into the next will be lost.

Next, the diviner should tell the client that if he hopes to bring sweetness back into his life, he must do the following five-week ebó: In the first week, he must make a list of all that he owns. The following week, he should make a list of all his spiritual possessions. The third week, he must create another list, writing down all the wonderful people he knows or has known. The fourth week, he must make a list of all the wonderful places he has gone. The fifth week, he must create a list of all the wonderful blessings he has had in his life. After five weeks of work, the client should check all these lists again to see if he has left out anything. The lists will be quite long, and the client must return to the orishas to make an adimú thanking them for all the blessings he has but has ignored.

If the client is a pregnant woman, she must offer special eboses to ensure her health and that of the unborn child. First, she must have a rogación before Obatalá's shrine. This will pull the spiritual poison from her body. Second, after the rogación, the priest must rub her abdomen with a white pigeon or dove and then feed the bird to Obatalá. It will save the life of both the mother and the unborn child. Finally, the client must have a rogación of the abdomen before Oshún's shrine so that the child has the orisha's blessings. If this series of cleansings is completed once a month for three months, all will go well.

Oché Ogbe is a letter of music, creativity, and artistic talent. Before attempting closure of this odu, the diviner should ask the client about his artistic talents and find out what creative outlet—music, writing, acting, comedy, painting—he gave up as a child. The orishas want him to take up again whatever creative passion he gave up as a child.

Once these eboses have been explained, the diviner has his first chance to close the odu. If it will not close, he must explore the following possibilities:

- The client could have further issues with Oshún. First, the diviner should remind this person that as a child he played or dreamed of playing an instrument. When the client agrees, the diviner must tell him Oshún demands that he play that instrument again. When he is not playing it, the client must leave it with her. Also, the client should give Oshún a music box. When the client is sad, crying, or depressed, he must play that music box and pray to Oshún for release and healing. Finally, the diviner should find out if Oshún requires any ebó in this odu, asking, "Ebó elese Oshún?" If the answer is yes, he uses the diloggún to mark the offering.

- If the odu still will not close, the client's egun may be demanding ebó. The diviner should ask, "Ebó elese egun?" If the answer is yes, he uses the diloggún to mark the offering.
- The client could have issues with Oba. To see if she will take an offering, the italero must ask, "Ebó elese Oba?" If the answer is yes, Oba is coming through Oché Ogbe to tell the client that she knows how he has suffered for love and affection, and she wants him to suffer no more. The ebó prescribed in this odu will help dry his tears and put him on the path to evolution. Using the shells, the diviner must mark an appropriate offering to this orisha.

Having come this far without closure, if the client is an aleyo or an aborisha, the diviner should turn to the eboses of the parent odu, Oché (see page 257). Something there is needed for the client's evolution.

For an initiate, there are further considerations for ebó:

- The diviner should prepare a niche osain for Oshún, packed into a clamshell. Two skeleton keys are attached to it. The diviner washes and feeds it with the client's Oshún, and it remains in her sopera. After this is done, the client should seek a competent babalawo to feed a red snapper to his head.
- Inle is a final consideration. To see what is required in this odu, the diviner must ask, "Ebó elese Inle?" and "Koshé Inle?" If an ebó is marked, he uses the diloggún to determine the appropriate offering.

If none of these satisfies the odu for an initiate, the diviner must turn to the eboses of the parent odu, Oché (see page 257). Something there is needed for closure.

# The Ninth Composite Odu of Oché, Oché Osá (5-9)

## The Proverbs of Oché Osá

- The good child has the blessings of Olódumare and his mother.
- Resolve the problems with your mother and give her respect.
- Better late than never.
- Cleverness is more valuable than force.
- Life is beautiful; do not destroy your own beauty.
- Calmness and coolness save from destruction.
- Yemayá, by her trustworthiness, became mother to the world.
- The horse throws his rider.
- No one knows the good he has until it is lost.
- Take care of what is yours.

## The Message of Oché Osá

When an initial cast of five mouths precedes a cast of nine mouths, the odu Oché Osá is open on the mat. The diviner says, "Maferefún Oshún! Maferefún Aganyú!" In this pattern, Oshún saved Aganyú's life. All the rivers in the world are Oshún's, but Aganyú is her ferryman; he carries mortals and orishas across her vast, deep waters. One day, however, Aganyú was careless and he fell into the river. Unable to swim, he almost drowned, but Oshún extended a single oar to the struggling orisha. She saved his life. It is also this odu in which Oshún and Aganyú first ate castrated goat together.

The diviner also pays homage to Orúnmila, saying, "Maferefún Orúnmila!" One day this mighty spirit was traveling to a party; he chanced upon a friend who was going the same way. "Come with me," invited his friend. "Share my horse. If you walk, you will be late." Feeling that danger was at hand, Orúnmila refused his friend's offer and asked, "I feel danger, my friend. Why do you not walk with me instead?" The friend refused, leaving Orúnmila alone on his path. Almost immediately, the horse on which he rode stumbled; he was thrown and killed.

Because he refused to ride, Orúnmila got to the party late, but safe.

Oché Osá is a letter of intrigue and danger, and it will take the intervention of all three orishas—Oshún, Aganyú, and Orúnmila—to save the client from harm. The diviner should tell him this: "Oché Osá says that, spiritually, you are all but lost. You wander aimlessly. You are an emotional wreck. While you've never tried to take your own life, you have thought about it. The orishas tell you this: Do not take your own life. It is forbidden." Even if the client has resolved to live, even if his suicidal ideation is a thing of the past, Oché Osá signals that he is surrounded by danger. Carelessness will cause an accident, just as Aganyú's carelessness almost cost him his life. The client must have faith, for Oshún will save him. For the rest of his life, he must begin, live, and end each day by paying homage to all three orishas: "Maferefún Oshún!" for she is his salvation; "Maferefún Aganyú!" for letting the client learn from his mistakes; and "Maferefún Orúnmila!" for just as his own intuition led him away from danger, so he will lead the client to safety.

In addition to the issues with these three orishas, the italero should explore with his client the following points:

- Oché Osá flags issues between the client and his lover. If this person is in a committed relationship, the diviner should tell him, "The odu says you are not with the right person. In time, you will find your true love. Be prepared to let go of what you have."
- This sign alludes to nervous disorders and psychiatric conditions. The diviner should tell the client to relax and take care of his mental health. If emotional or spiritual problems become all-consuming, he should seek professional attention immediately. Know that suicide attempts born under this sign's influence will result in failure.
- An osogbo of ano or ikú flags special concerns in this odu. Men will suffer impotence, which could have medical causes. Pains in the joints will come; arthritis will be the final result. The client in ano or ikú must take care of his cardiovascular health and be wary of heart conditions.
- In iré, this odu speaks of some luck in gambling, contests, and games of chance. However, the client must participate in these only in moderation or that luck will be lost.
- No matter its orientation, Oché Osá announces the following: There will be a death close to the client; his family may become estranged; and the client has a trunk at home in which something valuable, perhaps even a weapon, is hidden.

## The Prohibitions of Oché Osá

- The ocean demands respect. Do not bathe in it. Do not pollute its waters or shores.
- Respect must be given to those with red complexions; respect those of Native American descent as well.
- Danger comes through objects given as gifts; do not save small trinkets, and do not save the boxes in which they were given.

## The Eboses of Oché Osá

Oché Osá indicates that the client has many issues to resolve with his egun. To begin, this pattern tells the diviner that the client has investigated other religions during his life. In each he tried to be sincere and devoted, but none satisfied him. If Oché Osá has come in iré, the client has found his spiritual home in the Lucumí faith. If it has come in osogbo, he will wander more, but in time he will come to the orishas again.

This odu also indicates that one of the client's past "faiths" is on his mind. This is because a powerful spirit, a priest of that religion, is with him as a guide. The diviner must prescribe a spiritual investigation of this spirit (a mass devoted to this single spirit), for while it can help him, it also will hinder his present evolution. Until the mass and investigation can begin, the client should set up a bóveda for this spirit-guide alone; it must have plenty of fresh water, light, and religious symbols or books of its faith. This offering will give the dead priest coolness and freshness and help keep him happy, and it will give the client a space in which to sort out his religious affiliations. One cannot walk two paths; this client needs to learn to walk one, and the spirit must support him or go away. (Note that in houses maintaining strong Catholic ties, it is not unusual to prescribe the litany of San Luis Beltran for guidance in this matter. The litany should be recited at the client's bóveda nightly.)

Before proceeding any further with ebó in this sign, the diviner must now determine if the client's egun require anything, asking, "Ebó elese egun?" If the answer is yes, he marks the offering with the diloggún.

In Oché Osá, the following prescriptions must also be made:

- Daily, the client should give thanks to Oshún. If she has not already claimed larishe, the diviner should ask, "Ebó elese Oshún?" If the answer is yes, he marks the offering with the shells.
- The diviner prepares both a knife and a nail for the client's front door to protect it. He washes them in omiero and then feeds a rooster to Ogún, the knife, and the nail. He pounds the nail into the door frame and secretes the knife behind the door.
- As a spiritual charm, the client must always carry an African gray parrot feather with him.

Now the diviner has his first chance to close the oracle. If the prescriptions made thus far do not bring closure, he must consider the following eboses:

- The client's egun might be in need of additional ebó. To see what else is required by the client's ancestors, the italero should ask, "Ebó elese egun?" If the answer is yes, he marks the offering with the diloggún.
- Maferefún Yemayá! In this odu, she can save the client from osogbo, and she might need ebó in exchange for her help. To find out if she requires anything, the diviner should ask, "Ebó elese Yemayá?" If the answer is yes, he marks the offering.
- Oshún, Elegguá, and Shangó are all firm in Oché Osá; to bring the session to closure and give evolution to the client, ebó might be claimed by one or more of these spirits. The diviner should ask, "Ebó elese [orisha's name]?" If the answer is yes, he marks the offering with the diloggún.
- Finally, Oché Osá can point out pending debts with Babaluaiye. If the odu refuses closure, this orisha could be holding it open. The diviner should speak frankly with the client about his health and what he has suffered in the past. If any debts are pending, the diviner should direct that they be written in the reading's record as ebó. If the client cannot think of any debts he owes Babaluaiye, the diviner should ask, "Ebó elese Babaluaiye?" If the answer is yes, he marks the offering with the diloggún. If Babaluaiye will not take ebó, his reception might be necessary. The diviner then should ask, "Koshé Babaluaiye?" Until he receives the orisha, the client should wear his eleke every day; he may be given the eleke after having a rogación before Babaluaiye's shrine. The client should offer adimú to Babaluaiye after the rogación and investment of the eleke.

If these prescriptions are not enough to close the reading and the client is an aleyo or an aborisha, the diviner should turn to the eboses of the parent odu, Oché (see page 257). Something there is needed for this person's evolution.

An initiate who opens in this odu has special concerns. First, he must remove Oshún's oars from inside her sopera and cross them in front of her shrine, holding them in place with her mazo. He also should give her a gold crown. This custom is born of the patakís in which Oshún saved Aganyú's life. If the client has Aganyú, he should seat him next to Oshún, for in Oché Osá they have a pact to live and eat together. Also, the diviner must ask, "Ebó elese Oshún y Aganyú?" If they claim ebó together, an oriaté must feed both a castrated goat. If the reading is an itá, this sacrifice must be done yearly on this date. Finally, if the initiate does not have Aganyú, he is now marked for his reception. Only after he has received Aganyú may he undertake all these eboses. The yearly feeding of a castrated goat becomes due on the anniversary date of Aganyú's reception.

If these prescriptions are not enough to close the odu for a priest or priestess, the italero now turns to the eboses of the parent odu, Oché (see page 257). Something there is needed for the client's evolution.

## The Tenth Composite Odu of Oché, Oché Ofún (5-10)

### The Proverbs of Oché Ofún

- The orishas save you from death.
- The dead will respect the idé of Orúnmila, yet they are still after you.
- Your enemy will do you evil, yet through this will come much good.
- The dead try to take what the saints have.
- Do not pretend to be either dead or a saint; you will not be able to wake from your dream.

### The Message of Oché Ofún

When an initial casting of five mouths, Oché, is followed by a casting of ten mouths, Ofún, the odu Oché Ofún is open. This odu is a sign of reversal. It is dangerous, hot, and volatile, yet it will bring many blessings to the client if he listens to all the odu has to say.

The diviner begins by saying, "Maferefún Oshún!" She comes here to tell the client that no matter how sour his life has become, she wants to bring sweetness. Already, she has brought much good, but the client fails to acknowledge her gift. He must give thanks to Oshún and offer her sweet adimú. When he does, she will continue to bless him. The diviner also praises Shangó, saying, "Maferefún Shangó!" Oché Ofún speaks of treason and war, yet if the client lays all his battles at Shangó's feet, this powerful orisha will fight for him. The diviner next praises the client's guardian orisha, saying to this spirit, "Maferefún!" In this odu, he or she stands up to demand the client's head in ocha. Finally, the diviner says, "Maferefún Yewá!" She speaks only rarely in the diloggún, but when Oché Ofún comes, Yewá will not remain silent. She is close to the client. If this reading is a bajado, she gets the first chance to claim the client's head. And if this reading is not a bajado but for a client who does not know his guardian, Yewá is, nevertheless, a strong contender.

The diviner should begin this reading by telling the client, "You were in danger of death, for Death himself has been on your trail; because this odu has opened, you are saved from him. Death himself has been removed. The orishas have brought you salvation, a way to placate and change all that was brought to you, all that was after you. Still, while Death himself is no longer after you, the dead are; some spirit wants you to join him or her on the other side. As soon as possible, you must receive the idé of Orúnmila, for while the dead do not respect your right to live, they respect him!" At this point, the diviner's assistant should put the mazo of the client's guardian orisha (or of Obatalá, if the client's guardian orisha is not known) over the client's neck. The diviner must tell him, "You are now in bondage to ocha. Because this sign removes death from you, your new life from this moment on belongs to the orishas. You are bound to them. Dedicate your life to them or lose it again."

This client's financial situation may not allow him to make ocha now. However, until he can make ocha, he must make ebó. Every month, the client must have a rogación of ten things at the feet of his guardian orisha. After this rogación, the priest must wash the client's head in the herbs of ocha. If the client's health is bad, as soon as possible he must receive his orisha *lavado* (washed). This will settle his issues and debts until he can afford his crowning.

The diviner must also tell the client that none of his current relationships is "right." While friendships across racial boundaries are to be encouraged in this sign, romantic involvements with those who are darker in complexion are dangerous. This sign cautions that the client should date within his own race or in a race that is lighter than he is. Also, those with whom the client has formed stable friendships will not be in this person's life much longer; the odu will slowly take them away and replace them with others more suitable for the client. If this person has a lover or spouse, in time this relationship, too, will come to an end. A man in this odu may harbor thoughts of adultery, and he may act on these. A woman in this odu is chronically unhappy and looking for a peaceful way out. Both Oshún and Olófin know this person's pain, and they will bring someone new and more compatible into this person's life. However, the diviner must advise the client against random sexual encounters: Venereal disease is a danger in this odu, and such an infection could render men impotent and women sterile.

In addition, the diviner should explore the following points with the client:

- No matter the orientation of this sign, it always foreshadows death by accident, communicable illness, or chronic disease.
- This odu forebodes operations, especially to solve the complications of pregnancy.
- When the odu opens in an osogbo of ano or ikú, the diviner must tell the client that pains will come in the muscles and bones, especially in the feet, legs, and knees. When he experiences such pain, he must seek medical attention. Eventually, the blood and abdomen will decompose. When these illnesses come, the client must seek not only seek medical attention but also the help of the diviner again.
- The client is constantly cursing himself, his fortune, and others. This must stop, for sourness always brings more of the same.
- While Death no longer haunts the client, he now haunts someone close to him. If this person is not careful, a close friend or relative could die in his own home needlessly. Someone close to the client suffers now; this person must be identified and brought to ocha for help. One by one, all whom this person loves will come to the religion for salvation.
- Witchcraft has been, or will be, thrown at this person's front door. When the client finally notices something unusual at the front door to his home, he must return to the diviner to make ebó with okra. The slime from the okra must be rubbed all over the front door to keep negativity from entering.

## The Prohibitions of Oché Ofún

- One has much aché with dreams; they will contain important messages from egun and other sources. These dreams are for one's own benefit. Do not discuss one's dreams with others.
- Be careful with one's keys; they could be stolen if mislaid or handled carelessly, and later the home or car will be robbed. Do not leave one's keys by doors or windows. If one has keys to businesses, vaults, or places of importance, be vigilant. The minute one notices that they are missing, notify the proper authorities.
- Do not consume foods made with animal intestines, including sausages, hot dogs, and lunch meats.
- Do not ever breed chickens or pigeons. One may have them for ebó but may not raise them or keep them for longer than a day.
- Laxatives, except in dire emergencies, are taboo. Unless the doctor prescribes them, do not take them. If the bowels become bound, drink a natural purgative made of castor oil, coconut oil, and cocoa butter.
- For one who has not yet made ocha, be careful who crowns one's head. If the orishas themselves do not approve of one's godparent, yubonna, and oriaté, death will come after ocha. The godparents and oriaté must be very selective in who is allowed to touch one's head, giving one aché, during the asiento.
- For an initiate, before receiving anything of ocha from another priest or priestess, one must receive the blessing and approval of one's crowning orisha. If the crown does not like the priest or priestess giving the orisha or doing the work of ocha for one, do not receive anything from him or her. Instead, seek out someone whom one's crown approves of. The danger here is that one will fall after receiving the aché, and the one giving the aché will rise instead.

## The Eboses of Oché Ofún

The opening of Oché Ofún on the mat is a serious omen; this odu has many eboses that must be considered by the diviner. First, one ebó is marked for everyone in attendance: Saraeko (see the recipe on page 52) must be given to the diviner's warriors before anyone may leave, and when these attendees are home, they must give saraeko to their own warriors as well. The next morning, the diviner and the attendees should throw this ebó into the street.

All those who came to offer spiritual support to the client (the godparents, the diviner, and the priests and priestesses sitting at the mat) are in debt to Elegguá. For all, the day must begin and end with his placation. The diviner must ask, "Ebó elese Elegguá?"; "Ebó elese Ogún?"; and "Ebó elese Ochosi?" Whatever Elegguá claims must be given by all present to their own Elegguá, and whatever Ogún and Ochosi claim must be given to them by the client alone. Once the client has made all his eboses to the warriors, all present will evolve. The client must be encouraged to do his sacrifices as soon as possible.

Also, within twenty-four hours the client must return to the diviner's home with the following elements for a rogación and an ebó: a derecho, two white candles, two coconuts, a white plate, a box of gofio, honey, smoked fish and jutía, eight pennies, and a basket of fruit. The priest sits Elegguá at Oshún's feet, and the client presents his derecho, the two white candles, and the two coconuts, all on a white plate, to both orishas, paying foribale. Then the client makes a paste of the gofio, honey, and smoked fish and jutía, saving a bit of each in case they are needed in his rogation. From this mixture he forms eight balls and inserts one penny into each. He gives three balls to Elegguá and five to Oshún. The diviner then gives the client a rogación using ten items at the feet of Elegguá and Oshún. After the rogación is complete and the two white candles have been lit for the spirits, the client presents his basket of fruit. The next day, the client brings everything to the river.

After exploring all these eboses, the diviner has his first chance to close the session. If it will not close, he should explore the following possibilities:

- The ebó and rogación to Elegguá and Oshún might need to be reinforced with a sacrifice. The diviner should ask, "Eborí elese Elegguá y Oshún?" If the diloggún answers yes, before the rogación the diviner should feed the client's orí two white pigeons or doves. Be careful: Pigeon blood and feathers must not touch Elegguá. The diviner must then ask, "Eyebale elese Elegguá y Oshún?" If eyebale is needed, each orisha must be fed feathers after the rogación is given but before the basket of fruit is presented.
- The client could have issues with Oshún. First, in this sign she says that she has brought many blessings to the client's life; he made promises to her but kept few of them. Now Oshún demands payment for all the good that she has brought. If the client can remember any of these unkept promises, their fulfillment now must be prescribed. If the client cannot remember making any promises to Oshún, the diviner must determine what she will take, asking, "Ebó elese Oshún?" If the answer is yes, he uses the shells to mark the offering. Even if Oshún takes nothing, some adimú should be given from the heart to ensure her goodwill. An initiate who opens in this odu must consider giving her a party, for this is how she will bring blessings to his life.
- Next, issues with the client's home must be addressed. The client's house is spiritually dirty, hot, and vile; the home must be physically scrubbed from top to bottom and from back to front. No drawer, closet, or cabinet should be left untouched. Once cleaned physically, the home should be cleansed with two white doves or pigeons; they are set free to fly away out the front door. The last cleansing is a solid spiritual one with a floor wash; a bad egun has taken up residence in the home, and it must be removed. The floor wash is prepared with water, ammonia, *vericola* (an herb avaliable at botánicas), and oil of myrhh. The client must scrub all the floors and carpets of his home with this mixture.

If these prescriptions are not enough to close the odu and the client is an aleyo or an aborisha, the diviner must now turn to the eboses of the parent odu, Oché (see page 257), to bring closure to the odu. Something there is necessary to bring evolution. If none of the eboses given for the parent odu will close Oché Ofún, the diviner must come back to the considerations given for initiates below.

An initiate who opens in Oché Ofún also has issues with Yewá. The first question the diviner should ask is "Ebó elese Yewá?" If the answer is yes, he marks the offering with the diloggún. If Yewá will not take ebó, or if ebó will not close the odu, the next question he should ask is "Koshé Yewá?"

If the diviner is returning to this possibility for an aleyo or an aborisha, Yewá cannot be received outside of ocha. Unless this reading is a bajado, the diviner cannot ask if Yewá is claiming the head, either. He must simply tell the client that Yewá is close; the client has to either have a bajado or go to a planté to bring down the crowning orisha. Until this can be done, the proper ebó for an aborisha or aleyo is to have his head washed in Oshún's omiero, followed by a rogación at her shrine. This will help him evolve until more specialized help can be sought out.

An initiate who comes in this odu also should wear a red parrot feather in his hair at all times. Oché Ofún says that this person is a king (or queen, if the client is a woman) of santo; he is blessed, and the orishas want all to know just how blessed he is.

If the odu still refuses closure for an initiate, the diviner must turn to the eboses of the parent odu, Oché (see page 257). Something there is necessary for this person's evolution.

## The Eleventh Composite Odu of Oché, Oché Owani (5-11)

### The Proverbs of Oché Owani

- He who is watched will never escape.
- In heaven will be written the good that is done.
- The elders are betrayed.
- To deny alms to the poor is to deny your own prosperity.
- If you do not know the laws under which you live, and if you don't obey them, you will learn them in the next world.

### The Message of Oché Owani

When a casting of five mouths, Oché, is followed by a casting of eleven mouths, Owani, the odu Oché Owani, also known as Oché Oniguo, is open. When this odu falls, the diviner must deliver a stern warning to the client: He must go home and stay there for three days. Death is close; it is looking for him, and unless he hides, it will find him. He must cancel all nonessential commitments, leaving only for work—and even this should be avoided if possible. He must not accept any invitations to venture out. The reason for this severe prohibition is that in Oché Owani all the evil forces in the world tried to kill Orúnmila; they are now trying to destroy this person. While physical death might not come in three days, the client's conduct, his actions, and his location will affect what happens to him in the near future. Orúnmila saved himself in this sign by hiding for three days, and this will save the client's life as well. For this the diviner pays homage to Orúnmila, as well as to other spirits, saying, "Maferefún Orúnmila! Maferefún Oshún! Maferefún Elegguá! Maferefún egun! Maferefún Babaluaiye!" All these spirits come to bless, advise, and save the client, and in a letter as strong as this the aché of them all might be needed to solve his issues.

The italero must impress on his client this: The odu open on the mat speaks of intrigues and death. In this odu the world's first lover was poisoned, and a similar fate could await the client. Yet if he follows the advice of this odu and makes ebó, in the end the poisoner will become the one poisoned. The attempted poisoning could be a furtive physical assault (murder or actual poisoning) or a mental, emotional, or spiritual attack. The client must be on guard against intrigues from his significant other. The relationship he is in now is not healthy, and he must reconsider to whom he is giving his heart. The diviner must ask the client if he loves his significant other; if he answers yes, the diviner should consider the aspect of witchcraft. Oché Owani says the client could be bound to his lover by magic.

In addition, the diviner should explore the following points:

- If this person limped when he came into the session, he could have a scar on the foot that is causing this limp. If there is no scar, surgery on his foot could be imminent.
- The client suffers from indigestion and digestive disturbances. This is because he consumes heavy meals and spicy foods. If the abdominal disorders are severe, even if this sign has come in iré, the diviner should prescribe all the food prohibitions of this sign and of Oché as parent odu. These prohibitions will do much to heal him.
- If any strange symptoms come in the abdominal or genital area after this odu opens, the client must see a physician. Oché Owani presages decomposition of the blood, stomach, and genitals. The client should be vigilant over infections that could lead to impotence, sterility, and reproductive damage.
- In this pattern the elders are betrayed; the diviner must warn the client not to betray his religious elders. Doing this will cause his luck to leave.

## The Prohibitions of Oché Owani

- Remember the first prohibition of this odu: Go home and stay there for three days.
- Many invitations will be extended. Do not accept any of them, regardless of when the event to which one is invited will occur, for three days. Refuse politely. If the one who extends the offer changes the date to accommodate one's needs, refuse again. There is danger and intrigue involved.
- Avoid hot and spicy foods, home remedies, and animal intestines.
- Never raise one's hand against a woman.
- In a serious osogbo, Oché Owani demands that one move as soon as possible; something is not right about one's present home.
- Do not accept any business propositions extended for the next month. If this reading is a bajado, be leery of engaging in any business propositions until ocha is made. If this is an itá, one must always be leery of business propositions. Have all business agreements put in writing, and have an attorney approve all contracts before signing.
- Oché Owani has a prohibition for the diviner: This client may become enamored with him; he might lust after him. The diviner is prohibited from entering into any romantic relationship with this client. Do not accept this client as a godchild, for he will cause trouble. Never again should this client step foot into the diviner's home. He will steal something that belongs to this priest. Note that if the client is already the diviner's godchild, he must be very careful with this relationship.

## The Eboses of Oché Owani

Oché Owani carries warnings and eboses for the diviner; the client who has come to the mat is enamored with him. So serious is this crush that the client might be tempted to steal something of the diviner's, later using it for witchcraft. Remember that it is forbidden for lovers to exchange things of the orishas, and this client is now taboo to the diviner. He may never read for him again and may not make ebó on his behalf. Once the reading is over, any ebó mandated by this sign must be done by another priest or priestess.

After the client leaves the house, the italero must offer two coconuts to his own head, using them to cleanse it, and then present them to his guardian orisha. If another priest or priestess is in the house, that person should give the diviner a thorough rogación in front of his guardian orisha's shrine. The coconuts should remain at the shrine until their milk is dry. The diviner should use obí to determine the proper method of disposal for them.

Before asking the odu for closure, the diviner must prescribe to the client the following ebó: The client should hang a fresh bunch of leaves from the carob or locust tree behind his front door and allow them to dry. He must never remove them from this location, for they block all negativity and witchcraft sent to his home. If the client moves to a new house, he must leave behind the old bunch and hang a new bunch in the new dwelling. Occasionally, he should bathe with an infusion made of fresh locust leaves; this will remove any witchcraft he has picked up on the street.

The diviner may now ask the odu for closure. If the letter remains open, the diviner should explore the following possibilities:

- The client needs a niche osain for the orisha whose diloggún is being consulted.
- In this pattern, Elegguá can stand up for ebó. The diviner should ask, "Ebó elese Elegguá?" If the answer is yes, the ebó marked is automatic: Give Elegguá a rooster.
- If this odu remains open, the client could have issues with Oshún. To see if she will take anything, the diviner must ask, "Ebó elese Oshún?" If the answer is yes, the diviner uses the shells to mark the offering.

If none of these prescriptions is enough to close the reading, the diviner must turn to the eboses of the parent odu, Oché (see page 257). Something there is needed for the client's evolution.

## The Twelfth Composite Odu of Oché, Oché Ejila (5-12)

### The Proverbs of Oché Ejila

- Do not play with fire, for you will get burned.
- Heaven confirms that which you have done. [This proverb applies only in iré.]
- The good son has the blessings of both God and his own mother.
- Remember, and respect, your mother.

### The Message of Oché Ejila

When a casting of five mouths, Oché, is followed by a casting of twelve mouths, Ejila Shebora, the odu Oché Ejila is open. Oché Oturupon is another name for this sign. This letter gives a severe warning for the diviner: He must be very cautious in all his dealings with this person, because he will take his godchildren to another initiate, and all will part as enemies.

The diviner begins by saying, "Maferefún Oshún!" In this pattern Oshún married Orúnmila, and a woman for whom Oché Ejila falls could be destined to marry a babalawo. Definitely, she will have issues with Ifá, and these need to be explored. No matter the sex of this client, however, this person could be a child of Oshún. If this reading is a bajado, Oshún gets the first option to claim this person's head. The diviner also pays homage to Elegguá, Shangó, and Aganyú, saying to each, "Maferefún!" Before the odu closes, the diviner will have to explore what Elegguá wants as ebó. Both Shangó and Aganyú might choose to speak or claim ebó here; if they do, the diviner should warn the client to listen carefully. No matter its orientation, in Oché Ejila each is upset, and each will speak only once.

Having cast this sign, the diviner should tell his client the following: "This odu tells the story of a conflict in your life. You cannot resolve it alone; you need the help of the orishas. You are the object of much envy. Others are jealous because you seem so much more knowledgeable than they; you seem to have more than they ever will. While this envy can destroy you, it can also help you. Live by making ebó, and keep others guessing."

This letter indicates that two women are mortal enemies of this client, yet he might think they are his friends. Unfortunately, he is being slandered by their tongues. Because of this, his current relationship could end; they accuse him of having more than one lover, hiding each from the other. The client is not always honest with his mate, and when she hears these rumors they will give her cause to worry. She might even leave. The key to avoiding this tragedy is simple: The client must be honest with his lover about everything.

In addition, the diviner should explore the following points with the client:

- This odu warns that the client's current lover or spouse is not the perfect match the client believes her (or him) to be. Although the odu warns against infidelity, it foreshadows the arrival of a new relationship.

- This person's home is not healthy. Soon, the client will move; the orishas will see to that. When he moves, he must take all his belongings in one day. Five days after the last box is unpacked, he must give a housewarming party for Oshún.
- If Oché Ejila comes in an osogbo of ano or ikú, it flags serious health concerns. Tissues in the kidneys, stomach, or liver suffer degeneration from stress, vices, or disease. The client should see his physician for a complete checkup. Remember that Oché in any osogbo can flag decomposition of the blood and abdominal region. Impotence and sterility brought by infections are born here as well.

## The Prohibitions of Oché Ejila

- One's home is not healthy; one must not live there any longer than is necessary. When one moves, move all one's belongings in one day. Anything left behind may not be reclaimed another time.
- Do not play with fire; one will get burned.
- For a priest or priestess, one may not give readings unless the client pays a derecho.
- The diviner who gives this reading is prohibited from working for free. Even if the client says he is destitute, charge something.
- Oché Ejila forbids the consumption of hot, spicy foods.

## The Eboses of Oché Ejila

Oché Ejila is another odu that carries warnings for the diviner who is reading the client, especially if this client is an initiate of the religion. This odu foreshadows that one day the client and diviner will become enemies; a schism will arise, and the one at the mat will steal many godchildren from the diviner's house.

The diviner may not read for this client for free; he must charge, and he must charge well for his work. This prohibition will last a lifetime between these two. Second, the client's orí and the diviner's guardian orisha must be supplicated. This is done so that no war ever arises between the two. The diviner should tell the client that, as ebó, he must have his head fed with two white pigeons, and following this, the diviner must have his crowning orisha fed with feathers. While performing this ebó, the priest must pray that there is always peace between himself and the client's orí and peace between the client and the diviner's orisha. After making this ebo, the diviner must give the client's head a rogación so that the diviner's own crown will watch over the client, forbidding him to take even one godchild. Finally, after the rogación the client must cook an adimú in the diviner's house for the diviner's crown. This seals the pact between the client's head and the diviner's so that the client will never steal or cause a war. Although the client offers this ebó for the diviner's or godparent's benefit, the client must pay a derecho to have this done, and he must be charged well. It is his own head bringing the osogbo; the orishas have seen this brewing in his heart, and the problem must be corrected before it begins. Forewarned is forearmed.

If this client is an initiate, the odu also foreshadows wars, treason, and abandonment in his own ilé ocha. He should be told this information and should be taught the ebó to seal the pact with his own godchildren so that no wars arise. First, each of his godchildren must have a rogación before the shrine of the client's crowning orisha. Each must cook adimú for the client's crowning orisha once the rogación is done. Afterward, if treason arises among those in the client's house, his crown will squelch their evil before it can do any damage. If this reading is an itá for a iyawó or for any orisha, each godchild who comes to the client's house must offer this ebó for his patron.

The following ebó is mandatory when the client is an initiate: Carrying a piece of sackcloth or burlap, this person must go out into the street and beg alms to honor Babaluaiye. He must use the money he receives to make a sacrifice of a goat and a chicken to Elegguá (have itá the next day), two hens to Oshún, and four roosters to Shangó. Between the day this ebó is made and the twelfth day afterward, the client's head must be fed two white doves, and he should have a rogación immediately afterward. Unless the animals are used to cleanse this person, cook the aché for the orishas and the meat for those who help with the ebó.

If the client is an aleyo or aborisha, he must wear the sackcloth or burlap out into the street and beg for alms. However, the money he receives is instead presented to the diviner's Babaluaiye on a white plate with two white candles and two coconuts as ebó.

Now the diviner may attempt to close the odu. If Oché Ejila refuses closure, the diviner should consider the following:

- Shangó may be standing up for ebó. To determine if this is the case, the diviner asks, "Ebó elese Shangó?" If the answer is yes, he uses the shells to mark an appropriate offering. If, after marking ebó to Shangó, the pattern still will not close, the client must feed Shangó a ram. The sacrifice should be done in the morning; in the evening, the meat from the ram is used to cater a large party in his honor.
- Aganyú may also stand up for ebó. To see if he requires anything, the diviner should ask, "Ebó elese Aganyú?" If the answer is yes, he marks the appropriate offering. If the client is an initiate, he might have to receive this orisha. If ebó will not satisfy Aganyú, the diviner may ask, "Koshé Aganyú?"
- If this letter continues to remain open and the client is an aborisha belonging to Shangó, he is now marked to make ocha. This ceremony must be done flawlessly and extravagantly or else there will be no iré for those who participate.

If the letter still remains open, the diviner must turn to the eboses of the parent odu, Oché (see page 257). Something there is needed for this client's evolution.

# The Thirteenth Composite Odu of Oché, Oché Metanla (5-13)

## The Proverbs of Oché Metanla

- Do not play with fire, or you will get burned.
- Your enemies will do you evil, and yet through their actions will much good be brought.

## The Message of Oché Metanla

When a casting of five mouths, Oché, is followed by a casting of thirteen mouths, Metanla, the odu Oché Metanla, also known as Oché Irete, has come to the mat. It is a powerful sign, and through its aché was born the custom of offering obí, the coconut oracle, to the orishas. One who comes in this letter has aché for that oracle and should begin to study its meanings and methods.

In this odu, one must give homage to Oshún; the diviner should say, "Maferefún Oshún!" She speaks strongly here on the client's behalf. Opening in osogbo, this odu flags issues with Oshún, and the diviner must begin the investigation of Oché Metanla keeping this in mind. In the past, Oshún has brought the client much good; he needs to be thankful for this and offer her adimú. He has sickness in the stomach, and a rogación at her feet will soothe the symptoms. Negative energy, people, or circumstances could surround this person's home, and Oshún wants the client to move. Belongings should be packed and ready on the day of the move, and the transportation of personal possessions must be completed in one day. As soon as the new home is unpacked and organized, the client must give Oshún a housewarming party. The bad luck will then be left at the old residence, and good things will come to replace the bad.

The diviner should keep in mind and explore with the client the following points:

- Oba and Shangó are both firm in Oché Metanla, and no matter the orientation of this sign, they will try to bring some blessing to the client if he propitiates them.
- One day, this person will obtain either a public office (in politics) or a private position of power (in business). Here, he must always be on guard against treason and false testimony. Those who are jealous of his rise to power will try to make him fall to poverty and despair.
- The client will soon be presented with a business opportunity involving three people. Two will have honorable intentions, but one will have selfish designs. Before accepting any new

business deals, the client must have a session with the shells and make ebó.

## The Prohibitions of Oché Metanla

- Do not play with fire. The one who does so will get burned. This prohibition applies not only to literal fire but also to spiritual fire. Do not start intrigues or wars.
- This sign foreshadows battles over possessions. Remember that sometimes it is best to let things go. Do not fight over material things.
- Never raise one's hand against a woman.

## The Eboses of Oché Metanla

When this odu falls opens, three eboses are required of the client. Once all three eboses are done to satisfy this odu, evolution will come. First, before leaving the diviner's home he must split open a coconut. From the meat he should cut two large pieces; a single piece goes in each of the front pockets of his pants. As soon as he reaches the street in front of the diviner's home, he should throw one piece to the curb. Upon reaching the street in front of his own house, he should throw the other piece of coconut to the street. Immediately, he must go inside and not come back out until the next morning. This ebó will save him from an unmarked, unseen danger and will bring iré.

Second, in honor of Babaluaiye this person must never deny alms to the poor; they are watched over by this spirit, and he will bless the client as he blesses his chosen.

Third, this letter signals undetermined issues with Oshún. Although she may have already claimed an ebó in Oché, the client should still offer her something "from the heart." She has pampered the client in the past and expects to be pampered by him in return. As soon as possible, the client must bring a token adimú to the diviner's Oshún. *Note:* The client must try to remember if he has ever made a promise to Oshún that he has not kept, for in this odu she demands payment. The fulfillment of these promises is now marked as ebó, and the diviner adds them to the written record of the reading.

Now the diviner has his first chance to close the oracle. If it remains open, he must consider the following points:

- Oba and Shangó could be expecting ebó. To see what, if anything, they require, the diviner should ask, "Ebó elese Oba?" and "Ebó elese Shangó?" If the answer to either question is yes, he uses the diloggún to mark the required offering.
- The client could have additional issues with Babaluaiye. The diviner must ask the following series of questions to determine what this issue is: "Ebó elese Babaluaiye?"; "Koshé eleke de Babaluaiye?"; and "Koshé Babaluaiye?"

If none of these options brings closure to Oché Metanla, the diviner should turn to the eboses of the parent odu, Oché (see page 257). Something there is needed to bring the client's evolution and the letter's closure.

# The Fourteenth Composite Odu of Oché, Oché Merinla (5-14)

## The Proverb of Oché Merinla

- Where my head takes me, there I am.

## The Message of Oché Merinla

When an initial cast of five mouths, Oché, precedes a cast of fourteen mouths, Merinla, the pattern Oché Merinla, also known as Oché Ika, is open on the mat. An ebó must be made immediately to cool the heat of this hot sign; see "The Eboses of Oché Merinla" on page 253.

With this odu open, the diviner knows that something bad is coming for the client; he also knows that something good is coming for the client. No matter what comes, however, in this sign the arrival will be hot and will cause tragedy in the end.

In iré, one must pay homage to Oshún ("Maferefún Oshún!") again and again, for she blesses the client. In osogbo, one must be afraid of Oshún, for she is angry. The greater the osogbo and the greater the client's status in the religion, the more angry this letter says that she is. An initiate who opens in Oché Merinla in any osogbo is in grave danger, for Oshún has left the house; she has abandoned her otanes, and great numbers of eboses may be required to bring her back.

The diviner also pays homage to Babaluaiye, egun, Shangó, and Orúnmila when Oché Merinla falls on the mat, saying to each, "Maferefún!" All may speak or stand up to claim ebó during this session.

The diviner should explore the following points with the client for whom this letter has fallen:

- Here, the slave ascends to a throne because of the wrong done by his master. For the client in a lower-level position, promotions, money, new jobs, and more may come, but they will come because of a great evil done to the client. He will prosper, but he will have to walk through fire first.
- Likewise, the client in a position of power could lose his authority because of the evil he has done. Underlings will become this person's supervisors.
- Death is close. He will not take the client, but he will take someone known to him. When this death comes, the client must not go to the funeral. He may send flowers, cards, and condolences, but he must not go to the burial ceremonies. If he does, Death will then seek him out.
- Blessings come from across the sea, but these will bring osogbo in the end. Oché Merinla is a sign of reversal, so the client must be counseled to look for the good in the bad and the bad in the good. It will always be there.

## The Prohibitions of Oché Merinla

- Do not go to any funerals.
- Do not be a bore, a pest, or a "loudmouth." Remember that silence is a virtue, and secrecy is essential to evolution in this pattern.
- It is taboo to lie to one's elders. If one cannot tell the truth, say nothing at all.

## The Eboses of Oché Merinla

When this pattern opens on the mat, three eboses are mandated and must be done immediately. First, before the diviner delivers the reading, the diviner's assistant takes the gourd of fresh water to the front door. He opens the door wide and pours out the contents of the gourd just outside. He then replenishes the water in the gourd before returning to the mat. This letter brings spiritual heat and announces that something bad could soon be visiting not only the client but also the diviner. This osogbo follows both wherever they go. It is not immediately on their heels, but it is gaining momentum, and if it is not fought, it will soon catch up with them. When the negative energy and the client or the diviner are in the same place at the same time, something serious will happen.

To avoid this tragedy, within twenty-four hours of the reading the client needs two more eboses: First, he needs a rogación, and after this is done, he must dress totally in white for twenty-one days. Second, he must have an herbal bath with things sacred to Elegguá (the diviner should prescribe the herbs he feels are necessary). He must have this bath often over the next twenty-one days to bring luck and iré.

After explaining these eboses, the diviner has his first chance to close the odu. If the letter refuses closure and the client is an aleyo or an aborisha, the diviner should consider the following:

- If the client has received neither the elekes nor the warriors, the diviner should try to mark the elekes as ebó, asking, "Koshé los elekes?" Such is the power of the elekes ceremony that almost any osogbo brought by Oché can be overcome. If the oracle marks this as ebó, the commitment entailed by the initiation must be explained to the aleyo before attempting the oracle's closure.
- If the client already has the elekes, or if the client has not the elekes but the oracle will not mark them as ebó, the diviner should then ask, "Koshé los guerreros?" If the oracle marks the reception of the warriors as ebó, the diviner should explain what is involved in this ceremony and mark the path of Elegguá to be received

through Oché before attempting the oracle's closure.

If the oracle still will not close for an aleyo or an aborisha, or if the client is an initiate, the diviner should consider the following possibilities:

- The elekes of one or more orishas speaking in Oché (see the list on page 212) could be necessary for protection. To find out if this is necessary, the diviner should ask, "Ebó eleke de [orisha's name]?" After marking an eleke, the diviner should explain to the client why this spirit is offering his or her protection in this odu (using his own aché to deliver this information). After an eleke is marked and explained, the diviner should attempt closure again. Note that more than one orisha could stand up in this odu to offer protection through his or her eleke.
- If the oracle still will not close, those spirits who offered protection through their elekes might also be standing up for ebó. Each spirit who has marked his or her eleke as larishe to this osogbo must then be asked, "Ebó elese [orisha's name]?" If any stand up for ebó, the diviner should use the diloggún to mark an appropriate offering.
- If the letter still will not close, Elegguá might be standing up for ebó. The diviner should investigate this option by asking, "Ebó elese Elegguá?" If the answer is yes, he should use the diloggún to mark an appropriate ebó.

If these options are not enough to close the session, the diviner should now turn to the eboses of the parent odu, Oché (see page 257). Something there is needed to bring the client's evolution.

## The Fifteenth Composite Odu of Oché, Oché Marunla (5-15)

### The Proverbs of Oché Marunla

- Heaven confirms the things that are done.
- Olorún and Orúnmila know what you have done.
- Others are filled with envy because they believe you to be wise, yet you are no wiser than they.

### The Message of Oché Marunla

When a casting of five mouths, Oché, is followed by a casting of fifteen mouths, Marunla, the odu Oché Marunla is open. This sign is also known as Oché Iwori. It is hot and volatile, and all the health warnings given for the parent odu, Oché, apply here no matter the sign's orientation. Even if the client is in perfect health, the abdominal and perineal/genital areas are in danger of disease and decomposition; many diviners will prescribe for the client a rogación at Oshún's feet once the reading is closed to help avoid these complications. If strange symptoms develop in the reproductive organs or genitalia, the client must see a physician immediately for a full checkup. The blood, stomach, kidneys, and perhaps the liver are also potential sites of decomposition and, if Oché comes in severe osogbo, dysfunction. The client will have aches and pains in the knees, feet, ankles, and legs. The elderly should pay careful attention to these areas, for the pain may be arthritic. (Note that for the elderly, falls can lead to death.) For those who are younger, these pains will be the result of overuse or overextension.

The diviner should also explore with the client the following issues:

- The client is the subject of envy, for others believe him to be things that he is not. The client may believe these lies as well.
- Ruin is brought in this odu when one grants the random whims of another without caution. The client must not do favors for anyone. If he is not careful, he could become an unwitting slave in another's evil plot.
- When this odu comes in an osogbo, robbery is a danger for the client or his home. Oshún stands up here to protect the client. However, he must think hard about what he owes her. Past debts must be resolved immediately.

### The Prohibitions of Oché Marunla

- Do not do favors for another. Ruin comes by granting the whims of others carelessly, so it is best to do nothing and promise even less.
- Do not make promises to Oshún that cannot be kept.

## The Eboses of Oché Marunla

When Oché Marunla opens on the mat, two mandatory eboses must be completed within twenty-four hours. First, as soon as the reading is closed, the client should have a rogación at Oshún's feet to avoid the health osogbos predicted in Oché Marunla. Second, after the rogación, the client must begin taking spiritual baths using egg whites and *maloja* (an herb).

If the client is an aleyo or aborisha, the diviner must also consider the following:

- If the client has received neither the elekes nor the warriors, the diviner should try to mark the elekes as ebó, asking, "Koshé los elekes?" Such is the power of the elekes ceremony that almost any osogbo brought by Oché can be overcome. If the oracle marks this as ebó, the commitment entailed by the initiation must be explained to the aleyo before attempting the oracle's closure.
- If the client already has the elekes, or if the client has not the elekes but the oracle will not mark them as ebó, the diviner should then ask, "Koshé los guerreros?" If the oracle marks the reception of the warriors as ebó, the diviner should explain what is involved in this ceremony and mark the path of Elegguá to be received through Oché.

Now the diviner has his first chance to close the oracle. If it will not close, he should consider the following possibilities:

- The elekes of one or more orishas speaking in Oché (see the list on page 212) could be necessary for protection. To find out if this is necessary, the diviner should ask, "Ebó eleke de [orisha's name]?" After marking an eleke, the diviner should explain to the client why this spirit is offering his or her protection in this odu (using his own aché to deliver this information). After an eleke is marked and explained, the diviner should attempt closure again. Note that more than one orisha could stand up in this odu to offer protection through his or her eleke.
- If the oracle still will not close, those spirits who offered protection through their elekes might also be standing up for ebó. Each spirit who has marked his or her eleke as larishe to this osogbo must then be asked, "Ebó elese [orisha's name]?" If any stand up for ebó, the diviner should use the diloggún to mark an appropriate offering.
- If the odu still will not close, the diviner must ask, "Ebó elese Shangó?" If the answer is yes, he uses the diloggún to mark the appropriate offering. If the answer is no, the client should give Shangó an adimú anyway to ensure the orisha's goodwill.
- The diviner must recommend that this client go to a babalawo immediately for a complete assessment by Ifá.
- If this is not enough to close the odu, egun are standing up for ebó. The diviner should teach the client how to set up a bóveda to honor his egun. It must be given fresh water and light weekly. He also might consider asking, "Ebó elese egun?" If the answer is yes, he uses the diloggún to mark the appropriate offering.

If these options are not enough to close the session, the diviner should turn to the eboses of the parent odu, Oché (see page 257). Something there is needed for this person's evolution.

# The Sixteenth Composite Odu of Oché, Oché Merindilogún (5-16)

## The Proverbs of Oché Merindilogún

- The cat is a thief by nature.
- You once lifted your hand against your mother, and she died with this feeling.

## The Message of Oché Merindilogún

When the initial cast of five mouths, Oché, is followed by a cast of sixteen mouths, Merindilogún, the odu Oché Merindilogún, also known as Oché Otura, is open. When it falls, the diviner says, again and again, "Maferefún Oshún!" For it is in this pattern that Oshún first came down to the earth. She left heaven and set out for the mortal world to bring all the wealth, health, happiness, and love that heaven had to offer. When this sign unfolded, the world was a sad, corrupt place, but in time Oshún made life worth living for all of creation.

The diviner should know that the one for whom this sign has opened is the "master of aché." However, unless he is a priest or priestess, he knows not how to use his aché to its full potential. Much wisdom, knowledge, and experience is hidden within the client, yet he is skittish and afraid of the potential in his own life. Others around him are jealous, and they want to destroy the gifts that the orishas have given him. There is one way to avoid all this destruction and lock in the iré that Oché Merindilogún would bring: make ocha.

For men, the sign foreshadows one additional issue: Ifá. A man who comes in this pattern has a future as a babalawo. However, this can be explored only by another babalawo with Ifá.

The diviner should also explore the following issues with the client:

- This person will suffer constipation if his diet is not changed; he eats poorly, and this affects his health. The diviner should tell him that if his bowels do become "twisted," he may not take any home remedies. Instead, he must see a physician for a prescription; something serious could be wrong.
- The client does not sleep well; he suffers from insomnia. This is due to his poor health habits. He must take better care of himself.
- The client must always take care with legal matters and exercise caution around the law.
- Others are watching every move made by the client, and they will take advantage of his bad luck.

## The Prohibitions of Oché Merindilogún

- All the prohibitions of the parent odu, Oché (see page 257), apply here, even when this letter comes in iré.
- Do not take home remedies for any ailment. One's health is delicate; have all complaints examined by a physician.
- Do not guard or store anything for anyone. Those things that others bring into one's home could be stolen property.
- Never argue or fight with Oshún's children. Do this, and all the blessings of this odu are lost.

## The Eboses of Oché Merindilogún

When Oché Merindilogún falls on the mat for an aleyo or an aborisha and refuses closure, the diviner should consider the following possibilities:

- If the client has received neither the elekes nor the warriors, the diviner should try to mark the elekes as ebó, asking, "Koshé los elekes?" Such is the power of the elekes ceremony that almost any osogbo brought by Oché can be overcome. If the oracle marks this as ebó, the commitment entailed by the initiation must be explained to the aleyo before attempting the oracle's closure.
- If the client already has the elekes, or if the client has not the elekes but the oracle will not mark them as ebó, the diviner should then ask, "Koshé los guerreros?" If the oracle marks the reception of the warriors as ebó, the diviner should explain what is involved in this ceremony and mark the path of Elegguá to be received through Oché before attempting the oracle's closure.

If the oracle still will not close for an aleyo or an aborisha, or if the client is an initiate, the diviner should consider the following possibilities:

- The elekes of one or more orishas speaking in Oché (see the list on page 212) could be necessary for protection. To find out if this is necessary, the diviner should ask, "Ebó eleke de [orisha's name]?" After marking an eleke, the diviner should explain to the client why this spirit is offering his or her protection in this odu (using his own aché to deliver this information). After an eleke is marked and explained, the diviner should attempt closure again. Note that more than one orisha could stand up in this odu to offer protection through his or her eleke.
- If the oracle still will not close, those spirits who

offered protection through their elekes might also be standing up for ebó. Each spirit who has marked his or her eleke as larishe to this osogbo must then be asked, "Ebó elese [orisha's name]?" If any stand up for ebó, the diviner should use the diloggún to mark an appropriate offering.

Whatever the orishas mark as larishe should be done quickly. There are no other eboses for this odu beyond taking the client to see Ifá. If the letter will not close, the diviner should proceed with the eboses listed for the parent odu, Oché (see page 257).

## Closing the Reading: Further Eboses of the Parent Odu, Oché

Having exhausted the options of larishe and ebó in the composite odu, the diviner must turn to the parent odu to find a method of closure. This sign, Oché, contains within itself many offerings and rituals to placate both the letter and the orishas that speak in it. Before marking the more complex eboses of five mouths, the diviner should begin with one or more of the following cooling spiritual prescriptions for Oché. This odu can become hot, and the following offerings will help soothe the client spiritually.

- When Oché has come in osogbo and refuses closure, the diviner must turn to Oshún. Although the diviner will already have asked this, he must ask the client once, "Do you have any unresolved issues with Oshún?" If the client has made any promises to Oshún that remain unfulfilled, they must be resolved. The diviner can also examine this issue from another standpoint: Has the client offended any of Oshún's children? If so, he must seek resolution. If the client is an aborisha whose godparent is Oshún's initiate, there could be disrespect between the two, godparent and godchild. The diviner must examine this issue as well. If nothing else, the client should resolve to give Oshún a huge party in her honor. He should invite as many initiates and aborishas of Oshún as possible. If this client is an aborisha, the party must be given to the godparent's Oshún. The italero might also consider asking, "Tambor [or guiro] elese Oshún?"
- When Oché opens for a priest or priestess of Oshún and refuses closure, the client could have unresolved issues with his own crown. He must offer a small castrated goat to her (note that only an oriaté may make the actual sacrifice). After the sacrifice, the initiate must have itá with his crown. Through itá, Oshún herself will dictate what the issues are.
- If the client is an initiate, he must feed every year Oshún in her home, the river, on the anniversary of this reading. For this ebó, he must feed her two hens on the riverbank, and after the animal carcasses are laid to rest in her waters, he should pour plenty of fresh honey and honeycomb to her.
- Spiritual cleansings are important to Oché. The client should scrub his house thoroughly, beginning at the back and working toward the front so that all negative energies are forced out the front door. Afterward, for five consecutive days he should scrub his bare floors with a wash of clear water, five egg whites, and honey. After the fifth floor wash, he must make ebó to his front door by waxing it inside and out with fresh cocoa butter, then draping it inside and out with white cloth. Once these things are done, the client must never allow his home to become dirty again. It must be cleansed both physically and spiritually frequently.
- Daily, before leaving home, to calm his nerves the client should do the following ebó at his front door: He should rub his hands well with cocoa butter, saying, "Maferefún Oshún! Maferefún Obatalá!" Once his hands are well coated with cocoa butter, he should use them to rub his head from front to back. Start with the forehead and end at the nape of the neck. This massage will refresh his orí; the day will be blessed and his nerves will remain calm.

If these prescriptions are not enough to close the session, there are more serious issues at stake.

The diviner should consider the following options for ebó:

- The diviner must now consider Elegguá; he accompanies Oshún in all composites of Oché. He should ask, "Ebó elese Elegguá?" If he accepts ebó through this odu, the appropriate offering is a smoked fish head oiled with epó. If this is not enough to satisfy Elegguá, sacrifice a rooster first, and offer the oiled, smoked fish head the day after the sacrifice. One week after offering the rooster, the client should provide him with a basket of fresh fruits. The priest should use obí after each offering to determine the proper method of disposal.
- The client should offer five calabazas (pumpkins, squash, or gourds) to both Elegguá and Oshún. Put Elegguá at Oshún's feet and offer the five calabazas to them together. After five days, the client discards the ebó in the river.
- Oché can flag serious issues with the dead. One or more egun may be in need of masses and offerings; the dead need constant help so that they can help the client. The diviner should ask, "Ebó elese egun?" If the answer is yes, he must use the diloggún to mark what they require. After these offerings have been given, the client should vow to keep a bóveda with fresh water and candles at all times.
- Another protective charm that can be prescribed in this odu is the feeding of a nail to Ogún; after the diviner feeds the nail, he pounds it into the client's front door so Ogún may keep it from harm. If the diviner wishes to reinforce this charm, he may hang the plaque known as *ojo y lengua* ("eye and tongue") outside on the front door with this nail. It will nullify the effects of the evil eye and gossip that may be sent to this client by others.
- If the letter still refuses closure, the client could have issues with any of the orishas who speak in this sign (see the list on page 212). Depending on the severity of the osogbo, the ebó needed could range from the eleke of any orisha to an ebó or reception of an orisha. The diviner must proceed with these investigations slowly and cautiously, asking for the smaller eboses before continuing with the larger.

If this list is exhausted and the odu still refuses closure, the diviner has two options. First, he may call an elder in the religion, for something important in the sign could have been overlooked. Second, he may look at the list of eboses given for the omo odu as a parent odu. For example, in a casting of Oché Ogbe (5–8), the diviner would turn to the eboses of Eji Ogbe as the parent odu for closure.

# SEVEN

# THE FAMILY OF OBARA

## The Proverbs of Obara

- From legends are truths born.
- You are confused by your own lies: You know not what is real or what is false.
- The king does not die.
- The king does not lie.
- Money vanishes like smoke.
- The king did not hang.
- From the lie shall the truth be born.
- Watch your treasures. Guard them. Still, you will lose them.
- The right hand washes the left.
- When Oro sounds, men become silent.
- While humans are born sincere, all will die liars.
- The tongue can be a lion, and it can devour you.
- As intelligent as quail are, they still sleep on the ground.
- A patient man can become the king of the world.
- He who knows will not die like the one who does not know.
- If one does not speak, the tongue cannot destroy one.
- A wheel that can roll forward can also roll backward.
- With the tongue, you can save or destroy the town; control the tongue.
- The fly that flies high up in the air and is not tempted by the bait on the ground will not get caught in the fly trap.
- The one who does not know will die, while the one who knows will live.
- A single tree cannot make a forest.

## The Orishas Who Speak in Obara

| | |
|---|---|
| Shangó | Obatalá |
| Oshún | Osain |
| Orúnmila | Oyá |
| Elegguá | Ochosi |

## The Message of Obara

Opening with six mouths on the mat, the diloggún sits before the italero in a vibrant, volatile pattern. Obara simmers and seethes with energy. Its apocalyptic pronouncements can bring radical change to the client's life, yet it also centers on the creation and continuation of community, as well as one's personal evolution. It bears witness to one's desire to grow, to evolve into something greater than the sum of one's parts. The growth and enlightenment brought here, however, are filled with tears and deception; Obara's cycle builds on itself, yet brings subterfuge. Just as sudden illumination in a darkened room brings temporary blindness, so can Obara's illumination bring spiritual blindness. Fá'Lokun Fatunmbi writes of this odu, "[E]nlightenment is transient . . . enlightenment can bring deception, and a false sense of accomplishment. . . . There should be a time to acknowledge accomplishments, and consider the future implications regarding that which has been achieved."* While the sign itself will have much to say to the client on daily, mundane levels, the greater spiritual currents that have been brought into play cannot be ignored. They must be dealt with, and the greatness foreshadowed by odu tempered with humility.

Such is Obara's strength and majesty that once it is cast on the diviner's mat, the reading is suspended before the diviner casts a composite. Six mouths is born of Shangó's odu, Ejila Shebora (twelve mouths); because of this, Shangó's presence is felt fiercely in Obara. Unlike his harsh nature in Ejila Shebora, though, in Obara Shangó speaks more sweetly. Perhaps this is because his lover, Oshún, is Obara's true owner. Perhaps this is why Shangó calls Obara home, making six his own special number. Because of this, when Obara falls on the mat, the diviner lifts first his left buttock and then the right while saying, "Kawo kabiosile!" to honor Shangó. After performing this ritual gesture, he recites the sacred prayer to honor the sign:

*Obara.*
*Oni'bara ala'bara eye'bara.*
*Kikate efeyuye kikate lodafun.*
*Ofefun oloya chun.*

While the diviner intones this prayer, those present in the room will bow their heads in reverence. Many will follow the italero's movements, raising first the left and then the right buttocks and muttering, "Kawo kabiosile!" Many will also say, "Maferefún Shangó! Maferefún Oshún!" Before this sign closes out, both orishas will have much to say to this person.

In this letter many spirits might choose to speak. The one whose shells are cast has the first option, and if this is the first time Obara has opened for a client, this orisha's words will help this person regain his destiny. No matter this letter's orientation, the orisha consulted says this person is not well grounded. He moves aimlessly, without plans or goals; when he does set plans or goals, they are insubstantial, lacking both form and force. This person desires much; the child of Obara is not afraid to build grand schemes for the future. Yet he has not attained many, if any, of these dreams. And this failure leads to sourness, for the client was born to be a leader. However, until the tendency to dream is replaced with pure action, nothing will be accomplished in his life. One way to read this odu is this: The client was born with a special gift or destiny, and due to laziness, environment, and loss of connection with his higher self, he lost this talent, and his destiny was buried beneath the turmoil of his day-to-day existence. Opening in six mouths, the orishas tell the client that he still has these gifts and talents; his destiny can still be his. He will, however, have to work hard to attain it.

In this odu, the diviner proclaims, "Maferefún Shangó!" Shangó has led the client far in life, and he will continue to lead him if he receives due reverence and ebó. When this orisha speaks in any composite of Obara, the diviner has many considerations to explore. If the odu opens in iré, the diviner should tell the client, "Shangó says you are very clever and shrewd. You have a good head on your shoulders, but ask yourself if you are using your head to its fullest potential. He says you have many dreams and plans, yet none of these comes to fruition as it should because you do not work hard enough. You love travel. There are many places you want to visit. Now is the time for these things. Fulfill your heart's deepest desires, for the time will come when you cannot."

No matter the orientation of this odu, Shangó says the one at the mat thinks much about life and death. He cries tears of joy and misery. The orisha warns that he must focus on the good, not the bad. In this way will more goodness come. Obara advises two eboses that must be done immediately to ensure that goodness comes and evil leaves: Feed Shangó (adimú or eyebale) and make sure Ósun sits higher than the client's head. In this way can Ósun watch for danger and Shangó fight all his wars.

When Obara opens in osogbo, the advice of Shangó is darker and dire, and the client must heed it all lest he fall. The diviner should tell him, "You deceive yourself, and you deceive others. These

*Awó Fá'Lokun Fatunmbi, *Awó: Ifá and the Theology of Orisha Divination* (New York: Original Publications, 1992), 136–37.

deceptions must end or you will fall. None of your thoughts is focused. The orishas, in the past, have blessed you. They have led you. Yet you in your own selfishness have refused to pay them their due. The spirits are all mounting before you to collect what is theirs by right." Obara in osogbo tells the diviner that the one who sits at the mat does not believe in himself; he has low self-esteem. Nor does he believe in others, for they have lied to him many times. This person believes in one thing: wealth. For him, there is never enough of it. The diviner should tell the client that he lies. He does not ever need to lie, but he does so to spice up an otherwise dreary life. This person does not sleep well; insomnia plagues him and his dreams frighten him. When Shangó speaks through Obara in osogbo, the letter marks deception. But if the client listens to all that is said and follows the advice of the reading, he will persevere. Shangó has come not to punish: He is here to chastise, but he will also help.

While six mouths is home to Shangó, it is owned by Oshún, and rarely will it close out unless she has had her chance to speak and claim ebó. It is said that Shangó gave the ownership of all calabazas to Oshún in exchange for his use of this sign. Since then, this sweet river orisha uses calabazas to prepare and store her most powerful spells and trabajos, and within the pumpkin she hides all of her wealth. When Oshún speaks in Obara, the first thing the diviner should tell the client is this: "You are now forbidden to use, eat, pick, or give away any form of calabaza. They are sacred to Oshún and are now meant to be used by you only for ebó." This will be but the first of Obara's many stern pronouncements. To use calabazas for anything other than ebó would offend the sweet orisha and her lover, Shangó.

Orúnmila's influence is also felt in Obara, even though he will not speak directly in the shells. Although only a babalawo can mark this prediction for certain, this awesome orisha can foreshadow an eventual passage into Ifá. The delivery of this advice depends on the sex and initiatory status of the person being read. A man who does not have ocha must go to Ifá and receive mano de Orúnmila; once he is there, the babalawo will advise him if he must make ocha, Ifá, or both. A woman (especially if she is an orisha priestess) who has opened under this sign needs kofá.* If the client is a male iyawó sitting for the itá of initiation, the diviner must prohibit him from using the diloggún until a babalawo has consulted on this client's behalf with Orúnmila; the client could be one of Orúnmila's chosen. Since women may not pass to Ifá, this restriction will never apply to them. No matter the sex of the client, however, if Orúnmila stands up in Obara, the diviner may offer one solid piece of advice: "Orúnmila is firm; he affirms that Olófin watches over you from heaven. You will be great, and one day you will live as royalty." Note that if Orúnmila stands up in Obara for one who has not had a bajado, the client's guardian orisha must be pulled down by a babalawo and not an oriaté. For through six mouths a great reunion between God and this client will come, and only Orúnmila can facilitate this.

Elegguá is the next to speak in Obara, and he gives witness to all Shangó, Oshún, and Orúnmila have had to say. Although Obara is dominated by Shangó and Oshún, unless Elegguá is plied and propitiated, evolution will not come. After Elegguá, the spirits Obatalá, Osain, egun, Oyá, and Ochosi may all stand up to speak or claim ebó in this family of odu. Their issues, however, will be dependent on the composite odu opening. In any pattern of Obara, it is appropriate to say to each, "Maferefún!"

Because Obara brings so many issues and energies into play, the easiest way to study it is to examine it first in iré. Six mouths in iré is a pattern of evolution; it alludes to the client's head, to its inherent royal nature and the greatness it can achieve one day. The diviner should ask this person one simple question: "Are you living the life you once dreamed you would live?" Sadly, he will answer no. The diviner should then tell the client, "Obara has come to save you. If you heed the words of Shangó, if you follow the advice of odu, if you make ebó, and if you heed the taboos of this letter, life will get better. You will have the orisha's blessings." In this odu the source of iré is integral to the reading; it tells the client whence his

*If a composite odu of Obara marks kofá for a woman who has never had a reading or who has not had a bajado, she could be Shangó's daughter. Since Obatalá and Shangó are always close, Obatalá offers his protection as well.

spiritual strength and help comes. It is to this source that he must turn lest his blessings are lost.

Having determined the iré and its source, the diviner continues to question the oracle. If the iré is marked iré yale (firm iré), the odu tells this client that his source of blessing is strong; Shangó and Obara mount behind him, pushing him toward his destiny. If the iré is also marked iré yale timbelaye (firm iré manifest in the client's life), Obara gives closure to itself. It tells the diviner that this pattern's energy has been in effect for some time, and the client has navigated himself well through its energies. He is in alignment with his destiny. Six mouths has opened here to tell the client what forces are in effect and what he will walk away with.

When Obara opens in iré, the diviner should tell the client, "Obara is a sign of freedom brought by speaking the truth. Six mouths gives you a clean road at the feet of the orishas, but only if you continue to speak the truth. Be frank with your peers, for no matter what you do, the truth will always be known, and lies will always be discovered. When others find out about your lies, your evolution will falter." This sign speaks of the tongue and the aché it holds. The diviner should impress upon the client the following proverbs, because in iré they hold the key to his blessings: The king does not lie; from the lie shall the truth be born; while humans are born sincere, all will die liars; the tongue can be a lion, and it will devour you; if one does not speak, the tongue cannot destroy him; with the tongue, one can save or destroy the town, so control the tongue. All these proverbs allude to the client's own mouth and his own words; they emphasize that his adherence to the truth, and his gentle speaking, will ensure his future good fortune. To convince him of this, the diviner should tell the client that once he had a "kingdom," and he lost it through his own lies. Nevertheless, the lies he has told in the past will give birth to a new truth, a new life. Then the diviner should let the client work out the issues it raises on his own.

In any casting of Obara in iré, the diviner has many issues to consider. He should explore the following with the client:

- The client has a great fondness for music; it can uplift him or depress him. Many of his past joys and heartaches are tied up with favorite songs. The diviner should advise the client to fill his home with music, playing only that which uplifts him. The music will bring luck to his life.
- The client's iré will come from one origin (the orientation of odu); however, his luck is not in one place. To fulfill his destiny, he will have to travel and experience new things. He will move many times throughout his life. Love will lead him to new places and new domiciles. While he should follow his heart, his head should be his guide in unknown territory. Obara in iré says the client will prosper greatly by living in the country, away from the erratic vibrations of the city.
- Whenever he has doubts in any issue, this person should consult the orishas. They have great things planned for him and will keep him on the path of evolution.
- Generally, the client is happy, almost carefree, and for this others are envious. He will always be cleansing himself of malicious witchcraft.

Regardless of the odu's orientation, it marks the client as lacking grounding in life. A child of this odu tends to move aimlessly; he may build grand schemes for the future, but he will rarely follow through with them. He was born to be a leader, the head of those around him, but until he replaces his tendency to dream with pure action, nothing much will come of his life. All of Obara's children share one magical talent: divination. Depending on the omo odu extracted, that talent will be stronger in some than in others. At this time the client lacks the necessary wisdom and aché to become a competent diviner. Although the odu giving birth to the spiritualist is Oché Meji (5–5), the client for whom Obara has fallen might want to explore some of the spiritual methods of divination—tarot, crystal gazing, water gazing, and spiritism. These will open the channels for him to eventually become a diviner in this religion.

The personality of the one who opens in this sign is a bit of a paradox. On the surface, this person is amiable and carefree; he seems to know how to enjoy both life and himself. Yet the negative within him is under fire and boils, and it soon will come to the surface in a massive explosion of uncontrolled temper and anger. The diviner should advise the client that no matter how terrible things may seem, he must never allow his temper to surface uncontrolled. With a single outburst, he will forever ruin the impression his peers have of him. If the odu comes in any type of osogbo, now is the time that such an outburst could happen. An osogbo reveals that secret enemies are on either side of this person; they hide in shadows and whisper evil things behind his back. This gossip could be his downfall. The client's own stubbornness will soon be revealed, and his newly emerging argumentative attitude will also bring his downfall. The client should consider this advice to be a prohibition.

When six mouths opens in any type of osogbo, the diviner must work carefully to help his client turn all into iré. Any larishe given by the shells must be fulfilled immediately; the client, diviner, or godparent should not hesitate. This odu, in osogbo, marks a variety of health concerns that must be explained to the client. Depending on the type and degree of this sign's severity, these health concerns may be in various stages: future possibilities, current concerns, or progressive illnesses of which the client may or may not be aware. If the client does not monitor his health carefully, it will begin to break down. (If the osogbo is ikú or arayé, the client's body is already in danger, and he should go for a physical immediately. Although it may be minute, decay is already present in the flesh.) Generally speaking, the client's head is delicate physically and spiritually, and it must be protected at all times. This person must be vigilant against all types of accidents, and he must always wear headgear when involved in intense exercise or contact sports. Rafting, canoeing, cycling, skating, football, and jogging are all sports that should be avoided. Spiritually, the client's orí could pick up the negativity of others through random touches or strokes to the hair and scalp, so the client must allow no one (for a time, not even this person's lover) this privilege. He should allow no one to cut his hair unless his godparents are present, and he must always take the shorn hair away with him. Remember: The head is the seat of the soul. When anyone touches the head, that person is unconsciously trying to touch one's soul. The drowsiness, the light trance that ensues from this feeling, can leave the client open to danger.

The client is prone to insomnia and sleep deprivation, which will cause his health to fail. The cause of sleep disturbances must be removed, because lack of sleep leaves the head weak, the mind clouded, and the body prone to injury or disease. Because this letter prohibits the consumption of home remedies or over-the-counter medications, if the client finds that sleeplessness becomes unbearable he should consult with his physician for a prescription. Regardless of the doctor's recommendation, however, the client should use the medication for only a very brief period, because he may have addictive tendencies. The letter also forebodes an unwanted pregnancy. The client should avoid this, for a child conceived at this time will have abnormalities. Brief chills, hot flashes, or unexplained fevers are sign that something is amiss, and if he experiences these symptoms, the client should see his doctor for a full physical. If Obara's osogbo is arayé or ikú, many other afflictions are possible: renal failure, bladder infections, abdominal disturbances, testicular disorders, and female reproductive disorders. Also, keep in mind that if Obara opens in arayé or ikú during the late fall or winter months, the client must guard his health, being extra cautious and vigilant over the body. The systems are weakest when darkness is greatest.

While true to an extent for all the odu, when Obara falls in an osogbo, many of its forecasts apply not only to the client but also to his relatives (physical and spiritual). Those who are bound to the client by blood or by ocha often share the cyclic patterns of odu. The health of the client's loved ones must be watched closely, and if any of the afflictions flagged by this letter appear, they must be encouraged to seek medical attention. The client and his family should be very careful about what they eat, checking foods and drinks for expiration dates, foul odors, and strange tastes. Fire and electricity could also pose threats now, so the client should be cautious of all electrical appliances and open flames. Accidents involving these can be serious and sometimes fatal.

When Obara comes in any osogbo, the diviner should keep the following points in mind during the reading:

- The client suffers financial hardship; it is of his own making. He must establish a budget and follow it. While money may come easily to some who fall under this letter's influence, the tendency here is for money to dissolve like sugar in water. The client must guard every penny carefully lest poverty ensue. Financial opportunity comes under this sign; however, it will probably be lost. The diviner should advise the client to be vigilant for moneymaking opportunities. When one comes, he should seize it. To not accept the gifts of Obara is to lose one's luck.
- The odu speaks of entanglements with the law and legal complications. To become involved in lawsuits or criminal actions will drain the physical, emotional, spiritual, and financial resources of this person. If he observes something unusual, the client should not talk about the occurrence. Likewise, the client should refrain from being a witness in a legal dispute until the influence of Obara has passed. In this odu, being the only witness could come in handy.
- If the client is a man, he should avoid affairs or counsel from outside his marriage. He must love and honor his wife; she must be his partner in all things. Treating his wife with respect and asking her advice on important matters will bring luck and strengthen the home.
- If marital difficulties have brought a man to the oracle, Oshún should be petitioned to bring stability and love back into his home. The client must then adore Oshún by loving his wife. If the client is female, marital difficulties should be left at the feet of Shangó; he will keep her spouse from straying.

## The Prohibitions of Obara

Obara is a strong sign demanding respect; when it opens, especially if a volatile osogbo comes, the diviner may need to prescribe one or more taboos to keep the client from harm. The italero performing the divination must depend on his own aché and the diloggún to determine appropriate prohibitions for the client. This letter gives strict dietary restrictions that must be prescribed during an itá; they are not as pressing for those who have come only for readings. In cases of a severe osogbo for the uninitiated, the diviner may impose certain prohibitions for a length of time greater than the usual twenty-one to twenty-eight days.

- Be careful when eating away from home. Avoid restaurants. For business or unavoidable social occasions, eat only in those places that are well known and trusted in the community. Ask the server how the food was prepared and what is in it. If he refuses to answer, tell him that you have many life-threatening food allergies and need to know what is in the food you are about to eat.
- Crabs are taboo in Obara.
- Do not consume alcohol.
- Do not touch, cook, or eat squash or other calabazas. Pumpkins are especially volatile; to eat them amounts to eating one's own good fortune.
- When cooking food at home, make sure that extra is always available. If visitors come during one's dinner hour, there must be enough food on hand to feed everyone. This is how Obara became rich, and this is how one will find prosperity as well.
- Do not wear red except for religious functions in which red (such as the elekes and the apparel worn by Shangó's children) would be appropriate. Do not wear stripes, polka dots, checks, or plaids.
- If searching for a new job, do not take a position requiring a uniform. Also, be wary of those who must wear uniforms in their daily work, including police officers, firemen, security guards, and rescue workers.
- Do not emulate the dress styles of friends. Dress differently, or stay home.
- Fire is a danger in this sign. Do not leave burning candles unattended. Do not smoke in bed or in a chair in which falling asleep is a danger. Shangó abhors cigarettes, and if one smokes these, consider quitting. Be sure that electrical

appliances do not have frayed cords. If Obara comes in an osogbo, reconsider having pets in the house. Inadvertently, pets could cause fire by chewing on cords or knocking over sources of open flame.

- Do not use or carry weapons, and do not have guns or knives in the house. Not only could these be turned against one, but they also could create danger. Remember: In this odu, like attracts like.
- Do not mistreat cats, for they are sacred to Shangó. If this letter comes in an osogbo, do not take in a cat, although the ones that are in the home already may stay. Treat all cats well. If this letter opens in iré, for luck have a black cat, treating it like one's most prized possession.
- This odu can bring complications with the law. Do nothing illegal, questionable, or shady; stay on top of legal matters. Try not to be a witness to anything. Even if one observes a crime, do not tell the authorities. Always respect and honor the justice system, but do so from afar. If respect is not given and the law not followed at all times, one will become entangled in expensive legal proceedings. These are ways in which Obara can bring turmoil and devolution.
- If possible, do not sign legal papers. If one must sign a legal paper, have an attorney approve it first. Never cosign a contract, promissary note, or loan for another person.
- Review business offers suspiciously. Do not trust one's business partners; take an active interest in all business affairs.
- If one works in a profession besieged by lawsuits (such as health care), keep proper documentation of all events. If one does not keep sufficient documentation, some day one's professional licensing will come under scrutiny and one's mode of living will be lost.
- Do not fight, argue, or defend oneself or others physically unless there is no other option. Disputes can bring serious, even fatal, consequences. Those who want to argue want to win because they think that they are in the right and are better than others.
- One's social conduct should be beyond reproach when this odu is in effect. Give proper respect to the elders in one's religious and physical families. Avoid spreading lies about others, and do not get caught up in gossip or rumors.
- Always speak frankly and from the heart, but keep secrets secret and do not hurt another's feelings. Do not play jokes on anyone. Remember that in this sign, the tongue has aché, and the tongue must be under control at all times.
- If this reading is the itá of asiento for a child of Shangó, the iyawó may not initiate a child of Oshún, nor may he have as a godchild a child of Oshún. If this reading is the itá of asiento for a child of Oshún, the iyawó may not initiate or work for a child of Shangó. A priest or priestess of one may not date a child (initiate or aleyo) of the other orisha. The aché of these two spirits is too entangled through this sign, and one who does not follow this prohibition will lose iré.
- If this letter has come in ikú, it is extremely important that one does not go anyplace where ceremonies for the dead are being held. If this is the itá of initiation, one may never work with any spirit of the dead beyond one's own egun.

## Marking Ebó in Obara: Initial Considerations

Because the diloggún is a tool facilitating evolution, each sign gives many eboses to bring alignment with one's destiny. When Obara comes, no matter the orientation, it alludes to one's head as the source of goodness and salvation; it is a letter of royalty and destiny, and only one's orí can truly know all it was meant for on this earth.

To begin, the diviner must consider the client's status in the religion: aleyo, aborisha, or initiate. As ebó for an aleyo, he should prescribe a rogación at the feet of either Shangó or Oshún. The diviner may choose the orisha best suited for the rogación based on his own aché, or he may consult the oracle, asking, "Rogación elese [orisha's name]?" After the rogación, the client should offer an adimú of calabazas to the orisha who offered the blessing.

An aborisha or an initiate should also have a

rogación, but the spirit to whom this is done will vary. If the client's guardian orisha is known, he should be cleansed before that spirit; again, after the cleansing of orí, the client should offer an adimú of calabazas. If (for an aborisha), the guardian orisha is not known, the rogación should be performed before Shangó, Oshún, or the godparent's crown.

No matter what composite opens, the diviner should tell the client that as ebó he should offer a ceramic pumpkin to Oshún; there, he should offer her money as a devotion. He must not use this money except in the most dire emergency. With this ebó, Oshún will make sure that the client is never broke.

If the diloggún marks nothing for Elegguá, upon its closure the client should offer some small token adimú to him. The diviner must send the client, out of respect for Orúnmila, to a babalawo for a thorough assessment by Ifá. He should also prescribe a rogación at the feet of Obatalá and ask if the client's orí needs to be fed. The client should offer ebó to Obatalá after completion of the rogación. If Shangó demands any eboses during the course of this reading, the client would do well to employ one of his priestesses to make these offerings for him. Finally, the work of Obara is not complete until Oshún has been given an offering. Even if the shells mark nothing, the client should be directed to give something in her name.

Remember that Shangó has prominence in all composites of Obara; rarely will a reading in this pattern close out unless he has been propitiated. The most common eboses given to this orisha through Obara follow.

### Traditional Eboses in Obara

In each odu, certain types of offerings are symbolic and traditional of the letter that has opened, and when making any type of ebó or larishe, these items should be considered. In Obara, for eyebale the diviner should choose from the following list: one pigeon, a guinea hen, two roosters, and two hens. For adimú-type offerings, he should prescribe a small cane, sixteen pumpkins, sixteen coconuts, red cloth, smoked or fresh fish, jutía, a white sheet, a single cake, anisette, rum, two bottles of water, a single pumpkin, a single coconut, two candles, or old clothing that is exchanged for white after a rogación.

## Adimú

### *Six Guinea Eggs*

Smear six guinea eggs with epó, cocoa butter, honey, and cascarilla. Give these six eggs to Shangó and let them stay with him for six days. At the end of this time, the client returns to his godparent's house to be cleansed with them. He then takes the eggs to the foot of a palm or ceiba tree and leaves them there, along with a derecho of six cents.

### *Six Plantains or Pomegranates*

Another adimú favored by Shangó consists of six plantains or six pomegranates smeared with epó and honey. After six days, the priest removes the fruits from his shrine and cleanses the client with them. After the cleansing, the client discards the plantains or pomegranates at the foot of a palm tree.

### *Guinea Egg Omelette*

The eggs of the guinea hen are one of Shangó's delicacies, and a light omelette made of these will serve as adimú for this orisha. The client will need to provide six guinea eggs, milk, and six pieces of okra (whole).

Crack the eggs into a large mixing bowl and add a dash of milk. Whip the eggs well until blended. Lightly grease and preheat a skillet over medium heat; once it is heated, pour the egg and milk mixture into the pan. Let the eggs solidify slowly. Set the six pieces of okra on half of the egg "pancake," then fold the eggs over the okra. When the omelette is thoroughly cooked, remove it from the pan. Serve this to Shangó on a white plate, leaving the ebó with him overnight.

The day after offering this dish to the orisha, the client discards the food at the foot of a palm tree.

### *Obeguede*

This cold dish also may be served to Shangó as adimú. The client will need to provide 1 pound of okra and 2 pounds of cornmeal.

Finely cut and dice the okra. Combine the okra and the cornmeal in a large mixing bowl. Add water a little bit at a time, mixing and beating until a very thick paste forms. Shape this paste into six balls and serve to Shangó on a red platter.

To discard this offering, the client leaves it at the foot of a palm tree.

### *Mamey Fruits*

Mamey fruits can soothe Shangó in this odu. Put the pulp of six mamey fruits in a ceramic or earthenware cooking dish. Add to this enough boiled yam, epó, honey, smoked fish, and jutía to make a thick paste. Mash together all the ingredients and form into six balls of equal size. Give these to Shangó in a bowl and let them remain with the orisha for six days.

At the end of this time, wrap the entire adimú in red cloth, light two red candles to the orisha, then take the offering to the foot of a palm tree.

## Spiritual Cleansings

### *Pomegranate Seed Bath*

This bath may be combined with the six-pomegranate adimú not only to obtain blessings from Shangó, but also to cleanse the client's body of negative energies.

Combine equal amounts of the herbs álamo, jobo, and almácigo in a large quantity of water. Try to use as many different waters as possible; include rain, river, and sea water. Bring to a boil, then add the pomegranate seeds. Remove from heat. When the water cools, strain the herbal matter from the liquid using cheesecloth. Mix honey, six egg whites, and dry red wine into the liquid. Divide the entire bath into six equal parts; bottle five of these and keep them in the refrigerator and use one part immediately.

Every night for six nights, beginning on the night the bathwater is made (it is strongest on this night), the client sits in a tub of fresh water and pours the pomegranate water over his body from the shoulders down. He relaxes in the bath before showering and dressing in white. The first bath will remove all negative vibrations from the client; the remaining five will help maintain this period of freshness and coolness.

### *Guarapo Bath*

To soothe a hot osogbo, open Shangó's batea and put a bowl of *guarapo* (sugarcane syrup) over him. Burn two white candles to the orisha while this ebó sits on his shrine, and pray for peace and prosperity. Once the candles have burned out, bathe with this juice, soaking in the bath as long as possible. Finish by showering with fresh water, and dress in white for the entire day.

## Petitions to Shangó

### *In General*

Special petitions to Shangó may be made by writing a detailed letter to the orisha. Seal the letter inside an envelope and place it in the center of six green plantains. Tie this bundle securely together with red and white ribbons and hang it just behind the front door. The plantains should remain there until they turn yellow; do not let them turn brown. When they are yellow, take them to the foot of a palm tree, along with a derecho of six cents. Shangó will answer the requests.

### *A Petition for Love*

If this client came to the diloggún seeking love, or advice concerning love and matters of the heart, he can offer a special ebó to Shangó and the orisha will help him find the love he desires. On brown paper, the client writes a petition to Shangó; he puts the letter in an envelope and lays the envelope on a red or red-bordered plate. He cores six red apples and places them around the outer edge of the plate. He fills the hollow core of each apple with cinnamon, a clove, and honey and then puts the "lid" back on each fruit. Inside this circle of apples, and over the petition, the client places a red seven-day candle. He serves this ebó to Shangó, paying foribale to the orisha and then praying for the love desired. Finally, he lights the candle.

This offering should remain with Shangó until the candle is finally consumed by the flame. Then the client leaves the six apples at the foot of a palm tree, along with a derecho of six cents. He buries the petition in the earth beneath the palm tree.

### *A Petition for Financial Evolution*

If economic concerns have brought this client to the diloggún, and if Shangó stands up to help him in the reading, a special ebó may be done to bring financial evolution. The client opens a pumpkin and fills it with amalá (see the recipe on page 54) and epó. (He does not remove the contents of the gourd, for in this odu pumpkin seeds represent one's wealth.) He then inserts into the pumpkin six pieces of okra and puts the lid back on the pumpkin. He writes a petition to Shangó expressing his needs and places it on a red or red-bordered plate. He places the pumpkin over his petition and serves the ebó to Shangó while paying foribale to him. He lights a red seven-day candle in honor of the orisha and prays for all that he needs.

When this candle is consumed, the client takes the pumpkin to a palm tree, along with a derecho of six cents. He buries the petition there at the foot of the tree.

# The First Composite Odu of Obara, Obara Okana (6-1)

## The Proverbs of Obara Okana

- Be frank and speak your heart.
- The whim is the loss of everything.
- Be careful of outsiders to our faith.
- Even Obatalá has turned his back.
- Don't lose your head, or you will lose yourself.

## The Message of Obara Okana

When an initial cast of six mouths, Obara, precedes a cast of one mouth, Okana, the odu Obara Okana is open on the mat. This letter is also known as Obara Kana, Obara Kanran, and Obara Okanran. Having come to the room in this sign, the pattern and the orishas who speak in it must be honored. The diviner says, "Maferefún Shangó! Maferefún Obatalá! Maferefún Orúnmila!" Both Shangó and Obatalá speak strongly here. Their bond in Obara Okana is so tight that when this odu falls for a client whose crown is unknown, the diviner should tell him that, for now, he must consider himself a child of both. Orúnmila is silent in diloggún, but his presence in Obara Okana is so strong that before this session closes, the diviner might have to prescribe to the client a visit to Ifá for a consultation.

Obara Okana is an interesting letter. Its opening on the mat presages events far beyond the diviner's or the client's life. In one of their cities, an important political/government official will fall ill with little chance of recovery. Also, a tragedy, an unforseen event with many casualties, will occur in a nearby city. The diviner must offer these predictions to the client, for once they occur he will believe in the oracle and the orishas.

While this odu can bring fulfillment in iré, before good fortune is found the client will have to move through a period of strife and struggle. To ensure that the client does not miss his blessings, the diviner would be wise to treat the odu as if it had come in an osogbo. Obara Okana can be a sign of lies and liars; the client is not only surrounded and influenced by lies but also can become a liar. Obara is a sign of royalty demanding truth, peace, and goodness even when wars rage; the client must remember this. Wars are coming to his life on both a personal and a professional level. No matter what evil others do, the client should never stoop to their level. In this odu, Shangó will fight and Obatalá will work for peace. The diviner should encourage the client to leave all his troubles at the feet of these two orishas so his own hands will remain clean. To enlist the orishas' help, the diviner should offer two spiritual prescriptions. First, the client should give Obatalá a fly whisk, beaded in his colors and packed with his aché. It should be consecrated with the orisha's omiero before being given to his sopera. Obatalá will cleanse the client with this whisk. Second, the client should give Shangó a white ceramic horse. Shangó will use it to ride into battle.

The diviner should also explore the following issues with the client:

- This is not a time for pregnancy. The client and his partner must use birth control. If the client is a woman, she should abstain from sexual relations for a few weeks, if possible. Not only could a child born under Obara Okana be sick or deformed, but also the mother's health will suffer. Pregnancy at this time could even ruin a marriage. Those who are planning families should make ebó and wait a few months.
- The client has told many lies. Not all of them were big, and at the time he told them they were necessary for his survival, but now the lies are coming back to haunt him. When caught in his lies, the client must tell the truth so he can move on.
- The head is weak and easily influenced in this odu. The client must be cautious of whom he lets touch his head. If he suffers frequent headaches or eyestrain or if his judgment becomes poor, he should come back for a rogación at Obatalá's feet. Clarity will return.
- Finally, this odu recommends caution and slow progress in all things.

## The Prohibitions of Obara Okana

- Do not do favors for anyone, especially if another requests that one hold something in storage.
- Do not tell lies. If the truth cannot be told, do not speak.
- Violence will bring legal entanglements at this time. Avoid fights, arguments, and raising one's voice or hands to anyone in anger. Do not stand on street corners. Watch one's back at all times; someone may try to strike one in the back of the neck before this odu passes.
- Do not wear clothing with stripes. Wear as much white as possible; if one must attend a function in which white is not appropriate, wear the lightest solid colors possible.
- Do not mistreat cats. If Obara Okana comes in osogbo, one may not own a cat. If Obara Okana comes in iré, having a black cat will bring much luck to one's home.
- Be careful of fire. Never have more than two candles burning at home, and never leave these unattended.
- If Obara Okana comes in itá with Oshún for an initiate, the initiate may never crown that Oshún to another's head. If Obara Okana comes in itá with Oshún for an initiate who is Shangó's child, he may never lift Oshún's children from the floor, nor may he crown them in ocha. The child of Oshún will rise, and he will fall in that person's place.

## The Eboses of Obara Okana

Conception and pregnancy are dangerous in this sign, and the diviner will caution against it. However, if conception does occur, the following ebó will protect the health of both mother and child: Before the shrines of Yemayá and Oshún, the mother must have a rogación of the abdomen. Once this is done, the priest must cleanse her head as well. After both cleansings, the mother should receive a fresh set of Yemayá's and Oshún's elekes. Every month until the baby's birth, the rogaciónes of the abdomen and head should be repeated. If a caesarean becomes necessary, the woman must make ebó to Ogún as well, giving him a new, sharp knife with prayers that the metal will be healing, not harmful. The priest must present a rooster to the client at this time, rubbing it well over her abdomen before sacrificing it to Ogún.

Now the diviner has his first chance to close the odu. If it will not close, he should investigate the following possibilities:

- Yemayá and Oshún could have additional remedies. To determine if they require anything else, the diviner should ask, "Larishe si Yemayá?" and "Larishe si Oshún?" If the answer to either question is yes, he uses the diloggún to mark the appropriate offering.
- Shangó and Obatalá stand firm here; if the odu will not close out, the client could have issues with one or both of these spirits. To determine if this is the case, the diviner should consider asking, "Ebó elese [orisha's name]?" If the answer is yes, he uses the diloggún to mark the appropriate offering.

- The orisha whose diloggún is consulted could require six calabazas as an adimú; these are allowed to remain with this orisha until they begin to turn bad. The diviner should then ask the orisha (using obí) where to discard the ebó.
- If this odu still refuses closure, the diviner should tell the client two things: First, he must go to Ifá for a consultation. Second, his destiny lies in ocha, and one day he must be crowned.

If these prescriptions are not enough to close the sign, the diviner must now turn to the eboses of the parent odu, Obara (see page 297). Something there is needed for the client's evolution.

## The Second Composite Odu of Obara, Obara Ejioko (6-2)

### The Proverbs of Obara Ejioko

- There was a favor done for another, and this has set you back your whole life.
- The love of money will destroy you.
- Your servant wants to steal your lover.
- One can be fooled by looks and appearances.
- The orishas will bring a resolution.

### The Message of Obara Ejioko

When an initial casting of six mouths is followed by two, the odu Obara Ejioko has come to the mat. This odu is also known as Obara Oyekun and Obara Yeku. In this sign, we say the manservant wants to come and steal one's lover. Through Obara Ejioko, Obatalá gave his thanks to the monkeys, but they did not give him any thanks for the good they had; in time, they were cursed. The sign warns us to watch, to be wary, and always to give thanks for the good we have before it is taken away.

The diviner begins by saying, "Maferefún Obatalá! Maferefún Oshún! Maferefún Elegguá! Maferefún egun!" He pays homage to Obatalá for all the good he brings us. Oshún speaks here as well; the client must honor her not only directly, but also by treating her sons and daughters on the earth well. To disrespect any of them now is to incur her wrath. Elegguá in Obara Ejioko guides us through the darkness that must be traveled. Finally, Obara Ejioko speaks of debts with the dead; they are the client's foundation, but this foundation is weak. Before this reading closes, the client's ancestors may require extensive eboses from him.

The client who has come in this sign can be friendly, outgoing, and charitable at times; however, these qualities are not stable, and when they manifest, they are extended toward the wrong people. Outlaws, bandits, and con men are attracted to this person, and with their flattery, attention, and hard-luck stories they weasel their way into the client's life. He grants them too many favors and offers too much financial or emotional support. Often this client finds himself being used and left with nothing. The orisha whose diloggún is being read lays down a stern prohibition: The client must not make friends with those who live outside the law, or even with those who must spend their lives pretending to live outside the law (undercover law enforcement officers). The "outlaws" whom the client has befriended must be quickly weaned out of his life. Unfortunately, he lives and works close to these people. To get away from them, he must move away from his present home, and perhaps find a new job. And he should never fall into this trap again.

In addition, the diviner should explore the following points with the client:

- If Obara Ejioko comes in a severe osogbo, we say that the client loves his own money more than he loves his own life. Unfortunately, there is not a lot of money in his life, nor is there a lot of life left to live. To survive, this client must change his ways.
- Even in iré, many health concerns arise in this odu. It points out the possibility of leg injuries; swellings, bruises, ulcers, cuts, and broken bones are a danger. The client should be wary of heights and guard against falls.
- The client must always respect the children of Oshún, especially her daughters. He must not enter into a relationship with one unless he is certain he can get along with Oshún's child.

## The Prohibitions of Obara Ejioko

- Until this odu's energy has passed (three to six months), refuse to do three things: fight, argue, and scale heights. While these may seem unrelated, all can quickly turn the iré of this sign to an osogbo.
- Do not use elevators or escalators; do not ride in anything that lifts a lot of weight. Also, do not help anyone lift anything from the floor.
- Do not venture out alone in the streets for the next seven days; stay home if possible. Know that someone could be waiting at a crossroads with a knife.

## The Eboses of Obara Ejioko

In Obara Ejioko, one of the many health afflictions that can come to the client is a topical ulcer that will not heal. If the client has or develops an ulcer, the diviner should prescribe the following remedy as ebó:

Grind the leaves of the cundiamor plant (which is sacred to Babaluaiye) and *itamo real* [AU: Need definition] in virgin olive oil. Let the leaves soak for seventeen days. At the end of this time, strain the oil from the herbs. Wash the skin with water and cocoa butter soap, and smooth the oil over the ulcerated skin. It will heal.

No matter the orientation of Obara Ejioko, certain eboses are mandatory in this sign. First, the client must visit a babalawo to have a thorough session with Ifá; he must also receive mano (or kofá, if the client is a woman) of Orúnmila. He must give his egun at least two masses, one a month for two months, and follow the prescriptions of the espiritistas exactly. Finally, the Ibeyi are essential to the client's evolution; if he does not have them, he must be marked for their reception now.

After making these prescriptions, the diviner has his first chance to close the odu. If Obara Ejioko will not close, the diviner should explore the following:

- The client's egun might need ebó in addition to the masses. To determine if they require anything, the diviner should consider asking, "Ebó elese egun?" If the answer is yes, he uses the diloggún to mark the appropriate offering.
- If the client already has the Ibeyi, they might need ebó. To determine if they require anything, the diviner asks, "Ebó elese los Ibeyi?" If the answer is yes, he uses the diloggún to mark the appropriate offering.
- The client could have issues with Obatalá, Oshún, Elegguá, Ogún, or Ochosi. To see if any of these orishas will take ebó, the diviner should consider asking, "Ebó elese [orisha's name]?" If the answer is yes, he uses the diloggún to mark the appropriate offering.

If these prescriptions will not close the odu and the client is an aleyo or an aborisha, the diviner must turn to the eboses of the parent odu, Obara (see page 297). Something there is necessary for the client's evolution.

If Obara Ejioko refuses closure and the client is an initiate, the orisha whose diloggún is being consulted could be marking a tambor as the solution to the client's troubles. The diviner should first question if a tambor is needed. If the answer is yes, then he must determine which orisha will claim the tambor, beginning with the orisha whose diloggún is being consulted, then the other orishas that this priest or priestess has received, and then all the spirits who may speak in Obara. Remember the two rules for giving a drum: First, before the client can give any other orisha a drum, he must give a drum to his godparent's guardian orisha. Second, if an orisha that has not been received by the client wants a drum, the client must receive that orisha before the drum can be given.

If at this point the odu still refuses closure, the diviner must turn to the eboses of the parent odu, Obara (see page 297).

# The Third Composite Odu of Obara, Obara Ogundá (6-3)

## The Proverbs of Obara Ogundá

- The mountain believed that it was powerful and did not make ebó; thus did it fall.
- You work hard, and yet your work is always bad.

- He who does not want soup will drink three cups.
- Always return what one's visitor offers.

## The Message of Obara Ogundá

Having come to the mat in a pattern of six mouths followed by three mouths, the odu Obara Ogundá has come to the house. Here, both Shangó and Oshún speak; the diviner says to each, "Maferefún!" Elegguá is firm here as well, and the diviner should say, "Maferefún Elegguá!" If the client is an initiate of Ogún, or if Ogún's diloggún is being consulted, ebó must be made between Shangó, Elegguá, and Ogún; see "The Eboses of Obara Ogundá" below. The diviner must make sure this ebó is done.

This is a dangerous pattern. It brings up many concerns about women, the most important being this: Avoid pregnancy at this time. However, if the client is a man, he must not recommend an abortion to any woman, even his own lover. Both Ogún and Oshún forbid this. If the client is a woman, her next pregnancy must not end in abortion; she must try to take it to full term. (The child will probably be a child of Oshún). Many problems in this person's life will be brought by the hands of women. If the client is a married man, his wife is not pleased with him. She is cold toward him and does not like making love to him. He must give her a lot of attention or eventually she will leave. If the client has a daughter, she has either run off before or will soon leave with her own lover. Finally, the client must always measure the gossip brought by women; however, he must not seek to verify it, for thus will danger be found.

Malicious spirits set traps for this client, and he must offer a spiritual mass for them to find out why they wish to bring him harm. Tragedy will be wrought by the spirits' hands, and only the client can save himself, by making ebó. Even when it comes in iré, this letter marks death and sickness; if disease visits the client's house, the one stricken should see a physician immediately before a small health problem becomes a big health problem.

The client must avoid all forms of violence, even those displayed on television, and also avoid arguing with loved ones. He will have a strong temptation to strike another in anger, but he must refrain from doing so at all costs lest there be severe legal entanglements.

In addition, the diviner should note the following points:

- The client should be on guard against accidents, especially falls, in his home. Elderly people—himself or those who live with him—are prone to broken bones, especially in the hips.
- Unknowingly, the client is entangled with someone who has a loose tongue. There is only one remedy to this: He must keep his personal business to himself. He should trust no one with secrets. The client will be victorious in all things if he works alone.
- The client has a poor personal and business reputation. If he desires success, he must repair this.
- This letter indicates that the client's business concerns are or will soon be lagging. Making ebó will help. Also, the client might wish to approach the oracle of this orisha at a later time to determine a secret Lucumí name for the business; he might also wish to have a business Elegguá at his workplace to keep it prosperous.
- There is a special warning for the diviner in this letter: His spouse may be thinking about leaving. The remedy for this is simple: He must give his spouse more love and attention.

## The Prohibitions of Obara Ogundá

- Do not climb ladders, and never pass under one.
- Do not go to places frequented by the dead or places where ceremonies are being done for the dead. This includes, but is not limited to, funerals, wakes, nursing homes, hospitals, and graveyards.

## The Eboses of Obara Ogundá

Whenever this composite odu opens for an initiate of Ogún or Shangó, a special ebó must be done. Both Shangó and Ogún are placed on the floor; if this reading is being given with Elegguá's diloggún, the client's Elegguá sits between them. The priest cleanses the client with a white chicken and then sacrifices the bird to Elegguá. After Elegguá eats, the priest cleanses the client with two white roosters and one guinea hen; he then sacrifices the birds to Shangó and Ogún together. After the sacrifices, the priest places all the carcasses in a bag along with toasted corn, jutía, smoked fish, epó, honey, rum, dried coconut, and nine guinea peppers. The client takes this bag to the woods and cleanses himself with it before discarding it.*

In addition, this letter indicates that Ogún is causing many of the client's problems and demands appeasement. For some reason (and the client probably knows what this is), the client has many unresolved issues with Ogún. He must offer Ogún an adimú. If this is not enough to close the letter, Ogún might be standing up for ebó; the diviner should ask, "Ebó elese Ogún?" If the answer is yes, he uses the shells to mark the offering. If the client does not have Ogún, these eboses must be given to the diviner's orisha, and the client should receive the complete initiation of the warriors as soon as possible.

The diviner should also offer Yemayá the chance to claim ebó, asking, "Ebó elese Yemayá?" If she claims ebó, the diviner should mark what she requires with the diloggún. If Yemayá will not claim an ebó, the client should give her an adimú in her home, the ocean. After making this offering, the client and the diviner should cast a net into the ocean, dredging its underwater shelf. Use whatever is found in the net to make ebó at the diviner's shrine for Yemayá. Hang the net over the client's back door to bring iré and keep away osogbo.

Now the diviner has his first opportunity to close the odu. If it refuses closure, the client may have unresolved issues with Aganyú. The diviner should ask, "Ebó elese Aganyú?" If the answer is yes, he should use the diloggún to mark an appropriate offering.

*If Obara Ogundá comes for an initiate of Shangó during an itá in either Elegguá or Shangó, or for an initiate of Ogún during an itá in either Elegguá or Ogún, this ebó must be done every year on the initiate's birthday.

If the odu still will not close and the client is an aleyo or aborisha, the diviner must now turn to the eboses of the parent odu, Obara (see page 297). Something there is needed to bring this person evolution.

If the client is an initiate and the odu will not close, the reception of Aganyú could be necessary. The diviner should ask, "Koshé Aganyú?"

Finally, if this sign continues to refuse closure, it may mark one of two eboses: the giving of four legs and an itá or the reception of the knife. First, the diviner asks the oracle if an orisha needs four legs; if the answer is yes, he asks if the orisha speaking will take the four legs. If so, the sacrifice does not require an itá. If the orisha speaking does not claim the sacrifice of four legs, the diviner must try to mark it for another orisha, questioning first the orishas the client received in his ocha and then all those who may speak in the parent odu, Obara (see page 297).

If the oracle will not mark four legs for any of the orishas, the diviner should next try to mark the reception of the knife, asking, "Koshé pinaldo?"

If the odu still remains open at this point, the diviner must turn to the eboses of the parent odu, Obara.

## The Fourth Composite Odu of Obara, Obara Irosun (6-4)

### The Proverbs of Obara Irosun

- Always give respect to the orishas.
- [In iré] A prince is crowned while a king dies.
- You cannot walk to the ocean without leaving a trail in the sand.
- Cats walk on fences, but men should not; make up your mind.

### The Message of Obara Irosun

When an initial cast of six mouths, Obara, is followed by a second cast of four mouths, Irosun, the odu Obara Irosun is open on the mat. This is a solemn, volatile sign demanding much respect.

Immediately, the diviner should say, "Maferefún Obatalá! Maferefún Babaluaiye!" Both orishas are coming to visit this client: Obatalá to his house and Babaluaiye in the street. The client must be aware of this, for to disrespect either of these orishas, their children, or their priests will destroy the iré of this odu. The diviner also pays homage to Eleggua and the Ibeyi, saying, "Maferefún Elegguá! Maferefún los Ibeyi!" Both orishas come in this odu to bring blessings. He says "Maferefún Aganyú!" as well, for Obara Irosun gives birth to the lava that flows from the volcano. Next he says, "Maferefún Oyá! Maferefún Olokun! Maferefún Orisha Oko!" These three dark, mysterious orishas are firm in this odu as well. They know the secrets of life and of death, and these are secrets that touch the client, yet elude him. Finally, the diviner ends his homage by saying, "Maferefún Shangó! Maferefún Oshún!" These orishas, too, are here; Obara Irosun speaks of the squash and the vine, mandating eboses and baths with both, for with these Shangó and Oshún found their wealth in the world. This is also the odu in which the king was hanged, yet he "did not hang." The client must ensure that he, himself, does not get hanged.

In iré, this odu promises one blessing: great wealth. Beyond this blessing, however, even in iré the sign is bad, and the diviner must explore this composite as if it had fallen in osogbo. Only in this way may the client evolve. To begin, Obara Irosun points to death and sickness in the client's home. If the odu opens in an osogbo of ano or ikú, death or sickness may have already happened, and it can occur again. The client should be prepared for medical emergencies when this sign falls. A spirit one who died by suicide or suffocation may be close to this person. This spirit walks with the client; it wants to help him, but it is too earthbound to be of any service. The client must offer candles, prayer, and adimú to assist its elevation to another plane.

The diviner should tell the client that he is surrounded by enemies. Even his friends do not have his best interests in mind. This sign speaks of treason and of danger, and the one sitting at the mat must be cautious in all his dealings if he hopes to evolve.

In addition, the diviner should explore the following with the client:

- Obara Irosun speaks of the *abiku*, spirits from the bush that incarnate again and again to a single mother, punishing her by living for a brief time and then dying suddenly. The client must bring the next child born in his family to the diviner. He or she may need to be chained to the earth (to wear on the left ankle a chain that has been previously fed to the earth) so the spirit of the abiku will not take it away. If the client has had many children die, or even many miscarriages, the next child born definitely needs to be chained.
- In this odu, all the orishas stand up to complain about the client's lack of respect. Although he may not mean to blaspheme the religion, he does. Another person close to him does this as well. This must stop.
- This client has a very curious neighbor capable of causing trouble. Forewarned is forearmed.

## The Prohibitions of Obara Irosun

- Young girls and children are a source of misfortune; do not be alone with them.
- Do not leave doors, windows, blinds, or curtains open. At night, lock them.
- Do not leave candles or sources of fire unattended in the house. Extinguish them before leaving.

## The Eboses of Obara Irosun

When this letter falls on the mat, it automatically marks certain eboses and spiritual works for the client. First, Obara Irosun alludes to the squash and to the vine upon which it grows, and the client should take many spiritual baths using the squash and its vine. Second, this letter alludes to a troubled spirit (one who has died by suicide or suffocation) that has attached itself to the client, and this spirit must be given spiritual masses so that it can move beyond the plane on which it is stuck. Finally, Elegguá stands up in this letter to demand more attention from the client; he should be treated as if he were the client's guardian orisha. If the diloggún being consulted is Elegguá's, and if the client is an initiate of our faith, the diviner should check to see if Elegguá is standing up for a crown.

After making these initial prescriptions, the diviner has his first chance to close the oracle. If it refuses, the diviner should keep the following points in mind:

- Olokun is important in all composite odus that incorporate Irosun. If the client does not have Olokun and the letter refuses closure, the diviner should try to mark her reception with the shells, asking, "Koshé Olokun?" If the client has Olokun, the diviner should ask if the orisha needs ebó.
- The Ibeyi can be an integral part of this odu. If it refuses closure and the client does not have these orishas, the diviner must determine if their reception is needed, asking, "Koshé los Ibeyi?" If the answer is no, or if the client already has them, the diviner should determine whether they are standing up for ebó, asking, "Ebó elese los Ibeyi?" If the answer is yes, he should mark what they require using the diloggún.
- Babaluaiye stands up in this letter as well, and if it will not close, the client may need to make ebó to him. The diviner asks, "Ebó elese Babaluaiye?" If the answer is yes, he marks a suitable ebó. If the answer is no and the client does not have Babaluaiye, the diviner asks, "Koshé Babaluaiye?" If the answer is yes, until he can receive the orisha the client should have his eleke for protection.

If the letter still refuses closure, the diviner must consider the eboses of the parent odu, Obara (see page 297). If the eboses of the parent odu are not enough to close the odu and the client is an initiate, he could have issues pending with Osain. To determine whether the reception of this orisha is necessary, the diviner asks, "Koshé Osain?" Note that the reception of Osain in this odu is a last resort, to be questioned only when all else fails.

## The Fifth Composite Odu of Obara, Obara Oché (6-5)

### The Proverbs of Obara Oché

- If something does not help, it hinders; throw it away.
- While you may be planting the seeds of the squash, it is your neighbor who steals the fruit.
- The apprentice wants to surpass the teacher, yet is stupid and knows nothing.
- The tongue can bring your death.
- Sweep toward the front, toward the yard.
- If the heart is clean, it holds more value than money.
- Bells sound better in your own yard.

### The Message of Obara Oché

When an initial cast of six mouths, Obara, precedes a cast of five mouths, Oché, the odu Obara Oché is open on the mat. This odu is also known as Obara'che. This is the sign of those with curious natures and big heads. We say that the apprentice wants to observe the teacher; however, the teacher should be careful because his student wants to usurp his authority. In time, he will try, but soon he will discover that he knows nothing. The sign tells the story of a younger priest who did such a thing to his elder, but when he began to divine and teach, he realized how little he truly knew. His teacher would not take him back. Elder initiates who come in this sign must be warned: Their own godchildren have treachery in their hearts. Even Orúnmila's students, his babalawos, thought that they knew more than he, but when Orúnla retreated from their midst, the Ifá priests were helpless and blundered all their tasks. For this reason, the diviner begins by saying, "Maferefún Orúnmila!"

The diviner also pays homage to Shangó and Oshún in this odu, saying to each, "Maferefún!" They can save the client from evil and treachery, but he must listen to their advice. The sign itself tells the client that many things in his life are broken, useless, and meaningless. While each possession he has might carry sentimental value, marking an important period in his life, the fact that the possession is broken or useless shows that these parts of his life must be discarded as well. The diviner must advise the client to gather all these broken things; he must leave them at Shangó's feet overnight with an adimú. The next morning, he should throw them away. Obara Oché also signals that the client's house is untidy and filthy, and it must be scrubbed from top to bottom and kept that way forever. The orishas do not like to live in a dirty home.

In all castings of Obara Oché, certain individual issues must be kept in mind by the diviner:

- Obara Oché is, if nothing else, an odu of throwing things outside to the yard. A spiritual prescription the diviner may give to the client is to place large bowls of water in the center of each room before going to bed. In the morning, starting with the bowl of water farthest away from the front door, throw these into the yard. Empty boxes, bottles, and trash should be taken out daily before beginning morning prayers. The client must do all these things in silence.
- In this odu, the client plants his squash, but the neighbor comes to steal his fruit. With this, the sign is telling the client that while he works hard, it is his "neighbor" who benefits from his blood, sweat, and tears. This person must make ebó so that he and not his friends reaps his rewards.
- In this odu the tongue has aché, yet its aché works against its owner. It can even bring death. The client must measure all his words before speaking. If the sign opens in a serious osogbo, the client must make ebó to Shangó with a cow's tongue so he controls and blesses the client's speech. To avoid the effects of gossip, the client should bury this fixed cow's tongue outside his front door.
- The client must monitor the clocks in his house carefully and pay special attention to his wristwatch, if he wears one. If any of these stops, it must be restarted immediately.

## The Prohibitions of Obara Oché

- Even if this is a casual reading for a new client, Obara Oché signals that Shangó and Oshún forbid the purchase, sale, cutting, cooking, or consumption of all gourds and squash. They should be used for ebó and nothing else. To break this taboo is to destroy one's luck.
- An initiate must watch his godchildren warily; one is planning treason. In this odu it is forbidden to teach all that one knows on any subject.
- Do not keep broken, burned-out, or unused electrical appliances in the house.
- Oshún now controls one's comings and goings. If the need for travel arises, do not travel unless one has consulted with her first. For safety, one may need to make ebó to her.

## The Eboses of Obara Oché

When a casting of Obara Oché opens on the mat, certain eboses must be done no matter the orientation of this odu. The orisha whose diloggún is being consulted, Shangó, and Oshún must each be given calabazas as ebó. To Oshún give five, to Shangó give six, and to the orisha consulted give a number of gourds equal to his or her favorite number (three for Eshu, four for Obatalá, nine for Oyá). Leave the gourds at the shrines of these orishas until they start to turn bad. The client should also plant a single vine of squash indoors, and when the vine is big enough he should transplant it to a spot outside his back door. He must guard the vine well and tend it carefully. The fruit growing on it belongs to Oshún, and when it is ripe he must pick it and give it to her. The more squash that ripens, the more luck this ebó will bring. Also, a niche osain for Oshún must be packed into a large gourd. This charm remains beside Oshún's sopera. Finally, if the client is an initiate, he now must wear a red parrot feather in his hair at all times.

After making these prescriptions, the diviner may now attempt to close the oracle. If the odu will not close, he should consider the following:

- Shangó or the orisha whose diloggún is being consulted could also require a niche osain packed

in a gourd. The diviner should ask, "Niche osain elese [orisha's name]?" These charms must be kept with the orishas' shrines at all times.
- The client could have further issues with Shangó and Oshún. To see if they require anything, the diviner should consider asking, "Ebó elese [orisha's name]?" If the answer is yes, he marks the required offering with the shells.

If the odu will not close at this point, the diviner should consider the eboses of the parent odu, Obara (see page 297). Something there is needed for the client's evolution.

## The Sixth Composite Odu of Obara, Obara Meji (6-6)

### The Proverbs of Obara Meji

- He who doesn't know dies, while he who does know lives.
- The one who knows the truth does not die like the one who does not know.
- There is a full belly one day and an empty belly the next.
- With your tongue, you may save or destroy the town; control your tongue.
- He who does not know dies, but not the one who knows.
- The fly that does not become greedy never dies inside a wine bottle.
- The fly that flies high up in the air and is not tempted by bait on the low ground does not get caught in the fly trap.
- The soldier does not sleep in a time of war.
- When gold speaks, men become mute.
- Men are born sincere, but all will die liars.
- Old friends should not be abandoned for the new.
- The lie that you speak becomes the truth in time.
- Your tongue is a liar; if you allow it, it will devour you.
- The quail knows so much that it sleeps on the ground.
- The king dies while a prince is crowned.
- The patient man can become king of the world.
- He who knows does not die like one who does not know.
- The eye of the rider fattens the horse, so keep your eyes on your affairs.
- If you remain silent, you will not have to watch what you say.
- The head first created will not fail to prosper in the market.
- The spring is not deep enough to cover the gourd.
- The one who scolds a person with the past reveals his own dark secrets.
- Excess breeds envy; envy invokes animosity; animosity begets hatred.
- It is true that a wheel travels forward, but it can also roll backward.
- The woman who eats from two hands should be sentenced and condemned by her acts. [This proverb speaks of adultery.]
- He who doesn't know dies; but he who does know will live forever.

### The Message of Obara Meji

When a casting of six mouths, Obara, is followed by itself, the odu Obara Meji has fallen on the mat. This sign is powerful and gives birth to all the odu in this family. It marks a person who is a diviner by birth; even an aleyo opening in this sign will have this raw aché. Without proper guidance, however, he will miss his calling. This odu also speaks of the eventual separation between the godparent and the godchild; it suggests that the godchild's head will be more powerful and famous than the godparent's.

While in its mother's womb, before being born on the earth among mortals, Obára Meji revealed important dangers and truths to its earthly parents through dreams; thus, this odu gave birth to dreams. Before its existence, one slumbered at night not bothered by nocturnal visions. Shangó and Oshún are said to have issues with each other in this pattern, for once Oshún was rich but Shangó brought her to ruin. Because of him, her fortune was squandered. In this odu children of Oshún must be careful that Shangó's children do not do this to them.

This odu gave birth to the rabbit's digging at the earth and the custom of the first drum given to egun. It also gave birth to the custom of using white cloth to wrap the corpses of the dead. Obara Meji is the sign in which the Egbado people headed to the Congolese kingdoms, searching for the secrets of black magic and witchcraft. While the history of their journey is obscure, we do know that they never found that which they sought; they destroyed themselves in their quest for ultimate power. In this sign Shangó defeated the army of Arara with his own troops. In Obara Meji a treaty of sorts was formed between Shangó and Ogún: Shangó gave Ogún the dog and Ogún gave Shangó the ram. In this odu the Muslim people abandoned the worship of Ifá for that of Allah. Obara Meji is the "head" of the earth, and it gives her the mountains for her crown. Obara Meji is the place where all the roads of Obatalá are born. It is where Baba Ode, a road of Babaluaiye, was born. It is where the pyramids of Egypt were built and the funeral rites created for burying the pharaohs. For all it brought to the world, "Maferefún Obara Meji!"

In this sign many spirits stand up to offer advice and protection; they may also come to take ebó. The diviner should explore these issues with the client.

- "Maferefún Shangó!" In Obara Meji, he comes to bless this client, but the extent of his blessings is heavily dependent upon odu's orientation. Shangó says that no matter what the client is facing, he is here fighting for him. When the client prays to Shangó (and he should pray to him often), he must always give to him six squashes and a red seven-day candle on a white plate. Shangó will listen to his petitions. If he needs passage or travel to a safe place, the client should give Shangó a white ceramic horse. If he needs protection, he should give him a bat beaded in red and white. Shangó will never let down this client .
- "Maferefún Oshún!" Even in iré, she comes to warn the client about Shangó's children. In Obara Meji, we say that Oshún was once rich, but Shangó brought her to ruin. The children of Shangó can bring ruin to the client; they will make him fail financially. Shangó's children can be especially dangerous for Oshún's children. The client should pray to Oshún after giving her five small pumpkins and a yellow seven-day candle on a large white plate. She will protect the client from poverty. Note that when Obara Meji comes in an osogbo, it is not wise for Oshún's children to have any dealings with Shangó's children, nor is it wise for Shangó's children to have any dealings with Oshún's children.
- "Maferefún Obatalá!" This orisha stands up in Obara Meji to warn the client against slavery. He may not try to enslave others, nor should he let himself become enslaved. In both iré and osogbo, the client's head can become overwhelmed by this odu. When this happens, he must return to the diviner for a rogación before Obatalá's shrine.
- "Maferefún Elegguá!" He can settle all the client's issues, especially those that arise between Shangó and Oshún. If the client is a child of either Shangó or Oshún, the following ebó must be done: Put all three orishas on the floor, with Elegguá sitting between the other two. Feed the guardian orisha a sacrifice of feathers first, sharing this with Elegguá. Next, feed the other orisha a sacrifice of feathers, again sharing it with Elegguá. Finally, give Elegguá his own sacrifice of feathers. Afterward, put the carcasses in a brown paper bag, along with toasted corn, jutía, smoked fish, and six fresh gourds. Take the bag to a river in the woods.
- "Maferefún egun!" They are the client's true foundation, and they want to lift him up. The diviner should advise the client to host a series of six masses, one a week for six weeks. He must follow the prescriptions of the espiritistas exactly, for they will help both the client and his egun evolve.

## The Prohibitions of Obara Meji

- Fires, both indoors and outdoors, are a danger. One must be cautious of open flames. Leave none unattended. It would be wise to have no more than two candles lit at any time.

- Avoid overspending; conserve one's financial resources.
- One must avoid all vices. Reduce the consumption of alcohol and cigars, cigarettes, and other tobacco products. Do not curse. Do not blaspheme. Consumption of both legal and illegal drugs and over-the-counter remedies is prohibited.
- Retain respectful marital relations. Adultery is forbidden.
- Do not try to profit from illicit religious activities.

## The Eboses of Obara Meji

When a casting of 6-6 falls on the mat, several eboses are considered mandatory for the client. The diviner should advise him to complete the following sacrifices immediately:

- Shangó, Oshún, and Elegguá must be given an adimú of fresh squash. Once this ebó is done, the client may not pick, eat, pierce, cut, or give away this fruit. It holds the key to his future prosperity. Note that in iré, the ebó needs to be done only once. In osogbo, however, six squashes or fresh gourds must always be kept with Shangó. If Obara Meji has fallen through the diloggún of Elegguá or the client's crowning orisha, these squashes must always be kept in front of their shrines. If the client opens in Obara Meji feet to head (in the itá of ocha, Obara opened with Elegguá and again in the guardian orisha), all his orishas of santo must have squash at their shrines as adimú.
- If the client is an aleyo and his crowning orisha is known, he must have a rogación at the feet of this orisha. After the rogación, he must give the spirit an adimú. If the crowning orisha is not known, this rogación is done before the godparent's crowning orisha.
- The diviner must take the client's Elegguá deep into the woods; there, he must feed him a rooster, sitting Elegguá directly on the earth so some of the blood falls on it. He must then prepare a niche osain for this orisha, including some of the earth from the location of Elegguá's ebó in the forest. After receiving this charm, the client must always carry it with him.
- After all these things have been done, the client must go to an Ifá priest to receive the idé and eleke of Orúnmila.

Having made these prescriptions, the diviner may now try to close the oracle. If the odu will not close, the diviner should turn to the eboses of the parent odu, Obara (see page 297).

If after working through the eboses of the parent odu the diviner still is not able to close the oracle, the client, if he is an initiate, may need to receive Aganyú or Osain. The diviner should ask, "Koshé [orisha's name]?" Osain's initiation is very deep and involved, and this question should be asked only as a last resort to close the pattern.

If the odu still will not close, the client could have additional issues with Shangó, Oshún, Elegguá, Obatalá, or Ogún. To see what is required, the diviner should ask, "Ebó elese [orisha's name]?" If the answer is yes, he marks the offering with the shells.

Those who owe drums to the orishas or egun must now pay their debts.

# The Seventh Composite Odu of Obara, Obara Odí (6-7)

## The Proverbs of Obara Odí

- While a dog has four legs, it still walks only one path.
- You cannot be everywhere at the same time.
- One has to bribe only a few to overthrow them all.
- If secrets are told to others, they are no longer secrets.
- Do not promise something that you cannot deliver.

## The Message of Obara Odí

When the first casting of Obara, six mouths, is followed by one of Odí, seven mouths, the odu Obara

Odí has come to the house. This sign is also known as Obara'di. It is the odu giving birth to the urn, the earthenware vessel that was first used to hold water; when it opens, the orisha speaking, or perhaps one of the spirits living with the client, is asking for a new sopera. It is a letter of treason, the place where one enemy has to bribe only a few to overthrow the rest. Even in iré, it is dangerous for those in positions of authority. The sign alludes to the hook; something of ocha is hanging by a hook, and the diviner must help the client figure out what it is. Among the lore of Obara Odí it is said that a pact was made between Yemayá and Shangó to always live together. Yemayá was in need, unable to take care of herself, and Shangó took her in. He clothed and fed her for a time.

The diviner begins by saying, "Maferefún Shangó! Maferefún Yemayá! Maferefún Elegguá!" These three orishas protect the client now, and he must turn to them to resolve all his issues. These spirits offer three pieces of advice to keep the client from all harm: Do not incur debt; do not offer things that cannot easily or painlessly be given; do not be greedy. If the client heeds these three mandates, then no matter what happens he will come out ahead.

The diviner should also explore the following issues in conjunction with Obara Odí:

- One day this client will not only have made ocha but also have had a child. Through this child will much good be wrought; as soon as possible after its birth and the parent's crowning, the child must be crowned so that his destiny is not missed.
- In this sign, women can cause men much loss. If the client is male and is living with a woman, she will force him to move unless he is careful.
- When this sign fall in osogbo, it signals that great evils can befall the client. The diviner should tell the client that all of his troubles are to be left at the feet of Elegguá and Yemayá with a small adimú. They will fight the battles that need to be fought. In osogbo, Yemayá says that the client's head is in need of a rogación; it needs strength. The rogación should be done at her shrine with Elegguá as a witness. Beginning the morning after the rogación, this person's head should be bathed with water from both the river and the sea.
- Much evil will come through the hands of a brother by blood or by spirit. This, too, should be left to Yemayá. She will punish those who bring the client evil.
- Sickness could be brewing slowly in the client. If the odu opens in an osogbo of ano or ikú, sickness could already be upon him. Arteriosclerosis is the main danger of Obara Odí. The diviner must send the client to a doctor for a physical now so his health's baseline is established. When sickness comes, he must seek medical attention again and also come back to the diviner to make ebó. To remove an illness foretold in this sign, the ebó is as follows: The diviner cleanses the client with three eggs to Elegguá and then with a rooster. He sacrifices the rooster to Elegguá and gives the client a rogación immediately afterward. The next morning, the client takes all these elements to a crossroads.

## The Prohibitions of Obara Odí

- Have proper respect for one's lover or spouse; shun adultery.
- Do not tell secrets and do not make promises. Through these will much osogbo enter one's life.
- Gossip will bring fatal consequences. Do not gossip. Do not listen to gossip.
- Do not answer personal questions. Refuse them, but tactfully.

## The Eboses of Obara Odí

When a casting of Obara Odí has fallen on the mat, the client should be told to give thanks to Orúnmila, Elegguá, and Osain; they support him in all his endeavors. The odu points out that the client has issues with Ifá, and a competent babalawo should be sought out to consult with the client. At the very least, this person will have to receive the idé and eleke of Orúnmila. He should also consider receiving an Eshu from Ifá; this will bring him much luck, opening doors in his life that were once closed.

If the client is an aborisha, as ebó to Osain he must go to the woods with the following sacrificial ingredients: popcorn popped in epó and sprinkled with jutía and smoked fish, a bottle of rum, a cigar, and two pennies. At the edge of the woods, the client offers these to Osain; he will bless the client.

A specific niche osain should be made for this client. The client offers a green coconut to Elegguá and leaves it with him until it is dry. When it is dry, he fries the meat in coconut oil. He then sprinkles the floor heavily with cascarilla and places Shangó on this. An oriaté feeds Shangó a turtle, making sure that some of the turtle's blood falls into the cascarilla. Before cleaning up the remnants of the sacrifice, the client gathers up the blood-soaked cascarilla and toasts it in the oven. When it is dry, he wrap it all in cotton and packs it in the turtle's shell. He keeps the shell with Shangó, feeding it whenever he is fed.

The initiate who opens in Obara Odí must put Shangó and Yemayá together at one shrine and give them adimú together. Whenever Shangó is fed, Yemayá must be fed as well. Together, they will keep the client from hunger, poverty, and danger.

Having made these prescriptions, the diviner may now attempt to close the oracle. If it will not close, he should explore the following options:

- Yemayá and Shangó might require more ebo. To determine if this is the case, the diviner asks, "Ebó elese Yemayá y Shangó?" If the answer is yes, he uses the diloggún to mark the appropriate offering.
- The niche osain made for Shangó might also need to be made for Elegguá; the diviner should consider this.
- Elegguá might be standing up for ebó. To see what he might require, the diviner must ask, "Ebó elese Elegguá?" If the answer is yes, he marks the required offering with the shells.

If none of these will satisfy the composite Obara Odí, the diviner must now turn to the eboses of the parent odu, Obara (see page 297). Something there is needed to close this session and bring evolution to the client.

## The Eighth Composite Odu of Obara, Obara Ejiogbe (6-8)

### The Proverbs of Obara Ejiogbe

- A trifle grows where nothing else will sprout.
- The ears cannot top the head; therefore, respect the elders.
- Only the burro has ears that extend beyond the head, and he works only to carry.
- Even the walls have ears.
- The ears do not pass the head.

### The Message of Obara Ejiogbe

When a casting of six mouths, Obara, is followed by one of eight mouths, Eji Ogbe, the odu Obara Ejiogbe has come to the mat. This odu goes by many names: Obara Ogbe, Obara l'Ogbe, Obara Elleunle, and Obara Unle. It is a powerful odu that alludes to initiation. One day, this client will make ocha. Here is born the custom of apprehending the iyawó with a white sheet before the asiento begins. It is also a harsh odu; this composite warns against disrespect of the body, the family, and the elders, for this is how an osogbo can creep into the client's life. Many have named this pattern "the land of disobedience," because it forebodes that the client's final fall will come through disobedience. Both the diviner and the client must be very vigilant over the aged, for Obara Ejiogbe announces that someone known to either of them will soon die. They should give the elders as much attention as possible so that they have no regrets when this happens.

The diviner opens by saying, "Maferefún Obatalá! Maferefún Shangó!" Shangó adores his father in ocha, Obatalá, and the two stand firm in this sign to deliver specific warnings. They demand that not only the client's elders but also anyone who is elderly should be treated well. Obatalá is their patron, and he watches over them carefully. Shangó stands at his side, punishing those who abuse the aged. The client must neither taunt the elderly nor make fun of them, for if he does, the blessings of Obara Ejiogbe will abandon him. Obatalá warns that he is coming for an unannounced visit. He will come in the form of an elderly, weak person in need. The diviner must tell the client to make sure that this person's needs are met, because if they are not, he will be abandoning Obatalá himself. And if this elder comes to any harm, Shangó will punish the client for his lack of care, respect, or concern.

The diviner also says, "Maferefún Orúnmila! Maferefún Elegguá!" These orishas are firm in Obara Ejiogbe as well. Having come to the mat in this pattern, the client could have issues that can be resolved only with Ifá. The diviner must relay this information as if it were ebó, sending his client to a competent babalawo as soon as possible. At the very least, the idé and eleke of Orúnmila will be needed; at most, the client could have to take mano or kofá. When he goes to Ifá, he must be financially prepared for these things. They will facilitate his evolution in the religion. Elegguá comes here to say that the client thinks poorly of Ifá and its priests; no matter his thoughts, he must not put them into words. If he does so, Elegguá will close all the doors in his life, and he will be trapped in his present situation. If this person does not have an Elegguá of Ifá, he should receive one; if he does have an Elegguá from Ifá, he must take it to his godfather in Ifá. That Elegguá has issues, and he might need a sacrifice before he can resolve the client's conflicts.

In addition, the diviner should explore the following points with the client for whom Obara Ejiogbe has fallen:

- When this sign falls for an aborisha, it says that this person should have made ocha already. However, if the odu has come in an osogbo, the client is not ready for initiation. Together, the diviner and client must discuss this issue, determining why the client is not ready to evolve to the next step and become a iyawó. Once all the obstacles have been identified, and once plans and goals have been determined, the diviner sees if there is a remedy to help this person evolve, asking the diloggún, "Larishe si?" Remember, however, that only total commitment to the religion and faith in the orishas can bring this person into alignment with his destiny.
- Much of this pattern's osogbo is brought through disrespect. To whom has the client been disrespectful? The diviner must determine the answer to this question so that he can recommend that the client make amends.
- In this odu, it is said that even the walls have ears. Everything the client says is heard by others; all that he does is known. The diviner should advise the client to use caution and secrecy in all dealings.
- Someone is coming to tell the client to go someplace. He must not go. If the client is a man, he must not go because he will have an affair with someone he will meet; this will bring scandal. If the client is a woman, she must not go because she could be attacked in this strange place.
- This odu speaks of making ebó; the client will have to rely on the orishas for all his needs, making frequent eboses to them.
- This client has two close friends with whom he "runs the streets." These two friends are not good; their lack of morals will get him into trouble. For now, he must not be around them.

## The Prohibitions of Obara Ejiogbe

- Do not be outdoors at either noon or midnight. These are times of danger. Between midnight and sunrise, be safely behind locked doors, preferably one's own.
- If this reading is an itá for a iyawó of Shangó and the diloggún consulted belongs to Oshún, the iyawó can never have one of Oshún's children for a godchild. He will fall in life if he crowns her child; Oshún guarantees this.
- If this reading is an itá for a iyawó of Oshún and the diloggún consulted belongs to Shangó, the iyawó can never have one of Shangó's children for a godchild. He will fall in life if he crowns his child; Shangó guarantees this.

## The Eboses of Obara Ejiogbe

When Obara Ejiogbe has opened on the mat, and especially if it comes in osogbo, one of the most important considerations for ebó is the client's own head. It may be hot, tired, weak, or overwhelmed; the client will need a rogación to help him overcome what lies ahead. There are two options for where to give this rogación: If the client is an initiate, the rogación is given at the feet of his guardian orisha. If the client is an aborisha or an aleyo, the rogación should be given at the feet of either Obatalá or the godparent's crown. After this rogación, the client should present this orisha an adimú. The diviner should ask, "Ebó elese [orisha's name]?" to see if anything specific can be marked. If not, the adimú must come from the client's heart.

If the sign opens in an osogbo of ano or ikú, this person's orí must be fed two white pigeons. In this case, both the feeding of the orí and the rogación are to be done at Obatalá's feet. Afterward, adimú should be given to Obatalá.

Having made these prescriptions, the diviner may now attempt to close the oracle. If it will not close, the client could have additional issues with Obatalá, Shangó, Elegguá, or Orisha Oko. The diviner should consider asking, "Ebó elese [orisha's name]?" If the answer is yes, he uses the diloggún to mark the required offering.

If this consideration will not close the odu and the client is an aleyo or aborisha, the diviner should now turn to the eboses of the parent odu, Obara (see page 297). If the client is an initiate, Oké could be standing up. The diviner should ask, "Ebó elese Oké?" If the answer is yes, he uses the diloggún to mark what is required. If the sign still will not close, the diviner must now turn to the eboses of the parent odu, Obara.

# The Ninth Composite Odu of Obara, Obara Osá (6-9)

## The Proverbs of Obara Osá

- You are crazy, but you think you only pretend to be crazy.
- You are crazy; you act as if you were crazy. Do you truly want to be crazy?
- When you run, run with prudence.

## The Message of Obara Osá

When the first cast of Obara, six mouths, is followed by a cast of Osá, nine mouths, the odu Obara Osá has come to the house. The energies of this powerful letter can be overwhelming, and even in iré it can mark a variety of tragedies upon the client. His head can become hot; he needs clarity and coolness now. Fortunately, a variety of spirits stand up in this odu to offer their support and protection, and the diviner pays homage to them all, saying, "Maferefún egun! Maferefún Shangó! Maferefún Aganyú! Maferefún Yemayá! Maferefún Oyá! Maferefún Ochosi!"

Egun form the client's foundation in life. The diviner should prescribe much spiritual work for them. The client must have his bóveda and opá ikú, and with these he should placate, propitiate, and elevate his ancestors on a daily basis. If masses have not yet been given for this client's egun, they must be given now. His spiritual court must be identified; they must be given a chance to stand up and speak. Because so many issues are pending with egun in this odu, the prescriptions of the espiritistas could be involved and intense. Still, they must be fulfilled.

Shangó and Aganyú, father and son, are firm in this sign; it will not close out unless ebó has been prescribed to at least one, and perhaps both. They come here to warn the client about a scandal. To avoid suspicion and false testimony, he must be ethical in all his actions. He must avoid arguments, fights, and wars; if these things erupt, the client must run so he does not get involved. Involvement in these things will ensure his failure. Even though he could be innocent and without blame (which could be the case only if the sign opens in iré), he will end up being discredited by all involved. His mind is not quick enough nor is his tongue firm enough to argue in his own defense. Shangó says that this person's relationships will always be a source of despair for him. He must learn to deal with others romantically and properly. He must not even think about beginning a new relationship before the old one is ended; if he neglects this advice, both the old and the new will end in failure. Shangó says he has seen this happen in the client's life again and again. When will the client learn his lesson?

Although it might seem strange to honor both Yemayá and Oyá in the same breath, here both orishas are firm behind the client. Yemayá is life and the passage to life; Oyá is death and the passage to death. Right now, this person stands firm between both, and he must be cautious lest he stray too far to either side. If he gives an ebó to Yemayá, he must give something equal to Oyá, and vice versa. Each loves this client dearly. Yemayá announces many new things coming into the client's life: new friends, new lovers, new beginnings, and new family. A child could be born soon. Oyá announces that many things could be leaving the client's life right now: old friends, old lovers, even family. He could face abandonment, and the death of a relative could be imminent. If the life of someone dear to the client hangs in the balance, the client should make ebó to Oyá first so she closes the gates to the cemetery, and in a few days petition Yemayá that she heal the afflicted. In time, the afflicted one could have at least a partial recovery.

Even in the harshest osogbo, Ochosi is here defending the client and leading him down a path to evolution. The client, however, must sacrifice all areas of his life in which he is doing something wrong. He must not entertain con artists, thieves, or vagrants; he must not break the law; he must neither curse nor blaspheme. Because while Ochosi protects this person, he will also punish him for all wrongdoings he commits. This odu tells us that the client might need to "run" for his own safety. If he runs because of something he did wrong, a crime or immoral act, he will not get away. If he is running because of a crime or offense committed by another, Ochosi will take him to a safe place where he can recover. In time, he will be able to face his enemy and persevere. Even if nothing bad is happening in his life now, the client should give at least an adimú to Ochosi. When the evil threatens, he will have the orisha at his side.

In Obara Osá are many other issues for the diviner to explore with the client:

- The client's actions for the next seven days will influence the rest of his life. If he now exists amid chaos and turmoil, he should stay home if possible, resting, and speak to no one unless it is absolutely essential. He must pray for peace and evolution. If possible, the diviner should give the client's head a rogación before Obatalá's shrine. In Obara Osá, clarity is essential.
- While this odu speaks of thievery and robbery, the greatest danger lies in the client's own home. If he lives with others, they may be the greatest thieves in his life. Unfortunately, the client knows this, and his own weakness allows it to continue.
- Due to carelessness, a child could become sick or injured. The client will suffer if this happens; he must be careful.
- The client's younger brother is in danger. He must make ebó to avoid this danger. If he will not make ebó to save himself, make it for his brother. He will, however, still suffer to some degree.
- This odu alludes to masks. The client himself must wear one to hide the truth inside. He must try to ascertain who wears masks, and try to see beyond them. This odu also alludes to carnivals; the diviner should advise the client to go to one after making ebó to Oyá in order to find the luck that he lost. He should leave her an ebó outside the carnival's entrance. Also, to make the masks that others wear break, the client should have a set of Mardi Gras–type masks washed to Oyá and keep them by the front door. She will rip the masks off the faces of all who visit.
- If the client heeds the advice and prohibitions of Obara Osá, a financial blessing will come. He must be wary, for others will try to destroy this.

## The Prohibitions of Obara Osá

- For seven days and nights following this odu's opening, do not go out into the street. If one must travel, go in the company of at least one other person. There could be a scandal in a public place, so limit excursions for the next month.

- Do not sleep naked. Wear clothes, and have shoes next to the bed in case of an emergency.
- At night, make sure that all the curtains are drawn, and lock all the windows and doors. Do not have one's bed next to a window.
- Do not linger on street corners.
- Do not kill mice.

### The Eboses of Obara Osá

Beyond the spiritual prescriptions given as advice in this odu, there are more options for ebó that must be considered by the diviner. First, in this pattern of Obara the elekes are a necessity; such is the power of this baptism that it will help soothe most of Obara Osá's osogbo. In conjunction with the beads of Obatalá, Yemayá, Oshún, and Shangó, the elekes of Oyá and Ochosi must be given as well. If the client already has his elekes but not the warriors, the diviner must mark the warriors as ebó. They will fight to sustain him through the trials ahead.

Having made these prescriptions, the diviner may now attempt to close the oracle. If it will not close, ebó could be needed by one or more of the following spirits: egun, Shangó, Aganyú, Yemayá, Oyá, and Ochosi. Note that if egun stand up for a sacrifice (blood) as ebó, in Obara Osá the proper ebó to give is a sheep.

If none of these will close the odu and the client is an aleyo or aborisha, the diviner must now turn to the eboses of the parent odu, Obara (see page 297). Something there is needed for the client's evolution.

If the client is an initiate and the odu will not close, he could have further issues with Yemayá, Oyá, Aganyú, or Ochosi. A child of Oyá must receive Yemayá and a child of Yemayá must receive Oyá. Initiates might also need to receive Aganyú or Ochosi. To find out if this is needed, the diviner must ask, "Koshé [orisha's name]?"

If the odu still will not close, ebó is marked to Elegguá: a goat. For an initiate, itá must be given. Now, the diviner turns to the eboses of the parent odu, Obara. Something there is needed for the client's evolution.

## The Tenth Composite Odu of Obara, Obara Ofún (6-10)

### The Proverbs of Obara Ofún

- Two calves do not drink at the same fountain.
- Flies get caught in flypaper.
- Take only those things that you have brought.
- You are not well in the head.
- A man must not walk the fence.
- One should not say all one wants to do, nor should one do all one has said.

### The Message of Obara Ofún

When a casting of six mouths, Obara, is followed by ten mouths, Ofún, the odu Obara Ofún, also known as Obara'fún, is open on the mat. In this pattern the diviner says, "Maferefún Elegguá! Maferefún Eshu! Maferefún Shangó! Maferefún Yembo! Maferefún Olófin!" This is a harsh odu for the client and a difficult sign for the diviner. Danger is here, but unless the italero works hard with the orishas, something important will be missed; both he and the client will suffer. For Obara Ofún tells of the time when Olófin himself knew something was wrong in his life, yet so close to him was this tragedy that he could not see what was coming. He descended to the earth to seek out the orisha priests and the best diviners among them; all said he was fine and no ebó was needed. Olófin was relieved, but something still nagged him. The next day, his only son died. The diviner must be wary if Obara Ofún comes in a clean iré, for a tragedy will befall this client, and even if this odu takes no ebó, even if no orisha stands up to demand a sacrifice, something must still be given. From his tragedy do we all learn.

Obara Ofún also speaks of a near tragedy between the mighty king Shangó and his saintly mother, Yembo. Time and distance had parted mother and son; so busy was Shangó with his kingdom and his wars that he never had time to check up on Yembo. After a long, hard time away at war, Shangó returned home; his favorite white horse abandoned him and disappeared. The mighty one issued a decree: a reward to the man who found his horse and death to the one who stole it. Little did Shangó know that his horse had gone on a mission of mercy; Yembo, his mother, was sick, weak, and alone. She was old and not well; her memory was fading and she spent all her time wandering the forest. The world wept, but Shangó was too bitter over his losses to know what was happening. Alone, the horse found his mother, and Yembo, exhausted, climbed on its back. In a few days the soldiers found an elderly woman sitting astride Shangó's beautiful horse, and both were brought to the king's palace. At first he was angry, ready to command the woman's death, but then his heart broke when he saw it was his mother. In shame, and with love, he embraced her; Yembo was healed, and the two were never parted again.

Olófin, Yembo, and Shangó warn us of what lies ahead for this client. Even if the odu opens in iré, dangerous times are coming, and this person must be prepared. If the client is a parent, he could lose a child. The diviner should tell him this and, even if odu offers no larishe, ask for this warning: "Larishe si?" The resulting ebó must be fulfilled immediately, and the client must pray to God that he spare the life of his child. If the client's mother is living, this pattern says she is not doing as well as the client thinks. She suffers due to negligence on the part of her child. Mother and child must reunite and never part again. The initiate should give a white ceramic horse to Shangó, and as soon as possible, he must receive Yembo. He should keep these orishas side by side, with the white horse then placed at Yembo's shrine. Together these two orishas will see that the client and all those in his family always evolve.

Obara Ofún says to us that this client stands at a crossroads in his life. Elegguá will help him make the proper choice at this time. He is ready to act impulsively, on a whim, yet this odu says that acting on impulse will create failure. Standing still ensures his downfall as well. When the client is ready to make a change in his life, he must ask Elegguá about what he is to do and give ebó to to Elegguá; he must give the same ebó to Eshu at a crossroads. Only in this way will he make the proper decisions.

The odu tells the diviner that this person has made many offers to other people, yet none of these has been fulfilled. Many should not be fulfilled, for here we often say, "Do not do that which one has proclaimed." The key to deciphering proper action for this person is to examine the prohibitions of both Obara and Ofún. Once the client knows exactly what the orishas prohibit at this time, he will be able to make good, informed decisions.

There are also health concerns in this sign. The client should have a complete physical, especially if the letter comes in ano or ikú. Any pains in the skeletal or muscular system should send him for medical attention. He must protect his head at all times. He must not drink, use intoxicants, or let others touch or strike his head. If this person has not already been scarred by surgery, one day he will go under the knife. To avoid this, he must make ebó to Ogún.

Other pressing issues that must be explored by the diviner include the following:

- Marriage is a possibility, and pregnancy within the year is ensured unless proper precautions are taken.
- The client must be warned not to argue with his elders. He should spend more time with them, because within a year one could die.
- The orishas are upset: Someone living with the client does not belong there. He should clean house now.
- If a child in this person's house becomes sick, even if the sickness is only a minor cold, the client should take him to see a physician immediately. Something small could become something big.

## The Prohibitions of Obara Ofún

- Remove any open bottles or torn items from the house. Do not wear clothing made of lace or eyelets. One's luck escapes through open holes.
- The consumption of ñame is forbidden. It is to be used as ebó only. Do not buy it, pierce it, harvest it, cut it, cook it, or give it away unless it is for something of ocha.
- In a severe osogbo, consider the prohibitions of both Obara and Ofún as parent odu. Without these as guidelines, one will suffer tragedy.

## The Eboses of Obara Ofún

This odu mandates the reception of the warriors. Once they have been brought home by the aborisha, he should give a ñame to Elegguá, to Ogún, and to Ochosi. Eventually, vines will grow from these. They must not be allowed to grow longer than the client is tall. These remain with the orishas until they go bad; then the client should cleanse himself with them and give them to the garbage.

In this odu the client must also feed Eshu in the street. For the next three days, the client must save a portion of all his meals, putting them in a paper bag. In the morning following each of these days, just before sunrise, he must give the paper bag to Eshu at a crossroads. On the final day of this ebó, he should cleanse himself with three pennies before leaving the crossroads. Eshu will take something bad away.

Also, in this pattern the client must give all the warriors, together, a large jícara of saraeko (see the recipe on page 52). This should be left with them overnight. The following morning the client throws it into the street.

The last mandatory ebó in this odu is a rogación before Obatalá's shrine. Because of Ofún's influence, use ten things sacred to Obatalá.

Having made these prescriptions, the diviner may now attempt to close the oracle. If it will not close, the client could have additional issues pending with Elegguá, Shangó, or Yembo. To see what they might required, the diviner must ask, "Ebó elese [orisha's name]?" If the answer is yes, he uses the diloggún to mark the required offering.

If this is not enough to close the odu and the client is an aleyo or aborisha, the diviner must turn to the eboses of the parent odu, Obara (see page 297). Something there is necessary for the client's evolution. If the client is an initiate, the reception of Yembo might be necessary. The diviner should ask, "Koshé Yembo?" If this will not close the odu, he now turns to the eboses of the parent odu, Obara.

# The Eleventh Composite Odu of Obara, Obara Owani (6-11)

## The Proverbs of Obara Owani

- Avoid becoming a slave to envy.
- To learn, you must not say that you know when you do not know.
- The pawn will always know more than you.
- You do not live by that which you know.

## The Message of Obara Owani

When an initial cast of six mouths, Obara, precedes a second cast of eleven mouths, Owani, the sign Obara Owani is open at the mat. In this pattern the diviner says, "Maferefún Obatalá!" Obatalá knows that many evil eyes and tongues are upon this client, but if he does as he is told, these will be fooled and he will be safe. The day after this reading is given, the client should dress totally in red. He must go out in public, running his usual errands, drawing as much attention to himself as possible. Immediately, he must return home and dress himself totally in white, then go out and follow the same path he took in red, but now in silence. All of his enemies will be looking for the one in red, and from this moment on he will escape their notice. Going back to the diviner's house, he is given a rogación before Obatalá's shrine. With his head refreshed and strengthened, and with his enemies looking elsewhere, he will persevere over all trials and tribulations.

The diviner also says, "Maferefún Elegguá! Maferefún Ogún! Maferefún Ochosi!" In Obara Owani these three orishas are strong, fighting against all those who would bring tribulation to the client's life. After following the advice of Obatalá, the client must return to the diviner's home the second day after the reading with the charm known as *ojo y lengua* (a plaque found in botánicas and adorned with an eye and a pierced tongue). The charm is washed in omiero, and the client presents it, along with an adimú of cool fruits, to the warriors. If the osogbo of this odu is severe, afterward a rooster should be fed to the three orishas, allowing the blood to drizzle over the ojo y lengua as well.

Afterward, the client should hang the charm by his front door; his enemies will be struck dumb and blind as to his whereabouts or doings in the world. Thus, this client can evolve safely.

On the third day after this reading, the client must return to the diviner's house to complete any eboses marked by the odu or the orishas.

Even when this letter has opened in iré, the diviner should warn the client to be cautious in all his dealings; it is a heated, volatile pattern that moves quickly and brings random changes to one's life. Even amid blessings, there is always danger. The diviner should begin this reading by telling the one who sits at the mat that he should thank all his egun, all his spirits, and all the orishas for the good existing in his life. If he gives proper thanks for his blessings, more will follow. All around exists treason and despair, but most of this cannot touch him if he remains true to his heart and steadfast in his path. Many wish the client ill; they try to create havoc in his life. If he isolates himself from friends and family for a time, none of this will have the chance to affect him.

### The Prohibitions of Obara Owani

- Do not argue, fight, or gossip. Stay away from those whom one knows harbor evil and jealousy in their hearts; thus will much of this odu's osogbo be missed.
- Secrets, once told, are no longer secrets. Tell no secrets to anyone.
- The next three days must be reserved for spiritual renewal. Do not leave home except to make ebó.

### The Eboses of Obara Owani

This odu mandates that the client receive his warriors; if he already has them, he must pray daily to Elegguá, giving him frequent adimú. To see if he will take any specific adimú, the diviner should ask, "Ebó elese Elegguá?" If the answer is yes, he uses the diloggún to mark the required offering. The ebó marked here must be done within three days.

Also, Eshu must be given a part of the client's food daily for three days. The client should wrap a third of all his meals in a brown paper bag and take it to him at the crossroads the next morning.

Having made these prescriptions, the diviner may now attempt to close the oracle. If it will not close, the client could have issues with Elegguá, Shangó, or Obatalá. To determine if any of them require ebó, the diviner should aks, "Ebó elese [orisha's name]?" If the answer is yes, he uses the diloggún to mark the required offering.

If this is not enough to close the odu, the diviner should turn to the eboses of the parent odu, Obara (see page 297). Something there is needed to create evolution.

## The Twelfth Composite Odu of Obara, Obara Ejila (6-12)

### The Proverbs of Obara Ejila

- Your stubbornness will take you from failure to failure.
- There is much arguing in your life, and because of this you go from failure to failure.
- Two kings cannot govern the same town.
- Sweetness is what we are searching for.
- One's failures are caused by one's lies.
- The turtle, for lack of a wife, sleeps with his own daughter and blames the goat.

### The Message of Obara Ejila

When the first casting of six mouths, Obara, is followed by one of twelve mouths, Ejila Shebora, the odu Obara Ejila has opened on the mat. This odu is also known as Obara Oturupon. Before assessing this sign for the client, the diviner must assess it for himself. Obara Ejila forbids the prescription of anything beyond advice and ebó to this client. No medicines, herbs, or home remedies may be offered, nor may an ebó dealing with a physical complaint be prescribed. If the client inquires about a physical complaint, the diviner must refuse to speak about it and, instead, send the client directly to a physician. A major issue is about to arise in regard to this person's health, and even though most have the foresight to combine herbal cures with medical treatments, this client will not. Even if he does, something will still go wrong and he will blame the diviner. Forewarned is forearmed.

Obara Ejila marks the client as having programmed himself for failure. Stubbornness, rebelliousness, lying, slander, and evil gossip have all been driven into this person, and to change his life he must change these things. Witchcraft figures prominently in this odu and will be used both by and against the client. There is unfaithfulness between the client and his spouse, and both will suffer for this. When this letter opens on the mat, the diviner must warn the client that the way he is living his life must end lest he be brought down before the orishas. We say that two kings cannot govern the same town; this person is meant for ocha and has the potential to one day become a prominent priest, but he will never be able to live in the same town as the godparent. The farther apart they live, the better. Without some distance between them, there will always be jealousy and resentment between them.

## The Prohibitions of Obara Ejila

- Do not show disrespect to either your parents or your godparents.
- Do not curse or blaspheme, no matter the words or the religion.
- Do not become involved in romantic triangles.
- Never strike a child, especially on the head.

## The Eboses of Obara Ejila

When Obara Ejila opens on the mat, several initial considerations for ebó must be fulfilled by the client. To begin, this sign calls for frequent spiritual cleansings and baths. Daily, the client should cleanse himself to egun using cloths and perfumes over his bóveda; also, he should take eight white baths made of things sacred to Obatalá. All baths made for the client should include the leaves of flor de agua; this plant is important for cleansing any osogbo brought by Obara Ejila.

If the client does not have his elekes, he must be marked for their reception now. Such is the power of this ceremony that any bad fortune found in this sign can be overcome.

Finally, Babaluaiye stands firm in this pattern, and the client needs a rogación before his shrine. At the conclusion of this rogación, he should receive the orisha's eleke.

Having made these prescriptions, the diviner may now attempt to close the oracle. If it will not close, he should explore the following possibilities:

- Obatalá could be standing up for additional ebó in this letter. To find out what he might require, the diviner should ask, "Ebó elese Obatalá?" If the answer is yes, he uses the diloggún to mark the required offering.
- Babaluaiye could be standing up here to prescribe more than just a rogación and his eleke for the client. First the diviner should ask, "Ebó elese Babaluaiye?" If the answer is yes, he uses the diloggún to mark the required offering. Any ebó marked by this orisha must be given after the rogación is given and the eleke vested. If this is not enough to satisfy Obara Ejila, consider asking, "Koshé Babaluaiye?" If this is marked as the solution to the client's osogbo, he must be received as soon as possible.

If these considerations are not enough to close the oracle, the diviner should turn to the eboses of the parent odu, Obara (see page 297). Something there is needed for this client's evolution.

# The Thirteenth Composite Odu of Obara, Obara Metanla (6-13)

## The Proverbs of Obara Metanla

- He who does not listen to advice does not attain old age.
- Those who do not heed the advice of the elders will not attain old age.
- [There will be] separation, but all will end up under one roof.

## The Message of Obara Metanla

When the initial casting of six mouths, Obara, is followed by a casting of thirteen mouths, Metanla, the odu Obara Metanla, also known as Obara Irete, is open on the mat. Falling in this pattern, the diloggún directs the italero to pay homage to the orishas Olokun, Orúnmila, Ogún, Yemayá, Oshún, and Babaluaiye, saying to each, "Maferefún!" Each may stand up in this odu to speak or claim ebó. Depending on the odu's orientation (iré or osogbo) and the origin of its orientation, the advice of each orisha will alter drastically. The letter itself is the pattern in which the jícara was opened and used for the first time; the diviner must remember this when marking ebó, for any offering made through this sign will require the use of a jícara. This odu is hot and volatile, foreshadowing sickness, arguments, death, and infidelity; it will take all the diviner's aché to sort out the implications of this reading.

When a man comes to the mat in Obara Metanla, the diviner can make many assumptions about his life. He might be in a "monogamous" relationship; however, his current lover is not the only person on his mind. He has a wandering eye; he likes to look around and flirt, and if he has not cheated on his mate already, he will. The diviner should warn him against this, for the odu says that the person with whom he cheats will already have a lover on the side. When this person discovers the infidelity, he will want to kill the client.

Both Oshún and Babaluaiye are close to the client. If the client has not had a bajado, one of these might be his guardian angel. Even if neither claims his head, both are close to him.

In all castings of Obara Metanla, the diviner should explore with the client the following issues:

- The sign alludes to friends and lovers who do not get along, and if ebó is not made, they will never get along. The reason for this is that each is watched over by the same orisha; spiritually, they are so alike that they cannot help but get on each other's nerves. Many of the problems in this person's relationship stem from one simple fact: Both he and his lover have the same guardian orisha.
- When ano, ikú, or arayé come as the osogbo of this odu, serious health concerns are raised for the client. Pains could come suddenly in any part of the body; they could herald serious injury or disease. When unusual symptoms occur, the client must see a physician. This letter also warns against going under the knife. While the doctor's intention is to heal, the energies surrounding the client at this time are not conducive to healing. The diviner should tell the client that the food he eats is slowly making him sick. He must be careful what he consumes. He must watch his diet and eat healthy food. If his health fails, there is ebó to save him: making ocha. Nothing short of this will help him make a full recovery.
- A woman who opens in this sign is unhappy with her lover. She has not cheated on him yet, but she will. The diviner must advise her against starting a new relationship before the old one is ended; if she does not heed this advice, she will bring osogbo to her life.

## The Prohibitions of Obara Metanla

- Adultery is forbidden in this odu, because it will cause any iré brought by the sign to be lost. No ebó can correct this.
- This odu foretells of separation between friends and lovers, yet all will end up under one roof. Be careful: Do not live with anyone who is not related by blood unless it is a stable relationship.

## The Eboses of Obara Metanla

When Obara Metanla has opened on the mat, there are many considerations for ebó depending on the client's personal circumstances. The diviner should consider the following:

- If the client is trying to get along with a friend or lover but cannot, there is a reason for the difficulty, and there is ebó. The two involved have the same guardian orisha, and this causes conflict in their lives. To correct this negativity, giving the relationship a chance to flourish, both involved must come back to the diviner's house and have a rogación at the feet of their guardian orisha. Once the rogación is complete, both must vow at the feet of their orisha never to fight or argue again. This will bring peace back to their lives.

- If Oshún stands up strongly during the reading of this odu, the client has issues to resolve with her. The diviner must tell him (especially if the sign opens in a dangerous osogbo) that there is a war between him and her; he once made a promise to Oshún, and that promise was never kept. If the client can remember this promise, it is now ebó. If the client cannot remember having incurred any debts with this orisha, the diviner sees if she will accept ebó instead, asking, "Ebó elese Oshún?" If the answer is yes, he uses the diloggún to mark the required offering. If the answer is no, the diviner should prescribe aladimú to the client. He must give Oshún something "from his heart." The greater the gift he gives, the greater the forgiveness this orisha will give.
- If the client is ill, he could have issues with Babaluaiye. To see if a simple ebó will settle these issues, the diviner should ask, "Ebó elese Babaluaiye?" If the answer is yes, he uses the diloggún to mark the required offering. If the answer is no, or if the ebó is not enough to close the oracle, the diviner should ask, "Koshé eleke de Babaluaiye?" If the reception of his eleke and a simple ebó are not enough to soothe this sign, the client must receive this orisha. Until this can be done, however, he must still offer an adimú from the heart, and if it will be some time before he can afford the expenses of this initiation, he should receive Babaluaiye's eleke.
- No matter what the two orishas Babaluaiye and Oshún do or do not demand as ebó, the diviner should tell the client that he must live by making ebó to both orishas. As he pampers them, they will bless him.
- If the client is a man, he may be in danger of losing his wife or lover. If his current relationship is falling apart, the following ebó should be done: Give an ornate fan made of blue things to Yemayá, leaving it with her for seven days. At the end of seven days, replace the fan with a more expensive adimú. The man must now present this fan to his lover. Once this ebó is done, Yemayá will give him a second chance to make things right with his mate; she will bless the relationship and help smooth over difficulties if he treats her well.
- If the diviner has come this far into the odu and closure eludes him, he should consider asking, "Ebó else egun?" If egun stand up in this pattern for an aborisha, the proper offering is a single rooster. If the client is an initiate, the proper offering is first a sheep and then a single rooster.

If at this point the odu still will not close and the client is an aleyo or an aborisha, the diviner should now consider the eboses of the parent odu, Obara (see page 297). Something there is needed for the client's evolution. If the client is an initiate, Ogún is standing up for a guiro. Before the guiro is given, a sacrifice of a pigeon, a rooster, and a new machete must be made to him. He will use this offering, and the aché of the guiro, to destroy anyone and anything that stands in the way of his evolution.

If these eboses are not enough to close the odu for an initiate, the diviner should now turn to the eboses of the parent odu, Obara. Something there is needed for this client's evolution.

## The Fourteenth Composite Odu of Obara, Obara Merinla (6-14)

### The Proverb of Obara Merinla

- The youngest child of the house is really the eldest, for he has the greatest head.

### The Message of Obara Merinla

When the initial cast of six mouths, Obara, precedes a cast of fourteen mouths, Merinla, the odu Obara Merinla, also known as Obara Ika, is open. It is a hot, volatile odu, and no matter its orientation (iré or osogbo) it will bring all the bad that six mouths has to offer. When it opens, immediately the diviner should say, "Maferefún Shangó!" This orisha's intervention in this pattern is essential to the client's evolution. The diviner also says, "Maferefún Oshún! Maferefún Ogún!" The sweetness of Oshún will be needed to soothe any hot osogbo that comes, and the strength of Ogún will be needed to keep harm away. Finally, the diviner says, "Maferefún Orúnmila!" Although he cannot speak directly in the shells, Orúnmila's influence may be shadowed here, and before the reading closes out the diviner might need to tell his client, "Orúnmila is here, trying to bring both a message and a blessing; you need to be seen by his priests, the babalawos, for a reading with Ifá."

The italero must keep in mind that this pattern speaks of treason, traps, and entrapment. In this odu both the mouse and the fish came to the diviners for a reading. The diviners marked ebó, but neither the mouse nor the fish made ebó. The mouse was killed in the trap and the fish died in the net.

When assessing any reading of Obara Merinla, the diviner should consider the following points:

- If the client has children, the youngest has the greatest head; he will achieve many great things during his life. He is, however, in danger, and the parent must guard this child lest his destiny be cut short by death. Spiritually, the client must raise this child to understand the importance of making ebó to the orishas; they will bless him.
- The client either is planning a trip or will soon plan a trip. The diviner should tell him not to go, because he will encounter death in the place he travels to. He may not be the one to die, but the death that he comes across will affect his life in profound ways, none of them for the good.
- A war is coming that the client will not see coming. This war will be bigger than he can imagine. When arguments and strife come in his life, immediately he must return to the diviner for a rogación at the feet of his guardian orisha. If the guardian orisha is not known, the rogación must be done at the feet of his godparent's orisha.

## The Prohibitions of Obara Merinla

- When this odu opens, the diviner must prescribe the taboos of the parent odu, Obara (see page 297), regardless of the sign's orientation of iré or osogbo. These prohibitions are integral to one's safety.
- One's next option for travel is prohibited; one will encounter death in that place if one goes. After this, one is forbidden travel unless one consults first with the orishas. No matter the reason for the trip, if the orishas say not to go, one must not go.
- Lies, slander, and gossip are prohibited. Neither listen to nor speak these things.

## The Eboses of Obara Merinla

When a casting of Obara Merinla opens on the mat, the following are considerations for ebó:

- The client must have a rogación at the feet of his guardian orisha. If the guardian orisha is not known, the client must have a rogación before the diviner's or godparent's orisha. After the rogación, the client should offer an adimú of calabazas to the orisha that offered the blessing.
- The herb yagruma is essential to this person. He must include this herb in as many eboses as possible. If the sign Obara Merinla comes in a hot osogbo, this herb should be used in the rogación given; it will soothe this odu.

Having made these prescriptions, the diviner may now attempt to close the oracle. If it will not close, he should explore the following possibilities:

- The diviner must ask, "Ebó elese Shangó?" to see if this orisha will take anything from the client. If the answer is yes, he uses the diloggún to mark the required offering. If Shangó will not take ebó, the priest must direct this person to give something "from his heart." The goodwill and intervention of Shangó is necessary to overcome the volatile essence of Obara Merinla.
- Oshún and Ogún can stand up here for ebó as well. The diviner must ask, "Ebó elese Oshún?" If the answer is yes, he uses the diloggún to mark the offering. If she will not take ebó, or if the odu still refuses closure, he should ask, "Ebó

elese Ogún?" If the answer is yes, he uses the diloggún to mark the appropriate offering.

- If none of these three orishas will offer a blessing, or if the odu remains open, the diviner must insist that his client sit at the feet of Ifá for a thorough assessment. The issues brought up by this pattern of Obara are too deep to be revealed through the orisha's diloggún.
- Having considered the above options for ebó, if the odu still refuses closure for an aleyo who has received neither the elekes nor the warriors, diviner should try to mark the elekes as ebó. Such is the power of the elekes ceremony that almost any osogbo brought by Obara Merinla can be overcome. The proper question is "Koshé los elekes?" If the oracle marks the elekes as ebó, the diviner must explain to the aleyo the commitment entailed by the initiation before attempting the oracle's closure.
- If the client already has the elekes, nor if the client does not have the elekes and the oracle will not mark them as ebó, the diviner should determine whether the reception of the warriors is necessary, asking, "Koshé los guerreros?" If odu accepts this, the diviner should explain to the client what is involved in this ceremony and mark the path of Eshu to be received through Obara Merinla before attempting the oracle's closure.

If none of these will close the odu, or if the client already has the warriors and the elekes, the diviner should consider the following possibilities:

- The elekes of one or more orishas speaking in Obara (see the list on page 259) could be necessary for protection. To find out if this is necessary, the diviner should ask, "Ebó eleke de [orisha's name]?" After marking an eleke, the diviner should explain to the client why this spirit is offering his or her protection in this odu (using his own aché to deliver this information). After an eleke is marked and explained, the diviner should attempt closure again. Note that more than one orisha could stand up in this odu to offer protection through his or her eleke.
- If the oracle still will not close, those spirits who offered protection through their elekes might also be standing up for ebó. Each spirit who has marked his or her eleke as larishe to this osogbo must then be asked, "Ebó elese [orisha's name]?" If any stand up for ebó, the diviner should use the diloggún to mark an appropriate offering.
- If the letter still will not close, Elegguá might be standing up for ebó. The diviner should question this by asking, "Ebó elese Elegguá?" If the answer is yes, he should use the diloggún to mark an appropriate ebó.

If these prescriptions are not enough to close the session, the diviner should now turn to the eboses of the parent odu, Obara (see page 297). Something there is needed to bring about the client's evolution.

## The Fifteenth Composite Odu of Obara, Obara Marunla (6-15)

### The Proverbs of Obara Marunla

- Success does not come to those who lose their heads.
- If the head is heated, it will not think about its actions.

### The Message of Obara Marunla

When a casting of six mouths, Obara, falls on the mat followed by a casting of fifteen mouths, Marunla, the odu Obara Marunla is open. Obara Iwori is another name for this pattern. Having cast this letter, the diviner pays homage to Olófin, Odua, Olokun, Oroiña, Orí, Shangó, and Borosi, saying to each, "Maferefún!" The aché of one or more of these spirits could be essential to the client's evolution. This letter is wrought with volatile energies; it is dangerous and brings all the bad that Obara has to offer. When it falls on the mat, the diviner must consider all the health warnings that come through Obara in osogbo, even if this composite has come in iré. Even if the client is in perfect health, the groin, kidneys, bladder, abdomen, and testicles are in danger of disease and decay. A woman who opens in Obara Marunla has concerns in her womb; pregnancy now is not a healthy option, and in the past she may have lost children through abortion or miscarriage. The client will suffer from insomnia to some degree, and unless the cause of this symptom is dealt with, disease and decay will come quickly. Strange internal fevers, temperature spikes of unknown etiology, will come; the client must be cautious when eating because many of these fevers will be allergic and systemic reactions.

When this sign opens, the diviner should also investigate the following concerns with the client:

- The client's head is disturbed and overheated in this sign. The client cannot think clearly. This letter speaks of short-term memory loss. This person must learn to write things down and keep careful notes lest he forget something important. Witchcraft and malice surround this person; others are doing all they can to make him "lose his head." He must fight lest he become lost.
- This person has many bad habits and vices. This odu demands that he give them up.
- Enemies from this person's past and present are coming together; there is a reunion whose sole purpose is to make him fall.
- Within the next year, the client will have a sudden urge to move. He must follow his heart, for only in this way will he find iré.

## The Prohibitions of Obara Marunla

- Avoid large gatherings. One's enemies are coming together and will invite one to their group. If one goes, they will destroy one.
- Bad habits and vices are taboo. Do not use drugs, alcohol, or tobacco; they destroy one's health.

## The Eboses of Obara Marunla

When Obara Marunla opens on the mat, three mandatory eboses must be done as soon as possible. These three eboses will soothe and cool the heat rising in the client's life; they will save him from tragedy. First, the client cannot leave the diviner's home until he has had a rogación. His orí is hot and overwhelmed, and if he leaves in this state, he will find tragedy. The orisha before whom this rogación is done depends on the client's status in the religion. If the client does not know his guardian orisha, the rogación should be done before the godparent's orisha. If his guardian orisha is known, the rogación should take place before that orisha.

Second, within twenty-four hours, this client must return to the diviner's home with all the elements for another rogación and two white pigeons. The rogación is repeated, and the two pigeons are sacrificed to the top of his head.

Third, for eight days following this rogación, the client must dress in white and remain pure, avoiding all vices. Nightly before retiring, he should take a white bath prepared with *sandolo* (sandalwood perfume), cow's milk, goat's milk, holy water, cascarilla, white flower petals, honey, and coconut milk.

Having made these prescriptions, the diviner may now attempt to close the oracle. If it will not close, he should explore the following possibilities:

- Yemayá may require an ebó. The diviner should ask, "Ebó elese Yemayá?" If the answer is yes, the client must have a rogación before her shrine, after which a fresh eleke should be put around his neck. The client must then offer an adimú to Yemayá; the diviner should use the diloggún to determine what she requires.
- If this is a client who has received neither the elekes nor the warriors, the diviner should try to mark the elekes as ebó. Such is the power of the elekes ceremony that almost any osogbo brought by Obara Marunla can be overcome. The proper question is "Koshé los elekes?" If the oracle marks the elekes as ebó, the diviner must explain to the aleyo the commitment entailed by the initiation before attempting the oracle's closure.
- If the client already has the elekes, or if the client does not have the elekes and the oracle will not mark them as ebó, the diviner should determine whether the reception of the warriors is necessary, asking, "Koshé los guerreros?" If

odu accepts this, the diviner should explain to the client what is involved in this ceremony and mark the path of Eshu to be received through Obara Marunla before attempting the oracle's closure.

If none of these will close the odu, or if the client already has the warriors and the elekes, the diviner should consider the following possibilities:

- The elekes of one or more orishas speaking in Obara (see the list on page 259) could be necessary for protection. To find out if this is necessary, the diviner should ask, "Ebó eleke de [orisha's name]?" After marking an eleke, the diviner should explain to the client why this spirit is offering his or her protection in this odu (using his own aché to deliver this information). After an eleke is marked and explained, the diviner should attempt closure again. Note that more than one orisha could stand up in this odu to offer protection through his or her eleke.
- If the oracle still will not close, those spirits who offered protection through their elekes might also be standing up for ebó. Each spirit who has marked his or her eleke as larishe to this osogbo must then be asked, "Ebó elese [orisha's name]?" If any stand up for ebó, the diviner should use the diloggún to mark an appropriate offering.
- If the odu will not close, the diviner must ask, "Ebó elese Shangó?" If the answer is yes, the diviner should use the shells to mark the appropriate offering. If the answer is no, the client should give the orisha adimú anyway to ensure his goodwill.
- The next possible prescription is that the client needs to be taken to a babalawo immediately for a complete assessment by Ifá.
- If this is not enough to close the odu, egun are standing up for ebó. The diviner should teach the client how to set up a bóveda to honor his egun. He must give them fresh water and light weekly. The diviner should consider asking, "Ebó elese egun?" to see what else is required. If the answer is yes, he uses the diloggún to mark the required offering.

If this is not enough to close the session and the client is an aleyo or aborisha, the diviner should turn to the eboses of the parent odu, Obara (see page 297). Something there is needed for this person's evolution. If the client is an initiate, the diviner should consider the reception of Odua, Oroiña, Orí, or Borosia, asking, "Koshé [orisha's name]?" More than one orisha may be marked.

If the odu still remains open, the diviner must turn to the eboses of the parent odu, Obara.

# The Sixteenth Composite Odu of Obara, Obara Merindilogún (6-16)

## The Proverbs of Obara Merindilogún

- The war in government will surge throughout the city.
- Danger is close.

## The Message of Obara Merindilogún

When a casting of six mouths, Obara, falls on the mat followed by a casting of sixteen mouths, Merindilogún, the odu Obara Merindilogún, also known as Obara Otura, is open. When it falls, the italero says, "Maferefún Obatalá! Maferefún Yemayá! Maferefún Oshún! Maferefún Shangó! Maferefún Orúnmila!" All these spirits may speak here, and their aché is essential to the client's evolution and salvation. Babaluaiye, Olófin, Elegguá, Odua, and Olosa can speak here as well, and it is appropriate to say to each, "Maferefún!"

No matter its orientation, this letter is hot and volatile; it can bring all the good and all the bad of Obara depending on the client's character and his willingness to make ebó. The diviner must proceed with this reading carefully and cautiously. To make the one who sits at the mat believe in all the odu has to say, the diviner should give this one prediction: "A problem in the government will surge to a war in the city. Watch for this, for once it happens, if you have not made ebó, you will know that your demise is near." (Years ago, this odu opened for a reading six days prior to the racial riots in Saint Petersburg,

Florida; the client who received this letter did not make ebó as he should have, and much of his property was destroyed in the ensuing fights.)

## The Prohibitions of Obara Merindilogún

- Do not consume grains, grainy foods, or any food made from animal heads or intestines. These bring sickness to the client.
- Choking is a danger. If meat is served on the bone, cut the meat off the bone before eating. Do not gnaw or suck on the bone.
- Be careful of open flames and electrical appliances. Have no source of open flame in the home, and unplug all nonessential appliances when not in use.

## The Eboses of Obara Merindilogún

To soothe the volatile nature of this odu, the diviner must prescribe a series of spiritual baths using items sacred to Obatalá, followed by a series of spiritual baths made of things sacred to Yemayá. The aché of both orishas will be needed to cleanse the client. Once both series of baths are complete, the diviner must take the client into the woods. There, the priest cleanses him with a small dark chicken. After the cleansing, the animal should be set free.

The client must give ebó to Oshún as well, offering him a bottle filled with cornmeal and water and capped tightly so the water does not evaporate. Once the ebó is made, the diviner should ask Oshún (using obí) how long it is to stay with her and how it is to be discarded. If this reading is an itá, the bottle of cornmeal and water must stay with Oshún indefinitely.

Finally, the client's home must be thoroughly cleansed spiritually. Afterward, the diviner washes the front door with omiero and prays to the orishas there that they cleanse, refresh, and protect the home.

Having made these prescriptions, the diviner may now attempt to close the oracle. If it will not close, he should explore the following possibilities:

- If this is a client who has received neither the elekes nor the warriors, the diviner should try to mark the elekes as ebó. Such is the power of the elekes ceremony that almost any osogbo brought by Obara Merindilogún can be overcome. The proper question is "Koshé los elekes?" If the oracle marks the elekes as ebó, the diviner must explain to the aleyo the commitment entailed by the initiation before attempting the oracle's closure.
- If the client already has the elekes, or if the client does not have the elekes and the oracle will not mark them as ebó, the diviner should determine whether the reception of the warriors is necessary, asking, "Koshé los guerreros?" If odu accepts this, the diviner should explain to the client what is involved in this ceremony and mark the path of Eshu to be received through Obara Merindilogún before attempting the oracle's closure.

If none of these will close the odu, or if the client already has the warriors and the elekes, the diviner should consider the following possibilities:

- The elekes of one or more orishas speaking in Obara (see the list on page 259) could be necessary for protection. To find out if this is necessary, the diviner should ask, "Ebó eleke de [orisha's name]?" After marking an eleke, the diviner should explain to the client why this spirit is offering his or her protection in this odu (using his own aché to deliver this information). After an eleke is marked and explained, the diviner should attempt closure again. Note that more than one orisha could stand up in this odu to offer protection through his or her eleke.
- If the oracle still will not close, those spirits who offered protection through their elekes might also be standing up for ebó. Each spirit who has marked his or her eleke as larishe to this osogbo must then be asked, "Ebó elese [orisha's name]?" If any stand up for ebó, the diviner should use the diloggún to mark an appropriate offering.
- If the client is an initiate, he could need to receive Odua or Olosa. The diviner must ask, "Koshé [orisha's name]?"

There are no other eboses for this odu beyond taking the client to see Ifá. If the letter still will not close, the diviner should proceed with the eboses listed for the parent odu, Obara (see below). Something there is needed for the client's evolution.

## Closing the Reading: Further Eboses of the Parent Odu, Obara

Having exhausted the options of larishe and ebó in the composite odu, the diviner turns to the parent odu to find a method of closure. Obara contains within itself many offerings and rituals to placate both the letter and the orishas who speak in it. The eboses for the parent odu follow.

- In this family of odu, the most important spiritual issues center on Shangó. When Obara has come in osogbo and refuses closure, the diviner must turn to him. Although the diviner may already have asked the client this question, he must now ask again, "Do you have any unresolved issues with Shangó?" If the client made any promises to him that he has not kept, he must resolve them immediately. The diviner may also examine this issue from another angle: Has the client offended any of Shangó's children? If so, he must seek resolution. If the client is an aborisha whose godparent is Shangó's initiate, there could be disrespect between the two, godparent and godchild. The diviner must examine this issue as well. If nothing else, the client should resolve to give Shangó a party in his honor, inviting as many initiates and aborishas of Shangó as possible. If this client is an aborisha who has not made ocha, the party should be given to the godparent's Shangó. If the client is an initiate, the diviner might consider asking, "Tambor [or guiro] elese Shangó?"
- If the client has come to the oracle because of financial need, he should buy a ceramic pumpkin, fill it with honey, and leave it at Oshún's feet overnight, along with five small calabazas. The next day, he should take the pumpkin and calabazas to the river, along with five pennies. He should drop the calabazas and pennies into the river and wash the honey out of the ceramic pumpkin with river water. Then he should take home the ceramic pumpkin and put money in it every week as a devotion to Oshún. As long as he has the pumpkin in his home, he will never be poor.
- If the client has come to this oracle in desperation, there is ebó that must be done immediately. He must give to his warriors Ogún and Elegguá (or the diviner's warriors if he has not received his warriors) two beaded, forked garabatos (branches). Elegguá's garabato should be beaded in red and black and Ogún's in green and black. If the client is a priest or priestess who has received the knife, he should use clear green glass beads instead of green beads on Ogún's branch. Once these branches are presented to the orishas, the client should pray that his paths be opened and his doors unlocked. A priest finishes the ebó by giving Ogún and Elegguá a rooster each, making sure that the beaded branches are fed as well. The next day, the client offers each orisha epó, smoked fish, and jutía. Once seven days have passed, he gives each orisha a basket of cool fruits. The warriors will open all that have been closed.
- A client for whom this letter has fallen might need to receive the elekes as ebó. The diviner should ask, "Koshé los elekes?" If the oracle answers yes, the initiation should be scheduled as soon as possible.
- If the client for whom this letter falls has not received the warriors, he might need them now. The diviner should ask, "Koshé los guerreros?" If the answer is yes, the initiation should be taken as soon as possible.
- If the client already has the warriors, or if the letter does not dictate their reception, either Elegguá or Ogún could be standing up in this sign for ebó. To see what they might require, the diviner should ask, "Ebó elese Elegguá?" and "Ebó elese Ogún?" If the answer to either question is yes, he uses the diloggún to mark the required offering.
- To propitiate the orishas Shangó and Oshún, the client should make an ebó of six calabazas to

Shangó and five to Oshún. Note that if this ebó is prescribed, even if the client is an aleyo, he is forever prohibited from using calabaza except as ebó.

- Because Osain and Shangó are close, Osain's influence can be found to some degree in all composites of Obara. The diviner should ask, "Niche osain de Shangó?" If the oracle answers yes, the following should be made for the client:

 An oriaté must come and sacrifice first a turtle and then two guinea hens to Osain. Separate the turtle's shell from the carcass, and wash it in some of Shangó's omiero. Once clean, place the head, the legs, and the internal organs (the part known as the "aché" of the animal) of each animal sacrificed into the shell. Let all these dry in the sun. When they are dried, put the animal parts (but not the turtle shell) into a piece of red cloth, along with a small thunderstone washed in Shangó's omiero, a small black stone washed in Shangó's omiero, a small black stone washed in Elegguá's omiero, a piece of the palo abre camino tree, a piece of ceiba tree branch, algarrobo, *álamo*, *jaguey*, *framboyán* (herbs avaliable at botánicas), dirt from the base of a palm tree, dirt from the four corners of a crossroads, six sewing needles, six guinea peppers, a piece of gold, a silver coin, a piece of red coral, six of Shangó's herbs, an avocado seed, obí, ósun, kola, six uncut cowries that have been washed in Shangó's omiero, six fishing hooks, a bow and arrow of Ochosi, and a small machete. All this should be tied in the red cloth with white and red cotton threads and then packed into the turtle's shell. Cement the shell shut, and decorate the seam with cowries. Wash it in Shangó's omiero and feed it a feathered animal with him. Then bury this niche osain beneath either a royal palm or a ceiba tree for twelve days. At the end of this time, dig it up and feed the hole a rooster. When the shell is not being carried by the client, it should be left with Shangó on his batea.

- All things that are completely or partially broken or burned in the client's house should be left at the feet of Shangó with an adimú. This will take away the heat in the client's life and remove things that are broken from his environment.
- If the client suffers from abdominal problems and the letter refuses to close, he should have a rogación at the feet of Oshún. Afterward, he should give her an adimú incorporating squash.
- If the client has legal problems and the letter will not close, he should offer an ebó to Ochosi to solve the problem. Let Ochosi dictate the type and terms of the ebó.
- Finally, to close this sign for an initiate, the reception of one or more orishas could be necessary. Ochosi, Aganyú, the Ibeyi, Olokun, and Osain (as a last resort only) are all a possibility. The diviner should try to mark one of these orishas, and then close the odu. If the client is an aborisha, these same orishas should be considered, but only the Ibeyi and Olokun may be considered for reception; for the other orishas, the diviner should simply ask, "Ebó elese [orisha's name]?" If the answer is yes, he uses the diloggún to mark the appropriate offering.

If this list is exhausted and the odu still refuses closure, the diviner has two options. First, he may call an elder in the religion, for something important in the sign could have been overlooked. Second, he may look at the list of eboses given for the omo odu as a parent odu. For example, in a casting of Obara Ejiogbe (6-8), the diviner would turn to the eboses of Eji Ogbe as the parent odu for closure.

# EIGHT

# THE FAMILY OF ODÍ

## The Proverbs of Odí

- This is where the hole was first dug.
- In adultery, there will always be danger.
- The biggest fish will be caught in the biggest ocean with the best bait and a little luck.
- It will take more than luck to catch the biggest fish; it will take the biggest hook in the biggest ocean with the best bait to win.
- In Odí, the hole [the grave] is finally dug.
- While today it will seem small, tomorrow it will be big. [This refers to the inherent osogbo in all the signs.]

## The Orishas Who Speak in Odí

| | |
|---|---|
| Yemayá | Babaluaiye |
| egun | Obatalá |
| Ogún | Inle |
| Elegguá | Orisha Oko |
| Otín | Olokun |
| Ochosi | Korikoto |

## The Message of Odí

Opening with seven mouths on the mat, the diloggún sits before the italero in a dynamic, volatile pattern. Odí moves quickly, permeating every area of one's life. It alludes to nature, from the ocean and the earth to the heavens and all that they contain. Yet like nature, Odí has two sides: the creative and the destructive. Life and death, composition and decomposition, putrescence and purification—all these are found in Odí's energy. For the client, no matter the sign's orientation (iré or osogbo), it easily becomes a blessing or a curse. Odí's blessings come when the client listens well, following its advice exactly; it becomes a curse when the client does not give it what it demands. No matter how Odí falls, throughout this reading the diviner must explore not only the good but also the bad that this letter predicts. Know, however, that the one at the mat has faith in neither the orishas nor their religion; he may not believe in the diviner's skills and may not feel the need to follow his prescriptions. At best, even if this person is devout, he has lost his faith.

Odí is not only complex but also controversial; its origin and birth are a subject of contention among priests. In a previous book I wrote, "The sign that we know as Odí in the diloggún was born from Okana (one mouth). Just as the latter sign is an expression of harmony and justice (brought through radical or harsh change), Odí is the completion of that balancing and the seal that holds it firm."* In this school of thought, Ogundá and Osá are believed to have been born from Odí separately. Another school of thought in the religion regards Odí as

*Óchani Lele, *The Secrets of Afro-Cuban Divination: How to Cast the Diloggún, the Oracle of the Orishas* (Rochester, Vt.: Destiny Books, 2000), 185–86.

having no parent, having descended directly from heaven. In this case, it is no longer a seal; it is a beginning. Those who follow this school of thought believe that Odí gave birth to Ogundá and Osá simultaneously; these three energies are thought to be so closely related that when one sign opens on the mat, the diviner considers the energies and implications of all three during the consultation. In this second school of thought, the three odu are so dependent on each other that they overlap and overflow; they are inseparable. It is beyond the scope of this work to debate these two philosophies; however, the neophyte diviner should keep them in mind and follow the customs of the house from which his head was born.

When Odí is cast on the mat, the diviner suspends the reading before drawing a composite odu. This pattern's energy enfolds all present; therefore, the diviner honors its opening. While some insist that no sacred gesture be associated with Odí, others do the following pantomime: The italero folds his arms over his breast as if cradling and nursing an infant. This gesture alludes to Yemayá, who owns this odu in the diloggún. Realize, however, that few have seen the elders in Cuba make this gesture. Many say it is an American invention, created to fill a "liturgical gap" in the ritual of diloggún.*

The diviner continues with the sacred prayer of Odí:

*Odí, orí orisha adima.*
*Ashama adima adima shama dima.*
*Mamayo mama y orisha ibariwa mabaya.*
*Werin werin yinweriko abarun mabale.*
*Ogerige yeni iworiwe yin ibarenfo.*
*Mabaya iwo dinwesin wero ibareyo mabaya.*
*Iwori werin yin worike.*

Those present bow their heads in silence while the diviner chants this brief prayer. When he is done, to honor both the opening odu and the orisha who owns it, many will mutter, "Maferefún Odí! Maferefún Yemayá!"

*Some say Odí is so vast that no gesture is capable of encapsulating its mystery. For this reason, many associate no pantomime with its opening.

Within Odí several spirits might choose to speak. The orisha whose diloggún is being consulted has the first option, and adherence to his advice is essential to the client's evolution. Following this spirit is Yemayá; she owns Odí, and this sign never closes until she speaks. Her issues are heavily dependent on the composite cast. Elegguá is quite comfortable in seven mouths, and since this is a sign concerned with one's destiny and fate, his propitiation is essential to evolution. Otín, an orisha serving Yemayá, also comes here. However, she will not speak unless the client is an initiate, and rarely will she be of any use in this odu to those who are not Yemayá's priests. After Otín, the orishas Ochosi, Babaluaiye, Obatalá, Inle, and Orisha Oko can speak, claim ebó, or demand reception by the client; these issues, however, are heavily dependent on the composite odu opened and the client's status in the religion. Finally, throughout the family of Odí the orisha Korikoto can speak. He is a spirit of farming and abundance, living and eating with Orisha Oko. He speaks only for initiates, and while those who have ocha done can receive him, they must have received Orisha Oko first. Also, no matter the composite opened, the diviner must assume that the client has issues with egun; the exact issues brought out, and how to handle them, depend on the composite odu cast.

Before beginning a thorough study of this family, keep an important point in mind: While each composite will be marked as coming either in iré or in osogbo, treating this odu as if it had fallen in both iré and osogbo is important. Remember the two sides of Odí, life and death; the odu shadows these two qualities in every casting regardless of its orientation. The client's behavior and adherence to what it says during this session will determine what comes his way. Even in iré, a client who does not make ebó loses his blessings; in osogbo, obedience brings grace. In the end, this person's evolution lies with his own actions.

This letter also carries a very stern warning for the diviner. He must beware of malicious gossip and evil tongues. The client will leave the mat and carry what the priest says to those who do not need to hear. Also, the danger that another will eavesdrop on the reading exists so the diviner should secure the reading room from the eyes and ears of others.

The easiest way to begin a study of seven mouths is with it in iré. If the composite odu is marked as coming in iré, the diviner's next step is to mark the origin of this iré. This process is crucial because it helps the client focus on his source of spiritual strength. In Odí, while all sources of iré bring blessings, the spirits who speak through seven mouths favor some more than others. The following origins are especially propitious for the client: iré otonowá (blessings from heaven), iré elese ocha (blessings at the feet of the orishas), iré elese egun (blessings at the feet of one's ancestral spirits), iré elese ará onú (blessings at the feet of the spirits of heaven), iré dedewan t'Olokun (blessings at the feet of Olokun), iré elese araoko (blessings at the feet of the fertile land), and iré banda loguro (blessings from the depths of the earth). Likewise, in Odí some sources of iré are dangerous for the client. The following origins are especially volatile in this family of letters: iré elese eledá (blessings from one's head), iré elese elenú (blessings from the speaker's tongue), iré lowo (blessings from one's own hands), iré elese abure (blessings from a sibling of blood or of ocha), iré elese obini or okuni (blessings from women or men), iré elese omo (blessings from one's child), and iré elese arubo (blessings from the elders).

If the odu is marked with an especially favorable iré in Odí, the diviner knows the client is doubly blessed. Because this odu refers to the ocean, the earth, and the sky, anything related to these brings special blessings. Nothing under heaven or above earth can keep this person from his destiny. The orishas favor him. Egun are prominent in all seven mouths composites, yet if egun bring iré, the entire force of this sign mounts behind the client, pushing him toward evolution. The diviner should assume in every reading of this letter that they will claim ebó no matter Odí's orientation. However, he should be careful when prescribing for egun, for while Odí is the father of Espiritísmo (mediumistic practices), the manner in which one works with the spirits is heavily dependent on the composite opened.

In particular, the iré marked as elese ocha requires further manipulation by the diviner. When an orisha promises iré elese ocha, the diviner must dig deeper into the odu to determine which orisha brings this blessing. For an aleyo, he should ask the following: Yemayá, Ogún, Elegguá, and Obatalá. For an aborisha, the list of possible orishas expands: Yemayá, Ogún, Elegguá, Babaluaiye, Obatalá, and Olokun. For an initiate, the list expands even further: Yemayá, Ogún, Elegguá, Otín, Ochosi, Babaluaiye, Obatalá, Inle, Orisha Oko, Olokun, and Korikoto. Having determined the orisha bringing iré, the diviner must prescribe ebó to that spirit. The orisha offering the blessing, as well as the client's status in the religion, will determine the exact offering. (See "Marking Ebó in Odí: Initial Considerations" on page 305 for more details.)

In spite of all these possibilities, keep in mind that of all the orishas who speak in Odí, the one who brings the greatest blessings is Yemayá. This odu is her true home. She alone can travel, at will, through all the realms referenced here: ocean, land, and sky. For while she was born of Olokun's chaining to the bottom of the sea, she walks on land (creating lakes and sinkholes where she steps), and once she ascended into heaven by her own aché. Even if this client is not her child, he is well protected by this powerful orisha. Since Odí always marks issues with Yemayá, even when she does not stand up strongly, the diviner would be wise to pause during this reading to ask the client if he has any issues with her. The client must fulfill any unpaid promises so no debt exists between the two. If the client is unable to remember any unpaid promises to Yemayá, the diviner needs to consider, carefully, what ebó or eboses this person should give to lock in her goodwill and blessings. In addition, if Yemayá stands up for an aleyo or an aborisha, especially in the composite Odí Meji, the diviner must tell the client that Yemayá demands his asiento. He should throw a mazo of Yemayá (or of the client's guardian orisha, if it is known) over the client's shoulders and direct him to salute the orisha and his godparents. His lack of a crown, promised to him before birth, is the true cause of all his troubles. Yemayá herself will help him remedy this.

When a "dangerous" source of iré opens, the diviner can make many assumptions and prescriptions for his client. Remember that this family encompasses the opposites of life and death; the client's own actions, or lack of action, easily turn blessings into curses. Any reference to a blessing coming through the client's works, words, or head is dangerous. Odí foreshadows this person's own lack of faith, his own unwillingness to work or make ebó; it says that his head is hard, and he does not like to listen to advice. His hardheadedness is the root of his problems. When Odí signals a blessing from the client's own deeds, head, or heart, the diviner should tell him this: "That which is bad, in the end, can bring nothing but curses." He can promise the client that if he listens to what the orishas are saying and acts appropriately, all he does will prosper. Nevertheless, if he ignores his own source of help—himself—his life will crumble under Odí's weight. Finally, Odí flags issues with friends and family; relationships are, at best, strained in this person's life. Unless he works hard to heal these broken bonds, any blessing promised through one of the client's relationships will not manifest in his life. And chances are that the client will not work to heal these bonds.

Having determined the iré and its source, the italero continues to question the oracle. If the iré is marked iré yale (firm iré), the diloggún tells the client that his source of help is strong. Spiritual forces mount behind him, pushing him toward his evolution. If, furthermore, the iré is then marked iré yale timbelaye (firm iré manifest in the client's life), Odí gives closure to itself. It tells the diviner that the odu's energy has been in effect in this person's life for some time, and he is on the verge of entering into another life cycle.

Coming in iré, seven mouths is a sign capable of miracles. Healing the sick and creating prosperity are within its grasp, as is illustrated by the odu's patakís. Among them is told the story of an aborisha whose town was plagued with an epidemic; house by house, the disease spread, and none survived its fever. After days of death, the illness crept into the aborisha's own home. Terrified for the lives of those he loved, the man sought out a diviner for advice. "Maferefún Shangó! Maferefún Babaluaiye!" he said. The wise italero prescribed ebó: "To Shangó, sacrifice a single guinea hen using a wooden sword, and make the same sacrifice to Babaluaiye with a knife. Put the carcasses of both beside the front door, hanging one up high with a rope and leaving the other in front of the door's steps." Immediately, the aborisha did as he was told. At night, he remained with his family; all were locked in a deep slumber, hovering between life and death. The man himself was burning with fever; the plague had infected him. Unknown to this man, Ikú came, cloaked in silence and darkness. The scent of rotten flesh entranced him. Quickly, he ate the first guinea hen on the front step; great was his gluttony, and he coveted the guinea hen tied over the door. In hunger, he snapped the rope holding the hen; the noise startled the aborisha who lay waiting indoors. In a feverish delirium he grabbed the wooden sword used to make his ebó and stormed the front door. He thought a robber was trying to break in. Ikú, gorged on rotten flesh and helpless in his gluttony, froze when he saw the crazed man brandishing the strange weapon. As the aborisha bore down on the specter, Ikú ran in fear. That night, sickness left the man's home.

Odí also tells of two newlyweds who lived impoverished lives. Their home was in shambles; it needed repair, but they had no money to fix it. They were starving; they needed food, but they had no money to buy any. Both needed clothes, but they had no money to purchase cloth. The two argued constantly, and the neighbors in their town ridiculed them about how they lived. Both, however, had faith in the orishas, and they went to the town's diviner. There, the priest told them, "Do not argue. Do not fight. You need each other to overcome your poverty. Those who ridicule you now will one day beg you for money. Wealth and prosperity can be yours if only you listen to Odí." The diviner marked ebó: With a new machete, they were to sacrifice two roosters and two pigeons to Ogún. While the wife cooked the meat to serve the orisha, the husband was to go out into the forest; with the new machete, he was to cut dozens of palm fronds to make a bed for the orisha's ebó. Together, husband and wife made the sacrifice, and while she cooked the meat, he searched the forest for palm fronds. As he worked, he tired, and by accident he dropped the machete into a small crevice. Needing to finish his ebó, and having no more money to buy another cutlass, the man lowered himself down into the crevice. He discovered that it was not just a hole but an opening into a vast cave filled with treasure. Husband and wife finished the ebó to Ogún, celebrating their newfound riches. They never wanted for anything again.

When Odí opens in iré, all things are possible for the client. He may come from poverty and despair. If he listens carefully to the diviner's advice, however, he will discover the path from impoverishment to prosperity; it has been hidden from him, but Odí can reveal it. Many who come with seven mouths are sick; they suffer or have suffered. Sometimes they come not for themselves but for those whom they love. While this odu cannot promise full, rapid recovery, its eboses and cleansings can promote health and clean living. The diviner must tell the client that, to evolve, he must listen carefully, make ebó, and conduct himself according to the pattern's taboos. Evolution is a process beginning within. As the client commits himself to his own growth and healing, those spiritual forces bringing iré will mount behind him. They will complement his own actions, pushing him farther than he ever dreamed he could go. In the end, the client's willingness to work and grow will determine how far he progresses; with this letter, no limit to what he can achieve exists.

Regardless of its orientation, Odí raises issues with the client's family. During this session, the diviner should investigate the client's interaction with his mother. If she is still alive, problems from the past have strained their relationship; he must now try to resolve them. If the odu opens in a harsh osogbo, they might be lost to each other. Odí speaks of mothers and their love for their children; it enforces the child's duty to the one who gave him birth. Of all bonds that exist between humans, none is more sacred or intimate than that between a mother and her child. Likewise, Odí suggests that a gulf exists between this person and his father; he must try to heal this as well. The past is the past; the client's parent will never change, and he must forgive them both. To help the one at the mat understand his parents better, the diviner should tell him, "Your birth was both a strain and a joy to your family, and so it has remained until today. Even now, you judge your parents based on the mind and memory of a child, and while as an adult you try to understand what happened, an immature memory has glazed all. Try to move beyond this, and all three of you will heal."

If the client's mother is dead, the issues brought by Odí change. The diviner will know that a great sorrow exists in the client. Loss, guilt, fault, mournfulness, melancholy—all these feelings seethe within. He had unfinished business with his mother when she died, and many words remained unspoken. While this is not the issue bringing the client to the orishas, it is the root of his emotional suffering. Somehow he needs to find release. Odí brings issues with one's father to a lesser degree, and the client may have similar issues toward his father if he is deceased. The diviner must assure the client that death is not the end; while no longer among the living, those who have died are still close and can still hear our prayers. He should advise the client to begin work with a bóveda. There, he can pour out what remains in his heart and soul for both parents. He can give them light and evolution; in return, they can bless him and make up for the wrong they did when he was but a child. Let this serve as a warning for all who sit in on this session: They must love and honor blood, for life is not eternal, and things left undone or unsaid can come back to haunt them.

Envy permeates the client's life from many sources. It comes not only from his family but also from his friends; the closer the friend, the greater the envy. Although he has not been overtly aware of this situation, the client must accept it and learn to deal with it.

The diviner must tell the client that he takes "friends of convenience." He remains loyal to those from whom he needs something: money, knowledge, advancement, or fulfillment. Having fulfilled his needs, however, the client leaves those people behind as he seeks out new sources. The diviner should advise him, "Never abandon old, long-term friends for new ones. Keep those close who are close now, and make new friends slowly. Realize that growth involves giving, and not just taking. Usually you take and give little in return." In the client's dealings with others, the issues of gossip, violence, and false testimony may arise. Gossip comes in two forms: about others and about the client. To evolve, he must ignore all forms of gossip. There is something violent in this person's character, and if Odí comes with a harsh osogbo, this violent nature will make itself known. It will get him into trouble with others. False testimony comes out of jealousy; the diviner should tell the client that rumors and accusations will come, and if osogbo is open at the mat, his friends will abandon him when he needs them most. Forewarned is forearmed.

Odí speaks of one who lives in continual anxiety. This person suffers from insomnia, and this unhealthy lack of sleep causes his mental disturbances. When he sleeps, he wakes in agitation from a sensation of falling and then landing on the bed in the same position in which he went to sleep. In the night, he sees the dead, and when he dreams he usually dreams with the dead. In dreams Yemayá and her spirits come; if the client dreams of the ocean, he may be her child. Egun whisper in darkness and in sleep, and although many of the client's nocturnal visions may seem far-fetched or unrealistic, the diviner should tell him to keep their basic principles in mind. Many will warn him about the future. Through dreams, both Yemayá and her spiritual court have tried to tell him often that his mother's health may not be good; it will not be long before she becomes ill or even dies.

If the client is a woman (or a gay man), three men are in love with her: one is black, one is white, and one has gray hair. One of these men will be sick, possibly with a venereal disease, so the client must be careful with whom she has sexual relations lest she become infected.

When Odí comes in a severe osogbo for a woman, she may be suffering from illness or disease in the reproductive and sexual organs; this illness may be due to a past abortion or may have caused a miscarriage. The diviner should tell the woman for whom this letter falls that Yemayá claims her sexual organs now, and all sexual acts and conceptions that occur from this moment on are sacred to her; the client must treat them with love and respect. Abortions are now taboo. If the client is afraid of having an unwanted pregnancy, two options exist: Either abstain from sex or use adequate birth control. Yemayá is the mother of all, and to her no greater blessing exists than that of children. This person could become very blessed, so she must be careful. If the client becomes pregnant, complications will result from this pregnancy. She must make ebó to Yemayá to ensure both her health and the health of the unborn child. A woman whose session opens in Odí is weak during menstruation; she must protect herself during her period.

When Odí comes in an osogbo of ikú or ano, it brings serious health warnings for the client. The ears, lungs, eyes, head, stomach, and the reproductive system are all vulnerable. Severe blows to the head may cause permanent injury to the brain and skull, so the client should always protect his head when playing sports. Spiritually, the client should protect his head as well, not letting others touch him there. Venereal disease runs rampant in ano and ikú; gonorrhea, syphilis, human papillomavirus, and AIDS are common, and if the client lives frequently among the gay community, many of his friends could die within the next seven years. Men need to ensure that they protect their testicles, scrotum, and penis from injury, especially while playing sports. Women must address the cause of irregular periods. Disease can form in the liver and blood; the client should be on guard against colitis, constipation (in the elderly, it can kill), cirrhosis, and all forms of hepatitis.

Having explored all these issues with the client, the diviner should now discuss the following concerns with him:

- All who come with seven mouths have strong issues centering on children. If the client is childless, parenthood is foreshadowed. Women who open in Odí in an itá will care for children not their own; fostering and adoption are possibilities.
- When dealing with family, the client stands

alone. His relatives are envious; they will never have the client's best interests in mind.

- Odí can forebode kidnapping. If the client has children, he must watch them carefully so one is not lost. If the client does not have children, this danger falls on him; in a severe osogbo, someone could kidnap or illegally detain him some day. If Ogún speaks here in an osogbo and is the one to offer larishe to the client, the danger becomes more specific: carjacking.
- Odí promises that the client will find something he lost. It also foreshadows unexpected gifts. The client should accept these graciously but promise nothing to the giver in return.
- This sign brings danger from the police. The client should avoid altercations with the law.
- At its worst, this pattern speaks of mental disturbances and illnesses. The client must take good care of his mental, spiritual, and emotional health.

## The Prohibitions of Odí

The effect of Odí is dependent on the client's own actions and behaviors. Therefore, in seven mouths the prescription of taboo is urgent. Note that if the reading comes in an osogbo, the diviner must prescribe the prohibitions of the composite odu as well. Unless this reading is an itá, one must follow all prescribed taboos for twenty-one to twenty-eight days. If this reading is a bajado, the client should follow the taboos given until he makes ocha.

- Seafood and freshwater foods are taboo. Note that dietary restriction not only honors Yemayá and Oshún, but also preserves one's health. Odí predicts death from food-borne poisons. Do not eat in restaurants that serve any type of seafood, for contaminants spread among dishes. Limit one's consumption of Yemayá's sacred foods; if this is an itá or a bajado, Yemayá's sacred foods are taboo.
- Do not drink alcohol.
- Do not take home remedies (even herbal remedies) or over-the-counter medications. When illness comes, see a physician. In Odí, one must avoid all intoxicants or medicines that can cause addiction. If the doctor prescribes narcotics or antidepressants, take these only as directed, and only if the physician is unable to provide another remedy.
- Beware of those in uniform who visit the house. One should say that one is too busy to receive guests and not let them in.
- Avoid gossip, especially if it comes from a woman's mouth. Treat women who gossip like enemies. Avoid them.
- Show no disrespect toward one's parents or godparents; always respect the elders.
- Never strike a child, especially on the head.
- Do not jump over holes, look through holes, or wear things that have holes.
- Do not lift heavy objects alone; injury will result.
- Adultery is taboo in this letter. Remain faithful to one's lover.

## Marking Ebó in Odí: Initial Considerations

Because the diloggún provides a means for evolution, each odu prescribes many eboses to put a client back into alignment with his destiny. The initial considerations for eboses in Odí are several in number.

If the odu opens in the favorable iré elese ocha, the diviner must determine which orisha offers the blessing (as described in "The Message of Odí"). He must then prescribe ebó to this orisha. If the client is an aleyo, the odu requires a simple adimú. If the iré is not firm, or if the sign refuses closure, the aleyo must also have a rogación before that orisha's shrine and receive his or her eleke. If the client is an aborisha, the considerations for ebó might go beyond a simple adimú. If either Elegguá or Ogún offers a blessing, the reception of the warriors is necessary to lock it in. Likewise, if either Babaluaiye or Olokun offers the blessing, the orisha might demand reception. If the client is an initiate, the implications of iré are more complicated. Blessings from Ogún demand the washing of his diloggún; if he offers this iré through the composite Odí

Ogundá (7-3), he demands pinaldo. Iré brought to an initiate by Otín, Ochosi, Babaluaiye, Inle, Orisha Oko, Olokun, or Korikoto will demand that orisha's reception.*

Whenever Odí opens, regardless of its orientation, one collective force will always demand propitiation no matter the reason that has brought the client to the mat: egun. Many consider Odí to be the father of Espiritísmo and spiritual masses; it is the family of signs through which these practices were first born to the religion. The manner in which the client elevates his spiritual court, however, is dependent on the composite odu that opens. Before delving into the eboses of the specific composite odu, however, the diviner delivers certain prescriptions. First, the client needs a bóveda, an altar where he gives light and refreshment to his ancestors and spirit guides. If the client has never used a bóveda before, this table must have seven glasses of water, not nine as is traditional in most lines of Espiritísmo. Also, if the client does not have an opá ikú, he must find one. The godparent must take him to a place near a large source of natural water (for example, an ocean, a river, or a lake), and in the woods near there he searches for his staff. Once the client has found a staff, the godparent decorates it with seven ribbons of different colors and seven small bells. Because Odí marks the client's beginnings with egun, the mark of Odí (seven) must be in all that he does.

Before considering any other option for egun, after prescribing the bóveda and opá ikú the diviner should ask, "Ebó elese egun?" If the answer is yes, the diviner marks the required offering with the shells. Even if the client's egun claim nothing, he should give something. To show love in life, one often gives loved ones gifts for no reason beyond "just because"; even after death, the same principle applies.

*Note that a protocol exists between Orisha Oko and Korikoto. While those who do not have Korikoto may receive Orisha Oko, those who do not have Orisha Oko may not receive Korikoto. If the odu marks iré elese Korikoto, the client must receive Orisha Oko first. Only after his reception may the client receive Korikoto.

### Traditional Eboses in Odí

Certain traditional substances are used for eboses in Odí. When marking any sacrifice, the diviner should first choose from the following list: a turtle, a hen, a rooster, two pigeons, two roosters, a duck, and a small calf that was bred, born, and raised to honor Yemayá. Note that the offering of a calf to Yemayá is what we call, in our house, a "holocaust offering." Red meat is the hottest meat one may use, and it should almost never be used for sacrifice or consumed by humans. For adimú-type offerings, the diviner may prescribe one or more of the following: a gourd, two ears of corn, all types of beans, two coconuts, seven coconuts, seven ears of corn, seven cloths of different colors, seven cakes, and two gourds plus one red parrot feather.

## Ebó Elese Egun
## *(Ebó at the Feet of Egun)*

### *Family Dinner*

The simplest and most powerful adimú one can offer egun is a family dinner shared among both the living and the dead. If the diviner determines that this ebó goes to the egun of blood, the client should invite as many blood relatives as possible: parents, grandparents, brothers, sisters, aunts, uncles, and children. If the ebó goes to the egun of ocha, the client should invite as many as possible from his spiritual family: godparents, godbrothers, godsisters, and godchildren. If the dinner is for egun in general, both spiritual and physical, the client may invite his relatives of both blood and ocha.

While the client may ask all who come to bring a cooked dish, because this is his ebó he must prepare as much food as possible with his own hands. Before serving the guests he must serve the ancestors by laying out some of all the food that has been prepared at the bóveda; he should call the dead by name, inviting them to eat and refresh themselves with the offerings. After lighting a white candle, he may then sit with his live relatives for dinner. This offering will supplicate the egun for all his dinner guests.

Once dinner is over, the client uses obí to find out how long to leave the adimú at the bóveda and where to discard the food. He must follow their instructions exactly, as adherence to their wishes brings full iré for his efforts.

### *Fried Okra and Potatoes*

When making ebó to egun, it seems they prefer food to any other type of offering; this makes sense, as one's ancestors were once alive and loved to eat. My favorite ebó to offer them is fried okra and potatoes. To prepare this dish, obtain yellow rice, 1 pound of fresh okra, two large baking potatoes, one medium-size white onion, 1/2 cup of cornmeal, 1/4 teaspoon of ground black pepper, and 1/2 cup of epó.

Cook the yellow rice according to the package's directions (but do not use salt in its preparation). While the rice is cooking, cut the stems from the okra. Wash it and cut into 1/2-inch pieces. Put the seeds into a small dish and leave it on the bóveda to commemorate the ancestors who brought this religion, and the plant, from Africa.* Wash, peel, and dice the potatoes into 1/2 -inch squares. Wash, peel, and finely grate the onion. Combine the potatoes, okra, and onion in a mixing bowl. Sprinkle the cornmeal and pepper over this and toss well.

In a large cast-iron skillet, melt the epó over medium-high heat. Do not allow it to smoke; if it does, reduce the heat just a bit. Spoon the mixture of potatoes, okra, and onion into the oil carefully so that it does not splatter. Fry, stirring frequently, until everything is browned (this will take 10 to 15 minutes depending on how hot the epó is). When the potato and onion mixture is cooked, remove the pan from the heat. Spoon the yellow rice into a large serving dish, and spoon the contents of the skillet over the rice. Serve this to one's egun while still warm, allowing it to remain with them overnight. The next day, using the oracle obí, the diviner determines how egun want their food discarded.

*Okra is not native to American shores; it was brought over by slaves as they were forced to endure the Middle Passage. The seeds were smuggled onto the ships by a small group of African women; they hid the seeds in their hair, and if the traders saw them, they thought it was only "dirt" embedded in their curls. Once these women were in the New World, they planted the seeds of the okra to remind them of their native lands, and okra soon became an important element in many eboses to the orishas, especially Shangó, Aganyú, and egun. It also became a staple food in the Americas; whenever one eats okra or uses it in a recipe, it is available only because of the ancestors.

### *Oguidí*

Egun adore this homemade candy; Elegguá also favors it. Whenever I make this candy as an ebó for egun, I also prepare it for Elegguá; the two can work together closely in Odí, and having Elegguá's goodwill when propitiating the dead is always wise. For the recipe, see page 55.

### *Plátanos Borrachos*

Both Elegguá and egun adore *plátanos borrachos* ("drunken plantains"). Again, this recipe has been given earlier in this book; see page 55 for instruction in the preparation of this dish.

### *Arroz con Leche*

Another adimú for egun is *arroz con leche* ("rice with milk"). To prepare this recipe, obtain one cinnamon stick, the peel of one lemon, 1/2 cup of uncooked rice, 1/2 teaspoon of vanilla extract, 7 tablespoons of white sugar, and 1 1/2 cups of milk.

Drop the cinnamon stick and a bit of finely grated lemon peel into 2 cups of water and bring to a rolling boil. Add the uncooked rice, reduce the heat to low, and stir well until the boiling ceases. Cover the pot and allow the rice to simmer until it is tender.

In a small bowl, mix the white vanilla extract, sugar, and milk. Stir well. When the rice is tender, add the milk mixture to the rice; turn the heat back up to high and stir vigorously until it begins to boil. Reduce the heat to low again, continuing to stir the rice, uncovered, until it thickens. Be careful: Allow neither the milk to scald nor the rice to burn. It will take another 15 minutes of stirring and cooking before the rice thickens; when it does, the dish is done. Serve this to egun while still steaming hot. The food remains with them overnight; the following morning, with the oracle obí, the diviner determines how egun want their offering discarded.

## Ebó Elese Yemayá
## *(Ebó at the Feet of Yemayá)*

No matter how Odí falls or to whom the larishe is directed, in all composites of Odí propitiating Yemayá is wise. Here, she is an important orisha and can bring evolution to the client. The following eboses are native to Yemayá and this family of odu.* The diviner may prescribe freely from these when advising his client on how to placate this spirit.

### *Baked Red Snapper Fillets*

Like many orishas, Yemayá loves to eat. The more lavish the dish one provides, the greater the iré she will give. The following recipe is for one of her favorites: baked red snapper fillets. One can offer this dish to certain other spirits as well; however, this dish calls for watermelon salsa to make it distinctly Yemayá's. Since this recipe serves eight and her number is seven, one may serve a single red snapper to Elegguá (remember, it is always wise to propitiate him) or eat the extra fillet oneself, sharing dinner with Yemayá.

To prepare this recipe, gather the following ingredients for the salsa: 2 cups of diced watermelon (all seeds removed), 2 cups of diced star fruit (also known as carambola), 2 cups of trimmed and diced fennel, 1/2 cup of orange juice, two tablespoons of virgin olive oil, 1/2 cup of minced red onion, 6 tablespoons of minced tarragon, and 2 tablespoons of lemon juice.

To prepare the fillets, gather the following ingredients: 2 teaspoons of salt, ground black pepper (to taste), four cloves of minced garlic, 2 tablespoons of lemon juice, 1/2 cup of orange juice, 2 tablespoons of Pernod, 4 tablespoons of virgin olive oil, and eight 1/2-pound red snapper fillets.

The first step is to prepare the salsa. In a large plastic or glass dish (not metal, as it is reactive with the ingredients and alters the taste), combine the watermelon, star fruit, fennel, orange juice, olive oil, red onion, tarragon, and lemon juice, stirring lightly. Cover the dish and let the flavors mingle at room temperature for 30 to 45 minutes. Do not serve the salsa before this amount of time, as a slight aging is essential for taste.

Preheat the oven to 400 degrees Fahrenheit. While the oven preheats, prepare the marinade for the fillets by combining the salt, pepper, garlic, lemon juice, orange juice, Pernod, and olive oil in a large ceramic baking pan (again, do not use metal as this reacts with the ingredients and alters the marinade's flavor). Mix briskly; a thorough mixing is essential to flavor.

Place each fillet in the marinade with its skin side down. Allow this to soak briefly before flipping the fillet so that its skin side faces up. (The skin side must be facing up or the fillet will not cook properly.) Over the skin, put one slice of star fruit (taken from the salsa) on each fillet. Bake immediately for 10 minutes, then check the fillets. If they flake easily when poked with a fork, they are done; if not, cook an additional 2 minutes.

Offer Yemayá seven of these fillets on a large platter, with a bowl of watermelon salsa on the side. If one is serving Elegguá, give him his fillet and salsa first. The next day, the client discards the food in the ocean.

Note that if one gives a small dinner party in Yemayá's honor, this is a tasty delicacy to serve. The recipe is easily doubled to cater large groups.

### *Stuffed Gourds*

This is a simpler adimú that will also appease Yemayá. To prepare this offering, the client will need to provide the following ingredients: seven small jícaras, toasted corn, smoked fish, jutía, epó, seven guinea peppers, honey, molasses, and a large serving platter.

Fill each gourd with toasted corn; over this, sprinkle the smoked fish, jutía, and epó. Place one guinea pepper in each gourd and then cover each with the honey and molasses. Serve the stuffed gourds to Yemayá on a platter. The ebó stays with her for seven days. On the eighth day, the client removes the ebó and discards it in the ocean.

*These eboses for Yemayá should be discarded in the ocean. If the ocean is not nearby, any large body of water will do.

### *Ñame Balls*

Boil a large ñame until soft. Mash and mix this with molasses, epó, smoked fish, jutía, honey, and toasted corn. Form seven balls. Serve to Yemayá, along with two seven-day candles, and allow the offering to remain with her for seven days. At the end of this time, the client takes the ebó to the ocean.

### *Watermelon*

Take the pulp out of a large watermelon. Serve this, neatly sliced, to Yemayá on a platter. Fill the watermelon's shell with gofio, seven balls formed from boiled ñame, toasted corn, seven smoked fish, seven guinea peppers, honey, and molasses. Leave this with Yemayá for seven days. On the eighth morning, the client discards the ebó in the ocean.

### *Rogación for Elegguá and Yemayá*

When a client must propitiate Elegguá and Yemayá together and the odu marks a rogación, the following ebó will satisfy all these requirements, cleansing the client's orí and putting him under the guidance of these two orishas. To fulfill this ceremony, the client must come dressed in white, bringing two coconuts, two white candles, a white plate, the derecho, a grass mat, two white seven-day candles, and twenty-one fresh fruits. The priest puts Elegguá at Yemayá's feet; the client presents his derecho, and the priest gives the rogación before both orishas. After the cleansing, he offers the fruits to Elegguá and Yemayá, lighting the two white seven-day candles. The client gives foribale, praying for his heart's desires. After seven days the client removes the fruits and discards them in the ocean.

### *Peace in the Ilé Ocha*

If the client is a priest with many godchildren, Odí foreshadows separation and treason in his own house. There is ebó to solve this. First, he must plan a day to invite all his godchildren for dinner, letting everyone know that this is in honor of Elegguá and Yemayá and all are expected to attend. On the morning of that day, he should sacrifice two white roosters to both Elegguá and Yemayá. One goes to Elegguá, but he shares it with Yemayá; the other goes to Yemayá, but she shares it with him. Once sacrificed, the birds should be plucked, cleaned, and cooked in a dish (of the priest's choosing) to serve that evening for dinner. The priest also sets up a small throne for the two spirits, laying out a small offering of fruits to them.

Everyone who comes through the initiate's door that day must pay foribale to the two orishas. Before leaving, those who came to dinner must take some fruit from the orishas' throne. Once done, this ebó will bring peace back to the priest's house of ocha.

# The First Composite Odu of Odí, Odí Okana (7-1)

## The Proverbs of Odí Okana

- The rich will envy the poor.
- One who dreams with the dead or with the sea cannot fear either one.

## The Message of Odí Okana

When a casting of seven mouths, Odí, precedes a casting of one mouth, Okana, the odu Odí Okana is open. The diviner says, "Maferefún Yemayá! Maferefún Oshún! Maferefún Shangó!" Yemayá not only owns this family of signs, but also reigns supreme in this letter. Odí Okana is hot and volatile, but if placated, Yemayá will soothe what seeks to spoil the client's dreams. Even if this letter offers no larishe to her, the diviner must prescribe ebó. This odu signals that Oshún loves the client, and the client adores her; however, he loves Oshún for all the wrong reasons. The sweetness she brings enamors him, yet before this sign's energy passes his faith in her will be tested. Life will get bitter and tumultuous. No matter what happens, the client must continue to show her respect, for when this sign passes, she will shower him with love again. In this odu Shangó stands close to the client, protecting him and fighting his wars. No matter who claims this person's head, Shangó is his king, and the client must treat him well. The diviner should encourage the client to adorn Shangó's shrine as one would a king's throne; he should give him silken pañuelos and a crown. Shangó will see to it that the client overcomes all.

Odí Okana is a letter of stubbornness; it causes most of the client's problems. The diviner should tell the client, "Your own refusal to listen to advice is what has brought you to this point, yet even now, you are not truly listening to me. If you hope to evolve, you must seek good counsel in all your affairs." Men who come in this sign are adulterous; while the client might have a lover, his eyes wander. When the chance to cheat comes, he takes advantage of this. The diviner must advise him against adultery; conception will occur. If the client is a woman, he must advise her, too, against extramarital affairs, for she will become pregnant by her lover. Birth control is a necessity, and abortion is taboo. Birth defects are the scourge of Odí Okana, and any child conceived now is in danger. The diviner should inform the client that venereal diseases transmit easily with this sign's energy. Personal responsibility is the key to averting this osogbo. However, the diloggún says this client probably will not heed these warnings; he will get into trouble anyway.

In addition, the diviner should keep in mind the following points:

- "Maferefún Obatalá!" While Odí Okana tends toward unbalance, Obatalá restores the client's equilibrium. If nothing else is offered to Obatalá in this odu, the diviner should have the client pay foribale him. If the trials that come prove to be too severe or overwhelming for the client, he should return to his godparent's home for a rogación before Obatalá; after the rogación, he should give him an adimú of fresh fruits.
- Evil eyes watch this person; many tongues wag about his business, gossiping about what they see. The client must beware of this. While he might see himself as poor and suffering, others see him as well off, maybe even wealthy, and they are jealous. In truth the client is neither poor nor wealthy, but his life hangs in a delicate balance in which he could prosper or fail. The jealousy around him is gathering, almost as a curse, and if he is not careful, it will cause him to fall.
- If the client is a man and is dating a woman or is married, his lover suffered a miscarriage or abortion in the past. If conception is difficult now, she may be paying for past transgressions. He must offer ebó now and ensure that his wife or lover does not abort a child in the future.
- If this odu opens in strong iré, the next child conceived will bring blessings. The client should do all that is possible to ensure the well-being of both the mother and the unborn child.
- Infectious disease will destroy someone the client knows. When someone close to the client falls ill, he should take that person to a physician immediately.

## The Prohibitions of Odí Okana

- Abortion is taboo. Neither men nor women for whom this odu falls may recommend abortion to another.
- Adultery is forbidden in this odu. Avoid extramarital affairs.
- While discrimination and prejudice are prevalent in one's life, one may not discriminate against or judge others. Give up racial, sexual, and moral issues.

## The Eboses of Odí Okana

If the client is an aleyo without elekes, he must take this initiation quickly. He must receive the elekes of Elegguá and Ogún at this ceremony as well, since they have the aché to resolve many of his issues.

Odí Okana also mandates the reception of the warriors; if the client does not have them, he must make preparations to undergo this initiation as soon as possible.

Finally, Yemayá stands up to solve many of the client's problems. He must pray to her, leaving all the evil others have done at her feet with an adimú. She will protect the client from harm. If these eboses are not enough to close the session, the diviner must determine if she demands a specific ebó, asking, "Ebó elese Yemayá?" If the answer is yes, he uses the diloggún to mark the appropriate offering.

For a man, this odu can suggest that he left a

spouse or lover because he was not satisfied with her. However, he did not make a clean break. Instead, he left her only after falling in love with another woman. This second lover satisfies him, but now the first interferes with the relationship. She might even use witchcraft (unconscious or deliberate) against him and his current mate. Odí Okana gives an ebó to fight this: Find a spider's web spun close to one's front door. Wrap a picture or personal article of one's ex-lover inside this. Give the article, still wrapped in the web, to Elegguá. He will take away the witchcraft she sends.

If these eboses are not enough to close the session and the client is an aleyo, the diviner must turn to the eboses of the parent odu, Odí (see page 346). Something there is needed for the client's evolution. It the client is an initiate, the diviner has two more options for eboses to investigate:

- If this reading is an itá with a diloggún that does not belong to Elegguá, the diviner asks, "Ebó elese Elegguá?" If the answer is yes, he must feed the client's Elegguá a goat. The next day, Elegguá gives an itá. This ebó puts the initiate on the path to evolution.
- Aganyú's reception is a possibility. The diviner asks, "Koshé Aganyú?" If the answer is yes, the client must make arrangements for the lavatorio as soon as possible.

If the odu remains open, the diviner must turn to the eboses of the parent odu, Odí.

## The Second Composite Odu of Odí, Odí Ejioko (7-2)

### The Proverbs of Odí Ejioko

- Riches will come when the business is born.
- The sick are cured.
- He who eats a lot is killed by his own mouth.

### The Message of Odí Ejioko

When a cast of seven mouths, Odí, precedes a cast of two mouths, Eji Oko, the odu Odí Ejioko is open on the mat. There are two other names for this sign: Odí Oyekun and Odí Yeku. When it opens, the diviner says, "Maferefún Olófin!" Through Odí Ejioko's energy Olófin gave nature the power to renew itself again and again; Olófin blessed all the earth (but not the animals; that happened in the family of Ogbe) with the gift of regeneration and procreation. The diviner praises Yemayá, Obatalá, Shangó, and Elegguá here as well, saying to each, "Maferefún!" Yemayá is close to the client, so close that he might be her child. One of her spirits stands close to him, and if he is to evolve, he must give light and peace to that entity. Obatalá brings peace and refreshment to the client's orí when this letter becomes heated and volatile. This sign speaks of war and death, and when this person is caught up in these troubles, Shangó will defend him to the end. Finally, this person's life is caught up in a volatile cycle, and how he acts and reacts now will influence his future. Elegguá is fate and destiny; he alone can keep the client's feet on the road to evolution.

This hot letter gives much advice to the client; he must heed all of it if he hopes to evolve in life. To begin, the diviner should tell the client that he has much aché with dreams; he wakes frequently at night, remembering fragments, and as the days pass he realizes that these dreams were foreshadowing events in his life. Unfortunately, he doesn't always realize the prediction until it is too late. Large groups of people come to him when he dreams; he sees faces of those he has never met before. What he has yet to realize is that those faces belong to the dead. Although not all of these spirits belong to his spiritual court, they all are clamoring for his attention. They come to him because he embodies light and strength. One spirit, that of a black man, that comes to him in his dreams does belong to his spiritual court, and he takes him to these gatherings of the dead. This spirit is his protector and ally, and he will help keep the client from danger on his nocturnal journeys. The diviner should advise the client to cleanse himself every day over his egun; when he awakens in the morning, he carries heavy vibrations back from these foreign spirits. The client should attend frequent spiritual masses as well, for these will give light and strength to his own spiritual court.

The diviner may also explore the following issues with the client:

- If the client is a woman or a homosexual male, she or he is in love with an incompatible man. The client must not despair or cry over this inappropriate love, for someone more suitable is coming. This person must make an ebó of thanksgiving to Oshún.
- The client forgets about his godparents. Sometimes he speaks ill of them. This must stop now, and he must learn to be a better godchild.
- Odí Ejioko, especially in the osogbo of ano or ikú, warns of breast cancer in both men and women. The diviner must advise regular self-exams and impress upon the client the need for regular mammography. Men might scoff at this warning, but breast cancer is a danger for both sexes.
- This sign speaks of drugs and the damage they do. This damage extends beyond the drug user, for those close to addicts suffer as well. Danger could also come through a random attack or robbery from someone under the influence of drugs. The client must stay away from those who abuse drugs, and if the client lives with someone who has a drug problem, he should consider moving. Note that this warning applies not only to street drugs but also to prescription drugs.
- If the client comes seeking advice for one who is terminally ill (himself or another), Odí Ejioko promises a slow, gradual recovery or remission. The healing will not be easy, however, and the one who is ill will want to give up before the worst has passed. It will take massive amounts of medical intervention and ebó to save this life; the client must be prepared for a battle.
- Finally, this client must be wary of his own friends. Most of his misfortunes come by their hands, even though he may not be aware of this. Many of them do not mean him harm, but their own actions have serious implications for him.

## The Prohibitions of Odí Ejioko

- Do not make fun of anyone, especially those with handicaps, for they are Obatalá's true children.
- Do not be around drunks or those using illegal drugs. Do not become intoxicated.
- Avoid arguments, fights, and gossip with or about other priests in this religion. Do not make negative comments about initiates of this religion. The orishas see what their children do and will punish them on their own.
- Be wary of leftovers and reheated foods. Odí Ejioko brings sickness and death through food-borne poisons.

## The Eboses of Odí Ejioko

Regardless of its orientation, when this pattern opens three eboses are mandated. First, the client needs seven spiritual baths with the following ingredients: cascarilla, leaves from an orange tree, *flores cordiales*, and *quita maldición.* [AU: need definitions for 2 preceding terms]Crush these herbs in a large bowl seasoned for Yemayá; sing to Osain while making the omiero. Allow these leaves to soak overnight before straining them from the water. Once strained, add plenty of crushed cascarilla to the bath. The client should take one bath every night for seven nights in this mixture.

The second ebó marked by this letter is the reception of the elekes. If the client cannot afford the full initiation at this time, he must have Yemayá's necklace; the diviner should instruct the client to wear it every day.

Finally, Shangó figures prominently in this odu, and even if he offers no advice in this letter, the client should give him at least a token adimú. If after these prescriptions the letter will not close, Shangó might want something specific; to determine if this is the case, the diviner should ask, "Ebó elese Shangó?" If the answer is yes, he uses the diloggún to mark the appropriate offering.

If Odí Ejioko still will not close, the diviner should explore the following options:

- The client needs spiritual cleansings to egun weekly; this will keep him from danger.
- If Odí Ejioko will not close, Elegguá may need ebó. The diviner asks, "Ebó elese Elegguá?" If the answer is yes and the odu is in any type of

iré, he requires a simple adimú. If, however, the sign is in osogbo, give him a rooster. If Elegguá takes no sacrifice, the client must offer him something to keep his goodwill. A basket of fruits will cool and refresh this spirit.

- Ogún may be standing up for ebó. The diviner asks, "Ebó elese Ogún?" If he claims ebó here, give Ogún a rooster. If the osogbo of this odu is great, immediately after the sacrifice to Ogún one must feed the earth a feathered animal. These two eboses fight witchcraft and will help the client avoid an early grave.
- If the odu refuses closure, the client should provide a hollow plastic doll; the priest packs this doll with seven of Yemayá's herbs and dresses it in blue gingham to honor the orisha. The client should give this doll a place of prominence at home and give her frequent adimú. This is one of his main spiritual protectors and will lead him away from osogbo.
- If someone in the client's house is ill, that person must have a rogación before Obatalá's shrine. If the sick person cannot make it to the diviner's house, the client must come in his place, wearing something that belongs to the afflicted. The diviner rips the clothing off his body, bathes him in Obatalá's omiero, dresses him in white, and then gives him a rogación in the sick person's name. The following day, this client returns for another bath and rogación for himself.
- In this sign, it is important that the client have the Ibeyi; this does not need to be marked as ebó. If the client has the Ibeyi, however, and the odu refuses closure, the diviner should determine if they need ebó, asking, "Ebó elese los Ibeyi?" If the answer is yes, the client should give a party in their honor.

If these eboses are not enough to close the odu and the client is an aleyo or an aborisha, the diviner should turn to the eboses of the parent odu, Odí (see page 346). Something there is needed for this client's evolution. If the client is an initiate, the diviner should consider the following eboses:

- A tambor may hold the solution to the client's troubles. First, the diviner must ask if a tambor is required. If the answer is yes, he must then ask if the orisha whose diloggún is being consulted will claim the tambor. If this orisha refuses, the diviner must mark the tambor for Yemayá, Shangó, Obatalá, or Elegguá. If none of these will take the tambor, the drum is marked for egun.
- If this client is an initiate of Shangó, that orisha wants him to consider moving to the country, to a home with lots of land. There, he is to raise a white horse in honor of his crowning orisha.

If these are not enough to close the session, the diviner must turn to the eboses of the parent odu, Odí.

## The Third Composite Odu of Odí, Odí Ogundá (7-3)

### The Proverbs of Odí Ogundá

- Let others eat what you cannot finish.
- The orishas are angry.
- What is known is not questioned.
- Look at what is in front of your eyes.
- Guess the riddle.

### The Message of Odí Ogundá

When a casting of seven mouths, Odí, precedes a casting of three mouths, Ogundá, the odu Odí Ogundá is open on the mat. Of all composites existing in this family, none is more protean or martial than this one. The diviner must work quickly to avoid this sign's spiritual heat. First, he makes the sacred gesture of Ogundá, patting the abdomen three times with open palms and then blowing over them as if directing a delicate powder toward the client. This gesture sends the odu's full weight back on him; the essences aroused will not attach to any other initiate in the room. The diviner then pays homage to Ogún, Yemayá, Elegguá, and Inle, saying to each, "Maferefún!" The aché of all four will be needed to settle the client's issues. For Odí Ogundá is a caustic sign; it appears when severity is called for. It is harsh, never frivolous or flippant in nature. No matter whether it comes iré or osogbo, it emphasizes all the bad Odí has to give. There are issues of disrespect and disobedience not only with Yemayá but also with the client's orí. Before the session gives closure, all these issues need to be aired.

While the family of Odí is specific regarding issues with one's mother, Odí Ogundá flags serious complications between the client and his father. When this odu opens in iré, the orishas say that the past is irrelevant: No matter what happened between father and child, there is a spiritual need for one to forgive the other. But this odu also signals stubbornness, and the client will insist that all is well; he will say that there is nothing to heal. The diviner knows to trust the odu and not the client's words. If this pattern comes in an osogbo, the chasm between father and child is severe. The osogbo that has opened will give clues as to the problems the father and son face. If the osogbo is ano or ikú, the implications for this person's father are serious, indeed; the orishas are saying that the child's hate or disdain for his father is more than warranted. The father has led a vile life and hurt his own flesh and blood in many ways. He is all but beyond help now; here the orishas say he doesn't deserve help. But if the father is willing to change, the trials he suffers might be lessened. The diviner must tell the client that his father needs to see, urgently, a physician; his health is bad, and his time on the earth is coming to an end. He should be cautious about having surgery, however. His ill health is his punishment; he is paying for all the wrongs he has done in his life. The client must try to forgive him now so there are no issues after he passes; the orishas themselves are destroying him for what he has done to his family.

When a casting of Odí Ogundá opens on the mat, the diviner should also explore the following issues with the client:

- This client must live by making sacrifice and ebó; if he does this, he will grow to be very prosperous, for the orishas will bless all that he does.
- If the client is a married male, his wife is bored with him sexually; she may be thinking about leaving. He himself is thinking about having an affair, for he is bored with his wife. This marriage can be saved, but it will take a lot of the client's effort to do so.
- If the client is a married woman, she is being unfaithful to her husband in either body or mind. Adulterous thoughts are as bad as true adultery, for right now she is in the emotional state to carry out her fantasies. The diviner should tell the woman that of all the men she has ever loved, her current husband is the only one who will come back to her time and time again. If she opens honest communication with him and remains faithful, the marriage can be saved.

## The Prohibitions of Odí Ogundá

- In this odu, one must avoid all vices. Even if the client is healthy, the vices that he entertains are slowly killing him. They might take him to the operating table.
- Gossip among blood will destroy the family; do not gossip with relatives.
- There are food taboos in this letter. Do not eat rooster, and do not consume the inner parts of any animal.
- Do not carry weapons.

## The Eboses of Odí Ogundá

After Odí Ogundá has closed, no one, not even those aleyos present but uninvolved in the session, may leave until performing a specific ebó for Ogún. On behalf of everyone present, the diviner smears a piece of raw beef liberally with epó. He wraps the beef in brown paper, shows it to Ogún, and petitions him to cleanse all in the house. Beginning with himself and then moving from the client to the godparents, priests and priestesses in elder status, aborishas who have taken initiations, and then aleyos who have taken nothing of ocha, the diviner rubs everyone in the house from head to toe with the ebó. After all are cleansed, the diviner leaves the meat to sit with Ogún overnight. The next morning, he takes the ebó into the street, saying, "Eshu batie sode" ("Eshu takes the negativity [of the reading]"). After returning home, the diviner casts the oracle for himself to ensure that he does not suffer from Ogundá. In this way, the diviner is assured that neither he nor anyone else will be harmed by Ogundá's energies.

Note that if the oracle refuses closure no matter what the diviner tries to mark or discuss, this initial prescription of ebó might need alteration. The orishas may decide that it needs to be taken not to the street but to the trash, a crossroads, railroad tracks, a river, a lake, the ocean, or the woods. A diviner with the knowledge, aché, and experience will know when this needs to be altered to bring closure to odu. Also, those persons present at the reading who have received the warriors should perform this same ebó to their own Ogún when they return home to ensure that the harsh energies of Ogundá have been removed. Those aleyos who were in the diviner's home during the reading who have not received the warriors might consider sitting for a session with the diloggún soon. They may need to take the initiation of the warriors for their own spiritual protection.

Having made this prescription, the diviner then moves on to the eboses specific to the client. To begin, if the client does not have the elekes, he must take this initiation as soon as possible to avoid the inherent osogbos of this odu. If he cannot receive the elekes within a week, the client should at least receive Yemayá's necklace and wear it every day. Soon, he must also receive his warriors. If the client already has the warriors, the diviner must determine if they need ebó, asking, "Ebó elese Elegguá?" and "Ebó elese Ogún?" If the answer to either question is yes, he uses the diloggún to mark the appropriate offering.

This letter can be difficult to close. If the diviner attempts to close the oracle but is refused, he should consider the following:

- We say that in Odí Ogundá the orishas are unhappy or angry, even when the odu comes in iré. Any spirit that has spoken to the client during the course of this reading might demand an ebó as payment for past offenses. Examining them one by one, the diviner should ask, "Ebó elese [orisha's name]?" If the answer is yes, he should use the diloggún to mark what is required. If an orisha who has spoken does not demand ebó, the client should still present an adimú to soothe that spirit.
- If these eboses have been prescribed and the odu remains open, every week for the next seven weeks the client must have a rogación of the head before Obatalá's shrine. Use the following ingredients in each rogación: fruit, milk, coconut, water, and white bread. These rogaciónes will feed and strengthen his orí. If the osogbo of this letter is severe, the diviner may also consider eborí.
- Exactly three months from the date of the reading, the client must give to the orisha who offers larishe in this odu the same ebó that was marked in this reading.
- There are many African spirits around this client. He must have a spiritual mass to investigate them. He should follow the advice of the espiritistas exactly, for these are ways in which he will settle his spiritual court and find evolution.
- If a woman has opened in this odu, the diviner should tell her that some day in the future she will conceive. When she does, to guarantee both her health and that of her unborn child, she must have a rogación of the abdomen three times to Yemayá. She should have this series of rogaciónes immediately after discovering pregnancy. After each, she should offer ebó to Ogún so that the child is delivered naturally, and not by the knife.
- If osogbo has come and health issues have been identified for the client's father, there is ebó to save his life if the client wishes to make that ebó (remember—there is a serious rift in this relationship, and the odu says the father deserves what he is experiencing). To the orisha that stood up to offer a larishe for this sign, the client should make ebó in his father's name. With the diloggún, the diviner must mark what it will take to save the father's life. Realize, however, that this ebó will be no simple affair, and it will only lessen his pain and extend his life. It will

not be a cure, nor will it be a spiritual indulgence.

If the prescriptions made thus far do not end the session and the client is an aleyo or an aborisha, the diviner must now consider the eboses of the parent odu, Odí (see page 346). If the client is an initiate, the diviner should consider the following:

- The client could need to receive the diloggún of Ogún; make arrangements for this ceremony to happen as soon as possible. If the client cannot afford the expenses of this initiation now, he should offer a rooster and two pigeons to Ogún and receive this orisha's eleke. He must wear the eleke every day until he receives the diloggún.
- Odí Ogundá may mark the sacrifice of a four-legged animal (and an itá). The diviner should ask the oracle if an orisha needs four legs. If the answer is yes, he should ask if Yemayá will claim the ebó. If the answer is yes, the diviner must prescribe an itá and a huge feast cooked and given in her honor; the more people fed by the animal, the greater the iré that will come from the ceremony. If Yemayá does not want the four legs, the diviner should ask if the orisha whose diloggún is being consulted will claim it. If this spirit wants four legs, no itá is necessary. If this spirit will not accept the sacrifice, the diviner must question Ogún. If he will not take four legs, the sacrifice must be made to egun. A sacrifice to Ogún or to egun requires an itá.
- If the diloggún will not mark four legs, the diviner should try to mark the reception of the knife.
- If the odu still refuses closure, the diviner should consider for the client the reception of Inle or Osain. First, the diviner should ask, "Koshé Inle?" Then he should ask, "Koshé Osain?" The reception of one or both orishas may be required to successfully close this letter.

Barring closure for an initiate, the diviner must now consider the eboses of the parent odu, Odí. Something there is needed for the client's evolution.

# The Fourth Composite Odu of Odí, Odí Irosun (7-4)

## The Proverbs of Odí Irosun

- By my own hand, I made myself king.
- He who makes the law lays the trap.
- All the body sleeps except the nose, for it did not make ebó.
- A king is made by his own hand.
- No one knows what lies at the bottom of the ocean.
- Salt for the road; the orishas will be with you all your nights.
- The machete in my hands went when I made myself king.
- It was ocha that made me a king.

## The Message of Odí Irosun

When a casting of seven mouths, Odí, precedes a casting of four mouths, Irosun, the odu Odí Irosun is open on the mat. Three forces are prominent here: Yemayá, egun, and Olokun. The diviner honors all three, saying to each, "Maferefún!" The client who opens in this odu comes with a great need, a spiritual void consuming him slowly like a cancer. Such is the client's emotional suffering that his need must be fulfilled, and the three forces found here can help him do this. The diviner should tell the client that once even the earth was lacking. There was no food, no water, no money, and no aché. Creation had consumed all these in its greed. To save the world, Olófin gathered together all the orishas; he wanted to fix what was broken through their hands, not his. Olófin asked each, "What do you need to live?" Some spirits asked for food, and they were fed. Others asked for water, and their thirst was quenched. Money and riches, beauty and fame—all these were among their requests. Yet Yemayá, the last to be asked, wanted aché. Her wish was granted. Because all things have aché, and because aché gives all things, Yemayá became the richest of all the spirits.

Before telling the client this story, however, the diviner should ask him one question: "What do you need to live?" Because of the energy inherent in this odu, he will answer with the usual demands—food, water, clothing, shelter—or perhaps make a more specific request, identifying what brought him to the mat. However, to find fulfillment, the client must turn to Yemayá; she is the queen of aché, and by her grace he can have all his heart desires. The diviner should tell him, "You are empty inside; Yemayá tells me this. She also says that she loves you and will give you all that you need. But you must make ebó to her, and when you complete your sacrifice, you must not ask merely for what you want. Ask for the aché to achieve what you want. For aché is everything, and without it you have nothing."

Part of the client's longing can be filled spiritually by his egun. In Odí Irosun one's ancestors come clamoring for attention; the most ancient forces whose names have been forgotten by their descendants arise from the shadows. Obscured by generations of neglect, the client's ancient egun are still a part of him, and they demand what is theirs by right: worship and adoration. They also come bearing warnings of falsehood and treason. The client is surrounded by wicked people; they bear vehemence, and it drips off them like poison from a snake's fangs. But all his enemies wear masks; they masquerade as friends. Odí Irosun offers a solution with egun for this: The client must have a collection of seven masks hung over his bóveda. By giving the masks to egun, he prevents others from hiding. One powerful spiritual entity, in particular, has attached herself to the client. In death, she is very much like Yemayá, having great aché with the ocean. The diviner should tell the client that this spirit will bless him if he works with her.

In addition, the diviner should explore the following issues with the client:

- No matter Odí Irosun's orientation, sickness is foreshadowed. Someone ill might live with the client now. He must guard against respiratory ailments; asthma, asphyxiation, choking, and drowning are dangers.
- Odí Irosun marks one who hears the ocean in his head continually, the same sound one hears when a conch is held to the ear. Often, he feels like the ocean itself is inside his head. In iré, this is a blessing, and if he listens carefully to this sound, Yemayá's spirits (her deceased children) will whisper secrets to him. If the letter comes in osogbo, the client could lose his hearing one day. He must take care of his hearing.
- The client sleeps deeply at night but is awakened by fitful dreams. He sees his enemies in his dreams. He should remember these faces, for the dreams will save his life.
- This client must do all that he can spiritually to prepare himself for ocha. The orishas are coming to claim his head, and soon. If this person does not prepare to make ocha, he will have a war between his orí and his physical head and between himself and his guardian orisha. He will not win this war; he must make ocha, for it is his destiny.

## The Prohibitions of Odí Irosun

- Do not visit people in jail. Do not participate in any activity that makes one feel confined or jailed.
- Do not eat crabs or any animal that can walk backward. Do not consume spicy foods.
- Stay away from people who drink a lot of alcohol or use illegal drugs.
- Do not cheat on one's lover; if one cheats, the person who brings true happiness will be lost.

## The Eboses of Odí Irosun

When Odí Irosun opens, the diviner must prescribe a variety of eboses for egun, regardless of the sign's orientation. First, he must instruct the client on the construction of a bóveda. In all composites of Odí, it must have seven glasses of fresh water. The client must always keep a single white candle lit for the bóveda; he must never let it go dark.

If the client is an aborisha, the diviner must send him to a *palero* (a priest of Palo Mayombe) immediately for a thorough consultation; this person has much to do with *madre de agua* (a nkisi of Palo Mayombe) and may need the initiation known as rayado. If the client is an aborisha or initiate with rayado but lacking ngangas, he should consider receiving one. If this person already has a nganga, he or she should consider the reception of madre de agua. This nkisi has the potential to bring great things to the client's life. While Palo Mayombe is woven into our religious beliefs, it still functions as a religion separate from our own, and the diloggún can only hint as to what is needed from that faith. The word of the palero consulted is final on these issues.

In Odí Irosun, a very powerful spirit accompanies the client; so strong is she that he has felt her presence many times, but he has not realized who she is. This spirit has much to do with both Yemayá and madre de agua. If the client works with her, she will help him evolve. The diviner should prescribe the following: First, the client finds a hollow plastic doll that he feels best represents this spirit. The diviner packs at least seven and no more than twenty-one of Yemayá's herbs inside the doll. From the same number and kind of leaves, the diviner prepares an herbal infusion and washes the doll with it after packing it with aché. Then he dresses her in blue-and-white gingham. On the third day after her washing, the client receives her, takes her home, and hosts a mass in her honor. The espiritistas present will not only discover the spirit's name, but will also tell the client how he is to work with her. He must follow their advice exactly, for this is how both he and the spirit will evolve.

The client must also offer an ebó to Yemayá in order to gain the aché he needs to fulfill his life's desires. The sacrifice for Yemayá's aché in Odí Irosun is simple: a large basket, lined with blue cloth and filled with seven coconuts that have been sanded and painted blue and white. Covered with an elaborate pañuelo, this offering remains with Yemayá for seven days. On the night of the seventh day, the client cleanses himself with the pañuelo and puts it over Yemayá's sopera. She will remove what hinders his evolution. The client then discards the coconuts in the ocean.

When Odí Irosun opens with an osogbo, the diviner must prescribe additional eboses for Obatalá, Elegguá, and Olokun. First, the client must have a rogación to Obatalá using grated coconut, grated cocoa butter, crushed cascarilla, and four apple snails. After the rogación, he must offer to Elegguá an ebó of three baby chickens, feeding these to him behind the front door to seal it from evil. Finally, Olokun demands sacrifice. After feeding her, the client should have an agbán. These three eboses will save the client from osogbo.

Having made these prescriptions, the diviner may now attempt to close the oracle. If it will not close, he should explore the following possibilities:

- The rogación may need to be sodidé. The diviner should ask, "Rogación sodidé?" If the answer is yes, the rogación begins with the client's feet and ends with his head; this elevates his orí into ocha. The diviner might also consider eborí, asking, "Eborí?" If the answer is yes, the rogación should be followed by the feeding of two white pigeons or doves to the client's head.
- If this sign opens in an osogbo that speaks of curses of witchcraft, the following ebó must be done: The client should bring a single egg to the diviner, who prays to it over his Elegguá. The client then cleanses himself with the egg and takes it to a crossroads. There he must break it and leave without looking back.
- The client must love Elegguá dearly; he should have a pocket Elegguá that he carries with him always.
- If the client's mother has not passed away, she could fall ill very soon, and the child must make ebó quickly to save her. He should have a rogación of the head using four snails and give Yemayá that which she requires to save his mother's life. Even if this ebó is done, the mother could still become ill, and the client is advised to spend as much time with her as possible, ensuring that proper medical attention is given for all physical complaints. A small health concern can easily become a major health problem.
- If the client's mother is alive, she might soon die. This sign, however, does offer an ebó to save her life and possibly forestall illness: The client must pay for his mother to have a rogación of the head before Yemayá. The

rogación must use grated coconut, grated cocoa butter, crushed cascarilla, molasses, and seven live snails. If illness comes in spite of this rogación, the client's mother should sit for a session with the diloggún. The orishas are saying that her life can be spared if potent eboses are made.
- If the client's mother has already passed, this odu dictates that a sacrifice be given to the drains in the kitchen sink on her behalf, to Yemayá Asesu, for only then will his mother's spirit find peace and will he find evolution.

If these prescriptions are not enough to close the reading, the diviner must turn to the eboses of the parent odu, Odí (see page 346). Something there is needed for the client's evolution.

## The Fifth Composite Odu of Odí, Odí Oché (7-5)

### The Proverbs of Odí Oché

- One is absolved through lack of proof.
- All things are good to eat, but not all things are good to say.
- If the worms eat the eggs hens lay, the eggs will never hatch.
- If the head does not sell you, no one can buy you.
- The feet are taking the body to the auction block.
- The hen sits on an empty nest.
- If the hen abandons the nest, insects will eat her eggs.

### The Message of Odí Oché

When a casting of seven mouths, Odí, precedes a casting of five mouths, Oché, the odu Odí Oché is open on the mat. This is a powerful pattern that can bring great iré or great osogbo, depending on the client's own actions and his own head. Here is born the place where two waters meet, the ocean and the river, and the river and the lake. Those who open in this letter in an itá are known as the "children of two waters" and are especially blessed by both Yemayá and Oshún.

The diviner begins by saying, "Maferefún Yemayá! Maferefún Oshún! Maferefún Inle!" All three orishas offer grace to the client, and as soon as possible he must go to brackish water (where fresh and salt waters meet) to make ebó.

The diviner begins the reading by telling the client this: "No matter what you have done, the orishas forgive you; you are absolved because there is no proof for judging. But from this moment on, know that they watch all you do and say. The orishas want to know how you will conduct yourself with your newfound freedom and forgiveness, and they will judge you even more harshly the next time you are immoral."

Coming in iré, the client must be cautious; he is surrounded by parasites. He has many friends and acquaintances who are friendly for the sake of their own convenience. Each wants something in return for his or her friendship, and all will abandon him in his hour of greatest need. Iré, however, promises that if the client is cautious and makes ebó, the orishas will save him from harm. He will not be used by those who have their own interests in mind.

When the letter comes in osogbo, the meaning of this sign is greatly changed. The client is absolved of his past transgressions, but the orishas say that it is he who is the parasite. He uses others for his own pleasure and gratification, and if this behavior continues, the orishas themselves will put a stop to his actions.

Note that in any orientation, this sign speaks of parasitic infections. Ticks, fleas, lice, scabies, fungal infections, and internal parasites are all a danger. The client must be fanatical about his cleanliness; hygiene is key to avoiding these infestations.

This sign in any orientation presages many dangers beyond parasites and parasitic infections. Odí Oché speaks of the *abiku*, spirits who plague mothers by dying before their time. If children were recently born to the client's family, the diviner needs to check each one for the presence of abiku. If one is found, the diviner must offer ebó to the child's guardian orisha and chain the child to the earth (have the child wear on the left ankle a chain that has previously been fed to the earth) to prevent a premature death. For adults, impotence and sterility are a concern; not only should the client offer ebó to Yemayá and Oshún to prevent or reverse this, but also he should have a thorough physical, including an assessment of the reproductive organs. In the physical he should be tested for sexually transmitted diseases. If infertility is the reason the client has come to the mat, the diviner will know that he has tried many solutions already, and consulting the diviner now constitutes his last recourse. Also, the client could have an ill relative; as soon as the illness manifests, he must make ebó quickly on this person's behalf so it does not lead to death. He must take care of children now, for one could be hurt or killed in an unforeseen accident. He must also be good to his legs and feet; he must not stand or walk for long periods of time, and he should elevate his legs at night. There could be some swelling and edema in these areas; in the elderly, it could forebode heart and lung disease.

In addition, the diviner should explore the following with his client:

- During the course of his life, the client has spent much money on doctors and spiritual workers; he has looked to others to cure his mind, body, and soul. Odí Oché indicates that the spirits that support him say this is his last chance to be "cured." Enough aché and light exists here to remove those things that hinder the client, but he must make ebó, and he must make it quickly. If the client walks away from this reading unresolved to follow the advice of Odí Oché, his life will continue to unravel. There will be no hope.
- No matter the orientation of Odí Oché, the client must prepare for war. Someone or something is coming to harm him.
- In the osogbo of ano or ikú, impotence and sterility are dangers. Men must protect their genital area from sudden and hard blows, and women must avoid any activity that could strain their womb or abdominal area. Infections are a danger here, and any infection of the pelvic region (especially sexually transmitted diseases) will leave the client sterile. He must be careful.
- This letter forebodes separation between godparent and godchild; they have different destinies, and they cannot fulfill them together. If this reading is an itá, both should keep this prediction in mind and resolve to part as friends. One day they will need each other's help.

## The Prohibitions of Odí Oché

- There is a prohibition for the diviner when this pattern falls: He must not tell the client all that the orishas wish to say. He must keep some information for himself only. The full force of this odu could cause more problems than solutions; always, it will bring about arguments, especially between the diviner and the client.
- Do not gamble or spend money foolishly.
- Do not walk outdoors barefoot, for parasites and disease may cling to the skin.
- Do not share combs, hats, towels, clothing, or anything else that touches one's skin with another person.

## The Eboses of Odí Oché

Odí Oché is a complicated odu, and it can be difficult to mark ebó for those who open in this pattern. The diviner must consider the client's initiatory status: aleyo, aborisha, or initiate. The concerns of each will differ in this odu.

If the client is an aleyo or an aborisha, the diviner should consider the following list of eboses:

- Rarely will this sign open for one who was not born near a river, near an ocean, near a lake, near the joining of two waters, or during a rainstorm. The diviner should check to see if this is the case with his client. If so, this person is watched over by Oshún and Yemayá; he should consider himself a child of two waters and must care for both orishas equally. As ebó, the client should have a rogación before both Yemayá and Oshún using coconut, efun, water (from the soperas of both orishas), cocoa butter, honey, white bread, and molasses. At the completion of this rogación, the client should give a simple adimú to both Yemayá and Oshún, making sure the same thing is given to both in equal portions. From this moment on, for the rest of his life, whatever the client does for one orisha as ebó should be done for the other.

- This client's egun are in need of masses. The client must follow the advice of the espiritistas exactly, as they will elevate his spiritual court. At the end of each mass, the client should leave an adimú to egun.

Having made these prescriptions for the aleyo or aborisha, the diviner may now attempt to close the oracle. If it will not close, he should explore the following possibilities:

- Oshún and Babaluaiye may be standing up to claim ebó. The diviner should consider asking, "Ebó elese Oshún?" and "Ebó elese Babaluaiye?" If either claims ebó, the diviner should use the the diloggún to mark an appropriate offering. The client should fulfill this ebó as soon as possible, as both orishas hint at past promises to them that were left unfulfilled.
- The aborisha might need to receive Babaluaiye. To see if this is necessary, the diviner should ask, "Koshé Babaluaiye?"
- A woman who opens in this letter could have unresolved issues with Olokun. The diviner should consider asking, "Ebó elese Olokun?" If the answer is yes, he uses the diloggun to mark the required offering. If the answer is no, he asks, "Koshé Olokun?" If Olokun's reception is marked, the diviner knows that this woman's life is in danger; she must make arrangements to receive this spirit as soon as possible.
- In this odu, even an aborisha can have issues with Inle. The diviner should ask, "Ebó elese Inle?" If the answer is yes, a plaza of fruits should be laid out to him in brackish water, a place where salt water meets fresh water.
- The client may have unresolved issues with Yemayá, Oshún, Inle, Babaluaiye, Ochosi, or egun. To determine if any of these spirits will accept ebó, the diviner should consider asking, "Ebó elese [spirit's name]?" If the answer is yes, he uses the diloggun to mark the required offering.

If this list of eboses has been exhausted and the odu refuses closure for the aborisha, the diviner must turn to the list of eboses for the parent odu, Odí (see page 346). Something there is needed for this client's evolution.

When Odí Oché opens for an initiate, the issues it raises are more complex. The diviner should consider the following eboses:

- From now on, the client must adore Yemayá and Oshún together; they both stand up here to say that they love the client dearly, and he must be zealous and equal in the treatment of both. First, he must put the two orishas side by side and at an equal height. He must adorn their shrines equally. For example, if Yemayá has a mazo, Oshún must have one as well. If Oshún has a pañuelo, Yemayá must have one as well.
- This sign also marks the initiate for the reception of a special spiritual charm known as dos aguas. It has the aché of both Yemayá and Oshún. Arrangements for its reception should be made immediately; once received, it lives between both orishas.
- The client needs to receive Inle, for he lives in the place where the river and the ocean meet. This orisha should live at the feet of Yemayá and Oshún, standing between them.
- Odí Oché forebodes a split in the initiate's spiritual family, especially between his godfather and his yubonna. The following ebó will soothe the tension and bring reunion: For his own Oshún, the initiate must sew three silk pañuelos. He lays one pañuelo over Oshún and places five one-dollar bills over it. The second pañuelo goes over this; again he places five one-dollar bills over it. The third pañuelo goes over the second, with another five one-dollar bills over it. The initiate then prays to Oshún for his spiritual family to come together again. After five days have passed, the initiate removes one pañuelo and five one-dollar bills and takes them to his godparent's Oshún (the one who gave him birth). Afterward, he removes another pañuelo

and five one-dollar bills, taking this to his yubonna's Oshún. The third pañuelo and final set of one-dollar bills remain with his Oshún. This ebó will bring a divided family together again.

- Finally, the initiate must play a tambor for his godfather's crown first and his yubonna's crown second. Remember that Oshún and Yemayá must be adored equally, so if the godparent or yubonna has one of these two orishas crowned, the other spirit must be included in the tambor. Once this ebó is done, there will be peace, progress, and evolution.

Now the diviner has his first chance to close the oracle. If it remains open, the initiate might also have issues with Orisha Oko. To determine what this orisha requires, the diviner must ask, "Ebó elese Orisha Oko?" If the answer is yes, he uses the diloggun to mark the required offering. If the answer is no, he asks, "Koshé Orisha Oko?"

If these prescriptions are not enough to close the session, the diviner should turn to the eboses of the parent odu, Odí (see page 346). Something there is needed for this client's evolution.

## The Sixth Composite Odu of Odí, Odí Obara (7-6)

### The Proverbs of Odí Obara

- The peony cannot decide whether it is red or black.
- You destroy with your feet that which you made with your hands.
- Do not put off until tomorrow what you may do today, or else it will be too late to do anything.
- You have many impulses, both bad and good. Do not follow your bad impulses; go only with those that are good.
- Dogs have four legs but walk only one path.
- You cannot be everywhere at once.

### The Message of Odí Obara

When a casting of seven mouths, Odí, precedes a casting of six mouths, Obara, the odu Odí Obara is open on the mat. Immediately, the diviner pays homage to Obatalá, Yemayá, Oshún, Shangó, Ogún, Elegguá, Ochosi, and Orisha Oko, saying to each, "Maferefún!" The influence of this powerful odu depends on its orientation. When it opens in iré, it bestows all greatness upon the client's head. When it comes in osogbo, it brings all misfortunes to the client's head. The diviner must be cautious when delivering the reading. Of all that may be said or done in this sign, nothing is more important than the prescription of a rogación; if possible, the diviner should offer it before sending the client home. Afterward, the diviner should tell the client, "This sign brings greatness to one's head, yet one's head must be strong. Whenever there is doubt or indecision, return to Obatalá. Lay out all your troubles to him. While he cannot solve them all, he will keep your head cool so you can make proper, enlightened decisions."

Odí Obara gives birth to many things, and all will have some bearing on the client's life. Marriage is a child of this odu. Before its birth, there were no commitments between men and women. Carnal lusts burned in the loins of men, and they spent these upon the fairest sex as they would. For years, women were abused, beaten, and raped to fulfill men's burning desires. In heaven, Odí Obara awakened; he saw the evil erupting across the earth and descended to fight it. His first decree was marriage, and woe to those men who dominated their women mercilessly. Yet once this custom was institutionalized, a new war was born: the unspoken rivalry between the sexes. Odí Obara promises, however, that one day all will be equal.

In this sign, also, flower gardens were born for the delight of the living and of the dead. Through this odu the duck gained Yemayá's favor, then lost it, and became her favorite sacrificial food due to his own arrogance. This is also the odu of the great theft in heaven: Yemayá and Shangó were hungry, and only Ogún had food. A great field of plantains was his. Together, the two orishas stole all he had. Ogún accused both of them before Olófin, but there was no proof for the judging. Each said, simply, "It was not I." With that, thefts and robberies in which no one is implicated due to lack of proof were born.

Of all the stories told in this pattern, however, none is more significant than the patakís of the rosary bead plant. Because of its strength and raw beauty, this annual gained the favor of all the orishas. Through Odí Obara, it received the aché to replace any missing plant in Osain's omiero. Its seeds were red and black, like Elegguá's face, yet the rosary bead plant grew tired of its coloring. The seeds began to argue among themselves. "We are red," cried some. Others argued, "No, we must be black." The plants on the left of the rosary bead saw red in all its seeds, while the plants on the right of the rosary bead saw black in all its seeds, and soon the entire forest was arguing. The seeds themselves became divided, each struck by a manic illness that caused a single seed to war with itself. The noise was too much for the orishas, and Shangó was angry. From the plants nearest his house, he ripped out all the seeds and sealed them inside a thick gourd. He roared, "Now you are neither red nor black; you live in darkness. Be quiet!" The seeds, however, continued to quarrel, but their noise was now pleasing and invigorating: The maraca was born. Shangó shared this instrument with all the orishas, and soon most of them preferred this instrument above all others.

So it is with this person's life. It is filled with indecision. The client quarrels with others, but mostly he fights with himself. Every day opens myriad possibilities for him; he thinks, plans, and analyzes his goals constantly, yet he cannot make more than nominal progress in any one direction. The spiritual noise he makes is great. The diviner must tell him that Shangó hears his incessant whining and indecision, and just as he was with the rosary plant, he is angry. If the client does not make up his mind soon, Shangó will make it up for him; he will seal him up and force him to become something new. If the odu opens in iré, this will be a great blessing indeed, but in osogbo, the client will not like what his life becomes. The diviner should tell the client, "Until you settle down and set priorities for yourself, there will be no evolution. Do this for yourself, or Shangó will do it for you."

Odí Obara flags a variety of other issues in the client's life; the diviner must also examine the following, assessing the client appropriately:

- The client thinks about vengeance, for someone wronged him and he wants justice. A war is coming; it is beginning now. The key to winning is an impenetrable defense; the client must not mount an offensive. The client's enemy is strong and vicious, like a tiger, and without a plan he will lose.
- Those body parts that are soft and moist are vulnerable to disease and decay. The breasts, vagina, testicles, penis, and anus are entryways for disease. The mouth and throat could deteriorate. The client must have proper rest and nourishment, and he must have regular visits to see his physician. He also must frequently have rogaciónes at the feet of Obatalá, for mental illness and memory loss are foreshadowed.
- For a man to be blessed, he must honor and respect women. If the odu opens in iré, a man who seeks marriage will find happiness. In osogbo, a man who is engaged marries for the wrong reasons. This is a sign of quarrels between spouses.
- This odu demands respect for many types of commitments: with the orishas, with one's children, and with one's family (even spiritual). This odu also speaks of one's obligations to society. The client must respect these commitments and fulfill these obligations.
- If the odu opens in osogbo, great evils can befall the client. The diviner should tell the client to leave all his troubles at Yemayá's feet with an adimú. She, not the client, will fight the battles. In a severe osogbo, Yemayá says she can strengthen the client's head with a rogación. The client must have this rogación at her shrine with Elegguá as a witness. The next morning, the priest should bathe the client's head with water from both the ocean and the river.
- If the odu opens in an osogbo of ano or ikú, sickness breeds inside the client. He must see a physician now so the baseline of his health can be established. Also, the diviner must prescribe immediate ebó to Elegguá: a cleansing of the client with three eggs to Elegguá followed by a

cleansing with a rooster. After cleansing the client with the live animal, the priest sacrifices it to Elegguá. The next morning, the client takes all the elements of the ebó to a crossroads.

## The Prohibitions of Odí Obara

- For a woman in iré or a moderate osogbo, limit the wearing of pants. In a severe osogbo, especially if Shangó speaks, avoid pants altogether.
- Do not be like the peony seed and make too much noise; the neighbors will have one imprisoned if this happens.
- Do not grab anyone's buttocks. If this odu opens for a man, he will have the impulse to grab the buttocks of a large woman. She is Obatalá's child, and if he does this, he will lose all his luck and offend this orisha gravely.
- Never be around children alone; have someone else with one at all times when another person's child is present.
- This odu speaks of the duck that lost its religious position because of arrogance; do not be arrogant.
- Deer meat is taboo.
- No matter the circumstances, never steal.

## The Eboses of Odí Obara

Of all that may be said or done in this sign, nothing is more important than the prescription of a rogación. Before Obatalá, the client must have a rogación of the head with grated coconut, grated cocoa butter, crushed cascarilla, and white cotton. The diviner should perform this rogación, if possible, before sending the client home. After the rogación, the client should pay foribale to Obatalá.

In addition to the rogación before Obatalá, the diviner should prescribe the following eboses:

- The first ebó requires an oriaté. He will prepare a rosary bead necklace for the first orisha who spoke to the client in Odí Obara, stringing it on thick, absorbent cotton thread. He will also prepare omiero for this orisha, singing a full series of songs to Osain. He will wash both the necklace and the orisha in these sacred waters and, after the washing, feed the orisha a sacrifice of feathers. This necklace has potent aché; the client should wear it every day and leave it with the orisha's shrine at night. (If the client is an aleyo or an aborisha, he can keep this beaded necklace with the rest of his elekes at night.) The power of the necklace is this: As long as he wears it, he will never face indecision. The rosary beads absorb his problems during the day, and at night, the orisha to whom it belongs works to solve his problems. This ebó works only for those under Odí Obara's influence.
- Through this sign the custom of refreshing one's front door was born. For the rest of his life, the client (even if he is an aleyo or an aborisha) should keep an urn of fresh water behind his front door. Every morning before beginning his daily activities, the client throws this water to the street, replacing it with fresh water. Also, before praying to any spirit or orisha, the client begins all rituals by filling a jícara from this urn. In three dashes, he pours the water from the jícara onto the ground in front of his home's entrance, praying to Olófin, Olorún, and Olódumare for freshness. All libations made during the day should be taken from this same urn.
- The client should put a two-faced, wooden statue with his Elegguá. If the odu has opened in an osogbo, this doll must be washed and fed with Elegguá, or it is useless. The diviner must also determine if the orisha will take ebó, asking, "Ebó elese Elegguá?" If the answer is yes, he uses the diloggún to mark the appropriate offering.

When Odí Obara brings osogbo, there are other eboses to consider. They are not mandatory; however, the diviner should consider each in relation to the client's situation. One or more of the following might be appropriate.

- This odu has its own bath that will remove osogbo from the client, cleansing him. The priest makes an infusion from the leaves of the rosary bead plant, purslane, and canna lily (known as *platanillo de cuba* in Spanish). Once the juices are infused, he adds crushed cascarilla, grated cocoa butter, almond oil, and seven egg yolks. He divides this bath equally into seven containers. Once a night for seven nights, the client uses one container for a bath. After each bath, he dresses in white. On the eighth day, he returns to the diviner for a rogación at Obatalá's feet.

- Elegguá has a special ebó in this pattern that will remove osogbo: The client smears three fish with epó and broils them lightly. He serves them to the orisha on a platter of toasted corn. This ebó remains overnight; the next morning, the client discards it at a crossroads.
- To remove osogbo, the client may also give Elegguá a whole ñame smeared with epó. It remains with him until it begins to rot. The diviner uses obí to determine how the orisha wants the ebó discarded.
- A special ebó can be done with a balance scale to bring balance to the client's life, soothing the osogbo opened. If the client is an aleyo or an aborisha, he places the balance scale in the highest location in his house. Usually, this will be the same location in which his Ósun is kept. If the client is an initiate, he places the scale in one of two places: with the guardian orisha or with the orisha whose diloggún is being consulted. On one side of the scale, the client places a small bottle with sixteen peony seeds. On the other side, he places enough weight to keep the scale in perfect balance. If this scale ever goes off balance, it shows that the client's life is out of balance. He must immediately correct the scale; this is a temporary solution to keep his head from being overwhelmed. Afterward, he should seek out a reading with the diloggún immediately.

If the diviner has come this far into the list of eboses for an aleyo or an aborisha and the letter remains open, he must turn to the eboses of the parent odu, Odí (see page 346). Something in that list is necessary for the client's evolution. If the client is an initiate, the diviner should continue with the following list:

- The diviner prepares a niche osain for Shangó. He washes and feeds it with him; once done, the client should carry the charm with him. When he does not have it with him, he should keep it inside Shangó's sopera.
- The client should plant a rosary bead plant, keeping it indoors near the front or back door. This plant, in an emergency, can substitute for any plant missing in an osain. It can also bring much luck when well cared for.
- If these eboses are not enough to close the odu, the diviner should ask, "Ebó elese Yemayá?" If she claims ebó here, the proper offering is a new crown lined with seven red parrot feathers.
- The initiate might need to receive Ochosi or Orisha Oko. To determine if either is required, the diviner should ask, "Koshé [orisha's name]?"

If these are not enough to close the odu for an initiate, the diviner must turn to the eboses of the parent odu, Odí.

## The Seventh Composite Odu of Odí, Odí Meji (7-7)

### The Proverbs of Odí Meji

- Two people do not do things correctly.
- In adultery, there is danger.
- You are a child of envy, and your tongue can destroy your secrets.
- There is misery in the mother's womb.
- Do not leave your customs.
- Everyone makes sure that he does his things with care so they come out well.
- Two do not know how to do things properly.

### The Message of Odí Meji

When a cast of seven mouths, Odí, repeats itself, the odu Odí Meji is open on the mat. To honor Yemayá, Elegguá, Otín, Ochosi, Babaluaiye, Obatalá, Inle, and Orisha Oko in this odu, the diviner says to each, "Maferefún!" The aché of several will be needed by the client. Many oriatés believe that the aché of both

Ogundá Meji (3-3) and Osá Meji (9-9) is also present here; in their lines of ocha, the energy of all three patterns is believed to be intertwined inseparably. Odí Meji, according to these elders, not only gives birth to Ogundá Meji and Osá Meji simultaneously but bleeds into both as well. If the diviner is from a house following this custom, he pays homage not only to the spirits of Odí Meji but also to those orishas who speak through Ogundá Meji and Osá Meji. Because of this, the energy of Odí Meji is vast, and any spirit might choose to speak. The meanings of Ogundá Meji and Osá Meji are delivered after the diviner's interpretation of Odí Meji. While the proverbs, patakís, and eboses of the remaining two signs will not apply, their energy will, and it will form a substratum to the client's issues.*

For all it creates, "Maferefún Odí Meji!" From its vastness were born the sun, earth, and sky; some attribute all the stars to its power. This odu alludes to the beauty of these creations and the vastness they occupy. Just as the material world displays beauty and vastness, so can the client's life; he can achieve greatness if he heeds the advice and warnings of this odu. The diviner should tell the client that while the sun, earth, and sky are all great, here the sun became the greatest and most awesome star in the sky because he alone made ebó. If the client makes ebó, he will be as important to others as the sun is to life.

When it falls for the itá of a iyawó, Odí Meji's blessings are great.† A priest born of this sign is touched by grace. The diviner should tell the iyawó, "Before you were born, your mother cried; there were tears in her womb. You were almost lost, but the orishas brought you to life. Before your ocha, Yemayá cried for you. There were tears in her womb, and tears on your path to evolution. You were almost lost to this religion, but Yemayá herself moved heaven and earth to bring you here." Even if Yemayá is not this person's crown, the iyawó must live by making ebó to her.

While Yemayá might bless the client, here Oyá comes to warn him; if the client is Oyá's child, the odu is dire indeed, and the client must heed the moral of the following patakís. Here it is said that Oyá found death in the marketplace, and her children might find death there, too.‡ She was once happily married to Ogún, and together the two had a child: Elegguá. In the marketplace, she met Shangó, and he inflamed her heart with desire. Using a potion made with her knowledge of witchcraft, Oyá faked her own death, and her body was laid to rest deep in the forest. When the potion wore off, Oyá ran to her lover, Shangó. Because Shangó was not a tireless worker like Ogún, Oyá was forced to work, and she found employment in the marketplace where she and Shangó met. Months passed, and one day Ogún and Elegguá went shopping in the marketplace together. They saw Oyá. Infuriated, Ogún told all there the story of her treason while Elegguá cried. She was stoned there, in the marketplace, and her body buried deep under the earth so she could not rise up. Never before had the earth been opened to receive a corpse; thus began the custom of ritual burial.§

Odí Meji is a sexual odu, and those who open in this sign reflect this energy in their lives. It is said that after all things were created, the world was stagnant and sterile. Plants were unable to pollinate, but Odí Meji came from heaven and showed them how to fool insects into doing the work for them; she created their gentle fragrances, which enticed the insects to explore their petals. Animals were barren, but the odu created their cycle of heat and the scents by which males know the females are ready to breed. Men and women lived together; each knew the other was different. Yet men knew not what to do with their penises, and women remained virgin

**Author's note:* I myself do not follow this custom, yet it is so prevalent that it is worth explaining. As always, one must follow the customs of one's house.

†For a iyawó, this sign hints that he was born on a good Friday or during a solar or lunar eclipse. If this is true for the iyawó, he is destined for great things.

‡Keep in mind that life itself is often thought of as a marketplace. In an osogbo of ano or ikú, Oyá's children are in danger. If Oyá's dilogún is being consulted and gives Odí Meji during an itá, it is always a warning against lies, false love, and adultery.

§There is another version of this story in which Odí was the woman who faked her own death. Even though Odí tried to disguise herself, her son recognized her by her long, extravagantly painted nails. Those who tell this version of the story prohibit women from growing their nails long and painting them.

and chaste. Odí Meji taught the women to open their vaginas and she showed men how to enter. Thus was copulation born. But humans realized that sex felt good, and, unlike plants or animals, they had the intelligence to experiment. It was also Odí Meji who brought avarice and sodomy to humans' sexual practices, and homosexuality was born among men and women who cared not to bear young. For the pleasures this odu brought to our race, "Maferefún Odí Meji!"

In addition, the diviner should keep the following in mind when working through this letter:

- In iré, this odu marks the client as a diviner by birth; he will make an exceptional italero. This pattern also puts aleyos and aborishas in bondage to ocha.
- This is a dangerous odu for those who have children; the parent must care for the oldest child, because Odí Meji marks that one for danger. If there are three children, there could be incest between two of them or between one child and a parent. Note that the diviner must be very cautious when revealing this information, because the offender could be sitting at the mat. The diviner must caution the client to be wary of what he says and does around children and explain to him that when this sign comes, it is taboo to strike children. Also, the diviner should tell the client that he could have three to seven children in his life.
- This pattern, in osogbo, speaks of abortion and miscarriage.
- A single mother who opens in this sign must beware of sexual predators and the men whom she dates; she must be very cautious about marriage. This sign tells of a woman whose children fall prey to her lover. Remember: Pedophiles are attracted to single mothers, for while they blind them with love and attention, they can prey on their children behind their backs.
- During the menstrual periods, a woman in this odu will have headaches and severe cramps. If these continue to worsen, or if the period is excessively heavy or long, she should consult her physician. Something could be wrong.
- Odí Meji speaks of love triangles and extramarital affairs. To make sure that the client's luck and blessing is neither missed nor lost, he must never have more than one relationship at a time. He must end each relationship cleanly and completely before beginning another.
- Coming in the osogbo of ano or ikú, the client must pay careful attention to the eyes, kidneys, and reproductive organs. Disease could be brewing in those places.
- If ano falls in Odí Meji, mental derangement, psychosis, and nervous breakdowns or disorders are possibilities.
- If the letter falls in ikú, death may come by drowning, choking, or suffocation, especially at the ocean. The client must be careful.

## The Prohibitions of Odí Meji

- Do not leave one's own customs, especially one's religious customs. Even though one now participates in the Lucumí faith, continue to follow the religion of one's ancestors as long as it does not interfere with one's own practices. However, one must avoid that religion's sacraments, for this would amount to blasphemy. This odu forbids blasphemy of any faith.
- Do not reveal one's secrets to anyone; this odu marks one as a child of envy. People will use against one everything secret that one reveals.
- Gossip is taboo. Neither listen to it nor repeat it.
- Weapons are taboo. Do not carry them or use them.
- One must not have two sexual relationships at once, or else all iré brought by this odu will be lost.
- Do not consume alcohol or other intoxicants.
- Do not eat watercress.
- If the osogbo of this letter is severe, do not shop in an outdoor marketplace. A child of Oyá, in any orientation, should avoid outdoor marketplaces as well (where Oyá found death), unless one makes ebó first.

## The Eboses of Odí Meji

When Odí Meji opens on the mat, no matter its orientation, it is important for the client to make ebó. All who come in this sign should carry a niche osain of their guardian orisha. If the guardian orisha is not known, the diviner should prepare the osain for Elegguá, who is present in all odu, and a bajado should be had as soon as possible, for this client is marked for ocha.

The remaining eboses that must be prescribed will differ depending on the client's initiatory status: aleyo, aborisha, or initiate.

If the client is an aleyo or an aborisha, the diviner must prescribe the following eboses:

- If the client does not have the warriors, he must receive them as soon as possible. He should find the stone for his Elegguá in the ocean and seal its concrete representation with a piece of turtle shell. While Ogún is born with one machete, the client must give him three more as ebó upon bringing the orishas home; with these four machetes, Ogún will fight all the evil that comes to him from the four cardinal points of the world.
- Spiritual baths are a necessity when Odí Meji has come for an aborisha. The priest must make an omiero for the orisha whose shells have been consulted, and once a day for seven days this client must bathe with a portion of this. During this period of cleansing, the client dresses in white. After the seventh bath, he returns to the diviner's home for a rogación. If Odí Meji has brought osogbo, the priest must also feed the client's orí two white doves or pigeons.

If the client is an initiate, the diviner should prescribe the following eboses:

- Another path of Eshu must be prepared for this person; the stone for this must come from the ocean and be mounted in a shell. Obviously, the Elegguá thus made will be one of the paths that work exclusively with Yemayá or Olokun. Before closing this session, the diviner will have to determine which Eshu to prepare. Regardless of the path that is marked, this Elegguá must be sealed with a piece of turtle's shell (from the breastplate). The image must have an additional seven shells beyond those used in its face to mark it as having been born from Odí Meji.
- Spiritual baths should be made for this client using omiero made from his guardian orisha's sacred herbs. Once a night for seven nights, the client's godparent should bathe him in this spiritual bath. During this period of cleansing, the client must dress in white. After the seventh bath, the client should have rogación before this orisha's shrine. The diviner must determine if an ebó is required after this rogación, asking, "Ebó elese [crowning orisha's name]?"
- The client must carry a niche osain of his guardian orisha with him at all times. In addition, he must have a niche osain for Shangó.

Whether the client is an aborisha or an initiate, if the eboses prescribed thus far by the diviner are not enough to close the session, the diviner should investigate the following options:

- Egun may be demanding ebó. The diviner should ask, "Ebó elese egun?" If the answer is yes, the diviner must make a few prescriptions. First, the client's spiritual court must have a series of masses to advance them spiritually. The client must follow the advice of the espiritistas exactly, because they will help his egun evolve. These masses will also give egun the strength to overcome his enemies. Before the first mass begins, the client should offer a machete to his bóveda. The following day, he must place a portion of all his food with the bóveda in front of the machete. Before sunrise the next morning, the client must place all this food in a brown paper bag and leave it at the gates to a cemetery.
- If this letter has opened in the osogbo ikú, the client must move his bed immediately to a dif-

ferent portion of his bedroom so that Death will not find him in his sleep.
- If these eboses do not bring closure to the oracle, the client could have issues with Obatalá, Yemayá, Oyá, or his own guardian orisha. The diviner should consider whether any of them will take ebó, asking, "Ebó elese [orisha's name]?" If the answer is yes, he uses the diloggún to mark the appropriate offering.

If the odu remains open and the client is an aborisha, the diviner must turn to the eboses of the parent odu, Odí (see page 346). Something there is needed for this client's evolution. If the client is an initiate, the diviner should explore the following:

- The initiate may need to wear a red parrot feather in his hair at all times, especially when going to a festival for the orishas.
- To protect the front door, the client may need to sew a red flag in honor of Shangó. He should hang it over Shangó's batea overnight and then hang it prominently outside the front door.
- All the orishas that are considered warriors can speak in this sign, and if it will not close, the diviner should try to mark as many eboses as possible to them. Serious, unseen wars are being fought around this person, and he will need their protection.

If these prescriptions are not enough to close the odu for the initiate, the diviner should turn to the eboses of the parent odu, Odí.

# The Eighth Composite Odu of Odí, Odí Ogbe (7-8)

## The Proverbs of Odí Ogbe

- The goat that breaks the drum pays for it with his own skin.
- Something that was left behind cannot be picked up.
- The rooster is singing in another coop.
- Do not leave your customs.
- Do not return to what was once had; move on.

## The Message of Odí Ogbe

When a casting of seven mouths, Odí, precedes a casting of eight mouths, Eji Ogbe, the odu Odí Ogbe is open on the mat. This sign is also known as Odí Elleunle and Odí Unle. Coming with this pattern, the diloggún directs the diviner to pay homage to Yemayá, Orisha Oko, Inle, Ogún, and Obatalá, saying to each, "Maferefún!" These five forces form the client's spiritual foundation, and no matter the letter's orientation, he must make adimú to each. This letter is powerful, and it must be respected. For the strength it brought to the world, "Maferefún Odí Ogbe!" Through it was born our most precious instrument—the drum. After its birth, the drummers offered the world's first tambor to Shangó; he descended from heaven and into the bodies of his priests, blessing those who gave him music. When this pattern opens, Shangó demands music. Aleyos and aborishas must play orisha music in their homes; it honors the religion. Initiates born from Shangó or made to Shangó are required to give tambors frequently. For luck, no matter his initiatory status, the client must go to the next tambor offered to Shangó.

With the birth of the drum and the first tambor came man's most primitive form of long-distance communication: drumming between towns. For it was discovered that a properly made drum, strategically placed in the town's center, could transmit sounds for miles, much faster than any person could travel. It gave birth to the beats by which humans communicated as well. Some in the religion say that long-distance communication, no matter its form (mail, telegraph, radio, telephone, e-mail), was first conceived here. Elders say that the slave revolts of Haiti were born of this sign. The drums of the *loas*, spirits who are distant cousins to the orishas, spawned and strengthened the uprisings. Slaves played drums, and the drummers themselves were mounted by loas; the loas, in turn, put their music into the drumbeats, inspiring anger and revolution among their people. When Odí Ogbe falls, the orishas, and the client's entire ancestral court, are mounting behind him. Soon they will inspire him into action. Great changes are coming to his life, revolutions and upheavals that will change the course of his personal history.

"Maferefún!" to the Seven African Powers as well. When Odí Ogbe opens on the mat, the Seven African Powers stand behind the client, prepared to fight his battles. Their aché is integral to his spiritual court, and he must work with all seven entities if he hopes to evolve beyond the wars and strife occupying his life now. In this religion, however, there is much misconception about who these forces are. Many initiates equate the Seven African Powers with the orishas, yet this is untrue. These powers are seven spirits from the seven African tribes enslaved in Cuba: Yoruba, Congo, Takua, Kissi, Calabar, Dahomey, and Mandika. Although all the tribes were enemies in Africa, in Cuba they were forced to unite, to make personal treaties enabling them to survive the hardships of slavery. Among these, three became so close that they left spiritual imprints on each other's faiths: Yoruba, Congo, and Dahomey. Stories from all three were absorbed into the Yoruba religion, known as Lucumí in Cuba and beyond; and both the Congo and Dahomey absorbed Yoruba elements into their own ritual practices. Congo priests borrowed from all the ritual practices of the remaining six, influencing the religion that came to be known as Palo Mayombe or Palo Monte.

Here, the odu says that the client has one spirit from each tribe standing up to be a part of his spiritual court. Yet all seven cannot be equal; one will have prominence, taking the lead for the remaining six spirits. Behind each spirit is an army of lesser-developed entities, spirits that will fight for the client under the direction of their leader. The client must purchase seven statuettes into which these seven spirits can be seated. First he must buy a single, large statue of a black man. Immediately, he hosts a spiritual mass to investigate this one spirit. The espiritistas present must focus on this spirit and search all seven until the leader forming the core of this person's Seven African Powers is found. This first statue is washed and baptized to this spirit and dressed in the clothing of his tribe. The sexes of the remaining six, their names, and their respective tribes are also determined at the mass. Once this information is known, the client seeks out six smaller dolls (to give visual prominence to the head of all seven), dresses them in appropriate clothes, and puts them with their core spirit. As the years progress, each spirit will demand several smaller dolls dressed in the clothing of his or her tribe. As the client works with them, each will amass a powerful army. Yet no matter how large any one army grows, remember that they all have one leader; the client should always approach this spirit first, before approaching any other. To do otherwise is to unbalance this spiritual court.

Congo spirits are prominent in this odu, and many patakís tell about their interaction with the orishas. Once, the Congo tribes were in debt; they had no money or food, and poverty was destroying their kind. In despair they went to the orisha priests, and the odu Odí Ogbe was opened. The diviner told the Congolese to make ebó with a single jícara of saraeko to Elegguá; then they were to cut down all the trees in a field and destroy every plant but one: the strawberry plant. They did as the diviner told them and found only one strawberry plant in the entire field. The diviner brought the gourd with which the Congos had made ebó, and he covered that one plant with it. In days, one strawberry plant filled the entire field with strawberries, and the Congolese people became rich.

This letter also tells of the Congolese evil and disobedience, and what happened to them when they struck out at the orishas. Another patakís tells about the war fought between Obatalá and the Congos. Obatalá lived on one side of a lake and a tribe of Congo lived on the other. Both laid claim to the lake, but in truth, it belonged to Obatalá. The entire tribe warred against this one orisha, but Obatalá won by making a single ebó: He fed the earth. This odu says the client has strong issues to settle with Palo Mayombe; he must consult with a palero to determine what they are.

In addition, the diviner should explore the following issues with the client when Odí Ogbe falls:

- The client doubts everything that makes life worth living, especially love. The orishas are telling him never to doubt love, for it is coming to his life soon.

- This letter refers to one's bones. The client must take care of his bones; he must be careful when running or climbing because one could be broken. A woman in this sign is in danger of osteoporosis and softening of the bones; she should seek medical advice for this condition.
- When this letter comes in itá for a iyawó, the orisha speaking promises that one day he will become very famous and sought after in the religion; already, there is a town of people standing behind him, waiting for him to rule as their spiritual king.
- A santero for whom this pattern falls must guard his orishas well; someone is coming to steal something from one of his spirits, weakening his spiritual court.
- This person should be working now to strengthen himself, not to obtain fame and fortune. If he does otherwise, he will fail in life miserably.
- The pattern alludes to a mysterious woman in the client's life; this religion is her one, true object of devotion, and no matter what happens to her, she will triumph. This woman is so strange in her ways that the client will be afraid of her and might lose her. The diviner must caution him against this, because so powerful is this woman that she will save his life one day.

## The Prohibitions of Odí Ogbe

- Do not kill mice or other rodents.
- Stealing is taboo; theft of even the smallest item will destroy any iré brought by this sign.
- Do not abandon one's obligations to chase after more pleasurable pursuits. One must finish one's work first and play later.
- Never be alone in another person's house. Something could turn up missing, and that person will blame one.

## The Eboses of Odí Ogbe

When Odí Ogbe opens on the mat, the diviner should prescribe the following eboses:

- Once Odí Ogbe closes, all present must offer ebó to Elegguá. The diviner fills a brown paper bag with toasted corn, jutía, and smoked fish. Standing before Elegguá, he crosses himself with the bag, rubbing his body thoroughly to cleanse it. Once the diviner's cleansing is over, all present cleanse themselves with the bag. After everyone leaves that evening, the last guest departing the diviner's home takes the brown bag to a crossroads, discarding it there.
- Starting this evening, the client must offer ebó to his own Elegguá for three, seven, or twenty-one days. From every meal, the client wraps a small portion in brown paper, cleansing himself with it before giving the ebó to Elegguá. Every morning, before praying, the client walks this bag to a crossroads.
- Drums have prominence in this sign. If the client has his warriors, he must provide a set of small toy drums for his orishas. When talking to Elegguá, Ogún, or Ochosi about his problems, he taps out a basic beat to excite them into action. In addition to a toy drum, he should provide plenty of soothing music for the orishas' enjoyment.

Having made these prescriptions, the diviner may now attempt to close the oracle. If it will not close and the client is an aleyo or an aborisha, the diviner should turn to the eboses of the parent odu, Odí (see page 346). Something there is necessary for the client's evolution. If the client is an initiate, the diviner should consider the following options:

- The reception of Yembo is a possibility. The diviner must ask, "Koshé Yembo?" If the answer is yes, preparations for her ceremonies should begin as soon as possible. If the client already has Yembo, the diviner should determine if she requires ebó, asking, "Ebó elese Yembo?" If the answer is yes, he uses the diloggún to mark the appropriate offering.
- At this point, if the osogbo has not been resolved, this ebó will help: The initiate plays batá for Shangó. The orisha will solve many of his issues.
- Finally, this odu can mark the initiate for the

reception of the knife. The diviner asks, "Koshe pinaldo?" If the answer is yes, the odu marks this reception as a necessary ebó. If the expenses for this ceremony are too great at this time, the client's guardian orisha should receive a sacrifice of four legs; the day after, the client should have itá with this spirit. This will settle the client's affairs until he can afford the pinaldo.

If these eboses are not enough to close Odí Ogbe for a priest or priestess, the diviner must now turn to the eboses of the parent odu, Odí.

## The Ninth Composite Odu of Odí, Odí Osá (7-9)

### The Proverbs of Odí Osá

- Extend your hand only as far as it reaches.
- Stretch the sheet only as far as it can reach.
- That which was left will come back.
- Two people with big noses cannot kiss.
- That which was agreed upon has been fulfilled.

### The Message of Odí Osá

When a casting of seven mouths falls on the mat followed by nine mouths, the odu Odí Osá is open. When a client comes in this sign, the diviner pays homage to Yemayá, Oyá, Obatalá, Elegguá, and egun, saying to each, "Maferefún!" Here, however, no orisha is more prominent than Olokun, and the diviner must say, "Maferefún Olokun!" Olokun brings blessings to the client's life. Those enfolded by this letter have an awesome ally in this spirit; he is vast, a force encompassing most of the earth, and while his secrets in the sopera might seem finite, they open a gate to limitless strength and aché. When Odí Osá comes, Olokun's immediate reception is mandatory. Also, if the client has not had a bajado, he must have one soon. Such is this orisha's love and protection that the one at the mat might be his child. If this reading is a bajado, the aborisha at the mat is Olokun's; there is no need to ask or mark with ibó. Realize that when it comes to making a child of Olokun in ocha, one initiates the client to Yemayá *oro* (through) Olokun; thus both parents are already known.

This sign, in osogbo, also carries a warning: The client is a "child of the wind." While he will be a great spiritualist, he will be a poor priest unless he becomes more grounded and stable. By following the advice of this pattern, he can achieve this.

Spirits of the dead have strong ties with the one for whom this letter falls. The client may feel that he is psychic, having a chasm of untapped powers within himself. His belief is only partly true. His gift is clairvoyant and clairaudient, but it is focused not on the past or the future but on the present; his visions and voices are inspired by the dead. Without them, his gifts are useless, and he must live by adoring and placating egun if he hopes to develop his talents to any degree of usefulness. The diviner should question the client about his favored spiritual practices; the types he participates in will reveal his spiritual guides. Those who read cards, palms, or tea leaves work with a Gypsy very much like Oshún. Scryers, seers, crystal workers, and water gazers have a madam similar in character to Yemayá. Those who love witchcraft and spells are influenced by spirits who have a nature similar to Oyá's. The diviner should advise frequent attendance at spiritual masses; not only will these elevate the client's spiritual court, but also he will learn more about his guides and their powers.

In Odí Osá, Congo spirits and the Congolese religion Palo Mayombe are prominent. The diviner should tell the client that he has the spirit of a young Congolese man close to him. If the odu comes in iré, this spirit is wise and spiritually developed; in osogbo, it is young, impetuous, and rash. Regardless of the odu's orientation, the client needs a consultation with a *tata nkisi* (a high priest of Palo Mayombe), but in osogbo the client is in danger until this is done. The Congo spirit gets in the way of this person's egun; when the client prays to his spiritual court, it is this spirit who hears and rushes to get work done. He does love the client, but his well-meaning assistance causes trouble, and the client's more elevated egun spend time cleaning up the messes the Congo spirit creates. Other unseen souls are also around the client; they are attracted to his light and vibrant life force, and at times, to get his attention, they play tricks on him. To avoid this, the client should place a stalk of yucca next to the opá ikú at his egun shrine. The aché of this stalk ensures that the spirit called will be the one who answers.

The diviner should also explore the following issues with the client:

- For an initiate, Odí Osá alludes to his crown being "up in the air." The client is not stable and cannot think rationally. When this reading is over, the diviner must give the client a rogación. After the rogación, the diviner should give obí to the client's orí to see if it requires sacrifice. He must not attempt to ask this with the diloggún; the answer must come directly from the client's own head, and it cannot answer until the rogación has been given.
- This odu warns that the client will be intimately involved with the problems of his brother. Unless they make ebó, they will not have long together on the earth. The death of his brother will ruin the client's life. Only by making sacrifices can this person do his work on the earth.
- The diviner should tell a man who comes in this sign that he will battle for subsistence.
- If this person's mother is not a witch, he has a witch in his life who plays the role of a mother. He should make a sacrifice to Elegguá and to Ogún, place the inner parts of the animals known as the aché in a basket, and take it to a crossroads to feed the elders of the night, the witches.
- This person will not prosper in life if he settles down to live in the place where he was born. He must live in a different town or country to have luck.
- The diviner must give an initiate opening in Odí Osá a stern warning: Be wary of doing ebó for a pregnant woman. While the ebó will not harm the woman, this sign forebodes a miscarriage by one of the initiate's clients. If she makes ebó and then miscarries, she will blame the loss of her child on him.
- In iré, the orisha whose diloggún is being consulted is telling the initiate that he is going to be very big in the religion; however, he must always respect his elders. No matter what, this person must remember that his godparents love him, and he should love them in return. Even if this client came to ocha for his health, the orishas will give him fame and fortune if he always honors his religious beginnings.
- If the odu opens in osogbo, a great suffering exists within the client. He worries a lot and loses sleep over an important issue. He also has issues with both of his parents, and this causes much guilt. The diviner must ask the client to air out his concerns at the mat. The orishas do not want him to suffer, and if he bares his soul openly and honestly, they will help him overcome what bothers him.
- In an osogbo alluding to curses or witchcraft, Odí Osá says that someone in the client's own family has worked witchcraft against him. More than likely, this was done in a cemetery. The client must make ebó to Oyá at the cemetery gates so she closes these doors to him. With the diloggún, the diviner questions whether she will stand up to defend the client, asking, "Larishe si Oyá?" If the answer is no, the client must still supplicate her with an offering to retain her goodwill.
- In osogbo, this letter signals that the client begins all his projects with good intentions, but before he reaches the goal, he loses his momentum. If the client wants to evolve and persevere in life, he must always finish what he begins.

## The Prohibitions of Odí Osá

- One's home is not good for one; move. If one cannot do this immediately, but take advantage of the first opportunity to do so.
- Olokun must be clean and beautiful always. Do not allow her shrine to go unattended.
- Do not wear costumes. If one must wear a costume, do it as ebó.
- This odu warns that one might think about throwing away one's orishas or leaving the religion. Do not discard one's spirits. Instead, pack them away and put them in storage or give them

to one's godparents. One day, one will want them back and they will still be there, waiting.

- One may not work in the forest for anyone except oneself. If a client or godchild needs to make ebó in the woods, another priest or priestess must help that person do his sacrifice.
- Do not use or wear anything torn, ripped, or filled with holes. Do not dig or open holes in the earth.
- Do not lift anything or anyone from the floor. If one does this, that object or person will continue to rise and one will fall in his place. Also, back injury can be sustained when lifting heavy objects.
- For a santero, one must be cautious about taking young women for clients. If a young woman comes to one's home to make ebó, another older santera should be present. Never touch female clients in any way; thus will gossip and slander be avoided.

## The Eboses of Odí Osá

If the client is an aleyo or an aborisha, the diviner must explore the following:

- If the client's head has not been marked (his guardian orisha has not been identified), the diviner knows that the orisha Olokun is close to him. The client's bond with Olokun is so special that this orisha might claim his head in ocha. This, however, can be determined only in a bajado. As ebó, this person must receive Olokun; he will bring many blessings. If the client cannot afford this ceremony immediately, the godparent should give him a rogación before Olokun and give him Olokun's eleke. This will help him evolve in the religion.
- A Congo spirit is close to this person, and he must deal with it before he can evolve further in the religion. The diviner must seek out a competent palero to advise this client; he might need rayado (the initiation of palo mayombe) and a nganga. Also, the divener should prescribe a series of masses for this person's egun. During these masses, the Congo spirit will show himself to the mediums present, and they can better advise the client on how to deal with it.
- When possible, the client should give a yucca stalk to his egun. The yucca stalk will ensure that the proper spirits are present for the client's petitions.

If these prescriptions are not enough to close the odu for an aborisha, the diviner should turn to the eboses of the parent odu, Odí (see page 346). He needs something from that list for his evolution.

When Odí Osá opens for an initiate, after investigating the initial considerations for ebó in Odí (page 305), the diviner should ask the odu for closure. If it refuses closure, he must consider the following eboses:

- An initiate who does not have Oyá must now receive her; she speaks strongly in this odu and will bring many blessings to the client's life.
- Elegguá could be standing up for ebó in this odu. The diviner should ask, "Ebó elese Elegguá?" If the oracle answers yes, the proper ebó is an ornate mask. The client should place this in front of Elegguá so that when onlookers see the warriors, all they see of Elegguá is the mask. He does not want strangers looking at him.
- Next, the diviner should consider Ogún, asking, "Ebó elese Ogún?" If Ogún claims ebó in this sign, the proper offering is a bellows. This will keep him cool and help him advance the client spiritually.
- Finally, the initiate who opens in Odí Osá has many issues with egun; this sign tells him to work egun equally to santo.

If these eboses are not enough to close the reading, the diviner should turn to the eboses of the parent odu, Odí.

## The Tenth Composite Odu of Odí, Odí Ofún (7-10)

### The Proverbs of Odí Ofún

- You were born to be initiated.
- Those who practice deception are doing you a favor.
- Do not be ashamed to look at yourself.

### The Message of Odí Ofún

When a casting of seven mouths, Odí, precedes a casting of ten mouths, Ofún, the odu Odí Ofún is open on the mat. Having cast in this sign, the diviner pays homage to Ogún, Yembo, and Naná Burukú, saying to each, "Maferefún!" For Odí Ofún is the pattern in which the curse was born among the land of the orishas; it alludes to the beginning of time when the only spirits incarnated on earth were Obatalá, Yembo, Ogún, Shangó, Elegguá, Dada, Aganyú, Ochosi, and Ósun. Obatalá and Yembo were mother and father to all, and besides Yembo, all were male save one: Dada. Obatalá promised her in marriage to Shangó, and the other orishas were jealous, embittered that they had to spend their days in loneliness. Yet the rage of none grew like that of Ogún. Days passed, and he worked himself weary trying to provide for the orishas all the tools they needed to create civilization for the humans that were walking the earth. In time, his loneliness warped his mind, and he returned home to rape his own mother, Yembo. Obatalá tried to curse the two; he decreed that all of Yembo's male children from that day forth would be put to death. Yembo, in despair, broke open into a great flood, a column of water that rushed from the earth to the sky, and she became Naná Burukú, the one who protects women from the evils of men. Ogún cursed himself to work night and day ceaselessly and without rest; so it has been since this day that Ogún works and never stops. Ogún's tireless nature was born here of his own rage and loneliness; Naná Burukú came into existence by the overwhelming sorrow boiling inside Yembo.

This letter also gave birth to marriage ceremonies; while marriage itself was born in Odí Obara (7-6), in Odí Ofún the religious ceremony binding two people together came to be. This sign also gave birth to deception, and when it falls the diviner must be wary. If the odu comes in osogbo, the first words out of the diviner's mouth should be the question "Are you an initiate?" For this person may be a spy, coming to test the diviner's skills and knowledge. If the client is not a priest or priestess, there is still the chance that he has come to test the skills of the diviner. The italero must be careful of what he says and how the reading progresses. He must measure all his words before saying them, and he must mark ebó carefully. Also, if the client is not an initiate, the diviner should bring out a mazo and throw it around his neck, instructing him to prostrate himself before either the diviner or the godparent; he is now bound to make ocha. The diviner will note that one day this person may inherit many orishas from dead priests or priestesses, but he does not need to deliver this information during the reading.

The diviner should also keep the following points in mind when delivering a reading of this odu:

- When this letter comes in iré, every day of his life the client should say, "Maferefún Obatalá!" Obatalá loves him, blesses him, and elevates him. He should dress in white daily, show respect to the elderly every chance he gets, and make adimú to Obatalá frequently.
- Regardless of this letter's orientation, every day of his life the client should say, "Maferefún Shangó!" Shangó supports him through darkness; he tries to elevate him no matter what the client is going through. Every chance he gets, the client should go to his godparent's home and make some adimú to this orisha in thanks for his blessings.
- While rain is holy, in this sign rain can damage the client's luck. He must not go out in rainstorms. If he must go out, he should carry an umbrella, protecting the top of his head at all costs.
- The client has many around him who deceive him; they pretend to be friends but have only

their best interests in mind. The diviner should tell the client not to be angry, for those who practice deception are doing him a favor. In the end, they will fall and he will rise.

- This person is thinking about moving, and he should do so. Many enemies are around him now, and he needs to get away from them quickly.
- There have been many illnesses in this person's life, all of them brought as punishments from the hands of God. If this letter comes in an osogbo of ano or ikú, he must make ebó quickly as repentance for the evils he has committed; if he does not, he may die at a young age from disease.
- The diviner should tell the client this: If he continues to live a life of deception, he will end up living in the woods, under the stars. Homelessness will be his fate.

## The Prohibitions of Odí Ofún

- Do not get wet in the rain. If one allows rainwater to fall on one's head, it will wash away one's luck.
- Danger comes through unlocked windows and doors; keep these locked always. Do not have the bed under a window, and never sleep under an opened window.

## The Eboses of Odí Ofún

When Odí Ofún opens on the mat, the client must prescribe four eboses.

- First, if the client is a homeowner, he must paint the interior and exterior walls of his home white where possible. This honors Obatalá; he will bring peace and safety to the client's home.
- Second, if the client has children in his house, the youngest daughter must receive Olokun. This orisha will keep her from getting lost in life.
- Third, this client is a true espiritista; he has a talent for working with spirits. He must begin attending spiritual masses, studying how the espiritistas work. In time, he must be a host to his own masses, inviting others to come. He will gain notoriety and fame from this work.
- Finally, for the next ten days, the client must offer the following ebó to Olófin: Save the leftovers from the evening meal until sunrise the next day. Take the plate outside to the street, touching it to the head while saying, "Olófin, here I am, your humble child and servant, making my ebó. Have pity on me, for I am but a humble man." Once the ten days of ebó are complete, Olófin will bring back the luck that the client has lost in life.

Having made these prescriptions, the diviner may now attempt to close the oracle. If it will not close, he should explore the following possibilities. One or more might be needed to soothe the client's osogbo:

- If the client is an aborisha, the orishas are marking his head as a priest by right of birth. This client will neither find nor fulfill his destiny until he is crowned. If his guardian orisha is known, the diviner should drape this orisha's mazo over the client like a banner and lead him to salute the orisha, the godparents present, and the diviner. He is now in bondage to ocha.
- This letter refers to inherited orishas, spirits that others bequeath to a godchild or relative during a priest's *itutu* (funeral rite). The diviner should ask the client if he has received soperas left behind by the departed. If so, the orishas of these soperas might need ebó. For each spirit the client has inherited, the diviner must ask, "Ebó elese [orisha's name] de [deceased priest's name], ibaé?" If the oracle marks ebó, the diviner must then use the diloggún to mark the required offering.
- This pattern also refers to ngangas that the client has inherited. If the client possesses any such cauldrons, he must feed them immediately. They require attention.
- If the client's godparents are deceased, the diviner should ask him if he knows the names of their main *muerto*, or spiritual guide. The godparents' muerto might have sought out this

client to guide him and elevate him; however, this spirit needs ebó. The diviner should consider asking, "Ebó elese [muerto's name]?" If this spirit claims ebó, the diviner uses the diloggún to mark the offering, and the client must give it immediately. The client must now tend to this spirit as if it were his own guide; it will help him advance spiritually.

- If the client is an aborisha who does not have an Elegguá, he must receive one. While it would be best for him to receive Elegguá along with all the warriors, if he cannot afford the full initiation, he must still receive his Elegguá. Once Elegguá lives with the client, this orisha will open all the doors that were once closed to him.

If these eboses are not enough to close the odu, the diviner should consider the eboses of the parent odu, Odí (see page 346). The client needs something there for his evolution.

## The Eleventh Composite Odu of Odí, Odí Owani (7-11)

### The Proverbs of Odí Owani

- Stretch your hand only as far as it can reach.
- Those who laugh at you today will beg you tomorrow.
- To carry water in a basket is to let water run out.

### The Message of Odí Owani

When a cast of seven mouths, Odí, precedes a cast of eleven mouths, Owani, the odu Odí Owani has come to the mat. No matter its orientation, this is a dangerous sign. It gives birth to the deathwatch beetle, the insect that chirps when death is near. Listen well for this sound; it announces that the death of someone close to the client is imminent. Sexual diseases are born in this odu, and if the client is not chaste, he may become infected with one soon. Even those in monogamous relationships must be wary, for while one can be sure of one's own actions, how can anyone know what the lover does when he is away? Odí Owani also gives birth to the custom of the godchild giving the derecho to the godparent whenever something is done in the religion; no matter how much or how little work the client (if he is an initiate) does for others, he must never forget to put this derecho to his godparent's crown.

Having cast this pattern, immediately the diviner pays homage to Obatalá, Elegguá, Orúnmila, Olófin, and Yemayá, saying to each, "Maferefún!" The aché of all five orishas may be required to overcome the inherent osogbo of this sign.

The diviner must examine the following issues thoroughly with the client who has come in Odí Owani:

- Of all relationships considered holy in this faith, none is holier than that between godparent and godchild. This odu reinforces this relationship. A godchild must stand close to his godparent, and in return, the godparent must help elevate the godchild spiritually. One day, the godchild will save the godparent's life.
- The client is poor, and others laugh at him. Know, however, that one day this client will be rich, and others will ask him for help.
- If the client is a woman or a homosexual male, she or he is thinking about leaving a lover. The diviner should advise against this. The problems that the two have now are only temporary, and if they can work through these, they will be together a long time.
- Eshu stands close to this person, not to bless him but to punish him for his disobedience. Jail is the ultimate punishment. If the client does not change his ways now, he could spend a multiple of seven or eleven days, weeks, months, or years in jail.

### The Prohibitions of Odí Owani

- Vices that one entertains will cost one's life. The orishas want one to give up smoking, drinking, overeating, overworking, and drugs. Do this now, and they will give good health and a long life.
- Do not leave others unattended around one's orishas, and always keep the orishas in a secure,

safe place. They cannot take care of someone who does not take care of them. If the osogbo of this letter is severe, lock the shells in a safe place and move the otanes to a new location. The orishas might want the client to move them to a new permanent home, for only in this way will all be safe.

- Do not wear more than two necklaces, including orishas' elekes, at once.

## The Eboses of Odí Owani

When Odí Owani opens on the mat, the diviner must prescribe two mandatory eboses.

- If the client is an aborisha and does not have an opá ikú, he must go out and find one in the woods with his godparent. The godparent must prepare and feed it. From this moment on, egun should be the client's foundation both in the religion and in his life. To keep the relationship between him and egun strong, he should go for long walks outdoors using the staff as a walking stick. He should attend much to egun. The diviner should consider asking, "Ebó elese egun?" If the answer is yes, he uses the diloggún to mark the appropriate offering.
- This person must buy a straw basket and cut a hole in the bottom. He should give this basket to Elegguá so that he no longer carries things in "baskets with holes." If the client does not have Elegguá, he must receive him as soon as it is possible.

Having made these prescriptions, if the odu remains open, the diviner should consider the following options for ebó:

- In Odí Owani, Elegguá and Yemayá can help the client recover what he has lost spiritually, emotionally, and financially. If the odu refuses closure, the diviner should consider asking, "Ebó elese Elegguá y Yemayá?" If they will claim ebó, the diviner, must mark something that the two orishas can take together. Once the ebó is completed, they will lead the client gently to evolution.
- If the client is a man, he could have special issues with both Elegguá and Ogún; to see if they will take ebó, the diviner should ask, "Ebó elese Elegguá y Ogún?" If so, the diviner must mark an offering that the client can give to both simultaneously. Note that this sign foreshadows danger to men from women, and the help of these two orishas is needed to overcome this osogbo for the client.
- If the client is facing legal difficulties, remember that this letter promises jail time. To overcome this osogbo, the client should propitiate Elegguá and Obatalá; the diviner must ask, "Ebó elese Elegguá y Obatalá?" If they will take ebó, the diviner should mark an offering the two can take together. If they demand no ebó, the client is on his own to solve his legal difficulties.

If these considerations are not enough to close a session in Odí Owani, the diviner must turn to the eboses of the parent odu, Odí (see page 346). The client needs something there for his evolution.

# The Twelfth Composite Odu of Odí, Odí Ejila (7-12)

## The Proverbs of Odí Ejila

- The other world acts in this one.
- He who set you free may die; you cannot cry.
- The blind man made ebó and caught the thief.
- The ear is smaller than the head, yet it does not go through it.

## The Message of Odí Ejila

When a casting of seven mouths, Odí, precedes a casting of twelve mouths, Ejila Shebora, the odu Odí Ejila is open. This letter is also known as Odí Shebora and Odí Oturupon. Having cast this pattern, the diviner says, "Maferefún Shangó!" No matter the orientation of this odu, he is strong here, and he has come to advise the client and help him through his trials and tribulations. The diviner should tell the client this: "You are in great wanting of something; you know what will make you happy, yet you are afraid to go out and find it. Shangó tells you to go out and look for your happiness. Set your goal and work to achieve it. Once you have it, make ebó to him to seal this firm. Give him a ram and a drum. Thus, the things you seek will never abandon you." In iré, Shangó says that this search will be easy, and along the way the client will find fame and fortune. In osogbo, the quest will be difficult, and it will cost the client all he has to achieve his dreams and goals. Nevertheless, after making the ebó to Shangó, he will recover all that he lost on his quest.

The meaning of this odu is heavily dependent on its orientation. If it opens in iré (even if it is not firm), it brings promises of fortune and happiness if the client heeds the orishas' advice and if he does all eboses quickly. Unfortunately, this letter hints at the client's obstinance and unwillingness to follow advice, so the iré promised may be lost by his own hands. If the odu opens in an osogbo of eyo, it marks a person who talks too much for his own good, giving away both his secrets and the secrets of others; this person also commits adultery regularly and feels that any woman he encounters should not only want him, but also be with him at his whim. An osogbo of ano or ikú will bring all the illness and disease predicted in the sign Odí; in this osogbo, the client should be very careful of his abdomen and waist, avoiding tight pants, belts, and any other item of clothing that is restrictive in these areas, because they can damage internal organs.

The diviner should also keep in mind the following issues when delivering a reading of Odí Owani:

- Any osogbo marks the client as a target for malicious witchcraft, especially that sent by practitioners of Palo Mayombe. They will send the dead after him, and he must work daily to strengthen himself and his spiritual court.
- Regardless of its orientation, this sign marks the client as a target for fights and violence; however, he can avoid these things if he makes ebó and stays calm.
- Someone has recently set the client free, and he cries over this. The orishas say to cry no more; they are sending a blessing to wipe away his tears.

## The Prohibitions of Odí Ejila

- When this odu falls during an itá, one is forbidden ever to tell the sick that one can heal them or save them. If this reading is for a client with ocha but who is not an itá, someone sick is coming to one for healing; while one can work to cleanse and make ebó for that person, one must in no way promise a cure. Trouble will come from this, even if one cures the client. Finally, if this reading is for an aleyo or an aborisha, the diviner himself may not promise to cure any sickness in this person or anyone known to him. The diviner may prescribe ebó and help the client make it, but he must make no promises.
- Iron at one's work can be deadly; avoid working with metal, if possible. Always be cautious around metal instruments.
- Do not wear tight clothing, especially pants and belts that restrict the natural movement of the abdomen and waist.
- Avoid large crowds, and avoid places where violence happens frequently.

## The Eboses of Odí Ejila

When the odu Odí Ejila falls for an aleyo or an aborisha, the diviner should attempt to close the oracle after relaying to the client the appropriate prohibitions, determining the larishe (if any), and prescribing the mandatory eboses for the family of Odí (see "Marking Ebó in Odí: Initial Considerations," on page 305). If the oracle refuses closure, the diviner may explore a variety of eboses to soothe the osogbo.

- If the client is one of three brothers, Odí Ejila is warning that before the year is over, one of these three could die. Immediately, the client must have a series of three rogaciónes before Obatalá. One should be given in the name of each brother, with the last one for the client himself. This will keep heads of all three safe from death.

- Shangó speaks strongly for all who open in this sign. If he has not offered a larishe to the client's troubles, the diviner should determine if he will take anything, asking, "Ebó elese Shangó?" If the answer is yes, he uses the diloggún to mark the required offering. The client should give the ebó immediately.
- A woman who is trying to conceive should do the following ebó: Sacrifice a hen to Oshún, and give two more between the orisha and the client's womb. If this is not enough to satisfy the odu, the diviner should consider asking, "Ebó elese Oshún?" If the answer is yes, he uses the diloggún to mark the required offering. She might want additional adimús in exchange for her help.
- If the one who opens in Odí Ejila is seeking fame and fortune, the diviner may prescribe the sacrifice of a rooster to Elegguá. This client must have his own Elegguá for this sacrifice, and he must begin every day praying and propitiating him until his luck is found.
- If the osogbo of this letter marks witchcraft as the source of the client's ills, he must do the following ebó: Daily, he is to refresh his front doorstep with a libation of fresh water offered to Olófin, Olorún, and Olódumare, and he must keep the entrance to his home free of trash, dirt, and debris. He should also wash his front door daily. This will ensure that his day is blessed and will deflect most of the witchcraft aimed at him.
- Finally, the diviner should inquire about the religious charms or niche osains that the client has. This sign suggest that the client may possess many charms, especially of the orishas, and one of them has all but lost its power. The diviner must mark to which charm this letter refers, and then mark the eboses needed to recharge this item. The client must not throw it away.

If these considerations are not enough to close the odu for an aleyo or an aborisha, the diviner should turn to the eboses of the parent odu, Odí (see page 346). The client needs something there for his evolution.

When this pattern opens for an initiate, there is one initial mandatory ebó: He must give a ram to Shangó. The day after giving the ram, he is to have an itá, followed by a tambor. The luck he seeks will come.

If the oracle refuses closure for an initiate after the prescription of this ebó, the diviner must turn to the eboses of the parent odu, Odí.

## The Thirteenth Composite Odu of Odí, Odí Metanla (7-13)

### The Proverbs of Odí Metanla

- As a favor, the bull remains tied to his horns.
- See how much crackling is left after the fat is fried.
- Give everything its time and you will win.

### The Message of Odí Metanla

When a casting of seven mouths, Odí, precedes a casting of thirteen mouths, Metanla, the odu Odí Metanla is open on the mat. This pattern is also known as Odí Irete, Odí Lere, Odí Leke, and Odí Legue. No matter its orientation, this letter is dangerous for the client. It alludes to exchanges of the head, a process by which the destiny of one's orí is switched, either purposefully or accidentally, with the destiny of another's orí. If ocha is the client's destiny, he must crown soon, for this is the only way that he can lock in his luck. This letter is where the ox did a favor for the dog, and because of this he remained forever tied to his horns, a beast of burden, while the dog became a beast of pleasure.

When this letter falls on the mat, the diviner should pay homage to Obatalá, Naná Burukú, and Babaluaiye, saying to each, "Maferefún!" Although all three may not speak directly to the client in this sign, their influence will be felt throughout this odu. They will protect and lead him through the many osogbos predicted in this sign. Perhaps the greatest osogbo predicted is this: The world mocks this client. He has many enemies who would like to see him fall, but if he makes the eboses of the letter quickly, the ones who mock him will come to need him soon. The client should pray to Obatalá frequently; on a daily basis, once in the morning and again at night, he should say, "Maferefún Obatalá!"

Even if the letter brings iré, in regard to the client's health the diviner would be wise to treat the letter as if it had fallen in the osogbo of ano or ikú. Here, the client should monitor his body for changes, especially in the abdomen or womb. Women could suffer menstrual or reproductive problems, and men could suffer injury from blows to the pelvic region. Parasites that attack the intestines are also a danger. If the client has any moles or birthmarks on the skin, he must watch these for changes and see a physician immediately if any are noticed. If any new moles or spots develop on the skin, the client should see a physician to have them checked; they could become cancerous. Also, there is a warning given to the diviner in this odu: Watch what one tells during the reading, for the client's spouse could visit, bringing many problems. The client will disbelieve the italero's words and will repeat them to his spouse, bringing gossip, heartache, and despair.

The diviner should also keep the following points in mind:

- This odu raises issues with adultery. If the client is faithful in mind and body, he can be assured that his spouse is not. One of the two will stray soon.
- In this odu, sacrifice can cure lack of children, poor health, and disease. If one of these is a problem for the client, the diviner should have the client whisper his problem to the ibó, and then the diviner should ask the diloggún, "Larishe si?" If the diloggún offers a larishe to the condition, the diviner should mark the ebó carefully. The client must do this ebó immediately.
- Now is not a good time for marriage. If the client is single and thinking about marriage, he should reconsider or at least put it off for a time. The prospective spouse has secrets and brings danger. When osogbo comes in Odí Metanla, the danger could be death.
- If the client is male, he flirts with three women. One of these might have a child soon; the child might not be his. He should keep this in mind.

## The Prohibitions of Odí Metanla

- The first prohibition given in this odu is for the diviner: If the letter opens in an osogbo centered on the client's words or actions, this priest must be cautious, choosing his delivery carefully. Speak of odu, but not specifics, and reveal no personal secrets during this session. The client has come to cause problems for this priest.
- Do not do favors for others. Remember: The ox, because he did a favor for the dog, remained tied to his horns. He became a beast of burden. The orishas do not want this happening to the client.
- Do not climb winding stairs; do not descend stairs leading into a dark room or basement.
- Protect the head physically and spiritually; it is weak. Ensure that no one touches the head, and do not use a hat or a scarf that another person has worn.

## The Eboses of Odí Metanla

No matter what issues come up during this session and no matter the sign's orientation, Odí Metanla carries danger for the diviner. He must complete two eboses himself. First, immediately after the client leaves, he must have another initiate give him a rogación before his guardian orisha. Second, within seven days, while the diviner is sitting in a place where his feet cannot touch the floor (such as on top of the roof or seated in a chair in which the feet dangle freely), an elder priest or priestess should feed two guinea hens to his orí. Once he or she feeds the diviner's head, the priest or priestess must give him a rogación in that same place. After the rogación is complete and the signs of obí are satisfactory, that same priest or priestess should feed the diviner's Elegguá a rooster. Until both eboses are done, the diviner's head is hot, perhaps even in danger.

In addition, when possible, the diviner, the client, and the godparents should offer a cleansing to egun. For this ebó, the diviner prepares four balls of ñame incorporating honey, molasses, and epó; he places these four balls in a jícara with plenty of honey covering the adimú. He also obtains a large, dark rooster and nine strips of multicolored cloth. Taking his opá ikú, the priest goes with the client and his godparents to a dead, decaying tree in the woods. There, he prays to egun with his opá, calling his, the client's, and the godparents' egun. He places the jícara of sweet ñame balls at the foot of the tree and sacrifices the rooster over it. Laying the carcass at the tree's roots, the diviner then cleanses himself and everyone present with the multicolored cloths. Everyone should leave an adimú for his or her own egun. That night, at their own bóvedas, all involved in the ceremony should light candles and leave a sweet adimú.

For a client who is an aleyo or an aborisha, the diviner must also explore the following concerns:

- As soon as possible this client must go to a babalawo for a reading with Ifá; Orúnmila has issues with him.
- As ebó the client must bring seven red parrot feathers to the diviner's Yemayá; if the diviner's Yemayá has a crown, the client should put the feathers in her crown. If she does not have a crown, the client must save these feathers until he purchases a crown for her.
- Finally, the client should dress in burlap and beg alms in the street, doing this in honor of Babaluaiye. He should use the money he receives to give two guinea hens and an agbán to this orisha.

Now the diviner asks the oracle for closure. If it refuses to close, it marks that the client needs to pray frequently to Obatalá, making frequent adimú at his shrine for peace and evolution. If the client is an aborisha, he may need to receive Obatalá lavado. To determine if this is the case, the diviner should ask, "Koshé Obatalá?"

If these eboses will not close the odu for an aleyo or an aborisha, the diviner should turn to the eboses of the parent odu, Odí (see page 346). The client needs something there for his evolution.

When Odí Metanla opens for an initiate and refuses closure, the diviner should consider the following eboses:

- Before doing any other ebó, the client must give Yemayá a crown adorned with seven red parrot feathers.
- This letter can mark the reception of Naná Burukú. To find out if this is necessary, the diviner should ask, "Koshé Naná Burukú?" If the answer is yes, the client should make preparations immediately.
- The next question to ask the oracle is "Ebó elese Olokun?" If the answer is yes, the proper ebó to give her in this odu is a sacrifice of three roosters. Olokun will help the client clear his osogbos. If the client does not have Olokun, he is now marked for his reception.
- Finally, if nothing else will close the letter, the diviner should ask the oracle, "Ebó elese Ósun?" If Ósun needs ebó, the godparent must call in an experienced oriaté for the ritual. The oriaté will paint Ósun in his four colors and, at the end of the ceremony, put Yemayá on top of Ósun. Only the oriaté will know the secrets for doing this ceremony.

If these considerations are not enough to close the odu for an initiate, the diviner should turn to the eboses of the parent odu, Odí (see page 346).

## The Fourteenth Composite Odu of Odí, Odí Merinla (7-14)

### The Proverb of Odí Merinla

- Blood runs from the mouth.

### The Message of Odí Merinla

When a casting of seven mouths, Odí, precedes a casting of fourteen mouths, Merinla, the odu Odí Merinla, also known as Odí Ika, is open on the mat. In this pattern, the diviner pays homage to Yemayá,

Babaluaiye, Obatalá, Eleggúa, and egun, saying to each, "Maferefún!" The aché of all five may be needed to overcome any osogbos marked in Odí Merinla. In osogbo, this sign marks all the evil that Odí can bring. Its workings are swift and its prohibitions severe. To begin, a woman in the client's life cannot get pregnant or is already pregnant. If she cannot get pregnant, she should not now, for she will miscarry. If she is already pregnant, this odu warns that she might not carry the baby to term. Ebó may help, but it will not guarantee the safety of mother and child in this letter. The client himself is ill, suffering with disease in his abdomen. During the day his body aches, and at night his abdomen hurts. Before this sickness has passed, blood could come from the nose, mouth, or anus. The client must guard his health well, and if he experiences any abnormal symptoms, he must see a physician immediately.

The diviner should also keep the following points in mind:

- When this pattern opens, the diviner should tell the client not to imitate other people; he should mind his own business.
- If the roof of the client's house develops a leak, he must fix it immediately. Evil spirits are spying on him through this.
- This person's life is not settled, and this is mostly his own fault. When this odu comes, the orishas are telling him that he must strive for a settled existence.
- False accusations, false arrests, and imprisonment are predicted in this odu as well. The client must take care against enemies who could being confrontations with the law.
- Finally, great treason is coming to the client. He is thinking of traveling, and while this trip will be dangerous, he may go if he makes ebó. The place to which he is going harbors secret enemies, and if they know he is there, they will try to hurt him. The diviner should tell the client to go and return secretly.

### The Prohibitions of Odí Merinla

- Travel is taboo in this odu. If one is planning a trip for pleasure, do not go. If one is planning a business trip, make ebó and go cautiously. Enemies who will rob and kill are waiting at one's planned destination. If this reading is an itá or a bajado, one may never travel without first consulting the orishas.
- Do not live in a leaky house; if the roof leaks, repair it immediately.

### The Eboses of Odí Merinla

Having cast Odí Merinla, the diviner has many initial considerations for ebó to prescribe to this client. First, if he does not have either or both the elekes and warriors, he must commit to receiving them when possible. While the energies of odu will pass in time, the orishas cannot completely remove the osogbos wrought in this sign until he has these initiations. The client's life is at a turning point, but things will not turn, nor will they get better, until he is firmly seated in this religion with the orishas.

Second, in this pattern the orishas Yemayá and Shangó can stand up for ebó. To determine if this is the case, the diviner should ask, "Ebó elese [orisha's name]?" If the answer is yes, he uses the diloggún to mark the required offering.

Having made these prescriptions, the diviner may try to close the reading. If the diloggún remains open, he must turn to the eboses of the parent odu, Odí (see page 346). Something there is needed for this person's evolution.

## The Fifteenth Composite Odu of Odí, Odí Marunla (7-15)

### The Proverb of Odí Marunla

- In business, others will try to rob you.

### The Message of Odí Marunla

When a casting of seven mouths, Odí, precedes a casting of fifteen mouths, Marunla, the odu Odí

Marunla has come to the mat. This odu is also called Odí Iwori. This sign speaks of disaster and treason; in osogbo, it can bring out all the worst Odí has to offer. It also speaks of triumph and recovery; in iré, it can bring out all the best Odí has to offer. Regardless of its orientation, however, ultimately the client's own actions will determine how the energies of this odu will play out. In this sign is told the story of the blind priest who sold water lilies in the market; his enemies robbed him of all his money because he could not see them. Olorún once needed a mouse for ebó and he could not find one. He sent Elegguá, Ogún, and Shangó to find a mouse in the forest. All found mice, but Elegguá and Ogún were hungry, and they ate theirs. Shangó was starving as well, but he decided that bringing the mouse home to his father was more important. Because he alone succeeded in his quest, Shangó came to represent law on earth and in heaven. "Maferefún Shangó!" He alone has the aché to help the client overcome all the osogbos in this odu.

When Odí Marunla falls on the mat, it is important that the diviner discuss the following issues with the client:

- The client must be careful at work, especially if he is in a business that handles large sums of cash or valuables. Someone is coming to rob him.
- If the client is a palero, he has either a cauldron of mayombe or a spiritual shrine in his home from that faith that embodies a powerful spirit. He has, however, lost control of the muerto, and because it does not work for him, he no longer believes in it. Little by little, this spirit is consuming him. There is only one solution to this: becoming initiated to ocha. Without his guardian orisha crowned on his head, the client will slowly lose his life.
- A woman who opens in this sign will always have difficulty with conception. If she lives by making ebó, however, she can still conceive.
- Finally, this sign refers to an old family curse; so strong is this that it affects the client now. There is only one way to destroy this curse: The client must make ebó to Elegguá in the home where he was born. Once this has been done, his entire family will prosper again.

## The Prohibition of Odí Marunla

- Do not travel without first consulting the orishas and making ebó. Even if the orishas give their permission for one to travel and mark no ebó, one should still offer something to Elegguá. And avoid frivolous trips.

## The Eboses of Odí Marunla

To appease this letter, the client must be marked for the reception of the elekes, warriors, and the Ibeyi. If he has already taken these initiations, then the warriors or the Ibeyi might be standing up for ebó; the diviner should try to mark this.

Also, if someone in the client's family becomes ill, the odu requires, as an ebó, that he take this person to see a physician. He must do this even if there is no money available for medical treatment, and the one who became ill should come to the diviner when possible for a reading.

This odu marks the client to make frequent ebó and adimú to Ogún. If Ogún has not stood up for larishe in this sign, the diviner needs to mark several eboses to him before asking the odu for closure. The client should also offer sacrifices to Elegguá and Olokun. He should pray to Olódumare for evolution, for he is the one to bring it. Finally, the client should have a huge feast in honor of his ancestors.

If these prescriptions are not enough to close the odu, the diviner should turn to the eboses for the parent odu, Odí (see page 346). Something from that list is necessary for the client's evolution.

# The Sixteenth Composite Odu of Odí, Odí Merindilogún (7-16)

## The Proverb of Odí Merindilogún

- You want one thing for yourself, and the orishas want another for you.

## The Message of Odí Merindilogún

When a casting of seven mouths, Odí, precedes a cast of sixteen mouths, Merindilogún, the odu Odí Merindilogún is open. This sign is also known as Odí Otura, Odí Atago, and Odí Okparo. It is especially dangerous for those who refuse to make ebó. Here is told the story about the rooster who wanted to be general and the goat who wanted to be king. Both went to the diviners to mark ebó, but neither made his prescribed eboses. The two soon became food. In another storey, Obatalá once went to the diviners to mark ebó; they told him to have a rogación of his head with *seso vegetal* (avaliable at botánicas). The king of all the orishas felt this was foolish and refused to have the rogación. He soon died.

Because of disobedience, all who come in this odu fail to realize their dreams and aspirations. They lose because of disobedience. The diviner must tell the client that he has been disobedient as well. When the odu opens, the first words the diviner should offer are "Maferefún Elegguá!" For Elegguá speaks strongly about disobedience here. There are serious issues afoot between the client and his Eshu, and the diviner's job in this letter is to discover why the orisha is perturbed. From this moment on, Elegguá needs much care and attention; he has covered the client and all his roads are closed. No matter what the orishas promise the client here, this person will always want something different. His will is at odds with theirs, and consequently he has many problems with Elegguá.

The italero must also explore the following points in all readings of Odí Merindilogún:

- Soon, others will ask the client for four separate things that he owns only in single units. He must not hesitate to part with these even though he has only one of each. They will compensate him richly in the end.
- Assassination and murder are true dangers in this odu, especially if it opens in osogbo. The diviner must speak openly and honestly with the client about this; with inspired introspection, the two can discover from what place this danger comes.
- If pains arise in the groin or abdomen, the client must see a physician immediately. Pain in these areas signals serious illness brewing in his body.

## The Prohibitions of Odí Merindilogún

- All the prohibitions of the parent odu, Odí (see page 346), apply here, even when this letter comes in iré. Odí Merindilogún hides more than it reveals, and each orientation carries a bit of the other when it opens. Good fortune can quickly turn to bad, and vice versa.
- Home remedies for any ailment are forbidden. One's health is delicate; see a physician for all complaints.
- Do not guard or store anything for anyone. Those things that others bring into one's home could be stolen property.
- Never argue or fight with Yemayá's children, or else all the blessings of this odu will be lost.

## The Eboses of Odí Merindilogún

When Odí Merindilogún opens, it marks the client as being in danger and needing the initiation of the elekes desperately. If he does not have the elekes, he must receive them as soon as possible. After the initiation of the elekes, or if he already has the elekes, he will need to take the warriors. Only after taking both will his osogbo lift. If the client already has both initiations, the diviner should see if the warriors will take an ebó in exchange for fighting the client's battles, asking, "Ebó elese los guerreros?" If the answer is yes, he uses the diloggún to mark the appropriate offering.

Remember that five spirits—Yemayá, Elegguá, egun, Shangó, and Orúnmila—always speak in Odí Merindilogún. Each may stand up to claim ebó in this odu. If the sign will not close at this point, the diviner should consider asking of these orishas, "Ebó elese [spirit's name]?" If the answer is yes, he uses the diloggún to mark the appropriate offering.

If these orishas will not claim ebó, or if the oracle still refuses closure, the diviner must turn to the eboses listed for the parent odu, Odí (see page 346). Something there is needed to close the session.

## Closing the Reading: Further Eboses of the Parent Odu, Odí

Once the options for larishe and ebó have been exhausted through the composite odu, the diviner turns to the parent odu for closure. Odí is complex and demanding; at this point, not only the orishas but also the odu must be satisfied. Before examining the options in this list, the diviner examines what has been prescribed so far. If the session offered a larishe either to lock in iré or to avoid osogbo, the diviner should incorporate the number seven into that ebó. For example, he might add seven ingredients to the offering, seven days to the length of time it is offered, or seven other elements. Then he examines the eboses of the composite odu required for this client and incorporates the mark of seven into those as well.

If the odu remains open after this, the diviner should consider the following options for ebó in Odí. Not all are necessary, but the diviner might wish to prescribe one to cleanse the client of osogbo:

- The first ebó offered by the parent odu, Odí, consists of the following: a large pumpkin or calabaza, seven coconuts, seven ears of corn, a variety of grains and beans, and two feathered animals. The diviner should offer this ebó to the orisha whose shells have been consulted. To prepare for this, he digs a deep hole in the earth and places the orisha beside this hole. The diviner cleanses the client with the pumpkin, coconuts, corn, and grains, throwing each into the hole after using it. Finally, he cleanses the client with the birds, one at a time, sacrificing each after the cleansing to both the orisha and the earth. He throws the carcasses into the hole, then buries the ebó.
- The orisha whose shells are consulted may enjoy an ebó made from the following ingredients: several different types of grains, a large gourd, a chicken, and two pigeons. To begin, the diviner cleanses the client with the grains, placing them in the gourd after using them. Next he cleanses the client with the chicken, then sacrifices the bird to the orisha. He lays the carcass on top of the gourd. Finally, he performs a rogación for the client's head, feeding his orí the two pigeons. With obí, he determines where to discard the ebó.
- An ebó for Elegguá can be made with the following elements: a ñame, white thread, black thread, and a rooster. Before Elegguá, the client wraps the ñame in the threads, praying to him for evolution, protection, and strength. When the ñame is completely wrapped, the diviner cleanses the client with the root, offering it to the orisha. After this, he cleanses the client with the rooster and sacrifices the bird to Elegguá. The ñame stays with the orisha until it begins to rot; the bird's carcass is discarded in a dumpster.
- An ebó for Yemayá can be made with the following elements: a rooster, seven pañuelos, seven ears of corn, seven coconuts, and seven gourds filled with black-eyed peas. First, the diviner cleanses the client with the rooster and sacrifices the birds to Yemayá. After cleansing her otanes and shells, the diviner adorns her shrine with the seven pañuelos and lays the remaining elements of ebó before her shrine. The client discards the bird's carcass in a lake. In seven days, he removes all elements of ebó except the pañuelos; she keeps these forever.

Normally, one of the above eboses is enough to end a session that has been difficult to close. If, however, closure is not granted, the diviner should consider the following list of possible eboses:

- For an aleyo, the diviner should prescribe the reception of the elekes.
- An aborisha with elekes but without warriors must receive Elegguá, Ogún, Ochosi, and Ósun. The aché of these four orishas is essential to the client's evolution.
- If the client's mother is deceased, a priest feeds Yemayá Asesu in the drains of the kitchen sink in the client's home. After feeding her, the client must give his mother's spirit many spiritual masses.
- If the client's mother still lives, odu is demanding that she have a rogación with four live snails

to strengthen her orí. She will die if this is not done. If the client's mother is not in the religion, the client may have the rogación before Yemayá in her name. Once this is complete, he must sacrifice a hen to Yemayá to save his mother's life. The day following this ebó, the client should return to have a rogación to clear his head of his mother's osogbo.

- In any osogbo (especially ano or ikú), the client could need a rogación at the feet of Yemayá; his orí might need an ebó of two white pigeons as well. To determine if this is the case, the diviner must ask, "Rogación elese Yemayá?" If the answer is yes, he continues with the question "Eborí?" If both are marked, this person has seven days to make ebó. Once this cleansing is done, he should give Yemayá an adimú. If this letter still refuses closure, Yemayá might be standing up for something specific; to determine if she will take anything, the diviner should ask, "Ebó elese Yemayá?" If the answer is yes, he uses the diloggún to mark the appropriate offering.
- If the client is an aborisha or an initiate, he could have issues with Babaluaiye. The diviner should ask the following series of questions: "Ebó elese Babaluaiye?"; "Koshé eleke de Babaluaiye?"; and "Koshé Babaluaiye?" If Babaluaiye claims ebó, the diviner should use the diloggún to mark an appropriate offering, and the client must make it immediately. If the eleke of this orisha is marked, the client must have a rogación before his shrine; immediately after the rogación, he is cleansed with the orisha's broom and the eleke is vested on him. (Note that when the client receives the eleke, it would be in good taste for him to make an adimú to this orisha once the ceremony is complete.) Finally, if this orisha's reception is marked, the client must prepare for it immediately. An initiate will receive him with four legs and an itá, while an aborisha will receive him with only feathers.
- If the client is an aborisha or an initiate, Olokun may have issues with him. The diviner should consider asking, "Ebó elese Olokun?" and "Koshé Olokun?" If Olokun claims ebó, the diviner uses the diloggún to mark the appropriate offering, and the client must give it within seven days. If Olokun's reception is necessary, the client must prepare for this ceremony as soon as possible.
- If the oracle continues to refuse closure for an aleyo or anaborisha, he may have issues pending with Ogún, Elegguá, or Ochosi. One or more might need ebó.
- Also, for an aleyo or an aborisha this sign can point out the need for the client to make ocha as soon as possible. If this client has children, the youngest of them will need to make ocha soon as well. If the client is one of many brothers and sisters, this sign also marks issues pending between the youngest and ocha. The diviner should consider this aspect of the sign as well.
- If the client is an initiate, he could have issues pending with Orisha Oko, Otín, Ochosi, Inle, and Korikoto. Anything from a simple ebó to the spirit's reception could be necessary; the italero must consider this carefully.

If this list is exhausted and the odu still refuses closure, the diviner has two options. First, he may call an elder in the religion, for something important in the sign could have been overlooked. Second, he may look at the list of eboses given for the omo odu as a parent odu. For example, in a casting of Odí Okana (7-1), the diviner would turn to the eboses of Okana as the parent odu for closure.

# NINE
# THE FAMILY OF EJI OGBE

## The Proverbs of Eji Ogbe

- Remember: It is the head that carries the body; do not lose the head.
- When two snakes fight, they embrace each other.
- Young palm fronds grow more frondose than their elders.
- To not learn from one's mistakes: This is the biggest mistake.
- Do not destroy with your feet what you create with your head.
- Love yourself, for only then can you love others.
- One should never desire a hat more than a crown.
- You will be poor when the ocean is poor.
- To have everything is to lack all.
- Where there is life, there is always hope.
- Only one king can govern a town.
- When my head is on my shoulders, my feet in salty waters, and my thoughts extend beyond the horizon, there is no doubt in my mind that I stand facing the ocean.

## The Orishas Who Speak in Eji Ogbe

| | |
|---|---|
| Obatalá | Yemayá |
| Oduduwa | Naná Burukú |
| Orúnmila | Oba |
| Oshún | Ajé Shaluga |
| Oké | Iroko |
| Olokun | When necessary, all the orishas |

## The Message of Eji Ogbe

Having opened with eight mouths on the mat, the ritual of diloggún becomes a solemn but joyous occasion. The reading transcends to a time marking not only the beginning of creation but also the dissolution of all things. To borrow a metaphor from the Christian faith, one might call this odu the alpha and the omega; it is Baba (Father) Eji Ogbe, and its power is transcendent. Babalawo Fa'Lokun Fatunmbi writes of this odu, "[It is] the primal impulse for expansion, evolution, and ascension . . . a way of knowing that involved the whole being and not just the intellect."* This letter is the eldest of the elders, the raw energy expanding and awakening in the east, and it is the path by which all spirits began their descent to the earth. Its primal stirring created light, holy and infinite, a white fire consuming that void. Its movements birthed the Irunmole, those orishas who sprang from heaven with Olódumare's first thoughts. In short, Eji Ogbe is life, and life is Eji Ogbe.

After making this cast on the the mat, the diviner suspends the reading before drawing a composite letter. In reverence for the odu unveiled, he touches his forehead in an attitude of prayer, then crosses his arms tightly over his chest with his head bowed. The initiates present for the reading follow the

*Awó Fa'Lokun Fatunmbi, *Awó: Ifá and the Theology of Orisha Divination* (New York: Original Publications, 1992), 138.

italero's movements. If the client does not know our customs, he may not repeat this gesture. He will, however, know awe, for the energies unfolding at the mat combined with the reverence that the odu receives can kindle a feeling akin to ecstacy; this person will know peace, and tears, before the letter has closed. He will watch with curiosity as the initiates present touch their foreheads in an attitude of prayer, mirroring the diviner's movements. All will cross their arms tightly over the chest, their heads bowed and eyes closed, while the diviner's assistant blesses the heads of all present. Using efun, he marks the foreheads of everyone seated in the room, beginning with the diviner and the client and ending with the initiates present for the reading. Then he sprinkles slivers of cocoa butter over the crowns of everyone's head. No one moves until the priest giving the reading of Eji Ogbe finishes the sacred prayer of the sign:

*Dedele la boru, dedele la boya, dedele bochiche.*
*Tonti eko de dide inolori lodafunbe ibolotan.*
*Loda ewe Oke osese loda abonyu on'Ife.*
*Abonyu onofe abi tibi tire oku ele buburu.*
*Mubaye baba oro o to taye pa.*
*Dedele la boru, dedele la boya, dedele bochiche.*
*Tonti eko ode leri lodafun ibó, ibó leti loda.*
*Oke.*
*Elese lodafun aboru onife obi tibi tire*
*Okurun ni un baye.*

Even if this is a casual reading for a new client, many will continue their devotions by uttering, "Maferefún Eji Ogbe." Others will say, "Maferefún Obatalá"; Obatalá is the true owner of this odu, and before it closes he will have much to say. When eight mouths opens on the mat, it demands that the diviner drape Obatalá's mazo over the client, over his left shoulder and under his right arm, so that he wears it like a banner. Eji Ogbe binds this person to ocha, and one day he will be initiated. Even if this person has no plans of being initiated, initiation will come. Odu will drag this client to the asiento, kicking and screaming all the way if need be. It will not be immediate and many years might pass before the ritual takes place, but from this moment on all that the client goes through in life will prepare him for that one ritual, a glorious moment when seasoned priests put aché into his head. The diviner should explain these things during the reading. Once the diloggún gives closure, the client should pay foribale to his godparents, Obatalá, and his guardian orisha (if known) to receive their blessings.

If a bajado has already been done and the client knows his guardian orisha, the diviner can foretell the many blessings that initiation will bring. Initiation equals spiritual transformation, and once the client takes this step, his life will never be the same. Children of Elegguá will find stability, foundation, and a home; Elegguá was born through this family of odu, and through this letter his initiates will find their destiny unfolding. Oshún, who was once the poorest of the spirits, found her wealth in this sign, and she will share her wealth with her children if they heed the advice of this letter and take her as their crown. Shangó finds wisdom here, and he shares that with his children when his aché is put into their heads. Yemayá, mother to the world through this odu's power, will make her initiates the mothers and fathers to vast numbers of godchildren. Initiation ensures their immortality for centuries. Yet the blessings of none compare with what Obatalá brings to his children when they follow the path of progress laid out through Eji Ogbe: He gives all knowledge, greatness of the head, and the means to use these things in the service of humanity. The client should heed this odu's advice for initiation: If he does so, fame and fortune will follow.

Through this letter several orishas might speak to the client. The spirit whose diloggún is being consulted has the first option. If the odu has opened in iré, Olófin follows this orisha; all the orishas work for him in this sign, and it is he who directs them to bless the client. Obatalá owns this pattern, and rarely will it close unless he has spoken. Oduduwa and Orúnmila follow Obatalá. Although they will not speak directly through the diloggún, they are close to the client and could direct him to Ifá for an assessment. Oshún, Oke, Olokun, Yemayá, Shangó, Naná Burukú, Oba, Aye Shaluga, and Iroko might stand up to claim ebó. If the odu will not close, the diviner should question them in that order. Finally, because Baba Eji Ogbe gave birth to all things, any spirit, even egun, could choose to speak in this odu. The diviner must assess this sign carefully so that he misses nothing.

The easiest way to begin a study of Eji Ogbe is with an examination of it in iré. When eight mouths promises iré, it offers one of the greatest possible evolutions. This sign can create something out of nothing; it can fill the void with unlimited potential. No matter from where the client has come, this odu can destroy the old and create new possibilities in its place. Remember that once there was nothing: no earth, no stars, no sun, no moon, only a vast vacuum in which *not a single thing* existed. Olódumare unfolded; Eji Ogbe was his first manifestation, and from this did all things descend, coalescing from blackness and vacancy. So it will be with the client's life if he heeds the advice of eight mouths, giving the orishas due worship and reverence. His life can transform, and under Eji Ogbe's influence his entire mode of living can become one miracle after another.

Having determined the iré and its source, the italero continues to question the oracle. If the odu is further marked as iré yale (firm iré), Eji Ogbe is telling the diviner that the client's source of help is strong. Spiritual forces are mounting behind him, a wealth of strength that can carry him to new heights of existence if he is obedient. If the iré is also marked iré yale timbelaye (firm iré manifest in the client's life), Eji Ogbe gives closure to itself. It tells the diviner that the odu's energy has been in effect for some time, and the client is on the verge of obtaining all the blessings meant for him in this life.

When this pattern opens in any type of iré, the diviner may make many assumptions about this client, his life, and how it will progress. Being the primal cause of creation and the first letter of Olódumare's unfolding, Eji Ogbe marks spiritual alignment with orí in heaven, the immortal self. It rules the physical and mental orí (the head) as well, and the heart. It will affect all these areas in the client's life. At its best, it gives perfect alignment and flawless achievement. The one at the mat has an uncanny knack for knowing; material, emotional, mental, and spiritual truths come intuitively. Knowledge flows to this person, and he tries to soak it in like a sponge. The omo odu that opens, along with the orientation of the iré, will determine how these things manifest. In some, these blessings manifest as beauty and health; in others, as strength and magnificent form; in still others, as a razor-sharp mind. Some who open in this odu will blend so perfectly with an orisha that all who look will know, without a doubt, who claims the head. Note that all who heed this sign's advice will enjoy the unlimited blessings of Olófin and Obatalá. They generate coolness, health, fulfillment, and longevity here.

The diviner should examine and inventory the client's life at this time. Even in iré, this person has experienced devolution in one or more areas. His health may be failing; serious decay and disease develop slowly. Eventually it will consume him. Emotionally, this person is drained; relationships, marriages, and friendships could be strained to the point of loss. Financially, materially, and economically this person could be on the brink of disaster. Yet eight mouths with blessings guarantees an end to this. Evolution is coming. Until now the client has tended not to recognize blessings when they manifest, and the greatness of this odu demands recognition, humility, mirth, and reverence. The client must learn these lessons before iré can be given. The diviner should tell the client this: "There has been laughter, but more tears; there has been health, yet it faded. Now come rebirth and renewal. Plan to make ocha, for only in this way will happiness be found."* If the client is an initiate, Eji Ogbe in iré demands a token ebó that must be done occasionally (or for life if this reading is itá): The client must wear a red parrot feather in his hair at orisha rituals, giving it to Obatalá after the festival is done.

No matter the orientation of Eji Ogbe, however, the one for whom this odu opens is a paradox. He has many personality extremes buried deep within,

*Although it is said that in certain situations one should not make ocha, such as if one is elderly or chronically ill/weakened, this odu in iré demands that the client go through initiation in time. If the guardian orisha is too strong for the weakened head to receive, the client should be crowned with Obatalá and the true guardian orisha will step down to become the complementary mother or father of the iyawó.

each extreme manifesting as the environment changes. A child of eight mouths wants nobility, craves status, and spends much time projecting an image of caring and concern. The desire is for altruism, yet the reality is buried stinginess. He spends so much time acting selflessly (yet selfishly) for others that his own life deteriorates. Perfection is his ideal; he works toward clear dreams, astute aspirations, and delineated goals, yet he has little time left for rest. His exhaustion brings tears. Overwork and overextension of physical, mental, and emotional resources drive the client closer to his desires, yet an overwhelming lethargy from insomnia and lack of rest weakens and clouds his mind. Rarely will a child of Eji Ogbe make a mistake when working at his optimum level; however, overextension toward too many goals brings carelessness and recklessness. To achieve, to excel, as is this person's nature, he must choose one goal and accomplish it before he begins the next. The diviner should encourage this client to complete one project that he has started, leaving the rest for future attainment. This will bring evolution.

The italero should also tell the client this: Rarely does he give himself recognition and self-praise for the good works he has done. Seeking approval from others, he finds only disappointment; most people see his sly presentation of the goals he has achieved and the good works he has accomplished as vanity and bragging. Rewards will not come from without; the reward must first come from within. The client must learn to work hard, achieve superior results, and keep quiet. Others will see what he has done, and even if they remain quiet, the client should know that he impresses them.

This person also has an opportunistic nature. He sees what must be done and then completes those tasks. Perhaps this is why he achieves so much in spite of himself; perhaps this is why others are full of evil thoughts and jealousy. The diviner must warn the client that others are jealous. Envy exists around every corner. His peers believe themselves superior, yet they are not. Others work hard to emulate the client, yet it is their own jealousy that causes their failures. The diviner should warn the client to beware of jealousy and jealous people; he must not keep their company. He must realize that he has few real friends. Many talk behind his back. Everyone has his or her own plans for him, and he should harden himself toward these things; in this way he can never be used. The client must make ebó continually to ensure that this negativity does not manifest as a curse.

Perhaps the most important advice for the client's conduct is this: He must not become overwhelmed, overexhausted, or overworked. He must not let his head become heated, and he should never leave the company of gentle people for those who are harsh or coarse. Depression, exhaustion, and oppression will bring out the darker side of this client's personality and encourage him to curse, to blaspheme, and to leave the nobility of his own nature for something more selfish.

When this letter opens in an osogbo, many of its meanings become altered. It reveals the client as someone who suffers alone, sometimes in silence and sometimes noticeably, cut off from his orí, the higher self. His intuition is active, but the client has neither the faith nor the desire to follow these feelings. He wanders, led blindly by his environment. Physically, he behaves like those around him; often, coarse people surround him. Spiritually, he mirrors the beliefs of others, and those with whom he associates have little spirituality of their own. He seeks out knowledge for its own sake; the client does not apply what he knows, nor does he study what he should. Much of the time that he could spend in mental pursuits is spent in sloth and laziness instead. He never acknowledges his blessings. Instead of seeing beauty, the child of this odu who comes in osogbo will see only imperfections. Instead of promoting good health, this person entertains vices and bad habits. Unless this person modifies his behavior and thoughts, he will miss the blessings that originate here. The specific composite opening will tell the diviner just how much work the client has to do.

As with Eji Ogbe in iré, the diviner must begin a reading of this odu in osogbo by assessing the client's life. Devolution will come in one or more areas; most often, it began before the oracle was opened. The client's health has suffered or will suffer; aggressive decay and disease are possibilities.

Poor health habits and vices will damage healthy tissues, and he will notice the physical effects only when the most damage has been done. Emotionally, the client will become drained, and all his relationships will suffer. His finances are stretched; often an osogbo in this sign marks one who lives well beyond his means. Disaster comes slowly, unseen in this letter. When it shows itself, it will be too late for the client to correct it. Good and nobility may exist in this person's life; however, when he is exhausted, depressed, or oppressed he speaks ill of others. His head is too weak to handle life's extremes; it becomes heated, and in this state the client hangs all types of ills upon himself. He curses. He blasphemes. He speaks poorly of others and makes snide remarks behind their backs. Jealousy surrounds him. Those who are friendly to his face show another side when he turns his back; they wish him ill and plan his end.

In spite of all these things, Baba Eji Ogbe is the most forgiving of all the odu. To begin, the diviner must help the client explore his own osogbo; he must find a way to make this person assess his own life and actions. Before detailing eboses, the diviner should impress upon the client the value of behavior modification. If one is miserable yet smiles, others will smile as well, uplifting the soul. Darkness flees from light, and the aché of this letter is to create light out of nothing. Whenever the client is tempted to speak ill of another, he should say nothing. In that way, he does not release negativity to create more of the same. Similarly, he must not lie, gossip, or blaspheme. He must give up vices and bad habits; alcohol, intoxicants, sexual addictions, and other mindless vices can harm him now. Finally, Obatalá is always receptive to ebó through this pattern, and since he is the most forgiving of all the orishas, the client opening in osogbo should turn to him for help.

In any osogbo, Eji Ogbe foreshadows bitter arguments and heated combat if the client does not follow its advice and prohibitions. This person must avoid verbal, intellectual, physical, or spiritual combat, even from a distance. Those with whom he fights will only be brought closer into his life. Remember the proverb of this odu: "When two snakes fight, they embrace each other." In this letter, there is no such thing as safe combat from a distance, nor can one attack anonymously.

The osogbos ano and ikú bring special considerations for this client. In this orientiation, the letter no longer promises evolution and material progress; it will bring only ruin. These osogbos exaggerate health problems, and for the elderly they will bring death unless they make ocha. One who opens in these osogbos must make the prescribed eboses quickly and, once these are done, should see a physician for a complete physical. The diviner must advise caution and vigilance over the body. The client must not ignore pains that come in the legs, feet, or abdomen; these are the first signs that the serious health concerns predicted by Eji Ogbe are happening. The client could experience general aches, pains, and cramps, and the diseases foreboded by these symptoms could leave him bedridden for an extended period. Colic in infants and throat problems in both children and adults are common. If this letter falls in the darker months of the year, these concerns become critical. Exhaustion, mental breakdown, and physical paralysis are possible if the client does not care for his own health. If any symptoms of ill health manifest in the chest, thoracic, or cranial cavities, the client should see a physician, even if the complaints are minor.

Regardless of its orientation, the diviner can make other general predictions for the client who opens in this odu, and the diviner should spend time exploring them:

- While the client might be intuitive and emotional, this sign dictates that he must always put the head first. He should not be led blindly by the feet; he must think about the steps he is taking. When the client becomes excited, he must stand back, take a deep breath, and think about the situation for a few days. When his head is cool, calm, and clear, the situation might not appear as promising. Even if this letter has opened in the firmest iré, it suggests that being forced into quick decisions can destroy the good that exists in the client's life. He must not allow himself to be forced into giving quick responses to major decisions. The proper answer, for now, will always be "I need to think about that for a few days." Remember the proverb of this odu: "The head carries the body; do not lose the head."

- Eji Ogbe promises that the head will create great ideas and solid plans; yet it also promises that the feet will trample these. Thought moves faster than light, so the client must learn to think before moving. He must let rational thought pave the way for gentle movement.
- The client should beware of those who seek to touch, kiss, or embrace too often. They can become sources of despair.
- In this pattern, youth flourishes beyond the achievements of its elders. The client must keep in mind, however, that the elders fought wars and battles for this faith, and won. It is upon their achievements that youth stands. It is from them that youth is created, new ideas are born, and new growth is sought out. While youth implies energy and change, these changes must be wrought and energies expended with the elders' guidance. Only then is youth not squandered.
- Baba Eji Ogbe promises that the client will make mistakes. If he learns from those mistakes, future growth will come more easily. He should also learn from the mistakes of his elders and of his peers. This way, growth is positive, continual, and always fruitful.
- Eji Ogbe is growth, and growth promises movement. While the child of this odu has the potential to achieve greatness, those that gave his head birth will always be greater. To live up to his potential, this person must move away from those that gave him spiritual and physical birth. However, he must ensure that the physical separation does not include emotional or spiritual separation.
- When misfortune comes (and it will), the client must not cry or complain to others. He should wear a happy face, forcing himself to smile and hold his head high no matter the adversity he faces. Sweetness and assurance will always attract more of the same.
- This odu offers an ebó that can be used to lighten up the environment when things get too heavy or dark: laughing freely. Fake laughter will bring true laughter in time. The client should not let his environment become overly oppressive.
- No matter the orientation of odu, the digestive tract of one who opens in this sign cannot handle hot and spicy foods. For optimum health, this person should avoid heavy meats and peppers, herbs, and spices. He should eat a bland diet most of the time.
- Robbery can be a danger in this sign, and the client must ensure his personal safety always. A key to avoiding harm is this: If the client hears a disturbance outside, he should not check it out. Instead, he must make sure that the doors and windows are closed and locked, then call the police. He should not admit to witnessing the disturbance; he should say only that he heard a strange noise. He must allow the authorities to check it out for themselves.
- The child of this odu is adventurous and likes to travel; depending on the orientation, however, he may fulfill these desires in various degrees. One day, this person will venture outside the country.
- A single person who opens in this letter will one day get married. Odu says that the first child after marriage will probably be a daughter. If this person has reproductive difficulties, adoption is still a possibility for the future.
- Eji Ogbe predicts that this client will one day own property. The type of property he owns will depend on the client's desires and his willingness to work and save money. If, however, the client already owns property, he will sell some land first before purchasing more.
- This sign indicates that the client will not find rewards for the good things he does immediately; however, the rewards will come in time. The diviner should tell the client never to become discouraged and to continue to work hard.
- This sign points out that the elder in the family can be lost through disease or accident. The client must give much care to this person. Even if she is not the elder, the mother of the client

could also be in danger. If this sign comes in either the feet or the head in itá, the elder of the spiritual family could be lost, and eboses must be done to save that person.

## The Prohibitions of Eji Ogbe

Each of the sixteen parent odu of the diloggún offers specific prohibitions by which a client may or may not need to live by for a period of time. Each omo odu offers prohibitions that complement those of the parent. If a reading opens in a firm iré, these prohibitions are guidelines by which this person should consider living. If an osogbo comes with the letter, they are strict taboos that may not be broken if the client aspires to goodness and evolution. The aleyo or aborisha opening in Eji Ogbe should treat the reading as if it were an itá and follow these prohibitions until he is crowned with his guardian orisha. With a sign like this, he will make ocha.

- Eji Ogbe forbids blasphemy, cursing, lying, and gossip under any circumstances.
- Be respectful of elders, especially those who have gray hair. Some day, Obatalá could come to one disguised as an elderly or infirm person.
- Never make fun of anyone, especially those who are elderly or imperfect. One day, one of these will be Obatalá in disguise.
- Do not use anything that does not belong to one, including those items left in one's care. Do not steal. Never sleep with someone else's spouse or lover.
- One's home is one's temple. Keep it neat and orderly. Do not hide anything under the bed or in the corners of the house; make sure that these areas are kept tidy and free of clutter. One day, something hidden there could harm one.
- Whenever someone calls, do not answer unless one knows the identity of the caller. Let the answering machine pick up the phone or ask for identification before opening the door. If a visitor comes to the door in the night, after one has gone to bed, do not get out of bed to answer the door. We say that even if it is Olódumare knocking, he will come back another day.
- Do not visit the sick or frequent other places where Ikú might travel. One should also avoid places where ikú happens frequently. If a close friend or relative becomes ill, check with the orishas before going to visit. If they say no, ask if ebó may be done to facilitate a visit. Do not go alone; go with a godparent in the religion so that one's head is protected, and make sure that a thorough spiritual cleansing is done afterward.
- Do not sunbathe, and never get wet in the rain. If exposure to the elements is unavoidable, protect the head and face always.
- One's dreams prophesy future events; some are warnings from egun and the orishas. These are for one's own use; do not tell them to anyone or the dead will take away the dreams.
- Do not take anything that belongs to the dead. In this odu, many rituals of Palo Mayombe are forbidden, for they involve taking things from the dead from the cemetery.
- Do not handle broken or burned items, especially if they are blackened or reduced to ashes.
- If the hands become soiled or dirty, wash them immediately. Evil things come to the body through the hands.
- Do not wear tight clothing, especially if it is knotted or tangled. Keep the hair neat and untangled; it must be well groomed always. Do not put colognes, perfumes, or scented waters on the head. If any article of clothing becomes torn or damaged, do not mend it; instead, throw it away. Wear white frequently; avoid black.
- Stay out of basements; there is danger there. Do not climb stairs that are circular, winding, or broken.
- Be very careful of what one eats; food might be spoiled. Do not eat white beans or drink white beverages. Never eat intestines or sausages. Avoid reheated foods and leftovers. Do not eat sweet potatoes or peanuts.
- Avoid alcohol and other intoxicants; they will cloud the mind, induce foolish behavior, and bring ruin to one's life.
- Do not participate in passionate intrigues, liaisons, and adultery.

## Marking Ebó in Eji Ogbe: Initial Considerations

While Eji Ogbe is a sign in which any orisha may speak, one reigns supreme in all castings of this family: Obatalá. He is the "king of the white cloth" who wove all things in existence from a vast fabric of pure energy. While not everyone is meant to be Obatalá's child, every person's head, ultimately, belongs to him, for he is the one who crafted the human head for the body. When eight mouths opens on the mat in any combination, the client must turn to this awesome orisha and the client's own orí for evolution. If the orisha prescribes nothing else in this session, the italero must recommend a rogación before Obatalá for the one who sits at the mat. Once the rogación is complete, the client should offer him a simple adimú.

When attempting to supplicate Obatalá in any composite of eight mouths, the client may use the following eboses to help his evolution. All of them are native to this family of odu, and the diviner may prescribe from them freely using his own aché.

### The Traditional Eboses of Eji Ogbe

When marking ebó for this odu, the diviner should keep in mind that certain substances are traditional to this letter. For offerings that require the sacrifice of an animal, he should select from the following list if possible: two white pigeons, eight white pigeons, and eight snails (some say slugs, but in my ilé ocha but we use only snails). For adimú-type offerings, the diviner should try to use elements from this list: a stick of the consultant's height, cocoa butter, two red parrot feathers, eight red parrot feathers, cotton, eight feet or yards of white cloth, four or eight balls of efun, and anything that is silver or white. Other traditional offerings include four or eight coconuts and two, four, or eight white candles.

## Adimú

### *Nine Fish*

If the sign comes in an osogbo and the client has a special concern not addressed by the oracle, it is possible that he must appease Obatalá before evolution can be found. The proper adimú to offer is this: Fry nine small fish in sunflower oil; do not season them with salt. While the fish are frying, prepare a pan of white rice, again without salt. Form a bed of white rice on a small plate and place one of the fish on it; this portion goes to Elegguá. Even if Obatalá is upset with the client, if part of the adimú goes to Elegguá first, he will ensure that Obatalá listens. Place the rest of the rice on a large white serving platter and set the fish on top. Place this platter on top of Obatalá's sopera with two unlit white candles. The ebó must sit with the orishas for four days.

At the end of this time, wrap the two portions separately in brown paper. Take Elegguá's to a crossroads with a derecho of three cents, and take Obatalá's to either a small hill or a ceiba tree with a derecho of eight cents. After removing these adimús, return to light the two white candles to Obatalá and pray for one's special request.

### *Arroz con Leche*

When the orisha Obatalá requires an adimú, the diviner can prescribe the following dish, arroz con leche prepared with cocoa butter, to satisfy the requirements of odu. When the client comes to the diviner's home to make ebó to his Obatalá, he should bring the following ingredients: one cinnamon stick, finely grated lemon peel, 1/2 cup of rice, 1/2 teaspoon of vanilla extract, 8 tablespoons of sugar, 1 1/2 cups of milk (use goat's milk if the osogbo of this sign is severe), and 1 teaspoon cocoa butter.

In a large saucepan over high heat, bring 2 cups of water to a rolling boil. Add the cinnamon stick and a tiny amount of lemon peel. A few moments after the two ingredients have started to boil, add the rice. Cover the pan and reduce the heat to the lowest setting. Allow to simmer for 15 to 20 minutes, or until the rice is tender and the water absorbed.

While the rice is simmering on the stove, in another bowl combine the vanilla extract, sugar, and milk. Mix well, until the sugar is dissolved into the milk. Raise the heat under the rice to high again and stir in the milk mixture; keep stirring until the dish begins to boil. Reduce the heat to the lowest setting and continue to stir, uncovered, for 15 minutes, or until the milk is absorbed. Add cocoa butter and stir until it is melted.

When the dish is prepared, serve it to Obatalá on a white platter, placing the platter over his sopera. Light two white candles to the orisha, and pray for the evolution needed. The following morning, with obí the client must ask where Obatalá wants his food discarded; he should take it there immediately.

Note that one can dress up this dish in many ways. Some serve it on a platter lined with cotton and efun; others sprinkle the entire dish with efun, putting a white flag (or eight flags) into it so that Obatalá will "notice" the petition behind the ebó. The diviner should prescribe all these extras while the odu is still open so that the orisha will know what they are for.

### *Ñame-Rice Balls*

Another ebó that may be done to appease the orisha uses a ñame, white rice, cocoa butter, coconut milk, cascarilla, a large white serving platter, white cotton, eight pennies, and two white seven-day candles.

First, peel the ñame and drop it into boiling water. When the ñame is soft, remove it from the water, place it in a large mixing bowl, and mash it thoroughly. Then add the white rice, cocoa butter, coconut milk, and cascarilla and mash all ingredients together until they form a paste. Cover a large white serving platter with white cotton; sprinkle this liberally with cascarilla. Divide the ñame mixture into eight equal portions and roll each into a ball. Cover each ball in cascarilla then place it on top of the cotton. Insert one penny into each ball. Sprinkle the entire ebó with more cascarilla and cover it with more white cotton. Place the platter of ñame balls on top of Obatalá's sopera with two unlit, white seven-day candles.

The ebó stays with Obatalá for four days. At the end of this time, use obí to determine where to discard the ñame balls. Take them to that place immediately, wrapped in brown paper. Returning home, light the white candles and pray about one's needs. While the candles burn over the course of the next few days, spend some time each day praying to Obatalá.

### *White Tower*

If this letter came in a gentle osogbo and the client aspires only to personal evolution (whether it is spiritual, financial, emotional, or physical), he should make a tall white tower from cooked, unsalted white rice and cocoa butter. Serve this to Obatalá by placing it on a white plate and covering the entire ebó with a fine sprinkling of cascarilla. Light a white seven-day candle. Once the candle has burned out, ask the orisha with obí where he wants his ebó deposited.

To ensure that he always evolves, the client, after disposing of the tower, places a fresh ñame (the whole root, uncooked and unpeeled) coated with cascarilla on that white plate. A vine will grow from the root; when it begins to grow, the client's personal evolution will unfold. This root may eventually spoil, having absorbed the negativity holding this person back from his goals. With obí, the client should ask Obatalá where to discard the ñame and then give him a new one. He should continue this cycle, always leaving the orisha wish a fresh ñame indefinitely.

### *Eight Ñame Balls*

Put eight large balls of boiled, mashed ñame in a white bowl. Sprinkle this with smoked fish, smoked jutía, and toasted corn (use coconut or virgin olive oil, and not palm oil, for toasting the corn). Place one guinea pepper on each ball, along with melted cocoa butter. Sprinkle the dish liberally with cascarilla. Then pack the bowl with white cotton and offer it to Obatalá. The ebó should remain with the orisha for eight days. At the end of this time, the client takes it to a small hill or ceiba tree, along with two white candles.

If the osogbo is severe, sprinkle the entire dish with white sugar to sweeten Obatalá toward the client's desires.

## Spiritual Baths

### *White Baths*

If the diviner wishes to prescribe a bath for the client to help him remove negative energies, he may recommend several. The simplest baths involve things that are cool and white, which are pleasing to Obatalá. They may include, among other items, white sugar, cascarilla, goat's milk, cow's milk, white flowers, sandalwood oil or perfume, coconut milk, and any of the herbs sacred to Obatalá.

### *Meringue Bath*

If the odu opens in a more serious osogbo, when the diviner wishes to employ a spiritual bath he may combine it with an adimú. A common ebó in this category consists of a meringue; it is given to the orisha as ebó and then used to bathe the client and remove negative energies.

To prepare the adimú, the diviner breaks open eight chicken eggs (or sixteen pigeon eggs if the osogbo is hot), adds white sugar and plenty of cascarilla, and then whips this mixture, adding more sugar, until a stiff white meringue forms. He shapes this into a mountain and offers it to Obatalá on a white plate. Beside it, he lights a white candle.

The ebó remains with the orisha for four hours, with the client praying to Obatalá for luck and evolution. After four hours have passed, the diviner removes the meringue mountain and bathes the client with it. The client should soak in the sweet, sticky waters for some time before the diviner washes him anew with fresh water and dresses him in white.

If the oracle accepts this bath as ebó but it is not enough to bring closure, the diviner should consider prescribing a rogación for the client at Obatalá's feet once the bath is complete.

### *Milk Bath*

Another bath that can be done for Obatalá consists of the following ingredients: goat's milk, cow's milk, coconut milk, *bleo blanco*, *verdolaga*, quita maldición, cascarilla (all avaliable at botánicas), and one herb from the composite odu opened.

The priest prepares the bath by grinding, crushing, and mixing all the ingredients in a large basin. He sets the basin at Obatalá's feet, on a white cloth with two lit candles at its edges, along with the derecho and two coconuts. The offering remains with the orisha for four hours. At the end of this time, the diviner washes the client, allows him to soak, then washes him again in fresh water. He dries him with a white towel and dresses him in white clothes.

If this is not enough to close the oracle, give a rogación before Obatalá's shrine.

## Spiritual Cleansings

### *Eight Pigeon Eggs*

To heal mild sickness or to cleanse a client as he gives up a bad habit or vice, the client should bring eight pigeon eggs to the diviner's home (if the client has Obatalá, he may do this at his shrine). Coat each liberally with cocoa butter and then sprinkle each generously with cascarilla. Wrap the eggs individually in white cotton and place them on a plate coated with cascarilla and layered with cotton. Give these eggs to Obatalá, placing them on top of his sopera. Beginning the next day, for eight days the client should come before the orisha, take an egg from the platter, and rub himself with it from head to toe; afterward, he should place the egg on a bed of white cloth and cotton on the floor before the orisha. On the eighth day, after this person cleanses himself with the final egg, he must use obí to determine how Obatalá would like the ebó to be disposed of. He should tie the eggs in the cotton and white cloth and dispose of them immediately.

### *Eight Coconuts*

The client should sand eight fresh coconuts until they are stripped of their hairs and color each of them white with efun. Then he should bring them to Obatalá in a basket lined with white cloth, along with two seven-day candles. Before the godparent's shrine (or before his own, if he has Obatalá), he should rub himself from head to toe with the coconuts, praying for a solution to his problem. After lighting the two white candles to the orisha, he uses the obí to determine where the ebó should be discarded. Once the candles have burned out, the client should return to remove the coconuts from the orisha's shrine, taking them to where Obatalá dictated.

## Petitioning Obatalá

For a special petition to Obatalá, the client should write a letter expressing his desires. He places this letter between two clean white plates. On top of the plates, he builds a tower of cooked mashed ñame, cooked white rice (unsalted), and cocoa butter. While it is still hot, he sprinkles the tower liberally with efun and covers it in white cotton. He gives the ebó to Obatalá along with a white seven-day candle; before his shrine, he pays foribale and prays for what he desires. Once the prayer is complete, he sticks a handmade white flag (white cloth sewn to a toothpick or a popsicle stick) into the top of the tower to seal the prayer. Unless the request is for something big, it is usually granted before the candle is consumed.

## Ebó for the Dying

Eji Ogbe speaks of the two paths that should not be crossed: life and death. However, there are times when this sign comes in osogbo for the dying, signifying that life and death are about to cross and the client is destined to pass to the other side. Fortunately, in cases such as this, the odu offers an extreme ebó that may be used to uncross the two, buying more time for the one whose energy is fading. This sacrifice is extreme and dangerous; it involves a *cambio de cabeza*, or "switching of the head," between the dying human and a sacrificial calf. Only an experienced oriaté will have the aché and skill needed to make this ritual work. For the ebó, the client must provide the following elements: a white calf, a large white tureen (big enough to hold the calf's head), a stick of cocoa butter, plenty of crushed cascarilla, an ample supply of white cotton, four white pigeons, and the elements for a rogación.

If the client has the strength, he should care for the calf for twenty-four hours; at the end of this time, preparations for the sacrifice may begin. The first task is for the dying one to dress the white tureen with a liberal amount of cocoa butter. He should bite some off the stick. He holds this between his front teeth and lips and then sucks the moisture from the cocoa. Spitting it into his hands, he rubs it briskly until it begins to melt, then rubs it into the interior of the tureen. Next he places a large amount of white cotton in the bottom of the bowl and, over this, sprinkles a generous amount of crushed cascarilla. Now the bowl is ready.

The oriaté presents the calf to the client, touching the client's head to the calf's head, while praying that the destiny of the dying man's orí is transferred to the calf's. Immediately, he sacrifices the calf to Obatalá while the client pays foribale to the orisha. Once the calf's head is severed, the client puts it into the prepared bowl.

Immediately, both heads—first the client's and then the calf's—are given a rogación with grated coconut, crushed cascarilla, grated cocoa butter, cow's milk, goat's milk, white flowers, sandolo, and honey. The client's head is left uncovered, but the oriaté covers the calf's head in white cotton. He uses two white pigeons to cleanse the client, afterward sacrificing them to Obatalá and the calf's head together and throwing the birds' carcasses on top of the calf's head. Next, the oriaté uses two white pigeons to feed the client's orí and Obatalá; he throws their carcasses into the sopera as well. Finally, the oriaté seals the lid onto the bowl with a generous amount of white wax. The bowl stays beside the client's bed overnight, along with two lighted white candles.

The next morning, before removing the elements of the rogación, the client goes with the oriaté to bury the calf's head in the cemetery. After the burial, the oriaté removes the rogación from the client's head and lays it to rest over the grave of the calf's head. Immediately, the client goes home to bathe, dress in white, and rest. The ritual is complete, and the client begins the process of physical recovery. He should consider himself a child of Eji Ogbe and follow all the restrictions and taboos of this sign for the rest of his natural life.

## The First Composite Odu of Eji Ogbe, Ogbe Okana (8-1)

### The Proverbs of Ogbe Okana

- The water of the forest is like indigo dye.
- The head carries the body.
- The water of the grasslands is like palm kernel oil.
- Birds of a feather will flock together.
- Once an animal, always an animal.

### The Message of Ogbe Okana

When a cast of one mouth follows a cast of eight mouths, the odu Ogbe Okana is open. This sign is also known as Ejiogbe Okanran, Ogbe Okana, Ogbe Kanran, Elleunle Okana, and Elleunle Okanran. Opening thus, the diviner pays homage to Ogún, Elegguá, egun, Shangó, Yemayá, Obatalá, and Orí, saying to each, "Maferefún!" All may speak in this pattern, and before this session closes, one or more might stand up to claim ebó. This letter gives birth to many things: Masturbation was born here; the one for whom this pattern falls delights in its practice. Strangely enough, the birth of the holy table of Ifá is credited to this letter. The babalawo's divination tools were manufactured in this sign as well. Because the odu has so many patakís about the elephant, some have nicknamed Ogbe Okana "The Sign of the Elephant." Consequently, when it opens on the mat for a child of Obatalá, or if Obatalá chooses to speak in the letter, many will offer a white ceramic elephant to him as ebó. Children of this sign will put as many as eight elephants to their shrine and will often incorporate white elephant beads in the elekes made for Obatalá. The offering of a ceramic elephant is not a requirement of this pattern, but it does honor its stories.

The person who opens in this composite could have issues revolving around gossip, lies, deceit, treason, and adultery. The diviner should caution him to pay attention to what others say, but not repeat what they say. He must keep this information for personal use and knowledge.

In Ogbe Okana, ebó is one's salvation. The client must make ebó frequently.

In any reading of Ogbe Okana, the diviner should explore the following issues with the client:

- Regardless of the odu's orientation, the diviner should tell the client, "You were a diviner in heaven, and you are destined to be a diviner on earth."
- Even in iré, many of this letter's concerns focus on the client's home and those who live with him. Everyone needs personal space. Visitors will come knocking, yet the client should limit his guests, entertaining only the most important and trusted friends. Those who come to him now will come with issues in which he does not need to be involved.
- This person comes to the mat with an unspoken concern: a major purchase. Even if this was not the issue he presented to the orishas, it exists. To be happy, the client must make this purchase. After this, he must be very frugal with his money.
- In osogbo, sexual activities will peak for the client; this will bring danger. Even if the client has a lover, he masturbates frequently, fantasizing about those he knows. In the past, this person seduced another's lover, and in the future, he will do the same. A married woman who opens in this odu has two or more lovers on the side. A man who opens in this sign is adulterous. All these things will lead to danger.
- In the osogbo of ano or ikú, the diviner must deliver many health warnings to the client. Any health problem that the client has had in his life could return or become worse; this sign exacerbates physical ailments. The client must be particularly cautious against chicken pox, mumps, addictions, and vices; in the extremities, pain, blueing, clubbing, growths, and swellings are also a danger. If any of these symptoms appear, he must see a physician immediately.
- Also, an osogbo of ano and ikú forebodes the death of an elder in the client's family. Ebó will not save this person; timely medical care will. If anyone falls ill, the client must get that person to a physician immediately.

## The Prohibitions of Ogbe Okana

- Do not consume sweet potatoes, fowl, vulture, pigeon, undercooked meat (meat should always be well done to avoid sickness), black beans, red beans, pumpkins, squash, calabazas, alcohol, intoxicants, or sweets. If the odu opens in iré, sweets must be at least limited. Eat sweets sparingly. If the letter opens in any osogbo, one's stomach is weak and cannot tolerate acidic or spicy foods.
- Avoid eating in the house of strangers, and be wary when eating in a friend's home. Make sure one knows how all food is prepared before its consumption. Food poison is a danger for those under this sign's influence.
- Eji Ogbe forbids the lowering of oneself to meet others, and Okana prohibits one to rise to meet others. In this sign, Ogbe Okana, it is important that one realize one's true station in life. One can neither lower oneself to the standards of others nor rise above oneself to become something that one is not. Be happy with one's station in life, and stay there for now. Do not put on airs.
- Do not wear any type of mask or disguise. Do not dress in imitation of others.
- Do not accept gifts unless they are given on appropriate occasions (such as Christmas and one's birthday) by appropriate people (close friends or relatives).
- Plaster or stucco statues are taboo. Throw them away. Do not sell them or give them to another person.
- Do not walk in swamps or damp, muddy places.
- In this odu, there are restrictions against the types of plants one may grow indoors. Do not grow poisonous, carnivorous, or parasitic plants; these will draw those types of people into one's life.
- Respect the Iroko, and do not use any part of that tree, not even for an ebó. If one must offer ebó made with a part of the Iroko, another priest or priestess must prepare it. Never incorporate it into a bath.

## The Eboses of Ogbe Okana

When Ogbe Okana opens on the mat in an osogbo, the diviner must prescribe two eboses. In this sign, the cactus saved a man named Ekun when he stole the elephant's wife; the cactus can also save the client from all danger. To honor the patakís of this odu, this person should plant a cactus outside his front and back doors, and if this is impossible (if he lives in an apartment), he should keep one inside the front door and one inside the back door or on the patio. He should make this a habit for life. If either of the cacti dies, he must replace it immediately, as it has spent its aché saving his home from osogbo.

The second ebó involves Shangó. Early in the morning, the client should take his Shangó onto his back patio (or anywhere outside the back door) and give the orisha a bowl of freshly made amalá (see the recipe on page 54). This offering remains with Shangó overnight. The next morning, the client should give Shangó another bowl of freshly made amalá. When replacing the old adimú with the new, he should use obí to learn where Shangó wants his previous day's offering discarded. The client should repeat this offering every day for a total of six days; on the seventh morning, he should bring the orisha back inside. Using obí again, the client must ask Shangó if all is well, and if it is not, he must mark another adimú for him. If this reading is for an aleyo who does not have Shangó, he must return to the diviner's or godparent's house every morning for six days to fulfill this obligation.

Once the diviner has prescribed these two eboses for the odu in osogbo, or if the odu opened in iré, he should now attempt to close the oracle. If it will not close, the client could have further issues with Ogún, Elegguá, egun, Shangó, Yemayá, or Obatalá. To determine if any of these spirits requires ebó, the diviner should question, "Ebó elese [spirit's name]?" If the answer is yes, he must use the diloggún to mark an appropriate offering.

If after these eboses have been investigated the odu still will not close, the diviner must turn to the eboses of the parent odu, Eji Ogbe (see page 393). The client needs something from that list for his evolution.

# The Second Composite Odu of Eji Ogbe, Ogbe Ejioko (8-2)

## The Proverbs of Ogbe Ejioko

- The tongue must be restrained and the words must be measured carefully.
- The one who circumcises the tortoise must not circumcise the snail.
- It is false like the fog, bitter like a lemon, and the embarrassment on the house.
- The head that should not go naked will find a cloth seller when the market opens.
- One day you will use the calabash's lid to measure beads for your mistress.

## The Message of Ogbe Ejioko

When an initial cast of eight mouths, Eji Ogbe, precedes a second cast of two mouths, Eji Oko, the odu Ogbe Ejioko is open. Ejiogbe Oyekun, Ejiogbe Ejioko, Ogbe Oyekun, and Ogbe Yeku are other names for this sign. Having cast this sign on the mat, the diviner honors Eleggua, Obatalá, Ogún, the Ibeyi, Oshún, Ochosi, Oduduwa, Osain, and Orúnmila, saying to each, "Maferefún!" All influence this pattern, and before the session closes one or more might stand up to claim ebó. This letter gave birth to incest and incestuous desires in humans and animals; it the sign in which the goat "mounts" its mother. Precious metals also find their worth here; before metal left heaven, it went to the diviners in heaven to learn what it had to do for immortality. The diviners marked ebó and metal fulfilled this. Coming to earth, Olódumare's aché transformed metal into gold, silver, copper, lead, and all other metals found precious in life. The ebó gave his many forms the strength to withstand the ages. This is also the odu of life and death; while death is prominent, this sign can also give the gift of many years if one follows its advice and makes ebó. Through the pattern Ogbe Ejioko, mysteries are created and re-created daily; some of these mysteries will unfold in the client's life with malicious intent. It is the letter of sanity and insanity, maturity and immaturity. It brings serious consequences to those who argue with spouses or lovers, and it makes the client see himself as he is not. This person, in truth, is the opposite of what he believes himself to be. This odu refers to the tongue; it has aché, yet unless the letter comes in firm iré, the tongue will bring deadly consequences. The advice of this sign is simple: Restrain the tongue always, and avoid dangerous extremes.

When this letter opens on the mat, the diviner must explore many issues with the client:

- Many problems faced by a client who has opened in this odu come "elese elenú," or "by his own tongue." Even if this is not the orientation marked for the odu, its opening may imply it. To avoid trouble, the client must consider his words carefully before speaking. Not speaking at all would be best.
- The diviner should tell the client that those of "good breeding" will be known by their actions and manners, not by their words. Stance, demeanor, and mood always reveal a person's stature in life. Smooth words can never hide a coarse nature.
- In this letter, Obatalá stands up to say that the client must respect him always. Obatalá comes to us not as a mere orisha in a sopera, but in the heads of all people, especially the elderly. The client must not let the elderly be alone or suffer harm and must have respect for the heads of the elders; this shows love to Obatalá. People who are physically imperfect are Obatalá's special children, and the client must show these respect as well.
- Financial problems come and go like tides of the ocean. The client finds himself poor as often as he finds himself rich; he must work in his youth to have wealth in his old age. It is possible that others are working to ruin this person's finances, but this is not always the case. The diviner must determine if the jealousy of others is bringing this person harm. The client must thank the orishas for the financial blessings that he has in his life, even when he seems poor. The diviner should remind him: He never goes without a home. He never goes without food or clothes.

The client should give thanks for that which he has so more will come.

- It is important that this person does not cry in misery or let others cry in his home. Tears only bring more of the same. He must smile and try to be happy even when happiness seems elusive; it will bring more of the same.
- This odu raises family issues. The client has problems with his relatives, and he will never resolve all of them. One family member in particular always wishes ill of this person and always will wish ill of this person. The client must figure out who this relative is and beware of him or her. The client has done many good things for his family, but none of them appreciates his deeds. That is okay, because the orishas know the good that was done.
- Marriage is a concern in this sign for those who are single, but this odu promises that in time a mate will be found. Children will be born; if the client worries about conception, it will come in its own time. The next child born will more than likely be a daughter.
- This client abandoned the orishas once, yet they did not abandon him. He must not neglect them anymore or they will abandon him in the future.

## The Prohibitions of Ogbe Ejioko

- Do not eat honey, pork, liquor, fowl, or coconut. Do not accept food that has already been cooked (such as food another person brings from home). Do not eat at parties or social gatherings unless the food is served by a restaurant and one knows how the food is prepared.
- Do not go to funerals, hospitals, nursing homes, cemeteries, or dark places. Never travel at night.
- Do not wear masks or disguises. Never try to emulate the dress or customs of another. Always, just be oneself so one does not miss one's own luck or suffer a dire fate meant for another.
- Do not lend money or possessions. Do this and one's luck will be lost, and the items will not come back easily. Limit the giving of gifts to appropriate occasions.
- Hunting is taboo in this sign.

## The Eboses of Ogbe Ejioko

When this letter opens in an osogbo, the following three eboses are mandatory. First, the client should keep his refrigerator and pantry well stocked, for whenever he receives visitors (even if they are unexpected) he must entertain them well, offering plenty of food and drink. The happier his guests are with their visit, the more iré this ebó will bring. Second, for the next twenty-one days, the client should speak in a very low voice, never repeating anything that he has already said. Those that need to hear will hear, and those that should not hear will not. Finally, the diviner must prescribe a series of spiritual baths for the orisha offering larishe in this sign. To this bath he should add the herb zapote. The client should have one of these spiritual baths once a week for four weeks.

Having made these prescriptions, the diviner may now attempt to close the oracle. If it will not close, he should explore the following possibilities:

- The client could have issues with an orisha speaking in this sign: Elegguá, Obatalá, Ogún, Oshún, or Ochosi. To determine if they require anything, the diviner should question, "Ebó elese [orisha's name]?" If the diloggún marks an ebó to one or more orishas, the diviner must investigate what they require.
- The Ibeyi are important in this sign; the client may need to receive them. The diviner should ask, "Koshé los Ibeyi?" If the answer is yes, the client should make preparations for this ceremony immediately. If the client already has the Ibeyi, they might need ebó. The diviner should ask, "Ebó elese los Ibeyi?" If the answer is yes, he should use the diloggún to mark the required ebó.

The diviner may then attempt to close the odu again. If the client is an aleyo and the pattern will still not close out, the italero must then begin to explore the eboses of the parent odu, Eji Ogbe (see page 393). The client needs something in that list for his evolution.

If the client is an initiate and the odu will not close, the odu suggests that a tambor is the solution to all this person's troubles. The diviner should determine if this is the case. In Ogbe Ejioko, the proper order of questioning when trying to mark a tambor is Elegguá, Obatalá, Ogún, Ibeyi, Oshún and Ochosi, Yemayá, Oyá, Shangó, and Aganyú. Note that if the diloggún marks a tambor during an itá for a iyawó through either Elegguá or the guardian orisha, it automatically marks this client to give a drum to all the orishas in time.

If none of these will close the odu for a priest or a priestess, the italero must then turn to the eboses of the parent odu, Eji Ogbe.

# The Third Composite Odu of Eji Ogbe, Ogbe Ogundá (8-3)

## The Proverbs of Ogbe Ogundá

- Nobody knows what lies at the heart of the ñame except the knife that cuts it.
- Now that the bad is known, the good shall be known.
- The drum that speaks poorly does so because it does not have a mouth.
- The embarrassment of the diviner is in his mouth; it eats with addiction.
- The major fortune is to have, to be capable, and to know.
- The proud lagoon separated from the small brook as if the water was not the same between them. The lagoon dried up.
- When the goat is alive, his skin cannot be used for a drum.
- The sheep still dresses in the wool from last year.
- While we find money in this world, we must also leave it in this world.
- A gourd transported carefully will not break.
- The glutton enlarges his stomach and reduces his head.
- The male goat that breaks a drum pays for it with his hide.
- A newly sprouted frond is straight from tip to base.
- Patience is the father of good character.

## The Message of Ogbe Ogundá

When an initial cast of eight mouths, Eji Ogbe, precedes a cast of three mouths, Ogundá, the odu Ogbe Ogundá is open. Ejiogbe Ogundá, Ogbeyono, Ogbe Suru, and Ogbe Oligun are other names for this sign. Having cast this pattern, the diviner must honor Elegguá, Ogún, Oshún, Shangó, Yemayá, Obatalá, Orúnmila, Olokun, Babaluaiye, and Nanumé, saying to each, "Maferefún!" All may speak or claim ebó before this session closes. Oshún deserves special reverence here, for in this sign her children were first crowned. Her priesthood was born here. If the client at the mat has not yet had a bajado, Oshún might be his guardian orisha. While this reading might not be the proper time to impart such information (without a bajado one cannot be sure who claims the head), before the letter closes out she will demand many eboses.

This letter gives birth to several things, all of which are referenced and acknowledged through this odu: the penis and the vagina; the human conditions of blood, weeping, laughter, and patience; the secret of the Ajala (the one who crafts heads in heaven); and the secret of salt. Ogbe Ogundá is a deep, mystical odu; it gives birth to strange things. Mysterious occurrences and obscure phenomena that exist in our world without rational explanations are often credited to this sign. The client will experience much of this in his own life.

This letter speaks of the need for the client to act honorably, patiently, and ethically to avoid danger. His words must be soft spoken and well thought out, and he must never raise his hands toward another in anger. The sign also speaks of excessive vices, especially gluttony, and warns about the health dangers that come from them.

Ogbe Ogundá raises many issues for the client; the diviner should explore all of them:

- In iré, this letter promises gentle moderation in the client's life. He will not have much of any one thing, but he will have many things. Money will come to him from different sources, and not all these extend from his own hands or work. He must live by being thankful for all that others give to him.

- In osogbo, this sign marks greed and gluttony in all the senses. Anger and violence could lead a person to the use of weapons instead of using persuasion and communication.
- When an osogbo of ano or ikú comes, many health issues are flagged. The client must watch for stress, high blood pressure, hemorrhage, anemia, impotence, and infertility. Infectious diseases, strokes, leukemia, loss of memory, and surgery are a danger. He must see a physician for a full examination, and he must learn to take care of his health.

## The Prohibitions of Ogbe Ogundá

- Do not eat fish, breadfruit, yam, alcohol, coconut, manioc, or cassava. Also follow the food taboos given to children of Obatalá: Do not consume white foods, such as eggs, bread, and milk.
- Do not consume foods that others offer repeatedly or forcefully.
- Be mindful of sacrificial foods eaten, and avoid those of the orishas Elegguá and Ogún.
- Do not trust inebriated people. Even if they have one's best interests in mind, they will bring osogbo. Do not go to places where people drink or do illegal drugs. Do not let friends or acquaintances get drunk in one's home.
- This letter carries restrictions on one's mode of travel. When walking, walk alone or in pairs; do not walk in groups of three or more. Do not walk under ladders, over holes, or on broken pavements. Do not ride horseback; this will cause a serious accident, and one could lose the ability to walk (Ogbe Ogundá can bring paralysis of the legs). Do not skate, ride motorcycles, or even bicycles without proper safety equipment, and travel in these modes only during the day when the weather is good. Trains are hot in this sign; if the odu opens in osogbo, never travel in this fashion, and if it comes in iré, ask Ogún for permission first and offer ebó to him.
- Do not stand beside the door of a building with one's back turned to the street.
- Do not carry heavy loads. Do not rest or tip one's chair against the wall.
- Do not carry weapons.
- Do not argue or quarrel with others.

## The Eboses of Ejiogbe Ogundá

When Ogbe Ogundá opens on the mat in an osogbo, the diviner must prescribe four eboses to the client. The orisha whose diloggún is being consulted demands two of these eboses. First, prepare an osain for this spirit with an alligator's tooth, and second, give a stuffed alligator (the head and four feet are acceptable) to this spirit. Third, this sign in osogbo indicates that Olokun is angry. If the client has not received her, he is now marked for her reception. If he does have her, he must give her adimú immediately. Finally, when this sign falls in an osogbo, Ogún is demanding a sacrifice in the woods. If the client has not received the warriors, the client must seek out Ogún's otá in the forest and, after he is washed, take Ogún back to where he found him and feed him a feathered animal.

If these eboses are not enough to close the oracle and the client is an aleyo or an aborisha, the diviner must then turn to the eboses of the parent odu, Eji Ogbe (see page 393). If the client is an initiate, the diviner should explore the following options:

- Elegguá, Ogún, Oshún, Shangó, Yemayá, Obatalá, Olokun, Babaluaiye, or Nanumé could be demanding ebó. The diviner should consider each in turn, asking, "Ebó elese [orisha's name]?" If the oracle answers yes to any of these, the diviner should mark an appropriate ebó.
- If no orisha will take ebó, or if the letter still refuses closure, the next option is the sacrifice of a four-legged animal. The diviner should first ask the diloggún whether the sacrifice of four legs is required. If the answer is yes, he must then determine which orisha will claim it. The proper order of questioning is Elegguá, Ogún, Shangó, Yemayá, Obatalá, Olokun, Babaluaiye, and Nanumé. Once the orisha claiming the sacrifice has been determined, the diviner must

find out whether itá is necessary after the ebó is completed; he asks, "Itá elese [orisha's name]?" Note that if four legs and an itá are marked for an orisha that the client lacks, he must receive that spirit.

- If Olokun, Babaluaiye, or Nanumé do not claim the sacrifice of a four-legged animal, the client could need to receive one or more of them. To determine if this is the case, the diviner should ask, "Koshé [orisha's name]?"
- If none of these options is accepted, the next possibility in this odu is the reception of the knife.

If nothing will close the odu, the diviner must turn to the eboses of the parent odu, Eji Ogbe.

## The Fourth Composite Odu of Eji Ogbe, Ogbe Irosun (8-4)

### The Proverbs of Ogbe Irosun

- If the head is not sold, no one will buy it.
- A king saves a town.
- You were born to be the head and not the tail.
- You were born to be served and not to serve.

### The Message of Ogbe Irosun

When an initial casting of eight mouths, Eji Ogbe, precedes a second cast of four mouths, Irosun, the odu Ogbe Irosun is open on the mat. This letter is also known as Ogbe Iroso, Ogbe Roso, Ejiogbe Irosun, Ogbe Dawo Ósun Tele, Ogbe Masu, and Ogbe Masun. Having cast this letter, the diviner pays homage to Yemayá, Orí, Obatalá, Elegguá, Olokun, Osain, Ogún, Oyá, egun, and Shangó, saying to each, "Maferefún!" All may speak or claim ebó in this sign. The diviner should note that when this letter falls on the mat, the orisha whose dilog-gún is cast is giving a warning: The client has come to test both the diviner's skills and his knowledge, and everything that this odu demands must be said to this person lest he leave in disbelief.

In this odu were born two things: the plucking of birds after sacrifice and the *nangareo* made before itá. Iyerosun appeared for the first time here. The duties and relationships between fathers and their sons were born in this letter. When this odu comes in an osogbo, it indicates that there is a chasm between the client and his father, and this must be healed. It is usual for the one who opens in this pattern to be abandoned by his father; it is not unusual for this person to abandon his son. Daughters suffer in parental relationships as well. This odu demands that these relationships be healed, even if the client's father or son is dead.

Osogbo in this odu also reveals this person as wicked; he thinks wicked thoughts and does wicked things, although the extent of the wickedness of his actions depends on the severity of the letter's osogbo. In firm iré, the client is free of this and might even fight against wickedness.

This odu foreshadows initiation and tells the client that once his godparents put aché into his head he will achieve great things. From this moment on, the person at the mat must dedicate himself to learning as much about this religion as he can, especially its history, for he is destined to become a great oriaté.

### The Prohibitions of Ogbe Irosun

- Do not eat apples, cashews, red plums or prunes, rooster, red beans, red foods, red drinks, mango, the heads or tails of animals, sardines, fish, grains, seeds, grainy foods, grainy fruits, and tripes. Avoid the consumption of blood by making sure all animal meats are well cooked and drained of juices.
- Do not dress like friends or celebrities; dress only like oneself. Do not wear torn, ripped, or mended clothes or any item of clothing with holes (lace or eyelets, for example). Fringes are taboo, as is the color red.
- Avoid holes. Cover or repair all holes in the house. Do not look through holes, jump over holes, or keep things in holes. Do not get inside holes or tight spaces.
- Avoid adultery, especially with the spouses or lovers of other initiates. This will bring death.

- This odu forbids reading, studying, or working in poor light. One could go blind from this.

## The Eboses of Ogbe Irosun

When this letter opens in an osogbo, it demands that the client receive the warriors. Since most houses dictate the reception of the elekes first, before the reception of the warriors, if this person has not taken that initiation, he must do so now, before receiving the warriors.

If the client who opens in this odu in osogbo already has the warriors, Eshu is demanding a rooster. This sacrifice must be done as soon as possible.

In osogbo, this sign also calls for a rogación at Shangó's feet. The client must come back to the diviner's house immediately with two coconuts, two white candles, a brown envelope containing a derecho of twenty-one dollars, and a white plate. The coconuts, candles, and derecho should be offered to Shangó on the plate; after this, the italero must give the client a rogación so Shangó can clear all osogbo from this person's head.

In this sign, Elegguá, Obatalá, Yemayá, Shangó, and Orúnmila stand up to protect this person, and when the osogbo is severe the client should give each spirit a seven-day candle. The candles should remain lit for eight days. If the client does not have his own orishas to offer this ebó to, the client should offer it to his godparent's orishas. As they have light, so will his way be lit.

Also, if this client is not a priest or priestess, he or she must make ocha when possible.

Having made these prescriptions, the diviner may now attempt to close the oracle. If it will not close, he should explore the following possibilities:

- If the client is an initiate, he must receive both Dada and Bañaní.
- The Ibeyi can be an integral part of this sign. If the client has not received these orishas, the diviner should ask, "Koshé Ibeyi?" If the client already has them, the proper question to ask is "Ebó elese los Ibeyi?" If the answer is yes, the diviner must mark an ebó.
- If the client is an initiate and the diloggún being consulted belongs to Elegguá, Elegguá might be standing up himself; he could want a crown. The diviner should ask Elegguá if this is necessary as an ebó. If the answer is yes, from this moment on the client must treat him as if he were the orisha of the head. Note that when Elegguá stands up for a crown, he is telling the client that a kingdom awaits him. Once he receives the adoration he demands, he will bring the kingdom promised. This person will have many godchildren.
- Olokun is important in all composite odu that incorporate Irosun. If the client does not have Olokun and the letter still refuses closure, the diviner should ask, "Koshé Olokun?" If the client already has Olokun, she might be standing up for an ebó; the proper question to ask here is "Ebó elese Olokun?" If Olokun wants an ebó, the proper ebó to give her in this sign is a sacrifice and an agbán. Once the agbán is done, everything must go to the ocean in a basket with blue cloth.
- If the odu still refuses to close, the client may need a series of rogaciónes; let the oracle dictate how many and how often. These should be done at the foot of Shangó, for in this sign he stands up to fight the evil the client faces and to strengthen the head from all osogbo. A niche osain using Shangó's herbs should also be made and fed with him; this should be presented to the client at the end of the first rogación given.
- If the previous eboses are not accepted or are not sufficient to close the oracle, the diviner should determine if Yemayá, Obatalá, Ogún, Oyá, or egun need ebó, asking, "Ebó elese [spirit's name]?" If ebó is necessary, the diviner should use the diloggún to mark what is needed.
- Finally, if the letter will still not close, the odu mandates a rogación by a babalawo with a red snapper at the feet of Orúnmila. Only this will offer the client the strength that he needs to evolve. The client may also need to receive mano or kofá de Orúnmila. If the client is male, he may be marked for Ifá. Only the babalawo, however, can determine these things.

If all these eboses have been considered and the diloggún still refuses closure, the diviner must turn to the eboses listed for the parent odu, Eji Ogbe (see page 393). The client will need something in that list to clear the osogbo, close the sign, and bring evolution.

## The Fifth Composite Odu of Eji Ogbe, Ogbe Oché (8-5)

### The Proverbs of Ogbe Oché

- Lies bring revolution.
- Even the clothes you wear will betray you.
- The macaw sings in the woods, and the parrot sings in the city.
- The goat, slaughtered by the priest for food, was provided by the layman.
- You do not know the good that you have until you lose it.

### The Message of Ogbe Oché

When an initial casting of eight mouths, Eji Ogbe, precedes a casting of five mouths, Oché, the odu Ogbe Oché is open on the mat. This odu is also known as Ogbe'Che, Ogbe Sweoole, Ejiogbe Oché, Ogbe Sanwo, and Ogbe Kowojo. Having cast this sign on the mat, the diviner must say, "Maferefún!" to the following orishas: Oba, Elegguá, Ogún, Oshún, Olokun, Osain, Obatalá, Orúnmila, and Olófin. All may speak or claim ebó in this pattern. It gives birth to many things. Through it, Oba was born to the world, and she speaks silently but strongly in this sign. Music, premonition, and prophecy were all created by this odu's aché; a head born to this letter has the gifts of rhythm and prophecy embedded in its soul. Money came to settle down on the earth by the grace of Ogbe Oché, and it sought out those who were also born here. If this reading is an itá or a bajado, the child of this odu will one day become wealthy beyond his wildest dreams—if he follows all the advice of the sign. The orisha crowns using red parrot feathers appeared first in this sign. Here the pact between Osain and the enemies of the earth was made.

In this letter, the client cries a lot both secretly and openly; this is a letter of severity, and both bitterness and sweetness will come to this person, evoking emotional extremes. This client must find balance in his emotional life. When Ogbe Oché opens on the mat, even if this person is popular among peers, the diviner should tell him that he has no true friends in life. Others look upon him with greed and envy, and none has the client's best interests in mind. Even his lover can be false. Yet in this odu both Oshún and Elegguá stand up to defend the client; although the client has no true friends on the earth, they are the client's true friends in heaven. He must live life by relying on these two orishas.

### The Prohibitions of Ogbe Oché

- The following foods are taboo: meats and vegetables that are roasted or burned, canned foods, pumpkins, squash, calabazas, reheated foods, cold leftovers, beets, canistel, eggs, watercress, malanga, chopo, goat, fowl, red snapper, and shellfish (especially crabs).
- When eating, foods that are not part of a single dish must be kept separate; do not mix anything on one's plate.
- Have nothing to do with fireplaces, woodstoves, or bonfires. Do not play with fire and never stir ashes. Do not carry firewood, and if ashes stain the clothes, change immediately. Wash the hands and face if they become blackened by soot.
- Do not cage, imprison, or tie up anything, especially animals. Do not raise animals that must be caged in the home, such as small rodents, snakes, and birds. Do not work in positions that involve the imprisonment of people or animals (even nursing or veterinary clinics).
- In this letter, abortions are taboo. Do not have one, and do not recommend one.
- In this sign, a red parrot feather can become one's salvation. Never give anyone a red parrot feather; one must keep the feather for oneself.
- Respect all bodies of water. Do not jump or dive into pools, lakes, or the ocean. Never go swimming in the river, and ask permission before

driving or crossing over one. Enter all bodies of water feet first, never head first.

- Do not accept any invitations to go to private parties. If one is forced into accepting an invitation, at the last minute say that one's foot is injured, and stay home. Social gatherings bring disaster and traps under this odu.

## The Eboses of Ogbe Oché

In this sign certain eboses are automatically marked:

- When Ogbe Oché opens in osogbo, egun stand up for attention; the diviner does not need to ask if the spirits want ebó because it is mandated when the letter opens in an osogbo. Using the diloggún, the diviner should try to mark what is needed. If no ebó can be marked, then egun should be given a sheep. Since this sacrifice involves a four-legged animal, an initiate who has received the knife or an oriaté must be called in to do the ceremony.
- Another ebó that is mandatory when this letter opens in an osogbo is the preparation of a niche osain for the client. It is to be made to Oshún; it must be filled with her herbs, beaded, and then washed and fed with her. The client should carry this charm with him every day; he should give it respect equal to that of the elekes. If the client is an initiate, he may leave the niche osain in Oshún's sopera. The aleyo, however, does not have this option.
- The client could have issues with Oba, Elegguá, Oshún, Olokun, or Obatalá. To see if any will take ebó, the diviner should ask, "Ebó elese [orisha's name]?" If the answer is yes, he should use the diloggún to mark the required ebó.

Having made these prescriptions, the diviner may now attempt to close the oracle. If it will not close, he must turn to the appropriate list that follows. One is for aleyos and aborishas, while the other is for initiates.

When this odu opens in an osogbo for an aleyo or an aborisha and refuses closure, the diviner should consider the following eboses:

- The client needs to receive his elekes and then his warriors as soon as possible. He also needs to be given a rogación at the feet of Oshún. Since the initiations of the elekes and warriors are expensive and not readily affordable by all who come to the oracle, the rogación may be given first if the client commits to the rest of this ebó. Before having the rogación to Oshún, the client should place a derecho of twenty-one dollars in a brown envelope and present it to the orisha on a white plate with two coconuts and two white candles. Once the rogación is complete, this client must give Oshún a jar of honey with honeycomb inside; he should wrap this in yellow ribbon and give it to her with a yellow seven-day candle. Oshún will bless the client with sweetness.
- If the above ebó is chosen by the orishas, yet it is not enough to close the oracle, the diviner must then ask Oshún if she requires anything else as ebó, querying, "Ebó elese Oshún?" If the answer is yes, he should use the diloggún to mark the required ebó.

If the oracle will not accept these eboses, or if it will not close after their prescription, the diviner must consider the list of eboses given for the parent odu, Eji Ogbe (see page 393). Something there is needed to bring closure and the client's evolution.

When this odu opens in an osogbo for an initiate and will not close, the diviner must consider the following list of eboses carefully, marking only what is essential to close the session.

- The client might need to have a new path of Elegguá. In the odu of Eji Ogbe, four paths of Eshu can be marked when Ogbe Oché opens on the mat: Eshu Alagbana, Eshu Laroye, Eshu Ayé, and Eshu Ayé Belleburo. To see if one of these is needed, the diviner must ask, "Koshé [name of Eshu]?" If none can be marked and the initiate does not have a pocket Elegguá, the diviner might also attempt, "Koshé Elegguá?" If the answer to any of these questions is yes, the initiate must have the reception when possible.

- The next ebó to be considered must be done with the new path of Eshu, or the new Elegguá, received by the initiate. If no new Eshu or Elegguá was mandated by odu, this ebó is to be done with the initiate's own Elegguá. Take Elegguá to the ocean first, and then to the river. At each place feed him a rooster on clean sand. After each sacrifice, the client dances around Elegguá while playing a flute, concentrating hard on that which he needs. Once the orisha is brought home, the client must give him the flute, and he will make the client's dreams come true.*
- If the odu, in osogbo, continues to refuse closure, the client must throw a party for Oshún. At the party, he should give her a crown as a present, for from now on, she is the true queen of the client's home. To make this crown, before the party a priest must sacrifice a goat to Oshún and save the skin; it should be used to line the inside of the brass used to make her gift. (If the letter will not close, the client may need to have an itá with Oshún after this sacrifice; to determine if this is the case, the diviner should ask, "Itá elese Oshún?") Once the crown is made, the client should embed five red parrot feathers in the goat's skin just behind the five points of the crown. As time passes, increase the number of feathers until the crown has a total of fifty-five red parrot feathers. To do this and to solicit blessings from Oshún, add five more feathers to the crown every year on her birthday, each time giving a huge party and throne in honor of the mighty queen.
- The next ebó mandated by this sign is that the initiate must wear a red parrot feather in his hair or on his head always. Many priestesses attach a parrot feather to an earring, while priests should secret the feather in the hair somehow.
- Finally, this sign could mark the initiate for the reception of Oba; the diviner must ask "Koshé Oba?"

If all these eboses have been considered for an initiate and the letter will not give closure, the diviner should turn to the eboses listed for the parent odu, Eji Ogbe.

## The Sixth Composite Odu of Eji Ogbe, Ogbe Obara (8-6)

### The Proverbs of Ogbe Obara

In iré, we say of this sign:

- All is clear at the feet of the orishas.

In osogbo, we say of this sign:

- He who looks for problems is the one that must fix them.

Opening in the osogbo of ano or ikú, we say:

- The king will die when a prince is crowned.

The other proverbs associated with this sign, regardless of its orientation, are:

- When the lightning flashes, it touches sky and earth.
- The dove was once menaced by the snake, so he opened his wings and flew away.
- The tiger who eats the bone has satisfaction in his throat.
- The hen on top sits on the hen below.
- The lunatic will dance all types of dances.
- The idiot is happy with all kinds of excitements.
- The king is dead, but a new prince is crowned.
- The waters run deep.
- The bat, with its head down, can observe the manner in which the parrots behave.

### The Message of Ogbe Obara

When an initial cast of eight mouths, Eji Ogbe, precedes a second cast of six mouths, Obara, the odu

*This ebó works only in this odu, as Elegguá owns all wind instruments and would take this ebó as an offense at any other time! If this is marked in itá for Elegguá, it is a powerful spell that the iyawó may do whenever he is in dire need.

Ogbe Obara is open on the mat. This odu is also known as Ogbebara and l'Ogbe Bara. It is said that the world dethroned the true owner of this odu; thus, it has become known as the sign of the undesirable people. Through it was born the custom of sacrificing to the front door; this letter also gave birth to the herb yagruma (*Cecropia peltata;* Moraceae family). This is the sign in which Shangó made Ifá in heaven; he was poor, and the priest of Orúnmila did the initiation for free. The diviner should keep this in mind when prescribing expensive eboses for one who probably cannot afford them.

With this odu open on the mat, the diviner knows that the client is disrespectful of others; if he is an elder in the religion, he is very disrespectful of those younger than he in ocha, especially those who have not made ocha. Shangó wants this to stop, now. If this letter opens in an osogbo, such is his anger toward this person that he has all but left the house, and soon he might flee altogether.

This odu also speaks of traps, treason, and persecution; the client must be wary of all around him always. This person should remember that in times of stress and turmoil, sometimes it is both safer and wiser to flee than to fight. Heaven always provides an open road away from difficulties.

## The Prohibitions of Ogbe Obara

- Do not eat the following foods: pumpkin, squash, calabazas, ball-shaped foods, hard candy, cassava, alcoholic beverages, corn flour, rooster, okra, red beans, plantains, mutton, pork, and shellfish. Do not eat anything that is offered to one forcefully or insistently.
- The place in which one eats is as important as what one eats. Do not go to restaurants in which one has not eaten before, and do not dine in strange places or surroundings. Do not eat while standing or walking. Eat slowly and deliberately, for in this odu mindlessness while eating causes choking.
- Personal hygiene is important in this sign. Bathe frequently, but do not bathe or swim in the ocean or in lakes. Be respectful when bathing in the river.
- Do not use another's personal hygiene products, and do not share washcloths or towels. Bring one's own soap, shampoo, and toothpaste when staying overnight at another person's house. Do not share personal items with another, such as combs, brushes, makeup, and toothbrushes.
- Do not entertain guests or host parties and dinners in one's own home.
- Do not borrow or lend clothes.
- Do not wear clothing that has stripes, polka dots, checks, or plaids in the design. Do not wear the color red.
- Do not try on under garments before they are washed.

## The Eboses of Ogbe Obara

In Ogbe Obara, the diviner will attempt to close the oracle after determining the larishe (if any) and prescribing the eboses mandatory for the parent odu, Eji Ogbe. If the letter will not close, there are two considerations. First, the client should have a rogación at the feet of Shangó. If this is not enough to close the letter, the client should present an adimú of sweet amalá (see the recipe on page 54) to Shangó once the rogación is complete. This amalá should be cooked by the client's own hands. If he does not know how to make the amalá, the diviner and godparent can instruct during the process, but they may not help in any way.

If the sign's osogbo is severe, the diviner should consider asking, "Ebó elese Shangó?" If the answer is yes, he must use the diloggún to mark an appropriate offering. The orisha may require an additional ebó to defend the client and clear him from negative forces.

If after these considerations the session still will not close, the client could have issues with one or more of the following orishas: Shangó, Oba, Ogún, Elegguá, Obatalá, and egun. The diviner must ask, "Ebó elese [spirit's name]?" If ebó is needed, the diviner should mark the exact ebó with the diloggún.

If the session still will not close and the client is an aleyo or aborisha, the diviner must turn to the list of eboses for the parent odu, Eji Ogbe (see page 393), to find an ebó that will bring evolution. If the client is an initiate, the following four eboses are possibilities. They should be considered carefully by the diviner before they are prescribed to the client.

- Both the batea and odo of Shangó may need to be repainted in red and white. A leopard skin* should then be put to the orisha, for this is the true animal owner of this odu.
- If the client is a man, he may need to wear a special belt. It should be half red and half white; on the red side, embed eight cowrie shells in the leather, and on the white side, embed six cowrie shells. Sew a pocket into the inner part of the belt to contain an osain for Shangó. If the client is a woman, instead of this belt she should wear bloomers that are red on one side and white on the other.
- When this sign opens in a tragic osogbo, it shows that Shangó has left the house and may be brought back only thus: He must be offered a ram immediately. Until a ram can be found, the client should supplicate him at his shrine with two coconuts that have each been painted half red and half white. This will protect the client so that neither enemies nor the law can overcome him.
- If after these prescriptions the letter will still not close, the diviner should ask, "Koshé Oba?" The sign could be marking her reception.

If the diloggún refuses either to mark these eboses or to close after they have been prescribed, the diviner must turn to the eboses of the parent odu, Eji Ogbe.

## The Seventh Composite Odu of Eji Ogbe, Ogbe Odí (8-7)

### The Proverbs of Ogbe Odí

- There are no roses without thorns.
- One can never know all things, for Olódumare dispersed all knowledge evenly throughout the world.
- You make something out of nothing; make something good this time.
- Say something once and only once; that shall suffice.
- You rattle on, and you nag.
- All the fingers are brothers of the same hand, and none can work alone, or separate.
- Quietly I shall go, and quietly I shall come.

*Some houses make the mistake of giving a tiger skin to Shangó when this odu falls, and this is a big mistake! The tiger is of Indian origin, not African. The ancient Yoruba knew nothing about this animal and would never have offered it to Shangó.

### The Message of Ogbe Odí

When an initial cast of eight mouths, Eji Ogbe, precedes a cast of seven mouths, Odí, the odu Ogbe Odí is open on the mat. This sign is also known as Obedí. Having cast this sign, the diviner honors Oke, Elegguá, Dada, Ogún, Oshún, Shangó, Yemayá, Obatalá, Babaluaiye, and Orisha Oko, saying to each, "Maferefún!" All may speak or claim ebó in this letter.

This odu gave birth to many things. In osogbo, it brought nothingness, trashiness, and bragging into our world. In iré, it brought love (both its beginning and end), fertility, and marriage. Marriage is perhaps the greatest blessing brought in this sign, for in the beginning, men used and abused women as they would, and women were left on their own to bear and raise children.† When Ogbe Odí was born, it taught men to respect women; later it created the institution of marriage so that women and their children would be loved, honored, and protected. When this odu opens for a man, it flags one whose ways toward women are too casual and abusive, and this letter warns that if he does not stop this behavior, the wrath of heaven will be upon him. The patakís of this sign teach us that Orisha Oko was once married to Olokun (some say Yemayá), and these spirits enforced the institution of marriage and committed relationships. It is also said that when this pattern was born,

†Note that there are those who attribute the birth of marriage to the odu Odí Obara (7-6). Yet because Olokun and Orisha Oko were married in this letter (some say Yemayá and Orisha Oko), many attribute marriage to this pattern as well. As always, one should check the customs and beliefs of one's elders when exploring religious dogma.

the earth had become evil and rotten, and it took all the aché of Ogbe Odí to heal it. Wisdom and knowledge come to us through this odu, although both come divided. No one person can ever know all things. Orisha Oko himself was born here, and his influence is important in the client's life. The morning dew was born here, and when this pattern falls on the mat the client is told that he must bathe in it at least once. Ogbe Odí also speaks of Elegguá, who not only became the servant of Orúnmila but came to live outside the house as well. Obatalá lost a son in this letter when that child tried to avenge the injustices done to his father. Oshún became ill, and was healed, in this sign.

Beyond these concepts, in any casting of Ogbe Odí the diviner should explore the following issues with the client:

- Obatalá speaks strongly in this letter, and he says that no matter how far the client goes in life, there are always those better off than he. If he wants to evolve always, he must live by paying homage to Obatalá, Yemayá, and Shangó, saying to each every day, "Maferefún!"
- In any orientation of Ogbe Odí, a male client could end up being gay, even if he is heterosexual now. His homosexual tendencies have not yet been acknowledged or accepted. A woman who opens in this odu should—tactfully—be delivered this advice about her husband.
- In osogbo, this sign is harsh. It tells the diviner that the client's roads are all but closed; the orishas are covering him due to disobedience. They must be placated quickly before his life gets worse.
- When an osogbo of ano or ikú comes, the client must watch for skin eruptions, liver disease, abdominal problems, lung or chest pains, irregular menses (if the client is a woman), kidney disease, and psychological disorders. If any of these develop, he should see a physician immediately.

## The Prohibitions of Ogbe Odí

- Do not consume shellfish, rabbit, rooster, fish, alcohol, coffee, the tails of animals, or the heads of animals. Do not consume any food containing blood.
- Do not enter the woods without first offering a sacrifice to Osain.
- Do not do collective or volunteer work.

## The Eboses of Ogbe Odí

In Ogbe Odí, the diviner will attempt to close the oracle after determining the larishe (if any) and prescribing the eboses mandatory for the parent odu, Eji Ogbe. This letter is complicated, and when it refuses closure the diviner must consider the client's position in the religion. The eboses that are appropriate for aleyos differ from those that are appropriate for initiates, and even those that overlap differ in the method in which they are made. The lists for each follow.

When an aleyo or aborisha opens in Ogbe Odí and the letter refuses closure, the diviner should consider the following possibilities:

- If the client has received nothing of ocha, he is now marked for the reception of the elekes. The inherent osogbo of this sign is so severe that only a ritual of this strength can destroy the negativity that surrounds him. Because both Ogún and Elegguá stand up to defend this person through Ogbe Odí, their elekes must be given in this ceremony along with those of Obatalá, Yemayá, Oshún, and Shangó. The diviner should consider having the aleyo make a simple offering of a candle to each spirit once the investment of the necklaces is complete.
- The client who has nothing of ocha, or who has already received the elekes but nothing else, can also be marked for the reception of the warriors. This initiation should be take place as soon as possible.
- If the client already has the elekes and the warriors, Ogún must be fed so that he will have the strength to fight the osogbo upon this person's head. He must be given two roosters and two

pigeons as soon as possible. The diviner should ensure that the client does have Ogún's eleke so Ogún's protection is with him always.

- If these eboses are not enough to close the sign for an aleyo, the diviner should consider marking ebó Shangó, Eleggua, and Obatalá, asking, "Ebó else [orisha's name]?" If an orisha stands up here to claim ebo, the diviner uses the diloggún to mark an appropriate offering. Before that ebó is made, the client should be given a rogación at the orisha's shrine to cool and strengthen his head.

If these considerations are not enough to bring Ogbe Odí to closure for an aleyo, the diviner should turn to the list of eboses for the parent odu, Eji Ogbe (see page 393). Something there is needed to bring the client's evolution.

When the letter opens in an osogbo for an initiate and will not close, the diviner should consider the following possibilities:

- If the initiate has the orishas Dada and Bañaní, the diviner should mark ebó to them and to Shangó. If the client does not have those two orishas, he is marked for their reception. Before paying the derecho for them, however, a token adimú should be given to Shangó so he will keep the osogbo at bay until Dada and Bañaní are received.
- If this is not enough to close the sign, Obatalá is the next orisha to petition in this letter. The proper ebó to mark is a rogación at his feet. After the rogación, a ñame painted white with cascarilla should be put on a white plate and left at his shrine. Always, for life, the client's Obatalá should have this ebó with him. If the root begins to grow a vine, it must not be allowed to grow any longer than the client is tall. Once this root rots, it should be taken away and replaced with a new one. As long as Obatalá has this ebó, he will ensure that the client evolves in life.
- If this letter still refuses closure, the client may need one or more of the following orishas: Yembo, Ochumare, Orisha Oko, or Oba. The italero should ask of each, "Koshé [orisha's name]?" If one of these spirits is marked, the diviner should immediately try to close the oracle before moving on to the next orisha. If the client already has one of these orishas, before questioning about the reception of the others the diviner should ask, "Ebó elese [orisha's name]?" If the answer is yes, he should use the diloggún to mark the required ebó.*

If the letter continues to refuse closure, the diviner now deviates from his normal pattern of questioning and turns to the list of eboses given for the parent odu, Eji Ogbe (see page 393). If nothing in that list will bring closure to the oracle, he must return to the remainder of this list. The following possibilities are severe and have drastic implications. They must be prescribed only if necessary.

- When the osogbo is severe and the odu will not close out, the client must do the following annually. First, he must give the river proper recognition and tribute. Every year on the anniversary of this odu's opening, the client must sacrifice two hens to Oshún in her home, the river. Since Oshún lives in the river, the client's orisha does not need to be brought with him for this ebó. Once this is done, the client should feed Oba on the riverbank, for in Africa she owns a river as well. If the initiate does not have Oba, he is now marked for her reception. He will need to bring this orisha to the river to do this ebó. Within a week of doing the sacrifice at the river, the client will need to sacrifice to the earth, egun, and Orisha Oko, in that order. If this person does not have Orisha Oko, he is marked for his reception now. Also, since Oshún, Oba, and Orisha Oko are saving this person's life through this sign, he must celebrate their feast days yearly.
- If the osogbo is severe and the sign still will not close, the client needs to give a goat to the earth

*Note that if the reception of an orisha is marked and the godparent does not have that orisha, the initiate needing that spirit must pay two derechos: one for the godparent to receive the orisha and one so he can receive it himself.

and Orisha Oko immediately. This may be done before the reception of Orisha Oko, and even before the river is fed, since this sign is now signaling imminent death. Once this sacrifice has been completed, the client should feed Obatalá a female goat, and he should then have a rogación beside Obatalá, finishing up with his head being fed a guinea hen. The next day, the client should have itá with Obatalá.

- Having exhausted these options, if the diviner is still facing an open odu, he should consider further issues with the following orishas: Elegguá, Ogún, Oshún, Shangó, Yemayá, Obatalá, Babaluaiye, and Orisha Oko. Even if options with these orishas have already been explored and marked previously through this odu, one or more of these might want additional eboses. The italero must ask, "Ebó elese [orisha's name]?" If the answer is yes, he should use the diloggún to mark the required ebó.

If the oracle still does not bring closure, the diviner must now consult with an elder, even calling one by phone if none is present at the reading, for help in finding a way to bring closure. Remember: It is not a sign of weakness to ask for help and advice. It is a sign of wisdom.

## The Eighth Composite Odu of Eji Ogbe, Ogbe Meji (8-8)

### The Proverbs of Ogbe Meji

- Two inseparable friends will separate.
- Bit by bit, we eat the head of the rat.
- A cap will never be more famous than a crown.
- Bit by bit, we eat the head of the fish.
- None of us can ever be as large as the elephant, nor will we ever be as strong as the buffalo.
- The sash worn against the body is not as fine as the sash worn outside the clothes.
- One must measure the width and measure the height before the true measure is known.
- The head guides the body.
- Death does not, nor can it ever, wage war in Olófin's house.
- If I have everything, I will lack all.
- The hand can reach much higher than the head.
- We stand on the shoulders of those who have come before.
- The young palm fronds grow much higher than those that are older.
- The forest is dense, yet Iroko can still be seen standing high among the trees.
- No music is so loud that a gong cannot be heard over it.
- There is no sound strong enough to silence the bell.
- We have cut off our own heads in order to grow, like the banana tree.
- The hands belong to the body, and the feet belong to the body; however, all of these belong to the head.
- The king dies while another is crowned.
- He who owes the monkey cannot plant corn beside the river.
- The road is open for the dog to follow.
- A pig could spend his entire life sitting on the rock, yet he prefers to live under the rock.
- You are a prisoner of ocha.
- A king is dethroned, yet another is quickly put into place.
- There is separation between godparent and godchild.
- A fish dies through the mouth.

### The Message of Ogbe Meji

When a casting of eight mouths repeats itself, the odu Ogbe Meji is open. This odu is also known by the names Elleunle, Elleunle Meji, and Baba Eji Ogbe. Having cast this sign, the diviner offers praise to Olófin, Obatalá, Olokun, Shangó, Oduduwa, Babaluaiye, Ogún, Orúnmila, Orisha Nla, Oshún, Orí, Oyá, Yemayá, and Naná Burukú, saying to each, "Maferefún!" All may speak or claim ebó in this pattern.

This odu gives birth to many things: sexual perversion, the desert mirage, spinach, the lymphatic system, capillaries, and the sternum. Both Olokun and Naná Burukú were born here. It is the odu in which Oshún found her wealth, and it is the letter that put Elegguá behind the front door.

When this sign falls on the mat, the client is in bondage to ocha. No longer does the letter promise that initiation will come; instead, it enforces the fact that this person must be a priest or priestess of the orishas. Until that aché is put into his head, he will have no true happiness, and he will wander through life unfulfilled. In iré, this sign promises all the good that life has to offer, but in osogbo, it promises separation, divorce, loss, and tears. In Ogbe Meji, it is important that the diviner spend time with this client, laying out his life on the mat and offering good advice, yet it is equally important that the client heed all that is said, conducting himself according to the orishas' wishes. Their greatest wish in this letter is that he focus always on initiation, for this is how he will evolve.

Two proverbs sum up the influence of this letter: "We stand on the shoulders of those who have come before" and "The young palm fronds grow much higher than those that are older." These sayings are native to Yoruban religion, having been saved almost intact by the initiates in Cuba and passed on to those of us here in the States. In his book Ifá *Divination*,* the cultural anthropologist William Bascom noted that the tree to which the second sentence refers is the oil palm tree *(Elaeis guineensis)*. In this species of palm trees, the younger palm fronds grow not from the bottom of the tree but from its tops, while the older ones stay close to the ground, drooping and dropping with age. As time passes, the elder branches grow heavy, sagging to the ground and showing their age, while the crown of the tree renews itself with greenery. The tree grows yearly, reaching toward heaven, yet those leaves that are oldest will never brush the sky. It is youth destined for this honor. When compared with the first proverb, "We stand on the shoulders of those that have come before," these two sentences sum up the influence and power of this odu. The basis of our entire religion is ancestral reverence; both humans and orishas were brought to this world by the ancestors and elders. Their work makes our own possible. Each new generation of priests and priestesses comes closer to heaven, closer to making perfect the orishas' spiritual manifestation on earth. Yet this can be done only because of the sacrifices made by the elders before us.

When Eji Ogbe opens, it alludes to the fact that our sacrifices must be made properly and in timely fashion; they must be pure and strong in order to continue providing a foundation for the future. Those who come into this faith must rely on age and wisdom in their training. They must respect the elders and the lessons that they have to teach. The elders must be given a strong voice in this faith. They must have respect and honor, and they must themselves ensure that the newer generations are properly taught and instructed, for in time, youth itself will become aged, and the elders will be reborn as youth, coming even closer to fulfillment and attainment. This cycle began in this letter, and it is this cycle that will continue to unfold as Olódumare renews all daily.

Many issues must be explored in this letter. Depending upon the reason for which the client has come for divination, the diviner might wish to explore the following points with the one who sits at the mat:

- This letter, in any orientation, foreshadows broken and lost relationships. Under the influence of Eji Ogbe, all aspects of life could change. Friendships could be broken. Relationships could be lost. Family units could be destroyed. Even spiritual ties between godchildren and godparents could become strained. During the periods of evolution that come, this client must hold on to those things that he considers dear to his life. If human relationships are to persevere beyond the influence of this odu, they must be nurtured. None of us lives in a vacuum, and we need each other to continue in life. The client must make sure that those whom he loves are shown this love. He should reach out to others frequently, even when he does not need or expect anything from them. Only in this way will his interpersonal relationships continue to grow.
- Two proverbs in this sign warn the client that

*William Bascom, *Ifá Divination: Communication between Gods and Men in West Africa* (Indianapolis: Indiana University Press, 1991).

while opportunities for knowledge and growth will come unbidden, he must resolve to grow slowly. He will be offered massive amounts of information, and although he should study and digest this information, he should proceed carefully, and he should not put it to use before its time. Remember these two proverbs: "Bit by bit we eat the head of the rat" and "Bit by bit we eat the head of the fish." Both the rat and the fish were once considered delicacies of the Yoruba; while good to eat, they are filled with sharp bones that can cause problems if ingested, as might happen if one ate them in a rush. Knowledge is like the rat and the fish. Putting new knowledge into use before it has been properly assimilated or analyzed can bring more harm that good. As always, the client would be wise rely on the advice of the elders in his spiritual line.

## The Prohibitions of Ogbe Meji

- Many foods can become taboo in this sign. If the orientation of the odu is an osogbo, avoid eggs, sweet potatoes, peanuts, fruits with grainy seeds (like kiwi and strawberry), sesame seeds, white beans, pork, tripe, fish, any reheated foods, any powdered foods, animal heads, kola nuts, spinach, coffee, palm oil, corn and any other grains, elephant meat, white yams, white drinks, and palm wine. Alcohol may be consumed in moderation unless this reading is the itá of an initiate; in that case, it is forbidden for life. Sugar and sweeteners should be avoided unless they are cooked into a dish; in that case, limit the consumption of sweets.
- For the next seven days following the opening of this odu, do not leave the house between the hours of noon and 6:00 P.M.
- For the next three months (unless this reading is the itá of initiation, in which case, for life), the following places are considered taboo: funeral parlors, hospitals, burial sites, graveyards, dark places, spiral stairs, and attics.
- Avoid any place in which a dead body was discovered and any site at which there was a murder or accidental death.
- Do not travel in the rain or in a snowstorm. (In itá, these restrictions could become taboo for life.)
- Do not wish oneself or anyone else dead; this might happen.
- Do not desire another person's lover, and do not date anyone who is dating someone else. Make sure a prospective partner's marital status is known; if that person is divorced, especially if this sign came in severe osogbo, reconsider a possible relationship with him or her.
- Do not answer the phone if the caller is not known; likewise, do not open the door if one does not know who is calling. Do not allow visitors in the home once one has gone to bed or anytime after midnight.
- When in the street, if one's name is called, do not answer, even if the voice is that of someone known. Respond only to those in one's direct line of sight.
- Keep one's house immaculately clean. Do not let trash or empty bottles accumulate, and do not let anything gather in corners, under furniture, or under the bed. Keep closets neat and well lit; do not store unused or broken items in them.
- Ashes must be kept neither in the home nor on the person.
- Do not put anything artificial on the head or neck, such as perfumes or hair dyes.
- Do not kill mice.
- Do not wear mended clothes.
- Do not curse, blaspheme, or wish ill of others.

## The Eboses of Ogbe Meji

If this odu falls as the letter of the head during itá for a iyawó, the following eboses are mandated; they do not need to be marked. A white horsetail should be given to Obatalá. A pigeon should be fed to the front door and to Ogún for protection against harm. In general, the iyawó must make sure that no one steals any of the fundamentals of the orishas. He should dress in white often; depending on the severity of the osogbo, the iyawó may need to dress in white every day for the rest of his life. Finally, when the year of initiation is finished, this person needs to receive the knife and make the ebó of the year.

If the reading is not an itá of initiation, the above eboses are not prescribed.

This odu is complex, and if it refuses closure after the larishe (if any) and initial eboses of the parent odu have been prescribed, marking ebó will take much skill. The diviner must consider the client's position in the religion (aleyo, aborisha, or initiate) and must go through the following lists carefully and systematically so that he misses nothing. To simplify this, the lists of possible eboses in Ogbe Meji can be divided into three parts: one for aleyos, one for aleyos and initiates, and one for initiates only. They must be considered in this order.

When this odu opens on the mat for an aleyo or an aborisha and will not close, the diviner needs to explore the following list of eboses.

- If this client has nothing of ocha, Ogbe Meji is marking ocha as his true salvation. He will, one day, become an initiate. The diviner must respect this and must gently lead this person on his true path. The first step is the initiation of the elekes. These must be prescribed as ebó.
- If the client already has the elekes, or if the odu will not close out after the elekes have been prescribed, the warriors are the next initiation the client must have. The diviner should explain this initiation, and if he has the skill, he should now mark the path of Eshu the client will receive. Note that in an odu this strong, the elekes of Elegguá, Ogún, and Ochosi should be given when the warriors are received, if possible.
- If these eboses are not enough to close the session for an aleyo, he needs a rogación; in severe osogbos, his orí must also be fed two white doves or pigeons. If the letter will not accept this, then the client's godparent must give him a rogación every day for a total of sixteen days. The client should dress in white the entire time.
- As a last resort for a client who currently has nothing of ocha and, perhaps, has no intention of going further into the religion, the diviner should drape the mazo of Obatalá over his neck like a banner, so that it passes over his left shoulder and under his right arm. There, while odu is still open, the diviner should direct this person to pay foribale first to Obatalá, then to his godparent (if she or he is present), and then to the diviner to receive their blessings. This person is now in bondage to ocha, and the diviner must tell him this.

If the exploration of this list is not enough to bring closure to the oracle, the following list of eboses for aleyos, aborishas, and initiates should be considered.

When this odu opens for a client of any status—aleyo, aborisha, or initiate—and will not close, the diviner should explore the following list. (Note that these are the first eboses the diviner should consider for initiates.)

- In this odu, the strongest and holiest of all the Meji signs, the Ibeyi can stand up to claim ebó or demand reception. The diviner should first ask, "Ebó elese los Ibeyi?" If the answer is yes, he should use the diloggún to mark the required ebó. If they will not take ebó and the client does not have them, their reception may be necessary; the diviner should ask, "Koshé los Ibeyi?"
- Olokun was born in this odu, and she could stand up either to claim ebó or to demand reception. The diviner should first ask, "Ebó elese Olokun?" If the answer is yes, he should use the diloggún to mark the required ebó. If she will not claim an ebó and the client does not have her, the diviner should then ask, "Koshé Olokun?"
- In this odu, a conditional ebó may be offered to Olokun to solicit her assistance in resolving great problems or making life-altering decisions. The client should dress in black and pray to Olokun.* Then he should remove his cloth

*Having offered this ebó, the client is now prohibited ever to wear black again unless he is making this ebó.

and dress totally in white; the old clothes are then thrown into the ocean so Olokun can remove all blocks from the client's destiny. This ebó will only work for those for whom this odu has fallen.

- The client could have issues pending with Obatalá, Shangó, Babaluaiye, Ogún, Oshún, Oyá, Yemayá, or Naná Burukú. The diviner should ask, "Ebó elese [orisha's name]?" If the answer is yes, he should use the diloggún to mark the required ebó.

If these eboses are not enough to close the oracle for an aleyo or an aborisha, the diviner should turn to the eboses listed for the parent odu, Eji Ogbe (see page 393), to find a way to end the session and bring evolution.

If these eboses will not bring the oracle's closure for an initiate, the diviner should turn to the list of eboses that may be considered only for initiates.

If the client is an initiate and the eboses that are appropriate for any person—aleyo, aborisha, or initiate—are not enough to close the odu, the diviner should explore the following options:

- The initiate may need an itá with Elegguá. The diviner should now ask, "Ebó elese Elegguá?" If the answer is yes, the appropriate sacrifice is a goat. An oriaté should be called in to sacrifice the goat to Elegguá and give the itá.
- If the letter still refuses closure, the client may need to receive Oba or Orisha Oko. The diviner should ask of each, "Koshé [orisha's name]?"
- If the letter will not take any ebó or larishe, the following is mandated: An oriaté must give the client a rogación using an eel and two white doves at the feet of Obatalá.

If the diviner has considered all these options and cannot find a way to close the odu, he must turn to the eboses listed for the parent odu, Eji Ogbe (see page 393).

# The Ninth Composite Odu of Eji Ogbe, Ogbe Osá (8-9)

## The Proverbs of Ogbe Osá

- What the mouth swallows does not come out through the mouth.
- The bad that you did once, do not do again.
- The fowl does not refuse the call of the corn.
- When the padlock fastens, it does not release itself.
- Your best friend is a dollar in your pocket.
- The body cannot resist the sting of the bee.
- Do good and speak the truth; this is what the orishas want.
- The temptations will be many, so always be strong.
- The bad that was done once should not be done again.

## The Message of Ogbe Osá

When an initial casting of eight mouths, Eji Ogbe, precedes a casting of nine mouths, Osá, the odu Ogbe Osá is open on the mat. Having cast this pattern on the mat, the diviner must honor Shangó, Olokun, Orúnmila, Oduduwa, Yemayá, Olófin, Oshún, Ogún, Elegguá, Oyá, Obatalá, and Nanumé, saying to each, "Maferefún!" This odu is a sign of depth and mystery, and it gives birth to deep, mysterious things. We say that the moon was born here, as was the orisha who is the moon, Nanumé. Those who honor the feminine mysteries of the lunar cycle rely on the power of this odu for their strength. The flint, that stone in which fire hides to escape the rain, finds its origin in this pattern. Patakís told in this sign say that Shangó ate ram for the first time here, and Oduduwa, the supreme ruler and founder of the Yoruba empire, got his aché here. We say that Ogbe Osá made Yemayá fond of both seahorses and ducks, and this pattern may demand two eboses of her children when it opens on the mat. (See "The Eboses of Ogbe Osá" on page 381.) The lamb is also spoken of here. He was once a gentle yet cunning creature. Humans knew his meat was sweet, but the lamb was always running away, hiding where it could not be found. It had one weakness, however: coconut meat. Humans seduced the lamb from hiding with this. Thus was it first brought to the slaughterhouse.

Of all the orishas who speak in this sign, and of all the patakís existing in its lore, no one story has caused more controversy or confusion in our religion than the tale of Oyá's betrayal by the ram. For Oyá and the ram were once the best of friends; she trusted him with all her thoughts, her fears, and her secrets. Even when she could turn to no orisha for help or comfort, the ram was always there for her, and she loved him above all other things. In time, Oyá's enemies put a bounty on her head; her comings and goings in the world caused problems for them, and they coveted her head for their own. The ram heard rumors of their desires, but as the story was passed among those on the earth, the tale had changed. What the ram heard was that Olófin himself wanted to destroy Oyá, and he was offering the gift of immortality to the one who could bring her to his palace. In greed, the ram went before Olófin and told him, "Father, I have heard of your hatred for Oyá, and I can bring her here for you. I can trick her, and you can have her head as you wish."

Olófin was stunned; he, too, had heard that Oyá had great enemies who wanted her dead. He had also heard that of all things that walked on the face of the earth, the one being she loved beyond all others was the ram. "And how," Olófin asked, "are you able to bring her to me?"

"It is simple, father," he said. "Oyá trusts me with her very life; we are the best of friends. I will bring her to you, as long as you agree now to what you offered as her bounty."

"And what might that be, ram?"

"Eternal life. That is what you promised, is it not?"

Olófin was furious, but his face was calm. "Ram," he said, "bring Oyá to me and I will grant you what you wish, eternal life. Fail, and in place of Oyá's head I will have your own!"

He dismissed the ram; as the animal left his palace, Olófin transported himself to Oyá's home. "Oyá," he warned, "you have many enemies who wish you dead. Yet none can betray you like your best friend. The ram is coming to deliver you into their hands. You must not let him destroy you."

"Father," she said in disbelief, "surely you are not serious. He is my best friend, the one whom I favor above all things."

"It is true, Oyá. He will offer to take you to a safe place, and instead he will bring you to me. For, you see, the ram thinks that I want your head, and he came to me today to say he could bring you to me. In exchange for your head, he wants eternal life."

Anger seethed within Oyá. Olófin was beyond lies, but the ram was her greatest friend. He knew all her secrets. Lightning flashed in her eyes when she said, "I will destroy him!"

"No, Oyá," he soothed her with his gentle voice, "for friend should not betray friend, and you cannot curse what you once blessed. When the ram comes to betray you, go with him. But first, put your nine copper bracelets in a box. As you come to my palace walls, shake the box with your bracelets vigorously, and a huge whirlwind will come down to take you safely away. My guards will seize the ram at the palace walls, and I myself will punish him for his treason. He knows the cost of failure is great, for I will remove his head with my own hands." Olófin stopped for a moment, and then he reached out to embrace Oyá. "My child, mortal beings do strange things out of greed. But the ram knows you love him. Perhaps, even now, he is rethinking his vile plan. Perhaps he will not come. Perhaps he will not betray you. But forewarned is forearmed."

There was a loud banging at Oyá's door. "It is he," Olófin said. "I must go." And his figure melted away.

Oyá answered the door, and the ram, frenzied, burst inside. "My friend," he gasped, "your enemies are scattered in the forest, and there are many. They have come to kill you. Come with me, and I will take you to safety."

She stilled her anger as suddenly as a great wind can still itself. "I must get something first."

"There is no time!"

Before he could say another word, Oyá was in her chambers; she gathered her nine copper bracelets in a box as Olófin said, then hopped onto the ram's back. "Surely," she thought, "this is not real. This is not happening. Maybe . . . the ram is taking me to hide from Olófin?" The ram gathered Oyá on his back, and in an instant they were rushing through the forest. The familiar path was all around Oyá as she realized, "He is taking me to Olófin's palace." The gates to Olófin's home rose before them, and Oyá, as Olófin had instructed, shook the box vigorously. A vast tornado descended, whisking Oyá away into the skies, far from the ram's sight. He froze. As the tornado lifted, he was surrounded by Olófin's guards, who brought him before the throne.

"Ram," roared the normally soft orisha, "you committed the greatest of crimes today. You sought to destroy your best friend, the one orisha who loved you above all things. You thought I wanted Oyá's head, and in truth, I love her as I love all my children on the earth. She is a princess in my heart. Oyá has many enemies, it is true, but never was I her enemy. I could never curse what I once blessed!"

Olófin's anger rose to fill the vast chamber; it was solid, electrifying. "Because you were willing to deliver one of my most beloved daughters to Death's cold hands, I sentence you, ram, to death. Your head is mine, as do all heads belong to me, and I will take that head now!" It was thus that the ram found death for his betrayal of his best friend, Oyá. His head was delivered to Oyá's enemies, a sign that Olófin himself would not tolerate anyone harming her. Oyá's enemies fled; she was never betrayed again.

Since this betrayal, Oyá will not be in the same room with a ram; it was once her best friend, her confidant, and it tried to destroy her. Because of this patakís, Oyá's children cannot crown the children of Yemayá or Shangó, nor can either orisha crown a child of Oyá. Many attribute these customs to a "war" existing between Yemayá and Oyá and between Oyá and Shangó. Nothing could be farther from the truth. In fact, having studied this story, one will realize that the sole reason these customs exist comes not from any war but from Oyá's hatred of the ram. It is for this reason that children of Oyá will not crown Yemayá's or Shangó's children, for to give birth to them a ram must be present; it is the proper sacrifice. Oyá would need to be in the same room since she was giving birth to the iyawó. Because of her hatred of this creature, such a thing is not possible. Likewise, children of Shangó and Yemayá do not receive Oyá at their asiento, for this would be like the ram itself giving birth to Oyá, and such a thing is not possible. The entire reason for these customs extends from Oyá's hatred of the ram, and not because of her hatred for those that eat the ram.

When this pattern opens in a firm iré, it can become heated, disposing the client to violence (either his own or another person's). This letter cautions the one at the mat to be wary of violence. He must neither own nor carry weapons, especially guns, knives, sticks, and mace. He must not raise his hand to any in anger, and if he becomes caught up in a heated argument, he must make sure that words are not exchanged within hand's reach. In this letter, someone will be either killed or maimed through a forceful strike.

Once this person leaves the diviner's house, other elements of odu will affect him. To begin, those from beyond the house of ocha will come offering advice; he should heed none of it. Others, especially priests and priestesses, will say that this person's religious initiations are wrong. They will try to teach the client the "proper" way to work the religion, but their ways are no better than what the client's godparent has already taught. The diviner must caution the one at the mat not to listen to these people, for their words bring devolution, not evolution. If he bows to these people's insistence, the orishas who offer protection will become angry, and when the godparents' spirits turn away, he will have nothing left to rely on. Yemayá says that just as she is the mother to all, this person must honor those who act as both mother and father in the religion. He must live by leaning on his godparent's teachings, and she will take care of the rest. No one else, not even this person's best friend, will have his best interests in mind. It is important that this person learn to live his own life, sharing his home, his life, and his love with no one but immediate family (of ocha or of blood). To let anyone else in intimately is to invite personal disaster.

## The Prohibitions of Ogbe Osá

- Do not eat ram, rooster, liquor, white or red beans, mutton, or coconut. Coconut is especially volatile in this letter, for in Ogbe Osá it was used to seduce the lamb; by it, he was brought to the slaughterhouse. The consumption or offering of foods with coconut implies that one is being "seduced" into destruction.
- An initiate crowned with Yemayá may not kill, sacrifice, or eat duck. She favors these fowl and will punish those who harm them.
- Do not run.
- Do not own or carry weapons.
- Do not open doors after dark.
- Do not smoke.
- Do not go to places where ikú may be found or let sick people sleep in his house. When close friends or relatives become ill, one may not visit them unless it is essential, and even then, one must first consult the orishas and mark ebó to cleanse oneself of sickness once the visit is over.

## The Eboses of Ogbe Osá

When this odu opens in any orientation beyond the firmest iré, the following eboses become mandatory for the client.

- The practice of spiritualism is to be abandoned. The only forces beyond orishas that this person should work with are his own egun. He must avoid prendas, spirit guides, and the gods of other religions; they will lead the client astray in this odu. He should not have a bóveda in his house, and no other forms of ancestral reverence beyond those of the Lucumí faith are to be employed.
- This odu raises issues with Obatalá. This orisha says that the client once had some routine, maybe even an altar, for one or more of the orishas. Now, this altar and the spiritual routine have been abandoned. The orishas are reclaiming their due, and these old customs must be begun once more. Only when the client starts paying homage to them again will he evolve. Luck will come when and where it is least expected.

Having made these prescriptions, the diviner may now attempt to close the oracle. If it will not close, he should explore the following possibilities:

- Egun must be given sacrifice. If the osogbo is severe, an oriaté must be called in to sacrifice a sheep to them.
- Obatalá, Yemayá, and Shangó could all be standing up for specific eboses in this sign. The diviner must ask for each, "Ebó elese [orisha's name]?" If the answer is yes for Obatalá or Shangó, the diviner should use the diloggún to mark the required ebó. If Yemayá answers that she wants ebó, the appropriate offering is for the client to raise two baby ducks in her honor. When grown, these two ducks should be fed to Yemayá by an oriaté. If either Yemayá or Shangó stands up for an ebó in this sign, for the next month the client should try to spoil them both with many gifts and adimús.

If these options are not enough to close the letter and the client is an aleyo or an aborisha, the diviner should turn to the eboses of the parent odu, Eji Ogbe (see page 393), to find closure for the sign. If the client is an initiate, he should continue to explore the options given in this list.

- If the client is an initiate of Yemayá, he must raise a pair of breeding ducks; through this letter was her love of these animals born. Likewise, she came to favor the seahorse, and seven of these should be put to her shrine.
- This sign can raise issues with Shangó. Shangó stands up to offer his aid and protection from all the osogbos predicted in this sign; so that he may offer his full protection, the client should give him a beaded bat or club. It must be washed in omiero and fed with Shangó. In addition to this, a niche osain should be made for the client using Shangó's herbs; this should be washed and fed with the bat as well. In an orientation of ano or ikú, Shangó should be fed a ram, and the innards should be placed at the feet of the royal palm. Through obí, the orisha himself should be allowed to dictate what is to be done with the carcass.

- When this sign comes in an itá, every year the client must feed Oyá two hens; once she has been fed, Shangó must be given a ram. If the client does not have Oyá, the iyawó must receive her before the week is over. After Shangó is fed the ram each year, the oriaté must ask with obí if the client is to sit for itá. If this sign does not come during an itá, then the sacrifice of a ram and the possible itá may need to be done only once; to determine if the odu will mark it, the diviner should ask, "Ebó elese Oyá y Shangó?"

If these considerations are not enough to close the odu, the diviner should turn to the list of eboses given in the parent odu, Eji Ogbe.

## The Tenth Composite Odu of Eji Ogbe, Ogbe Ofún (8-10)

### The Proverbs of Ogbe Ofún

- In darkness, the feline sees best.
- Two fight for one thing, but only one will win.
- The polar opposites; the war of the poles.
- Do not go by the sayings of others; listen only to yourself.

### The Message of Ogbe Ofún

When an initial casting of eight mouths, Eji Ogbe, precedes a second casting of ten mouths, Ofún, the odu Ogbe Ofún is open on the mat. Ejiogbe Ofún and Ogbe Kulejo are other names for this pattern. Immediately, the diviner must pay homage to Elegguá, Ogún, Oshún, Obatalá, and Orúnmila, saying to each, "Maferefún!" All may speak or claim ebó here. In this pattern, it is said that Ofún and Eji Ogbe fought a terrible war; eight mouths won, and Ofún, embittered, put a curse on the world. Since this day, both good and evil have come to this realm. Obatalá rules this odu, and before it closes he will have claimed many eboses. Many also say that Ikú is the mother of this sign. Death is found here; it is marked here. The client must be cautious that death does not come to him. He must be wary of arguments and passionate intrigues. He should also avoid the color red; he should wear white more often so that he sides more with Eji Ogbe and not Ofún, who loses all in this pattern.

This letter often speaks of a client who is in love and is planning a marriage or a partnership. While things look good now, infidelity (either real or implied by another) will destroy this relationship. The diviner must tell the client to make sure no one puts him into any compromising situation or in a place that could imply an affair. Egun are around this client continually, and they demand many spiritual masses; if this is not done, the client could begin to lose sleep at night. Also, this odu speaks of fighting and wars, and the client could become involved in a battle with another for a job, a promotion, a lover, or something similar. The client will win only if his determination is strong and he works continually to have what he wants.

### The Prohibitions of Ogbe Ofún

- Do not eat entrails, tripe, white beans, peanuts, eggs, sweet potatoes, rooster, or mushrooms.
- Do not consume alcohol.
- Avoid places in which many people have died or places where both egun and Ikú travel. Do not go to funerals, cemeteries, hospitals, nursing homes, wakes, or memorials. Limit the time one spends in dark or poorly lit places. Make sure that one's home is well lit always so that the dead do not gather, and keep the home clean and immaculate. When eating, remember to feed the dead first so that they do not feast on one's plate.
- Do not open the door during mealtime, or else evil comes in. Do not sleep in total darkness, and do not get up to open the door or answer the phone after retiring for the night.
- When going out during the day, do not wear ripped, torn, or mended clothes.
- Be careful when walking that one does not step on blood.
- Here, Obatalá suffered mental illness. In his condition he went to war, but he wore black robes instead of white. Because of this, he lost

the war. Do not wear black, or else one will lose one's mind.

## The Eboses of Ogbe Ofún

In Ogbe Ofún, the diviner will attempt to close the oracle after determining the larishe (if any) and prescribing the eboses mandatory for the parent odu, Eji Ogbe. If the odu refuses to close, the further investigation of eboses will depend on the client's initiatory status: aleyo, aborisha, or initiate.

If this letter opens in osogbo for an aleyo or an aborisha and will not close, the diviner should consider the following eboses:

- The diviner should prescribe a rogación at the feet of Obatalá; he can save this person from all osogbo. Note that a rogación marked in any composite incorporating Ofún should include ten elements in its performance.
- If the prescription of a rogación is not enough to bring closure to the oracle, the diviner must mark an ebó to Obatalá. He should first ask, "Ebó elese Obatalá?" If the answer is yes, the diviner must mark what he requires. If Obatalá will accept nothing of his own volition, the diviner should direct the client to make an offering from the heart. The orisha is waiting to see how much his help is worth to the client.
- If the odu still will not close, the client could have issues pending with Elegguá, Ogún, or Oshún. The diviner must ask if any of them need ebó. If any claim an offering, the diviner must mark what the orisha requires.

If these considerations are not enough to close the letter for an aleyo, the diviner must then turn to the eboses listed for the parent odu, Eji Ogbe (see page 393), to find a way to bring closure to the oracle.

When this letter will not close for an initiate, the diviner must consider the following options for ebó:

- The client could have various issues with Elegguá, Ogún, Oshún, or Obatalá. The diviner should determine if any of these spirits require ebó.
- The diviner should prohibit this person to kill or sacrifice pigeons. When he can, he must build a coop stocked with white pigeons; this should be dedicated to Obatalá.
- The client should tend to all his orishas well, for Obatalá is watching his conduct with them.
- If the client is looking for his happiness, he should offer the following ebó: Offer a pigeon's nest in which the eggs have hatched to Obatalá. Leave this next to him permanently as a symbol of that which he seeks. Whenever the client has a special request from this orisha, he should put a ceramic egg in the nest to represent his desire. In time, Obatalá will grant it.
- The client should give two small silver machetes, one sharp and one dull, to Obatalá. They should be kept in Obatalá's tureen.
- If this letter still refuses to close, it may mark the reception of Ochanlá. The diviner should ask, "Koshé Ochanlá?"

If the diviner has explored all these options and the letter continues to refuse closure, he should turn to the eboses listed for the parent odu, Eji Ogbe.

# The Eleventh Composite Odu of Eji Ogbe, Ogbe Owani (8-11)

## The Proverbs of Ogbe Owani

- Be generous: Share what you have with others, and you will never be in need.
- Overeating causes sickness; you will become ill, and blood will come from your mouth.
- One should attend first to his own affairs before taking care of his neighbor's business.

## The Message of Ogbe Owani

When an initial casting of eight mouths, Eji Ogbe, precedes a casting of eleven mouths, Owani, the odu Ogbe Owani is open on the mat. Ejiogbe Owani and Ogbe Hunle are other names for this odu. Having cast this sign, the diviner must honor Ogún,

Elegguá, Babaluaiye, Orúnmila, Naná Burukú, Osain, Shangó, Obatalá, and Ochosi, saying to each, "Maferefún!" All may speak or claim ebó in this letter. A custom is born of this sign, and the client must follow it for the rest of his life if he hopes to avoid any osogbo: The client must invite guests who come uninvited during mealtime to the table, to dine.

When this pattern opens on the mat, it marks the arrival of the supernatural, things that one knows exist not in the material world but in the spiritual world. It can bring confinement, and before it passes the client could find himself confined. Ogbe Owani is also the odu in which Oshún ate her first hen, and when this letter opens and refuses closure, many mark a hen to her as ebó. We say that egun traveled naked through the world until this pattern emerged, and then they received their clothing. To commemorate this, many offer cloth to their egun shrine.

Note that when this letter opens on the mat, it tells the diviner that the client is not listening to what he is saying. He hears selectively, if at all, and thinks that the diviner is either lying or making up the reading as he goes along. He may not make ebó at all, for he believes that this italero is just after his money. Therefore, in this odu the diviner becomes a soothsayer, for when the client heeds not what the diviner says and does not make ebó, all the bad told to him will come true. This person will return later to have his life straightened out by the orishas.

The diviner must also consider the following when Ogbe Owani opens on the mat:

- If an aleyo preparing for initiation sits at the mat, the diviner must tell him that financial difficulties are coming, but he may not use money that he has been saving for ocha to get out of these troubles. If he does, the orishas will punish severely, perhaps even putting this person in jail for a time.
- The client is undeserving of his godparents' goodness; they have been very kind, gentle, and fair with him, and he has done nothing for them in return. This person is filled with disbelief of the things told to him by his elders; he will believe only once what they have said has happened. This is what causes many of his troubles.
- If osogbo comes, the client must be careful when praying. Prayers that are too emotional or fervent will attract supernatural forces with which he is not prepared to deal.
- If an osogbo of ano or ikú opens in this odu, back pain, nervous disorders, tuberculosis, and pigmentation problems are all possible. If any of these arise, the client must see a physician immediately.

## The Prohibitions of Ogbe Owani

- Sesame seeds, grains, and fruits with grainy seeds are all taboo. Do not consume alcohol, corn, and red foods.
- When making any meal, prepare extra portions in case unexpected visitors show up. If visitors do not come, give some of the extra food to egun.
- The roads are too hot and volatile to travel on when this letter appears, and danger comes early in the morning. To avoid an accident, do not drive before noon.
- Do not despise anyone; treat all equally well. Be gracious to those who visit unexpectedly.
- At all costs, avoid promiscuity.

## The Eboses of Ogbe Owani

In Ogbe Owani, the diviner will attempt to close the oracle after determining the larishe (if any) and prescribing the eboses mandatory for the parent odu, Eji Ogbe. If the odu refuses to close, the diviner needs to explore the following options for ebó.

- The client's egun are standing up to speak. They have been all but ignored. He has abandoned the routines he once had with them. The client needs to reinforce his relationship with the dead. To strengthen his ties with them, he must put freshly cut lilies on their shrine; once these die, the client should consider keeping potted flowers with the egun, using lilies whenever they are obtainable. Depending upon the osogbo of this sign, the client's egun could also require additional eboses; to see what they require, the diviner should ask, "Ebó elese egun?" If the answer is yes, he uses the diloggún to mark the appropriate offering.

- Elegguá and Babaluaiye can stand up in this odu to claim ebó. To see if one or both require an offering, the diviner must ask, "Ebó elese Elegguá?" and "Ebó elese Babaluaiye?" If the answer is yes, he uses the diloggún to mark the appropriate offering. If neither Elegguá nor Babaluaiye will claim ebó, the diviner should advise the client that giving them an offering anyway would be wise, ensuring their goodwill.
- If this letter will still not close and Babaluaiye did claim ebó, he might wish to be in the client's home. The diviner should check this by asking, "Koshé Babaluaiye?" If the answer is yes, this person should arrange to receive the orisha when possible. If finances do not permit this immediately, the diviner should give the client a rogación at the feet of Babaluaiye and place the eleke of that orisha around the client's neck.
- Ogún, Naná Burukú, Shangó, Obatalá, and Ochosi can also stand up in this odu to claim ebó. The diviner should determine if any of these require offerings.

If these considerations are not enough to close the oracle and the client is an aleyo, the diviner should turn to the eboses of the parent odu, Eji Ogbe (see page 393) to find closure. If the client is an initiate, the diviner should explore the rest of the items in this list. He may not ask for closure until he has investigated all of them.

- The orisha whose diloggún is being consulted might want ebó of a female goat that has recently given birth. The diviner should check this by asking, "Ebó elese [orisha's name]?" If the answer to this is yes, the ebó has been marked and an oriaté must be found to do the ceremony. The oriaté who performs this sacrifice must give the client an itá.
- This odu can mark the reception of Orisha Oko, Yembo, and the diloggún of Ogún. The diviner should investigate each of these options. If the initiate already has any or all of these, those spirits could be standing up for ebó. The diviner must consider that as well.

If these options are not enough to close the oracle, the diviner must then turn to the eboses of the parent odu, Eji Ogbe.

## The Twelfth Composite Odu of Eji Ogbe, Ogbe Ejila (8-12)

### The Proverbs of Ogbe Ejila

- A blessing received was paid for by a curse.
- A wasp bites hard, and yet the pain will soon pass.
- Ogbe Tun Omo Pon: Ogbe puts a child on the back again.
- Today cannot be like tomorrow.
- Nobody knows what he will do tomorrow.
- The one who raises water in a flat pan invites water to pour over his head.
- The enemy eats and drinks from the same place as you.
- Those that work will be paid, but those that do not work will be left without a salary.
- When a child goes to play outside, that child never forgets to return home.
- One who sows the seeds of hatred will see his children harvest the fruits.

### The Message of Ogbe Ejila

When a casting of eight mouths, Eji Ogbe, precedes a casting of twelve mouths, Ejila Shebora, the odu Ogbe Ejila is open on the mat. This odu is also known as Ejiogbe Oturupon, Ejiogbe Ejila, Ogbe Trupo, Ogbe Tun Omo Pon, and Ogbe Tomokpon. Having cast this sign, the diviner must praise Oyá, Elegguá, Orúnmila, Shangó, Obatalá, and Babaluaiye, saying to each, "Maferefún!" All may speak or claim ebó in this letter. This letter gives birth to taboo, its prescription and reception. When this sign opens on the mat in anything but iré, the diviner must warn the client that throughout his religious life he has been given many prohibitions. Some were long term, while the orishas mandated others for only a short period. He heeded few, if any, of these. He is now expected to abide by them for a certain period; see "The Prohibitions of Ogbe Ejila."

Ogbe Ejila is also known as the odu of doubts. The client doubts the diviner, the religion, the orishas, and even himself at times. He doubts those whom he calls his friends, and he doubts his own blood. The diviner should know that the one sitting at the mat also doubts that the reading is valid and that ebó will do any good. He also knows this: This odu forbids the "giving away" of the religion, and the priest must charge well for any work prescribed in this sign.

This letter is explosive and volatile, a paradox within the family of Eji Ogbe, and even when it comes in iré the client must be forbidden to handle things that are hot, spicy, explosive, or volatile if he hopes to avoid accidents and hardships. He must be cautious of fire, gunpowder, alcohol, electricity, kerosene heaters, and gas-powered and other combustible engines. The danger of explosions is severe in this sign, and this must be considered always.

The diviner must also tell the client that financial difficulties are coming, even if he has plenty of money now. When they come, he must not spend that which he is saving for ocha. If he does, he will end up in jail, or dead, for through Ogbe Ejila ocha is his only true salvation. Focusing on that leaves much of life's hardships behind. Finally, the client should beware one with whom he dines regularly; he has an enemy there.

## The Prohibitions of Ogbe Ejila

Because this client has, in the past, ignored prohibitions that were given to him, odu now digs into this person's past and asks him to remember all that the orishas once prohibited. After the client has recalled these prohibitions and told them to the italero, the priest must tell the client that they are now taboo again, and if this person hopes to avoid osogbo, he must heed them without fail. If this reading is an itá, these prohibitions now hold for life; if this is only a reading with the orishas, they must be followed for three months. Consider this an ebó whose fulfillment will affect the rest of this person's life.

In addition, the diviner should consider the following prohibitions for the client:

- Do not eat ram, eel, fowl, okra, pumpkins, squash, calabazas, and papaya. Observe all taboos traditionally given to initiates of Oyá, especially food prohibitions. In this odu, Oyá can be one's salvation if one gives her proper respect.
- If a stranger, client, or coworker offers food or drink, accept it but do not consume it.
- Do not argue, fight, baby-sit, gossip, travel, or stop fights.
- When the child of another cries, do not comfort it. Others will make accusations.
- Throw anything broken in the trash. Do not keep broken or burned items in one's home.
- When it rains, do not get wet.
- Do not handle explosives or gunpowder.

## The Eboses of Ogbe Ejila

When this odu opens for a client, it marks an ebó for the diviner: He must give a rogación to the next initiate who comes to visit his house. If any priests and priestesses are present at this reading, they do the same when an initiate comes to visit their houses. The diviner and the priests attending may not fulfill this ebó by giving rogaciónes to each other's heads when the oracle is closed. That will not fulfill their obligations to the odu that has opened.

Having made this prescription, the diviner will attempt to close the oracle. If it refuses closure and the client is an aleyo, the diviner must first consider the potential eboses that are common to Ogbe Ejila (8-12) through Ogbe Merindilogún (8-16), as described beginning on page 392.

- If the client is an aleyo and the eboses described in "The Eboses of Ogbe Ejila" (8-12) through "The Eboses of Ogbe Merindilogún" (8-16) are not enough to close the oracle, he may of issues with Oyá, Elegguá, Shangó, Obatalá, or Babaluaiye. Any of these spirits could require ebó, and the italero must consider this.
- If the client is an initiate, he may need to receive Eshu Eshun Irirke (who walks with Osain), Oba,

or Osain. The diviner should ask of each, "Koshé [orisha's name]?"

If these eboses are not enough to close the letter (or if odu will accept none of them), the diviner must turn to the eboses of the parent odu, Eji Ogbe (see page 393).

## The Thirteenth Composite Odu of Eji Ogbe, Ogbe Metanla (8-13)

### The Proverbs of Ogbe Metanla

- Be humble.
- On one's knees, beg Olódumare.

### The Message of Ogbe Metanla

When an initial casting of eight mouths, Eji Ogbe, precedes a second casting of thirteen mouths, Metanla, the odu Ogbe Metanla is open. This letter goes by many other names: Ejiogbe Irete, Ejiogbe Metanla, Ogbe Ate, and Ogbe Irete. Having cast this sign, the diviner must honor Orúnmila, Oduduwa, Olokun, Ogún, Elegguá, egun, Oshún, Osain, Shangó, Babaluaiye, and Yewá, saying to each, "Maferefún!" All may stand up to speak or claim ebó. This sign brings many clashes and personal reprisals, altercations with others that come without provocation. Conflicts, plights, travesties, and treasons begin here. It is a pattern of reversal, and those who come in iré will suffer osogbo before it passes, while those who come in osogbo will eventually emerge with iré in their lives. Most who open with Ogbe Metanla on the mat suffer bad fortune, but before this letter has passed their fortunes will be reversed; life will change for the better. In Ifá, this odu directs the babalawos to feed each other's heads, and in santo, initiates should do the same. Know that Ogbe Metanla abandoned Ifá at the river but returned to save it later. Abandonment, exile, and poor character can all be found here, but initiation can reverse these things. This odu marks the client as one who must live by making ebó; he must offer the eboses prescribed by this odu quickly to find salvation. This is a sign of deterioration in the mouth and tooth decay. The client must measure his words carefully and should go see a dentist soon.

### The Prohibitions of Ogbe Metanla

- Do not eat hen, banana, okra, black-eyed peas, corn, or corn flour.
- Beware of adultery. Do not seduce another's spouse, and do not flirt with those who are married, for this will bring osogbo into one's life.
- Date no one whose complexion is lighter than one's own.
- If dating another who has recently broken up with a lover, ensure that the former relationship is over before beginning something new. In this letter, the old lover comes back to reclaim the former; often, the old one wins.
- Do not entertain guests. If guests are in one's home, do not throw things to them; hand things to them instead. Do not let guests sleep in one's home overnight, because in this letter someone who does not live with one could die in one's house.

### The Eboses of Ogbe Metanla

After prescribing the initial larishe (if any) for Ogbe Metanla, the diviner will attempt to close the oracle. If it refuses closure and the client is an aleyo, the diviner must first consider the potential eboses that are common to Ogbe Ejila (8-12) through Ogbe Merindilogún (8-16), as described beginning on page 392.

Next, if the odu has come in an osogbo for either an aleyo or an aborisha and refuses closure, the diviner has immediate options to explore:

- This first option is mandatory. The client must pray daily on his knees to Olódumare for help and guidance. If this ebó is fulfilled each morning, the help this person needs will be given. Once he skips a day, all help will be withdrawn. He won't be able to restart the ebó.
- The second option must be marked by the shells. Babaluaiye speaks in this letter and could be demanding one of three things. First, the

client might need to make ebó to him; the diviner must ask, "Ebó elese Babaluaiye?" If the answer is yes, the diviner must mark what the orisha requires. The second option is the reception of his eleke; the diviner must ask, "Ebó eleke de Babaluaiye?" If the answer is yes, the derecho for this must be presented to the orisha on a white plate with two white candles and two coconuts. The client should have a rogación before receiving the eleke.

- The final option is the reception of Babaluaiye; the diviner must ask, "Koshé Babaluaiye?" If the answer to this is yes, the client must arrange to receive this orisha when possible.

If the oracle will not close after these eboses have been prescribed, the client could have issues to resolve with Olokun, Ogún, Elegguá, Oshún, Shangó, or Yewá. The propitiation of one or more of these is essential to the client's evolution. To determine if any of these orishas will accept ebó, the diviner asks, "Ebó elese [orisha's name]?" If the answer is yes, he uses the diloggún to mark the appropriate offering.

If these options are not enough to close the letter for an aleyo or an aborisha, the diviner must then turn to the lists of eboses given for the parent odu, Eji Ogbe (see page 393).

If this sign falls for an initiate, it automatically marks him to receive both Babaluaiye and Naná Burukú. Until he can receive them, the diviner should give the client their elekes, along with a rogación before their shrines, and the initiate must make monthly eboses to both of them.

If this is not enough to close the letter, the italero must turn to the eboses given for the parent odu, Eji Ogbe, to find closure for the reading.

# The Fourteenth Composite Odu of Eji Ogbe, Ogbe Merinla (8-14)

## The Proverb of Ogbe Merinla

- Even if you have done nothing wrong, pretend that you have and watch your back.

## The Message of Ogbe Merinla

When an initial casting of eight mouths, Eji Ogbe, precedes a second casting of fourteen mouths, Merinla, the odu Ogbe Merinla is open on the mat. Ejiogbe Ika, Ejiogbe Merinla, Ogbe Ika, Ogbe Eka, and Ogbe Karele are additional names for this odu. When it falls, the diviner should honor Ochumare, Elegguá, Ogún, Orúnmila, Obatalá, and the Ibeyi, saying to each, "Maferefún!" Here, all may stand up to speak or claim ebó. Through this sign, the world once accused Orúnmila of being a thief, and to prove his innocence he commanded Eshu to create fingerprints. With these, the true culprit was found. Many go so far as to say that the current phenomenon of DNA testing finds its origin in this pattern's energy; it gives birth to personal identification.

If the client is living both legally and ethically at this time, others could falsely accuse him of wrongdoing. Osogbo often marks this person as a criminal, however, and the diviner must be careful. In Ogbe Merinla, one is never innocent until proven guilty; others will always assume this person is guilty. This pattern brings gossip, lies, slander, and false testimony. Only by making ebó can the client forestall these negative influences. To keep himself out of legal trouble, he must touch nothing he finds on the street, buy nothing secondhand, and do his best to keep himself out of compromising situations.

## The Prohibitions of Ogbe Merinla

- Do not eat pork and monkey meat.
- When dining, do not eat or drink from small bowls. When someone serves food in a small bowl, if it is appropriate, ask for a large mug instead. If it is not appropriate, do not consume the food.

- This letter enforces fidelity to one's spouse. If this letter opens and one is considering a divorce, reconsider, and stay in the relationship for at least another three months. Let the spouse instigate divorce if he or she wants to leave. If this reading is an itá, one must choose one's mate wisely, for divorce is now taboo for life.

## The Eboses of Ogbe Merinla

This odu requires two eboses:

- The client must have a rogación at the feet of his guardian orisha. If the guardian orisha is not known, the rogación must be done before Obatalá. At the end of this ceremony, the diviner should feed two white doves or pigeons to the client's head.
- The warriors must be fed two roosters so that they have the strength to fight all of the client's osogbos.
- Having made these prescriptions, the diviner has his first chance to close the oracle. If it will not close and the client is an aleyo, he must next consider the potential eboses that are common to Ogbe Ejila (8-12) through Ogbe Merindilogún (8-16), as described beginning on page 392, before returning to the list of possible eboses listed below.
- The diviner should next consider offerings to Elegguá, Ogún, Obatalá, and the Ibeyi, asking, "Ebó elese [orisha's name]?" If the answer is yes, he marks the offering with the shells.
- This sign can mark the client for the reception of Ochumare, the Ibeyi, or both. The diviner should consider this option.

If these eboses are not enough to close the oracle, the diviner should turn to the eboses of the parent odu, Eji Ogbe (see page 393), to find closure for the oracle.

# The Fifteenth Composite Odu of Eji Ogbe, Ogbe Marunla (8-15)

## The Proverbs of Ogbe Marunla

- Trust your secrets to no one.
- There is a war of witchcraft, and it is strong.
- One weaver bird does not settle in town because its kind flocks in multitudes.
- When the elephant dies, we cut it up.
- When the buffalo dies, we cut it up.
- A dead goat sounds louder than a live goat.
- The blessings will come to your house, but you will not be there: Do not miss your blessings.
- An elder, sitting but not leaning back, looks like one standing.
- Honor finds wealth wherever it turns.
- Wasps have painful stings, but the pain soon subsides.

## The Message of Ogbe Marunla

When an initial casting of eight mouths, Eji Ogbe, precedes a second casting of fifteen mouths, Marunla, the odu Ogbe Marunla is open on the mat. Ogbe Guene, Ogbe Weyin, Ogbe Wehin, Ogbe Iwori, Ejiogbe Iwori, and Ejiogbe Marunla are other names for this sign. When it opens on the mat, not only the ritual gestures of Eji Ogbe but also an additional series of gestures must be done. Both the diviner and the client (the priest might have to instruct the client to do this, since he may not know our customs) should turn their heads to the side, first to the right and then to the left, while the diviner says, "May the battle of the rear not overcome us." This pantomime and chant are born of the patakís in this odu. The letter Ogbe Marunla tells of a war that happened in Cuba, the war of the Ifá priests (babalawos) and the Palo Mayombe priests (mayomberos). This was a war not of weapons and bloodshed but of magic and death. The nfumbe and nkisi of the mayomberos were pitted against the mysteries of Orúnmila, and the babalawos won, for the mysteries of Ifá are greater than any other on the earth. To this day, a bitter chasm exists between these two priesthoods. When this sign opens on the mat, especially if the client has been initiated to Palo Mayombe, it speaks of one who has used magic and witchcraft to attack those who have made either ocha or Ifá, and the orishas are not happy with this. The italero must ask the palero to admit his wrongdoings, and then the oracle will give eboses to atone for his evil. Once these are done, they will heal those who have been hurt by his evil, releasing them from harm. The italero must warn the palero never to use his religion for evil again, especially against those in the Lucumí faith, for the orishas will destroy him.

If the sign opens in an osogbo, and if the client has not been cut to palo, the diviner must tell him that a war of witchcraft exists around him, and it is strong. Either someone has employed a palero to attack him or a palero has become irate with this person and is sending his spirits to attack, maim, or destroy. The eboses prescribed through this letter, especially the gesture (a larishe) given as the sign was opened, will destroy all these things. They will release the client from what has been sent, and the one doing the sending will be destroyed by his own spirits.

No matter the orientation of this pattern, when it opens on the mat it marks a person who is both happy and proud with himself. Evil comes. He is oblivious to it, preferring to be an optimist and thinking that things could be worse and will get better in time. There are plenty of reasons for this person to be happy, and his many accomplishments in life might give him good reason to be proud. However, the odu says he must not be so obvious about either his happiness or his pride. The opening of Ogbe Marunla says that this person must keep his accomplishments, plans, dreams, and goals quiet. To do otherwise is to invite jealousy, and with jealousy come slander, gossip, and even the evil eye. Odu says that others will find out about the client's good works when the time is right.

Something else to keep in mind when this pattern falls is this: Rain usually falls within seventy-two hours of this pattern's opening. The client and the diviner should not get wet in this rain; if either the client or the diviner must go out in it, he must keep his head, hair, face, and neck dry. Rain will bring much evil if it touches these parts of the body.

## The Prohibitions of Ogbe Marunla

- Do not eat yam, rooster, corn, or corn flour. Respect the sacrificial foods of the orishas.
- When dining in the house of strangers, be wary of what one eats, and make sure one knows how the food is prepared. Do not eat things that are raw or not well cooked. If a person offers food with insistence, do not consume it; whether it is intentional or unintentional, something could be wrong with it.
- Do not buy, carry, or own weapons. If weapons, such as clubs and knives, are already in the house, they may be kept if they stay in the house. Be very wary of guns around children and teenagers, because there could be a fatal accident. If one has a handgun, sell it or dispose of it; if one has a rifle or shotgun, keep it unloaded and under lock and key.
- Do not take or borrow the belongings of others. Do not pick up, use, or carry an item that belongs to another.
- Do not lend out one's personal possessions. Do not be generous with either one's money or one's possessions.
- Going out in the first rain is taboo after this odu opens; stay home. After the first rain, one may go out, but do not get wet in the rain for three months (or for life, if this reading is an itá).
- Do not seduce another's spouse or lover. Before having sex, make sure one knows one's lover. This person could have another lover on the side.
- Do not pretend to be rich or have money, and do not carry valuables or wear expensive jewelry in public. This will attract thieves.
- Have nothing to do with holes. Do not wear them, buy them, dig them, or walk over them.

## The Eboses of Ogbe Marunla

After prescribing the initial larishe (if any) for Ogbe Marunla, the diviner will attempt to close the oracle. If it refuses closure and the client is an aleyo, the diviner must first consider the potential eboses that are common to Ogbe Ejila (8-12) through Ogbe

Merindilogún (8-16), as described beginning on page 392, before returning to the list of possible eboses described below.

- When this odu opens in osogbo and refuses closure, two eboses must be done. First, the diviner must feed the warriors two roosters; he should feed Elegguá and Ogún side by side behind the front door so that they protect not only the client but his home as well. He must be sure that some blood from the sacrifice is rubbed on the door and also on the door's frame. Second, the diviner reinforces Ósun's carga and feeds him two white pigeons behind the front door. This will give him the strength to guide the client's head away from danger.
- If the odu still will not close, the diviner should consider eboses to the following orishas: Shangó, Obatalá, Oshún, Olokun, and even egun.
- If the odu continues to refuse closure and the client is an initiate, it marks this person as an *osainista* (one who has the natural ability to work with herbs and plants); by receiving Osain and studying his herbal lore, this person will find evolution and salvation. The diviner should fulfill this ebó as soon as possible, for only once he has brought Osain into the client's life will things begin to clear.

If the oracle still refuses closure at this point, it is directing the diviner to consider the eboses for the parent odu, Eji Ogbe (see page 393).

## The Sixteenth Composite Odu of Eji Ogbe, Ogbe Merindilogún (8-16)

### The Proverbs of Ogbe Merindilogún

- Do not be nosy.
- Ogbe does not have a lawsuit.
- Ogbe is the owner of the white cloth.
- Do what you are told, no more and no less.

### The Message of Ogbe Merindilogún

When an initial cast of eight mouths, Eji Ogbe, is followed by a second cast of sixteen mouths, Merindilogún, the odu Ogbe Merindilogún is open on the mat. Ogbe Kosejo, Ogbe Otura, Ejiogbe Otura, Ejiogbe Merindilogún, Ogbe-Alaso Funfun, Ogbe Etura, Ogbe Alaara, and Ogbe Kunle are other names for this sign. Many elder santeros credit this odu for giving birth to the lighting of two white candles upon the completion of a sacrifice. Also, note that when this odu opens, it predicts strange earthquakes at sea. This is the letter giving a crown to the earth.

Before the italero determines whether this sign comes with iré or osogbo, he should tell the client to leave the house and then come back. Upon returning, the diviner should ask what he saw. The client will tell a lie. The opening of this letter tells the italero that the client is a liar and a cheat. He is not telling the italero the true reason that he came to the mat. No matter how much is said, this person will not come clean. This will be his own downfall. The letter speaks of major losses and setbacks, and once this person leaves the diviner's house, his life will begin to fall apart; definitely, he will not make all the eboses prescribed. This person will come back. He might also suffer blood loss before the aché of this odu has passed.

### The Prohibitions of Ogbe Merindilogún

- Do not consume alcohol, corn, yam, pork products, rooster, rabbit, turtle, crab, and animal meats from scavengers.
- Do not smoke cigarettes or cigars; in this sign, they are poison, and deadly. A lifetime smoker who opens in this odu should have a physical and chest X ray immediately; there could be something wrong with his lungs.
- One must not work for free; one will lose one's luck. Do not participate in volunteer programs, mentoring programs, relief programs, blood drives, fund-raising, or any type of work in which one does not get paid.
- Do not give gifts unless it is an appropriate

occasion (such as Christmas or a birthday).

- Control the tongue and measure one's words carefully. Do not lie or gossip. These things will bring osogbo.

## The Eboses of Ogbe Merindilogún

After prescribing the initial larishe (if any) for Ogbe Merindilogún, the diviner will attempt to close the oracle. If it refuses closure and the client is an aleyo, the diviner must first consider the potential eboses that are common to Ogbe Ejila (8-12) through Ogbe Merindilogún (8-16), as described beginning on this page, before returning to the list of possible eboses described below.

- When this odu opens in osogbo for an aleyo or aborisha and will not close, it is marking one of two things: Either ebó must be made to Olokun or the client must receive her. The diviner should ask, "Ebó elese Olokun?" If the answer is yes, he uses the diloggún to mark the required offering. If she requires no ebó and the client does not already have her, Olokun now marks him for her reception. Only the strength of this orisha can turn this person's life around.
- If this prescription does not close the odu for an aleyo or aborisha, the diviner should consider issues with the following orishas: Olokun, Yemayá, Elegguá, Oyá, Ogún, Obatalá, Oshún, and Iroko. One or more might require eboses before closing this sign.

If this does not bring resolution for an aleyo or aborisha, the diviner must turn to the eboses of the parent odu, Eji Ogbe (see page 393). The client needs something there for his evolution.

An initiate who comes in an unresolved osogbo must purchase a jutía and offer it to Elegguá as ebó. After the sacrifice, he must skin the animal and give the pelt to the orisha. Because jutía is a four-legged animal, only an oriaté can perform this sacrifice. One day, the client will need this pelt for a special ebó. Elegguá will tell him when; the client should call an oriaté for this as well.

After explaining this prescription to the initiate, the diviner should attempt the oracle's closure. If it remains open, he must turn to the eboses of the parent odu, Eji Ogbe.

## Aleyo Eboses of Ogbe Ejila (8-12) through Ogbe Merindilogún (8-16)

If Ogbe Ejila (8-12), Ogbe Metanla (8-13), Ogbe Merinla (8-14), Ogbe Marunla (8-15), or Ogbe Merindilogún (8-16) comes in an osogbo and will not close for an aleyo, the diviner knows that the odu is hot and volatile. While Ogbe Ejila is not as dangerous as the later composites, working through it is difficult. Those signs beyond 8-12 can become explosive for the diviner, client, and those present at the mat if they are not manipulated skillfully. Remember that once odu is opened at the mat, the implications of that letter enfold all present until the pattern is placated and closed. Once closed, the energies rest again with the one who brought them to the mat—the client present for a reading. If the sign is not closed properly, those energies remain open and will affect all who were present. The ritual of diloggún is not one to be taken lightly. When the signs beyond Ogbe Owani open, it is important that the diviner impress upon the client that his true salvation lies in making ocha. It is his destiny, and any eboses prescribed will only hold negativity at bay until he takes that step.

Having refused closure for an aleyo, the composites 8-12, 8-13, 8-14, 8-15, and 8-16 demand that the diviner consider the following eboses before any others:

- Because Obatalá and Elegguá are found in all 256 odu, the diviner attempts to mark ebó to these two orishas first. He asks, "Ebó elese Obatalá?" and "Ebó elese Elegguá?" If the answer is yes, the orishas are telling the diviner that they will stand up and defend the client, clearing the osogbo. He must use the diloggún to mark the required offering, and the client must give whatever they mark quickly. Obatalá is the most forgiving of all the spirits, and he embodies all things that are cool and refreshing, easing evolution. Elegguá is fate or destiny, and while he cannot erase what one consents to in heaven, he can bend it, making it either gentler or more harsh. He is essential to evolution in these signs.

- If this client has nothing of ocha, Eji Ogbe is marking ocha as his true salvation. One day, he will become an initiate. The diviner must respect this and must gently lead this person on his true path. The first step is the initiation of the elekes. The diviner must prescribe these as ebó.
- If the client already has the elekes, or if the odu will not close after they have been prescribed, he must receive his warriors. The diviner should explain this initiation, and if he has the skill, he should now mark the path of Eshu the client will receive. Because of the strength of this odu, the client should receive the elekes of Elegguá, Ogún, and Ochosi when he receives the warriors, if possible.
- If these eboses are not enough to close the session for an aleyo, he needs a rogación. In severe cases of osogbo, the diviner might also need to feed his head two white doves or pigeons. To check this, he should ask, "Eborí?" If the letter will not accept this, then the client's godparent must give him a rogación every day for a total of sixteen days. The client must dress in white the entire time.
- Before letting this person leave his house, the diviner must drape the mazo of Obatalá over his neck so that he wears it like a banner, over his left shoulder and under his right arm. He must then pay foribale to Obatalá, the godparents, and the diviner to receive their blessings.

If at this point the odu still will not close, the diviner may continue his assessment with the eboses of the particular composite odu open on the mat.

## Closing the Reading: Further Eboses of the Parent Odu, Eji Ogbe

Having exhausted the options of larishe and ebó in the composite odu, the italero must turn to the parent odu to find a method of closure. This sign, Eji Ogbe, contains within itself many offerings and rituals to placate both the letter and the orishas speaking in it. The eboses for this pattern follow.

- If Eji Ogbe will not give closure, the diviner must prescribe a series of four spiritual baths that should be done on four consecutive Thursday evenings. The bath must contain water (from a natural source, such as rain, river, sea, holy lake, or brook), milk (goat's milk if a serious osogbo has opened), efun, cocoa butter, prodigiosa leaves, coconut milk, white flowers, and grated coconut. If the osogbo of this letter is ano or ikú, the water should be left out and Obatalá's omiero used instead. At night before retiring, the client should stand in a tub of warm water, pouring the bath over himself from the shoulders down. He should then soak in the waters for as long as possible. After taking a quick shower to remove the sticky residue, he should dry off with white towels and dress in white clothing. The morning after this bath, he should rub cocoa butter and efun into the soles of his feet and the palms of his hands. When opening the front door for the first time that day, he must blow cascarilla off his hands and into the street, saying, "Maferefún Obatalá!" This will clear all obstacles from his path.
- When it will not close, this sign also marks that the client should bring a bolt of white cloth to the diviner's Obatalá as ebó. We know Obatalá as the "king of the white cloth," for it is from this color that he weaves both the world and the destiny of all things within it. The client should present to Obatalá the white cloth, along with with a white plate, two coconuts (which may be painted white with efun), two candles, and a derecho. After the presentation of ebó, the client should have a rogación at Obatalá's feet; if the osogbo is severe, the diviner might wish to wash the client first in omiero to cleanse him of all dangerous energies. For eight days after this ebó is done, the client should dress totally in white. If the letter will not close off these eboses, the diviner should determine if Obatalá requires any further ebó, asking, "Ebó elese

Obatalá?" If the answer is yes, he uses the diloggún to mark what the orisha needs. Keep in mind that when making ebó to Obatalá, the number eight should mark all offerings.

- If a rogación is marked in this sign, yet the letter will not close, Eji Ogbe may be trying to mark a sacrifice to the orí. The diviner should check this by asking, "Eborí?" If the answer is yes, the client needs to have two white pigeons or doves fed to his head during the rogación.
- Olokun speaks strongly in this sign; the client could have issues pending with her. First, the diviner should ask, "Ebó elese Olokun?" If the answer is yes, he should use the diloggún to mark a specific ebó to her. Her reception could also be necessary; to determine if this is the case, the diviner should ask, "Koshé Olokun?"
- Note that if this sign comes for the head of a iyawó during itá, he will need to put eight red parrot feathers in a silver crown and offer it to Obatalá. If the odu opens in iré, the client must wear a red parrot feather to all orisha rituals, returning it to Obatalá upon returning home. A serious osogbo marks that the client needs to wear a red parrot feather on his head always. Note that since the ebó of the crown marks the head sign of itá, the client should allow only close friends and family members to salute this orisha. Even then, he must not allow them to see the crown. It gives others who know odu too much information about the client's relationship with the orisha to whom he was made. The ebó of the red parrot feather, on the other hand, can come from any reading at any time and may be worn openly among other priests or priestesses without enabling them to guess the head sign of this initiate.
- If the oracle continues to refuse to close, it can mark issues with any number of orishas, for any orisha can speak in Eji Ogbe. At this point the inexperienced diviner must call/consult with his elders on the reading being given. If the diviner is secure in his skills, he may ask the following questions, or any questions that his own aché dictates for the omo odu that has opened: "Ebó elese [orisha's name]?"; "Eleke de [orisha's name]?"; and "Koshé [orisha's name]?" The marking of ebó for any orisha in a composite odu adds to the initial implications of the letter. If an orisha claims ebó, the diviner must explain the orisha's attributes to the client, and using his aché and knowledge of odu and ocha, the diviner should then explain why this orisha is standing up for the client and the benefits to be gained by honoring the spirit with ebó.
- If the letter still will not close, its implications become more serious. First, the orisha that guards the client's head could be standing up for ebó. If this spirit is not known, the reading must mark the head before it can be ended. The diviner, having determined this information, should then ask, "Ebó elese [guardian orisha]?" If the answer is yes, the diviner should use the diloggún to mark the ebó, which should be done as soon as possible to placate both orí and orisha. If no ebó can be marked, then the diviner should ask, "Koshé [guardian orisha]?" If the answer to this is yes, the client needs santo lavado, or "the washing of the saint." He must receive both the guardian orisha and Obatalá; the guardian orisha wants to be in the client's home/heart immediately, and if Obatalá is not the parent, he must be received to keep the client from being overwhelmed by the spirit.*

Further refusal on the part of the oracle for closure could be pointing the diviner to the eboses of the omo odu as a parent odu. For example, if Ogbe Okana will not close at this point, the diviner may need to explore the prohibitions and eboses listed under the parent odu Okana to find closure for the letter. And even if the diviner is experienced with the diloggún, at this point he should consult an elder.

*When santo lavado is given, the guardian orisha is given *to* the head but not *into* the head. This is a mystery that can be done only when ocha is made. The spirit, however, will want to be inside the client's head, and unless Obatalá, who is the owner of all heads, is also given and first put to the head, the guardian orisha's desire will cause problems for the client. At the very least, the guardian orisha's desire to make ocha will be overwhelming. At its most dangerous level, the guardian orisha can cause overwhelming mental disturbances. Obatalá will ensure that only iré, and not osogbo, comes from the reception of the parent.

# TEN

# THE FAMILY OF OSÁ

## The Proverbs of Osá

- You have left behind many things; do not recover them.
- That which has been left behind should be left behind.
- Your friend is great; the evil that he brings will be great as well.
- You have many friends, yet none is true.
- Your best friend is your worst enemy.
- Change is coming.
- Falsehood, revolution, torments, and treason are coming.
- You have no friends.
- If the friend is great, the traitor shall be great as well.
- You can be your own worst enemy.

## The Orishas Who Speak in Osá

| | |
|---|---|
| Oyá | Oké |
| Ayao | Yewá |
| Aganyú | Babaluaiye |
| Obatalá | Oduduwa |
| Elegguá | Olokun |
| egun | |

## The Message of Osá

Opening with nine mouths on the mat, the diloggún sits before the italero in an explosive yet mysterious pattern. Osá is open. This odu represents the destructive side of nature, the forces that cause one quality to mutate into its opposite. Floods, hurricanes, tornadoes, typhoons, earthquakes, volcanic eruptions, and forest fires all derive their destructiveness from this sign. While its aggressive nature may seem frightening, in truth it is only a part of the renewal of Olódumare's designs. Our world is neither stable nor stagnant; everything moves in a continual cycle of change, destruction, and creation to revive and revitalize the earth. To grow, there must be decay; this feeds new growth. Birth guarantees death. Osá ensures that this cycle moves continually but randomly. To understand this sign's power, meditate on its symbols: the wind, the market, the cemetery gates, and the moment between life and death. Each of these shows an eternal yet ephemeral transition, something predictable in occurrence but not in time. Osá warns us that all things will change, and there is nothing we can do to avoid it.

Born of Odí, seven mouths, Osá is linked with the energy of its parent; so similar are their symbols that in nature their actions are all but inseparable. In chapter 8 I wrote of Osá's parent, "[Odí] alludes to nature . . . yet like nature, Odí has two sides: the creative and the destructive." Osá inherited this duality from her mother, and she relies on it in her work. Yet the function of duality changes in its endowment from mother to daughter. Metaphorically, nine mouths alludes to the two sides of one coin, opposite extremes similar to that embodied by seven mouths. Within Osá, each half is a separate entity, yet each is but half of an essential whole. Life and death, dark and light, male and female—they are found in Osá as well as Odí. While the symbolism is similar, each sign manipulates these symbols differently. By working with raw materials, Odí uses her opposing forces to create something new and then sets a seal to hold it firm. By destroying the seals created in Odí, Osá destroys the mother-sign's spawn, turning them back into raw material with the potential to become anything. Odí can show both extremes at once, while Osá can show only one, holding the other within as an unrealized potential. Acting alone, one letter would unravel the earth's balance. Acting in concordance, both nurture nature.

It is important to acknowledge here that many novice diviners and inexperienced priests feel that the energies of these two signs are in opposition, just as they say that a "war" exists between the two owners of these signs, Yemayá and Oyá. Neither could be farther from the truth.* In my first book, I wrote of Osá, "This letter is similar to the metaphor of yin and yang . . . light balanced by darkness, yet each carrying the seed of the other."† While this metaphor borrowed from Chinese philosophy does illustrate Osá's internal mechanics, it also illustrates the relationship between seven and nine mouths. Odí carries the seed of Osá within; Osá carries the seed of Odí within. Between the two there is balance, and each essential is to the other. Their relationship seems like a war only when one watches the energy in separation of the bigger picture; when one steps back and watches the cycle occur, one sees only the process of creation. Like Odí and Osá, the orishas Yemayá and Oyá are two halves of a whole process. The energy flowing between them may seem destructive, but in truth both are working together for the benefit of the world.

To honor the vastness and royalty of this sign, the diviner suspends the reading before drawing a composite odu. This pattern enfolds all present, its currents emanating blindly from the mat. Immediately upon casting this sign as a parent odu, the italero honors it by whipping his head from side to side. All familiar with the odu follow suit in this gesture. Once done, the italero prays to placate the letter:

*Osá niko, Osá wo iworiwo awo.*
*Aforiku owo loso.*
*Osá, Osá wo iwori awo.*
*Aforiku Osá wo abati oleya.*
*Aloban un mu.*

The priests and priestesses present in the room bow their heads in silence during this prayer. No one speaks or whispers while the italero intones the chant. Once he is finished, to honor both the odu and the orisha owning it, many will mutter, "Maferefún Osá! Maferefún Oyá!" Those who truly know nine mouths will continue their adoration with "Maferefún Yemayá!" Not only does Yemayá speak here, but also she received her crown through this family of signs. Both Osá and Yemayá are integral to this sign's aché.

When Osá opens on the mat, it stimulates the air currents both within and without the diviner's home. Those most susceptible to this letter, and especially the client, will have trouble focusing. Throughout this reading the diviner will have to redirect everyone's attention to the task at hand: the ritual of divination. To soothe the atmosphere in his house, the diviner directs someone to open all windows and doors, allowing Osá to disperse into the world. The earth is vast, more than capable of handling the energies evoked by the dilogggún. From time to time during the reading, all should pause to gaze outside, reflecting on the sky. Osá brings a variety of atmospheric disturbances; light breezes, strong winds, tornadoes, and angry storms of unexplained energy are all possible. The closer the composite comes to Osá Meji (9-9), the more pronounced these atmospheric disturbances

*For more information on how this religious misconception arose, see the description of the composite odu Ogbe Osá (beginning on page 378). Knowledge of the patakís told there is essential to understanding how the erroneous belief in a war between Yemayá and Oyá arose; it is also essential to understanding the true reason why priests of one orisha cannot initiate children of the other.

†Óchani Lele, *The Secrets of Afro-Cuban Divination: How to Cast the Diloggún, the Oracle of the Orishas* (Rochester, Vt.: Destiny Books, 2000), 233.

become. Note that once a session of Osá closes, the diviner will find himself exhausted; the varying currents of this Odu will drain his strength while he divines. He will need a brief rest or nap after closing the letter. If the sign brings overwhelming lethargy or exhaustion, he should consult Elegguá's diloggún after a brief rest, marking eboses to cleanse Osá from his head.

Through this letter many orishas might choose to speak. The spirit whose diloggún is being consulted has the first option, and adherence to his advice is essential to the client's evolution. Oyá is the next to stand up in Osá. This is her kingdom, her home; she reigns supreme here and has the aché to resolve most of this person's problems. Her issues with the client are heavily dependent on the composite cast. Yemayá speaks next. She is comfortable in Osá's conflicting currents; often, what Oyá cannot solve, she can. If the client is a child of Oyá or of Yemayá, Osá says that the other is his crutch in life. Ogún is fierce here; he comes not to chastise but to defend, and before any composite in this family closes he might demand placation with one or more eboses. Aganyú is present as an explosive force bringing destruction to the client's life; however, anything he destroys leaves more room for growth. Obatalá is present in every odu, and when no other orisha will forgive the client in nine mouths, the client must turn to him for a blessing. Finally, Elegguá, egun, Oké, Yewá, Babaluaiye, Oduduwa, and Olokun also influence this family of odu. Their issues are heavily dependent on the composite opened.

Before beginning a specific investigation of Osá in either iré or osogbo, once he has completed the initial manipulations of the diloggún the diviner sets all this aside momentarily. In any composite odu of Osá, one must keep in mind the simile of a coin: It has two sides, two faces, either of which is displayed at random. So it is with this client. No matter how nine mouths presents itself, in either iré or osogbo, each quality carries a seed of the other. If the client is blessed by ocha, he still has the potential for utter ruin; if he ignores the advice, taboos, and eboses of this letter, he will nurture and grow his own osogbo regardless of what the spirits want for him. Likewise, even if the orishas mark the client with misfortune, a seed of blessing comes with it. In this case, the diviner must tell the client that to sprout that seed, he must nurture not only himself but also the orishas. If he follows taboo, makes ebó, and listens to all the diviner says, in time the client will achieve all his hopes and dreams. It will not be easy; hard labor will be his lot in life. Most things worth having, however, are worthy of the effort to obtain them.

With that in mind, the easiest way to begin a study of nine mouths is with it in iré. If the odu is marked as coming in iré, the diviner's next step is to mark the origin of this iré, which will help the client focus on his source of spiritual strength. While all sources of iré have their own aché, in Osá some are more favored. The following origins are especially propitious for the client who opens in this odu: iré arikú (blessings of health, vitality, and immortality); iré otonowá (blessings from heaven); iré elese egun (blessings from one's ancestors); iré elese ará onú (blessings from the spirits of heaven); iré ayé (blessings through an increase of fortune); iré aláfia (blessings of peace); iré elese ocha (blessings from the orishas); and iré ashegunota (blessings from the orisha's otanes).*

Because nine mouths refers to the market, the cemetery gates, the wind, and the moment between life and death, any iré coming from the dead, ancestors, increase of fortune, or peace (often amid chaos) brings special blessings. Nine mouths brings change, but the odu itself promises that the changes will be for the better; nothing in this world or the next can keep the client from achieving his destiny. Iré elese ocha and iré ashegunota, the final two iré that can be marked in this list of propitious signs, are the strongest; they are also the most difficult for

*Unless the client is an initiate or an aborisha who has been involved in this religion for quite some time, the diviner should not consider this option when divining with the diloggún. While iré ashegunota can bring vast blessings, it creates too many issues for an aleyo who is new to the religion or a casual client who does not wish to go deeply into our mysteries. Remember: An aleyo is a client with nothing of ocha. Often, an aleyo will not have the loyalty, love, or respect for this religion that an aborisha or initiate would have; to put such sacred objects into the hands of such a person can bring more harm than good.

the diviner to explore. In both cases, the diviner must determine which orisha offers the blessing. First, he must consider the client's status in the religion: aleyo, aborisha, or initiate.

- For an aleyo, the following orishas can stand up for iré elese ocha: Oyá, Obatalá, Yemayá, Ogún, and Elegguá. It is not wise to ask iré ashegunota for an aleyo.
- For an aborisha, the following spirits can stand up for iré elese ocha: Oyá, Yemayá, Ogún, Obatalá, Elegguá, Babaluaiye, and Olokun. If iré ashegunota has been marked, the aborisha might receive his blessing from one of the following: Elegguá, Ogún, Babaluaiye, or Olokun.
- An initiate opening with either iré elese ocha or iré ashegunota might receive blessings from Oyá, Yemayá, Ogún, Aganyú, Obatalá, Elegguá, Oke, Yewá, Babaluaiye, Olokun, Ayao, or Oge.

The orisha offering the blessing, as well as the client's status in the religion, will determine the exact offering. (See "Marking Ebó in Osá: Initial Considerations" on page 402 for more details.)

In spite of all these possibilities, keep in mind that of all the orishas who speak in Osá, the one who brings the greatest blessings is Oyá. This odu is her kingdom. She alone can travel and influence all the realms referenced here: the cemetery gates, the marketplace, the wind, and the moment between life and death. She is queen of all these. Because Osá always mark issues with this orisha, even if she does not stand up individually, the diviner would be wise to pause during this reading to ask his client if he has any issues with her or if he has made any promises to her that he has not kept. Now is the time to placate her and make sure there is no debt between them. If the client does not owe or cannot remember owing a debt to Oyá, the diviner will need to consider, carefully, what ebó or eboses this person should give to lock in her goodwill and blessings.

If Oyá does stand up and the client is an aleyo or an aborisha, the diviner must tell him that Oyá demands he be crowned soon, especially if the composite Osá Meji opens on the mat. The diviner should drape the mazo of Oyá (or of the client's guardian orisha, if known) over the client's shoulders and directs him to salute both the orisha and his godparents. His lack of a crown is the true cause of all his troubles. Oyá herself will help him remedy this.

Throughout nine mouths, egun are referenced; while they might not speak openly, the client's ancestors (of ocha and of blood) whisper quietly. The diviner should tell the client that there are times he can feel the dead close to him. During the day, the client shivers as if chilled and feels a light, gentle stroking along his spine. He thinks he is cold or that a slight chilly breeze or draft has found its way down his shirt. He shakes off this feeling. When this happens, however, he is not cold or feeling a breeze; the dead are calling hiim to attention. He must be aware of his surroundings. Danger, despair, or evil could be waiting for him, or an unforeseen opportunity could be coming his way. The diviner should tell the client to pay attention when the hairs on the back of his neck stand up; this is a sign of Eshu ni pacuó, the Eshu that forms the link between the orí and the body, the path of Elegguá that lives in the client and tells him when the dead are near. It is a warning, for good or bad, and must not be ignored. At night, sometimes this person awakes from his sleep, a dream fragment just eluding his consciousness. He must lie still and try to remember. Something in that dream is a message from egun. He will hear whispers; he will see shadows. These mark the presence of the dead, and they are warnings; the client's egun are trying to get his attention in order to alert him to something unusual.

Nine mouths also flags difficulties within relationships; the closer the client is to any one person, the more strained that friendship becomes. It is as if the energy of Osá tests each bond, straining it to the point of breaking; those who falter are not worth keeping, while those who work hard to stay together in spite of Osá's meddling are meant for each other. Marriages and sexual relationships are the hardest hit with this sign's power.

No matter its orientation, when Osá comes the diviner knows this: Treason, betrayal, and false friends permeate the client's life. No one other than himself has his best interests in mind, and even his greatest friend could hurt him by talking too much. Surrounding this person are many miserable people. Their own relationships do not work well, and their judgment is tainted by their own horrible experiences. They are not happy, and they feel no one else should be happy around them. They like to spread their misery by breaking up their friends' relationships. They do not work openly; they are subversive, preferring to spread doubt and deceit behind one's back. They delight in separation and divorce. Ironically, when spouses and lovers scorn their friends, they are among the first at the scene to offer comfort. The client must beware of these friends, for they are dangerous. The diviner can be assured that the client is already aware of these things; he is just afraid to acknowledge them. Most of his friends are not loyal, and he knows this as well. Even his spouse might stray. In this case, the client must not be like his lover, no matter how great the temptation. Osá forbids adultery, adulterous designs, and even the casting of the eyes toward another. As long as one spouse remains faithful, there is hope that a marriage can be saved with ebó and perseverance. Once the relationship is secure again, the one who remained faithful will hold all the power. Some things are worth the fight; the client must fight honorably and remain ethical.

No matter the client's sex or sexual orientation, this person for whom Osá has fallen would be happier and more prosperous living alone than with a lover. This sign dictates that all aspects of a one's life should be given the counsel of the orishas, so if the client decides to take a lover, he should consult the diloggún first to divine the parameters of the relationship. If this client is currently single, the italero must deliver this warning: Do not insist on taking a lover too quickly. The guardian orisha will bring one in time, and the one the client hopes for will come when the orishas are ready to provide. The client must not force a new relationship to progress with either wiles or witchcraft. Without the orishas' approval, this could bring death to the desired lover. Some things are just not meant to be. If this reading is an itá for a child of Oyá, the taboos about marriages and relationships may be even stronger: Oyá says her children are best unmarried, and although she allows them to take lovers, often they wind up widows of divorcées. If her children marry without her consent, she will destroy or drive away their spouses.

Although relationships between men and women figure prominently in this sign, family issues are addressed here as well. At best, the social structure of the client's family is tangled and stressed; at worst, it is worn and falling apart. Osá speaks of children who are related but have different biological mothers and fathers. These children may have come to the family from previous marriages, lovers, or even extramarital affairs. Not all may know each other or even be known, but one day these stray branches of the family tree will come together. The parents of one child must respect and love both half siblings and step-siblings of their own children and spouses; to withdraw their love would anger the orishas. The client is also warned to give both honor and respect to his own brothers and sisters, half siblings, stepchildren, and relatives by ocha. The client's own guardian orisha will punish falsehood. Although friends will not remain loyal under the influence of this odu, family will always offer love no matter what. Even if there are strong arguments in the family unit now, the client must not separate from his blood. He must learn to stick with them through the good and the bad.

In the religion, Osá directs the client to become more involved with both his spiritual family and the orishas; in this way the inherent osogbos of the letter may be overcome in full and turned to iré. The aborisha who opens in nine mouths is searching for a religious home. So long and so far has he traveled in search of this religion that he will stay with the first priest or priestess who offers him any type of attention or concern. However, he must remember that false faces and friends abound in this sign. The diviner should advise the client to settle into a house of ocha with a godparent whom he can trust, love, and honor. Once the aborisha settles with a godparent, he must have a bajado soon if he has not already had one. Note that the odu marking his orí will define the parameters of the godchild/godparent relationship. The settling into an ilé and the reception of his orishas will give the client more than his physical family to fall back on. He will now have a sound spiritual family to help him go through his trials and introduce him to his spiritual family in the world of the orishas. If the client already keeps his religious responsibilities, the diviner should direct him to pay more attention and respect to his godparent. He offers love in exchange for respect. Someone else in this person's family will soon come to the orishas, and the godparent of this client should be his as well. This dual connection will help strengthen family ties. The italero should warn the one who sits at the mat, however, that his relative would probably make ocha before he does. He must harbor no jealousy; rejoice! This will make his own path easier.

An initiate who opens under the guidance of Osá is wandering; if he has not left his godparent, he will. The ephemeral nature of Osá shows that he has learned all he can learn, and he has received all that he can receive, from his godparent. While in an ideal world both godchild and godparent would continue to grow and nurture each other, this sign, especially if it opens with any osogbo, shows that the godparent is not concerned with his protégé's growth, and the godchild does not have true love in his heart for the godparent. A great spiritual chasm has opened between the two, and at this time it is irreparable. If the client cannot be with his godfather, the diviner should advise him to work with his yubonna for a time, and if this is not possible, he should seek out the guidance of his oriaté. If none of these three is accessible to him, the client must not settle into another house of ocha too quickly. The diviner should advise him to look up those who were present at his ocha and at his itá of ocha. He must circulate and work with other initiates of other houses; he will learn by working. In time, another will come offering guidance. When he finds this person, he must plan to receive the knife as soon as possible. Not only will this enforce the separation from his original godparent, but also it will put him under the protection of his new godparent's orishas. Realize that once the knife is received, the client will have nowhere else to go; if this relationship does not work out, he will be alone, without spiritual guidance.

When any composite of Osá brings osogbo, the diviner has many issues to explore with the client. The proverbs sum up most of these, making it clear what the client is or is not to do. This person dwells on the past; he longs for lost things. Family, places, possessions, lovers—he thinks about all these from time to time. Often, Osá refers to mothers who have put up their own children for adoption, and it speaks of the adoptive child's longing for his own blood. People who bring Osá in osogbo have lost much, but through their losses, they have grown. Unsuitable lovers and broken marriages could be in this person's past; he himself could have been unwanted, unloved, or abused as a child. A vast gulf separates him from the things he has lost, and while his life has given him much to fill the longing in his heart, he sees that chasm as a curse and not a blessing. If the client has these issues, the diviner must tell him, "You have left behind many things; do not recover them." These things were left behind for a reason. The diviner must emphasize, "That which is left behind should be left behind." If the client does otherwise, he will suffer.

Osogbo indicates that change is coming for this client; every day, new traumas, trials, and tribulations will befall him, and his reactions to these will determine what his life becomes. Yet the changes themselves are unpredictable. It is as if destiny flips that coin which is Osá, and even the world's foremost psychic cannot foretell each cast. The greater the osogbo, the greater the changes. The diviner should tell the client, "Falsehood, revolution, torments, and treasons are coming." The degree to which these come, however, depends on the client's actions. He must heed the advice of this odu. He must follow the sign's prohibitions strictly, for they will help him avoid danger. Finally, he must make ebó; only by placating the orishas will he have their protection. Unfortunately, Osá tells us that the client can be his own worst enemy. He will undermine himself, not believing all the diviner has said until his life begins to crumble.

An osogbo in Osá can also mark tragedy in this client's life. Someone could die in his home; he must not let sick or injured guests visit for extended periods, and he must be careful of children and the elderly when they visit. Electricity and heat can be a hazard in this sign as well, so the client must thoroughly assess all appliances in his home. He should keep nothing plugged in unless it is being used, and he must extinguish all sources of flame when leaving the home. Robbery, theft, slander, and random violence both within and outside of the home are possible, so the client must take extra steps to ensure personal safety. He should lock doors and windows, travel only in large groups, and avoid excursions after dark. If the client must travel alone at strange hours of the night, he should make sure that others know his itinerary and anticipated hour of return. If the osogbo is severe, the diviner should tell his client this: Life is sometimes hard, yet it is not worth destroying oneself. The diviner should suggest some form of professional counseling, because this person might take his own life.

An osogbo of ano demands special consideration by the italero. Ano in Osá speaks of death and disease that rises from the earth. The client should not eat grains, roots, or vegetables that grow touching the ground (such as celery, lettuce, and cabbage). They will provide a channel for sickness to enter the body. Osá speaks of the air that we breathe and the lungs with which we breathe. From this moment on, the client cannot smoke any type of tobacco product. To do so would be to offend Oyá, who owns his lungs. Both the flu and the common cold could prove fatal to one who has opened in an osogbo of ano; at the first sign of respiratory distress, this person should see a physician immediately. He must not take home remedies. Both food and drink should be fresh and properly stored; consuming spoiled goods will bring death. The client must avoid stress and excitement at all costs, because they hurt the heart and brain. The diviner must caution him against becoming angry, for this will make his blood hot and it will rush to the head, causing a stroke, even if the client is a young person.

Any composite of Osá that opens in ikú is to be feared, and ebó must be made quickly. The italero should consider carefully the origin of ikú. The client will have to make ebó and modify his behavior drastically to avoid the disasters inherent in this sign if ikú comes from one of the following origins: otonowá (heaven), eledá (his head), egun (ancestral spirits), ará onú (spirits of heaven), ocha (orisha), or lowo (his own hands). Orientations of lowó arayé (arguments and gossip), tiya-tiya (stubbornness), and elenú (tongue) will demand behavior modification on the client's part; ebó will not help. The remaining origins for ikú show that the client has either angered those close to him or is associating with undesirables. Those orientations require that the client remove himself from his present environment to avoid the osogbo of ikú.

While giving this reading, regardless of the odu's orientation the italero should keep in mind the following points. Odu will often refer to many of these issues in the client's life.

- Osá falls often for those who are involved in metaphysical and spiritual pursuits; however, those in these systems of magic often use their studies for cursing and not healing. If this client wants evolution in his life, he must use his spiritual studies to benefit himself and others. The cursing must stop.
- The client finds himself filled with brilliant ideas, yet he quickly forgets these and does not act on them. He should write down random thoughts as they come, judging later if they are worth the effort to attain.
- A malicious entity may be following this person; the client will hear his name called out frequently, especially at night. Unless the one calling for the client is in full view (and is known), he must not answer. It could be Death (Ikú) calling for him.
- The client will have many opportunities for reunions with family, friends, and coworkers. He must not go to these; there will be danger. Nor should he spend time at parties. Now is a time to be alone.
- Many opportunities will come for the client to reclaim things that he has lost. These may involve property, jobs, and people. He must turn down these opportunities. These things were lost for a reason.
- If someone close to the client is offering home remedies, medicines, or homemade foods, the client should not accept them. They are laced with bad intentions.

- If the opportunity comes to purchase property, the client should take advantage of it.
- Under the influence of Osá, it is possible that a poor man can become rich. A rich man, however, will lose his fortune.
- Unless ebó is made, a relative of the client could die before a year has passed.
- The client will soon plan to go on a trip, yet this trip will not be taken.
- Osá speaks of the dead and danger from the dead. Do not go to places where death or the dead are known to frequent. Darkness hides many things; never walk alone in the dark. Keep a night-light lit in the house.
- Do not help anyone lift anything from the floor: That person will rise while one will fall.
- Do not accept gifts from strangers.

## The Prohibitions of Osá

If a reading opens in iré, this list of prohibitions becomes a guideline for the client's conduct. If the reading opens in osogbo, these prohibitions become mandatory, and he should not break them. The diviner will determine the duration for which the client must abide by these prohitibions. (See chapter 1 for a more detailed breakdown of the prescription of prohibitions.)

- All forms of fish and seafood, including freshwater fish, are taboo. Do not eat in a restaurant that serves any type of seafood, for contaminants can be spread among dishes.
- The consumption of rooster, ram, and pigeon is forbidden.
- Be careful when eating in another person's home. Food could be spoiled or improperly prepared.
- Do not drink alcohol.
- Dress conservatively. Avoid gaudy or bright colors, checks, and plaids.
- Avoid falsehood to one's relatives.
- Do not argue; anger could cause blood to rush to the brain, bringing stroke or hemorrhage. Be calm under pressure, and never speak harsh words.
- Never sweep one's house with an old broom. Instead, every month buy a new one. Never take a broom from an old home into a new one.
- Osá can point toward travel, although the trip one most desires might not be taken. If extended journeys are begun while under the influence of this sign, consult with the orishas and make ebó before going.

## Marking Ebó in Osá: Initial Considerations

No matter its orientation, when Osá comes the diviner knows this: Treason, betrayal, and false friends permeate the client's life. No one other than himself has his best interests in mind, and even his greatest friend could hurt him by talking too much. Yet for all who come in this sign, Osá offers three powerful eboses, three spiritual prescriptions that the diviner can make to protect this person. First, the orisha whose diloggún is being consulted demands a mask for him- or herself. The client should dress the mask in the spirit's favorite colors and wash it with omiero before presenting it. With this ebó, the client's true intentions are hidden from the world. Second, the client should give to Elegguá a wooden, two-faced doll. With this offering, the client's Elegguá is empowered to watch both in front of and in back of the client for danger. Finally, the client should purchase a special pendant: a small, silver set of theatrical masks. The client washes it in Oyá's omiero and wears it on a silver chain around his neck continually. The diviner must tell him never to take it off. With this, the client can hide his true feelings from others, appearing happy or sad as his wishes and not as his emotions dictate; they will keep his true intentions secret and unknown.

Osá also demands that client work with his egun. Before ending this session, the diviner must instruct the client on how to set up and work a bóveda. If he has already has a bóveda, it must be strengthened. If the client has used seven glasses on his altar, he must now fortify it with two more glasses for a total of nine. For nine days, he must perfume each chalice with a separate perfume and put in it a flower (of a different color for each chalice). While many burn white candles to the dead, during these nine days the client should keep a nine-colored seven-day candle burning in honor of Oyá and egun. If the client does not have an opá ikú, he must receive one; if he has one, it must be reinforced with nine ribbons of different colors and nine small bells, and it must be fed a rooster. On the bóveda itself, the client should place photographs of his ancestors, making sure that no one living, other than himself, appears in them. Every day during this nine-day period, the client must pray in either Lucumí or his native tongue, asking Olódumare to bring light, peace, and refreshment to his spiritual court. While praying, he must call each spirit by name, tapping the opá ikú as he calls them. The final ebó to be done for egun when Osá comes is this: The client must begin a collection of masks, hanging a total of nine on the wall over his bóveda. With these, not only will his egun hide his true face from the world so that enemies cannot harm him, but also they will rip the smiling masks worn by his enemies. In time, the client will overcome all.

For bringing rapid, unexpected changes to one's life, no odu moves more swiftly than Osá. Even in iré, when Osá pushes one toward evolution, the speed at which its energies travel can overwhelm one unprepared for its actions. This letter can bring heat to the client's orí; overwhelmed by the vast spiritual chasm spinning around him, the client can lose his focus. Even if no ebó is marked by nine mouths, the diviner should prescribe a rogación. It will soothe and strengthen a head engulfed by chaos. To whom this rogación is done, however, depends on the client's initiatory status. An aleyo should have the rogación before Obatalá. All heads are his, although not all heads are meant for his priesthood. Obatalá will give calmness and clarity while the elements of the rogación will strengthen the client's orí. An aborisha whose guardian orisha is unknown should have the rogación before his godparent's guardian orisha. From this spirit his soul is nourished, and from this spirit will he evolve. As ebó, this client must have a bajado soon. Knowing to whom one's head belongs will bring stability. An aborisha whose guardian orisha is known should have the rogación before that spirit. It is leading him toward ocha, and the rogación will strengthen the bond between both mortal and immortal. Evolution will come more easily. Finally, an initiate should have the rogación before his godparent's crown, for from that sopera was his spiritual head born, and it is to that sopera that the client must turn to find stability. The orisha before whom the rogación is given will mark the appropriate method of disposal for the rogación.*

For a rogación to be accepted in Osá, it must incorporate nine separate elements. Having fewer elements than this will not give the client's orí the strength it needs to persevere. The diviner should use the following: grated coconut, cocoa butter, cascarilla, white flowers, and five grated fruits. The fruits must be those favored by the orisha before whom the rogación will be given. The priest giving the rogación adds his aché to it by chewing the coconut, cocoa butter, and fruits before they are put on the client.

When a composite odu of Osá opens in the propitious iré of iré elese ocha or iré ashegunota, the diviner must determine which orisha offers the blessing. Having made this determination, the diviner prescribes ebó to that spirit. For an aleyo, a simple adimú is all odu requires. If the iré is not firm, or if the odu will not close, a rogación before that orisha's shrine plus the investment of his or her eleke might lock in the blessing for the aleyo. For an aborisha, the considerations for ebó might go beyond a simple adimú. If either Elegguá or Ogún offers the blessing of iré elese ocha, the reception of the warriors is necessary to lock it in. If either Babaluaiye or Olokun offers the blessing of iré elese ocha, that orisha demands reception. Iré ashegunota for an aborisha always marks the reception of an orisha; if this orisha is not one of the

*In Osá, the diviner should try to mark the disposal of the rogación in a place representative of Osá's energy, such as a cemetery, flea market, outdoor fruit stand, mall, carnival, or a place of commerce or quick change. For orí, the diviner should try to mark the disposal of eborí in a place representative of the client's guardian orisha, such as the woods for Obatalá, the river for Oshún, or the sea for Yemayá. Places that tend to absorb negativity—hospitals, nursing homes, police stations, trash receptacles—are also beneficial for the disposal of eborí.

warriors, Babaluaiye, or Olokun, this person is marked to make ocha. It must be done soon.

The implications of iré elese ocha and iré ashegunota for an initiate might prove more complicated. Blessings from Ogún could demand the washing of his diloggún; if this iré is offered through the composite Osá Ogundá (9-3), the odu demands pinaldo. An iré brought to an initiate by Aganyú, Yewá, Babaluaiye, Olokun, Ayao, or Oge will demand that orisha's reception. Note that in some composites other orishas, beyond those who speak in the parent odu, will speak. If an omo odu comes with spirits not mentioned here, the diviner should consider their reception for the initiate as well.

The final consideration for ebó in Osá is this: In all composites, Oyá rules supreme. Osá is her true home, and rarely will it close unless at least some small token adimú is marked to her. The most common sacrifices to Oyá in Osá are given below.

### The Traditional Eboses of Osá

When marking ebó for this odu, the italero should keep in mind that certain substances are traditionally used as ebó. When marking any type of eyebale in Osá, the diviner should try to select from the following: two hens, two pigeons, and one rooster. If an adimú-type offering is required, he should try to select from the following: a small machete, nine honey cakes, two stones from the client's property, nine red parrot feathers, nine coconuts, and nine candles of different colors.

## Adimú

### *Aguidí*

When propitiating Oyá with adimú, the dish known as aguidí is a favorite. To prepare this, the client must bring the following ingredients to the diviner's or godparent's home: 2 pounds of yellow cornmeal, water, 3 tablespoons of vinegar, a sour orange, 1 cup of milk, 1½ cups of brown sugar, 2 cups of raisins, 1 tablespoon of vanilla extract, one cinnamon stick, and one lemon.

Mix the cornmeal with 3 cups of water, the vinegar, and the juice of the sour orange. For two days, allow this mixture to soak uncovered; it must ferment. At the end of the second day, drain off the liquid and add 3 cups of fresh water. Cook over low heat, stirring frequently, until all the water evaporates. Add the milk, brown sugar, raisins, vanilla extract, cinnamon stick, and juice of one lemon. Continue to stir while cooking over low heat. When all the liquid is consumed, cool the aguidí and form into nine balls of equal size. Serve these to Oyá on a multicolored platter; they should remain with her for nine days. If the client is praying for sweetness to return to his life, he can drizzle honey lightly over these balls while praying to Oyá.

To discard this ebó, the client uses the oracle obí to ask the orisha where she wants it taken.

### *Olelé*

This is another of Oyá's favored foods. The client must provide the following ingredients: 1 pound of black-eyed peas, two eggs, a pinch of saffron, a medium-sized onion, one red bell pepper, six cloves of garlic, 3 tablespoons of epó, ½ cup of tomato sauce, ¼ teaspoon of black pepper, and a roll of aluminum foil.

Soak the black-eyed peas overnight. The following day, rub them gently between the fingers to remove the shells. Mash the peas into a paste, adding a few drops of water as needed. Once a thick paste is created, add two raw eggs and a pinch of saffron. Mix well, then set aside. Peel and dice the onion, pepper, and garlic. Melt the epó in a saucepan over medium heat, and fry the onion, pepper, and garlic in it until the onion becomes translucent. Immediately add the tomato sauce and black pepper. Cook, stirring continuously, for 3 minutes, or until the tomato sauce becomes a shiny red. Then add the bean mixture and mix well. Remove from the heat.

Cut nine evenly sized squares from the aluminum foil. Divide the peas mixture into nine even portions. Drop each in the center of one square of aluminum foil and wrap tightly like a tamale. Boil these squares in water for 30 minutes. When done, remove the foil-wrapped packages from the water and allow them to cool before opening.

Serve to Oyá on a multicolored platter; they should remain with her for nine days. At the end of this time, the client discards the ebó at the gates of a cemetery.

### *Natilla*

Natilla is a traditional staple for Oyá.* When she demands adimú, many times this simple ebó will sate her. This is an adaptation of the traditional recipe; natilla's preparation can be time-consuming, and this microwave dish is acceptable to Oyá. If the client desires, he may instead prepare instant chocolate pudding for her; it is the same dish, although more convenient. To prepare this recipe, the client brings the following ingredients to the diviner's or godparent's home: 3/4 cup of evaporated milk, 1/4 cup of water, one cinnamon stick, 1 1/2 tablespoons of sugar, a pinch of salt, 1 1/2 tablespoons of cornstarch, one egg yolk, a tin of cocoa, and 1/4 teaspoon of vanilla extract.

To make natilla, mix together the evaporated milk and the water. Stir thoroughly. Divide this mixture into two portions: a 3/4-cup serving and a 1/4-cup serving. Set the 1/2-cup serving to the side. Pour the 3/4-cup serving into a microwave-safe bowl. Mix into this the cinnamon stick, sugar, and salt. Stir well. Microwave this mixture on high for 1 minute and 40 seconds. While those ingredients are cooking in the microwave, add to the 1/4-cup serving of evaporated milk and water the cornstarch and the egg yolk. Stir well, blending all ingredients thoroughly. Pour into the mixture that has just finished warming in the microwave. Stir well. Slowly stir in the cocoa one teaspoon at a time until a dark, rich chocolate color is obtained. Put the bowl back in the microwave, and cook on medium-high for 2 to 3 minutes, or until the mixture becomes thickened. Remove, then stir in the vanilla extract. Pour this into a serving bowl for Oyá; leave it with her overnight. The next day, discard the natilla at the cemetary gates.

*This adimú is also a staple for one's egun.

### *Sofrito Beans*

Prepare a large saucepan of kidney beans following the directions provided on the package. To these add the following ingredients liberally and to taste: cooked cabbage, pork shoulder, smoked pork sausage, bacon, and the Latin seasoning known as sofrito. Let this simmer for a couple of hours so all the flavors come together. Serve this to Oyá in a large serving bowl and leave with her overnight. The following day, take the adimú to either a cemetery or a marketplace.

### *Fried Eggplant*

Eggplant is one of Oyá's favorite staples. For this simple adimú, the client should provide the following ingredients: a large eggplant, almond oil, and toasted corn or brown rice. Slice the eggplant lengthwise into nine even portions. Heat a small quantity of almond oil in a skillet; lightly fry these nine pieces. Once done, the client gives this adimú to Oyá over a bed of either toasted corn or brown rice. Using obí, he should determine how long the orisha wants to keep the ebó, and where to discard it once it is removed.

### *Grilled Onions*

Peel nine dark onions and smear them with both epó and cocoa butter. Roast these on a grill or over an open flame until they are lightly browned. Open the onions and insert some cascarilla and one guinea pepper into each. On a large, terra-cotta dish, arrange a bed of toasted corn, with a liberal sprinkling of smoked fish, smoked jutía, and grated coconut and a light drizzle of both honey and molasses. Put the nine grilled onions on the dish in a circle and serve to Oyá. The ebó remains with her overnight. The following day, take the ebó to a cemetery or marketplace for disposal.

## Cleansings

### *Nine-Eggplant Cleansing*

If the client needs a thorough cleansing to Oyá, this ebó will satisfy both her and the odu, removing osogbo from the client. The client should provide the following items: a large basket, nine multicolored cloths, nine large eggplants, two multicolored candles, and a pañuelo for Oyá. If possible, the client should make the pañuelo with his own hands.

Place the basket before Oyá's shrine. Wrap each eggplant in one of the cloths and place them in the basket. Place one candle on either side of the basket, and lay the pañuelo over this. Leave the ebó to Oyá overnight.

The next evening, the diviner cleanses the client with the pañuelo, rubbing and whipping it over his body to remove negativity. When he is done, he lays the pañuelo over Oyá; it remains with her indefinitely. Next he gives the client's head a rogación with nine ingredients: grated coconut, grated cocoa butter, cascarilla, cotton, nine flower petals of different colors, honey, coconut milk, and two grated fruits. After wrapping the client's head with white cloth, he cleanses him with one of the wrapped eggplants. He should send this eggplant home with the client; the next day, he discards it with the elements of the rogación. For the next eight days, the client dresses in white and returns each evening to the diviner's house so the diviner can cleanse him with an additional eggplant. Using obí, the diviner asks Oyá each time where he is to discard the ebó. After the ninth cleansing, the client fills the basket with fruits and lights the two candles. This adimú remains with Oyá until the candle burns out. Then the client takes the basket of fruits to the gates of a cemetery, along with a derecho of nine cents.

### *Brown Bag Eggplant Cleansing*

A simpler cleansing can be made to Oyá with eggplant if the odu has opened in iré or a gentle osogbo. The client should provide the following: nine small brown paper bags, one eggplant, toasted corn, eighty-one pennies, eighty-one pieces of hard candy, eighty-one guinea peppers, jutía, smoked fish, honey, and nine pieces of cloth in different colors.

Cut the eggplant into nine equal portions. Put one piece of eggplant in each brown bag. Add to each bag a handful of toasted corn, nine pennies, nine pieces of hard candy, nine guinea peppers, a dash of jutía and smoked fish, a drizzle of honey, and one piece of cloth. Seal the bags.

Before Oyá, the client cleanses himself with each bag, rubbing his body thoroughly from head to toe. These bags remain with Oyá overnight. The next morning the client collects the bags, taking one to each of the following places: the gates to a cemetery, the marketplace, an outdoor fruit stand, a church, a river, a lake, the woods, a crossroads, and a railroad track.

## Offerings to Combat Gossip

### *When the Loose Tongue Is Known*

When gossip and loose tongues cause problems for the client and he knows the identity of the people who gossip and speak badly of him, the following ebó to his godparent's Oyá will force those who talk too much to be quiet or make them suffer with their own words. For this ebó, the client must provide the following elements: a dark platter, a cow's tongue, a piece of brown paper, nine guinea peppers, smoked fish, jutía, epó, a sewing needle, and nine threads of different colors.

Before Oyá's shrine, the client puts the beef tongue on the platter. Using a sharp knife, he makes nine slashes across the width of the tongue and a large slash lengthwise down the center of the tongue to open it up. On the brown paper, he writes the names of all his enemies, the people who gossip and speak badly about him. He folds this paper lengthwise and pushes it deep inside the meat. Over the paper, he inserts the nine guinea peppers, smoked fish, jutía, and epó. With needle and thread, he sews both the lengthwise and widthwise cuts, using all nine colors. He places this ebó with Oyá's sopera; it remains with her for nine days. The night of the ninth day, he removes it and takes to the gates of a cemetery, where he leaves it, along with a derecho of nine pennies.

### *When the Loose Tongue Is Not Known*

When Osá marks gossip as the source of the client's osogbo yet the client cannot determine who the loose tongue belongs to, he should make the above ebó of cow's tongue with a few changes. First, Ogún should sit at Oyá's feet while the tongue is being prepared, for the assistance of both orishas is needed. The client puts no names inside the tongue; he leaves the brown paper blank so Oyá and Ogún will seek out those trying to harm the client. He places the prepared tongue on the floor in front of both orishas. The client should now have a rogación sodidé at the feet of these two orishas. The client and the tongue remain at the godparent's house for nine hours. At the end of this time, the godparent cleanses the client with the tongue. The godparent takes him and the tongue to the gates of a cemetery; again, he cleanses his godchild with the tongue. Next, he takes the client to a railroad track. Both wait for a train to pass. As the train passes, the client cleanses himself with the tongue. He leaves the tongue there, along with the elements of the rogación. With the passing of the train, all osogbo is removed from the client; his enemies will fall one by one.

## The First Composite Odu of Osá, Osá Okana (9-1)

### The Proverbs of Osá Okana

- One consumes more with the eyes than with the mouth.
- A fight between man and wife always brings tragedy.
- Envy brings gossip.

### The Message of Osá Okana

When a cast of nine mouths, Osá, is followed by a cast of one mouth, Okana, the odu Osá Okana is open on the mat. This letter is also known as Osá Okanran, Osá Kana, and Osá Kanran. When it falls, the diviner says, "Maferefún Olokun! Maferefún Orisha Oko! Maferefún Shangó! Maferefún Yemayá! Maferefún Obatalá!" Although all signs of Osá are owned by Oyá, in this pattern Olokun and Orisha Oko take prominence. Depending on his initiatory status in this religion, the client has a variety of issues with these two to settle. An aleyo who has not had a bajado is blessed by both orishas; his spiritual tie with them is so strong that they are fighting for his head in ocha. If this reading is a bajado, the italero must ask if Olokun is the guardian orisha first; if Olokun will not claim the client's head, he then asks if Orisha Oko will. Once these two have had their chance to claim the client's orí, the diviner may then question the other orishas who speak in this sign and Osá as parent odu.

An aborisha who opens in Osá Okana is marked to receive Olokun; this must be done immediately. If the client already has Olokun, the diviner must direct him to live by making ebó to him, for he is the client's strength. Finally, the client, whether an initiate or an aborisha, might have to receive Orisha Oko to settle the issues brought by Osá Okana. True, it is rare for an aborisha to receive such a powerful orisha outside of ocha, but the opening of a letter with this strength for the uninitiated is equally rare.

Shangó comes here to warn the client, and his warning can save him. The diviner must tell this person, "You must learn to eat more with your eyes than with your mouth if you hope to survive. You must make ebó with your own two hands so your mouth does not kill you with what you eat. And to save your own head, in time you must make ocha." Gluttony is a vice that consumes the client; his appetites must be curbed. Those things in which he indulges can kill him. The diviner should tell the one at the mat to open his eyes and look around, for there is much to see. Evil and treason come unbidden and without warning; and while the client indulges himself, his enemies will gain the upper hand. The client must bring to Shangó an adimú, anything from the heart. He must give this ebó with his own two hands to receive the orisha's blessing. As he gives to Shangó, so will Shangó give to him.

In Osá Okana, Yemayá is the client's crutch in life, the one who will love him and bless him when all others fail him. Although the client has many disappointments and setbacks in his life, he still has his luck. The diviner should tell him that he overcomes most of what tries to bring him down only because Yemayá, together with Obatalá, blesses him every day of his life. He should thank them both again and again, beginning and ending every day by saying to each, "Maferefún!" Whenever the client is undecided, is overwhelmed, or cannot cope, he should go to his godparent's house with two white plates, two coconuts, two white candles, and a derecho; there, before Obatalá's shrine, his godparent should give him a rogación. This will bring clarity back to his life. When the client cannot trust anyone, when there is no one to whom he can confide his thoughts, his fears, or his hopes, it is to Yemayá he must turn. Before her he must make ebó and pray, and she will lift all the confusion from his life. By leaning on these two awesome orishas, the client can have evolution.

In addition, the letter Osá Okana brings up several additional concerns. The diviner should explore these with the client:

- Often, those who open with Osá Okana are proficient at witchcraft and sorcery. This letter tells the italero that his client is contemplating love magic. The diviner must warn him against using these types of spells. Now is not the time for love; that time will come, but if it is rushed, the client will miss his true partner. He should, instead, pray to Yemayá that love comes quickly and leave this concern there at her feet.
- Before the client walked through the diviner's door, many of the "doors" to greater opportunity were closed and locked to him. Once the client walks back out of the diviner's door, many doors will unlock and open to him, especially chances for travel. He must be careful, however, for while doors are opening to greater opportunities, doors are also opening to dangerous places. The client must be selective in what he chooses for himself.
- If this letter comes in osogbo, the diviner should ask the client about his past involvement in this religion. He may have received elekes once and later threw them away. If so, the diviner should replace these necklaces. The client must make ebó to every orisha he offended when he got rid of them.
- Finally, in osogbo the client's children are marked for danger. One could be abducted or lost; he must watch them carefully.

## The Prohibitions of Osá Okana

- Do not cast love spells or use magic geared toward obtaining love; one has abused these powers in the past, and for this reason they are taken away now.
- Do not destroy or throw away anything given to one in this religion, such as charms and elekes. Otherwise, one destroys one's own life.

## The Eboses of Osá Okana

A woman who opens in Osá Okana with osogbo must receive Olokun; this is mandatory and does not need to be marked with the shells.

Regardless of its orientation, the odu Osá Okana mandates two other eboses. First, if the client does not have the elekes, he must receive them immediately; with these elekes, the client must also have the eleke of Orisha Oko. If the godparent does not have Orisha Oko, an initiate present at the reading who does have this orisha should present it to the client. (If this happens, the godparent is now marked to receive this orisha as soon as possible, for the godchild cannot possess an aché that the godparent lacks. The proper protocol is for the godparent to receive the orisha from the same initiate who put Orisha Oko's eleke around his godchild's neck.*)

Second, this client's head is weak, and it must be refreshed and strengthened. If the client's guardian orisha is known, this ebó should take place before that orisha. If the client's guardian orisha is not known, the ebó should take place before the godparent's guardian orisha. First, the diviner washes the client's head in omiero made of that orisha's herbs. Then he places one leaf from each plant used in the omiero on the client's head. Immediately, he gives the client a rogación with nine different items: coconut, cascarilla, cocoa butter, honey, molasses, and four grated fruits sacred to the orisha before whom this ebó is done. After his rogación, the client makes a simple adimú to the orisha in return for the cleansing.

*Another option is for the godparent to receive Orisha Oko immediately. With his reception, he should have several elekes already prepared to wash with this orisha. This way, no one but the godparent has to touch the client's head.

Having made these prescriptions, the diviner now has his first chance to close the odu. If it remains open, he should ask, "Eborí?" If eborí is marked, the diviner should feed two white pigeons to the client's head after the washing and before the rogación.

- Osá Okana demands many masses for the client's egun. The diviner should prescribe at least one, but nine would be better. He should also determine whether the egun will take a specific offering, asking, "Ebó elese egun?" If the answer is yes, he uses the diloggún to mark the appropriate offering. The client should make this ebó before each mass.
- If the client is a man, he may have serious issues with Shangó; the diviner should recommend that the client make ebó to him frequently.
- If the client is a man, he may need to receive Olokun. The diviner might consider asking, "Koshé Olokun?"
- If this is not enough to close the odu Osá Okana, the client could have further issues pending with Orúnmila, Shangó, Yemayá, or Obatalá. If Orúnmila stands up, the diviner should send the client to a babalawo for a full assessment; the client has issues with this orisha that can be resolved only by his priesthood. For the other orishas, the diviner should ask, "Ebó elese [orisha's name]?" If the answer is yes, he should use the diloggún to mark the appropriate offering.

If the odu continues to remain open and the client is an aleyo or an aborisha, the diviner turns to the eboses of the parent odu, Osá (see page 436). Something among the list is needed for this client's evolution.

An initiate who has reached this point might have additional concerns with two orishas: Orisha Oko and Orí. For Orisha Oko, the diviner should ask, "Ebó elese Orisha Oko?" and "Koshé Orisha Oko?" For Orí, there is only one question to ask: "Koshé Orí?" If Orí's reception is marked, the client must make arrangements to have the ceremony as soon as possible. His head is overwhelmed spiritually, and only the reception of this orisha can save him.

If this is not enough to close the odu for an initiate, the diviner must turn to the eboses of the parent odu, Osá.

## The Second Composite Odu of Osá, Osá Ejioko (9-2)

### The Proverbs of Osá Ejioko

- There will be revolution with the spouse; there will be revolution with a friend.
- Your best friend wants your woman.
- There will be confusion among your friends and family.

### The Message of Osá Ejioko

When a cast of nine mouths, Osá, is followed by a cast of two mouths, Eji Oko, the odu Osá Ejioko is open. This sign is also known as Osá Yeku and Osá Oyekun. When this letter falls, the diviner says, "Maferefún Shangó! Maferefún los Ibeyi! Maferefún egun!" These four orishas are working to bless the client. In iré, all is well, and he needs only to pray and make infrequent adimú to them to keep happy. In osogbo, however, he must live by making ebó to them. Before this letter closes, one or more eboses will be claimed by all four.

Osá Ejioko is always a letter of debt. This person has debts with himself, his friends, his family, and the orishas. He might even be lost in financial debt, and his own standard of living far exceeds what he brings in as income. To help his client and end the reading, the diviner must work carefully through this letter to ensure that all the client's debts are exposed, for only then can they be resolved. Even if the client has a debt to a person who has died, he must pay it; just as the dead have a pact to assist the living, so must the living honor and assist the dead.

In addition, the diviner should keep the following points in mind when delivering a reading of Osá Ejioko:

- The client may have a close friend or relative who is terminally ill; he may be praying for his healing. While this letter has nothing to say about the diseased, it has much to say about the client. First, his constant worrying is draining his strength. It affects his appetite, his sleep, and his own health. Second, while the spirits appreciate his prayers, they are doing little to help the one suffering, because his affliction equates with his own karma. The outcome of this illness has been decided by God himself, and nothing can be done to sway the forces of life or death. What will be will be. The diviner should tell this client that he can do little more now than to offer his support and sympathy.

- This person has much aché with dreams. The diviner should tell him to pay attention to them carefully, for in time the faces of all his enemies will be revealed there.
- While the orientations of ano and ikú can aggravate health issues brought up through Osá, this letter flags health issues no matter its orientation. Insomnia plagues the client; if this continues, he should have a rogación before Obatalá to settle and clear his mind. Exhaustion aggravates muscle pains, back aches, and pains in the chest, so even when he cannot sleep, the client should spend time relaxing so his strength is not drained. Often, the best advice the diviner can give the client is that he should take a short vacation. Stress levels are too high in his life, and his health will continue to suffer.

## The Prohibitions of Osá Ejioko

- Do not lend anything. Do not pawn personal items. Do not charge; the use of credit is prohibited except for emergencies. Do not borrow anything from others. Here, when one lends out something, one also lends out one's luck, and neither the item loaned nor the luck will come back. When one borrows from others, one will take on their osogbo; it will come with the items borrowed.
- No one beyond one's family or lover should live in one's home; if possible, avoid having even these people in one's home.
- The law is hot and already on one's trail. Do not break the law in any way lest one be taken into the court system and Ochosi's home, the jail. Do not let lawbreakers into one's home, and do not associate with those who must hide to make a living. Do not argue, fight, or even make simulated actions of violence. If someone attacks, one must not fight: Run. Do not associate with those who work in legal professions, and do not talk to anyone in a uniform. Even as a law-abiding citizen, one must pretend as if one had something to hide, and hide.
- If a court appearance is scheduled during the next twenty-one to twenty-eight days, one must do everything legal to avoid it. Try not to be called as a witness, and do all that is possible to stay out of jury duty. Do not step foot in a police station, a police car, a court, or a jail, if avoidable. Avoid civil litigation as well.

## The Eboses of Osá Ejioko

When a casting of Osá Ejioko falls on the mat, no matter its orientation certain eboses are mandatory. Here, egun stand up; they whisper of death and the dead and secrets the client has yet to learn about himself. The diviner must prescribe a series of nine masses for the client, one a month for the next nine months. Before each mass, the client should offer the following ebó: Early in the day before the ceremony, the godparent takes the client to make a simple adimú at one of the following places: a church, a river, the ocean, a marketplace, the railroad tracks, a crossroads, the woods, a cemetery, and a place where river and ocean meet (brackish waters). The two should visit a different place before each mass, so that after the ninth mass the client has offered adimú at all nine locations. The diviner should warn the client to follow the advice of the espiritistas exactly, for their prescriptions will elevate his spiritual court. Also, the client must have a bóveda in his home, and he must have his godparent prepare his opá ikú.

The next consideration is a series of nine cleansings for orí. Once a week for the next nine weeks, the client must have a rogación before his guardian orisha. If this orisha is not known, the rogación should take place before Obatalá; the client's head is hot, and Obatalá has the aché to cool it down. The rogación should use the following nine ingredients: grated coconut, cascarilla, cocoa butter, a dash of cow's milk, a dash of goat's milk, white flower petals, grated pears, white bread, and honey. The client discards each rogación at a separate place in nature, following this list: a church, a river, the ocean, a marketplace, the railroad tracks, a crossroads, the woods, a cemetery, and the place where the river and the ocean meet.

Having made these prescriptions, the diviner has his first chance to close the oracle. If it will not close, he should consider the following possibilities:

- Egun could be standing up for ebó; the diviner should ask, "Ebó elese egun?" If the answer is yes, he uses the diloggún to mark the appropriate offering.
- The client's orí may need to be fed; the diviner should ask, "Eborí?" If eborí is marked, the diviner should feed two white pigeons or doves to the client's head before giving the rogación that has already been prescribed. Discard the animal carcasses with the rogación the following morning.
- If the oracle still will not close, the client may have debts with Shangó and the Ibeyi. The diviner should try to mark what is needed to pay the debts, asking, "Ebó elese Shangó?" and then "Ebó elese los Ibeyi?" If the answer to either question is yes, he uses the diloggún to mark the appropriate offering. If either of these orishas does not stand up for ebó, the diviner should advise the client to offer them an adimú to retain their goodwill and explain what the spirits like as offerings.
- This letter enforces the importance of the Ibeyi. If the client does not have them, he is now marked for their reception.
- The client could have issues pending with Oyá, Yemayá, or Elegguá. The diviner should consider asking, "Ebó elese [orisha's name]?" If the answer is yes, he uses the diloggún to mark the appropriate offering.

If these considerations are not enough to close the odu and the client is an aleyo or an aborisha, the diviner must turn to the eboses for the parent odu, Osá (see page 436). Something there is needed for the client's evolution.

An initiate who has reached this point could have additional issues. First, the diviner must prescribe that the intiate offer to egun the following ebó: a stick the client's own height wrapped in nine cloths of different colors, with nine ribbons and nine small bells attached to it. The client's godparent must feed this stick a rooster; the initiate keeps this at his egun shrine.

Second, Osá Ejioko marks a tambor as the solution to the client's difficulties. To whom this tambor is given depends on whether or not the client has played fundamento batá for his own godparent's crown. If he has not, then a tambor to his godparent's guardian orisha is marked as ebó. If this requirement has been fulfilled, the drum goes to the client's own crown. If he has already played a batá to his own crown, the diviner must now use the diloggún to determine to whom this drum goes, asking, "Tambor elese [orisha's name]?"

If this is not enough to close the odu for the initiate, the diviner must turn to the eboses of the parent odu, Osá.

## The Third Composite Odu of Osá, Osá Ogundá (9-3)

### The Proverbs of Osá Ogundá

- The man is keeping a secret from his wife.
- The war of the papers [is being fought].
- He who collects the most knowledge wins the war.
- The storehouse of knowledge.
- Blackmail lives in you.
- Humility will win the battle.
- Flies cannot enter a closed mouth.
- Stay to yourself.

### The Message of Osá Ogundá

When a cast of nine mouths, Osá, falls on the mat followed by three mouths, Ogundá, the sign Osá Ogundá is open. Of all the letters in this family, few are more volatile than this. It requires strong ebó for everyone present in the house once the session closes; see "The Eboses of Osá Ogundá" on page 413.

When the letter opens, the diviner pays homage to Ogún, Oyá, Shangó, Oge, Ayao, and Obatalá, saying to each, "Maferefún!" No matter the orientation of this letter, Ogún comes hot and fierce, a force fighting for justice in the client's life. In iré, his anger is directed at those who have done the client wrong—not just his known enemies, but all those who have attacked him in secret. The diviner should tell the client to open his eyes and watch who suffers around him; those who suffer were not his friends, for they had only evil in their hearts for him. If this reading opens in osogbo, the client's own life might be in danger, for Ogún's machete could be raised against him. The diviner should ask the client if he is hiding from the law or if he has broken any laws. Ogún might put him in jail. If the client lives by hurting others, he will get hurt himself. This letter does not come without hope, however, for it says the client already suffers, and Ogún can be propitiated. If he changes his behavior, and if he makes frequent ebó to Ogún, the orisha's wrath might be stilled. The diviner should tell the client that this will be his last chance to improve himself and save his own life.

Oyá and Shangó are strong in this pattern; they both stand up for the client's defense, and before it closes they may claim many eboses. Oge is here as well. He was once the world's physician, but in time he became forgetful and was lost. Shangó took him in, and now he stands up as the protector and patron of the world. He is, in many ways, the earth's stability. An initiate who does not have Oge might now need to receive him; those who have Oge might need to feed him. Ayao is Oyá's sister, and she speaks fiercely in Osá Ogundá. It was with her aché that the ritual of human sacrifice was finally abandoned in the land of the orishas. As with Oge, those with ocha might need to receive this powerful orisha to save their own lives. Finally, Obatalá is also found here; while this pattern is hot, he is always cool and always forgiving. If no one else in this sign will stand up to save the client, he will. The client should live by making ebó to him.

Having come in this sign, the letter first cautions the client about the necessity of secrecy and virtue: He should do nothing that would bring shame, and his secrets should not be told to another, especially his lover. He must avoid illicit activities and should not become entangled in violence or arguments. He must avoid any type of intoxicants, for they will cause him to act in ways that will give away his secrets and make him prone to violence. He must also safeguard his personal possessions, for there is an increased danger of robbery or theft at this time. Some type of imprisonment or slavery is predicted in this odu, so the client must be wary.

In addition, the diviner should investigate the following with the client:

- If the client is male, he keeps many secrets from his wife, and if she found out about them, she would leave him. The man, however, will one day reveal all to her in a drunken fit. If the client wishes to avoid this, he must not drink, ever.
- Even if the client witnesses a huge disaster, he must be careful about the promises he makes. He must not offer something that he has no intention of delivering.
- The client wants to be handsome; he wants others to think he is handsome. However, in this letter the client must be cautious against vanity. It will be his downfall.

## The Prohibitions of Osá Ogundá

- Avoid involvement in romantic triangles and intrigues; they are so dangerous that they could cause one to lose one's life. If one is involved in adultery, it must stop now. Avoid extramarital affairs. Have no more than one lover. End one relationship cleanly before another is begun. To evolve, in matters of the heart one must always think about the other half.
- Intoxicants, whether legal or illegal, are taboo. One needs full control of one's faculties at all times.
- Do not carry weapons or sharp objects. Do not hunt or fish. Also, forbid one's children to hunt or fish; an accident during this activity may claim the life of one's child.

- This letter forbids cosigning anything for anyone. This includes credit cards, loans, guarantees, bail bonds, and anything else that involves legal documentation or contracts.

## The Eboses of Osá Ogundá

Osá Ogundá requires an ebó for everyone who was in the diviner's home when the odu was cast; they must all come together to pay homage to Ogún. The diviner oils a piece of red meat with epó and sprinkles plenty of jutía and smoked fish over it. He sprays it with rum and cigar smoke and then wraps it tightly in a piece of brown paper. Beginning with himself and then moving on to the client and then the rest of those present, in elder to younger status, the diviner cleanses all with the piece of wrapped beef. He leaves the package with Ogún overnight, and the following morning he discards it at the railroad tracks. This simple ebó removes much of the heat arising from Osá Ogundá's opening. The diviner must tell all present for the reading that any who have warriors must perform this same ebó before retiring for the night; in the morning, it is essential to complete the ebó by taking the wrapped meat to the railroad tracks. If there are any aleyos present in the diviner's home who have not received warriors, they must sit for a session with the diloggún immediately to make sure they have not suffered from its opening.

The diviner must then prescribe the following to the client:

- Oyá and Shangó require ebó. The client must offer them adimú together. The diviner should use the diloggún to determine what the client is to give.
- Ogún requires the sacrifice of a rooster and two pigeons to him immediately, as he stands up here to destroy that which threatens the client.
- The client is required to offer a turtle to an orisha. However, it is up to the diviner to determine to whom this turtle goes. Unless the diviner or a godparent has received pinaldo, an oriaté must be called in for this ceremony.

Having explained all these eboses to the client, the diviner may attempt closure of the oracle. If the letter remains open, the diviner should consider the following possibilities:

- If the client has an enemy who is slowly destroying his life, Ogún stands up here to defend him. As ebó, the client must give Ogún a machete, a rooster, and a tambor or guiro. He will crush this enemy once the ebó is made.
- The client could have issues with both Oyá and Aganyú. The diviner should consider asking, "Ebó elese Oyá y Aganyú?" If the answer is yes, he should use the diloggún to mark the required ebó, and the ebó must be offered to the two together. If no ebó can be marked, or if the letter still remains open, the exploration with these two orishas ends here for the uninitiated. For those who have ocha, the diviner then must determine if the reception of one or both of these orishas is needed, asking, "Koshé Oyá?" and "Koshé Aganyú?"

If these considerations are not enough to close the odu and the client is an aleyo or an aborisha, the diviner must turn to the eboses of the parent odu, Osá (see page 436). This person needs something from that list to facilitate his evolution. If the client is an initiate, the diviner should proceed to investigating the following options:

- For an initiate, the next concern brought by Osá Ogundá centers on the tambor. If the client has not played a fundamento for his godparent's crown, he must do so. If he has done this already, he must play for his own crown and then for Elegguá. If the client has already fulfilled all these requirements, the diviner must determine which orisha the client will play for, asking, "Tambor elese [orisha's name]?" until the proper spirit is determined.
- The orishas Ayao and Oge were born in Osá Ogundá, and the client could need to receive one or both. The diviner should ask, "Koshé Ayao?" and "Koshé Oge?"
- If Osá Ogundá still refuses closure, it may be marking the sacrifice of four legs (and perhaps

an itá). The diviner should first ask the diloggún if the sacrifice of four legs is needed. If the answer is yes, he should ask if the orisha whose diloggún is being consulted will claim the sacrifice. If the answer is yes, the ebó is marked and no itá is required. If the orisha of the diloggún will not claim the sacrifice, the diviner tries to mark it for one of the orishas given in the client's ocha.
- If the diloggún will not mark the sacrifice of four legs, the diviner should try to mark the reception of the knife.

If these eboses will not close the odu, the diviner must turn to the list of eboses given for the parent odu, Osá.

## The Fourth Composite Odu of Osá, Osá Irosun (9-4)

### The Proverbs of Osá Irosun

- Always look to see what is before you and what is behind you.
- Look forward and look back, taking care where you walk.
- There are revolutions in love.
- Three cards sit at the table.
- Watch where you walk.

### The Message of Osá Irosun

When a cast of nine mouths, Osá, precedes a cast of four mouths, Irosun, the odu Osá Irosun is open on the mat. The diviner pays homage to Shangó, Obatalá, Oyá, Elegguá, and Olokun, saying to each, "Maferefún!" All five are strong here, and the aché of all five may be needed to overcome the client's osogbo. Among the lore of this sign, it is said that Shangó became angry with the world and its evil ways; so annoyed was he that he prepared to destroy all things with fire. Obatalá saw his rage and calmed the impetuous orisha before he began his destruction. When this letter falls in iré, Shangó is angry with all who try to harm the client, and he will destroy his enemies once ebó is made. In osogbo, however, Shangó is angry with the client, and the diviner must discover why.

This pattern reveals a variety of issues, and the diviner must explore all of them with his client:

- Because of witchcraft, the client has all but lost everything important in his life. This odu is specific as to how the witchcraft was sent and how the client should fight it: Someone has placed a powder, charm, oil, or cursed object at his front door. He must search for this object. When he finds it, he should carry it to a graveyard so Oyá can deal with it. Upon his return, he should prepare an infusion with nine of Oyá's herbs, nine flowers of different colors, and nine perfumes, and he should use it to wash the front door every day for nine days. Those of a Catholic persuasion may also hang a picture of Saint Teresa, lady of flowers and one of Oyá's Catholic personas, inside the house, over the front door.
- If the client lives with a lover or has a spouse, he must always seek that person's advice in all important matters. This will bring luck back to his life.
- The client must watch his front door carefully, because someone is going to "prepare" (with witchcraft) a nail to harm him and leave it there. When he finds the nail, he should remove it immediately. And he should make ebó to Elegguá to protect the front door.
- In the client's house comes a woman who wants to be with him; he must be wary of her, for she will start a revolution there until she gets what she wants.
- If this letter comes in iré and if the issues with Shangó have been settled, the client should play the lottery occasionally. He will have luck with numbers.

### The Prohibitions of Osá Irosun

- Live a disciplined life; allow nothing to go to waste.
- Cover all open holes in one's house so that evil does not enter unbidden.

- Do not eat grains, grainy foods, or any food containing animal heads or intestines.
- If the meat served at a meal has bones, do not gnaw or suck on them. Choking is a danger.

## The Eboses of Osá Irosun

If the odu opens in osogbo, it reveals that Shangó is angry with the client, and he must be appeased. The diviner should ask, "Ebó elese Shangó?" If the answer is yes, he uses the diloggún to mark the required offering. If Shangó will not accept ebó, the diviner should ask, "Ebó elese Obatalá?" Often, when one cannot appease Shangó's anger, Obatalá can. If nothing else suffices in this odu, the diviner should recommend that Obatalá and Shangó be fed a single white rooster together. This ebó will save the client's life.

If the osogbo marks witchcraft or curses as the source of all the client's ills and the diloggún prescribes a larishe to solve this, that ebó is the first one to make. The client must make it quickly. For Osá Irosun says that the curse is strong, and slowly it kills the client.

Regardless of its orientation, when this letter falls on the mat for an initiate, the diviner should prescribe the following three eboses to the client. They are mandatory.

- When Osá Irosun comes, Shangó is angry, and the only way to appease him is to offer a ram and have itá the following day. A large party should be given to Shangó the day of itá; serve the ram's meat to all who come.
- For blessings, the client should buy a guinea hen and let it roam free in his backyard. If it runs away, he should buy another. This ebó is done to honor Shangó.
- Once these two eboses are done, the client should play the lottery, sparingly but regularly. Iré will come.

Having made these prescriptions, the diviner now has his first opportunity to close the odu. If it remains open, he should explore the following:

- The client should take many spiritual baths using Shangó's herbs. The diviner should depend on his own aché and knowledge of odu to prescribe what is appropriate.
- Olokun is important in all composite odus that incorporate Irosun. If the client does not have Olokun and the letter refuses closure, the diviner should ask, "Koshé Olokun?" If the client already has Olokun, the diviner should determine if the orisha needs an ebó. If the answer to this is yes, the diviner must mark the ebó, and it should be given immediately.
- The Ibeyi can also be an integral part of this odu. If it refuses closure and the client does not have the twins, the diviner should ask the oracle if their reception is needed. If the client has the Ibeyi, the diviner should ask if they need ebó. The ebó marked must be given immediately.

If these considerations are not enough to close the odu and the client is an aleyo or an aborisha, the diviner should turn to the eboses of the parent odu, Osá (see page 436). Something there is needed for this client's evolution. If the client is an initiate, the diviner should explore the following options:

- If the shells being consulted belong to Elegguá, Elegguá might be standing up for a crown. The divine should ask Elegguá this question, marking it as ebó with the shells.
- If the letter remains open, the client could have additional issues with Oyá. The diviner should consider asking, "Ebó elese Oyá?" and "Koshé Oyá?"

If these considerations are not enough to close the session for an initiate, the diviner must turn to the eboses of the parent odu, Osá.

# The Fifth Composite Odu of Osá, Osá Oché (9-5)

## The Proverbs of Osá Oché

- If you don't learn how to live here, you will learn how to live there.
- If you don't learn how to live in this world, you will learn how to live in the next.

- No one knows what he has until it is lost.
- Take care of what is yours.
- Changes and falsehood follow.

## The Message of Osá Oché

When a cast of nine mouths, Osá, is followed by a cast of five mouths, Oché, the odu Osá Oché is open on the mat. Having cast this sign, the diviner says, "Maferefún Olokun! Maferefún Yemayá! Maferefún Oshún!" Olokun rules this pattern. Among its many patakís, it is said that Olokun once went to a diviner to discover the secret of prosperity on the earth. This letter opened, and Olokun was told to make ebó to his own head, and to do it quickly. Before leaving the diviner's home Olokun served his head two coconuts and three roosters. Once his ebó was complete, Olokun became the owner of the ocean and all that was in it. As he took his place in the ocean's depths, all the world came to pay tribute to him. Osá Oché says that this person's head is destined for greatness, like Olokun's, and one day others will pay tribute to him. The client, however, must be like Olokun and make ebó quickly. If he does not, he will lose what the orishas are trying to bring to his life.

In this pattern, Yemayá stands up to say that she is bringing much luck to the client. This luck will come through the hands of one of her daughters. If the client is to lock in this blessing, he must honor Yemayá and those who have her aché in their heads.

Whenever Osá Oché falls on the mat, the diviner should keep the following issues in mind, exploring the ones that are relevant with the client:

- The client must guard his orishas well; someone is coming who will steal something from his shrines.
- Oshún has brought many blessings to the client in the past, and she will continue to bless him if he pays his debts to her. (See "The Eboses of Osá Oché.")
- When Osá Oché comes in an osogbo, the diviner knows he is sitting before a liar. He must tell the client this: "You are not always honest, and sometimes you lie outright. This must stop, for the orishas are angry with you. The more you lie, the more you will lose your luck." This person also does not keep his word, and he skirts his responsibilities. This must end as well.

## The Prohibitions of Osá Oché

- Do not consume alcohol or illegal intoxicants.
- One must never say to one's elder these two words: "I know." Say these words, and no one will ever teach one anything.

## The Eboses of Osá Oché

When this letter opens on the mat in osogbo, the diviner's first concern is settling the client's issues with Oshún. For Osá Oché marks a serious debt between the two. If the client cannot remember making any promises to her that he has not kept, the diviner must determine if the orisha will accept an offering, asking, "Ebó elese Oshún?" If the answer is yes, he uses the diloggún to mark the appropriate offering. If the answer is no, the diviner must direct this person to make an adimú "from the heart." Somehow, issues between human and orisha must be settled or he will not evolve.

The diviner's second concern centers on egun. The diviner must prescribe a series of nine masses, at least one per month, to help him elevate his spiritual court. He should warn the client that all the prescriptions of the espiritistas present must be followed exactly if he hopes to evolve.

Having made these prescriptions, the diviner may now attempt to close the oracle. If it will not close, he should explore the following eboses:

- Olokun is prominent in Osá Oché, for it is in this odu that the entire world had to pay homage to him. This client must offer something to Olokun in the sea.
- If after making the above prescription the diviner still cannot close the sign, the client might need to receive Olokun. The diviner should ask, "Koshé Olokun?"
- Yemayá can also stand up in this letter for ebó to clear the client's osogbo. The diviner should

consider asking, "Ebó elese Yemayá?" If the answer is yes, he uses the diloggún to mark the appropriate offering.

If these considerations are not enough to close Osá Oché and the client is an aleyo or an aborisha, the diviner should turn to the eboses of the parent odu, Osá (see page 436). Something there is vital to the client's evolution.

If the odu will not close and the client is an initiate, he might need to receive Ajé Shaluga, the orisha of riches and the owner of the market. The diviner should ask, "Koshé Ajé Shaluga?" If the answer is yes, the client should plan for this ritual as soon as possible, for only after Ajé's reception will his fortune increase.

If the reception of Ajé Shaluga is not marked, or if the oracle refuses to close after it has been marked, the diviner should turn to the eboses of the parent odu, Osá.

## The Sixth Composite Odu of Osá, Osá Obara (9-6)

### The Proverbs of Osá Obara

- Different characters will cause separation.
- Two rams cannot drink together at the same fountain.
- You are not crazy, but you pretend to be crazy.
- Pretend to be crazy, and you will become crazy.
- Jail, imprisonment—life will be lived behind bars.

### The Message of Osá Obara

When a casting of nine mouths, Osá, is followed by a casting of six mouths, Obara, the odu Osá Obara is open on the mat. This is a powerful, volatile sign, and no matter its orientation it will bring both iré and osogbo to the client's life. Having made this casting, the diviner should say, "Maferefún Oshún! Maferefún Aganyú!" For through Osá Obara is born the custom of feeding Aganyú castrated goat. It is said that when he first emerged from the woods and entered civilization, he was wild and untamed; he had no concept of how to behave in either the land of the orishas or the land of mortals. The first city he entered belonged to Oshún; all were afraid save her, and she cooled his primal instincts with her sweetness and grace. While he was entranced by her, Oshún fed Aganyú the meat of a castrated goat; its meat was delicate and sweet, and its magical flavor soothed the last vestiges of wildness within him. Since that day Aganyú has been civilized, and he never returned to his wild ways. In osogbo, the client is like Aganyú in many ways; he is wild and untamed, harboring a bad temper that must be soothed. If he does not control his temper, he will suffer tragedy after tragedy before meeting his demise. In iré, this person is more like Oshún; he is surrounded by those of quick tempers and violent natures and will have to soothe them to keep himself, and others, safe. Either way, iré or osogbo, this letter raises serious issues about the client's safety and security, and the diviner must explore the implications of this patakís with him.

There are many issues raised in a casting of Osá Obara; the diviner should explore each of these with the client during the course of this reading.

- The client dreams about and yearns for wealth. Money and prosperity drive him, yet no matter how hard he tries, he never seems to have enough. The diviner should tell the client to make ebó, and make ebó often. His luck will come, and he will have what he desires.
- The client must be cautious in his dealings with others, because a war is coming. When it comes, he must turn to Shangó for help.
- If the osogbo of ano or ikú comes, this letter flags mental illness. Depression, acute schizophrenia, and paranoia are all possible. The client must take himself to a physician immediately if he begins to doubt his sanity.

### The Prohibitions of Osá Obara

- Do not share glasses or eating utensils with others.
- Do not fight with anyone: family, friends, or relatives. Do not carry weapons, and never raise one's fists in anger.

- In osogbo, one is forbidden to drink alcohol or to be in places where alcoholic beverages are served. Do not go to nightclubs or bars, for someone there will want to attack and rob one.

## The Eboses of Osá Obara

When Osá Obara falls on the mat, the following eboses are marked automatically for the client:

- The client must have a rogación at the feet of the orisha who spoke first in this odu. It is this spirit who will work to clear the osogbo hanging over the client's head. Because Osá marks nine things in all eboses and cleansings, there must be nine ingredients included in the rogación: grated coconut, cascarilla, cocoa butter, white flower petals, a few drops of cow's milk, a dash of goat's milk, some honey, and two grated fruits favored by the orisha before whom the rogación will take place.
- This person has weak connections to his egun. He needs to strengthen ties with his ancestral spirits. The client must host at least nine masses in his home. In addition, if he does not have his opá ikú, he must find and feed one.
- If the client dreams of money, the next morning he should offer an adimú to Elegguá to seal the iré of the dream.
- If this client enters a war, Shangó stands up to save him. He should give this orisha a single ñame smeared with epó and a red seven-day candle. With this simple adimú, Shangó will fight all the client's battles.

Having made these prescriptions, the diviner may now attempt to close the oracle. If the letter remains open, the diviner should consider the following options for ebó:

- The client's head may need to be fed. The diviner should ask, "Eborí?" If the answer is yes, the diviner should feed two white pigeons to the client's head immediately before the rogación that has already been prescribed.
- The client's egun may be standing up for ebó. The diviner should ask, "Ebó elese egun?" If the answer is yes, he uses the diloggún to mark the appropriate offering.
- Oyá, Babaluaiye, or Aganyú could be standing up for an ebó. Beginning with Oyá and ending with Aganyú, the diviner should ask, "Ebó elese [orisha's name]?" If the answer is yes, he should use the diloggún to mark the required ebó.
- If Oyá, Babaluaiye, and Aganyú do not want ebó, or if the letter remains open and the client does not have Babaluaiye, the diviner should consider asking, "Koshé Babaluaiye?"

If these considerations do not close the letter and the client is an aleyo or an aborisha, the diviner must turn to the eboses of the parent odu, Osá (see page 436). Something there is needed for the client's evolution.

If the client is an initiate and the letter will not close, the next questions the diviner should consider are "Koshé Oyá?" and "Koshé Aganyú?"

If the client already has Oyá, note that in this odu she might be standing up for an ebó of four legs; the diviner should consider this. If the sacrifice is marked for her, the client must sit for itá the day after the sacrifice.

If the client already has Aganyú, an ebó must be done to fulfill the aché of Osá Obara in his life. Sit Oshún and Aganyú on the floor with Elegguá before them. Feed these three orishas a castrated goat; all three, beginning with Elegguá, are to share in the same sacrifice. This honors the pact that was made between Oshún and Aganyú when she tamed him of his wild ways.

If these considerations are not enough to close the odu for an initiate, the diviner must turn to the eboses of the parent odu, Osá.

# The Seventh Composite Odu of Osá, Osá Odí (9-7)

## The Proverbs of Osá Odí

- No one understands you.
- Two people with big noses cannot kiss.
- He who works alone gets paid alone.

- One born to use a hammer will see nails from heaven.
- A single stick does not make a forest.
- The hammer and the anvil [work together].

## The Message of Osá Odí

When a casting of nine mouths, Osá, precedes a casting of seven mouths, Odí, the odu Osá Odí is open on the mat. This is a powerful sign, and many orishas can stand up to offer advice or claim ebó. Immediately, the diviner honors Oyá, Yemayá, Ogún, Aganyú, Elegguá, egun, Olokun, Obatalá, and Osain, saying to each, "Maferefún!" This letter gives birth to many things. The pier extending over the sea was first built here. (When marking ebó in Osá Odí, the diviner should keep this in mind, because any sacrifices made to Yemayá or Olokun might need to be done over the edge of a pier.) The world's first hurricane formed here. It is the sign where Ogún enslaved the bellows and the hammer first struck the nail. Many say that it was in this odu that Olokun tried to rise from the ocean and Obatalá had to chain him a second time. In this pattern Yemayá once was in danger, and while fleeing through the woods her crown fell off her head. Oba was in the forest and saw Yemayá lose her crown; she put it on herself and ran the other way so Yemayá's enemies would chase her instead. When they caught Oba they realized that they had chased the wrong woman, but it was too late; Yemayá was safely hidden away.

There are a variety of issues to explore when this sign falls, and the diviner must investigate them all with his client:

- Contrary to most of Osá's composites, this letter says that the client is neither insistent nor stubborn; instead, he is calm. While calmness is a good quality to have, there are times when he borders on complacency. This person must learn to be more assertive.
- This person has a close friend who is really an enemy. He harbors jealousy and wants the client to fall. Most of the client's tragedies come through the hands of well-meaning friends. He must be cautious in his dealings with others.
- Osá Odí speaks of one who practices magic and dabbles in the occult sciences. The client may work magic to get what he wants, not what he needs, and never to better himself spiritually. There is danger in this, so the client must be careful.
- Married couples fight over children, and a lack of them. The man should know that although his wife would never admit it, she does not want more children. If the couple is childless, she does not want children at all. Difficulty with conception stems from this. It is an issue that the two must work out together.
- This sign emphasizes that others around the client want him to be their slave. The client must be cautious lest he be enslaved (emotionally, physically, mentally, or spiritually) by his peers.

## The Prohibitions of Osá Odí

- This sign indicates that one nags about the same things to the same people over and over, and this must stop immediately. The people one nags are tired of one's complaints and will soon turn against one.
- Do not lift heavy objects, for this will cause injury.
- Avoid drinking dark fluids outside one's home. If eating in another person's home and the consumption of a dark liquid is unavoidable, make sure one watches the host pour the drink. The danger here is that something could be slipped into the glass, and the dark fluid will obscure it.
- The initiate who opens in Osá Odí is warned: Be cautious of whom one accepts as a godchild. Be selective. This letter does promise a huge house of ocha; however, it will grow slowly over a period of months and years, and the priest will have his choice of godchildren.

## The Eboses of Osá Odí

When this sign falls on the mat, regardless of its orientation it marks two mandatory eboses for all clients and an additional ebó that initiates must fulfill. First, all who open in Osá Odí must have a niche osain prepared for the orisha who first claimed ebó in this odu. No matter to whom this charm is made, it must be seated in a large gourd and hung high in the client's home. Its aché will keep him from harm and slavery. In time of great need or distress, the client cleanses himself with this gourd; it will eat the negativity surrounding him. At least once a year, the niche osain must be fed.

Second, Olokun must be offered a sacrifice in his home, the ocean. The client's godparent should give him three roosters in his waters, and over the edge of a pier if possible. Do not venture into the ocean after this offering is made, for Olokun will rise up in one of his many forms to claim the sacrifice. If the client does not have Olokun, after this ebó is done he must make preparations to receive him.

Finally, Yemayá requires initiates to offer a new crown to her. If she already has a crown, the initiate has two options: Add more ornate tools and red parrot feathers to it or buy her a more elaborate piece.

Having made these prescriptions, the diviner may now attempt to close the oracle. If the diloggún refuses closure, the diviner should consider the following points:

- The client may have a strong affinity with the religion Palo Mayombe. He must erect a bóveda immediately to honor the Congolese spirits surrounding him; they are hot and volatile and come seeking light and elevation. The aleyo or aborisha must offer these spirits nine spiritual masses to investigate who they are and what they want. The diviner should consider taking this person to a tata nkisi, for the client might need rayado (the initiation to the religion Palo Mayombe), and until he has this done there will be little peace in his spiritual court. Those who are rayado (no matter their initiatory status in ocha) need to receive the nganga.*
- A strong female spirit with strong ties to Oyá accompanies this client. He must purchase a dark-skinned female doll and dress her in a skirt of nine colors. If the doll is hollow, the godparent should stuff it with nine herbs of Oyá to give it strength. The diviner prepares a niche osain in a gourd for this doll; it sits and eats with this spirit always. The client should cleanse himself weekly to this shrine with a scarf of nine colors; when he is not using the scarf, he should leave it draped over the osain. Whenever this client is in trouble or needs to be cleansed, he prepares a bath before this spirit using nine of Oyá's sweet herbs. This spirit is very much a "madam"; she cleanses him continually and will take away most of the client's worries if he prays to her frequently.
- Ogún could have issues in this pattern. The diviner should ask, "Ebó elese Ogún?" If he stands up to take an ebó, in Osá Odí the proper adimú is a bellows, placed inside his cauldron. Ogún is hot, and the bellows will help cool him down. The client should also give cool, fresh fruits to him frequently.

If these considerations are not enough to close the letter for an aleyo or aborisha, the diviner should turn to the eboses of the parent odu, Osá (see page 436). Something there is needed for this person's evolution. If the client is an initiate and Osá Odí will not close, the diviner should consider the following eboses:

- First, the client could have issues with Oyá. The diviner must ask, "Ebó elese Oyá?" If the answer is yes, he uses the diloggún to mark the appropriate offering. If Oyá does not require ebó, the client might need to receive her. The diviner should ask, "Koshé Oyá?"
- In Osá Odí, initiates must adore Oyá and Yemayá equally; the two orishas work together in this letter to help the client evolve.† If one orisha is the client's mother in ocha, the other adores him as well and should be given equal

*If the italero is also tata nkisi, during the course of this reading he may make definitive judgments on the client's need for rayado or a nganga. If the italero is not a tata nkisi, he may only suggest these as options flagged by odu, and he should have the client consult with a tata as soon as possible on these matters.

†While many priests in this religion feel that there is animosity between Yemayá and Oyá, this is not true; the misunderstanding arises from Oyá's betrayal by the ram in Ogbe Osá; see page 379.

honor. Each offers the child of the other the blessings that his orisha mother is not able to provide. Whether or not the client is a child of Oyá or Yemayá, as ebó he should keep both at an equal height, adorn their shrines equally, pray to both daily, and make adimú to both frequently. The diviner should mark some type of ebó that can be shared between them from time to time to reinforce the importance of both in the client's life.

- The next consideration is Oba. The diviner should ask, "Ebó elese Oba?" If an offering is necessary, the diviner should mark the appropriate offering and have the client give it immediately. Next, the diviner should ask, "Koshé Oba?" If Oba's reception is marked, she must be received immediately.
- Finally, in Osá Odí a pact exists between Oba and Yemayá, and an ebó reinforces this pact for those who have Yemayá crowned. Whenever Yemayá's priest is at war or is being pursued by enemies, Yemayá's crown should be put at Oba's feet for nine days with a sacrifice of a feathered animal. At the end of nine days, the priest should put a basket of fruit at Oba's feet, and Oba should wear the crown for nine days. After this time, the priest removes the crown from Oba, places it on Yemayá, and feeds Yemayá feathers. This ebó honors the patakís in which Yemayá, pursued by enemies, lost her crown in the woods and was saved by Oba. In this odu, Oba is as much a crutch for Yemayá's children as Oyá is, and with this ebó, Oba will throw all the client's enemies now and forever off track.

If these eboses are not enough to close the odu for an initiate, the diviner must consider the eboses of the parent odu, Osá.

## The Eighth Composite Odu of Osá, Osá Ogbe (9-8)

### The Proverbs of Osá Ogbe

- After the fat is fried, the cracklings that are left will be seen.
- One should not repeat the evil that was committed.
- Treason among friends [is certain].

### The Message of Osá Ogbe

When a cast of nine mouths, Osá, precedes a cast of eight mouths, Eji Ogbe, the odu Osá Ogbe is open. Osá l'Ogbe and Osá Unle are other names for this sign. It is dangerous; never will it bring blessings even when iré is marked. The diviner must treat this pattern as if it has fallen in an osogbo. When the sign is cast, immediately the diviner pays homage to Eshu, Elegguá, Oyá, Obatalá, Ogún, and Shangó, saying to each, "Maferefún!" All are prominent, and the aché of one or more might be needed to solve the client's issues.

In this sign, the client must always propitiate Oyá, for she is so close to him that she treats him as if she were his mother. Be warned, however, that if the issues brought to the mat are too severe, Oyá herself might try to take the client away to a safer place, her own world—the cemetery. The diviner must tell the client that, no matter how harsh or tragic life becomes, he may turn to Oyá for help, but he must not cry to her. She will see his tears and embrace him too tightly. Obatalá is behind Oyá; he is the client's final salvation. The diviner should tell him to dress in white when approaching Oyá; Obatalá will hold him in this world if she tries to take him to the next. After the client offers ebó to Oyá, the diviner would be wise to give the client a rogación before Obatalá.

Many things are born in Osá Ogbe, and many of them will have some bearing on the client's life. Through this letter, the first sacrifice of sheep to egun was made; the diviner may need to prescribe this for the client. Wicked temptations, evil impulses that lead all astray, were born here; the client must beware of them. Musical instruments were born here, but not music itself; as ebó, the client should give an instrument to the orisha whose diloggún is being consulted. The eternal war between Ogún and Shangó was born here; children of either could find themselves in the midst of a spiritual battle if one or both are not placated.

Griyelu, the path of Eshu with two faces, was born here. This letter speaks of investigation, and others will soon examine all the client's personal dealings. Here is where the dog came to live with the hunter; the man treated the animal well and was blessed with the dog's tracking skills at the hunt. But one day, the hunter grew angry at the animal and, in anger, struck it. The dog ran away, and in time the hunter starved because alone he could track no game. This is also the sign in which the dog betrayed the king hidden in an earthenware jar.

In addition, the diviner should keep the following issues in mind when exploring the odu Osá Ogbe:

- Life is entering a chaotic phase, and the client will be tested with fire. The diviner should tell him to fight the battle, for when it is over what is left over will truly be his.
- There are two people fighting for the same thing; they both desire the same goal. Yet neither will win, for the need of a third party is greatest.
- Parents must take good care of their children; something bad is coming their way.
- If this sign opens in any osogbo, Eshu is waiting for the client in the house of Oyá, the cemetery. He must be placated quickly. Sickness is brewing in the client's body, and he might have a venereal disease. He must see a physician immediately.

## The Prohibitions of Osá Ogbe

Remember: This odu never brings iré, even when iré is promised. Therefore, the italero must prescribe all the prohibitions of Osá. These will help keep the client from harm.

- Dogs are a source of blessings and troubles in this sign. If one has a dog, treat it well; however, one must keep it tied up so it does not stray or follow one. Osogbo will come if one does not follow this taboo. If one does not own a dog, one is forever prohibited to have one. If one ignores this prohibition, someday the animal will turn on one, bringing evil to his home.
- Do not fight or argue with women.

## The Eboses of Osá Ogbe

Even when Osá Ogbe is marked as iré, the following eboses are mandatory:

- First, this client needs the elekes. If he has them, he must refresh Obatalá's and wear it daily. All the client's children must receive the elekes; if this is a financial impossibility now, they should have at least the eleke of Obatalá.
- The client should have a rogación before Obatalá's shrine with grated coconut, cocoa butter, cascarilla, honey, grated ñame, grated pears, white flowers, mashed banana, and a dash of cow's milk. Before tying the white scarf on the client's head, the priest should wrap his head thoroughly with white cotton. Immediately after this rogación, the client must give an adimú to Obatalá.
- The client must use sweet baths using Obatalá's herbs and white baths incorporating the herb espanta muerto once a day for eight days. The diviner may prepare a large quantity of both baths at one time, instructing the client to bathe first with the herbs and second with the white bath, and to take a shower afterward. The diviner should tell the client to dress in white each day until after the eighth bath is done.
- Finally, if the client is in a war, this ebó will overcome all adversity: He must feed Shangó two guinea hens in the middle of his godparent's patio. Before this can be done, however, the client must complete the previous three eboses.

If these are not enough to close a session that has opened in Osá Ogbe, the diviner may consider the following eboses. One or more may be needed by the client.

- If the client does not have the warriors, he must receive them as soon as possible. He needs the aché of Elegguá, Ogún, Ochosi, and Ósun to overcome his osogbo.
- To see if Elegguá will take a specific adimú or offering to defend the client, the diviner should consider asking, "Ebó elese Elegguá?" If the answer is yes, he uses the diloggún to mark the appropriate offering.

- The client could have issues with Olokun. The diviner should ask, "Ebó elese Olokun?" If the answer is yes, he uses the diloggún to mark the appropriate offering. If the answer is no, the diviner asks, "Koshé Olokun?"
- Finally, the diviner should ask, "Eborí?" If the answer is yes, the diviner must prescribe that, in conjunction with the rogación that odu has already mandated, the client's orí must be fed two white pigeons or doves.

If these considerations are not enough to close the odu and the client is an aleyo or an aborisha, the diviner should turn to the eboses of the parent odu, Osá (see page 436). Something there is vital to the client's evolution.

If Ogbe Osá remains open for an initiate, he must turn to Oshún and Olódumare to save his life. The godparent must take the client to a river to make ebó: two hens and plenty of honey to Oshún. While there, the client must ask Oshún to pray for him before Olódumare. After making ebó, the client takes a large urn of water back home. There, the godparent must prepare an omiero for Oshún, and the initiate must bathe well in this.

If this prescription is not enough to close the odu for an initiate, the diviner should turn to the eboses of the parent odu, Osá (see page 436).

## The Ninth Composite Odu of Osá, Osá Meji (9-9)

### The Proverbs of Osá Meji

- Friend kills friend.
- Your best friend can be your worst enemy.
- The greater the friend, the greater the enemy.
- A friend who kills a friend, or a brother who kills a brother, cannot be pardoned; his crimes will not be forgotten.

### The Message of Osá Meji

When a casting of nine mouths repeats itself, the odu Osá Meji is open. The letter is volatile. For women, even in osogbo, it can bring increased blessings. For men, even in iré, it creates problems.

Having cast this sign, the diviner must take measures to protect himself. First, he gives the sacred gesture of this odu, whipping his head side to side to disperse its energies. Once done, he waves his right hand rapidly over the top of his head nine times, giving a snap of his wrist after each pass so negative energy is thrown off his orí. This additional gesture serves to keep osogbo off his own head. Finally, he crosses both arms over his chest, bowing his head while saying, "Maferefún Yemayá! Maferefún Oyá!" In Osá Meji, the energies of these two orishas are tightly intertwined, the forces of life and death coiled around each other, inseparable. Although Oyá owns this odu, Yemayá was crowned in this sign, and they exist here as sisters, even though the aché of each is vastly different. So close are these two that there is a spiritual "war" of sorts over the client's head; each loves him dearly, and each wants to be the focus of his life. However, if this reading is a bajado, Yemayá gets the first chance to claim the client's head, and Oyá is asked second. If this is not a bajado, but the client has not had a bajado, keep the casting of this odu in mind when that ritual is done. No matter the sign falling, these two orishas are given first choice over the client's head.

The power of Osá Meji is vast; it gave birth to many things. Born in this sign were funeral ceremonies, the spiritual liturgies by which one's soul is sent into the afterlife. In the beginning of time, blacks were the only race who walked on the earth, but this letter gave birth to the whites who soon migrated to the darker, colder climates. Here Obatalá battled with witches, the children of Iyami Osorongo; it was an embittered fight, but in the end Obatalá won, because the powers of light were greater than those of darkness. This is the sign in which the rich began to rob the poor to increase their own wealth; if the client is not careful, what little he has could be lost. The cotton plant, so this sign tells us, was at one time the last plant left on earth that the witches could not destroy. They called upon Iyami Osorongo and made pacts with all of nature to destroy the cotton plant. Yet he himself made a pact with Obatalá, who had once defeated the witches. Obatalá made certain that the witches could not destroy the cotton plant's seeds. He lived forever through his children, and the witches, once again, did not become omnipotent. The diviner should tell the client all these things, for some will have bearing on his own life.

In all castings of Osá Meji, the diviner should keep the following points in mind:

- In this letter, one is betrayed not only by one's best friends, but also by oneself. The client should trust no one, not even himself. The diviner should tell him to keep his secrets to himself; even still, in the end a trusted friend will bring betrayal.
- All who open in this letter might have low self-esteem and many bad vices. The diviner should tell the client to care for himself better.
- If the client has the means to buy property or stocks or make other investments, he should do so at this time. Eventually, they will increase his wealth greatly.
- In osogbo, the letter speaks of mental illness and wasting diseases of the brain.
- When this odu opens for anyone at the beginning of the year, it will mark a year besieged by bad weather and natural disasters. All present for the reading have been warned, and all must take appropriate precautions.

## The Prohibitions of Osá Meji

- This sign prohibits covetousness, enviousness, fighting, and cursing.
- In this odu, one may not wear spotted, stained, or splattered clothes. If one is out in the street and is splashed or gets dirty, return home immediately and change.
- When dressing, wear only solid colors; do not wear checks or plaids. Clothing should not be too bright unless the brightness comes from the amount of white being worn.
- Do not help others lift things from the floor. Otherwise, the one that helps lift will be the next to fall.
- Do not invite those who are sick or dying into one's home. Death follows these, and they will bring Ikú himself to one's front door.

## The Eboses of Osá Meji

When this odu opens on the mat, there are specific eboses marked that must be done by the client.

- Once a month for the next nine months, the client should have a rogación before Obatalá using grated coconut, cascarilla, cocoa butter, grated pears, mashed banana, honey, white flower petals, grated ñame (raw), and a dash of cow's milk. If a harsh osogbo has opened in Osá, the diviner should prescribe a white bath that the client will take the morning after the rogación, when it is removed from his head. The white bath should incorporate cow's milk, goat's milk, coconut milk, white flower petals, grated coconut, grated cocoa butter, efun, and sandolo.*
- Immediately, the client should hang a white flag to honor Obatalá at the front door, offer an ornate mask to the first orisha who spoke in Osá Meji, and give a two-faced doll to Elegguá. The white flag draws Obatalá's attention and protection to his home, while the mask will help the orisha speaking to hide the client's true feelings and intentions from his enemies. The two-faced doll given to Elegguá will help him watch for danger in all directions.
- Finally, the client needs to tend his egun well. He must erect a spiritual bóveda with nine glasses of water, a white candle, and nine cigars individually wrapped tightly in a ribbon; each ribbon should be a different color. The diviner should also consider asking, "Ebó elese egun?" If the answer is yes, he uses the diloggún to mark the appropriate offering.

---

*The rogación uses nine items sacred to Obatalá; nine items are used because Osá Meji marks nine in its eboses. However, Obatalá's sacred number is eight, and so eight items are used in the white bath to provide the client with more of Obatalá's cool, forgiving essence. Still, nine of these baths should be taken, one every morning after a rogación.

Having made these prescriptions to the client, the diviner now has his first opportunity to ask the oracle for closure. If he is refused, the diviner should proceed with the following line of questioning:

- The client could have issues pending with Babaluaiye. The diviner asks, "Ebó elese Babaluaiye?" If the answer is yes, he should use the diloggún to mark the required ebó. In this case, the client must pay the derecho for his ebó by begging alms. Wearing a piece of burlap or sackcloth, he should go out into the street and beg alms from strangers for a day. *Note:* If this odu comes in a severe osogbo, the client should be given a rogación and the eleke of Babaluaiye before going out into the street. The client should present the money he collects to Babaluaiye on a white plate with two coconuts and two white candles. Once this is done, the ebó to satisfy him may be given by the diviner. From this moment on, the client may not make fun of vagrants or beggars, and he can never refuse to give alms to the poor.
- The diviner should next ask, "Koshé Babaluaiye?" Again, if his reception is marked, the client must obtain part or all of the money for the derecho by begging alms in the street.
- The client may need to offer ebó to Shangó as well. The diviner may ask, "Ebó elese Shangó?" and mark what is required or prescribe an adimú with his own aché.

If these considerations are not enough to close the odu and the client is an aleyo or an aborisha, the diviner should turn to the eboses of the parent odu, Osá (see page 436). Something there is needed for the client's evolution. If the client is an initiate, the diviner should consider the following eboses:

- If Babaluaiye's reception is marked, the initiate must receive him with the sacrifice of a four-legged animal. The client must have itá and give a tambor to Babaluaiye before bringing him home.
- Osá Meji is the sign in which Yemayá received her crown. If the odu will not close, the initiate must buy Yemayá the most ornate, expensive crown he can afford. In return, this orisha will give him a kingdom to rule.
- The client could have additional issues with Oyá and Aganyú in this letter. To see if one of them will claim an ebó, the diviner should ask, "Ebó elese [orisha's name]?" If the answer is yes, he uses the diloggún to mark the appropriate offering. If the answer is no, the diviner should consider asking, "Koshé [orisha's name]?"

If these eboses are not enough to close Osá Meji for the initiate, the diviner should turn to the eboses of the parent odu, Osá.

# The Tenth Composite Odu of Osá, Osá Ofún (9-10)

## The Proverbs of Osá Ofún

- Be calm; things will come.
- Butterflies don't go to the city because children will kill them.
- Rain is God's water; wash in it.

## The Message of Osá Ofún

When a cast of ten mouths, Ofún, follows a cast of nine mouths, Osá, the odu Osá Ofún is open on the mat. Having cast this pattern, the diviner must pay homage to Olófin, Obatalá, Elegguá, and Oyá, saying to each, "Maferefún!" This is the letter in which butterflies learned to stay deep in the countryside; every day, they would venture into the city, and children, in their impetuousness, would kill them. The butterflies went to the diviner and were told, simply, to stay out of the city. The diviner should tell the client this story, for he goes places that he should not. If he wants to avoid trouble, he should stay away from those places in which others mean him harm.

Osá Ofún also alludes to the race between the turtle and the dog; the turtle had a bet with the dog that he was the faster, the more intelligent, and the wiser of the two, and the dog challenged him to a race. The turtle accepted, but he went to the diviners first to make ebó. He was told to sacrifice three roosters to Elegguá and to carry the animal carcasses with him on his journey. Starting at the beginning of the race, and every third of the way, he was to drop one carcass. The dog stopped to eat at each point, which gave the turtle time to win the race. The diviner should tell the client to be like the turtle and make ebó, not like the dog who gets sidetracked easily. If he does this, he will always win in life.

When this pattern opens on the mat, all the orishas are standing up here to make one bold statement: "Do not speak to us in the manner to which you have become accustomed, nor treat us as your slave." Many times this client has approached these spirits with arrogance, making unrealistic demands and speaking in an irreverent tone of voice. The orishas will no longer tolerate this, and they will punish him if it continues. Through his own negligence, the client has developed a relationship with the spirits that is either too friendly, too subservient, or too demanding, and it is up to the diviner to open an honest communication about this issue with the client. The client must remember that the orishas are in more than the sacred shells and stones; they are in nature and in the heads of their priests. To develop an honest, open relationship with them is to honor their manifestation in all things. To speak ill of the rain is to dishonor Yemayá and Oshún; to pollute the air is to poison the body of Obatalá. Littering the earth in any form is to desecrate the body of Osain. Our faith comes from the earth, and that, too, must be honored at all times.

In addition, the diviner should keep the following points in mind when this odu falls:

- A woman who comes in this sign will suffer menstrual problems. If the odu opens in a serious osogbo, there will be more intense complications in the reproductive system and cycles. This letter recommends a thorough physical, followed by many eboses and cleansings before Yemayá and Oshún. They can heal this woman.
- The letter speaks of a person who is about to cast witchcraft on someone. The client must not do such a thing because the victim, when he becomes ill, will cause the caster to feel sorry for him. The illness will leave the victim then and come home to roost.
- If this client has left his previous house of ocha, and if this is his first reading since, the diviner should tell him that his previous elders taught him poorly; now they realize this, and now they want him to come back. The diviner should advise the client against this.
- The client is thinking about taking a trip; he must make ebó before he goes. If he fails to do this, the reception he receives will be poor, and he might be in danger.

## The Prohibitions of Osá Ofún

- Do not speak to the orishas in a loud or harsh tone of voice; never speak to them when there is anger in one's heart.
- If one is involved in any form of the occult, do not use one's powers to harm anyone regardless of what he has or has not done to others.

## The Eboses of Osá Ofún

Two eboses must be prescribed by the diviner for any client who opens in Osá Ofún:

- First, the client must collect rainwater every time it rains and prepare spiritual baths with it under the diviner's guidance.
- Second, Obatalá wants the client to have evolution in his life; the orisha can assist with this only if the client performs ebó. This ebó, however, does not need to be directed to Obatalá. The diviner should try to mark a larishe for the client's evolution, beginning with the question, "Larishe si Obatalá?" If the answer is yes, the diviner should mark what he requires. If Obatalá will not offer the larishe, the diviner should then ask, in turn, Oyá, Elegguá, Aganyú, egun, and Babaluaiye.
- Also, if the client is a woman, she must feed Elegguá three roosters and to Obatalá sacrifice a bolt of white cloth.

If these prescriptions are not enough to close the pattern for an aleyo or an aborisha, continue with the eboses of the parent odu, Osá (see page 436). Something there is needed for the client's evolution.

If the letter remains open for an initiate, the client must host a dinner party in honor of Obatalá. The dishes served must be foods that Obatalá can enjoy with the guests. Before dinner, the client should play traditional orisha music. During dinner, he should play soft, soothing rhythms.

If this prescription is not enough to close the sign, the diviner should ask, "Tambor elese Obatalá?" For serious osogbos, this might be needed to bring the client back into balance.

If the oracle still will not close, the diviner must turn to the eboses of the parent odu, Osá.

## The Eleventh Composite Odu of Osá, Osá Owani (9-11)

### The Proverbs of Osá Owani

- Things that are buried should be left buried.
- You can't dig a hole where one is already dug.
- Leave what is buried, or you will suffer great shame.

### The Message of Osá Owani

When a cast of eleven mouths, Owani, follows the initial cast of nine mouths, Osá, the odu Osá Owani is open on the mat. This letter is volatile, and although it applies strictly to the client who has come to be read, the diviner and godparent can be in danger as well, when they begin to make ebó on the godchild's behalf. Immediately, the diviner should say, "Maferefún Oshún! Maferefún Babaluaiye! Maferefún Shangó!"

Oshún's presence here is fierce; however, no matter the orientation of this odu she is not here to bless the client. She comes bringing *ona*, and even if this letter comes in iré the diviner must tell his client, "While Osá Owani brings blessings, here Oshún says she is giving you ona, afflictions of your body and closed roads in your life. You have offended this orisha by your actions, by your words, and if you hope to evolve, you must placate her well and change the way you live." In any orientation of ona, the propitiation of Elegguá is essential as well; he is destiny and fate, and if he is happy, Elegguá can make any orisha happy.

While Oshún is angry with this client, Babaluaiye is only mildly perturbed. The client has a debt to him, and the diviner must work to determine what this debt might be. If the client cannot remember having made any promises to Babaluaiye that he has not kept, the diviner must prescribe an ebó to settle the issues. Here, Babaluaiye issues stern warnings. First, the diviner should tell the client that things buried must be left buried. This is a literal warning: The client must not open holes to unearth anything, no matter the circumstances. This is also a figurative warning: The client must not unearth what was left behind in the past. People, places, things—all were lost for a reason and must not be reclaimed no matter how great the temptation. Babaluaiye warns that very dangerous enemies exist around this person, and all are working, secretly, to bring his demise. Even illness could be brewing in the client's body, and when it comes, it is to Babaluaiye that he must turn to regain his health.

Though Oshún brings ona to the client and Babaluaiye demands payment of a debt, Shangó comes because he has heard the client's pleas, and he stands up in this letter to defend him. His help, however, does not come without cost: The client must live by making ebó to Shangó continually. The diviner should tell the client, "Shangó loves you. He has heard your cries and your pleas for help. But his help is not free; the more you give to him, the more he will give you in return." The diviner should tell the client that in this odu, Shangó says he is envious and ungrateful, and he lacks respect for anyone or anything, and this is what has brought his life to such a volatile point. For now, he must live his life in secret, covering well all the things that he does so others do not find out what he is up to. If the client is a man, Shangó says he has not been a good father or a good husband. If the client is a woman, she is warned to hone her parenting skills as well; her children cause many problems for her because she has been a bad mother.

In addition, the diviner should investigate the following with the client:

- If this reading is the itá of a iyawó, the godchild will fight with the godparent always because he was not meant to be born from this priest's head. While the godchild might be innocent in this, the godparent is not; many times, the orishas have told this person that he or she should not do any work for the client. Yet the godparent did it for the money involved; the godchild was treated unfairly and was perhaps overcharged for everything. Unless the godparent makes ebó and makes this up to the godchild, osogbo will fall on his or her entire house of santo soon, and the godchild will rise higher in life than the godparent could ever dream of rising.
- If this reading is a bajado, the diviner should tell the godparent that this child is not meant to be born from his or her head. The diviner should tell him that if he initiates this aleyo or gives him anything else of ocha, there will be major problems later that no ebó will solve.
- If Osá Owani opens for an aleyo in any osogbo, he or she must make ocha quickly; this is one of the few letters of diloggún that mandates an ocha, must be done as of yesterday. If the client does not crown, he could lose his life soon. Note that in a harsh osogbo, even if he makes ocha, the client's life will be in danger. In this case, the itá is important and must be followed exactly if the client hopes to live a long life.
- Someone will soon give this client money. However, the person who gives the client money will watch closely to make sure it is being spent properly and wisely.
- Illness is carried on drafts; the client must watch out for them.
- This odu carries a stern warning for the diviner: He must be careful of what is said and how it is said. When this client leaves his house, it will bring a large scandal.

## The Prohibitions of Osá Owani

- Things buried must be left buried; do not uncover them, and never reclaim them.
- If one is called to court, refuse to testify. If forced to give witness, say as little as possible, telling the lawyer and judge, "I don't know; I'm not sure. I don't wish to bear false witness." If one is forced to say anything beyond these words, say as little as possible. The orishas will forgive and save one if one does this.

## The Eboses of Osá Owani

When this odu opens on the mat, the diviner should prescribe the following eboses to the client:

- In any osogbo, Oshún is angry and brings ona to the client. To see if the diloggún will prescribe an ebó to make things right between mortal and immortal, the diviner should ask, "Larishe si elese Elegguá y Oshún?" If no larishe is offered for this, the diviner must have an honest talk with his client to determine why Oshún is angry, and then, together, the two must come up with an ebó that will placate her.
- In this odu a special ebó can be done to open all the client's roads in life, bringing iré. The diviner cuts a piece of rope as long as the client is tall; he ties nine knots in it and gives the rope to Elegguá. On a staff of bamboo the client's height, the diviner ties nine strands of multicolored ribbons; he ties a small bell at the end of each strand. He then feeds the staff, which becomes the client's opá ikú, a rooster, Elegguá a chicken, and Oyá three hens. Once all these eboses are complete, the client needs a rogación with nine things at the feet of Oyá. If this sign has come in osogbo, it becomes necessary to use four apple snails in the rogación to strengthen orí. For the rest of the day and night, the client remains in the godparent's house. While he is there, the godparent must also have a rogación at the hands of an elder priest or priestess. After all these things are done, the elder priest must ask Obatalá (with obí) if all is well. If not, the

diviner must consult the shells himself to determine what he must do to free himself from the osogbo of Osá Owani.

- If the osogbo of this odu is severe, the day before the above ebó is offered the client must have a rogación before Obatalá using grated coconut, cascarilla, grated cocoa butter, white flower petals, four snails, grated pears, mashed banana, grated ñame (uncooked), and a dash of coconut milk. Immediately before the rogación, the priest should feed the client's orí two white pigeons or doves.
- Finally, the client should offer two fresh coconuts to Shangó as adimú. After making this prescription, the diviner should see if there is anything else the orisha requires, asking, "Ebó elese Shangó?" If the answer is yes, he uses the diloggún to mark the appropriate offering.

Having made these prescriptions, the diviner may now attempt to close the oracle. If it will not close, he should explore the following possibilities:

- If the client does not have the elekes, he needs them now. The diviner should recommend this to the client, noting that the eleke of Babaluaiye should be included in the ceremony if the osogbo of this sign predicts bad health or death through disease.*
- Oshún offers her sweetness and love if this letter comes in any type of iré, but she will not make these things manifest unless she is properly placated. To see if she is standing up for an ebó, the diviner should question, "Ebó elese Oshún?" If the answer is yes, he uses the diloggún to mark the appropriate offering. If the answer is no, the diviner should instruct the client to offer her a token adimú anyway to ensure her goodwill.
- Finally, Babaluaiye might need ebó. The diviner should question, "Ebó elese Babaluaiye?" If the answer is yes, he uses the diloggún to mark the appropriate offering. If the client has not received this orisha, the diviner should also consider asking, "Koshé Babaluaiye?"

If these considerations are not enough to close the session, the diviner must turn to the eboses of the parent odu, Osá (see page 436). Something there is needed for this client's evolution.

## The Twelfth Composite Odu of Osá, Osá Ejila (9-12)

### The Proverbs of Osá Ejila

- By your own actions you will enter the cemetery.
- Rebelliousness brings disaster.
- Someone wants to see you dead.
- You are a failure because you are a troublemaker.
- Your own head will put you in the cemetery.

### The Message of Osá Ejila

When an initial casting of nine mouths, Osá, precedes a second casting of twelve mouths, Ejila Shebora, the odu Osá Ejila, also known as Osá Oturupon, is open on the mat. Having cast this sign, immediately the diviner praises Shangó, Yemayá, Obatalá, Ogún, Aganyú, and Oyá, saying to each, "Maferefún!" All may stand up to speak or claim ebó, and the aché of more than one could be essential to this person's evolution.

When this odu falls on the mat, the diviner sits before a person whose life is in turmoil; disaster comes, and as soon as one crisis has ended, another comes to take its place. All these things are caused by the client's own rebelliousness and warring nature, and if he wants coolness and peace in his life, he must begin by cooling his own head. His personality is so troublesome that some of this person's friends wish him dead, and if the osogbos are severe, someone might even want to kill him. It is not uncommon for others to use witchcraft against one who opens in this odu, and usually the method employed is the placing and blowing of powders

*Note that if the godparent does not have Babaluaiye, he must find an initiate who does to give this necklace. Additionally, this marks the godparent for this orisha's reception, as the godchild may not possess an aché that the godfather does not.

behind the client's back. The quickest way to solve this person's problems is for him to adjust his own attitudes. Also, the client thinks himself to be handsome; the diviner must gently remind this person that there is always someone more beautiful than he is.

In addition, the diviner should explore the following with the client:

- Disaster comes due to the client's own rebelliousness; he does not listen to advice and may not listen to what is said in this reading. The diviner should tell him that obedience is essential to his evolution.
- If the client comes in a severe osogbo, his own actions will put him in the cemetery.
- Here, one has envious, hidden enemies. The client should be cautious.

## The Prohibitions of Osá Ejila

- When Osá Ejila opens on the mat, no matter its orientation, the diviner must prescribe all the prohibitions of the parent odu, Osá (see page 436).
- By doing favors, one can lose one's own life; do not do favors for others.
- Never raise one's hand against a lover or spouse in anger or play; otherwise, one will lose one's luck and suffer.

## The Eboses of Osá Ejila

- When a man opening in Osá Ejila suffers reproductive problems, especially swelling or inflammation in the genitals, there is ebó to solve this: He must have eborí before Shangó, using a guinea hen and two white doves or pigeons. Immediately after eborí, the client must have a rogación using grated pears, grated apple, mashed banana, mashed plantain, grated coconut, cascarilla, cocoa butter, honey, and molasses.
- Always, this letter flags serious issues with Shangó. If the client is an initiate, he must give a tambor or guiro in his honor to regain his favor. An aleyo or an aborisha must make ebó to him. The diviner must ask, "Ebó elese Shangó?" If the answer is yes, he uses the diloggún to mark the appropriate offering. If the answer is no, the aleyo or aborisha should still offer the orisha some token ebó, an offering from his heart (based on the diviner's knowledge of what Shangó likes). Shangó's placation is essential in this odu.
- If the osogbo of Osá Ejila is severe, the diviner should send the client to a babalawo for a rogación with red snapper.

If these considerations are not enough to close the odu for an aleyo or an aborisha, the diviner must turn to the eboses of the parent odu, Osá (see page 436). Something there is needed for this client's evolution. If the client is an initiate, the diviner should continue with the following list:

- In Osá Ejila, the reception of Oyá or Aganyú could be mandated. The diviner should consider asking, "Koshé [orisha's name]?"
- Aganyú might be standing up for a tambor in this letter. The diviner should ask, "Tambor elese Aganyú?"

If these considerations are not enough to close the letter, the diviner must turn to the eboses of the parent odu, Osá.

# The Thirteenth Composite Odu of Osá, Osá Metanla (9-13)

## The Proverbs of Osá Metanla

- In your house, under your bed, is where you will find your enemy hidden.
- Adultery [of one's spouse is a danger].
- He who knows nothing divines a lot.
- There is a hidden enemy in the house; there is a hidden enemy under the bed.

## The Message of Osá Metanla

When a cast of nine mouths, Osá, precedes a cast of thirteen mouths, Metanla, the odu Osá Metanla, also known as Osá Irete, is open on the mat. Having cast this pattern, immediately the diviner must praise Elegguá, Shangó, Oyá, Obatalá, and Orúnmila, saying to each, "Maferefún!" This odu is active, and its energies reference many things. This is the letter in which the toads were dying of thirst, and Obatalá, out of his concern for them, gave them water to drink. The diviner should tell the client that Obatalá hears his cries and sees his needs; if he makes ebó, this orisha will give him what he truly needs to survive. Orúnmila was once at war with his enemies and was losing the battle. He went to the diviners to mark ebó, and this odu was the one that fell to the mat. He was told to make sacrifice to Shangó with two roosters, and he did so immediately. Orúnmila won the war with Shangó's help. This is the letter in which the mouse was lost in the field; the young python came upon the mouse and ate him. The python then became lost in the field, and the African gray parrot saw him and killed him. The client must be warned to be like the parrot, not like the mouse or the python.

Osá Metanla is a dangerous odu for one who is married or involved in a monogamous relationship; it marks adultery and prohibits adultery at the same time. If the client sitting at the mat is married, this letter points out that the enemy to his marriage may be in his own home at this time. Perhaps the enemy has even been hidden in his home while he was there. His wife is not to be trusted, yet if the client wants to save his marriage, he may not let her know that he suspects her of adultery. He should spend more quality time with her and treat her well; only then will she have no reason to roam and no chance in which to cheat. If the wife is loyal, the client may be the one with the roaming eyes, and his behavior will bring about his own demise. In this case, there is already a man who comes to the house when the husband is away, and if the wife suspects adultery, she will cheat with this person. If the client wants to save his relationship, he must begin to heal it now.

In addition, the diviner should keep the following in mind when Osá Metanla comes to the mat:

- The diviner should tell the client that when he goes home, he should check under his bed. Something could be hidden there. He also must clear out the area under the bed, because one should not sleep on top of anything.
- If the client is an initiate, he must live by divining with the orishas on all the important issues in his life.
- In this odu, Shangó is angry because the client has declared war on one of his children. The client must make ebó to Shangó and end the war; he will take care of his own.
- This odu prohibits the client to complain about his lot in life and how others treat him. If he is obedient, both Elegguá and Shangó will take care of all the issues in his life.
- In this letter, hot winds bring death. Sickness will come to the house because of a hot wind; the client should clean it well to get rid of the illness before he is infected.

## The Prohibitions of Osá Metanla

- This odu, no matter its orientation of iré or osogbo, requires the prescription of all the parent odu's prohibitions. By following these, one will avoid many of the tragedies foretold.
- It is forbidden to have anything under one's bed. Check nightly before sleeping to make sure nothing is there.
- Adultery is forbidden. If one cheats on one's lover, one will lose all iré.

## The Eboses of Osá Metanla

When a casting of Osá Metanla opens on the mat, there are many options for ebó. The diviner should consider the following:

- Shangó holds the keys to the client's evolution. However, before the client can evolve, he must resolve the serious issues he has pending with this spirit. The diviner should ask the client if he has any unresolved issues with this orisha; there may be a promise unfulfilled. If he can remember nothing, the diviner should see if the orisha will claim an ebó, asking, "Ebó elese Shangó?" If the answer is yes, he uses the diloggún to mark the appropriate offering. The diviner should tell the client that Shangó is demanding this offering not to help him evolve but to resolve debts owed him for past blessings. After this ebó is made, the client must live by pampering Shangó; he will bless him every time the client gives the orisha an adimú.

- If the osogbo of Osá Metanla is harsh, the client may have declared war on one of Shangó's favored children. The diviner should lead him to talk about those with whom he argues and quarrels and try to determine not only if any of these are in the religion, but also if any of these are Shangó's chosen. If so, the orisha is sending "fire" to the client's life because he curses those Shangó loves. The client must end this situation immediately. He must sacrifice two guinea hens to the orisha and talk to him about the problems his child causes. Shangó will deal with his own children harshly, and as he sees fit.
- The client has issues with Babaluaiye. To begin, the diviner must ask, "Ebó elese Babaluaiye?" If he stands up for ebó, the diviner should use the shells to mark something appropriate. He might also consider asking, "Koshé Babaluaiye?" If this is marked, the client should begin preparations for this ceremony as soon as possible. If receiving him is a financial impossibility now, the client should have a rogación before Babaluaiye's shrine using grated coconut, cascarilla, cocoa butter, honey, molasses, coconut milk, white bread, a few grains of toasted corn, and a few leaves of cundiamor. After the rogación, the client should receive this spirit's eleke. This will put him under Babaluaiye's protection until he can receive the orisha.

Having made these prescriptions, the diviner may now attempt to close the oracle. If it will not close and the client is an aleyo or an aborisha, the diviner must turn to the eboses of the parent odu, Osá (see page 436). The client needs something from that list to facilitate his evolution. If this patterns refuses closure for an initiate, the diviner should consider the following eboses:

- An initiate who comes in this odu should keep an African gray parrot in his home. As the tail feathers shed, he should put them in a crown for his guardian orisha. If the orisha is one who does not take a crown, the initiate should use the feathers to decorate the orisha's sopera instead.
- Remember: In this letter, the frogs were dying of thirst and Obatalá sent life-giving water to save them. To honor this letter, an initiate should keep one or more ceramic frogs inside his home; this spiritual charm will bring luck, as Obatalá will never let him suffer. Those who do this must follow an additional prohibition for life: Never kill frogs or toads.
- For luck, the client should buy a thunderstone for Shangó. He should wash this in Shangó's omiero. The initiate should feed Elegguá a rooster and then feed two guinea hens to the thunderstone with Shangó. The client might also want to wear a small thunderstone pendant that has been washed and fed with Shangó.

If these considerations are not enough to close Osá Metanla, the diviner should turn to the eboses of the parent odu, Osá.

## The Fourteenth Composite Odu of Osá, Osá Merinla (9-14)

### The Proverbs of Osá Merinla

- You break one plate, and you pay with another.
- You live without peace.

### The Message of Osá Merinla

When a cast of fourteen mouths, Merinla, follows the initial cast of nine mouths, Osá, the odu Osá Merinla is open on the mat. Osá Ika is another name for this sign. Here, the diviner should pay homage to Ogún, Oyá, and Babaluaiye, saying to each, "Maferefún!" All three speak freely in this letter, and the aché of all might be needed to clear the client of osogbo.

When this sign opens on the mat, the diviner faces a client for whom most of the negative meanings of Osá will apply. He is a man without peace. All aspects of his life that come under scrutiny in this reading will be soured. He has no stable place of residence, no stable friends, no stable relationships. Poverty and despair figure prominently, due not to the orishas or malicious witchcraft but to the client's own head. He has made many bad decisions and mistakes in his life, and slowly they are catching up with him. The key to overcoming the osogbos in this odu is for the client to make all his prescribed eboses quickly, for the orishas are promising a way out of the evil that has come home to roost.

### The Prohibitions of Osá Merinla

- When Osá Merinla comes to the mat, no matter its orientation the diviner must prescribe all the prohibitions of the parent odu, Osá (see page 436). With these, one can avoid many of the inherent osogbos of this odu.
- Neither borrow money nor use credit; that which one uses one will never be able to pay back.

### The Eboses of Osá Merinla

When Osá Merinla opens on the mat, the diviner should consider the following eboses:

- The client needs the initiations of the elekes and warriors immediately. With these, he must receive the eleke of Oyá. He must wear Oyá's eleke daily.
- Ogún will remove many of the client's obstacles with this simple offering: The diviner should boil and mash a ñame, mix it with plenty of epó, and place the ebó in a brown paper bag. He then should instruct the client to clean himself to Ogún thoroughly. With obí, the diviner asks Ogún how long the ebó remains with him and where to discard it.

Having made these prescriptions, the diviner may now attempt to close the oracle. If it will not close, the client could have issues pending with Babaluaiye. To see if this orisha requires an ebó, the diviner should ask, "Ebó elese Babaluaiye?" He might also consider asking, "Koshé Babaluaiye?"

If these considerations are not enough to close Osá Merinla, the diviner must turn to the eboses of the parent odu, Osá (see page 436). Something there is needed for the client's evolution.

## The Fifteenth Composite Odu of Osá, Osá Marunla (9-15)

### The Proverbs of Osá Marunla

- By doing favors, you will lose your head.
- By doing favors, you will lose your life.
- You have no friends.

### The Message of Osá Marunla

When an initial cast of nine mouths, Osá, precedes a second cast of fifteen mouths, Marunla, the odu Osá Marunla is open on the mat. Osá Iwori is another name for this odu. Immediately, the diviner must pay homage to Oyá, Babaluaiye, Elegguá, Ogún, and Ochosi, saying to each, "Maferefún!" All may stand up to offer advice or claim ebó, and the aché of all may be needed to settle the client's issues.

When this letter falls on the mat, the diviner is facing one who determines his self-worth by how much he can do for others; this person gives so much of himself away for free that his own resources are strained to the point where he can do nothing for himself. Now the client comes before the diviner almost in tears, because he does not know where to turn, or what to do, to straighten out his own affairs. The diviner should point out that he has few true friends. Those who stand by his side do so only as long as they are getting something in return, and when this person has nothing left to give, they leave. The diviner should encourage the client to take stock of all the favors that he has done for others, all the things that he has given for free. He should ask him, "Where are those people now?" No one offers help to the client. In serious cases of osogbo, he is on the verge of losing his job, his luck, his peace, and his spouse or lover. The easiest way to reclaim his luck is for him to do nothing for another unless something is offered in return. Only then will the client's luck return.

In addition, the diviner should explore the following issues:

- The diviner must emphasize that doing favors for others will cause the client to lose his luck. If this letter comes in iré, the diviner should tell him that he may help his friends, family, and lover with their issues and problems only if he gets something in return. If this letter opens with any osogbo, the diviner should explain that it is by doing a favor that he will lose his life: In Osá Marunla with osogbo, favors equal death. The client must understand this.
- The diviner should question the client's living arrangements. The orishas are saying that someone lives there who should not be there. Somehow, the client must secure new living arrangements for either himself or this person. In this letter, it is best for the client to live alone.
- Slavery is an issue in this odu. The client should not let himself become a slave, nor should he enslave others.

## The Prohibitions of Osá Marunla

- When Osá Marunla falls on the mat, the diviner must prescribe the prohibitions of the parent odu, Osá (see page 436). These will keep one from suffering many of the odu's inherent osogbos.
- Do not do favors for others.
- Do not let anyone else live in one's home. Here, the visitor becomes the king, and the former king becomes a slave.

## The Eboses of Osá Marunla

When Osá Marunla opens on the mat, there are three considerations for ebó.

- First, the client needs the initiation of the elekes immediately. Because they are marked in such a hot and volatile sign, the rogación given before the ceremony must include nine ingredients: grated coconut, cascarilla, cocoa butter, grated pears, grated, raw ñame, a dash of cow's milk, a dash of goat's milk, and honey.
- Second, this client needs his warriors immediately after he receives his elekes. If this ceremony is a financial impossibility, the diviner must mark ebó to Elegguá and Ogún so they will bless him with the means to achieve this. Note that when these orishas are received, the client must have the elekes of both Elegguá and Ogún placed around his neck.
- Finally, the following ebó must be done as soon as possible: The client should sew an apron with two front pockets. He puts some freshly toasted corn in one pocket and some gravel in the other. The client visits one of his friends while wearing this apron. While there, he starts eating the corn. When the friend asks what he is eating, the client must hold out a handful of stones and say, "Stones. Would you like some?" Because Osá Marunla is an odu in which one's friends are envious and jealous, this will cleanse the client of the evil vibrations they send to him. His roads in life will open.

Having made these prescriptions, the diviner may now attempt to close the oracle. If it will not close, he should consider the following options for ebó:

- The client may have issues with Oyá and Babaluaiye. The diviner should ask, "Ebó elese [orisha's name]?" If the answer is yes, he uses the diloggún to mark the appropriate offering. If an ebó can be marked, the client must give it immediately.
- If the client is an aborisha or an initiate, he might need Babaluaiye to lift the curse he has been living under. The diviner should ask, "Koshé Babaluaiye?" If the reception is marked, the client should make preparations for this ceremony as soon as possible. If the client cannot afford this ceremony's expenses now, he must have a rogación before Babaluaiye's shrine and receive his eleke.
- Finally, if the client is an initiate who does not have Oyá, he is now marked for her reception.

If these considerations are not enough to close the composite Osá Marunla, the diviner must turn to the eboses of the parent odu, Osá (see page 436). Something there is needed for this client's evolution.

## The Sixteenth Composite Odu of Osá, Osá Merindilogún (9-16)

### The Proverbs of Osá Merindilogún

- Your worth is measured in what you have.
- He who gives away what he has loses what is left.

### The Message of Osá Merindilogún

When a cast of sixteen mouths, Merindilogún, follows the initial cast of nine mouths, Osá, the odu Osá Merindilogún is open on the mat. Osá Otura is another name for this sign. Opening thus, the diviner must pay homage to Oyá, Obatalá, Oshún, Ogún, and Orí, saying to each, "Maferefún!" The aché of one or more might be needed to settle this client's issues.

This letter's true meaning may be found in its proverbs: "Your worth is measured in what you have" and "He who gives away what he has loses what he has left." The diviner should advise the client to take stock of the things—material, physical, mental, emotional, and spiritual—that he has in his own life. These are what make him a unique individual, and once he realizes just how important his self-worth is, he must never give away these things for free. He must not do favors for others, work for free, or loan out material possessions or money unless something is given in return. Things loaned out to others will never be replaced. To give away the very things that make up his self-worth or importance will reduce the amount of worth he has.

There are various issues found in this sign, and the diviner should explore all with the client:

- This odu speaks of memory loss, forgetfulness, schizophrenia, and split personalities. In iré, this letter says the client cannot remember minor details. In a severe osogbo, the client could get so lost in his own world that he will not want to return to this one. Head injuries and emotional traumas will exacerbate this. The diviner must emphasize the need for the client to protect both his physical head and his emotional health.
- The client is in danger of losing his job due to carelessness or laziness. The diviner should tell the client to do no favors for anyone at work unless his own duties are complete. He must avoid heavy lifting at work; this will cause injury.
- In this letter, spirits engulf the client. He must have a strong breaking from these; they drain his physical and mental strength.
- Through witchcraft, someone may have rendered this person unable to have sex. This must be fought.
- In Osá Merindilogún, we say that Obatalá apprehends the one at the mat. Even if the client is not in the religion, he one day will be and must be initiated. The diviner should throw a mazo on this person and have him salute Obatalá and his godparent.
- If the client is married, his true luck lies with the current spouse, and this odu points out that she may be a child of Oshún. To increase his material success, the client must treat his spouse with love and respect. If she is lost, so is the client's luck. She also will one day need initiation.

### The Prohibitions of Osá Merindilogún

- When this letter opens on the mat, the diviner must prescribe all the prohibitions of the parent odu, Osá (see page 436). These will help one avoid the inherent osogbos of Osá Merindilogún.
- In this letter it is said that he who gives away what he has loses what is left; therefore, one is forbidden to give away any of one's possessions.
- Do not perform favors for anyone.

### The Eboses of Osá Merindilogún

When Osá Merindilogún opens on the mat, there are three initial considerations for ebó:

- First, this letter says that the client suffers some form of sexual dysfunction. To correct this, he must sacrifice three guinea hens to Ogún. Following this sacrifice, he must have a physical.
- The sign also speaks of husband and wife and the problems that exist between them. Osá Merindilogún says that these problems stem from their heads; the orí of both is bad. To correct this, husband and wife must both have a rogación at the feet of Obatalá using grated coconut, cascarilla, grated cocoa butter, grated ñame, mashed bananas, grated pears, a dash of cow's milk, a dash of goat's milk, and honey. Note that the honey is the last ingredient added to this rogación, and it must be shared between both heads liberally.
- Finally, the client who comes in this sign must honor Obatalá by wearing white frequently, and he must honor Oshún by considering his lover or spouse in all things.

Having prescribed these eboses, the diviner may now attempt to close the oracle. If it remains open, the diviner should consider the following possibilities with the client:

- The client could have further issues pending with Ogún, Oshún, or Obatalá. If the initiation of the elekes has not been taken, the client must receive these plus the eleke of Ogún. Also, the diviner must check to see if any of these orishas are standing up for ebó, asking, "Ebó elese [orisha's name]?" If the answer is yes, he uses the diloggún to mark the appropriate offering.
- If the osogbo of Osá Merindilogún is severe, the client must have a rogación with nine ingredients before Obatalá's shrine every week for eight weeks. The morning after each rogación, he must have a white bath. The rogación should use grated coconut, cascarilla, grated cocoa butter, honey, molasses, white sugar, grated pears, mashed bananas, and a dash of cow's milk. The white baths should use cow's milk, goat's milk, sandolo, white flower petals, grated cocoa butter, cascarilla, grated coconut, and coconut milk.

If these considerations are not enough to close the session, the diviner must turn to the eboses of the parent odu, Osá (see next section). Something there is needed for the client's evolution.

## Closing the Reading: Further Eboses of the Parent Odu, Osá

Having exhausted the options of larishe and ebó in the composite odu, the diviner must turn to the parent odu to find a method of closure. This sign, Osá, contains within itself many offerings and rituals to placate both the letter and the orishas that are speaking in it. The eboses of this pattern follow.

- The diviner should add to the rogacion of nine elements that he has already prescribed (see "Marking Ebo in Osa: Initial Considerations," on page 402). First, he should ask, "Rogación sodidé?" A rogación normally begins at the head and ends with the feet, but a rogación sodidé begins at the feet and ends with the head. This elevates the client closer to his orí and crowning orisha. Next, the diviner should question whether the orisha before whom the rogación is given needs ebó, asking, "Ebó elese [orisha's name]?" If the answer is yes, the diviner uses the shells to mark the appropriate offering; it should be given immediately after the rogación. Finally, the diviner asks, "Eborí?" If eborí is demanded for a normal rogación, the diviner should feed the client's head two white pigeons or doves before beginning the cleansing. Eborí made during a rogación sodidé is given after the cleansing, before the priest wraps the client's head in cotton. Since eborí is done to benefit the orí, the diviner must ask the orí, using obí, where to dispose of the animals' carcasses.
- The most important spiritual prescriptions concern the client's issues with Oyá. When Osá comes in an unresolved osogbo, the client must turn to her for help. Although the diviner may already have asked the client this question, he must now ask again, "Do you have any unresolved issues with Oyá?" If the client has made but not kept any promises to her, he must

resolve them now. The diviner may examine the client's relationship with Oyá from another standpoint: Has the client offended any of Oyá's children? If so, he must seek resolution. Note that if the client is an aborisha whose godparent is Oyá's initiate, there could be disrespect between the two, godparent and godchild. The diviner must examine this issue as well. If the client is an initiate, the diviner might consider asking, "Tambor (or guiro) elese Oyá?" If nothing else, the client should resolve to give Oyá a huge party in her honor. He should invite as many initiates and aborishas of Oyá as possible. If the client has not made ocha, he should give this party to his godparent's Oyá.

- The client must make ebó to Oyá at the gates to a cemetery. Dressed in white, the client should go to the cemetery gates with a multicolored cloth or grass mat. He lays this just outside the gate and over this lays out nine different dark-colored fruits. As he sets up his ebó, he should cleanse himself with each piece of fruit, praying to Oyá for cleansing. After doing this, he turns around and leaves the cemetery, not looking back. If he looks back, those things he cleansed from himself will follow him home.
- While many consider the cemetery gates to be Oyá's home, in truth it is just one place in which she may be found. Her true home is the marketplace. Oyá is the lady of commerce, and she rules the financial transactions of the world. The client should make ebó to her in an open-air market, such as a flea market. At the four corners of this market he should leave nine pieces of fruit, nine pennies, and nine pieces of hard candy. After making his ebó, he should go inside the flea market and shop, buying something to give to his egun. This ebó will bring him much luck, and it will elevate his spiritual court.
- Osá marks heavy issues between the client's orí and his guardian orisha. If the client's guardian orisha is known, the following eboses should be done before that orisha's shrine. If the guardian orisha is not known, these should be done before the godparent's crown. First, the client's head must be washed in the orisha's omiero to cleanse and consecrate the orí. Once this is done, the client should have a rogación with the mark of nine. Use plenty of grated coconut, efun, cocoa butter, cotton, a dash of goat's milk, and a dash of coconut milk. These things are sacred to Obatalá, who owns all heads; they will refresh his orí. To this add three more items sacred to the orisha before whom the head is rogated, such as three different grated fruits. If this is not enough to satisfy Osá, the diviner should ask, "Eborí?" If eborí is marked, the priest must feed the client's head two white pigeons immediately before the rogación. Depending on the severity of the osogbo opened, the diviner should consider prescribing one rogación a week for nine weeks.
- The client should consider putting out pinwheels to catch the wind, placing them outside the front and back doors of his home and inside each window. Osá is Oyá's home, and it is a pattern alluding to the wind. The client should make sure that the pinwheels are placed in places where the wind can catch them.
- The tongue is also important in Osá, and many times to placate the osogbo that has opened the client must make ebó with a cow's tongue. First, the diviner should try to mark this for the orisha whose shells have been consulted. If that spirit will not take an ebó of tongue, the diviner should try to mark it to Oyá. If neither of these will take the ebó, the offering must go to egun. The client should give a prepared cow's tongue to egun; it remains with them for nine days. At the end of this time, the client must take it to a cemetery.
- The diviner must always consider egun in Osá. At the very least he should prescribe a single mass; in more volatile osogbos, he should prescribe nine masses. Before each, the client gives a basket of nine different fruits to the client's bóveda.*
- The godparent should use obí before the mass

*If the client does not have a bóveda or an opá ikú, he must have these prepared for him by his godparent.

to determine the proper place in nature for disposal of the fruits. The last person leaving each ceremony carries these away to the predetermined place. The diviner should counsel the client to follow the advice of the espiritistas exactly, for these are ways that he will elevate his spiritual court.

- The diviner should also consider whether the client's egun will take a specific ebó to remove osogbo from the client, asking, "Ebó elese egun?" If the answer is yes, he uses the diloggún to mark the appropriate offering.
- Remember that although Osá is a letter of fertility (through it, Oyá became the mother of nine children), it is also a sign of the abiku. If the sign comes in osogbo for a parent, if the woman (the client or the client's partner) has sustained many miscarriages or sudden infant deaths (SIDS), each living child should see the diviner as ebó. The presence of abiku must be ascertained. If abiku is found, that child must make ebó to its guardian orisha. Afterward, the priest should chain the child to the earth (have him or her wear on the left ankle a chain that has previously been fed to the earth). If the child is too young to make ebó on his own, the parents must do this in the child's name. As the child outgrows the chain, the priest must prepare a new one before removing the old one.
- If the client is an aleyo or an aborisha, one or more of the following orishas could be standing up for ebó: Oyá, Obatalá, Elegguá, Babaluaiye, and Olokun. To see if any will take ebó in exchange for their blessings, the diviner should ask, "Ebó elese [orisha's name]?" If the answer is yes, he should use the diloggún to mark the appropriate offering.
- If the client does not have Olokun or Babaluaiye, he might be marked to receive these two orishas in Osá. The diviner should consider asking, "Koshé [orisha's name]?"

If the diviner has come this far into the odu and it still refuses closure, the pattern itself, Osá, could be standing up for propitiation. To clear the heat from this odu, both the letter and the orishas must be placated. Every ebó that has been marked thus far should be adjusted to include the mark of nine. Instead of marking one fruit, the diviner must mark nine; instead of marking one cleansing, the diviner should mark nine. Somehow the number nine must be incorporated into everything done on the client's behalf.

If after this prescription the letter remains open and the client is an aleyo or an aborisha, the diviner has two options. First, he may look at the list of eboses given for the omo odu as a parent odu. For example, in a casting of Osá Ejiogbe (9-8), the diviner would turn to the eboses of Eji Ogbe as the parent odu for closure. Second, he may call an elder in the religion; he may have missed something important during the session, and a second opinion might be needed to close the diloggún.

If, however, the client is an initiate, there are more options for ebó in the parent odu Osá.

- Yemayá or the initiate's guardian orisha could be standing up through Osá for a crown. First the diviner should try to mark this as ebó for Yemayá. Her crown must have seven red parrot feathers, one on each point. Then the italero should attempt to mark this ebó for the client's orisha. Note that while the initiate must buy the crown for Yemayá himself, the one to be given to his crown must be bought by his godchildren. As ebó, they should decorate it lavishly in red parrot feathers. Thus will the priest obtain the respect of all his godchildren, and thus will the house of ocha prosper and grow.*
- Initiates must make frequent offerings to Oge, who lives with Shangó, and rub camwood on his horns daily to propitiate him. To see if this spirit requires anything else as ebó, the diviner should consider asking, "Ebó elese Oge?" If the answer is yes, he uses the diloggún to mark the appropriate offering. To make ebó to Oge, the initiate must remove him from Shangó's batea and put

*Through Osá one of the initiate's godchildren can be marked for ocha, and this might be the reason his own guardian orisha is standing up for a crown. If the diviner wants to pursue this, he should try to mark one of the heads of those who are already in the client's ilé. The person marked is said to have a mazo thrown over his neck.

him on a white plate. The ebó is made to him there. If eyebale is marked, the only option for feeding him consists of two white pigeons while he sits on the white plate. For any other type of adimú, all offerings suitable for Obatalá are suitable for Oge. Never feed Shangó while Oge sits in his batea, and never feed Oge while he rests with Shangó.

- Those who are children of either Yemayá or Oshún might need to make ebó to both together. The diviner should ask, "Ebó elese Yemayá y Oshún?" If they require ebó, he should mark something suitable for both.
- Initiates could have additional issues with Oyá, Aganyú, Oke, Yewá, or Ayao. First, the italero should try marking eboses, asking, "Ebó elese [orisha's name]?" If this is not enough to close the odu, he should consider asking, "Koshé [orisha's name]?"

At this point, if the oracle still refuses to close, the diviner has two options: He may turn to the eboses of the secondary odu as parent odu or he may call an experienced elder in the religion for a second opinion on the reading.

# ELEVEN

# THE FAMILY OF OFÚN

## The Proverbs of Ofún

- [Ofún is] where the curse was born.
- The one who curses shall be the one who is cursed.
- Whatever is thrown into the ocean will sink to the bottom; it cannot be recovered.
- Your position was lost at birth.
- When a snail dies, it forgets its shell; when a chicken dies, it leaves a pile of down; and when a great man dies, he leaves his bones on the earth.
- All that we find in this world we leave in this world.
- Because of one's chin, the sun will not strike the bottom of the jaw.
- Even deep in the forest, a fire cannot hide.
- Beside the river, the silk cotton tree cannot hide.
- When one leg steps forward, the other leg must follow.
- When the father leads, his child follows.
- If the father lets the child walk in front of him, the child will be honored as greater than his father ever was.

## The Orishas Who Speak in Ofún

| | |
|---|---|
| Obatalá | Iroko |
| Elegguá | Yewá |
| Oshún | Naná Burukú |
| Oyá | Babaluaiye |
| Odua | Osain |
| egun | Ogún |

## The Message of Ofún

Opening with ten mouths on the mat, the diloggún sits before the diviner in a numinous, almost inscrutable pattern: Ofún has come to the house. Always, it hides more than it reveals; it is delphic in nature, leading the client on a journey of self-discovery. The energies opened here will help this person discover talents, traits, and secrets once hidden in obscurity. All its composites are profound, for Ofún itself was born of heaven's emergence and Olódumare's unfolding. Its symbols are vast but vague; the act of doubting, the state of darkness, and the image of the egg sum up its attributes. Ponder these. While many consider Ofún to be the giver of knowledge and wisdom, in our house we call it the confuser. It is here that one begins one's first spiritual quest, and although this quest might begin as an active, delineated process, Ofún does not guarantee enlightenment; instead, it promises more unease, more questions, and more searching. As is inherent in its symbols, a true spiritual journey raises more doubt; it leads the voyager to examine arcane truths unpondered by most. And like the age-old question "Which came first, the chicken or the egg?" the initiate will become lost in a cycle that has no beginning and no end.

When this letter opens on the mat, the italero placates and honors Ofún with a solemn series of rituals. First, with cascarilla the diviner marks his own forehead in the area above and between both eyes (known as the "third eye"). Then he marks the client's forehead in the same manner, and all the initiates present mark their own heads as well. Second, the diviner makes the series of sacred gestures attributed to this letter: He covers both eyes with the palms of the hands; his right palm covers his right eye and his left palm covers his left eye. This simple gesture alludes to Ofún's shielding nature; it will always hide more than it reveals. With the eyes alone, one cannot know its mysteries. Then the diviner pats both palms gently on his stomach; this symbolizes how the odu's truths may be felt only intuitively, never intellectually. Finally, he balances both palms together just below his chin as if holding a delicate powder, and he exhales from his mouth, sending a slow, steady puff of air over them as if he were blowing that powder onto the client. This is purely a defensive measure. It symbolizes that what the client has brought into the room remains only with him.

Once he has made these gestures, the italero prays the sacred chant associated with this odu:

*Ofún mafun yega ki mafun Ikú.*
*Ki mafun Ano, ki mafun Ofo,*
*Ki mafun Eyo, ki mafun Tiya.*
*Elese oranfun filedi onide Imale.*
*Dede dedi afaye kole pamiku.*

Those present bow their heads in silence while the diviner chants this brief prayer. When he is finished, to honor both the opening odu and the orisha owning it, many will mutter, "Maferefún Ofún! Maferefún Obatalá!" Others will continue their devotions with "Maferefún Elegguá!" Elegguá is a spirit of mystery, quite comfortable in this mysterious odu. He, like Obatalá, knows all it holds, and the aché of both is essential to all composites in this family.

The series of rituals designed to placate Ofún does not end with these. By its opening, the odu indicates that the orishas Obatalá and Elegguá are heated. Before continuing the diloggún's manipulations, the diviner honors both by making ebó. He (or his assistant) prepares a porridge known as saraeko by combining in a large bowl or gourd a large amount of fresh, cool water with cornmeal and honey. Everyone present for the reading must sip the saraeko, in the following order: the diviner, the client, and the initiates present in the order of eldest to youngest. After all drink from the gourd, the diviner fills two smaller bowls with saraeko for Elegguá and Obatalá. He retains a portion in the original bowl; it sits by the front door until the end of the reading. Once the session closes, the diviner throws that portion into the street with the words, "Eshu batie sode." ("Eshu takes the heat [of the reading].")

Having made ebó, the diviner may safely open Ofún's composite letter. Keep in mind that many of these signs have their own special rituals designed to further placate and cool ten mouths' complex energies. (If a composite requires such eboses, they will be detailed in the text of that specific pattern.)

Within Ofún several spirits might choose to speak or claim ebó. The orisha whose diloggún is being consulted has the first option, and adherence to his advice is essential to the client's evolution. Following this spirit is Obatalá. He owns Ofún, and no orisha is better empowered than he to navigate its currents. Rarely will this sign close unless ebó has been marked to him. Oshún is the next to speak; she is quite comfortable amid Ofún's sour notes, for she uses its energies to remind the client that without bitterness, one could not know sweetness. Though her issues are heavily dependent on the composite opened, she is the client's salvation, his eternal hope. After Oshún, the spirits Oyá, egun, Babaluaiye, Elegguá, and Ogún may stand up to offer advice, prescribe taboo, or claim ebó; their exact natures depend on the composite unfolding. For initiates, Odua, Iroko, Yewá, Naná Burukú, and Osain might also intervene in this pattern. Though they speak freely throughout this family, their exact natures and requirements depend on the composite sign cast.

The easiest way to begin a study of ten mouths is with it in iré. When a composite odu is marked as coming in iré, the next step is to mark the origin of this iré; this step is crucial because it helps the client focus on his source of spiritual strength. While iré through Ofún always offers some type of blessing, in this family certain sources are strong, but others can bring osogbo if the client is not careful. The following origins of iré are especially propitious in Ofún: iré elese ocha (goodness from the orishas), iré ashegunota (goodness from the otanes of the orishas), iré dedewan t'Olokun (goodness from Olokun), iré elese egun (goodness from the feet of ancestral spirits), and iré elese ará onú (goodness at the feet of the spirits of heaven). The following origins of iré are volatile in Ofún: iré elese eledá (goodness from one's orí), iré lowó (goodness from the client's hands), iré iyeku (blessings through tragedy), iré elese orí yoko (blessings from initiation), and any iré dealing with people such as abure (brother/sister), obini (women), okuni (men), omo (children), arubo (elders), babatobi (godfather), and iyátobi (godmother).

Opening with a favorable iré in Ofún, the client faces many initial considerations. Through ten mouths, intimate relationships are woven with both the orishas and egun. The spirit offering iré is this person's strength and salvation, and he or she must be treated as such. Two sources of iré given by the orishas, iré elese ocha and iré ashegunota, demand further exploration by the diviner. While in these orientations all the orishas bless the client, the italero must determine with whom the client has the strongest bond; this spirit offers the most light and evolution and must be honored. In all composites of Ofún, the following orishas may stand up to defend the client and offer the blessings of iré: Obatalá, Oshún, Oyá, Odua, egun, Iroko, Yewá, Naná Burukú, Babaluaiye, Osain, Elegguá, and Ogún. The orisha offering the blessing, as well as the client's status in the religion, will determine the exact offering. (See "Marking Ebó in Ofún: Initial Considerations" on page 449 for more details.)

Having determined the orisha offering iré, the diviner must prescribe ebó to that spirit. If the client is an aleyo, this letter requires only simple adimú. Later, if it is determined that the iré is not firm or if the odu refuses closure, a rogación before that spirit's shrine plus the investment of his or her eleke might help lock in the blessing for the client. If the client is an aborisha and the orisha offering the blessing is Elegguá or Ogún, he might need to receive that orisha. Finally, if the client is an initiate and he receives a blessing from an orisha he does not possess, he must receive that spirit. The need to receive this spirit is not a spiritual emergency, but it will lock in the blessings meant for him. Note that in all cases of iré ashegunota, the client must receive that orisha to lock in his blessing.

While iré dedewan t'Olokun brings transcendent blessings through Ofún, the diviner must be very cautious and very strict when reading for this client. Olokun comes to bring blessings and evolution, but he does so at a cost. Immediately, the client must begin propitiating him, even if the iré is later marked as firm. The diviner should detail several adimús that the client can offer this orisha; his placation and worship must be fervent and continual. If the client does not have Olokun, he must receive him immediately. True, his expenses are vast, but so are the blessings that he will bring through Ofún. If the client cannot afford him at this time, he must offer this weekly ebó to this orisha: On the same day of every week, the client must bring an offering. The first ebó he brings must be a large basket of fruit, and in this basket he leaves a small sum of money. Thereafter, the weekly ebó can be anything appropriate, even if it is just a blue seven-day candle. To show his continued devotion to this spirit, every week that he makes ebó he must leave another derecho in the basket. All the money put into this basket goes toward his derecho for Olokun's initiation. By doing this, he shows Olokun his devotion and obtains his blessing as he works to receive him.*

The blessings brought by the dead, as marked by iré elese egun or iré elese ará onú, are strong sources of strength for the client. In Ofún are found the most powerful espiritistas, spiritual workers who can call and command entire armies of the dead with no more than a fervent plea and a single lit cigar. Within this client is a strong source of light, a powerful aché to which the dead are drawn; they crave this light for their own evolution and will do what it takes to obtain it from the client. Offering his love and prayers freely, from the heart, this person will

*The seriousness of iré dedewan t'Olokun in the family of Ofún arises from the unfinished business between the babalawos and Olokun in the odu Ofún Ogbe. See page 470 for an explanation of what happened in 1958 when this odu opened as the letter of the year for Cuba.

find that egun form the focus of his spiritual court; they will work hard to bring him what he needs so he, in turn, can give them what they require. When one of these two types of blessings comes through any composite of Ofún, the diviner must demand that the client keep and maintain a spiritual bóveda. Daily, he should pray in front of this, asking God to uplift his spiritual court.

There is a special consideration for iré elese ará onú: When it comes, it hints at an elevated spirit who is not tied to the client by blood or by ocha but wants to form a symbiotic relationship with him. This spirit will guide the client as he makes ebó to it. The diviner should prescribe a series of spiritual masses in the client's home. He should invite as many talented mediums to these events as possible. As the client reaches out to this entity, it will make itself known.*

When a "dangerous" source of iré opens, the diviner can make many assumptions and prescriptions for his client. First, remember that this odu is owned by Obatalá, the owner of all heads; it is also a letter that creates confusion. Its very nature can overwhelm the client until he cannot see straight. If iré elese eledá has come, the goodness of Ofún emanates through the client's own head, yet the nature of Ofún in its raw state is confusion. Here the diviner must prescribe a rogación before Obatalá; it is to him that one turns for clarity. The rogación should use ten cool white things sacred to this orisha: grated coconut, coconut milk, cocoa butter, grated ñame, white flowers, cascarilla, cow's milk, goat's milk, cotton, honey, and sandolo. To gain this spirit's favor, the client should give a simple adimú to Obatalá after completing the rogación. He must wear white for sixteen days, and on the eve of the sixteenth day he should return for another rogación. He must avoid any place or activity that would cause him shame or confusion, for by keeping his orí clear the client will evolve. Later, if the reading refuses closure, the diviner might consider adding to this ebó, asking, "Eborí?" If eborí is marked, the diviner should feed two white pigeons or doves to the client's head during each rogación.

Iré lowó (goodness from the client's hands) and iré iyeku (goodness through tragedy) are so dangerous in Ofún's family that the diviner might consider them osogbos in themselves. Iré lowó indicates that the client receives his blessings through his own works; he reaps what he sows, and he will have to work hard to evolve beyond what he is now. Those who open in Ofún are innately lazy. They have worked so hard in the past that at this point they are exhausted; clients under this sign's influence tend to give up and lie by the wayside. The diviner should tell the client that, no matter what, he must continue to work hard, even harder than he has worked in the past. Blessings will follow, but not immediately. Also, the diviner should tell the client that he will reap from what he has planted in the past before he will reap what he sows now. If the client has been hostile and treacherous in the past, even if he ends this behavior now he will reap from the treachery and hostility he has planted before goodness comes. This prediction should not encourage him to return to his old ways; instead, the diviner should tell him that it should provide encouragement for change—the future can become brighter.

The second iré, iyeku, reinforces the volatile and hostile nature of Ofún in relation to the client's evolution. Ofún in this orientation is beset by tragedy and change, and while the orientation of this sign says this is not a permanent state, the client will evolve only after he has suffered even more tragedies and setbacks. The diviner should tell him not to give up; he must encourage him to persevere with goodwill and good character. The end to all tragedy will soon be in sight.

No source of iré can bring more danger than those dealing with people. No matter how it falls or the composite odu opened on the mat, Ofún marks despair, deceit, and tragedy by the hands of others and oneself. While an odu now, Ofún was once

*Note that the composite opened will give clues as to what type of spirit this is. If the omo odu speaks heavily about the faith Palo Mayombe, the entity guiding the client could be a Congolese spirit. Also, the secondary letter that modifies Ofún will give clues as to this spirit's nature. For example, if iré elese ará onú opens for the sign Ofún Oché (10-5), the diviner may assume that this spirit has qualities similar to those of the orisha Oshún. If Ofún Ejila opens, the spirit could have qualities similar to those of Eleggúá. And in the case of Ofún Ogbe, an elevated spirit sharing Obatalá's nature could be close to this person.

mortal; he walked the earth and lived a long, lonely life studying the mysteries of magic and witchcraft. Yet he was kind and gentle; he spent his powers in the service of others, cleansing and removing evil from the world. All that he cleansed he kept safely locked in a room, amid his cauldrons and pots and secreted under a white sheet. Others knew him as a great healer, but in truth Ofún was a witch. Though his powers were great, when old age came he was a miserable, lonely man; wanting to end his solitary existence, one day he opened both his home and his heart to parents with but a single daughter, Ananagun. So sweet and beautiful was she that Ofún doted upon her, and all four lived together in Ofún's home as an extended family. The parents were poverty-stricken and unemployed, but Ofún used his charms to help them find work. By day he was entrusted with the young girl's care while her mother and father labored in the marketplace.

As he told the child, Ofún's house had only one rule: "Behind that locked door, in the corner of that room, are many objects covered with a white cloth. No matter what, never go in that room. No matter what, never lift that cloth. What lies there is for my eyes only. Obey me, and I will give you all that you want and desire, beautiful child." Ananagun agreed, and Ofún loved her even more. Every day while her parents worked, he left the child at home; he shopped in town, buying her the most beautiful and extravagant gifts. And every day he was pleased that she had not even touched the locked door. Ananagun's curiosity grew daily, but Ofún never saw this, so blinded was he by his love for the child. One day he forgot to lock the door to the forbidden room before leaving the house. That day the child's curiosity got the best of her. Ofún was at the market; she was alone, and the mysterious room beckoned. She opened the door. Dozens of white candles burned therein, and she saw the huge white sheet with mysterious, moving shapes under it. Cautiously, excitedly, she lifted the sheet. She screamed in fright when she saw the terrible implements of Ofún's witchcraft beneath it. Awakened by her cries, the evil trapped there awoke, and all the pestilence, curses, and diseases that Ofún had trapped during his life flew past the girl and into the world. She fell back into a faint, and such was her shock that when she awoke, she only stared blankly at the white sheet. She knew neither who nor where she was.

When all the great evils besieged the world at once, the skies darkened and the earth rumbled. Men, women, and children panicked and ran while great hordes of shadows, beasts, and insects ravaged the earth. Ananagun's mother was frightened; she left work in a hurry. Ofún was angry; he stopped shopping at once. Both the old man and the mother arrived home at the same time, and both ran to the opened, forbidden room. The girl still sat there, in a stupor, pointing at the white sheet. It billowed and boiled beneath; one final evil remained in its grasp, unable to escape—hopelessness. Ofún roared, "Child, I forbade you to enter this room. What evil have you wrought?" As the mother held her child and saw the cursed implements lying in the room, mere emptied shells, she seethed, "Evil, wicked man! We trusted you. And you are but a witch! You have cursed my child and the world with your evil." Before Ofún could explain that he spent his entire life capturing evil, not creating it, the mother ran from the house with her daughter; the two were never seen again. Thus did the curiosity of Ananagun bring her own fright and ruin to the world of Ofún. He died a poor, maligned, lonely man. And it is for this reason that the one who opens in Ofún must be wary, continually on guard against others. For while they might not wish to cause harm, their own human nature will bring harm. Yes, this iré does promise a blessing, but the client must be careful and keep the advice of Ofún at all times if he hopes to avert tragedy before his blessings come.

Having determined the iré, its source, and its initial advice, the diviner continues to question the oracle. If the iré is marked iré yale (firm iré), the odu is telling this client that his source of blessing is strong; Obatalá and Ofún mount behind him, pushing him toward his destiny.* If the iré is then marked as iré yale timbelaye (firm iré manifest in the client's

*If the odu is marked for a volatile iré in Ofún, that source is equally strong. Spiritually, the client must brace himself for the worst before the best will come.

life), Ofún gives closure to itself. It tells the diviner that this pattern's energy has been in effect for some time, and the client has navigated himself well through its energies. He is in alignment with his destiny. Ten mouths has opened to tell the client what forces are in effect and what he will walk away with.

Whenever Ofún comes in any iré, it is a letter of evolution, an energy removing all blockages from the client's paths if he heeds the letter's advice and makes ebó. The patakís of Ofún illustrate this. This family speaks of the elephant; while he was the largest creature of the forest, he was being eaten alive by the smallest: mosquitoes, gnats, and flies. Although minuscule to the behemoth mammal, they brought him sickness and disease, and the elephant had no way to fight back. Unable to bear their torture, the elephant went to the diviners and made ebó as they recommended. Awakening the next morning, he was still attacked by flying insects, but he discovered that he now had a long, powerful tail. With this, he could swat and kill the insects; their torment was no more. Another story tells of Ochanlá, the mightiest and eldest avatar of Obatalá, who was frail and ignored before the opening of Ofún in his life. He went to the diviners; he made ebó. With his age came wisdom, and that wisdom proved to be his strength. The morning after his ebó, Ochanlá descended to the earth clothed by rays of the sun, and all the world paid homage to him with the brilliance of a new day. He was worshiped and adored forever thanks to Ofún's aché.

Yet even if the client makes ebó through Ofún in iré, he must abide by many taboos. He must not stay out late, nor go out alone during the day. He must avoid all intoxicants to keep his mind focused at all times. For Ofún was once first among all odu; he was king, worshiped by all. But when the sixteen holy odu descended to the earth, Ofún stopped many times along the way to dance, party, drink, and fraternize with strangers. Months later, when Ofún arrived on the earth, he found that Eji Ogbe had taken his place as king. The other odu assented: Ofún was once their leader, but he lagged behind while Eji Ogbe picked up the slack. Their order was forever changed by Ofún's own mistake. Now, to keep his iré firm, Ofún warns the client to stick to his goals and keep his head even.

Regardless of the odu's orientation, the diviner has many issues to explore when any composite of ten mouths opens on the mat. This is a pivotal odu. It changes all that it touches, and it can touch every aspect of the client's life. The nature of the changes he will experience depends on which composite has come to the mat. The diviner must realize that over the coming days and weeks, the client will doubt what is told to him now, for the changes themselves are in the future; however, the events shaping these changes are happening in his life now. Each single event might seem minor, small, or insignificant, but like a pebble thrown into a pond, it will cause ripples that spread outward, making immediate changes in every aspect of his life. Because Ofún's nature can be erratic, the client must make ebó to lock in his blessings. The diviner should tell him, "Ofún has opened on the mat. Everything that you do starting this moment will affect the rest of your life. Nothing happening now is insignificant. Your circumstances, events, actions, and reactions will shape your life in subtle ways that will seem insignificant at first, but they will be felt more intimately in years to come."

Ofún references the client's home. It is not as serene, quiet, or beautiful as the orishas would like it to be. Consider each of the following pieces of advice to be ebó; the client must fulfill them exactly if he hopes to make his life more comfortable and pleasing. First, the diviner should tell the client that his residence needs a thorough cleansing to remove both physical and spiritual dirt. In many orientations and composites of ten mouths, curses and powders have been placed by enemies. The client must be sure to air out the sleeping place well; he should also look under the bed and separate the mattresses, making sure there is neither dirt nor clutter there. These things cause turmoil during his sleep, bringing insomnia, and already the client sleeps fitfully. He should now cleanse his home spiritually with two white doves, beginning at the back of the house and working through to the front. Outside the front door, he should pour a copious amount of fresh, cool water while praying to Olódumare and all the orishas for renewal and protection, and then he should let the two doves fly free. When they take to the air, they will take all the evil with them. Now, there is a taboo to enforce: Once the client's home is clean physically and spiritually, it must stay that way. The client should not quarrel or fight in his home. It must be kept peaceful. While one's home is a refuge, the client's home must be the client's refuge. He should never let friends or relatives move in, for then the client will be tempted to move away from his own house.

In any orientation of Ofún, the diviner should give many medical and health warnings to the client. Ofún brings disturbances and disaster by water. Anything that holds water in reserve could be a source of decay, and this includes rivers, the ocean, rain, dams, plumbing, and the human body. The client must respect all natural sources of water and the orishas or spirits that live in them. If the household plumbing begins to leak, he should call a plumber immediately, before a small problem becomes a big problem. Diseases of the body that involve dehydration or fluid retention could become a source of discomfort and severe illness. The client must be on guard against chronic obstructive pulmonary disease, pneumonia, edema, nausea, digestive discomfort, and diarrhea. He should see a physician if any strange symptoms develop. Women in the client's family who are of childbearing age should not conceive now. If any of them becomes pregnant, she should go immediately for an exam and proper neonatal care. The danger here is that an imperfect child will come to the family, if one has not been born already. Although there is no prohibition against abortion in this odu, Oshún has a soft place in her heart for the imperfect children of Obatalá; she might later stand up to demand that a pregnancy in which the child is known to be imperfect in some manner be carried to term. The best option for now is either abstinence or proper birth control.

When Ofún opens in any osogbo, it becomes a dangerous sign, and the diviner must proceed carefully with the reading if he hopes to help his client evolve. In osogbo, this letter focuses on three major misfortunes: sickness, witchcraft, and death. If any of the following osogbos present themselves, the unbalanced nature of Ofún is ripe in the client's life and he must make ebó immediately: ikú (death), ano (illness), arayé (arguments, gossip, witchcraft), ogo (witchcraft), fitibo (sudden death), and epe (curses). When these come, the client will be fortunate if the odu has prescribed a larishe, a remedy to help the client not only avoid the misfortune but also align himself properly with ten mouths' energy. If the odu has not prescribed a larishe, a careful reading of the composite should provide an ebó to help this person. No matter the osogbo opened, however, the origin of the misfortune is more important than the misfortune itself. Once identified, the source can be avoided, placated, or worked through.

The osogbo origins of elese otonowá (from heaven), elese eledá (from one's head), and elese ocha (from the orishas) mark their own difficulties through Ofún. How the diviner proceeds with these depends on the client's initiatory status. For an aleyo or an aborisha, these sources of osogbo indicate that undefined issues of anger exist between the client and an orisha. Elese otonowá flags issues between the client and the prime owner of a composite odu. For example, if Ofún Obara (10-6) opens with osogbo elese otonowá, the diviner knows Shangó is angry with the client, and his propitiation is essential to the client's physical and spiritual safety.

Elese ocha indicates that the osogbo comes from an orisha, and the diviner must determine which orisha this is, questioning, in turn, each of the orishas that speak in Ofún. Once the orisha is identified, the diviner can mark eboses to bring the client back into alignment with him or her. If this orisha is not the primary owner of the odu, the issue is not as serious; it shows a serious lack of aché, but not real anger. To illustrate this, consider the example of Ofún Obara (10-6) again. Shangó speaks foremost in this composite; here, an osogbo elese Oshún is not as serious as an osogbo elese Shangó. Oshún is here to tell the client that most of his troubles come from his lack of alignment with her, yes, but one cannot say she is as angry as she might be if she were speaking in her true odu in this family, Ofún Oché (10-5). Finally, if an osogbo elese eledá opens through any composite of Ofún, disaster is brought by the client's own head. Many rogaciónes and eboses will be needed to settle the client's orí. If his guardian orisha is not known, he must have a bajado soon. An osogbo through Ofún elese eledá marks disrespect between the client and his own guardian orisha, but until this spirit is identified, the spiritual issues cannot be settled.

The problems flagged by elese otonowá, elese eledá, and elese ocha are similar for the initiate, but they are handled in a different manner. First, if the initiate sits at the mat with Elegguá's dilog-gún, an osogbo elese otonowá or elese eledá in any composite odu flags issues between the client and his own guardian orisha. The head is one's connection with not only the orisha but also heaven, and to get to the powers in heaven, one must go through one's crown in prayer. These issues are not necessarily anger; however, something is out of alignment between the initiate and the orisha installed in his head. The diviner must investigate this odu from that angle, determining what needs to be fixed. At the very least, the client must make ebó not only to his orisha but also to his head, and he might require several rogaciónes before that spirit's shrine to correct the imbalance. If the osogbo brought by Ofún for an initiate is elese ocha, and the spirit who brings this osogbo is the client's own crown, the diviner knows that the spirit is angry with his protégé. In Ofún, this anger stems from disobedience. While involved eboses will be required to settle this, before attempting to mark any ebó to the client's guardian orisha, the diviner and client must discuss the itá of initiation. For this sign suggests that the client is not following his itá as he should, and these recorded words are the key to his evolution as a priest or priestess. If any orisha speaks to an initiate with *any* osogbo or origin in Ofún, that orisha is not pleased; even if this spirit is not the client's crown, he or she is displeased and must be placated.

When the osogbo marked in Ofún is ano or ikú, the letter becomes very dangerous, and it will take severe prohibitions and frequent ebó to save this client from danger. The diviner should tell him that serious illnesses are creeping up on him; not only must the eboses prescribed be done immediately, but also the client must run, not walk, to see a physician for a thorough exam. The orishas will guide the physician in offering treatment and diagnosis. A woman who opens in ano in Ofún will tend to have reproductive difficulties. She must not try to get pregnant now, for there are too many problems in the uterus and ovaries to carry a healthy baby to term. She may also experience retention of the period (delayed menstruation) and difficulties with menstruation that cause cramping and discomfort; under Ofún's energy, these things will only worsen. In both men and women, illnesses will occur in the stomach (pains from constipation or menstruation), and the client may also suffer from blockages in the digestive or circulatory tract, as well as tumors. The brain and eyes are vulnerable; the diviner must caution the client to protect these regions. He must also be meticulous about personal hygiene, for many rare illnesses are spread through filth and sloth. Even if the client feels no pain and experiences no symptoms, the diviner must mark a medical checkup as one of the eboses and insist that this person go. If the orientation is ikú, however, the physician could be the one to bring unnecessary danger through unwarranted medical procedures. Ikú announces that death is near, usually through illness but not always. In this osogbo, invasive surgeries will be risky and can be the cause of death.

Note that Ofún in any osogbo forbids cosmetic surgery. It is unwise to operate on healthy tissue, for the aging process is not a disease state.

In addition, there are various issues flagged by osogbo that the diviner will need to convey to his client. The italero should frankly discuss each of these issues and their relation to the client's life at this time.

- In a severe osogbo, the following dangers exist for the client: rape, spousal abuse, assault and battery, legal complications, injustice, unemployment, emergency operations, and economic loss. If the osogbo is mild, these things will likely happen to another, but they will still affect the client's life (by occurring to a close friend or a relative). The client must take steps to ensure his own personal safety, and he should perform marked eboses as soon as possible.
- If the osogbo is severe, there is also a chance

that a body could be found near the client's home. It may even be buried under or beside this person's house.

- If the client has mused about moving to a new home, an orientation of osogbo marks that move as ebó. The diviner should ask the client first if he has thought about finding a new house or apartment and then should relay this information so there is no chance that the client will lie. For the client to stay in the house now would be to court disaster. The orishas should be given the final say as to where the client moves.
- If the orientation of Ofún makes it clear that a curse has been cast upon the client, only the intervention of Obatalá will remove what has been sent. The italero must work the diloggún until an ebó is marked to this orisha, and this offering or set of rituals must be done immediately lest the client suffer irreversible harm.
- The elderly who open in any orientation of Ofún will have degenerative disease of the muscular, cardiovascular, and skeletal systems. Progressive diseases of this nature cannot be reversed, yet their advancement can be slowed with exercise, good nutrition, and proper medical care. The diviner must encourage an elderly client to have a complete physical.
- If the client does not have a place of his own to call home, Obatalá stands up again to demand that the client work harder to acquire one.
- Finally, any type of osogbo in Ofún will mark the client as one who can become potentially ill, exhausted, or depleted. He will overextend his resources, and it is only through more hard work that they will be renewed. The client must learn to set priorities so that no one part of his life is out of balance with the next. Sickness brought by exhaustion will leave the client bedridden for a long time, so he must be sure to give himself adequate rest, care, and nutrition.

Remember that once the reading is over and the oracle has allowed closure, the italero should remove the gourd of saraeko from beside the front door and throw it out into the street. When this is done, it is customary for all those present at the reading to go out into the street with the diviner and then leave immediately once the porridge has been cast forth. The diviner must take care not to throw the saraeko into the path that those leaving must travel; the energies might latch on to them again and follow them home. Once home, those priests and priestesses should perform this entire ritual of saraeko for themselves to ensure that no negative energies remain from the opening of Ofún. The diviner, in honor of Obatalá, should leave his gourd sitting with the orisha's shrine until midnight. At that time, he removes it and throws it far away from the house so that the last vestiges of Ofún are cleansed. If the osogbo of the letter was severe, before retiring the diviner should give a cool offering to both Elegguá and Obatalá. Only then is the work of Ofún complete and the heat that could bring disaster and discord removed from the diviner's home in full.

## The Prohibitions of Ofún

Ofún is an extremely volatile odu, and through experience with this pattern our house has developed a unique way of prescribing its prohibitions. Normally, in iré the taboos of a sign are considered guidelines; they are not mandatory but should be contemplated so one does not miss one's blessing. When Ofún comes in iré, the prohibitions of ten mouths are still guidelines; however, the prohibitions of the secondary sign as a parent odu are strict taboo. For example, if the letter Ofún Odí (10-7) comes in iré, the taboos of Ofún are recommended as guidelines, and the taboos of Odí are mandatory. The rationale for this is simple: Ofún hides more than it reveals, but the secondary letter modifies the casting of the first. It flags the core of the client's issues with Ofún; therefore, strict enforcement of these taboos will keep the client from danger.

Any type of osogbo demands that the prohibitions of Ofún be prescribed. The diviner must use his own common sense and aché to determine which ones from the list apply to the client sitting at the mat.

If the letter refuses closure, no matter what eboses are prescribed by the orishas, then the prohibitions from the composite odu are given to ensure that the client avoids all harm.

- The food taboos of Ofún are as follows: Avoid alcohol and other intoxicants, whether legal or illegal. Do not consume intestines, white beans, sweet potatoes, gritty fruit (that which includes its seeds in its flesh), and pears. Before consuming fruits or vegetables, wash them thoroughly to remove all traces of dirt and pollutants from the skin.
- Elegguá says that the streets are his home, not one's own, and one spends too much time in them. At night, stay home. During the day, do not go out alone. If travel after dark is a necessity, do not walk; go by car and in the company of a trusted friend.
- In any osogbo, one's home has been marked as a target for robbery, burglary, violence, and loss. Keep one's home well lit; at night, keep exterior lights on. Keep doors and windows locked, even during the day. This taboo is urgent for the next twenty-one to twenty-eight days.
- This letter says many strangers will knock at one's door during odd hours of the day and night. While one may answer the knock, never open the door until the caller has been properly identified. Unless the caller is a close friend or relative, say that now is a bad time; one has guests, and one cannot talk. Call the police immediately to let them know there are strangers or solicitors in the neighborhood going door to door.
- When sitting down to a meal, do not open the door or answer the phone for anyone until the meal is over. After going to bed, answer neither the door nor the phone. Even God will come back another day!
- Use no color other than white on one's bed. Do not sleep in any stripes or patterns, ever. Dress in white when sleeping, and wear white frequently during the day. Even if one is wearing clothing of some other color, wear white somewhere on the body to promote coolness.
- Do not let anyone, especially those of another sex, stay in one's house for an extended period.
- Remove trash on a daily basis. Gather it into one receptacle, and have no more than one trash can in the home.
- Cover any holes in the house. Do not allow bottles to accumulate; cap, cover, or throw them away.
- When walking in either the rain or moonlight, cover one's head or else madness will come.
- Avoid funerals and wakes that are not for family members. If someone in the family dies, consult with the orishas before going, and make ebó. Ikú himself could be at this ceremony, waiting to take another life. If anyone outside of one's family becomes gravely or terminally ill, do not go to visit without first making ebó.
- Do not argue with anyone who is a child of Ofún from itá. Avoid children of Ofún as much as possible.
- Be cautious when dealing with young children. Always have another adult present; do not be with a child alone. Otherwise, accusations will be made.

## Marking Ebó in Ofún: Initial Considerations

Once the diviner has marked Ofún as coming in either iré or osogbo and has determined the source of this orientation, he must prescribe to the client the eboses that are needed to propitiate or assuage that source. Not all sources of iré and osogbo require eboses; the diviner must make a careful study of the different types of iré and osogbo and their influences on the client in Ofún. (See the study of Ofún in iré, beginning on page 441, and in osogbo, beginning on page 446.)

In the family of Ofún, the aché of three spirits is essential in all composites: Obatalá, Oshún, and Oyá. When ten mouths opens on the mat in any combination, the client turns to these three orishas for help and resolution. If none of these spirits claims ebó in the session, the italero must recommend a rogación before Obatalá for the one who sits at the mat. After the cleansing, the client should offer all three of these spirits a simple adimú.

When attempting to supplicate these spirits in any composite of ten mouths, the client may use the following eboses to assist his evolution. All are native to this family of odu, and the diviner may prescribe from them freely using his own aché.

### Traditional Eboses in Ofún

Keep in mind that certain elements of ebó are considered traditional in Ofún. Because Ofún marks ten in all things, each ebó marked with the shells should incorporate this number somehow so that the letter itself is placated with the orisha. Additionally, whenever a sacrifice is needed through this sign, the diviner should try to pick the animals used from the following list: two pigeons or doves, a single rooster, a single hen, and four white pigeons. Any rogación given might also include snails, because they are sacred to Obatalá and their secretions cool and refresh the orí. Adimú-type offerings can include cascarilla, cocoa butter, coconuts, coconut oil, and horse's hair (in the form of the fly whisk given to the orishas considered to be royalty).

## Ebó Elese Obatalá
## *(Ebó at the Feet of Obatalá)*

The first rule of marking ebó to Obatalá or any orisha through Ofún is this: Try to include cascarilla in all eboses one makes. If cascarilla cannot be used in the ebó itself, before making the offering mark the forehead with it and coat the hands liberally in the white powder. The reason for this is twofold. First, cascarilla is the only substance we have in our religion that truly resembles Olófin's nature, and he is the most powerful orisha, the one who can literally make something out of nothing. Cascarilla is soft and white, yet it is easily dispersed throughout the atmosphere until it becomes invisible; it is still there, but in particles too small to be seen. So it is with Olófin; even though he cannot be seen, he is with us always. Second, while it resembles Olófin's nature, cascarilla is owned by Obatalá, becauses he owns all white things. By using cascarilla in all our eboses, the cool, eternally forgiving nature of this orisha is called to witness what is done. Obatalá is the true owner of Ofún, and he should be present in all that is done to placate ten mouths.

### *Ten Coconuts Cleansing*

If Ofún marks the need for a cleansing before Obatalá, this ebó will satisfy both ten mouths and the orisha. The client sands ten coconuts smooth. He then rubs them with cocoa butter and sprinkles them heavily with cascarilla. He brings them to the diviner's home with a basket big enough to hold all ten; he lines the basket with enough white cloth to not only cover the basket but also provide some extra material overlapping the floor. Immediately, he presents these to Obatalá, setting the ten coconuts outside the basket, on the white cloth overlapping the floor. Every day for the next ten days the client cleanses himself with a single coconut, putting it in the basket when he is done so that he does not reuse it. After the tenth coconut has been used, the client ties all ten in the white cloth and takes the bundle to the door of a church.

### *Ten-Biscuit Petition*

If the client came to the shells with a specific request or concern and Obatalá stands up to help, this ebó will enlist the orisha's aid on the client's quest. On a brown piece of paper, the client writes a petition to Obatalá. He coats the paper in cocoa butter and sandwiches it between two sheets of rolled cotton. He places the cotton package on a large white serving platter. On top of this, he places a circle of ten white, freshly baked biscuits, each buttered freely with cocoa butter. In the center of the circle goes a single white seven-day candle. Paying foribale to Obatalá, the client prays for what is in his heart, sprinkles cascarilla liberally over the entire ebó, and lights the candle before placing it on top of Obatalá's sopera. The ebó remains with the orisha until the candle burns out. At the end of this time, the client discards the biscuits by the front door of a church.

### *Meringue Bath*

If Ofún marks a bath for cleansing and Obatalá stands up in the composite to defend the client, this ebó will satisfy both Ofún and the orisha. Beat the whites of ten eggs with a mixer until they are foamy; to this, add five heaping tablespoons of sugar. Continue to beat the eggs and sugar until they form a thick foam; the meringue is done when the egg whites will hold the mixer's imprint. Divide the meringue into ten small baking cups, swirling the top so that a pretty peak is formed. Before the meringues "set," sprinkle the tops with white sugar. Serve these to Obatalá on a white plate, leaving them with him for ten hours. At the end of this time, the client bathes with all ten meringues, scrubbing himself from head to toe with the sweet confection. After showering to remove the sticky residue, he must dress in white for the remainder of the day.*

### *Spiritual Baths*

If Ofún marks an osogbo for which no other cleansing can be found, the diviner may mark a series of ten spiritual baths for the client. The diviner makes these baths with ten ingredients, including Obatalá's omiero, which must be prepared fresh before the orisha's shrine. To the omiero, he adds cow's milk, goat's milk, cocoa butter, grated coconut, coconut milk, white flowers, cascarilla, sandolo, and a macerated snail. He divides the bath into ten equal parts and gives them to the client, who stores them in the refrigerator. Every night for ten nights the client bathes in one part. He must dress in white the entire time.

## Ebó Elese Oshún
## *(Ebó at the Feet of Oshún)*

### *Cornmeal Balls with Honey*

When Oshún stands up in a casting of Ofún, the following ebó will satisfy and placate her. To make this adimú the client must provide the following ingredients: cornmeal, honey, cascarilla, smoked fish, jutía, and toasted corn.

In a mixing bowl, combine the cornmeal, honey, cascarilla, smoked fish, and jutía; mix well, forming a paste. Cover a serving platter with plenty of toasted corn, and slather it with a generous amount of honey, enough to cover all the corn. From the cornmeal paste, form ten balls, and place them on the serving platter. Serve them to Oshún, allowing them to remain with him for ten days. At the end of this time, the client discards the ebó in a river.

Note that if a cleansing is marked in Ofún, this ebó to Oshún may be used to satisfy that requirement as well. When discarding the ebó in the river, the client uses each ball to cleanse himself. Holding one ball in each hand, he rubs himself, beginning with the head and ending with the feet, and then casts both into the river.

### *Pumpkin Leaf Bath*

If Oshún stands up in the reading to offer a cleansing, the diviner may prescribe this bath. The client must provide the following ingredients: river water, water from Oshún's sopera, ten pumpkin leaves, ten perfumes, and honey.

Mix a large amount of river water with a small amount of Oshún's water. Into this, crush the pumpkin leaves until the water is tinted green. Add equal amounts of each perfume and a liberal amount of honey. Divide the water into ten equal parts and store them in the refrigerator. Every night for ten days, the client bathes with one part of this bath, dressing in white when finished. This will help cleanse him of Ofún's osogbo.

## Ebó Elese Oyá
## *(Ebó at the Feet of Oyá)*

### *Ten Egg Cleansing*

If Oyá stands up in the reading to offer a cleansing, one may use the following ebó for this. The client must provide the herbs cascarilla, verdolaga, bleo blanco, sauco blanco, almendra, siempre viva, and antiponla, as well as ten guinea eggs.

The priest seasons a large bowl with a liberal sprinkling of cascarilla and fills it with fresh, cool

*Obatalá's number for ebó is eight; however, one placates not only him but also Ofún with this ebó. Therefore, ten meringues are made and presented to the orisha for his blessing before administering the bath.

water. In the water, he crushes the herbs, wringing them until all the juices are infused into the bath; it should be a dark green color. That night, he bathes the client with a portion of the bath, dresses him in white, and has him remain in white for the next ten days. Before leaving the priest's home, the client should place the ten guinea eggs in the remaining bathwater and leave the ebó in front of Oyá overnight.

The next morning, the client removes one egg from the bath and cleanses himself from head to toe with it, rubbing his body thoroughly with the egg. Immediately, he takes that egg to the gates of a cemetery. This continues every day for ten days, until the last egg is used. On the tenth day, the client takes the bowl with the herbal water to the graveyard as well and pours it over the last egg at the cemetery gates.

## The First Composite Odu of Ofún, Ofún Okana (10-1)

### The Proverbs of Ofún Okana

- Ofún Okana is evil and treason.
- Sickness is close to you.
- He who is fond of gold never has any.
- He who embraces a lot cannot squeeze hard.
- If the leopard walks at high noon, he is only looking for a fight.
- The one who provokes the leopard is only looking for a fight.
- [In iré] I am not going to die yet, for my time has not come.
- A bell without a sound is of no use to Obatalá.
- A bell that has no clapper cannot call anyone's attention.

### The Message of Ofún Okana

When a cast of ten mouths is followed by a cast of one mouth, the odu Ofún Okana is open on the mat. Immediately, the diviner must say, "Maferefún Shangó!" Here this orisha stands beside the client; he is a potent force bringing safety from turmoil and evolution amid crisis. This letter, no matter its orientation, marks the client for many difficulties, obstacles, and illnesses; this person has come to the mat not because of his faith in the orishas, but because his situation has become desperate. He seeks help, but he is not sure that the orishas can help. To settle the client into this reading and make him listen, the diviner should tell him, "Shangó says you have an unusual mark or scar on your body. It is from either birth or injury. You could have died; the injury could have been much worse, and Shangó says that he is the one who saved you." The diviner should give the client a moment to rationalize this, and agree, and then continue, "Shangó also says that someone you know has recently lost a daughter. Due to problems at home, she has run away. Your friend should not worry, for she will come back on her own." If the client acknowledges that his own daughter has run away, the diviner must forbid him to curse her or call the police; she has many things to work out on her own, and she will return in her own time. He should encourage the client to pray for her; Shangó will keep her safe from harm. After exposing these two truths, the client will settle into the reading and listen to its advice.

While all Ofún has to say should be related to the client, investigate each of the following items thoroughly as well; to some degree, all will apply to the client who has opened in Ofún Okana.

- In this odu, "Maferefún Obatalá!" While Shangó blesses the client, Obatalá blesses all those whom he cares about; he watches over them and keeps them safe from harm. The diviner should tell the client that no matter what happens in his home, to his family, or to those whom he loves, he can protect all of them by praying to Obatalá and making ebó.
- The client must guard his head and his face at all times, especially when outdoors or playing sports. An injury can occur while this letter is in effect, and any injury to these regions will be disfiguring.
- If the client experiences any pain in his muscles or bones, he should seek medical attention. He can avoid serious disease or decay if he catches

problems in these areas while they are still minor.

- The client must be on guard against pregnancy. The combination of Ofún and Okana presages reproductive troubles, miscarriages, abortion, and birth defects. Pregnancy will invite a host of medical difficulties for both the mother and the unborn child. The client must use adequate contraceptives or practice abstinence for the next ten months. At the end of this time, if the client and his partner wish to conceive, they must come together and make ebó to the orishas.
- By avoiding gossip, lies, deceit, and adultery, the client can avoid the inherent osogbo of this sign.

## The Prohibitions of Ofún Okana

- Do not have sex on Thursdays. If this reading is an itá or a bajado, sex on Thursdays is prohibited for life.
- During holy week, cover the mirrors in one's house. During this time, do not work the religion for any but oneself; only prayer is allowed.
- The consumption of rabbit is taboo.
- If one comes because one's daughter has left, neither curse her nor send the police after her. She will come back on her own time.
- Do not go out of the home for seven days for anything other than essentials, such as work and grocery shopping. Going out at night during this time is strictly forbidden.

## The Eboses of Ofún Okana

Special considerations for aleyos and aborishas: When Ofún Okana opens on the mat in an osogbo from Elegguá's diloggún, the diviner should pay careful attention to the misfortune's origin. If an osogbo elese egun (at the feet of one's ancestral spirits) or elese ará onú (at the feet of heaven's inhabitants) opens, the client is in danger from the dead that surround him. An osogbo elese Otonowá (from heaven) always marks serious issues between the client and Shangó. Elese ocha (at the feet of the orishas) from Shangó, Aganyú, or Elegguá is extremely dangerous; for some reason, the aché between this client and that spirit is so strained and tense that one might say the spiritual force is angry at him. The diviner must work slowly and skillfully to determine the reason for this. He prescribes a series of offerings to propitiate that spirit, giving obí after each to ensure acceptance. Once the orisha gives *aláfia* or *etawa* in response to the eboses, the client should have a rogación before that spirit's shrine. Until these things have been done, the client is in danger.

After marking the larishe (if any) and prescribing the appropriate eboses of the parent odu and as determined by the source of iré or osogbo, the diviner should attempt to close the oracle. If it refuses closure, the first option for ebó goes to Obatalá. The client returns to the diviner's house the next day for a rogación, bringing the following ingredients: grated coconut, cascarilla, cotton, cocoa butter, cow's milk, goat's milk, white flowers, grated pears, mashed bananas, and sandolo. The diviner gives him a rogación before Obatalá. After the rogación, the client must dress in white for ten days; this seals the cleansing and brings blessing from Obatalá.

If the osogbo of Ofún Okana is severe and the letter still refuses closure, the diviner should ask, "Rogación sodidé?" If the odu marks this type of rogación as ebó, instead of beginning with the client's head and ending with his feet, the diviner begins with his feet and ends with his head. This will elevate his orí toward Obatalá. The diviner might also consider asking, "Eborí?" Marking this as ebó, the diloggún directs the diviner to feed the client's orí two white pigeons or white doves immediately after the rogación but before wrapping his head in cotton and white cloth.

Obatalá may claim other eboses in this letter; the diviner should ask, "Ebó elese Obatalá?" If he takes an ebó through Ofún Okana, the proper offering is a series of rituals done with the rogación already prescribed. Before the rogación, the diviner crushes and sprinkles eight balls of efun on the floor, forming a thick circle. He places a silver bowl on this circle and lines the inside of it with white cotton. He then brings Obatalá down into the bowl. There, the diviner feeds him four white pigeons, covering the blood with cascarilla. After the sacrifice, he shrouds the entire bowl in white cloth with the orisha still inside. Without cleaning Obatalá, the diviner lifts him up and gives the client a rogación before him. After the client leaves, the diviner may bring Obatalá down once more, washing him in either fresh, cool water or omiero. Once the client completes his ten days in white, he returns to the diviner's home, and the diviner sacrifices to Obatalá again. He prepares the floor with efun as before and brings Obatalá down in a silver bowl lined with white cotton. This time, the diviner sacrifices four pigeons and a single white rooster. Then he covers Obatalá with white cloth and lets him rest overnight in his sacrifice. The next morning, the diviner washes the orisha and elevates him once more.

If Obatalá will not stand up to elevate the client in Ofún Okana, the diviner should see if Shangó has the solution to the client's osogbo, asking, "Larishe si Shangó?" If answer is yes, the diviner performs the same ritual just described for Obatalá for Shangó instead, with some minor changes. First, the rogación must include grated coconut, cascarilla, cotton, cocoa butter, grated pears, mashed bananas, grated apples, red flowers, honey, a touch of epó, and a dash of jutía and smoked fish. The red flowers, epó, jutía, and fish are considered hot ingredients, so the diviner must use them sparingly on the client's head. The diviner must ask, "Rogación sodidé?" If the oracle answers yes, the rogación begins at the client's feet and ends with his head. Next, the diviner asks, "Eborí?" If eborí is marked, after the rogación the diviner feeds two white pigeons or white doves to the client's head before wrapping it with cotton and white cloth. Finally, the diviner asks, "Ebó elese Shangó?" Any ebó marked to this orisha must be given immediately before the rogación and again after the ten days in white are completed. The client discards any ebó made to Shangó at the foot of either the royal palm or a ceiba tree.

This sign has other mandatory considerations for ebó:

- The client needs a series of masses for egun. The first mass is for the most recently deceased member of his family; the remaining masses are given to his ancestors as a whole.
- If the client is pregnant, ebó must be made to Elegguá immediately. After sacrificing to him, the diviner should give a rogación of the client's abdomen before both Yemayá and Oshún. Sacrifice two pigeons to the unborn child after the rogación; give plenty of epó and honey as well.

If these considerations are not enough to close the session, the diviner must turn to the eboses of the parent odu, Ofún (see page 489). Something there is needed for the client's evolution.

## The Second Composite Odu of Ofún, Ofún Ejioko (10-2)

### The Proverbs of Ofún Ejioko

- Wherever you turn, there are traps and prisons.
- With your eyes, you will get into trouble.
- The one who curses is cursed.
- He who rises early has money in his pocket.

### The Message of Ofún Ejioko

When an initial cast of ten mouths, Ofún, precedes a second cast of two mouths, Eji Oko, the odu Ofún Ejioko is open on the mat. Ofún Oyekun and Ofún Yeku are other names for this sign. The diviner says, "Maferefún Obatalá! Maferefún Elegguá!" These two orishas can be the client's salvation; he must live by making ebó to both. He also praises Oyá, saying, "Maferefún Oyá!" for she knows the secrets of this letter, and by her graces the client can avoid many of its dangers.

The diviner should tell the client that this letter speaks of traps, deception, treason, and prison. If the client hopes to avoid these things, there are many pieces of advice that he must keep in mind. First, he must never loan out personal articles or money, for they will be almost impossible to get back without some type of legal action. If the client needs money, he must not borrow it or take out a loan because he will not be able to pay it back. The use of or extension of credit in this odu is one's financial demise. He must be more reserved in his behavior; he should not argue, fight, or raise his hands toward anyone in anger, for in these ways will the law be brought to his front door. Others may ask the client to store personal articles or packages in his home, and he should refuse. He also should not buy any secondhand items from another; they could be stolen property.

Keep in mind that the client for whom this odu has fallen is a dreamer; however, his dreams are centered on the dead, and one spirit in particular causes trouble. The diviner should mark eboses and spiritual masses to appease the dead, and they will work for, and not against, the client. If the identity of the troublesome spirit cannot be determined, the diviner should ask him what item he has in his home that belongs to the dead. The spirit will be the former owner of that item.

The diviner should also explore the following points with the client:

- If he is a man, the client must be careful about the women he dates, and he must avoid infidelity at all costs.
- If the client is a woman, she should not play with her man, for this will bring violence.
- If the client is a woman, she will one day date, and perhaps marry, a babalawo. Oshún might be her crown.

## The Prohibitions of Ofún Ejioko

- There is a prohibition for the italero in this odu: He may not make an ebó for the client unless he first makes ebó for himself. Ofún Ejioko promises danger for the priest who breaks this taboo.
- Do not loan either money or possessions. Do not use credit cards or borrow money; one will never be able to pay back the loan and will ruin one's credit.
- Do not store anything for anyone; these could be stolen items and will bring the law to the front door.
- Do not do favors for others, or one will end up in jail.
- Avoid infidelity and adultery.

## The Eboses of Ofún Ejioko

Special considerations for aleyos and aborishas: When Ofún Ejioko comes from Elegguá in an osogbo, the diviner must pay careful attention to the misfortune's origin. If it comes elese otonowá (from heaven), there are dangerous issues between this client and Ochosi. Elese ocha (at the feet of the orishas) from Elegguá, Ogún, or Ochosi is extremely dangerous; for some reason, the aché between the client and that spirit is so strained and tense that one might say the spiritual force is angry with the client. Carefully, the diviner must work to determine the reason for this rift and then prescribe several eboses to placate the orisha. After each offering, the priest uses obí to determine if the spirit accepts the offering in good faith. Once obí gives good letters and the eboses are complete, the client should have a rogación before that spirit's shrine. Until these things are done, the one sitting at the mat is in danger from the very spirits he has turned to for help.

The sign Ofún Ejioko is volatile; its opening on the mat enfolds the diviner in dangerous currents, and before he makes any ebó for the client he must make ebó for himself. The first step is to have another priest or priestess give him a rogación using ten ingredients before his guardian orisha. Grated coconut, efun, cocoa butter, cotton, honey, and molasses are staples in this cleansing; to this the diviner should add four of his guardian orisha's favorite fruits, all grated. Next, the diviner reviews the eboses marked for the client carefully; once the rogación is done, he gives a simple adimú to each orisha who has claimed ebó. A libation of fresh water, a colored seven-day candle, and a prayer will suffice. If a harsh osogbo came with this sign, the diviner must consult Elegguá's diloggún for himself. He may need more potent eboses to cleanse himself of what the client brought to the mat.

Note that if any initiates came to this session, they, too, must offer some token adimú to each orisha who stood up for the client; they do this to their own spirits. Remember, odu is a symbiotic creature, and by sitting at the mat all have participated in this client's life vicariously. Now, all must make ebó to cleanse themselves of what has opened around them.

For the client opening in Ofún Ejioko, some eboses are mandatory. This letter marks the client for a session with Ifá; Orúnmila has issues to settle with him. If the client is a woman, she must prepare to receive kofá de Orúnmila; if the client is a man, he needs mano de Orúnmila. The diviner should encourage the client to go to Ifá within ten days.

The Ibeyi are a necessity. If the client does not have them, he must receive them. If the client does have them, the diviner should determine if they require a sacrifice, asking, "Ebó elese los Ibeyi?"

Finally, for twenty-one days the client must wear a red parrot feather in his hair; after this, he must wear the feather whenever he attends any orisha function. Note that if Ofún Ejioko comes in an itá, the client must wear this feather for life.

Now the diviner asks the odu for closure. If it remains open, he should consider the following eboses:

- Ofún has much to do with the dead. The client must host a series of masses in his home for egun.
- If Oyá has marked a larishe to Ofún Ejioko's osogbo, yet the letter refuses closure, the client should have a rogación sodidé before her shrine. This rogación, however, is complex, requiring the help of ten initiates (including the diviner). Each priest employed to help must prepare and bring one of the following ten ingredients: grated coconut, grated cocoa butter, cascarilla, cotton, honey, molasses, nine flowers of different colors, grated eggplant, and two fruits sacred to Oyá, grated. The client comes to the diviner's home dressed in white, bringing two multicolored seven-day candles and a length of burgundy ribbon cut so that its length matches his own height. Beginning with the client's feet and ending with his head, each priest adds the one ingredient he has brought for the rogación, placing it on each center of aché. As he places his ingredient, each priest offers the entire litany of prayers for the rogación, as if he were the only one doing the ceremony; this adds the full strength of each initiate to the ebó. After all have worked to elevate the client, the diviner gives obí to ensure the ceremony is complete; he then wraps the client's head in cotton and white cloth. All leave the room, allowing the client time to pray before Oyá for his elevation and protection. When he is done, he lights the two candles to her and wraps his ribbon around her sopera. Later, the diviner will put that ribbon inside Oyá's tureen, and it stays with her for an indefinite period.
- If Ofún Ejioko comes in an itá, the following ebó must be done: At his godparent's home, in front of the orishas, the client sleeps with a chain and lock around his hands (the lock must be the type using a key). In the morning, after being wakened by his godparent, he goes outdoors holding a rooster in his chained hands. The godparent carries the client's Elegguá. At the first door or gate found, the godparent unlocks the lock and unties the chain. Both the lock and the chain are left there. Elegguá is fed the rooster in front of this gate. (If the client is an initiate, he does this under his godparent's supervision. If he is an aborisha, the godparent does it for him.) The rooster is left before this gate. Next, godparent and godchild go to the ocean. Elegguá sits on the shore while the client walks with the key out into the ocean. When he can safely walk no farther, he throws the key as far out as he can. Elegguá is then washed clean of the sacrifice in the ocean water. Later that same day, with Elegguá as a witness, the godparent gives the client a rogación before his guardian orisha using ten separate ingredients. For the next sixteen days, the client dresses in white from head to toe and wears a red parrot feather in his hair.

If these considerations are not enough to close the session for an aleyo or an aborisha, the diviner must turn to the eboses of the parent odu, Ofún (see page 489). Something there is needed for the client's evolution.

If Ofún Ejioko refuses closure for an initiate, the orisha speaking here could be marking a tambor as the solution to all his troubles. The diviner must try to mark this tambor first to the orisha whose shells are being consulted. If that orisha refuses the drum, he should try to mark it to Obatalá, Elegguá, Oyá, Ochosi, or Orisha Oko.*

If these are not enough to close Ofún Ejioko for an initiate, the diviner must turn to the eboses of the parent odu, Ofún.

## The Third Composite Odu of Ofún, Ofún Ogundá (10-3)

### The Proverbs of Ofún Ogundá

- You have been cursed from the womb.
- Forgive those who curse you, for he who forgives is saved.
- A bad hunter will use poisoned arrows.
- Mud is mushy, stiff, and wet.
- Ofún tastes palm oil.
- It bears fruit, but we cannot pick it; the fruit falls, and we cannot gather it.

### The Message of Ofún Ogundá

When a cast of ten mouths, Ofún, precedes a cast of three mouths, Ogundá, the odu Ofún Ogundá is open. This odu is powerful; immediately, the diviner must dip his finger in epó and put his finger in his mouth. He should direct the client to do the same and then pass the palm oil throughout the room so all may taste it. This gesture honors the odu open on the mat. The diviner also honors Shangó, Ogún, Orisha Oko, Olokun, Yewá, and Obatalá, saying to each, "Maferefún!"

Ofún Ogundá requires many eboses of the client, and all will prove a financial hardship for him. The diviner, however, must charge well for his work. This pattern opens because the client has put himself in this situation. No one but he is responsible for his life. This person has gossiped, laid traps, slandered, and lied to those who are closest to him. He has been deceitful and has poor character. Even though he wants to change and evolve, he must pay for his past transgressions. The expense of ebó is not an indulgence but a deterrent. The orishas will help, but their help does not come without cost. The diviner should tell the client, "What is prescribed for you will help absolve you, but it is not absolution itself. Continue to conduct yourself as you have, and one day you will pay the most expensive derecho: your life."

Shangó is here to defend the client; if he listens to the advice of Ofún Ogundá and makes ebó, Shangó will destroy those who seek to hurt him. Yemayá nurtures the client. She offers the support of a mother, yet she is no doting mother; her support comes in the form of advice and discipline. Ogún and Orisha Oko are also found here. It is said that through this odu, Orisha Oko was once working to sustain the growing population on the earth, trying to keep humans from hunger, but his meager wooden tools of agriculture could not adequately till the hardened soil. He plied Ogún with epó, and Ogún created iron tools to till the earth. Both work hard to benefit civilization, and both will work hard to support the client. Olokun and Yewá are also found here; while the client hides his true intentions from all, including the diviner and the orishas, he cannot hide anything from these two titanic forces. They know all secrets, including the client's, although neither will reveal them to the diviner. The diviner should say, "These two know your heart; they know what lies in you, the thoughts you think, and the evil you have done. Even though I may not know, they know. They watch. They wait." Finally, of all the orishas, Obatalá is the most forgiving. If the client commits to change and evolution, in time Obatalá himself will cleanse his past transgressions.

We say that one who comes in Ofún Ogundá has

*Note that if the tambor is marked during a iyawó's itá through either Elegguá or the orisha of the head, that client is marked to play to all his orishas in time. Also, proper protocol must be followed in giving this ebó: The godparent's orisha (from whom the iyawó's head is born) must be given a drum before the client can play for his own orishas.

been "cursed since the womb"; this is a person whose life has been filled with illness, tragedy, and bad luck. Now that the odu has opened on the mat, it not only points out that his life has become extremely hard and filled with danger, but it also says that these things may come to an end soon if the client follows the advice of the reading and performs quickly any prescribed eboses. Although many may try to harm this client now (physically, emotionally, and spiritually), under the influence of Ofún this person may not lash out in vicious acts, and under the influence of Ogundá he may not enter into arguments, violence, or any type of gossip. To make it through the influence of this odu, the client must remain cool and calm. He should take care when going out into the street at night. Avoid threesomes at all costs, and take precautions against robbery, rape, and accidents. Realize that a woman who comes in this letter has already been or will soon be raped or molested. A man who opens in this odu, as well, should be on guard against some type of sexual violation. Now is not the time to become pregnant, for the mother and child will be in danger; unfortunately, if a woman who opens in this sign is pregnant and thinking about an abortion for health reasons, this surgical procedure could bring health complications.

There are many severe warnings that come in this letter. First, he who mimics others finds danger. The client should avoid get-rich, pyramid, and illegal schemes; for the client they will bring only ruin. Many secret enemies surround this person, and he must be on guard constantly. He should keep his back against the wall so that no one can sneak up on him from behind. Danger can come from in front as well, but if the back is against a strong foundation, the client can be more vigilant. No matter the orientation of this letter, it can bring little iré, and if it falls in osogbo, even the most minor afflictions can become severe. The client must give up vices and bad habits and monitor the health closely. Any complaints in the muscles, bones, stomach, or genitals warrant a trip to the physician. Small complaints will flare into large symptoms if they are not treated. A woman who opens in this sign will have problems in her reproductive system. Also, until this odu passes, elective surgery is not wise. If a health problem demands emergency treatment and the client is allowed to choose between medical (pharmaceutical and other noninvasive treatments) and surgical interventions, he should opt for medical and not surgical. If no option other than surgery is offered, the client should try to get a second opinion. If surgery is imminent, he should see the diviner to mark ebó.

## The Prohibitions of Ofún Ogundá

- When this letter opens on the mat, the italero is warned not to work for free. He must charge when he does ebó for the client, and he must charge well. Once the session is closed, he must not refer to this odu again unless he charges a derecho. The client will come back for more information, and it is by reciting the proverbs and patakís for free that danger will come to the italero.
- Be careful when going out into the street at night. Avoid threesomes of any sort at all costs, and take precautions against robbery, rape, and accidents.
- Do not loiter at street corners. One must protect one's back at all times.

## The Eboses of Ofún Ogundá

Special considerations for aleyos and aborishas: When Elegguá opens Ofún Ogundá in an osogbo, the diviner must pay careful attention to the origin. If it comes elese otonowá (from heaven), Ogún is angry and the forces of heaven give witness to his wrath. If it comes elese Ogún, he is upset with the client. Carefully, the diviner examines this letter and all the client brings to the mat to determine the reason for Ogún's wrath. He must appease him with several eboses. After each ebó, the priest must use obí to determine whether it has been accepted. Once the coconut's letters come out clean (aláfia or ejife), the client may sit for a rogación before Ogún's shrine to correct the aché between him and the spirit. Until these things are done, the client will remain in danger; Ogún is not to be toyed with.

When Ofún Ogundá opens on the mat for an aleyo who has nothing of ocha, the diviner must prescribe the elekes. These are needed for his protection and evolution. The diviner should tell the client, however, that the problems he has in life will grow; he will be safe from harm, but things around him will continue to broil. In time, the orishas will draw him closer to protect him, and he will have to take many initiations to clear his osogbo.

If the client is an aborisha, he should already have the the warriors (Elegguá, Ogún, Ochosi, and Ósun), the Ibeyi (the twins Taewó and Kaindé), and Olokun. The diviner should tell him that as soon as he goes home, he must give the following adimús to his orishas: a saraeko of water, cornmeal, and honey to Elegguá, Ogún, and Ochosi; cocoa butter to Ósun (the client should rub him with it); a dish of candy to the Ibeyi twins; and a mat with fruits to Olokun. Note that if the aborisha lacks any of these orishas, he must make preparations for their reception as soon as possible. Without this intervention in his life, he cannot overcome the osogbos of Ofún Ogundá. Until he receives them, however, he may make these eboses to the diviner's orishas.

Now the diviner has his first chance to close the oracle. If it will not close, he investigates the following ebó:

- The client may have issues with Shangó, Obatalá, Ogún, or Oshún. To see if any will take ebó, the diviner should consider asking, "Ebó elese [orisha's name]?" If the answer is yes, he uses the diloggún to mark the appropriate offering.

If this consideration is not enough to close the odu for an aleyo or an aborisha, the diviner must turn to the eboses of the parent odu, Ofún (see page 489). If the client is an initiate, however, the diviner should investigate the following possibilities:

- If the client does not have Ogún's diloggún, he must receive it now. The itá of Ogún will separate him from past difficulties, bringing many solutions.
- Because Ogún and Orisha Oko made a pact in this odu to work together, an initiate who does not have Orisha Oko must receive him. These two orishas must live side by side so they can work together on the client's behalf.
- If the client's osogbo is severe, the diviner may prescribe the reception of the knife (the initiation known as pinaldo). The itá given after the client has received the knife will illuminate the path the priest is to walk for the rest of his life.
- If this client has already taken pinaldo, or if the oracle will not close after the knife has been prescribed, the last option for ebó is itá with Elegguá and the client's own crown. The diviner should have an oriaté feed both orishas four legs; the next day the oriaté must give this client itá from both. Their advice will get him back on track.

If these do not close the reading, the diviner must turn to the eboses of the parent odu. Something there is needed for the client's evolution.

## The Fourth Composite Odu of Ofún, Ofún Irosun (10-4)

### The Proverbs of Ofún Irosun

- Jealousy brings tragedy.
- Within the family, siblings fight.
- No one listens to a boaster.

### The Message of Ofún Irosun

When an initial cast of ten mouths is followed by one of four mouths, the odu Ofún Irosun is open on the mat. Having made this cast, the diviner pays homage to Orúnmila, Obatalá, Yemayá, Olokun, Yewá, and egun, saying to each, "Maferefún" All six spirits are fierce in this pattern, and it will take the aché of each to surmount the client's problems and push him toward his destiny.

Although Orúnmila will not speak directly in the diloggún, Ofún Irosun is the odu in which the hen, for her rudeness and arrogance, was sacrificed to Orúnmila for the first time. Since that day, he has preferred to eat hen over all other animals. The diviner should warn the client not to be like the hen; instead, he must be kind and gracious to his visitors, friends, and loved ones lest life consume him for his arrogance.

This sign speaks of Obatalá's elder paths and the elderly. To turn misfortunes into blessings, and to hold his iré firm, the client must be kind and gentle to the elderly, watching over them and attending to their needs. Likewise, he must respect his religious elders if for no other reason beyond the seasoned aché in their heads. Not only do the elder priests and priestesses have the strength of ocha in their heads, but also they have spent years in this religion learning, studying, praying, and praising the spirits. Though each might not know everything, all have something to teach. The client must soak in this knowledge as it is offered, respectfully, so that there can be evolution.

Ofún Irosun also alludes to the ocean, from whose ceaseless waves Yemayá was born. Like the ocean, this letter is deep and mysterious; Olokun, queen of the depths, knows intimately the secrets it holds. The diviner should tell the client that Olokun knows all about him, even things he does not know himself; secrets that he hides even from the diviner cannot be hidden from Olokun. He must propitiate this orisha well, for she will punish or bless as she feels is deserved. Yewá, queen of the grave, is important here because Ofún Irosun whispers of death and the dead. The client must pray to her that his grave is not opened; Ikú is near, and he stalks him stealthily. This also speaks of ancient secrets; here the spirits of the dead clamor for attention and respect. Those whose names and faces have been obscured by the centuries rise beneath the client. They come for offerings, for sacrifices, and for propitiation. All these are theirs by right of the client's birth. It must be given.

When this pattern displays itself on the mat, the diviner knows that a great darkness, an overwhelming chasm of boredom and loneliness, arises within the client. Day by day this grows greater, threatening to plunge him into despair. He is thinking about giving up, about running away, about losing himself in a new environment that may or may not be any better for him. If the client follows his heart on this and the sign has opened in any type of osogbo, the adventure will bring more disappointment than happiness. In osogbo, he would do better to change his routine than his lifestyle at this time. He should not alter his dwelling, town, friends, lover, spouse, and customs; he should not abandon the life he has created. Tragedy will enter this person's life soon from both friends and family, but if he makes the eboses prescribed in a timely manner, he can avoid many of these things. Boredom can motivate one to better things, yes, but unlike the cliché "The grass is always greener on the other side," the client will discover, in the end, that his current life really isn't that bad.

In all castings of Ofún Irosun, the diviner should keep the following considerations in mind during the session:

- The client's eyes are vulnerable; they could become weak or damaged. If any redness, irritation, or blurry vision is noted, the client must go to an ophthalmologist immediately. A serious condition is developing that needs treatment. If the client participates in athletics, he must wear proper eyewear to avoid an accident. If the osogbo of ano or ikú has opened, not only could the client's sight be compromised, but also a severe blow to the eyes could result in death.
- The orishas are not happy with the client's home. It is too dark, dirty, unkempt, or oppressive. The client must clean his house thoroughly, emptying it of all that is not beautiful or uplifting. He should give his home more light and warmth, making it a place to entertain and receive loved ones. Iré will come to him when he does this.
- Ofún Irosun speaks of a spirit and a box; this is a riddle that the client must figure out for himself. The diviner should merely tell him the riddle, letting him rationalize it himself.
- A great spiritual entity is close to this person; it wants to bring great light and evolution to his life. The diviner should tell the client to spend more time with his egun. The more he works with them, the closer this spirit will come, and the greater its influence will be.

- Finally, this letter can be summed up in one word: mystery. The diviner should tell the client that he is a mysterious person to whom mysterious things happen. If he heeds the advice of this reading, those mysteries will be pleasant: If he ignores the advice of Ofún Irosun, these mysterious currents will unveil sinister influences in his life.

## The Prohibitions of Ofún Irosun

- Do not abandon one's religious customs. While one may love the orishas, one must also love the religion from which one comes. This odu does not require one to take the sacraments of the former faith, for such would be blasphemy and this letter prohibits sacrilegious acts. However, for the sake of one's spiritual court, continue to honor one's previous faith.
- Do not argue with elders, including those in one's family and those in one's faith.
- Avoid violence and harsh words.
- Do not use alcohol or illegal intoxicants.

## The Eboses of Ofún Irosun

Special considerations for aleyos and aborishas: When Ofún Irosun opens on the mat in an osogbo through Elegguá's diloggún, the diviner must pay careful attention to the misfortune's origin. An osogbo elese otonowá (from heaven) marks serious issues between the client and Olokun. Elese Olokun is extremely dangerous. For some reason, the aché between this client and that spirit is so strained and tense that one may say the spiritual force is angry with the client. The diviner should prescribe a series of offerings to propitiate Olokun, giving obí after each to ensure acceptance. Once the orisha gives aláfia or etawa in response to the eboses, the client should have a rogación before his shrine. Until these eboses are done, he is in danger.

When the letter Ofún Irosun opens on the mat, no matter the orientation of odu or the initiatory status of the client, the diviner must prescribe certain eboses:

- The client must immediately give the warriors—his own if he has them, or the diviner's if he doesn't—saraeko. He should mix fresh water, honey, and cornmeal in a gourd, taste it, and then give it to Elegguá, Ogún, and Ochosi. The next morning, he should discard this ebó in the street.
- The night after giving this offering to his warriors, the client must return to the diviner's home. Before Obatalá, the diviner must give the client a rogación with ten ingredients: grated coconut, cascarilla, grated cocoa butter, white flowers, grated ñame, peeled, mashed bananas, grated pears, sandolo, cow's milk, and goat's milk.
- After the rogación, the client must offer ebó to the earth, the ocean, and his egun. Simple foods and fruits will suffice for these, and the priest must preside over the offerings.
- The diviner must instruct the client to take nightly spiritual baths for the next sixteen days using the same ingredients that were included in the rogación. After each bath, he must dress in fresh white clothes.

These four eboses will only soothe what was opened at the mat; they will not solve the client's more complicated issues. After the initial sixteen days of eboses and baths are complete, more will need to be done. Before attempting closure, the diviner should consider the following eboses:

- For all who open in Ofún Irosun, Oshún, Yemayá, egun, and Yewá might stand up to demand ebó. To determine if any of these spirits will take ebó, the diviner should ask, "Ebó elese [orisha's name]?" If the answer is yes, he should use the diloggún to mark the appropriate offering.
- Egun are integral in all composites of Ofún; the diviner should prescribe a series of spiritual masses to be done in the client's home. This letter hints at a spirit of great spiritual elevation. The espiritistas present during the mass must be

aware of this; they must search for its presence. By working with this one spirit, the client will evolve above his osogbo.

- Both the Ibeyi and Olokun are important in this sign. If the client does not have them, he must receive them; if he has them, he must lay out a plaza of fresh fruits to both.

If these prescriptions are not enough to close the reading for an aleyo or an aborisha, the diviner must turn to the eboses of the parent odu, Ofún (see page 489). Something there is needed for the client's evolution. If the diloggún remains open for an initiate, he should consider the following options:

- In Ofún Irosun, no matter to whom the client's head belongs Elegguá says he is king of this client's home. If the client's Elegguá does not have a crown, he needs one. If Elegguá has a crown, the diviner should mark ebó to this orisha.
- Initiates who have not received Yewá might need this orisha. The diviner should consider asking, "Koshé Yewá?"

If after exploring these options for the initiate the diviner still faces an open odu, he must turn to the eboses of the parent odu, Ofún.

## The Fifth Composite Odu of Ofún, Ofún Oché (10-5)

### The Proverbs of Ofún Oché

- The dead despoil the saints.
- The dead do not bother when the orishas are present.
- The dead are before and apart of the orishas.
- The needle pulls the thread.
- In the house of the soapmaker, everyone slips.
- A bird in the hand is worth two in the bush.
- You believe yourself to be very wise, but only Olorún and the orishas are truly wise.
- The dead steal from the saints.
- Pretend to be neither dead nor a saint; you will not like the wake.
- The river is disgraced when it fills with mud.
- The river's disgrace is to become muddy and murky.
- Even in the house of a wealthy man, old water turns stale.

### The Message of Ofún Oché

When the initial cast of ten mouths is followed by five mouths, the odu Ofún Oché is open on the mat. In this letter the diviner praises Elegguá and Oshún, saying, "Maferefún Elegguá! Maferefún Oshún!" When this sign opens, the diviner sits before one who was destined to make ocha. His calling, however, has been missed. If the client is an aleyo, he has been exposed to these mysteries before and, even though his heart told him to follow the religion, his own thoughts were at odds with his feelings. An aborisha who comes in this pattern has been told many times that his calling was ocha, but he did not listen. If this signs comes in iré, both Elegguá and Oshún are forgiving but strong in their pronouncement that the asiento is the aborisha's only salvation. In osogbo, they are angry, and they must be placated if the aborisha hopes to evolve. If the client is an initiate, no matter the sign's orientation both orishas announce their displeasure. This person has not taken his priesthood as seriously as he should; this must change. When aché was put into his head, a whole town was waiting for its newly crowned king. This town disintegrated because the king never came. His own problems are caused because he did not help those whom he should have helped. It will take some time to overcome his past and reclaim his destiny.

The diviner also praises the client's ancestral spirits, saying, "Maferefún egun!" They come in Ofún Oché to say that while they should be this person's foundation, they are not; the client knows this, because it has been told to him many times. He avoids the dead and refuses to give them their due. When this letter opens, the italero must prescribe a large amount of spiritual work for the client's egun. If he does not have a bóveda, he must have one, and when he prays to the dead he must mark his forehead and palms with cascarilla. An opá ikú is necessary to strengthen his ties with the ancestors, and daily he must mark it with cascarilla before he prays. The one for whom Ofún and Oché come together could be a great espiritista, but his talents are undeveloped. The diviner should advise him to attend masses regularly, for he will learn by watching other espiritistas work. One day, he will achieve greatness on his own.

Beyond the primary meanings of Ofún, this sign brings some serious health concerns to the client no matter the odu's orientation. He could have problems in the abdominal, intestinal, and genital regions. Women will suffer either infertility or difficult pregnancies, and men may experience temporary impotence or sexual dysfunction. Now is not the time to conceive, for this letter marks the birth of an imperfect child into the family; it also marks dangerous ectopic pregnancies. The client may have a scar on his body from surgery; the diviner should impress upon the client that if he does not change and monitor his health habits, another surgery could be in the near future. Cysts and fibromas may form throughout the body; the client must monitor himself for strange lumps or pains in soft tissues. The more serious the osogbo, the more serious the health concerns will become, and once they manifest, without prompt treatment the client's condition will worsen.

In addition to the health concerns of Ofún Oché, the diviner should explore the following points during the reading:

- Danger is coming through the front door of the client's house. He must be careful about whom he lets inside. He should not sit in or near the doorway and should never leave any door or window unlocked. If entry is barred, the danger will go elsewhere.
- This letter, no matter its orientation, marks great tragedy and loss. Financial setbacks could be devastating; the client must learn to save and should build an emergency fund.
- Know that this client lusts for results in lieu of hard work, and Ofún Oché says that this will never happen. If the client wants to achieve anything worthwhile, he will have to work hard.
- Finally, realize that in spite of this letter's volatility, both egun and the orishas have tried twice to bring a special blessing to the client. He lost it due to his own negligence. They will try to bless him a third time; he must be careful lest this is lost as well.

## The Prohibitions of Ofún Oché

- Conception is taboo for the next six months. Abstain from intercourse or use proper birth control. An imperfect child will be conceived during this time if one is not careful. Note that if a woman does conceive, she may not abort the pregnancy. It must be carried to term.
- Do not sit beside one's front door. Danger is coming.

## The Eboses of Ofún Oché

Special considerations for aleyos and aborishas: When the diloggún of Elegguá opens Ofún Oché in an osogbo, the diviner must pay careful attention to its origin. If it comes elese otonowá (from heaven), Oshún is angry and the forces of heaven give witness to her wrath. If it comes elese Oshún, she is angry with the client. Carefully, the diviner must examine this letter and all the client brings to the mat to determine the reason for Oshún's wrath. Then he should appease her with several eboses. After each ebó, the priest must use obí to determine whether it has been accepted. Once the coconut letters come out clean (aláfia or ejife), the client sits for a rogación before Oshún to correct the aché between himself and the orisha. Until these things are done, the client will remain in danger.

When Ofún Oché opens on the mat, the diviner must prescribe three mandatory eboses:

- As soon as the client returns home, he must give a saraeko to his warriors. He should mix fresh water, cornmeal, and honey in a gourd, taste it, and give it to Elegguá, Ogún, and Ochosi. If the client does not have the warriors, he may offer this ebó to the diviner's orishas. He is now marked to receive them and must do so within sixteen days.

- The next morning, the client returns to the diviner's home for a rogación with ten ingredients: grated coconut, cocoa butter, cascarilla, grated ñame, white flowers, cow's milk, goat's milk, sandolo, and two grated fruits favored by Obatalá. For the next sixteen days, the client must dress in white completely; no other colors are allowed.
- At the end of the sixteen days in white, the client must make the following sacrifices to his warriors: Elegguá, Ogún, and Ochosi are each given a rooster. Ogún, Ochosi, and Ósun are each given a pigeon. After all four are washed clean, the client should give a bunch of bananas to Elegguá, Ogún, and Ochosi. He should rub Ósun with fresh cocoa butter and put him back on a high shelf. Remember: If the client does not have his warriors, this is the final day of the time period in which it was prescribed that he receive them. The diviner should tell the client that if he does not at least present his derecho to the diviner on this day, the osogbo of Ofún Oché will overwhelm him.

Having made these prescriptions, the diviner may now attempt to close the oracle. If it will not close, the diviner should consider the following options:

- One of the proverbs of this letter is "The needle pulls the thread." The diviner should instruct the client to sew pañuelos for both Obatalá and Oshún. He must make them as ornate as his skills allow. When these two cloths are presented to the orishas, the diviner cleanses the client with them before draping them over their tureens. They remain indefinitely.
- Together, Oshún and Elegguá might claim ebó. The diviner must ask, "Ebó elese Oshún y Elegguá?" If they take ebó, the diviner must mark something suitable for both. It should be offered to both at the same time.
- The diviner may prescribe a series of masses to the client's egun in the client's home. To see if they will claim anything as ebó to clear the client's osogbo, the diviner should consider asking, "Ebó elese egun?" If the answer is yes, he should use the diloggún to mark the appropriate offering.

If these considerations are not enough to close the oracle and the client is an aleyo or an aborisha, the diviner must turn to the eboses of the parent odu, Ofún (see page 489). Something there is needed for the client's evolution. If the sign remains open for an initiate, the diviner should continue with the following list:

- The initiate now needs the staff known as *ariku babawa*. The diviner should prepare this for him as soon as possible.
- The client might have issues with Iroko. The diviner should first ask, "Ebó elese Iroko?" If the answer is yes, he uses the diloggún to mark the appropriate offering. If this does not close the letter, he should then ask, "Koshé Iroko?"

If the odu still will not close for the initiate, the diviner must turn to the eboses of the parent odu, Ofún.

## The Sixth Composite Odu of Ofún, Ofún Obara (10-6)

### The Proverbs of Ofún Obara

- Secrets are not meant to be told.
- Two calves will not drink from the same fountain.
- The new moon rises in a clear sky. [This proverb applies in iré].
- In a darkened sky, we cannot see the new moon rise. [This proverb applies in osogbo.]
- The broken calabash will break again.
- It is time for each to find his true path.

### The Message of Ofún Obara

When an initial cast of ten mouths, Ofún, precedes a cast of six mouths, Obara, the odu Ofún Obara is open on the mat. In this sign the diviner pays homage to Shangó, Yembo, Oshún, Iroko, Ogún, and Yemayá, saying to each, "Maferefún! The support of all these orishas is needed if the client hopes to overcome his osogbo, and one or more might stand up to claim ebó before allowing closure. In this odu there once was separation between Shangó and Yembo, and it was the loss of Shangó's horse that brought them back together. Their reunion began in shame and betrayal, but it ended in joy; so have these two orishas remained joyous ever since. Oshún and Iroko also figure in the stories of this odu. Saddened by her lack of children, Oshún went to the Iroko to pray for a child. In return, she promised that offspring in service to him. Iroko granted Oshún's petition, but in time Oshún forgot the promise she had made. One day, while mother and daughter were walking in the woods, they passed the forgotten tree, and Iroko, remembering Oshún's promise, reached out and took the daughter away.

Ogún stands strong in this pattern to defend the client from all harm. If the client propitiates him, no force on earth will be able to hold the client down. Yemayá comes in this pattern to nurture and support the client through what afflicts him. Her help, however, will not come without cost, for the client has offended her in the past. If approached with love, Yemayá will forgive.

Ofún Obara speaks of family, relationships, and promises unfulfilled among these. If the client is a man, the diviner should question him about his relationship with his mother; there is distance between the two, and this rift must be healed. The mother's health may not be good, and before the energy of this sign passes she could fall ill. If the client is a woman, the diviner should question her about her children; separations could come if she is not vigilant. Those with young children must watch their health: Disease and decay could take a child before his time. Abduction is a possibility; the client must guard his young ones against kidnapping and molestation. A mother of grown children will find that the time between visits grows greater, and she will be tempted to arrive at her child's house unannounced. The diviner must advise her against this. If she plans to visit an estranged child, she must announce her arrival in advance. If she does not, she will find despair and treason. The diviner should speak openly to the client about unfulfilled promises to his relations. If he has any debts to them, no matter how small, the client must repay them immediately. If he does not, he will soon lose something dear to him.

Women in this sign have issues with conception, pregnancy, and children. Those for whom this letter falls need to care for and monitor their reproductive organs. If the client is pregnant, the diviner should mark eboses to the orishas so that she will have a safe pregnancy. If the client is not pregnant, the diviner should advise her that now is not the time to conceive, for there will be complications. A woman who is having trouble with conception will be affected differently by the energies in this odu. For this type of client, the letter offers an ebó to Iroko that will help her conceive after this odu's energy has passed and then carry a child to term. Women with children will need to recall the conditions of each child's birth, for this letter speaks of a mother whose children were almost lost at or before birth. During the pregnancy, even if she was not in this religion, she made many promises and prayers to God to guarantee the safety of her children, and now that she has come to the feet of the orishas, Iroko is standing up to claim those promises as his own. Unless Iroko is fed and given ebó, he may claim the life of a child.

In addition, the diviner should explore the following issues with the client when Ofún Obara opens on the mat:

- The children in this client's family are spoiled and ungrateful. They should not be given everything that they want or desire, or else their ungratefulness will only worsen with age.
- The orishas are telling this person that his affairs, especially his finances, have been poor. He must not despair, because if he does the prescribed eboses quickly, before this year is up things will turn for the better.
- No matter what happens, the client must never appear sad or cry in misery. Instead, he should smile and be sweet, for sweetness only brings more of the same into his life.
- The client must respect his elders and always turn to them for advice; they have a vast amount of wisdom from which he may draw.

## The Prohibitions of Ofún Obara

- Never make a promise to the orishas that cannot be kept. They will give the blessing asked for, but when one's promise is not kept, they will then take it away.
- Secrets told are no longer a secret, and they will destroy one. Do not confide in anyone.
- Crying in misery is taboo; tears will draw more of the same, and one's life will fall apart. No matter how bad things are, smile.

## The Eboses of Ofún Obara

Special considerations for aleyos and aborishas: When the diloggún of Elegguá opens Ofún Obara in an osogbo, the diviner must pay careful attention to its origin. If it comes elese otonowá (from heaven), Shangó is angry and the forces of heaven give witness to his wrath. If it comes elese ocha (from the orishas) from Shangó, he is angry with the client. Carefully, the diviner must examine this letter and all the client brings to the mat to determine the reason for Shangó's wrath. Then he must appease him with several eboses. After each ebó, the priest must use obí to determine whether it has been accepted. Once the coconut's letters come out clean *(aláfia* or *ejife)*, the client sits for a rogación before Shangó's shrine to correct the aché between himself and the orisha. Until these things are done, the client remains in danger.

When Ofún Obara opens on the mat, the diviner must prescribe the following eboses:

- If the client has his warriors, he must have the diviner sacrifice to all of them: a rooster shared between Elegguá and Ogún, and a pigeon shared among Ogún, Ochosi, and Ósun. Seven days after the sacrifice, the client should present a large basket of fruits to all four orishas. If the client does not have the warriors, he must offer this ebó to the diviner's orishas. He is now marked for their reception and must have this initiation within sixteen days.
- After the ebó to the warriors is complete, the client offers a fresh ñame smeared with epó and sprinkled with smoked fish and jutía to Elegguá. He gives another ñame smeared with cocoa butter and sprinkled with cascarilla to Obatalá. These offerings should remain with the orishas until they begin to rot. If a vine or root grows from the ebó, do not cut it back; let it grow as long as it will.
- The same day that the ñames are put to Elegguá and Obatalá, the client gives an offering of fresh green plantains to both Shangó and Aganyú.

After explaining these eboses to the client, the diviner may attempt to end the session. If it remains open, he should consider the following:

- Iroko is important to all who open in Ofún Obara. The diviner should prescribe an offering of fresh fruits to the Iroko tree. The priest must preside over this offering, cleansing the client with each piece of fruit before presenting it to Iroko. If the diviner has Iroko, he may consider asking, "Ebó elese Iroko?" If this orisha claims ebó, the diviner uses the shells to determine the required offering; it must be given only after the mandatory eboses of this sign are completed. Note that women who open in Ofún Obara often have come to the mat for help with conception. Iroko brings the blessing of children here. If this is the case, but the diviner does not have Iroko, the client must pay the derecho for him to receive this orisha. After he has received her, the diviner may give the woman a rogación of the abdomen before Iroko. He should use plenty of grated coconut, cascarilla, and cocoa butter on the woman's abdomen, ending with a sacrifice of two pigeons over her womb. After her belly is wrapped in white cotton and white cloth, she must present a huge basket of fruits to the orisha, adorning Iroko as if it were a birthday shrine. After her baby is born, every year on the child's birthday she must come to make this same ebó of fruits to Iroko. The diviner must warn her that if she does not, Iroko will take away the child she gave. Also, after this woman makes ocha (remember, this odu foreshadows

initiation), regardless of what she is told during itá she must return to this priest to receive Iroko before receiving any other orisha.
- The diviner may also consider asking, "Ebó elese Ogún?" If Ogún claims an ebó, the diviner should mark what he requires with the diloggún. In addition, the client must give a red melon to Ogún. After making this ebó, he is prohibited from eating any type of melon; he may use them only for ebó.

If at this point the sign remains open for an aleyo or an aborisha, the diviner must turn to the eboses of the parent odu, Ofún (see page 489). Something there is needed for the client's evolution. If the client is an initiate, the diviner should continue with the following options:

- If the client does not have Aganyú, his reception is now mandated. The client should make preparations for this ceremony as soon as possible.
- Iroko's reception may also be necessary. The diviner should ask, "Koshé Iroko?" If his reception is marked, the client must receive this orisha after receiving Aganyú.
- Finally, if the odu still will not close, the client must plant an Iroko tree in his yard. If he is not a homeowner, he must plant the tree somewhere in the forest nearest his home. An oriaté will be needed to preside over this ceremony.

If these considerations are not enough to end the session for the initiate, the diviner must turn to the eboses of the parent odu, Ofún.

## The Seventh Composite Odu of Ofún, Ofún Odí (10-7)

### The Proverbs of Ofún Odí

- Things thrown into the ocean sink to the bottom.
- He who grasps at everything will lose it all.
- Your position was lost at birth.
- Never be ashamed to look at yourself.
- If the wall collapses at home, the farm is spared.

### The Message of Ofún Odí

When a cast of ten mouths, Ofún, precedes a cast of seven mouths, Odí, the odu Ofún Odí is open on the mat. Ofundí is another name for this sign. As soon as the letter opens, but before its orientations are determined, the diviner must offer an ebo to cleanse his home and all those present at the mat of this powerful sign's heat. (See "The Eboses of Ofún Odí" on page 468.)

This odu is powerful, giving birth to many things in nature. Through it, Yemayá created the sun and the moon; for giving the world such gifts, "Maferefún Yemayá!" Together, the sun and the moon had many children, the stars, who chose to follow their mother at night and not their father during the day. The moon gave order to her children, and the constellations were born in the night sky. It is here that one must pay homage to the moon and all her children, honoring the ancient patterns in the sky. Ofún Odí made Obatalá a king; "Maferefún Obatalá!" One should praise the elephant as well, for after Obatalá became king the elephant gave him his ivory tusks as a symbol of royalty. After his ascension to king, Obatalá and Ikú made a pact and because of this efun must be present whenever egun are invoked. Finally, egun are powerful here, and the custom of sacrificing to egun under the kitchen sink was born through this letter; "Maferefún egun!"

This letter raises many issues, and the diviner must explore them all with his client:

- If the sign opens in iré, it indicates that the client has become too vain; he looks at himself in the mirror too much. If the sign opens in osogbo, the client is overly concerned about his appearance and might think himself ugly; however, he still contemplates himself too much in mirrors. The client must learn to let others be his true mirror, watching how the eyes of others react to what he presents to the world. A mirror is a two-dimensional, subjective representation, but the reflection this person finds in others will be more objective and three-dimensional. It is this reflection the client should worry about, and no other.

- Ofun Odí focuses on the eyes, the stomach, the respiratory system, and the reproductive system. It foreshadows illnesses to these regions brought by contact with others. The client must guard his health well and follow proper hygiene precautions.
- In all patterns of Ofún, Obatalá is spoken of as an elder, an aged man. If this reading is an itá of initiation and the sign comes for the client's head or for Obatalá (if Obatalá is not the crown), the path of this orisha will be one of the eldest ones. To honor Obatalá in this odu, the client should not speak ill about or toward anyone of elder status, whether in religious or secular functions. Children of Obatalá figure prominently in this sign, and through one of his children the client will find much iré. When the children of the other orishas let the client down, the children of Obatalá will always be there to offer help, comfort, or support.
- The dead are inside this person's house. Only egun should be present. To remove the dead that are not egun, the client must clean the house well, getting rid of all empty, uncovered containers. In the more serious osogbos, Ikú can hide in these places.
- The client has "friends of convenience," and they can do the most damage to his life now.

## The Prohibitions of Ofún Odí

- For a woman, do not go out at night alone or travel alone. Do not keep the company of strange men in strange places.
- Be wary of fire and open flames. Extinguish all candles burning at home, and do not relight them for ten weeks.
- Avoid mirrors. One is vain and gazes at oneself too much. Use mirrors only when necessary.
- Do not get wet in the rain; it will wash away one's luck.
- If this reading is an itá for a iyawó using the diloggún of either Elegguá or the iyawó's crowning orisha, the iyawó must wear white for life. If a social function comes in which white is not appropriate, the iyawó must ask the orisha giving Ofún Odí for permission to wear a more appropriate color. If permission is not given, one may not go.
- In Ofún Odí, those with ngangas may not keep their pots in the house; their power is too vast and will heat up one's environment. They must be kept in a shed outdoors.

## The Eboses of Ofún Odí

Special considerations for aleyos and aborishas: When the diloggún of Elegguá opens Ofún Odí in an osogbo, the diviner must pay careful attention to its origin. If it comes elese otonowá (from heaven) or elese Yemayá (from Yemayá), Yemayá is angry and the forces of heaven bear witness to her wrath. Carefully, the diviner must examine this letter and all the client brings to the mat in order to determine the reason for Yemayá's malcontent. Then he must appease her with several eboses. After each ebó, the priest must use obí to determine whether it has been accepted. Once the coconut's letters come out clean (aláfia or ejife), the client may sit for a rogación before Yemayá's shrine to correct the aché between himself and the orisha. Until these things are done, the client will remain in danger.

Ofún Odí is an active letter, filled with many eboses that must be done by all who open under its influence. As soon as the letter opens, but before its orientations are determined, the italero must prepare a saraeko for Obatalá from cornmeal, cocoa butter, efun, and a single leaf of the prodigiosa plant. (This variation of saraeko replaces the saraeko one normally prepares when Ofún opens.) Beginning at the mat and then circling through the entire house, he sprinkles a bit of this mixture throughout the home to cleanse it, cooling the harsh energies of odu. Once done, all in attendance must sip a bit of the saraeko; the diviner then places it at Obatalá's feet. Only after completing this ritual may the diviner continue his manipulations of the diloggún. Once the diloggún is closed, the diviner lifts the saraeko from Obatalá and throws the entire mixture to the street with the words, "Eshu batie sode." When the client returns home, he must cleanse his home with this same saraeko. If he is an aleyo or an aborisha, he throws what remains to the street after the cleansing; if the client is an initiate, he leaves the saraeko with Obatalá overnight and throws it to the street the next morning. If this reading is an itá, the client must perform this cleansing occasionally throughout his life; Ofún Odí is a major player in his life, and this cleansing will keep much osogbo at bay.

For all who open in this letter, the following eboses are mandatory and must be done as soon as possible:

- First, if the client who comes to the mat is planning a marriage, he must have two ceremonies: an African-style ceremony to satisfy the orishas and a wedding done in the custom of his ancestors to placate his egun. Any other type of wedding commitment will not satisfy these spirits, and the marriage will end in divorce.
- If a young girl lives with the client, he must pay for her to receive Olokun immediately. If the child does not have her warriors, he must pay for her to receive Elegguá as well, for no orisha may be born unless Elegguá is firstborn. This ebó will save the girl from rape, molestation, and death.
- Finally, the client must pamper his godparent's Yemayá, buying her an expensive, ornate gift. Yemayá brings both iré and osogbo in Ofún Odí, so the greater the gift, the lesser the osogbo and the greater the iré.

Now the diviner has his first chance to close the odu. If it remains open, he should consider the following options for ebó:

- If the client is an aleyo or an aborisha, he could have issues with Yemayá, Olokun, Oshún, or the warriors (Elegguá, Ogún, Ochosi, and Ósun). If the client is an initiate, he could have issues with these orishas as well as Ochanlá and Yembo. Keeping the client's initiatory status in mind, the diviner should determine if any of these orishas will stand up to claim ebó, asking, "Ebó elese [orisha's name]?" to see if any will take ebó. If an orisha claims ebó, the diviner should mark one from the following lists:

- For Yemayá, prepare a boat in her honor. The client should purchase a model kit and build the boat with his own hands. Next he must prepare, under his godparent's direction, twenty-one small packages to be distributed throughout this boat. Each package should contain an item such as herbs, money, grains, or aché de Yemayá. Once the boat is prepared with its packages, the client should display the boat prominently in his home. If the client is an initiate, he should hang the boat above Yemayá's sopera. Note that if the initiate is a "child of two waters," he should prepare this boat for Oshún as well.
- If Olokun claims ebó, the client must receive her. If he already has her, inside Olokun's urn he must put a thin chain cut to his own height; she will use this to protect him always. After making that ebó, he should wrap her in a fishing net that has been soaked in seawater overnight. With this, she will catch all the blessings that are meant for him.
- If Oshún claims ebó, she must be fed a hen and two pigeons. Note that if the client is a child of two waters, he must also feed Yemayá.
- If the warriors claim ebó, the diviner should prepare a saraeko for them using water, cornmeal, and honey. This stays with them overnight; the next morning, discard it in the street. Coat Ósun with plenty of fresh cocoa butter.
- If Ochanlá claims ebó, the client must receive him. Once he has Ochanlá, an ornate mazo and pañuelo must be made for this orisha.
- If Yembo claims ebó, the client must receive her. Once he has her, an ornate pañuelo and beaded fishing net must be prepared for her.
- Because egun are prominent in all composites of Ofún, the client must host a series of masses in his home for them. The diviner

should consider asking, "Ebó elese egun?" If they claim ebó, feed them a rooster under the kitchen sink before the first mass is given.

If these eboses are not enough to close the odu for an aleyo or an aborisha, the diviner must turn to the eboses of the parent odu, Ofún (see page 489). Something there is needed for this client's evolution.

If it remains open for an initiate, he might have additional issues with the orisha Babaluaiye. The diviner should ask, "Ebó elese Babaluaiye?" If he claims ebó, the diviner should mark what he requires using the diloggún. Also, the diviner should tell the client that since Babaluaiye has claimed ebó in Ofún Odí, he must receive this orisha in conjunction with his mother, Naná Burukú. The client should make preparations for this ceremony as soon as possible.

If this prescription does not close the reading for an initiate, the diviner must turn to the eboses of the parent odu, Ofún.

## The Eighth Composite Odu of Ofún, Ofún Ogbe (10-8)

### The Proverbs of Ofún Ogbe

- Obatalá loves you for free.
- You are old before your time.
- Those who speak nonsense are not to be followed.
- When a vulture is hungry, catastrophe will feed him.
- Catastrophe feeds the vulture.
- Iron hooks do not break.

### The Message of Ofún Ogbe

When an initial cast of ten mouths precedes a cast of eight mouths, the odu Ofún Ogbe is open on the mat. Ofún Elleunle, Ofún l'Ogbe, and Ofún Shogbe are other names for this odu. Immediately, before continuing with his manipulations of the shells, the diviner should say, "Maferefún Elegguá! Maferefún Obatalá! Maferefún Olokun!" The influence of all three orishas is severe in this sign.

Ofún Ogbe is often referred to as the letter of "revolution and upheaval." When this sign falls on the mat, the danger here is that either the client or those present will not perform ebó, and this danger is innate, latent yet flowering in this sign. The random heat of this sign becomes especially dangerous if any type of osogbo is predicted. Many elder italeros like to tell the story of New Year's Eve 1958 in Cuba as a historical illustration of what can happen when the orisha's oracle is consulted but not heeded. On New Year's Eve in 1958, the babalawos in Cuba assembled for the annual calling down of Ifá. Orúnmila and Odu herself were brought down, and this sign was opened in osogbo. By manipulating Ifá, the babalawos ascertained that political treason and revolution were coming to the nation, and Cuban President Fulgencio Batista, who was currently in power, would be overthrown. Batista was reputed to be an adherent of orisha worship (although no one in our house is sure how deep his involvement was). The orishas were all gathering themselves for a spiritual war to be fought in heaven and earth, a war that directly involved Batista and indirectly affected all the Yorubas' spiritual descendants on the island.

Ebó was marked: Orúnmila declared that Olokun would save the island from the rule of a new dictator if the five babalawos gave him a tambor and danced his sacred dance with masks. Those present at the reading sighed in relief, for the orishas would save them from political revolution (Batista was loved by many). But the babalawos were frightened. To dance Olokun's dance is no easy task; the spiritual strain is so great that it drains physical energy. And whenever Olokun is called upon in the New World through this dance, one of the dancers will die before the year has turned. The babalawos did not dance; they offered alternate eboses to appease this mighty spirit. While the lesser oracles indicated that those eboses were accepted, revolution still came (although it did not immediately ruin the island and the Cuban people). Batista, being devoted to the orishas, was saved from execution at the hands of Fidel Castro, the new dictator of the island. As the story is told, the former president sat in his chambers with a gun to his head while Fidel's men tried to gain entry into his room; the plan was that once they broke in, they would watch as he took his own life. The orishas had other plans for his loyalty and worship. Just before the door was broken in, his own soldiers came through a window and whisked him to a waiting helicopter. With millions of dollars at his disposal, Batista was saved and taken to Spain, where he lived the rest of his life in comfort. Fidel took control of the island due to the babalawos' disobedience, and things have gone rancid economically and politically ever since.

While not every client who comes to the mat in Ofún Ogbe will face such severe trials and tribulations in his life, the odu guarantees that unless the eboses prescribed are done as the oracle dictates, there can be no evolution. Consider the other patakís told in this letter: Here, it was ordained that the vulture could never be tired, sick, or hungry, and he would always prosper and feed off the misfortunes of others. Here, urine, saliva, and semen went to the diviners to make ebó for long life and success. Urine did not make ebó; he sank into the ground when he touched it. Saliva did not make ebó; he, too, disappeared into the ground when he touched it. Semen made ebó; when he touched the earth, he became a healthy child.

Before beginning the reading, the diviner should tell his client this: Everything he does from this point on will affect everything else that happens in his life. Like a pebble thrown into a pond, every action will cause ripples that creep outward, changing the surface both near and far. Even if the advice given through this reading seems to have no bearing on the client's present circumstances, he should still act upon it. The spiritual forces at work in this letter are attempting to lay a stable foundation for the future. The rugged cornerstones and rigid, inflexible base being built now can be either infinite or finite, depending on the client's faith in the orishas. The larger the foundation built in the spiritual world, the greater the accomplishments of the client.

Obatalá is prominent in this odu. This letter speaks of Obatalá's elderly paths, and if the client desires evolution and true goodness in his life, he must not neglect the needs of the elderly at this time. He must make sure the elders in his family are well cared for; then he must tend to the elders in his religious family, including even those who have ocha but are now living in retirement and nursing homes. The client must see to it that the elders in his families are never alone or in need. He should go out of his way to help even those senior citizens who are not part of his secular or religious family; any elderly person could be Obatalá in disguise. The client must not make fun of those who are old and infirm or those with physical or mental imperfections. He must never argue with an elder, and he should always pay attention to the advice elders give. If the client listens to the advice of an elder and does not agree with it, he should keep his mouth shut and just acknowledge politely that he has heard what was said. He must not discuss his disagreement with anyone.

In more serious osogbos, Obatalá is speaking up to say that the client spends too much time in the street away from home: He wants to tell him, "Go home and stay there." If the client does not have a home, he should make one.

In addition, the diviner should also explore the following points with this client:

- In osogbo, Ofún Ogbe can mark certain types of illness whose certainty and severity will increase with the severity of the osogbo. Keeping this in mind, the diviner should recommend that the client protect his head at all times, both physically and spiritually. Through some type of mental or physical illness, this person could be in danger of "losing his head."
- This person should abstain from dangerous activities. In addition, he should monitor his body for any symptom of disease. This letter can mark a serious operation, although the letter promises recovery if the doctor's advice is followed. The client should see a physician immediately if he experiences any pains in the bones or muscles, and especially in the back.
- There will be an argument between brothers. The client must not let this get out of hand.
- Three children of the same mother must all

make ebó or only the youngest will live.

- Before a month has passed, two others will fight over the client's affections.

## The Prohibitions of Ofún Ogbe

- Ofún Ogbe enforces responsibility toward the elderly. Do not let them suffer. Cater to their needs.
- Pork products are now taboo for life, even for the aleyo. An ebó of pork will save one's life one day.
- Those with ocha crowned who receive this sign may never sacrifice pigeons. Eborí with two live pigeons will save one's life one day.
- Clear or white liquors are taboo; do not consume them.
- Do not linger in the street.

## The Eboses of Ofún Ogbe

Special considerations for aleyos and aborishas: When the diloggún of Elegguá opens Ofún Ogbe in an osogbo, the diviner must pay careful attention to its origin. If the osogbo originates elese otonowá (from heaven), two spiritual forces are angered with this client: Obatalá and Olokun. When the osogbo comes elese ocha (from the orishas), the diviner should pay careful attention to the orisha marking this; that spirit is angry with the client. Remember: All the orishas, when necessary, may speak through Ofún Ogbe. Carefully, the diviner must examine the letter and all the client brings to the mat in order to determine the reason for this spirit's wrath. Then he must appease the orisha with several eboses. After each ebó, the priest must use obí to determine whether it has been accepted. Once the coconut's letters come out clean (aláfia or ejife), the client may sit for a rogación before that orisha's shrine to correct the aché between himself and the spirit. Until these things are done, the client will remain in danger.

Ofún Ogbe marks three immediate eboses: If the client does not have his warriors, he must receive them. If he does not have Olokun, he must receive her. And if he does not have ocha, he is marked for the asiento. Before letting the client leave his home, the diviner should drape Obatalá's mazo over his neck and have him pay foribale to the orisha.

If many castings of Ofún open during this session, after closing the diloggún another ebó is mandated: The diviner must prepare a special saraeko for Obatalá. He mixes water, cornmeal, cocoa butter, efun, and a leaf of prodigiosa in a gourd and sprinkles this mixture liberally throughout the house. He gives what is left to Obatalá, and the next morning he throws it to the street with the words, "Eshu batie sode." When the client returns home, he must cleanse his home with this same saraeko. If he is an aleyo or an aborisha, he throws what remains to the street after the cleansing; if the client is an initiate, he leaves the saraeko with Obatalá overnight and throws it to the street the next morning.

Of all the orishas who might speak in this casting of Ofún, none is more important that Olokun. Just as he sought to protect Cuba, and then cast it into despair when his eboses were not done in 1958, so does he seek to protect the client. He will, however, cast him into despair if the client does not placate him immediately. (If the client does not have Olokun, he offers this ebó to the diviner's orisha.) The client prepares an adimú of gofio and molasses for Olokun, forming seven balls out of this mixture, and places it over Olokun's urn in a simple gourd. The ebó remains with him for seven days; at the end of this time, the client replaces the ebó with a blue candle and discards the balls in either the ocean or the largest body of water available.

By making this ebó, the client puts himself in bondage to Olokun, and he must receive him as soon as possible. Those initiates in attendance who do not have Olokun are now marked to receive him as well. If the client already has Olokun, he should purchase five beautiful, ornate masks to acknowledge the dance he required of the babalawos in 1958; these are given to him in remembrance of the worship he was denied.

Olokun demands ebó of the italero's ilé ocha as well: an agbán in his honor. The diviner must require the client's attendance, for it is his osogbo that brought this to the diviner's home.

Having made these prescriptions, the diviner may now attempt to close the oracle. If it will not close, he should explore the following possibilities:

- Olokun may require further ebó. The diviner should ask, "Ebó elese Olokun?" If the answer is yes, he uses the diloggún to mark the appropriate offering.
- The client must rely on his spirits for evolution. The diviner should consider eboses for Elegguá, Ogún, Ochosi, Ósun, Obatalá, and Yemayá. One or more might claim something from this reading.
- In all composites of Ofún, egun are prominent. The diviner should now prescribe a series of masses for them and consider asking, "Ebó elese egun?" If the answer is yes, he uses the diloggún to mark the appropriate offering.
- No matter the client's initiatory status, if he lives in the country, the sign marks him for the following ebó: To honor Obatalá, the client must keep a coop filled with white pigeons. The diviner should tell him that within eight months, all these birds might die. If they do, the ebó is finished; there is no need to begin again, because Obatalá has taken their lives. If the coop continues to thrive (and the client should work hard to ensure the birds' health), then he must keep up this ebó for life in honor of Obatalá. Note that if this reading is an itá of initiation or if the client is an initiate, once this pen is built he may never again sacrifice pigeons for any reason. Someone else must do this on his behalf.

If these considerations are not enough to close the odu and the client is an aleyo or an aborisha, the diviner must turn to the eboses of the parent odu, Ofún (see page 489). Something there is needed for the client's evolution. If the client is an initiate, however, the diviner should continue with the following list:

- If the right to sacrifice pigeons has been removed by this odu, the client may offer the following ebó in times of overwhelming need: Dedicate two white pigeons to Olorún with prayers and a libation of water (some recommend making nangareo before this ceremony). Once this is done, the initiate may sacrifice the two pigeons to Obatalá (but no other orisha). He will then have the blessings of both Obatalá and Olorún. Note that he may make this ebó only for himself; odu still removes the right to sacrifice pigeons on behalf of any other person.
- In addition, if the initiate's orí ever stands up for an ebó, having another priest or priestess offer two pigeons first to Olorún and then to the client's head will bring increased strength, blessings, and luck. This should be done only during a "holocaust"—a time of great need—when no other method of cleansing will help.
- The initiate must wear the necklaces of Obatalá and Olokun every day, exclusively, for a period of time determined by the diloggún. If this reading is an itá, the initiate must wear these two beads every day (but not exclusively) for life.
- Finally, the initiate must see a competent babalawo to receive the eleke and idé of Orúnmila. While the eleke may be worn at will, the idé should be worn daily and never removed unless it breaks. If it does break, the client should return to his godfather in Ifá to have a new one tied on his wrist.

If these considerations are not enough to close the session with Ofún Ogbe for the intitiate, the diviner must turn to the eboses of the parent odu, Ofún.

## The Ninth Composite Odu of Ofún, Ofún Osá (10-9)

### The Proverbs of Ofún Osá

- The monkey cannot trust even his own tail.
- You will see that which you never wanted to see.
- Do not let yourself become another's monkey.
- Dress yourself first, and then you may dress others.
- Rain is God's water; bathe in it.
- One who knows how to sweep does not use a broom to clean the sky.

- When rain falls, it does not miss the plants by the lake.
- If one has it easy, he will always have it easy. [This proverb applies in iré.]
- If one has it hard, he will always have it hard. [This proverb applies in osogbo.]
- Ofún applies medicines and then looks to see if they will heal.

## The Message of Ofún Osá

When an initial cast of ten mouths, Ofún, precedes a cast of nine mouths, Osá, the odu Ofún Osá is open on the mat. It is here that the sisters Yemayá and Oshún nurtured the parched earth by giving birth to rain, the sweet waters that fall from the sky. This is also the sign that created greed, the love of money and wealth that infects evil hearts; this sign also brings all the tragedies that befall those who love money above all else. It is the letter in which Orúnmila's son made a bet with Ikú's child over whether or not the moon would rise that night; Ikú's child knew that it was time for the moon to rise, but Orúnmila's son did not and said that it would not. To save his child's life, Orúnmila made ebó to stall the moon's awakening. Also in this letter the monkey, Obatalá's confidant, thought he saw the orisha drinking palm wine; wanting to usurp the orisha's authority and gain special favors from God, the monkey accused Obatalá of being drunk to Olófin. Olófin made Obatalá appear before him, and he saw that the orisha had only been making ebó with the liquor. The monkey was cursed on that day to live in the forest like an animal, separated from both humans and the orishas.

When this letter falls on the mat, the diviner says, "Maferefún Obatalá! Maferefún Oyá!" Both demand much respect, and they give the client many severe warnings dealing with both health and conduct. In all composites of Ofún, Obatalá speaks in his elder path, and he demands that the client give his ancestral priests and priestesses prayers, respect, offerings, and homage. Now is the time for the client to center his thoughts on egun, praying to them for light, health, and guidance, and in return he should give these same things back to them. The diviner should instruct the client to set up a bóveda with nine glasses of water and a perpetual light; he can use this as a special place to pray for the dead, offering them coolness and refreshment. In addition to this, the client should work egun with the opá ikú, as is common in our faith. These acts of workship will ensure that the dead have the strength to guide and lead the client through darkness and turmoil.

With the energy of this odu in his life, the client should be on the lookout for signs of illness and disease in the respiratory system, the bones, the muscles, the head, and the reproductive system. Unless the sign opens in a severe osogbo, these will be minor complaints, but the client should monitor his health closely so that he can notice symptoms early enough that they don't develop into a serious health problem. Oyá is the wind and the breath, and in this pattern she demands that the client give up any vice affecting the respiratory system. If the client gives up smoking, she just might let him keep his lungs! Women in this sign will suffer retention of the menses and might think that they are pregnant, even if they are not; nevertheless, they should engage only in safe sex and have a pregnancy test just in case.

Yewá is strong in this letter as well, and the client must refuse to argue or enter into treason against her children. In serious osogbo, the diviner might wish to mark ebó to her to ensure Yewá's goodwill.

In addition, the client should also keep the following in mind:

- Every day, the client should cleanse himself spiritually, or else he will see that which he does not want to see, and it will affect his life adversely.
- The client must be watchful over his friends, for there is danger that someone close to the client could violate a daughter or young girl while drunk in his house.

## The Prohibitions of Ofún Osá

- Smoking and drinking are now taboo. Give them up the moment one rises from the mat.
- Neither argue nor fight; these will bring per-

manent separations between family, friends, and lovers.

- There is danger in the streets. Do not linger in them, and do not walk them at night.

## The Eboses of Ofún Osá

Special considerations for aleyos and aborishas: When the diloggún of Elegguá opens Ofún Osá in osogbo, the diviner must pay careful attention to its origin. If it comes elese otonowá (from heaven) or elese Oyá (from Oyá), Oyá is angry with the client and heaven gives witness to her wrath. Carefully, the diviner must examine the letter and all the client brings to the mat in order to determine the reason for Oyá's wrath. Then he must appease her with several eboses. After each ebó, the priest must use obí to determine whether it has been accepted. Once the coconut's letters come out clean (aláfia or ejife), the client sits for a rogación before Oyá's shrine to correct the aché between himself and the orisha. Until these things are done, the client remains in danger.

Ofún Osá requires ebó no matter the sign's orientation. First, the diviner should tell the client he must cleanse his home with a saraeko made of water, cornmeal, honey, cocoa butter, efun, and a prodigiosa leaf. The client should sprinkle this throughout the house and then take a sip before casting the mixture to the street. That night, the client must sleep in white clothes with a single mark of cascarilla on his forehead.

Second, three orishas accompany the client: Obatalá, Yemayá, and Oshún. Obatalá blesses the client continually; in return, he should honor him with frequent offerings. Just as Yemayá and Oshún created the life-nurturing rain for the earth in this letter, so do they wish to nurture the client. He must, however, pamper them as queens, honoring them with mazos, crowns, pañuelos, red parrot feathers, and cooked foods. The more he pampers the two together, the more they will give in return.

Finally, if this sign comes in an itá with Oyá, every year the client must feed her two hens on the anniversary of this reading. If this letter comes as the itá for a iyawó in any orisha, Oyá is his crutch in life; he must live by making ebó to her. Children of Yemayá and Shangó, who do not receive Oyá in asiento, are now marked to receive Oyá before their week in the throne is completed. The godparents of this iyawó must ensure that the godchild does not leave without her.

Having made these prescriptions, the diviner may now attempt to close the oracle. If it will not close, he should consider the following:

- This is a letter of spiritualism and strong spiritualistic tendencies. The client must spend some time every night at his bóveda, calling upon egun and telling them what he needs in life. Strong offerings are not required to accomplish this; by lighting a candle and smoking a cigar, this person has the spiritual strength to accomplish much with little.
- If an osogbo promising sickness or untimely death has opened, it falls not only on the client but also on his youngest child. If the letter has given a larishe, that ebó will protect the client. Ebó must be made separately on the child's behalf. The diviner should tell the client to bring his youngest for a session with the diloggún so appropriate ebó can be marked.
- In any osogbo, Oshún may require a castrated goat immediately. The diviner should ask, "Eyebale elese Oshún?" If the sacrifice is marked and the client is an initiate, he is also marked for itá. If the client is an aleyo or an aborisha, however, the diviner must question whether an itá is necessary, asking, "Itá elese Oshún?" While it is unusual for Oshún to give itá to the uninitiated, in this letter she must have that option. Ofún Osá in osogbo is bitter, and this orisha wants to bring sweetness to the client's life.
- Finally, if the client is an aleyo or an aborisha, he may need to receive the elekes and the warriors. The diviner will use his own aché to determine if this is the case. Because Oyá is prominent in all odu incorporating Osá, if the

diviner decides that the client must have the elekes, the ceremony must also include the investment of Oyá's eleke.

If these considerations will not close the session for an aleyo or an aborisha, the diviner must turn to the eboses of the parent odu, Ofún (see page 489). Something there is necessary for the client's evolution. If the client is an initiate, however, the diviner should consider his relationship with Oyá. If the client does not have this orisha, he is now marked to receive her; she has many blessings to give, but she cannot bring them until she is seated in this person's house. If the client already has Oyá, she may need ebó; the diviner should ask, "Ebó elese Oyá?" If the answer is yes, he uses the diloggún to mark the appropriate offering.

If these eboses do not close the session with Ofún Osá, the diviner must now consider the eboses of the parent odu, Ofún.

## The Tenth Composite Odu of Ofún, Ofún Meji (10-10)

### The Proverbs of Ofún Meji

- The one who gambles with what he owns will lose the things he owns.
- The gambler loses his money and his home.
- By greed, you will lose everything, even your own life.
- Because there is no one to guard the orchard when our apples grow, we will always pick them unripened.
- While you lived on the earth, you broke your oath; what happens now concerns the oath that was made.
- A straight road has no curves.
- You will laugh until hunger kills you.

### The Message of Ofún Meji

When the initial cast of ten mouths, Ofún, repeats itself, the odu Ofún Meji is open on the mat. Of all the letters in this family, Ofún Meji is the most volatile. It requires a series of eboses even before the diviner can determine its orientations. First, from the gourd the italero fills his mouth with fresh water; looking at the ceiling, he sprays this water through his clenched teeth so that it falls back on his face, refreshing him. He fills his mouth with water again and sprays it over the shells. The italero (or his assistant, if he has one) prepares a saraeko of cornmeal, water, and honey for the warriors and Obatalá. After closing this session, the priest must excuse all from his home so he may cleanse it with another special saraeko made of water, cornmeal, honey, cocoa butter, cascarilla, and a prodigiosa leaf. After this cleansing, the diviner gives this saraeko to Obatalá while he consults Elegguá's diloggún for himself. He keeps his house locked down until midnight; others may neither come nor go, and the diviner is forbidden to open odu for any other clients. At midnight, all the saraekos are taken to the street, where the diviner discards them with the words, "Eshu batie sode."

Many stories are told in this letter, and through it are many customs born. The mother of the Muslim faith, Nana, lay dying; she was Yoruba, and she called upon all the priests in the land to divine for her and prescribe ebó. Ofún Meji opened on the mat, and the diviners told Nana to sacrifice twenty thousand cowries, the clothes on her body, and a white hen to Obatalá. Nana was too sick to make ebó on her own, and she was too poor to pay the priests to do it for her, so she called upon all her children for help. None would part with the cowries she needed (for cowries were money) to make the sacrifices. Instead, they ministered to her needs as she lay in her bed, dying. They fed her gruel in the morning as they went to work and gruel at night as they came home to see if she still breathed. The last thirty days of her life she could not eat; disease had weakened her, and she sipped only water. On the night of the thirtieth day of her death-fast, she called to her children, and all of them came. "Selfish children," she croaked, "because you would not make sacrifice for the one who gave you life, the one who gave you life lies dying. For as long as you live, you will all remember me and suffer as I have suffered. Every year, you will fast for thirty days if you hope to receive blessings from me and God. As you suffer in life, so shall I rejoice in my death." This odu gave birth to the Muslim custom of fasting, and woe to those who do not keep their faith.

In Ofún Meji, it is also said that the entity known as Coldness was embittered at his lot in life. He was born in this odu and was almost an orisha in his own right, but he was ignored by those who lived on the earth. None made sacrifice to him. No one was afraid of Coldness because he was only a spirit; he was amorphous, without body or substance, and he could do nothing to influence the world. The day came when this forgotten entity grew angry and wished to harm those who denied him sacrifice. Coldness went to the diviners in heaven and asked, "What can I do to punish those who refuse to give me my due?" Ofún Meji opened on the mat, and the diviners told Coldness to make sacrifice with all that he had and all that he was. Coldness did as he was told, and he sacrificed his whole life to his own vengeance. With anger, he descended upon the earth with the wind as his guide, an invisible cloud of frigid anger and arrogance. As he enveloped the earth, people shivered; they felt the cold, and they ached. Sickness came with his wrath. Slowly, he crept over the earth one piece at a time, and whatever he touched felt him and acknowledged his presence. Coldness made his ebó, and through it he became one of the most feared presences on the earth.

Many other entities were born in this letter as well. Olokun, while chained in the ocean by Obatalá and Olorún, rose to power in this sign; she became the true queen of all waters, and her strength empowers the weather of the world. This is also the sign in which Ikú descended upon the earth to find his own followers and made pacts with all of them. These *curanderos* (healers) became his godchildren, and by accepting the pact with Death they were given the power to overcome illness, disease, and decay. With a word from a curandero, one marked to die and feed Ikú can be freed from that fate, for a time. Ofún Meji also brought to the earth a great void, the chasm that forever separates the earth physically from heaven, and created loneliness among mortal beings by causing their separation from God. It also alludes to Christ's passion, the fear and loneliness he felt when facing his own divine fate.

In this sign the diviner says, "Maferefún Obatalá! Maferefún Odua! Maferefún Yewá!" Here, these orishas hold the keys to life and death itself. Even an aleyo could have issues with these three mysterious forces. To honor them, the client must refuse to have any argument with their children, especially elder priests and priestesses, and he must follow any advice an elder priest or priestess of these orishas gives. These three orishas demand respect for themselves and for the rest of the orishas; until now, the client has not been in alignment with the spirits, treating them more as servants or slaves than as reflections of Olódumare. If he is to have evolution in this lifetime, the client must put his relationship with the orishas into proper perspective. He must avoid greed, for this vice will bring devolution, and neither gamble nor bet, for in this way will all his blessings be lost.

The opening of this letter indicates that a child of Oshún is near this client. This child has been almost lost to the religion or perhaps never truly found it. But the client will find this person and perhaps even bring him or her to the diviner. This person will be known and marked easily, because he will be in trouble with the law and will try to flee. The client must not let this person flee, for Oshún will save him or her if ebó is made.

This letter normally marks the client as being very loud, boisterous, and flirtatious. He likes to party and go to parties, and he likes to drink, but partying and drinking are the worst enemies and vices this person could have. To ensure spiritual and material evolution, Ofún Meji demands that the client settle his lifestyle. Here, the diviner should tell the client that Obatalá says, "You live in the streets, but you do have a home. Go home, and stay there." Yewá wants to tell the client that the grave has been opened for him, but not by her hands. This osogbo comes from his own actions and conduct. The diviner should tell him, "Death is not yet near, but it is foreboding; to escape, make ebó to Yewá and then stay home!" From this moment on, the client must not keep things of the dead in his home beyond his own egun. If the client has a nganga, it should be disinterred and buried. He may not have a prenda or be initiated to Palo. If he does not obey this advice, the dead will consume him, for he does not have the spiritual strength to control these powerful forces. If he practices any spiritual form of witchcraft, he may not use this power to curse, for only the orishas have that right, and they will take care of his enemies for him. The curse that he casts on another will not only come home to roost but also affect those who are closest to him, those whom he loves.

In addition, the diviner should keep the following points in mind:

- The client must take good care of his body, monitoring the chest region for signs of decay or illness, being careful of muscle strains and broken bones, and guarding the throat against illness. At the first sign of sickness, and especially during the colder months of the year, the client should see a physician.
- Somewhere in the client's spiritual or religious family, an imperfect child will be conceived. The client must avoid pregnancy or impregnating women lest this osogbo fall on her- or himself. Note that Oshún forbids an abortion; even if an imperfect child is conceived, it must be carried to term.
- Ofún Meji can mark a period in the client's life in which there will be many opportunities for fatal accidents. The client should stay home as much as possible and be very cautious when going out. He should wear the elekes often so the orishas can offer their protection at all times.

## The Prohibitions of Ofún Meji

- Do not argue with the children of Obatalá, Odua, or Yewá; this will anger these orishas.
- Avoid avarice; do not covet the possessions of others.
- Neither gamble nor bet, or else one will lose all that one owns.
- Do not linger in the streets; there is danger there.
- One's home should be painted no color other than white. Have only white sheets and pillowcases on one's bed; any other color will draw osogbo while one sleeps.
- Avoid hospitals, nursing homes, funerals, and wakes unless family obligations require attendance. Before going, however, consult with Elegguá and make ebó.
- If Ofún Meji comes during an itá, the initiate must live with the following prohibitions: Wear white every day. Do not use perfumes, colognes, scented soaps, or scented shampoos. Do not dye the hair; do not pluck gray hairs. Avoid alcohol, tobacco, and intoxicants. Do not allow trash or empty bottles to accumulate indoors. Do not have more than two candles lit in the house at one time. Never sleep without a shirt.

## The Eboses of Ofún Meji

Special considerations for aleyos and aborishas: When the diloggún of Elegguá opens Ofún Ogundá in an osogbo, the diviner must pay careful attention to its origin. If it comes elese otonowá (from heaven) or elese Obatalá (at the feet of Obatalá), Obatalá is angry and the forces of heaven give witness to his wrath. Carefully, the diviner must examine this letter and all the client brings to the mat in order to determine the reason for Obatalá's anger. Then he must appease him with several eboses. After each ebó, the priest must use obí to determine whether it has been accepted. Once the coconut's letters come out clean (aláfia or ejife), the client may sit for a rogación before Obatalá's shrine to correct the aché between himself and the orisha. Until these things are done, the client will remain in danger.

Ofún Meji is a sign demanding strong eboses regardless of its iré or osogbo. The key to averting disaster in this letter is for the diviner to prescribe everything possible under its influence.

Of prime importance is the client's orí: A strong head will bring him blessings, while a weak head will bring him misfortune. Before Obatalá, the client should have a rogación with grated coconut, grated cocoa butter, cotton, cascarilla, honey, white flowers, cow's milk, goat's milk, sandolo, and grated ñame. After giving the rogación, the diviner must prohibit the client from wearing any color except for white for sixteen days (a number sacred to Obatalá). These sixteen days will be a period of cleansing for the client. Every night before going to bed, this person must take a spiritual bath prepared with cow's milk, goat's milk, coconut milk, sandolo, grated coconut, grated cocoa butter, and cascarilla. Because egun are active in Ofún Meji, these ancestral spirits must form the client's spiritual foundation. After each bath he should go before his bóveda and light a single white candle to egun. These eboses will do much to calm and soothe the client's life.

The diviner should next consider the client's initiatory status in the religion. If he is an aleyo or an aborisha, he will need both the elekes and the warriors; if he lacks either or both, the diviner should prescribe them as ebó. In addition to the beads of Obatalá, Yemayá, Oshún, Shangó, and Elegguá, this client needs the beads of Ogún and Ochosi. If the client has already received these intiations, the elekes must be strengthened and refreshened, and a sacrifice of two roosters and three pigeons should be made to the warriors.

If the client is an initiate, he could have issues with Obatalá, Yemayá, Oshún, Shangó, Elegguá, Ogún, or Ochosi. To find out what these spirits may require, the diviner should consider asking, "Ebó elese [orisha's name]?" If the answer is yes, he uses the diloggún to mark the appropriate offering.

Now the diviner has his first chance to ask the oracle for closure. If it remains open, he should consider the following options:

- If the odu has opened in an osogbo of ano, ikú, or araye, which would indicate that the grave has been opened for the client, the priest must feed the earth, Orisha Oko, and Yewá for him. The diviner must use the diloggún to mark the particular eboses to be fed. There is no need for the diviner to ask if ebó must be done; he may assume that it is necessary and mark what is required. If this ebó is prescribed for an initiate, he must receive Orisha Oko as soon as possible.
- Iroko is of prime importance to all who open in this odu; even an aborisha might need to receive him (in conjunction with Obatalá, if he has not made ocha). First the diviner should determine if a simple offering or sacrfice will suffice, asking, "Ebó elese Iroko?" If the answer is yes, he uses the diloggún to mark the appropriate offering. If the answer is no and the client is an aborisha or an initiate, the diviner should ask, "Koshé Iroko?" (He should not ask this question for an aleyo.)
- Finally, if the client is an initiate, he might need to receive Yewá. The diviner should ask, "Koshé Yewá?" If this reception is marked by the shells, the client should make preparations for this ceremony as soon as possible.

If these considerations are not enough to close Ofún Meji, the diviner must turn to the eboses of the parent odu, Ofún (see page 489). Something there is needed for the client's evolution.

## The Eleventh Composite Odu of Ofún, Ofún Owani (10-11)

### The Proverbs of Ofún Owani

- That which is cheap comes out expensive.
- In the fight between the sun and the wind, the sun won; be like the sun.

### The Message of Ofún Owani

When an initial casting of ten mouths, Ofún, precedes a second casting of eleven mouths, Owani, the odu Ofún Owani is open on the mat. The letter speaks of a war fought between the wind and the sun; each thought it was the most powerful, and each wanted to dominate the earth. The sun won the war, and the wind was forced to wander in loneliness both day and night. Be like the sun, and not the wind!

Opening in this odu, the diloggún is directing the diviner to pay homage to Obatalá, Yemayá,

Oshún, and Iroko. He should say to each, "Maferefún!" This odu reveals a strong bond between the client and Obatalá; it is so strong that the client might be this orisha's child. While only a bajado can accurately determine the client's guardian orisha, the diviner should tell the client, "Obatalá loves you as if you were his own. Indeed, you could be his child. Praise this mighty one on a daily basis. Say, 'Maferefún Obatalá!' when you awake and before you sleep; say it several times a day. Make ebó to him; spoil him; give him frequent adimú. Obatalá will bring you all that you lack."

In any orientation of Ofún Owani, the client is having troubles sleeping at night due to disturbing dreams. A few of these dreams are nightmares, but most of the trouble is caused because he dreams of either Obatalá or Oshún. The client should heed these nocturnal visions, for they carry messages and warnings from the orishas. He may share these dreams with his godparents, who can help him interpret them, but with no one else.

If the client is a married man or a man involved a monogamous relationship with a woman, Oshún wants to tell him that his partner might be leaving him because of his actions; he must take part in no adultery, no infidelity, nor any wandering eyes if he wants to hold on to his lover. If she is the most important thing in his life, he should treat her in that manner. He should offer to Oshún an ebó of an expensive bottle of sweet perfume, which remains with her for five days. Once the five days have passed, the client should give the bottle of perfume to his wife or lover and devote time and energy to her as if this effort were an ebó for Oshún; the woman will not stray as long as he gives her total attention.

Yemayá wants to warn both men and women that a dangerous pregnancy is forebode for the near future, and Obatalá is near as well to say that an imperfect child might soon be born into the family. Under the odu Ofún, now is not a propitious time for conception. If proper measures are not taken, a dangerous pregnancy will soon begin that will put the mother's life in danger or even create an imperfect fetus. The client must keep this in mind, for Oshún is conception, and with her influence felt so strongly in this odu, she forbids an abortion.

## The Prohibitions of Ofún Owani

- Do not argue with one's elders. Respect the elderly.
- There is danger in the streets, and one spends too much time in them. Go home and stay there for seven days. After this period, do not go out at night.
- Black and dark colors are taboo. Wear white daily.
- Adultery and infidelity are taboo; wandering eyes will bring osogbo.
- Unless one is a tata nkisi, one may have nothing of the Congos or the nkisi in one's house. Ofún Owani prohibits rayado for aleyos and aborishas.
- Do not walk under stairs or ladders. Do not climb winding stairs or go into basements.

## The Eboses of Ofún Owani

Special considerations for aleyos and aborishas: When the diloggún of Elegguá opens Ofún Owani in an osogbo, the diviner must pay careful attention to its origin. If it comes elese otonowá (from heaven) or elese Elegguá (from Elegguá), Elegguá is angry with the client and the forces of heaven give witness to his wrath. Carefully, the diviner must examine this letter and all the client brings to the mat in order to determine the reason for Elegguá's wrath. Then he must appease him with several eboses. After each ebó, the priest must use obí to determine whether it has been accepted. Once the coconut's letters come out clean (aláfia or ejife), the client may sit for a rogación before Elegguá's shrine to correct the aché between himself and the orisha. Until these things are done, the client will remain in danger; there can be no evolution for one who does not have Elegguá's goodwill and assistance.

When Ofún Owani opens on the mat, the following eboses are mandatory no matter the letter's orientation:

- This client may not have anything of witchcraft or palo in his home. The initiation of Palo

Mayombe is now taboo; the client is not meant to walk that path. If the client already has a spiritual nganga, yet is not a palero, he should disinter that cauldron; the nfumbe that lives within is eating him alive. If the client is a palero, he is forbidden to use his powers for wicked ends. Even though he is a priest of Palo, from this moment on he must rely more on the orishas than on the dead or nature spirits.

- In the client's house is a stick that trips people from time to time. If the client can find it, he should bring this stick to the diviner; if he cannot find it, he should go into the woods, find a stick equal to his height, and bring it to the diviner instead. Along with the stick, the client should bring to the diviner a pouch, a belt, and anything else marked by the orisha whose diloggún is being consulted. The diviner fills the pouch with the ingredients for the ebó and ties it to the stick with the belt. He then drives the stick into the earth so it stands upright and feeds it a feathered animal in the name of the orisha being consulted.
- In any type of osogbo, Oshún or Yemayá (or possibly both) is standing up to claim an unpaid debt. If the client can remember what the debt is, he should pay it immediately as one of the eboses for this letter. There is no need for the diviner to mark it. But if the client cannot recall incurring a debt to either of these orishas, the diviner must mark a larishe so that the debt does not go unpaid. Iré from that orisha will follow once the ebó is complete.

If the letter remains open after he has explored these options, the diviner should investigate the following eboses:

- The client should give a beaded cane to Obatalá. If the client does not have Obatalá, he should offer this ebó to his diviner's or godparent's Obatalá. Before the client presents the cane, the client's godparent washes it in Obatalá's omiero and feeds both the orisha and the cane four white pigeons.
- If this letter remains open and the client is an initiate or an aborisha, he needs to receive Iroko. If he already has this orisha, the diviner should ask, "Ebó elese Iroko?" If the answer is yes, this spirit might have the solution to all the client's troubles, but he requires ebó before solving them. The diviner uses the diloggún to mark the appropriate offering.

If these considerations are not enough to close the letter, the diviner must turn to the eboses of the parent odu, Ofún (see page 489). Something there is necessary for the client's evolution.

## The Twelfth Composite Odu of Ofún, Ofún Ejila (10-12)

### The Proverbs of Ofún Ejila

- The drunks do not know what they are doing and cannot meet.
- Drunks do not know what they are doing even when they pay attention.
- They come to buy something for a penny and then sell it for one hundred pennies.

### The Message of Ofún Ejila

When the initial cast of ten mouths, Ofún, precedes a second cast of twelve mouths, Ejila Shebora, the odu Ofún Ejila is open on the mat. Ofún Oturupon is another name for this sign. For a parent, this letter can be one of the more disastrous and one of the most heartbreaking. For in this letter, one's child suffers because of one's own sins. This odu speaks of a person who does devious things on a regular basis, perhaps breaking the law, perhaps ignoring the unspoken ethical laws of society. It talks of one who has changeable or loose morals. While the "law of karma" says everything one does affects everything else and always comes home to roost upon the one who does wrong, in this pattern that law has been warped, and a parent will find that his child will be affected directly by all the wrongs he himself has done. Indeed, the punishments of Ofún Ejila are severe, for even if this client does not love himself, he has a strong bond with his children, and having to watch them suffer for the wrongs he has committed is one of the most terrible punishments the orishas can offer. To help the child evolve, to keep the child safe from harm, this person must straighten out his life immediately. There is no other way.

A heterosexual male who opens with this sign is promiscuous, and if he does not already have a woman pregnant, one will soon be with child. Unfortunately, if he does not change his ways, the danger here is that more than one woman will become pregnant by him. A woman who falls in this odu is of the mind-set to trap her lover through pregnancy, but this will bring only disastrous consequences. Ofún, in any pattern, warns that now is not the time to conceive; now is not the time to plan a pregnancy or to become pregnant. The elder paths of Obatalá that one finds in this letter warn that an imperfect child might be born soon; although many parents might find this a curse, for Obatalá it would be a blessing, for the imperfect are his true children. He is sworn to love and protect them at all costs. And although pregnancy right now is a health risk to the mother, Oshún stands up in this letter to forbid abortion. The client must either abstain from sex or use proper precautions at this time. He should also remember that under the influence of Ejila, sexual diseases are a strong possibility.

There are many other strict warnings that the diviner must deliver when this letter opens on the mat. To begin, the client has unresolved issues with Yemayá, and he should pray to and make an offering either to this titanic orisha in her home (the ocean) or to the godparent's Yemayá. The offering should be a watermelon, the most sacred of her foods, and from this moment on, the client must not eat watermelon. Also, there are, or soon will be, many fights in this person's life. Some will be with lovers, others will be with family or friends, and the advice of this odu is that the client should walk away peacefully from any sudden altercations. Arguments under the influence of this letter tend to get bloody quickly. The client must also be aware of the path he walks, for there is danger of a fall that could cause serious injury or death. To avoid all these osogbos and promote peace, the client must make every ebó prescribed to him as quickly as possible.

## The Prohibitions of Ofún Ejila

- Avoid adultery, infidelity, and promiscuity. These things will cost one's life. Conception is taboo; an imperfect child will be conceived. Use proper birth control, or abstain from sexual relations for six months. Note that if pregnancy occurs, abortion is taboo. Instead, return to the orishas and make ebó.
- Neither argue nor fight. Disputes will cause permanent separation between friends, family, and lovers, and one could end up in jail.

## The Eboses of Ofún Ejila

Special considerations for aleyos and aborishas: When the diloggún of Elegguá opens Ofún Ejila in an osogbo, the diviner must pay careful attention to the origin. If it comes elese otonowá (from heaven) or elese Shangó (from Shangó), Shangó is angry with the client; if it comes elese Aganyú (from Aganyú), Aganyú is angry with the client. Carefully, the diviner must examine this letter and all the client brings to the mat in order to determine the reason for the orisha's wrath. Then he must appease him with several eboses. After each ebó, the priest must use obí to determine whether it has been accepted. Once the coconut's letters come out clean (aláfia or ejife), the client may sit for a rogación before that orisha's shrine to correct the aché between himself and the spirit. Until these things are done, the client will remain in danger; he cannot evolve.

When Ofún Ejila opens on the mat, no matter the sign's orientation the following eboses are required:

- The client needs a rogación at Obatalá's feet with ten ingredients: grated coconut, grated cocoa butter, crushed cascarilla, white flowers, cotton, coconut milk, cow's milk, sandolo, honey, and grated pears. If osogbo came with this letter, the diviner should include eborí in this ebó: two white pigeons or white doves fed to the client's head.
- Strong eboses are needed for this letter. The

client should have both the elekes and the warriors; if he does not have them, he should receive them as soon as possible. The orisha who first spoke and claimed ebó in this sign demands that the client wear his or her eleke every day.

- The client must give saraeko (made from honey, cornmeal, and water) to the warriors.

If these considerations are not enough to close the sign, the diviner must turn to the eboses of the parent odu, Ofún (see page 489). Something there is needed for the client's evolution.

# The Thirteenth Composite Odu of Ofún, Ofún Metanla (10-13)

## The Proverbs of Ofún Metanla

- By mistake, the man was almost buried alive.
- He who rests under a strong tree benefits from the shade.

## The Message of Ofún Metanla

When a casting of ten mouths, Ofún, precedes a cast of thirteen mouths, Metanla, the odu Ofún Metanla is open on the mat. Ofún Irete is another name for this sign. Opening with this pattern, the diviner honors Babaluaiye, egun, Elegguá, Ogún, and Oyá, saying to each, "Maferefún!" Here, each is firm and each may speak; however, none speaks as strongly as Babaluaiye. He warns of sickness, diseases in the blood, and illnesses spread by sexual contact. This warning, however, is not only for the client but also for all those seated at the mat. As soon as possible, each present for the reading must light a white candle for Babaluaiye and supplicate him with toasted corn, epó, grated coconut, smoked fish, and jutía. Once this offering is complete, each supplicant must return to the diviner's home with a feathered animal for Babaluaiye. The diviner should cleanse the supplicant with the animal before sacrificing it to Babaluaiye.

This odu is very hot and volatile, and if the diviner is to help the client avoid the dangerous osogbo it brings, he must not fail to prescribe everything possible when it comes to eboses and larishes. The letter itself brings fires and tragedies to this person. He should go through his home, his office, his car, and any other place in which he spends a lot of time and remove all trash, empty bottles, and sources of flame. He should unplug all electrical appliances when they are not in use, and he must not keep sources of flame, such as matches, lighters, and cigarettes, near his sleeping place.

Relationships are flagged in this odu. The client should keep the following points in mind:

- If he has not had three marriages already, he will have three in his life. With the opening of this odu, he is either in or about to be in one of these marriages.
- When the client leaves home, another sneaks in behind his back. His current relationship will end in adultery.
- If the client is a woman, she will become pregnant if she is not careful.

## The Prohibitions of Ofún Metanla

- Avoid adultery, infidelity, and promiscuity. These things will bring osogbo to one's life.
- Do not let trash or empty bottles accumulate in one's home, office, or car.
- Have no more than two candles lit at home, and extinguish them when leaving. If they are not in use, unplug electrical appliances before sleeping or leaving home.
- Sleep clothed and with shoes next to the bed; danger could come in the middle of the night. Never sleep naked.

## The Eboses of Ofún Metanla

Special considerations for aleyos and aborishas: When the diloggún of Elegguá opens Ofún Metanla in an osogbo, the diviner must pay careful attention to its origin. If it comes elese otonowá (from heaven) or elese Babaluaiye (from Babaluaiye), Babaluaiye is angry with the client. Carefully, the diviner must examine the letter and all the client brings to the mat in order to determine the reason for this orisha's wrath. Then he must appease him with several eboses. After each ebó, the priest must use obí to determine whether it has been accepted. Once the coconut's letters come out clean (aláfia or ejife), the client may sit for a rogación before Babaluaiye's shrine to correct the aché between himself and the orisha. Until these things are done, the client will remain in danger.

When Ofún Metanla opens on the mat, no matter the sign's orientation three eboses are mandated by the odu:

- First, the client must have a rogación before Obatalá with the following ten ingredients: grated coconut, grated ñame, grated cocoa butter, two grated pears, crushed cascarilla, white bread, cow's milk, goat's milk, white flower petals, and cotton. If the osogbo is severe, promising death or disease, the diviner should consider sacrificing to the client's orí and ask the oracle, "Eborí?" Finally, if the session does not close out, a rogación sodidé might be necessary.
- Second, the client needs both the elekes and the warriors. If he does not have them, he must now be given them. If he already has the elekes, the diviner should consider bestowing the beads of every orisha that has spoken in Ofún Metanla; a rogación must precede this.
- Finally, before retiring for the night, this client must give a saraeko of cornmeal, water, and honey to the warriors. If he does not have his warriors, he should make this offering to the diviner's orishas before he leaves his home. The next morning, the client should throw the saraeko to the street with the words, "Eshu batie sode."

In addition, if the client is an aborisha who has Oyá as a guardian orisha, he is now marked to make ocha. This must be done as soon as possible, for it is the only way that he will evolve in life.

Having made these prescriptions, the diviner now has his first chance to close the oracle. If it refuses closure, he must investigate the following options for ebó:

- The rogación before Obatalá that the diviner has already prescribed may need to be strengthened. The diviner should ask, "Rogación sodidé elese Obatalá?" If the answers is yes, the rogación begins with the client's feet and ends with his head; this will elevate his entire consciousness toward his orí and Obatalá.
- The client could have issues with Babaluaiye. First, the diviner must ask, "Ebó elese Babaluaiye?" If the answer is yes, he should use the diloggún to mark the required ebó. If Babaluaiye takes no ebó, the diviner should ask, "Eleke de Babaluaiye?" If this is marked as the solution to the client's troubles, the diviner should invest the eleke upon the client after a rogación with the following ten ingredients: grated cocoa butter, grated coconut, crushed cascarilla, cotton, smoked fish, jutía, honey, coconut milk, white bread, and mashed plantains. The morning after the rogación, the client takes all the elements to the cemetery, because this ebó is intended to save the client from death. Finally, if neither of these satisfies the diloggún, the diviner should ask, "Koshé Babaluaiye?" If the reception is marked, the client should make preparations for this ceremony as soon as possible. Because this initiation is so expensive, however, the diviner may give the client the orisha's eleke to tide him over until he has the finances to proceed with the initiation.
- Ofún Metanla also brings unresolved issues with Oyá. If the client is an aleyo or an aborisha, the diviner should ask, "Ebó elese Oyá?" If the answer is yes, he uses the diloggún to mark the appropriate offering. If this will not solve the issues, the diviner should consider asking, "Eleke de Oyá?" If the answer is yes, the client should have a rogación with ten ingredients sacred to Oyá.

If these considerations are not enough to close the oracle for an aleyo or an aborisha, the italero must investigate the eboses of the parent odu, Ofún (see page 489). Something there is needed for the client's evolution. If the client is an initiate, however, and he does not have Oyá, he may need to receive her. The diviner should attempt to mark this by asking the shells, "Koshé Oyá?" If the answer is yes, preparations for her reception should be made as soon as possible. If the answer is no, or if the odu still will not close, the diviner must turn to the eboses of the parent odu, Ofún.

## The Fourteenth Composite Odu of Ofún, Ofún Merinla (10-14)

### The Proverb of Ofún Merinla

- There is a great war.

### The Message of Ofún Merinla

When an initial cast of ten mouths, Ofún, precedes a second cast of fourteen mouths, Merinla, the odu Ofún Merinla, also known as Ofún Ika, is open on the mat. When it comes, the diviner praises Babaluaiye, Obatalá, egun, and Orúnmila, saying to each, "Maferefún!" The influence of all four is strong in this odu, and each must be given proper homage. Orúnmila does not speak directly through the diloggún; however, this sign represents him as saying, "I have issues with this client; send him to my priests so that I may speak with him." The diviner should prepare the client: This letter foreshadows expensive eboses and initiations at the hands of Merlinla. Ofún Merinla says that the client will need to be cleansed thoroughly before Ifá; there is strong witchcraft on him, and it will take all the strength of the babalawo to fight it. Also, Orúnmila wants this person to evolve into a new life filled with blessings, but for this the client needs the Eshu of Ifá and either mano de Orúnmila (for a man) or kofá de Orúnmila (for a woman). If the client can afford these expensive initiations now, direct him to take them immediately.

Even in iré, Ofún Merinla is one of the most volatile letters in this family. When it comes, it is dangerous and will exaggerate all the warnings and prohibitions of Ofún. There may be robbery, confrontations, violence, and sickness in the client's life. His own karma is mounting a slow, subtle attack. He walks a path that is scorched by magic and sorcery; others have thrown powders and witchcraft at his feet, and he takes these vibrations with him wherever he goes. A spiritual prescription to cool his path may be made when this sign falls: The diviner should tell the client to rub the soles of his feet daily with cocoa butter while praying to Obatalá for peace and coolness. Inside his shoes, he should sprinkle cascarilla. For while he cannot avoid what others throw secretly in his path, he can take steps to lessen its effects. There is a war of Palo Mayombe; this person has attracted the scorn of powerful mayomberos, and they wish him dead. If he works frequently with Babaluaiye, Obatalá, and his own egun, he will survive these attacks. But before they are over, he will suffer. The secret to clearing the negativity of this sign is that the diviner must not fail to mark all possible eboses. He must work the diloggún thoroughly until all possible eboses have been marked.

### The Prohibitions of Ofún Merinla

- This sign gives a prohibition to the diviner: He must hold the derecho for this reading, and the derechos for any eboses performed, for four days. If he spends the money before this amount of time passes, he will absorb the client's osogbo. Also, he may not spend the money on himself. He must spend it on his orishas.
- Neither the diviner nor the client may work the rituals of Palo Mayombe for sixteen days. If there is a war, rely on the orishas, not the Congo spirits or the nkisi.
- Also, for the next sixteen days the client may not touch anything spiritually "hot" such as epó, peppers, and liquors. He must promote coolness in his life, and these things betray that quality.

### The Eboses of Ofún Merinla

When Ofún Merinla falls on the mat, regardless of its orientation it marks two eboses the diviner must do for himself before he can make ebó for the client. First, this odu announces a danger for the diviner: If he makes ebó for this person, the law will come to his front door. He must protect himself. As soon as possible, an elder priest must give the diviner a rogación sodidé before his guardian orisha. After all elements of the rogación are in place, this priest must feed the diviner's head two white pigeons. Second, after the rogación, the elder priest consecrates three arrows to Ochosi by feeding both the arrows and the orisha three dark pigeons. After feeding the arrows, wash them and mount them on the front door. The points of all three arrows must be turned upward, facing the sky; one is vertical so that it points directly to heaven from the earth, while the other two form an X over it. Once all these things are done, the diviner may make ebó for his client.*

In any orientation the diviner must prescribe the following eboses:

- The client must have a rogación before Obatalá with the following ingredients: grated coconut, grated ñame, grated pears, mashed plantains, grated cocoa butter, crushed cascarilla, bread, honey, coconut milk, white flowers, and cotton.
- For the sixteen days after the rogación, the client must dress in white. (If the dress code at his workplace prevents this, he may dress appropriately for work but immediately before and after he must dress in white.) During this sixteen days, the client must work hard to obtain the derecho needed for the initiation of the elekes of Obatalá, Yemayá, Oshún, Shangó, and Elegguá, if he does not have them; if he has these elekes, he must prepare to receive the eleke of Babaluaiye. On the seventeenth day, he returns to the diviner to receive this initiation.
- After the reception of the elekes, the client must spend another sixteen days in white. During this time he prepares to receive the warriors, if he does not have them. On the seventeenth day, he returns to the diviner's home for this initiation. If the reception of the warriors is a financial impossibility, at this time the client must present at least part of the derecho for this initiation. When Ofún Merinla has opened in a volatile osogbo, if the client cannot afford the entire initiation, the diviner should suggest that he receive at least Elegguá. And if the client already has his warriors, he must offer them an ebó of saraeko at this time.
- If this sign opened in osogbo, the client must offer eboses of a rooster to Elegguá at the street corner and in the house.
- If the odu still will not close, the diviner should prescribe the reception of Babaluaiye; the client needs this orisha for his health.

At this point, if the odu remains open, the diviner must turn to the eboses of the parent odu, Ofún (see page 489). Something there is needed for this client's evolution.

*Note that because the client brought Ofún Merinla to the diviner's home, he must pay for the priest to make this ebó; until it is done, the diviner can do nothing for the client. Also, if the diviner does not make ebó for the client, the law will not come.

## The Fifteenth Composite Odu of Ofún, Ofún Marunla (9-15)

### The Proverbs of Ofún Marunla

- The ones you deceive will discover the deception.
- While the machete clears the land for planting, it is the scythe that reaps the harvest.
- A full silo brings happiness to the farmer.
- The one who gets into trouble and does not beg forgiveness denies his guilt.

### The Message of Ofún Marunla

When an initial cast of ten mouths, Ofún, precedes a cast of fifteen mouths, Marunla, the odu Ofún Marunla is open on the mat. Ofún Iwori is another name for this sign. The letter brings up issues with Yemayá, and the client is forever forbidden to eat her sacred fruit, the watermelon. This letter speaks of a woman who has two men in her life; each thinks that he is the only one, and that she loves only him. This, however, is a lie, and before much time has passed the woman will be left all alone, on her own. In addition, Ofún warns against pregnancy; it will bring illness and possibly an imperfect child, and if the woman is careless in her methods of birth control, she will conceive under the influence of this letter. She also will be unsure about the parentage of her unborn child.

Many of the sicknesses and illnesses marked by Ofún Marunla are brought about through sex and the reproductive organs, so the client must monitor this area carefully for signs of disease and decay. Also, in both men and women there is danger of kidney problems and general body weakness.

## The Prohibitions of Ofún Marunla

- When Ofún Marunla opens, all melons are taboo. One may not eat, pick, pierce, or give them away. They are for ebó only.
- Cover one's head with a white hat or scarf when going out.
- Avoid extremes of temperature.
- Do not let sunlight, moonlight, or rainwater fall on one's head.

## The Eboses of Ofún Marunla

When Ofún Marunla opens, no matter its orientation the diviner must prescribe three eboses:

- The client needs a rogación before Obatalá using ten ingredients sacred to the orisha: grated coconut, grated ñame, grated cocoa butter, grated pears, mashed plantains, crushed cascarilla, white flowers, honey, goat's milk, and cotton. In a serious osogbo, the diviner must also feed the client's head two white pigeons. After the rogación, the priest uses a white silk scarf to cleanse the client's body of any remaining negativity; afterward, the scarf is given to Obatalá on an indefinite basis. For the next sixteen days, the client must dress in white.
- On the seventeenth day, the client must prepare a watermelon and take it to Yemayá in the ocean. To prepare this ebó, he should cut seven holes out of the melon, filling each hole with a penny, honey, molasses, gofio, jutía, smoked fish, and a pork rind. He then caps the holes with the "plugs" of rind he cut out and wraps the melon in a large blue cloth. He should throw this package as far out into the ocean as possible.
- The client must have the elekes, the warriors, and Olokun. Whatever he lacks he is now marked to receive.

If after making these prescriptions the diviner asks the letter for closure and is refused, he should consider whether the rogación he has prescribed for the client before Obatalá needs to be a rogación sodidé. He asks the shells, "Rogación sodidé?" If this is marked, the cleansing begins at the client's feet and ends at his head.

If after this question the letter still will not close for the client, the diviner must turn to the eboses of the parent odu, Ofún (see page 489). Something there is needed for this client's evolution.

# The Sixteenth Composite Odu of Ofún, Ofún Merindilogún (9-16)

## The Proverbs of Ofún Merindilogún

- Remember to pay your debts or you will get sick.
- This is the odu of phenomena.

## The Message of Ofún Merindilogún

When the initial cast of ten mouths precedes a cast of sixteen mouths, the odu Ofún Merindilogún is open on the mat. Ofún Otura is another name for this sign. Falling in this pattern, the diloggún demands strict ritual attention. The italero must suspend the reading before determining the orientation of the letter. First, the diviner puts the shells in the jícara of fresh water that was used to make a libation to the spirits when he first opened the reading, and while the shells soak all present for the reading, in the order of diviner, client, and then eldest to youngest initiates, taste a dab of epó. After all have tasted the palm oil, the diviner's assistant carries the gourd to the front door. Opening it wide, he flings the water as far out into the street as he can without losing any of the shells. He refills the gourd with cool water and returns it to the diviner. The shells remain submerged in this fresh water until the ritual of saraeko has been done for Obatalá and Elegguá. After completing all these rituals, the diviner continues the session.

Even if it comes in iré, the diviner treats Ofún Merindilogún as if it were in osogbo; it is a hot, volatile letter, and iré means only that the client will escape his difficulties in time if he follows the eboses and advice of this reading. This sign speaks of one who likes to tell others his personal business, even if his activities are illicit. Eventually, this will land him in trouble with the law, and the door to Ochosi's house has been practically thrown open to him. The diviner must advise the client to keep his mouth shut, telling him to keep his personal business to himself lest someone turn him in to the authorities. If he is participating in anything illegal, he must stop now.

Sickness is near the client, seeking him out; yet it cannot easily find him. The client should spend more time at home in "spiritual hiding" or retreat; the warriors should live with him in his home so that they can protect his front door from negativity. If the person at the mat is involved in witchcraft, the occult, or any type of spiritual system beyond this religion, he is warned never to use his skills for healing; he may never speak words of healing or offer advice for spiritual healing. The sicknesses he tries to cure by these means are incurable, and the forces that mount these diseases will then mount an attack against him.

In addition, Shangó stands up in this sign to offer a warning: "Do no favors, for the favors that are done will bring one's downfall." "Favors" here includes help solicited by brothers of blood and of ocha.

Finally, once this reading is done and the letter allows closure, the diviner would be wise to take this client to the feet of Ifá for a more thorough assessment.

## The Prohibitions of Ofún Merindilogún

- This odu carries a warning for both the italero and the client (if he is an initiate): Never allude to being able to cure illness. Many with incurable disease will come for healing, and great tragedy will result for the initiate. Make ebó, but make no promises.
- Refuse to do any favors for one's brother until the energy of this sign passes. Those favors, if done, will bring osogbo to one's life.

## The Eboses of Ofún Merindilogún

The diviner must prescribe an ebó for everyone present at the reading: Before midnight that night, they must each give a saraeko of water, cornmeal, and honey to their own warriors. At the first stroke of midnight, they must discard the saraeko into the street. Ofún Merindilogún will remain with someone in the room in addition to the client; it is said that either the first or the last to remove saraeko from his or her warriors will take the osogbo upon him- or herself. The diviner should also advise all the initiates present to return for a session with Elegguá's diloggún before too much time passes. He himself must also seek out another italero for a reading to make sure Ofún Merindilogún has brought no misfortune on him.

For the client, when Ofún Merindilogún opens on the mat in an osogbo, the odu says that he has serious issues with Shangó. These issues revolve around petitions the client has made to Shangó, promising ebó in exchange for a blessing. The orisha says that the blessing was brought, but the client never gave him what he promised. Now the diviner must speak honestly with the client, encouraging him to try to remember any promises he made to Shangó but did not keep. As ebó, he must now fulfill these promises. If the client cannot remember any unkept promises to Shangó, the diviner must determine if the orisha will accept ebó to settle the debt, asking, "Ebó elese Shangó?" If the answer is yes, he uses the diloggún to mark the appropriate offering. If the answer is no, the italero must lead the client to offer to Shangó something "from the heart." Without an ebó, there is no way to settle these issues, and he will not evolve.

In any orientation, Ofún Merindilogún requires that the client have a rogación to clear his orí of negative energies. The diviner should give this rogación before Obatalá with the following ingredients: grated coconut, grated ñame, grated cocoa butter, crushed cascarilla, white flowers, mashed plantains, coconut milk, cow's milk, goat's milk, and cotton. If a serious osogbo is open, the diviner may consider two further options: a rogación sodidé and eborí. They may be needed to soothe the misfortune brought by Ofún Merindilogún.

If the prescriptions made thus far are not enough to close the odu, the diviner should consider the following eboses:

- If the client is an aleyo or an aborisha, he must now have the elekes and the warriors. If he lacks either, he is now marked for their reception. If the client already has both, the diviner should see if the warriors will take an ebó in exchange for fighting the client's battles, asking, "Ebó elese los guerreros?" If the answer is yes, he uses the diloggún to mark the appropriate offering.
- Five spirits speak in this sign: Yemayá, Elegguá, egun, Shangó, and Orúnmila. Each may stand up to claim ebó in this odu. If the sign will not close, the diviner should consider whether any of these spirits (except for Orúnmila) will take an offering, asking, "Ebó elese [spirit's name]?" If Yemayá, Elegguá, egun, and Shangó will not take ebó, the diviner should recommend that the client go to Ifá for a thorough assessment.

If none of these will close the odu for the client, the diviner must turn to the eboses listed for the parent odu, Ofún (see below). Something there is needed to close the session.

## Closing the Reading: Further Eboses of the Parent Odu, Ofún

Having exhausted the options of larishe and ebó within the composite odu, if the letter remains open, the italero must turn to the eboses of the parent odu, Ofún, to bring closure. This sign contains many eboses to placate both the letter and the spirits that speak through it. The possible offerings and sacrifices follow.

To begin, remember that in Ofún the orishas Obatalá, Oshún, and Oyá can solve almost any osogbo. If nothing has been marked for them in the session thus far, the italero must consider each and what his or her issues might be. Ofún itself can mark unpaid debts to the three orishas, so the diviner must talk with his client honestly: Has he ever prayed to any of these for a special blessing in exchange for ebó? If the ebó was not made, or if it was not made in a timely or acceptable manner, that ebó is marked as ebó now. If the client remembers no such promises, the diviner should ask for each of the three, "Ebó elese [orisha's name]?" If the answer is yes, he uses the diloggún to mark the appropriate offering. Anything marked at this point must be given immediately.

Note also that within Ofún are five "conditional" eboses that must be done if the diviner has come this far without closing the oracle and the client comes under one of the following circumstances. The diviner should consider each carefully:

- First, if the client is a woman with children, she should make a votive offering to the first orisha who spoke to her in this sign. This will ensure that her children come to no harm either in the house or in the street. Remember: Ofún marks tragedies for children related to the client. Normally, this ebó is given to Elegguá, because his diloggún is read for the aleyo and initiate alike, but if an orisha who embodies some sort of motherhood (like Yemayá or Oshún) stands up, the offering should be directed to her. If there is any confusion, the diviner should mark the orisha taking the ebó and the ebó itself with the shells.
- Second, if the client is a married man, having any type of osogbo mandates that he make a votive offering to Oshún lest his wife be influenced by this letter. The worst-case scenario under this sign is that she will feel impelled to leave her husband while he is under Ofún's

influence. The diviner must mark the ebó to Oshún so her acceptance is ensured.

- Third, if the client possesses the warriors, immediately upon returning home he should give a saraeko made from water, cornmeal, and honey to Elegguá, Ogún, and Ochosi. This offering should be left with the orishas overnight and thrown to the street the next morning. The client should repeat this offering every day for three days. If the osogbo is severe, the client should add a dry white wine to the saraeko.
- Fourth, if the client opens in an osogbo in Ofún and the letter will not close after the initial larishe (if any) and the eboses of the composite odu have been prescribed, for the next ten days he should use a spiritual bath made of quita maldición. If the osogbo is severe, fifteen different herbs sacred to the first orisha to speak in this letter should be added to this bath. If the letter still will not close, the baths should be repeated for a total of sixteen days, and during this time the client must dress totally in white.
- Finally, until the energy of Ofún has cleared, the client should mark both his feet and his hands with cocoa butter and cascarilla before going out his front door the first time in the morning. This will help him encounter only coolness and freshness throughout his daily journeys.

Having prescribed the eboses from the list above that apply, the diviner may attempt to close the oracle again. If it continues to refuse closure, he must pursue the following options:

- The diviner should now review the eboses that have been prescribed during the course of the reading. At this point, the diviner needs to placate not just the orishas but also the letter Ofún. Ofún marks the number ten in all its offerings; all eboses that have been prescribed must be adjusted to incorporate the number ten in their composition. For instance, if a single rogación was mandated, the diviner should incorporate ten elements into that rogación. If a single cleansing was prescribed, the diviner should turn this into a series of ten cleansings. Offerings made with multiples of ten will soothe this odu.
- If the composite did not prescribe a rogación, the diviner should ask, "Rogación elese Obatalá?" If this is accepted as ebó, the diviner continues by asking, "Rogación sodidé elese Obatalá?" and then "Eborí?" Ten elements sacred to Obatalá must be used in this rogación: grated coconut, grated ñame, grated cocoa butter, crushed cascarilla, white flowers, coconut milk, goat's milk, cow's milk, white bread, and white cotton. The diviner should also consider asking, "Ebó elese Obatalá?" Give any adimú marked at this point immediately after the rogación is complete.
- Still barring closure, the client's orí needs more reinforcement. The diviner should give a rogación with the mark of ten every day for four days and demand that the client dress totally in white during this time. The following prohibitions must be added to any already given: Avoid dark places, and avoid places where the dead frequent (hospitals, nursing homes, funeral homes, and cemeteries).
- If the rogación cannot be marked, Obatalá needs ebó with four cool fruits. The diviner should let the oracle mark the fruits to be given. If either Obatalá or Ofún demands more, the same four fruits should be given anew every day for four days, and after the last set of fruits is taken away from him, two doves or white pigeons are offered in sacrifice to the orisha. Note that if some type of cleansing has been marked previously, the client may cleanse himself with the fruits before discarding them and replacing them with new ones; he may also be cleansed with the pigeons before the sacrifice.
- Through Ofún, the client might have additional issues with Odua, egun, Iroko, Yewa, Naná Burukú, Babaluaiye, Osain, Elegguá, or Ogún. At this point, the diviner should consider marking ebó for the orishas, asking, "Ebó elese [orisha's name]?" If the answer is yes, he uses the diloggún to mark the appropriate offering.

- If the odu still will not close, the diviner should consider the reception of Babaluaiye, asking, "Koshé Babaluaiye?"
- If the client is an initiate, the diviner may consider the reception of Oyá, Odua, Iroko, Yewá, Naná Burukú, and Osain, asking, "Koshé [orisha's name]?" He may also consider the reception of the diloggún of Ogún, asking, "Koshé caracoles de Ogún?"
- If the oracle still will not close and this reading is an itá for a iyawó using the shells of either Elegguá or the crowning orisha, every month, on a Friday, this person must have a white bath and, immediately afterward, give a spiritual mass in his home for egun. The ancestors form the foundation of his spiritual court, and he must elevate them. The white bath should be made with white lilies, goat's milk, river water, cocoa butter, and cascarilla. He should prepare this bath once a month on Thursday night and leave it with Obatalá until Friday morning. Immediately upon awakening, the client bathes with this; afterward, he dresses in white and has the mass for egun. He should remain in white for the rest of the day.

After these options have been exhausted, the diviner may turn to the eboses of the omo odu as a parent odu. For example, in a casting of Ofún Obara (10-6), the diviner would now turn to the eboses of the parent odu Obara for closure. If, however, the reading has progressed this far and Ofún will not close out, there could be some error or oversight on the diviner's part. He should call an experienced elder diviner for a second opinion.

# TWELVE

# THE FAMILY OF OWANI

## The Proverbs of Owani

- Two words sum one up: ungrateful and mistrustful.
- When water is carried in a basket, it drips between the reeds.
- When money is scarce, the search for work begins; when one feels thirst, one travels to the well; when hunger pangs are felt, one seeks out food: Only when a need becomes known does one begin his search, for need is the beginning of fulfillment.
- Famine comes when food is scarce.
- Thirst comes when the well runs dry.
- Poverty comes when money is scarce.
- When there is more on the ground than in the basket, one has wasted his blessing.
- The hurt that one causes others is the hurt that they will cause him.
- Those who break taboo suffer in their own ignorance.
- Water cannot be carried in a basket.
- Only the coconut knows if it has worms inside.
- You are one who is ungrateful and full of mistrust.
- You try to carry your water in a basket.

## The Orishas Who Speak in Owani

| | |
|---|---|
| egun | Ogún |
| Elegguá | Ochosi |
| Oshún | Naná Burukú |
| Babaluaiye | Osain |
| Olokun | Shangó |
| Oyá | |

## The Message of Owani

Having opened with eleven mouths on the mat, the ritual of diloggún becomes an earnest, solemn occasion; Owani has come to the house. It is a powerful sign demanding the utmost in respect, thoughtfulness, and consideration from the diviner. It was born of Metanla (thirteen mouths), an angry, fulminating sign whose dynamics are lost to diviners who have not the skill of an oriaté. To understand the primal energy of Owani, however, one must examine, briefly, the implications of Metanla. While the orisha Babaluaiye speaks freely throughout the diloggún, Metanla is the only family of letters he owns; it is the sign through which he began his sojourn to the earth and in which he received his aché as an emissary of Olódumare. With Babaluaiye's ascension came disease and terminal illness, and it is Metanla giving him that power. Many know Metanla as the letter giving birth to "the hot winds that bring infectious disease . . . tropical epidemics [that] will blow through an area and strike at random."* Even in its most gentle orientations, thirteen mouths brings Babaluaiye's wrath: disease of the skin,† immune disorders, famine, poverty, and communal catastrophes. Yet the iré of Metanla is this: That which does not kill us makes us stronger. That which does not destroy our species evolves it. Metanla is an integral part of life, for it destroys weakness and strengthens survivors.

Metanla began in creation as a primal concept, an idea, a force that had no form, and as it evolved, it coalesced upon itself. Yet so vast were its energies that Metanla could not keep up with itself; it could not encompass itself. The odu overflowed with energy; the outpouring of Olódumare's strength was too much for it to hold. Much like the contents of a cup thoughtlessly filled to the brim and beyond, these energies and unrealized potentials spilled away from their container, their mother sign, and they puddled to themselves. From this puddle was Owani born. All the potentials that thirteen mouths could not hold to itself were lost, and these evolved; they became something new. Of Owani, Fatunmbi writes, "Once the past has become solidified in the present moment, it lays the foundation for that which is to come . . . every present moment carries the potential to change the future as an act of will."‡ The odu Owani is rooted in the past and geared toward the future, yet its fulfillment is found in one's present actions. It is a letter of introversion and introspection, and it encourages the sacrifice of all superfluous for the accomplishment of one goal.

Already, before casting a composite on the mat, the diviner knows much about the client who has opened with eleven mouths. This sign was born of affliction, poverty, sickness, and unrealized dreams; all these exist within the client now. This person has survived the worst in his life, and he is stronger for it. He will need this strength to continue his evolution, becoming what he was truly meant to be. All his unrealized dreams and crushed aspirations are still with him, and with an eloquent reading of eleven mouths the diviner can help this person live up to his destiny. It is a formidable pattern, one of fulfillment through growth; its energy brings the final realization of one's hopes and dreams. Yet it brings them to fruition only with the ultimate sacrifice: total commitment to growth.

A major crossroads lies before the client. His entire life has pushed him to this one point. Now is a time for both introspection and introversion, but the diviner should not let the client remain motionless for too long or his momentum will be lost. To help the one who has come to the mat understand these things, the diviner should have him visualize a crossroads. For years he has traveled a long, arduous road, and now four options face him: Stand still, turn right, turn left, or forge ahead. If he stands still, all avenues of choice remain open but unfulfilled; remaining still for too long, someone will overtake him from the rear. Picking one of the other three options sacrifices the remaining two, and he will never know what lay at the end of those roads. The choice he makes now will alter the course of his life forever, and eleven mouths is here to help him navigate.

The italero can be assured that the client's past is a shadow, a blurred memory, a fragment of light that he shares with no one but himself, and that the weight of the present bears down on him ominously. He is so lost in the past and blocked by the present that there seems to be no future. He is frozen. These feelings are borne by all those who open in Owani. To evolve, the client must perceive all his major choices to be decisive crossroads in his life. He must consciously, deliberately, choose the direction to travel; once he has made his choice, he must follow through with no hesitation. Unlike a real crossroads, in which one may turn around and go back if a wrong turn has been made, the philosophical crossroads of life do not offer this option. Time

---

*Awó Fá'Lokun Fatunmbi, *Awó: Ifá and the Theology of Orisha Divination* (Bronx, N.Y.: Original Publications, 1992), 144.

†Author's note: Because of the syncretism of Babaluaiye with the Catholic saint Lazarus (the poor man from the parable of the rich man and the poor man), many associate leprosy with Babaluaiye. In truth, leprosy is a scourge of Orisha Oko, who suffered as a leper while living among mortals. Babaluaiye was afflicted with smallpox, and he spread this disease around the globe when humans and orishas made fun of him. From this disease he received one of his many names: Sòpònná (the Yoruba word, and spelling, for smallpox). While Babaluaiye can be associated with leprosy because he has aché over all skin afflictions, he was never a leper.

‡Fatunmbi, *Awó,* 141.

stands still for no one, and the chance to alter one's course in life does not come often. Once a major, life-altering event occurs, life is forever transmuted. There is no "going back" to make another choice. One's mistakes cannot be corrected. Owani encompasses the mystery of sacrifice, and the client will have to sacrifice everything to reach his goals. Remember: Metanla destroys weakness so that strength may prevail, and Owani uses this power to further evolution. While the client might feel weak, the diviner knows that he is strong. The odu ensures this. Such is the sign's power that Fatunmbi makes one final assertion: "[Owani] incarnates great prophets, those who have the courage to deviate from the past in search of a better future, in search of deeper levels of understanding and harmony."* If he heeds all this session reveals, the client can achieve all this, and more.

When Owani opens on the mat, as a measure of respect for its depth, the diviner temporarily suspends the reading to give the sacred sign of this odu: Placing both hands on the mat with the palms facing up, he wiggles the fingers of both several times in succession. Note that Owani is sometimes called "wiggly," for those born under it have soft, weak backs; however, although the sacred gesture alludes to this, no one would dare call eleven mouths by this name while it is open.

After giving this sign, the diviner bows his head and chants the odu's prayer:

*Owani Shogbe egbe Eshu wa sisa.*
*Chimi chi awo obe ofe ilu agana.*
*Chemi che adie dane lore kana mofe tani.*

While the diviner is intoning this, to honor the opening odu and the orisha who owns it many will mutter, "Maferefún Owani Shogbe! Maferefún Elegguá!" Those who know this sign well continue their devotions with "Maferefún Babaluaiye!" Because Babaluaiye rules the parent of Owani, Metanla, his energy is reflected here. Metanla could not hold all the mystery that Babaluaiye is, and some of it overflowed into this family of odu. Finally, some will say, "Maferefún Olokun!" In a letter as deep and mysterious as this, no spirit can see what it hides in its depths better than he.

Once the prayer is complete, many italeros and oriatés perform a short series of rituals to honor the odu; being a sign of great mystery and depth, Owani demands both respect and placation. First, the diviner gathers all the shells from the mat, open mouths first and closed mouths second. He puts these in the jícara of water that was used to pour a libation to the orishas before the ritual of diloggún began. Eleven mouths is hot, and its display on the mat opens a spiritual vortex channeling Owani's energy into the reading room. Water cleanses and filters this. Water alone, however, is not enough to bring freshness back to the shells; some of Owani's energy has escaped into the italero's home, and he must remove it. The diviner gives the gourd to his assistant, if he has one, and directs him to take the shells to the front door. The assistant opens the door wide and, using one hand to cover the open gourd, with his fingers fanned loosely so water may flow out, he dashes the water as far away from the front door as possible. Thus is the heat of Owani removed from the diviner's home. Odu is now spiritually "cool" enough to be handled, and the assistant returns the shells to the diviner so he can proceed with the casting of the composite. (Note that if no assistant is present, the diviner must do all these things himself.)

The diviner then casts the omo odu. If the secondary letter exceeds twelve mouths, showing Metanla (thirteen mouths), Merinla (fourteen mouths), Marunla (fifteen mouths), or Merindilogún (sixteen mouths), the initial heat of Owani is doubled. A novice italero has neither the training nor the skill to handle this sign. While an elder priest might read these letters, and while an oriaté will always investigate these letters, those inexperienced with the diloggún must not work with these composites.† Again, the assistant is called to perform a brief series of rituals to cool the orisha's

*Fatunmbi, *Awó*, 142.

†For this reason, this chapter does not deal with any composites beyond Owani Ejila. These signs contain too many variables with which a book of this scope cannot deal. Only training with an elder oriaté will give the initiate the skills necessary to manipulate these composite odu.

diloggún, bringing this session to closure. The diviner puts all the shells in a gourd of fresh, cool water; the assistant takes this gourd to the front door and casts the water as far away from the house as possible, without losing any of the shells. Note that in some houses, the custom is to have a virgin child, if possible do the ritual of cooling Owani's heat the second time, for children are, by nature, innocent, and innocence placates Owani. When the assistant returns the shells to the priest, the priest gathers the shells in his cupped palms and blows on them. He then seals the diloggún in a covered plate and returns the client's derecho. Later, after the client leaves, the priest casts a large quantity of cool water into the street after him to remove all possible harm from his front door. For a proper consultation, this diviner takes his client to a more experienced oriaté or a babalawo.*

If a secondary odu opens that is numerically less than twelve mouths, the session with Owani proceeds normally. Both diviner and client manipulate the cowries and the ibó in tandem, determining the qualities of iré or osogbo and their orientations. Once all this information is gathered, the reading is interrupted for a brief series of rituals designed to placate the owner of this odu, Elegguá. If it has opened in iré, Owani demands that a saraeko of water, cornmeal, and honey be given to this orisha. If the odu has opened in osogbo, Owani demands the same saraeko for Elegguá, but with the additional ingredients of epó, jutía, and smoked fish.

In this letter many orishas might choose to speak. The one whose shells have been cast has the first option. Since this is the spirit who has marked Owani, this is the one to whom the client must turn for spiritual help; this orisha has identified the major decisions that must be made and will guide the client to proper action. Egun follow this orisha. Since the ancestors form one's spiritual foundation, in eleven mouths there is no force that can provide greater guidance. The diviner should have the client reflect for a moment on the ancestors that he knows by name; then he should have him think about all those who have been forgotten. It has taken hundreds of souls and thousands of years to create the client's current incarnation. Nothing is born of pure chance; while life might seem chaotic, there is a plan behind this chaos. The diviner might ask him, "Why do you think you are here? Why has so much gone into creating your one life?" The ancestors have a selfish interest in this person's evolution. Through Owani, the propitiation of egun is essential; they will help unravel this person's destiny.

Elegguá's influence is felt next. He owns this sign, and without him little good can come of it. To pick apart the many prophecies in this pattern, the diviner should determine if the client knows his guardian orisha. The client's orí could be Elegguá's, and it is through him that the client must work to understand Owani's implications. Even if the client is an aborisha with a guardian orisha other than Elegguá, in Owani the propitiation and adoration of Elegguá is essential, for he is so close that he might as well own the client's head. If the client has not received the warriors, the reception of Elegguá is mandatory. Any other initiation such as the elekes or warriors can wait for a time. For whatever reason, Elegguá wants to be in the client's life; he will have little evolution until he is there. An initiate will have the same issues in this odu as an aleyo or aborisha; however, if this letter opens in an osogbo it hints at a lack or respect between the two, between mortal and immortal. The guardian orisha comes first and foremost; but the diviner should caution the initiate client that without Elegguá's goodwill, there is no communication between humans and the divine. The client must adore this spirit; he will bring about evolution.

Oshún and Babaluaiye are the next orishas who speak through this odu. As the client makes his life-altering decisions under the influence of Owani, he should spend time pampering Oshún; even if he makes the wrong decisions, with her goodwill he can still reap the blessings of her sweetness. Babaluaiye can forgive the poor choices the client has made in the past, especially ones directly affecting his health. While Babaluaiye may not completely

*The diviner is cautioned to not read for anyone else that day until after he has read for himself; the eboses prescribed in his own reading will serve to remove all harm that the volatile energies these last four composite odu can bring.

heal, he can soothe, and sometimes this minor release from pain is all it takes to make life livable again. If one or both of these orishas speak in an osogbo, they come to claim debts owed to them. If the client is a child of either spirit, his problems here deepen; the orishas are angry, and this anger must be appeased. The client must clear these debts immediately. The diviner should counsel the client on this issue, helping him determine if any promises have been broken. If the one at the mat remembers nothing, mark eboses to the orisha. The clearance of debt is essential to evolution.

Oyá, Ogún, Ochosi, Naná Burukú, Osain, and Shangó may speak through Owani's composites, but their issues will be dependent on two things: the reason bringing the client to the mat and the composite odu opened before him. When others try to bring scandal, intrigue, or treason to the client, Oyá, Ogún, and Elegguá take prominence. If the client gives the three ebó, they will help him. With the shells, the diviner should mark an ebó to satisfy all three spirits. When invoking them with ebó, the diviner should bring the three orishas together: He sets Oyá on a small throne with Elegguá and Ogún before her, and then gives the client a rogación before all three spirits. After the rogación, he leads the client in making his ebó. For eleven days this miniature throne stands; the diviner should keep at least one white seven-day candle burning to the orishas. On the twelfth day, he may take it down and return the orishas to their normal shrine, knowing that all three are focused on the client's problems.

Ochosi defends those destined for incarceration; however, the diviner should assure the client that he will face some punishment for his crimes. Making ebó, followed with behavior modification, will lessen the client's punishment. The client should do the following: With twenty-one dollars in his pocket, he should go to the jail in which he is destined to spend time if found guilty of his crimes. At the front desk, he should ask the attending officer if he himself (the client, using his full name) is in the facility at this time. When the attendant answers no, the client should politely ask the attendant to check one more time. And when the attendant again answers no, the client should ask if he was there recently. Three is one of Ochosi's numbers, and once the client's question has been answered three times negatively, the client should go out into the street until he finds a beggar or indigent at a crossroads, and he should then give the person his derecho, promising Ochosi that he will never again break the law. Elegguá, as fate, will be appeased by these actions, and Ochosi will close the doors to his house for a time. To continue his crimes after this, however, will once again bring the wrath of these two spirits, and the ebó will then be useless. The client must resolve within himself to give up all shady dealings.

Shangó walks closely with Obatalá in Owani. Shangó is the client's defender. When the one at the mat feels that his life is in danger at the hands of another, he should go to Shangó for protection, offer him adimú, and pray that he fights in all wars the client is facing. Through Obatalá, the client opening in Owani can find peace. He should cleanse himself and his house with two white pigeons and then feed the birds to Obatalá. He also should have a rogación at Obatalá's feet to soothe his orí; afterward, a white hen or rooster (depending on the client's path of Obatalá) should be given to the orisha in thanksgiving. If the help of either Shangó or Obatalá is enlisted, both should be honored.

Finally, the diviner must emphasize again the importance of honoring and propitiating Elegguá until Owani has passed. He is of integral importance. Owani can be placated only by continual ebó. The diviner must ensure that the client understands this and follows through with his religious responsibilities.

The easiest way to begin a study of Owani is with an investigation of it in iré. If the odu is marked as coming in iré, the diviner can make many assumptions about the client and how he will progress. This odu has come as one of evolution; the client's life will change, but the changes that occur, and how he will benefit from them, depend on the choices that he makes now. Again, consider the illustration of a crossroads—while one may travel any road, only one of the paths available will lead the client to his proper destination. His entire life has been spent building up to this one point, and now he must make an informed decision. The diviner must emphasize the quality of sacrifice in making these choices, for travel on any one path bars travel on any other. Also, even in iré Owani emphasizes the need to focus and find stillness within, and it marks commitment to the achievement of one goal. While the client might feel that he can be or do anything he wants, in truth he can be no more than himself, and he can accomplish only one thing at a time. If he follows this bit of advice, Owani in iré promises attainment.

When the diloggún promises iré, the diviner's next step is to mark the type of iré promised by the sign. Given the action of Owani, which pushes one to make rapid choices, the origin of one's blessings is integral to proper action; the diviner must mark the origin so the client does not miss his blessing. Of the twenty-five possible origins for blessings, in Owani some are more favored than others. Those that bring favorable graces in eleven mouths are iré otonowá (blessings from heaven), iré elese ocha (blessings from the orishas), iré elese egun (blessings from the ancestors), iré elese ará onú (blessings from the inhabitants of heaven), and iré ashegunota (blessings from the orisha's otanes). Likewise, in Owani some sources of iré can equate with osogbo; they are not firm in the letter's energies and can cause travesty and turmoil to the client if the diloggún marks them as the source of his grace. These irés of misfortune are iré elese eledá (blessings from one's orí), iré arikú (blessings of a long life), iré lowó (blessings through one's hands or works), iré ibujoko (blessings through change), and iré iyekú (blessings through death, accident, or inheritance). The manner in which the diviner proceeds with the reading depends on the type of iré that opens.

When a propitious iré comes for the client, the diviner must keep the following points in mind:

- **Iré otonowá.** When iré otonowá opens through Owani, it shows that blessings shower upon the client from Olódumare and from all the spirits who sit at his feet. In eleven mouths, this is a favorable grace to have. While the orishas may seem, in comparison to humans, to be omniscient, they are in truth limited in their knowledge; God, however, never makes a mistake. He is vast, knowing all that exists in heaven, on the earth, and beyond. Iré otonowá through eleven mouths shows that the client stands at a crossroads, yes, but this point in his life can bring him all that he was destined for. The diviner must encourage the client to follow through with the prescribed taboo and ebó, for with adherence to these the client will make no mistakes as he pursues his goals.
- **Iré elese ocha.** When iré elese ocha opens in Owani, blessings come from a specific spirit. The diviner's next job is to determine who offers the blessing. In Owani, the orishas who may offer blessings are Elegguá, Oshún, Babaluaiye, Olokun, Oyá, Ochosi, Naná Burukú, Osain, and Shangó. The diviner questions each in turn, asking, "Iré elese [orisha's name]?" until he determines the proper orisha. If none of these offers a blessing, the diviner should next consider the spirits speaking through the composite odu open on the mat. It is important to determine the orisha who offers blessings, for the client must focus all his love, adoration, and propitiation upon this force. As the client navigates what Owani throws at him, this one orisha will protect and guide him on his journey.
- **Iré elese egun.** Through Owani, one's egun often clamor for attention. When they mark iré at their feet, they have a vested interest in the client's evolution. What he attains now is, in part, the fulfillment of many of their dreams. While alive, they did not accomplish all they set out to do, but through this person, much of what remained undone will be finished. Egun can form a vast spiritual foundation in Owani, one that the client must rely on in the trials that lie ahead. When iré elese egun comes, he must focus on their worship and propitiation.
- **Iré elese ará onú.** Promising iré from the spirits in heaven, Owani emphasizes a spiritual current similar to iré elese egun. However, in this case the spirits pushing the client toward evolution are not his ancestors but spirits unrelated to him physically and spiritually; they are foreign souls that for whatever reason have taken an interest in this person. Somehow, the client's

evolution fulfills some part of their own work on the earth, and they will labor ceaselessly until his fulfillment is realized. They can come from any cultural or spiritual background, for heaven does not discriminate on the basis of religion, and in the end, we all worship one creative force. While the client must focus on ará onú in manners similar to egun, he must realize that there is a difference in the spiritual forces with which he works.

- **Iré ashegunota.** This orientation of iré points out that the good fortune predicted will be brought by one of the otanes, or sacred stones, of the orishas. First, the diviner must determine which orisha brings the blessings to the client, asking, "Elese [orisha's name]?" If the client is an aleyo or an aborisha, the diviner asks this question of Elegguá, Ogún, Ochosi, and Babaluaiye. If iré ashegunota comes from Elegguá, Ogún, or Ochosi, it is necessary for the client to receive the warriors; if it is offered by Babaluaiye, the client must receive him. If the client is an initiate, the diviner asks this question of Elegguá,* Babaluaiye, Oyá, Ogún, Ochosi, Naná Burukú, and Osain. If the client does not have the orisha who stands up to offer iré, he must receive him or her.

When Owani opens with one of these favorable graces, it is a letter of great achievement, maximum evolution, and riches, for no matter the client's current status in life (poverty, despair, or illness), eleven mouths shows the road toward destiny. The many patakís found among its lore illustrate this. Here, it is said that Oshún, the mother of all sweetness and richness on the earth, fell down on hard times; she was enveloped in poverty and despair, and no matter how hard she tried, all that she touched withered. Helpless and hopeless, Oshún went to the earthly diviners to learn what she had to do to prosper once more. Owani opened for her on the mat, and the odu itself stood up to bless the spirit. "Owani is here," said the diviner, "and it has come to bless you. Yet your sacrifice is no simple thing, and not only will it take all that you possess materially, but also all your faith will be tested. Take every last bit of money you have, and go to the market. Use every penny to buy all the epó and all the honey you can find. Before sundown, pour this into the river. Owani will bring all that you desire, and more." Oshún despaired, for she had so little left and was loath to part with it, yet she had faith in the diviner's skills and the decree of the odu. Immediately, she took all that she had to the marketplace, and there she bought all the epó and honey she could find. Knowing who she was, the merchants even gave her extra. At the river's edge, she prayed to Olódumare as she poured all that she had left into the river, giving each drop to make her offering. At the riverbank, forlorn with nothing else in life, Oshún sank down and cried; she cried so much and so hard that she was exhausted and fell into a deep sleep. When she awoke the next morning, she saw that her tears lay beside her, but each had turned into a perfect jewel. The river itself was transformed. The epó had become brass, and the honey gold. Olódumare made Oshún the owner of that river, and with its treasure, she became the richest orisha on earth.

Even Dada, Shangó's crown, found wealth and prosperity through the odu Owani. When he came to the earth, he was surrounded by many spirits whose names have now been lost to history. All of them were poor, for Olódumare provided only those things that they would need their first few days in this world. Wanting to live long, prosperous lives, they sought out the earthly diviners, and the odu Owani opened for each. The diviners told them, "Make ebó to Shangó with all that you have, holding nothing back. He comes to bless you, but he requires total commitment and total faith. Feed the orisha a ram, a rooster, and a guinea hen. Do not waste the meat; prepare a huge feast from the animals in Shangó's honor, serving him no less than half of all that is cooked. Although you are poor, you must save nothing from this selfishly for yourselves—feed as many people as possible with what is left over. Sometimes, it is better to appear wealthy

*The initiate will have already received Elegguá. However, through Owani, Elegguá might stand up to demand that the initiate receive a new Eshu. If this is the case, as part of the ebó the diviner must mark the path of Eshu to be received.

and generous than it is to actually be wealthy. Once Shangó is sated, make ebó to the odu Owani in your backyards. With all the money you have, buy eleven of the largest baskets you can afford. Purchase enough toasted corn to fill each basket to overflowing, and on top of each, leave eleven cowrie shells in honor of this odu. Do this, and you will never want for anything in life again. Shangó will bless you, and this odu will make you rich!" Dada and all the spirits made ebó to Shangó, and that evening the entire town was fed. All came to honor Shangó, and the orisha himself, sated on the flesh of so many animals, blessed all who came to his feast. Only Dada, however, finished his ebó to honor Owani with the baskets, corn, and cowries. The other spirits spent almost all that they had on the sacrifices to the orisha, and all but Dada were leery to part with what little money they had left. Dada was broke and penniless after laying the baskets with corn and cowries outdoors, but he had faith in Owani, Shangó, and the diviner. When he awoke the next morning, the corn in the baskets was gone, and in its place were thousands of gold coins, jewels, and other precious things. As promised by the odu, Dada became rich beyond his wildest dreams.

When one of the less favorable graces of Owani opens at the mat, the diviner should carefully consider the following issues for each:

- **Iré elese eledá.** This promises goodness from one's orí, or head. However, in Owani the head is not always strong or clear. Rapidity of decisions is called for, and if the client's head is overwhelmed by the choices laid out, he will miss the goodness promised. Some of the composites themselves emphasize that the client's head is bad (a "bad head" signals that one is born to fail in life) no matter the orientation of this odu, and if his head is bad, goodness cannot be forthcoming. Yet there is a solution to this: The client must have a rogación, or a series of rogaciónes, before his guardian orisha. (If his guardian orisha is not known, the rogación should be given before Obatalá.) During the reading, if issues of weakness come up, the diviner should prescribe eborí, the feeding of the head. When iré elese eledá is marked for an aleyo whose guardian orisha is not known, the diviner should prescribe a bajado as ebó; the determination of who guides his orí is essential to the client's evolution. If iré elese eledá opens for an aborisha who knows his guardian orisha, he must now commit to making ocha; this is the crossroads foreshadowed spiritually. If iré elese eledá opens for an initiate in any composite of Owani, it marks the need for the initiate to receive the orisha Orí. Those who have ocha have already passed an important milestone, the crowning of the guardian orisha, and by its nature Owani puts the client at a crossroads to greater spiritual evolution: the reception of his own spiritual head.
- **Iré ariku.** In Owani, iré ariku is difficult to work with. This type of blessing promises that the client will not suffer an untimely death. However, the crossroads to which Owani alludes can mark vast spiritual transitions, and death could be one of the roads open to this person. As promised by the blessing, if the client chooses this road, his death will not be untimely; it is one of the possibilities preordained for him at birth. The diviner should pay careful attention to the composite opened, for if the letter speaks of death as a possibility, the client is already walking down death's road. Each letter, however, prescribes eboses to forestall this, and they must be done immediately if the client hopes to change his destiny.
- **Iré lowó.** This orientation of iré points out that the client is in control of his own blessings. The proper translation for this phrase is "evolution through works, the client's own hands." In some ways, this blessing is almost a taunt, because the client has come for help and enlightenment from the orishas, and they tell him, "Your help is in your own hands." Also, by its nature Owani does not bring evolution through hard work initially; it brings evolution by careful thought and wise decisions. Once those are made carefully, the hard work begins. When reading a letter that promises iré lowó, the diviner must glean the composite odu that has opened for hints as

to what decisions the client should make. The diviner should tell him to have blind faith in the orishas and forge ahead. Unfortunately, the client may not do this, and in the end he will be working even harder because he made the wrong life choices.

- **Iré ibujoko.** This type of iré brings "the goodness and blessings of change." When iré ibujoko is marked for the client through Owani, it shows that once his decisions are made and his goals are set, life will no longer be the same for him. These are no minor changes; major alterations are foretold. Eleven mouths, unfortunately, speaks of one who cannot withstand any more major changes; he is tired, weary, and worn. It marks someone who is a creature of habit and seeks solace in an unchanging world. Yet it is by embracing and accepting change that blessings come. The diviner should tell the one who sits at the mat that the changes coming will be almost catastrophic, and he must adapt or be lost. There is no other way to evolve.
- **Iré iyekú.** This blessing marks many tragedies before it will manifest. Almost always, it brings a financial windfall through death, accident, or inheritance. It also marks lawsuits and personal injury claims. The danger here is that the client will doubt that a blessing will come; Owani is a hot, harsh odu, and this iré increases what the client must endure. Already, he may be pushed to the limit. Adherence to taboo will forestall many tragedies. However, the client will have to endure much before he attains anything.

When Owani opens in one of these less favorable graces, it is still a sign of evolution, but that evolution will not come easily; it will require much work, ebó, and thought on the client's part. He will be in danger; he will suffer at the hands of perverse friends, and they will commit treason against him no matter what he does or does not do. But if the client placates the letter, making ebó and following all the advice the diviner gives him, their treason will come to naught. The universe itself, and the orishas, will intervene on his behalf, and while he will still face suffering and fear, neither will be great. The client does not need to fear osogbo brought by another's evil. For no matter the hostility found from others, this odu will intervene with infallible protection. There is no danger that cannot be overcome. For here is told the patakís of two young married women who were friends: One was kind, gentle, and fair, the mother of many children, while the other was stingy, coarse, and evil, a woman who could not bear children to her husband no matter what she tried. Every week, the two went to the river together to do their laundry. There, they talked about their husbands and the work they did, and the evil woman always lamented the fact that she could not have children. She was jealous of the other's most recent child; it was young, not even weaned, and this one accompanied her whenever she went to the river. This day, however, the evil woman's jealousy got the best of her, and while the young mother was engrossed in her work, paying no mind to her baby, the jealous friend quietly slipped the sleeping infant into the water. Helpless, its mouth filled with water, and it began silently to drown. This young one would have died that day had not a stray dog come running down the riverbank, barking deliriously at the infant. The mother watched, in horror, as the animal jumped in and pulled her baby out by the scruff of its neck. It was wet but not hurt, and the evil woman's treason was discovered before the baby died.

Having determined iré and its source, the italero continues to question the oracle. If the iré is marked as iré yale (firm iré), Owani is telling the diviner that the client's source of help is strong; the orishas are mounting behind this person to thrust him toward evolution and his destiny. If the iré is also marked iré yale timbelaye (firm iré manifest in the client's life), Owani is giving closure to itself. It tells the diviner that its energy has been in effect for some time, and the client has conducted himself well through its energies. The force of his conduct, his prior good deeds, and his adherence to his own destiny and the worship of the orishas have already given him the tools to facilitate his own evolution. The letter has opened here to tell him what forces are in effect and what is coming his way.

When Owani falls on the mat with osogbo, many

of its meanings are altered. The client is out of alignment with the sign's energy, and a variety of ills can befall him. It becomes a sign of destruction, ruin, treason, scandal, and scarcity. Much of this danger stems from the orishas themselves, and the diviner must be certain of his client's initiatory status to determine the full extent of this. First, consider the aleyo who opens with eleven mouths; while he does not know his guardian orisha, and while he might not be deeply involved in the religion's mysteries, he does have an orí, a spiritual head, and it accompanies him on all his journeys. One of the spiritual concerns in this odu is not only lack of alignment with one's head but also the "bad" head—one who is born to fail in life. Yet each letter of this oracle carries a glimmer of hope, and even those born to fail can rise above a bad head; they can create something powerful with their lives.* If this is the case with the aleyo who opens in this family of signs, Owani again points to a crossroads; this, however, is a crossroads that can change his very destiny. It will take a lot of spiritual work to help the client evolve. At the very least, a series of rogaciónes are needed before Obatalá, and soon the client must have a bajado. The determination of this client's guardian orisha will place him under that spirit's protection, and with the spiritual advice of the bajado, this person can begin to change his life.

An aborisha (who knows his guardian orisha) and an initiate (who is crowned with his guardian orisha) can have more pressing concerns in Owani. In osogbo, this sign indicates that the client's guardian orisha has turned his or her back on him; that spiritual force is angry and demands placation. Here, the diviner must assess the composite odu thoroughly; he must not fail to prescribe every taboo and every ebó that the letter offers. If the odu that was cast during the aborisha's bajado is known, the diviner should consider that sign. It gave very specific guidelines for this client's conduct, and Owani tells the diviner that the client is not conducting himself as he should. For an initiate, the diviner should consider the itá of ocha, and specifically the letters that fell for Elegguá (who owns Owani) and the head (the guardian orisha). He should also consider the odu under which this priest or priestess is said to be born: the first letter of Elegguá's itá combined with the first letter of the guardian orisha's itá.† Finally, speak honestly with the client. Ask him if the guardian orisha has ever asked him for ebó, and if that ebó remains unfulfilled. Question him about his conduct related to past sessions with the diloggún; determine if he followed all his taboos, prohibitions, advices, and eboses. Somewhere there has been disrespect between mortal and immortal, and until this rift is healed, there can be no evolution. All debts demand payment.

Consider, also, the client's relationship with both Oshún and Babaluaiye. When any composite of Owani brings osogbo, one or both of these orishas may speak to announce displeasure. Not only do they give witness to the rift existing between the client and his orí or his guardian orisha, but also they come to say that they themselves have issues with this client. To heal this rift, the client must do several things. First, he must pay whatever debts he owes his orí or his guardian orisha. He must pay careful attention to Elegguá and incorporate him into any eboses made. For Elegguá is the doorway to the divine, and with his goodwill, one can open the gates of heaven even if they have been locked. Once these spirits are pleased and placated, the client must live by making ebó to Oshún. With her blessing, all the sourness in his life can be replaced with something beautiful, and once his life transforms, he will be all the more thankful for all the blessings he receives. Normally, the one sitting at the mat is an ingrate; he is never thankful for the good life gives him or the good things others do for him. Oshún sees this, and it saddens her. Finally,

*If one could not change one's destiny or environment, there would be no need for an oracle such as this. Always, the diloggún is a tool for transformation, and even those who are hopeless have hope when they come to the orishas for help.

†Remember: While all the odu of itá are important, three signs outweigh all the rest. The first is Elegguá's odu. The second is the guardian orisha's odu. The third consists of Elegguá's first letter (this becomes the parent odu of the client's destiny) paired with the first letter of the guardian orisha's odu (this becomes the omo odu of the client's destiny). For example, 6-2 in Elegguá and 5-8 in the guardian orisha equates to the iyawó being born under 6-5.

within any letter of Owani the reception of Babaluaiye is a possibility. Until the client can afford the expenses of this ceremony, however, he must live by making ebó to this orisha.

Of all the osogbos that can fall in this odu, none demands more careful consideration or attention than ano and ikú. This is a desperate letter when ano falls, for no matter its origin, it tells the diviner that illness is already present in the client's body. He is under attack from within his own tissues, and only his strong constitution keeps him from experiencing symptoms. His lifestyle and vices have brought decay to his internal organs. It is possible that the illness is only at its weakest initial stages, but it is there, and it will worsen if the client does not care for his body. Behavior modification can do much to repair or reverse the damage already done. Owani marks the scourge of sexually transmitted diseases upon the client. The diviner should caution the client against unwise sexual encounters and send him to see a physician immediately. Many of these illnesses are asymptomatic for years, and some can leave the afflicted invalid for years after the infection is gone. The diviner should tell him that he must have a full battery of tests run for venereal disease—syphilis, gonorrhea, HIV, human papillomavirus, chlamydia, and any others that the doctor recommends. If the client has a lover, the diviner should insist that person go as well; the risk of transmission from one lover to the next is foretold in this sign. In addition to the taboo against unwise sexual encounters, the diviner should prescribe two more: The client must not get wet in the rain, nor may he live in high humidity. If any sickness is found, he must make ebó immediately to both Oshún and Babaluaiye, and if he has not received Babaluaiye, this is now necessary as ebó.

When ikú comes, Owani is predicting the death of the client or of someone whom he will become angry with. The diviner must caution the client against violence, for ikú in this family of signs announces a violent death. If the client is not killed himself, he will kill another. Jail and imprisonment are foreshadowed here. For those facing jail, death behind bars is the ultimate punishment brought by this letter. The diviner should tell the client that there is salvation: When ikú is marked in any composite of this family, ebó is marked automatically to both Elegguá and Ochosi. The diviner will let these two orishas dictate what they require.

Regardless of Owani's orientation, iré or osogbo, all of its composites share many qualities. To help this client evolve, the diviner must investigate all these issues at the mat; each will have some relevance for this person. The diviner should tell him, "You are not now as you once were; your life changes quickly, and know that in a few months you will not be as you are now. The changes you have gone through—you know these, and they are all part of the reason you are here. The changes that are in the future, and whether they are for good or bad, are entirely up to you and how you conduct yourself. Elegguá knows what is coming; this is his sign, and you must live by making ebó to him. Through Owani he tells us what must be done to save you and keep you from harm." If the client is an aleyo or an aborisha whose guardian orisha is not known, the diviner knows this: Elegguá is on top of him. So strong is the bond between these two, mortal and immortal, that the client could be his child. The ownership of this client's head can only be inferred, however, and not assumed; only an oriaté performing a bajado can determine this information for sure. As ebó, the client needs a bajado immediately. The determination of his guardian orisha is a vital part of his destiny; ocha is in his future, and one day he will wear his orisha's crown. Regardless of the client's initiatory status, Elegguá is his crutch in life; he must live by making ebó to him.

When dealing with Elegguá, one must keep in mind that the spirit known as Eshu is an integral part of his energy. In Owani, while Elegguá blesses the client, Eshu comes behind Elegguá to test him. As long as this odu's influence is felt in the client's life, he must be careful regarding the relationship of these two orishas, and he must be cautious in his daily conduct lest he be tested severely. Remembering that Eshu is always listening and watching, he should keep the following points and prohibitions in mind: No matter how prosperous or happy the client, he must never brag, especially to those less fortunate. Blessings need no proclamation. One who announces his good fortune will find it soon ruined and squandered; this is Eshu, testing him. Initially, Owani speaks of happy marriages and solid relationships; however, the tendency of one involved in these is to engage in public displays and pronouncements among friends. Eshu hears this, and he will test the strength of that love. This odu indicates that punishment is coming because of past transgressions, and even in iré, Eshu has marked this client for jail. He must be careful, making sure that when imprisonment comes, it is for something minor.

In all the client's dealings with others, Eshu is behind him, and the greatest hindrance to the client's life is his own lack of communication skills. Eshu owns the tongue as well as the alphabet and all words created from those letters. When the client finds himself at a loss for words, when others continually misunderstand the nature of his words and his actions, he must turn to Eshu and Elegguá for resolution. Owani provides an ebó that will remove the client's blockages in communication and will help others understand the true meaning of his words; he will become a better communicator. To Elegguá, who is very much like a child, the client should give an ebó of alphabet blocks, making sure that each letter of the alphabet, and all the essential numbers from one to ten, is included. After giving him the blocks, the client should make an adimú of alphabet soup, filling a huge bowl or tureen with it. He should leave the soup with Elegguá briefly and then take it to the nearest crossroads. With obí, he must make sure that Eshu accepts the offering there in the street. With Elegguá and Eshu both placated, the client will find that the avenues to good communication with others are open; blockages will be removed.

In all castings of Owani, the diviner can make many assumptions about the client's character. This person is very strong, decisive, and hardheaded; when his mind is made up about anything, an act of God would be needed to change it. In some ways this is good, for the client pursues his goals ruthlessly, almost recklessly. Yet it is also bad, because in the pursuit of his wants and needs, the client rarely thinks about how his actions affect others. More than any other character trait, this brings his demise. At his best, the client has bad character; he treats others as it suits him, not as they should be treated. At his worst, he is a user; he sees others not as equals or companions in his life, but as opportunities and resources. He is willful and ill-tempered, and his attitude will bring his destruction if he does not bring it under control.

The client's head is so hot that one day his temper will get the best of him. Again, the diviner should tell him that Owani is a letter of imprisonment and incarceration; one day, the client will be arrested and he will go to jail. And Owani guarantees that jail will be worse than sickness. He should do all that he can to make sure his jailing is for something minor, so that his time incarcerated is brief. He must never try to kill someone or even say that he wants to kill someone. He should not be meddlesome or irritated. He must avoid anger and violence. He should avoid scandals; he has constant problems because of these. He must also be wary against gossip, slander, and libel. Someone will invite him to commit an illicit or illegal act; he must decline, or else he will wind up facing trial in court. Now, he must get rid of all who he thinks could cause him harm. He should never try to take revenge on anyone, for no matter how hard he tries to destroy someone, his odu says that the final destruction will be of himself. At the very least, a quarrel will come in the client's life that will require the intervention of the police, and once they come, the client will know that he has lost all his luck. If he does not act properly, his life will be in ruin.

This letter flags family concerns, and the client must heed this advice well if he hopes to keep a strong, stable family unit. The client for whom this sign falls faces one of many possibilities concerning children. First, a woman in this sign either has or will have children by different fathers. It is not uncommon for a married woman in this sign who has committed adultery to be unsure of the parentage of at least one child. A man in this sign might have children by different women, and there is the possibility that these children have never met. He might even be unaware that he has fathered a child by one of his past lovers. In family units with children of different parentages, especially those involving adoptions or stepchildren, it is imperative that both spouses love all of their children equally. The children are innocent of their parent's mistakes and should not suffer emotionally, mentally, or physically because of them. Human nature, especially when influenced by eleven mouths, dictates otherwise; however, Owani demands equality. If the client and his spouse follow this advice, a brief period of good fortune will follow among all family members. However, sickness in the family is marked here as well, even if the sign opens in iré. Only ebó will save those who fall gravely ill. Eventually arguments will arise between those who are married, and they will destroy the family.

This letter alludes to someone who was born next to a river or an ocean, or perhaps on a rainy day. If this was not the circumstance of the client's birth, then this person is someone close to him in his immediate family. This person is blessed. The diviner should advise the client to treat this person well, for then blessings will shower on him.

In addition, Owani can bring a huge variety of issues. The italero should explore with his client the following points:

- Manifestations of the dead will occur in the client's life. He will see strange shadows, hear faint noises or voices, smell foreign scents and aromas, taste things in his mouth that are not there, and feel faint brushes against his skin. All these sensory illusions are from the dead. In iré, the client is developing latent psychic powers and should learn to work with these. In osogbo, this person is haunted and tormented; *ropimientos* (spiritual breakings and beatings using herbs) and spiritual masses are needed to clear this phenomenon.*
- This letter forebodes that the client has no home. If he is not careful, he could become homeless. It is a sign in which the child moves in with the parent; if this happens to the client, he will know that he has lost all his luck.
- Surrounding this client are many people who wish to harm him. The client knows this, but he does nothing about it. Owani directs him to remove himself from the company of coarse people—he must do this immediately.
- The client likes to do the exact opposite of what he is told. Rarely does he handle his affairs as he should. Before attempting closure of the oracle, the diviner should tell him this: If he does not handle himself properly, beginning now, his entire life will be in ruins.

## The Prohibitions of Owani

When Owani falls on the mat, the diviner has several taboos to discuss with the client. Although most signs demand taboo only with osogbo, in Owani the diviner would be wise to prescribe prohibitions even in iré. These religious and mundane restrictions guide the client in the proper direction. (Remember: In this sign choices are made once and cannot be unmade.) Like other odu, Owani requires that the client follow these prohibitions for a period of twenty-one to twenty-eight days. It will take at least this much time for Owani to settle in the client's life, and the immediate choices he makes during this period will be crucial. After the first month, he must keep these prohibitions, if not as strictures, then at least as guidelines for conduct.

Note that each of the sixteen composites of Owani also contains specific prohibitions that the diviner does not need to prescribe unless the reading is in osogbo. In osogbo, the prohibitions of the composite odu will keep the client from further mental, emotional, physical, or spiritual harm.

- Do not leave others unattended around one's orishas. Keep them in a secure, safe place. If the osogbo of this sign is severe, lock the orishas' shells in a safe place. The danger here is that someone will disrespect the orishas (in both iré

*Note that adolescents and prepubescent children who come under Owani's influence are marked for poltergeist phenomena. These intrusions come from not only spirits but also the child's innate psychic powers. Puberty is a time for physical, emotional, and spiritual development. The vast reservoir of energy in this child will attract many foreign spirits, some malefic. The diviner must deal with these as they occur; he should make sure the child has adequate spiritual and emotional support. Many children outgrow these powers, but if they can be contained and controlled, they can be maintained, usefully, into adulthood.

and osogbo) or steal something from their soperas (in osogbo). A tragedy in one's home, such as robbery, fire, or other natural disaster, might deprive one of one's shrines.

- Works of destruction are forbidden. Do not use one's orishas or spirits to harm another person. Curses cast under Owani's influence often return home to roost.
- In osogbo, the orisha whose diloggún is being consulted prohibits one's consumption of his or her foods. The diviner will detail these.
- Romantic relationships bring danger. Do not lie, argue, or fight with one's lover. Do not become involved with another person's lover or spouse. Avoid three-ways of the heart. Communicate clearly with one's lover; make sure he or she understand what one is trying to say. By following these rules, one will avoid scandal in one's personal relationships.
- Because this letter emphasizes that the law looms close by, do not accept gifts from strangers or acquaintances, and do not hold on to anything for anyone. Such items could be stolen and will bring incrimination.
- Do not keep broken pots, and do not plant seeds in pots that are broken, cracked, or chipped.
- Avoid parties, large groups of people, and places in which people "party" and use intoxicants. The orishas say that these things are not meant for one now.
- Street corners are sources of danger; stay home.
- Initiates who open in Owani are forbidden to wear necklaces, even elekes. If one must wear elekes, wear no more than two, and wear them only on special occasions.

## Marking Ebó in Owani: Initial Considerations

Because the diloggún is a tool for human evolution, each odu prescribes many eboses to put a client back into alignment with his destiny. When someone opens in Owani, the letter requires much spiritual work to avoid and overcome its inherent osogbo.

First, if the client's guardian orisha is not known, as ebó the client must have a bajado immediately. The determination of his guardian orisha is a vital part of his destiny; ocha is in his future, and one day he will wear his orisha's crown.

If the client is an aleyo or an aborisha and does not have the elekes, he must receive these necklaces as ebó. The aché bestowed by this baptism and the beads of Obatalá, Yemayá, Oshún, and Shangó negate much of Owani's volatility. Many decisions will be made in the client's life now, and these orishas will help him make the proper decisions on his journey. A prescription of the elekes plus the larishe eleven mouths offers (if any) might be enough to close out the reading.

In Owani, the diviner may also need to prescribe the eleke of the orisha whose diloggún is being consulted or the eleke of an orisha who speaks in this sign. To determine if this is necessary, he should ask, "Ebó eleke de [orisha's name]?" If an orisha marks his or her eleke and later the odu still refuses closure, each spirit who has offered an eleke might need ebó. To see if this is necessary, the diviner should ask, "Ebó elese [orisha's name]?"

If the client has received his elekes, in Owani the initiation of the warriors is the next consideration. The reception of Elegguá, Ogún, Ochosi, and Ósun is a powerful way to leave this odu's osogbo behind. When the odu mandates the reception of the warriors, the diviner must keep some important points in mind. First, houses that give Eshu to noninitiates must mark the path of Eshu required before bringing Owani to closure. Second, the elekes of Elegguá and Ogún must be prepared and washed with these warriors. The diviner should not prescribe the beads of Ochosi unless the oracle will not close; there are other odu and other circumstances for which one should save these. Finally, if Owani has already prescribed the initiation of the elekes for the client, the diviner should not prescribe the initiation of the warriors in the same session unless there is absolutely no other way to settle the sign's osogbo. He should, instead, wait for another reading before considering this initiation. Initiations are potent, powerful milestones in one's life. They should not be given haphazardly but, rather, at specific points in a client's evolution. In this way, they can make the monumental changes for which they are meant.

Regardless of the client's initiatory status, Elegguá is his crutch in life; he must live by making ebó to him. If the reception of the warriors is a financial impossibility, the diviner should encourage the client to receive at least Elegguá. An aborisha who has already received Elegguá should be directed to take better care of his Elegguá; even in the firmest iré, the diviner knows that the client does not live up to all his religious responsibilities. To facilitate this person's evolution, the diviner must prescribe several eboses to Elegguá, for in Owani, ebó is the key to success. Finally, when this family opens for an initiate, no matter to whom this person is crowned Elegguá loves him as if he were his child. The diviner must enforce the need for the initiate to treat Elegguá as if he were his guardian orisha, plying and propitiating him daily. If this is the first time Owani has opened for an initiate, the odu demands the reception of another Eshu. With the diloggún, the diviner marks the path to be received. The client should make preparations for this ceremony immediately. This new path of Eshu is for the client only; he is never to use it to work for a godchild or client. Once received, it will guide him on greater roads of evolution.

Remember that in Owani, Eshu stands behind Elegguá, testing the client's adherence to the advice and worship of the orishas. To help the client avoid Eshu's testing, the diviner must prescribe ebó immediately: At the crossroads, the client should feed this spirit a rooster, smoked fish, jutía, and plenty of toasted corn. When he is done, he should give obí. If a solid ejife does not come from this ebó, the client should continue to placate Eshu with ebó until he is satisfied.

When Owani opens in osogbo, certain other eboses become mandatory. To begin, Owani in osogbo demands that everyone in the diviner's house perform an ebó to Elegguá at the conclusion of the reading. The diviner should fill three small brown paper bags with three pennies each, toasted corn, jutía, smoked fish, and epó. Attendees at the reading use these bags to cleanse themselves before Elegguá, and then everyone else who was in the diviner's house at the time of the reading must do the same. The bags remain with Elegguá until the diviner has finished all his readings for the day; at the end of the day, he takes the bags to the street and discards them, saying, "Eshu batie sode."

The diviner must also consider the client's relationship with Oshun and Babaluaiye. When Owani opens in osogbo, they come to claim debts owed to them. If the client is a child of either spirit, his problems here deepen; the orishas are angry, and this anger must be appeased. The client must clear these debts immediately. The diviner should counsel the client on this issue, helping him determine if any promises have been broken. If the one at the mat remembers nothing, the diviner should mark eboses to the orishas. The clearance of debt is essential to evolution. From this point on, the client must live by making ebó to Oshún. With her blessing, all the sourness in his life can be replaced with something beautiful, and once his life transforms, he will be all the more thankful for all the blessings he receives. Normally, the one sitting at the mat is an ingrate; he is never thankful for the good life gives him or the good things others do for him. Oshún sees this, and it saddens her.

When Owani opens in osogbo, the reception of Babaluaiye is a possibility. The diviner may ask, "Koshé Babaluaiye?" Until the client can afford the expenses of this ceremony, however, he must live by making ebó to this orisha. Note that any ebó prescribed to Babaluaiye through Owani requires the use of a basket. When presenting ebó, the diviner or client should present it in a small basket: When giving a cleansing, the diviner should make sure the elements he uses end up in a basket. The entire basket used for ebó should be discarded according to this orisha's wishes.*

The osogbos ano and ikú demand particular eboses. If the osogbo is marked as ano and the client has any sickness, he must make ebó immediately to

*Keep in mind, always, these two proverbs for Owani: "When water is carried in a basket, it drips between the reeds" and "Water cannot be carried in a basket." Baskets are an important part of ebó to any orisha in this family of odu. One gives the orisha the basket so that the client does not carry empty baskets, or baskets with holes, in his life.

both Oshún and Babaluaiye. If he has not received Babaluaiye, this is now necessary as ebó. When ikú is marked in any composite of this family, ebó is marked automatically to both Elegguá and Ochosi. The diviner will let these two orishas dictate what they require.

The next option is Olokun's reception; the diviner asks, "Koshé Olokun?" If Olokun's reception is marked, the client must make preparations immediately. Owani demands that the client retain the basket used in the orisha's agbán and the twenty-one plates used at the ceremony. Olokun sits inside this basket, with the plates around him. Any future eboses made to him are given inside this basket or in a smaller basket set on top of his urn. No matter how ragged or worn this basket becomes, the client must never replace it; if any of the plates break or chip, he must not throw them away. They represent the client's luck and health, and Olokun retains them all so that he, and not the client, carries all the client's loads in life.

### The Traditional Eboses of Owani

Certain elements of ebó are considered traditional to Owani, and the diviner should try to mark these in the offerings as much as possible during the consultation. If eyebale is called for, the diviner should try to pick from the following list: two roosters, one hen, one rooster, and a single rat or jutía. If the rat or jutía is chosen, no matter which orisha accepts the sacrifice, the diviner must cut off the animal's head, oil it with epó, and give it to Elegguá. Also, the sacrifice of jutía must always be accompanied by smoked fish. For adimú-type offerings, the diviner should try to choose from a bottle of water, a bottle of rum, three pots, eleven needles, and any of the adimú described in "Ebó Elese Elegguá (Ebó at the Feet of Elegguá)." Fruits are desirable when the odu demands coolness.

## Ebó Elese Elegguá
## *(Ebó at the Feet of Elegguá)*

Readings in any composite of Owani are dominated to some degree by one orisha: Elegguá. He owns this family of signs, and rarely will any session close unless something has been offered to him as ebó. When Owani comes and Elegguá demands placation, any of the following will satisfy him.

### *Eyebale*

Two sacrifices will placate Elegguá when eyebale is necessary. First, to improve the client's luck, the diviner takes both Elegguá and the client deep into the woods; there, he feeds the orisha a single dark chicken. Instead of discarding the bird's carcass, the diviner brings everything back to the client's home. Elegguá remains beside the front door with the fowl at his feet; the diviner lights a single white candle for him. At midnight, the diviner places the chicken in a brown paper bag and discards it in a dumpster far from the client's home. Finally, the diviner washes Elegguá and puts him back in his clay tray. Once the rooster is discarded, all that hinders the client in his life will be discarded with it.

If the diloggún hints that the client needs a strong cleansing, this sacrifice will accomplish that and appease the orisha. The diviner and the client go far out into the woods, bringing with them Elegguá, two white roosters, and a clean set of white clothing for the client. There, the diviner uses both roosters to cleanse the client, singing to Elegguá while rubbing the client from head to toe with both animals. He then sacrifices the roosters to the orisha. He pulls several handfuls of feathers from the birds and uses them to rub the client from head to toe, leaving no part of his body untouched and singing to Elegguá the entire time. Next he rips the off the clothes the client is wearing and continues to cleanse him with feathers. Once all the client's clothes have been torn away, the diviner dresses him in the whites that they brought. The diviner and client leave the animal carcasses and the old clothing at this spot of the sacrifice. They return home with Elegguá and leave him by the front door with two white candles, which they light. They neither clean nor remove Elegguá from that spot until both candles consume themselves.

### *For Luck in the Home*

This sacrifice can be given in the client's home to improve his luck. The diviner places Elegguá beside the client's trash; there, he feeds him three baby chicks. He places the carcasses of all three in the trash can and lights a white candle to Elegguá there; he puts another lit white candle beside the front door. The diviner neither washes nor removes Elegguá until both candles burn out. When they do burn out, the diviner removes the trash immediately, taking it to a dumpster far away from the client's home. Only after the trash is removed may Elegguá be washed and returned to his normal place of residence.

### *Eleven Gourds Basket*

This is a simple adimú to prepare for Elegguá. The client greases eleven gourds with plenty of epó and then fills them with toasted corn, smoked fish, jutía, cornmeal, grated coconut, rum, honey, molasses, three pieces of hard candy, cascarilla, and grated ñame. He lines a basket with red and black cloth and puts the eleven gourds inside this basket. He then lights both a red and a black seven-day candle for Elegguá, and he keeps them burning for eleven days.

On the morning of the twelfth day, the client removes the basket. He visits eleven different places (such as a crossroads, the river, the ocean, the woods, a cemetery, a palm tree, and a dumpster). At each place, he removes one gourd from the basket and cleanses himself from head to toe with the gourd and then discards it. After all eleven gourds have been used and discarded, he takes the basket back to Elegguá and gives him an adimú of fresh fruits. This basket remains with the orisha; whenever the client makes ebó to him, it should go inside this basket.

### *Caramel Basket*

This is another simple adimú that can be used to placate Elegguá. The client should follow these steps: First, buy a large gourd and a basket just large enough to hold this gourd. Line the basket with red and black cloth, leaving enough overhang to cover the basket's opening. Put the gourd inside this. Fill the gourd with toasted corn, cornmeal, honey, twenty-one guinea peppers, smoked fish, jutía, and rum. Cover the gourd with enough unwrapped caramels that the gourd cannot be seen. Cover the contents of the basket with the cloth overhanging the basket. Leave this basket with Elegguá for three days; at the end of this time, remove the gourd and discard it at a crossroads. Leave the basket with Elegguá. In the future, when the client makes ebó he should put it inside the basket.

### *Coconut Basket*

This simple adimú can also be given to Elegguá. The client should follow these steps: Purchase a basket large enough to hold three coconuts. Line it with red and white cloth. Poke one eye out of each coconut; do not lose the milk inside. Through the open eye, drop into each coconut eleven guinea peppers, eleven grains of toasted corn, smoked fish, jutía, honey, epó, three pennies, and rum. Seal each eye shut with white wax. Place the coconuts in the basket, then set the basket before Elegguá. Every day for three days, burn a single white candle to Elegguá. The morning of the third day, take one coconut to the woods, one to a crossroads, and one to a cemetery. At each place, the client cleanses himself with the coconut and discards it. Bring the basket back to Elegguá; in the future, when the client makes ebó to the orisha, he should put the offering in the basket.

### *Sugar-Water Petition*

The client may make a special petition of Elegguá with the following ebó: In a crystal cup, mix fresh water with plenty of sugar. Stir well so that all the sugar is dissolved. On a piece of brown paper, the client writes one wish that he would like the orisha to grant. Fold this, and put it in the water. Put a white saucer on top of the glass and turn the entire ebó upside down; the saucer will form a bond with the glass, and the water will not escape. Keep a white candle burning on top of this glass every day for seven days. On each of the seven mornings, the client prays for what he desires. At the end of seven days, he pours out the water and the paper at a crossroads.

### *Broiled Ñame*

For Elegguá, this simple adimú is a favored ebó; it will propitiate and sate him when he requires an offering. The client should follow these steps: First, obtain a large ñame, epó, and honey. Wash and peel the ñame; cut it in slices 1/3 to 1/2 inch thick. Brush each piece lightly with first epó and then honey, and lay the pieces in a 3-inch-deep baking pan. Broil until the slices brown. Remove, and serve to Elegguá while still hot. Leave the offering with the orisha overnight, and the next morning, with obí, determine how he wants his ebó discarded.

### *Rejuvenating Elegguá*

If the client received his warriors but became lax in taking care of his Elegguá, he must begin a new routine every Monday morning if he hopes to reclaim his luck. Early on this day, he should wash Elegguá with fresh water from the tap. In Elegguá's clay dish, he should mix a little water with dry white wine and rum. Taking Elegguá to the front door and opening it wide, the client should smear the orisha's face with epó and honey. Then the client chews three guinea peppers and takes a swig of rum. Through clenched teeth, he blows the peppers and rum onto Elegguá's face. He follows this up by blowing cigar smoke into Elegguá's face. Finally, he sprinkles the top of Elegguá's head with smoked fish, jutía, and crushed spearmint and leaves him in a sunny place for the rest of the day. The client must perform this ebó every Monday morning until his luck returns; when it does, he must never fail to take care of Elegguá again.

## Ebó Elese Babaluaiye
## *(Ebó at the Feet of Babaluaiye)*

Beyond Elegguá, another orisha holds prominence in this family of signs: Babaluaiye. While he remains silent in many of the composites, his influence extends throughout this family. Rarely will odu close unless something has been prescribed to him.

### *Rogación*

A rogación before Babaluaiye's shrine will strengthen the client's orí, and his head needs all the strength and clarity it can get to survive what lies ahead. To determine if this cleansing is necessary, the diviner asks, "Rogación elese Babaluaiye?" If the answer is yes, the rogación is marked as ebó. In a rogación before Babaluaiye, after wrapping the client's head in white cotton, some priests and priestesses forgo wrapping the client's head in white cloth and wrap it, instead, in burlap or sackcloth. These materials symbolize the humility Babaluaiye embodies and the humility required of the client in his daily life. The diviner should remember that there are two other options to consider when marking a rogación: a rogación sodidé and eborí. If the oracle will not close after a rogación before Babaluaiye has been marked, the diviner should consider these two possibilities.

### *Amibo*

Amibo is a delicious way to prepare guinea hen for Babaluaiye. After a sacrifice to this orisha, one can prepare this recipe to complete the ritual, sharing with all who were present (including the orisha) for the ceremony, or one can prepare this adimú to placate Babaluaiye alone. When making this as an ebó itself (and not as part of an animal sacrifice), if possible, use a guinea hen that was saved from a previous sacrifice to this orisha. It will have more aché. The client will need to provide the following ingredients: a guinea hen, two medium onions, five garlic cloves, 1 tablespoon of salt, 1/2 cup of dry cooking wine (unsalted), 1/2 cup of grated ginger, four hot peppers (finely diced), 2 tablespoons of epó, and half of a box of yellow cornmeal.

Cut the hen into small, bite-sized portions and put the pieces in a large saucepan. Peel and dice the onions and scatter them over the guinea hen. Peel and mince the garlic, placing this in the pan over the meat. Sprinkle over the meat the salt, cooking wine, and ginger. Add 5 cups of water to the saucepan, and place over high heat. Bring to a rolling boil, then reduce the heat and let simmer for 45 minutes. Remove the soup from the heat, allowing it to cool. The meat will be tender; remove it from the broth and place it into a separate bowl.

To the soup, add the hot peppers, epó, and cornmeal. Put the saucepan back on the stove, turn the heat to low, and stir continually until the soup is completely warmed and cooked. The cornmeal will thicken to a paste. Add the meat and keep stirring until it is heated evenly. Serve this to Babaluaiye in a gourd, including with it another gourd of unsalted dry white wine. Leave the adimú with him overnight, and the next morning, use obí to determine how he wants his ebó discarded.

#### *Cleansing*

If the diloggún marks that a cleansing needs to be done before Babaluaiye, this bath will remove the osogbo obstructing the client's evolution. The client should purchase the herbs romerillo, cundiamor, and bleo blanco (available from botánicas) as well as seven ears of roasted corn, sackcloth, honey, epó, dry white wine, a paper bag, a cigar, and seventeen pennies.

Shred the herbs into a large vat and soak them overnight in fresh water. The next day, wring out the herbs until the liquid turns a dark green. Strain the herbs from the water and discard the plant material. Pour the herbal water into seven jars.

Every night for seven nights, the client must bathe with the liquid from one jar. While bathing, he should scrub himself with one of the ears of corn. Once the bath is done, he should place the ear of corn on the sackcloth before Babaluaiye. After the seventh bath, the client smears all seven ears of corn with the honey and epó. He sprays the wine over them and places them in the paper bag, then seals the bag with smoke from the cigar. The next morning, the client should leave everything by the gates of a cemetery with seventeen cents as Babaluaiye's derecho.

#### *Roasted Corn*

When financial concerns have brought the client to the oracle, if Babaluaiye stands up for ebó, the following adimú might help solve these problems. The client must bring two white seven-day candles, seven fresh bread rolls, seven ears of corn roasted in epó, a white plate, and sackcloth to the orisha. Before presenting the ebó, the candles are lit and the client must pray, silently, for the abundance that is needed.

When he has finished his prayers, he should set the food on the white plate and place this on top of the sackcloth. The adimú remains with Babaluaiye for as long as the candles burn. When the candles burn out, the client wraps the food in the sackcloth with a derecho of seventeen cents. He leaves all this under a bush in the woods, allowing the earth to consume the offering.

## The First Composite Odu of Owani, Owani Okana (11-1)

### The Proverbs of Owani Okana

- There will be a massacre if you do not watch your back.
- If there is nothing bad, there can never be anything good.
- He who is troublesome and stubborn comes to a bad end with his bones in jail.

### The Message of Owani Okana

When a casting of eleven mouths precedes a casting of one mouth, the odu Owani Okana is open on the mat. While the sign comes for the client, it gives a warning to the diviner, and he must act quickly and speak honestly if he is to avoid the evil that it brings. First, the diviner must offer ebó: He oils a jícara with plenty of epó both inside and out and places the client's derecho inside it. Immediately, he takes this jícara to Elegguá, offering it to him. This ebó remains with the orisha for eleven days; the diviner must not remove or spend the money before this amount of time has passed. Returning to the mat, the diviner says, "Owani Okana has opened for you, but it has also opened to warn me. Maferefún Elegguá! He says that while you have come here as a friend seeking help, before long you will leave this house as an enemy. You will spread lies and rumors, and you might even try to hurt me. Elegguá dares you to part as my enemy. You have come for help; if you listen, you will get the help you desire. Hurt me, the one who is trying to help you now, as you have done to others in the past, and Elegguá says you will be punished severely."

In addition to Elegguá, the diviner pays homage to Ogún and Ochosi, saying to each, "Maferefún!" To overcome the osogbos of Owani Okana, the propitiation of all three is essential. While only one might stand up in the reading to claim an offering, part of that offering must be shared among all three so that they work as a powerful team to defend the client. Elegguá is fate and destiny; he lives at the crossroads, so no spirit knows better than he what the client faces. Ogún wields his machete in this sign, and if properly worshiped, he will use that tool to cut down anyone or anything that tries to block this person's path to evolution. Ochosi is justice, and the client has lived immorally and illegally. While Ochosi will punish this person for the wrongs he has committed, if the client makes ebó, changes his behavior, and shows true sorrow for his transgressions, Ochosi will forgive. He might even lessen that which is dealt to the client. In the end, it all depends upon this person's own willingness to change.

Understand that this letter brings no true iré. If it is marked as coming in iré, it promises only an arduous journey through troubles if the client adheres to the advice, prohibitions, and eboses. Any ebó that is marked must be done quickly, and if the osogbo is severe, the diviner must not fail to mark all the eboses that are possible through this letter. Otherwise, the client will have only torment, tears, and treason.

The influence of Okana here brings issues with the client's mother. She has saved this child's life many times; she has cried over this child's life many times. In return, she has received little. Any chasm that exists in this relationship must be healed; the child must repay his mother for all the good she brought to him. No matter who sits at the mat, the diviner should deliver a stern warning: This sign says that all good in his life is almost lost. The letter promises incarceration, and this sentence can be either literal, figurative, or both. At best, the client will be "jailed" by his circumstances; he will be caught in a prison of his own making and will not find escape. At worst, he will be thrown in jail, and his sentence could last for a very long time. The diviner can sum up this letter in one word: desperation. This is all the client will understand. No matter how many eboses are marked, and no matter how quickly the client tries to change his life, it is too late for him. He is lost, and he will spend most of his life trying to find his way again.

This letter also brings the following concerns and issues:

- Illness comes with the opening of Owani Okana. How the client deals with this illness depends on many factors. If others, especially children, live in his house, he must monitor their health carefully. This sign flags witchcraft thrown upon him by those he has slighted. Unfortunately, it will miss its mark and latch on to someone who is innocent. If a child becomes ill, no matter how small the disease may seem, the client must take him to see a physician immediately. Even terminal illness begins with a minor complaint. When possible, the client should bring the child to this diviner so he might make ebó on his behalf.
- Owani Okana speaks of the throat and its weakness. Death can come through the obstruction of the client's airway. He should not chew, suck, or eat meat off bones. He must be careful and thoughtful when chewing food and should not talk when eating. He should never eat alone; he should have another person with him in case there is an emergency. To protect the throat from illness, the client should wear shirts with collars when outdoors and, if the weather is cold, a scarf. If any unusual symptoms arise in his throat, he should see a physician at once.
- Women opening in this sign have increased vulnerability in both the upper and lower abdomen. If any unusual pains or swellings develop in those areas, women should consult a physician immediately.
- If any osogbo suggesting a deliberate curse or malicious witchcraft opens, it must be fought; however, it must be fought with more than ebó. Here, the attacks of a palero are continual and constant, and witchcraft is best fought with witchcraft. Depending on the severity of the

osogbo, the client might need rayado to clear all sent his way.

- In osogbo, Elegguá is not happy with this person, and he will give him nothing without a price. Not only is his life hard, but also for now hard labor will be his lot in life. He must continue to work hard to overcome these things, and the client must live by making ebó to Elegguá, not to improve his luck but to propitiate and placate him. Remember: Without Elegguá's goodwill, nothing in this religion can be accomplished.
- Finally, keep in mind that this letter speaks of murder and unwarranted massacre. The prescription of taboo is integral to the client's safety. Even if he has no enemies who want him dead, if he does not follow the prohibitions of this sign, he will suffer a tragic demise.

## The Prohibitions of Owani Okana

- This letter indicates that one is often angered by those one loves and can be abusive on many levels (physical, emotional, and verbal). Suppress violence, and never show it. When angry, take care that the arms stay close to the body. Touch no one. Watch children carefully, and treat them well. Measure one's words before addressing a child.
- In relationships, avoid adultery. Owani Okana says one may have only one lover, and no more.
- Do not keep the company of thugs, con artists, drunks, liars, thieves, or drug abusers. They will bring down all types of misfortune on one's head.
- Do not enter into any discussion or conversation that could escalate into an argument.
- One's lover will ask one to go shopping soon; do not go. For seven days following this request, do not go into any public places with one's lover, or else something will happen that will cost one's relationship, and maybe one's life.
- Never go outdoors alone during the day, and never go outdoors at night. Tragedy searches for the one who breaks this taboo.

## The Eboses of Owani Okana

To begin, the diviner must consider the client's relationship with Elegguá. If Owani Okana has opened in osogbo, he is angry with the client, and he must be appeased. To begin this process, the diviner should prescribe two sacrifices. First, he will feed Elegguá a chicken in the client's home; immediately afterward, he will feed him a chicken in the woods. After giving this sacrifice, the client must live by making ebó to this orisha. Until Elegguá's goodwill is obtained, there can be no evolution.

In addition, it is imperative that ebó be made to the warriors together. After the initial sacrifices to Elegguá are complete, the client should offer an ebó of cool fruits to the warriors. He should repeat this offering weekly until the issues that brought him to the mat are resolved.

Having made these prescriptions, the diviner may now attempt to close the letter. If it will not close, he should explore the following possibilities:

- The client might have issues with Babaluaiye, Oyá, or Shangó. If the letter will not close, the diviner should consider asking of each, "Ebó elese [orisha's name]?" If the answer is yes, he uses the diloggún to mark the appropriate offering.
- The reception of Babaluaiye is a possibility for both aborishas and initiates who open in this sign. The diviner should consider asking, "Koshé Babaluaiye?" If the diloggún marks this as ebó, preparations for this ceremony must begin immediately.
- Because this sign marks future issues between the diviner and the client, another ebó to ensure the diviner's safety might be necessary. The diviner should ask, "Rogación elese [diviner's guardian orisha]?" If the orishas mark this as ebó, this rogación must be done before any other sacrifice is made. The diviner should give the rogación sodidé, beginning with the client's feet and ending with his head; this elevates his orí toward the diviner's guardian orisha. In this way, if the client attempts to harm the diviner in any way, his own guardian orisha will destroy him before he can hurt the diviner. The diviner should tell the client that he must return weekly

to pray to the diviner's guardian orisha, bringing a simple adimú or a token derecho each time he comes. As long as the client remains loyal to the diviner, this orisha will continue to bless him; the moment the client turns upon the diviner, the orisha will destroy all that he or she has given.

If these considerations are not enough to close the letter for an aleyo or an aborisha, the diviner must turn to the eboses of the parent odu, Owani (see page 534). Something there is necessary to elevate the client. If the client is an initiate, the diviner should continue with the following list.

- The diviner should next prescribe the sacrifice of two goats to Elegguá. The first sacrifice should take place deep in the woods and the second, immediately after, in the client's home. The next day, this person must sit for an itá with Elegguá. The godparent must be present to record the results of this itá in the client's libreta.*
- If the client has not received Oyá, he might need her. The diviner should ask, "Koshé Oyá?"

If these considerations are not enough to close the session for an initiate, the diviner must turn to the eboses of the parent odu, Owani (see page 534).

## The Second Composite Odu of Owani, Owani Ejioko (11-2)

### The Proverbs of Owani Ejioko

- Obatalá has you in bondage to ocha.
- Elegguá comes as a beggar.
- Just as birds will die in cages, so will one's children; do not not imprison one's children.

### The Message of Owani Ejioko

When an initial cast of eleven mouths, Owani, precedes a second cast of two mouths, Eji Oko, the odu Owani Ejioko is opened on the mat. This odu is also known as Owani Oyekun and Owani Yeku. Having cast this pattern, the diviner must say, "Maferefún Elegguá! Maferefún Eshu! Maferefún Orúnmila! Maferefún Oyá! Maferefún [client's guardian orisha]! Maferefún egun!" Here, Elegguá comes as a trickster; he will appear to the client as a beggar to test him. Over the next few months, vagrants will come to beg money of the client, and he must not fail to help them in some small way because each could be an "Eshu" in the street. A small kindness will be repaid many times over. Orúnmila does not speak directly through the diloggún, but Owani Ejioko indicates that this person could have issues with Ifá; the diviner should send him to a babalawo for a thorough consultation. As for Oyá, if this client is not her child, she loves him as if he were. The client must propitiate Oyá frequently so she will continue to bless him. The client should also pay homage to his guardian orisha or, if his guardian is not known, his godparent's guardian orisha. This spirit blesses him frequently and is pushing him to make ocha.

Of all these spirits, however, none is closer to the client than his own egun. Over the next few months, this person must work closely with egun to obtain all that he desires. Lacking a bóveda, he must set one up; he must provide his bóveda with fresh water, flowers, and candles daily. If he lacks an opá ikú, the diviner dresses one for him. As ebó, he should go walking with this stick frequently, leaning on it for support as he goes. Egun will walk with him and inspire him to greater things in life. The diviner should tell the client that one of his ancestors died with a secret; absolutely no one in his family knows what this is. The client should attend masses frequently; while there, he should open his mind and contemplate this spirit and the secret he or she took to the grave. In time, it will become known. Depending on the orientation of Owani Ejioko, the discovery of this secret can bring great wealth or blinding despair. Regardless, its discovery will lead the client to greater evolution.

There are many issues additional issues addressed in Owani Ejioko, and the diviner must explore each with his client:

*This sacrifice may be prescribed for an aborisha as well, but only as a last resort.

- An unexpected visitor is coming to the client's house. This person has lost everything; he is destitute. The client must offer food, drink, and rest. The more he takes care of this one person, the more iré this act of kindness will bring to his life.
- The client's head—physically and spiritually—is delicate and easily overheated. He must take care of his head; the diviner should advise him to guard against depression, mental illness, and nervous breakdowns. Exhaustion is found in Owani Ejioko, and the client must give himself adequate time for rest and sleep. He needs mental clarity.
- The client's blood pressure is a concern in this sign. Both high and low blood pressure could plague the client; he must monitor this and see a physician for a thorough physical.
- A child in this person's house will fall. If the child falls from a great height, he will break a bone, endangering his life. The diviner should advise this person to "child-proof" his home immediately, even if he does not have children (this sign says he has friends who do, and they will come to visit). In osogbo, a child could die in his house. He must be wary.
- In osogbo, the client suffers many tragedies. If he is an aborisha, he is blaming his troubles on witchcraft, and he has come to the mat looking for a remedy for this. The diviner should tell him there is no remedy because there is no witchcraft on him (unless, of course, the orientation of osogbo points out deliberate witchcraft or curses that have been sent his way). Because of his troubles, he has all but abandoned the orishas; even his own guardian orisha is troubled by this. Unless he regains his faith and makes ebó, he will continue to suffer. In this odu, there is no ebó greater than behavior modification. Act properly, and life falls into place. Act immorally, and life unravels. In Owani Ejioko, it is as simple as that.

## The Prohibitions of Owani Ejioko

- Do not fight with one's lover. Even a simple disagreement is enough to bring great tragedy to one's life. Try to be loving and agreeable at all times. Walk away from fights.
- Travel at this time is not recommended. Travel for pleasure is forbidden. If one's business requires travel, ask Elegguá first. If he says go, one may go, but the trip will not be all that one expects. If he says not to go, bargain with him; try to mark an ebó that will appease him. Be very careful, however; there will still be danger.
- Do not go to places frequented by the dead: hospitals, nursing homes, cemeteries, funeral homes, or wakes. Ikú will be there; he will be looking for someone else to take.

## The Eboses of Owani Ejioko

In Owani Ejioko, the reception of the Ibeyi is mandatory. If the client already has the Ibeyi, the diviner should determine if they require ebó, asking, "Ebó elese los Ibeyi?" If the answer is yes, he uses the diloggún to mark the appropriate offering.

Having made this prescription, the diviner next asks the odu for closure. If he is refused, the diviner should consider the following options for ebó:

- The client may need a rogación to strengthen his head. Before whom this is given depends upon the client's initiatory status. An aleyo without a godparent (a casual client of the diviner) needs a rogación before Obatalá. If the client is an aborisha for whom the guardian orisha is not known, the godparent should give him a rogación before the godparent's own crowning orisha. If the client is an aborisha for whom the guardian spirit is known, he must have a rogación before that orisha. If the client is an initiate, he must return to his godparent's home to have a rogación before that priest's or priestess's crown; from that sopera was the head born, and in Owani Ejioko, to that sopera must the head return for strength.
- If a rogación will not settle this odu's issues, the diviner should consider asking two more questions: "Rogación sodidé?" and "Eborí?" If the diloggún marks either as ebó, they must be incorporated into the rogación.

- If the client is an aborisha or an initiate, he might have further issues with egun, Elegguá, or Oyá. To see if one or more of these spirits will take ebó, the diviner should ask, "Ebó elese [spirit's name]?" If the answer is yes, he uses the diloggún to mark the appropriate offering.
- If none of these eboses soothes the odu for an aborisha, the diviner should ask, "Mazo de [guardian orisha's name]?" If the client's guardian orisha is not known, he should ask, "Mazo de Obatalá?" If the answer is yes, the diviner should immediately drape the appropriate mazo over the client's neck. He is in bondage to ocha. If he cannot afford the expenses of this ceremony immediately, he should consider giving his orisha "lavado" (or washing) until he can make ocha.

If these considerations are not enough to close the sign for an aleyo or an aborisha, the diviner must turn to the eboses of the parent odu, Owani (see page 534). One of the sacrifices there will bring evolution to this person and closure to this odu.

If the client is an initiate and Owani Ejioko refuses closure for an initiate, the orisha speaking in this sign could be marking a tambor as the solution to all the client's troubles. The diviner must first ask if a tambor is required. If the answer is yes, he must then ask if the orisha whose diloggún is being consulted will claim the tambor. If that orisha refuses batá, the diviner must try to mark the tambor for one of the orishas the client received in his ocha. If all of these refuse the drum, the diviner should question the orishas speak through Owani (see the list on page [000]). Note that if a tambor is marked during a iyawó's itá through either Elegguá or the orisha of his head, that client is marked to give a drum to all his orishas in time. Also, proper protocol must be followed in giving this ebó: The sopera from which the client's head was born must be given a batá before any of his own orishas may have one.

If this does not close the sign for an initiate, the diviner must consider the eboses of the parent odu, Owani (see page 534).

# The Third Composite Odu of Owani, Owani Ogundá (11-3)

## The Proverbs of Owani Ogundá

- While only one man throws the stone, it is the whole town that will be blamed.
- The tiger changed his clothes so that the hunters would not catch him.
- One leader throws the stone, and all his people are blamed.
- Why take on the troubles of others when one has problems of one's own?

## The Message of Owani Ogundá

When a cast of eleven mouths, Owani, precedes a cast of three mouths, Ogundá, the odu Owani Ogundá is open on the mat. When it falls, the diviner pays homage to the warriors, saying, "Maferefún Elegguá! Maferefún Ogún! Maferefún Ochosi! Maferefún Ósun!" These four spirits stand as warriors behind the client; they offer their support through the trials, tribulations, and decisions that this person faces, and they will work hard to remove this sign's osogbo if they are propitiated.

This is the sign in which the tiger was first hunted; others wanted to steal his skin, and he ran to the diviners to make ebó. They told him to change his clothes; this he did, and his life was saved because no one recognized him. To save his own life, the client will have to change his own clothes, and a whole lot more. First, as ebó the diviner should tell him that he must dress in white for sixteen days; during this time, he is to stay at home, venturing out for no more than the most essential items. After the sixteen days in white, he must change not only his daily habits but also his personal dress, adopting a more conservative style. For Owani Ogundá is the sign of mistaken identity; it is also the letter of false imprisonment, and by being mistaken for another the client could lose all his liberties. False testimony abounds in this pattern, and by word of mouth he could lose all. Almost always, those who open in this letter are currently in or facing some sort of litigation. Even if the client is innocent, Owani

Ogundá insists he will be found guilty of something unless strong eboses are made. If the client is not caught in the legal system now, he will be. Between now and then (and odu gives no clue as to when this will be), he must conduct himself well so any future court proceedings are for something minor. He must live by placating Elegguá, Ogún, and Ochosi; they will save him.

In addition, the diviner should explore the following issues with the client:

- This letter hints at relatives the client has never met. While he might be the biological child of the mother and father who raised him, both have had lives that he knows nothing about; he may have siblings in another state or country. One day he will meet them.
- Before the next year ends, death will come to the client's family. This sign, however, gives no further clues as to whom this relative might be. The client should resolve family issues now so that there are no regrets when death comes.
- Disobedience to the orishas will be this client's downfall. He must profess his faith not only with his mouth but also with his actions. There is no other way for him to evolve.
- Owani Ogundá speaks of a tragedy that can happen in or be brought to the client's house. If the client follows the taboo of not entertaining strangers or letting strangers into his home, much of this osogbo can be avoided. If he keeps his doors and windows shut and locked, his safety will be further ensured. Something, however, will come; he must pray that it is minor.

## The Prohibitions of Owani Ogundá

- Of all the prohibitions and warnings given in this letter, this is the most important: Never speak ill of this religion's priests and priestesses. The odu marks one as being opinionated, and because of what one has suffered in the past at the hands of unscrupulous initiates, one often degrades the most devoted adherents. This must stop now. If one has nothing good to say, say nothing at all; one's silence on certain "heads" amid one's praise of others will speak for itself. All deserve some respect, if for no other reason than the orisha seated in their head.
- Secrets told are no longer secret; confide in no one.
- Do not dress in red. It will attract death.
- Do not keep or guard things in one's home for others. Do not accept presents given by strangers or casual acquaintances. If one is afraid of upsetting the gift-bearer, quietly and thankfully accept the item and then dispose of it quickly. Do not buy used goods unless their true origin is known; they might be stolen.
- This letter forebodes evil from strangers; be wary of those who approach unknown. Do not invite strangers to one's home; if strangers come, do not entertain them for any length of time. If someone unknown knocks on one's door, do not open it. Simply say, "Now is a bad time. I cannot accept guests," and apologize. Under no circumstances should one open the door. If the caller insists, call the police, and let the caller know that the police are en route. Keep all doors, windows, and other entrances to the home closed and locked, especially when home alone and at night. If these taboos are followed strictly, most of the osogbo inherent in Owani Ogundá can be avoided.

## The Eboses of Owani Ogundá

Immediately after closing the reading, an ebó must offered to the client's warriors or, if he does not have the warriors yet, to the godparent's warriors.* The diviner places the orishas together on the floor. He feeds two roosters to Elegguá and Ogún together; two pigeons to Ogún; and one pigeon to Ósun and the otá that represents Ochosi.† The next day, he cleans all of the warriors, oiling

*If this ebó is offered to the godparent's warriors, do not include the godparent's Ósun in the ebó. Ósun is a personal symbol and works only for its owner.

†In some lines of Lucumí it is customary to give a light brown otá to Ogún's cauldron to represent Ochosi as he walks with Ogún. In this case, the two pigeons for Ogún are shared with Ochosi's otá as well. If no otá is present for Ochosi, feed the crossbow and arrow that represent Ochosi with Ogún's otá.

Elegguá and Ogún with epó and Ósun with cocoa butter. Seven days after the sacrifice, the client should offer cool, fresh fruits to all four orishas.

Having prescribed the closing ebó, the diviner next asks the oracle for closure. If he is refused, the following series of eboses must be done immediately. Until all are complete, the client will not be safe:

- First, the client must have a rogación. If the client is an aleyo or an aborisha whose guardian orisha is not known, the rogación should be given before Obatalá, as all heads belong, ultimately, to him. If the client is an aborisha whose guardian orisha is known, the rogación should be done before that spirit. If the client is an initiate, he must return to his godparent's home; the rogación is done before that priest's or priestesses's sopera. After the rogación, the client remains in white for sixteen days.
- After spending sixteen days in white, the client must have another rogación, and his orí should be fed two white pigeons. After another day in white, the client may return to his normal dress.
- Once the rogaciónes are complete, the client must feed Ogún two pigeons at his home, the railroad tracks.
- If the client now or ever faces a lawsuit, this odu gives him an ebó to help win. First, on behalf of the client the diviner feeds the warriors: a rooster to Elegguá, a rooster to Ogún, two pigeons for Ogún, and two pigeons for Ósun. The day after this ebó, the client gives a small party (a tambor) to Elegguá, Ogún, and Ochosi. These three orishas will ensure that all comes out well. If the client is an initiate, he is marked to receive Ochosi immediately before the tambor.

After detailing all these prescriptions to the client, the diviner may again attempt closure of the oracle. If the odu remains open, he should fortify the ebó offered to Ogún. Following the feeding of two pigeons at the railroad tracks, the client should take Ogún deep in the woods and there feed him a rooster.

If these considerations are not enough to close the odu for an aleyo or an aborisha, the diviner must turn to the eboses of the parent odu, Owani (see page 534). Something there is needed to soothe this letter's osogbo. If the client is an initiate, however, the diviner should continue with the following considerations for ebó:

- If the initiate does not have Ogún's diloggún, he might need it. The diviner should ask, "Koshé diloggún de Ogún?"
- Next, an orisha might be standing up for four legs and an itá. The diviner should consider asking, "Ebó de cuatro patas?" If the diloggún marks the sacrifice, the diviner must determine which orisha, of those who speak in Owani (see page 492), will accept this ebó. An oriaté must preside over the sacrifice ceremony, for the day after four legs are offered the client must sit for itá with that orisha.
- Finally, the knife is a consideration in this sign. The diviner must ask, "Koshé pinaldo?" If odu marks this, preparations for this ceremony begin immediately.

If none of these is enough to close the odu for an initiate, the diviner must turn to the options for ebó in the parent odu, Owani.

## The Fourth Composite Odu of Owani, Owani Irosun (11-4)

### The Proverbs of Owani Irosun

- That which makes you dirty, wash yourself to take it away.
- [This is the odu of] The greatest revenge.
- [This is the odu of] The greatest lie.
- The same fire that is on top is below.
- If you cannot love yourself, you cannot love anyone else.
- White is beautiful; wear it more often.

### The Message of Owani Irosun

This odu opens when a casting of one mouth, Owani, is followed by a casting of four mouths, Irosun. This sign is also known as Owani Iroso and Owani Hermoso (beautiful Owani). For of all the predictions found in this letter, none is more important than these: It speaks of a child that was born or is about to be born, and the mother doubts its paternity. She must raise this child anyway, never telling others her doubts. This baby will grow to be healthy, beautiful, strong, wise, and famous. His natural aché will bring great changes to the world. His family must nurture this. Also, within this client is beauty; while it may not show on the outside, it exists within. Unlike the other odu found in Owani's family, which can be hot and volatile, this sign is cool and soothing; it acknowledges that the client has always had the power to achieve great things even though he never tapped it to its fullest. He cannot make great use of it now because he does not acknowledge what is within, so his potential lies dormant and fallow. Once this person perceives the goodness and vibrant energy within, once he begins to nurture it on his own, others will see it and they, too, will nurture him. That within will manifest without, and the client will be desired by the world.

When this sign falls on the mat, the diviner hugs himself and directs the client to do the same. He then pays homage to Shangó, Obatalá, and Orúnmila, saying to each, "Maferefún!" These three spirits take an interest in the client; they will lead him to evolution. Of all three, Shangó is the most involved. He tells the client that he is dirty; others have stained him and spoiled him with gossip and witchcraft. Yet for all the bad that has been thrown his way, the client still emerges unscathed. This evil, however, must be fought. The diviner should tell the client that, to fight this evil, he must bathe himself thoroughly from head to toe, afterward dressing in white and offering an adimú to Shangó. No other cleansing—no herbs, no potions, no chants—is needed. So powerful is the client's inner strength that the witchcraft and gossip pale in relation to him, and all will be washed away with fresh water. The diviner should tell him to clean his house as well, in case something nasty has been dropped there. It cannot hurt him. Shangó also warns the client to take great care with fire and electrical appliances; something in his house has gone bad, so he must check all cords and wires for frays. He should not leave burning candles unattended. If he follows these simple rules, no osogbo can destroy what he has worked so hard to obtain.

In addition, the diviner should explore the following issues with the client:

- At times this client is proud, and at times he is down on himself. The diviner should tell him to avoid extremes of emotion, especially over his own life. They will affect his head; blood could rush to his brain, and he could suffer a stroke. He must focus on maintaining calmness and mental clarity.
- Owani Irosun says that this client may either be a twin or have been born after twins. If this is so, special blessings are coming for the one who sits at the mat.
- This person could have a destiny with Ifá. The diviner should send him to a babalawo for a thorough consultation as soon as possible.
- In any type of osogbo, this letter brings up specific health issues. Owani Irosun alludes to the urinary system: kidneys, ureter, bladder, prostate, and outer organs (vagina for women and penis for men). Renal failure, kidney disease, and bladder infections are all possibilities. Stones and blockages will occur. To avoid this, the client should drink plenty of fresh, cool water, and he should give up dark drinks and sodas. If any unusual symptoms arise in the urinary tract, he must see a physician immediately.

## The Prohibitions of Owani Irosun

- Do not consume dark drinks, sodas, coffee, apples, cashews, red plums or prunes, red beans, red foods, red drinks, mango, the heads or tails of animals, sardines, fish, grains, seeds, grainy foods, and tripe. Avoid the consumption of blood by making sure that all meats are drained of their fluids.
- All clothing worn must be in good repair. Do not wear torn, ripped, or mended clothes or clothing with lace, holes, or eyelets. Fringes are taboo, as is the color red.
- Never have more than two open flames in the house, and when leaving home, extinguish

them. Examine all cords to electrical appliances for breaks or frays. When leaving home, unplug all electrical appliances that are not in use.

- Do not go to the woods unless it is to make ebó. When going, go with a second person. Danger lies there.

## The Eboses of Owani Irosun

Obatalá is present in this odu to lead the client gently to ocha. Because the road to his asiento has many obstacles, Obatalá mandates that the client do the following ebó. On a large white platter, he must present two coconuts, two soles from old shoes, two small fish, two small dolls, three scarves (white, red, and yellow), a small toy house, two bunches of plantains, and two full packets of confetti. On the day that this ebó is made, the client dresses in old clothes and comes to his godparent's house with this ebó and another change of new white clothes. The godparent presents the client to Obatalá and then gives him a thorough washing in Obatalá's omiero. When the washing is complete, the client changes from his old clothes to his new white clothes. He takes the platter with the ebó and his old, torn clothes to the foot of the Iroko tree, where he leaves it, with a prayer for initiation. Obatalá and Iroko will move heaven and earth to make sure that this client is initiated soon.

There are other spiritual issues that must be explored; however, the manner in which these are considered will depend upon the client's status in the religion. First, if the client is an aleyo or an aborisha whose head has not been marked (his guardian orisha is not known), he has issues pending with Obatalá, Shangó, his own orí, and his godparent's crown. To settle these issues, the client should have a rogación before Obatalá's shrine to strengthen his orí. Afterward, he should present an adimú to Shangó and to his godparent's crown. When these adimús or eboses are lifted, they must be replaced immediately with eight white candles: two for Shangó, two for Obatalá, two for the client's orí (placed on the floor before Obatalá), and two for the godparent's crown. Until all the client's issues are settled, these candles should remain, being replaced with new candles when they burn out.

If this client is an aborisha whose head has been marked or is an initiate, the rogación given previously to Obatalá is done before the sopera of the client's crowning orisha instead, and the eboses are distributed among Shangó, Obatalá, and the client's guardian orisha.

The final issue that demands exploration is the client's relationship with Elegguá. In Owani Irosun, ebó must be made to Elegguá on the client's behalf, any of the eboses described in "Ebó Elese Elegguá (Ebó at the Feet of Elegguá)." This ebó sits with Elegguá for three days, and each night the client must come before him and pray for evolution and all the things he considers necessary in his life.

Having made these prescriptions, the diviner has his first chance to close the odu. If it will not close, he should consider the following possibilities:

- Shangó and the client's godparent's crown (if his own guardian orisha is not known) or his crown (if his own guardian orisha is known) might want a specific ebó in place of a simple adimú after the rogación before Obatalá is given. To determine if this is the case, the diviner asks, "Ebó elese [orisha's name]?" If the answer is yes, he uses the diloggún to mark the appropriate offering.
- Elegguá might be standing up for more ebó. To see what he requires, the diviner must ask, "Ebó elese Elegguá?" If the answer is yes, he uses the diloggún to mark the appropriate offering.
- If the letter continues to refuse closure, the client could have issues pending with the first two Ibeyi, the twins Taewó and Kaindé. Remember that Owani Irosun hints that the client might be a twin or have twin births in his family. If the client does not have these two orishas, the diviner should ask, "Koshé los Ibeyi?" If the client has them, the diviner should determine if they will take ebó, asking, "Ebó elese Taewó y Kaindé?" If the answer is yes, he should use the diloggún to mark the appropriate offering.
- The Ibeyi born after the twins, Ideu, can be integral to the client's aché, even if he has not made ocha. If the client does not have Ideu, the

diviner should ask, "Koshé Ideu?" If the answer is yes, preparations for this ceremony begin immediately. If the client is an initiate who already has Ideu, he might need ebó. To see what is required, the diviner should ask, "Ebó elese Ideu?" If the answer is yes, he uses the diloggún to mark the appropriate offering.

- Olokun is important in this odu. Remember that this client has great untapped reserves of beauty and strength within, and not even he knows how great this aché is. Olokun, however, knows, and he will show the client his strength if he receives him. This orisha's reception may be required; to determine if this is the case, the diviner asks, "Koshé Olokun?" If the client has Olokun, he needs ebó before he can work with the client. To see what he might require, the diviner should ask, "Ebó elese Olokun?" If the answer is yes, he uses the diloggún to mark the appropriate offering. In the rare occasion that Olokun stands up for ebó but will not mark any, the proper offering is a sacrifice of feathers and then an agbán. He will clear all osogbo from the client with this.
- If the client has Eleggúa, this orisha might be standing up for more carga and reinforcement into his clay tray; the diviner must try to mark this. If this offer is accepted and the client is an initiate, after strengthening Eleggúa he must give him a crown. Once he has his crown, he will give the initiate a kingdom to rule.
- Finally, the diviner should ask, "Ebó elese los guerreros y Shangó?" If the diloggún marks this as ebó, sacrifice a rooster to Eleggúa and Ogún together, and then two roosters to Shangó. These three orishas will fight all the wars that need to be fought in the client's life.

If Owani Irosun remains open for an aleyo or aborisha, the diviner must turn to the eboses of the parent odu, Owani (see page 534). Something there is necessary for the client's evolution. If the client is an initiate, however, the diviner should consider the following eboses:

- The reception of Iroko is a possibility; the diviner should ask, "Koshé Iroko?" If the answer is yes, the client must make preparations for this ceremony immediately. If the client already has Iroko, the diviner should ask, "Ebó elese Iroko?" If the answer is yes, he uses the diloggún to mark the appropriate offering.
- This letter enforces the initiate's need to feed Yewa and then Shangó. As soon as possible after this ebó is done, the client must make preparations to receive Yewá. She has much to bring to his life.

If these prescriptions are not enough to close the odu for an initiate, the diviner must consider the eboses of the parent odu, Owani.

## The Fifth Composite Odu of Owani, Owani Oché (11-5)

### The Proverbs of Owani Oché

- The ocean would overflow but for the goodness of one.
- If one does not know the laws under which one lives, one will learn them in prison.
- If one does not know the laws of life, one will learn them in death.

### The Message of Owani Oché

When a casting of eleven mouths, Owani, is followed by a casting of five mouths, Oché, the odu Owani Oché is open on the mat. Immediately, the diviner must praise the two orishas who own this sign, saying, "Maferefún Eleggúa! Maferefún Oshún!" Eleggúa is here as fate or destiny, the master of the crossroads who knows what path the client must travel to obtain all he desires. Oshún is the mistress of sweetness, those things that make life worth living. With these two spirits at his side, there is little that the client cannot accomplish. Such is Oshún's love that if the one at the mat is not her child, she still cares for him as if he were.

The diviner also praises egun, Obatalá, and Olokun, saying to each, "Maferefún!" Through this letter was born *bobowaniche*, the custom of sacrificing to one's ancestral spirits. Before this session closes, egun will demand to be fed. Obatalá once chained Olokun to the bottom of the sea; Olokun, embittered, spent the centuries plotting to regain what she lost. One day, she challenged Obatalá to a contest; the greatest orisha would display the greatest beauty, and the one most handsome would win the world. "Maferefún Alaguemu!" Obatalá gave Alaguemu, the chameleon, the gift of all the world's colors; he wove them from his own tapestry of white cloth, which contained all shades perfectly balanced in its brilliance. With this, Alaguemu won the contest for Obatalá, and Olokun remained chained in the sea.

Of all the issues found in this letter, none is more pressing than this: Someone learned in the arts of magic and witchcraft has cursed the client, and because of this, all his roads are closed. Oshún stands up here to defend him, but before she will release him from harm, the diviner must determine one thing: the debt that exists between this client and this orisha. He must explore this concern with the client carefully. (See "The Eboses of Owani Oché.)

When this letter opens on the mat, there are many issues to be explored with the client. While all seem unrelated under this sign's energy, all will have some bearing no matter the orientation of Owani Oché. The diviner should carefully discuss the following points:

- Just as there was a war between Obatalá and Olokun, if this person is Obatalá's child, he will soon have a war with one of Olokun's children. Under no circumstances is he to fight this battle himself. He must give an adimú to Obatalá and ask him to deal with the issues at stake. Just as Obatalá defeated Olokun when she wanted to reclaim the world, so will Obatalá defeat the one trying to hurt his child.
- The client's body harbors disease; he must take care of himself lest this erupt into a life-threatening illness. If any unusual symptoms arise, he should see a physician immediately. With proper rest and nutrition, however, the body will heal itself before this disease overtakes him.
- If the client's child becomes sick, he must bring him to the orishas immediately. While the initial illness might be minor, in time disease could take this child's life. It is by making ocha that his life will be saved.
- In osogbo, this letter flags illness in the urinary tract. The kidneys, ureter, bladder, and urethra could all suffer trauma. Kidney stones and bladder infections will damage this person's body severely. At the first sign of trouble in these areas, he must see a physician immediately. Also, the diviner should caution the client to be wary of lower back pain toward his sides. If he suffers any discomfort in this area, especially in the morning when awakening or after long periods of no urination, he must consult his physician. Lower back pains mask kidney trouble and renal failure.
- The key to evolution in this sign is this: The client must see himself, not others, as the source of all his problems. He believes himself to be without blame in all his troubles, but in truth he causes them all. Victory will come when this person learns to defeat the enemy within—himself.
- A woman who comes in ano or ikú must monitor her menstrual cycles, reproductive organs, and vagina for disease. In Owani Oché, it is not unusual for asymptomatic, sexually transmitted diseases to ravage a woman's body silently. If it has been more than six months since her last physical, and if she is sexually active, the diviner should encourage her to go for a health screening. She may discover a sexually acquired disease before it has the chance to harm her body permanently.
- The client's wife, or the client herself, will have a child who brings luck. Even if pregnancy comes under the most dire circumstances, in this odu Oshún forbids both abortion and adoption. This child is her gift, and the client must not only carry it to full term but also raise it.
- Finally, in any orientation Owani Oché marks the development of stones and hardened areas in the body. Noncancerous tumors are also a possibility. The client should monitor his body for signs of these.

## The Prohibitions of Owani Oché

- When bad happens, one will be tempted to accuse and blame others. Do not bear false witness; before pointing a finger of blame at anyone, be certain that one speaks the truth. False accusations will destroy one.
- The following foods are taboo: roasted or burnt meats and vegetables, canned foods, pumpkin, squash, calabazas, reheated foods, cold leftovers, beets, canistel, eggs, watercress, malanga, chopo, goat, fowl, red snapper, and shellfish. When eating, foods that are not part of a single dish must be kept separate; do not mix anything on the plate. The sacrificial foods of the orisha who stood up to claim larishe (if one was offered), plus the foods of Oshún, may be limited or taken away altogether if the diviner chooses.
- Do not enter into altercations with Oshún's children. If any of her priesthood starts trouble, take it up with the orisha; she will punish her own.

## The Eboses of Owani Oché

When Owani Oché opens on the mat, it flags three eboses that must be done by the client no matter the odu's orientation. First, this person must clean his house, beginning at the point farthest away from the front door and working toward it, not forgetting to clean closets, drawers, cabinets, and under furniture. He should open any dark, closed areas that are infrequently visited and let them air out thoroughly; shampoo carpets; and blow out all heating and cooling vents. To move negative energy out of the house, he should keep open all windows and doors while cleaning. Once the house is physically cleaned, he should cleanse it spiritually with white candles, holy water, floor washes, and incense. If the osogbo of Owani Oché is severe, the client should do a cleansing with two white doves and then set them free at the front door so they can take away any remaining negativity. Once this cleansing is complete, the client is ready to receive his egun into his home. He should have both a bóveda and an opá ikú. He should feed egun a rooster and that same night host a mass in his home. After all these things are done, his issues with egun are settled. The diviner should encourage him to live by offering them frequent prayers and adimú.

Second, the client must receive Olokun. Although normally one would not attend to Olokun too often, after his reception this odu says that the client must pamper him, praying to him and offering frequent adimús. Remember: Without the grace of one, the ocean would have overtaken the world. Without the grace of Olokun, the client will drown in his own problems. Note that if Olokun is received through this odu, he must be kept in a room apart from Obatalá. The two once fought a war in Owani Oché, and the client would not want them to repeat this war in his life.

Third, the client must settle his debts with Oshún, who stands up to defend him against witchcraft but demands the repayment of a debt the client owes her. The diviner must ask the client if he ever asked any blessings from Oshún in exchange for ebó; he must then determine if the client offered that ebó in a timely manner. If he did not, that ebó must now be prescribed. If the client remembers no such promises to Oshún, the diviner should allow Oshún to dictate what she requires, asking, "Ebó elese Oshún?" After this ebó is offered (and it must be made quickly), the client may do the following to wash away the curse that is on him and send it back to the witch or sorcerer who cast it. First, he obtains a large gourd of honey, a hemp sponge, a large bar of cocoa butter soap, and a change of white clothes. At the edge of a river he prays to Oshún, dripping the honey slowly into her waters. He removes his clothes, throwing them into the river, and then goes out as deep as he can. There, he scrubs himself thoroughly with the hemp sponge and soap until he is clean. Returning to the shore, he dresses in white, and returns to his godparent's house.

Before Oshún's shrine, the godparent gives the client a rogación with grated coconut, grated cocoa butter, crushed cascarilla, honey, and yellow rose petals. Before wrapping the client's head in white cotton and white cloth, he feeds two white pigeons or white doves to the client's orí. Once all these are complete, not only is the curse removed, but also any future curse cast to the client will return to its sender.

Note that for some, this ebó may not be enough to remove all the witchcraft. If the letter refuses closure, the diviner should consider asking, "Rogación sodidé?" If the diloggún marks this as the remedy, the godparent begins the rogación at the client's feet and ends with his head. Instead of removing the ingredients from the client's feet at the end of the ceremony, however, he wraps his feet in white cotton and then again in white cloth before letting him don his socks and shoes. This remains on his feet as long as the rogación remains on his head. This way, the path that the client walks will be sweetened, and his feet will be safe from any witchcraft or evil powders thrown in his path.

If the client is ill, this odu offers eboses to solicit the help of the orishas in healing. If the disease is in the blood, stomach, legs, feet, or internal organs of the body, he should have two rogaciónes before Oshún, using a generous amount of honey. The first should cleanse his head and the second his abdomen. Once both are complete, the diviner should cleanse the client with two pigeons and a hen and then feed the birds to Oshún. If the client is ill and an operation is imminent, the diviner should ask the diloggún, "Larishe si Ogún?" If Ogún offers a remedy, the diviner should let the diloggún dictate what to give. If Ogún offers no remedy, the diviner should encourage the client to pamper him with frequent adimús between now and the date of his operation; each time he brings something for Ogún, he should pay foribale to him and ask for his health. Plying and propitiating Ogún in this manner will ensure that the physician's hands are directed by his grace; iron will be healing, not harmful.

If the diviner has considered all these eboses and the odu remains open, he must explore the eboses for the parent odu, Owani (see page 534). Something there is needed for this client's evolution.

# The Sixth Composite Odu of Owani, Owani Obara (11-6)

## The Proverbs of Owani Obara

- You act like one of the dead to see what your funeral will be like.
- Do not be envy's slave; beware those who are envious.

## The Message of Owani Obara

Owani Obara is the letter opened when an initial casting of eleven mouths, Owani, precedes a cast of six mouths, Obara. Having cast this odu, the diviner says, "Maferefún egun!" This sign is full of aché from the dead. The diviner should tell the client that his ancestors form his foundation; it is strong, and if he works hard, he can build an empire. The client should have both an opá ikú and a bóveda, and he should tend the latter well. Also, the diviner should recommend that the client attend spiritual masses weekly if possible. As he watches the espiritistas work, he will learn; one day he will have great spiritual gifts of his own. The songs, prayers, and chants will also reinforce his spiritual court, and to survive the erratic vibrations Owani brings, the client will need strength.

In his opening homage, the diviner also says, "Maferefún Palo Mayombe! Maferefún Nkuyu Nfinda! Maferefún Siete Rayos!" Although Palo Mayombe is a religion separate from Lucumí, Owani Obara is one of the few signs in the diloggún that tell the client he must seek initiation into this cult. The nkisi Nkuyu Nfinda (also known as Lucero, the crossroads) and Siete Rayos (the storm) have much to give him. Already, the client has felt this pull to the Congo religion, but he has not investigated what it is that pulls him to it. He is meant to be rayado (cut, or initiated, to the religion), and until he has this initiation he will not evolve. Quickly, the diviner must take this client to a tata nkisi (father of the spirit) so that his issues can be divined. Owani Obara says that the client has a Congo spirit very close to him; it walks just behind him, not with him, and if the client has this nfumbe seated into a nganga, it will grant him the gifts of clairvoyance and clairaudience.

The issue of initiation to Palo Mayombe becomes more complicated for a Lucumí initiate. The mysteries of the dead come before the mysteries of ocha, and rayado must be done prior to the asiento. Once an orisha is seated in the head, nothing else can be put to the body. Yet another rite of Palo known as jubilation may solve this problem. Because jubilation involves the drawing of chalk marks on the body, as opposed to cuts with razors, the Lucumí initiate may take this ceremony even after he has made ocha. Before doing this, however, he must seek permission of not only the nkisi (the forces of nature) but also the orisha crowned on this person's head.

In addition to the client's issues with both egun and muerto (spirits of no relation to the client), the diviner has many other things to explore in relation with this sign. He should discuss the following carefully with his client:

- The diviner should tell the client that each morning and each evening he should sit for a few moments just outside his front door and relax, watching the people who walk by. One of these will be his enemy. When evil is done to him unexpectedly, he should consider who walks by his house on an almost daily basis. If he is obedient and does all this odu says, one day he will see the body of his enemy go by; death will take that person away.
- Owani Obara is a materialistic odu. The one who opens in this sign desires material things; these are what will make him happy. In iré, the letter promises fulfillment; in osogbo, the letter promises failure. Yet the client can change his lot in life, and even increase his blessings, if he commits to hard work now. One must help oneself first. When the orishas see the client helping himself, they will double the effects of his actions. He will have all that he needs.
- This person needs more peace in his life. He likes to fight with his friends, lovers, and family members. While for him argument is entertaining and psychologically empowering, it brings too much heat in his life. The diviner should ask him to assess his life honestly and then tell him that after each argument, no matter how minor, he suffers setbacks. Once the client realizes the truth in this, he can change his ways. His lot in life will improve.
- Finally, this odu says the client's main problem is this: He is confused about life. The reason that he has come to the mat is simple: He is looking for someone to give him wisdom and understanding. These things, however, cannot be found here. The client must look within himself for wisdom; he must learn from his experiences. And he must look to the orishas for guidance. If he does this, all his troubles will slowly melt away.

## The Prohibitions of Owani Obara

- The first prohibition of this odu is for the diviner: He may not spend the derecho for this reading on himself. He must give it away to someone in need. A portion of any money that he charges for the eboses must be given away as well.
- For the next three months, avoid the color red; it brings danger. If this reading is an itá, red becomes taboo for life.
- Give up all vices. Tobacco, alcohol, drugs, smoking, and gluttony all destroy one bit by bit.

## The Eboses of Owani Obara

When Owani Obara opens on the mat, no matter its orientation the diviner must prescribe the following eboses:

- The diviner should prepare both a bóveda and an opá ikú for the client. Weekly, the client should provide fresh water and fresh flowers to his bóveda. It must always have light; he should keep a white seven-day candle lit for it, replacing it just before it burns out. Every week, he must place a plate of freshly cooked food before his opá ikú and otá de egun (a stone for egun). To see what elese these spirits might require, the diviner should ask, "Ebó elese egun?" If the answer is yes, he uses the diloggún to mark the appropriate offering.
- As soon as possible, the diviner should take this client for a consultation with a tata nkisi. He has issues with the religion Palo Mayombe. An aleyo or an aborisha might need rayado, while

an initiate might need jubilation. If the client is a palero, Owani Obara directs him to receive a nganga. This will bring him power, strength, and luck.

- In Owani Obara, Elegguá stands up not to bless but to demand something of the client. The diviner must speak honestly about this, questioning the client and his relationship with the orisha. If the client may any promises to Elegguá that he did not keep, he must fulfill those promises now. If the client cannot remember any unkept promises to Elegguá, the diviner should see if Elegguá will accept a sacrifice, asking, "Ebó elese Elegguá?" If Elegguá refuses a sacrifice, the client must placate him daily with prayers and adimús until these issues are resolved. Without his goodwill in Owani, there can be no evolution.
- In this sign, Elegguá, Shangó, Aganyú, Oyá, or Ogún might need ebó. To determine if one or more of these orishas requires an offering, the diviner asks, "Ebó elese [orisha's name]?" If the answer is yes, he uses the diloggún to mark the appropriate offering.

Now the diviner has his first chance to close the oracle. If these considerations are not enough to close the odu for an aleyo or an aborisha, the diviner must turn to the eboses of the parent odu, Owani (see page 534). Something there is necessary for the client's evolution.

If Owani Obara remains open for an initiate, Elegguá requires a four-legged sacrifice and an itá. If this prescription is not enough to close the odu for the initiate, the diviner must turn to the eboses of the parent odu, Owani.

## The Seventh Composite Odu of Owani, Owani Odí (11-7)

### The Proverbs of Owani Odí

- The whim is one's loss.
- Elegguá saves you from death.
- Your two friends are your enemies.
- Stretch out your hand as far as it will reach.

### The Message of Owani Odí

When a cast of eleven mouths, Owani, precedes a cast of seven mouths, Odí, the odu Owani Odí is open on the mat. Having cast this pattern, the diviner pays homage to the orishas who speak in this odu, saying, "Maferefún Elegguá! Maferefún Shangó! Maferefún Oshún! Maferefún Yemayá! Maferefún Obatalá!"

This odu gave birth to the construction of the fundamento batá, the sacred drums by which the orishas are called to the earth. When this pattern appears on the mat, the diviner must immediately prescribe, as ebó, the gift of a small set of toy drums to the orisha whose diloggún is being consulted. A tambor and fundamento batá might be required by the orishas who speak in this odu. (See "The Eboses of Owani Odí" on page 526 for a more thorough explanation.)

The diviner must also explore the following points with the one for whom Owani Odí has fallen:

- The client has two close friends, one rich and one poor, with whom he spends much time. Unfortunately, neither of these is a true friend; each is evil and has his sights on the client's destruction. While the two are not working together, in time each will create chaos in this person's life. The reason for their treason is simple: envy. The client has accomplished much on his own, and neither wants him to rise. To overcome this osogbo, the client must learn to discern the true nature of his friends. He must make them prove themselves to him. There is no other way.
- Four people around the client want to be his lover. One of these four likes to drink to excess; if this person is not an alcoholic, alcoholism is not too far away. None of these four is suitable for the client. He must let go of three and keep the one who likes to drink close to him, but only as a friend. He will be integral to that person's recovery. Owani Odí promises that in time, someone more suitable as a lover will be brought into the client's life.
- The client is bored; however, he does not have the money to entertain himself as he wants to be

entertained. Finances are tight, and the client is inherently lazy. The diviner should tell him to work hard; money will come. In the meantime, he should make adimú to both his guardian orisha and his godparent's crown. The two orishas will work together to bring him what he lacks in life.

## The Prohibitions of Owani Odí

- Do not live in high places. If one must dwell in an apartment, it must be on the first floor, never on top.
- Never offer what is not easily given. One makes too many empty promises and gives too much of oneself away for free. This must stop now.
- The consumption of ham or other pork products is forbidden.
- Of all the prohibitions of Owani, this is the most important: Do not go out into the street for eight days. Death, murder, rape, and robbery are out there, and they will find the one for whom this odu opens if this taboo is broken.

## The Eboses of Owani Odí

Owani Odí is complex, and the diviner needs to keep several points in mind. First he must consider the ebó of the drums. The client must give a small set of toy drums to the orisha whose diloggún is being consulted. When the client is at war, as ebó he should tap out a simple rhythm while speaking to the orisha. The drumming will incite the orisha into action. If the client is an initiate, he must also give Elegguá, Shangó, Oshún, Yemayá, or Obatalá a tambor with fundamental batá. The diviner must determine which orisha will claim this tambor. The initiate must hire a priest or priestess to dance at that tambor as a mount (someone who becomes possessed by his or her guardian orisha), for that orisha must come down and speak to the client. At least a week before the tambor, the client must feed that mount's guardian orisha. Also, if this reading is an itá, the initiate must learn to play the drums and must have a set constructed for his own use.

Once the diviner has settled these issues with the client, he must prescribe an ebó that must be done before the client can go home. At Obatalá's feet, the diviner must give the client a rogación using grated coconut, water, grated cocoa butter, crushed cascarilla, white flowers, honey, and milk. As soon as he has wrapped the client's head, the diviner should tell him, "Obatalá forbids you to go out of your house for eight days. Dress in white during this time, and stay home." If Owani Odí has opened in a severe osogbo, the diviner should ask the diloggún, "Rogación sodidé?" If the answer is yes, the rogación must be a rogación sodidé. In this case, the diviner should not remove the ingredients from the client's feet. Instead, he must wrap the client's feet in white cotton and white cloth. The client must leave his feet wrapped as long as the rogación remains on his head.

Note that if both Elegguá and Oshún stand up during this reading for ebó, the client must make his offerings to them together. He should place Elegguá at Oshún's feet to do so. Together, they will help the client prosper.

Having made these prescriptions, the diviner now has his first chance to close the odu. If it remains open, he should consider the following eboses:

- Owani Odí is called the odu of the "monkey with nine tails." The diviner must prepare a niche osain for the client. On this charm he must place a small monkey (such as the kind found in the child's toy called Barrel of Monkeys), with nine multicolored ribbons hanging from the monkey's buttocks. The client should carry this charm with him every day for luck.
- Another ebó may be done with the monkey for Elegguá. The client should purchase Barrel of Monkeys and give that toy to Elegguá; he should open the barrel and let the tiny toys hang from its edges. This is done so that no one can make a "monkey" out of the client in front of others.
- The client might have issues with Elegguá, Shangó, Oshún, Yemayá, Obatalá, or Ochosi. If the letter refuses closure, the diviner should

consider marking ebó to one or more of these spirits, asking, "Ebó elese [orisha's name]?" If the answer is yes, he uses the diloggún to mark the appropriate offering.

- If this letter comes with a serious osogbo and Elegguá stands up for ebó, the diviner should offer him three chickens. If he accepts this as a sacrifice, the diviner should feed him the chickens deep in the woods. If the client does not have Elegguá, it is acceptable for him to offer this ebó to his godparent's Elegguá. The client, however, is bound to receive the warriors (which include Elegguá) quickly. He must make preparations for this ceremony immediately.

If these considerations are not enough to close the session for an aleyo or an aborisha, the diviner must turn to the eboses of the parent odu, Owani (see page 534). Something there is necessary for the client's evolution.

If the client is an initiate, however, there is one more option for ebó in this composite odu: the reception of Ochosi. The diviner should ask, "Koshé Ochosi?" Marking this as ebó, the diloggún demands that preparations for this ceremony be made immediately. If the sign will not accept this ebó, or if it still remains open after Ochosi's reception has been prescribed, the diviner must turn to the eboses of the parent odu, Owani.

## The Eighth Composite Odu of Owani, Owani Ogbe (11-8)

### The Proverbs of Owani Ogbe

- Instantaneous imprisonment [is coming for you].
- Do not cry in misery over what you spend or your things will not come out well.
- He who eats too much will get sick.
- You will not regret sharing what you have with the needy.

### The Message of Owani Ogbe

When a casting of eleven mouths, Owani, precedes a cast of eight mouths, Ogbe, the odu Owani Ogbe is open. This letter is also known by the names Owani Unle and Owani l'Ogbe. Having made this cast, the diviner says, "Maferefún Elegguá!" This odu signals issues between the client and Elegguá; the client must settle these so he may evolve. For here is told the story of the farmer who bargained with Elegguá for a bountiful harvest. His crops flourished, yet he did not sacrifice. Angered, Elegguá set a trap for the farmer and caused him to destroy his own planting. This is also the sign in which two good friends boasted that nothing in heaven or on the earth could destroy their friendship. Elegguá tested their faith by walking between them: One side of his hair was well styled and the other side was ill-kempt. The two friends argued over the orisha's hairstyle, and their friendship ended.

Other stories are told in this odu as well. Here it is said that Owani once had a child; when young, he placed a golden chain around his son's neck, fastening it so he could not take it off and lose it. The child grew quickly, and the chain became too tight. Owani could not remove it without breaking it, and he almost lost his son. In another story, Ogbe was a farmer who raised many fruit trees, and in an act of kindness to Owani, he often took him a bundle of plantains. Having opened in this sign, the client is now marked for two taboos and one ebó. To the orisha whose diloggún is consulted he must give a bundle of plantains. And from this moment on, he is never to eat plantains himself, and he may never wear chains or clothing with tight collars. Break these taboos, and all the osogbo of Owani will fall upon him.

In addition, when Owani Ogbe falls on the mat the diviner must investigate the following issues:

- The diviner should tell the client that he has betrayed a friend by having an affair with that person's lover. If this relationship continues, it must end now. He cannot be a friend to this person anymore, nor can he continue to sleep with his lover.
- Soon, good news will come to the client. It may involve a job change or a new house. When the blessing comes, the client should take advantage

of it and give thanks to the orishas.

- Over the next few months, this person will incur debt, and a lot of money will be spent. He must not cry over this. If he does, no good will come.
- To avoid tragedy, the client must live with his eyes and ears open at all times. In this way he will save his own head.

## The Prohibitions of Owani Ogbe

- In Owani Ogbe, the following foods become taboo: eggs, peanuts, alcohol, grainy fruits, and white drinks. Do not consume beans, pork, tripe, fish, or reheated foods. The heads and tails of animals are taboo. Do not pick, eat, or give away plantains unless making ebó.
- Do not wear necklaces or chains around one's neck. Clothing with a tight collar is forbidden.
- Do not help anyone to rise. For just as one helps that person rise, so shall one fall in his place.
- Neither take revenge nor talk about revenge. Avoid gossip. Leave all the evil that others do to the orishas, especially Elegguá. He will punish those who harm one.

## The Eboses of Owani Ogbe

There are many eboses to consider in this letter. The diviner should investigate the following:

- When this pattern falls, it issues a stern warning: The police are coming, so be prepared. For whom the law comes, however, is not foretold. Because Owani Ogbe opens for the client, this osogbo is a danger for him, yet the energy enfolds all present for the reading. This sign offers a remedy—make ebó to Ochosi with two pigeons. If this ebó can be done immediately upon closing the session, the diviner can cleanse all the initiates in addition to the client with the birds; but if the sacrifice cannot be made this night, all present at this session must return as soon as possible with their own pigeons to make ebó. The diviner should enforce the need to sacrifice immediately, for when the police come imprisonment is instantaneous.
- If the client is having legal difficulties, we say that it will not be long before the police come to take him away. This odu, however, gives an ebó that promises escape from the legal system: On behalf of the client, the diviner should offer Ochosi two pigeons, and then he should give the client a rogación at the orisha's feet. The derecho for this work is twenty-one dollars, Ochosi's number. The diviner may not keep this fee for himself or else the law will come to knock at his door. Instead, he must seek out a beggar in the street; this will be Eshu in disguise to test the italero. He should give the client's derecho to that beggar.
- To the orisha whose diloggún is being consulted, the client must give a bundle of plantains.
- The diviner must investigate the client's relationship with Elegguá; this odu signals that the client made a promise to Elegguá that he has not kept. If the client cannot recall making such a promise, the diviner should see if Elegguá will accept ebó instead, asking, "Ebó elese Elegguá?" If the answer is yes, he uses the diloggún to mark the appropriate offering. Elegguá's propitiation is essential; the client needs his goodwill.
- Even if the client thinks that he attends to his Elegguá well, he should still, as soon as possible, offer this orisha a rooster so that he does not incur any debt to him.
- The client has many difficulties, and these should be left at Elegguá's feet. The diviner marks ebó to this orisha using the shells, and when the client comes to make his ebó, he first tells Elegguá about all the people and situations in his life that are troubling him and then offers him the prescribed ebó.
- This odu mandates that the client care for Elegguá frequently; he should also care well for a child of Obatalá living in his house.

At this point the diviner has his first opportunity to close the oracle. If all these eboses have been considered and the odu remains open, the diviner must turn to the eboses of the parent odu, Owani (see page 534). Something there is necessary for the client's evolution.

## The Ninth Composite Odu of Owani, Owani Osá (11-9)

### The Proverbs of Owani Osá

- A flag planted will help win the war.
- You have many eyes upon you.
- You cannot dig a hole where one is already dug.
- What is buried must stay buried; it will be rotten when it is dug up.

### The Message of Owani Osá

When a casting of eleven mouths, Owani, precedes a cast of nine mouths, Osá, the odu Owani Osá is open on the mat. Having made this cast, the diviner must say, "Maferefún Elegguá! Maferefún Oyá! Maferefún Shangó! Maferefún Aganyú!" All four spirits speak strongly here, and the aché of all four may be needed to save the client from this odu's osogbo. Their propitiation is essential, and the sign closes rarely without all of them claiming ebó. Elegguá and Oyá take a special interest in the client; even if this client is an initiate of another orisha, their love for him is so strong that he could be a child of either. To find iré and achieve evolution, the client must pamper both, bringing them together and offering a sacrifice to be shared between the two. The gifts they bring will be immense.

Owani Osá is a hot letter. Even if the odu is marked as coming in iré, its energies can bring little goodness. It points out a person who is victimized by himself and others; this client has many enemies who are always close, and some of these could appear to be well-meaning friends. Their constant meddling and interference will bring this person's best-laid plans to ruin. The client becomes so confused by the good intentions of others that he does not heed even good advice, and because of this, many of his plans do not come out well. There is an evil eye laid upon him from others who are jealous, and this unnoticed sorcery brings him failure. The first key to averting danger in this odu is secrecy; everything the client hopes to accomplish must be done silently and alone; he should not tell even his best friend about his plans. Second, the client must reconsider whom he calls "friend." Too many people around him wear masks.

In addition, the diviner must explore the following points with the client:

- This person often finds himself in a period of evolution followed by sudden decline. This erratic pattern permeates all areas of his life: finances, career, relationships, and travel. Before beginning any new project, this person must consult with the orishas and make ebó. They will help him stabilize his affairs.
- The diviner should caution the client against buying used or secondhand goods. If he finds anything of value in the street, he must not bring it home. No good will come of it.
- The client's head is weak; his thoughts are not good. The diviner should tell him never to act on a whim, for whimsy will be his destruction.
- There are too many evil eyes and tongues upon this person. Because Elegguá and Shangó both speak in this sign, if gossip and rumors become too harsh, the client should make an ebó to both together with a cow's tongue. They will destroy the tongues of those who speak harshly about him.
- While the client will have to work hard once this odu has fallen, the sign itself says that hard work will pay off in the end. It is important that amid all the change and chaos that comes, the client keep his eyes set on one important goal. If he does this, he will not be overwhelmed.

### The Prohibitions of Owani Ogbe

- Ram, rooster, liquor, white and red beans, mutton, miniestra, and coconut are forbidden. Do not consume these foods.
- Do not deny alms to a beggar in the street, especially at a crossroads. He could be Elegguá in disguise.
- Do not walk barefoot, even indoors. Getting

out of bed barefoot could cause a serious sickness. Wear socks to bed.

## The Eboses of Owani Osá

The following eboses must be prescribed when Owani Osá opens on the mat:

- The orisha speaking in this odu demands that a flag in his or her colors be flown over or near the front door to client's house. This will put everyone within the home under that spirit's protection.
- If the client is expecting a new child in the family, ebó must be made to save the unborn baby. The diviner should determine which orisha stands up for the child, and what the orisha requires in return.
- If someone ill comes to the client's house, he can make ebó on that person's behalf so that death will not take the sick one before his time.
- This letter prescribes that the client bathe many times with an infusion of sage. He should also fumigate the home with sage so that no evil can rest within its walls.
- The client should have a rogación before Obatalá's shrine. Afterward, before wrapping the client's head in white cloth, the diviner feeds his orí two white pigeons.

Having made these prescriptions, the diviner may now attempt to close the oracle. If the sign refuses closure, the diviner should continue with the following items:

- The letter now demands that a niche osain be made for the orisha speaking up in this reading. The client should carry this charm with him at all times, following the taboos that one would follow for the elekes.* Whenever he does not carry this niche osain, he should keep it with his orishas.
- Elegguá and Ogún could be standing up for their own eboses to clear the client's paths in life and to keep his travels safe. The diviner should ask, "Ebó elese Elegguá?" and "Ebó elese Ogún?" If the answer is yes, he uses the diloggún to mark the appropriate offering.

If these considerations are not enough to close the session, the diviner must turn to the eboses of the parent odu, Owani (see page 534). Something there is needed for the client's evolution.

# The Tenth Composite Odu of Owani, Owani Ofún (11-10)

## The Proverbs of Owani Ofún

- Only the coconut knows the worms that it has within.
- That which has never happened can happen.
- That which comes cheaply will one day cost a lot.

## The Message of Owani Ofún

When an initial cast of Owani, eleven mouths, precedes a cast of Ofún, ten mouths, the odu Owani Ofún is open on the mat. Having made this cast, the diviner says, "Maferefún Elegguá! Maferefún Afra! Maferefún Babaluaiye!" These three orishas dominate this sign, and their propitiation is essential to the client's evolution. For here is told the story of Babaluaiye and the coconut palm. Babaluaiye and Elegguá were once out walking together, and the two chanced upon a coconut palm. Babaluaiye paid foribale to her but did not notice that the tree did not acknowledge him in return. When Elegguá pointed out the tree's transgression, Babaluaiye was angered; he pointed a single finger at her and said, "Only the coconut knows the worms it has within." He wandered off, but Elegguá stayed behind, puzzled. He saw the coconuts, unripe, fall to the earth. A scourge of worms rose from the ground, consuming the tree. It fell. For its lack of respect, the beautiful

*Many taboos accompany the wearing of elekes or carrying of any charm of the orishas. One must not go to bars or "seedy" places while they are in one's possession. One should not drink or take illegal intoxicants while wearing them. Nor should one wear them when engaging in sexual activity or during one's menses. After sex or after the menses, one should shower or bathe before wearing them again. One must observe proper legal, ethical, and moral conduct when wearing or carrying anything of ocha.

coconut palm was reduced to dust, consumed by a cancerous scourge. Elegguá was pleased.

When this letter opens in iré, both Babaluaiye and Elegguá come to bless the client; they will free him from the osogbos that have held him down. If he heeds all this odu tells him, tears will be replaced with laughter, sickness with health, and poverty with wealth. The extent of these blessings, however, rests with the client's actions. To thank these orishas, he must make ebó to Afra, the Eshu that walks with Babaluaiye, and to the orisha himself. Daily, he should say, "Maferefún Elegguá! Maferefún Afra! Maferefún Babaluaiye!" In osogbo, however, Babaluaiye is angry; Elegguá points out the client's transgressions and the debt he owes to Babaluaiye. Carefully, the diviner must work through these issues. Debts, disrespect, and unethical behavior—all these are flagged when Owani Ofún comes in osogbo. If he refuses to work these out, the client could die.

In addition, the diviner should consider the following issues with the client:

- In any orientation of Owani Ofún, terminal or wasting diseases are a danger. Even if the client is not sick now, soon he could be. In iré, Babaluaiye will help the client. In osogbo, his help will not come easily.
- This client's mother is in poor health. He must make ebó on her behalf. Ulcers, tumors, cysts, cancers, and parasitic infections are a danger.
- The client's lover is in danger of mugging, robbery, rape, and other violent crimes.
- Owani Ofún marks various forms of imprisonment: mental, emotional, and physical. Incarceration and kidnapping are dangers.
- The client's hands are in danger. He should never put them in tight, awkward places. If he is involved in manual labor, he could lose a hand.

## The Prohibitions of Owani Ofún

- The following foods are taboo: alcohol, mushrooms, rooster, eggs, peanuts, tripe, and entrails.
- Do not go to funerals, cemeteries, hospitals, nursing homes, wakes, or memorials. Avoid places where death is found.
- One must not be nosy. Do not get involved in others' business, even when invited. The troubles of others are not one's concern.
- Here, one may lose one's life in a fight. Do not fight.

## The Eboses of Owani Ofún

When this odu opens on the mat, the diviner should consider the following:

- In this sign, Babaluaiye is removing his blessings from the client's life due to disrespect. The client has debts with him, and the orisha is demanding payment. The diviner should mark what the orisha requires, asking, "Ebó elese Asohano?" If the answer is yes, he should use the diloggún to mark the required ebó. If no ebó can be marked, the diviner should advise the client to spoil Babaluaiye in return for his goodwill and future blessings. As the client gives to the orisha, so shall the orisha forgive him.
- The diviner should offer Elegguá a rooster to retain his blessings in the client's life.

Having made these prescriptions, the diviner may now attempt to close the oracle. If it will not close, the sign could be marking the client for the reception of Babaluaiye. To determine if this is necessary, the diviner asks, "Koshé Babaluaiye?"

If these eboses are not enough to close the session, the diviner must turn to the eboses of the parent odu, Owani (see page 534). Something there is necessary for the client's evolution.

# The Eleventh Composite Odu of Owani, Owani Meji (11-11)

## The Proverbs of Owani Meji

- The bad that you have made is now on top of you.
- Cats see in the dark, but they cannot see themselves.
- Only Olorún will bring justice.

- You will see your enemy's corpse from your front door.
- Do not curse those who wish you evil.

## The Message of Owani Meji

When a cast of eleven mouths, Owani, precedes another casting of eleven mouths, the odu Owani Meji is open on the mat. Immediately, the diviner pays homage to Elegguá, Babaluaiye, and Osain, saying to each, "Maferefún!" Once the determination of iré or osogbo has been completed, the diviner suspends the reading to offer ebó to Elegguá. If the odu has been marked as iré, the ebó is a saraeko of water, cornmeal, and honey. If the odu has been marked as osogbo, the same saraeko is prepared, but the diviner adds to it epó, jutía, and smoked fish. Regardless of the odu's orientation, as ebó some of the food cooked at the italero's home that day must be given to Elegguá before the diviner gives the reading. When the reading is finished and the odu has closed, the diviner takes all these eboses to the street and discards them, saying, "Eshu batie sode." Using obí at the street corner, the diviner should ask Eshu if all is well. If the answer is no, there he must use the coconuts to mark a suitable ebó. Whatever Eshu claims is given immediately.

This letter is hot and volatile. Here the war between Osain and Orúnmila was born. Osain tried to destroy Orúnmila with his knowledge of herbs and witchcraft, while Orúnmila fought his war by making ebó. The power of his sacrifices proved to be greater, and Osain was maimed. It is also the letter in which the cat and many animals descended from heaven to the earth. Before leaving, they all went to the diviners to mark ebó; they were told to carry black cloth with them to the earth and to be prepared to use it as ebó. Only the cat heeded this advice. Together, they left for the earth, only to find that witches blocked the way. The witches asked each of the animals for black cloth before they would let any pass, and when an animal had none to give, the witches feasted on his flesh. Only the cat had what they desired. They marveled at his large, gorgeous, glowing eyes and were surprised that he carried what they needed. The witches accepted him as one of their own and let him pass.

This odu is the most dangerous composite of Owani, and the diviner must work carefully though the meanings, prohibitions, and eboses of this letter to help the client avoid danger. Even in iré, it foreshadows justice, jail, tragedy, and death. Intentional poisoning is a danger. If the client does not follow the taboo to the letter and do the prescribed eboses immediately, the orishas can do nothing to limit the spiritual currents at work in this person's life. Perhaps the biggest impediment to evolution comes from this person's own spiritual court: There is an egun that does not let him progress easily. Just as this spirit had to work hard in his own life to get ahead, he wants his descendant to work hard in his, and at times this desire amounts to no more than interference. Somehow, the client must placate this spirit. Until it is satisfied, there can be little evolution.

In addition, the diviner should explore the following with the client:

- This person has the tendency to make impossible, unreasonable demands on others. For this reason, his own friends will abandon hm when he needs them the most.
- In Owani Meji, it is said that the child will kill his own mother. Worry and doubt can bring her an early death.
- The letter is one of "reversed heads." This client's fortune could be replaced with another's.
- This letter speaks of inheritances and how they could be lost. If the client has many siblings, one day they will cheat the client out of what is his. If a parent or other family member dies, the client must ensure that his interests are protected or he will be left with nothing.

## The Prohibitions of Owani Meji

- Sesame seeds, grains, grainy fruits, alcohol, corn, and red foods are all taboo.
- Here, it is said that one cursed someone and the curse came back. For now, do not curse anyone.
- Do not share hats, scarves, combs, or brushes. The danger here is that one could "switch heads" with another person.

## The Eboses of Owani Meji

In addition to the eboses that must be given to Elegguá during the course of the reading, Owani Meji offers the following possibilities:

- No matter how many eboses the client makes to the orishas, his life will remain difficult due to a spirit (egun) that likes to make him work hard for what he gets. This spirit must be placated so that it interferes no more, and the diviner should mark what it will take to keep this egun from being so troublesome.
- After placating egun, the client must tend to Babaluaiye. The diviner marks what this orisha requires. In severe cases of osogbo, the client will have to receive him.
- The diviner should feed Elegguá three baby chickens at a crossroads so that all the roads in the client's life are open.

If these prescriptions are not enough to close the session, the diviner must turn to the eboses of the parent odu, Owani (see page 534). Something there is necessary to the client's evolution.

# The Twelfth Composite Odu of Owani, Owani Ejila (11-12)

## The Proverbs of Owani Ejila

- A united family is a strong family.
- In a tempest, all the world will be scarred.
- After the tempest, there is only peace.

## The Message of Owani Ejila

When an initial casting of eleven mouths, Owani, precedes a second cast of twelve mouths, Ejila Shebora, the odu Owani Ejila is open. Owani Oturupon is another name for this sign. Having made this cast, the diviner says, "Maferefún Shangó! Maferefún Aganyú!" Here, both speak strongly; they advise the client to listen well because they will give their advice only once. The proverbs of this letter sum up most of what Owani Ejila has to say. A united family is a strong family: Right now, issues and calamities of which the client is unaware are brewing. Family units will be strained to the point of destruction unless all are united in love. Tragedy, revolution, entanglement, evil, and bad luck are foreshadowed, so the client must be prepared. When danger strikes, it will come as a tempest, and all whom this client loves will suffer. A violent death is foreshadowed—someone could be lost through this tragedy. The closer the family is before this evil strikes, the more easily they will all be able to pick up the pieces and continue with their lives. When all has settled, there will be peace: If the client and his family stand strong, they can survive.

The diviner should also explore the following points with the client:

- Owani Ejila is an odu of hypochondria. The client always complains about minor health issues, and many of these are not issues at all. He must be careful or he will bring real sickness upon himself.
- In this sign, the client's worst enemy drinks from the same cup as he; he should be wary.
- If moles and pimples have not formed on the client from the waist down, they will. Without proper medical intervention, some could become cancerous.
- Owani Ejila marks a gathering of many people. Some of the client's friends will want him to go to this social occasion. He must agree to go, but he must say he will meet them there. Then he must not go. The diviner should tell the client that if he goes, there will be tragedy, but if he stays home, all will be safe.

## The Prohibitions of Owani Ejila

- The following foods are taboo: ram, eels, fowl, okra, and papaya. Do not eat food offered by either a coworker or a stranger.
- Do not mingle with or use the service of a prostitute.
- Do not be stubborn, do not argue, and do not fight.

## The Eboses of Owani Ejila

When Owani Ejila opens on the mat, the diviner should prescribe the following eboses:

- The client should offer an adimú of cool fruits to Ogún to placate him; if this orisha remains spiritually hot, the client will soon be injured by metal. The diviner should mark what is needed to cool the orisha, how long the offering is to stay with him, and what is to be done with it after the ebó is complete.
- Shangó stands up to help this person, but he demands an ebó in return. The diviner should mark what is needed so that this orisha may begin his work.

If these prescriptions are not enough to close the session, the diviner must turn to the eboses of the parent odu, Owani (see page 534). Something there is necessary to the client's evolution.

# Closing the Reading: Further Eboses of the Parent Odu, Owani

Having exhausted the options for larishe and ebó in the composite odu, the diviner turns to the parent odu to find a method of closure. This sign, Owani, contains within itself many offerings and rituals to placate both the letter and the orishas who are speaking in it. Before considering these, however, if Owani has opened in osogbo, the diviner should investigate the client's issues with Elegguá. Although the diviner may have already asked the client this question, he must ask again, "Do you have any unresolved issues with Elegguá?" If the client made any promises to the orisha that he did not keep, he must fulfill them now. Elegguá is, by nature, a trickster; if he strikes a bargain with one who does not hold up his end of the deal, Elegguá sometimes finds a way to get what he was promised and more by testing that person. At this point, if the client remembers any unfulfilled promises, he must give Elegguá double what he promised. For example, if he promised Elegguá a basket of fruit in exchange for a blessing, he now owes Elegguá two baskets of fruit. In addition, or if the client cannot remember any unkept promises, the diviner should ask, "Ebó elese Elegguá?" Now that the client has admitted his debt, the orisha might want something else to resolve the disrespect that existed between the two.

Once he has investigated this issue in depth, the diviner should prescribe the following eboses:

- The orisha whose shells were cast and the odu eleven mouths demand placation together. The diviner should prescribe for each eleven gourds filled with eleven separate foods adored by the orisha. This spirit has marked Owani as the odu in effect; the supplication of this spirit with the number eleven is essential to the client's evolution. This ebó should remain with the orisha for a number of days equal to his sacred number. For example, in an ebó of eleven gourds made to Elegguá, the diviner will choose three, seven, or twenty-one days as the amount of time the sacrifice remains with him. If Oshún was consulted, the gourds should remain with her for five days. Making ebó to Shangó demands that the sacrifice be left for six days. At the end of this time, dispose of the ebó in a manner suitable for both Owani and the orisha. Remember that Owani refers to the crossroads; this symbol is a necessary part of the ebó. For example, the client might take Oshún's gourds to a river near a crossroads or Shangó's to a palm tree planted near a crossroads.
- The diviner must placate the client's guardian orisha as well. First, the client should have a rogación at that spirit's feet. After the rogación, the client should give to that orisha a basket lined with that orisha's favorite colors and filled with eleven coconuts. Every day for the next eleven days, the client should return to cleanse himself with one coconut, discarding it when he is finished. On the eleventh day, after the last coconut is used, the client should fill the basket with eleven different types of fresh fruits and leave the basket at the orisha's feet for a number

of days equal to his or her sacred number. At the end of this time, the client should discard the basket at that orisha's place in nature.

- If any orisha has demanded a cleansing for the client through the reading, the diviner must adapt that cleansing to represent Owani. Instead of one cleansing, he might prescribe eleven, using eleven different materials. The eleven cleansings should take place on consecutive days so that the erratic vibrations of Owani are removed and stabilized during this time.

Having prescribed these eboses with the necessary adaptations, the diviner now has another chance to close the oracle. If it remains open, he should prescribe the following four eboses:

- First, if the client does not have Elegguá, he must receive him now; the diviner should keep in mind that the client sitting before the diloggún might be Elegguá's child. If the client already has Elegguá, the diviner should make an additional Eshu for him, marking the path needed with the diloggún. This will be the path of Elegguá to solve all the problems the client faces.
- Second, the client's ancestors stand up now to claim what they have not received: prayer, veneration, fresh water, light, and devotion. The client must have an opá ikú fed, and he should use it regularly. He also must have a spiritual bóveda.
- Third, the client should give a large amount of epó to Elegguá on a daily basis; epó is one of his favorite staples, and it will give him the strength to keep the client's life moving smoothly.
- Finally, the diviner must prescribe a rogación and eborí for the client at Obatalá's feet. Before wrapping the client's head in the white cotton and cloth, the diviner should feed the client's orí two white pigeons or doves; he needs this to strengthen his head.

Now the diviner again asks the oracle for closure. If it refuses closure, the diviner must determine if Elegguá or the client's egun require anything else, asking, "Ebó elese Elegguá?" and "Ebó elese egun?" If the answer is yes, he uses the diloggún to mark the appropriate offering.

If Elegguá will not claim an ebó, or if the ebó marked is not enough to satisfy Owani, the following ebó is mandatory: the sacrifice of a rooster, followed by a showering of toasted corn, jutía, and smoked fish. The client cooks the fowl's aché for the orisha and prepares a meal with the rooster's meat. If this does not close the session and the client is an initiate, the diviner should prescribe the sacrifice of four legs and an itá with Elegguá.

If the odu still will not close, the diviner should consider, in turn, the following possibilities:

- With any type of osogbo in Owani, Babaluaiye might claim ebó. It is possible that the client has debts with this orisha, for he has bailed him out of trouble many times. To determine if ebó is necessary, the diviner asks, "Ebó elese Babaluaiye?" If the answer is yes, he should use the diloggún to mark the required ebó. If Babaluaiye will not take ebó, the diviner should prescribe a rogación for the client at the orisha's feet and, afterward, the investment of the orisha's eleke. The client must wear Babaluaiye's eleke every day.
- If the diviner has come this far into the odu and it will not close, he must take into account the orishas that have stood up in this sign. Normally, Elegguá will speak in Owani in tandem with one or more orishas, the most common being Oyá, Ochosi, Babaluaiye, and Oshún. The two spirits could be standing up together for ebó, and the diviner must ask each combination, "Ebó elese Elegguá y [orisha's name]?" If the answer is yes, he should use the diloggún to mark the required ebó, and the two orishas should be given the ebó at the same time. If eyebale is called for and the client is an initiate, the diviner should keep in mind that four legs and itá could be marked for these spirits as the solution to all his problems.
- If the composite letter opened in ano or ikú and will not close, it mandates eboses to Elegguá and Ochosi. Also, an ebó should be marked to

Oshún to save this person from illness if the illness has not yet manifested.

- Finally, if the odu still will not close, the client may need to receive Oyá, Babaluaiye, or Ochosi. The diviner should ask of each orisha, "Koshé [orisha's name]?"

Having come this far without being able to close the oracle, the diviner at this point will want to call a more experienced elder. He has two options at this point: First, he might explore eboses with the remaining orishas that speak in this odu; second, he might explore the eboses of the secondary odu as if it were the parent odu. Before proceeding with either option, however, the diviner should pause to reflect upon the advice of a more experienced elder. The odu's continued refusal to close could indicate that the diviner has missed something in the process of divination.

# THIRTEEN

## THE FAMILY OF EJILA SHEBORA

### The Proverbs of Ejila Shebora

- It is better to drown than to burn.
- Shangó says, "I am the only one of all the orishas who eats and speaks fire!"
- Only one king can govern a single town.
- In your house, you must act like a king.
- A ship will sink.
- During times of war, a soldier will not sleep.
- No one knew when Eghurun married the vulture, nor did anyone know when she left him.
- When rough waters come, even a ship will sink.
- When one does not welcome visitors to one's home, the house will never receive a greeting.
- The high hill with a narrow peak will never tumble over.
- There are no arms so strong that they can hold the sun; there is no mouth so powerful that it can command the day.
- Those who sacrifice to the orishas will accomplish their destinies.
- One lights a single candle to the orishas; it becomes the light of blessings, the light of wealth, and the warmth of children.
- A knife, no matter how long or how sharp, cannot cut itself.
- A knife, no matter how long or how sharp, can never carve its own handle.
- A wise man will never try to be king; he will be the adviser to the king, and no more.
- Only a brave man will take the crown of ocha.

### The Orishas Who Speak in Ejila Shebora

| | |
|---|---|
| Shangó | Osain |
| Aganyú | Iroko |
| Oshún | Obatalá |
| Dada | Orúnmila |
| Oyá | Oké |
| Oba | |

### The Message of Ejila Shebora

Opening with twelve mouths on the mat, the diloggún sits before the italero in a controversial pattern. Ejila Shebora has come to the house, and this odu is dangerous to read. Its essence seethes with conflicting spiritual currents, energies borne not only by the pattern itself, but also by each priest's individual preferences. To fathom the risks of this sign, one must understand the history of Lucumí divination, the slow, essential evolution of our oracle. Those who have read the works of William Bascom, *Sixteen Cowries* and *Ifá Divination*, know that orisha priests and priestesses in Africa before the 1900s did not read composite odu as they are now read in the New

World.* Instead, they employed a simple system based on the sixteen parent odu of the diloggún. The sixteen African parent odu had the same names as the sixteen Cuban parent odu: Okana, Eji Oko, Ogundá, Irosun, Oché, Obara, Odí, Eji Ogbe, Osá, Ofún, Owani, Ejila Shebora, Metanla, Merinla, Marunla, and Merindilogún.† However, these African cowrie shell diviners cast composite odu only to determine the degree of iré or osogbo at each session; they used only the parent odu to divine a client's destiny. Composites were in the sole possession of the babalawos.

It is common knowledge that slavery brought orisha worship to Cuba. Due to the political climate in Africa, however, most babalawos remained in Nigeria; few were brought to the New World in chains. On the island of Cuba, orisha priests proliferated while Ifá priests dwindled.‡ Without the cult of Ifá, orisha worshipers needed a more advanced oracle to manage religious and spiritual affairs. Since most Yoruba were, and still are, immersed in Ifá mythology and verse from early childhood, such a task did not prove insurmountable; their own knowledge and aché added to the diloggún's growth. Yet this system remained incomplete until the priest Obadimelli made the Middle Passage to Cuba. As was described in chapter 1, Obadimelli had been in training to be a babalawo, although he had not made that initiation, and he brought to Cuba a thorough knowledge of Ifá. Under Obadimelli's guidance the final reformations of divination were completed and a new oracle was born: the diloggún and its 256 composite odu.

While originally a survival mechanism, the composites grew in popularity among orisha worshipers. However, as Ifá slowly gained prominence in Cuba, a schism in the faith arose. Some say this chasm was created by the late Ferminita Gomez, a powerful priestess of Yemayá. A faction of ilé ocha arose that separated from the babalawos entirely; all aspects of the religion were handled by orisha priests, and an office known as the *oriaté* came into existence. Oriatés mastered all aspects of the faith, including the knowledge of all 256 composite odu. Santeros who were not oriatés, on the other hand, mastered all composites except those of Metanla (thirteen mouths), Merinla (fourteen mouths), Marunla (fifteen mouths), and Merindilogún (sixteen mouths).§ A separate faction arose in which priests and priestesses worked hand in hand with Ifá. Diviners in this faction continued to work with composite odu, but the oriatés among them were ordained by Ifá priests, and even they were loath to study any composite beyond Ejila Meji (12-12). Their skills as diviners were relegated to the level of an italero. Now a third faction has come into existence; ilé ocha of this faction believe that those with the skill (mainly oriatés and their students) may read freely beyond twelve mouths, but the advice and knowledge of the babalawos still have their place. It is to the beliefs of this third faction that I ascribe; however, as a wise mentor once told me, "The babalawos live from *us*, and not us from *them*."

*An acquaintance of mine, the late Dr. Mary Curry (ibaé), assured me of this: In Lagos, Nigeria, it is now the custom of many Yoruba cowrie shell diviners to read composite odu as they are read in Ifá. While some say it is the Lucumí influence that caused this development (Dr. Curry's own godfather moved to Lagos for business reasons almost twenty years ago and began working the religion there in the Lucumí style), others say that it was brought about by the inevitable evolution of orisha worship. Dr. Curry told me that her godfather found this composite divination style already in place when he moved to Lagos, and while he shared Lucumí doctrine and methods with some of his friends there, they, in turn, shared their methods and information with him.

†In most areas of Nigeria, the names of the parent odu are similar to those of our diloggún. In his works, William Bascom documents, to the best of his ability, minor regional variations, some of which carried over to Cuba. Realize, however, that many credit these variations to poor scholarship on the part of Bascom and one of his research subjects, Salako.

‡Our sister religion in Brazil, Candomblé, evolved in a similar fashion to Lucumí, without Cuban intervention. There, Ifá disappeared entirely; there were no babalawos, and many said that Orúnmila fled the nation for his home, Nigeria. The Candomblé system of divination, known as *los buzios*, evolved to include composite odu similar to that of the diloggún.

§By now, the reader should have realized that in my writings, I identify a santero without the skill of an oriaté as an italero. Some believe the titles of *italero* and *oriaté* to be interchangeable, but I have been taught that an italero is a diviner without the skills of an oriaté. It is the italero that this book aspires to inform. Therefore, it teaches all composites from Okana through Owani, plus those numerical composites Owani Okana (11-1) through Owani Ejila (11-12) and Ejila Okana (12-1) through Ejila Meji (12-12).

Therefore, one must keep in mind that for many branches of the Lucumí faith Ejila Shebora is the last family of odu that a diviner without the skill of an oriaté can read for his clients. While there are historical and political reasons for this development, there are also mythological reasons found in Ejila Shebora's patakís. Some of these stories are traditional Yoruba, and several acquaintances, among them the late Dr. Mary Curry, have assured me that they exist in the motherland, Nigeria. Among these is a story about the marriage of Oshún and Orúnmila. While the two were married, only Orúnmila had the right to divine. In the beginning, he used the sixteen cowries as his oracle, and with these he could access all 256 odu offered by the system. Yet the cowries had one flaw: When Opira (no open mouths) would open, Orúnmila was helpless to advise his clients.* So rare was Opira's appearance, however, that this flaw never bothered the wise diviner. It came to pass that the mighty one was called away on business, and he left Oshún in charge of his household. Orúnmila realized that his absence would be a hardship for his hundreds of clients, but he told Oshún that if any clients came for divination, she was to reschedule them for when he returned from his trip. Oshún assented, and Orúnmila went away to tend his business.

After Orúnmila left, however, a severe drought came to his village. Orúnmila did not return as he was scheduled to, and people were dying from thirst and starvation. Oshún felt sorry for all the people in the town, and, not knowing when her husband was going to return, she pulled the cowries from Orúnmila's divining bag and cast odu. Although she did not know all the secrets of the diloggún, she knew enough to mark ebó, and the townspeople made this ebó immediately. Rains came the next day; all were saved. With her limited knowledge of the oracle, she saved the lives of many. Orúnmila returned soon thereafter, and while he was happy that his people survived the drought with his wife's help, he was angry that another could divine with cowries as well as he could. He took Oshún before Olódumare, and God himself acknowledged that Oshún was a great diviner in her own right. There, Olódumare decreed that Oshún had the right to divine with the sixteen-cowrie-shell oracle, but because only Orúnmila was the true master of divination, he gave him a new tool for divination: the opele. In Oshún's hands, the diloggún would always have a small margin of error and would always close in Opira, but with his new tool Orúnmila would always be able to divine in all of the 256 odu; the opele would never fail to speak. Olódumare also charged Orúnmila to teach Oshún how to use the sixteen cowries while they were married, and to this he agreed, but their marriage did not last long after this. Oshún learned only the meanings of the sixteen meji odu from Orúnmila. This came to be the system used among Yoruba orisha priests, and it was this system of divination that first came to the New World with the slave trades.

Later in the corpus of Ejila Shebora's patakís, it is said that Orúnmila was married to Yemayá.† She was a diviner in her own right, having learned the basics of sixteen shells from her sister, Oshún, but Yemayá was very attentive to her husband and his work, and daily she watched him as he cast his opele for clients. She loved how this simple tool always talked and was more accurate than her own work with the sixteen cowries. She learned, from observation, the meanings and methods of the composite odu, committing them all to memory so she could use them in her own work with the cowries. Again, Orúnmila was called away on business, and while he was gone, clients continued to show up for sessions with the opele. Not wanting to turn anyone away, and wanting to try her own hand at her husband's

*It is important to note that in Cuba and the United States, Opira is recognized as an odu, and a powerful one. The oriaté, however, is the only priest who has both the knowledge and the skill to manipulate this sign. Therefore, it is not covered in this book.

†Although this patakís is well known in the Lucumí religion, no one can offer any evidence that it existed across the Atlantic, among the Yoruba. Perhaps it is one of the stories born from our own religious evolution. It is true, however, that the Yoruba believed Orúnmila and Yemayá were married; their marriage, however, did not last long. The story of Yemayá's usage of Orúnmila's opele was adapted into the diloggún from Cuban Ifá, so perhaps it was conceived by babalawos to explain why an orisha priest should not divine beyond Ejila Shebora.

tool, Yemayá cast opele for all who came to see her. She had learned well from watching her husband and was almost as skillful as he with the chain's manipulations. She divined for all of Orúnmila's clients, and all were as impressed with her as they were with her husband. Yet Orúnmila returned home in the middle of one of Yemayá's sessions, and he caught her casting for a client. He saw that Ejila Shebora lay open with the chain, and there he cursed her. "Woman," he roared, "the opele is mine and mine alone. Because you have tried to steal my tool, I curse you! In your own system of divination, the diloggún, you will have the right to cast up to twelve mouths on the mat, and no further. Any number of mouths beyond that belongs to me, and when they open for you, you will have to send all your clients to my feet for them to ascertain their destiny."

Because of our history, evolution, and patakís, each initiate brings his or her own preconceived notions to the reading. Even if the diviner is an oriaté, less experienced priests will be afraid of him making a mistake that will affect everyone. Some will expect him to close Ejila Shebora, and others will expect him to proceed. While it is true that the odu falls only for the client, its energies expand to encompass all present at the mat, and sometimes all in the diviner's home. As with the other volatile odu in this system, however, there are a series of rituals designed not only to placate and cool the letter, but also to close the session safely if the diviner has not the skill to proceed. Immediately upon its opening, to placate the letter the diviner gives the sacred gesture for twelve mouths: He lifts first his right buttock and then the left, saying, "Kawo! Kabiosile Shangó!" to honor both the orisha Shangó, who owns Ejila Shebora, and the sign itself. Initiates in the room follow suit, for the royal nature of this letter demands the utmost in respect. Having honored its opening, the italero now bows his head and prays:

*Agangaya agaba gaya oka kan.*
*Ayaba bada koini orisha kinchete.*
*Timbalota lorifa kinchete.*
*Iba kimashete Ikú, kimashete Ofo.*
*Kimashete Eyo, ariku babawa.*

While the diviner prays, those in the room bow their heads as well, and while he intones the chant, many will mutter, "Maferefún Ejila Shebora! Maferefún Shangó! Maferefún Aganyú!" to honor the odu and the spirits found in its realm.

At this point, the diviner deviates from his normal procedure; while he must cast a composite odu to begin the session, he must also deal with the spiritual heat radiating from the orisha's diloggún. Gently, the diviner lifts each shell, those with open mouths first and those with closed mouths next, and places them in the gourd of fresh, cool water used to pour a libation. The diviner then asks the youngest child (a virgin) in the house or, if a child is not available, the youngest initiate to lift the gourd from the mat and take it to the front door. (Innocence placates Ejila Shebora's heat, and children are innocent by nature.) The child or initiate opens the front door wide and, covering the opening of the gourd loosely with one hand so the shells cannot fly out, flings the water far out into the street. This action cools the spiritual vibrations brought by the letter; they are then flung back into the world, which is large enough to handle and cleanse these energies. The child or initiate then refills the gourd with water and brings the shells back to the diviner, who proceeds to cast the composite odu.

Because this letter is dangerous, novice diviners may not wish to continue the consultation. If this is the case, now is the time to close the diloggún, before more complex energies are marked on the mat. To end the session now, the diviner cups all sixteen shells in his hands; he blows over them, dismissing the spirit invoked. He then places all the shells, including the adele laid to the side of the mat, back onto a plate, covers them with a second plate, and returns the derecho to the client. The energy exchange begun is returned to its original state, and the oracle is closed. Either the client seeks out a more competent diviner or the diviner takes this person to an oriaté or babalawo for a more thorough assessment.

If the diviner chooses to proceed with the reading, he now casts the omo odu to form the composite odu of the reading. If Ejila Meji falls, the diviner must do the ritual of saraeko for Shangó before marking the orientations, larishes, and eboses for the composite odu. In all the composites except for Ejila Meji, this ritual is optional, but the diviner may want to consider it also for other hot letters, such as Okana, Ogundá, Obara, Osá, and Owani.* Some diviners wait to see if the letter falls in osogbo before deciding to make saraeko. In my own ilé ocha, we make saraeko out of items that are cool and sacred to Obatalá, for he and Shangó are close, and while Obatalá cannot partake of all things sacred to Shangó, Shangó can partake of all things sacred to Obatalá. With Obatalá's cooling influence, one can turn the heat of Ejila into a blessing. Once the saraeko is prepared (see the recipe on page 52), the diviner heats up a piece of metal until at least part of it has turned red. He places the saraeko at the feet of Shangó and then drops the heated metal into the cool fluids; he removes the metal once its heat has been quenched. Each person, beginning with the diviner and moving on to the client and then the priests and priestesses present in order of elder status, should kneel before Shangó and dip the index finger of the left hand into the saraeko. Each uses his dampened finger to make an equal-armed cross on the roof of his mouth, saying, "It is better to drown than to burn." Once everyone present at the mat has made this gesture, the iyawós present in the diviner's home, and then the aleyos and aborishas, do this short ritual before Shangó as well. Now, everyone returns to the mat and the reading continues.

For the sake of this book, and for those houses that do not deal with any composite in this family beyond Ejila Meji (12-12), the diviner must pay careful attention to the omo odu that falls. If it exceeds twelve mouths, showing Metanla (thirteen mouths), Merinla (fourteen mouths), Marunla (fifteen mouths), or Merindilogún (sixteen mouths), the initial heat of Ejila Shebora is doubled. A novice italero has neither the training nor the skill to handle this sign. While an elder priest might read these letters, and while an oriaté will always investigate these letters, those inexperienced with the diloggún must not work with these composites.† Again, the young child or youngest initiate is called to perform a brief series of rituals to cool the diloggún, bringing this session to closure. He puts all the shells in a gourd of fresh, cool water and takes this gourd to the front door, where he casts the water as far away from the house as possible without losing any of the shells. He then returns the shells to the diviner. The diviner gathers the shells in cupped palms and blows on them. He seals the diloggún in a covered plate and returns the client's derecho. As before, this gesture returns the opened energies to their original state; odu is sealed, and its energies are banished. Later, after the client leaves, the priest casts a large quantity of cool water into the street after him to remove all possible harm from his front door. For a proper consultation, the client must consult with a more experienced oriaté or a babalawo.‡

If one proceeds with the reading, know that although this letter is initially unstable, it is capable of tempering itself so that new creative processes can begin. This odu is as supportive as it is destructive; its sole purpose is to carry evolution through new thresholds and completions. Of this sign, Fá'Lokun Fatunmbi writes, "Ejila Shebora is the metaphysical principle used to represent all things which stand on the threshold of completion. As we move towards the completion of any task, a moment comes when we begin to sense the consequences of our effort even before it is fully manifest."§ This family is the most volatile of all a diviner may read. Born from Ogundá, a pattern filled with struggles, wars, and bloodshed, Ejila Shebora shares in its parent's martial essence. What is born of war bears the scars of war. Yet there is temperance in Ejila

*It is important to make this saraeko if Ejila Shebora falls as an orisha's birth odu cast after lavatorio (the single "birth cry" given by an orisha when born, consisting of a single cast of the diloggún). The spirit just born has come to fight a war, and this war will get hot. Always, it is better to drown than to burn!

†For this reason this chapter does not deal with any composites beyond Ejila Meji. These signs contain too many variables with which a book of this scope cannot deal. Only training with an elder oriaté will give the initiate the skills necessary to manipulate these odu.

‡The diviner is cautioned not to read for anyone else that day until after he has read for himself; the eboses prescribed in his own reading will serve to remove all harm that the volatile energies from these last four letters can bring.

§Awó Fá'Lokun Fatunmbi, *Awó: Ifá and the Theology of Orisha Divination* (Bronx, N.Y.: Original Publications, 1992), 142.

Shebora, and it becomes a threshold to greater things. Unless the client aggravates its energy, this pattern cools slowly over time; eventually, it becomes neither too hot nor too cold. Through it, nature becomes supple and supportive, but the forces creating homeostasis are always severe. Order comes to chaos. Peace emerges from struggle. Harmony coalesces amid discord. Before this pattern runs it course, the client will see the end result and understand the reasons for life's harshness.

Twelve mouths alludes to the molten earth, the viscous, thick lava gyrating beneath the earth's core. One finds it in the action of fire; while destructive, fire also brings transformation and release. Its consumption of any material destroys, yes, but through its violent nature energy is released and new material forms are created. Electricity, which flashes and flickers briefly before dissipating, represents Ejila Shebora's ephemeral nature. All of Ejila's actions find summation in one phrase: the wrath of heaven. For heaven is not always kind; heaven strikes briefly, and creation coalesces, but the vast energy expended destroys what hinders its work. Whenever this sign is open, its actions represent this nature. Of Ejila Shebora's connections with both thresholds and completions, Fatunmbi writes, "In nature, one of the places that stood on the threshold of completion was the fire at the center of the earth. There was a point in the past when the fire at the center of the earth was too hot to sustain life. There will be a point in the future when the fire at the center of the earth will be too cool to sustain life. At the moment when the great oceans began to form, the Earth stood at the threshold of evolution."* One's life aspires to this moment—a threshold in which all transmutes—yet the road to this point is fraught with danger and despair. Ejila Shebora's energy is overwhelming; it will take perseverance to evolve amid its influence.

Through this letter many spirits might choose to speak. The one whose shells are being consulted has the first option, and what he has to say will be harsh. If this person has never opened in this sign before, the orisha consulted has much to say. First, this person can be summed up in one word: paradox. While sharply intelligent, the child of Ejila pays little attention to his environment. This results in poor choices. He loves adventure, excitement, and the unusual, yet this desire for exotic experience leads him astray. Rarely does this client look at, listen to, or evaluate others. Enemies are hidden, and they do all they can to bring ruin to his plans. Traps need not be well laid, for under this odu the client tends to be forward focused. He does not watch his back, nor does he look to either side to see what dangers, or blessings, await there. When his goals are unattained or plans shattered, he knows not why. When blessings approach from unknown, unseen sources, he does not claim them. A responsible italero will spend time carefully explaining this information. He must tell the client, "Your eyes must be opened to other people and other places; watch where you walk and always look in all directions at once. Do not trust anyone save yourself. Only in this way will harm be avoided."

The orisha whose diloggún is being consulted says those things that bring trouble to the client could also become his salvation. While opening his eyes to look in all directions, the client should always keep his focus; if he is aware of the environment, there is little that can stop him or turn him aside. The goals he has attained so far have not been achieved without struggle, and he is stronger for this. The diviner should tell the client this: "There was once a time when life was sour and difficult. You had dug yourself into a hole, and you had to climb out alone. Poverty and danger were all around. There was even imprisonment or danger of being jailed. Maybe you even had thoughts of suicide. Yet this momentum, the impetus built up by your motion and struggles, kept you moving when nothing else could. Listen to this reading. Heed the advice of the orishas. You will never be that low again." The diviner should advise the client to clean house within himself. He is to control all his negative traits with an iron fist; bad temper, violent tendencies, foul language, pride, vanity, recklessness, and promiscuity must all be tamed. The client must be open to suggestion rather than hardheaded and stubborn. Thus will he have evolution.

*Fatunmbi, *Awó*, 143.

Shangó stands up next to speak and claim ebó; behind him stands his father, Aganyú. If the client is having his first reading, or if his guardian orisha has not yet been determined, this strong letter suggests that he might be a child of either orisha. Keep in mind that the child of one is followed closely by the second, and both will figure prominently in the casting of Ejila Shebora. Falling for an aleyo or for one who has a different guardian orisha, both Shangó and Aganyú are standing up here to offer advice and protection. Through twelve mouths, both become aggressive; Shangó is said to be angry in orientations of osogbo. The diviner should deliver this stern admonition: "Shangó is now speaking to you, and he speaks only once! Listen carefully lest his protection be withdrawn and you are left to deal with your problems alone." Even if this oracle has marked larishe, and even if the eboses for odu have not yet been marked, the diviner should instruct the client about Shangó's nature and the adimús that he likes to receive. This orisha's placation is essential at this time.

Spiritual prescriptions involving the orisha Shangó may be given at this time. To clear away all the broken promises, plans, and effects of his enemies, the client should go through his home to find all items that are broken, burned, or worn out; he should bring them to Shangó, along with an adimú. The orisha will remove all blocks from the past that impede future progress. Since much of the negativity surrounding the client originates with the "bad tongues" around him, he should make an ebó to Shangó with a fresh cow's tongue. If his enemies are known and can be named, the client should write down their names on a piece of brown paper, smear it with epó, and then sprinkle it with a liberal amount of hot peppers. He should make a thin slit in the cow's tongue and then fold the paper tightly and place it inside the slit. Using threads that are red and white (Shangó's colors), the client sews the cut tightly. He sets the ebó on a white plate and gives it to the orisha, along with two seven-day white candles and two coconuts. While lighting the two white candles, the client prays to Shangó, asking him to sew shut the mouths and bind the tongues of those who speak evil. Everything is left at the shrine until the candles burn out, and then the client removes everything and leaves it at the foot of a royal palm tree with six pennies, the orisha's derecho. The italero should note to the client that once this ebó is done, the client may not participate in gossip lest Shangó sew his own mouth tightly.

Through Ejila, this client's destiny has become so tightly bound with the mighty Shangó that all future work and placation done with this spirit will serve to further his own evolution. Yet he must always heed the orisha's advice and words. The diviner should relay to the client this information: "Perhaps your strongest qualities are those that you share with Shangó; even when your mind, body, and soul are weak, your head, the orí, is still strong! It makes action a way of life for you and drives you to achieve even when all the odds are against you. Yet the orisha from whom these things come reminds you to slow down. Do not mirror his negative traits. Carry his good aspects in your heart at all times." If the italero is familiar with any of the patakís of this sign that involve the two orishas Obatalá and Shangó, now is the time to explore them. If he is not familiar with these patakís, the diviner must explain some of the more admirable traits bestowed by Obatalá, the most desirable being respect. Throughout Shangó's adventures as both a human and an orisha, Obatalá has brought him coolness, calmness, and wisdom. In ocha, we often say that whenever Obatalá is present, Shangó is there as well, attending to his father and learning by his actions. There are even times when a child of Obatalá's younger aspects is easily mistaken for a child of Shangó, and vice versa. This client must learn to depend on the coolness of Obatalá to balance the excessive energy of Shangó that runs through his veins.

Obatalá, of course, has the next option to speak in this sign. He stands up in this odu to tell the client that while there are times when the unquenchable heat and energy of Shangó are needed to get by in life, there are also times when coolness, purity, and spiritual chastity are needed to keep life running smoothly. Now is such a time. While Ejila Shebora will keep the client working and moving at a frantic pace to achieve his goals and his evolution, he must also spend time each day in seclusion and quiet contemplation. The body must rest, and the mind must be stilled so that exhaustion is not overwhelming. This letter whispers of one who becomes overwhelmed by exhaustion; he will not recuperate. The client can depend on Obatalá to guide the strength that Shangó has given and look to him for a way to cool the passionate, heated vibrations of the odu Ejila Shebora. If the client is in obvious distress or a state of exhaustion when the reading is given, the italero should offer a cool rogación at the feet of Obatalá before allowing him to leave his home. Remember: Obatalá, though the eldest of the orishas, is also the strongest, and his strength comes from both age and wisdom. The client should look to the elders of his ilé ocha for Obatalá; their age and wisdom will help him find a passage from all osogbos in this sign. Their advice is integral to the safe passage within this odu.

Elegguá speaks in this odu as well, and while what he has to say is heavily dependent on the composite odu opened, the diviner may make many spiritual prescriptions with this orisha to help the client overcome osogbo. First, the client should employ Elegguá to trap this person's enemies. He paints three mousetraps red and black and washes them in Elegguá's omiero. He gives the mousetraps to Elegguá with a white candle and some rum, asking that he capture his enemies before they capture him. Before leaving, he sets the traps, leaving them alone until something trips their springs. Each trap sprung shows that one of the client's enemies has been subdued. He must remove it and throw it in the trash, which Elegguá owns. After removing the traps, the client should give three more to the orisha and leave them there indefinitely. To keep the evil eye off the client's home and to stop evil gossip from spreading, an ojo y lengua (a plaque with an eye and tongue) should also be washed in Elegguá's omiero and hung prominently on the front door. Again, a white candle should be lit to Eshu, and the client must pray for the protection he desires. Finally, the client must wear Elegguá's eleke at all times so his protection is bestowed in all walks of life.

After the first four orishas—Shangó, Aganyú, Obatalá, and Elegguá—speak in this odu, many others may stand up to speak. Oshún is next; while Ejila Shebora is a hot odu, she is still a sweet orisha who can bring blessings amid turmoil. When life becomes sour and unbearable, the client can turn to her to reclaim what was lost. If she is pampered, she will pamper in return. Dada, Oyá, Oba, Osain, Iroko, and Oké are all found in this series of signs; however, what they have to say is dependent not only on the composite opened but also on the client's initiatory status. When delivering advice from these orishas, the diviner will have to consider their issues carefully.

The easiest way to begin a thorough study of Ejila Shebora is with it in iré. If the odu is marked as coming in iré, it comes as one of evolution. However, in twelve mouths evolution is not a simple process. The volatility of this sign says that the client's environment is feverish; at this moment, spiritual forces surround him that are favorable, but their overwhelming strength renders them more harmful than helpful. The client is at a threshold, but he cannot take advantage of it yet. He must first work to cool himself and his environment; he must soothe those forces arising and overwhelming him. He may keep in mind that the nature of Ejila Shebora is to cool down; just as the earth was once too hot to support life, so is the client's environment too hot to support him. But in time, like that energy of the earth, the energy in the client's life will expend itself. Those things useless and outworn will be destroyed in this process, and the client will find himself in a supple, supportive environment. The key to surviving this period of time is ebó. By making ebó, and by following the taboos and prescriptions given to him by the diviner, the client will speed Ejila's cooling process, and he will find himself thrust farther and faster toward his goals by the sign's nature.

Having determined that this sign brings iré, the italero continues to question the oracle. If the sign is marked as being iré yale (firm iré), Ejila Shebora tells the diviner that the client's source of help is strong; the orishas mount behind him, thrusting him toward his evolution and destiny. If the sign is further marked as iré yale timbelaye (firm iré manifest in the client's life), Ejila is giving closure to itself. It tells the diviner that this odu's energy has been in effect for some time, and the client has conducted himself well through its energies. The force of his conduct, his prior good deeds, and his adherence to his own destiny and his worship of the orishas have given him the tools to facilitate his own evolution. The letter has opened here to tell him what forces are in effect and what is coming his way.

When this letter comes in iré, Ejila Shebora can still bring a period of great suffering, but it also can create miracles for those who work through their tribulations. Those who open under its influence often promise grand things and accomplish them through sneaky or stealthy means. Those who suffer under its tutelage come to achieve great wealth and renown. The patakís of Ejila Shebora illustrate these characteristics. Among them is told the story of twins born to a single impoverished mother. Wanting the best in life for her children, yet unable to provide, she put up the infants for adoption immediately after their birth. Yet no one wanted to take on the responsibilities of twins, and the children were separated. One child, a girl, went to live with the priestesses in Ilé Ifé, while the other child, a boy, went to live with the priests in Oyó. Each compound acted as an extended family, but each child, as it grew, served the eldest priest as a servant. So attentive and bright were the children that the eldest of both cities loved them dearly, and when each passed, they left all their worldly goods to each child. With their wealth, the children were initiated into their respective orisha's mysteries, and the spirits blessed them with all the aché they had to give. Neither knew of the other, yet the two rose to fame among all the Yoruba and were sought out for advice on all matters.

When Ejila Shebora opens in iré, all things are possible for the client. He may come from poverty and despair. If he listens carefully to the diviner's advice, however, he will discover the path from impoverishment to prosperity; it has been hidden from him, but Odí can reveal it. Many who come with seven mouths are sick; they suffer or have suffered. Sometimes they come not for themselves but for those whom they love. While this odu cannot promise full, rapid recovery, its eboses and cleansings can promote health and clean living. The diviner must tell the client that, to evolve, he must listen carefully, make ebó, and conduct himself according to the pattern's taboos. Evolution is a process beginning within. As the client commits himself to his own growth and healing, those spiritual forces bringing iré will mount behind him. They will complement his own actions, pushing him farther than he ever dreamed he could go. In the end, the client's willingness to work and grow will determine how far he progresses; with this letter, no limit to what he can achieve exists.

Regardless of its orientation, Ejila Shebora addresses many concerns and problems that can arise in the client's home, in particular issues that exist between the client and his father. At best, the client's childhood relationship with his father was rocky; the diviner should ask the client if there were issues of spiritual, emotional, or physical abuse. These concerns need to be addressed now. The client has some type of resentment that needs to be aired out at the mat. The orishas are listening, and this initial release of negative energy will begin the long process of healing. Right now, Ejila Shebora demands that the client give more attention to his father. As long as he is alive, the client must have open, active communication with him so that when he eventually passes, the client does not have any feelings of guilt or resentment. There is already the foreshadowing of poor health for the father, and if he is elderly, Death could be strolling about looking for him. If the father falls ill, the client should make ebó on his behalf if he is not in the religion; if the father is in the religion, he should be encouraged to seek the counsel of the orishas. Although the father might never truly change, he is not now the person that he once was, and the client should forgive him any unresolved issues and put them in the past. Thus may the future come new and bright. Also, if the client has any brothers or sisters, he must not fail to set a good example for them, especially if they are younger, for they look to the older one for support and guidance in their life.

Issues in the home center on secret, unknown enemies. Others are using witchcraft to bring harm to the client. While this sign often points to deliberate cursing, even those who are not in the occult sciences can bring malicious magic by their deliberate wishing of harm. Making ebó will do much to quell these negative thought patterns manifesting in the client's life. However, if the orientation of this letter is such that it points out a curse, the diviner must investigate ways of fighting the witchcraft. Slander is evident. Someone in the family or in the home has been deceptive about an inheritance or a benefit. In time, the client will realize what this deception was. The most dangerous enemy lives in this client's home; if he has roommate, he should consider living alone or having no one in the house who is not a blood relative, a spiritual relative, or a lover. The enemy shares with this person; he could even share this person's lover right now.

Beyond having an enemy in his home, for the client danger also comes from fire. He should keep no lit candles or sources of open flame in his home, especially in the bedroom. He should unplug all electrical appliances when they are not in use. During electrical storms, he should stay inside the house, away from doors and windows. Also, he should check the smoke detectors in his home and make sure there is one in every room. He must also have fire extinguishers handy at all times and have a predetermined plan of escape from the home in case of a fire. If there are young children in the client's home, all these precautions become even more imperative.

Depending on the sex and sexual orientation of the client, Ejila Shebora can give specific advice. First, heterosexual men have voracious appetites in this letter; so strong is their sex drive that it is not uncommon for them to have two or three lovers, and in many cases, none of them knows about the others. Yet while the client roams about sexually, he loves only one with his heart, and it is to this woman that he will turn in times of troubles. Should she find out about his other affairs, she will leave; perhaps she would even do something desperate to keep her man. The client is mirroring the more negative qualities of Shangó's dalliances with women, and Shangó wants this to stop. The client must learn from, and not repeat, Shangó's mistakes. Here, Shangó also warns that one of the women with whom the client will have an affair will try to tie him to her, perhaps through witchcraft, but more likely through a pregnancy or feigned pregnancy. The client must use proper birth control at all times, especially if the composite odu is Ejila Okan (12-1), Ejila Ogundá (12-3), or Ejila Oché (12-5). The danger in Ejila Okana is that the health of both mother and child could be compromised. The same warning applies in Ejila Ogundá, but here the death of the mother or the unborn baby is also foreshadowed. In Ejila Oché the desire for abortion will be strong, yet Oshún forbids the woman to have an abortion, and the man may not suggest this option. He must be on guard against this trap.

A man who is homosexual is very promiscuous in this letter; and while none of the client's lovers may know about the others, eventually one will find out. The one who discovers the unfaithfulness could become unbalanced and unstable, and odu promises that this person will do something desperate to either get back at the client or keep him close. Also, some of the secondary odu will foreshadow sexual diseases, and this is always a strong deterrent to sexual activity.

A heterosexual woman who opens in any combination of Ejila Shebora is dealing with a man who is unfaithful, and she should open her eyes to what is going on. Homosexual women are extremely masculine in this letter. While masculinity is not itself a problem, in this odu the homosexual woman will often carry it to excess, mirroring the worst characteristics of heterosexual men. Shangó demands that the homosexual woman in this situation soften for a time.

Finally, no matter the orientation of this odu, when in the street the client must be cautious. The streets hold the potential for both danger and good fortune. If the client is careful, he will encounter someone or something in the street that will bring about his own good fortune and salvation. He must guard this object or person and treat it or the person well.

When Ejila Shebora opens in any type of osogbo, it marks a variety of tragedies on the client's head. The key to averting these dangers comes not only by making ebó but also by observing the many prohibitions and warnings that are given in this letter. First, much bad news could come to the client over the next month or so, and he should handle each delivery with caution, calmness, and coolness. Others will depend on the client's strength and reactions for support. The client's current life situation is bad, and the client must be cautious in all things so that he is not hurt. He should watch well the actions of others, especially close friends, for there could be scandal, gossip, and treason; definitely, at the time this odu fell on the mat someone was planning a trap, something that would hinder the client from achieving his personal goals. Poisoning, by intention or accident, is always a danger in osogbo, so the client must pay attention to how his food is prepared both within and without the home. If the osogbo of this letter is severe, the diviner can be assured that Shangó is angry with either the client or his actions, and any eboses demanded by this orisha must be done quickly to appease him. The client must pay Shangó what is needed and owed so that the bad times can be left behind for the good ones.

The osogbos of ano and ikú demand special attention in Ejila Shebora. When the reading predicts ano (sickness), the client must be careful with his heart. He should not eat heavy foods, such as red meat and pork, or high-fat foods. And he must see a physician as soon as possible for a medical assessment. The danger here is that the client could have some sort of myocardial infarction or congestive heart disease, and if these are already a danger or present, the symptoms will soon bring disability. The client could become bedridden for some time. If the client is already gravely ill, the orishas say that no remedies may be offered for twelve hours. If after twelve hours have passed the client is still alive, ebó may be marked and made. This will help save the person's life for a time. Ikú (death) in this letter is the most dangerous of all the diloggún's pronouncements. Be aware that before too much time has passed, someone with whom the client is familiar, if not the client himself, will die.

In addition, the diviner may wish to explore the following issues when Ejila Shebora opens in osogbo:

- Over the next month or so, the client will become more intimately aware of violent acts that are done without provocation: robberies, assaults, rapes, and murders. Some of these could strike those with whom he is familiar, and if he is not careful, some of these things could affect him. The diviner must impress upon him the need for personal security, as well as for security for those he loves.
- This client has spoken ill of this religion and the orishas. He must never do this again.
- The diviner should tell the client that he is, indeed, a child of the orishas; they love him. Yet because of his past indiscretions, he must live his life by making ebó to them. In particular, he has incurred debts to Shangó, and he must now pay them. He should look to Obatalá for advice and encouragement and pamper Oshún, for she can bring sweetness back into life when it has become sour.
- There is a lot of physical and spiritual fire around this client.
- This client is a friend to one who likes to play cruel practical jokes. The client must realize that cruel jokes are never funny, and sometimes more than a person's feelings can be hurt. The client must never emulate this friend, and if possible, he should distance himself from him for some time. The friend will cause problems.

After the consultation has ended, the diviner must have the client leave his home immediately, and then he must make an ebó. If the diviner had to prepare saraeko for Shangó at the beginning of the reading because Ejila Meji or another hot letter opened, he must now take this offering from Shangó and throw it far out into the street with the words "Eshu batie sode" ("Eshu takes the negativity [of the reading]"). Next, the diviner must pour a large quantity of fresh water at his front door to ensure that no negativity from this saraeko can return to his house. After closing a reading in Ejila Shebora, the diviner no longer has the aché to divine for anyone else on this day. The effects of Ejila Shebora drain the power of divination away from the orisha priest until sufficient rest has recharged his strength. He should, however, immediately open the oracle for himself using Elegguá's diloggún to see if any of this letter's effects remain with him. It is important that the priest mark as many eboses as possible so that the full effects of Ejila Shebora may be cleansed from himself, his home, and those who live in his house. Only once this reading has been done is the work of odu complete and the diviner able to relax and recharge for the remainder of the day.

## The Prohibitions of Ejila Shebora

As was described in chapter 1, within the diloggún in general a reading in iré offers prohibitions as guidelines by which the client should consider living. If an osogbo comes with the letter, the prohibitions become strict taboos that the client should not break if he aspires to goodness and evolution. However, because Ejila Shebora is such a heated and volatile odu, even if this sign opens in iré the prohibitions described below should be enforced to some degree to keep the client on the path to evolution.

- The most important taboo is this: Do not argue with the children of either Shangó or Aganyú. In this family of letters, these two orishas reign supreme, and both demand the utmost respect. If the client is an initiate, even if the child of Shangó or Aganyú whom he faces is an aborisha, he must treat that person as if he had ocha made and as if he were the initiate's elder. If arguments and wars arise with the children of these orishas, it is in the client's best interests to turn the other cheek. In this case, he must go before Shangó and tell him the evil that his children do; the orisha will deal with them harshly. Shangó promises to protect the client no matter who tries to harm him; however, he wants to be the one to mete out punishment.
- Out of respect for Shangó and Aganyú, do not eat their favorite foods; these are now taboo. Avoid red foods, reheated foods, and canned foods. Do not consume alcohol or any illegal intoxicants.
- If one has a lover, in that person's home restrict what one eats, and watch the preparation of the food. One's lover may be filled with jealousy, insanity, or anger and may poison one's food or lace it with witchcraft.
- Do not drink dark liquids away from home. In restaurants, ask for unopened bottles.
- Neither borrow clothing nor purchase it secondhand. Do not allow another to borrow or wear personal items, including combs, brushes, towels, bedsheets, hygiene products, and anything else that has intimate contact with one's body.
- Do not wear clothing with stripes, polka dots, checks, plaids, eyelets, or lace. Avoid the color red.
- Do not work in an environment where a uniform must be worn. Do not become involved with anyone who must wear a uniform at work.
- If one has bad intentions toward another person, do not carry out one's plans. Harbor no jealousy or evil thoughts. Shangó stands up in this letter to offer his protection, and the evil that others do or have done should be left at his feet; he will deal with these himself.
- Do not arouse hot emotions in others; someone in whom one arouses strong emotions will bring much harm and disaster. Be careful with one's heart and to whom it is given. Make no false statements of love, friendship, or fealty to another person.
- Do not argue with those in positions of authority or power.
- Do not carry or be near weapons. Do not associate with anyone who must carry a weapon for either work or protection; danger comes from such people.

## Marking Ebó in Ejila Shebora: Initial Considerations

When Ejila Shebora opens in iré, the larishe offered (if any) and a simple adimú to Shangó will keep the client on the path to evolution, and often these simple eboses, in addition to the mandatory eboses of the composite odu, are enough to close the oracle. Yet there are times when a great osogbo opens, and the session radiates heat and volatility, or perhaps no larishe is offered, or else the letter opened is so urgent that there seems no way to soothe its intensity. When this happens, there is an initial solution to explore: a rogación. Within this family of signs are several special rogaciónes. When Ejila Shebora opens in an unmanageable osogbo, a diviner turns first to these rogaciónes to find resolution.

The diviner should consider asking three questions in regard to these cleansings. The first is "Rogación elese Shangó?" If the diloggún marks this as a solution, a rogación before Shangó is necessary. The second question is "Rogación sodidé?" If this is marked, the diviner prescribes a rogación sodidé, which begins at the client's feet and ends with his head. The third question is "Eborí?" Marking eborí, the oracle directs the diviner to feed the client's head once the rogación is complete. Note that some of these rogaciónes are complex, and some require that ebó be prepared before, during, or after the cleansing. Each gives specifics within the directions. The rogaciónes most often used in Ejila Shebora follow.

### The Traditional Eboses of Ejila Shebora

Certain elements are considered traditional eboses in this sign. Whenever prescribing an ebó that involves eyebale, the diviner should try to choose from the following list: two roosters, red meat (such as steak), and twelve turtles. For adimú-type offerings, he should choose from these: jutía and smoked fish, cornmeal, twin gourds of cooked beans and rice, a piece of tiger skin, cocoa butter, pigeon peas, a small beaded bat, and red and white cloths.

## Rogaciónes for Ejila Shebora

### *Rogación from Yemayá*

When a rogación is called for in any composite of Ejila Shebora, this one is usually the appropriate one to administer. Twelve mouths can fill one's life with fire; this rogación will quench that fire so that the client can evolve. Only a priestess of Yemayá can perform this ritual. Yemayá is the queen of all waters; her aché is needed to soothe the heat devouring this person, and it takes a woman to placate Shangó's anger. If no priestess of Yemayá is available, this rogación may not be done.

The day before the rogación, the client goes to this priestess's house to pay his derecho; he wraps it in brown paper, on a white plate accompanied by two white candles and two coconuts. He also makes ebó to Yemayá; however, it is the priestess, and not the godparent or the diloggún, who determines the ebó given. This derecho belongs only to Yemayá; neither the godparent nor the diviner may claim any money from it for his or her own.

The next day the client and the priestess present themselves before her Shangó (not the diviner's or the godparent's). Before Shangó, the Yemayá priestess lights a large brazier of coals, praying, "Ican aiña odemaso aiña ican manyaina oña ican aiña." ("I [Shangó] am the only one of all the spirits who eats and speaks fire.") Both stand beside Shangó while the flames consume the coals, and when only red embers remain, together the two walk over them. The priestess seats the client on a stool for the rogación and pours copious amounts of fresh water over the coals to extinguish them. Immediately, while steam still rises from the coals, she begins the rogación, using grated coconut, grated cocoa butter, coconut milk, and cotton. After wrapping the client's head in white cotton and white cloth, the priestess keeps the client seated until the coals are completely cooled. Only then may he be raised from his stool. For the next twelve days, the client dresses in white, keeping his head covered with a white hat.

### *Obeguede and Amalá Rogación for Shangó*

This is another of Ejila Shebora's traditional rogaciónes. When preparing for this rogación, the client must offer two adimús: obeguede and amalá. Beforehand, he should set up the plate for the rogación, placing on it grated coconut, grated cocoa butter, crushed cascarilla, and plenty of white cotton.

To prepare the obeguede, the client follows these steps: First, obtain 1 pound of okra, 2 pounds of cornmeal, and some honey. (Honey is added here to sweeten both Shangó and the client's head; it is integral to this ebó.) Dice the okra, removing all the seeds. Put this in a large mixing bowl with the cornmeal. Add a dash of water and stir, adding small amounts of water and honey while mixing until a thick paste forms. Put a small amount of the paste on the white plate to use in the rogación. From the rest of the mixture, form twelve small balls. Place these on a serving platter and present them to Shangó, along with a red seven-day candle. The client may drizzle honey over the balls after giving Shangó foribale; while drizzling the honey, he prays for sweetness and evolution.

To prepare amalá, provide 2 pounds of yellow cornmeal, salt, and 3/4 cup of epó. Combine the cornmeal and a dash of salt in a large pan with 8 cups of water. Place the pan over medium-high heat and stir until the mixture boils. Turn down the heat to low and continue to stir until the mixture thickens. Then remove the pan from the stove and stir in the epó. Set aside a small amount of amalá in a small bowl on the white plate for the rogación. Serve the rest to Shangó in a serving dish, at the same time lighting a white seven-day candle for him. While praying for evolution, the client drizzles honey over the amalá, just as he did for the obeguede.

After presenting these adimús, the client sits for a rogación before Shangó. All elements on the plate are used on his body and head in the following order: grated coconut, grated cocoa butter, crushed cascarilla, obeguede, and amalá. The priest should drizzle honey lightly over all points of aché before adding the white cotton. The next morning, when the rogación is discarded, the adimús of obeguede and amalá are discarded as well. For the next twelve days, the client dresses in white.

### *Rogación for Elegguá and Shangó to Clear Osogbo*

This rogación should be used when both Elegguá and Shangó stand up to advise the client in a serious osogbo. It repeats the rogación described in Obeguede and Amalá Rogación for Shangó, above, with the following additions: Elegguá sits with Shangó throughout the procedures, sharing his adimú and witnessing the cleansing. For the entire twelve days that the client dresses in white, Elegguá remains at Shangó's feet; they work together to remove blockages to the client's progress. On the twelfth day, the client sits for another rogación before Shangó and Elegguá. The priest uses only the following elements: grated coconut, grated cocoa butter, crushed cascarilla, and white cotton. Immediately afterward, he feeds Elegguá a chicken and Shangó two roosters. After the sacrifice, the client must again dress in white for twelve days.

If Yemayá stands up during the reading, she demands ebó at this time as well. Before cleaning the blood off the otanes of Shangó and Elegguá, the client should present her with a small basket of fruits. She will bring freshness to the client's life while Elegguá and Shangó fight his wars.

### *Rogación and Twelve-Coconut Cleansing for Shangó*

This rogación demands an adimú of twelve coconuts, which the client must prepare at home before coming to the priest's house. He sands the coconuts until no hairs remain on them; each must be smooth as glass. He paints each coconut half red and half white. Then he lines a large basket with one red and one white pañuelo and places all twelve coconuts in the basket.

Arriving at the priest's house, he presents the basket of coconuts to Shangó. Then the priest gives him a rogación with grated coconut, coconut milk, grated cocoa butter, crushed cascarilla, and cotton. Every day for the next twelve days, the client dresses in white, and each day he must return to the priest's house for a cleansing with one coconut. After using a coconut, the client takes it to the foot of a royal palm (a different tree every day). On the twelfth day after the rogación, when all the coconuts are gone, the priest cleanses his client with both pañuelos, afterward draping them over Shangó. The orisha keeps these cloths indefinitely. The client fills the basket with fresh fruits; they remain with the spirit until they start to turn bad. The priest then uses obí to determine where Shangó wants the fruits taken when they are removed. The basket is discarded at this time as well.

### *Rogación and Twelve-Pomegranate Cleansing for Shangó*

This rogación requires a simple adimú: twelve pomegranates for Shangó. The client presents these to the orisha before the rogación; after the rogación, the priest cleanses the client with each piece of fruit. They remain inside Shangó's batea for twelve days. During this time, the client dresses in white. After the twelve days of dressing in white are complete, the priest uses obí to determine where Shangó wants his fruits discarded; they are taken there immediately, along with a derecho of twelve pennies.

### *Rogación and Twelve-Calabaza Adimú for Shangó*

This rogación also requires an adimú: twelve calabazas for Shangó. After presenting these to the orisha, the client sits for a rogación with the following ingredients: grated coconut, grated cocoa butter, crushed cascarilla, and white cotton. After the rogación, the client dresses in white for twelve days. After this period of time, the twelve calabazas go to the foot of a royal palm.

### *Rogación of Plantains and Bananas for Shangó*

This ebó requires an offering of twelve green plantains and twelve green bananas for Shangó. The client presents himself to the orisha, giving foribale, and while he prostrates himself, the priest places the plantains and bananas over the orisha's batea. Then the priest gives the client a rogación. In six days, the client returns with twelve more plantains and twelve more bananas. Removing the old ones while the client pays foribale, the diviner places the new ones over his batea. Again, he administers a rogación, this time using on the client's head one banana and one plantain from those that he just removed from Shangó's batea. In six more days, the client again returns for a rogación and the priest again uses a banana and a plantain from the previous rogación's offering; this time, however, the client does not offer a new adimú. Throughout this time, for the twelve days from the time of the first rogación to the time of the last, the client dresses in white. The rogación and adimú, once removed, are discarded at the foot of a palm tree.

### *Rogación of Coconuts and Mamey Fruits for Shangó, Oshún, and Obatalá*

When Shangó, Oshún, and Obatalá all stand up to speak to the client in any composite of Ejila Shebora, this is the appropriate series of eboses and rogaciónes to give. First, the client presents an adimú of six coconuts and six mamey fruits to Shangó. Every day for the next six days, the client comes to have a rogación before Shangó with one whole coconut and one whole mamey fruit; no other elements are used in these rogaciónes beyond the white cotton and white cloth used to bind the client's head.

On the sixth night, before the priest gives the final rogación with coconut and mamey, the client presents five specially prepared jars of honey to Oshún. Each jar has both honeycomb and cinnamon. Every day for the next six days, the client returns to the priest's home for a rogación before Oshún with one jar of honey. No other elements are used in these six rogaciónes except for the white cotton and cloth used to bind the client's head. On the eleventh day, before the fifth rogación, the client presents a white plate with two coconuts, two white candles, white cotton, cascarilla, and cocoa butter to Obatalá.

On the twelfth day, the client returns for a final rogación at Obatalá's feet using the elements he presented to the orisha the day before. Throughout this time, for the twelve days from the time of the first rogación to the time of the last, the client dresses in white, and he continues to dress in white for twelve days after the final rogación.

## Ebó Elese Shangó
## *(Ebó at the Feet of Shangó)*

No matter the client's initiatory status, all who open in Ejila Shebora should placate Shangó. The following eboses of Ejila Shebora will do just that; the diviner should prescribe at least one.

### *Six-Plantain Adimú*

This simple adimú to appease Shangó through Ejila Shebora can be made of the following ingredients: six plantains, smoked fish, jutía, honey, toasted cornmeal, and guinea pepper.

First, peel and boil the plantains until they are soft. Strain them from the water, mashing them to form a paste with the smoked fish, jutía, honey, and cornmeal. From this paste form twelve balls. In each ball, insert one guinea pepper and smear with a liberal amount of honey. Serve these to Shangó on a white or red serving platter, lighting two seven-day candles, one white and one red. Leave the adimú for twelve days, and then discard it at the foot of a palm tree.

### *Ñame Tower with Cowrie Shells*

In Ejila Shebora, Shangó accepts towers as adimú. Provide the following ingredients for the ebó: a fresh ñame, honey, a platter (white or red), eighteen cowrie shells, a red and white flag (a construction paper cutout mounted on a toothpick is fine), and two seven-day candles, one white and one red.

Wash, peel, dice, and boil the ñame until it is soft. Strain the pieces from the water and mash them with honey until a paste forms. On the platter, form a tall tower with this paste. Place twelve of the cowrie shells around the base and six around the peak. Insert the flag at the tower's highest point. Leave this ebó over Shangó's sopera for either six or twelve days; during this time, keep the two candles lit at the base of his shrine.

At the end of nine days, wrap the tower in brown paper and discard it at the foot of either a palm or a ceiba tree.

### *Plantain Tower with Cowrie Shells*

If the diviner chooses, the ñame tower just described may be made of plantains instead. Use six plantains in place of the ñame; the rest of the ebó remains unchanged.

### *Sweet Amalá*

To appease Shangó, prepare a dish known as sweet amalá (see the recipe on page 54). Serve to Shangó while it is still warm. The dish remains with the orisha overnight; the next morning, using obí, the priest determines how Shangó wants his ebó discarded.

If Elegguá's diloggún was consulted for this session, one may share this ebó between Shangó and Elegguá. Put Elegguá at Shangó's feet, then give both an equal serving of amalá. When discarding the food, let each dictate separately where his ebó should be taken.

### *Sweet Amalá with Plantains*

The recipe of sweet amalá may be enhanced if the osogbo of Ejila Shebora is severe. Note that with this ebó, both Shangó and Elegguá are appeased. To enhance this dish, and the ebó, provide all the ingredients necessary for making sweet amalá, as well as waxed paper, 3/4 cup of epó, and nine peeled bananas.

After making the sweet amalá, let it cool. Once cool, brush nine pieces of wax paper lightly with epó. Divide the sweet amalá into nine equal potions, and roll each flat with a greased rolling pin (use epó to grease the pin). Place one banana on each flat piece of amalá. Roll the banana in the amalá tightly and squeeze the ends shut so the bananas are totally enclosed. Place three of these bananas on a small platter for Elegguá and the remaining six on a serving plate for Shangó. Leave the adimús with them overnight, and the next morning, with obí, determine how the orishas want the ebó discarded.

### *Pumpkin with Sweet Amalá*

This ebó may also be made to appease Shangó if the osogbo of the letter is severe. Several items are needed: sweet amalá (see the recipe on page 54), a pumpkin, a white plate, okra, and two white seven-day candles.

Prepare the sweet amalá first; give Elegguá a small portion, then take the rest of the items for ebó before Shangó's shrine. Put the pumpkin on the white plate and cut off the top. Pour the sweet amalá into the pumpkin. Cut the okra into six pieces of equal size and place them over the amalá. Light the two white candles to Shangó, and pray to him while giving foribale. The plate with the pumpkin remains over Shangó's batea for six days; at the end of this time, the pumpkin is discarded at the foot of a palm or ceiba in the woods.

# The First Composite Odu of Ejila Shebora, Ejila Okana (12-1)

## The Proverbs of Ejila Okana

- If there is nothing bad, there can never be anything good.
- The speaker dies by his own words.
- One cannot put out a fire with a mouthful of water.

## The Message of Ejila Okana

When the initial cast of twelve mouths, Ejila Shebora, precedes a cast of one mouth, Okana, the odu Ejila Okana is open on the mat. Having made this cast, the diviner pays homage to Elegguá, Ogún, his own guardian orisha, the client's guardian orisha, and the guardian orisha of this client's godparent, saying to each, "Maferefún!" Because Ejila Shebora and Okana, two volatile patterns, have crossed here, their union demands caution by the diviner. He must immediately prepare saraeko as ebó for Shangó (as described on page 52, and he must prescribe for everyone present at the reading a cleansing ebó for Elegguá and Ogún. (See "The Eboses of Ejila Okana" on page 554.)

The diviner's guardian orisha, the client's guardian orisha, and the guardian orisha of this client's godparent are three spirits that stand up in this odu to bring blessings; they also come to fight the osogbos inherent in this sign. Before Ejila Okana closes, eboses may be needed for all three. In any orientation, this letter marks bad luck, gossip, and slander; unfortunately, these osogbos come from not one person but many people. Even those whom the client thought were his friends speak maliciously behind his back. Enemies exists where least expected, so in all personal and business dealings the client must be cautious. The diviner should deliver the following warnings to the client so he can avoid danger:

- Because of exhaustion and insomnia, this person cannot think clearly or rationally. The diviner must impress upon him the importance of caution in his most important decisions. He should avoid unplanned changes. When a need to accomplish something drastic arises, the client should procrastinate, if possible, and return to the diviner to consult with the orishas.
- This pattern tells the client that his friends are involved in personal wars and disputes. He may get caught in these. There is danger here: His friends, relations, and acquaintances might tell him lies or half-truths, hoping to make him take sides.
- Relationships in this sign are tricky. In iré, they can be bad, but in osogbo they can be even worse. The client should treat his lover carefully and thoughtfully. Even then there will still be problems.
- Conception and pregnancy under this odu's influence will be not joyous but, instead, full of despair. For now, the client should use proper birth control or abstain from sexual activities.
- In any osogbo, this odu can bring blood loss through disease or injury. In ano or ikú, the loss of blood is imminent and may occur as a result of internal bleeding, anemia, or accidents. Blood-borne pathogens introduced by injury, intestinal disease, renal disease, and back pains are also a danger.

## The Prohibitions of Ejila Okana

- Ejila Shebora and Okana both speak of fires in one's home. Do not have any lit candles in one's home, and ensure that all ovens and hot plates are turned off and unplugged before leaving the home. Older homes should have their electrical wiring assessed by an electrician. Have no more than one appliance plugged into any outlet, and examine all cords for fraying.
- Avoid violence and violent people. While under this odu's influence, one given to dramatic outbursts could become even more boisterous.
- Do not store anything for anyone. There is the chance that one will take in stolen property, and in this sign conflicts with the law are to be avoided.
- Either abstain from sexual relations or use proper birth control. Women must not conceive

under this odu, because it will result in unfortunate, undesirable pregnancies; men must be careful not to impregnate women for the same reasons.

- Alcohol clouds one's mind and impairs good judgment; if one consumes alcohol, it will turn out to be at times when one is in need of one's faculties. Do not consume alcohol. Avoid illegal intoxicants as well.

## The Eboses of Ejila Okana

In Ejila Okana, the first ebó to consider, beyond the saraeko the diviner may give during the reading to Shangó, are the cleansings to Elegguá and Ogún. Once the odu gives closure, the diviner should oil two pieces of beef with epó and wrap them separately in brown paper. All who were present in the house at the time of the reading should gather before the diviner's warriors while he prays to both Elegguá and Ogún to lift the heat of this sign. Once the prayers are finished, the italero cleanses himself with one piece of meat to Elegguá and with the other to Ogún. He then cleanses the client in the same manner. Once they are done, the initiates present cleanse themselves to both orishas. Finally, aborishas and aleyos are allowed to cleanse themselves. Once everyone in the house has finished this ebó, the diviner should open the room, and all should leave. Those who have their own warriors should do this same cleansing to their own orishas once they are home. The next morning, all should discard Elegguá's ebó at a crossroads and Ogún's at the nearest railroad track. Note that all present for this reading should return for a session with the diloggún as soon as possible.

After prescribing this ebó, the diviner must tell the client the rest of the eboses that he must complete to bring this odu to closure. First, Elegguá and Ogún demand sacrifice. Elegguá protects the client from all the harm his enemies wish upon him, while Ogún is planning a trap for them himself. If the client walks nobly, in good character, one by one his enemies will fall. The diviner prescribes the sacrifice of a single rooster to Elegguá, which he will share with Ogún. He also prescribes the sacrifice of two pigeons to Ogún. One week after these sacrifices, the client must give both orishas a huge basket of fresh fruits.

In addition to these eboses, one mandatory ebó remains: The client must offer two coconuts to his own orí and two to his guardian orisha (or to his godparent's guardian orisha, if his own is not known). Ejila Okana clouds the mind, and this simple sacrifice brings clarity.

After explaining these options to the client, the diviner has his first chance to close the oracle. If it remains open, he should consider the following eboses:

- Although this odu advises against pregnancy, if the client is pregnant she should make the following ebó to Yemayá and Oshún: She lies on a mat before both orishas, and the diviner gives her a rogación of the abdomen, using grated coconut, grated cocoa butter, crushed cascarilla, honey, and molasses. He then sacrifices a hen and two pigeons over her belly before wrapping it in white cotton and white cloth. After this, the diviner gives the client a rogación of the head, using the same ingredients and also feeding two white pigeons or doves to her orí. If the client does not have her elekes, after doing all these eboses the diviner should put the necklaces of Yemayá and Oshún around her neck. She must wear both every day during her pregnancy.
- If the client is pregnant and faces a caesarean birthing, in her eighth month she should make the following ebó: The client gives Ogún a very sharp knife, praying that he guide the surgeon's hands. The diviner presents a rooster to the client, rubbing her abdomen well with the animal, and then sacrifices the rooster to Ogún. Seven days after the sacrifice, the client should give Ogún a basket of fresh fruit.
- If the client faces legal difficulties, the diviner sacrifices three pigeons to Ochosi. He impales the heads on the orisha's crossbows and leaves them with him for three days. On the third day, the client takes the pigeon heads to the courthouse where his case is to be tried. He discards the heads there in a trash can. Upon returning

home, the client should present Ochosi with a basket of fresh fruits. To determine if this orisha might require anything else, the diviner should consider asking, "Ebó elese Ochosi?" If the answer is yes, he uses the diloggún to mark the appropriate offering.

- The client could have additional issues with Shangó. To see what this orisha might require, the diviner should ask, "Ebó elese Shangó?" If the answer is yes, he uses the diloggún to mark the appropriate offering.
- If the client is an initiate, the diviner may ask, "Koshé Aganyú?" and "Koshé Ochosi?" One or both orishas might be necessary for the client's evolution.

If Ejila Okana remains open after the diviner has explored these options, he must turn to the eboses of the parent odu, Ejila Shebora (see page 58). Something there is necessary for this client's evolution.

## The Second Composite Odu of Ejila Shebora, Ejila Ejioko (12-2)

### The Proverbs of Ejila Ejioko

- The brothers are enemies.
- He who does not petition the orishas will fail in all things.

### The Message of Ejila Ejioko

When the first casting of cowries opens in twelve mouths, Ejila Shebora, and the second casting of cowries brings two mouths, Eji Oko, the odu Ejila Ejioko is open on the mat. There are two other names for this pattern: Ejila Oyeku and Ejila Yeku. Having made this cast, the diviner says, "Maferefún Shangó! Maferefún Ogún! Maferefún Obatalá!"

Shangó's influence is strong in this odu. However, he comes to issue the client a warning: Do not fight with him. Many times in the past, this orisha has given the client advice; he has stood up to protect him and to fight his wars. Yet the client did not pay his debts to Shangó as he should have, and many times he did not heed Shangó's words. To Shangó, this is a fight, and the diviner should tell the client that he will not win this fight. This person is surrounded by many of this orisha's children, and he might be close to some of his priests. Those who have made ocha embody Shangó; he lives in their heads. When the client argues with these people, he shows disrespect to Shangó, and the orisha tolerates this no more. The diviner should emphasize the following: "Shangó speaks to you now, and he speaks only once. He will never warn you again. So listen, and heed his words."

In Ejila Ejioko, all of the client's relationships are under the orishas' scrutiny. In iré, this scrutiny will be gentle, but the diviner must advise caution. This person must learn to live by a simple rule: He must treat others as he would have them treat him. Bring good intentions and honorable actions, and those will be given back. Give evil, and evil will be returned swiftly. Lies, deceit, gossip, and treason will dissolve even the most solid relationships. If Ejila Ejioko comes with any osogbo, many of the client's closest friends could abandon him. Many of these relationships are almost dissolved now, and they will only worsen unless the client changes his ways. Monogamous relationships, especially marriages, will suffer. If an osogbo is present, the diviner knows that lovers and spouses lie to each other; even the client's friends participate in lies. Treachery, deceit, despair, jealousy, and adultery are all being hidden. Odu tells the one at the mat that if he values his significant other, all this behavior must end now. He should also be aware that his lover has lied to him many times. Those who lie deserve their losses, and in a volatile osogbo the relationship is already unsalvageable.

If the client does all as he should, Ogún will fight for him; Ogún will destroy all who try to hurt him. From this moment on, the client lives by making ebó to Ogún; this orisha is his salvation from all that others try to do to him.

Of all the orishas, none is stronger, wiser, or more forgiving than Obatalá; yet it will take all of Obatalá's strength to help the client evolve. He must have a rogación before this orisha and then offer him adimú (as described in "The Eboses of Ejila

Ejioko"). With proper propitiation and supplication, this spirit will give him a second chance at life, a new beginning free from osogbo.

After exploring these issues, the diviner should consider the following points, discussing each thoroughly with the client:

- The orishas are not pleased with the client's current living conditions. His home is too cold, sterile, dark, and unkempt. He must both physically clean and spiritually cleanse his house, and afterward he must make sure that it has more light and warmth.
- There could be witchcraft buried at the client's front door. To fight it, the client should pour copious amounts of fresh water at his doorstep daily, praying to Olófin, Olorún, and Olódumare for strength and blessing.
- In this odu, neighbors are nosy; they want to know what goes on behind closed doors. Someone is envious and wants the client to move.
- While members of his immediate family can bring tears and depression to the client's life, the members of his extended family will eventually bring him physical and emotional harm. He must keep his immediate family's problems home so that no one else becomes involved; others will use these issues to destroy him if he does not.
- If anyone in the client's family or close circle of friends falls critically ill, the first twelve hours are of utmost importance. The client must immediately consult the diviner and make ebó; if the afflicted one survives the first twelve hours, there might be a recovery. The diviner should tell the client, however, that before the next twelve months have passed, two people known to him will die.

## The Prohibitions of Ejila Ejioko

- This odu prohibits the pawning of one's valuables. If one has jewelry, gold, or anything else valuable in hock, buy it back immediately, even if one has to borrow the money from another person to do so. Items pawned take one's luck bit by bit, and when an item is lost, one's luck will go altogether. Pawning one's belongings is tantamount to pawning one's life.
- One's words affect one's life. Therefore, profane language must not be used. Do not take God's name in vain; do not curse or blaspheme. Bragging is also taboo in this odu. Do not speak of one's good fortune to others, for here one's words dissipate into thin air.
- Do not keep religious icons made of plaster. Have no religious imagery not made of a more expensive material such as wood, ivory, metal, or glass. Plaster icons draw bad energies to one's home. The diviner may ask the orishas if plaster icons one already owns must be thrown away; one should not give them away unless one wants the recipient to suffer.

## The Eboses of Ejila Ejioko

This odu speaks of death and the dead; therefore, when faced with this pattern on the mat, the diviner must first consider the client's relationship with egun. Here, the most ancient and forgotten spirits, forces whose names have been forgotten by their descendants, clamor for attention. There is also heavy aché with twins here, and the client's relationship with twins must be established. The diviner should question this person about when the last set of living twins were born to his family or if twinning is common among his ancestry. If the twins were born in the client's own generation, and both are still alive, one might suffer an untimely death unless ebó is made. If either or both are deceased, this odu marks that many masses and prayers should be said in their honor.

If the client does not have a bóveda, he must set one up. If he lacks an opá ikú, one must be found and fed. The diviner must also prescribe a series of spiritual masses; the client must follow the advice of the espiritistas exactly, for this is how he will evolve. This odu also reveals that within this client's family a child was lost, and he was almost lost as well. After the bóveda is established, the client should buy a baby doll and have the diviner pack it for him.

Finally, the diviner should give the client's egun a chance to personalize the eboses done in this odu, asking, "Ebó elese egun?" If the answer is yes, he uses the diloggún to mark the appropriate offering.

The client who opens in Ejila Ejioko must also reinforce Ogún's cauldron. First, he should give him a bigger cauldron, as large as the client can find and afford. Also, he should maximize Ogún's implements, giving him twenty-one horseshoes, twenty-one railroad spikes, and at least three iron railroad ties. This odu also calls for four machetes to be placed in the cauldron; with these, Ogún will fight the evil that comes from all four directions. The client's godparent should wash all these implements with a piece of raw iron ore, place them in Ogún's pot, and then feed him a rooster and two pigeons.

Once the client has fulfilled all the eboses prescribed in this odu, he should return to the diviner's home for a rogación at the feet of Obatalá. The rogación should use grated coconut, grated cocoa butter, grated ñame, grated pears, crushed cascarilla, white flowers, four apple snails, and cow's milk. After the rogación, the client should give a simple adimú to Obatalá and commit himself to wearing white for at least sixteen days. This is done as a "penance" to the orisha; as he supplicates Obatalá and propitiates him, this spirit will give him a second chance at life, a new beginning free from osogbo.

Now the diviner has his first chance to close the oracle. If these prescriptions are not enough to close the session, the diviner should consider the following:

- The Ibeyi are an integral part of this letter's aché and are an important part of the client's evolution. Now, if he does not have them, after taking care of his issues with egun, the client must receive them. If he already has the Ibeyi, he should make ebó. To determine what they might require, the diviner should ask, "Ebó elese los Ibeyi?" If the answer is yes, he uses the diloggún to mark the appropriate offering.
- If the client is an aleyo or an aborisha and Ejila Ejioko still refuses closure, it marks the need for him to attend a tambor. When the spirits come down at the tambor, they will have much advice to give.

If these considerations are not enough to close the letter for an aleyo or an aborisha, the diviner should explore the options for ebó in the parent odu, Ejila Shebora (see page 581). If the client is an initiate, however, the diviner should explore the rest of this list.

- Having fallen for an initiate, the orisha speaking here could be marking a tambor as the solution to all the client's troubles. Using the diloggún, the diviner should ask if the orisha whose shells are being consulted will claim the drum. If this spirit refuses, the diviner should mark the drum for one of the spirits the initiate received in ocha. If a tambor is marked as an ebó and this reading is an itá of either Elegguá or the client's crowning orisha, the client is marked to give all his spirits a drum during the course of his life. The playing of the first sacred drum will put this person on the path to spiritual evolution. However, before giving a drum to any of his own orishas, the client must give one to his godparent's crown.
- If this client's osogbo is great and his lot in life already tragic, there is a severe ebó that can be used to bring luck back into his life quickly: two jutías sacrificed to Elegguá. Only an oriaté may give this ebó, as it involves the sacrifice of four legs. This ebó is expensive, as jutía must be imported, and it can be used as a last resort when all else fails.

If nothing in this list will satisfy the odu for an initiate, the diviner must turn to the eboses of the parent odu, Ejila Shebora. Something there is needed for the client's evolution.

## The Third Composite Odu of Ejila Shebora, Ejila Ogundá (12-3)

### The Proverbs of Ejila Ogundá

- Tragedy is wrought by making the wrong decisions.
- Tragedy, deception, and despair are near.
- One person will throw the stone and all will carry the blame.

- Put your heart in what you do so that all things will come out well.

## The Message of Ejila Ogundá

When an initial cast of twelve mouths, Ejila Shebora, precedes a cast of three mouths, Ogundá, the odu Ejila Ogundá is open on the mat. When it falls, the diviner immediately says, "Maferefún egun!" The diviner offers this expression of homage not only for the client's egun but also for the egun of all present at the mat, the priests and priestesses seated for the reading. Everyone must make ebó to his or her own egun when the letter closes, and the diviner will explain that ebó now. (See "The Eboses of Ejila Ogundá" below.) After this explanation, the diviner pays homage to Shangó, Elegguá, Ogún, Ochosi, Oshún, and Obatalá, saying to each, "Maferefún!" The aché of all six is strong in this pattern, and the client may need the help of all of them in order to evolve.

Oshún and Ogún are the strongest orishas in this sign. They stand together to deliver many warnings and prohibitions. The client's life has become bitter and sour, and Ogún says that this is due to his own laziness and his own lack of personal counsel. To accomplish anything at this time, the client must work hard through all his difficulties, and he must work alone, keeping secret all his goals and plans. There is no other way. Too many loose tongues and evil eyes surround the client; although his best friend might be his most trusted friend, under this odu there is a tendency for others to gossip.

Ejila Ogundá also foreshadows death, sickness, and disease. If the odu opens in an osogbo of ano or ikú, the client should offer an ebó to Ogún now so he will not put the client "under the knife." The diviner must also prescribe that the client see a physician. If the client is not careful, a minor health issue can easily become a major health problem.

Oshún brings up issues for women in this letter. The diviner should advise the client that pregnancy is not desirable at this time; the client should either abstain from sexual relations or use proper birth control at all times. If pregnancy results at this time, there are too many dangers and issues that could result. Unwanted pregnancy, deformed children, revelations of lies and deceit—all these are strong possibilities. Ignore this warning and Oshún delivers another: The mother may not have an abortion. Nor may the father suggest one. Also, if anyone with whom this client is familiar becomes pregnant, he may not recommend an abortion as a solution. He should do all he can barring the restriction of free will to save the unborn child's life. Additionally, if the client is a man, Oshún is upset with how he treats women in general. Her anger must be appeased by modifications in behavior.

In addition to these issues, the diviner should explore the following with the client:

- If the client is a man, no one can help him more in his darkest hour than his own lover. Sexually, he should not stray from the one who has his heart. All the rest with whom he engages in amorous affairs will bring him ruin.
- When others bring harm to this client, he should not lash out in anger at them. Instead, he should leave their wrongdoings at the feet of Ogún with an adimú; the orisha will deal with it.
- Ogún says that this client's thoughts are not clear. He should wait at least a month before acting on any new goals or plans so that his mind can clear.

## The Prohibitions of Ejila Ogundá

- Being the third party to any activity is taboo. Do not accept any item from anyone thirdhand. Avoid threesomes of the heart, especially with someone who is already married or dating.
- Be cautious of papers and contracts. Do not sign anything unless it is first approved by an attorney.

## The Eboses of Ejila Ogundá

The diviner must make his first prescription of ebó immediately upon the opening of Ejila Ogundá, but this ebó will not take place until after the letter closes. The diviner explains that all the priests and priestesses seated for the reading must make ebó to their own egun. Deep in the woods, beside a hollow tree, all must come together with offerings for the dead: rum, cigars, honey, molasses, cooked food, and a single rooster. While calling all of their blood and spiritual ancestors, the diviner sacrifices the rooster to the tree for egun. Once the sacrifice is done, one by one all leave their individual offerings for the dead. If this ebó is not done, those sitting in on the session will find that their own egun will demand more elaborate eboses as they, in turn, sit for sessions with the diloggún.

Once the reading of Ejila Ogundá closes, the diviner makes ebó immediately on behalf of all present for the reading. He oils a large piece of beef with epó, coating it well on all sides. He then wraps the beef, along with twelve guinea peppers, twelve dashes of smoked fish and jutía, and twelve pennies, in brown paper. The number twelve appeases the odu Ejila Shebora. With this meat, the diviner cleanses himself, the client, and all present in his house—everyone in the house, not just those seated for the reading—to Ogún. After this short ritual is complete, he encourages everyone to leave his home immediately, then casts copious amounts of water outside the front door after the last person leaves. The ebó sits with Ogún overnight, and the next day the diviner discards it at a crossroads with the words, "Eshu batie sode." Note that those with warriors must do this ebó to their own Ogún upon returning home, and those aleyos without warriors must return for a reading as soon as possible.

No matter this sign's orientation, when it opens the diviner must prescribe the following two eboses:

- First, the client must have a rogación at Obatalá's feet; this letter heats one's orí, and Obatalá brings coolness and clarity amid turmoil. This rogación should use grated coconut, grated cocoa butter, crushed cascarilla, grated ñame, honey, white flowers, four apple snails, and a dash of cow's milk.
- Immediately after the rogación, the client should offer to Oshún and Ogún together this adimú: Combine gofio, honey, jutía, smoked fish, and molasses until they form a thick paste. From this paste form twelve balls. Put five in a jícara and serve them to Oshún; put the remaining seven in a jícara and serve them to Ogún. Before these two orishas, the client should petition Ogún to destroy his enemies and Oshún to sweeten his life.

Having made these prescriptions, the diviner may now attempt to close the oracle. If Ejila Ogundá refuses closure, he should consider the following options for ebó:

- Oshún and Ogún might demand more complex eboses. To determine if this is the case, the diviner should ask, "Ebó elese [orisha's name]?" If the answer is yes, he uses the diloggún to mark the appropriate offering.
- The client's Ósun might need reinforcement. To determine if this is the case, the diviner should ask, "Ebó elese Ósun?" If the answer is yes, the diviner adds additional carga to his cup and feeds him a pigeon.
- If the client is an aborisha or an initiate, he might need to make ebó to Elegguá, Ochosi, Shangó, Yemayá, or Aganyú. The diviner should ask of each, "Ebó elese [orisha's name]?" If the answer is yes, he uses the diloggún to mark the appropriate offering.

If these considerations are not enough to close the odu for an aleyo or an aborisha, the diviner must turn to the eboses of the parent odu, Ejila Shebora (see page 581). The client needs something there for his evolution. When a casting of Ejila Ogundá remains open for an initiate, however, the diviner should explore the following options:

- The reception of Aganyú is a possibility. The diviner should ask, "Koshé Aganyú?" If this orisha's reception is marked, preparations for the ceremony must begin immediately.
- The sacrifice of a four-legged animal might be necessary. The diviner should try to mark this. If the sacrifice is accepted, the diviner should question whether the orisha whose diloggún is being read will accept it. If the answer is yes, the sacrifice does not also require an itá; this reading is considered to be the orisha's itá. If the answer is no, another orisha might need four legs; the diviner must consider this. If the answer is yes, an itá is given.

- An initiate without Ogún's diloggún must receive this now.
- Finally, if these eboses cannot be marked, or if they will not close the odu, the client could need the initiation of pinaldo (knife). The diviner must ask, "Koshé pinaldo?"

If none of these will close the odu, the diviner now turns to the list of eboses for the parent odu, Ejila Shebora. Something there is needed to bring evolution for the initiate.

## The Fourth Composite Odu of Ejila Shebora, Ejila Irosun (12-4)

### The Proverbs of Ejila Irosun

- Only Olokun and Olorún know what lies at the bottom of the sea.
- Chickens were born to lay eggs. You were born to have children; do not avoid it.

### The Message of Ejila Irosun

When an initial cast of twelve mouths, Ejila Shebora, precedes a cast of four mouths, Irosun, the odu Ejila Irosun is open on the mat. To honor this sign, the diviner pays homage to Obatalá, Shangó, Yemayá, Olokun, and Olorún, saying to each, "Maferefún!" This sign is dangerous for both the diviner and the client, but the majority of Ejila Irosun's heat falls on the italero who cast it. As soon as this session closes, he must offer a sacrifice for both himself and the client as protection. (See "The Eboses of Ejila Irosun" on page 561.) This letter's counterpart in Ifá is known as Trupon Roso; when it falls, the babalawo who cast the odu must initiate the client to Ifá whether or not the client has any money for the ceremonies. Many feel the italero should do the same with ocha when this pattern opens on the mat.

When Ejila Irosun opens in iré, the diviner knows that all the blessings heaven and earth have to give are coming for the client; vast karmic debts are about to be repaid, and this person will reap all that he has sown throughout his life. The client will find this hard to believe. His past has been rough, and at times his conduct has been less than ethical. He did what he had to do to survive. This, however, was part of his learning process, and the bad that he did was part of his karma. He had to go through these "trials by fire" as part of his learning process; it was, in many ways, a cleansing. The diviner should tell him to learn from his mistakes, to never repeat them, and to be proud of the good he did in spite of all that was happening around him. Obatalá stands here to forgive him; the diviner should encourage the client to make an adimú to this orisha. Shangó is here to fight his wars; there will be no more trouble and turmoil. Yemayá is here to bless him; she will offer her wealth. And Olokun stands here to reveal all that the client has yet to see within himself. Over all these stands Olorún; in Ejila Irosun, all the orishas are directed by him. They work for him and him alone. Olorún demands that they bless this client.

In osogbo, the meaning of this sign changes drastically. Intrigues and danger are coming for the client. Gossip, envy, intranquillity, hypocrisy, insomnia, and slander exist all around him. These misfortunes are not only directed at the client but also instigated by the client. Odu demands that he stop his negative actions, for only then will the negative actions of others cease. The client must not listen to gossip, become entangled in gossip, or bear false witness. He must treat everyone with equal respect. In this way will many of this letter's osogbos be cleared.

With this odu open, the diviner knows that the client sitting at the mat is a mystery to everyone, including himself; he thinks he knows himself well, yet he has only begun the plunge within himself to discover who he is. To many of the orishas, he is a mystery as well, but Olokun and Olorún know him. Olokun will help him decipher his life into a coherent whole. His reception is integral to this sign. The Ibeyi, as well, are standing up in this letter to offer their help and protection against the enemies known and unknown who wish him ill. They should be received as soon as possible.

This odu brings up additional issues that the diviner should explore with the client:

- The client must guard against depression in this odu. Even in iré, Ejila Irosun marks suicide and suicidal ideation. Unfortunately, this is a letter in which one cries inwardly, not showing the world one's true feelings. This is also a pattern of memory loss, and if it comes in a severe osogbo, the client's head will be affected.
- This letter speaks of murder. Someone close to the client might die. Note that in Ejila Irosun, murders are made to look like suicides, and the truth will not be forthcoming easily. If anyone known to the client seems to have taken his own life, the client should make ebó so that the truth is discovered.
- Here, Elegguá demands that the client make peace within his family. While the client's relationship with his mother might seem good, in truth it is not. Yet he does not have problems with his mother; it is his father who has caused the rift. Because this client and his father do not get along, his mother suffers. If he wants to assuage her suffering, he must make peace with his father.
- The client must protect his eyes. An accident or injury could take the sight of at least one. Diseases that affect the ocular organs, such as macular degeneration, myelinated nerves, glaucoma, and cytomegalovirus (CMV), are a danger. At the first sign of trouble, the client must see an ophthalmologist.

## The Prohibitions of Ejila Irosun

- Keep no empty bottles or open containers in one's home. Discard these immediately, for negative energies can gather therein.
- Do not wear ripped or torn clothing. Either mend these items or throw them away. Do not store them at home. Shirts and pants that incorporate lace or eyelets are also taboo in this letter.
- All weapons—guns, knives, clubs, and gases—are prohibited. Violence is one of the means by which the heat of this letter will escalate, so avoid areas and situations in which one would feel the need to carry a weapon.
- Do not let strangers or those with whom one is not familiar into the home. These people will bring danger to those who live under that roof.

## The Eboses of Ejila Irosun

To relieve some of the heat this sign radiates on the one who cast it, as soon as he closes this session the diviner must obtain a rooster. Outside his home, another priest or priestess must sacrifice this rooster to the earth; once the bird's head is severed, and just before pouring water or honey, the diviner steps on the blood, grinding it forcefully into the dirt. He does this so no one may harm him; as he tramples the rooster's blood, he tramples on the blood of his enemies. After completing this ebó, the diviner does the same for the client, who must come back to the diviner's home for this ritual with another rooster. However, no money changes hands for this sacrifice. It is done for free, as part of the diviner's ebó.

Having made this initial prescription, the diviner now attempts to close the oracle. If it remains open, he should explore the following:

- The warriors Elegguá and Ogún now require sacrifice together. Elegguá takes two chickens; Ogún takes two roosters. On his own, Ogún also takes two pigeons. After the sacrifice, the client lights two white candles to the orishas.
- To help the client achieve his goals, the diviner makes the following ebó to Ogún: He places an iron ladder on the side of Ogún's cauldron and feeds him two pigeons, making sure that some of the blood drips over the ladder. After the sacrifice, the diviner covers Ogún's cauldron with a bunch of green plantains and bananas.
- Olokun is important in all composite odu that incorporate Irosun. If the client does not have Olokun and the letter refuses closure, the diviner should attempt to mark his reception with the shells, asking, "Koshé Olokun?" If the client already has Olokun, the diviner must determine if the orisha needs ebó, asking, "Ebó elese Olokun?" If the answer is yes, he uses the diloggún to mark the appropriate offering.

Marking either of these, the orisha whose diloggún is being consulted dictates that the ceremonies be done immediately.

- The Ibeyi are an integral part of this sign; if it refuses closure and the client does not have these orishas, the diviner should ask, "Koshé los Ibeyi?" If the answer is no, or if the client already has them, the diviner asks, "Ebó elese Ibeyi?" If the answer is yes, he should use the diloggún to mark the required ebó.
- Babaluaiye stands up in this letter, and if it will not close, the client may need to make ebó to him. The diviner asks, "Ebó elese Babaluaiye?" If the answer is no and the client does not have Babaluaiye, the diviner asks, "Koshé Babaluaiye?" If the answer to this question is yes, preparations for this ceremony begin immediately.

If these considerations are not enough to close the session for an aleyo or an aborisha, the diviner must turn to the eboses of the parent odu, Ejila Shebora (see page 581). If the client is an initiate, however, the diviner investigates the following issues:

- The client could have issues with Shangó. In osogbo, the initiate is accused of disobedience, and Shangó may have left him. To determine if this is the case, the diviner should ask, "Ebó elese Shangó?" If the diloggún marks ebó, the only way to bring Shangó back is to feed his otanes a ram and have the client sit for itá with the orisha.
- If the letter still refuses closure, this client might need the orisha Osain. The diviner asks, "Koshé Osain?" If the answer is yes, preparations are made as soon as possible.

If this letter remains open for the initiate, the diviner must turn to the eboses of the parent odu, Ejila Shebora.

# The Fifth Composite Odu of Ejila Shebora, Ejila Oché (12-5)

## The Proverbs of Ejila Oché

- Everything in this life has its time.
- The good son has God's and his mother's blessings.
- One should remember his mother, and bless her.

## The Message of Ejila Oché

When the initial cast of twelve mouths, Ejila Shebora, precedes a cast of five mouths, Oché, the odu Ejila Oché is open on the mat. This is the odu in which the guinea hen became one of Olófin's favorite birds after the fowl's enemies tried to destroy him and everything else. Just as the guinea hen gained God's favor above all other birds, so can this client gain his favor if he leads a noble, pure life.

Having made this cast, the diviner says, "Maferefún Shangó! Maferefún Oshún!" In this sign, both are strong, and they come to fight on the client's behalf. In iré, both orishas predict that the client will receive favorable communications from others. Brief visits, telephone calls, and letters will bring good news from near and far. Life will lighten up just a bit, but only if the client follows the advice and prohibitions and makes the eboses for this letter. Iré yale brings good news as well, but Shangó and Oshún promise that life's struggles will soon end. The client's life will progress slowly, and he will have spiritual evolution. Yet these things will come only if the client listens to Shangó; the diviner should tell him to listen well, for Shangó speaks only once.

The diviner also pays homage to Elegguá and Ogún, saying to each, "Maferefún!" Ejila Oché, no matter its orientation, is filled with strife. Literally, the client's enemies are out to destroy his world, but in the end the client will win. What Shangó and Oshún cannot settle, Elegguá and Ogún will. Note that this odu brings revolution, tragedy, and accidents; to ignore the taboos given in Ejila Shebora will ensure these osogbos.

The diviners should also explore the following issues with the client:

- Someone may have died in the client's home. If the client is unaware of any death in his home, it happened before he came to live there. This spirit still lives in the house, although it has no right to do so. A series of spiritual masses are required to release this spirit.
- The client had a confrontation or tragedy involving someone with darker skin. He thinks this is over, yet he will have more problems with this person in the future.
- The client may have already had an operation. He will have another in the future. If the operation deals with the heart or the abdomen, an ebó to Oshún will preserve his health. Note that the client must follow Ejila Shebora's food taboos. These will help him preserve his health.
- If osogbo came with Ejila Oché, it marks all of the following on the client: disappointments, disillusionment, depression, despair, hypocrisy, envy, gossip, and deception. Remember that Ejila says the client deserves the bad it brings; he will have to make up for all the evil he has done.
- The diviner should tell the client the following, and let him rationalize it himself: "There is a 'house' that you desire, and you go there a lot to visit the 'person' that lives there. This house is neither yours nor is it meant for you. Stay away from it." The meaning of this is more than literal, and the client will figure it out.

## The Prohibitions of Ejila Oché

- Police and imprisonment are a danger in this sign. Have nothing to do with anyone in uniform. Discuss nothing with the authorities. Carry no weapons. Do not argue, and do not fight. Follow these guidelines, and most of the legal difficulties presaged by Ejila Shebora are avoidable.
- Have only one lover at a time; sex outside this relationship is forbidden.
- The following foods are taboo: grains, grainy fruits, the heads and extremities of animals, red foods, red drinks, and all dark liquids. Do not consume calabazas, gourds, and squashes; use them only for ebó.
- Do not say negative things about others. Oshún reminds one that sweetness is favored over sourness; the negative words one speaks affect one's own life.
- A woman may never cut her hair short; she must allow it to grow forever. If a man wishes to shorten the length of his hair, he must consult with Oshún first.

## The Eboses of Ejila Oché

In Ejila Oché, the diviner has several initial considerations for ebó.

- First, the diviner must prescribe a rogación to strengthen the client's orí. If the client's guardian orisha is known, the rogación takes place at the feet of that spirit. The client should give this spirit an adimú of calabazas afterward. If the client's guardian orisha is not known, the rogación takes place at the feet of Obatalá. If possible, the diviner should do this rogación in his home after the reading, before the client leaves. If Ejila Oché opens with any osogbo, before attempting closure the diviner should consider asking "Rogación sodidé?" and "Eborí?" If either of these options is marked, the diviner should adapt this prescription accordingly, calling for a rogación sodidé or the feeding of two white pigeons or doves to the client's orí.
- Second, Shangó and Oshún demand ebó together. The client should give Shangó six calabazas with a red seven-day candle and Oshún five calabazas with a yellow seven-day candle.
- The final ebó goes to Elegguá and Ogún; the diviner feeds a rooster to the two orishas and gives two pigeons to Ogún alone. Seven days after the sacrifice, the client gives three calabazas to Elegguá and seven to Ogún.

For all three eboses prescribed thus far, the diviner notes that the adimús made to all the orishas remain until the gourds start to spoil. At this point, the client discards them.

Now the diviner has his first opportunity to close the reading. If the letter refuses closure, he should consider the following options:

- The first possibility to consider is that Shangó, Oshún, Elegguá, and Ogún could be standing up for additional eboses. To determine if this is the case, the diviner should ask, "Ebó elese [orisha's name]?" If the answer is yes, he uses the diloggún to mark the appropriate offering. After each ebó that is marked, the diviner should attempt to close the oracle before moving on to the next ebó.
- If the oracle still will not close and illness afflicts the client's abdomen, the diviner should prescribe a rogación of the abdomen before Oshún. The rogación should use grated coconut, grated cocoa butter, crushed cascarilla, and honey. Before wrapping the client's stomach with cotton and white cloth, the diviner should feed two pigeons and one hen to the abdomen. If the sign's osogbo is great, he should share this sacrifice between the client's abdomen and Oshún.
- Next the diviner might ask, "Ebó elese egun?" If the answer is yes, he should use the diloggún to mark the required ebó. In addition, the diviner should make sure the client has an opá ikú and otá de muerto and assist him in maintaining a bóveda. All are necessary for his spiritual evolution.
- For luck, the client may offer to Elegguá a sacrifice of plenty of toasted corn, yellow cornmeal, a rooster, and plenty of honey.
- To Ogún, the client should present a knife with a machete. If he has received pinaldo, the client may place these implements in the orisha's cauldron; if he has not, he should place them on the floor in front of Ogún. Then he should give Elegguá and Ogún plenty of toasted corn and sacrifice two chickens to Elegguá and a rooster with two pigeons to Ogún. Seven days after this sacrifice, the client should give both orishas plenty of fresh fruit. When the fruits start to spoil, he discards them in the woods.
- If the letter still remains open, the client could have issues with Babaluaiye. The dininer should ask, "Ebó elese Babaluaiye?" and "Koshé Babaluaiye?" If either is marked, preparations for these ceremonies should begin immediately.

Having explored all these possibilities, if the letter still will not allow closure, the diviner must now turn to the eboses of the parent odu, Ejila Shebora (see page 581). Something there is needed for the client's evolution.

## The Sixth Composite Odu of Ejila Shebora, Ejila Obara (12-6)

### The Proverbs of Ejila Obara

- From the lie shall the truth be born.
- With the tongue, one may destroy the town, and with the tongue, one may save the town: Control the tongue.
- The one who knows will not die like the one who does not know.
- Old friends are not to be abandoned for the new.
- One's stubbornness will take him from failure to failure.

### The Message of Ejila Obara

When an initial cast of twelve mouths, Ejila Shebora, precedes a cast of six mouths, Obara, the odu Ejila Obara is open on the mat. Having made this cast, the diviner pays homage to Yemayá, Shangó, Dada, and Ainá, saying to each, "Maferefún!"

Ejila Obara is hot and volatile, an odu of duty and inescapable karma. Once, even the goat tried to escape his destiny in this sign. He heard that Obatalá was throwing a grand party in his palace, and the goat was to be sacrificed to Elegguá in the evening. Obatalá's palace was far away from Elegguá's home, and the goat had a plan: He would befriend Elegguá and do him a great favor. He walked for three days and three nights from Obatalá's palace to Elegguá's humble abode, and then, with Elegguá on his back, he walked again to Obatalá's palace. The goat was exhausted and weary when they arrived; suddenly, he was surrounded by priests brandishing knives and ropes, and Elegguá, rested and refreshed from his journey, stepped off the goat's back. "But I am your friend!" wailed the weary goat. "For days I carried you on my back while you rested." Sadly, Elegguá reached out and petted the animal. "I am sorry, goat," he said. "But destiny is unalterable, and it is in your destiny to feed me." Yet Elegguá had pity, and the goat was sacrificed quickly and painlessly; so has his goat been killed to this day. If Ejila Obara teaches us nothing else, it shows us that destiny is tricky, and one can never escape its grasp.

In spite of this patakís, when Ejila Obara opens on the mat with iré, it says that the client's destiny is not only good but also obtainable. This client comes from an impoverished past; finances were bad, love was nonexistent, and the client, at times, lost faith in the orishas for the hardship life brought. Now, the client is coming to a point full of bounty, and he must give thanks for his blessings. Yemayá loves this client dearly; she will navigate him through life's storms and tumultuous currents to the port of bounty that Ejila Obara promises. Even if she claims no ebó here, the client should offer adimú to her in thanksgiving. Shangó is here to fight all this person's wars. Shangó reminds the client that he lifted himself to orisha once by his own works and will, and the client should do no less in his own life. He should lift himself up at all times, refusing to be brought down by the tragedies life brings. Goodness is coming, and he must fight hard to attain it. Dada and Ainá are here to bless the client, although they speak up mostly for initiates in Ejila Obara. The client has issues with these two orishas, and before the sign closes the client might have to commit to their reception to lock in his blessings.

Whenever osogbo is predicted in this composite of Ejila, the implications for the client become severe, indeed; it is an odu of karma, of reaping what one has sown. Throughout his life, this client has cast a shadow over all in his life. Now, like the goat, he comes to the mat trying to escape his destiny, but it is unalterable. He should pray that the forces mounting against him are kind. The diviner should try to impress upon the client that he has many enemies around him. Some will overtly try to hurt him and cause distress; they will stop at nothing to destroy the good that he tries to create in his own life. Others are more subtle, working covertly to destroy what has been created. The client also has enemies who do not know they are enemies; their own loose lips and interference have brought calamity to this person's life. Sometimes even his best friend can bring unintentional disaster by telling the client's business to those who have no business knowing about it. The client must learn to keep his own counsel, to keep things to himself until they have been achieved. Thus will others not be able to interfere in his plans. When Ejila Obara opens in an osogbo, the discovery of a larishe is of utmost importance, for just as the sign marks karmic disaster upon the client, if larishe is found, it shows that the client has a solution to all his ills. Ejila Obara in osogbo with no larishe is a dangerous combination; in this case, no matter what eboses are done, the client will suffer.

This sign also addresses issues in the immediate family unit. There are divisions between father and child. This chasm exists spiritually and emotionally, and the client must mend it as soon as possible so that later in life he does not have regrets about it. Ejila Obara indicates that the client is not an only child; he has brothers and sisters, although some of them might be dead (some might have died at or before birth). If the client has siblings still alive who are younger than he, they look up to him for guidance on how to live. He should make sure that he always sets a good example for them. If the client has siblings who are older than he is, there is a bit of a chasm in that relationship as well, and Shangó says that the client must work to mend it. The family unit must be strong, for there will come a time when family is needed.

In addition, the diviner should address the following points during the reading:

- Shangó wants the client to stop worrying and crying in misery. This only makes his present situation worse.

- The client should be frank and speak from the heart when with his lover; this will improve communication in the relationship. He must not have any affairs or commit adultery even with his heart.
- The client must respect his elders at all times. His mother and father have good advice to give, and he must seek it out in times of difficulty. Whenever he is uncertain about what path to travel in the religion, the client should talk to his godparent, for he or she has already suffered these things. He must always take his problems and concerns to the feet of the orishas, for they want what is best.
- Anyone who tries to start an argument with the client at this time only wants to win. The client should not enter into arguments with anyone for any reason. When one starts, he should merely walk away.

## The Prohibitions of Ejila Obara

- Do not discuss personal business with one's roommates or with family members living in one's home. In Ejila Obara, one's worst enemy lives under the same roof.
- If an elder (of the family or of the religion) makes a reasonable request, one may not refuse it.
- An initiate must not refuse to have godchildren. Others will come for help, and he must help them.
- Many who open in Ejila Obara with osogbo have lifted their hands in anger toward Shangó; never do this again. While he tolerated it once, he will tolerate it no more.
- Once this letter opens for an initiate, even if this reading is not an itá, the initiate must give up tobacco and alcohol for life. These two vices are the initiate's destruction.

## The Eboses of Ejila Obara

When Ejila Obara opens on the mat, regardless of its orientation the diviner must prescribe the following eboses:

- Elegguá and Ogún know the evil that others do. They also know the evil the client has done. While he must suffer for his transgressions, these two orishas will not let him suffer at the hands of others. Ogún prepares a trap for this person's enemies. As ebó, the client must give three mousetraps to Elegguá and a machete to Ogún. The two orishas should be fed a single rooster together. The next day, the client cleans his head with two coconuts, giving them to the warriors when he is done. The fruits remain until the milk dries up inside them, at which point the client discards them in the woods.
- The godparent must give the client a rogación before the client's guardian orisha (if it is known) or before Obatalá (if the guardian orisha is not known). The rogación should use grated coconut, crushed cascarilla, grated cocoa butter, and white flowers.
- To Oshún, the client must sacrifice a single hen. One week after the sacrifice, he should provide her with a small basket of oranges. When the oranges begin to spoil, the client takes them to the banks of a river and leaves them there.

Now the diviner has his first opportunity to close the odu. If it remains open, he investigates the following possibilities:

- The client could have issues pending with Shangó; remember the prohibition against raising one's hands in anger toward him. If the client has done this before, Shangó is angry. There might be a way to make amends, however. To see if the orisha will take anything as an apology from the client, the diviner should ask, "Larishe si Shangó?" If the answer is yes, he must use the diloggún to mark the appropriate offering.
- In osogbo, this sign mandates the following ebó: To Shangó and Oshún, the client must give an adimú of fresh squash. He must ensure that there is always some type of gourd or calabaza sitting with these two orishas. After making the ebó, this sign delivers a further prohibition: The client must not eat, pick, pierce, cut, or give away any type of gourd. They hold the keys to the client's future prosperity, and they should be used only for making ebó.

- In Ejila Obara, one's guardian orisha tries to bring a special blessing; however, without ebó this blessing will never come. To find out what the client's guardian orisha will accept as ebó, the diviner must ask, "Ebó elese [guardian orisha's name]?" If the client is an aborisha whose guardian orisha is unknown, a bajado is now marked as ebó. It must be done by an oriaté as soon as possible.

If these considerations are not enough to close the sign for an aleyo or an aborisha, the diviner must turn to the eboses of the parent odu, Ejila Shebora (see page 581). Something there is necessary for this client's evolution.

- If the sign remains open for an initiate, he has issues pending with Osain. First, the diviner asks, "Ebó niche osain?" If the answer is yes, the diviner must then determine to which orisha this niche osain belongs. If no niche osain is required, the diviner asks, "Koshé Osain?" If the answer is yes, preparations for his reception begin immediately.

If after these prescriptions the odu still remains open for the initiate, the diviner must turn to the eboses of the parent odu, Ejila Shebora.

## The Seventh Composite Odu of Ejila Shebora, Ejila Odí (12-7)

### The Proverbs of Ejila Odí

- In adultery there will always be danger.
- You are a child of envy, and your tongue will destroy your secrets.
- The ear is smaller than the head, but it does not go through it.

### The Message of Ejila Odí

When an initial cast of twelve mouths, Ejila Shebora, is followed by one of seven mouths, Odí, the odu Ejila Odí is open on the mat. Immediately, the diviner says, "Maferefún Obatalá! Maferefún Shangó! Maferefún Ochosi! Maferefún Yemayá!" All four orishas dominate this pattern. They offer their protection and have much advice to give the client. Obatalá is here to say that the client must lean on him. Spiritually, this person is not clean, and Obatalá wants to cleanse him of his past and of all the things that stand in his way. Shangó cares for this client as if he were his own child, and if the client spoils him with frequent adimú, he not only will save the client but also will lift him up. Ochosi is the bearer of justice; he sees what others have done to the client and he will punish them all for their transgressions. The client himself, however, has wrought much evil himself, and Ochosi might be here to punish him as well. After his punishment, Ochosi will lift him up again. Yet in Ejila Odí, no orisha protects the client as fiercely as Yemayá. She has watched over this person; she has seen how others have tried to beat him down when he was only following his spiritual path. She tells the client, "Keep dreaming your dreams; keep working. I support you all the way." So strong is her love that if the client's guardian orisha has not been identified, he might be her child.

No matter its orientation, Ejila Odí speaks of witchcraft sent to and from the client. If he is involved in any occult science, he must give this up. The "spells" he casts never reach their intended mark and always return home to roost. He does, however, have strong psychic powers, and he has much aché with the dead. Specifically, two spirits are close to him, working for his evolution. One is a spirit similar to Shangó, while the other belongs to Yemayá. "Maferefún!" to both spirits, for as the client works with them, he will find spiritual strength. If an osogbo of araye, ogo, or epe comes, the diviner may be certain that others are using witchcraft against the client. The initial larishe prescribed by this letter is essential to dispelling the sorcery; it must be the first ebó done. If no larishe was prescribed, the diviner must help his client fight the evil by prescribing trabajos (magical works) to help cleanse the witchcraft that has been sent for him. This odu provides clues as to who sent the curse: It began with the work of a man whose complexion is darker than the client's. The curse brings small accidents to the client's life, and in time what is small will grow bigger. After closing the odu, the diviner should advise the client on ways to fight witchcraft.

Ejila Odí also raises a variety of other issues that the diviner should explore with the client:

- Although there are many difficulties in the client's life now, hard work and persistence guarantee that he can overcome them.
- If the client is involved in politics, he must not carry weapons. However, he must ensure his security at all times. This is a sign of political assassination. For his own protection, a client who opens in this odu during an itá may not work for political clients.
- While the client's home, until now, has been safe, peaceful, and secure, something is coming that will shake him up. Something will try to destroy his peace, safety, and security. By following the taboos of both Ejila Shebora and this composite, he can avoid or lessen this tragedy.
- While the client professes faith with his mouth, in truth he has little faith in the orishas. In time, however, so many miracles will unfold around him that he will have no choice but to believe.

## The Prohibitions of Ejila Odí

- For an aleyo or an aborisha, seafood is prohibited for the next seven days. For an initiate, seafood is taboo for life. If this reading is a bajado, the consumption of seafood is prohibited until one makes ocha. If this reading is an itá, seafood is prohibited for life. This does not, however, remove the right to consume freshwater fish.
- There is a risk of venereal disease causing sterility. Have no more than one lover at a time. Do not engage in amorous liaisons outside of one's current relationship.
- Do not eat homemade foods, candies, or cookies that are offered with insistence. They may result in intentional or accidental poisoning.
- Lies and gossip will bring fatal consequences. Do not listen to or participate in these things.

## The Eboses of Ejila Odí

When Ejila Odí opens on the mat, two eboses are mandatory, and if the client is an initiate, a third ebó becomes mandatory as well.

- In the woods, before a dead tree and with the client's opá ikú, make the following ebó to egun: The diviner nails four scarves (red, yellow, blue, and green) to the trunk with a single nail. He then pours plenty of toasted corn in a circle around the tree and sprays rum and cigar smoke over the tree's trunk and then over the elements of the ebó. Finally, he sacrifices a single rooster to both the tree and the client's staff, making sure that the client's shadow falls on both the tree and the staff. Only the opá ikú comes home with the client; the rest of the ebó stays with the tree.*
- Because Ochosi comes to make justice, his propitiation is essential. Give him three arrows. Sacrifice three pigeons to him, putting the heads on the arrow tips. Sacrifice a rooster, leaving the head at his feet. Remove the birds' carcasses immediately, but leave the heads with Ochosi for three days. Afterward, the client disposes of the heads in the woods. If the client is an initiate, after making this ebó to Ochosi he must receive this orisha immediately.
- If the client is an initiate, after receiving Ochosi he must give a tambor in honor of his own and his godparent's Ochosi. On the throne, he should display the four colors of Ósun prominently. The ideal way to do this ebó is as follows: On the first day, the initiate receives Ochosi with four legs; on the second day, he gives the tambor; on the third day, he sits for itá with the orisha. When the client brings his Ochosi home, he must always display the four colors of Ósun in this spirit's shrine.
- If Ejila Odí opened in an osogbo, a rogación sodidé at the feet of Obatalá is necessary. The rogación should use grated coconut, grated

*If the client has an otá de muerto, the diviner feeds it with the tree and the staff and makes sure that the client's shadow falls on it during the sacrifice. The client takes the otá home with him as well.

cocoa butter, crushed cascarilla, four apple snails, white flowers, cow's milk, honey, and coconut milk.

Having made these prescriptions, the diviner may now attempt to close the oracle. If it will not close, he should explore the following possibilities:

- The client's orí may need to be strengthened. The diviner should consider asking, "Eborí?" If the odu demands eborí, before wrapping the client's head in white cotton or cloth in the rogación sodidé that has already been prescribed, the diviner should sacrifice two white pigeons or white doves to the client's orí.
- If the client does not have his warriors, he now needs to receive them. Inside Ogún's cauldron there must be four machetes. These will give the orisha the strength to protect the client from harm in all four cardinal points of the world.
- To clear the osogbo of this letter, the client must take many spiritual baths with herbs sacred to the orisha whose diloggún is being read. Also, the diviner must make for the client a niche osain for this same spirit, using herbs sacred to him or her.
- If this is not enough to close the letter, an aleyo or an aborisha must wear a red parrot feather in his hair daily for the next month; an initiate must do so for life.
- Somehow, this client may have incurred a debt with Obatalá. If he can remember what this debt is, he should pay it now. If he cannot remember having incurred a debt, the diviner must see what this orisha will require, asking, "Ebó elese Obatalá?" If the answer is yes, he uses the diloggún to mark the appropriate offering.
- All the orishas considered warriors can speak in this odu, and if it will not close, the diviner should try to mark eboses to as many of them as possible. There are serious, unseen wars being fought around the client, and he will need the protection of all these spirits.
- If the letter remains open, the diviner must turn to Elegguá and Yemayá for resolution. Every day, the client must wear Yemayá's eleke so that she can watch over him wherever he goes. Also, the client needs to be cautious with his head; no one should touch it. If the oracle still will not close, the client should offer ebó to Elegguá and Yemayá together. To see what they might require, the diviner should ask, "Ebó elese Elegguá y Yemayá?" If the answer is yes, he uses the diloggún to mark the appropriate offering.
- Because Yemayá and Shangó are considered by many to be mother and son, here the two might demand ebó together. To see if ebó is needed, the diviner must ask, "Ebó elese Yemayá y Shangó?" If the answer is yes, he uses the diloggún to mark the appropriate offering.
- Finally, if the client is an initiate, he might need to receive Osain. The diviner should ask, "Koshé Osain?" If the answer is yes, he must begin preparations for this ceremony immediately.

If the odu still remains open, the diviner must turn to the eboses of the parent odu, Ejila Shebora (see page 581). Something there is needed for the client's evolution.

## The Eighth Composite Odu of Ejila, Ejila Ogbe (12-8)

### The Proverbs of Ejila Ogbe

- The head must carry the body and not the tail.
- Love yourself so that you can love others.
- While the wasp has a fierce sting, the pain of its bite soon passes.

### The Message of Ejila Ogbe

When a casting of twelve mouths, Ejila Shebora, precedes a cast of eight mouths, Eji Ogbe, the odu Ejila Ogbe is open on the mat. This sign is also known as Ejila Unle, Ejila l'Ogbe, Ejila Elleunle, and Trupo Congua. Many know this as the odu of the tiger and the hunter, for it tells many stories of both. Once, the hunter felt sorry for the tiger, and he did a favor for him; the tiger took advantage of the hunter's kindness and ate him. Later, the tiger himself did favors for his small friends in the forest, and they, in return, trapped him under a rock. He lost his life that day. Two hunters who never made ebó went to the forest in search of game; they found none. By chance, they happened upon a farmer's field of ñame and stopped to dig some up. While they were digging, a tiger crept up on them from behind. The animal killed both and feasted well that night. When this odu comes, no matter its orientation, the diviner should tell the client, "There are predators and there are prey; neither should help the other. Do favors for no one, for always your kindness will be repaid with evil."

When this letter comes, the diviner pays homage to Olófin, Shangó, Obatalá, Aganyú, Elegguá, Olokun, and Oshún, saying to each, "Maferefún!" These seven spirits are fierce in this sign, and the aché of all seven is essential to the client's evolution. When this session opens for a client whose head has not been marked (his guardian orisha has not been determined) with a bajado, the diviner can be almost sure that this is Shangó's child sitting at the mat. Many diviners say that when the omo odu is eight mouths, Obatalá stands up to affirm that the owner of the parent odu is the aborisha's parent. If this reading is a bajado, the diviner would ask Shangó first, followed by Aganyú. If neither orisha accepts this client as his child, Obatalá would be asked next; the omo odu is his. Here is the confusion that priests say exist between the children of Obatalá and Shangó: Before the head is marked, where one sees Obatalá one also sees Shangó, and vice versa, for they are close. Although Aganyú is Shangó's father, it is Obatalá who gives him coolness, strength, and wisdom. The division among the aché of these three orishas in this odu is fine indeed.

The diviner should explore the following issues with the client:

- Robbery figures prominently in this odu. If the client is not a thief, he will be a victim of theft.
- Recently, the client has done three favors for other people. The diviner should tell him to consider each of these an enemy, for in time each will bring great treason to his life. If he makes ebó quickly, only they will suffer, falling victim in their own evil plans.
- In spite of all the difficulties and tribulations in this person's life now, he must always have patience and resignation. Only time will make life better.
- If Ejila Ogbe comes with an osogbo, the client's current mode of living does not match his true nature and constitution. He must promote coolness and clarity or else his health will suffer.

## The Prohibitions of Ejila Ogbe

- Even if the odu opens in iré, one must not do favors for others. All the good one does will be returned with evil.
- If this reading is an itá of inititation, the iyawó may never leave any of his orishas unattended, even around his own godparent. If the letter comes with a severe osogbo, the iyawó must dress in white for life.
- One's temperament is delicate, and nowhere is this better seen than with the stomach and bowels. All things must be done and taken in moderation. Do not consume hot, spicy foods. Consume meals at the same time every day, and limit between-meal snacks. Gluttony is taboo; do not overeat.
- Drugs, cigarettes, alcohol, and other intoxicants are taboo.
- Beware of passionate liaisons; do not engage in adultery.

## The Eboses of Ejila Ogbe

When Ejila Ogbe opens on the mat, ebó is required, but the ebó to be done depends on the letter's orientation, the client's initiatory status, and whether or not the client's guardian orisha is known. Carefully, the diviner must consider the following:

- If the client is an aleyo, he must have a rogación before both Elegguá and Obatalá. The priest's Elegguá sits at his Obatalá's feet during this ceremony. This rogación should use grated coconut, grated cocoa butter, crushed cascarilla, and white flowers. If the letter opens with osogbo, the diviner should determine whether the rogación needs to be sodidé and whether it needs to include eborí. In osogbo, the aleyo must also present an adimú to Elegguá and Obatalá immediately after the rogación. The client himself, with advice from the diviner, will determine what he wants to give.

- If the client is an aborisha, he must have the same series of eboses as an aleyo. However, if his guardian orisha is known, that spirit replaces Obatalá in the prescription. If the aborisha's guardian orisha is not known, a bajado is now ebó. If possible, an oriaté should perform the ceremony immediately after the aborisha's rogación and adimú are complete.
- If the client is an initiate and Ejila Ogbe brings iré, he must have a rogación sodidé before his crowning orisha, with Elegguá sitting at the orisha's feet, and he must present an adimú to the two orishas immediately afterward. If the odu opens in osogbo, eborí is mandatory. After these eboses are done, an oriaté feeds Shangó a ram. The next day, the client sits for itá.

At this point, the diviner has his first chance to close the oracle. If it remains open, the diviner should explore the following:

- The orishas who will be propitiated with the mandatory eboses may require further ebó. If the client is an aleyo or an aborisha whose guardian orisha is not known, the diviner asks, "Ebó elese Elegguá y Obatalá?" If the client is an aborisha whose guardian orisha is known, the diviner asks, "Ebó elese Elegguá y [guardian orisha]?"; he asks the same question for an initiate who opens in iré. If the client is an initiate who opens in osogbo, the diviner asks, "Ebó elese Elegguá y Shangó?" If the answer is yes, he then uses the diloggún to mark the appropriate offering.
- In this sign, the reception and propitiation of Olokun can be essential. If the client does not have him, he must receive him. If he has Olokun, the diviner should ask, "Ebó elese Olokun?" If the answer is yes, he uses the diloggún to mark the appropriate offering. At the least, the client should feed Olokun and host an agbán for her.

If these considerations are not enough to close the odu for an aleyo or an aborisha, the diviner must turn to the eboses of the parent odu, Ejila Shebora (see page 581). Something there is necessary for the client's evolution. If the client is an initiate, however, the diviner should continue with the following list:

- If the circumstances of the sign prescribe a ram and itá with Shangó, before giving this ebó the diviner feeds a goat to Elegguá, and the client should have an itá with him as well.
- If this letter falls during the itá of a iyawó, the following eboses are necessary: Before allowing the iyawó to leave his throne, the priest washes two white horsetails in Obatalá's omiero. He feeds these, along with Obatalá, two white pigeons and a white hen or rooster. When taking the iyawó home, the godparent uses the horsetails to whisk Death away from his house. He brings in Ogún but stops with him at the front door. Before taking him to his proper place, the godparent feeds Ogún three pigeons, one at a time. After sacrificing each pigeon, before putting its carcass on the floor the godparent smears some of the blood from the neck over the door frame. No one must wash this off; it must be allowed to dry. Finally, when the year in white is over, this initiate must receive the knife before taking any godchildren.
- Finally, if the osogbo of Ejila Ogbe is severe and the sign still refuses closure, the ebó to Shangó is altered again. The day after he is fed a ram, the client must host a tambor for Shangó. He must ensure that he has a private room where Shangó can consult with the initiate; he will have much to say, and these words must be written down. The day after the tambor, the client should sit for an itá with Shangó.

If these considerations are not enough to close the odu for the initiate, the diviner must turn to the eboses of the parent odu, Ejila Shebora.

# The Ninth Composite Odu of Ejila Shebora, Ejila Osá (12-9)

## The Proverbs of Ejila Osá

- If the friend is great, the traitor will be great as well.
- You have no true friends.
- One fails when one makes trouble.
- One's own hands will put one in the cemetery.

## The Message of Ejila Osá

When an initial cast of twelve mouths, Ejila Shebora, precedes a cast of nine mouths, Osá, the odu Ejila Osá is open on the mat. When it falls, the diviner honors Aganyú, Oroiña, Oyá, Shangó, Iboku, Ainá, Obatalá, and egun, saying to each, "Maferefún!" This is an explosive sign, and if it opens in osogbo, the aché of all these spirits will be needed to heal the client's life. For here is where the wind met the volcanic explosion; together, their power was awesome, each feeding the other, and volcanic night spread over the land.* Aganyú and Oyá have a pact in this sign; this is where the aumba used for their asiento was born, and here they share the nine colors sacred to Oyá, egun, and Ayao.† Ejila Osá is the odu of Ainá's birth; she is Shangó's fire, the flame erupting from his mouth and striking from heaven, born of the union between Shangó and Oyá. This is the sign where the slave murders his master. In iré, the sign portends that the client will destroy all those who bring enslavement and even bad habits to which one becomes enslaved. Yet in osogbo, Ejila Osá says the client is the master, and if he is not careful, someone will destroy him. The coup d'état is born here, and one could be murdered in the street.

This sign is one of the more heated and negative patterns of Ejila. Oyá and Elegguá stand up in this sign to let the client know that many roads may be closed to him now, and many secret enemies speak badly behind his back. He should always watch his back, keep his secrets, and trust no one until the energy of this odu has passed. Before beginning any new projects or work, the client must take these ideas to the feet of the orishas, for they are the ones who care right now. If he asks their advice in all things, all things will come out well. Currently the client wonders why some of the things for which he works so hard come out well while others crumble around his feet. He should petition and depend upon Elegguá for evolution in all the roads and paths that he walks. Elegguá says there is one path this person wishes to tread that must not be taken: He should not leave his current residence, and he should not run away from his troubles. Those things that affect the client now will follow him no matter where he goes, and he needs to deal with them now.

In addition, the diviner needs to explore the following with this person:

- An osogbo of ano or ikú brings serious health warnings for the client. Ejila Osá speaks of strokes and aneurism. The client must put aside all vices: smoking, alcohol, and gluttony. Severe lifestyle changes are in order. The diviner must advise a complete physical. The throat and lungs are weak; any infection in these regions, even a simple sore throat, can have devastating effects on the client's health.
- If the client listens to the advice of Ejila Osá, the diviner can assure him that those who mock him today will beg him for help in the future. Here, younger initiates are ridiculed by their elders, but in time, even the elders prostrate themselves before youth.
- Those who maintain strong Catholic ties in this religion believe that Ejila Osá is a sign of San Francisco. For these, he is a powerful egun, an ally in the times of desperation that this letter can bring. If the client is a Catholic, he should make the spiritual prescription of San Francisco's oration. He will guide the client through danger.
- This person often acts on the bad thoughts and

*When a volcano erupts at midday, the atmospheric currents gather fine ash, spreading it thickly and blotting out the sun. This is volcanic night; and it is born here of Aganyú and Oyá's union.

†Oyá shares her nine colors with her sister, Ayao, and her children, egun; but here she and Aganyú made the pact to use all nine together as well.

impulses that he has, and the orishas are warning him to stop this behavior immediately. Due to exhaustion, the client's mind is continually clouded; the thoughts he has on a daily basis are not good. He does not think through his actions or decisions. Again, the key to accomplishing anything in this sign is to consult first with the orishas.

- This client is also a habitual liar, and the diviner must keep this in mind while delivering the reading.
- The client's head is bad, and it can be lost (decapitated) through disaster. The client must ensure his safety at all times.
- Someone with whom this client deals acts like a fool, yet this is only a front. Once this person knows the client's business, he will reveal it to the world. Again, the client must trust no one.

## The Prohibitions of Ejila Osá

- For an initiate, Ejila Osá forbids the opening of four-legged animals in any ocha ceremony. The handling of intestines or blood is taboo. Even to be around this can inflame the initiate's orí miserably, and tragedies will befall him.
- Any client who comes in Ejila Osá is prohibited from eating raw or undercooked meats, sausages (especially blood sausage), the heads and feet of animals, the internal organs of animals, poultry, and eggs.
- Those with complexions darker than one's own plot against one. Be reserved and cautious when dealing with such people until their full intentions are understood.

## The Eboses of Ejila Osá

For all concerned, this is an intense odu, and there are many eboses to consider. No matter Ejila Osá's orientation, the diviner must consider the following works and sacrifices:

- The client must have three rogaciónes exactly twelve days apart. If the client is an aleyo or an aborisha whose guardian orisha is unknown, the rogaciónes should take place before Obatalá. If the client is an aborisha whose guardian orisha is known or an initiate, the rogaciónes should take place before his guardian orisha. During this period of cleansing, the client dresses in white. The rogaciónes should use four macerated apple snails, grated coconut, grated cocoa butter, and crushed cascarilla.
- Twelve days after the third rogación, the client must have another rogación, this time before Oyá. The priest should cleanse him with a pañuelo of nine colors and then drape this over the orisha's sopera.
- If the client is an initiate, he must receive both Oyá and Aganyú. These two orishas live side by side. Each must have a pañuelo of nine colors, and behind them, a large pañuelo of nine colors should be hung and shared between the two. Between them should rest the aumba, the one prepared to initiate their children to ocha.
- No matter the client's initiatory status, he must do the following three eboses immediately: Over the front door, hang a white flag in honor of Obatalá; give an ornate mask to the orisha whose shells are being consulted; and give a two-faced doll to Elegguá. The white flag alerts the spiritual world that this person's house is under Obatalá's protection; the mask hides the client's true face from his enemies; and the two-faced doll helps Elegguá watch for danger from the front and back.
- All who come with Ejila Osá must tend egun well. On his bóveda, the client must have nine glasses of water, a white candle, and nine cigars wrapped tightly in nine ribbons of different colors.

Having made these prescriptions, the diviner may now ask the letter for closure. If he is refused, the client's egun could be demanding more ebó. The diviner should ask, "Ebó elese egun?" If the answer is yes, he uses the diloggún to mark the appropriate offering.

In osogbo, if egun refuse more ebó, or if they accept but the letter still will not close, the diviner should consider the following options for ebó:

- To each orisha who spoke in this odu, the client

should offer a cool, refreshing adimú. Fresh fruits, coconuts, white rice, and sweet candies (nothing red) are all appropriate. The diviner should not prescribe a blood sacrifice unless there is no other way to close the odu. In this pattern, all the spirits are hot, and blood will only make them more volatile.

- The client could have issues pending with Babaluaiye. To see if he is standing up for anything, the diviner needs to ask, "Ebó elese Babaluaiye?" If the answer is yes, he should use the diloggún to mark the required ebó. The client, however, must pay for his ebó in the following manner: Wearing a piece of burlap or sackcloth, he should go out into the streets and beg alms from strangers for a day. (If this sign came in a severe osogbo, he should be given a rogación and the eleke of Babaluaiye the night before he does this. He should wear this eleke while begging.) He then presents the money he receives to Babaluaiye on a white plate with two coconuts and two white candles as a derecho. Once this is done, the diviner may perform the ebó to satisfy the orisha. From this moment on, the client must not make fun of vagrants or beggars, and he can never refuse alms to anyone.
- If the client is an initiate, this letter can also mark the reception of Osain. To see if this is needed, the diviner should ask, "Koshé Osain?"

If closure cannot be found with these eboses, the diviner must turn to the eboses of the parent odu, Ejila Shebora (see page 581). Something there is necessary for the client's evolution.

# The Tenth Composite Odu of Ejila Shebora, Ejila Ofún (12-10)

## The Proverbs of Ejila Ofún

- The one who curses is the one who will be cursed.
- By your own greed you will lose everything, even your own life.
- A drunk does not know what he is doing when he does not want to know what he is doing.

## The Message of Ejila Ofún

When an initial cast of twelve mouths, Ejila Shebora, precedes a cast of ten mouths, Ofún, the odu Ejila Ofún is open on the mat. Of all the patterns found in Ejila's family, this composite is perhaps the hottest. Although different houses deal with this energy in myriad ways, our own house has a series of short rituals designed to alleviate the spiritual heat that encompasses the diviner's home at this time. First, it is assumed that when twelve mouths presented themselves on the mat, the diviner performed the ritual of cooling the odu by placing the shells in a gourd of cool water and having his assistant throw that water out the front door so the volatile vibrations left the diviner's home, going back out into the world from which they coalesced. Now that this composite has presented itself, the diviner begins a new series of rituals: He marks his head, the client's head, and the heads of all present in order of elder status with cascarilla. This mark is to be the size of a small circle made firmly in the area of the third eye. While the diviner marks everyone's forehead, he directs his assistant to prepare a special saraeko made of water, cornmeal, honey, cocoa oil, cascarilla, and a leaf of prodigiosa. White ingredients such as cow's milk, coconut milk, and goat's milk may also be added to this mixture, if desired.

Once the saraeko has been made, the diviner takes a sip, then passes it to the client so that he may drink from the gourd; and then each priest or priestess present in order of elder status sips from the saraeko. The diviner or his assistant fills another gourd with the saraeko and gives it to Elegguá, then Obatalá, and then Shangó. The assistant heats a piece of metal until it is red hot. The diviner dips this piece of metal in the cool fluids of the saraeko, saying, "It is better to drown than to burn!" The diviner then dips his finger in the saraeko and marks an equal-armed cross on the roof of his mouth. The client and all the priests and priestesses present, in order of elder status, do the same. Every other person present in the diviner's home now is called to come do this short ritual, and just before he or she dips his or her finger into the saraeko, the diviner places the mark of cascarilla on his or her forehead. Once this ritual is complete, the divination session continues.

Once this session is closed, the client must leave the diviner's home immediately. The saraeko is then taken from Elegguá, Obatalá, and Shangó, in that order, and thrown to the street with the words "Eshu batie sode." Having given a reading in this composite, the diviner *must* have a rogación at Obatalá's feet as soon as possible.

The diviner opens the reading by saying, "Maferefún Orí! Maferefún Obatalá! Maferefún Elegguá! Maferefún Shangó!" All four orishas are prominent in this sign. The diviner should pay homage to the client's guardian orisha as well, for that spirit speaks here on behalf of his protégé. With this sign open, the diviner can be certain of one thing: An orisha is not pleased with the client. Even Shangó is often angry here; if the client has not directly incurred his wrath, he may be upset over past indiscretions and current behaviors. Now Shangó stands up to take control of the reading, and his advice must be heeded, for he speaks only once. If the client is an aleyo whose guardian orisha is not known, he could be Shangó's child. If the client belongs to another orisha, the heat of Ejila Ofún becomes even more explosive—the guardian orisha is angry as well. If the osogbo in this sign is severe, these feelings may move from anger to direct hostility on the part of the spirits. There is loss and there is disobedience, and the things that can cause this anger are many. The client has been disrespectful in his relationships to the orishas, his parents or children, his godparent or his godchildren, his youth or his elders. He has broken promises on all these levels, and he has ignored and not properly propitiated all the spirits. In all avenues of personal conduct, the orishas disagree with how the client acts, and there will soon be a spiritual war fought between human and orishas if the client does not correct the situation. The diviner must tell the client that he must listen to the advice of this odu, for he cannot win in a war against God!

In addition, the diviner should explore the following issues with the client:

- White is a beautiful color; the client should wear it more often. He must not ever wear the color red.
- The client is lazy and always finds himself in dire straits; the orishas say that no amount of ebó will improve this person's life until he begins to work hard. Before the energy of this odu has passed, he will work hard!
- There may be problems occurring in the muscles and bones of the client's body; if pain develops in these areas, he should see a physician as soon as possible.
- The client has a tendency to become romantically involved with more than one person or to begin one relationship before the existing one has ended. This tendency must cease now.
- This letter brings a variety of tragedies, revolutions, intrigues, and treason to the client's life. Many of these things are deserved, brought about by the client's own actions. He must account for what he has done before the orishas and commit to never doing them again. Only in this way will they help him.

## The Prohibitions of Ejila Ofún

- One must respect one's elders, not only those of blood or of ocha but also any elderly persons one might know or meet.
- Do not make fun of those who are infirm, fragile, handicapped, crippled, or mentally or emotionally disabled. These are all children of Obatalá, and his goodwill is needed in this sign.
- If orishas are in one's home, do not neglect them; treat each spirit well, praying daily and tending their shrines.
- Avoid arguments and wars with Shangó's children, for he will destroy the one who tries to harm his chosen.
- Do not consume alcohol, intoxicants, white beans, sweet potatoes, or gritty fruits. Entertain no vices.

## The Eboses of Ejila Ofún

When Ejila Ofún opens on the mat, the diviner must consider a variety of offerings, sacrifices, and eboses.

- If the client lacks either the elekes or the warriors, he must receive them immediately so that he is under the orishas' full protection. Once Elegguá is in his home, the client should give him a ñame to eat. Soon, it may begin to grow a vine; however, the client must not allow this vine to grow longer than the client is tall. From this moment on, ñame is one of this person's food taboos—he may not consume it. After giving a ñame to Elegguá, the client must give all the warriors saraeko, made from cornmeal, water, and honey, in a gourd. The gourd remains with them overnight. Once these eboses are complete, the client must tend Elegguá well, living by making ebó to him constantly.
- If this person already has the elekes and warriors, he must strengthen and refresh the elekes with omiero and offer sacrifice to the warriors; with this ebó, they will help bring the client through the severity of the letter.
- In addition, the client's godparent might want to give him the elekes of the orishas to whom he has to make ebó and the elekes of Ogún and Ochosi so he might be protected by them on a daily basis. The key to averting disaster in this odu is to prescribe everything possible under its influence.
- As soon as possible, the client should have a rogación to strengthen the orí. Unless the oracle dictates otherwise, this ebó should be done at the feet of Obatalá so the client is always under his protection.

After considering all these options, the diviner has his first chance to close the oracle. If it remains open, he should continue working with the following list of eboses. One or more might be necessary for the client's evolution.

- Before attempting to mark any other eboses, the diviner should now prescribe that the client clean his house thoroughly, putting all empty bottles and containers in the trash and removing them immediately from his home. Bad spirits and energies can hide in these things. The client must dress in white every day for the next twelve days, and thereafter he should dress in white often. Over the next twenty-eight days, the client should take many spiritual baths with the plant known as prodigiosa. The leaves of this plant should be ripped and shredded into cool, fresh water and allowed to soak overnight. The next evening, the client should draw a tub of warm water; while standing in the bathtub, he should pour the herbal waters over himself from the shoulders down. He should then lie back and relax in this mixture.
- If this sign has come in either ano or ikú and will not close, the client must feed the earth, Orisha Oko, and Yewá. This will save him from death.
- Obatalá can stand up in this letter to claim ebó. To see what he might require, the diviner should consider asking, "Ebó elese Obatalá?" If the answer is yes, he uses the diloggún to mark the appropriate offering.
- If the client is an initiate who has opened in a severe osogbo, Shangó might need four legs and an itá. The guardian orisha might need this as well. The diviner should attempt to mark this ebó with the shells. The day of itá, a huge feast should be prepared from the animals and fed to as many people as possible; the more who are fed, the greater the iré from this ebó.
- If the client is an aborisha or an initiate, he may need to receive Iroko; the diviner should ask, "Koshé Iroko?" If the client already has this orisha, the diviner should mark eboses to him to ensure this orisha's goodwill.*

If these considerations are not sufficient to close the odu, the diviner turns to the eboses of the parent odu, Ejila Shebora (see page 581). Something there is needed for this client's evolution.

## The Eleventh Composite Odu of Ejila Shebora, Ejila Owani (12-11)

### The Proverbs of Ejila Owani

- You are ungrateful and full of mistrust.

*If the client is an aleyo and the diviner exhausts the options for eboses under the parent odu, the diviner may then question the reception of Iroko.

- The bad you have made is now on top of you.
- A united family is a strong family, so unite your family.

## The Message of Ejila Owani

When the initial cast of twelve mouths, Ejila Shebora, precedes a second cast of eleven mouths, Owani, the odu Ejila Owani is open on the mat. A variety of rituals and eboses must be done to alleviate the spiritual strain brought by this pattern. While the exact nature of this varies from ilé ocha to ilé ocha, all are based on the following set of rituals. First, it is assumed that when twelve mouths presented themselves on the mat, the diviner cooled the odu in a jícara of water and threw its heat outdoors. Once done, the preparation of saraeko is necessary. In iré, the diviner prepares saraeko from water, honey, and cornmeal. He gives this simple mixture to Elegguá as ebó and, the next morning, throws it to the street. In osogbo, the diviner makes two bowls of saraeko—one for Elegguá and one for Shangó. He prepares Elegguá's saraeko using water, honey, cornmeal, epó, jutía, and smoked fish and gives it to him immediately. He then prepares Shangó's saraeko using water, honey, cornmeal, and a prodigiosa leaf. After presenting the saraeko to Shangó, the diviner heats a piece of metal until it is red hot and then submerses it in the liquid, saying, "It is better to drown than to burn." The diviner then dips his finger in the saraeko and marks an equal-armed cross on the roof of his mouth; he encourages everyone present for this reading to do the same, saying the same words.

When this odu opens, the diviner says, "Maferefún Elegguá! Maferefún Shangó!" While Ejila Shebora is Shangó's odu, Elegguá rules Owani, and here he comes before all other orishas. Both demand equal time and equal respect. Elegguá tells this person that while there are many inherent osogbos in his life right now (even if this letter comes in a type of iré, it brings much osogbo), if the client respects him and treats him well, he will evolve over all that hinders him. In the meantime, there will be grief, economic devolution, and perhaps sickness. Yet all these can be overcome with Eshu's goodwill. The client should placate him frequently with adimú, especially cool fruits so that Elegguá is calm. Instead of rum, the client should give him cool white wine (unsalted). If the diviner believes this client's Eshu is too heated and active, an offering of grated coconut sprinkled over his stone will cool him down a bit. The client must also pamper Shangó with unsolicited ebó, something that the client can give with his own two hands under supervision from either his godparent or the diviner. This will ensure the orisha's goodwill.

Of all things that can be said in this sign, perhaps the greatest hindrance to this person's personal evolution is his own strong character. There is nothing wrong with strength, but this person is so hardheaded that all good advice falls on deaf ears. There is little under heaven or on the earth that can sway him from his chosen path, barring sickness and death; however, if sickness or death is needed to put the client on his proper path, that is exactly what the orishas will send his way. Shangó tells this person to open his ears and to listen well to these words, for he speaks only once. After that, he will be moved to act against the client's erring ways. If Shangó sends sickness, it may strike not the client but someone in his own family; the severity of this will depend on the afflicted one's personal constitution. If the letter opens in either ano or ikú, the diviner should advise the client to spend as much time as possible with his family, especially his father and all elder male relatives, for one of them could become seriously ill. Let there be no regrets—the client should say what must be said and do what must be done, now.

In addition, the diviner should explore the following points with the client:

- The client is lazy and always finds himself in dire straits; the orishas say that no amount of ebó will improve this person's life until he begins to work hard. Before the energy of this odu has passed, he will work hard!
- There may be problems occurring in the muscles and bones of the client's body; if pain develops in these areas, he should see a physician as soon as possible.
- The client has a tendency to become romantically

involved with more than one person or to begin one relationship before the existing one has ended. This tendency must cease now.

- This letter brings a variety of tragedies, revolutions, intrigues, and treason to the client's life. Many of these things are deserved, brought about by the client's own actions. He must account for what he has done before the orishas and commit to never doing them again. Only in this way will they help him.

## The Prohibitions of Ejila Owani

- The color red is taboo in one's home, food, and clothing. Incorporate white into one's life as much as possible, especially one's clothes.
- Do not become entangled in lies; this client is one whose life could become caught up in lies until all that he is, says, and does becomes a lie.
- Be careful of fires and untended sources of flame at home. Never leave burning candles unattended. Do not smoke in the bedroom, or in any other place in which one might fall asleep.
- Neither argue nor fight; never raise the fists in anger.

## The Eboses of Ejila Owani

When Ejila Owani opens in osogbo, it demands that everyone in the diviner's house (all those present for the reading as well as every other person in the home) perform an ebó to Elegguá at the conclusion of the reading. The diviner should fill three small brown paper bags with three pennies each, toasted corn, jutía, smoked fish, and epó. In order, the diviner, the client, and then everyone else, in order of eldest to youngest, use these bags to cleanse themselves before Elegguá. The bags remain with Elegguá overnight. If any food is or was cooked in the diviner's house that day (up until midnight), part of what remains must go to Elegguá. The diviner must encourage the client to leave once these eboses are complete. He should pour copious amounts of fresh water outside the front door once the client is gone, and also after each person who was present during this reading leaves. The next morning, the diviner takes all the eboses, including the saraeko prepared for Elegguá and Shangó at the beginning of the reading, to the street with the words "Eshu batie sode." There, at the street, the diviner uses obí to see if Eshu is happy or if he requires another ebó. Make the eboses marked with the coconuts immediately.

Having explained the cleansing ceremony to everyone present for the reading, the diviner now prescribes and explains the eboses that the client will have to fulfill.

- No matter how many eboses he offers to the orishas, the client's life will remain difficult due to an egun that likes to make him work for what he gets. This spirit must be placated so that it interferes no more, and the diviner should mark what it would take to keep this egun from being so troublesome.
- After the egun is placated, the client should tend to Babaluaiye. The diviner must mark what this orisha requires. In severe cases of osogbo, the client will have to receive him.
- Elegguá should be fed three baby chicks at a crossroads so that all the roads in this client's life are opened.
- This odu mandates the following ebó: The client should dress in red after he goes home and walk out into the street, calling as much attention to himself as possible. Immediately afterward, he should go home, dress all in white, and then head back out, walking the same path he walked before but now in silence. This is done so that his enemies will always be looking for the one who is dressed in red; they will never find him. From this moment on, the client may never again wear red.
- Many of the tragedies in this sign can be avoided by working with Elegguá and Ochosi. The diviner should see if they need ebó, asking, "Ebó elese Elegguá?" and "Ebó elese Ochosi?" If the answer is yes, he uses the diloggún to mark the appropriate offering.

At this point, the diviner has his first chance to close the oracle. If it remains open, the client may need to receive Ochosi. The diviner should ask, "Koshé Ochosi?"

If these considerations are not enough to close the odu, the diviner turns to the eboses of the parent odu, Ejila Shebora (see page 581). Something there is necessary for the client's evolution.

## The Twelfth Composite Odu of Ejila Shebora, Ejila Meji (12-12)

### The Proverbs of Ejila Meji

- During times of war, a soldier will not sleep.
- Cleanse yourself, then you can cleanse others.
- In your home, you must govern yourself like a king.

### The Message of Ejila Meji

When a casting of twelve mouths repeats itself, the odu Ejila Meji is open on the mat. This is a powerful sign, the most awesome of all found in this family of odu; when it opens, it demands recognition. Immediately, before determining the qualities of iré or osogbo, the diviner uses the tips of his right fingers to touch the earth and then his heart, saying, "Ilé re o!" This gesture calls for the blessings of the earth and the safety that is hers to give. Next he pays homage to Babaluaiye, Obatalá, Ochumare, Ogún, Shangó, Yemayá, and the Ibeyi, saying to each, "Maferefún!" All these spirits may speak or claim ebó before the session closes. In this odu Babaluaiye deserves special reverence, for it is here that his diseases strike unbidden and at random, and it is here that he can cure all he causes. If the client has not yet had a bajado, Babaluaiye is a strong contender for his head. While this reading is not the proper time for a diviner to impart such information (without a bajado one cannot be certain of which orisha claims a client's head), before the letter closes out Babaluaiye will demand many eboses.

This letter gives birth to many things. All things rotund and protuberant are born here; the sign alludes to pregnancy and the pregnant woman. In iré, conception is blessed, but in osogbo, the letter becomes the scourge of the expectant mother. Tumors, cancers, boils, carbuncles, and hernias all come from this letter's energy, and hence its connection with Babaluaiye. This pattern also controls and directs many forces on the face of the earth. Under the direction of Ofún Meji, Ejila Meji gave form to that existing in the void; it made the earth come together. Under Ejiogbe Meji's command, Ejila Meji caused the mountains to rise from flat lands (shocks, tremors, and tectonic changes in the earth's crust are under this letter's command). Even the buttocks are controlled by this letter. (But it does not control the anus; that is created and controlled by Odí Meji.)

In addition, the diviner should keep the following in mind when Ejila Meji opens on the mat:

- In all orientations of this odu, the diviner must work through the reading slowly and carefully to help his client evolve. All the meanings and prohibitions of the parent odu, Ejila Shebora, apply to the one who has come to the mat. Even if the sign opens in iré, the diviner should detail all the osogbos this letter can bring. In this way will the client avoid much of its danger.
- This is one of the signs in the diloggún referring to the *iyamí* (the witches) and the punishments they bring. Diarrhea is their scourge. Any illness that causes loose bowels is serious under this odu's influence; the client must see a physician immediately. This is also a letter of heart attacks, HIV infection, and other serious illnesses such as tumors, boils, and hernias. The client must be on guard against these things.

### The Prohibitions of Ejila Meji

- When this odu opens in an osogbo, conception is forbidden for twenty-one to twenty-eight days; now is not the time to bring new life into the world. If this letter opens during a bajado or itá, before planning pregnancy the client must come to the orishas to make ebó. This is the only way to ensure the birth of a healthy child for those who are born of this sign.
- Do not lift heavy objects alone. Try not to lift at all if possible. Herniation of the bowels and vertebrae is possible.

- Unless one receives Babaluaiye, one may never have a dog as a pet. Even then, one must pamper and spoil the animal or risk this orisha's wrath. Note that if one already has a dog, the immediate reception of this spirit is necessary.
- When this letter falls in itá for a child of Oshún in Elegguá, Shangó, or the iyawó's head, this person can never initiate a child of Shangó.
- When this letter falls for a child of Shangó in Elegguá, Oshún, or the iyawó's head, this person can never initiate a child of Oshún.
- Eboses made with okra, papaya, melon, and calabaza can be one's salvation in this odu. Save these items for ebó; do not eat them.

## The Eboses of Ejila Meji

When Ejila Meji opens on the mat, two eboses are mandatory regardless of the letter's orientation.

- First, this is a sign of constant cleansing, and if the client hopes to evolve, he must cleanse himself spiritually, on a daily basis if possible. This odu has a special bath made with flor de agua (its aché is strong here) and eight herbs of Obatalá. The diviner should make enough liquid to administer eight baths; the client takes these consecutively on eight nights, dressing in white after each.
- All who come in this sign must have the elekes. In addition to the necklaces of Yemayá, Oshún, Shangó, and Obatalá, the client should have the eleke of Babaluaiye. Every day until the influence of this odu passes, the client wears the beads of Obatalá and Babaluaiye; these two orishas will keep him from harm.

Having made these prescriptions, the diviner now has his first chance to close the odu. If it remains open, he must also investigate the following:

- The Ibeyi known as Taewó and Kaindé (the twins) are an essential part of this letter's aché. If the client does not have the Ibeyi, he must receive them. If he has them, the diviner must determine if they require ebó, asking, "Ebó elese los Ibeyi?" If the answer is yes, he uses the diloggún to mark the appropriate offering. Even if the twins demand nothing, the client should still offer them a token adimú. The blessings that these two orishas can bring in Ejila Meji are vast.
- Babaluaiye, Shangó, Yemayá, and Ogún can require ebó from the client. To see if any of these orishas will take an offering or a sacrifice, the diviner asks, "Ebó elese [orisha's name]?" If the answer is yes, he uses the diloggún to mark the appropriate offering. The client must fulfill what these spirits demand immediately. Note that if Ogún will not take ebó, the client should offer an adimú of cool fruits to placate him. If this orisha remains hot, the client will be injured by metal.
- The client might need to receive Babaluaiye to overcome this letter's osogbo. The diviner should ask, "Koshé Babaluaiye?" If the diloggún marks his reception, the client must make preparations for this ceremony immediately.

If these considerations are not enough to close the odu for an aleyo or an aborisha, the diviner must turn to the eboses of the parent odu, Ejila Shebora (see page 581). Something there is needed for this client's evolution.

If the client is an initiate, he has one final possibility: Ochumare's reception. The diviner asks, "Koshé Ochumare?" If the shells mark this as ebó, the client must begin preparations for this ceremony immediately. If Ochumare's reception is not marked, or if it is marked but the letter remains open, the diviner must turn to the eboses of the parent odu, Ejila Shebora.

## Closing the Reading: Further Eboses of the Parent Odu, Ejila Shebora

Having exhausted the options of larishe and ebó in the composite odu, the diviner turns to the parent odu to find a method of closure. This letter, Ejila Shebora, contains within itself many offerings and rituals to placate both the letter and the orishas that are speaking in it. The eboses for this pattern are as follows:

- At this point, the letter indicates that the client is in desperate need of a rogación at Obatalá's feet. During the rogación, the diviner should feed the client's orí two white pigeons or white doves. Immediately after the rogación, the client should offer Obatalá an adimú. The diviner should mark the ebó to be given now, with the shells, before attempting closure of the oracle.
- If this will not close the letter, the diviner asks, "Ebó elese Shangó?" If the answer is yes, the diviner should make a new saraeko for Shangó every day for six days, with the client present each time. For each batch of saraeko, the client should dip his finger in the saraeko and then use that finger to mark a cross on the roof of his mouth, saying, "It is better to drown than to burn." Each time he gives the new saraeko to Shangó, the diviner should remove the old saraeko and use obí to determine how Shangó wants it discarded. If the client does not discipline himself for this daily routine, the diviner must still make the ebó so that he comes to no harm. After prescribing this ebó to placate Shangó, the diviner should check to see if he needs anything else. Also, the client must wears Shangó's eleke every day.
- The diviner should attempt to mark ebó to Oshún, asking, "Ebó elese Oshún?" If the answer is yes, he should use the diloggún to mark the required ebó. Oshún will bring money and economic evolution to this client. Even if Oshún demands no ebó in this sign, the client should give her frequent adimú so that he is assured of this orisha's goodwill.
- To calm spiritual heat and violence, the client should make an ebó to Obatalá and then wear his necklace every day. The diviner should explain the things this orisha likes as adimú, letting the client decide what he will give the spirit.
- If the client has come for advice about his projects, career, or personal goals, Shangó is demanding sacrifice so that all will come out well. The diviner should mark what is needed, and once the ebó is fulfilled, the client should take many spiritual baths with infusions of Shangó's herbs. If he fulfills this ebó, his projects will come out well.
- If the osogbo that fell forebodes wars and injuries, the diviner should pack a baseball bat with some of Shangó's herbs, cover it with red and white beads, wash it in omiero, and feed it with Shangó. He should leave the bat with the orisha so he can defend the client from harm.
- If any of the warriors stand up during the reading in Ejila Shebora, the diviner must now prescribe the sacrifice of two roosters to them; give Elegguá some smoked fish and jutía.

If these eboses are not enough to close the oracle, then the client has further issues pending with the orishas who speak in this sign; to solve these issues, eboses can range from the simple reception of an eleke, to an ebó, to the reception of the orisha. The diviner should progress with this line of questioning slowly, not marking anything more than what is truly needed in the odu. If the diviner has come this far, however, and the letter will not close, he could have made some mistake in the process of divination, and he should call in an elder for advice on how to handle the reading in Ejila Shebora now.

When Ejila Shebora refuses closure for an initiate, the diviner has a few more eboses to consider.

- To Shangó, one or more of the following eboses is necessary: a ram, jutía, a turtle, two roosters, amalá, two large platters of black-eyed peas, twelve young ears of corn, and twelve turtle shells. Note that if Shangó requires a four-legged animal, an oriaté must give the ebó, and additional eboses must be prepared with this offering. First, the oriaté opens the animals, preparing the aché for Shangó. The day after the sacrifice, the client hosts a party or tambor in honor of the orisha, and the oriaté must preside over this as well. On the third day after the initial sacrifice, the client sits for itá with Shangó; he has much to say.
- To Obatalá, an offering of one or more of the

following might be required: an amalá made with honey and milk (no epó), a white rooster, two white pigeons, white cloth, and a large array of cool fruits.

- To the warriors, one or more of the following eboses might be necessary: a goat, two roosters, four pigeons, an arrow, three arrows, and twelve young ears of sweet corn. Note that if either Elegguá or Ogún requires a goat of the client, an oriaté must perform this ceremony; itá is required by the orisha. Also, if the client does not have the diloggún of Ogún, the reception of this is marked as well. One cannot have itá with Ogún if Ogún cannot speak.

After these options are exhausted, some diviners turn to the eboses listed for the omo odu as a parent odu. For example, in a casting of Ejila Owani (12-11), the diviner now turns to the eboses of the parent odu Owani for closure. If, however, the reading has progressed this far and Ejila Shebora will not close out, there could be some error or oversight on the diviner's part. He should call in an experienced elder for advice.

# APPENDIX

## THE ODU BEYOND EJILA SHEBORA

Humans fear the unknown; it sends us all to the orishas for divination. Coming for help, there is only disappointment, perhaps vulnerability, when one of the four "forbidden" odu opens and the client is told the orishas have nothing to say through the diloggún. Many forget that the diviner must also have a diviner, just as the doctor has his own physician. In time, all must seek out Ifá, even the oriaté. Our own orishas have sought Orúnmila's help when their own lives seemed futile. While those who have ocha know these things, while the italero knows these things, while the oriaté knows these things, the uninitiated does not. To be given back a derecho when one has come for help and told "Orisha sends you to Ifá; they cannot speak on your problems here" can be frustrating. Frightening. The odu beyond Ejila Shebora do not always signal disaster for the client, although some diviners will say otherwise. These signs do bring blessings. They do have iré. They have beauty, light, and abundance for us all. In the diloggún, however, they have no meaning beyond "Go to Orúnmila," and no existence beyond a shadowing of odu Ifá. These letters have aché, aché that can be explored only by Orúnmila's priests.

Having opened the orisha's diloggún in one of these letters (Metanla, Merinla, Marunla, and Merindilogún), the diviner must now follow a specific pattern for ending the reading. Immediately, the session is considered closed; the orisha consulted has declared that this person's evolution will come through Ifá. Orúnmila has issues to discuss, and only the Babalawo has the right to work with him. The shells are gathered together and put into the gourd of cool water to refresh them. Next, the youngest child, initiate, or a virgin (someone who is already in the diviner's house) is called to take the gourd to the front door. There, the water is flung out as far into the street as possible while not allowing any of the shells to fly out. The shells are then brought back to the diviner, who blows on them and sets the diloggún back on the covered plate to dry. The Spirit has been dismissed. The derecho is then returned to the client; no work was done, so no charge can be incurred. Odu's one piece of advice is delivered: "Orisha says you must go to Orúnmila; he has issues to discuss with you, and it is through Ifá that your current life situation must be assessed." No fear, worry, or dismay should be encouraged. No osogbo or evil may be implied.

The only imminent danger that should be assumed when one of these signs falls is upon the diviner; until he checks himself with the diloggún of Elegguá, he should not read for any other client that day. Once he is alone, he should divine to make sure that the orishas have not delivered a warning for him. Many will not open the diloggún for this; instead, using the oracle obí, they will ask Elegguá if all is well. If not, ebó must be marked immediately, and performed as soon as possible to clear the sign from the diviner's home. If Eleggúa will not speak or mark ebó through obí, the italero has no choice but to open his diloggún for a session.

If the client has come to the oracle for a serious, life-threatening condition, or if the diviner's aché tells him this person is in danger, there is ebó to relieve the assumed osogbo until Ifá is consulted. A rogación should be given at the feet of that person's orisha. If the patron is not known, do the work at Obatalá's shrine; his calming influence can bring coolness to all the odu. Within twenty-four hours, the client should come back to the diviner dressed in old black clothing; he must come with a derecho, wrapped in brown paper, on a white plate with two coconuts and two white candles. A complete change of white clothing should be brought as well: undershirt, underpants, shoes, long-sleeved shirt, pants, and a white cloth to cover the top of the head. The black clothing is to be cut off the client, not merely removed, after the initial rogación is given. All should be put into a brown bag that is then sealed. The client must dress in white and have fresh coconut, cocoa butter, and efun put back on the head, which is then wrapped first in cotton and then with the white cloth. The next morning, all these things on the head are added to the brown bag, and they are left to rot by a river at the soggiest ground that can be found.

For those who insist on knowing what things these odu can foreshadow, I have provided the following lists of meanings. They are not exhaustive; and although they will not provide enough material to provide a proficient reading, they will give the student of odu an idea of what these signs can bring.

## Metanla— Thirteen Mouths on the Mat

- Take the water from the river, you destroy the home of fish.
- Only strength can destroy evil.
- The earth cannot fall ill.
- The stone will not die.
- It pays to stoop to conquer.

This odu can, and often does, bring disaster to the client when it opens in Ifá; however, because the italero has not the right to read this sign, he has not the right to impress this information upon the client. Metanla is the first letter owned by Asohano; it is his odu. It refers to the hot, African winds that fly the entire globe bringing infectious disease and death to the very young, the very old, and the very weak. Sickness, however, has its own aché and the implication of destruction in this sign goes beyond the rotting of flesh. Anything weak or useless in the client's life can be destroyed, leaving room for evolution and spiritual/material progress. This is the iré of the sign. Because Metanla can be read by the oriaté (who has been given Ogún's knife and many years of intimate instruction with other oriatés and Babalawos) and because it is not only so volatile, but also close to Ejila Shebora (and giving birth to Owani), many novice italeros do attempt to continue a session in Metanla, pulling up a composite odu to finish the sign. But this is not wise; the odu must be closed using the ritual described in the beginning of this appendix, and the derecho must be returned to the client. It is very important that the rogación previously mentioned is done; however, there are a few alterations. It is to be done before Babaluaiye's shrine, and the head should be wrapped in sackcloth before it is wrapped in white. To the bag must be added three items: jutía, red palm oil, and three eggs that have been rubbed with red palm oil and sprayed with rum and cigar smoke. The morning after the rogacíon, seventeen cents should be added, and the client should be cleansed with the contents of the bag.

There are many issues that can be addressed in this letter. First, those who are building homes will find that their construction is delayed; even if the entire edifice has been going on schedule, unforeseen delays will come. The client should now have a backup plan in case he is desperate to move. Those who are planning to move, but have not yet made commitments to move, should stop. Now is not a good time to be changing residences. Anyone involved in the construction industry should be careful; there is danger of accidents that would prevent this person's ability to work. Hospital administrators should not begin construction on their buildings now, and those who work in areas under construction must be cautious at all times. There is danger of falling or being fallen on. Be careful of hot and cold drafts; avoid the wind. Stay away from others who are sick, if possible. Disease can be found in old buildings that are undergoing renovation; avoid these as well.

Those who are wealthy or in positions of power also must exercise caution now. The danger in this sign is that those who are subservient will rise; the master will fall. Trust no one with secrets, and do not gossip about coworkers. Watch the back at all times. Those who are lower on corporate ladders are jealous and vile, and they will stop at nothing to get ahead. Many will lie to the boss. Many will steal from the boss. Many will not do a good job. The boss must stay on top of this, for in the end it is he who will be held accountable.

Parents must watch over children carefully. If they become sick, take them to the doctor immediately. Do not follow home remedies, for these will not be effective. Do not give the children over-the-counter medicine. Take them to a physician who can treat their illnesses effectively before something small becomes something big. If the client has an even number of children, sacrifice should be made now so that half of them will not die before their time. A woman has or will suffer the same number of miscarriages, if not more, than she has living children. Her womb is not as strong as she believes it to be. An infertile woman can become pregnant under this odu; however, the child born must one day be initiated as a priest or he will die. Parents must live by making ebó for their children, praying for their safety and well-being lest they grow up to be servants and not masters. Those who are born under this odu will grow up to be brewers, chemists, mixers of elements, dyers; they will be great masters only if ebó is made. It is in this sign that Orúnmila learned all the secrets of prosperity, and the children of Metanla can do the same.

This sign flags travels, wanderings, and goals set with no plan on how to attain them. One day, this person might leave the country for a time, traveling to far-off places that others only dream of. Opening in this sign, the client could have a total of three spouses over the course of one lifetime. If the current marriage is strong, there will be two affairs, and the same goes for the spouse.

## Merinla—<br>Fourteen Mouths on the Mat

- Although you lost the battle, you have won the war.
- Hot winds bring disease.
- Things come suddenly; you will miss your opportunities.

Within this letter, one learns the story of how the lamp received his own servant to watch over him and tend him for the rest of his life. Before the lamp was born, there was only a string of cotton and a vial of oil; the two of them were close, and went to the diviner (awó) to learn how they could prosper together all their days. Merinla was the sign that opened, and the awó told the two companions that the oracle declared they should live together as one for life. Immediately, a rooster and a he-goat were sacrificed to Elegguá. After eating his ebó, Elegguá put the cotton into the vial of oil and lit them both with the fire from his home. He sent the two who were now one to earth, naming them "lamp." Soon, humans saw that the lamp was good: It gave them light, and it gave them fire to cook their meals. Lamp could not take care of himself, however, so soon humans were appointed in each household to tend the fire. Thus did the cotton and the thread live all their days together as one, and they acquired mortal servants to tend them eternally. Those who receive this sign can have the same blessings of the lamp—eternal love and gratitude, service and tending from others—if ebó is made and the client spends his time offering useful service to his peers.

Merinla also tells the story of the cat. Before she came to earth, she went for divination; cat wished to prosper in life, to become a wild and vicious hunter whose prey would never escape. In heaven, she was soft, fluffy, and weak. Being an animal who would have to survive on her own wits, she needed help. Ebó was marked for her: a pigeon to strengthen the head, and a knife, scissors, and rooster to Eleggua. Cat made her ebó and set off for earth. When she arrived, she discovered that she was cunning, and stealthy; her mind was brilliant and she was blessed with the gift of tracking game. From her paws grew long, sharp claws, and anything she trapped was helpless in their grip. Her eyes were razor sharp, able to see in darkness and reflective of even the faintest light so that any animal who gazed at her stare was hypnotized, unable to move. She prospered because she made ebó. Under the influence of this odu, even the weak can become strong, the dull razor sharp, and the unlucky lucky. All that is needed are goals, determination, and ebó. Success can be attained.

Sacrifice to Eleggua is one of the keys to success under this sign; with his goodwill, almost any obstacle can be overcome, and success in moderate degrees can be obtained even when the world seems to have turned against the client. Warn this person that he must strive to become the master and not the servant, yet he must become master by offering those beneath him the use of his time, skills, and talents. When Merinla comes out in a reading for a man, it foreshadows the arrival of a new romantic interest, a woman who will be loyal and devoted to him all the days of his life. When his health is bad, she will nurture him; when he is tired and weak, she will watch over him. The man will die before his wife, and she will serve him even unto death. This loyalty will not come without cost. The man must build his life around her; she is to be his light, his warmth, his best friend, and his only lover. To betray her even once would be to send her away forever. The same advice should be told to the woman; however, she must still be attentive to all her man's needs lest he stray. To let him stray once would be to lose him forever.

Under this letter, the client must live his life by making ebó, placating and tending the orishas so all his affairs will come out well. Great problems will come, insurmountable odds that seem unreachable; yet ebó will make all things manageable. Life will be difficult; this person will live among powerful enemies who try to destroy him, but in the end their efforts will be for naught. He will rise above all adversity.

## Marunla—Fifteen Mouths on the Mat

- A good general does not send his best soldiers into battle.
- Strong people work to make others strong.
- Divine shrines will always be shrouded in mystery.
- My father told me to carry the bag of success on my neck, and so I will not surrender this bag of prosperity to anyone.

Under this odu, the client has many gifts; he also has many curses. There are wars and battles being fought, many he is not aware of. While strength is this person's best asset, the sign warns that he should not use all his strength at once. Save "heavy artillery" for the final battles of conquest. Act as if in a war: Do not send the strongest soldiers into the first battles. Rather, defend oneself with the weaker weapons in the arsenal. Those who are trying to destroy this person will assume his weakness to be his strength. Spend time trying to strengthen the weakest parts of one's character, nurturing unused or atrophied talents in the fight to achieve greatness. Once those are exhausted, go into battle with the heaviest artillery you have. Thus will success be attained in all things.

It is very important that this client go to the babalawos to sit with Ifá as soon as possible. Marunla promises great things for this person if he worships Orúnmila, making ebó to him through his priests. If mano de Orúnmila or kofá is not had, it would be wise to receive it. Orúnmila has great things in store for this person. Ask if the one at the mat is the third child in the family. If so, he is the reincarnation of the mother's previous miscarriage, or of a child that died soon after birth. He is lucky to have lived this long, and he must make ebó soon so that his life continues. The children of this third child could be in danger as well, and readings must be done for each to mark ebó and ensure that they live full lives themselves. A woman who has just had a miscarriage will soon be pregnant again; the soul of that lost child wants to return. Before her womb dries up, she will have at least three children. She must make ebó to Orúnmila after the third child arrives.

## Merindilogún—Sixteen Mouths on the Mat

- The person you met once you will meet again, and you will meet him as an elder.
- Patience brings great rewards.
- A single holy word does more good than a load of profane speeches.
- Trouble comes on the day of sleeping.

Merindilogún (also known as Etura, Otura) is perhaps the most powerful of these four odu. The *kasan* is its symbol, a billowing shirt worn by the Yoruba's most influential political advisers. Saved for only the highest-ranking officials, it denotes one who has no power of his own, no rule to hold sway, yet has the innate qualities to influence those who do have the power to change, to create. While there are many who would prefer to be king, sometimes it is better to be confidant to the king, to hold political clout rather than power. For while one cannot openly command the masses, there is satisfaction and safety behind another's authority.

Although the kasan is this letter's symbol, words are its power, spoken words enlivened by intelligent thought. Those under this sign's influence carry a spark within them that can ignite history's most potent flames; the course of world events can be changed. The extent of this sign's influence depends on the individual's position in life. Words have power, yes; but their power extends only as far as the speaker's audience, and it creates change only when the words reach the ears of those capable of making change. This is Merindilogún's iré: to have the vision, the ideals, and the intelligence to create change. This is also the letter's osogbo: to lack an audience or listener who can create change. It is the most frustrating of signs.

The voice of this odu is responsible for the creation and dissolution of our world's many religions: Christianity and Islam both have roots deep within this sign. Both are powerful faiths that have brought many changes to this world. They have done much good. They have created much evil. Both have frustrating pasts in which powerful orators struggled for an audience, and when those audiences were found, they were moved to go forth, conquer, convert, and crusade for their religious causes. Anyone influenced by this letter can do the same, but on varying levels. Children born to Merindilogún often grow up to become orators, teachers, politicians, lawyers, judges, and even presidents. Those who choose a profession not based on politics or teaching but go the route of other, more mundane professions easily rise the corporate ladder to command their own empire. It is the stuff that dreams are made of.

Opening on the mat in sixteen mouths, the orisha consulted has much to say to this client. First, to rise beyond life's tragedies, this is one who must live his life by making ebó; the orishas must be consulted in all things if the client is to evolve. Social, political, and economic well-being all depend on this. Under Merindilogún, one can either rise to the heights of heaven or crash to the depths of earth. Following the advice of this odu ensures that others will always flock as subservient to this person. One's family will grow large in this generation and beyond; someday, this client's descendants can number in the thousands. Unfortunately, some of those born to this generation will have darkness within them. One will definitely be a "bad seed" and will bring much dismay to the family. He will be filled with greed, envy, and avarice. If the client is expecting a child now, this is the one marked for the osogbo. If the client is not currently expecting but is planning another child in the future, that will be the one. Ebó made will save him from this. This letter also flags danger to the client's mother; if she is still alive, she may soon die from malnutrition and starvation. Much attention should be paid to her, and she must go immediately to the doctor if she falls ill. Sacrifice should be made to her head if she is alive, and if she is not in this religion, the sacrifice must be done to the client in her name.

Merindilogún is the home of unfulfilled dreams. The client has many of these; none will come to pass unless he works closely with Elegguá. For some reason, this orisha is upset in this letter. The diviner must speak frankly with the client to determine the reason for this, and he must then work the diloggún until a sacrifice pleasing to the orisha can be found. Once Elegguá's anger is resolved, this person's luck will change and slowly he will climb socially and economically. Things that were previously denied to him will become his. Finally, this letter may not close out unless the client resolves to receive Ifá. It is in this odu that Orúnmila brought much wealth to the world, and once he is brought into this person's life, the client's world will become prosperous.

# GLOSSARY

Lucumí, and the original Yoruba from which it evolved, is a tonal language, like Chinese. Because the Afro-Cubans had neither the time nor the opportunity for formal education during slavery, many of these words have no consistent spelling. While I have tried to keep my own spellings consistent throughout my work, my spellings will differ from those of other authors in the field. However, the pronunciation of the words will be similar. For any Lucumí or Spanish term that does not have an accent mark, the proper emphasis goes on the second-to-last syllable in the word. To facilitate proper pronunciation, I have included the appropriate accent for all words that vary from this pattern. Vowel sounds for all non-English words will approximate those of the Spanish language.

Keep in mind the following points when pronouncing words:

- The *ch* sound is used in Lucumí and Spanish words; these languages have no sh sound.
- The ñ character (*enye* sound) is used only in Spanish words, and not in Lucumí words.
- The *y* sound in Spanish has a slight edge to it, so that it sounds more like the English and Yoruba *j.* I have used *j* here whenever possible.

Also note that in each glossary entry one or more words may be italicized. The italicization of a word indicates that it can be found in the glossary as well.

**abiku:** Spirits who plague mothers by dying before their time.

**aborisha:** One who worships the *orishas* of the religion *Santería;* an aborisha has taken at least the initiations of the *elekes* and *warriors.*

**abure:** A sibling of blood or of *ocha.*

**aché:** A very dynamic universal force; the spiritual power of the universe. It has many meanings, among which are grace, life, fate, power, talent, and wisdom; the meaning intended depends on its usage in speech. Most *santeros* will agree that life is aché, and aché is life.

**Achotele:** The four colors of *Ósun*—white, yellow, blue, and red.

**adimú:** Any type of offering that does not include the sacrifice of an animal. Adimú is usually prescribed during a session with the *diloggún.*

**Afra:** An *avatar* of *Elegguá* who works specifically with the *orisha Babaluaiye.*

**Aganyú:** The *orisha* of volcanoes, born from *Oroina,* the molten center of the earth. He is also the father of *Shangó.*

**agbán:** A special ceremony done during the reception of *Babaluaiye, Orisha Oko,* or *Olokun* or as a cleansing before an *ebó* offered to one of the three orishas. It involves ritual cleansing with various types of foods and grains. At the end of each agbán, the *aché* of the *orisha* being received is passed from *godparent* to godchild.

**Ainá:** One of the seven *Ibeyi;* she is the fire of *Shangó.*

**Ajé Shaluga:** This *orisha* controls all aspects of luxury and wealth. Her normal guise is that of a beautiful woman, but when she wants to appear as a man, she does so. Often, she accompanies *Oshún* on her travels in the world.

**akoba:** A type of *osogbo* in which one's life in general is not good.

**Akoda:** The second disciple or *babalawo* of *Orúnmila.*

**aladimú:** A *Lucumí* contraction meaning any type of offering except a sacrifice. See *adimú.*

**aláfia:** A *Lucumí* word that translates into "peace" or "blessings"; it also denotes a letter in the African system of *obí* that means "coolness" when the response is positive. In the New World version of obí, aláfia brings blessings, peace, and coolness from the mighty *orisha Obatalá.*

**alaleyo:** A *Lucumí* contraction meaning "those who are outsiders to the faith."

**aleyo:** One who follows *Santería* but is not initiated as a *priest* or *priestess;* a noninitiate or an outsider.

**amalá:** A staple food of the *orisha Shangó;* it is normally made of okra and cornmeal, but other ingredients may be added.

**amalá-ilá:** One of many staple *Lucumí* dishes favored by *Shangó;* it is based upon *amalá* and includes among its ingredients onion, garlic, cumin, oregano, tomato sauce, red wine, okra, and *epó.*

**ancestral spirits:** Also known collectively as *egun;* they may include the practitioner's blood and spiritual ancestors. Spirit guides, *nfumbés,* Congolese spirits, Native American spirits, and other spirits of the dead are recognized in the religion *Santería,* but unless one is descended from them, they are not egun or ancestral spirits.

**ano:** A *Lucumí* word that means "illness" or "disease."

**apadí:** One of the eight *ibó* used in the divination system called *diloggún;* it is a piece of broken pottery, and it symbolizes loss, defeat, and marriage.

**ará onú:** The citizens of heaven; those spirits that rest with *Olódumare.*

**Arara:** An area in Dahomey, Africa, now known as Benin; it is the origin of *Naná Burukú* and her son, *Babaluaiye.*

**arayé:** Envy, ill will, arguments, evil tongues, and witchcraft.

**Asheda:** The first disciple and *babalawo* of *Orúnmila* on the earth.

**asiento:** See *ocha.*

**Asohano:** Another name for the *orisha Babaluaiye.*

**avatar:** Many *orishas,* including *Obatalá, Yemayá, Oshún, and Elegguá,* have different avatars, also known as paths, which could be thought of as different incarnations of the same spirit. Each avatar is related to one of an orisha's many incarnations on the earth (many orishas have spent mortal lives among humans). Only those incarnations of significant religious, historical, or political importance are remembered specifically and become avatars or paths of that orisha. One of the mysteries of the *ocha* is that when an *aleyo* is crowned (the *guardian orisha* is literally put on the head) and becomes a *iyawó,* he or she also, in some ways, becomes an avatar of the guardian orisha. Note that while many *ilé ocha* agree about the origins of most avatars, the subject itself is one of considerable debate.

**Ayao:** This *orisha* is the sister of *Oyá;* she is said to be the cyclone that touches the earth.

**ayé:** A *Lucumí* term that means "hardship." It is also a letter in the African system of *obí,* as well as one of the eight *ibó* used in the *diloggún.* As ibó, it denotes any type of elongated saltwater seashell.

**Baba Eji Ogbe:** See *Ejiogbe Meji.*

**babalawo:** An initiate of *Orúnmila.* A babalawo is always male because only men may enter Orúnmila's mysteries. Also known as "father of the secrets."

**Babaluaiye:** This *orisha* originates in the land of *Arara,* an area of Africa. He is the father of smallpox, disease, and afflictions of the skin.

**bajado:** *A divination* ritual done by an *oriaté* to determine a client's *guardian orisha.*

**Bañaní:** An orisha; this spirit is a sibling of Dada (some say Bañaní is female while others say male). This orisha is *Shango's crown* and brings physical, mental, and spiritual maturity to his children.

**batá:** A drumming festival held in honor of the *orishas;* also, the drums used at that festival.

**batea:** The wooden tureen in which *Shangó's* secrets are housed.

**batie sode:** A *Lucumí* phrase meaning "removes the negativity."

**Boromu:** An *orisha* who is one of *Odua's* companions and guardians. She is the younger sister of *Borosia.* While she lives deep in the forest, Boromu also exerts control over the ocean. Some say she is the ocean's currents. When angered, Boromu can cause a ship to be lost at sea. She can also take sailors home safely.

**Borosia:** An *orisha;* the older brother of *Boromu* and another of *Odua's* protectors. He guides the *orí* of the children of *Obatalá.* Unlike his younger sister, Borosia lives only on land and exerts no control over the ocean. Some, however, say he exerts influence over the wind.

**botánica:** A religious supply store; often found in Latin-American communities.

**bóveda:** An altar set up to honor and propitiate *egun.* Although it properly belongs to the practice known as *Espiritísmo,* the bóveda has been integrated into the practice of *Santería* because of the loss of the *egungun* cults in the New World. A bóveda can be set up to honor any spirit, even if that spirit is not one's own egun. Certain *odu* will dictate the creation of a bóveda as *ebó.*

**calabaza:** Gourds, pumpkins, or squashes. All are sacred to *Shangó* and *Oshún.*

**caracol:** The Spanish term for *cowrie* shell; it refers to the shells (caracoles) used in each *orisha's diloggún.*

**carga:** The secret ingredients packed into an *orisha's* physcial image to strengthen his or her *aché.*

**cascarilla:** A loosely packed soft chalk made from crushed eggshells.

**composite odu:** A pairing of *odu* that combines a *parent odu* with an *omo odu.* Each of the sixteen parent odu in the *diloggún* has sixteen composite odu; there are 256 composite odu in total.

**cowrie:** The type of shell that is used to create the *diloggún* of an *orisha.*

**crown:** See *guardian orisha.*

**crowning orisha:** See *guardian orisha.*

**Dada:** An *orisha;* the brother of *Shangó.*

**derecho:** The ritual fee paid to a *priest* or *priestess* for spiritual services.

**diloggún:** The system of *cowrie* divination by which a *priest* or *priestess* of *Santería* learns the will of the *orishas;* also, the eighteen or twenty-one cowrie shells that contain the soul of an orisha; also, the set of sixteen shells an *italero* casts to perform a *divination.* The exact meaning of the words depends on the context in which it is used.

**divination:** The act of uncovering the will of the *orishas,* the desires of *egun,* and the trends of the future. *Santería* employs three mains systems of divination: *obí, diloggún,* and *Ifá.*

**diviner:** One skilled in the art of *divination* who knows the secrets of *obí* and *diloggún.*

**ebó:** An offering made to an *orisha.*

**ebó keun edun keun:** A daily cleansing done before an *orisha's* shrine.

**ebó kere**: A set of spiritual cleansings.

**ebó misi:** A spiritual bath (in herbal waters).

**eborí:** A *Lucumí* contraction of two words: *ebó* (offering) and *orí* (head). The word is used to denote a blood offering to one's physical head and one's spiritual head (or consciousness).

**eboses:** The plural form of *ebó.* Although the *Yoruba* use "ebó" as both the plural and singular form, in Cuban *Santería* "eboses" has become accepted as the plural.

**eboshure:** An offering of anything edible. Normally, eboshure consists of fruits, grains, or vegetables, as opposed to cooked foods.

**efun:** A loosely packed, powdered chalk made from crushed eggshells. It is one of the eight *ibó* in the divination system known as the *diloggún.*

**égba:** A *Lucumí* term that means "paralysis."

**egun:** The many *ancestral spirits* related to one through one's blood relatives or one's spiritual relatives.

**egungun:** One who is possessed by *egun.* In Cuba, it often refers to the now-dead cult of egun—*priests* and *priestesses* who dealt only with the *ancestral spirits* and not the *orishas.*

**ejife:** The strongest response that one may receive in the oracle known as *obí;* it consists of two white coconut rinds and two black coconut rinds. In a divination session, it always signifies that the answer to the question asked is "yes, the world is in balance."

**Ejila Ejioko:** One of the sixteen *composite odu* found in the family of *Ejila Shebora;* it opens when a casting of twelve mouths (Ejila Shebora) is followed by a casting of two mouths *(Eji Oko).* This *odu* is also known as Ejila Oyeku and Ejila Yeku.

**Ejila Elleunle:** See *Ejila Ogbe.*

**Ejila Irosun:** One of the sixteen *composite odu* found in the family of *Ejila Shebora;* it opens when a casting of twelve mouths (Ejila Shebora) is followed by a casting of four mouths *(Irosun).*

**Ejila l'Ogbe:** See *Ejila Ogbe.*

**Ejila Meji:** One of the sixteen *composite odu* found in the family of *Ejila Shebora;* it opens when a casting of twelve mouths (Ejila Shebora) repeats itself.

**Ejila Obara:** One of the sixteen *composite odu* found in the family of *Ejila Shebora;* it opens when a casting of twelve mouths (Ejila Shebora) is followed by a casting of six mouths *(Obara).*

**Ejila Oché:** One of the sixteen *composite odu* found in the family of *Ejila Shebora;* it opens when a casting of twelve mouths (Ejila Shebora) is followed by a casting of five mouths *(Oché).*

**Ejila Odí:** One of the sixteen *composite odu* found in the family of *Ejila Shebora;* it opens when a casting of twelve mouths (Ejila Shebora) is followed by a casting of seven mouths *(Odí).*

**Ejila Ofún:** One of the sixteen *composite odu* found in the family of *Ejila Shebora;* it opens when a casting of twelve mouths (Ejila Shebora) is followed by a casting of ten mouths *(Ofún).*

**Ejila Ogbe:** One of the sixteen *composite odu* found in the family of *Ejila Shebora;* it opens when a casting of twelve mouths (Ejila Shebora) is followed by a casting of eight mouths *(Eji Ogbe).* This *odu* is also known as Ejila Elleunle, Ejila l'Ogbe, Ejila Unle, and Trupo Congua.

**Ejila Ogundá:** One of the sixteen *composite odu* found in the family of *Ejila Shebora;* it opens when a casting of twelve mouths (Ejila Shebora) is followed by a casting of three mouths *(Ogundá).*

**Ejila Okana:** One of the sixteen *composite odu* found in the family of *Ejila Shebora;* it opens when a casting of twelve mouths (Ejila Shebora) is followed by a casting of one mouth *(Okana).*

**Ejila Osá:** One of the sixteen *composite odu* found in the family of *Ejila Shebora;* it opens when a casting of twelve mouths (Ejila Shebora) is followed by a casting of nine mouths *(Osá).*

**Ejila Oyeku:** See *Ejila Ejioko.*

**Ejila Owani:** One of the sixteen *composite odu* found in the family of *Ejila Shebora;* it opens when a casting of twelve mouths (Ejila Shebora) is followed by a casting of eleven mouths *(Owani).*

**Ejila Shebora:** One of the sixteen *parent odu* in the *diloggún;* it consists of twelve mouths open on the mat. *Oturupon* is another name for this *odu*. It is the twelfth and final odu that a *santero* who has not the skill of an *oriaté* may read in the diloggún.

**Ejila Unle:** See *Ejila Ogbe.*

**Ejila Yeku:** See *Ejila Ejioko.*

**Eji Ogbe:** One of the sixteen *parent odu* in the *diloggún;* it consists of eight mouths open on the mat.

**Ejiogbe Ejila:** See *Ogbe Ejila.*

**Ejiogbe Ejioko:** See *Ogbe Ejioko.*

**Ejiogbe Ika:** See *Ogbe Merinla.*

**Ejiogbe Irete:** See *Ogbe Metanla.*

**Ejiogbe Irosun:** See *Ogbe Irosun.*

**Ejiogbe Iwori:** See *Ogbe Marunla.*

**Ejiogbe Marunla:** See *Ogbe Marunla.*

**Ejiogbe Meji:** See *Ogbe Meji.*

**Ejiogbe Merindilogún:** See *Ogbe Merindilogún.*

**Ejiogbe Merinla:** See *Ogbe Merinla.*

**Ejiogbe Metanla:** See *Ogbe Metanla.*

**Ejiogbe Obara:** See *Ogbe Obara.*

**Ejiogbe Oché:** See *Ogbe Oché.*

**Ejiogbe Odí:** See *Ogbe Odí.*

**Ejiogbe Ofún:** See *Ogbe Ofún.*

**Ejiogbe Ogundá:** See *Ogbe Ogundá.*

**Ejiogbe Okana:** See *Ogbe Okana.*

**Ejiogbe Okanran:** See *Ogbe Okana.*

**Ejiogbe Osá:** See *Ogbe Osá.*

**Ejiogbe Otura:** See *Ogbe Merindilogún.*

**Ejiogbe Oturupon:** See *Ogbe Ejila.*

**Ejiogbe Owani:** See *Ogbe Owani.*

**Ejiogbe Oyekun:** See *Ogbe Ejioko.*

**Eji Oko:** One of the sixteen *parent odu* in the *diloggún;* it consists of two mouths open on the mat.

**Ejioko Ejila:** One of the sixteen *composite odu* found in the family of *Eji Oko;* it opens when a casting of two mouths (Eji Oko) is followed by a casting of twelve mouths *(Ejila Shebora).* This odu is also known by the names Oyekun Ejila and Yeku Ejila.

**Ejioko Ejiogbe:** One of the sixteen *composite odu* found in the family of *Eji Oko;* it opens when a casting of two mouths (Eji Oko) is followed by another casting of eight mouths *(Eji Ogbe).* This odu is known as Ejioko l'Ogbe, Ejioko Unle, Oyekun l'Ogbe, and Oyekun Unle.

**Ejioko Ika:** See *Ejioko Merinla.*

**Ejioko Irete:** See *Ejioko Metanla.*

**Ejioko Irosun:** One of the sixteen *composite odu* found in the family of *Eji Oko;* it opens when a casting of two mouths (Eji Oko) is followed by another casting of four mouths *(Irosun).* This odu is also known as Oyekun Iroso, Oyekun Irosun, Yeku Iroso, and Yeku Irosun.

**Ejioko Iwori:** See *Ejioko Marunla.*

**Ejioko l'Ogbe:** See *Ejioko Ejiogbe.*

**Ejioko Marunla:** One of the sixteen *composite odu* found in the family of *Eji Oko;* this odu opens when a casting of two mouths (Eji Oko) is followed by a casting of fifteen mouths *(Marunla).* This sign also goes by the names Ejioko Iwori, Oyekun Iwori, Oyekun Marunla, Yeku Iwori, and Yeku Marunla.

**Ejioko Meji:** One of the sixteen *composite odu* found in the family of *Eji Oko;* this odu opens when a casting of two mouths (Eji Oko) is followed by another casting of two mouths. It is also known as Oyekun Meji and Yeku Meji.

**Ejioko Merindilogún:** One of the sixteen *composite odu* found in the family of *Eji Oko;* this odu opens when a casting of two mouths (Eji Oko) is followed by a casting of sixteen mouths *(Merindilogún).* It is also known as Ejioko Otura, Oyekun Merindilogún, Oyekun Otura, Yeku Merindilogún, and Yeku Otura.

**Ejioko Merinla:** One of the sixteen *composite odu* found in the family of *Eji Oko;* this odu opens when a casting of two mouths (Eji Oko) is followed by a casting of fourteen mouths *(Merinla).* The sign is also known as Ejioko Ika, Oyekun Ika, Oyekun Merinla, Yeku Ika, and Yeku Merinla.

**Ejioko Metanla:** One of the sixteen *composite odu* found in the family of *Eji Oko;* this odu opens when a casting of two mouths (Eji Oko) is followed by a casting of thirteen mouths *(Metanla).* It is also known by the names Ejioko Irete, Oyekun Irete, Oyekun Metanla, Yeku Irete, and Yeku Metanla.

**Ejioko Obara:** One of the sixteen *composite odu* found in the family of *Eji Oko;* this odu opens when a casting of two mouths (Eji Oko) is followed by another casting of six mouths *(Obara)*. It is also known by the names Oyekun Obara and Yeku Obara.

**Ejioko Oché:** One of the sixteen *composite odu* found in the family of *Eji Oko;* this odu opens when a casting of two mouths (Eji Oko) is followed by five mouths *(Oché)*. It is also known as Oyekun Oché and Yeku Oché.

**Ejioko Odí:** One of the sixteen *composite odu* found in the family of *Eji Oko;* it is formed when a casting of two mouths (Eji Oko) is followed by seven mouths *(Odí)*. This odu is also known as Oyekun Odí and Yeku Odí.

**Ejioko Ofún:** One of the sixteen *composite odu* found in the family of *Eji Oko;* it is formed when a casting of two mouths (Eji Oko) is followed by a casting of ten mouths *(Ofún)*. This odu is also known as Oyekun Ofún and Yeku Ofún.

**Ejioko Ogundá:** One of the sixteen *composite odu* found in the family of *Eji Oko;* it is formed when a casting of two mouths (Eji Oko) is followed by a casting of three mouths *(Ogundá)*. This odu is also known as Oyekun Ogundá and Yeku Ogundá.

**Ejioko Okana:** One of the sixteen *composite odu* found in the family of *Eji Oko;* this odu opens when a casting of two mouths (Eji Oko) is followed by a casting of one mouth *(Okana)*. It is also known as Oyekun Kanran, Oyekun Okana, Oyekun Okanran, Yeku Kanran, Yeku Okana, and Yeku Okanran.

**Ejioko Osá:** One of the sixteen *composite odu* found in the family of *Eji Oko;* this odu opens when a casting of two mouths (Eji Oko) is followed by a casting of nine mouths *(Osá)*. It is also known as Oyekun Osá and Yeku Osá.

**Ejioko Otura:** See *Ejioko Merindilogún.*

**Ejioko Owani:** One of the sixteen *composite odu* found in the family of *Eji Oko;* this odu opens when a casting of two mouths (Eji Oko) is followed by a casting of eleven mouths *(Owani)*. It is also known as Oyekun Owani and Yeku Owani.

**Ejioko Unle:** See *Ejioko Ejiogbe.*

**ekru-aro:** A staple *Lucumí* dish favored by *Olokun.* Its two ingredients are black-eyed peas and eggs.

**Elegbara:** One of the praises given to *Elegguá;* it means "owner of power."

**Elegguá:** Also known as *Eshu.* He is often portrayed as fate, a young child, and an old man. Elegguá is the messenger of all the *orishas* and the first and last to be honored in every ceremony performed. Without Elegguá's goodwill, one may not accomplish anything in the religion *Santería.* In *Ifá*, it is said that there are 256 paths of Elegguá, one for each *odu.* Each of these paths is known as Eshu and has a specific name, such as *Eshu Ayé*, *Eshu Bi*, and *Eshu Laroye.* In *ocha*, there are 101 paths of Elegguá (each also known as Eshu). In many *ilé ocha*, when an *initiate* receives the *warriors*, he is told the name of Eshu that his Elegguá enshrines.

**eledá:** The connection between one's *orí* and one's *guardian orisha.*

**eleke/elekes:** The beaded necklaces given to both *aleyos* and *santeros.* The bead colors denote not only the *orisha* to whom they are consecrated, but also the path of that orisha. In the initiation of the elekes, unless the *diloggún* specifies otherwise, an aleyo will generally receive four elekes: the elekes of *Obatalá*, *Yemayá*, *Oshún*, and *Shangó.* Sometimes, the eleke of *Elegguá* is also given.

**Elleunle Meji:** See *Ogbe Meji.*

**Elleunle Okana:** See *Ogbe Okana.*

**Elleunle Okanran:** See *Ogbe Okana.*

**epe:** Curse.

**epó:** A thick, viscous red palm oil used in African cooking and also as an *adimú* offering for certain *orishas;* for example, *Elegguá*, *Ogún*, and *Ochosi* often take epó on their sacred stones.

**Eshu:** See *Elegguá.*

**Eshu Alagbana:** The *avatar* of *Elegguá* compared with the lonely spirit (the soul in purgatory).

**Eshu Aniki Olokun:** The *avatar* of *Elegguá* said to live in the bottom of the sea with *Olokun.* He is the only *orisha* other than Olokun who may travel into the ocean's depths. Eshu Aniki Olokun dredges up the ocean's wealth and puts it into the hands of *Eshu Ayé Belleburo.*

**Eshu Ayé:** This *avatar* of *Elegguá* is said to walk on the shoreline where waves lap at the sand. He works closely with the *orisha Olokun.*

**Eshu Ayé Belleburo:** This *avatar* of *Elegguá* is said to live between the realms of *Eshu Ayé* and *Eshu Aniki Olokun.* Belleburo's job is to take the wealth from Eshu Aniki Olokun's hands and give it to Eshu Ayé, who spreads it throughout the world. This path of Eshu works closely with *Olokun.*

**Eshu Bi:** This *avatar* of *Elegguá* is both a young child and an old man; he is forceful and stern. It is said that this Eshu walks with the first two *Ibeyi*, the twins who were born of *Shangó* and *Oshún.* He is the protector of twins and also of small children.

**Eshu Laroye:** This *avatar* of *Elegguá* works closely with *Oshún* and is her constant companion; he is often referred to as the "little talkative one." He is one of Elegguá's most important and popular paths, being the one addressed and refreshed before any invocation or prayer to the *orishas.*

**Eshu ni pacuó:** The *avatar* of *Elegguá* that forms the link between the *orí* and the body; the path of Elegguá that lives in one's neck and tells one when the dead are near.

**Espiritísmo**: A Spanish term describing the collective mediumistic practices begun in France by Allan Kardec. In *Santería*, these practices are among the many used to make up for the loss of the *egungun* cults in the New World.

**espiritista:** A practitioner of *Espiritísmo;* a medium. It describes both male and female practitioners.

**ewe:** A *Lucumí* term for "herb"; it denotes any of those plants, roots, or trees that are used in the making of herbal baths, mixtures, medicines, or *omiero.*

**ewon:** Imprisonment.

**eyebale:** An offering that includes the sacrifice of an animal.

**eyo:** A *Lucumí* word that means "tragedies"; in the context of divination, it points out those tragedies that come through legal complications, gossip, and accidents.

**fitibo:** A *Lucumí* term denoting an impending, tragic death.

**fly whisk:** A horse's tail mounted in a wooden handle; the handle is beaded in the same colors as the *eleke* of the *orisha* it is given to. Orishas given fly whisks—*Oyá, Obatalá, Yemayá, Oshún*, and *Shangó*—are considered royalty in the pantheon.

**foribale:** One of the two methods of salutation to an elder or an *orisha;* the form of salutation depends on whether the *guardian orisha* is male or female.

**fundamento:** Spanish for "foundation," this term is used throughout this book to represent that which gives strength to an orisha. It also denotes the sacred drums, anya.

**godparents:** In *Santería*, one's godparents are one's sponsors in the religion, the *priests* or *priestesses* who will give the initiations of the *elekes, warriors*, and *ocha.* They are the aspirant's spiritual guides in both life and religion, and they are consulted on all matters of spiritual importance.

**guardian orisha:** The *orisha* that claims an *aleyo*, guiding him or her to the ritual of *ocha.* Once initiated, the aleyo becomes a *iyawó* (bride) of the guardian orisha, and after a year, he or she becomes a *santero* (priest) or *santera* (priestess) in *Santería.*

**guiro:** A ceremonial drumming and singing given to any *orisha* that does not use the consecrated drums of the religion.

**gungun:** One of eight *ibó* used in *divination;* it consists of a bone from the left hind leg of a goat used to feed *Elegguá.*

**ibaé:** A *Lucumí* phrase translating as "I give homage [to the dead]."

**Ibeyi:** The divine children of *Shangó* and *Oshún.* There are seven *Ibeyi*, also known as the "children of miraculous birth." The first two Ibeyi are twins whom *Oshún* gave to her sister *Yemayá* to raise. It has become common usage in *Santería* for practitioners to refer to these first two children as "the Ibeyi." They are the patrons of both twins and the mothers of twins. See also *Taewó* and *Kaindé.*

**ibó:** When reading the *diloggún*, these are the tools the *diviner* uses to determine orientation and *larishe.* There are a total of eight ibó: *otá, efun, ayé, owó, apadí, gungun, osán/sesán*, and *orí ere.*

**idé:** A bracelet beaded in the colors of the *orisha* to whom it is dedicated.

**Ideu:** The third *Ibeyi*, a child of *Oshún.* It is male, but generally it is accompanied by a doll dressed as a small girl.

**Ifá:** The original oracle of the *Yoruba* upon which both the African and Afro-Cuban forms of *diloggún divination* are based. This system includes 256 *odu*, revealed by *Orúnmila* to his disciples *Asheda* and *Akoda.* Only the priests of Orúnmila, the *babalawos*, may read Ifá.

**igbodu:** The sacred room where *orishas* are born and *initiates* are crowned.

**ikú:** Physical death or the personification of Death.

**ilé ocha:** The spiritual house of *ocha* or of the *orishas*, headed by either a *priest* or a *priestess* who has many years of experience in the religion.

**initiate:** One who has made *ocha* in *Santería.* It may refer to a *iyawó, priest*, or *priestess.*

**Inle:** An orisha envisioned as a beautiful, androgynous youth; he is the patron of homosexuals and fishermen. At one time he was a mortal, but *Yemayá* was so taken by his beauty that she made him immortal and stole him away to the bottom of the sea. There, she tired of him, yet he learned all of her secrets. Yemayá removed his speech by cutting out his tongue, and then she set him free to walk among the rest of the *orishas.* To this day, Inle will speak only through her. He is also seen as the great physician, the one who can cure any illness with his extensive knowledge of the medicinal uses of all *ewe* in the forest.

**inya:** War.

**iré:** Any type of blessing or good fortune that can befall one who sits for a session with the *diloggún.*

**iré aláfia:** Goodness through peace.

**iré arikú:** The blessing not to see an untimely death.

**iré ashegunota:** Goodness from an *orisha's* sacred stones.

**iré ayé:** Goodness or blessing of money.

**iré banda loguro:** Goodness from the earth.

**iré dedewan t'Olokun:** Goodness from *Olokun;* goodness from the depths of the ocean.

**iré elese abure:** Goodness from the hands of a brother or sister in *ocha.*

**iré elese araoko:** Goodness at the feet of the fertile land; goodness from the country.

**iré elese ará onú:** Goodness from the denizens of heaven.

**iré elese arubo**: Goodness at the feet of elders.

**iré elese babatobi:** Goodness at the feet of one's godfather.

**iré elese egun:** Goodness at the feet of *egun.*

**iré elese eledá:** Goodness at the feet of one's *orí.*

**iré elese elenú:** Goodness from the speaker's tongue.

**iré elese ewe:** Goodness from games of chance.

**iré elese iyátobi:** Goodness at the feet of one's godmother.

**iré elese obini:** Goodness from the hands of a woman.

**iré elese ocha:** Goodness at the feet of the *orishas.*

**iré elese okuni:** Goodness from the hands of a man.

**iré elese omo:** Goodness from children.

**iré elese orí yoko:** Goodness at the feet of a tied head (in other words, from making *ocha*).

**iré ibujoko:** Goodness through change.

**iré iyekú:** Goodness through tragedy.

**iré lowo:** Goodness through one's own hands.

**iré ni:** A *Lucumí* phrase meaning "blessings are predicted."

**iré otonowá:** Goodness from heaven.

**iré yale:** A *Lucumí* phrase meaning "firm goodness."

**iré yale timbelaye:** A *Lucumi* phrase meaning "firm goodness to manifest in this life."

**Iroko:** In Nigeria, Iroko refers to a specific tree that is sacred to the *orishas* and *Olódumare.* Iroko is also a powerful orisha who assisted the descent of *Obatalá* from heaven to the earth. Iroko spans the sky and the earth; he is the sacred tree before which all the orishas gather. The *diloggún* made the Middle Passage from Africa to the New World with Iroko's *priests* and *priestesses,* and he claimed the silk cotton tree as his native shrine in the New World.

**Irosun:** One of the sixteen *parent odu* of the *diloggún;* it is opened when four mouths fall face-up on the mat.

**Irosun Ejila:** One of the sixteen *composite odu* found in the family of *Irosun.* It forms when a cast of four mouths (Irosun) is followed by a cast of twelve mouths *(Ejila Shebora).* Irosun Oturupon is another name for this pattern.

**Irosun Ejioko:** One of the sixteen *composite odu* in the family of *Irosun.* It is formed when a casting of four mouths (Irosun) is followed by a casting of two mouths *(Eji Oko).* This odu is also known as Irosun Oyekun and Irosun Yeku.

**Irosun Ika:** See *Irosun Merinla.*

**Irosun Irete:** See *Irosun Metanla.*

**Irosun Iwori:** See *Irosun Marunla.*

**Irosun Kana:** See *Irosun Okana.*

**Irosun Kanran:** See *Irosun Okana.*

**Irosun l'Ogbe:** See *Irosun Ogbe.*

**Irosun Marunla:** One of the sixteen *composite odu* found in the family of *Irosun.* It forms when a cast of four mouths (Irosun) is followed by a cast of fifteen mouths *(Marunla).* Irosun Iwori is another name for this sign.

**Irosun Meji:** One of the sixteen *composite odu* found in the family of *Irosun.* It forms when a cast of four mouths (Irosun) repeats itself.

**Irosun Merindilogún:** One of the sixteen *composite odu* found in the family of *Irosun.* It opens when a cast of four mouths (Irosun) is followed by a cast of sixteen mouths *(Merindilogún).* Irosun Otura is another name for this sign.

**Irosun Merinla:** One of the sixteen *composite odu* found in the family of *Irosun.* It forms when a cast of four mouths (Irosun) is followed by a cast of fourteen mouths *(Merinla).* Irosun Ika is another name for this pattern.

**Irosun Metanla:** One of the sixteen *composite odu* found in the family of *Irosun.* It forms when a cast of four mouths (Irosun) is followed by a cast of thirteen mouths *(Metanla).* Irosun Irete is another name for this sign.

**Irosun Obara:** One of the sixteen *composite odu* found in the family of *Irosun.* It forms when a casting of four mouths (Irosun) is followed by a casting of six mouths *(Obara).*

**Irosun Oché:** One of the sixteen *composite odu* found in the family of *Irosun.* It forms when a casting of four mouths (Irosun) is followed by one of five mouths *(Oché).*

**Irosun Odí:** One of the sixteen *composite odu* found in the family of *Irosun.* It forms when a casting of four mouths (Irosun) is followed by a casting of seven mouths *(Odí).*

**Irosun Ofún:** One of the sixteen *composite odu* in the family of *Irosun.* It is formed when a casting of four mouths (Irosun) is followed by a casting of ten mouths *(Ofún).*

**Irosun Ogbe:** One of the sixteen *composite odu* found in the family of *Irosun.* It forms when a casting of four mouths (Irosun) is followed by one of eight mouths *(Eji Ogbe).* This odu is also known as Irosun l'Ogbe, Irosun Umbo, and Irosun Unle.

**Irosun Ogundá:** One of the sixteen *composite odu* found in the family of *Irosun.* It forms when a casting of four mouths (Irosun) is followed by one of three mouths *(Ogundá).*

**Irosun Okana:** One of the sixteen *composite odu* found in the family of *Irosun.* It opens when a casting of four mouths (Irosun) is followed by a casting of one mouth *(Okana).* Irosun Kana, Irosun Kanran, and Irosun Okanran are other names for this pattern.

**Irosun Okanran:** See *Irosun Okana.*

**Irosun Osá:** One of the sixteen *composite odu* in the family of *Irosun.* It is formed when a casting of four mouths (Irosun) is followed by one of nine mouths *(Osá).*

**Irosun Otura:** See *Irosun Merindilogún.*

**Irosun Oturupon:** See *Irosun Ejila.*

**Irosun Owani:** One of the sixteen *composite odu* in the family of *Irosun.* It is formed when a casting of four mouths (Irosun) is followed by a casting of eleven mouths *(Owani).*

**Irosun Oyekun:** See *Irosun Ejioko.*

**Irosun Umbo:** See *Irosun Ogbe.*

**Irosun Unle:** See *Irosun Ogbe.*

**Irosun Yeku:** See *Irosun Ejioko.*

**Irunmole**: The first *orishas* born in heaven from *Olódumare* and *odu.*

**itá:** A major divination ceremony, given either to a *iyawó* after the rites of *ocha* or to a *priest* or *priestess* who has fed an *orisha* a four-legged animal as *ebó.* The information, eboses, and prohibitions prescribed during an itá are followed by an *initiate* for life. Always, one's itá is written in the libreta given when ocha is made.

**italero:** A Spanish word that denotes an expert in the reading of the *diloggún.*

**iyawó:** A *Lucumí* term for the *initiates* of an *orisha.* It translates as "bride," no matter the initiate's sex. For at least a year after one's initiation, the rest of the initiates in one's *ilé ocha* will refer to one by this term.

**jícara:** A dried gourd that is cut open to resemble a bowl. It is used to give offerings and to pour libations to the *orishas.*

**jutía:** An African bush rat, a large rodent; it is a staple offering for many of the *warrior orishas* such as *Elegguá*, *Ogún*, and *Ochosi.*

**Kaindé:** The second *Ibeyi* born to *Oshún* and *Shangó.* The name means "the final to be born." Kaindé is female and is dressed in blue gingham due to her close association with *Yemayá.*

**Kana'yeku:** See *Okana Ejioko.*

**Kanran Ejioko:** See *Okana Ejioko.*

**Kanran Iroso:** See *Okana Irosun.*

**Kanran Irosun:** See *Okana Irosun.*

**Kanran Obara:** See *Okana Obara.*

**Kanran Oché:** See *Okana Oché.*

**Kanran Ofún:** See *Okana Ofun.*

**Kanran Ogundá:** See *Okana Ogundá.*

**Kanran Oyekun:** See *Okana Ejioko.*

**kariocha:** See *ocha.*

**kaure:** Prayers.

**kawo kabiosile:** A praise given to *Shangó.* It refers to the fact that the king (Shangó) did not hang (kill himself by suicide). He ascended before death to become an *orisha.*

**koborí eledá:** An offering made to one's *orí.*

**kofá:** See *kofá de Orúnmila.*

**kofá de Orúnla:** See *kofá de Orúnmila.*

**kofá de Orúnmila:** A rite given to women who need the protection of *Orúnmila.* This initiation can be given only by the *babalawos.*

**Korikoto:** This is the brother of *Orisha Oko;* while Orisha Oko takes care of his crops during the day, this spirit is said to guard them at night.

**koshé:** A *Lucumí* phrase meaning "to receive" or "to be had."

**larishe:** One of the hundreds of remedies that any one *odu* can prescribe to overcome *osogbo* and bring *iré* to the client sitting for a session with the *diloggún.*

**lavado:** Washed.

**lavatorio:** The birthing ceremony of an *orisha* in which the *otanes*, shells, and implements of that orisha are washed in *omiero* and are born from the *godparent's* orisha. See also Osain, *making osain*, and *niche osain.*

**Lazarero:** A title given to those *priests* and *priestesses* who have received the *orisha Babaluaiye.*

**letter:** Another term for *odu.*

**libation:** An offering of water, wine, rum, or other liquid given to nourish and refresh the spirits.

**libreta:** A Spanish word that translates as "notebook." When this word is used in *Santería*, it usually refers to the notebook a *iyawó* receives once his year in white is finished. Inside this libreta will be recorded the names of the *santeros* present at his initiation, the names of the *orishas* he received at his initiation, and the *odu* that opened at his *itá.* From itá will be listed the complete meaning of each odu and its orientations, *larishes*, and *eboses* that are to be performed by this *initiate* on a regular basis. This libreta will grow as he receives more orishas and as he progresses in the religion. Sometimes, the santero will keep personal libretas that list the secrets of Santería as he learns them. No libretas, theoretically, are ever seen by outsiders. They are passed down between initiates of an *ilé ocha* so that the knowledge they contain is not lost.

**l'Ogbe Bara:** See *Ogbe Obara.*

**lowo:** One's own hands or one's own works.

**Lucumí:** The word *Lucumí* is a contraction of various *Yoruba* words and translates as "my friend." As a people, the Lucumí are the physical, and now spiritual, descendants of the black Yoruba slaves in Cuba. This word also refers to language that is now used in *Santería.*

**maferefún:** A term meaning "Praise be to" or "All power be to."

**making osain:** The sacred ritual of making *omiero*, the herbal fluids used to bathe and consecrate people in this religion. Without *Osain* and his *ewe*, nothing in *Santeriá* is possible. See also *niche osain*.

**maní:** A Spanish word for peanuts.

**mano de Orúnla:** See *mano de Orúnmila*.

**mano de Orúnmila:** The initiation given only to men by *babalawos*.

**Marunla:** One of the sixteen *parent odu* in the *diloggún;* it is said to be opened when fifteen mouths fall face-up onto the diviner's mat.

**mass:** A ritual of *Espiritísmo*, sometimes called a séance, performed to honor the dead and heavily absorbed into the *Lucumí* faith. It involves prayers, offerings, and the possession of mediums by spirits.

**matanza:** The sacrifice of animals during an initiate's rites of *ocha*.

**mayombero:** An initiate of the religion *Palo Mayombe*.

**mazo:** A heavily beaded necklace draped over an *orisha's* shrine. When worn by an adherent, it is draped over the left shoulder and under the right arm, like a banner. The bead colors for an orisha's mazo are the same as those of an orisha's *eleke*.

**meji:** Twin, double.

**Merindilogún:** One of the sixteen *parent odu* in the *diloggún;* it consists of sixteen open mouths and no closed mouths on the mat.

**Merinla:** One of the sixteen *parent odu* in the *diloggún;* it is said to be opened when fourteen mouths fall face-up on the diviner's mat.

**Metanla:** One of the sixteen *parent odu* in the *diloggún;* it is said to be opened when thirteen mouths fall faceup on the diviner's mat.

**misa:** See *mass*.

**mojubando:** An invocation given by an *italero* to gently awaken the *orisha* whose *diloggún* is being cast; it pays homage to *Olódumare*, the earth, the ancestors, and that particular orisha.

**mouths:** In *diloggún* divination, "mouth" refers to the natural serrated opening of the *cowrie shell*.

**ñame:** A root vegetable, in the same family as yams.

**Naná Burukú:** In some mythologies, this *orisha* was born from *Yembo* when she ascended by her own aché to the palace of *Olódumare;* historically, she comes from the land of *Arara* in Africa and is not *Yoruba*. She was later syncretized into the *Santería* pantheon during the time of the *cabildos* in Cuba. She is the mother of *Nanumé* and *Babaluaiye*.

**nangareo:** A ritual performed to honor *Olorún* and *egun* before *itá;* it can also be done infrequently as *ebó*.

**Nanumé:** A very old female *avatar* of *Babaluaiye;* she is so dissociated from him that many consider her to be not only an aspect of this *orisha* but his sister and a separate entity as well (similar to the relationship between *Yemayá* and *Yembo*). She is the daughter of *Naná Burukú*, and she is said to be the moon in the night sky by elder *santeros*.

**nfumbé:** This Congolese term denotes the spirit that lives within a *palero's* cauldron or *nganga*.

**nganga:** A Congolese word meaning "priest" or "magician." In both Cuba and the United States it denotes the pot or cauldron that contains the *palero's* medicines, and it is also the home for the palero's *nfumbe*. Each nganga is based on one of the *nkisi* and is filled with items that contain the nkisi's *aché* (such as dirt, herbs, animals, minerals, metals, and tree branches). The Spanish term for nganga is *prenda*.

**niche osain:** An amulet made of herbal, mineral, and animal substances; it is beaded in the colors of the *orisha* to whom it is consecrated. Every niche osain is made for a specific purpose. Protection, blessings, prosperity, health, and longevity are among the most basic. See also *Osain* and *making osain*.

**nkisi:** Collectively, these are the forces of nature in the Congolese religion *Palo Mayombe*. There are several types of nkisi; for example, Siete Rayos (the storm), Kalunga (the ocean), Mama Chola (the river), Tiembla Tierra (the mountain), and Mariwanga (the cemetery). It is upon the nkisi that the *nganga* of the *palero* is based.

**Oba:** An *orisha* considered to be *Shangó's* only official wife. She is one of his three lovers; the other two are *Oshún* and *Oyá*.

**Obara:** One of the sixteen *parent odu* of the *diloggún;* it is opened when six mouths fall faceup on the diviner's mat.

**Obara'che:** See *Obara Oché*.

**Obara'di:** See *Obara Odí*.

**Obara Ejila:** One of the sixteen *composite odu* in the family of *Obara*. It forms when a casting of six mouths (Obara) is followed by a casting of twelve mouths *(Ejila Shebora)*. Obara Oturupon is another name for this odu.

**Obara Ejiogbe:** One of the sixteen *composite odu* found in the family of *Obara*. It forms when a casting of six mouths (Obara) is followed by a casting of eight mouths *(Eji Ogbe)*. Other names for this pattern are Obara Elleunle, Obara l'Ogbe, Obara Ogbe, and Obara Unle.

**Obara Ejioko:** One of the sixteen *composite odu* in the family of *Obara;* it forms when a casting of six mouths (Obara) is followed by a casting of two mouths *(Eji Oko)*. It is also known as Obara Oyekun and Obara Yeku.

**Obara Elleunle:** See *Obara Ejiogbe*.

**Obara'fun:** See *Obara Ofún*.

**Obara Ika:** See *Obara Merinla*.

**Obara Irete:** See *Obara Metanla*.

**Obara Irosun:** One of the sixteen *composite odu* found in the family of *Obara;* it forms when a casting of six mouths (Obara) is followed by a casting of four mouths *(Irosun).*

**Obara Iwori:** See *Obara Marunla.*

**Obara Kana:** See *Obara Okana.*

**Obara Kanran:** See *Obara Okana.*

**Obara l'Ogbe:** See *Obara Ejiogbe.*

**Obara Marunla:** One of the sixteen *omo odu* found in the family of *Obara.* It forms when a casting of six mouths (Obara) is followed by a casting of fifteen mouths *(Marunla).* Obara Iwori is another name for this odu.

**Obara Meji:** One of the sixteen *composite odu* found in the family of *Obara.* It is formed when a cast of six mouths (Obara) is followed by another cast of six mouths.

**Obara Merindilogún:** One of the sixteen *composite odu* found in the family of *Obara.* It is formed when a casting of six mouths (Obara) is followed by a casting of sixteen mouths *(Merindilogún).* Obara Otura is another name for this odu.

**Obara Merinla:** One of the sixteen *composite odu* found in the family of *Obara.* It forms when a casting of six mouths (Obara) is followed by one of fourteen mouths *(Merinla).* Obara Ika is another name for this odu.

**Obara Metanla:** One of the sixteen *composite odu* found in the family of *Obara.* It is formed when a casting of six mouths (Obara) is followed by a casting of thirteen mouths *(Metanla).* Obara Irete is another name for this odu.

**Obara Oché:** One of the sixteen *composite odu* in the family of *Obara.* It is formed when a cast of six mouths (Obara) is followed by a cast of five mouths *(Oché).* Obara'che is another name for this odu.

**Obara Odí:** One of the sixteen *composite odu* found in the family of *Obara.* It forms when a casting of six mouths (Obara) is followed by a casting of seven mouths *(Odí).* It is also known as Obara'di.

**Obara Ofún:** One of the sixteen *composite odu* found in the family of *Obara.* It forms when a casting of six mouths (Obara) is followed by a casting of ten mouths *(Ofún).* Obara'fun is another name for this odu.

**Obara Ogbe:** See *Obara Ejiogbe.*

**Obara Ogundá:** One of the sixteen *composite odu* in the family of *Obara.* It forms when a casting of six mouths (Obara) is followed by a casting of three mouths *(Ogundá).*

**Obara Okana:** One of the sixteen *composite odu* in the family of *Obara.* It forms when a casting of six mouths (Obara) is followed by a casting of one mouth *(Okana).* It is also known as Obara Kana, Obara Kanran, and Obara Okanran.

**Obara Okanran:** See *Obara Okana.*

**Obara Osá:** One of the sixteen *composite odu* in the family of *Obara.* It forms when a casting of six mouths (Obara) is followed by a casting of nine mouths *(Osá).*

**Obara Otura:** See *Obara Merindilogún.*

**Obara Oturupon:** See *Obara Ejila.*

**Obara Owani:** One of the sixteen *composite odu* in the family of *Obara.* It forms when a casting of six mouths (Obara) is followed by a casting of eleven mouths *(Owani).*

**Obara Oyekun:** See *Obara Ejioko.*

**Obara Unle:** See *Obara Ejiogbe.*

**Obara Yeku:** See *Obara Ejioko.*

**Obatalá:** An *orisha* considered to be king of all the orishas and the creator of humans.

**Obedí:** See *Ogbe Odí.*

**obí:** The system of *divination* based on the coconut; also the coconut itself.

**Obí:** The man who became an *orisha* and then fell from grace because of his own pride, becoming the coconut used in *divination.* Despite this, Obí is still an orisha and treated with respect in the religion *Santería.*

**obini:** Woman.

**ocha:** A shortened form of the word *orisha.* It denotes the major *initiation* ceremony of *Santería,* a series of rites through which an *aleyo* becomes a iyawó. The ceremony is also known as *asiento* or *kariocha.* To "make ocha" means that one engages in the ocha ceremony, becoming a iyawó. Ocha is also sometimes used to mean Santería in general.

**Oché:** One of the sixteen *parent odu* in the *diloggún.* It is opened when five mouths fall faceup on the diviner's mat.

**Oché Ejila:** One of the sixteen *composite odu* that can fall in the family of *Oché.* It forms when a casting of five mouths (Oché) is followed by a casting of twelve mouths *(Ejila Shebora).* Oché Oturupon is another name for this sign.

**Oché Ejiogbe:** See *Oché Ogbe.*

**Oché Ejioko:** One of the sixteen *composite odu* that can fall in the family of *Oché.* It forms when a casting of five mouths (Oché) is followed by a casting of two mouths *(Eji Oko).* Oché Oyekun and Oché Yeku are other names for this odu.

**Oché Ika:** See *Oché Merinla.*

**Oché Irete:** See *Oché Metanla.*

**Oché Irosun:** One of the sixteen *composite odu* that can fall in the family of *Oché.* It forms when a casting of five mouths (Oché) is followed by a casting of four mouths *(Irosun).*

**Oché Iwori:** See *Oché Marunla.*

**Oché Kana:** See *Oché Okana.*

**Oché Kanran:** See *Oché Okana.*

**Oché l'Ogbe:** See *Oché Ogbe.*

**Oché Marunla:** One of the sixteen *composite odu* that can fall in the family of *Oché.* It forms when a casting of five mouths (Oché) is followed by a casting of fifteen mouths *(Marunla).* Oché Iwori is another name for this sign.

**Oché Meji:** One of the sixteen *composite odu* that can fall in the family of *Oché.* It forms when a casting of five mouths (Oché) is followed by another casting of five mouths.

**Oché Merindilogún:** One of the sixteen *composite odu* that can fall in the family of *Oché.* It forms when a casting of five mouths (Oché) is followed by a casting of sixteen mouths *(Merindilogún).* Oché Otura is another name for this odu.

**Oché Merinla:** One of the sixteen *composite odu* that can fall in the family of *Oché.* It forms when a casting of five mouths (Oché) is followed by a casting of fourteen mouths *(Merinla).* Oché Ika is another name for this sign.

**Oché Metanla:** One of the sixteen *composite odu* that can fall in the family of *Oché.* It forms when a casting of five mouths (Oché) is followed by a casting of thirteen mouths *(Metanla).* Oché Irete is another name for this pattern.

**Oché Obara:** One of the sixteen *composite odu* that can fall in the family of *Oché.* It forms when a casting of five mouths (Oché) is followed by a casting of six mouths *(Obara).*

**Oché Odí:** One of the sixteen *composite odu* that can fall in the family of *Oché.* It forms when a casting of five mouths (Oché) is followed by a casting of seven mouths *(Odí).*

**Oché Ofún:** One of the sixteen *composite odu* that can fall in the family of *Oché.* It forms when a casting of five mouths (Oché) is followed by a casting of ten mouths *(Ofún).*

**Oché Ogbe:** One of the sixteen *composite odu* that can fall in the family of *Oché.* It forms when a casting of five mouths (Oché) is followed by a casting of eight mouths *(Eji Ogbe).* Oché Ejiogbe, Oché l'Ogbe, and Oché Unle are other names for this sign.

**Oché Ogundá:** One of the sixteen *composite odu* that can fall in the family of *Oché.* It forms when a casting of five mouths (Oché) is followed by a casting of three mouths *(Ogundá).*

**Oché Okana:** One of the sixteen *composite odu* that can fall in the family of *Oché.* It forms when a casting of five mouths (Oché) is followed by a casting of one mouth *(Okana).* Oché Kana, Oché Kanran, and Oché Okanran are other names for this odu.

**Oché Okanran:** See *Oché Okana.*

**Oché Oniguo:** See *Oché Owani.*

**Oché Osá:** One of the sixteen *composite odu* that can fall in the family of *Oché.* It forms when a casting of five mouths (Oché) is followed by a casting of nine mouths *(Osá).*

**Oché Otura:** See *Oché Merindilogún.*

**Oché Oturupon:** See *Oché Ejila.*

**Oché Owani:** One of the sixteen *composite odu* that can fall in the family of *Oché.* It forms when a casting of five mouths (Oché) is followed by a casting of eleven mouths *(Owani).* Oché Oniguo is another name for this sign.

**Oché Oyekun:** See *Oché Ejioko.*

**Oché Unle:** See *Oché Ogbe.*

**Oché Yeku:** See *Oché Ejioko.*

**Ochosi:** An *orisha;* one of the *warriors* and said to be patron of the hunt.

**Ochumare:** An androgynous *orisha* born from *Naná Burukú.* S/he is the rainbow, the crown of *Yemayá.* Some say that this is the patron spirit of gays, lesbians, and bisexuals. For half of the year, this orisha lives deep in the river water and never touches dry earth; in the other half of the year, this orisha lives on the earth and never touches water.

**Odí:** One of the sixteen *parent odu* of the *diloggún;* it is opened when seven mouths fall faceup on the diviner's mat.

**Odí Atago:** See *Odí Merindilogún.*

**Odí Ejila:** One of the sixteen *composite odu* found in the family of *Odí.* It opens on the mat when an initial casting of seven mouths (Odí) precedes a second casting of twelve mouths *(Ejila Shebora).* Odí Oturupon and Odí Shebora are two other names for this odu.

**Odí Ejioko:** One of the sixteen *composite odu* found in the family of *Odí.* It opens when an initial cast of seven mouths (Odí) precedes a second cast of two mouths *(Eji Oko).* Odí Oyekun and Odí Yeku are other names for this odu.

**Odí Elleunle:** See *Odí Ogbe.*

**Odí Ika:** See *Odí Merinla.*

**Odí Irete:** See *Odí Metanla.*

**Odí Irosun:** One of the sixteen *composite odu* found in the family of *Odí.* It opens on the mat when an initial casting of seven mouths (Odí) precedes a second casting of four mouths *(Irosun).*

**Odí Iwori:** See *Odí Marunla.*

**Odí Legue:** See *Odí Metanla.*

**Odí Leke:** See *Odí Metanla.*

**Odí Lere:** See *Odí Metanla.*

**Odí Marunla:** One of the sixteen *composite odu* found in the family of *Odí.* It opens on the mat when an initial cast of seven mouths (Odí) precedes a cast of fifteen mouths *(Marunla).* Odí Iwori is another name for this odu.

**Odí Meji:** One of the sixteen *composite odu* found in the family of *Odí.* It opens on the mat when an initial cast of seven mouths (Odí) repeats itself.

**Odí Merindilogún:** One of the sixteen *composite odu* found in the family of *Odí.* It opens when the first cast of seven mouths (Odí) precedes a second cast of sixteen mouths *(Merindilogún).* Other names for this pattern include Odí Atago, Odí Okparo, and Odí Otura.

**Odí Merinla:** One of the sixteen *composite odu* found in the family of *Odí.* It opens on the mat when an initial cast of seven mouths (Odí) precedes a second cast of fourteen mouths *(Merinla).* Odí Ika is another name for this odu.

**Odí Metanla:** One of the sixteen *composite odu* found in the family of *Odí.* It opens on the mat when an initial cast of seven mouths (Odí) precedes a second cast of thirteen mouths *(Metanla).* Odí Irete, Odí Legue, Odí Leke, and Odí Lere are other names for this odu.

**Odí Obara:** One of the sixteen *composite odu* found in the family of *Odí.* It opens on the mat when an initial cast of seven mouths (Odí) precedes a second cast of six mouths *(Obara).*

**Odí Oché:** One of the sixteen *composite odu* found in the family of *Odí.* It opens on the mat when an initial cast of seven mouths (Odí) precedes a second cast of five mouths *(Oché).*

**Odí Ofún:** One of the sixteen *composite odu* found in the family of *Odí.* It opens when the initial cast of seven mouths (Odí) precedes a second cast of ten mouths *(Ofún).*

**Odí Ogbe:** One of the sixteen *composite odu* found in the family of *Odí.* It opens on the mat when an initial cast of seven mouths (Odí) precedes a second cast of eight mouths *(Eji Ogbe).* Odí Elleunle and Odí Unle are other names for this odu.

**Odí Ogundá**: One of the sixteen *composite odu* found in the family of *Odí.* It opens when an initial cast of seven mouths (Odí) precedes a second cast of three mouths *(Ogundá).*

**Odí Okana:** One of the sixteen *composite odu* found in the family of *Odí.* It opens when an initial casting of seven mouths (Odí) precedes a second casting of one mouth *(Okana).*

**Odí Okparo:** See *Odí Merindilogún.*

**Odí Osá:** One of the sixteen *composite odu* found in the family of *Odí.* It opens when an initial cast of seven mouths (Odí) precedes a second cast of nine mouths *(Osá).*

**Odí Otura:** See *Odí Merindilogún.*

**Odí Oturupon:** See *Odí Ejila.*

**Odí Owani:** One of the sixteen *composite odu* found in the family of *Odí.* It opens on the mat when an initial cast of seven mouths (Odí) precedes a second cast of eleven mouths *(Owani).*

**Odí Oyekun:** See *Odí Ejioko.*

**Odí Shebora:** See *Odí Ejila.*

**Odí Unle:** See *Odí Ogbe.*

**Odí Yeku:** See *Odí Ejioko.*

**odu:** The many patterns, or letters, that can fall when using the divination system known as *diloggún.* There are a total of sixteen *parent odu* and 256 *composite odu.* Each of these has its own proverbs, *patakís,* meanings, and *eboses.* The word *odu* is both singular and plural in *Lucumí* and *Yoruba* usage.

**Odua:** An elder *avatar* of *Obatalá.* Many believe Odua to be female.

**Oduduwa:** The founder of the *Yoruba* empire. He is also a *warrior orisha.*

**ofo:** Loss.

**Ofún:** One of the sixteen *parent odu* of the *diloggún;* it is opened when ten mouths fall on the diviner's mat.

**Ofundí:** See *Ofún Odí.*

**Ofún Ejila:** One of the sixteen *composite odu* found in the family of *Ofún.* It opens when the initial cast of ten mouths (Ofún) precedes a cast of twelve mouths *(Ejila Shebora).* Ofún Oturupon is another name for this odu.

**Ofún Ejioko:** One of the sixteen *composite odu* found in the family of *Ofún.* It opens when the initial cast of ten mouths (Ofún) is followed by a cast of two mouths *(Eji Oko).* Ofún Oyekun and Ofún Yeku are other names for this odu.

**Ofún Elleunle:** See *Ofún Ogbe.*

**Ofún Ika:** See *Ofún Merinla.*

**Ofún Irete:** See *Ofún Metanla.*

**Ofún Irosun:** One of the sixteen *composite odu* found in the family of *Ofún.* It opens when the initial cast of ten mouths (Ofún) precedes a cast of four mouths *(Irosun).*

**Ofún Iwori:** See *Ofún Marunla.*

**Ofún l'Ogbe:** See *Ofún Ogbe.*

**Ofún Marunla:** One of the sixteen *composite odu* that exist in *Ofún's* family. It opens when an initial cast of ten mouths (Ofún) is followed by a cast of fifteen mouths *(Marunla).* Ofún Iwori is another name for this odu.

**Ofún Meji:** One of the sixteen *composite odu* found in the family of *Ofún.* It forms when the initial cast of ten mouths (Ofún) repeats itself on the mat.

**Ofún Merindilogún:** One of the sixteen *composite odu* found in *Ofún's* family. It opens on the mat when the initial cast of ten mouths (Ofún) precedes a second cast of sixteen mouths *(Merindilogún).* Ofún Otura is another name for this odu.

**Ofún Merinla:** One of the sixteen *composite odu* found in the family of *Ofún.* It opens when the first cast of ten mouths (Ofún) precedes a cast of fourteen mouths *(Merinla).* Ofún Ika is another name for this odu.

**Ofún Metanla:** One of the sixteen *composite odu* found in the family of *Ofún.* It opens when the first cast of ten mouths (Ofún) precedes a cast of thirteen mouths *(Metanla).* Ofún Irete is another name for this letter.

**Ofún Obara:** One of the sixteen *composite odu* in *Ofún's* family. It opens when the initial cast of ten mouths (Ofún) precedes a cast of six mouths *(Obara).*

**Ofún Oché:** One of the sixteen *composite odu* found in the family of *Ofún.* It opens when the initial cast of ten mouths (Ofún) precedes a cast of five mouths *(Oché).*

**Ofún Odí:** One of the sixteen *composite odu* found in the family of *Ofún.* It opens when a casting of ten mouths (Ofún) is followed by a casting of seven mouths *(Odí).* Ofundí is another name for this sign.

**Ofún Ogbe:** One of the sixteen *composite odu* found in the family of *Ofún.* It opens when the initial cast of ten mouths (Ofún) precedes a cast of eight mouths *(Eji Ogbe).* Ofún Elleunle, Ofún l'Ogbe, and Ofún Shogbe are other names for this odu.

**Ofún Ogundá:** One of the sixteen *composite odu* found in the family of *Ofún.* This letter is open when the initial cast of ten mouths (Ofún) is followed by a cast of three mouths *(Ogundá).*

**Ofún Okana:** One of the sixteen *composite odu* found in the family of *Ofún.* It opens when the initial cast of ten mouths (Ofún) is followed by a cast of one mouth *(Okana).*

**Ofún Osá:** One of the sixteen *composite odu* existing in the family of *Ofún.* It opens when the initial cast of ten mouths (Ofún) precedes a cast of nine mouths *(Osá).*

**Ofún Otura:** See *Ofún Merindilogún.*

**Ofún Oturupon:** See *Ofún Ejila.*

**Ofún Owani:** One of the sixteen *composite odu* found in the family of *Ofún.* It opens when the initial cast of ten mouths (Ofún) precedes a cast of eleven mouths *(Owani).*

**Ofún Oyekun:** See *Ofún Ejioko.*

**Ofún Shogbe:** See *Ofún Ogbe.*

**Ofún Yeku:** See *Ofún Ejioko.*

**Ogbe Alaara:** See *Ogbe Merindilogún.*

**Ogbe-Alaso Funfun:** See *Ogbe Merindilogún.*

**Ogbe Ate:** See *Ogbe Metanla.*

**Ogbebara:** See *Ogbe Obara.*

**Ogbe'che:** See *Ogbe Oché.*

**Ogbe Dawo Ósun Tele:** See *Ogbe Irosun.*

**Ogbe Ejila:** One of the sixteen *composite odu* found in the family of *Eji Ogbe.* It opens when the initial cast of eight mouths (Eji Ogbe) is follwed by a cast of twelve mouths *(Ejila Shebora).* It is also known as Ejiogbe Oturupon, Ogbe Tomokpon, Ogbe Trupo, and Ogbe Tun Omo Pon.

**Ogbe Ejioko:** One of the sixteen *composite odu* found in the family of *Eji Ogbe.* It forms when a casting of eight mouths (Eji Ogbe) precedes a casting of two mouths *(Eji Oko).* Ejiogbe Oyekun, Ogbe Oyekun, and Ogbe Yeku are other names for this sign.

**Ogbe Eka:** See *Ogbe Merinla.*

**Ogbe Etura:** See *Ogbe Merindilogún.*

**Ogbe Guene:** See *Ogbe Marunla.*

**Ogbe Hunle:** See *Ogbe Owani.*

**Ogbe Ika:** See *Ogbe Merinla.*

**Ogbe Irete:** See *Ogbe Metanla.*

**Ogbe Iroso:** See *Ogbe Irosun.*

**Ogbe Irosun:** One of the sixteen *composite odu* found in the family of *Eji Ogbe.* It forms when an initial casting of eight mouths (Eji Ogbe) precedes a casting of four mouths *(Irosun).* Ejiogbe Irosun, Ogbe Dawo Ósun Tele, Ogbe Iroso, Ogbe Masu, Ogbe Masun, and Ogbe Roso are other names for this odu.

**Ogbe Iwori:** See *Ogbe Marunla.*

**Ogbe Kanran:** See *Ogbe Okana.*

**Ogbe Karele:** See *Ogbe Merinla.*

**Ogbe Kosejo:** See *Ogbe Merindilogún.*

**Ogbe Kowojo:** See *Ogbe Oché.*

**Ogbe Kulejo:** See *Ogbe Ofún.*

**Ogbe Kunle:** See *Ogbe Merindilogún.*

**Ogbe Marunla:** One of the sixteen *composite odu* found in the family of *Eji Ogbe.* It opens on the mat when the initial cast of eight mouths (Eji Ogbe) precedes a cast of fifteen mouths *(Marunla).* Ejiogbe Iwori, Ejiogbe Marunla, Ogbe Guene, Ogbe Iwori, Ogbe Wehin, and Ogbe Weyin are other names for this odu.

**Ogbe Masu:** See *Ogbe Irosun.*

**Ogbe Masun:** See *Ogbe Irosun.*

**Ogbe Merindilogún:** One of the sixteen *composite odu* found in the family of *Eji Ogbe.* It forms when an initial casting of eight mouths (Eji Ogbe) precedes a second cast of sixteen mouths *(Merindilogún).* Other names for this odu include Ejiogbe Merindilogún, Ejiogbe Otura, Ogbe Alaara, Ogbe-Alaso Funfun, Ogbe Etura, Ogbe Kosejo, Ogbe Kunle, and Ogbe Otura.

**Ogbe Merinla:** One of the sixteen *composite odu* found in the family of *Eji Ogbe.* It opens on the mat when the initial cast of eight mouths (Eji Ogbe) precedes a second cast of fourteen mouths *(Merinla).* Ejiogbe Ika, Ejiogbe Merinla, Ogbe Eka, Ogbe Ika, and Ogbe Karele are other names for this odu.

**Ogbe Metanla:** One of the sixteen *composite odu* found in the family of *Eji Ogbe.* It opens on the mat when the initial cast of eight mouths (Eji Ogbe) precedes a cast of thirteen mouths *(Metanla)*. Ejiogbe Irete, Ejiogbe Metanla, Ogbe Ate, and Ogbe Irete are other names for this odu.

**Ogbe Obara:** One of the sixteen *composite odu* found in the family of *Eji Ogbe*. It forms when an initial cast of eight mouths (Eji Ogbe) is followed by a second cast of six mouths *(Obara)*. This odu is also known as Ogbebara and l'Ogbe Bara.

**Ogbe Oché:** One of the sixteen *composite odu* found in the family of *Eji Ogbe*. It forms when an initial cast of eight mouths (Eji Ogbe) precedes a cast of five mouths *(Oché)*. Ejiogbe Oché, Ogbe'che, Ogbe Kowojo, Ogbe Sanwo, and Ogbe Sweoole are other names for this odu.

**Ogbe Odí:** One of the sixteen *composite odu* found in the family of *Eji Ogbe;* it forms when an initial cast of eight mouths (Eji Ogbe) precedes a cast of seven mouths *(Odí)*. Obedí is another name for this odu.

**Ogbe Ofún:** One of the sixteen *composite odu* found in the family of *Eji Ogbe*. It forms when the first cast of eight mouths (Eji Ogbe) precedes a second cast of ten mouths *(Ofún)*. Ogbe Kulejo is another name for this odu.

**Ogbe Ogundá:** One of the sixteen *composite odu* found in the family of *Eji Ogbe*. It forms when an initial cast of eight mouths (Eji Ogbe) precedes a cast of three mouths *(Ogundá)*. Ejiogbe Ogundá, Ogbe Oligun, Ogbe Suru, and Ogbeyono are other names for this pattern.

**Ogbe Okana:** One of the sixteen *composite odu* found in the family of *Eji Ogbe*. This odu opens when a casting of eight mouths (Eji Ogbe) is followed by a casting of one mouth *(Okana)*. It is also known as Ejiogbe Okana, Ejiogbe Okanran, Elleunle Okana, Elleunle Okanran, Ogbe Okana, and Ogbe Kanran.

**Ogbe Oligun:** See *Ogbe Ogundá*.

**Ogbe Osá:** One of the sixteen *composite odu* found in the family of *Eji Ogbe*. It opens on the mat when the initial cast of eight mouths (Eji Ogbe) precedes a second cast of nine mouths *(Osá)*.

**Ogbe Owani:** One of the sixteen *composite odu* found in the family of *Eji Ogbe*. It opens on the mat when the initial cast of eight mouths (Eji Ogbe) precedes a second cast of eleven mouths *(Owani)*. Ejiogbe Owani and Ogbe Hunle are two other names for this odu.

**Ogbe Oyekun:** See *Ogbe Ejioko*.

**Ogbe Roso:** See *Ogbe Irosun*.

**Ogbe Sanwo:** See *Ogbe Oché*.

**Ogbe Suru:** See *Ogbe Ogundá*.

**Ogbe Sweoole:** See *Ogbe Oché*.

**Ogbe Tomokpon:** See *Ogbe Ejila*.

**Ogbe Trupo:** See *Ogbe Ejila*.

**Ogbe Tun Omo Pon:** See *Ogbe Ejila*.

**Ogbe Wehin:** See *Ogbe Marunla*.

**Ogbe Weyin:** See *Ogbe Guene*, *Ogbe Iwori*, *Ogbe Marunla*, and *Ogbe Wehin*.

**Ogbe Yeku:** See *Ogbe Ejioko*.

**Ogbeyono:** See *Ogbe Ogundá*. Ejiogbe Ogundá is another name for this sign.

**Oge:** This *orisha* is the messenger of *Shangó*.

**ogo:** A witch, a sorceror, or witchcraft.

**Ogún:** One of the *warrior orishas;* the patron of ironworkers and civilization.

**Ogundá:** One of the sixteen *parent odu* in the *diloggún;* it is opened when three mouths fall on the diviner's mat.

**Ogundá'di:** See *Ogundá Odí*.

**Ogundá Ejila:** One of the sixteen *composite odu* found in the family of *Ogundá*. It falls when a casting of three mouths (Ogundá) is followed by a casting of twelve mouths.

**Ogundá Ejiogbe:** One of the sixteen *composite odu* found in the family of *Ogundá;* it forms when a casting of three mouths (Ogundá) is followed by a casting of eight mouths *(Eji Ogbe)*. This odu is also known as Ogundá l'Ogbe, Ogundá Ogbe, and Ogundá Unle.

**Ogundá Ejioko:** One of the sixteen *composite odu* in the family of *Ogundá*. It falls when a casting of three mouths (Ogundá) is followed by a casting of two mouths *(Eji Oko)*. This odu is also known as Ogundá Oyekun and Ogundá Yeku.

**Ogundá Ika:** See *Ogundá Merinla*.

**Ogundá Irete:** See *Ogundá Metanla*.

**Ogundá Irosun:** One of the sixteen *composite odu* in the family of *Ogundá*. It falls when a casting of three mouths (Ogundá) is followed by a casting of four mouths *(Irosun)*. This odu is also known as Ogundá Roso.

**Ogundá Iwori:** See *Ogundá Marunla*.

**Ogundá Kana:** See *Ogundá Okana*.

**Ogundá Kanran:** See *Ogundá Okana*.

**Ogundá l'Ogbe:** See *Ogundá Ejiogbe*.

**Ogundá Marunla:** One of the sixteen *composite odu* found in the family of *Ogundá*. It is formed when a casting of three mouths (Ogundá) is followed by a casting of fifteen mouths *(Marunla)*. This odu is also known as Ogundá Iwori.

**Ogundá Meji:** One of the sixteen *composite odu* found in the family of *Ogundá*. It falls when a casting of three mouths (Ogundá) repeats itself.

**Ogundá Merindilogún:** One of the sixteen *composite odu* found in the family of *Ogundá*. It falls when a casting of three mouths (Ogundá) is followed by a casting of sixteen mouths *(Merindilogún)*. This odu is also known as Ogundá Otura.

**Ogundá Merinla:** One of the sixteen *composite odu* found in the family of *Ogundá.* It falls when a casting of three mouths (Ogundá) is followed by a casting of fourteen mouths *(Merinla).* This odu is also known as Ogundá Ika.

**Ogundá Metanla:** One of the sixteen *composite odu* found in the family of *Ogundá.* It falls when a casting of three mouths (Ogundá) is followed by a casting of thirteen mouths *(Metanla).* This odu is also known as Ogundá Irete.

**Ogundá Obara:** One of the sixteen *composite odu* found in the family of *Ogundá.* It falls when a casting of three mouths (Ogundá) is followed by a casting of six mouths *(Obara).*

**Ogundá Oché:** One of the sixteen *composite odu* found in the family of *Ogundá.* It is formed when a casting of three mouths (Ogundá) is followed by a casting of five mouths *(Oché).*

**Ogundá Odí:** One of the sixteen *composite odu* found in the family of *Ogundá.* It is formed when a casting of three mouths (Ogundá) is followed by a casting of seven mouths *(Odí).* This odu is also known as Ogunda'di.

**Ogundá Ofún:** One of the sixteen *composite odu* found in the family of *Ogundá.* It is formed when a casting of three mouths is followed by ten mouths *(Ofún).*

**Ogundá Ogbe:** See *Ogundá Ejiogbe.*

**Ogundá Okana:** One of the sixteen *composite odu* in the family of *Ogundá.* It falls when a casting of three mouths (Ogundá) is followed by a casting of one mouth *(Okana).* This odu is also known as Ogundá Okanran, Ogundá Kanran, and Ogundá Kana.

**Ogundá Okanran:** See *Ogundá Okana.*

**Ogundá Osá:** One of the sixteen *composite odu* in the family of *Ogundá.* It falls when a casting of three mouths (Ogundá) is followed by a casting of nine mouths *(Osá).* This odu is also known as Ogundá'sa.

**Ogundá Otura:** See *Ogundá Merindilogún.*

**Ogundá Owani:** One of the sixteen *composite odu* in the family of *Ogundá.* It falls when a casting of three mouths (Ogundá) is followed by a casting of eleven mouths *(Owani).*

**Ogundá Oyekun:** See *Ogundá Ejioko.*

**Ogundá Roso:** See *Ogundá Irosun.*

**Ogundá'sa:** See *Ogundá Osá.*

**Ogundá Unle:** See *Ogundá Ejiogbe.*

**Ogundá Yeku:** See *Ogundá Ejioko.*

**ojo y lengua:** Translates as "the eye and the tongue"; a spiritual charm that keeps away evil eyes and gossip.

**Okana:** One of the sixteen *parent odu* in the *diloggún;* it is opened when one mouth falls on the diviner's mat.

**Okana Ejila:** One of the sixteen *composite odu* in the family of *Okana.* It is formed when an initial casting of one mouth (Okana) is followed by a casting of twelve mouths *(Ejila Shebora).* Okana Oturupon is another name for this sign.

**Okana Ejioko:** One of the sixteen *composite odu* in the family of *Okana.* It is formed when an initial casting of one mouth (Okana) is followed by a casting of two mouths *(Eji Oko).* This odu is also known as Kana'yeku, Kanran Ejioko, Kanran Oyekun, Okana Oyekun, Okanran Ejioko, and Okanran Oyekun.

**Okana'fun:** See *Okana Ofún.*

**Okana Ika:** See *Okana Merinla.*

**Okana Irete:** See *Okana Metanla.*

**Okana Iroso:** See *Okana Irosun.*

**Okana Irosun:** One of the sixteen *composite odu* in the family of *Okana.* It is formed when an initial casting of one mouth (Okana) is followed by a casting of four mouths *(Irosun).* Kanran Iroso, Kanran Irosun, and Okana Iroso are other names for this odu.

**Okana Iwori:** See *Okana Marunla.*

**Okana l'Ogbe:** See *Okana Ogbe.*

**Okana Marunla:** One of the sixteen *composite odu* in the family of *Okana.* It is formed when an initial casting of one mouth (Okana) is followed by a casting of fifteen mouths *(Marunla).* Okana Iwori is another name for this odu.

**Okana Meji:** One of the sixteen *composite odu* in the family of *Okana.* It is formed when an initial casting of one mouth (Okana) is followed by another casting of one mouth.

**Okana Merindilogún:** One of the sixteen *composite odu* in the family of *Okana.* It is formed when an initial casting of one mouth (Okana) is followed by a casting of sixteen mouths *(Merindilogún).* This odu is also known as Okana Otura.

**Okana Merinla:** One of the sixteen *composite odu* found in the family of *Okana.* It is formed when an initial casting of one mouth (Okana) is followed by another casting of fourteen mouths *(Merinla).* Okana Ika is another name for this odu.

**Okana Metanla:** One of the sixteen *composite odu* in the family of *Okana.* It is formed when an initial casting of one mouth (Okana) is followed by a casting of thirteen mouths *(Metanla).* Okana Irete is another name for this odu.

**Okana Obara:** One of the sixteen *composite odu* in the family of *Okana.* It is formed when an initial casting of one mouth (Okana) is followed by a casting of six mouths *(Obara).* This letter is also known by the names Kanran Obara and Okanran Obara.

**Okana Oché:** One of the sixteen *composite odu* in the family of *Okana.* It is formed when an initial casting of one mouth (Okana) is followed by a casting of five mouths *(Oché).* Okanran Oché and Kanran Oché are other names for this odu.

**Okana Odí:** One of the sixteen *composite odu* in the family of *Okana*. It is formed when an initial casting of one mouth (Okana) is followed by a casting of seven mouths *(Odí).*

**Okana Ofún:** One of the sixteen *composite odu* in the family of *Okana*. It is formed when an initial casting of one mouth (Okana) is followed by a casting of ten mouths *(Ofún).* This odu is also known as Kanran Ofún, Okana'fun, and Okanran Ofún.

**Okana Ogbe:** One of the sixteen *composite odu* in the family of *Okana*. It is formed when an initial casting of one mouth (Okana) is followed by a casting of seven mouths *(Eji Ogbe).* This odu is also known by the names Okana Unle and Okana l'Ogbe.

**Okana Ogundá:** One of the sixteen *composite odu* found in the family of *Okana*. It is formed when the initial casting of one mouth (Okana) is followed by a second casting of three mouths *(Ogundá).* Kanran Ogundá is another name for this odu.

**Okana Osá:** One of the sixteen *composite odu* found in the family of *Okana*. It is formed when the initial casting of one mouth (Okana) is followed by a second casting of nine mouths *(Osá).*

**Okana Otura:** See *Okana Merindilogún.*

**Okana Oturupon:** See *Okana Ejila.*

**Okana Owani:** One of the sixteen *composite odu* found in the family of *Okana*. It is formed when the initial casting of one mouth (Okana) is followed by a second casting of eleven mouths *(Owani).*

**Okana Oyekun:** See *Okana Ejioko.*

**Okana Unle:** See *Okana Ogbe.*

**Okanran Ejioko:** See *Okana Ejioko.*

**Okanran Obara:** See *Okana Obara.*

**Okanran Oché:** See *Okana Oché.*

**Okanran Ofún:** See *Okana Ofún.*

**Okanran Oyekun:** See *Okana Ejioko.*

**oke:** Mountain.

**Oké:** Referred to as *Orisha Oké*, he is the spirit of the mountain, the first point of land that rose from *Olokun's* watery domain. Orisha Oké is the first point where *Obatalá* came down to earth; it is his foundation and strength, and Oké acts as his messenger between heaven and earth.

**okuni:** Man.

**Olódumare:** A *Yoruba* contraction that translates into "owner of the womb"; this is the supreme deity of the Yoruba and *Lucumí.*

**Olófin:** It is said among the *Lucumí* that Olófin is "god on earth"; he is the eldest *avatar* of *Obatalá* and can be received only by the priesthood of *Orúnmila*, the *babalawos.*

**Olokun:** The androgynous *orisha* who rules and owns the deepest parts of the sea.

**Olorún:** A *Lucumí* contraction of two words: *olo*, "owner," and *orún*, "the sun." It means "owner of the sun." It is a name for God, his symbol being the sun in the daytime sky.

**Olosa:** This is the *orisha* of lakes and lagoons. When *Olokun* is said to exist as a male, Olosa is said to be his wife.

**omiero:** Any number of herbal waters made by *initiates* of *Santería;* it is used in bathing the *iyawó* and giving birth to the *orishas.*

**omo:** Child.

**omo odu:** This translates into "children of odu." The omo odu is cast after the *parent odu;* as a pair, they form the *composite odu.*

**ona:** Afflictions.

**oni:** Owner.

**onire:** A *Lucumí* contraction meaning "[to give a blessing] to clear a sign."

**opá ikú:** Staff of the dead.

**Opira:** Although many call Opira an *odu*, it is not an odu in the *diloggún*. It is a shadow that falls on the mat when the *orishas* do not wish to speak about the client's concerns. One says that Opira has come to the house when the shells fall so that no mouths are open; they are all facedown on the *italero's* mat. The *ebó* is automatic: The diviner must send the client to *Ifá.* If Opira falls during a reading but is not the opening odu, there are rituals that can be done to pacify this sign so that the diviner can continue with his reading.

**oracle:** A tool of divination. In the religion *Santería*, there are three oracles: *obí*, *diloggún*, and *Ifá.*

**oran:** Moral and legal crimes.

**orí:** A *Yoruba* word that means "head" or "consciousness"; it is used to refer to the spiritual consciousness of the client.

**Orí:** Refers to the part of one's spiritual consciousness remaining in heaven; it is a part of every person but never manifests on earth. As such, it is regarded as an *orisha*, and it may be received like any other orisha.

**oriaté:** An expert not only in the reading of the *diloggún*, but also in all ceremonies of *Santería.*

**orisha:** A *Yoruba* contraction that means "select head"; it denotes any of the myriad spirits in the pantheon of *Santería* that are an extension of *Olódumare's aché.*

**orisha of the head:** Denotes one's guardian, or patron, *orisha;* it is the spirit that one will be crowned with at the rites of ocha. While an initiate may receive many orishas, the initiate will be a *priest* or *priestess* of only this orisha.

**Orisha Nla:** One of the many *avatars* of *Obatalá.*

**Orisha Oko:** The *orisha* who controls the fecundity of the earth. He has two forms: During the day he is envisioned as a handsome black male; at night be becomes a terrifying presence in the darkness. Traditionally, this orisha lives in the *santero's* home for the six months that the fields lie fallow, and then he goes outdoors with the beginning of the planting season (our house does this on the spring equinox and takes him back inside during the autumn equinox).

**Oroiña:** The *orisha* who lives at the center of the earth; she is its molten core. She gave birth to the orisha *Aganyú.*

**Orún:** Heaven; the invisible world.

**orún:** A *Lucumí* word for "sun."

**Orúnla:** See *Orúnmila.*

**Orúnmila:** The *orisha* of *Ifá* and its *priests*, the *babalawos.* Only men are called to his priesthood. He does not speak directly through the *diloggún;* however, certain *composite odu* indicate that he would like the one at the mat sent to his priests so that he may speak with him. He is also known as Orúnla.

**Osá:** One of the sixteen *parent odu* of the *diloggún;* it is opened when nine mouths fall on the diviner's mat.

**Osá Ejila:** One of the sixteen *composite odu* found in the family of *Osá.* It opens when nine mouths (Osá) are followed by twelve mouths *(Ejila Shebora).* Osá Oturupon is another name for this odu.

**Osá Ejioko:** One of the sixteen *composite odu* found in *Osá's* family. It opens when nine mouths (Osá) are followed by two mouths *(Eji Oko).* This odu is also known as Osá Yeku and Osá Oyekun.

**Osá Ika:** See *Osá Merinla.*

**Osain:** One of the most mysterious *orishas.* Osain was created after creation; he sprang forth from the earth the moment the first green thing began to grow. He is the lord of *aché* on the earth, knowing all the secrets of the *ewe.* Without Osain, none of the orishas can work its magic, nor can its children be initiated, nor can the orishas be born on earth. He will live until the last green thing on this planet perishes. Anyone born with either six fingers or six toes is said to be an *osainista* from birth. See also *niche osain* and *making osain.*

**osainista:** A *priest* or *priestess* of the *orisha Osain;* an osainista is either claimed by Osain in the *diloggún* or claimed by birth (his mark being six fingers or toes).

**Osá Irete:** See *Osá Metanla.*

**Osá Irosun:** One of the sixteen *composite odu* found in the family of *Osá.* It forms when the initial cast of nine mouths (Osá) precedes a cast of four mouths *(Irosun).*

**Osá Iwori:** See *Osá Marunla.*

**Osá Kana:** See *Osá Okana.*

**Osá Kanran:** See *Osá Okana.*

**Osá l'Ogbe:** See *Osá Ogbe.*

**Osá Marunla:** One of the sixteen *composite odu* found in the family of *Osá.* It opens when the initial cast of nine mouths (Osá) is followed by a cast of fifteen mouths *(Marunla).* Osá Iwori is another name for this odu.

**Osá Meji:** One of the sixteen *composite odu* existing within the family of *Osá.* It forms when nine mouths *(Osá)* repeats itself, creating a twin.

**Osá Merindilogún:** One of the sixteen *composite odu* found in the family of *Osá.* It opens when the initial cast of nine mouths (Osá) precedes a cast of sixteen mouths *(Merindilogún).* Osá Otura is another name for this odu.

**Osá Merinla:** One of the sixteen *composite odu* found in the family of *Osá.* It forms when an initial cast of nine mouths (Osá) is followed by fourteen mouths *(Merinla).* Osá Ika is another name for this odu.

**Osá Metanla:** One of the sixteen *composite odu* found in *Osá's* family. It opens when the initial cast of nine mouths (Osá) is followed by a cast of thirteen mouths *(Metanla).* Osá Irete is another name for this odu.

**osán:** One of the *ibó* used in *divination.* It is a guacalote seed used to represent children and their concerns. Sometimes it is used in questions dealing with illness, because before a seed can take root, the fruit holding it must rot. This ibó will always respond in the negative.

**Osá Obara:** One of the sixteen *composite odu* found in *Osá's* family. It is open when the initial cast of nine mouths (Osá) is followed by a second cast of six mouths *(Obara).*

**Osá Oché:** One of the sixteen *composite odu* found in the family of *Osá.* It forms when the initial cast of nine mouths (Osá) precedes a cast of five mouths *(Oché).*

**Osá Odí:** One of *Osá's* sixteen *composite odu.* It forms when the initial cast of nine mouths (Osá) is followed by a second cast of seven mouths *(Odí).*

**Osá Ofún:** One of the sixteen *composite odu* found in the family of *Osá.* It forms when a cast of nine mouths (Osá) precedes a cast of ten mouths *(Ofún).*

**Osá Ogbe:** One of the sixteen *composite odu* found in the family of *Osá.* It forms when the initial cast of nine mouths (Osá) precedes a cast of eight mouths *(Eji Ogbe).* Osá l'Ogbe and Osá Unle are other names for this odu.

**Osá Ogundá:** One of the sixteen *composite odu* found in the family of *Osá.* It forms when the initial cast of nine mouths (Osá) precedes a cast of three mouths *(Ogundá).*

**Osá Okana:** One of the sixteen *composite odu* found in the family of *Osá.* It forms when a cast of nine mouths (Osá) is followed by a cast of one mouth *(Okana).* There are three additional names for this odu: Osá Okanran, Osá Kana, and Osá Kanran.

**Osá Okanran:** See *Osá Okana.*

**Osá Otura:** See *Osá Merindilogún.*

**Osá Oturupon:** See *Osá Ejila.*

**Osá Owani:** One of the sixteen *composite odu* found in *Osá's* family. It forms when a casting of nine mouths (Osá) precedes a casting of eleven mouths (Owani).

**Osá Oyekun:** See *Osá Ejioko.*

**Osá Unle:** See *Osá Ogbe.*

**Osá Yeku:** See *Osá Ejioko.*

**Oshún:** The *orisha* bringing love, sweetness, money, prosperity, fertility, conception, and all the things that make life worth living to humans. She is sister to *Yemayá* and one of *Shangó's* three wives. She is also referred to as the "mother of twins."

**osogbo:** Negative influence; any of the evils that may be predicted for a client through the oracle known as *diloggún.*

**Ósun:** Some in the New World consider Ósun a minor *orisha*; however, there are many types of Ósuns that can be given in different initiations, including that of the warriors, *Babaluaiye, Naná Burukú,* and *Inle.* Ósun is an orisha in one sense, the spirit that guards the orí of the client from danger. Yet more properly, Ósun is the herbal staff of *Osain,* which is packed with herbs and secrets specific to the orisha given to an adherent.

**otá:** When referring to the *ibó*, otá is a smooth, black pebble that the *priest* or *priestess* has found in the woods. It represents the strength and immortality of one's soul. In divination, the otá can be paired with any ibó and will always answer in the negative.

**otá de muerto:** A stone used to give material basis to the dead; it receives the blood offerings given to one's *egun.*

**otanes:** The sacred stones that house the spirit of the *orisha* to whom they are consecrated. Their number and color will depend on the orisha embodied.

**Otín:** An *orisha* whose sole purpose is to serve *Yemayá.*

**otonowá:** From heaven.

**Owani:** One of the sixteen *parent odu* of the *diloggún;* it is opened when eleven mouths fall on the mat.

**Owani Ejila:** One of the sixteen *composite odu* found in the family of *Owani.* It is open when the initial cast of eleven mouths (Owani) precedes a cast of twelve mouths *(Ejila Shebora).* It is also known as Owani Oturupon.

**Owani Ejioko:** One of the sixteen *composite odu* found in the family of *Owani.* It forms when the initial cast of eleven mouths (Owani) is followed by a cast of two mouths *(Eji Oko).* Owani Oyekun and Owani Yeku are two other names for this odu.

**Owani Hermoso:** See *Owani Irosun.*

**Owani Iroso:** See *Owani Irosun.*

**Owani Irosun:** One of the sixteen *composite odu* found in the family of *Owani.* It forms when the initial cast of eleven mouths (Owani) precedes a cast of four mouths *(Irosun).* Owani Hermoso and Owani Iroso are other names for this sign.

**Owani l'Ogbe:** See *Owani Ogbe.*

**Owani Meji:** One of the sixteen *composite odu* found in the family of *Owani.* This odu forms when the initial cast of eleven mouths (Owani) presents itself a second time.

**Owani Obara:** One of the sixteen *composite odu* found in the family of *Owani.* This odu forms when the initial cast of eleven mouths (Owani) is followed by a cast of six mouths *(Obara).*

**Owani Oché:** One of the sixteen *composite odu* found in the family of *Owani.* It opens when the initial cast of eleven mouths (Owani) precedes a cast of five mouths *(Oché).*

**Owani Odí:** One of the sixteen *composite odu* found in the family of *Owani.* It opens on the mat when the initial cast of eleven mouths (Owani) precedes a cast of seven mouths *(Odí).*

**Owani Ofún:** One of the sixteen *composite odu* found in *Owani's* family of odu. It forms when the initial cast of eleven mouths (Owani) precedes a cast of ten mouths *(Ofún).*

**Owani Ogbe:** One of the sixteen *composite odu* found in the family of *Owani.* It opens when the initial cast of eleven mouths (Owani) is followed by a cast of eight mouths *(Eji Ogbe).* Owani Unle and Owani l'Ogbe are other names for this odu.

**Owani Ogundá:** One of the sixteen *composite odu* in *Owani's* family. It consists of an initial cast of eleven mouths (Owani) preceding a cast of three mouths *(Ogundá).*

**Owani Okana:** One of the sixteen *composite odu* found in the family of *Owani.* It opens when the initial cast of eleven mouths (Owani) precedes a cast of one mouth *(Okana).*

**Owani Osá:** One of the sixteen *composite odu* found in the family of *Owani.* The letter is open on the mat when the initial cast of eleven mouths (Owani) precedes a cast of nine mouths *(Osá).*

**Owani Oturupon:** See *Owani Ejila.*

**Owani Oyekun:** See *Owani Ejioko.*

**Owani Unle:** See *Owani Ogbe.*

**Owani Yeku:** See *Owani Ejioko.*

**owó:** Money *(derecho); cowrie;* hand. When referring to the *ibó,* owó may take one of two forms: a single uncut cowrie shell or two cut cowries shells that have been attached so that their mouths face outward. Owó is used as ibó in any question dealing with money or finances. It can be paired either with *efun* to represent the loss or with *otá* to represent the gain. The use of this ibó is not taught in most houses.

**Oyá:** This female *orisha* is the patron of "the fire in the sky" or lightning that does not touch the earth. She is the gatekeeper to the cemetery, *Shangó's* partner in battle, and the lady of the marketplace. She is also the orisha of fast change and tumultuous cycles. Some also see her in the action of the tornado. This is Shangó's third wife, and his favorite even over *Oshún*.

**Oyekun Ejila:** See *Ejioko Ejila*.

**Oyekun Ika:** See *Ejioko Merinla*.

**Oyekun Irete:** See *Ejioko Metanla*.

**Oyekun Iroso:** See *Ejioko Irosun*.

**Oyekun Irosun:** See *Ejioko Irosun*.

**Oyekun Iwori:** See *Ejioko Marunla*.

**Oyekun Kanran:** See *Ejioko Okana*.

**Oyekun l'Ogbe:** See *Ejioko Ejiogbe*.

**Oyekun Marunla:** See *Ejioko Marunla*.

**Oyekun Meji:** See *Ejioko Meji*.

**Oyekun Merindilogún:** See *Ejioko Merindilogún*.

**Oyekun Merinla:** See *Ejioko Merinla*.

**Oyekun Metanla:** See *Ejioko Metanla*.

**Oyekun Obara:** See *Ejioko Obara*.

**Oyekun Oché:** See *Ejioko Oché*.

**Oyekun Odí:** See *Ejioko Odí*.

**Oyekun Ofún:** See *Ejioko Ofún*.

**Oyekun Ogundá:** See *Ejioko Ogundá*.

**Oyekun Okana:** See *Ejioko Okana*.

**Oyekun Okanran:** See *Ejioko Okana*.

**Oyekun Osá:** See *Ejioko Osá*.

**Oyekun Otura:** See *Ejioko Merindilogún*.

**Oyekun Owani:** See *Ejioko Owani*.

**Oyekun Unle:** See *Ejioko Ejiogbe*.

**palero:** A *priest* of *Palo Mayombe*.

**Palo:** A religion of magic and mysticism that is based on the spiritual practices of those who came from the Congo in Africa.

**Palo Mayombe:** One of the two mains sects of *Palo*.

**Palo Monte:** One of the two main sects of *Palo*.

**pañuelo:** An intricate silk or satin cloth used to cover and decorate the *soperas* of the *orishas*. Normally, it is made of the colors sacred to the spirit for whom it is prepared.

**parent odu:** The sign giving birth to all sixteen *composite odu* in a single family. For instance, *Okana* is a parent odu; it gives birth to the signs *Okana Ejioko*, *Okana Ogundá*, and *Okana Irete*.

**patakís:** The many sacred stories and legends found in the *diloggún;* some of these are about the *orishas*, while others are about the actions of historical/mythological humans who lived and died in both Africa and Cuba. All patakís teach spiritual truths found in *odu*. Note that the word is both singular and plural in usage; in pronounciation, the *s* at the end is dropped off.

**path:** See *avatar*.

**pinaldo:** Refers to the initiation of the knife, the ceremony giving a *priest* or *priestess* the right to sacrifice four-legged animals.

**prenda:** See *nganga*.

**priest:** Refers to a male initiate of *Santería* who heads an *ilé ocha* and cares spiritually for godchildren.

**priestess:** Refers to a female initiate of *Santería* who heads an *ilé ocha* and cares spiritually for godchildren.

**proverbs:** One of the many refrains found in the *odu* of the *diloggún;* a wise saying that encapsulates the meaning of an odu.

**rayado:** Initiated, or cut to, the *nganga* of the Congolese religion *Palo Mayombe*.

**rogación:** A cleansing of the head or *orí;* grated coconut is the main ingredient. It incorporates a series of prayers to strengthen and support the head. The specifics of each rogación are given in each *odu* of the *diloggún*.

**rogación sodidé:** A *rogación* that begins at the feet and ends with the head. Its purpose is to elevate the client back under the guidance of his *orí* and heaven.

**saint:** Although the saints are the elevated, canonized souls of the Catholic faith, in the religion *Santería* the term *saint* is used, lovingly, to denote the *orishas* of the *Lucumí*. It is a practice stemming from the syncretization and amalgamation of Catholic practices into orisha worship. In Spanish, the word used is *santo*.

**sandolo:** Sandalwood perfume.

**Santería:** The name of *orisha* worship as it developed in Cuba; the English translation from the Spanish is "worship of the saints." The name derives from the syncretizing of the Catholic saints and the orishas of the *Yoruba*.

**santero/santera:** A *priest* or *priestess* of *Santería*.

**santo:** A Spanish term for the *Lucumí* word *ocha*. See also *saint*.

**santo lavado:** A Spanish term for "washing of the saint." While all *orishas* must be washed in *omiero*, the use of this phrase refers to the reception of one's *guardian orisha* outside the ritual of *ocha*.

**saraeko:** A porridge normally made of water, cornmeal, and honey. It is a simple *adimú* appropriate for most orishas.

**sarayeye:** A spiritual cleansing.

**Shangó:** The fourth king of *Oyó*, and the *orisha* of the storm, thunder, and lightening.

**sodidé:** A *Lucumí* word meaning "to arise."

**sopera:** A Spanish word for "tureen"; it denotes the bowls where the *otanes* and implements of the *orishas* are kept.

**Spiritism:** See *Espiritísmo.*

**spiritual investigation:** A practice of *Espiritísmo* in which several mediums focus on the *egun* and spirit guides of an individual; it is a mass centered on one person. Through the mass, the spirits assisting this client's spiritual evolution are identified, and the needs and wants of those spirits are determined.

**taboo:** A prescription made during divination with the *diloggún;* it prohibits a client from certain actions, foods, or situations.

**tambor:** The sacred festival of an *orisha* in which the drums are played and the *priests* and *priestesses* are mounted or possessed by their orishas.

**tata nkisi:** A Congolese term for "father of the spirit." It refers to a high *priest* in the religion *Palo Mayombe.*

**thunderstone:** A sacred stone belonging to *Shangó* and believed to be created when lightning touches the earth.

**tiya-tiya:** Arguments, gossip, and slander.

**Trupo Congua:** See *Ejila Ogbe.*

**warriors:** The four *orishas* that are received together in one initiation: *Elegguá, Ogún, Ochosi,* and *Ósun.* A simulacrum of Ochosi is received with Ogún in the form of an iron crossbow.

**Yeguá:** See *Yewá.*

**Yeku Ejila:** See *Ejioko Ejila.*

**Yeku Ika:** See *Ejioko Merinla.*

**Yeku Irete:** See *Ejioko Metanla.*

**Yeku Iroso:** See *Ejioko Irosun.*

**Yeku Irosun:** See *Ejioko Irosun.*

**Yeku Iwori:** See *Ejioko Marunla.*

**Yeku Kanran:** See *Ejioko Okana.*

**Yeku Marunla:** See *Ejioko Marunla.*

**Yeku Meji:** See *Ejioko Meji.*

**Yeku Merindilogún:** See *Ejioko Merindilogún.*

**Yeku Merinla:** See *Ejioko Merinla.*

**Yeku Metanla:** See *Ejioko Metanla.*

**Yeku Obara:** See *Ejioko Obara.*

**Yeku Oché:** See *Ejioko Oché.*

**Yeku Odí:** See *Ejioko Odí.*

**Yeku Ofún:** See *Ejioko Ofún.*

**Yeku Ogundá:** See *Ejioko Ogundá.*

**Yeku Okana:** See *Ejioko Okana.*

**Yeku Okanran:** See *Ejioko Okana.*

**Yeku Osá:** See *Ejioko Osá.*

**Yeku Otura:** See *Ejioko Merindilogún.*

**Yeku Owani:** See *Ejioko Owani.*

**Yemayá:** Born when *Olokun* was chained to the bottom of the ocean by *Obatalá,* Yemayá arose to become mother to the world and to the *orishas.* She is the patron of motherhood and of the fresh waters of the world.

**Yembo:** There is confusion over exactly who this female *orisha* is. Some say she is an elder path of *Obatalá;* however, because she was once the wife of Obatalá, our house believes her to be an ancestral *Yemayá.* She is the mother of the orishas and gave birth to all the waters of the world. *Naná Burukú* was born after Yembo was raped by *Ogún.* Yembo ascended to *Olódumare's* palace by her own grief and *aché,* creating the moon and Naná Burukú to watch over women and punish those who commit crimes against them.

**Yewá:** A very young, very gorgeous *orisha,* perhaps the most beautiful of them all; however, she is also the most chaste of them all, eternally virgin. She demands no less of her *priestesses* (men may never be initiated to her mysteries). Many know her as the devourer of the dead; she decomposes the bodies that lie in the earth's grasp. She is also known as Yeguá.

**yoko ocha:** This is a Lucumí term denoting that one's salvation is found by being initiated to his or her guardian orisha.

**Yoruba:** The native Africans who originally settled in the southwestern parts of the area known today as Nigeria; their deities, the *orishas,* form the basis of the religion *Santería.* The word *Yoruba* also denotes the language shared by these peoples, the native tongue that mixed with Cuban Spanish to become *Lucumí.*

# SUGGESTED READING

For those who desire more general information about the religion Santería and its basic beliefs, the following books are highly recommended.

**Angarica, Nicolas V.** ***Manual del Oribate, Religión Lucumí.*** **Havana, Cuba: Private printing, 1955.**

This is one of my favorite underground texts; it is available only through botánicas and is somewhat hard to obtain as it is continually mimeographed and republished by individuals, not publishers. While attributed to the work of Angarica (a godchild of Octavio Sama, omo Aganyú, Obadameji), Angarica was mostly illiterate. One of his godchildren (name unknown to this author) wrote the book based on Angarica's teachings. It teaches the reading of composite odu; however, unlike the method taught in this book, it bases its teachings on the "marriage" of two signs. For example, when one reads about the odu 3-6 in *Manual del Oribate,* it is a combination of the meanings of the parent odu Ogundá and the parent odu Obara. While this is a valid way to read composites, there is far more to the aché of each letter than this. Its study, however, will enrich the reader's knowledge of diloggún. This book is published only in Spanish.

**Bascom, William R.** ***Ifá Divination.*** **Bloomington: Indiana University Press, 1969.**

**———.** ***Sixteen Cowries.*** **Bloomington: Indiana University Press, 1970.**

William Bascom is the American authority on African spirituality. Although none of his books provides the instructional material needed to work any of the oracles, his writings are filled with scholarly information about the African traditions. His two books are filled with a wealth of patakís for each odu, and our diviners are continually turning to these volumes as a source of information and clarification.

**Cabrera, Lydia.** ***El Monte: Igbo, Finda, Ewe Orisha, Vititi Nfinda.*** **Miami: Ediciones Universal, 1975.**

**———.** ***Ochún y Yemayá.*** **Miami: Ediciones Universal, 1970.**

Lydia Cabrera was a "cultural anthropologist" who did her field work in Cuba. While not an initiate of Santería at the time she was researching, most of her work is accurate. Priests and priestesses often refer to these works, and other books she wrote, for information. All of her books are published only in Spanish.

**Canizares, Raul.** ***Walking with the Night: The Afro-Cuban World of Santería.*** **Rochester, Vt.: Destiny Books, 1993.**

This book is a wonderful testament to the power of Santería from a man who not only was raised in the religion but also was initiated at a very young age. It is filled with anecdotes and personal stories that illustrate the intervention of the orishas in his life. It is an inspirational must-read for those involved in all levels of the religion.

**Castillo, J. M.** ***Ifá en Tierra de Ifá.*** **Newark, N.J.: Castillo House, 1976.**

This is an interesting book. The title makes one think that it is about the odu Ifá; however, the author promotes himself on the book's cover with the title "Oba, Oriaté." These are titles of an orisha priest or priestess who has mastered the ceremonies of ocha. They have nothing to do with Ifá. Most of the information contained therein is about odu diloggún, although Castillo refers to them by their markings and names in Ifá. While the book can be confusing, it is a good read; like Cortez's book (below), it is also an underground classic and rarely sold to those who are not initiates known to the botánica owner. This volume is published only in Spanish.

**Cortez, Enrique.** ***Secretos del Oriaté de la Religión Yoruba.*** **New York: Vilaragut Articulos Religiosos Corp., 1980.**

This book is difficult to obtain. It is privately published and distributed through botánicas. It is often hidden behind counters where none can see them; most of these businesses will sell the book only to those who they know "have aché" or initiation. If one can obtain this volume, it is excellent. Published in poorly written Spanish, it is still a wealth of information about the odu diloggún, and it is well worth the inflated price one will have to pay for it. Some sell copies for as much as $100, so be prepared.

**Fatunmbi, Awó Fá'Lokun.** ***Awó: Ifá and the Theology of Orisha Divination.*** **Bronx, N.Y.: Original Publications, 1992.**

While this book is often criticized by orisha priests and priestesses for its innovations on the casting of four cowries in the place of four coconut rinds to read the oracle obí, it is also praised for its detailed metaphysics. A book that brings controversy also brings much thought; I recommend it for its provocative content.

**Flores, Ysamur.** ***Santería Garments and Altars.*** **Jackson: University Press of Mississippi, 1994.**

This book was written in conjunction with Peña and Roberto J. Evanchuk. It is an exceptionally wonderful overview of the faith's religious elements. Unlike other books written today that promise to teach the religion by a series of "how-to's" that read like an esoteric cookbook, this volume instructs the reader about the faith and its orishas by depicting various coronation gowns and suits, along with a variety of celebration and anniversary altars for the orishas. It gives a wonderful feel for the religion and its celebrations. It is a hardback filled with color plates and photographs, and although it is costly and a bit difficult to get, it is well worth the reader's investment in time and money.

**González-Wippler, Migene.** ***Introduction to Seashell Divination.*** **Plainview, N.Y.: Original Publications, 1992.**

**———.** ***Legends of Santería.*** **St. Paul, Minn.: Llewellyn Publications, 1994.**

**———.** ***Powers of the Orishas.*** **Plainview, N.Y.: Original Publications, 1992.**

**———.** ***Rituals and Spells of Santería.*** **Bronx, N.Y.: Original Publications, 1984.**

**———.** ***Santería: African Magic in Latin America.*** **Bronx, N.Y.: Original Publications, 1993.**

**———.** ***The Santería Experience.*** **St. Paul, Minn.: Llewellyn Publications, 1994.**

**———.** ***Santería, the Religion.*** **St. Paul, Minn.: Llewellyn Publications, 1994.**

Although many have criticized her for popularizing the magical side of Santería and downplaying the religious elements, González-Wippler has corrected much of this in the later editions of her work, especially those published by Llewellyn Publications. If not for her writings, many of those now in the religion never would have found Santería.

**Idowu, E. Bolaji.** ***Olódumare: God in Yoruba Belief.*** **New York: Original Publications, 1995.**

This is the best book available about the supreme deity of Yoruba belief; it also sheds light on the original practices that spawned the religion we now practice. It is essential reading for those either in the faith or about to enter it.

**Neimark, Philip John.** ***The Sacred Ifá Oracle.*** **New York: HarperCollins, 1995.**

**———.** ***The Way of the Orisa.*** **New York: HarperCollins, 1993.**

Neimark's descriptions of the orishas (he spells them orisa) and the attributes are among the best I have read; however, I cannot help but disagree with his conception of Yemayá/Olokun as being one and the same orisha. Although I am an initiate of Santería, I have met a few African priests in my lifetime and none of them agrees with his conception of "how things are done in Africa." Yet his book, as a whole, is a wonderful testament of the orishas as seen from the eyes of a newly initiated babalawo.

**Popoola, Solagbade.** ***Practical Ifá Divination.*** **New York: Athelia and Henrietta Press, 1997.**

This book was originally marketed as volume three of a proposed eighteen-volume set; however, the remaining seventeen books never materialized, at least on the open market. It is a wonderful overview of the composite odu in the family of Eji Ogbe.

# INDEX